W9-AQL-793

DISCARD

ENCYCLOPEDIA *of*
Small Business

SECOND EDITION

J-Z
VOLUME 2

Kevin Hillstrom
Laurie Collier Hillstrom

ENCYCLOPEDIA *of*
Small Business

SECOND EDITION

J–Z
VOLUME 2

GALE GROUP

THOMSON LEARNING

Detroit • New York • San Diego • San Francisco
Boston • New Haven, Conn. • Waterville, Maine
London • Munich

R

Kevin Hillstrom and Laurie Collier Hillstrom, *Editors*

Gale Group Staff

Jane A. Malonis, *Senior Editor*

Erin Braun, *Managing Editor*

Paul Lewon, *Technical Training Specialist*

Mary Beth Trimper, *Production Director*

Evi Seoud, *Assistant Production Manager*

Cynthia Baldwin, *Product Design Manager*

Eric Johnson, *Art Director*

Library of Congress Cataloging-in-Publication Data

Hillstrom, Kevin, 1963-

   Encyclopedia of small business / Kevin Hillstrom, Laurie Collier

Hillstrom. —2nd ed.

     p. cm.

   Includes bibliographical references and index.

   ISBN 0-7876-4906-6 (set : hardcover : alk. paper)—ISBN 0-7876-4907-4 (vol.

1)—ISBN 0-7876-4908-2 (vol.2)

    1. Small business—Management—Encyclopedias. 2. Small business—

Finance—Encyclopedias. I. Hillstrom, Laurie Collier, 1965— II. Title.

HD62.7 .H5553 2001

658.02'2-dc21

2001033781

CONTENTS

J

JOB DESCRIPTION

At the heart of the recruitment process lies the general concept that a company needs to hire people to complete certain tasks or group of tasks within the organization. The description of the various responsibilities of each position can usually be found within the ''job description'' or ''job specification'' that is typically put together by business owners or managers.

Recruiters and personnel managers rely on clear and concise job descriptions to streamline the application and interviewing process and to judge work performance after a person has been hired. Job descriptions and specifications usually include known duties and responsibilities, required levels of education and work experience, salary and benefits provided to employees in exchange for their labor, and information regarding the work environment. Job descriptions also may include helpful details addressing other work-related issues, such as the position's travel obligations, normal work schedule, physical location where duties of position will be carried out, union status, supervisory relationships, bonuses, and any other information directly pertinent to the execution of any and all responsibilities associated with the job. In essence, wrote Philip B. Crosby in *The Eternally Successful Organization,* effective job descriptions let employees know what is expected of them: ''If people are going to perform their assigned task, then they obviously have to know what it is, how to do it, and how to measure the results. Either someone has to explain it all to them or they have to figure it out themselves.''

Researchers, executives, and small business owners all agree that job descriptions—if studied and created carefully and used appropriately as a productivity measurement tool—can help organizations, especially in the early stages of a worker's employment. ''Job descriptions are potentially one of the most powerful tools available to help managers improve employee performance and productivity,'' stated Philip C. Grant in *Supervision.* ''They have great utility for every phase of human resource administration. From designing jobs and reward systems, through staffing and training to performance evaluation and control, the job description is literally indispensible if the human resource is to be managed properly. A recent analysis of job description usage uncovered 132 major management uses for job descriptions. Probably no other management tool has such potential for usage in such a wide variety of significant ways.''

JOB DESCRIPTIONS AND COMPANY CULTURE

The level of detail utilized in the creation of job descriptions and the monitoring of employee execution of the duties articulated therein can vary tremendously from organization to organization. A multinational corporation, for example, may have job descriptions that are far more formal and detailed in their contents than those used by a small local business. Companies in different industries tend to approach the issue of job descriptions differently as well (tool and die manufacturers, for example, are more likely to institute job definitions for various positions than are fishing charter services). And, finally, some business owners and management teams simply institute and nourish different company cultures that may have dramatically different conceptions of job descriptions and their utility. For example, companies that operate in a flexible working environment in which employee roles are fluid and expectations change may find the quest to define various job parameters to be a daunting one. ''The essence of the problem is how clear directives, where these are needed, can be reconciled with flexible work systems,'' wrote Belbin, Watson, and West in *People Management.* ''One approach to this is for a manager to set up a job as a working hypothesis on how the work should be carried out. Added to this is a system of continuing feedback to check whether the job is proceeding as expected. Thus, the boundaries and content of the job can be defined through an interactive communication process.''

But researchers note that on the whole, larger organizations will often, out of either real or imagined necessity, institute more formalized job description/ monitoring procedures. Still, in many companies with detailed plans in this area, ''job descriptions are usually thought of as something for the lower-level people in an organization,'' said Crosby. ''Higher-ups have 'mission statements' which sound good but are hard to measure. So we have all these people doing things which we may or may not have agreed to do. It doesn't take very long before a great deal of the organization's work has very little to do with the main objectives of the business.'' He and other business consultants contend that job descriptions can help business enterprises maintain their focus at all job levels, including top management and ownership positions. Owners of family establishments or very small business enterprises, meanwhile, may simply decide that formal job descriptions are unnecessary. Ultimately, each small business owner needs to consider the unique aspects of his or her own business situation when deciding how to define and monitor the responsibilities of each work position.

JOB DESCRIPTIONS AND PERFORMANCE APPRAISALS

One major advantage associated with formal job descriptions is that it provides business owners and supervisors with a useful tool of performance measurement. ''Fundamentally, productivity means producing—getting the work done with the most advantageous results using the best possible methods,'' observed Levesque. ''Doing work and getting results is a measurement of *what* we do, while the methods used to carry out work is a measurement of *how* we conduct ourselves and our work transactions. Therefore, each job is represented by what is within the defined scope of the position (job description) in relation to others we work with, and how each job function is carried out. . . . What does good communications of performance criteria constitute? At the very

minimum it means giving employees copies of their job description and appraisal form, then explaining what kinds of job functions are evaluated against performance dimensions and standards.'' In addition, job descriptions are often used to provide potential job applicants with a sense of the various obligations and rewards of that position, to help businesses develop salary grades, and to help maintain a recognizable organizational structure.

But while the benefits that accrue to businesses that take the time and effort to devise and update job descriptions are numerous, consultants note that firms still need to be cognizant of the potential for legal difficulties therein. ''I'd be willing to wager that there's a potential legal nightmare lurking in your office. It's probably hiding where you would least expect it, tucked away in a file folder or notebook you haven't opened in months or years. It's called a job description,'' said Allen Halcrow in *Folio: The Magazine for Magazine Management.* ''In today's litigious climate . . . those seemingly innocuous documents can come back to haunt you on issues such as overtime, performance reviews, and terminations.'' According to Halcrow, ''the fundamental problem is that the job descriptions you may consider merely guidelines about work tasks and expectations may be seen as much more definitive by attorneys and the courts.''

PERFORMANCE REVIEWS Annual or semi-annual performance reviews are fixtures in most establishments, and they are useful to both employee and employer for many reasons. But employers should know that they can also run into trouble here if they give an employee poor marks for their work on tasks that are not delineated in their official job description. ''You're at legal risk if you hold employees responsible for work that has not been defined in writing,'' Halcrow flatly stated. He noted that this problem is most likely to crop up in situations where a reorganization or attrition has prompted a reallocation of responsibilities within the organization. Of course, bestowing praise on an individual who takes on responsibilities not mentioned within his or her job description is unlikely to have unwanted repercussions. ''The key,'' said Halcrow, ''is to be careful not to tie negative outcomes (such as discipline or denial of a raise) to duties outside the job description'' or to unduly focus on those duties at the expense of those responsibilities that are specifically mentioned.

OVERTIME Practically all employers are aware of the differences in classifying employees as exempt or non-exempt in the area of overtime compensation. But Halcrow noted that many employers are not aware that overtime liability can be linked to an employee's duties *as they are described in his or her job description,* not according to what tasks the employee actually performs: ''For example, suppose you decide that one of your supervisors should be moved to a larger office, or to one closer to the production department. If the employee comes in over the weekend to pack or move boxes, you may be liable for overtime—even if the employee is exempt—because packing and moving are not part of the employee's usual job activities. . . . This principle applies to any tasks not normally performed by the employee, or to tasks that are not directly related to his or her normal job duties [such as going to the post office or addressing envelopes]. The important issue to consider isn't whether the activity is a one-time event, but whether the task relates to the employee's usual job duties.''

EMPLOYEE DISMISSALS Small business owners that decide to terminate an employee for poor performance have to make sure that they are doing so because of their dissatisfaction with the targeted employee's work on tasks that are discussed in the job description.

USING AND MAINTAINING JOB DESCRIPTIONS

Job descriptions can be valuable business resources when used correctly. But many companies do not take full advantage of these documents, either because they are ignorant of their possibilities or because of company-wide perceptions that they are of limited use. Grant noted several factors that can limit the effectiveness of these documents:

- Managers unfamiliar with purpose and usage of job descriptions.

- Vague, inaccurate, outdated, or incomplete job descriptions.

- Managers not motivated to utilize job descriptions.

- Job descriptions arranged in format that is not standardized or friendly to managers or employees.

- Job in question "escapes definition" because of fluidity, variety of tasks, etc.

Entrepreneurs and managers, then, need to attend to all of these potential pitfalls when creating job descriptions for their workforce. In addition, human resource management experts hasten to point out that job descriptions are only effective if they are subject to continuous review and revision.

1) Continuous updating—"Each employee's job description should be amended when his or her duties change,'' observed Halcrow. "Reassigning tasks or simply letting them drift until someone steps in to do them is not a good idea. It doesn't matter that everyone in the company know who's doing the work, and that the situation is 'understood.' '' One commonly overlooked aspect of this re-

quirement is that employers should react quickly when an employee quits or is terminated. In such instances, each task formerly carried out by the ex-employee should be formally reassigned in writing to another person's job description.

2) Proper classification—Employers who remain cognizant of job descriptions and classifications when assigning various tasks are far less likely to get tripped up on overtime hassles than businesses that are careless about such issues.

3) Communication—In addition to regularly scheduled performance reviews, employers should make sure that employees who find their duties and responsibilities undergoing change have the opportunity to ask questions—and even raise objections.

FURTHER READING:

Arthur, Diane. *Recruiting, Interviewing, Selecting & Orienting New Employees.* New York: AMACOM, 1991.

Belbin, Meredith, Barrie Watson, and Cindy West. "True Colours." *People Management.* March 6, 1997.

Crosby, Philip B. *The Eternally Successful Corporation: The Art of Corporate Wellness.* New York: New American Library, 1990.

Degner, Jim. "Writing Job Descriptions that Work." *Credit Union Executive.* November-December 1995.

Dorf, Paul, and Ethel P. Flanders. "Classify Jobs Properly to Avoid Overtime Trap." *HRMagazine.* April 1994.

Grant, Philip C. "Why Job Descriptions are Not Used Anymore." *Supervision.* April 1998.

Halcrow, Allan. "Hidden Traps in Job Descriptions." *Folio: The Magazine for Magazine Management.* December 1, 1992.

Levesque, Joseph D. *The Human Resource Problem-Solver's Handbook.* New York: McGraw-Hill, 1992.

"Reality Doesn't Have a Job Description." *Workforce.* December 1999.

Wanous, John Parker. *Organizational Entry: Recruitment, Selection, Orientation and Socialization of Newcomers.* New York: Addison-Wesley, 1992.

JOB SHARING

Job sharing is a flexible work option in which two or possibly more employees share a single job. For example, one person may work in a certain position Monday and Tuesday, and a second person may occupy that same position Thursday and Friday. The two people may both work on Wednesday and use that time to update each other on the current status of the various projects on which they collaborate. A variety of other arrangements are possible as well.

Job sharing is a somewhat controversial alternative to telecommuting, flexible working hours, compressed work weeks, and other arrangements used by small businesses looking to offer their employees a bit more flexibility while maintaining productivity. It is aimed at the small number of employees in the work force who do not have a problem with earning less money if it offers them the opportunity to pursue the other interests in life that are important to them. A job sharing position should not to be confused with a part-time job. These types of employment opportunities are usually ones that require all the attention and dedication that is standard to the typical work day and week.

Job sharing offers small businesses a chance to retain valued employees that they would normally be in danger of losing if not for the flexible schedule. It can also help eliminate the need to train new employees if a valued employee were to leave the company. Job sharing can seem intimidating to managers, who may fear that it could lead to confusion, more paperwork, and a host of other hassles. If a proper plan is in place and each job sharer is held accountable for their duties, however, these issues can be avoided.

PLANNING A JOB SHARING POSITION

In order for a job sharing program to succeed, a solid plan must be put in place to ensure that the work gets done properly. Managers must pay close attention to how the system is working. Solid communication between work partners and management, as well as other employees who are not in the job sharing program, is a must. Done right, job-sharing can lead to a high level of productivity—perhaps even higher than the level contributed by a single, traditional employee.

The first step in implementing a job sharing program is to decide whether the job can be shared and if there are likely candidates with whom to share it. Most often, these candidates already exist within the company, although potential job sharers can be recruited from the outside workforce. Jobs with clearly defined individual tasks are the best to consider for job-sharing. Those that are more complex have a tendency of failing under this type of arrangement. Above all, management has to be committed to the job sharing program, as do the employees who are participating in it.

JOB SHARING AND EMPLOYEES

It is important to find partners in a job sharing position that have work styles, habits, preferences, quality standards, and communications skills that are compatible and closely matched. Many times, it can be advantageous if the employees select their own partners to ensure that these conditions are met. Most often it is important for employers to find job sharing partners with comparable skill levels, but there are still possible benefits if they do not. For instance, a more experienced worker can train an up-and-coming employee in a job sharing situation. When this happens, the employer can cut back on the time and money it would normally take to train the new employee, while also paying them a lower salary than the veteran worker during this time.

Employees who participate in job sharing divide their responsibilities in several different ways. They can share the job evenly or separate it into individual tasks that better suit each individual. If the job has unrelated tasks, those can also be divided. The work week can be split in half and shifts can be alternated so one employee works three days one week and two the next. Job sharing employees must be able to coordinate their schedules to make sure someone is always on the job when they are required to be.

THE ADVANTAGES OF JOB SHARING

It would seem that the one who benefits most from job sharing is the employee. This type of arrangement allows the employee to work part-time in order to spend more time with their families, attend school, or pursue other personal interests. New mothers find that it is a way to continue their careers while not having to deal with the stress and guilt that comes with putting their child in full-time day care. Experienced senior workers who wish to cut back a bit while still continuing their careers also benefit from job sharing, as do employees who wish to pursue more than one career opportunity at the same time. In addition, job sharing employees often find that this type of arrangement helps them to cut down on work-related stress and burnout.

Despite its often intimidating nature and the possibility of large-scale confusion, job sharing can also be seen as advantageous and desirable to small business owners and managers. First, there is the simple theory that two or more individual employees can bring a greater variety of abilities to the job than a single employee can. In some instances, job sharing can also lead to extended work days and therefore more productivity without having to pay employees overtime. Employers can also ask job sharers to work more during busy times, therefore eliminating the hassles of having to hire and train temporary employees.

Job sharing can also help to cut back on lost time due to vacations, sick days, and other personal situations that can cause someone to miss a day of work. Job-sharing employees might be more inclined to help work around the schedules of their partners to not only keep the work flowing smoothly, but also to accumulate time for when these type of situations come up for them and require the assistance of the job-share partner to ensure that the job gets done. Finally, because this type of arrangement allows a company to have more employees while not requiring them to be in the office at the same time, it is also an effective way to deal with a lack of office space, which can be a problem for many small businesses.

HOW TO KEEP A SHARED JOB RUNNING SMOOTHLY

Employees who share a job have an arsenal of resources at their disposal to communicate with each other and ensure that the job is getting done. These resources include e-mail, phone and fax messages, checklists, and daily logs.

It is probably in the best interest of small business owners to conduct performance reviews of employees involved in a job sharing program to ensure that things are going smoothly. These reviews can either be individual evaluations of each worker or take the form of a team review. If one person is carrying the weight of the team and the other is not doing their fair share, it is up to management to decide if this is just an isolated problem with that particular team or if the job sharing program is just not a successful one for their business.

If a meeting that is pertinent to the job comes up, the employees and management must decide if both employees should attend or just one. It often helps if the job sharing employees who work on the same days are able to overlap their schedules in order to interact and keep things running as smoothly as possible.

Benefits for employees who participate in jobsharing can be handled in a variety of different ways. Full or partial benefits can be given to the job-sharer according to the specific situation. Benefits such as insurance and pension plans are easier to negotiate and are often prorated. Vacation time, personal and sick days, and even salary can be also be prorated to the amount of time each employee spends on the job. In order to avoid any unwanted difficulties, these issues should be established before the job-sharing program is implemented. A guide or formal contract is suggested to make sure everyone involved understands these issues. Usually job sharing results in a slight increase in benefit costs, mainly in covered statutory benefits like Social Security and employment taxes. Small business owners must decide if the assumed increase in productivity is enough to offset these costs. Since job sharers work fewer hours than typical employees do, overtime pay is rarely an issue in these types of situations.

FURTHER READING:

Laqueur, Maria, and Donna Dickinson. *Breaking Out of 9 to 5: How to Redesign Your Job to Fit You.* 1994.

SEE ALSO: Flexible Work Arrangements

JOB SHOP

A job shop is a type of manufacturing process structure where small batches of a variety of custom products are made. In the job shop process flow, most of the products produced require a unique set-up and sequencing of processing steps. Examples of a job shop include a machine tool shop, a factory machining center, paint shops, a French restaurant, a commercial printing shop, and other manufacturers that make custom products in small lot sizes. Volume and standardization is low and products are often one of a kind.

CHARACTERISTICS OF A JOB SHOP

LAYOUT In the job shop, similar equipment or functions are grouped together, such as all drill presses in one area and grinding machines in another in a process layout. The layout is designed to minimize material handling, cost, and work in process inventories. Job shops use general purpose equipment rather than specialty, dedicated product-specific equipment. Digital numerically controlled equipment is often used to give job shops the flexibility to change set-ups on the various machines very quickly. Job shops compete on quality, speed of product delivery, customization, and new product introduction, but are unlikely to compete on price as few scale economies exist.

ROUTING When an order arrives in the job shop, the part being worked on travels throughout the various areas according to a sequence of operations. Not all jobs will use every machine in the plant. Jobs often travel in a jumbled routing and may return to the same machine for processing several times. This type of layout is also seen in services like department stores or hospitals, where areas are dedicated to one particular product (men's clothing) or one type of service (maternity ward).

EMPLOYEES Employees in a job shop are typically highly skilled craft employees who can operate several different classes of machinery. These workers are paid higher wages for their skill levels. Due to their high skill level, job shop employees need less supervision. Workers may be paid a standard hourly wage or by an incentive system. The role of management is to bid on jobs and to establish prices for customer orders. The key activity in a job shop is processing information.

INFORMATION Information is the most critical aspect of a job shop. Information is needed to quote a price, bid on a job, route an order through the shop, and specify the exact work to be done. Information begins with quoting, then a job sheet and blueprint are prepared before the job is released to the floor. Once on the production floor, employees complete job sheets and time cards for labor cost calculations and to update records for quoting future jobs when variances are present.

While it is often easy to bid on jobs the shop has manufactured before, new jobs require accurate costing of labor, materials, and equipment as well as accurate assigning of overhead to the job. Tickets follow each job through the shop, where time and activities are recorded. Because the job shop makes specialty, custom items, it competes on quality and customer service and not on price. The job shop has little if any raw materials inventory because customers bring in the parts and materials to be worked on. The job shop has work-in-process inventory while jobs are being completed, but typically the customer is waiting on the order and expects prompt delivery, so there is no finished goods inventory in this make-to-order environment. Some job shops, like many small businesses, thrive on managing cash flow. They may work on small jobs to complete them by the end of the month so they can bill customers for the work.

SCHEDULING A job is characterized by its route, its processing requirements, and its priority. In a job shop the mix of products is a key issue in deciding how and when to schedule jobs. Jobs may not be completed based on their arrival pattern in order to minimize costly machine set-ups and change-overs. Work may also be scheduled based on the shortest processing time.

Capacity is difficult to measure in the job shop and depends on lot sizes, the complexity of jobs, the mix of jobs already scheduled, the ability to schedule work well, the number of machines and their condition, the quantity and quality of labor input, and any process improvements.

JOB SHOPS AS AN EARLY FORM OF MANUFACTURING ORGANIZATION

Most manufacturers today began as job shops and grew into the other manufacturing processes as volume allowed. The job shop allows entrepreneurs the most flexibility in making a variety of products to meet customer quality and service standards. As customers request repeat jobs and as volumes grow, the job shop may group machines into work cells to process batches of like jobs.

Job shops are one of the first structures for a manufacturer in the process life cycle. As volume increases and manufacturers reduce or standardize their product offerings, structures change from the job shop to a batch flow to an assembly line and then to a continuous flow. Over the life cycle, flexibility decreases due to high volume and standardization, but unit costs decrease. The job shop is organized by process, where assembly lines or continuous flow operations are organized in a product layout. In the latter layout, equipment or work processes are arranged according to the exact steps in which the product is made and the path for each part resembles a straight line.

FURTHER READING:

Chass, R.B., N.J. Aquilamo, and F.R. Jacobs. *Operations Management for Competitive Advantage.* 9th ed. Burr Ridge, IL: McGraw-Hill Irwin, 2001.

Schmenner, Roger W. *Plant and Service Tours in Operations Management.* Saddle River, NJ: Prentice Hall, 1998.

JOINT VENTURES

A joint venture is a business enterprise undertaken by two or more persons or organizations to share the expense and (hopefully) profit of a particular business project. ''Joint ventures are not business organizations in the sense of proprietorships, partnerships or corporations,'' noted Charles P. Lickson in *A Legal Guide for Small Business.* ''They are agreements between parties or firms for a particular purpose or venture. Their formation may be very informal, such as a handshake and an agreement for two firms to share a booth at a trade show. Other arrangements can be extremely complex, such as the consortium of major U.S. electronics firms to develop new microchips. . . . A joint venture is, in effect, a form of partnership that is limited to a particular purpose.'' Joint ventures have grown in popularity in recent years, despite the relatively high failure rate of such efforts for one reason or another. Creative small business owners have been able to use this business strategy to good advantage over the years, although the practice remains one primarily associated with larger corporations.

Most joint ventures are formed for the ultimate purpose of saving money. This is as true of small neighborhood stores that agree to advertise jointly in the weekly paper as it is of international oil companies that agree to work together for purposes of oil and gas exploration or extraction. Joint ventures are attractive because they enable companies to share both risks and costs.

TYPES OF JOINT VENTURES Equity-based joint ventures benefit foreign and/or local private interests, groups of interests, or members of the general public. Under non-equity joint ventures (also known as cooperative agreements), meanwhile, the parties seek technical service arrangements, franchise and brand use agreements, management contracts, rental agreements, or one-time contracts, e.g., for construction projects. Participants do not always furnish capital as part of their joint venture commitments. There are, for example, non-equity arrangements in which some companies are more in need of technical services or technological expertise than they are capital. They may want to modernize operations or start new production operations. Thus, they limit partners' participation to technical assistance. Such arrangements often include some funding as well, albeit limited.

LEGAL STRUCTURE OF JOINT VENTURES

As Lickson observed in *A Legal Guide for Small Business,* joint ventures are governed entirely by the legal agreement that brought them into existence. "Unless the joint venture is formalized by creation of a corporation or partnership, it never ripens into a tax-paying, legal entity on its own. Instead, the joint venture functions through the legal status of the venture participants, known as co-venturers or venture partners," Lickson wrote. "Since the joint venture is not a legal entity on its own, it does not hire people, enter into contracts, or have its own tax liabilities. These matters are handled through the co-venturers. Corporate law, partnership law, and the law of sole proprietorship do not govern joint ventures; contract law governs joint ventures." And as Marc J. Lane noted in the *Legal Handbook for Small Business,* "since the venture ends at the conclusion of a specific project, issues of continuity of life and free transferability become moot."

WHY JOINT VENTURES FAIL

Small business owners should not engage in joint ventures without adequate planning and strategy. They cannot afford to, since the ultimate goal of joint ventures is the same as it is for any type of business operation: to make a profit. Experience dictates that both parties in a joint venture should know exactly what they wish to derive from their partnership. There must be an agreement before the partnership becomes a reality. There must also be a firm commitment on the part of each member to the project and to one another. One of the leading causes for the failure of joint ventures is that some participants do not reveal their true business agendas, or mislead their partners about their ability to uphold their agreed-upon responsibilities.

Many small business consultants counsel clients to approach joint ventures cautiously. They acknowledge that such partnerships can be most valuable in nourishing a company's growth and stability, but also point out that smaller businesses usually have far less margin for error than do multinational corporations, or even mid-sized companies. Some experts recommend that business owners considering a joint venture with another establishment (or establishments) launch a small joint venture first. Such small projects allow companies to test the relationship without committing large amounts of money. This is especially true when companies with different structures, corporate cultures, and strategic plans work together. Such differences are difficult to overcome and frequently lead to failure. That is why a "courtship" is beneficial to joint venture participants.

Other factors that can have a debilitating impact on joint ventures include marketplace developments, lagging technology, partner's inability (rather than reluctance or refusal) to honor their contractual obligations, and regulatory uncertainties. Another problem with joint ventures concerns the issue of management. The managers of one company may be more adept and/or decisive with their decisionmaking than their counterparts at the other company. This can lead to friction and a lack of cooperation. Projects are doomed to failure if there is not a well-defined decisionmaking process in place that is predicated on mutually recognized goals and strategies.

BENEFITS OF JOINT VENTURES

Among the most significant benefits derived from joint ventures is that partners save money and reduce their risks through capital and resource sharing. Joint ventures also give smaller companies the chance to work with larger ones to develop, manufacture, and market new products. They also give companies of all sizes the opportunity to increase sales, gain access to wider markets, and enhance technological capabilities through research and development (R&D) underwritten by more than one party. Until relatively recently, U.S. companies were often reluctant to engage in research and development partnerships, and government agencies tried not to become involved in business development. However, with the emergence of countries that feature technologically advanced industries (such as electronics or computer microchips) supported extensively by government funding, American companies have become more willing to participate in joint ventures in these areas. In addition, both federal and state agencies have become more generous with their financial support in these areas. Government's increased involvement in the private business environment has created more opportunities for companies to engage in domestic and international joint ventures.

FURTHER READING:

Johnson, Howard E. "Reducing the Risks in Joint Ventures." *CMA Management.* December 2000.

Lane, Marc J. *Legal Handbook for Small Business.* AMACOM, 1989.

Lickson, Charles P. *A Legal Guide for Small Business.* Crisp Publications, 1994.

Lynch, Robert Porter, *The Practical Guide to Joint Ventures & Corporate Alliances.* John Wiley and Sons, 1989.

Moeller, Bud. ''Becoming a Corporate 'Partner of Choice.' '' *Corporate Board.* November 2000.

Nueno, Pedro. ''Alliances and Other Things.'' *R&D Management.* October 1999.

K

A Keogh Plan is an employer-funded, tax-deferred retirement plan designed for unincorporated businesses or self-employed persons, including those who earn only part of their income from self-employment. Covered under Section 401(c) of the tax code, Keogh plans are named after Eugene Keogh, the congressman who first came up with the idea. Keogh plans feature relatively high allowable contributions—25 percent of salary to a maximum of $30,000 annually, in some cases—which makes them popular among sole proprietors and small businesses with high incomes. In general, however, Keoghs are more costly to set up and administer than similar retirement programs, such as Simplified Employee Pension (SEP) plans, because they require annual preparation and filing of IRS Form 5500. This long and complicated document usually requires a small business to obtain the services of an accountant or financial advisor. In addition, financial information becomes available to the public under Keogh Plans.

As is the case with other common types of retirement programs, Keogh contributions made on employees' behalf are tax-deductible for the employer, and the funds are allowed to grow tax-deferred until the employee withdraws them upon retirement. The funds held in a Keogh may be invested in certificates of deposit, mutual funds, stocks, bonds, annuities, or some combination thereof. Withdrawals are not permitted until after the employee has reached age 59 ½, or else the amount withdrawn is subject to a 10 percent penalty in addition to regular income taxes. Usually only the employer may contribute to a Keogh plan. In addition, the employer can establish a vesting schedule through which employees gradually gain full rights to the funds in their accounts over a number of years. Keogh accounts must be opened by December 31 in order to qualify for tax deductions in a given year, but funds can be contributed until the company's tax deadline.

TYPES OF KEOGH PLANS

Keogh plans can be structured in a number of ways. Although it is possible to design a Keogh as a defined benefit plan (which determines a fixed amount of benefit to be paid upon retirement, then uses an actuarial formula to calculate the annual contribution required to provide that benefit), most Keoghs take the form of a defined contribution plan (which determines an amount of annual contribution without regard to the total benefit that will be available upon retirement). The three most common types of Keoghs are profit-sharing, money purchase, and combination plans—all of which fall under the category of defined contribution plans.

Profit-sharing Keoghs are the most flexible, allowing the employer to make larger contributions in good financial years and skip contributions in lean years. This type of plan enables the employer to contribute a maximum of 15 percent of compensation, or $22,500 per employee, annually. In contrast, money purchase Keoghs are highly restrictive, requiring the employer to make a mandatory annual contribution of a predetermined percentage of compensation. For this reason, many smaller businesses or those with variable levels of income shy away from this type of plan. On the positive side, money purchase Keoghs allow the highest possible contribution—25 percent of compensation, to a maximum of $30,000 per employee, annually. Combination Keogh plans, as the name suggests, blend some of the features of the other two primary types. Combination plans allow the employer to designate a fixed percentage of mandatory annual contribution, then supplement this amount with additional, discretionary contributions in years when profit levels are high. The total annual contributions in a combination plan cannot exceed 25 percent of compensation or $30,000.

Though Keoghs give small business owners valuable tax deductions and enable them to provide a valuable benefit to their employees, the plans also have some disadvantages. Business owners who employ other people are required to fund a retirement program for nonowner employees if they establish one for themselves. But because the owner's contributions to his or her own plan are based upon the net income of the business—from which self-employment taxes and contributions to employees' retirement accounts have already been deducted—the owner's allowable contributions are reduced. In the case of a money purchase or combination Keogh plan, for example, the business owner is only able to contribute 20 percent (rather than 25 percent) to his or her own retirement fund. But many companies find that the benefits of Keogh plans outweigh the drawbacks. Small businesses that offer such plans can use them to attract potential employees and deter current employees from leaving the company to work for a larger competitor. With their high allowable contribution levels, Keogh plans also give the business owner a good opportunity to achieve a financially secure retirement.

FURTHER READING:

Blakely, Stephen. ''Pension Power.'' *Nation's Business.* July 1997.

Crouch, Holmes F. *Decisions When Retiring.* Allyear Tax Guides, 1995.

Jones, Sally M. ''Maximizing Deductible Contributions to a One-Participant Retirement Plan.'' *The Journal of Taxation.* February 1998.

Nadel, Alan A. ''Self-Employment Tax Treatment of Keogh and SEP Contributions and Unreimbursed Business Expenses.'' *The Tax Adviser.* November 1995.

Pedace, Frank Jr. ''Keoghs: Unlocking the Key to Retirement Planning.'' *Air Conditioning, Heating and Refrigeration News.* September 16, 1996.

SEE ALSO: Retirement Planning

L

LABOR SURPLUS AREA

A labor surplus area is an economic region in which the number of prospective—and qualified—employees for positions with a company or companies exceeds the number of jobs available. This state of affairs can be an important component in business success, for businesses operating in labor surplus areas can typically find the personnel they need to conduct their operations at lower payroll expense than can businesses that may have to offer more generous compensation packages to secure even mediocre employees. "Although many factors relating to labor are essential, with respect to location decisions, the primary factor is the availability of labor in the region," confirmed Howard Weiss and Mark Gershon in *Production and Operations Management.* "Typically, a company wants to see a high ratio between the number of potential employees and the number of jobs available. The reason for this is twofold. First, this gives the company a large pool of applicants to screen, allowing the company to be selective in hiring those it feels will best fits its needs, which leads to a productive work force. In addition, if there is competition for the positions due to the large labor pool, there will be less chance of the company's losing workers. Second, typically, a company does not want a region to be dependent on it. If most workers in the region depend on Company X and the company then moves or goes out of business, the entire region will be affected adversely, which reflects poorly on the company."

Business experts note, however, that a true labor surplus does not truly exist unless there exists a surplus of prospective employees who possess the necessary skills, background, and experience to handle the responsibilities of the jobs that need to be filled. While some companies engage in industries that require only semiskilled or unskilled labor, others—such as high technology companies—rely on a highly educated and skilled work force. Such a business may be located in a region in which large numbers of people are looking for employment, but unless those people also have the necessary training and skills to meet the company's needs, the business is not operating in a true labor surplus environment.

Many analysts and business consultants point out that the labor availability disparities that are evident in certain industries will continue to exist—and possibly widen—over the next few years. Some manufacturing and technology sectors, for example, are expected to operate with periodic shortages of labor talent for the next several years; this partially accounts for the high salary levels that skilled practitioners in these areas can currently command. But other geographic and industry sectors are expected to be able to take advantage of labor surpluses, and many observers contend that the current tight labor market that some industries are experiencing will ease in the coming years. "The labor force will grow in number for the next few years," predicted Anne Fisher in *Fortune.* "More people will be more highly educated than ever before. Market forces will kick in—albeit gradually—and guide people toward the growing number of high-skilled jobs that pay above-average wages. And, perhaps most important, employers will wake up" and recognize the importance of training their current work force. Fisher cited the growing number of "retirement-age" people staying in the work force, the dramatic growth in continuing education among adults, and the computer-literate character of today's youth as evidence of possible future labor surpluses in high-skilled industry areas.

FURTHER READING:

Edmondson, Brad. "Work Slowdown." *American Demographics.* March 1996.

Fisher, Anne. "What Labor Shortage?" *Fortune.* June 23, 1997.

Fullerton, Howard N., Jr. "Labor Force 2006: Slowing Down and Changing Composition." *Monthly Labor Review.* November 1997.

Henricks, Mark. "Labor Pains." *Entrepreneur.* April 1998.

Lyne, Jack. "The Skills Gap: U.S. Work-Force Woes Complicate Business-Location Equation." *Site Selection.* August 1992.

"Scientists, Engineers—Shortage or Surplus?" *Research-Technology Management.* July-August 1996.

Weiss, Howard J., and Mark E. Gershon. *Production and Operations Management.* Boston: Allyn and Bacon, 1989.

LABOR UNIONS

A labor union is an organization of wage earners or salary workers established for the purpose of protecting their collective interests when dealing with employers. Though unions are prevalent in most industrialized countries, union representation of workers has generally declined in most countries over the past 30 to 40 years. In the United States, unions represented about one-third of all workers in the 1950s. Today, unions represent less than 15 percent of the labor force—and less than 10 percent of the labor force in the private sector (unions represented between 35-40 percent of public-sector workers in the late 1990s). But although labor unions are not as strong a force in the United States economy as they have been in earlier decades, they continue to be an important factor in American business.

TYPES OF UNIONS

Unions can be categorized according to ideology and organizational forms. A distinction is often made between political unionism and business unionism. Although the goals and objectives of politically oriented unions may overlap those of business unions, political unions are primarily related to some larger working-class movement. Most political unions have some formal association with a working-class political party; these types of unions are more prevalent in Europe than they are in the United States. Contemporary American labor unions are best viewed as business unions. Business unions generally support the capitalist economic system and focus their attention on protecting and enhancing the economic welfare of the workers they represent, usually through some

form of collective bargaining. According to U.S. law, unions can bargain with employers over wages, hours, and working conditions.

But while most American unions are classified as business rather than political unions, U.S. business unions often do have some involvement in nation's politics. Most large national unions are involved in lobbying and electoral activities at various levels of government, including the national level. However, such political efforts serve to supplement their principal economic goals. For example, many unions campaigned against passage of the North American Free Trade Agreement (NAFTA). The labor movement feared that NAFTA would undercut jobs of union workers and weaken the ability of unions to negotiate favorable contracts with employers.

The earliest unions in the United States were known as craft unions. Craft unions represent employees in a single occupation or group of closely related occupations. The members of craft unions are generally highly skilled workers. Examples of craft unions include the various skilled trades in the construction industry, such as carpentry, plumbing, and electrical work. Craft unions are most common in occupations in which employees frequently switch employers. A construction worker is usually hired to complete work at a specific job site and then moves on to work elsewhere (often for another employer). In addition to collective bargaining, craft unions often serve as a placement service for members. Employers contact the union's hiring hall and union members currently out of work are referred to the job.

Closely related to craft unions, though distinct in many respects, are professional unions. A professional is generally understood to be an employee with advanced and highly specialized skills, often requiring some credentials, such as a college degree and/or a license. Professional unions are much more recent than craft unions and are most common in the public sector. Teacher's unions are one of the most visible examples of this kind of union.

Most unionized workers in the United States belong to industrial unions. An industrial union represents workers across a wide range of occupations within one or more industries. A good example of a typical industrial union is the United Automobile Workers (UAW). It represents skilled craft workers, assembly-line workers, and unskilled workers in all of the major American automobile companies. The UAW negotiates separate contracts for workers in each of these companies. Although most industrial unions began by organizing workers in a single industry or group of related industries, most have diversified over the past 30 to 40 years. For example, the UAW also represents workers in the tractor and earth-moving equipment industry (e.g., Caterpillar and John

Deere) and in the aerospace industry (e.g., Boeing), and in the late 1990s it added such disparate groups as the Graphics Artists Guild (3,000 members), the National Writers Union (5,000 members), and various service, technical, and graduate student employees at more than 20 colleges and universities across the country. In addition, the UAW and other national unions have increasingly sought to expand their influence into emerging high-tech sectors of the economy.

Another organizational form is the general union. General unions organize workers across all occupations and industries. Although some highly diversified unions, such as the Teamsters, may appear to be general unions at first glance, this form of organization does not really exist in the United States. Because they are typically politically oriented, general unions are more common in Europe and developing countries.

OPEN SHOP AND CLOSED SHOP The term ''open shop'' refers to a company policy that does not restrict the business's employee work force to union members. ''Closed shop,'' on the other hand, refers to a company that hires only union members. Under this latter arrangement, employees are required to join the existing union within a specified time after they have been hired.

UNION GROWTH AND DECLINE

Union membership in the United States has varied considerably throughout the country's history. Although unions have been in existence in some form in the United States for nearly 200 years, they did not attain any meaningful level of power and influence until the 1930s, when several factors combined to spur a dramatic rise in union growth (the unionization rate went from about 12 percent of the labor force in 1935 to between 32 percent and 35 percent in the mid-1950s):

1) The American economy shifted from an agricultural to an industrial base; industrial workers, who were concentrated in urban areas and increasingly shared the same language (English), were thus able to create a common culture that was absent among earlier generations of workers.

2) The Depression created a backlash against big business entities, who were viewed as the chief culprits for the country's economic difficulties.

3) Changing political dynamics also played an important role. Active support for organized labor was an integral part of Roosevelt's New Deal, and the passage of the National Labor Relations Act (NLRA) in 1935 was a potent new weapon for union organizers.

The NLRA provided a means for official recognition of labor unions. Once recognized, an employer was legally bound to bargain with the union, enforceable by government action.

4) Economic growth during World War II and in the post-war era was an important facilitator of union growth.

By the mid-1950s, the most union-prone sectors of the American economy had largely been organized, and millions of workers saw improvements in their living standards as a direct result of union activity. Many economists observed that this rise in union fortunes helped non-union workers as well. ''Collective bargaining has significantly improved the wages and working conditions of unionized and nonunionized workers,'' contended Levitan, Carlson, and Shapiro in *Protecting America's Workers*. ''Other benefits of union representation include increased leisure, better medical coverage, and more secure pensions. . . . Finally, unions have helped nonunion workers by lobbying for legislation that grants all workers such protections as equal employment, safe and healthy workplaces, and secure pensions.''

Unions maintained their strength at around one-third of the labor force until about 1960. Union membership declined gradually, decreasing to about 25 percent of the labor force in the mid-1970s. The rate of decline was much sharper in the 1980s, and by the year 2000 private sector union membership had declined to less than 10 percent of the total.

Factors often cited for the decline in union membership include the following:

- Changing nature of the global economy. International competition has increased significantly over the past few generations, especially in sectors of the economy that were heavily unionized (e.g., automobiles, steel, and textiles). As these industries became more competitive globally, employer resistance to unions often increased. In addition, it became feasible for employers to relocate production facilities to areas of the country which have traditionally been less supportive of unionism (such as the southern and Mountain states) or overseas to less developed countries that have low wages and few unions. Finally, employment in traditionally nonunion industries expanded, while employment in heavily unionized sectors declined.

- Shifting demographics of the labor force. In the 1930s, ''blue collar'' workers represented a large proportion of the labor force. Now ''white collar'' workers (i.e., managers, professionals, and clericals) are a very large component of the labor force. Historically, white collar workers have been more difficult to organize (except in the public sector).

- Changing attitudes of government. As early as 1947, amendments were added to the NLRA that significantly expanded employer rights and limited the rights of unions. The best-known of these laws was the Taft-Hartley Act. Moreover, appointees to the National Labor Relations Board, which enforces the NLRA, became more promanagement in outlook during the 1970s and early 1980s. This trend, however, was slowed—and in some areas reversed—during the generally union-friendly Clinton administration (1993-2001).

- Growing public and management perceptions that some union demands and attitudes were unreasonable.

- Ineffective union organization efforts, despite continued belief in the legitimacy of labor unions among the American workforce.. ''Labor leaders are partly to blame for the disconnect between pro-union sentiment and dwindling membership,'' charged *Business Week*. ''For decades, they have focused on preserving jobs rather than organizing the fastest-growing parts of the economy, such as services and high tech.''

By the mid-1990s, however, there were indications that America's leading unions had adopted more proactive measures in order to shore up existing membership and expand the presence of unions into high-tech ''New Economy'' sectors and other areas. This ''revival'' of organized labor, as some observers have dubbed it, is being studied closely by all sectors of American business and academia.

INDUSTRIES FEATURING STRONG UNION PRESENCE

Unions have traditionally been strong in four sectors of the American economy: manufacturing, mining, construction, and transportation. They have lost substantial ground in all four of these sectors in the last few decades, however. In the transportation sector, an important factor has been deregulation, particularly in the trucking and airline industries. Substantial increases in competition in those industries have made it difficult for unions to negotiate favorable contracts or organize new units. In construction, the growth of nonunion contractors, able to hire qualified workers outside of the union hiring hall system, undercut union contractors. At one time, more than 80 percent of all commercial construction in the United

States had been unionized; today, however, the percentage of workers engaged in construction that belong to unions is a fraction of that. Foreign competition, technological change, and played-out mines, meanwhile, have all weakened mining unions. In manufacturing, the whole range of factors previously discussed has been responsible for union decline. The only sector of the economy where unions have gained strength in recent years has been public employment. In the late 1990s, almost 40 percent of public employees at all levels of government—local, state, and federal—were unionized.

INTERNAL STRUCTURE AND ADMINISTRATION

Labor unions are complex and vary considerably with respect to internal structure and administrative processes. It is easiest to differentiate among three distinct levels within the labor movement: local unions, national unions, and federations.

LOCAL UNIONS Local unions are the building blocks of the labor movement. Although there are some free-standing local unions, the vast majority of locals are in some way affiliated with a national or international union. Most craft unions began as local unions, which then joined together to form national organizations. Some major industrial unions also began as amalgamations of local unions, though it was generally more common for national organizations to be formed first, with locals to be established later.

The duties of a local union almost always include the administration of a union contract, which means assuring that the employer is honoring all of the provisions of the contract at the local level. In some instances, local unions might also negotiate contracts, although unions vary considerably in terms of the degree to which the parent union is involved in the negotiation process.

Another important function of the local union is servicing the needs of those represented by the union. If a worker represented by the union believes his or her rights under the union contract have been violated, then the union may intervene on that person's behalf. Examples of such situations include the discharge of an employee, failure to promote an employee according to a contract seniority clause, or failure to pay an employee for overtime. Virtually any provision of a contract can become a source of contention. The local union may try to settle the issue informally. If that effort is not successful, the union may file what is known as a *grievance*. This is a formal statement of the dispute with the employer; most contracts set forth a grievance procedure. In general, grievance procedures involve several different steps, with higher levels of management entering at each step. If the grievance cannot be settled through this mechanism, then the union may, if the contract allows, request a hearing before a neutral arbitrator, whose decision is final and binding.

Most craft unions have *apprenticeship programs* to train new workers in the craft. The local union, usually in cooperation with an employers' association, will be responsible for managing the apprenticeship program. In addition, local unions with hiring halls are responsible for making job referrals.

The jurisdiction of a local union depends to a large extent on the organizational form of the parent organization. Locals of industrial unions most often represent workers within a single plant or facility of a company (and thus are termed *plant locals*). For example, in the case of the UAW, each factory or production facility of each automobile manufacturer has a separate local union. In some instances, a factory may be so big that it requires more than a single local, but this is not usually the case.

In contrast to plant locals, local craft unions (as well as some industrial unions) are best described as *area locals*. An area local represents all of a union's members in a particular geographical region and may deal with many different employers. Area locals are typically formed for one of two reasons. First, members may in the course of a year work for a number of different employers, as in the case of craft unions. Consequently, it would be difficult, if not impossible, to establish and maintain a separate local in each work location. Second, members may work continuously for a single employer, but each employer or location may be too small to justify a separate local union. The latter case is more typical of some industrial unions. The size of the region served by a local union depends on the number of members available. In large metropolitan areas, an area local might serve only members in a particular city. In less densely populated regions, an area local may have a jurisdiction that covers an entire state.

Internal structures and administrative procedures differ between plant and area locals. In almost all local unions, the membership meeting represents the apex of power, as the officers of the union are accountable to the members much as the officers of a corporation are accountable to stockholders. However, in practice, membership participation in union affairs may be quite limited. In such instances, local union officers often enjoy considerable power.

Plant locals have a number of elected officials—usually a president, vice president, secretary, and treasurer. In almost all cases, the officers are full-time employees of the company the union represents, and the contract generally allows some release time for union affairs. In addition to the principal officers of the local, there are also a number of *stewards*. Stewards may be elected or appointed, depending upon the union. The steward serves as the everyday contact between the union and its rank-and-file members. If members have concerns about the affairs of the union, these may be voiced to the steward. The steward's most important responsibility is handling grievances. Should a worker represented by the union have a dispute with the employer over his or her rights under the contract, the steward has the initial responsibility of representing the worker. Usually the steward will discuss the matter with the employee's supervisor to see if the dispute can be resolved. If not, then a formal grievance may be filed, and it then proceeds through the grievance system. At higher levels in the grievance system the employee may be represented by a chief steward or union officers.

Area locals typically have more complex internal structures than plant locals. This is usually because of the large geographical region under the local's jurisdiction, along with the greater dispersion of members within the region. As in the case of plant locals, area locals hold periodic meetings in which the officials of the union are accountable to members. There are also elected officers in area locals, as well as stewards for the various work sites in the local's jurisdiction. The principal difference between a plant local and an area local is that the latter typically employs one or more full-time staff members to handle the affairs of the union on a daily basis. These staff members are usually called *business agents*. Given the dispersion of members over a large geographical area and the possibility that the local may be responsible for administering many different contracts, it is the business agent's responsibility to visit work sites regularly and deal with problems that may arise. The business agent may also be responsible for managing any apprenticeship programs and the union's hiring hall. Contracts are often negotiated directly by local unions and the business agents are usually responsible for these negotiations. In some unions, elected officers may serve as business agents, but normally business agents are separate staff members. Depending on the size of the local union, there may be a number of assistant business agents.

NATIONAL UNIONS National unions are composed of the various local unions that they have chartered. Some unions have locals in Canada and therefore call themselves *international* unions. However, the terms *international union* and *national union* are generally used interchangeably.

As with local unions, the administrative structures of national unions vary considerably in complexity. One important factor is the size of the union: larger unions are structurally more complex. Structural complexity also differs between craft and industrial unions. Craft unions tend be smaller organizations that feature a decentralized decision-making structure. With craft unions, contracts usually have a limited geographical scope and are negotiated by local unions. The parent union can be of significant assistance, however. The national union pools the resources of local unions, thus helping out with things such as strike funds, and it may also provide research services and serve as the local union's voice in political matters at the national and state levels. In general, there are few intermediate units between the national office and the local craft unions. National officers, elected periodically, generally work on a full-time basis for the union. Such unions also hold national conventions, most often every couple of years. The officers of the national union are accountable to the convention, much as the officers of a local are accountable to membership meetings.

National industrial unions are typically more complex. They tend to be larger and have a more heterogeneous membership than craft unions (both in terms of skills and demographic traits). Although there are exceptions, contracts in industrial unions tend to be negotiated primarily by staff members from the national office. In many cases, the bargaining unit will include all locals from a particular company (across the entire country). Even if contracts are negotiated by locals, representatives from the national union will often participate in talks to assure that the contract conforms to patterns established by the national organization.

As with craft unions, national unions have periodic conventions and national officers. Depending on the union, the national officers may be elected directly by rank-and-file members or by some other body (such as convention delegates). National unions generally have a substantial paid staff who provide a variety of different services (e.g., research, legal representation, organizing new members, negotiating contracts, and servicing locals). National unions may also have one or more layers of hierarchy between the local unions and the national offices. For example, in the case of the UAW, there are different divisions responsible for the major industries in which that union represents workers. Within the automobile industry, there are divisions that correspond to each of the major manufacturers. There are other divisions that deal with the needs of special groups within the union (such as minority workers and skilled craft workers). Consequently, the structures of large industrial unions are often as complex as the companies with which they deal.

FEDERATIONS A federation is an association of unions. It is not a union in the usual sense of the term. Rather, it provides a range of services to affiliated unions, much as an organization such as the National Association of Manufacturers provides services to its member firms.

FURTHER READING:

''All's Not Fair in Labor Wars.'' *Business Week.* July 19, 1999.

Dole, Carol. ''The Effect of Unions on Hours and Employment.'' *Atlantic Economic Journal.* June 1998.

Lawler, J.J. *Unionization and Deunionization: Strategy, Tactics, and Outcomes.* Columbia, SC: University of South Carolina Press, 1990.

Levitan, Sar A., Peter E. Carlson, and Isaac Shapiro. *Protecting American Workers: An Assessment of Government Programs.* Washington, DC: Bureau of National Affairs, 1986.

Mills, Daniel Quinn. *Labor-Management Relations.* 5th ed., New York: McGraw-Hill, 1994.

Trombly, Maria, and Kathleen Ohlson. ''Unions Take Aim at High-Tech Workers.'' *Computerworld.* August 14, 2000.

Troy, Leo. ''Beyond Unions and Collective Bargaining.'' *WorkingUSA.* January/February 2000.

Troy, Leo. ''Why Labor Unions are Declining.'' *Journal of Commerce and Commercial.* September 1, 1994.

''Unions and Strikers: A Huge Nonproblem.'' *Fortune.* May 31, 1993.

Worsham, James. ''Labor's New Assault.'' *Nation's Business.* June 1997.

LABOR UNIONS AND SMALL BUSINESS

Labor unions are commonly associated with big business and giant industries, but many small business owners find that unions are not limited to the government sector or to corporate behemoths such as General Motors, UPS, and Boeing. Labor unions are not as powerful or as plentiful as they were a few generations ago. But they remain a vital component of the American business landscape, and many small businesses rely on union employees for their operations. Indeed, all small business owners who employ workers should have a basic familiarity with the fundamentals of U.S. labor laws, since they offer protections to union and nonunion employees alike.

The likelihood that a small business will employ a unionized work force is predicated on a wide range of factors, including industry, geographic location, traditional strength of union presence, and the nature of the work involved. A Midwest-based business involved in the transportation industry, for example, is more likely to utilize union employees than a restaurant nestled in the heart of the traditionally non-union American South.

But whether the business is unionized or not, owners must recognize that they and their employees are, to some degree, destined to exist in what Marc J. Lane, author of *Legal Handbook for Small Business,* characterized as a state of conflict. ''You and your co-owners . . . are dedicated to effecting cost economies wherever you can, and, as owners of capital, you may claim both the right and the obligation to decide how best to use that capital,'' wrote Lane. ''Your rank-and-file employees, on the other hand, are striving for the best compensation package and working conditions they can, and, since their jobs may be lost to business reverses, they may feel that they are entitled to have some influence on decisions.'' It is this desire for compensation and influence that are the underpinnings of labor unions' attraction, for as Lane noted, ''generally speaking, no one employee can usurp managerial authority, but a united organization of employees can effectively bargain with employers to gain a major role in business decision making.''

CORNERSTONES OF LABOR LAW

Hundreds of U.S. laws have some bearing on employee and employer rights and obligations in one area or another, but experts agree that six cornerstones of American labor law are the National Labor Relations Act of 1935 (NLRA), the Labor Management Relations Act of 1947 (LMRA), the Fair Labor Standards Act of 1938 (FLSA), the Labor-Management Reporting and Disclosure Act of 1959 (LMRDA), the Civil Rights Act of 1964, and the Occupational Safety and Health Act of 1970.

THE NATIONAL LABOR RELATIONS ACT This act, which created the National Labor Relations Board (NLRB), gives employees the right to organize and bargain collectively with their employers—in essence, it gives them the right to unionize. Importantly, it also confers legal protection on employees who try to organize their fellow workers into a union. It is worth noting, however, that this legislation also protects nonunion employees from being forced or otherwise coerced into joining a labor organization or engaging in collective bargaining. The act ensures that employees can choose their own representatives for the purpose of collective bargaining, establishes procedures for secret-ballot elections, and defines unfair labor practices, to which both employers and unions are subject. This law is also known as the Wagner Act.

LABOR MANAGEMENT RELATIONS ACT Also known as the Taft-Hartley Act, this legislation amended the National Labor Relations Act in ways that are generally thought to benefit business owners and management. While it forbade businesses from launching unwarranted or sudden lockouts of union employees, it also imposed restrictions on some union activities in the areas of organizing, picketing, striking, and other activities. It also outlawed the ''closed shop'' (which required that employers hire only union members) and gave the government the power to obtain injunctions against strikes that ''will imperil the national health or safety'' if they take place or continue.

FAIR LABOR STANDARDS ACT This act, also known as the Wage-Hour Act, ''establishes fair labor standards in employments in and affecting interstate commerce, and for other purposes,'' wrote Donald Weiss in *Fair, Square, and Legal.* ''It protects all workers, including children and women, by establishing minimum hourly wages and distinguishing between nonexempt employees (those to whom you must pay overtime for hours in excess of forty hours a week) and exempt (those to whom you do not have to pay overtime).'' Weiss noted that many employers view this law as pro-worker, but he added that the Act does provide employers with a significant freedom to shape ''specific forms of compensation or benefits not covered by the law,'' including gifts, special bonuses, travel and other reimbursable expenses, retirement/pension plans, and insurance plans.

LABOR-MANAGEMENT REPORTING AND DISCLOSURE ACT The Landrum-Griffin Act, as this legislation is sometimes known, was in large measure shaped to regulate the internal affairs of unions and to provide additional safeguards to ensure that the rules laid out in the Labor Management Relations Act of 1947 were adhered to.

CIVIL RIGHTS ACT OF 1964 This landmark legislation prohibited employers from discriminating in their hiring practices on the basis of race, religious beliefs, gender, or natural origin.

OCCUPATIONAL SAFETY AND HEALTH ACT OF 1970 This legislation, which created the Occupational Safety and Health Administration (OSHA) established guidelines and regulations to make workplaces safer and healthier for employees. ''Each employer shall furnish to each of his employees employment and a place of employment which are free from recognized hazards that are causing or are likely to cause death or serious physical harm to his [or her] employees,'' read one portion of the Act.

UNION ORGANIZATION EFFORTS AND THE SMALL BUSINESS OWNER

''If workers exercise their right to organize, employers should know what their rights are,'' wrote Harrison G. Darby and Margaret R. Bryant in *HRMagazine.* Indeed, some analysts believe that smaller business establishments may be more likely to encounter union organizing activities in the late 1990s than in previous years, given the AFL-CIO's stated intentions of approaching the work forces of smaller firms with greater zeal.

Historically, most business owners have not greeted unions with open arms because of concerns about their impact on bottom-line profitability and operational control. This viewpoint remains prevalent today, which has led consultants to make a number of recommendations to small- and mid-sized business owners hoping to ward off union organizers. "Employers need to make preparations now—before there are any signs of union activity—and teach their managers how to immediately and lawfully respond to union organizing efforts," wrote Darby and Bryant. "As union leaders commit serious money, time, and attention to organizing new members, employers should heed any warning signs and take steps to prepare for a union campaign. The best preparation is to anticipate issues that a union would be likely to raise and minimize the potential for union support. By identifying and correcting vulnerabilities, employers can blunt the edge of a union's strategy."

Darby and Bryant also noted that there are certain solicitation and distribution rules that union organizers and supporters must adhere to, but they added that such rules "must be promulgated before the start of union activity to avoid a charge of unlawful retaliation." These rules include bans on union literature, restrictions on internal efforts to convince employees to sign union authorization cards, and prohibitions expressly forbidding outside organizers from any activity on company property.

UNIONIZATION BIDS AND POSSIBLE MANAGEMENT RESPONSES If a union is able to garner sufficient interest from a business's employees (30 percent of the work force is a rule of thumb), then it may petition the National Labor Relations Board for an election by secret ballot to determine whether the work force will join the union in question (a 50 percent response may result in union recognition even without the holding of an election). Writing in the *Legal Handbook for Small Business*, Lane indicated that "if you [the small business owner] and your lawyer have any reasonable doubt that the union is the collective bargaining choice of a majority of the workers in a legally organizable bargaining unit, he will draft a refusal to recognize the union. Although your refusal to recognize a union that legitimately represents a majority can lead to later charges of unfair labor practices, recognizing a union that does not represent the majority is also illegal. When in doubt, opt for the refusal and let the NLRB conduct a secret election to determine the union's true status."

In instances where an agreement is made to hold a union election, consultants note that anti-union business owners do have certain rights to make their case to the workers in their employ, provided that they do not violate any laws. "Be careful to avoid any unfair tactics," wrote Lane. "Improper conduct can induce the NLRB to set aside a management victory; and your repeated violations of the National Labor Relations Act can force union recognition even without an election." Darby and Bryant point out that according to U.S. labor law, "management personnel have the right to express their views on unionization when answering questions or making statements about the union, its supporters, or its campaign communications. . . . [But] despite this broad right to free expression, managers and supervisors must never threaten or interrogate employees, promise them benefits or improved working conditions, or place employees' union activities under surveillance." Other tactics held to be unfair, said Lane, include the following:

- Polling employees about their attitudes toward the proposed union.

- Threatening or otherwise implying that a union victory will spell a loss of employment or benefits.

- Withholding of employee names and addresses from union organizers once an election agreement has been made.

- Visiting employees at their homes to lobby against the union.

- Unequal application of rules about solicitation on company grounds and company time (regarding pro- and anti-union forces).

- Favoritism toward antiunion employees.

- Discrimination against prounion workers.

In the weeks leading up to a union election, small business owners may also communicate the advantages of the current non-union arrangement with their employees, provided they do so in a lawful manner. Lane pointed to several factors that might be used to the owner's advantage (provided, of course, that they actually exist in the business):

- Delineation of current benefits enjoyed by workers.

- Advantages of "one-to-one" interactions between employees and owners/managers.

- Highlight areas in which employees' wages, benefits, and working conditions are already above the norm.

- Highlight aspects of unions that might not be as palatable to some members of the work force, such as seniority systems that are sometimes interpreted as penalizing younger, ambitious employees.

- Explain that signing an authorization card does not mean that the employee has to vote for unionization.

- Explain the various difficulties associated with decertifying a union if the workers become unhappy with it.

- Maintain a high level of integrity in addressing various issues associated with unions. "Correct any rumors, misrepresentations, or distortions of fact with clear rebuttals,'' counseled Lane.

DEALING WITH ELECTION OUTCOMES Once the NLRB-supervised election has been held, the small business owner is confronted with one of two outcomes, each of which come with their own unique challenges. The outcome that most small businesses would prefer to deal with is a management victory in which the union organization effort is defeated. But even in this situation, management will likely have to deal with disappointed employees who had hoped for unionization and the lingering residue of what is almost always a stressful event. In addition, the election does not necessarily conclude the episode; the union may apply for a nullification of the results (based on allegations of unfair labor practices, etc.) or simply regroup and make another attempt down the line.

If the unionization drive is a successful one, the small business owner can proceed in one of four ways, according to Lane:

- Charge the union with unfair labor practices and, if the allegations have merit, attempt to have the election results set aside.

- Sell your business, leaving the purchaser with any liability for pending charges of unfair labor practices as well as the burdens of a union shop.

- Go out of business.

- Recognize the union and enter into collective bargaining arrangements in good faith.

The collective bargaining agreement is basically a contract between the business and the union that explicitly states how workplace issues between management and employees will be handled.

UTILIZING LABOR UNIONS FOR BUSINESS SUCCESS

As indicated above, many businesses and industries try to avoid unions, convinced that their presence too often results in unwelcome sacrifices in the realms of profitability and control. But analysts point out that thousands and thousands of businesses that feature a unionized work force are tremendously successful. They note that the primary determinants of business success continue to be in the realms of business planning, marketing strategy, operational capabilities, technological advancement, and other areas, not in whether or not the business is unionized.

In fact, some observers contend that labor unions can provide often-unappreciated benefits to both individual companies and larger economies. "It may take some creative thinking and strategy, but unions can be a valuable ally when it comes to keeping top management aware of production issues,'' wrote Jim Treace in *Production*. "Outside the company, unions have political clout as well. At a time when state governors are delighted to shower tax breaks, training funds, and other goodies on anyone bringing a new factory into their state—even a direct competitor of yours—the unions' voting power can be a useful agent to make sure your existing plant gets its share. Second, union officials from the top down have an interest in some of the issues that can improve your operations: safety programs, ergonomics, and worker education.''

The Economist concurred with this evaluation, noting that "by giving workers a collective voice, unions do not just push up wages. They can also improve a plant's, and hence an economy's, productivity and efficiency. They do this by establishing grievance procedures, helping to reduce staff turnover, and promoting stability in the work force. They can be an effective mechanism through which employers can consult workers, and can help to organize the training so crucial for honing the work force's skills.''

FURTHER READING:

Black, John, Anne-Marie Greene, and Peter Ackers. "Size and Effectiveness: A Case Study of a Small Union." *Industrial Relations Journal.* June 1997.

Chapman, Elwood N. *Human Relations In Small Business.* Menlo Park, CA: Crisp Publications, 1994.

Dannin, Ellen, and Terry Wagar. "Impasse and Implementation: How to Subvert the National Labor Relations Act." *Working USA.* Fall 2000.

Darby, Harrison G., and Margaret R. Bryant. "When Unions Knock, How Should Employers Answer?" *HRMagazine.* July 1997.

"The Future of Unions." *The Economist.* July 1, 1995.

Lane, Marc J. *Legal Handbook for Small Business.* Rev. ed. New York: AMACOM, 1989.

Schupp, Robert W. "When Is a Union Not a Union? Good Faith Doubt and its Limitations in Collective Bargaining." *Labor Law Journal.* June 1997.

Treece, Jim. "On Unions." *Production.* April 1994.

Weiss, Donald H. *Fair, Square, and Legal: Safe Hiring, Managing & Firing Practices to Keep You & Your Company Out of Court.* New York: AMACOM, 1991.

SEE ALSO: Employee Strikes; Grievance Procedures; National Labor Relations Board

LAYOFFS AND DOWNSIZING

Layoffs and downsizing are both terms that refer to reductions that companies make in the number of employees on the payroll, although the term "layoff" is used more often to refer to temporary displacement, while "downsizing" generally has more permanent connotations. Other terminology sometimes used in this regard include reductions in force (RIF), right-sizing, restructuring, and reorganization. Employee terminations in such cases are usually the result of surplus labor caused by economic factors, changing markets, poor management, or some other factor unrelated to worker behavior. Because work force reductions make a company vulnerable to many of the same legal risks inherent in behavior-related terminations, companies usually terminate workers by means of a carefully planned and documented process. The process is typically conducted in two stages: 1) selecting the workers to be dismissed and then terminating them according to the above process; and 2) providing benefits to ease the transition, including severance packages, unemployment compensation, and outplacement services.

Prior to the 1980s, layoff/downsizing initiatives were typically associated with business cycle downswings, with laid-off workers recalled as business conditions improved. Beginning in the 1980s, a greater proportion of layoffs resulted from plant and office closures and were, therefore, permanent. Many of these downsizing efforts were intended to make U.S. firms more profitable in the face of intensified global competition. As the U.S. economy improved in the 1990s, large-scale layoffs continued even at highly profitable firms, indicating a break with historical patterns. These layoffs, many of them resulting from re-engineering and restructuring efforts, impacted managerial positions to a greater degree than ever before. Conversely, displacement rates fell for blue-collar groups that have historically been most vulnerable to layoffs/downsizing. Today, primary causes of layoffs and downsizing initiatives include rapid technological change, increased international competition, changing customer demands, regulatory changes, regional economic downturns, and poor company leadership.

STEPS INVOLVED IN DOWNSIZING

Companies that engage in a study of their workforce prior to initiating layoffs or downsizing need to proceed carefully. After all, organizations must weigh the impact of such actions on company efficiency, morale, and public image. But care must also be taken to ensure that the reductions do not violate state and federal laws. As with behavior-related terminations, downsizing terminations cannot be based on bias against protected minorities, or even unintentionally result in an inequitable outcome for a protected group. In fact, extensive legislation exists to protect disabled workers, racial minorities, workers over the age of forty, women, and other groups. In addition to bias-related laws, moreover, companies must comply with a battery of laws specifically directed at cushing the

blow for employees who are victims of corporate layoffs.

The actual termination of employees as a result of downsizing, however, should follow the same general procedures used when employees are terminated for behavioral reasons. That is, the situation should be reviewed carefully ahead of time and a plan established; the criteria for dismissal should be well documented (options include eliminating positions by job title or classification, reducing each area or department by a certain percentage or number of employees, and determining which resources will be needed to handle future work); the employees should be informed of their termination during a personal, face-to-face meeting that is not scheduled on a Friday afternoon or just before a holiday; the employees should be presented with a letter outlining the assistance and benefits they will receive; and then other employees and customers should be notified. "The exiting process is contingent on a variety of factors," said Richard Bunning in *Personnel Journal*, "including whether employees have volunteered to exit, the potential danger of sabotage (such as in the computer area), the potential for vandalism and the importance of the employees' continued presence in the organization. With a partial downsizing, quicker usually is better. . . . With a complete plant closure, a phased exit process may be necessary."

DOWNSIZING AND INTERNAL COMMUNICATION

Downsizing, which may eliminate the jobs of many employees all at once, requires a more extensive communication effort on the part of management than does a single employee termination. As a result, it is essential that business owners and managers clearly explain the reasons for the action to their remaining employees. As Bunning remarked, "as the necessity to downsize becomes clear, management should openly acknowledge the difficulty it had making this decision, which is required to restore (or maintain) the organization's health."

The personal announcement should be followed with written communication, such as newsletters and bulletin-board postings, to help keep employees informed, eliminate rumors, and maintain morale and productivity. Dealing with the media is another consideration in downsizing, since the loss of jobs may be of interest to the community. Deems noted that companies might find it helpful to prepare press releases ahead of time and choose one person as a contact.

The final stage of the downsizing process, outplacement, helps maintain the morale of remaining employees, enhance the public image of the company, and reduce the amount of unemployment compensation owed. Whenever possible, outplacement programs should be conducted by professional counselors in a neutral location, beginning as soon as possible after the downsizing occurs. Outplacement usually includes two activities: counseling and job search assistance. Both are necessary to help the displaced workers: 1) develop a positive attitude; 2) assess their career potential and direction, including background and skills, personality traits, financial requirements, geographic constraints, and aspirations; 3) develop job search skills, such as resume writing, interviewing, networking, and negotiating; and 4) adjust to life in transition or with a new employer. "The outplacement process often can be coordinated with local governmental and social service agencies," noted Bunning. "That way, employees may sign up for unemployment benefits, receive information about retraining programs, hear about other employment opportunities, receive financial planning tips and so on when they're told about benefits and receive severance pay."

ALTERNATIVES TO DOWNSIZING

Considering the mixed results large corporations have had with layoffs, some small businesses have adopted formal or informal no-layoff policies. In fact, the American Management Association reported in 1997 that small firms (defined as those with less than 500 employees) are half as likely as large ones to lay off employees. According to Harvey Meyer in *Nation's Business*, avoiding layoffs can offer small businesses a number of benefits, including "retention of highly trained, skilled, and productive workers; elimination of the need to spend time and money on

recruiting; payroll savings in those instances when employees agree to small and generally temporary wage reductions in return for employment security; the superior customer service that results from a loyal and upbeat work force; and reductions in turnover and absenteeism." Moreover, avoiding layoffs prevents adverse situations from arise in which employees who are *not* laid off are forced to handle both their usual responsibilities and those that were previously the prevince of laid off workers. Employees who are "swamped" in this manner almost always suffer from declines in both performance and workplace satisfaction.

A no-layoff policy can have pitfalls, however. It reduces the small business owner's ability to respond to a cash crunch, for example, and it may encourage employees who have been terminated to contest their firing in court (given this reality, small business owners should avoid putting no-layoff policies in writing). In addition, such a policy is unlikely to work for companies that have volatile sales levels or employ low-skilled workers who could be replaced easily.

For small companies that must compete with larger ones to attract and retain a highly trained and skilled work force, however, a no-layoff policy can be a valuable tool. Some small businesses that promote no-layoff policies keep employees busy during slow periods with training sessions or painting, maintenance, and repair work. Others choose alternatives that cut costs and eliminate the need to downsize, such as hiring freezes, restrictions on overtime, pay reductions, job sharing, and shortened work weeks.

FURTHER READING:

Aaronson, Daniel, and Kenneth Housinger. "The Impact of Technology on Displacement and Reemployment." *Economic Perspectives.* Summer 1999.

Bunning, Richard L. "The Dynamics of Downsizing." *Personnel Journal.* September 1990.

Cameron, Kim. "Downsizing Can Be Hazardous to Your Future." *HR Magazine.* July 1991.

Crofts, Pauline. "Outplacement: A Way of Never Having to Say You're Sorry?" *Personnel Management.* May 1992.

Cross, Michael. *U.S. Corporate Personnel Reduction Policies: An Edited Collection of Manpower Layoff, Reduction and Termination Policies.* Gower, 1981.

Eisen, Rebecca D. "Devising a Layoff Contingency Plan." *HR Magazine.* June 1993.

Meyer, Harvey. "Avoiding Pink Slips." *Nation's Business.* June 1997.

Noer, David M. *Healing the Wounds: Overcoming the Trauma of Layoffs and Revitalizing Downsized Organizations.* Jossey-Bass, 1995.

"Study: Layoffs Haven't Boosted Profits, Productivity." *Washington Post.* September 26, 1993.

SEE ALSO: Constructive Discharge; Employee Termination

LEARNING CURVES

Learning curves graphically portray the costs and benefits of experience when performing routine or repetitive tasks. Also known as experience curves, cost curves, efficiency curves, and productivity curves, they illustrate how the cost per unit of output decreases over time as the result of accumulated workforce learning and experience. That is, as cumulative output increases, learning and experience cause the cost per unit to decrease. Experience and learning curves are used by businesses in production planning, cost forecasting, and setting delivery schedules, among other applications.

Learning curves are geometric curves that can be graphed on the basis of a formula. Typically the X (horizontal) axis measures cumulative output, and the Y (vertical) axis measures the cost per unit. The curve starts with a high cost per unit at the beginning of output, decreases quickly at first, then levels out as cumulative output increases. The slope of the learning curve is an indication of the rate at which learning becomes transformed into cost savings.

An 80 percent learning curve is standard for many activities and is sometimes used as an average in cost forecasting and production planning. An 80 percent learning curve means that, for every doubling of output, the cost of new output is 80 percent of prior output. As output doubles from one unit to two units to four units, etc., the learning curve descends quite sharply as costs decrease dramatically. As output increases, it takes longer to double previous output, and the learning curve flattens out. Thus, costs decrease at a slower pace when cumulative output is higher.

One can explain the shape of learning curves another way. When a new task or production operation begins, a person or system learns quickly, and the learning curve is steep. With each additional repetition, less learning occurs and the curve flattens out. At the beginning of production or learning, individuals or systems are said to be ''high'' on the learning curve. That means that costs per unit are high, and cumulative output is low. Individuals and systems ''move down'' the experience or learning curve by learning to complete repetitive tasks more efficiently, eliminating hesitation and mistakes, automating certain tasks, and making adjustments to procedures or systems.

Some theorists believe that learning curves are not actually curves, but more like jagged lines that follow a curving pattern. They assert that learning occurs in brief spurts of progress, followed by small fallbacks to previous levels, rather than in a smooth progressive curve. Such a model of learning, however, does not affect the usefulness of learning curves in business and production applications.

FURTHER READING:

Chambers, Stuart, and Robert Johnston. ''Experience Curves in Services: Macro and Micro Level Approaches.'' *International Journal of Operations and Production Management.* July 2000.

Henry, Jane, ed. *Creative Management.* Sage Publications, 1992.

Lapre, Michael A., Amit Shankar Mukherjee, and Luk N. Van Wassenhove. ''Behind the Learning Curve: Linking Learning Activities to Waste Reduction.'' *Management Science.* May 2000.

Waterworth, Christopher J. ''Relearning the Learning Curve: A Review of the Derivation and Applications of Learning-Curve Theory.'' *Project Management Journal.* March 2000.

Weiss, Howard J., and Mark E. Gershon. *Production and Operations Management.* Allyn and Bacon, 1989.

LEASING PROPERTY

A lease is a contract between an owner and a user of property. In business lease agreements, the owner (commonly known in lease arrangements as the lessor) receives financial compensation and in exchange, the tenant (also known as lessee) is given the right to operate his or her business on the property. There are many different types of property lease arrangements that can be made, and many different considerations that business owners should weigh before entering into such a contract. But leasing is very popular with small business owners, in large measure because such arrangements allow new or financially-strapped businesses to divert their capital to other business needs. Indeed, many small businesses operate in leased facilities for their entire existence.

TYPES OF PROPERTY LEASES

FULL SERVICE LEASE This type of lease is used primarily in multi-tenant office buildings. In essence, lessees who agree to such arrangements pay a single lump sum for a wide range of supplementary services in addition to the lease payment. Under the terms of full service leases, the landlord is responsible for providing a number of different services for his or her tenants, including security, maintenance, janitorial, and various utilities (water, electricity, air, heat).

GROSS LEASE Under the terms of a gross lease contract, the lessee pays the lessor a gross amount for rent (as well as sales tax when applicable). Property costs such as property taxes, insurance, and maintenance are the responsibility of the landlord, while the tenant is responsible for utilities that it uses. Sometimes the lease contract will include provisions that require the tenant to cover property costs that go over a certain specified level.

Variations of this basic lease arrangement include the flat lease and the step lease. The flat lease is the most basic type of agreement, and generally the most popular with small businesses. It calls for the lessee to pay a flat set price for a specific period of time. The step lease, on the other hand, calls for a gradual escalation of the base rent payment over time in recognition of the likely rise in owner expenses in such areas as taxes, insurance premiums, and maintenance. A related lease contract, usually known as the cost-of-living lease, includes rent increases based on general inflation figures rather than increases in specific expenses.

NET LEASE The net lease is the most ubiquitous of the various lease contract types. Under the terms of a net lease, the tenant pays the landlord a base rent as well as an additional sum that covers the tenant's share of property taxes on the facility. When taxes increase, it is the responsibility of the tenants to cover those costs. The obligations of each tenant are figured by determining what percentage of the total facility is occupied by each tenant. If a business occupies 20 percent of a facility that has just been hit with a rise in property taxes, for example, that tenant is responsible for paying 20 percent of that increase.

Variations of the basic net lease include the "double-net" lease and the "triple-net" lease. Under the terms of a double-net lease, the terms of the contract are such that the tenant is responsible for picking up added insurance premiums as well as tax increases; under triple-net leases, tenants are responsible for covering insurance premiums, tax increases, *and* costs associated with maintenance and/or repairs of the building, the parking lot, and other areas used by the lessee. The triple-net lease is popular with landlords for obvious reasons, and small business owners should note that such arrangements sometimes make landlords less attentive to upkeep in these areas than they might be if they had to foot the bill themselves.

PERCENTAGE LEASE This arrangement calls for tenants to pay a base rent and/or a percentage of the lessee's gross revenue. This percentage, which can run as high as 10-12 percent in some contracts, is paid on an annual, semiannual, or quarterly basis (some malls and shopping centers, however, call for even more frequent payments). This lease arrangement is a favorite of lessors with property in coveted retail areas; the percentage lease is not favored by tenants, but the laws of supply and demand often make it possible for owners of desirable property to insist on it. For small business owners who sign such leases, it is important that they fully understand what the contract defines as "gross revenue." "Be specific in how you define gross sales," wrote Fred Steingold in *Legal Guide for Starting & Running a Small Business*. "Depending on your type of business, certain items should be deducted from gross sales before the percentage rent is determined. Here are some possibilities:

- returned merchandise
- charges you make for delivery and installation
- sales from vending machines
- refundable deposits
- catalog or mail-order sales
- sales tax

In short, make sure your lease excludes all items that overstate your sales from the location you're renting."

ADVANTAGES AND DISADVANTAGES OF LEASING

The Small Business Administration (SBA) counsels small business owners to consider a variety of factors when weighing whether to lease or buy property. These considerations include:

- Operating requirements—if the business's operating requirements are expected to change significantly over the next several years, leasing would probably be preferable, since it allows businesses to move more easily.

- Capital supply and capital needs—leasing frees up a greater percentage of a small business's capital for other operating needs (advertising, production, equipment, payroll, etc.). If the business does not have a lot of extra cash on hand (and few small businesses do), then leasing may be the more sensible choice. This is probably the biggest reason why small companies lease.

- Financing and payment flexibility—It is generally easier to secure financing to lease rather than purchase a property. In addition, leases can be spread out over longer periods than loans and can be structured to compensate for cash flow variations (the latter can be an important factor for seasonal businesses).

- Resale value—Is the value of the property likely to increase? If so, how much? Many small business owners choose to purchase rather than lease—even if they have to accrue significant debt—if they decide that the asset is a worthwhile long-term investment.

- Equipment—Many lease agreements include stipulations that provide lessees with increased flexibility in terms of upgrading and/or maintaining equipment.

- Taxes—Property owners enjoy tax benefits such as depreciation and investment tax credits that are not open to tenants.

OTHER LEASE TERMS

In addition, there are other elements of a lease agreement that can weigh heavily on a contract's overall acceptability. Indeed, the details of lease contracts can vary enormously. "In theory," noted Steingold, "all terms of a lease are negotiable. Just how far you can negotiate, however, depends on economic conditions. If desirable properties are close to full occupancy in your city, landlords may not be willing to negotiate with you over price or other major lease terms. On the other hand, in many parts of the country where commercial space has been over-built, landlords are eager to bargain with small businesses to fill empty units."

LEASEHOLD IMPROVEMENTS Small business owners who find themselves in negotiations with property owners over lease terms should make sure that they pay attention to a variety of issues that, if overlooked, can be costly. For example, leases will usually cover any remodeling that needs to be done to the property and specify who will pay for it. Most of this remodeling falls under the category of "leasehold improvements": carpeting, insulation, plumbing and electrical wiring, lighting, windows, ceiling tiles, sprinkler and security systems, and heating and air conditioning systems all fall under this heading. Small business owners should try to ensure that the lease specifies each improvement that the landlord will make to the property and when those improvements will be made (ideally, they should be completed before the move-in date). The landlord's willingness to fit the bill for such improvements typically depends on several factors, among them the length of the lease agreement; the business's value to the landlord as a tenant ("anchor" tenants typically have more clout in these areas); and the likely long-term economic benefits harvested by the landlord from the improvements (in terms of property value and future rentals). However, as Steingold noted, "if you [the small business owner] have specialized needs—for example, you're running a photo lab or a dance studio—and your darkroom or hardwood floor would be of limited value to most future tenants, don't expect the landlord to willingly pick up the costs of the improvements. The landlord may even want to charge you something to cover the cost of remodeling the space after you leave." Some leases provide tenants with the option of making improvements themselves, provided that they adhere to certain guidelines and restrictions.

LENGTH OF LEASE Negotiations between tenants and landlords often snag on the question of lease length. As Craig Melby and Jane Utzman noted in their book *Site Smart*, "the length of the lease is usually a very important issue. Some landlords may want a long lease for financial stability, others may prefer a short lease because of hopes that rental rates may rise in the short term future. Tenants may want a short lease in case of a decline in their business, or if their business becomes more profitable and they need more space for expansion purposes. Other tenants may want a longer term lease because of their large investment in tenant improvements, amount of money spent advertising a new location, as well as moving costs if their lease isn't renewed. Depending on what the landlord wants, the length of the lease will effect all other concessions offered." Generally, small business owners try to secure leases with mid-range lengths. Leases of less than a year can leave them more vulnerable than they would like, but multi-year terms can be dangerous as well, especially if the business is new and unproven. A common compromise is to include an "option clause" in the contract so that the lessee can stay if he or she wishes at the conclusion of the original lease period.

EXCLUSIVITY Many small business owners quite reasonably insist that any lease agreement they sign contain what is commonly known as an "exclusivity clause." This clause provides the tenant with an exclusive right to sell his or her product or service on the property, "thus obligating the landlord to prevent other tenants from selling those same goods or services," wrote Melby and Utzman.

INSURANCE Landlords often ask lessees to secure insurance in the event that 1) the tenant damages the leased property, or 2) customers or others suffer injuries on the premises. "The landlord may specify the specific dollar amount of liability coverage required by the tenant," noted Melby and Utzman. "The landlord will also insure the building in respects to liability and property damage. While the landlord's and tenant's liability coverage may overlap, the property insurance covered by the landlord includes everything except the interior contents of the tenant's space. Most leases require [tenants] to provide the landlord with proof of insurance."

USE OF PREMISES Shopping center/strip mall landlords typically include language in the lease contract providing specific details on approved uses of the premises that is being rented. Such stipulations often serve to protect the businesses of other tenants. For example, the owner of a cafe in a strip mall may be quite unhappy if his neighbor, who formerly ran a quiet sports memorabilia shop, decides to change gears and launch a tattoo parlor. "The use of the space definitely affects the tenant mix of the [shopping center] and may directly affect the neighboring tenants as well," explained Melby and Utzman. "If the tenant changes their scope of business or products they sell, the image of the center might suffer. In many retail centers, landlords spend a significant amount of time and money attracting the right mix of tenants to the center that will attract a specific type of shopper. To maintain the center's value, the use must conform to the tenant mix that will most benefit the center."

In addition, lease contracts provide stipulations and regulations on a plethora of other issues of interest to both lessors and lessees. These include:

- Signage (regulates the size, style, and brightness of tenant advertising signs)
- Compliance with various zoning laws, permits, restrictions on use of space

- Compliance with other local, state, and federal laws

- Subletting or assigning the lease

- Definition of the space being leased

- Security deposit

- Landlord's right to enter leased space

- Relocation (wherein the landlord relocates a tenant to another space because of remodeling or expansion by a neighboring tenant)

- Default provisions

- Hours of operation

- Incidents of damage or destruction from natural causes

- Repairs

- Indemnification provisions

- Abandonment (by the tenant, either through outright abandonment, diminished hours of operation, etc.)

- Condemnation (cases where all or part of the property is taken by city, county, state, or federal government for other use, such as road, right-of-way, or utility easement)

- Bailout clauses (in the event of catastrophic developments—tornadoes, riots, wars, floods, droughts, etc.)

- Cotenancy clauses (allows the business owner to break the lease if an anchor store closes or moves)

- Recapture clauses (also known as a cancellation clause, this allows landlords to evict tenants for breach of contract if the tenant is unable to meet minimum rent requirements)

CHOOSING BETWEEN EXISTING AND PLANNED BUILDINGS

Most start-up businesses move into already existing facilities. Many small business owners who have built up profitable, established enterprises, however, often have more options when they decide that the time is right to move. Indeed, some choose to arrange a lease in a building or facility (office center, shopping center, or industrial park) that is still in its planning stages. The savvy small business owner will consider the potential benefits and drawbacks of both choices before deciding. "Leasing in an existing building provides the Lessee . . . with more known at the time new space is occupied than any other facility option provides," said Wadman Daly in *Relocating Your Workplace.* "More so than in any other circumstances, the [lessee] is in a position to closely inspect both the facility and the terms of proposed leases in a number of competing locations. However, the nature of the lease in an existing building signifies minimum tenant control over the potential variables in either lease or facility. Rental rates, maintenance and escalation costs, utilities and building features are fixed or relatively non-negotiable. Landlords may vary in their abatements and finish-to-suit clauses, however their basic price structure, like that of the building and mechanical systems, remains unchanged. Of course, there are no investor implications with this option."

But Daly cautions that leasing in a planned building contains its own mix of attractive features and uncertainties: "Building features [in a planned building] will be new, up-to-date and, to a certain minimal extent, capable of adjustment to tenant need. If your lease is important enough to the developer, you may receive some attention when it comes to special requests for identification, parking, security, a prime location in the building, etc." Nonetheless, small business owners should be cautious when approaching such leases, for both the final appearance and utility of the building—as well as its costs—remain unseen and untested when the building is in its planning stages. "Proposed rental rates must be examined in the light of comparable projects with similar advantages," Daly wrote. "Descriptions of less obvious features like parking, air handling systems, security, maintenance, etc., should be clear and complete. The track record of the developer making the offer should be inspected carefully. Is there a history of quality construction at the rental rate asked, or one of build for quick re-sale? Is there a reputation for good maintenance or benign neglect? Regardless [of] the size of the lease or the duration of the proposed tenancy, these and related questions should be probed."

FURTHER READING:

Daly, Wadman. *Relocating Your Workplace: A User's Guide to Acquiring & Preparing Business Facilities.* Crisp Publications, 1994.

"For Existing and New Properties: Protect Yourself When Renting to Your Company." *The Business Owner.* September-October 1998.

Kahn, Jeremy. "Disownership is Everything." *Fortune.* March 30, 1998.

Steingold, Fred S. *Legal Guide for Starting & Running a Small Business.* Nolo Press, 1997.

Weber, Fred I. *Locating or Relocating Your Business.* Small Business Administration, n.d.

LEGAL SERVICES

Legal services are an important consideration for any business owner, but especially for small business owners, who often face a number of legal hurdles. Protecting the owner's personal assets from lawsuits against the business, ensuring protection for the business against discrimination, wrongful termination, and sexual harassment lawsuits, and handling employee contracts, copyright claims, and incorporation are just a few of the legal issues that commonly face small business owners.

The high costs of retaining a lawyer often make it seem as if competent legal services are out of reach of most small business owners. But there are reasonably priced methods of obtaining such services, such as pre-paid plans and legal software. In addition, experts emphasize the dangers of entering into legal agreements without first obtaining advice from a qualified attorney. In many cases, this attempt to cut corners can turn small problems into big problems for small business owners. "Perhaps your tax structure is not to your best advantage, or you are not adequately protected from liability," Charles Poling noted in the *New Mexico Business Journal.* "If you're in a regulated business, you might run afoul of the law simply because you haven't gotten educated by your lawyer. Failing to consult with a securities or financial lawyer when you're raising capital can cause serious problems."

The type of legal services a small business should obtain varies with the size and age of the business. "Exactly what type of lawyer you need depends on what business you're in, and what stage it's at," Poling wrote. "A general business lawyer can help you as day-to-day questions come up, reviewing contracts and tax questions. But for more complicated matters, you might need a specialist. . . . Just starting up? Find someone who specializes in forming corporations or partnerships. Going public? Find a securities lawyer. Other specialties include environmental law, banking, patenting, copyrighting, medicine, nonprofit corporations, employment law, and so on."

According to Michael Barrier in *Success,* the best way to find a good attorney is by getting referrals from people you trust, especially those with similar legal needs. Before signing a retainer, small business owners should inquire about the attorney's experience, charges, and potential conflicts of interest. It may also be helpful to check your insurance policy, because certain litigation expenses may be covered.

PRE-PAID LEGAL SERVICES

Perhaps the most cost-effective way for small business owners to obtain legal advice is through a pre-paid legal services plan. These plans provide companies with affordable access to legal advice and attorney's services for one low, monthly fee. Pre-paid firms are being compared to health maintenance organizations (HMOs) because they offer a wide range of services at one low, set price.

"This concept is where health insurance was in the '50s or where HMOs were 15 years ago," said Nashville attorney Jack Bufkin in an article in the *Memphis Business Journal.* "Prior to the '50s, people could go to the hospital and pay for it out of their pocket. You can't do that anymore. Today, people are expected to pay for the cost of a lawyer out of their pocket, but it's quickly getting to the point where most people can't afford the cost of going and getting a lawyer."

This prepaid concept was pioneered by Caldwell Legal, U.S.A. in 1967. It is still one of the largest prepaid firms. It offers Caldwell's Business Protector Program, which is available in all 50 states. At each Caldwell field office, attorneys provide telephone consultation, document review, letter, and other services, all for $20 per month. The plan includes unlimited hours of toll-free telephone consultation. That seems like a lot of service for very little money, but research done by Caldwell shows that 73 percent of legal problems can be solved with a single phone call. If more extensive services are needed, additional fees are applied as they are accrued.

Another company that has become one of the largest and best-known pre-paid legal firms was founded in 1972 in Ada, Oklahoma. PrePaid Legal Services, Inc. has set up a program that essentially allows small business owners to purchase "legal insurance," much like they would purchase health insurance. The program is called the Pre-Paid Small Business Legal Defense Plan and is available only to for-profit companies that have fewer than 20 employees and $2 million or less in gross income.

PrePaid contracts with one law firm in each state in which it does business, usually a very well regarded firm that might otherwise be inaccessible to small business owners. Just like with health insurance, the small businesses pay a monthly premium, usually less than $100 per month. For that fee, PrePaid clients are guaranteed many services, including 10 primary benefits. Other legal firms offering similar services typically provide a package that includes some combination of the following:

- Legal consultation services—Includes toll-free calls to an attorney and up to one hour of research.

- Legal correspondence services—The company will, on behalf of the business owner, write one letter per legal subject matter per year as part of the plan. Additional letters are available at a 25 percent discount.

- Designated consultations—An attorney will provide free telephone consultations for designated legal matters. Also included are two additional telephone consultations of up to 30 minutes each, for certain legal situations.

- Basic contract review—Includes up to three contracts of 15 pages or less reviewed each month before the business owner signs.

- Executed document review—An attorney will review one signed contract up to 10 pages in length each month and advise (by phone) what options the business owner has regarding the signed document.

- Legal document review—Attorney will review three business documents of up to 15 pages each month.

- Initial debt collection letters—Attorney will write up to 10 initial debt collection letters each month.

- Trial defense—Includes up to 60 hours of the attorney's time when the business is named as a defendant or respondent in a lawsuit. Every year that the business stays in the plan, an additional 60 hours are made available for free, with a maximum of 300 hours reached after five years in the plan.

- Reduced fee services—Provides a 25 percent discount off the attorney's normal corporate hourly rate for legal services.

- Reduced contingency fee services—Provides for a five percent discount off the attorney's corporate contingency fee for contingency-type cases.

ADVANTAGES OF PRE-PAID SERVICES

The primary advantage associated with pre-paid legal services is savings. ''The greatest benefit of a pre-paid legal plan is that it provides a way to reduce the cost of legal services for small business owners while providing greater access to the legal system,'' said Bufkin. ''Small business people are being hammered by legal issues. The time is right to offer a product like this.'' For example, a typical pre-paid plan might charge $125 per hour for attorney's fees, plus the monthly premium, which can range from $40 to $100 per month. Without the plan, the attorney's fees skyrocket to $180 to $350 per hour, with a retainer fee of several thousand dollars often demanded up front.

Quality service is another promise of most pre-paid plans. For example, one plan requires its attorneys to have a minimum of 15 years service, experience in business law, a favorable rating from Martindale-Hubbel (the rating service of the American Bar Association), and a clean record that shows no indication of ethical or malpractice claims against the attorney. Of course, these services vary in quality, just as attorneys as a group vary in quality. Small business owners should do their research before signing up with a service. There are new ones joining the industry each year. For example, the Lawyers Assurance Group of America maintains 20 franchises throughout the United States.

Another benefit of pre-paid plans is their size. Because they pool together hundreds of small businesses, they instantly become one of the largest clients of whatever firm handles the plan's account. This is a huge benefit for small business owners. One owner on his or her own will be a very small part of any law firm's business. As one business owner in Ohio said of his former legal firm, ''I felt I wasn't important enough to them.'' As part of the pre-paid plan, however, the small business becomes one part of a very important client that the law firm wants to keep happy to ensure continued business. Like HMOs, pre-paid plans offer collective bargaining power, as lawyers find it worth their while to offer low cost services to plan members because of the high volume of business that is generated.

Pre-paid plans also make it easier for small businesses to practice preventive law instead of reacting to crises. Without the plan, a business owner is more likely to take his or her chances in any given situation and hope that no legal problems arise. This is because asking for legal advice can be so expensive. The plan, however, makes advice readily available and encourages owners to make use of it so that small problems do not become big problems.

HOW TO SELECT THE PLAN THAT IS RIGHT FOR YOU

The most important thing to look for is the number and type of services offered at a reduced rate as part of the plan. The number of services might be lower than what you expect, so make sure the plan has what you need. Also find out what the plan charges for services that are not covered as part of the basic plan. A set fee for additional work may be cheaper in the long run than receiving a discount on the firm's ''usual fee'' for such services.

Other factors to consider include:

- Deciding whether you would prefer to work with just one lawyer over the years, or whether the service can provide a different lawyer for each legal matter.

- Do your homework. Obtain a list of clients and ask them if they have been satisfied with the quality of the legal work they have received.

- Ask how the law firm handles conflicts of interest when the person or business with a case against you uses the same pre-paid plan.

LEGAL SOFTWARE AND ONLINE ADVICE

Small business owners can also gain expertise and reduce risks and costs by utilizing one of the legal software packages that are designed just for small businesses. McGraw-Hill offers the *Small Business Lawyer,* a CD-ROM that contains more than 320 customized legal forms and agreements that cover such things as power of attorney, partnerships, loans, real estate, leases, and the sale of business assets. Once the software is installed, the business owner enters information about his business just once, after which all of the forms can be generated using that information.

A CD-ROM from Nolo Press called *Small Business Legal Pro Deluxe* includes the full text of four books published by Nolo, each targeted at the small business owner. The books, which are fully searchable, address hundreds of legal situations that are common to small businesses. Fifty forms are also included on the disc. Another CD-ROM from Nolo called *Law on the Net* provides descriptions of and links to thousands of resources available on the Internet. The disc is updated quarterly. Observers note that the demand for this subject, coupled with the ever-changing legal landscape and continued advances in computer technology, are likely to ensure that an expanded list of titles will be available to choose from for some time to come. However, it is often a good idea to have off-the-shelf forms reviewed by a practicing attorney to make sure they are adequate for your particular industry, state, or deal.

Another potential source of legal forms and advice is the Internet. A number of Web sites exist that provide directories of attorneys, sources for legal research, samples of various types of forms and documents, and even free legal advice in chat rooms. For example, the American Bar Association site provides the addresses of state and local bar associations and lawyer referral services at www.abanet.org/referral. Martindale-Hubbel also sponsors an online "lawyer locator" at http://lawyer.martindale.com/marhub. The Web site www.uslaw.com offers overviews of the law as it affects small business and also provides a directory of affiliated lawyers.

But according to Carol Ebbinghouse in *Searcher,* small business owners should approach online legal services with caution. Obtaining legal advice online makes it difficult to establish a recognized attorney-client relationship, which may leave a small business without the protection of confidentiality and with no recourse in cases of malpractice or conflict of interest. Another potential pitfall is that online attorneys may not be licensed in the business owner's state. They may even be law students or otherwise lack the necessary experience or qualifications to provide good advice. For those who do use online legal services, Ebbinghouse recommends making sure the site is in compliance with Internet privacy and security protocols, reviewing all disclaimers and conditions, and double checking the advice received.

FURTHER READING:

Bahls, Steven C. and Jane Easter Bahls. "Cover Charge: Prepaid Plans Put Routine Legal Services Within Your Budget." *Entrepreneur.* August 1996.

Bahls and Bahls. "Got It Covered?" *Entrepreneur.* February 1998.

Barrier, Michael. "The Maw of the Law." *Success.* October 2000.

Bell, David M.M. "Ethics and the Internet: In a Chaotic Dot-Com World, Internet Use Presents Many Practical, Ethical, and Regulatory Questions for Lawyers." *California Bar Journal.* July 2000.

Ebbinghouse, Carol. "Medical and Legal Misinformation on the Internet." *Searcher.* October 2000.

Perenson, Melissa J. "Navigating the Law." *PC Magazine.* December 17, 1996.

Poling, Charles. "Is Your Lawyer Doing Right for You?" *New Mexico Business Journal.* March 1997.

"PrePaid Legal Services Announces New Venture to Benefit Small Business Owners." *PR Newswire.* May 21, 1997.

Sewell, Tom. "Pre-Paid Legal Services Offered to Small Businesses." *Memphis Business Journal.* May 26, 1997.

Taylor, Dennis. "Hear Ye! These Legal Services Won't Leave Firms Bankrupt." *The Business Journal.* September 30, 1996.

LETTER OF INTENT

A letter of intent is essentially a document that summarizes the major ingredients of a proposed transaction, including the price, payment method, and important target dates (for contract signing and closing). In most cases, the letter of intent is not legally binding, but it is nonetheless regarded as a useful tool. As Charles F. Claeys observed in *Small Business Reports,* "the non-binding letter confirms that the buyer and seller have reached a sufficient 'meeting of the minds' to justify the time and expense of executing a final purchase and sale agreement." A letter of intent is most often utilized in situations in which one party is selling a business or facility to another, but the document may also be used to delineate the relationship in a supplier/customer agreement.

Although letters of intent are nominally non-binding, business and legal experts still counsel business owners to be careful in crafting and using them. Claeys noted that ''the case law of ever state is replete with disputes over the meaning of letters of intent. Most of these disputes stem from misperceptions about whether or not the letter binds one side or the other to complete the deal. In some cases, the courts have deemed the documents to be binding due to mistakes in their execution, forcing sellers to sell and buyers to buy when they wanted to back out of the deal.''

CONTENTS OF A STANDARD LETTER OF INTENT

There are a few basic steps that small business owners should make sure when putting together a letter of intent to make sure that the document is not a legally binding one. First of all, you should make certain that the letter of intent specifically states that the letter will eventually be superseded by a definitive purchase-and-sale contract that will be legally binding, and that the letter also includes a explicit statement that the letter itself is not legally binding. ''If you neglect to state in the letter that you will not be bound legally until you sign a contract, the seller possibly could hold you against your will to the terms of the letter of intent,'' wrote Mark Pestronk in *Travel Weekly*. Another big mistake that small business owners sometimes make in fashioning letters of intent is to agree to a statement that says that they will negotiate toward a purchase and sale agreement ''in good faith.'' According to Claeys, ''it's virtually impossible to get out of a deal once you've included this language, since the seller need only ask for reasonable terms to meet the 'good faith' criteria. Therefore, the letter should never include the good faith provision in any form.''

Non-binding letters of intent may also include most or all of the following elements:

- Total compensation offered, including breakdown (size of security deposit, down payment, seller-financed debt, bank debt)
- Warranties of clear and marketable title
- Detailed list of all liabilities and assets to be purchased
- Assurances of the validity and assumability of contracts (if applicable)
- Tax liability limitations

- Operating condition of all equipment and machinery at time of purchase
- Stipulations allowing buyer to adjust the purchase price in the event that: 1) undisclosed liabilities come due after settlement, and 2) actual inventory purchased does not match amount specified in sale agreement
- Provisions that the business passes any and all necessary inspections
- Provisions that final sale is contingent on verification of financial statements, license and lease transfers
- Provisions that final sale is contingent on obtaining financing for purchase
- Restrictions on business operations until final settlement
- Non-competition and advisory clauses (these are sometimes arranged in a separate document)
- Allocation of purchase price
- Date for settlement (may also include ''drop dead'' date at which both sides agree to discontinue negotiations)

Business experts say, however, that most letters of intent are primarily concerned with delineating only the major terms of the transaction. Indeed, a small business owner who ends up negotiating numerous minor details in a letter of intent may as well skip the step entirely and proceed directly to a binding purchase and sale agreement.

Major terms that should be included in a letter of intent, however, include total price to be paid, including down payment and installment payments; description of assets or stock to be sold; tax allocation of the price among fixed assets, goodwill, noncompete covenants, and consulting fees; and target dates for contract signing and closing. Of these components, price and payment terms are easily the most important elements of the letter.

ADVANTAGES AND DISADVANTAGES OF LETTERS OF INTENT

There are certain advantages associated with signing letters of intent for sellers. After all, a signed letter—even if legally non-binding—does signal that the prospective buyer is truly interested in making a deal, thus saving the seller from incurring unnecessary expenses to accountants and attorneys. Indeed, if a seller consents to sign a letter of intent, he or she can take comfort in the fact that it gives the prospective buyer a better chance of securing financing for the purchase (lenders tend to be favorably inclined toward borrowers who arrive armed with letters of intent).

But according to Claeys, "the disadvantages of the letter [for the seller] usually outweigh the advantages." He pointed out that once a prospective buyer has a signed letter in hand, he or she "tends to terminate its 'courtship' of the seller and toughen its stance on the details that remain to be worked out, including the seller's representations and warranties about how the business is doing, the indemnities for a breach of these representations, and covenants about how the business will be run prior to the change of ownership." Of course, the above-mentioned factors also tend to make letters of intent popular with buyers.

Some prospective buyers request that a "no-shop clause" be inserted into the language of the letter of intent. This clause, when implemented, basically means that the seller agrees not to offer the assets or stocks that are for sale to anyone else for a set period of time. Sellers often refuse to include such a clause, because it means that they are turning away other potential buyers for the duration of the agreed-upon period (usually 60 or 90 days) even though the buyer making the no-shop request is not yet obligated to make the purchase (remember the letter of intent, when constructed correctly, is nonbinding).

One option for sellers who face this type of request is to ask the buyer for a deposit in return. This money can be used by the seller to cover his or her legal and accounting expenses if the deal ultimately fails to come together. Buyers may balk at this condition, however, reasoning that both parties are responsible for their pre-transaction costs.

LETTERS OF INTENT FOR SUPPLIERS AND CUSTOMERS

Although letters of intent are primarily associated with purchases of entire businesses, they can also be used to delineate expectations between business suppliers and customers. These can be especially useful to businesses that have suppliers upon which they are particularly reliant. Such a letter is "a guide rather than a contract," admitted Ernest L. Anderson Jr. in *Purchasing,* "but it does make clear the outlines of the partnership." Anderson and other business consultants note that customer/supplier letters of intent can discuss all aspects of the relationship, including:

- Supplier and purchasing obligations associated with maintaining adequate inventories of goods and materials

- Order-handling, billing, and delivery procedures

- Handling of price changes

- Allocation of responsibilities in such areas as material quality and acceptance

- Efforts to reduce costs (of materials purchased, for instance)

- Treatment of gifts, gratuities, and other perks to and from suppliers (most are rejected outright)

- Duration of agreement

FURTHER READING:

Anderson, Ernest L., Jr. "A Sample Letter of Intent." *Purchasing.* October 6, 1994.

A Basic Guide for Buying and Selling a Company. John Wiley, 1996.

Claeys, Charles F. "The Intent to Buy." *Small Business Reports.* May 1994.

Furmston, Michael. *Contract Formation and Letters of Intent: A Comparative Assessment.* John Wiley, 1998.

Pestronk, Mark. "Get It in Writing." *Travel Weekly.* May 6, 1996.

LEVERAGED BUYOUTS

The term leveraged buyout (LBO) describes an acquisition or purchase of a company financed through substantial use of borrowed funds or debt. In fact, in a typical LBO, up to 90 percent of the purchase price may be funded with debt. During the 1980s, LBOs became very common and increased substantially in size, so that they normally occurred in large companies with more than $100 million in annual revenues. But many of these deals subsequently failed due to the low quality of debt used, and thus the movement in the 1990s was toward smaller deals (featuring small- to medium-sized companies, with about $20 million in annual revenues) using less leverage. Thanks to low stock prices, looser regulatory restrictions, and a rally in high-yield bonds, *Barron's* predicted that 2001 would be the biggest year since the 1980s for LBOs.

The most common leveraged buyout arrangement among small businesses is for management to buy up all the outstanding shares of the company's stock, using company assets as collateral for a loan to fund the purchase. The loan is later repaid through the company's future cash flow or the sale of company assets. A management-led LBO is sometimes referred to as "going private," because in contrast to "going public"—or selling shares of stock to the public—LBOs involve gathering all the outstanding shares into private hands. Subsequently, once the debt is paid down, the organizers of the buyout may attempt to take the firm public again. Many management-led, small business LBOs also include employees of the company in the purchase, which may help increase productivity and increase employee commitment to the company's goals. In other cases, LBOs are orchestrated by individual or institutional investors, or by another company.

According to Jennifer Lindsey in her book *The Entrepreneur's Guide to Capital,* the best candidate for a successful LBO will be in growing industry, have hard assets to act as collateral for large loans, and feature top-quality, entrepreneurial management talent. It is also vital that the LBO candidate post a strong historical cash flow and have low capital requirements, because the debt resulting from the LBO must be retired as quickly as possible. Ideally, the company should have at least twice as much cash flow as will be required for payments on the proposed debt. The LBO debt should be reduced to 50 percent of overall capitalization within one year, and should be completely repaid within five to seven years. Other factors improving the chances for a successful LBO include a strong market position and an established, unconcentrated customer base.

In order to improve the chances of success for an LBO, Lindsey noted that the deal should be undertaken when interest rates are low and the inflation rate is high (which will make assets more valuable). It is also vital that a management, employee, or outside investment group wants to own and control the company. Many LBOs involving small businesses take place because the owner wants to cash out or retire and does not want to sell to a larger company. LBOs can be very costly for the acquiring parties, with expenses including attorney fees, accounting evaluations, the printing of prospectus and proxy statements, and interest payments. In addition, if either the buyer or the seller is a public company, an LBO will involve strict disclosure and reporting requirements with both federal and state government agencies. Possible alternatives to an LBO include purchase of the company by employees through an Employee Stock Ownership Plan (ESOP), or a merger with a compatible company.

ADVANTAGES AND DISADVANTAGES

A successful LBO can provide a small business with a number of advantages. For one thing, it can increase management commitment and effort because they have greater equity stake in the company. In a publicly traded company, managers typically own only a small percentage of the common shares, and therefore can participate in only a small fraction of the gains resulting from improved managerial performance. After an LBO, however, executives can realize substantial financial gains from enhanced performance. This improvement in financial incentives for the firm's managers should result in greater effort on the part of management. Similarly, when employees are involved in an LBO, their increased stake in the company's success tends to improve their productivity and loyalty. Another potential advantage is that LBOs can often act to revitalize a mature company. In addition, by increasing the company's capitalization, an LBO may enable it to improve its market position.

Successful LBOs also tend to create value for a variety of parties. For example, empirical studies indicate that the firms' shareholders can earn large positive abnormal returns from leveraged buyouts. Similarly, the post-buyout investors in these transactions often earn large excess returns over the period from the buyout completion date to the date of an initial public offering or resale. Some of the potential sources of value in leveraged buyout transactions include: 1) wealth transfers from old public shareholders to the buyout group; 2) wealth transfers from public bondholders to the investor group; 3) wealth creation from improved incentives for managerial decision making; and 4) wealth transfers from the government via tax advantages. The increased levels of debt that the new company supports after the LBO decrease taxable income, leading to lower tax payments. Therefore, the interest tax shield resulting from the higher levels of debt should enhance the value of firm. Moreover, these motivations for leveraged buyout transactions are not mutually exclusive; it is possible that a combination of these may occur in a given LBO.

Not all LBOs are successful, however, so there are also some potential disadvantages to consider. If the company's cash flow and the sale of assets are insufficient to meet the interest payments arising from its high levels of debt, the LBO is likely to fail and the company may go bankrupt. Attempting an LBO can be particularly dangerous for companies that are vulnerable to industry competition or volatility in the overall economy. If the company does fail following an LBO, this can cause significant problems for employees and suppliers, as lenders are usually in a better position to collect their money. Another disadvantage is that paying high interest rates on LBO debt can damage a company's credit rating. Finally, it is possible that management may propose an LBO only for short-term personal profit.

CRITICISM OF LBOS

Ever since the LBO craze of the 1980s—led by high-profile corporate raiders who financed takeovers with low-quality debt and then sold off pieces of the acquired companies for their own profit—LBOs have garnered negative publicity. Critics of leveraged buyouts argue that these transactions harm the long-term competitiveness of firms involved. First, these firms are unlikely to have replaced operating assets since their cash flow must be devoted to servicing the LBO-related debt. Thus, the property, plant, and equipment of LBO firms are likely to have aged considerably during the time when the firm is privately held. In addition, expenditures for repair and maintenance may have been curtailed as well. Finally, it is possible that research and development expenditures have also been controlled. As a result, the future growth prospects of these firms may be significantly reduced.

Others argue that LBO transactions have a negative impact on the stakeholders of the firm. In many cases, LBOs lead to downsizing of operations, and employees may lose their jobs. In addition, some of the transactions have negative effects on the communities in which the firms are located.

Much of the controversy regarding LBOs has resulted from the concern that senior executives negotiating the sale of the company to themselves are engaged in self-dealing. On one hand, the managers have a fiduciary duty to their shareholders to sell the company at the highest possible price. On the other hand, they have an incentive to minimize what they pay for the shares. Accordingly, it has been suggested that management takes advantage of superior information about a firm's intrinsic value. The evidence, however, indicates that the premiums paid in leveraged buyouts compare favorably with those in inter-firm mergers that are characterized by arm's-length negotiations between the buyer and seller.

FURTHER READING:

Fox, Isaac, and Alfred Marcus. "The Causes and Consequences of Leveraged Management Buyouts." *Academy of Management Review*. January 1992.

Franecki, David. "Here's the Deal: Leveraged Buyout Revival." *Barron's*. February 12, 2001.

Kaplan, Stephen. "The Effect of Management Buyouts on Operating Performance and Value." *Journal of Financial Economics*. October 1989.

Latif, Yahya. "What Ails the Leveraged Buyouts of the 1980s." *Secured Lender*. November/December 1990.

Lindsey, Jennifer. *The Entrepreneur's Guide to Capital: The Techniques for Capitalizing and Refinancing New and Growing Businesses*. Chicago: Probus, 1986.

"Return of the LBO." *Business Week*. October 16, 2000.

SEE ALSO: Mergers and Acquisitions

LIABILITIES

A liability is a debt assumed by a business entity as a result of its borrowing activities or other fiscal obligations (such as funding pension plans for its employees). Liabilities are paid off under either short-term or long-term arrangements. The amount of time allotted to pay off the liability is typically determined by the size of the debt; large amounts of money usually are borrowed under long-term plans.

Payment of a liability generally involves payment of the total sum of the amount borrowed. In addition, the business entity that provides the money to the borrowing institution typically charges interest, figured as a percentage of the amount that has been lent.

A company's liabilities are critical factors in understanding its status in any industry in which it is involved. As John Brozovsky noted in *Journal of Commercial Lending*, "a basic understanding of accounting for liabilities is necessary to assess the viability of any company. Companies are required to follow certain accounting rules; however, the rules allow considerable flexibility in how a company accounts for liabilities."

TYPES OF LIABILITIES

CURRENT LIABILITIES Current liabilities are short-term financial obligations that are paid off within one year or one current operating cycle, whichever is longer. (A normal operating cycle, while it varies from industry to industry, is the time from a company's initial investment in inventory to the time of collection of cash from sales of that inventory or of products created from that inventory.) Typical current liabilities include such accrued expenses as wages, taxes, and interest payments not yet paid; accounts payable; short-term notes; cash dividends; and revenues collected in advance of actual delivery of goods or services.

Economists, creditors, investors, and other members of the financial community all regard a business entity's current liabilities as an important indicator of its overall fiscal health. One financial indicator associated with liabilities that is often studied is known as working capital. Working capital refers to the dollar difference between a business's total current liabilities and its total current assets. Another financial barometer that examines a business's current liabilities is known as the current ratio. Creditors and others compute the current ratio by dividing total current assets by total current liabilities, which provides the company's ratio of assets to liabilities. For example, a company with $1.5 million in current assets and $500,000 in current liabilities would have a three-to-one ratio of assets to liabilities.

LONG-TERM LIABILITIES Liabilities that are not paid off within a year, or within a business's operating cycle, are known as long-term or noncurrent liabilities. Such liabilities often involve large sums of money necessary to undertake opening of a business, major expansion of a business, replace assets, or make a purchase of significant assets. Such debt typically requires a longer period of time to pay off. Examples of long-term liabilities include notes, mortgages, lease obligations, deferred income taxes payable, and pensions and other post-retirement benefits.

When debt that has been classified as long-term is paid off within the next year, the amount of that paid-off liability should be reported by the company as a current liability in order to reflect the expected drain on current assets. An exception to this rule, however, comes into effect if a company decides to pay off the liability through the transfer of noncurrent assets that have been previously accumulated for that very purpose.

CONTINGENT LIABILITIES A third kind of liability accrued by companies is known as a contingent liability. The term refers to instances in which a company reports that there is a possible liability for an event, transaction, or incident that has already taken place; the company, however, does not yet know whether a financial drain on its resources will result. It also is often uncertain of the size of the financial obligation or the exact time that the obligation might have to be paid.

Contingent liabilities often come into play when a lawsuit or other legal measure has been taken against a company. An as yet unresolved lawsuit concerning a business's products or service, for example, would qualify as a contingent liability. Environmental cleanup and/or protection responsibility sometimes falls under this classification as well, if the monetary impact of new regulations or penalties on a company is uncertain.

Companies are legally bound to report contingent liabilities. They are typically recorded in notes that are attached to a company's financial statement rather than as an actual part of the financial statement. If a loss due to a contingent liability is seen as probable, however, it should be included as part of the company's financial statement.

FURTHER READING:

Brozovsky, John. ''A Review of Changes Affecting Accounting for Liabilities.'' *Journal of Commercial Lending*. March, 1994.

Williams, Georgina, and Thomas J. Phillips, Jr. ''Cleaning Up Our Act: Accounting for Environmental Liabilities.'' *Management Accounting*. February 1994.

Winicur, Barbara. ''Long Term Liabilities.'' *National Public Accountant*. January 1993.

SEE ALSO: Assets

LICENSING

According to Pat Upton, author of *Make Millions in the Licensing Business,* licensing is ''the practice of allowing a manufacturer (also called the licensee) to affix or associate the idea, character, design, or other representation owned by another (licensor) to his products.'' In the most basic terms, licensing is the legal act of granting rights to a certain property in exchange for payment. Although licensing is often referred to as an industry, many experts claim that it is actually a marketing tool or concept.

Examples of licensing arrangements can be found in a wide variety of products and services. For instance, a you might wear a sweatshirt bearing an NFL logo, purchase a child's sleeping bag with a cartoon character on it, or relax on bed sheets or other home furnishings by Ralph Lauren. ''As more companies—from Fortune 500 ones to startup companies—incorporate licensed products into their lines, licensing has become the marketing strategy of the future,'' Vanessa L. Facenda wrote in *Supermarket Business.* Some of the benefits a company might gain from licensing include increasing its revenues with a minimum of expenditure, exploiting its technology, and opening new markets for its products and services.

Licensing applies to small businesses in two main ways. First, small businesses may participate in arrangements known as *licensing-in.* In this case, the small business becomes the licensee and acquires the rights to a product or brand name from another company. This type of arrangement can help a small business reduce internal product development costs, get a faster start in an industry, and increase its stature based on its association with the licensor. The second way small businesses may participate in licensing arrangements is known as *licensing-out.* In this case, the small business is the licensor and reaches agreement with another company allowing that company to produce and market one of its products, apply its brand name, or use its patented technology. This sort of arrangement can help a small business underwrite its research and development costs, increase its visibility as well as that of its products, spread its marketing costs across more items, and add volume to its manufacturing operations.

Retail sales of licensed products in the United States and Canada reached $110 billion in 1998. The largest segments in the licensing business were entertainment (including character licensing), corporate brand licensing, fashion, and sports licensing. While licensing arrangements continue to increase in value each year, the field is becoming more competitive. ''The industry has learned from the lessons of the past,'' Ralph Irizarry and Cory Bronson noted in

Sporting Goods Business. ''More and more, we're seeing a contraction in the number of licensees, thus, eliminating fringe manufacturers and product categories. We're also seeing licensors develop partnerships with their licensees, strategic relationships, whereby the licensee essentially becomes a marketing partner.''

Analysts cite several reasons for the changes and consolidations taking place in licensing. Retailers have limited shelf space, and thus are unwilling to take on untested products or characters. In the meantime, consumers are becoming more fickle and trend-conscious, which makes it more difficult to predict hot new entertainment trends. This has put a premium on licensing rights to ''classic'' characters like Winnie-the-Pooh, which offer lasting value and provide consistent business. In the late 1990s, other trends in licensing included: licensed goods based on established brands and trademarks, like Jeep heavy-duty baby strollers; retail stores dedicated exclusively to a corporate brand; cross-promotions featuring two licensed properties, like movie tie-ins with fast-food restaurant meals; authorized Web sites; and sports licensing, especially of video and computer games.

DECIDING WHETHER OR NOT TO LICENSE

Given the popularity of licensing, many small businesses today must face the question of whether to manufacture a new product itself or license the production to another company. Major factors entering into this decision are the nature of the product and the relative strengths of the small business and its potential licensee. Experts recommend that small businesses examine their core competencies when deciding whether to license a product. For example, an in-depth assessment of the company's unique skills and abilities may indicate that it could make more money by licensing its manufacturing process than it could by manufacturing and marketing a finished product. Basically, if your company has the expertise and resources needed to make the product profitably in-house, then you should probably do so. If not, then it makes sense to find a licensing partner who can contribute the needed resources and expertise.

According to Dianne M. Pagoda in an article for *WWD,* the following factors may indicate that a small business would be best served by launching a new product in-house rather than licensing it to another manufacturer: 1) the new product is a fairly straight-forward extension of an existing product or brand; 2) the new product will be sold through the same channels of distribution used for existing products; 3) the new product shares similar production and sales cycles with the company's core business; 4) making the new product will not require special technical or mar-

keting and sales skills that would require the small business to seek expertise it does not already possess; and 5) the small business possesses sufficient resources and production capability to manage the larger operating base required to produce the new product. When these conditions are met, it is likely that the company would benefit from producing its own goods rather than licensing them to another company.

BECOMING A LICENSEE

Some small business owners worry that they will not be taken seriously when they attempt to enter licensing arrangements for the first time. They assume that individuals and companies that own licensable properties prefer to work with larger, well-established licensees. But experts claim that, in most cases, successful small businesses have good opportunities to obtain licensing rights. ''Manufacturers looking to become first-time licensees can expect fair but intensive negotiations and ongoing participation by the licensor during the life of the product,'' Teresa Salas noted in *Playthings.* In general, licensors like to see that potential licensees have a solid track record of making quality products, including some that are similar to the property being licensed. Small businesses interested in obtaining a license must be willing to submit to financial scrutiny, provide references, describe their available sales force and retail accounts, and make sales projections.

In the *Playthings* article, Licensing Industry Merchandisers Association Director Murray Altchuler made some suggestions for small businesses interested in becoming licensees. First, small businesses should try to license properties that are similar to their existing products or services, or that add an extra dimension to their core business. Second, small businesses should make sure that the licensor has a good reputation and a history of supporting the property and protecting it through legal means. Third, the small business should examine the provisions of the contract to ascertain its length, the renewal options available, and the amounts of guarantees and royalties expected.

LICENSING AGREEMENTS

The arrangements between the licensor and the licensee are typically laid out in a legal document known as a licensing agreement. This formal agreement is an important component in a successful business venture. ''While it is impossible to determine the future success of a product, much can be done in the earliest stages to ensure that a licensed product gets the best chance possible,'' Salas wrote. ''One might even say that the entire future of a licensed product is laid out, at least in part, during the process of negotiating a licensing contract.''

Licensing agreements usually include a number of provisions designed to protect the interests of both parties. Some of the most common elements of licensing agreements are outlined below:

Financial Provisions: Payments from the licensee to the licensor usually take the form of guaranteed minimum payments and royalties on sales. Royalties typically range from 6 to 10 percent, depending on the specific property involved and the licensee's level of experience and sophistication. Not all licensors require guarantees, although some experts recommend that licensors get as much compensation up front as possible. In some cases, licensors use guarantees as the basis for renewing a licensing agreement. If the licensee meets the minimum sales figures, the contract is renewed; otherwise, the licensor has the option of discontinuing the relationship.

Time Frame: Many licensors insist upon a strict market release date for products licensed to outside manufacturers. After all, it is not in the licensor's best interest to grant a license to a company that never markets the product. The licensing agreement will also include provisions about the length of the contract, renewal options, and termination conditions.

Quality Control: In order to ensure quality, the licensor may insert conditions in the contract requiring the licensee to provide prototypes of the product, mockups of the packaging, and even occasional samples throughout the term of the contract. Another common quality-related provision in licensing agreements involves the method for disposal of unsold merchandise. If items remaining in inventory are sold as cheap knockoffs, it can hurt the reputation of the licensor in the marketplace.

LICENSING OF PATENTS

In addition to products and brand names, another popular type of licensing relates to patented technology. Licensing of patents involves granting another entity the right to use an original process or type of equipment. It is important to note that licensing of patents does not necessarily require a company to give up the underlying know-how that led to creating the invention. The licensing arrangement may stipulate that the licensee only gains the right to use the invention, rather than the technical knowledge that contributed to its development. The main benefit to companies in licensing patented technology to other companies is that the fees generated may help offset the costs of developing the technology. In some cases, companies end up licensing patented technology to other entities that have already commercialized the technology. For example, the engineer who invented time-delayed windshield wipers for automobiles successfully sued the major American car makers for royalties on his patented technology years after the manufacturers had incorporated it into nearly every car on the road.

More typically, however, companies will develop manufacturing processes or other technologies that are peripheral to their core business, patent the non-core technologies, and then seek to license them in order to gain a source of revenue to help offset their development costs. In an article for *CMA,* Alistar G. Simpson and Martin Langloi recommended that companies look for licensing opportunities for patents that extend beyond the core of their business. Companies may have some such patents as a result of an acquisition or left over after a divestiture. The next step is to identify potential licensees, which are likely to be companies already involved in that area of business. Before contacting potential licensees, Simpson and Langloi suggest that companies study the market to see how important the patented technology is and to gauge the level of profit margins generally available. These factors will influence the life expectancy of the patented technology as well as the royalties that might be expected from licensing it.

Licensing patented technology—particularly when it involves patent infringement litigation—can be costly and time consuming. In addition, potential licensors may find that they lack sufficient knowledge of their target companies and industries to conduct good negotiations. But there are also several advantages to licensing non-core technologies. For example, companies may gain an opportunity to enter new areas of business, and they may develop strong relationships with licensees that open up further business opportunities. Finally, licensing non-core technologies is not likely to have a negative effect on the company's normal, core business.

LICENSING AND THE INTERNET

An emerging challenge for companies involved in licensing in the twenty-first century is how licensing agreements will handle the question of online rights. The fast growth of electronic commerce on the World Wide Web has exposed a completely new area of licensing with no established rules to guide agreements. ''How can you enforce geographic restrictions on a technology that is global and borderless?'' Lisa Vincenti pointed out in an article for *HFN.* ''How can you maintain exclusivity of your crown jewels if any Tom, Dick, and Harry can get your goods and put them up for sale on the Web? How can you control pricing if some Web peddlers are auctioning off your prize possessions?''

Many companies with long-standing licensing arrangements are approaching Internet licensing with caution. In some cases, large-scale, highly publicized licensing agreements simply do not include online rights. For example, the domestic expert Martha Stewart reached an agreement to develop exclusive lines of furniture, clothing, and other goods for the discount retailer K-Mart. But none of these popular items appear on the K-Mart Web site because the licensing agreement between the parties did not include online rights. In the future, Vincenti predicted that licensors will make separate licensing deals with traditional and online vendors.

FURTHER READING:

Bloomgarden, Kirk. ''Craze or Classic? Licensing Agents Rely on Profits from Long-Running Classic Rights to Survive the Shift Toward Brand Licensing.'' *Marketing.* September 2, 1999.

Burns, Stuart. ''Definition Is the Key.'' *Accountancy.* March 2000.

Facenda, Vanessa L. ''The Power of the License.'' *Supermarket Business.* July 1999.

Heicklen, Michael J. ''Licensing Your Restaurant's Name, Trademark.'' *Nation's Restaurant News.* June 29, 1998.

Irizarry, Ralph, and Cory Bronson. ''A License to Operate.'' *Sporting Goods Business.* September 14, 1998.

Lazar, Bart A. ''Licensing Gives Known Brands New Life.'' *Marketing News.* February 16, 1998.

Pogoda, Dianne M. ''To License or Not.'' *WWD.* May 27, 1998.

Salas, Teresa. ''Building a Lasting Licensing Contract.'' *Playthings.* October 1988.

Simpson, Alistar G., and Martin Langloi. ''Potential Patent Profits.'' *CMA: The Management Accounting Magazine.* September 1998.

Stodder, Gayle Sato. ''License to Win.'' *Entrepreneur.* February 1995.

Upton, Pat. *Make Millions in the Licensing Business.* Monarch Press, 1985.

Vincenti, Lisa. ''Licensing Online: An Emerging Parallel Universe.'' *HFN: The Weekly Newspaper of the Home Furnishing Network.* June 7, 1999.

SEE ALSO: Inventions and Patents; Royalties

LICENSING AGREEMENTS

A licensing agreement is a legal contract between two parties, known as the licensor and the licensee. In a typical licensing agreement, the licensor grants the licensee the right to produce and sell goods, apply a brand name or trademark, or use patented technology owned by the licensor. In exchange, the licensee usually submits to a series of conditions regarding the use of the licensor's property and agrees to make payments known as royalties.

Licensing agreements cover a wide range of well-known situations. For example, a retailer might reach agreement with a professional sports team to develop, produce, and sell merchandise bearing the sports team's logo. Or a small manufacturer might license a proprietary production technology from a larger firm to gain a competitive edge, rather than expending the time and money trying to develop its own technology. Or a greeting card company might reach agreement with a movie distributor to produce a line of greeting cards bearing the image of a popular animated character.

Whatever the type of licensing arrangement, the formal licensing agreement is an important component in a successful venture. ''While it is impossible to determine the future success of a product, much can be done in the earliest stages to ensure that a licensed product gets the best chance possible,'' Teresa Salas wrote in *Playthings.* ''One might even say that the entire future of a licensed product is laid out, at least in part, during the process of negotiating a licensing contract.''

ELEMENTS OF A TYPICAL LICENSING AGREEMENT

Because of the legal ground they must cover, some licensing agreements are fairly lengthy and complex documents. But most such agreements cover the same basic points. ''In general, contracts contain the same provisions,'' Salas noted. ''Outlined clearly in the contract are such things as advances, royalties, guarantees, market dates, renewal options, length of contract, monitoring rights, procedures for quality control, inventory, and returns and allowances.''

One of the most important elements of a licensing agreement covers the financial arrangement between the two parties. Payments from the licensee to the licensor usually take the form of guaranteed minimum payments and royalties on sales. Royalties typically range from 6 to 10 percent, depending on the specific property involved and the licensee's level of experience and sophistication. Not all licensors require guarantees, although some experts recommend that licensors get as much compensation up front as possible. In some cases, licensors use guarantees as the basis for renewing a licensing agreement. If the licensee meets the minimum sales figures, the contract is renewed; otherwise, the licensor has the option of discontinuing the relationship.

Another important element of a licensing agreement establishes the time frame of the deal. Many licensors insist upon a strict market release date for products licensed to outside manufacturers. After all, it is not in the licensor's best interest to grant a license to a company that never markets the product. The licensing agreement will also include provisions about the length of the contract, renewal options, and termination conditions.

Most licensing agreements also address the issue of quality. For example, the licensor may insert conditions in the contract requiring the licensee to provide prototypes of the product, mockups of the packaging, and even occasional samples throughout the term of the contract. Of course, the best form of quality control is usually achieved before the fact—by carefully checking the reputation of the licensee. Another common quality-related provision in licensing agreements involves the method for disposal of unsold merchandise. If items remaining in inventory are sold as cheap knockoffs, it can hurt the reputation of the licensor in the marketplace.

Another common element of licensing agreements covers which party maintains control of copyrights, patents, or trademarks. Many contracts also include a provision about territorial rights, or who manages distribution in various parts of the country or the world. In addition to the various clauses inserted into agreements to protect the licensor, some licensees may add their own requirements. They may insist on a guarantee that the licensor owns the rights to the property, for example, or they may insert a clause prohibiting the licensor from competing directly with the licensed property in certain markets.

FURTHER READING:

Heicklen, Michael J. ''Licensing Your Restaurant's Name, Trademark.'' *Nation's Restaurant News.* June 29, 1998.

Salas, Teresa. ''Building a Lasting Licensing Contract.'' *Playthings.* October 1988.

Stodder, Gayle Sato. ''License to Win.'' *Entrepreneur.* February 1995.

Upton, Pat. *Make Millions in the Licensing Business.* Monarch Press, 1985.

LIFE INSURANCE

In general, life insurance is a type of coverage that pays benefits upon a person's death or disability. In exchange for relatively small premiums paid in the present, the policy holder receives the assurance that a larger amount of money will be available in the future to help his or her beneficiaries pay debts and funeral expenses. Some forms of life insurance can also be used as a tax-deferred investment to provide funds during a person's lifetime for retirement or everyday living expenses.

A small business might provide life insurance to its workers as a tax-deductible employee benefit— like health insurance and retirement programs—in order to compete with larger companies in attracting and retaining qualified employees. In addition, there are a number of specialized life insurance plans that allow small business owners to reduce the impact of estate taxes on their heirs and protect their businesses against the loss of a key employee, partner, or stockholder. Group life insurance is generally inexpensive and is often packaged with health insurance for a small additional fee. Companies that provide life insurance for their employees can deduct the cost of the policies for tax purposes, except when the company itself is named as the beneficiary.

Life insurance is important for individuals as well, particularly those who—like many entrepreneurs—are not covered by a company's group plan. Experts recommend that every adult purchase a minimum amount of life insurance, at least enough to cover their debts and burial expenses so that these costs do not fall upon their family members. The insurance industry uses a standard of five times annual income in estimating how much coverage an individual should purchase. In her book *Health Insurance: A Guide for Artists, Consultants, Entrepreneurs, and Other Self-Employed,* Lenore Janecek claims that entrepreneurs should determine the minimum amount of coverage they need by calculating how much they spend annually and how much debt they have, then adding the cost of funeral arrangements and, if applicable, college tuition for children.

The cost of life insurance policies depends upon the type of policy, the age and gender of the applicant, and the presence or absence of dangerous life-style habits. Insurance company actuaries use these statistics to determine an individual's mortality rate, or estimated number of years that person can be expected to live. Policies for women usually cost less than those for men, because women tend to live longer on average. This means that the insurance company will receive premiums and earn interest on them longer before it has to make a payment. Experts recommend that companies or individuals seeking life insurance coverage choose an insurance agent with a rating of A or better, and compare the costs of various options before settling on a policy.

TYPES OF LIFE INSURANCE POLICIES

TERM INSURANCE Term life insurance is the simplest and least expensive type, as it pays benefits only upon the policy holder's death. With annual renewable term insurance, the policy holder pays a low premium at first, which increases annually as he or she gets older. With level term insurance, the premium amount is set for a certain number of years, then increases at the end of each time period. Experts recommend that people who select term insurance make sure that their policies are convertible, so they can switch to a cash-value plan later if needed. They also should purchase a guaranteed renewable policy, so that their coverage cannot be terminated if they have health problems.

Term insurance typically works best for younger people with children and limited funds who are not covered through an employer. This type of policy enables such a person's heirs to cover mortgage and college costs, estate taxes, and funeral expenses upon his or her death.

WHOLE LIFE INSURANCE With whole life insurance, the policy holder pays a level premium on an annual basis. The policy usually covers until the end of the person's life—age 90 or 100. In most cases, the policy holder is overcharged for the premium, and the extra amount goes into an interest-bearing dividend account known as a cash value account. The individual can use the money in this account to pay future premiums, or can withdraw it or borrow against it to cover living expenses. With a variable whole life policy, the individual controls the investments made with his or her cash value account. Selecting certain types of investments, such as mutual funds, may allow the policy holder to increase the balance in the account significantly. Regardless of the performance of the investments, however, the amount of the insurance benefit can never drop below its original value. When choosing a whole life policy, experts note, it is important to analyze the fund's past performance and inquire about commissions and hidden costs. Although whole life insurance can provide added security upon retirement, it should not be considered a replacement for retirement savings. In fact, Janecek revealed that, on the average, whole life policy holders only yielded between 2 and 4.5 percent on their investments over a twenty-year period.

UNIVERSAL LIFE INSURANCE Universal life insurance was introduced in the 1980s as a higher-interest alternative to whole life insurance. Universal life premiums are based not only on the cost of the insurance, but also on the interest rate offered on investments. Still, they are usually less expensive than whole life policies. Universal life policies provide individuals with a wider array of investment choices and higher projected interest rates. They are essentially similar to a term policy with a fixed rate of interest guaranteed for a year at a time.

CURRENT ASSUMPTION LIFE INSURANCE Current assumption life insurance features a fixed annual premium for the duration of the plan. This type of policy pays a set interest rate on premiums received, less the actual cost of the insurance. They can be useful as a tax-deferred investment vehicle, since they usually pay 2 to 4 percent more than banks. Policy holders may elect to overpay their premiums early in the plan period to accumulate cash value. They can withdraw or borrow from the funds later for any purpose, including retirement income, or can use the cash value to pay the premiums for the remainder of the plan period.

RIDERS AND OPTIONS Most types of life insurance policies give individuals the opportunity to add optional coverage, or riders. One popular option is accelerated benefits (also called living benefits), which pays up to 25 percent of the policy value to the holder prior to their death if they are struck by a serious illness. Another option, known as a waiver of premium, allows an individual to continue coverage without paying premiums if he or she becomes disabled. Many policies also provide an accidental death and dismemberment option, which pays twice the amount of the policy if the insured dies or loses the use of limbs as a result of an accident.

KEY PERSON PROTECTION

Small businesses tend to depend on a few key people, some of whom are likely to be owners or partners, to keep operations running smoothly. Even though it is unpleasant to think about the possibility of a key employee becoming disabled or dying, it is important to prepare so that the business may survive and the tax implications may be minimized. In the case of a partnership, the business is formally dissolved when one partner dies. In the case of a corporation, the death of a major stockholder can throw the business into disarray. In the absence of a specific agreement, the person's estate or heirs may choose to vote the shares or sell them. This uncertainty could undermine the company's management, impair its credit, cause the flight of customers, and damage employee morale.

Life insurance can help small businesses protect themselves against the loss of a key person by providing a source of income to keep business running in his or her absence. Partnership insurance basically involves each partner acting as beneficiary of a life insurance policy taken on the other partner. In this way, the surviving partner is protected against a financial loss when the business ends. Similarly, corporate plans can ensure the continuity of the business under the same management, and possibly fund a repurchase of stock, if a major stockholder dies. Although life insurance is not tax deductible when the business is named as beneficiary, the business may deduct premium costs if a partner or owner is the beneficiary.

FURTHER READING:

Anastasio, Susan. *Small Business Insurance and Risk Management Guide.* U.S. Small Business Administration, n.d.

Bury, Don. *The Buyer's Guide to Business Insurance.* Oasis Press, 1994.

Janecek, Lenore. *Health Insurance: A Guide for Artists, Consultants, Entrepreneurs, and Other Self-Employed.* Allworth Press, 1993.

Kirwan, Roberta. "How Much Insurance Do You Need?" *Money.* April 1, 1999.

Kurylo, Steve. ''Choosing the Most Appropriate Insurance Policy and Company.'' *Estate Planning.* October 1996.

Lynn, Jacquelyn. ''A Quick Guide to Insurance.'' *Entrepreneur.* June 1997.

Stettner, Morey. ''Your Money or Your Life: A Guide to Term Insurance.'' *Working Woman.* April 1998.

Wolpoff, Charles R. '' 'Key Man' Life Insurance Helps Companies Survive.'' *Washington Business Journal.* September 5, 1997.

LIMITED LIABILITY COMPANY

The Limited Liability Company (LLC), a hybrid of the partnership and the corporation, has become a popular legal alternative for business owners. Now available in almost all states, the LLC combines the benefits of limited liability and pass through taxation, much like an S corporation. But the LLC's legal structure is much looser, allowing many companies that find S corporation status too restrictive to take advantage of its benefits. Small business owners are taking advantage of the LLC because it is easier to set up and maintain than a corporation.

Because the LLC is a fairly new option in the United States (it first became available in Wyoming in 1977, but most other states did not follow suit until the 1990s), the laws governing this business form are largely uninterpreted by court cases. In addition, each state has its own statutes concerning LLCs. Therefore, learning and keeping up with the laws that govern LLCs, which are still being fine-tuned, can be a tricky business. When considering the LLC option, consulting knowledgeable and up-to-date legal and tax advisors is a must.

ADVANTAGES OF FORMING AN LLC

LIMITED LIABILITY Like corporations, the LLC provides its members (owners) with protection from being personally responsible for the debt liabilities of the company. Members are only liable to the extent of their investments in the company. If a customer slips and is injured on company property, a law suit may still bankrupt the business, but it cannot touch the personal assets of the LLC's members. This limited liability, then, is a great advantage over partnerships. In general partnerships, all members are liable for the company's debts, and in a limited partnership, at least one member must still be liable.

AVOIDING DOUBLE TAXATION Like S corporations, LLC's enjoy exemption from the double taxation required of C corporations. In other words, the LLC's profits pass through to the company's members, who report their share of the profits on their personal federal tax returns. The company itself does not pay a federal tax before the money is distributed to the members, as in the case of C corporations. But state and local taxes may still be levied against the LLC.

FLEXIBILITY OF INCOME DISTRIBUTION One of the biggest benefits that small businesses enjoy when choosing LLC status, according to Fred Steingold, author of *The Legal Guide for Starting and Running a Small Business*, is that it is ''easier to allocate profits and losses for tax purposes.'' Whereas the amount of profits the S corporation's shareholders report on their federal tax returns must be proportional to their share of stock, an LLC's members can determine amongst themselves how to divide their income as long as they follow the Internal Revenue Service's rules on partnership income distribution.

SIMPLICITY Another great advantage of LLCs over corporations is the ease of setting up and running one. Whereas incorporation can be an involved and costly process, all that is required to start an LLC is the filing of an Articles of Organization and the drafting of an Operating Agreement defining the company's policies and procedures (a filing fee, though, will still be required of LLCs). And whereas a corporation requires a board of directors, officers, and regular shareholders' and directors' meetings, an LLC is not required to observe such formalities in its operation. An LLC can be run from day to day essentially as if it were a partnership.

NO OWNERSHIP RESTRICTIONS The biggest drawback of forming an S corporation—the restrictions on the type and number of shareholders the corporation may have—is avoided by forming an LLC. The members of an LLC may be foreign nationals or other companies, both of which are prohibited from owning stock in an S corporation. In addition, there is no limit on the number of members an LLC may have, as there is with an S corporation.

MEMBER INVOLVEMENT IN THE COMPANY One problem with limited partnerships is that those partners who wish to protect themselves with limited liability (which may be all but one of the members) are prohibited from direct involvement in running the company. These partners may have only a financial investment in the firm. All members of an LLC may be directly involved in the company's management without jeopardizing their limited liability.

ATTRACTIVE TO FOREIGN INVESTORS Because LLCs have been in existence in Europe and Latin America for over a century, investors from those parts of the world are particularly knowledgeable about this business form. According to *The Essential Limited Liability Handbook*, ''LLCs often prove to be the most familiar and least imposing business structure for foreign entrepreneurs who wish to enter the American market.''

DRAWBACKS OF FORMING AN LLC

NEWNESS LLCs are still a very new option in most states (only Wyoming and Florida had LLC statutes on the books prior to the 1990s). This means that the statutes governing the establishment of LLCs are still evolving. And there is virtually no case history in the courts to indicate how these laws will be interpreted. The Internal Revenue Service is also still working out its position concerning LLCs, so it will be imperative for small business owners to solicit legal and tax advice on the current laws before making a decision about whether or not to form an LLC. And because the laws may change while the LLC is in existence, it will be important to keep on top of the developments in LLC statutes to determine whether it remains in the company's best interests to operate as an LLC.

INTERSTATE BUSINESS MORE COMPLICATED Laws governing LLCs can vary widely from state to state, complicating the conduct of business across state lines. There are, as of yet, no uniform laws concerning LLCs, so an even greater knowledge of the state laws will be required of the company that does business in more than one state.

NO PERPETUAL EXISTENCE Most states require that an LLC's Operating Agreement set a limit to the company's existence (usually 30 years). And in the absence of a clause in the Operating Agreement providing for the continuance of the LLC in the event of the death or withdrawal of a member, the LLC will cease to exist when such events occur. The transfer of ownership is also more restricted for an LLC (like a partnership) than for a corporation.

CREATING AN LLC

It is important that the organizer(s) of a prospective LLC follow the ''enabling statutes'' or formation laws of the state in which the company will be formed in order to be designated as an LLC. Without this designation, the company will lack the protection of limited liability and will be treated as a general partnership. Therefore, the first step in creating an LLC is to find out your state's specific enabling statutes.

The organizer does not have to be one of the company's members. The organizer's function is to file the articles of organization, a task which can be accomplished by a lawyer, a hired agent from a service company specializing in such business, or a manager of the prospective company.

NAMING AN LLC Before forming an LLC, the company name must be reserved with the secretary of state or its equivalent. Most states require that the words ''Limited Liability Company'' or the abbreviation ''LLC'' be included in the name of the company. In some states, ''Limited Company'' or ''LC'' is the preferred designation. In all states, though, the name of the LLC must not resemble the name of any other corporation, LLC, partnership, or sole proprietorship that is registered with the state.

THE ARTICLES OF ORGANIZATION This form, called the articles of organization or certificate of formation, must be obtained from the secretary of state's office or its equivalent, filled out by the organizer(s), and filed with the same office. A filing fee, which varies from state to state, will also be charged. This simple document requires, at minimum, the company name and address, a description of the business to be conducted, the name and address of the registered agent (the contact to whom notices of lawsuit or other official matters can be served), the names of the company's members and managers (usually the members themselves), and the dissolution date. Other information may be required, depending on which state the articles of organization are filed in. It is important that the articles describe the business in a way that will allow the Internal Revenue Service to designate the company a partnership for tax purposes, and not a corporation. In order for the I.R.S. to do so, the articles must show that the company possesses no more than two of the following four characteristics (which describe a corporation):

- Perpetual existence
- Centralized management
- Free transferability of ownership interest
- Limited liability

One of the easiest ways to show that the LLC is not a corporation is to limit its existence. In fact, most states require that a dissolution date be determined in the articles of organization. On this date the LLC's assets will be liquidated and its business will cease (occurrences such as the mutual written agreement of the members or the death or retirement of a member may also terminate the LLC's existence before the dissolution date). If no date is specified, a default period of usually 30 years will be enacted. However, the members may decide to continue the LLC's existence at a later date.

FEES Filing fees vary from state to state, from $50 to $500. In addition, some states require the LLC to publish an announcement of its creation to the public in a generally circulated newspaper. This latter requirement can be very expensive, ranging from $500 to $2,000.

THE OPERATING AGREEMENT At the first meeting of the members, called the organizational meeting, an operating agreement should be drafted. Although each state has laws governing how LLC's should be operated, the members should create their own operating agreement to document that all members agree on how the company should be run. It should be carefully constructed with an eye to preventing future disagreements and deadlocks. Most basically, the agreement should address the division of profits, members' voting rights, and company management. A good operating agreement will address the following issues:

- Who the members are and how they will be elected in the future.

- Grounds on which members may be terminated, and procedures to execute such terminations.

- Stipulations regarding allocation of business shares after the death of a member.

- If a member becomes disabled, how will the company provide for him/her (with disability insurance or out of its own funds)?

- How managers will be selected and what their duties, salaries, and grounds for dismissal will be.

- How major decisions will be made. (Which decisions will require unanimous approval of the members and which a simple majority vote? Which decisions can be delegated to the manager in charge of daily affairs?)

- How often meetings will be held and how much notice members must receive.

- Who will keep records and how they will be kept.

- How members will invest in the LLC: will only cash contributions be allowed, or can members contribute services as well? If so, which services will be accepted and how will they be valued?

- How profits and losses will be allocated to members.

- How compensation (salary) for actively participating members will be determined.

- How new capital should be acquired should the company need it.

- What procedures must be followed to transfer interests in the company.

- What banking procedures should be followed.

- Penalties, if any, if members or managers fail to act in accordance with the operating agreement.

FURTHER READING:

Borofsky, Jeffrey Mark. ''Converting a Corporation to an LLC.'' *CPA Journal.* March 1998.

Byrd, Stephen, and Brett Richey. ''The Choice of Entity for the Small Business Owner.'' *Mid-Atlantic Journal of Business.* December 1, 1998.

Damman, Gregory C. *How to Form and Operate a Limited Liability Company: A Do-it-Yourself Guide.* Self-Counsel Press, 1995.

The Essential Limited Liability Handbook. Oasis Press, 1995.

Friedman, Scott E. *How to Profit by Forming Your Own Limited Liability Company.* Upstart, 1995.

Handmaker, Stuart A. *Choosing a Legal Structure for Your Business.* Prentice Hall, 1997.

Mancuso, Anthony. *Form Your Own Limited Liability Company.* Nolo Press, 1996.

Shenkman, Martin M., Samuel Weiner, and Ivan Taback. *Starting a Limited Liability Company.* Wiley, 1996.

LIQUIDATION AND LIQUIDATION VALUES

Many factors can contribute to tough financial times for a small business, including a struggling economy, hostile takeover, natural disaster, or illegal activity such as theft or fraud. When a business encounters this type of financial turmoil, it may be forced to claim bankruptcy and liquidate some of its assets (including property, furniture, and computers) in order to regain some of its investment. The liquidation value is the approximate amount a business can expect to get back when this type of sale takes place.

Usually, this amount is less than the retail value (sometimes as much as 20 percent less) as well as the book value (which is the actual amount paid for the assets). The reason for this decrease in value is that liabilities are subtracted from the value of the assets in order to determine the liquidation value of the business. The liquidation value is usually determined by a qualified professional appraiser, who will provide an estimate so that the company can decide if it actually wants to go through with the process.

Another factor that can influence liquidation values is the state of the market at the time of the liquidation. According to an article by Andrei Shleifer and Robert W. Vishny that appeared in the *Journal of Finance,* ''When a firm in financial distress needs to sell assets, its industry peers are likely to be experiencing problems themselves, leading to asset sales at prices below value in best use. Such illiquidity makes assets cheap in bad times.''

There are two types of liquidation values, depending on the urgency of the situation. Orderly liquidation value applies to a business that can afford to take its time to field offers from a multitude of bidders in order to get the best price for its assets. Often, in these cases, the business can sell items individually instead of selling the whole collection of assets at one time. Distress liquidation values come into play when a business is desperate to liquidate its assets. Usually the assets are sold all at once and often to firms or dealers who specialize in purchasing liquidated items. Distress liquidation values are always lower than orderly liquidation values, and in some instances drastically lower.

Recently, many of the most publicized business failures have been those of online retailers (also known as dot-coms). Inexperience, technological difficulties, poor customer relations, and changes in consumer tastes have contributed to the demise of many of these types of companies. But the rollercoaster rise and fall of dot-com companies has lead to new trends in liquidation: that of online e-liquidators. Many new dot-coms are starting up that specialize in buying up the assets of their failed competitors and selling them online at deep discounts. This trend leads to increased sales for the e-liquidators as well as great bargains for consumers.

It should be noted that liquidations are not necessarily a sign of failure. While many liquidations occur during poor financial times, others do not. Often a business may be forced to liquidated some of their assets in an effort to keep up with changes in the marketplace. For example, new products or technologies can come out that make older ones obsolete and therefore force a business to buy the new products in an effort to keep up. Some experts contend that some form of liquidation is taking place even amongst the most successful companies. If these trends are closely monitored and quickly dealt with, a company should be able to stay ahead of the game and avoid any negative financial repercussions.

TYPES OF LIQUIDATIONS

While there are two main types of liquidation values, there are three main categories for the liquidations themselves. A foreclosure or Chapter 7 liquidation takes places when a creditor gets a court order to take possession of a company's assets. An agent is usually appointed by the creditor to tend to this type of liquidation. A voluntary (or orderly) liquidation occurs when the business agrees to sign over possession of its assets and cooperates with its lender (or lenders) in an amicable fashion. During this type of situation, the debtor and lender work together to see that the liquidation goes smoothly.

Unfortunately, some liquidations fall under the category of hostile. This situation takes place when the business in question fails to cooperate with its lender. Many times the debtor will refuse to provide necessary information and act in an unprofessional manner in an effort to sabotage the liquidation. These situations tend to get ugly and often lead to further legal proceedings. Despite these differences, the only way any type of liquidation can be considered successful is if outstanding debts are settled between the business and the lender.

When a company decides to go into liquidation, it either does so immediately or opts to proceed with the process over an extended period of time. A cease and desist liquidation is one that takes place rather quickly. Once it is determined that this is the route that will be taken, the business stops operating and debtors are immediately contacted to begin the liquidation proceedings. In this type of situation it is usually understood that the business and the lender are ending their relationship and both parties move quickly to tie up loose ends and avoid dragging the situation out. During a winding down liquidation, the business continues to operate while working with the lender to find buyers willing to give them top dollar for their assets.

ALTERNATIVES TO LIQUIDATION

Instead of going into formal liquidation proceedings, a business may want to explore other avenues of liquidating their assets. They can opt to sell items such as vehicles, computers, furniture, or remaining inventory themselves through auctions or by simply placing ads in appropriate publications.

A company can also contact their competitors directly to see if there is any interest in buying them out or participating in a bulk sale. Both parties stand to benefit when a company sells out to a competitor. As Eric Shaw noted in an article for *Business Credit,* ''There is an intrinsic value to a competitor to purchase the goodwill and customer list of a company that is liquidating. Once verification of the sales volume and gross margins is established, a competitor can be induced to purchase the intangible assets. . . . The bank benefits by receiving the value paid for the goodwill and trademark. It is also easier for the outside party to collect receivables from customers that are being serviced by a new company with the blessing and cooperation of the liquidating debtor.''

LIQUIDATION AND SMALL BUSINESSES

In the small business world, many companies are sold to other entrepreneurs who wish to take them over. This is another situation where liquidation comes into play that is not necessarily negative. There are many reasons why a small business owner would want to sell his or her company. These reasons includes retirement, changing career goals, frustration with the marketplace, illness, and even death. Often, this situation is a very emotional one for the seller because they have a lot of personal interest and time built into their business. On the other hand, an established small business would be an attractive entity to a prospective buyer for many reasons as well. A loyal customer base, experienced employees, working assets, and a prime real estate location are some of the things that would attract a buyer to this type of situation.

When a small business is put up for sale, the buyer and seller must work together to determine fair market value of the assets. The seller must document the history of the business and describe how it operates, including relationships with employees, suppliers, and competitors. The book value of the assets and property should discussed. It is recommended that 3 to 5 years worth of financial statements are provided as well. At the same time, the buyer must secure the proper financing so the transaction goes off smoothly. Like any type of liquidation, this type of transaction will be considered successful only if both the buyer and the seller are satisfied with the results.

FURTHER READING:

Shaw, Eric. ''Understanding the Art of Liquidation from a Lender's Point of View.'' *Business Credit.* January 1995.

Shleifer, Andrei, and Robert W. Vishny. ''Liquidation Values and Debt Capacity: A Market Equilibrium Approach.'' *Journal of Finance.* September 1992.

SEE ALSO: Bankruptcy; Business Failure and Dissolution

LOAN PROPOSALS

Loan proposals are formal, written documents that small businesses must prepare when they approach potential lenders or investors for funding. A complete loan proposal package should consist of completed loan application forms (if required), and a comprehensive business plan with complete financial statements. Ideally, the loan proposal should present information about the small business, its future prospects, and its financing needs in a straightforward manner. All the pertinent information the lender or investor might need in making a decision should be provided in a logical format. Loan proposals must be thorough yet concise, convincing yet honest. The aim is to answer all the questions that a lender or investor is likely to ask without overstating the facts and figures.

Preparing a solid loan proposal can be very time consuming, but it has proven to be the best way for a small business owner to demonstrate his or her understanding of the business and its financial demands to potential lenders and investors. Furthermore, the business plan portion of the loan proposal can serve as a sort of handbook for running the business. It presents criteria against which management's strategy and decisions can be continually evaluated. Overall, a formal loan proposal should illustrate why the small business is a good credit risk by placing it within the context of its market and competition, explaining any peaks and valleys in cash flow, and emphasizing the strengths of the management team.

ELEMENTS OF A LOAN PROPOSAL

The Small Business Administration publication *Handbook for Small Business* outlines some of the elements that should be included in a good loan proposal. It should begin with a summary page that provides contact information for the company, the amount of the loan request, the company's intended purpose for the funds, and the proposed repayment terms.

The next section should feature a description and summary of the business, including a brief history. The description should also include information on the size and potential for growth of the business's main markets, an analysis of the competition, and notes on any emerging industry trends. Other useful information might include an explanation of any unique aspects of the business's product or service, information on local advertising efforts, and a long-term growth plan.

The next major section of the loan proposal features information on the company's management team, including brief resumes outlining the experience of key employees. This section might also include notes on the business's current staffing level, along with an analysis of future staffing needs. The names and contact information for accountants and attorneys should also be provided.

The next section consists of the loan request itself. This section should provide the potential lender with details about the amount of funds needed, how they will be used, what collateral is available to secure the loan, the company's proposed repayment terms, and evidence of the small business's ability to repay the loan.

Another section should include supporting financial data, including a current balance sheet and income statement, three years of historical financial statements (for existing businesses), projections of cash flow for the next year, and personal financial statements for the business's primary owners or investors. Another important loan-related section should supply information on the business's current sources and uses of credit, including the names and contact information for lenders and trade creditors.

The final section of the loan proposal can include a variety of miscellaneous information that might help the lender to reach a favorable decision. For example, the small business owner could attach business licenses, copies of the partnership agreement or articles of incorporation, copies of tax returns, lease information if renting facilities, and information on insurance coverage.

MAKING THE PROPOSAL

In his book *Doing Business with Banks,* Gibson Heath recommended that the loan proposal be written using layman's terms, and illustrated with computer-generated graphics and charts that highlight key areas of the proposal and provide a visual representation of the ideas presented. Overall, the loan proposal must anticipate any objections the lender or investor might have to providing funds for the small business, and then provide the information needed to overcome the objections.

In an article for *Inc.,* Bruce G. Posner solicited comments from bankers regarding the most glaring weaknesses they saw in small business loan proposals. They all expressed a desire to see evidence that the business owner had thought the loan proposal all the way through. "Business owners come in with these beautiful three-ring binders. The numbers are in nice, straight columns, but a lot of these people haven't though about the assumptions they've made and what it will take to do what they say they'll do," said Jeffrey C. Gardner of U.S. Bancorp. "We need to know where the numbers come from. The sad part is that many people don't know what the projections are about because their accountant made all the assumptions."

Dev Strischek of Barnett Bank of Palm Beach County echoed these comments, noting that "The biggest weakness I see is a lack of specificity and a lack of preparation. A lot of people don't really know what they need the money for or how much they need. . . . We like to see a cash-flow analysis—how much they plan to sell, how much they spend on overhead, how much for inventory, and what's available for debt service. It's easier to do business with people who've thought things through."

After creating a formal, written loan proposal, the next step is to present the proposal to a potential lender. Heath recommended that the small business owner take one last look at the loan proposal before taking it to the bank, in order to verify the numbers and be ready to answer any questions with confidence. It is important that, rather than just dropping the loan proposal off, the small business owner meet with the lender to review the loan proposal in detail. The in-person presentation should focus on just a few key points of the proposal. It is intended to improve the lender's understanding of the business and the loan request, so that he or she will be able to defend the proposal before other decision makers. At the conclusion of the meeting, the small business owner should ask when a decision might be expected. It is also important for the small business owner to be available during that time period to answer any follow-up questions.

FURTHER READING:

Dawson, George M. *Borrowing for Your Business: Winning the Battle for the Banker's "Yes."* Upstart Publishing, 1991.

Heath, Gibson. *Doing Business with Banks: A Common Sense Guide for Small Business Borrowers.* DBA/USA Press, 1991.

"Make Preparations Before Approaching Bank for Your Loan." *Memphis Business Journal.* November 3, 2000.

SCORE. *Handbook for Small Business.* U.S. Small Business Administration, 1989.

Posner, Bruce G. "Plugging Holes in Loan Proposals." *Inc.* April 1992.

Whittemore, Meg. "Creative Financing That Succeeds." *Nation's Business.* April 1995.

LOANS

A loan is the purchase of the present use of money with the promise to repay the amount in the future according to a pre-arranged schedule and at a specified rate of interest. Loan contracts formally spell out the terms and obligations between the lender and borrower. Loans are by far the most common type of debt financing used by small businesses. Loans can be classified as long-term (with a maturity longer than one year), short-term (with a maturity shorter than two years), or a credit line (for more immediate borrowing needs). They can be endorsed by co-signers, guaranteed by the government, or secured by collateral—such as real estate, accounts receivable, inventory, savings, life insurance, stocks and bonds, or the item purchased with the loan. The interest rate charged on the borrowed funds reflects the level of risk that the lender undertakes by providing the money. For example, a lender might charge a startup company a higher interest rate than it would a company that had shown a profit for several years.

CHARACTERISTICS OF LOANS

Loans have the following distinguishing characteristics:

1) *Time to maturity.* Time to maturity describes the length of the loan contract. Loans are classified according to their maturity into short-term debt, intermediate-term debt, and long-term debt. Revolving credit and perpetual debt have no fixed date for retirement.

Banks provide revolving credit through extension of a line of credit. Brokerage firms supply margin credit for qualified customers on certain securities. In these cases, the borrower constantly turns over the line of credit by paying it down and reborrowing the funds when needed. A perpetual loan requires only regular interest payments. The borrower, who usually issued such debt through a registered offering, determines the timing of the debt retirement.

2) *Repayment Schedule.* Payments may be required at the end of the contract or at set intervals, usually on a monthly or semi-annual basis. The payment is generally comprised of two parts: a portion of the outstanding principal and the interest costs. With the passage of time, the principal amount of the loan is amortized, or repaid little by little until it is completely retired. As the principal balance diminishes, the interest on the remaining balance also declines. Interest-only loans do not pay down the principal. The borrower pays interest on the principal loan amount and is expected to retire the principal at the end of the contract through a balloon payment or through refinancing.

3) *Interest.* Interest is the cost of borrowing money. The interest rate charged by lending institutions must be sufficient to cover operating costs, administrative costs, and an acceptable rate of return. Interest rates may be fixed for the term of the loan, or adjusted to reflect changing market conditions. A credit contract may adjust rates daily, annually, or at intervals of 3, 5, and 10 years. Floating rates are tied to some market index and are adjusted regularly.

4) *Security.* Assets pledged as security against loan loss are known as collateral. Credit backed by collateral is secured. In many cases, the asset purchased by the loan often serves as the only collateral. In other cases the borrower puts other assets, including cash, aside as collateral. Real estate or land collateralize mortgages. Unsecured debt relies on the earning power of the borrower.

COMMON TYPES OF LOANS

Consumers and small businesses obtain loans with varying maturity periods to fund purchases of real estate, transportation, equipment, supplies, and a vast array of other needs. According to W. Keith Schilit in *The Entrepreneur's Guide to Preparing a Winning Business Plan and Raising Venture Capital,*

they receive these loans from a number of sources, including friends and relatives, banks, credit unions, finance companies, insurance companies, leasing companies, and trade credit. The state and federal governments sponsor a number of loan programs to support small businesses. Following are examples of some common types of loans.

SHORT-TERM LOANS A special commitment loan is a single-purpose loan with a maturity of less than one year. Its purpose is to cover cash shortages resulting from a one-time increase in current assets, such as a special inventory purchase, an unexpected increase in accounts receivable, or a need for interim financing. Trade credit is another type of short-term loan. It is extended by a vendor who allows the purchaser up to three months to settle a bill. In the past it was common practice for vendors to discount trade bills by one or two percentage points as an incentive for quick payment.

A seasonal line of credit of less than one year may be used to finance inventory purchases or production. The successful sale of inventory repays the line of credit. A permanent working capital loan provides a business with financing from one to five years during times when cash flow from earnings does not coincide with the timing or volume of expenditures. Creditors expect future earnings to be sufficient to retire the loan.

INTERMEDIATE-TERM LOANS Term loans finance the purchase of furniture, fixtures, vehicles, and plant and office equipment. Maturity generally runs more than one year but less than five. Consumer loans for autos, boats, and home repairs and remodeling are also of intermediate term.

LONG-TERM LOANS Mortgage loans are used to purchase real estate and are secured by the asset itself. Mortgages generally run between ten and forty years. A bond is a contract held in trust with the obligation of repayment. An indenture is a legal document specifying the terms of a bond issue, including the principal, maturity date, interest rates, any qualifications and duties of the trustees, and the rights and obligations of the issuers and holders. Corporations and government entities issue bonds in a form attractive to both public and private investors. A debenture bond is unsecured, while a mortgage bond holds specific property in lien. A bond may contain safety measures to provide for repayment.

LOAN CONSIDERATIONS FOR SMALL BUSINESSES

When evaluating a small business for a loan, Jennifer Lindsey wrote in *The Entrepreneur's Guide to Capital,* lenders ideally like to see a two-year operating history, a stable management group, a desirable niche in the industry, a growth in market share, a strong cash flow, and an ability to obtain short-term financing from other sources as a supplement to the loan. Most lenders will require a small business owner to prepare a loan proposal or complete a loan application. The package of materials provided to a potential lender should include a comprehensive business plan, plus detailed company and personal financial statements. The lender will then evaluate the loan request by considering a variety of factors. For example, the lender will examine the small business's credit rating and look for evidence of its ability to repay the loan, in the form of past earnings or income projections. The lender will also inquire into the amount of equity in the business, as well as whether management has sufficient experience and competence to run the business effectively. Finally, the lender will try to ascertain whether the small business can provide a reasonable amount of collateral to secure the loan.

Experts indicate that borrowing can be a useful strategy, particularly for companies with good credit and a stable history of revenues, earnings, and cash flow. But small business owners should think carefully before committing to large loans in order to avoid cash flow problems and reduced flexibility. In general, a combination of loans and other types of financing is considered most desirable for small businesses.

In the Small Business Administration publication *Financing for the Small Business,* Brian Hamilton listed several factors entrepreneurs should consider when choosing between their various financing options. First, the entrepreneur must consider how much ownership and control he or she is willing to give up, not only at present but also in future financing rounds. Allowing the founders to retain ownership and control of the company is a major advantage of loans over equity financing, or selling stock to outside investors. Second, the entrepreneur should decide how leveraged the company can comfortably be, or its optimal ratio of debt to equity. Third, the entrepreneur should determine what types of financing are available to the company, given its stage of development and capital needs, and compare the costs and requirements of the different types. Finally, as a practical consideration, the entrepreneur should ascertain whether or not the company is in a position to make set monthly payments on a loan.

No matter what type of financing is chosen, careful planning is necessary to secure it. The entrepreneur should assess the business's financial needs, and then estimate what percentage of the total funds must be obtained from outside sources. A formal business plan, complete with cash flow projections, is an important tool in both planning for and obtaining financing. Lindsey noted that small businesses should consider loans as a financing option when federal interest rates are low, they have a good credit history or property to use as collateral, and they expect future growth in earnings as well as in the overall industry.

The main disadvantage of loans is that they require a small business to make regular monthly payments of principal and interest. Very young companies often experience shortages in cash flow that may make such regular payments difficult. Most lenders provide severe penalties for late or missed payments, which may include charging late fees, taking possession of collateral, or calling the loan due early. Failure to make payments on a loan, even temporarily, can adversely affect a small business's credit rating and its ability to obtain future financing. Another disadvantage associated with loans is that their availability is often limited to established businesses. Since lenders primarily seek security for their funds, it can be difficult for unproven businesses to obtain loans. Finally, the amount of money small businesses may be able to obtain via loans is likely to be limited, so they may need to use other sources of financing as well.

FURTHER READING:

Anderson, Tom. "Choosing a Corporate Bank for Business Loan, Partnership." *Memphis Business Journal.* November 3, 2000.

Evanson, David R. "B-B-Bad to the Loan." *Entrepreneur.* February 2000.

Hamilton, Brian. *Financing for the Small Business.* U.S. Small Business Administration, 1990.

Heath, Gibson. *Doing Business with Banks: A Common Sense Guide for Small Business Borrowers.* DBA/USA Press, 1991.

Lindsey, Jennifer. *The Entrepreneur's Guide to Capital.* Probus, 1986.

"Make Preparations Before Approaching Bank for Your Loan." *Memphis Business Journal.* November 3, 2000.

Schilit, W. Keith. *The Entrepreneur's Guide to Preparing a Winning Business Plan and Raising Venture Capital.* Prentice Hall, 1990.

Timmons, Jeffrey A. *Planning and Financing the New Venture.* Brick House Publishing Company, 1990.

LOCAL AREA NETWORKS (LANS)

In the modern office environment, each worker is equipped with a personal computer, containing its own disk drives and processor. Each of these computers can communicate with another by the way of a local area network (LAN), which is a computer network that covers a small area, usually a single building or group of buildings. In addition, the LAN may also connect the network of computers with a series of printers, a mainframe computer or file server with even greater processing power and memory storage, and with other devices that can send messages from the network over telephone lines to another location.

As the name suggests, a LAN is local, meaning that it is a proprietary system limited to a finite number of users. It generally serves an area of less than one mile. It is also a network, affording users both functional and communicative diversity through a distribution of resources. A LAN permits workers—isolated in separate offices—to operate off the same system, as if they were all sitting around a single computer.

One of the great attributes of a LAN is that it may be installed simply, upgraded or expanded with little difficulty, and moved or rearranged without disruption. LANs are also useful because they can transmit data quickly. Perhaps most importantly, anyone familiar with the use of a personal computer can be trained to communicate or perform work over a LAN. But despite their great potential and capabilities, LANs have yet to demonstrate an increase in office productivity. They have certainly eliminated paper and speeded the flow of information, but in many cases they have also created additional work in terms of organization, maintenance, and trouble-shooting.

THE HISTORY OF LANS

The advent of personal computers changed the type of information sent over office computer networks. Terminals were no longer ''dumb,'' but contained the power to perform their own instructions and maintain their own memories. This took considerable pressure off mainframe devices, whose energies could now be devoted to more complex tasks.

LANs allowed for the transmission of data between workers. In turn, they enabled this shared data to be directed to a common printer, serving a larger group of users. This eliminated the need for each worker to have a printer and ensured that the one printer provided was not underutilized. In addition, LANs allowed data to be called up directly on other workers' computers, providing immediate communication and eliminating the need for paper. The most common application was in interoffice communications, or electronic mail (e-mail). Messages could be directed to one or several people and copied to several more over the LAN. As a result, an e-mail system became something of an official record of communications between workers. Addressees became obligated to respond to e-mail messages in a timely manner because their failure to answer could be easily documented for supervisors.

Personal computers transformed LANs from mere shared processors to fully integrated communication devices. With processing power distributed among several computers, the mainframe's main role was eclipsed and complex processing, administrative functions, and data file storage became the job of a new device, the file server. Today, there are many different types of LANs. For example, many Macintosh computers use Appletalk, while IBM computers commonly use Ethernets.

PHYSICAL COMPONENTS OF LANS

The physical properties of a LAN include network access units (or interfaces) that connect the personal computer to the network. These units are actually interface cards installed on computer motherboards. Their job is to provide a connection, monitor availability of access to the LAN, set or buffer the data transmission speed, ensure against transmission errors and collisions, and assemble data from the LAN into usable form for the computer.

The next part of a LAN is the wiring, which provides the physical connection from one computer to another, and to printers and file servers. The properties of the wiring determine transmission speeds. The first LANs were connected with coaxial cable, the same type used to deliver cable television. These facilities are relatively inexpensive and simple to attach. More importantly, they provided great bandwidth (the system's rate of data transfer), enabling transmission speeds initially up to 20 megabits per second.

Another type of wiring, developed in the 1980s, used ordinary twisted wire pair (commonly used for telephones). The primary advantages of twisted wire pair are that it is very cheap, simpler to splice than coaxial, and is already installed in many buildings. The downside of this simplicity is that its bandwidth is more limited.

A more recent development in LAN wiring is optical fiber cable. This type of wiring uses thin strands of glass to transmit pulses of light between terminals. It provides tremendous bandwidth, allowing very high transmission speeds and because it is optical rather than electronic, it is impervious to electromagnetic interference. Still, splicing it can be difficult and requires a high degree of skill. The primary application of fiber is not between terminals, but between LAN buses (terminals) located on different floors. As a result, fiber distributed data interface is used mainly in building risers. Within individual floors, LAN facilities remain coaxial or twisted wire pair.

When a physical connection cannot be made between two LANs, such as across a street or between buildings, microwave radio may be used. However, it is often difficult to secure frequencies for this medium. Another alternative in this application is light transceivers, which project a beam of light similar to fiber optic cable, but through the air rather than over cable. These systems do not have the frequency allocation or radiation problems associated with microwave, but they are susceptible to interference from fog and other natural obstructions.

LAN TOPOLOGIES

LANs are designed in several different topologies, or physical patterns, connecting terminals. These shapes can range from straight lines to a ring. Each terminal on the LAN contends with other terminals for access to the system. When it has secured access to the system, it broadcasts its message to all the terminals at once. The message is picked up by the one or group of terminal stations for which it is intended. The branching tree topology is an extension of the bus, providing a link between two or more buses.

A third topology, the star network, also works like a bus in terms of contention and broadcast. But in the star, stations are connected to a single, central node (individual computer) that administers access. Several of these nodes may be connected to one another. For example, a bus serving six stations may be connected to another bus serving 10 stations and a third bus connecting 12 stations. The star topology is most often used where the connecting facilities are coaxial or twisted wire pair.

The ring topology connects each station to its own node, and these nodes are connected in a circular fashion. Node 1 is connected to node 2, which is connected to node 3, and so on, and the final node is connected back to node 1. Messages sent over the LAN are regenerated by each node, but retained only by the addressees. Eventually, the message circulates back to the sending node, which removes it from the stream.

TRANSMISSION METHODS USED BY LANS

LANs function because their transmission capacity is greater than any single terminal on the system. As a result, each station terminal can be offered a certain amount of time on the LAN, like a time-sharing arrangement. To economize on this small window of opportunity, stations organize their messages into compact packets that can be quickly distributed. When two messages are sent simultaneously, they could collide on the LAN causing the system to be temporarily disrupted. Busier LANs usually utilize special software that virtually eliminates the problem of collisions by providing orderly, non-contention access.

The transmission methods used on LANs are either baseband or broadband. The baseband medium uses a high-speed digital signal consisting of square wave DC voltage. While it is fast, it can accommodate only one message at a time. As a result, it is suitable for smaller networks where contention is low. It also is very simple to use, requiring no tuning or frequency discretion circuits. This transmission medium may be connected directly to the network access unit and is suitable for use over twisted wire pair facilities.

By contrast, the broadband medium tunes signals to special frequencies, much like cable television. Stations are instructed by signaling information to tune to a specific channel to receive information. The information within each channel on a broadband medium may also be digital, but they are separated from other messages by frequency. As a result, the medium generally requires higher capacity facilities, such as coaxial cable. Suited for busier LANs, broadband systems require the use of tuning devices in the network access unit that can filter out all but the single channel it needs.

THE FILE SERVER

The administrative software of the LAN resides either in a dedicated file server; in a smaller, less busy LAN; or in a personal computer that acts as a file server. In addition to performing as a kind of traffic controller, the file server holds files for shared use in its hard drives, administers applications such as the operating system, and allocates functions.

When a single computer is used as both a workstation and a file server, response times may lag because its processors are forced to perform several duties at once. This system will store certain files on different computers on the LAN. As a result, if one machine is down, the entire system may be crippled. If the system were to crash due to undercapacity, some data may be lost or corrupted.

The addition of a dedicated file server may be costly, but it provides several advantages over a distributed system. In addition to ensuring access even when some machines are down, its only duties are to hold files and provide access.

OTHER LAN EQUIPMENT

LANs are generally limited in size because of the physical properties of the network including distance, impedance, and load. Some equipment, such as repeaters, can extend the range of a LAN. Repeaters have no processing ability, but simply regenerate signals that are weakened by impedance. Other types of LAN equipment with processing ability include gateways, which enable LANs operating dissimilar protocols to pass information by translating it into a simpler code, such as ASCII. A bridge works like a gateway, but instead of using an intermediate code, it translates one protocol directly into another. A router performs essentially the same function as a bridge, except that it administers communications over alternate paths. Gateways, bridges, and routers can act as repeaters, boosting signals over greater distances. They also enable separate LANs located in different buildings to communicate with each other.

The connection of two or more LANs over any distance is referred to as a wide area network (WAN). WANs require the use of special software programs in the operating system to enable dial-up connections that may be performed by a telephone lines or radio waves. In some cases, separate LANs located in different cities—and even separate countries—may be linked over the public network.

LAN DIFFICULTIES

LANs are susceptible to many kinds of transmission errors. Electromagnetic interference from motors, power lines, and sources of static, as well as shorts from corrosion, can corrupt data. Software bugs and hardware failures can also introduce errors, as can irregularities in wiring and connections. LANs generally compensate for these errors by working off an uninterruptable power source, such as batteries, and using backup software to recall most recent activity and hold unsaved material. Some systems may be designed for redundancy, such as keeping two file servers and alternate wiring to route around failures.

Security problems can also be an issue with LANs. They can be difficult to manage and access because the data they use is often distributed between many different networked sources. In addition, many times this data is stored on several different workstations and servers. Most companies have specific LAN administrators who deal with these issues and are responsible for the use of LAN software. They also work to backup files and recover lost files.

PURCHASING A LAN

When considering if a LAN is suitable for a business, several things must be considered. The costs involved and the administrative support needed often far exceed reasonable predictions. A complete accounting of potential costs should include such factors as purchase price of equipment, spare parts, and taxes, installation costs, labor and building modifications, and permits. Operating costs include forecasted public network traffic, diagnostics, and routine maintenance. In addition, the buyer should seek a schedule of potential costs associated with upgrades and expansion and engineering studies.

The vendor should agree to a contract expressly detailing the degree of support that will be provided in installing and turning up the system. In addition, the vendor should provide a maintenance contract that binds the company to make immediate, free repairs when performance of the system exceeds prescribed standards. All of these factors should be addressed in the buyer's request for proposal that is distributed to potential vendors.

LANs can also be purchased for home use. Initially, these kits were expensive and slow and transmitted data via the phone lines in the home. New products have emerged that is faster, more affordable and uses wireless technology such as radio waves to allow multiple computers to share printers and perform other LAN functions. This technology allows phone lines and LANs to be used simultaneously and is perfect for a small business owner that works out of his or her home.

LANS AND SMALL BUSINESSES

A 1996 *Business Week* article estimated that only 70 percent of small businesses own PCS, and that of those, only 20 percent operate computer networks. But today, many companies offer products designed specifically to help small businesses install and use LANs simply and affordably. Many major software and network providers are planning products tailored toward the small business market as well. As a result, many more small businesses should soon be able to gain access to the advantages of LANs.

FURTHER READING:

Arnst, Catherine, et al. ''Wiring Small Business.'' *Business Week*. November 25, 1996.

Derfler, Frank J., and David Greenfield. ''Beyond the LAN.'' *PC Magazine*. December 20, 1994.

Feltman, Charles. ''A Reality Check on Virtual LANs.'' *Business Communications Review*. July 1996.

Green, Harry James. *The Business One Irwin Handbook of Telecommunications*. 2nd ed. Business One Irwin, 1991.

Seitel, Peter. ''Realistic Expectations Are Linchpins of Decent LAN.'' *Puget Sound Business Journal*. September 16, 1994.

SEE ALSO: Wide Area Networks

LOSS LEADER PRICING

Loss leader pricing is an aggressive pricing strategy wherein a store sells certain goods below cost in order to attract customers who will, according to the loss leader philosophy, make up for the losses on highlighted products with additional purchases of profitable goods. Loss leader pricing is employed by retail businesses; a somewhat similar strategy sometimes employed by manufacturers is known as penetration pricing. Loss leader pricing is, in essence, a bid to lure customer traffic away from the businesses of retail competitors. Retail stores employing this pricing strategy know that they will not make a profit on those goods that are earmarked as loss leaders. But such businesses reason that the use of such pricing mechanisms can sometimes attract large numbers of consumers who would otherwise make their purchases elsewhere. In the world of e-commerce, loss leader strategies are intended to draw consumer traffic to an online retailer's Web site.

In recent years, loss leader pricing has been practiced with considerable success, especially by large national discount retailers. The strategy is not without controversy, however. Indeed, many states have passed laws that severely limit—or explicitly forbid—selling products below cost. Lawsuits alleging that some loss leader pricing strategies amount to illegal business practices have increased in recent years, though the plaintiffs have not always been victorious. Opponents of loss leading pricing practices argue that the strategy is basically predatory in nature, designed to ultimately force competitors out of business.

Defenders of the practice contend that loss leader pricing is simply one of many measures that retail establishments take to increase in-store traffic and, ultimately, their financial well-being. They note that U.S. antitrust and trade regulation statutes are designed to protect competition, not individual competitors, and that legitimate marketplace competition inevitably results in economic winners and losers. The furor over the practice is not expected to subside any time soon, since many small businesses have been economically damaged over the past several years by larger competitors willing to take losses or razor-thin profit margins on some products in order to expand their customer bases.

Business experts note that suppliers sometimes object to loss leader pricing as well, despite the greater volume of sales that the practice often spurs within a given store. These increases may be offset by drops in sales at the stores of other clients. Such developments can strain relations between supplier and customer, and in worst case scenarios, bring pressure on the supplier to lower its price for the good(s) in question. Loss leader pricing has its greatest impact, though, in the retail community. It is there, noted *Super Marketing,* that "retailers may find themselves caught up in a downward spiral on price when one of them breaks rank and loss-leads on a product."

In recent years, retail industries have acknowledged a side effect of loss leader pricing known as "Cherry Picking." This is a practice wherein customers move from store to store, making purchases only on those products that are priced near or below acquisition cost. Such purchasing patterns effectively foil the strategy underlying loss leader pricing—to lure customers who will also buy products with healthier profit margins—but to date the practice is not deemed to be sufficiently widespread as to be of concern.

FURTHER READING:

Berry, Leonard L., and Manjit S. Yadav. "Capture and Communicate Value in the Pricing of Services." *Sloan Management Review.* Summer 1996.

Hamilton, David P. "The Price Isn't Right: Internet Pricing Has Turned Out to Be a Lot Trickier Than Retailers Expected." *Wall Street Journal.* February 12, 2001.

Harrison, Keely. "Rebels Without a Cause?" *Super Marketing.* February 10, 1995.

Zettelmeyer, Florian. "Expanding to the Internet: Pricing and Communications Strategies When Firms Compete on Multiple Channels." *Journal of Marketing Research.* August 2000.

SEE ALSO: Pricing

M

MAILING LISTS

Mailing lists are compilations of the names and addresses of actual and potential buyers of a product or service. These lists are created by companies for their own marketing initiatives (e.g., lists of all past and present customers), or they are purchased or rented from list brokers—companies that specialize in making list compilations. Indeed, some mailing lists contain information that enables businesses to target very narrow niche markets. It is possible to rent or purchase mailing lists that include the names, addresses, and phone numbers of people in categories as specific as museum curators or people who have recently purchased kayaks (or even museum curators who have recently purchased kayaks).

The importance of the mailing list has been well documented over the past few decades. Indeed, accurate, appropriately defined lists can serve as launching pads for tremendously successful direct mail advertising campaigns. Conversely, poorly chosen lists—those with outdated information or inappropriate targets for the company's advertising message—can cripple a campaign from the outset. ''You can make lots of mistakes in direct mail,'' said Jeffrey Dobkin in *Direct Marketing*. ''You can create a terrible package that no one will open. You can set your price too high—or too low—and people will not buy. You can offer your products at the wrong time. . . . But nothing in as bad as mailing to the wrong list.''

Obtaining and utilizing mailing lists for direct mailing campaigns is a favorite tactic of small business owners because of the relatively light expenses associated with it, but larger companies rely on direct mailings as well. Indeed, direct mail is used by more advertisers than any other medium, and more dollars are spent on it than on any other form of advertising. According to the Direct Marketing Association, direct mail accounted for nearly $40 billion of advertising expenditures in the United States in the late 1990s. Studies also indicated that sales figures for direct mail are continuing to expand at a healthy rate in both the consumer and business-to-business markets.

TYPES OF MAILING LISTS

There are three primary types of mailing lists, each of which are compiled in a different fashion:

RESPONSE LISTS Response lists consist of names and addresses of individuals at home or in the workplace who have responded to an offer of some kind (by mail, telephone, billing inserts, etc.). Because these people are known responders, their names are generally priced higher than those in lists compiled by other means. However, individuals on response lists may have responded to a media other than direct mail (e.g., telephone solicitation) and may not even open their ''junk mail.'' Thus it is important for the small business owner to know what percentage of a list was direct-mail compiled. And always, the business owner's most valuable response list is the ''house list'' of current and past customers.

COMPILED LISTS Compiled lists contain names and addresses of individuals gleaned from the White Pages and Yellow Pages, often enhanced with information gathered from public records (e.g., auto registrations, birth announcements, business start-ups). A very popular method of list compilation is through magazine subscriptions, since lists of readers provide an excellent means of targeting individuals in specific industries (e.g., *Institutional Investor*), or within distinct areas of interest (e.g., *Field and Stream*). Lists may also be compiled based on zip code when the small business owner seeks to reach consumers in a particular geographic area or income level (as dictated by the zip code). Credit card lists are also an effective means of list compilation.

COMPILED LISTS FROM RESPONSE MEDIA If a compiler creates a list from a professional association directory, this may be called a compiled list. However the association may well have brought in members via a mail solicitation. Thus an apparent compiled list is actually a compiled list of mail-responsive professionals.

THE LIST TEAM

Small business owners seeking to obtain and/or use a mailing list can turn to a variety of sources to help execute that task:

The List Broker. Many small business owners utilize the services of a list broker when performing direct-mail marketing campaigns. In direct mail parlance, the broker is an agent who rents the prospect lists of one business to another. The broker is paid a commission, usually 20 percent, by the list owner each time a list is rented; the renter does not pay for the broker's service. It is important to note that the broker represents the mailer and not the list owner. Since the broker researches, analyzes, and evaluates the tens of thousands of individual lists available, the broker is a marketing consultant—not just a source of list rentals.

The List Compiler. The list compiler is usually a broker who rents a number of lists from published sources and combines them into composite lists, then rents them out. The compiler performs his or her own individual alchemy on a list, adding overlays and enhancements, and often refining it down to a manageable niche. Most compilers specialize in either consumer or business lists. Large compilers maintain large staffs to verify data.

The List Manager. The list manager represents the list owner just as the broker is the agent for the mailer. The primary job of the list manager is to maximize income for the list owner by promoting the lists to as many brokers and list users as possible.

The Service Bureau. The primary function of a service bureau is constantly improving the lists—a process called "list enhancement." A primary step in list enhancement is merge/purge, the elimination of duplicate names (which can be costly to the advertiser and annoying to the customer). Service bureaus are most commonly utilized in instances where large lists are involved.

The Letter Shop. Mechanically performing a mailing can be costly and time consuming. Thus small business owners often "farm out" their mailings to letter shops. These companies not only address the envelopes, but also mechanically insert the materials, seat and stamp the envelopes, and deliver them to the post office according to mailing requirements.

THE COST OF A LIST

The small business owner shops for a list that will provide the greatest number of responses at the lowest cost. Like most purchased items, lists vary in quality and price-generally, the more expensive the list, the better the quality. The least expensive lists are known as unqualified lists; these consist of a rundown of occupants in a specified geographic area. But many lists—such as a list of another establishment's identified customers—are much more expensive. Other factors can impact the cost of a list as well. For example, lists rented for one-time mailings will cost more than multiple-use lists.

THE MAILING PROCESS

Small business owners typically rent lists rather than purchase them outright. The reason for this is the upkeep needed to keep lists current. Lists typically go bad at the rate of 2 percent per month—-at the end of the year about a quarter of most lists are out of date. Further, the more often a list is used, the less effective it becomes. Thus assuring that a list is current and "fresh" is normally left to the expertise of an experienced list compiler.

Many list brokers prefer not to actually give out a rented list, but instead will arrange to have the pieces mailed through an independent mailing house. According to *Agency Sales Magazine*, when dealing with a reputable broker there is no need to fear-the broker provides receipts from the letter house assuring that the mailing was handled as agreed.

Successful use of a mailing list is a multistep process:

DEVELOPING A CUSTOMER PROFILE The process begins with developing a profile of the ideal customer. "The more precisely you can define your target audience, the better you will be able to aim your mailing, and the better your response will be," noted Dobkin. This means that the advertiser needs to determine customer motivations, income levels, and other considerations. A precise profile allows the broker to provide a list tailored to the needs of the small business owner. This customization helps assure the highest possible response rate.

FINDING THE RIGHT LIST Once an advertiser has defined the market it wishes to target, it begins the process of culling the herd of available lists to find the best one for its particular campaign. Listings of available mailing lists can be found in advertisements in leading marketing periodicals. Trade and business associations also maintain potentially valuable membership lists. Another good source of listings is the subscription database maintained by magazine publishers, who typically use the services of a list broker to maintain this information.

As the list research and selection process unfolds, small business owners should consider the following factors when weighing the ultimate value of a list:

- How often is the list updated and/or cleaned (a "cleaned" list is one that has been processed by the U.S. Postal Service to flag recent changes of address and remove old non-deliverable addresses)?

- How frequently do people on the list make purchases, and how much do they spend?

- Have earlier customers rented or purchased the list after initial test mailings?

- How frequently has the list been rented by other companies? Business owners should avoid lists at either end of the rental spectrum, for heavily used lists are often played out, while lightly used lists generally indicate poor quality.

- What is the list company's policy on returns? Will it pay for postage on returns or is the company who purchased the list obligated to absorb the cost of mail that never reaches its intended target?

SHOPPING FOR THE LIST BROKER Many businesses utilize the services of list brokers, who vary considerably in the quality of service they provide. Reputable list brokers will provide the list pedigree, which states when the list was last purged, who else used the list, and the success rate of previous mailings. Businesses should find another list broker if discussions reveal that the firm has only sketchy knowledge of list revision and update processes, limited contacts with the list management community, limited knowledge of developments in the industry, or incomplete information on pricing, test, and roll-out potential for lists under consideration. Small business owners should also make sure that their list broker does not engage in the practice of "aging" the money that is paid them for 30 days or more before they make payment to the list management company. This practice enables the list broker to earn interest on the client's money prior to payment, but it can jeopardize the small business's credit and reputation at list management companies.

But while some list brokers do not earn their fees, others can be invaluable in ensuring that their client purchase only top-tier lists and take advantage of changing conditions in the direct mailing world. Indeed, owners of small businesses should recognize that some list brokers may not be particularly interested in adding them to their client base. Small companies that place relatively small list orders (less than two million names annually) will not be seen as a source of significant profit by list brokers. "If you order fewer than this quantity of names from a broker who is doing a good job for you, you are very fortunate," commented *Target Marketing*. "In general, forget trying to save on broker commissions. If you find a good list broker, count your blessings."

In addition to the above considerations, small business owners should weigh the following when purchasing mailing lists:

Purchase several lists if necessary—"When you are launching a new product that is heavily dependent on direct mail, make sure you have a universe of lists available large enough to support your circulation goals," counseled *Target Marketing*. "Don't put your trust in a few lists that are obviously good for your product but represent too small a universe."

Look ahead—Mailing houses typically schedule runs months in advance. For introducing a new product or service, improper planning can be disastrous. Thus small business owners are advised to plan ahead, taking into account the list broker's billing cycle: brokers typically bill their customer with 30 days to pay, and will not put out a piece of mail before receiving payment.

Utilize technology—Pioneering list brokers are establishing Internet sites to provide information about their products and services. Although many web sites are merely electronic versions of the broker's printed catalogue, some sites actually enable a small business owner to generate and purchase a mailing lists of up to 10,000 names while online. Internet mailing lists have emerged as another route for small business owners looking to publicize their product or service line.

EXPANDING A CURRENT CUSTOMER LIST

While a rented list can pay handsome dividends, the small business owner's most valuable resource is usually its list of existing customers—this serves as a starting point for any mailing. But business enterprises that are content to rely solely on such a list are courting trouble, say business experts. Indeed, list updating is a relatively inexpensive way of shoring up a company's marketing efforts. The cost of expanding a list can be offset by renting the list to non-competing businesses. An owner may choose to manage the list in-house, or hire an outside list management company. The small business owner also has the option of securing a list brokerage firm to handle the rental process in exchange for a percentage commission, usually 20 percent or so of the total price.

FURTHER READING:

Beresford, Lynn. "Pushing the Envelope." *Entrepreneur.* February 1996.

Dobkin, Jeffrey. "How to Buy a Great Mailing List." *Direct Marketing.* December 1997.

"Entrepreneur's Guide to Direct Mail Advertising." *Entrepreneur.* February 1994.

Fallek, Max. *How to Set Up Your Own Small Business.* American Institute of Small Business, 1995.

Goldsborough, Reid. "Internet Mailing Lists Offer Targeted Discussions." *Link-Up.* May-June 1999.

Hatch, Denny. "The Business of Business Lists: A Look at this Incredibly Unbelievably Complex World." *Target Marketing.* January 1997.

"How to Get and Use Mailing Lists." *Agency Sales Magazine.* March 1991.

"The MIN Top 100 (Largest Mailing Lists)." *Target Marketing.* January 1997.

Raphel, Murray. "The Name of the Game Is the Name." *Direct Marketing.* August 1989.

Scott, Howard. "Targeting Prospects with Direct Mail." *Nation's Business.* September 1997.

"32 List Laws." *Target Marketing.* September 1997.

MAIL-ORDER BUSINESS

A mail-order business is one that receives and fulfills orders for merchandise through the mail. The terms "mail-order," "direct mail," and "direct marketing" are sometimes used as if they were synonymous, but in fact they have different meanings. While a mail-order business may solicit orders using a variety of direct mail packages and catalogs, there are also many businesses, organizations, and agencies that use direct mail that are not mail-order businesses. Direct mail is simply an advertising medium, just as television, radio, newspapers, and magazines are advertising media. With direct mail, a business attempts to sell its product through the mail by means of specifically addressed advertising.

Direct marketing, meanwhile, is actually an advertising/marketing methodology employed both by mail-order enterprises and other businesses. Direct marketing may be distinguished from other types of general advertising, noted Alexander Hiam and Charles D. Schewe, authors of *The Portable MBA in Marketing,* by "the following characteristics: 1) A definite offer is made; 2) all the information necessary to make a decision is provided; and 3) a response mechanism is given—a toll-free telephone number or a mail-in coupon, for example." But while direct marketing makes heavy use of direct mail, it also employs a range of other advertising options—catalogs, coupons, periodicals, newspapers, telephone, radio, and television—to reach its target audiences.

A mail-order business, on the other hand, is simply a kind of commercial enterprise. A mail-order establishment is a business primarily engaged in soliciting sales via various media—often through direct marketing methodologies (catalogs being the best known)—and delivering, by mail, the merchandise that is ordered by customers (either via the mail or the telephone) as a result of those sales efforts. Mail-order businesses originally took orders primarily through the mail, but lower long-distance telephone rates and the advent of toll-free telephone calls (800 numbers) made it more convenient for customers to place orders over the telephone (the mail-in option is still generally offered, however). More recently, most mail-order companies have also instituted online ordering options for customers.

MAIL-ORDER BUSINESSES TODAY

Mail-order businesses date back to pre-Revolutionary War days, when gardeners and farmers ordered seeds through catalogs. Indeed, several of America's largest modern-day retailers first established themselves as mail-order enterprises back in the nineteenth century. This trend, in which retail enterprises establish themselves via catalog sales before venturing into the nation's malls and other centers of commerce, is still evident today. Other businesses are primarily retail-oriented, and use mail-order campaigns to supplement store sales. But while some studies indicate that a mail-order establishment that also cultivates a presence in the retail world is more likely to be regarded as a viable enterprise by potential customers, many businesses exclusively engaged in mail-order sales enjoy fine reputations.

Mail-order shopping is popular in modern America for a variety of reasons. Historically, mail-order businesses became successful because they offered a wider variety of goods than could be found in local retail outlets. In addition, goods purchased through the mail were often less expensive than those available locally, in part because mail-order houses, blessed with the capacity to maintain far larger inventories than many of their retail competitors, could afford to offer more sizable discounts. Mail-order shopping also offered consumers more convenience than shopping at retail stores. Indeed, for consumers in remote rural sections of the country, their isolation from commercial centers made catalog or mail-order shopping a necessity. Finally, individuals pursuing a hobby or special interest were more likely to locate those hard-to-find items in a specialty catalog than in a store.

By the latter half of the twentieth century, several socioeconomic factors had further contributed to the growth of "at-home shopping." Possibly the single most important factor was the dramatic increase in the number of women working outside the home. This change gave some families more discretionary income, but perhaps more tellingly, the trend also meant that women had less time to make purchases. Shopping convenience subsequently became a larger concern, and mail-order purchases that could be executed at home—without driving to a mall or other retail outlet—became more attractive. The emergence of credit cards and telephone-based ordering systems also helped mail-order businesses.

Mail-order businesses today offer consumers a wide array of products and services that they can order from their own home. Magazine subscription sales represent the largest segment of mail-order sales, while books and newspapers also account for a significant portion of mail-order business. The fastest-growing segment of the mail-order business, however, is that of specialty catalogs. Specialty catalogs are fast replacing the large general merchandise catalogs with which American consumers of earlier generations were familiar. In fact, several of the major merchandise catalogs have been discontinued and replaced with a series of specialty catalogs. The list of specialty goods sold through the mail is seemingly endless, encompassing hundreds of categories. Kitchenware, furniture, gourmet foods, outdoor clothing, health products, gardening products, sports equipment and apparel, music, collectibles, and computer software and equipment are but a few of the more popular categories of goods sold through specialty catalogs today.

CATALOG MARKETING

There are three major categories of catalogs: business-to-business catalogs, consumer catalogs, and catalog showrooms. Business-to-business catalogs provide merchandise to be used in the course of business, including everything from office supplies to computers. In industrial settings, business-to-business catalogs are used to sell everything from heavy machinery to hand tools. Business-to-business catalogs are mailed to individuals at their place of business, with most purchases being made on behalf of the business rather than the individual.

Consumer catalogs are mailed to consumers at home. In her book *Catalog Marketing*, Katie Muldoon identified eight types of consumer catalogs. Unaffiliated catalogs are stand-alone ventures—not affiliated with any retailer or manufacturer—whose primary purpose is to sell merchandise by mail. The next type of consumer catalogs are retail catalogs, which include traffic generators, independent profit centers, and combination catalogs. Traffic generator catalogs are designed to build store traffic rather than to generate mail order sales. On the other hand, a retailer might set up a catalog as an independent direct mail operation that is expected to produce a profit on the basis of the sales it generates. Hybrids that are designed to generate store traffic as well as mail order sales combine the best of both worlds.

A third type of consumer catalog is the manufacturer-supported catalog. These may be designed to generate mail order sales, build store traffic, or simply create an image for the maker of a product. Incentive catalogs—which are often issued by credit card companies—offer consumers discounted name-brand merchandise with some proof of purchase of a particular product or use of a particular credit card. Catalogs issued by nonprofit organizations represent yet another type of consumer catalog. Museums have successfully used catalogs to increase sales of gift shop items, for example. Co-op catalogs are used to highlight merchandise from a variety of companies. These catalogs are relatively inexpensive to produce and are often found in non-traditional distribution channels such as bookstores and newsstands.

Syndicated consumer catalogs carry the name of a particular company, usually one that is well known and prestigious. However, the company whose name is on the catalog is not involved in its production and does not carry the merchandise listed in the catalog. Instead, the syndicator pays a commission to the company for use of its name and handles all of the aspects of the catalog business. Another category of consumer catalog is the international catalog. With improved telephone service, it is possible to order by telephone or fax from virtually anywhere in the world.

Catalog showrooms combine retail marketing with catalog marketing. A catalog showroom is essentially a retail outlet. The catalog, usually quite large, serves primarily to build traffic in the showroom. The trend in catalog showrooms has been to de-emphasize the mail order aspect of the catalog and present the showroom as a retail outlet with the added benefit of being able to place catalog orders from the showroom.

Industry analysts forecast continued growth within the mail-order business, although they caution that competition has increased in the industry. In addition, the growth in mail-order purchases has brought, perhaps inevitably, an attendant increase in concerns about a minority of establishments who engage in deceptive mailing practices or disregard commonly adhered to customer privacy parameters. Concerns over such issues have spurred discussion of increased regulation of mail-order businesses.

STARTING A MAIL-ORDER BUSINESS

Mail-order's current popularity, as well as the almost uniformly positive assessments of its future prospects, have made it an attractive area for entrepreneurs. But while some entrepreneurs have been highly successful in mail order ventures, those who enter the business are not guaranteed to succeed. Indeed, the prospective mail-order business owner needs to consider a variety of factors before launching his or her enterprise.

The single most important factor to consider is whether the product (or products) that would be featured in your mail-order business is a strong one. In assessing the strength of a product line, factors that should be weighed include the product's availability in other mediums (such as retail outlets), its intended demographic audience, and its unique qualities. Of course, just because a product is unique does not mean that it will be popular. A unique product that is of little use to customers will not be successful; conversely, some of the most profitable mail-order businesses concentrate on providing commonly available goods such as kitchen appliances. They are successful because they are able to convince customers that their products offer advantages in price, performance, or aesthetics. Still, some of the most spectacularly successful mail-order establishments have been ones that take advantage of previously untapped consumer niches by introducing products that are unique in one respect or another.

Another important consideration when weighing whether to launch a mail-order business is the cost of doing business. Catalogs are quite expensive to print and mail, and the nature of other direct mail advertising options, such as coupon mailings or newspaper advertising, precludes presentation of more than a couple products. This is not a deterrent if you are only selling one or two products, but if you have a sizable product line, such advertising avenues are far less attractive. The prospective mail-order business owner, then, must determine if he or she will sell sufficient quantities of their product(s) to compensate for marketing/ advertising costs and other expenditures. In addition, he or she also must gauge whether the product is suited for sale through mail order. If it is a delicate product, or one that might spoil or otherwise lose its attractiveness in a relatively short time span, then it may not be one that should be subjected to the rigors and shipment schedule realities of mail order.

If the business owner determines that mail order is the route to go, then a catalog will almost certainly be the centerpiece of the firm's advertising efforts. To best ensure that their catalog is effective in sparking sales and long-term profitability, experts urge entrepreneurs to consider the following:

- Establish toll-free ordering for catalog users, especially if competitors' catalogs publicize such a convenience.

- Establish live, 24-hour service. This is not yet commonplace in many industries, but in others it may loom as an imperative. Small mail-order companies should note, however, that introducing this feature may be impractical if their line is highly technical and/or requires trained customer service representatives.

- Review ease and speed of ordering, especially when compared to competitors.

- Review return and refund policies and their level of user-friendliness. Again, this is another area that can build or destroy customer loyalty.

- Compare your prices with those of direct and indirect competitors.

- Consider special offers for customers who make bulk purchases.

Since many mail-order establishments rely on the mail to reach customers, it is vitally important for them to secure and maintain useful and reliable mailing lists. For many mail order businesses, their internal customer database is one of their most valued commodities. "The fastest way to make money in the catalog business is to mail more frequently to your known customers," stated one mail order consulting executive in *Entrepreneur*. Given the importance of this information, many owners of small mail order companies outsource management of this data so that it can be maintained at a high standard (professional database managers can ensure uniformity and accuracy of information). In the meantime, the owners can turn their energies to aspects of the business to which their talents are better suited (marketing, workforce management, etc.) In addition to internal lists of customers, good mailing lists can also be secured from list brokers, magazine publishers, or trade associations. Of course, even the best mailing list is of little long-term use if the mail-order enterprise provides shoddy goods or customer service. "Dissatisfaction with the product or a poorly conducted return program can cause enough bad will to ruin your business reputation or simply destroy your profit margin by the extra postage and handling charges involved," observed the editors of *How to Run a Small Business*.

Another business option for the prospective mail-order business owner is to sell goods that are actually manufactured by other establishments. Entrepreneurs who opt for this kind of mail-order business should make every effort to purchase the goods they are selling from the manufacturers themselves. Purchasing from secondary sources is significantly more expensive, for those establishments need to push up the price of the goods in order to realize a profit. Experts acknowledge, however, that in some instances—such as scenarios where an offered product dramatically exceeds estimated sales—it may be necessary to deal with secondary sources in order to meet customer orders.

Some mail-order businesses even arrange for their suppliers to ship the goods themselves. Under this system, mail-order outfits accept paid orders on behalf of the manufacturer, then pay the manufacturer to mail the product directly to the customer. Some mail-order houses shy away from this arrangement, however, for while such systems eliminate most inventory costs, they also compromise the independence of the mail-order house and its ability to ensure quality service. If a manufacturer proves incompetent or engages in questionable business tactics—such as using the addresses supplied by the mail-order business to compile its own mailing list, thus cutting the mail-order house out of the action down the road—a mail-order enterprise can find its very existence threatened.

REGULATIONS THAT AFFECT MAIL-ORDER BUSINESS

Mail-order businesses must comply with the regulations of the Federal Trade Commission (FTC) and the U.S. Postal Service (USPS). In addition, mail-order businesses may be subject to applicable state laws, especially concerning the collection of sales tax.

The FTC has issued several directives, guidelines, and advisory opinions concerning mail-order businesses. These and other relevant regulations are published in the Code of Federal Regulations (CFR), Title 16, Chapters 1 and 2, which is available in most large libraries or directly from the FTC. Among the most important of these FTC rules is the Mail-Order Merchandise Rule. This regulation, also known as the 30-Day Rule, is designed to protect consumers from unexpected delays in receiving merchandise ordered through the mail. It allows the customer to cancel any order not received within the time period advertised or, if none is stated, 30 days of order. According to the rule, in those instances in which shipment of goods is delayed, a customer must be notified within 15 days of placing his or her order. Moreover, if shipment is delayed past the agreed-upon delivery date (or 30 days), then the business must send a postage-paid return notice notifying the buyer that he or she may terminate the order for a full refund, which must be received within seven business days.

Another FTC rule requires all mail-order advertising to indicate the country of origin of the product being advertised if the product has a fabric as part of its content. This rule was designed to protect domestic textile and wool producers. Mail-order business are also subject to FTC guidelines concerning product guarantees and warranties that apply to all businesses.

Mail-order advertising frequently contains endorsements or testimonials. Under FTC guidelines, any endorsement must reflect the views of the endorser, and must not be reworded or taken out of context. In addition, the endorser must be a genuine user of the product. If the endorser has been paid, the ad must disclose that fact, unless they are celebrities or experts. Additional FTC rules apply specifically to endorsements by average consumers and expert endorsements.

The FTC has also issued guidelines to curb deceptive pricing by some mail-order businesses. These rules affect two-for-one offers, price comparisons, and other issues. The practice of advertising products that have yet to be manufactured, while legal, is subject to FTC requirements as well. FTC regulations call for this advertising practice, also called dry testing, to clearly state that sale of the product is only planned and that it is possible that consumers who order the product may not receive it. In addition, if the product is not manufactured, consumers who ordered it must be notified within four months of the original ad or mailing, and they must be given the opportunity to cancel their order without obligation.

In addition to FTC regulations, mail-order businesses must also be aware of USPS regulations. Lotteries, for example, are illegal under USPS regulations. As defined by the USPS, a lottery includes the element of chance, consideration—a term that means that one must make a purchase to enter—and a prize. In recognition of this definition, mail-order businesses instead organize sweepstakes that do not require any consideration, payment, or purchase on the part of the consumer. While sweepstakes have proved to be an effective method of advertising mail-order merchandise, many states have laws affecting their use.

Post office operations can impact on a mail-order enterprise in other ways as well. A mail-order house that presorts direct mailings by zip code can sometimes lower its postage costs, for example, while business-reply cards are subject to the approval of your postmaster. For complete information on postal rates, regulations, and requirements that could potentially impact a mail-order (or any other) business, contact your local post office or the Customer Programs Division of the U.S. Postal Service in Washington, DC.

FURTHER READING:

Beresford, Lynn. "Pushing the Envelope." *Entrepreneur*. February 1996.

Hiam, Alexander, and Charles D. Schewe. *The Portable MBA in Marketing.* Wiley, 1992.

J.K. Lasser Institute. *How to Run a Small Business.* Simon and Schuster, 1994.

Keup, Erwin J. *Mail-Order Legal Guide.* Oasis Press, 1993.

McIntyre, Susan. "Cataloging for Entrepreneurs: Doing Your Own Competitive Analysis." *Direct Marketing.* January 1999.

Muldoon, Katie. *Catalog Marketing.* American Management Association, 1988.

Simon, Julian L. *How to Start and Operate a Mail-Order Business.* McGraw-Hill, 1993.

Small Business Administration. *Selling by Mail Order.* No. MT09. SBA, na.

Sroge, Maxwell. *Inside the Leading Mail-Order Houses.* NTC Business Books, 1989.

MANAGEMENT INFORMATION SYSTEMS (MIS)

According to Kenneth C. Laudon and Jane Price Laudon in their book *Management Information Systems: A Contemporary Perspective,* an information system is "a set of procedures that collects (or retrieves), processes, stores, and disseminates information to support decision making and control." In most cases, information systems are formal, computer-based systems that play an integral role in organizations. Although information systems are computer-based, it is important to note that any old computer or software program is not necessarily an information system. "Electronic computers and related software programs are the technical foundation, the tools and materials, of modern information systems," Laudon and Laudon wrote. "Understanding information systems, however, requires one to understand the problems they are designed to solve, the architectural and design solutions, and the organizational processes that lead to these solutions."

Though it is sometimes applied to all types of information systems used in businesses, the term "management information systems," or MIS, actually describes specific systems that "provide managers with reports and, in some cases, on-line access to the organization's current performance and historical records," Laudon and Laudon noted. "MIS primarily serve the functions of planning, controlling, and decision making at the management level." MIS are one of a number of different types of information systems that can serve the needs of different levels in an organization. For example, information systems might be developed to support upper management in planning the company's strategic direction or to help manufacturing in controlling a plant's operations. Some of the other types of information systems include: transaction processing systems, which simply record the routine transactions needed to conduct business, like payroll, shipping, or sales orders; and office automation systems, which are intended to increase the productivity of office workers and include such systems as word processing, electronic mail, and digital filing. Ideally, the various types of information systems in an organization are interconnected to allow for information sharing.

SYSTEMS DEVELOPMENT

The development of effective information systems holds a number of challenges for small businesses. "Despite, or perhaps because of, the rapid development of computer technology, there is nothing easy or mechanical about building workable information systems," Laudon and Laudon stated. "Building, operating, and maintaining information systems are challenging for a number of reasons." For example, some information cannot be captured and put into a system. Computers often cannot be programmed to take into account competitor responses to marketing tactics or changes in economic conditions, among other things. In addition, the value of information erodes over time, and rapid changes in technology can make systems become obsolete very quickly. Finally, many companies find systems development to be problematic because the services of skilled programmers are at a premium.

Despite the challenges inherent in systems development, however, MIS also offer businesses a number of advantages. "Today, leading companies and organizations are using information technology as a competitive tool to develop new products and services, forge new relationships with suppliers, edge out competitors, and radically change their internal operations and organizations," Laudon and Laudon explained. For example, using MIS strategically can help a company to become a market innovator. By providing a unique product or service to meet the needs of customers, a company can raise the cost of market entry for potential competitors and thus gain a competitive advantage. Another strategic use of MIS involves forging electronic linkages to customers and suppliers. This can help companies to lock in business and increase switching costs. Finally, it is possible to use MIS to change the overall basis of competition in an industry. For example, in an industry characterized by price wars, a business with a new means of processing customer data may be able to create unique product features that change the basis of competition to differentiation.

The impetus to develop a new information system can grow out of end-user demands, the availability of new technology, or management strategy. A variety of tools exist for analyzing a company's information needs and designing systems to support them. The basic process of systems development involves defining the project, creating a model of the current system, deriving a model for the new system, measuring the costs and benefits of all alternatives, selecting the best option, designing the new system, completing the specific programming functions, installing and testing the new system, and completing a post-implementation audit.

Information systems designers, whether internal to the company or part of an outside firm, are generally responsible for assuring the technical quality of the new system and the ease of the user interface. They also oversee the process of system design and implementation, assess the impact of the new system on the organization, and develop ways to protect the system from abuse after it is installed. But it is the responsibility of small business owners and managers to plan what systems to implement and to ensure that the underlying data are accurate and useful. "The organization must develop a technique for ensuring that the most important systems are attended to first, that unnecessary systems are not built, and that end users have a full and meaningful role in determining which new systems will be built and how," according to Laudon and Laudon.

KNOWLEDGE MANAGEMENT

Knowledge management (KM) is a relatively new form of MIS that expands the concept to include information systems that provide decision-making tools and data to people at all levels of a company. The idea behind KM is to facilitate the sharing of information within a company in order to eliminate redundant work and improve decision-making. KM becomes particularly important as a small business grows. When there are only a few employees, they can remain in constant contact with one another and share knowledge directly. But as the number of employees increases and they are divided into teams or functional units, it becomes more difficult to keep the lines of communication open and encourage the sharing of ideas.

Knowledge management is a way of using technology to facilitate the process of collaboration across an organization. A small business might begin sharing information between groups of employees by creating a best-practices database or designing an electronic company directory indicating who holds what knowledge. Larger companies, as David Coleman wrote in *Computer Reseller News,* can implement KM systems through targeted pilot projects or through a broader strategy involving the firm's technical infrastructure. Many companies have installed intranets—or enterprise-wide computer networks with databases all employees can access—as a form of KM. A number of software programs exist to facilitate KM efforts. Some of the leaders in the field include Lotus Notes,

Microsoft Exchange Server, and a variety of systems based on XML.

FURTHER READING:

Coleman, David. "Taking the Best Approach to Knowledge." *Computer Reseller News.* June 1, 1998.

Laudon, Kenneth C., and Jane Price Laudon. *Management Information Systems: A Contemporary Perspective.* 2nd ed. New York: Macmillan, 1991.

Schwartz, Jeffrey. "Collaboration—More Hype Than Reality; True Knowledge Management Remains the Province of an Intrepid Few Organizations." *Internet Week.* October 25, 1999.

MANAGEMENT BY OBJECTIVES

Management by Objectives (MBO) is a process in which a manager and an employee agree upon a set of specific performance goals, or objectives, and jointly develop a plan for reaching them. The objectives must be clear and achievable, and the plan must include a time frame and evaluation criteria. For example, a salesperson might set a goal of increasing customer orders by 15 percent in dollar terms over the course of a year.

MBO is primarily used as a tool for strategic planning, employee motivation, and performance enhancement. It is intended to improve communication between employees and management, increase employee understanding of company goals, focus employee efforts upon organizational objectives, and provide a concrete link between pay and performance. An important factor in an MBO system is its emphasis on the results achieved by employees rather than the activities performed in their jobs.

IMPLEMENTING AN MBO PROGRAM

To be successful, an MBO program should be part of a small business's overall system of planning and goal setting. The first step in implementing MBO is to establish long-range company goals in such areas as sales, competitive positioning, human resource development, etc. A small business owner may find it helpful to begin by defining the company's current business and looking for emerging customer needs or market trends that may require adaptation. Such long-range planning provides a framework for charting the company's future staffing levels, marketing approaches, financing needs, product development focus, and facility and equipment usage.

The next step in establishing an MBO system is to use these long-range plans to determine company-wide goals for the current year. Then the company goals can be broken down further into goals for different departments, and eventually into goals for individual employees. As goal-setting filters down through the organization, special care must be taken to ensure that individual and department goals all support the long-range objectives of the business. Ideally, a small business's managers should be involved in formulating the company's long-range goals. This approach may increase their commitment to achieving the goals, allow them to communicate the goals clearly to employees, and help them to create their own short-range goals to support the company goals.

At a minimum, a successful MBO program requires each employee to produce five to ten specific, measurable goals. In addition to a statement of the goal itself, each goal should be supported with a means of measurement and a series of steps toward completion. These goals should be proposed to the employee's manager in writing, discussed, and approved. It is the manager's responsibility to make sure that all employee goals are consistent with the department and company goals. The manager also must compare the employee's performance with his or her goals on a regular basis in order to identify any problems and take corrective action as needed.

Formulating goals is not an easy task for employees, and most people do not master it immediately. Small business owners may find it helpful to begin the process by asking employees and managers to define their jobs and list their major responsibilities. Then the employees and managers can create a goal or goals based upon each responsibility and decide how to measure their own performance in terms of results. In the Small Business Administration publication *Planning and Goal Setting for Small Business,* Raymond F. Pelissier recommended having employees create a miniature work plan for each goal. A work plan would include the goal itself, the measurement terms, any major problems anticipated in meeting the goal, a series of work steps toward meeting the goal (with completion dates), and the company goal to which the personal goal relates.

Small business owners may also find it helpful to break down employee goal setting into categories. The first category, regular goals, would include objectives related to the activities that make up an employee's major responsibilities. Examples of regular goals might include improving efficiency or the amount and quality of work produced. The second category, problem-solving goals, should define and eliminate any major problems the employee encounters in performing his or her job. Another category is innovation, which should include goals that apply original ideas to company problems. The final category is development goals, which should include those goals related to personal growth or the development of employees. Dividing goal setting into categories often helps employees think about their jobs in

new ways and acts to release them from the tendency to create activity-based goals.

Another requirement for any successful MBO program is that it provide for a regular review of employee progress toward meeting goals. This review can take place either monthly or quarterly. When the review uncovers employee performance that is below expectations, managers should try to identify the problem, assign responsibility for correcting it, and make a note in the MBO files.

SMALL BUSINESS OWNER INVOLVEMENT

Given that MBO represents an unusual way of thinking about job performance for many employees, small business owners may find it best to introduce MBO programs gradually and to include a formal training component. A small business's managers can be introduced to MBO through a classroom seminar taught by the small business owner or by an outside consultant. Either way, it is important that the managers be allowed to express any doubts and reservations they may have, and that the training include preparation of an actual goal by each participant. When MBO is brought back to the small business, it may be best to start slowly, with each employee only preparing a few goals. This approach will allow employees to learn to prepare goals that are achievable, develop ways to measure their own performance, and anticipate problems that will prevent them from attaining their goals.

Another factor determining the success of MBO programs is the direct involvement of the small business owner. Pelissier noted that the small business owner needs to champion the MBO system from the beginning, as well as set an example for the company's managers, in order for it to succeed. Since managers have a natural tendency to focus their attention upon their own functions rather than on the goals of the overall organization, it can be difficult to educate them about MBO. It is also important for the small business owner to remain patient during the implementation phase: in fact, Pelissier claimed that it may take three to four years before an MBO program creates quantifiable results in a small business. As David Dinesh and Elaine Palmer indicated in their article for *Management Decision,* partial implementation is one of the major potential problems associated with MBO programs.

Implemented correctly, however, MBO can provide a number of benefits to a small business. For example, MBO may help employees understand how their performance will be evaluated and measured. In addition, by allowing them to contribute to goal setting, it may increase the motivation and productivity of a small business's employees. MBO also stands to provide a small business's employees with the means to prioritize their work on a daily basis. Although employee performance evaluation is still a complex task under an MBO system, MBO can also provide an objective basis for evaluation. However, it is important to note that an employee's failure to meet preestablished goals can be attributed to many things besides personal failure. For example, the failure to meet goals could result from setting the wrong objectives, not taking into account company restrictions that may impinge upon performance, establishing an improper measures of progress, or a combination of all of these factors.

Overall, establishing an MBO system in a small business may be difficult, but it is usually worth it. The most difficult aspect of implementing MBO may be simply getting people to think in terms of results rather than activities. Even when an MBO system is implemented well, a small business may encounter problems. For example, employees may set low goals to ensure attainment. Similarly, managers' objectives may focus on the attainment of short-term rather than long-term goals. Finally, employees and managers alike may fall victim to confusion and frustration. Some of the most common reasons for the failure of an MBO program include a lack of involvement among the top management of a small business, inadequate goal setting on a company-wide basis, implementation of an MBO system that occurs too rapidly, or the failure to instruct a company's managers and employees in the basics of MBO. But even though establishing an MBO program may be problematic, it can also offer significant rewards to small businesses.

FURTHER READING:

Bateman, Thomas S., and Carl P. Zeithaml. *Management: Function and Strategy.* Homewood, IL: Irwin, 1990.

Dinesh, David, and Elaine Palmer. ''Management by Objectives and Balanced Scorecard: Will Rome Fall Again?'' *Management Decision.* July-August 1998.

Pelissier, Raymond F. *Planning and Goal Setting for Small Business.* Washington, D.C.: Small Business Administration, n.d.

MANAGER RECRUITMENT

Nearly every successful small business starts out the same way—with a hardworking business owner who has a dream that he or she believes in and the work ethic to make that dream become a reality. If everything goes according to plan, that owner founds a business, the business grows, and new employees are hired. Even as those first employees are hired, however, the owner is still the ultimate decision maker, the person who maintains power over the direction and strategy of the firm. During this period of expansion, however, an unhealthy dynamic can take root. ''As the company grows, many [owners] are still leading their organizations alone and continue to take hands-on control of all areas of the operation,'' observed Mike Knowlton and Alexis Candalino in *Canadian Business Review.* ''This leads to a strangling effect on the development of the company.'' The savvy small business owner is the one who knows when to stop trying to do it all and when to expand his or her management team, either by promoting existing employees to new positions of authority and responsibility or by recruiting managers from outside the company.

In almost every growing business, the owner eventually reaches a point where he or she has to go outside the company to hire a new officer, a new part of the management team. This is an inevitable development once a business reaches a size in which responsibilities become fragmented and specialized. In the early days, it might have been easy for the owner and one or two other people to manage everything, from the hiring to marketing to inventory control. Business expansion, however, especially if it takes place at a pace that outstrips existing facilities and operational procedures, makes that ''do it all'' approach unworkable—handling hiring and firing on the fly might be manageable when there are six employees in the whole company, but not when there are 60.

Business experts cite several major advantages associated with the development and institution of effective management teams in enterprises that previously relied on a single individual for guidance. One of the most frequently mentioned benefits of promotion from within, for instance, is that it serves to increase motivation and improve morale throughout the workforce, which recognizes that hard work and contributions to the company's success will be rewarded in tangible fashion. But proponents of hiring management personnel from outside the organization contend that such practices help to provide diversity at the company's highest level. Laurence Weinzimmer contended in the *Journal of Small Business Management* that having a variety of voices from different professional backgrounds on the management team leads to an atmosphere that fosters constructive criticism and reduces complacency. According to this argument, the different perspectives foster company growth and ''produce better decision making because whereas members with many years in a particular industry can offer insights based on rich experience, newcomers can provide fresh perspectives.''

Different voices also create a system of checks and balances on the management team. A team comprised of long-time company insiders might suffer because the owner still views the company as being in the start-up phase and might be reluctant to delegate authority, which increases the likelihood that a single person will exert too much influence over the strategic direction of the entire company. Many business experts believe that outsiders, once they are acclimated to the company, are more likely to challenge the status quo and act as a balancing influence to the existing management team. In addition, outsiders are usually specialists in a certain area that they were hired to oversee. This knowledge base often means that their opinion carries more weight than that of a longtime employee who is not a specialist in that field.

FURTHER READING:

Beech, Wendy M. "Choosing the Team: The Management Plan Can Help Outline and Define the Duties of Your Key Personnel." *Black Enterprise*. January 1998.

Candalino, Alexis W., and Mike Knowlton. "Small Companies as Business Laboratories." *Canadian Business Review*. Spring 1994.

Carrier, Camille. "The Training and Development Needs of Owner-Managers of Small Businesses with Export Potential." *Journal of Small Business Management*. October 1999.

Dauten, Dale A. *The Gifted Boss: How to Find, Create and Keep Great Employees*. Morrow, 1999.

Half, Robert. *Finding, Hiring & Keeping the Best Employees*. Wiley, 1993.

Nelson, Robert B. "Empowering Employees Through Delegation." *Small Business Reports*. June 1994.

Weinzimmer, Lawrence G. "Top Management Team Correlates of Organizational Growth in a Small Business Context: A Comparative Study." *Journal of Small Business Management*. July 1997.

SEE ALSO: Span of Control

MANAGING ORGANIZATIONAL CHANGE

Organizational change occurs when a company makes a transition from its current state to some desired future state. Managing organizational change is the process of planning and implementing change in organizations in such a way as to minimize employee resistance and cost to the organization, while also maximizing the effectiveness of the change effort.

Today's business environment requires companies to undergo changes almost constantly if they are to remain competitive. Factors such as globalization of markets and rapidly evolving technology force businesses to respond in order to survive. Such changes may be relatively minor—as in the case of installing a new software program—or quite major—as in the case of refocusing an overall marketing strategy. "Organizations must change because their environments change," according to Thomas S. Bateman and Carl P. Zeithaml in their book *Management: Function and Strategy*. "Today, businesses are bombarded by incredibly high rates of change from a

frustratingly large number of sources. . . . Inside pressures come from top managers and lower-level employees who push for change. Outside pressures come from changes in the legal, competitive, technological, and economic environments."

Organizational change initiatives often arise out of problems faced by a company. In some cases, however, companies are encouraged to change for other, more positive reasons. "Change commonly occurs because the organization experiences some difficulty," Bateman and Zeithaml wrote. "But sometimes the most constructive change takes place not because of problems but because of opportunities." The authors used the term "performance gap" to describe the difference between a company's actual performance and the performance of which it is capable. Recognition of a performance gap often provides the impetus for change, as companies strive to improve their performance to expected levels. This sort of gap is also where many entrepreneurs find opportunities to begin new businesses.

Unfortunately, as Rick Mauer noted in an article for *HR Focus*, statistics show that many organizational change efforts fail. For example, 50 percent of quality improvement programs fail to meet their goals, and 30 percent of process reengineering efforts are unsuccessful. The most common reason that change efforts fail is that they encounter resistance from employees. Change appears threatening to many people, which makes it difficult to gain their support and commitment to implementing changes. Consequently, the ability to manage change effectively is a highly sought-after skill in managers. Companies need people who can contribute positively to their inevitable change efforts.

AREAS OF ORGANIZATIONAL CHANGE

Bateman and Zeithaml identified four major areas of organizational change: strategy, technology, structure, and people. All four areas are related, and companies often must institute changes in the other areas when they attempt to change one area. The first area, strategy changes, can take place on a large scale—for example, when a company shifts its resources to enter a new line of business—or on a small scale—for example, when a company makes productivity improvements in order to reduce costs. There are three basic stages for a company making a strategic change: 1) realizing that the current strategy is no longer suitable for the company's situation; 2) establishing a vision for the company's future direction; and 3) implementing the change and setting up new systems to support it.

Technological changes are often introduced as components of larger strategic changes, although they sometimes take place on their own. An important aspect of changing technology is determining who in the organization will be threatened by the change. To be successful, a technology change must be incorporated into the company's overall systems, and a management structure must be created to support it. Structural changes can also occur due to strategic changes—as in the case where a company decides to acquire another business and must integrate it—as well as due to operational changes or changes in managerial style. For example, a company that wished to implement more participative decision making might need to change its hierarchical structure.

People changes can become necessary due to other changes, or sometimes companies simply seek to change workers' attitudes and behaviors in order to increase their effectiveness. "Attempting a strategic change, introducing a new technology, and other changes in the work environment may affect people's attitudes (sometimes in a negative way)," Bateman and Zeithaml wrote. "But management frequently initiates programs with a conscious goal of directly and positively changing the people themselves." In any case, people changes can be the most difficult and important part of the overall change process. The science of organization development was created to deal with changing people on the job through techniques such as education and training, team building, and career planning.

RESISTANCE TO CHANGE

A manager trying to implement a change, no matter how small, should expect to encounter some resistance from within the organization. Resistance to change is a normal reaction from people who have become accustomed to a certain way of doing things. Of course, certain situations or tactics can increase resistance. "Individuals, groups, and organizations must be motivated to change. But if people perceive no performance gap or if they consider the gap unimportant, they will not have this motivation. Moreover, they will resist changes that others try to introduce," Bateman and Zeithaml explained.

The authors outlined a number of common reasons that people tend to resist change. These include: inertia, or the tendency of people to become comfortable with the status quo; timing, as when change efforts are introduced at a time when workers are busy or have a bad relationship with management; surprise, because people's reflex is to resist when they must deal with a sudden, radical change; or peer pressure, which may cause a group to resist due to anti-management feelings even if individual members do not oppose the change. Resistance can also grow out of people's perceptions of how the change will affect them personally. They may resist because they fear that they will lose their jobs or their status, because

they do not understand the purpose of the change, or simply because they have a different perspective on the change than management.

Fortunately, Bateman and Zeithaml noted, there are a number of steps managers can take to help overcome resistance to change. One proven method is education and communication. Employees can be informed about both the nature of the change and the logic behind it before it takes place through reports, memos, group presentations, or individual discussions. Another important component of overcoming resistance is inviting employee participation and involvement in both the design and implementation phases of the change effort. "People who are involved in decisions understand them better and are more committed to them," Bateman and Zeithaml explained. Another possible approach to managing resistance to change is through facilitation and support. Managers should be sure to provide employees with the resources they need to make the change, be supportive of their efforts, listen to their problems with empathy, and accept that their performance level may drop initially.

Some companies manage to overcome resistance to change through negotiation and rewards. They offer employees concrete incentives to ensure their cooperation. Other companies resort to manipulation, or using subtle tactics such as giving a resistance leader a prominent position in the change effort. A final option is coercion, which involves punishing people who resist or using force to ensure their cooperation. Although this method can be useful when speed is of the essence, it can have lingering negative effects on the company. Of course, no method is appropriate to every situation, and a number of different methods may be combined as needed. As Bateman and Zeithaml stated, "Effective change managers are familiar with the various approaches and capable of flexibly applying them according to the situation."

TECHNIQUES FOR MANAGING CHANGE EFFECTIVELY

Managing change effectively requires moving the organization from its current state to a future desired state at minimal cost to the organization. Bateman and Zeithaml identified three steps for managers to follow in implementing organizational change:

1) Diagnose the current state of the organization. This involves identifying problems the company faces, assigning a level of importance to each one, and assessing the kinds of changes needed to solve the problems.

2) Design the desired future state of the organization. This involves picturing the ideal situ-

ation for the company after the change is implemented, conveying this vision clearly to everyone involved in the change effort, and designing a means of transition to the new state. An important part of the transition should be maintaining some sort of stability; some things—such as the company's overall mission or key personnel—should remain constant in the midst of turmoil to help reduce people's anxiety.

3) Implement the change. This involves managing the transition effectively. It might be helpful to draw up a plan, allocate resources, and appoint a key person to take charge of the change process. The company's leaders should try to generate enthusiasm for the change by sharing their goals and vision and acting as role models. In some cases, it may be useful to try for small victories first in order to pave the way for later successes.

"Successfully changing an enterprise requires wisdom, prescience, energy, persistence, communication, education, training, resources, patience, timing, and the right incentives," John S. McCallum wrote in the *Ivey Business Journal*. "Successfully leading and managing change is and will continue to be a front-burner responsibility for executives. Prospects are grim for enterprises that either cannot or will not change. Indeed, no industry member is quite so welcome as the one that steadfastly refuses to keep up."

FURTHER READING:

Adebanjo, Dotun. "Corporate Restructuring: Managing the Change Problem from Within." *Leadership and Organization Development Journal*. September 1996.

Austin, Mary Ruth. "Managing Change." *Manage*. August 1997.

Bateman, Thomas S., and Carl P. Zeithaml. *Management: Function and Strategy*. Homewood, IL: Irwin, 1990.

Dove, Rick. "The Principles of Change." *Automotive Manufacturing and Production*. March 1997.

Hurst, David K. "When It Comes to Real Change, Too Much Objectivity May Be Fatal to the Process." *Strategy and Leadership*. March-April 1997.

Maurer, Rick. "Transforming Resistance." *HR Focus*. October 1997.

McCallum, John S. "The Face Behind Change." *Ivey Business Quarterly*. Winter 1997.

Recardo, Ronald J. "Overcoming Resistance to Change." *National Productivity Review*. Spring 1995.

Schwartz, Andrew E. "Eight Guidelines for Managing Change." *Supervisory Management*. July 1994.

Trahant, Bill, W. Warner Burke, and Richard Koonce. "Twelve Principles of Organizational Transformation." *Management Review*. September 1997.

Wallington, Patricia M. "Making Change." *CIO*. April 1, 2000.

MANUFACTURERS' AGENTS

Manufacturers' agents or representatives are independent contractors who work on commission to sell products for more than one manufacturer. They are not under the immediate supervision of the manufacturers—typically called principals—that they sell for, so their relationship generally falls into client-customer patterns.

Manufacturers' agent firms range from businesses operated by a sole entrepreneur to considerably more extensive organizations armed with numerous salespeople covering specific territories. As of 2000, the Manufacturers' Agents National Association (MANA) estimated that there were 150,000 agents operating in the United States. The typical agency was a corporation that employed six people (including both sales personnel and office personnel), MANA research showed. These firms, which are concentrated in major metropolitan areas but can be found in all 50 states, represent every conceivable product line, including goods produced in the automotive, plastics, electronics, food and beverage processing, apparel, lumber and wood, paper, chemical, and metals industries. Virtually any product that is made and sold can be handled by a manufacturers' agent.

Manufacturers' agents generally represent several different companies that offer compatible—but not competing—products to the same industry. This method reduces the cost of sales by spreading the agent's costs over the different products that he or she pitches. Consequently, manufacturers' agents view themselves as a cost-effective alternative to full-time salaried sales forces, and this is an evaluation that is shared by thousands of small- and medium-sized manufacturers in the United States. Indeed, manufacturers' agents are particularly popular among companies that do not have the financial resources to launch their own sales team. In addition, since manufacturers' agents are generally paid by commission, the small manufacturer incurs no cost until a sale is made.

SMALL BUSINESSES AND MANUFACTURERS' AGENTS

ADVANTAGES In addition to the above-mentioned financial benefits that manufacturers' agents offer to small business owners, they also provide relocating or start-up firms with immediate front-line information on marketplace trends and demographics. By contracting with a manufacturers' agent, a company gains instant access to industry expertise or knowledge of a particular country or region.

There are other distinct advantages as well. For manufacturers with a narrow product line, agencies offer one of the best ways to access the market. Because they normally sell compatible products to a single market, the manufacturers' agent firms usually are well-connected with the manufacturers' principal market targets. This offers manufacturers immediate entry to markets that may be hard to reach with a direct sales force. In addition, rep firms can provide new businesses with ideas about where to advertise, comment on what the competition is doing, and give estimates of a given territory's potential.

DISADVANTAGES Consultants and business owners note, however, that while using manufacturers' agents may make a lot of sense to the small company that needs to allocate its financial resources carefully and learn about the marketplace quickly, there are drawbacks associated with the practice as well. Lack of control over the agent is easily the most frequently mentioned complaint that business owners cite when discussing rep firms. Since the manufacturers' agent is not an employee of the company, the company's ownership cannot dictate how he or she goes about business. Certainly, the small business owner can negotiate for certain things in his or her business dealings with the agent, just as any client can do with any vendor. But in the final analysis, the agent has far greater freedom to operate as he or she feels fit than do salespeople that are actual employees of the company.

Some critics also claim that since manufacturers' agents conduct business on behalf of more than one manufacturer, they are not always able to devote the necessary time to one single product line. Finally, some agents also may be reluctant or unable to provide service beyond the point of sale. Fundamental elements of customer service, such as start-up assistance and follow-up service, often must be supplied by the manufacturer even if the goods were sold through a manufacturers' agent.

Another concern frequently raised about manufacturers' agents is that they add to the cost of sales by acting as a middleman in the process. But as Bob Trinkle pointed out in *Agency Sales Magazine,* ''reps are an alternative (or substitute) to direct sales. They should be looked upon as a form of outsourcing of the sales function.'' Therefore, hiring a manufacturers' agent should eliminate the need to maintain an in-house sales staff for a particular region or product line. In this way, the agent may actually help a small business reduce its administrative costs.

SELECTING A MANUFACTURERS' AGENT

Manufacturers have many factors to consider when they being the process of selecting a manufacturers' representative. Small business owners should look for someone who shows an ability and a willingness to become knowledgeable about their products and applications, as well as someone who will re-

spond quickly to calls and present the product in terms of how it will meet customer needs. A good agent will also represent the various product lines he or she markets in a just fashion, giving each line the attention it deserves, regardless of how much income it accounts for (this latter concern is especially acute for small and start-up businesses).

The best rule of thumb for manufacturers is to be patient and do plenty of preliminary research. After all, the choice is going to be the primary link between the company and its target audience. A poor selection can ruin a company; conversely, a good choice can help launch a new manufacturer to long-term financial stability. Given the stakes involved in this choice, then, MANA suggested in its *Directory of Manufacturers' Sales Agencies* that business owners consider doing the following when weighing their choices.

- Create a profile of the ideal agency—Make the profile clear, but also be flexible and realistic. Perfect agencies are nonexistent, but there are many that will do a good job if given the opportunity.

- Create a profile of the manufacturing firm—Manufacturers are encouraged to compile a profile of their target customers, a rundown of the business's needs, and a summary of the governing philosophy of the business. Many agencies can be selective in terms of who they will add to their client list, so it makes sense to inform them about the business and its goals and prospects. The profile should be honest and touch on growth plans, real advantages of the product(s) it manufacturers, and previous history.

- Secure referrals from other agencies—Manufacturers' representatives are a close-knit fraternity in the United States, and many can provide the names of several agencies that would be a good fit for the line.

- Get referrals from other manufacturers—Companies in the same area that sell similar but noncompetitive products can be a good source of information in locating potential representatives. Some may even recommend their own agencies, although others may be reluctant to have their agents take on additional product lines and responsibilities.

- Be patient—While manufacturers do not have the luxury of waiting forever when filling rep openings, doing preliminary research usually is a good idea. Many manufacturers who have been burned in this regard later admit that they did not devote sufficient time to exploring their options and learning about the agent they did select. It is better to take the needed time to select the right prospect than to rush into a bad situation and have to rectify it later.

- Be flexible in setting up territories—Agents must have exclusive rights within a territory, but rather than assign arbitrary territories based on geography, it is often preferable to select the agents that best fit your line and let their coverage determine the territories.

''Manufacturers should always recognize that independent reps choose independence because they want to do what they want to do, not what any one manufacturer wants them to do,'' Harold J. Novick wrote in *Agency Sales Magazine*. ''Therefore, the key to success with independent reps is finding that one high-performance rep who comes closest to doing what you want done in the marketplace now. Recruiting a rep with even one key characteristic missing may substantially reduce your market share possibilities in that territory. Finding the right rep creates a high probability for a true win-win situation, as both 'partners' have common objectives.''

DEALING WITH AGENTS

Manufacturers must remember that their rep firms are independent sales agencies that are not employees of any of its principals, but business partners with each of them. As such, the manufacturers cannot have the same type of direct control as they do over their own personnel. From a legal standpoint, it is important to remember that the manufacturers pay nothing to a rep until a sale is made. They also pay no withholding taxes or Social Security. Using manufacturers' agents also means that some of the manufacturer's bookkeeping needs will be taken care of by non-employees. This is an important distinction for the Internal Revenue Service, which frowns mightily upon arrangements in which companies disguise employees under the veil of independent agencies or contractors. When judging this, the IRS typically uses as one of its tests the amount of direct control exercised over sales reps. If regular reports are demanded of independent agents, the IRS can declare the rep an employee and require the various withholding taxes that apply.

Communication remains an integral part of the relationship between agents and their clients. Both parties need to keep the other appraised about their operations. Agents should let their principals know what they are doing for them in the field, regardless of the level of sales at that particular moment, while agents need updated information on matters such as product specifications and pricing. Ultimately, both parties simply need to recognize that a cohesive working relationship is in their shared best interests. In their dealings with representatives, manufacturers expect: loyalty; knowledge of the territory and/or industry; knowledge of product lines after a reasonable amount of exposure; quick response to suggestions; regular follow-up; and a fair share of the agent's time. Agents, meanwhile, have every right to expect: a fair contract that recognizes performance and rewards success and longevity; access to customer service, training, and technical back-up; a quality product; timely delivery; and a true commitment to build business in their territory.

FURTHER READING:

''How to Work Successfully with Manufacturers' Agencies.'' Special Report in *Directory of Manufacturers' Sales Agencies*. Manufacturers' Agents National Association, 1994.

Gibbons, James J. ''Recruiting Agents: Do it Right and You'll Never Have to Settle for Second Best.'' *Directory of Manufacturers' Sales Agencies*. Manufacturers' Agents National Association, 1993.

Marshall, Michael, and Frank Siegler. ''Selecting the Right Rep Firm.'' *Sales and Marketing Management*. January 1994.

Novick, Harold J. ''Rep Search and Selection: The Foundation of Outstanding Performance.'' *Agency Sales Magazine*. March 1999.

Trinkle, Bob. ''Defining the Value of the Rep.'' *Agency Sales Magazine*. December 1998.

MARKET ANALYSIS

Market analysis is a tool companies use in order to better understand the environment in which they operate. It is one of the main steps in the development of a marketing plan. The first step is to conduct market research—or gather information through direct mail, telemarketing, focus groups, online surveys, etc. Then comes market analysis, which involves critically reviewing and organizing the data collected so that it can be used in making strategic marketing decisions. ''Just as one would not build a house on sand, one should never undertake a marketing program that is not built on a firm foundation of market knowledge,'' David J. Freiman stated in his book *What Every Manager Needs to Know about Marketing*. ''It is remarkable and alarming how little managers of businesses really know about their markets and the other elements of their outside environments.''

A good market analysis should include information on industry trends, an assessment of major competitors and their strategies, a review of the channels of distribution, and a wide variety of data on current and potential customers. The market analysis provides the input for the next step in developing a marketing plan—market segmentation, or dividing an overall market into key customer subsets, or segments, whose members share similar characteristics and needs. The company then selects from among these segments the particular markets it wishes to target, and creates a marketing plan that will appeal to the target customers. "Small businesses that identify the needs of specific target markets—existing and potential customers who are the focus of marketing efforts—and work to satisfy those needs, are more effective marketers," according to Gloria Green and Jeffrey Williams in *Marketing: Mastering Your Small Business*.

Most market analyses begin with a broad study of the overall industry and conclude with a narrow definition of the company's target market. Some of the industry factors that might be mentioned in a market analysis include the relative market share held by various competitors, the rate of new product introductions, the technological environment, and the impact of significant laws or regulations. A market analysis would also include overall market information such as sales history, current demand, and expected future trends. It is particularly important to know whether demand is increasing, decreasing, or remaining constant.

The next area of a market analysis involves creating an in-depth portrait of customers. Through market research, the company tries to answer such questions as: who are the primary decision makers and purchasers; what are their main motivating factors; and when and where do they tend to buy? The key is to understand how customers make their purchasing decisions in order to be able to influence those decisions. Market research might assess such demographic features as age, gender, income level, educational background, financial situation, marital status, household size, and ethnic or religious background. Once this information has been broken down through market analysis, the company then creates a detailed description of the most desirable segment of the market to be included in the marketing plan. The market analysis should demonstrate why the target market chosen is more favorable than other segments, since the company will be investing its limited resources in marketing to that target market.

In addition to its role in developing the marketing plan, market analysis has numerous other implications for company strategy. "Once we understand the phenomena that underlie the behavior of our markets, we can assess our strengths and weaknesses relative to those phenomena. External threats and opportunities need to be carefully examined so that we can apply our strengths to areas with high potential and avoid major environmental pitfalls. Finally, we must link the resulting diagnosis to our corporate capabilities, strategies, and constraints in order to ensure a good fit between our marketing strategy and major corporate goals and objectives," Glen L. Urban and Steven H. Star explained in their book *Advanced Marketing Strategy*.

FURTHER READING:

Freiman, David J., ed. *What Every Manager Needs to Know about Marketing*. New York: AMACOM, 1986.

Malburg, Chris. "Brave New Product Worlds." *Industry Week*. November 6, 2000.

Sherman, Andrew J. *The Complete Guide to Running and Growing Your Business*. New York: Random House, 1997.

Stevens, Berni. "Save Money with Online Analysis." *Marketing News*. November 6, 2000.

Urban, Glen L., and Steven H. Star. *Advanced Marketing Strategy*. Englewood Cliffs, NJ: Prentice Hall, 1991.

SEE ALSO: Advertising Strategy

MARKET QUESTIONNAIRES

Market questionnaires are a form of quantitative, primary market research that can provide small business owners with specific information about their customers' needs. Whether conducted over the telephone, through the mail, over the Internet, or in person, market questionnaires are designed to survey a sample group of respondents whose opinions reflect those of the business's target customers.

Like other forms of market research, questionnaires are designed to connect marketers to consumers through information gathering and evaluation. Market research is commonly used to identify marketing problems and opportunities, as well as to develop and evaluate the effectiveness of marketing strategies. Small business owners, because of their usually limited financial resources, have a particular need for adequate, accurate, and current information to aid them in making decisions. Market research can help entrepreneurs evaluate the feasibility of a start-up venture before investing a great deal of time and capital, for example, as well as assist them in effectively marketing their goods and services.

"Questionnaire construction is one of the most difficult steps in marketing research," Gloria Green and Jeffrey Williams noted in their book *Marketing: Mastering Your Small Business*. "Yet, many people seem to think putting together a good questionnaire is easy. That's why there are so many terrible questionnaires—full of confusing or incomprehensible questions all but guaranteed to produce worthless results."

In general, a good market questionnaire will consist of a screening or qualifying question, an introduction, demographic questions, closed-ended questions, and open-ended questions. Each of these elements serves a particular purpose. The screening question, which should usually be posed first, makes sure that the respondent is a member of the target group and thus is qualified to participate in the survey. For example, a home remodeling and repair company might ask whether the person has had any work done in the previous six months. The introduction then informs qualified respondents what company is conducting the survey and why, and explains the benefits answering might have on their future business relationship with that company. Demographic questions—which cover such basic information as age, gender, marital status, education level, income level, etc.—allow the business to categorize responses. Since some respondents may be hesitant to answer such personal questions, demographics should usually be addressed near the end of the questionnaire.

Closed-ended questions ask respondents to select from a limited set of answers. This enables businesses to collate responses and analyze results more easily. Closed-ended questions may require a ''yes'' or ''no,'' or ''true'' or ''false'' answer. They may also be set up as a multiple-choice question, so that respondents choose one possible answer from a list. Finally, closed-ended questions may involve a scaled response, such as rating a product or service on a scale of one to ten or on the basis of categories such as ''strongly like,'' ''like,'' ''neither like nor dislike,'' etc. In contrast, open-ended questions enable respondents to provide a more lengthy response in their own words. Although open-ended questions can provide valuable information, the results can also be difficult for companies to analyze and categorize.

According to Green and Williams, there are a number of guidelines small business owners should follow in order to create good market questionnaires that are likely to produce meaningful responses. First, the survey should be as short as possible and collect only necessary information. Second, questions should be clearly worded and concise, without excessive technical jargon. Third, questions should be objective, so that they do not imply a correct answer. Fourth, questions should be limited so that they only seek one piece of information, and answers fall into distinct categories. Finally, questionnaires should be arranged so that they begin with easier questions and progress into more difficult ones after a measure of trust has been achieved. It may be helpful to test a market questionnaire on a small group and then make any necessary refinements before using it in a large-scale market research effort.

FURTHER READING:

Green, Gloria, and Jeffrey Williams. *Marketing: Mastering Your Small Business.* Chicago: Upstart, 1996.

Hayes, Lallie. ''Questionnaire Design, Printing, and Distribution.'' *Technical Communications.* November 2000.

MARKET RESEARCH

The term market research encompasses a number of activities that are designed to connect marketers to consumers through information gathering and evaluation. Market research provides businesses with information about their customers, their competitors, and their overall industry. It is commonly used to identify marketing problems and opportunities, as well as to develop and evaluate the effectiveness of marketing strategies. Small business owners, because of their usually limited financial resources, have a particular need for adequate, accurate, and current information to aid them in making decisions. Market research can help entrepreneurs evaluate the feasibility of a start-up venture before investing a great deal of time and capital, for example, as well as assist them in effectively marketing their goods and services. Employing such marketing strategies as market segmentation and product differentiation would be nearly impossible without first conducting market research.

Although market research can be costly, it is often even more costly to make erroneous decisions based upon bad or inadequate information. In fact, an average business spends between 25 and 50 percent of its annual marketing budget on research activities. Conducting large-scale market research in-house is not possible for many small businesses, since it requires a comprehensive understanding of the problem to be addressed, the market, and the application of research procedures. But there is a great deal of helpful information available to entrepreneurs who know where to look, and there are many consultants, advertising firms, and market research specialists who offer their services to small businesses for a fee.

The information gathered through market research can be divided into two main categories. The first category—primary information—generally does not exist in a coherent form before the marketer gathers it in response to a particular question or problem. The most common methods of gathering primary market research information are through direct mail, telemarketing, and personal interviews. The other category—secondary information—has already been compiled and organized by a source other than the marketer. Rather than looking at a specific marketing problem faced by an individual company, secondary information generally tracks trends within a market, an industry, a demographic group, or a geographic region. A great deal of valuable secondary information is available to small business owners at little or no cost. Some possible sources of secondary market research information include government reports, trade association records, newspaper and magazine surveys, university-sponsored research, local chamber of commerce records, on-line services, and competitors' annual reports.

Market research can provide small business owners with the information they need to answer a wide range of questions, including: Who are my customers? Where are they located? How much and how often will they buy? and What product attributes do they prefer? Given the importance of market research—and its potential cost—experts recommend that businesses follow a step-by-step approach in order to gain the most benefits from their research activities.

The first step in the market research process is to define the marketing problem to be addressed. Next, a marketer should determine what information is needed to solve the problem, as well as what sources should be used to acquire the information. Many businesses make a preliminary investigation at this early stage in order to give their definition of the problem more focus and to develop tentative answers that can be tested during the next stage of the process. The third step involves planning the research. This step includes selecting the techniques to be used for gathering data and deciding on an appropriate group, or sample, to be included in the research. Fourth, a marketer actually gathers the necessary data. The fifth step involves analyzing and interpreting the information that has been gathered. Finally, the marketer reaches a conclusion about the marketing problem and translates the findings into changes in the firm's overall marketing strategy.

There are three general types of market research suppliers that can assist small businesses with one or more steps in the above process. Some firms specialize in conducting overall market research that they release to a variety of clients for a fee. This type of firm includes syndicated services such as A.C. Nielsen and Company, which provides viewership ratings for national television programs. There are also custom market research firms that handle all aspects of the process, from defining the marketing problem and designing research techniques to evaluating results and formulating new marketing strategies. In contrast, smaller, specialty line suppliers usually concentrate on one aspect of the process. Marketers who wish to secure the services of a market research firm usually obtain bids from a number of suppliers. The following sections provide more information about the various types of market research that such suppliers perform.

TYPES OF MARKET RESEARCH

AUDIENCE RESEARCH Research on who is listening, watching, and reading is important to marketers of television and radio programs and print publications—as well as to advertisers who wish to reach a certain target audience with their message. Television and radio ratings demonstrate the popularity of shows and determine how much stations can charge for advertising spots during broadcasts. Publication subscription lists, which are audited by tabulating companies to ensure their veracity, are important in determining the per page rate for advertising.

PRODUCT RESEARCH Product research includes simple, in-person research such as taste tests conducted in malls and in the aisles of grocery stores, as well as elaborate, long-term ''beta testing'' of high-tech products by selected, experienced users. The objective of product research can be simple; for example, a company may tweak the taste of an existing product, then measure consumers' reactions to see if there is room in the market for a variation. It can also be more extensive, as when a company develops prototypes of proposed new products that may be intended for market introduction months down the road.

In product research, as in all market research, there is a danger to paying too much attention to the wrong things. For instance, the introduction of New Coke was based on the outcome of taste tests that showed the public wanted a sweeter product. But later an angry public, outraged that Coca-Cola was planning to change the familiar formula, forced the company to ignore its taste tests and leave the original Coke on the market. The company had put too much stock in the results of the taste test studies, and had failed to factor in research that showed consumers were happy with the product as it was.

BRAND RESEARCH Brands, the named products that advertising pushes and for which manufacturers can charge consumers the most money, are always being studied. Advertisers want to know if consumers have strong brand loyalty (''I'd never buy another brand, even if they gave me a coupon''); if the brand has any emotional appeal (''My dear mother used only that brand''); and what the consumer thinks could be improved about the brand (''If only it came in a refillable container'').

Brand research, too, has its perils. Campbell's Soup once convened a focus group comprised of its best soup customers. One of the findings was that those customers saw no need for a low-salt alternative soup Campbell's wanted to market. Concerned that the general public seemed to want low-sodium products, Campbell's retested groups other than their best customers. This research found a market interested in a low-sodium soup. The loyal Campbell's customers loved the saltier product, while a larger group of potential customers preferred the low-salt alternative.

PSYCHOLOGICAL RESEARCH Perhaps the most controversial type of market research is psychological research. This type of research tries to determine why people buy certain products based on a profile of the way the consumers live their lives. One company has divided all Americans into more than 60 psychological profiles. This company contends the lifestyles these people have established, based upon their past buying habits and their cultural upbringing, influences their buying decisions so strongly that individual differences can sometimes be negated.

Psychological research is controversial because it measures attitudes about buying rather than the buying itself. Critics point to conflicting information uncovered through other market research studies. In one series of research projects, researchers asked people what they were planning to buy before they entered a store. After the people surveyed left the store, the same researcher examined what was actually in their shopping carts. Only 30 percent of the people bought what they had said they planned to buy just a half hour earlier.

SCANNER RESEARCH In contrast, there is no fooling the checkout scanner at the supermarket or the department store: it records what was actually purchased. This is valuable information an advertiser can use to help plan an ongoing marketing strategy. Scanner technology has changed the way advertisers track the sale of consumer products. Before scanners, advertisers received sales information only when retailers reordered stock, generally every two weeks. This meant that the advertisers had no way to quickly measure the effect of national advertising, in-store sales promotions, or the couponing of similar products by their competitors. Now, computer technology can send scanner information to advertisers within days or even hours.

DATABASE RESEARCH Virtually every type of consumer—credit card holders, smokers, drinkers, car buyers, video buyers—shows up on thousands of lists and databases that are regularly cross-referenced to mine nuggets of marketing research. Database research is growing in popularity among marketers because the raw data has already been contributed by the purchaser. All the marketer has to do is develop a computer program to look for common buying patterns.

Database research can be thought of as the ultimate tool in market segmentation research. For example, from zip code lists, marketers may determine where the wealthy people live in a city. That list can be merged with a list of licensed drivers. The resulting list can be merged with another list of owners of cars of a certain make older than a certain year. The resulting list can be merged with another list of subscribers to car enthusiast magazines. The final list will deliver a potential market for a new luxury car soon to be introduced and profiled in the car magazines. The people on the potential buyers' list could then be mailed an invitation to come see the new car.

Database research also allows companies to build personal relationships with people who have proven from past purchases that they are potential customers. For example, a motorcycle manufacturer such as Harley Davidson may discover from database research that a family with a motorcycle has a teenage son. That son is a potential new customer for everything from clothes to a new motorcycle of his own. Maintaining a personal relationship with customers also provides businesses with a basis for more detailed and economical market research than might be possible through random sampling.

POST-SALES OR CUSTOMER SATISFACTION RESEARCH Most companies no longer believe that a sale ends their relationship with a customer. Nearly one-third of the research revenues generated by the leading American market research firms concern customer satisfaction. Many companies now wait a few days or weeks, then contact customers with survey questionnaires or telephone calls. Companies want reassurance that the customer enjoyed the buying experience and that the product or service has met the buyer's expectations.

The reason behind post-sales research is to ensure that current customers are happy, will consider themselves future customers, and will spread positive word-of-mouth messages about the product and company. One study found that 70 percent of customers believed it was important for companies to stay in contact with them, but less than one-third of those same customers reported that they had heard from companies whose products they purchased. Nearly 90 percent of those surveyed said they would be more likely to choose a company's products if it stayed in touch with them and sought their satisfaction.

PERSONAL RESEARCH METHODS

CLOSED-END QUESTIONNAIRE A closed-end questionnaire is the type of market research most people have experienced. It includes such common activities as filling out a comment card at a restaurant or responding to a telephone survey. In closed-end questionnaires, the person being surveyed cannot expound on their answers. Such surveys usually ask for ''yes'' or ''no'' responses or for measures of multiple choice opinion (e.g., ''extremely interested,'' ''somewhat interested,'' ''not interested''). This type of market research is generally conducted to elicit the opinions and beliefs of the public. It is commonly used for political polling and to determine the awareness or popularity of a product or service.

The inherent problem with multiple-choice questionnaires that ask for clear-cut answers is that many people do not think in a clear-cut fashion. If not carefully prepared, closed-ended questions may elicit answers that do not provide a clear view of the person being surveyed. Sometimes, the company conducting the survey may intentionally or inadvertently write questions that elicit the answers it wants to receive, rather than answers that provide a true picture of what is happening in the marketplace.

OPEN-ENDED QUESTIONNAIRE Over time, market researchers have grown increasingly aware that people often have opinions that do not fit into a multiple-choice questionnaire. To capture these opinions and try to analyze them, researchers are shifting toward open-ended research—asking people to say exactly what is on their minds. For example, manufacturers are giving customers plenty of space on questionnaires to explain their likes and dislikes about products and services, and telephone researchers will frequently mix closed-end and open-end questions on the same survey to try to delve deeper. A ''no'' response to whether a person watches a particular cable television station may trigger a follow-up question of ''Why not?,'' for instance, and the answer will be taken down word for word.

A problem with both closed- and open-ended questionnaire research, particularly when conducted over the telephone, is that people gradually become bored or annoyed and stop providing their true opinions. In addition, some studies have shown that a large percentage of Americans refuse to answer marketing research surveys.

FOCUS GROUPS In-person, sit-down discussions around a table with groups of consumers, would-be consumers, never-buyers, or any other demographic group a company wishes to bring together are called focus groups. This can be the least expensive type of market research when handled on a local basis by a small business wanting to get a handle on its customers. Or, it can be one of the most expensive if a major corporation wants to test its plans in various sections of the country. Small, local businesses may invite a focus group to a neighborhood home to sit around the dinner table and discuss how the company can develop new markets. In contrast, most major corporations conduct their focus groups in a controlled environment, usually with a one-way mirror at one end of the room. This allows executives to observe the proceedings unobtrusively or to videotape the session for further study.

The key to gathering good information from a focus group is for the moderator to keep the conversation flowing freely without taking a side. The moderator's job is to involve everyone in the discussion and prevent any individuals from dominating the conversation. Most market research experts agree that focus group research should be accompanied by other types of research and not be the sole basis for launching new products. The reason is that opinions expressed among strangers may not always reflect the way people would react when alone. For example, a focus group discussing low-fat foods may garner an enthusiastic response from people who want to be publicly perceived as being concerned about their health. The same people, however, might say they never buy low-fat products if questioned during an anonymous phone interview.

FURTHER READING:

The Entrepreneur Magazine Small Business Advisor. Wiley, 1995.

Haim, Alexander, and Charles D. Schewe. *The Portable MBA in Marketing.* Wiley, 1992.

Lehmann, Donald R. *Marketing Research and Analysis.* 3rd Ed. Irwin, 1988.

Lury, Giles. ''Market Research Cannot Cover for the 'Vision Thing.' '' *Marketing.* November 9, 2000.

''Market Research Is Accessible, Rewarding to Small Retailers.'' *Knight-Ridder/Tribune Business News.* January 19, 2000.

Stevens, Mark. *The Macmillan Small Business Handbook.* Macmillan, 1988.

Westfall, Tina Cook. ''Market Research: Nothing Is as Convincing as Hard Numbers.'' *Atlanta Business Chronicle.* August 29, 1998.

SEE ALSO: Focus Groups

MARKET SEGMENTATION

Market segmentation is the science of dividing an overall market into key customer subsets, or segments, whose members share similar characteristics and needs. Because it involves significant market research, market segmentation can be costly. But it is particularly important for small businesses, which often lack the resources to target large aggregate markets or to maintain a wide range of differentiated products for varied markets. Market segmentation allows a small business to develop a product and a marketing mix that fit a relatively homogenous part of the total market. By focusing its resources on a specific customer base in this way, a small business may be able to carve out a market niche that it can serve better than its larger competitors.

Market segmentation lies somewhere near the middle of a continuum of marketing strategies that range from mass marketing—in which a single product is offered to all customers in a market—to one-to-one marketing—in which a different product is specifically designed for each individual customer in a market. Most businesses realize that since no two people are exactly alike, it is unlikely that they will be able to please all customers in a market with a single product. They also realize that it is rarely feasible to create a distinct product for every customer. Instead, most businesses attempt to improve their odds of attracting a significant base of customers by dividing the overall market into segments, then trying to match their product and marketing mix more closely to the needs of one or more segments. A number of customer characteristics, known as segmentation bases, can be used to define market segments. Some commonly used bases include age, gender, income, geographical area, and buying behavior.

MARKETING STRATEGIES

Though mass marketing (also known as market aggregation or undifferentiated marketing) cannot fully satisfy every customer in a market, many companies still employ this strategy. It is commonly used in the marketing of standardized goods and services—including sugar, gasoline, rubber bands, or dry cleaning services—when large numbers of people have similar needs and they perceive the product or service as largely the same regardless of the provider. Mass marketing offers some advantages to businesses, such as reduced production and marketing costs. Due to the efficiency of large production runs and a single marketing program, businesses that mass market their goods or services may be able to provide consumers with more value for their money.

Some producers of mass market goods employ a marketing strategy known as product differentiation to make their offering seem distinct from that of competitors, even though the products are largely the same. For example, a producer of bath towels might embroider its brand name on its towels and sell them only through upscale department stores as a form of product differentiation. Consumers might tend to perceive these towels as somehow better than other brands, and thus worthy of a premium price. But changing consumer perceptions in this way can be very expensive in terms of promotion and packaging. A product differentiation strategy is most likely to be effective when consumers care about the product and there are identifiable differences between brands.

Despite the cost advantages mass marketing offers to businesses, this strategy has several drawbacks. A single product offering cannot fully satisfy the diverse needs of all consumers in a market, and consumers with unsatisfied needs expose businesses to challenges by competitors who are able to identify and fulfill consumer needs more precisely. In fact, markets for new products typically begin with one competitor offering a single product, then gradually splinter into segments as competitors enter the market with products and marketing messages targeted at groups of consumers the original producer may have missed. These new competitors are able to enter a market ostensibly controlled by an established competitor because they can identify and meet the needs of unsat-

isfied customer segments. In recent times, the proliferation of computerized customer databases has worked to drive marketing toward ever-more-narrowly focused market segments.

Applying a market segmentation strategy is most effective when an overall market consists of many smaller segments whose members have certain characteristics or needs in common. Through segmentation, businesses can divide such a market into several homogeneous groups and develop a separate product and marketing program to more exactly fit the needs of one or more segments. Though this approach can provide significant benefits to consumers and a profitable sales volume (rather than a maximum sales volume) to businesses, it can be costly to implement. For example, identifying homogeneous market segments requires significant amounts of market research, which can be expensive. Also, businesses may experience a rise in production costs as they forfeit the efficiency of mass production in favor of smaller production runs that meet the needs of a subset of the market. Finally, a company may find that sales of a product developed for one segment encroach upon the sales of another product intended for another segment. Nonetheless, market segmentation is vital to success in many industries where consumers have diverse and specific needs, such as homebuilding, furniture upholstery, and tailoring.

SEGMENTATION BASES

In order to successfully implement a market segmentation strategy, a business must employ market research techniques to find patterns of similarity among customer preferences in a market. Ideally, customer preferences will fall into distinct clusters based upon identifiable characteristics of the population. This means that if customer requirements were plotted on a graph using certain characteristics, or segmentation bases, along the axes, the points would tend to form clusters.

To be pursued by a marketer, according to Alexander Hiam and Charles D. Schewe in *The Portable MBA in Marketing,* the customer segments should be: 1) identifiable and measurable; 2) large enough to be profitable; 3) reached effectively (for example, its members must tend to view the same television programs, read the same publications, or shop in the same places); 4) responsive to marketing; and 5) stable and not expected to change quickly. A company might elect to serve a single market segment or attempt to meet the needs of several segments.

Determining how to segment a market is one of the most important questions a marketer must face. Creative and effective market segmentation can lead to the development of popular new products, but unsuccessful segmentation can cost a great deal of money and still not yield the desired results. There are three main types of segmentation bases for businesses to consider—descriptive bases, behavioral bases, and benefit bases—each of which breaks down into numerous potential customer traits.

Descriptive bases for market segmentation include a variety of factors that describe the demographic and geographic situation of the customers in a market. They are the most commonly used segmentation bases because they are easy to measure, and because they often serve as strong indicators of consumer needs and preferences. Some of the demographic variables that are used as descriptive bases in market segmentation might include age, gender, religion, income, and family size, while some of the geographic variables might include region of the country, climate, and population of the surrounding area.

Behavioral bases for market segmentation are generally more difficult to measure than descriptive bases, but they are often considered to be more powerful determinants of consumer purchases. They include those underlying factors that help motivate consumers to make certain buying decisions, such as personality, lifestyle, and social class. Behavioral bases also include factors that are directly related to consumer purchases of certain goods, such as their degree of brand loyalty, the rate at which they use the product and need to replace it, and their readiness to buy at a particular time.

Businesses that segment a market based on benefits hope to identify the primary benefit that consumers seek in buying a certain product, then supply a product that provides that benefit. This segmentation approach is based upon the idea that market segments exist primarily because consumers seek different benefits from products, rather than because of various other differences between consumers. One potential pitfall to this approach is that consumers do not always know or cannot always identify a single benefit that influences them to make a purchase decision. Many marketers use a combination of bases that seem most appropriate when segmenting a market. Using a single variable is undoubtedly easier, but it often turns out to be less precise.

THE SEGMENTATION PROCESS

Hiam and Schewe have identified six steps that companies should take in the market segmentation process. The first step is to determine the boundaries of the market. In completing this step, a marketer should use a formal business plan to develop a broad definition of their business, and then consider the offerings of both direct and indirect competitors to gain information about the basic needs of consumers in the market. The second step in the process is to decide which variables to use in segmenting the market. Many companies fall into the trap of collecting data on as many variables as possible and then attempting to sort through it later to draw meaningful conclusions. Instead, Hiam and Schewe recommend that marketers use their knowledge of the market to select a few relevant variables in advance. This approach is generally less expensive and will likely provide more useful results.

The third step in the market segmentation process is actually collecting and analyzing data, which involves applying market research tools. The goal in analyzing the data is to identify market segments that are internally homogeneous, yet are distinctly heterogeneous with respect to other segments. The fourth step is to develop a detailed profile of each market segment, which involves selecting those variables that are most closely related to consumers' actual buying behavior.

The fifth step in the market segmentation process is to decide which segment or segments to serve. In targeting a particular segment, a marketer should look for opportunities (i.e., customers with unsatisfied wants and needs) that provide a good match for the organization and its resources. It is important that the marketer consider not only the size and potential profitability of a market segment, but also whether the company's skills, technologies, and objectives would enable it to meet the needs of that segment better than its competitors. The sixth and final step is to develop a product and marketing plan that will appeal to the selected market segment. This involves identifying the product attributes that are most important to consumers in the segment, and developing a marketing strategy that will attract their attention. In fact, market segmentation can be usefully applied during the earliest stages of product design, when a company first identifies who its target customer will be in terms of demographic, geographic, and behavioral characteristics.

In general, customers are willing to pay a premium for a product that meets their needs more specifically than does a competing product. Thus marketers who successfully segment the overall market and adapt their products to the needs of one or more smaller segments stand to gain in terms of increased profit margins and reduced competitive pressures. Small businesses, in particular, may find market segmentation to be a key in enabling them to compete with larger firms. Many management consulting firms offer assistance with market segmentation to small businesses. But the potential gains offered by market segmentation must be measured against the costs, which—in addition to the market research required to segment a market—may include increased production and marketing expenses.

FURTHER READING:

Dickson, Peter R., and James L. Ginter. ''Market Segmentation, Product Differentiation, and Marketing Strategy.'' *Journal of Marketing* 51: 1-10.

Gabriel, Angela. ''Single Message May Not Hit All Markets.'' *Phoenix Business Journal.* November 20, 1998.

Hiam, Alexander, and Charles D. Schewe. *The Portable MBA in Marketing.* Wiley, 1992.

Kelner, Brad, et al. ''Market Segmentation Strategies and Service Sector Productivity.'' *California Management Review.* Summer 1999.

Millier, Paul. ''Intuition Can Help in Segmenting Industrial Markets.'' *Industrial Marketing Management.* March 2000.

Sandhusen, Richard L. *Barron's Business Review Series, Marketing.* 2nd Ed. Barron's Educational Series, Inc., 1993.

SEE ALSO: Demographics; Target Market

MARKET SHARE

Market share refers to the percentage of the overall volume of business in a given market that is controlled by one company in relation to its competitors. For example, if the total sales of a certain product in a market is $100,000, and the company in question sold $20,000 worth of that product, then the company had 20 percent market share. Market share is most meaningful in a relative sense; that is, when a company compares the market share it commands to the percentage held by its largest competitors. ''The important factor in computing relative market share is not the exact number associated with the sales volume,'' Kenneth J. Cook wrote in his book *The AMA Complete Guide to Strategic Planning for Small Business.* ''Your position relative to the competition is more important. You want to know basically if they dominate you, if you are relatively equal in size, or if you dominate them.''

To calculate market share, a small business owner first needs to determine the total sales of a product in a target market over a specific time period, usually one year. Then the small business owner needs to calculate the total sales achieved by his or her company in that market over the same time period. It may also be useful to find out the sales level achieved by the company's largest competitors and then use that information to compute relative market share. Information on the overall size of markets is usually available through industry associations, which commonly track both sales and growth rates. If competing firms happen to be publicly owned, their sales figures can usually be gleaned from their annual reports. Otherwise, the small business owner may be need to make an educated guess based on his or her knowledge of each competitor and on information provided by the company's customers and sales staff.

APPLICATIONS OF MARKET SHARE INFORMATION

Many companies use market share as a managerial objective—i.e., a company might try to gain a specified share of the market by a certain time. Market share can be a useful objective in that it forces small business owners to pay attention to the overall market and to the actions of competitors. It is also easier to measure than some other common objectives, such as maximizing profits. But there are some potential pitfalls associated with setting a company objective of increasing market share. For example, a company may be tempted to set too low a price to achieve this goal, even though a larger sales volume does not always lead to higher profits.

Another application of market share information is in evaluating a company's competitive position in an industry in order to formulate an effective strategy. Information on a firm's relative market share—which indicates its competitive position—can be combined with information on the growth rate and attractiveness of the industry to determine the best future positioning of the firm. The attractiveness of an industry can be determined through an industry analysis, which points out the threats and opportunities facing competitors. The growth rate of an industry can be determined by measuring trends in customer spending levels. As Michael E. Porter outlined in his classic book *Competitive Strategy: Techniques for Analyzing Industries and Competitors,* the results of these measurements can be plotted on a quadrant diagram. The horizontal side of the matrix represents the firm's competitive position and the vertical side represents the growth rate and attractiveness of the industry, both ranging from weak to strong.

If both the company's competitive position and the industry's attractiveness and growth rate are strong, then the company occupies a fortunate position and is known as a ''star.'' The most appropriate strategy for star companies is to exploit their competitive advantage and protect themselves against new competitors entering the industry. If both the company's competitive position and the industry's attractiveness and growth rate are weak, then the company is in an unfortunate position and is known as a ''dog.'' The potential for market growth is limited, and the company's future prospects in the industry do not appear promising. The most appropriate strategy for a dog company is to limit spending, generate as much cash as possible in the short term, and consider exiting the industry.

If a company holds a strong position in a weak industry, it is known as a ''cash cow.'' The best strategy for companies in this situation is to milk the market for cash while not expending too many resources. Finally, if a company occupies a weak competitive position in a strong industry, it is known as a ''question mark.'' The business owners have important strategic decisions to make. Although there is strong future potential in the industry, the company's weak position means that it will have to make a significant investment to take advantage of the opportunity presented. In this case, it is particularly important for the business owner to understand his or her customers and competitors to determine whether it will be possible for the company to develop a competitive advantage.

FURTHER READING:

Cook, Kenneth J. *The AMA Complete Guide to Strategic Planning for Small Business.* Chicago: American Marketing Association, 1995.

Green, Gloria, and Jeffrey Williams. *Marketing: Mastering Your Small Business.* Chicago: Upstart Publishing, 1996.

Porter, Michael E. *Competitive Strategy: Techniques for Analyzing Industries and Competitors.* New York: Free Press, 1980.

Urban, Glen L., and Steven H. Star. *Advanced Marketing Strategy.* Englewood Cliffs, NJ: Prentice Hall, 1991.

MARKETING

Marketing is a general term used to describe all the various activities involved in transferring goods and services from producers to consumers. In addition to the functions commonly associated with it, such as advertising and sales promotion, marketing also encompasses product development, packaging, distribution channels, pricing, and many other functions. The modern marketing concept, which is applied by most successful small businesses, is intended to focus all of a company's activities upon uncovering and satisfying customer needs. After all, an entrepreneur may come up with a great product and use the most efficient production methods to make it, but all the effort will have been wasted if he or she is unable to consummate the sale of the product to consumers.

The importance of marketing in the modern business climate cannot be overstated. In fact, management guru Peter F. Drucker has claimed that marketing ''is so basic it cannot be considered a separate function. . . . It is the whole business seen from the point of view of its final result, that is, from the customer's point of view.'' Marketing is the source of many important new ideas in management thought and practice—such as flexible manufacturing systems, flat organizational structures, and an increased emphasis on service—all of which are designed to make businesses more responsive to customer needs and preferences. This suggests that small business owners must master the basics of marketing in order to succeed.

In the *Macmillan Small Business Handbook,* Mark Stevens discussed four main areas of marketing in which entrepreneurs should concentrate their efforts: 1) determining the needs of customers through market research; 2) analyzing their own competitive advantages and developing an appropriate market strategy; 3) selecting specific target markets to serve; and 4) determining the best marketing mix to satisfy customer needs. The first three tasks are most appropriately performed when a start-up business is preparing to enter a market, or when an existing business is considering entering a new market or promoting a new product. The marketing mix, on the other hand, includes the main decision areas that an entrepreneur must consider on an ongoing basis. Some elements of the market environment, such as the general economic conditions, are beyond a small business owner's control. But he or she can adjust elements of the company's marketing mix—which consists of the ''four Ps'': product, place, price, and promotion—to better fit the market environment.

BACKGROUND

The term ''marketing'' is derived from the word ''market,'' which refers to a group of sellers and buyers that cooperate to exchange goods and services. The modern concept of marketing evolved during and after the industrial revolution in the 19th and 20th centuries. During that period, the proliferation of goods and services, increased worker specialization, and technological advances in transportation, refrigeration, and other factors that facilitated the transfer of goods over long distances resulted in the need for more advanced market mechanisms and selling techniques. But it was not until the 1930s that companies began to place a greater emphasis on advertising and promoting their products and began striving to tailor their goods to specific consumer needs. By the 1950s, many larger companies were sporting entire marketing departments charged with devising and implementing marketing strategies that would complement, and even direct, overall operations. Since the 1970s, the primary marketing trend has been a greater focus on providing benefits, rather than products, to customers.

MACRO-MARKETING AND MICRO-MARKETING

Macro-marketing refers to the overall social process that directs the flow of goods and services from producer to consumer. It is the economic system that determines what and how much is to be produced and distributed by whom, when, and to whom. E. Jerome McCarthy and William D. Perreault, Jr. identified eight universal macro-marketing functions that make up the economic process: 1) buying, which refers to consumers seeking and evaluating goods and services; 2) selling, which involves promoting the offering; 3) transporting, which refers to the movement of goods from one place to another; 4) storing, which involves holding goods until customers need them; 5) standardization and grading, which entails sorting products according to size and quality; 6) financing, which delivers the cash and credit needed to perform the first five functions; 7) risk taking, which involves bearing the uncertainties that are part of the marketing process; and 8) market information, which refers to the gathering, analysis, and distribution of the data necessary to execute these marketing functions.

In contrast, micro-marketing refers to the activities performed by the individual providers of goods and services within a macro-marketing system. Such organizations or businesses use various marketing techniques to accomplish objectives related to profits, market share, cash flow, and other economic factors that can enhance their well being and position in the marketplace. The micro-marketing function within an entity is commonly referred to as marketing management. Marketing managers strive to get their organizations to anticipate and accurately determine the needs and wants of customer groups. Afterward they seek to respond effectively with a flow of need-satisfying goods and services. They are typically charged with planning, implementing, and then measuring the effectiveness of all marketing activities.

THE TARGET MARKETING CONCEPT

Micro-marketing encompasses a number of related activities and responsibilities. Marketing managers must carefully design their marketing plans to ensure that they complement related production, distribution, and financial constraints. They must also allow for constant adaptation to changing markets and economic conditions. Perhaps the core function of a marketing manager, however, is to identify a specific market, or group of consumers, and then deliver products and promotions that ultimately maximize the profit potential of that targeted market. This is particularly important for small businesses, which more than likely lack the resources to target large aggregate markets. Often, it is only by carefully selecting and wooing a specific group that a small firm can attain profit margins sufficient to allow it to continue to compete in the marketplace.

For instance, a manufacturer of fishing equipment would not randomly market its product to the entire U.S. population. Instead, it would likely conduct market research—using such tools as demographic reports, market surveys, or focus groups—to determine which customers would be most likely to purchase its offerings. It could then more efficiently spend its limited resources in an effort to persuade members of its target group(s) to buy its products. Perhaps it would target males in the Midwest between the ages of 18 and 35. The company may even strive to further maximize the profitability of its target market through market segmentation, whereby the group is further broken down by age, income, zip code, or other factors indicative of buying patterns. Advertisements and promotions could then be tailored for each segment of the target market.

There are infinite ways to address the wants and needs of a target market. For example, product packaging can be designed in different sizes and colors, or the product itself can be altered to appeal to different personality types or age groups. Producers can also change the warranty or durability of the good or provide different levels of follow-up service. Other influences, such as distribution and sales methods, licensing strategies, and advertising media also play an important role. It is the responsibility of the marketing manager to take all of these factors into account and to devise a cohesive marketing program that will appeal to the target customer.

THE FOUR PS

The different elements of a company's marketing mix can be divided into four basic decision areas—known as the ''four Ps'': product, place, promotion, and price—which marketing managers can use to devise an overall marketing strategy for a product or group of goods. These four decision groups represent all of the variables that a company can control. But those decisions must be made within the context of outside variables that are not entirely under the control of the company, such as competition, economic and technological changes, the political and legal environment, and cultural and social factors.

Marketing decisions related to the product (or service) involve creating the right product for the selected target group. This typically encompasses research and data analysis, as well as the use of tools such as focus groups, to determine how well the product meets the wants and needs of the target group. Numerous determinants factor into the final choice of a product and its presentation. A completely new product, for example, will entail much higher promotional costs to raise consumer awareness, whereas a product that is simply an improved version of an existing item likely will make use of its predecessor's image. A pivotal consideration in product planning and development is branding, whereby the good or service is positioned in the market according to its brand name. Other important elements of the complex product planning and management process may include selection of features, warranty, related product lines, and post-sale service levels.

Considerations about place, the second major decision group, relate to actually getting the good or service to the target market at the right time and in the proper quantity. Strategies related to place may utilize middlemen and facilitators with expertise in joining buyers and sellers, and they may also encompass various distribution channels, including retail, wholesale, catalog, and others. Marketing managers must also devise a means of transporting the goods to the selected sales channels, and they may need to maintain an inventory of items to meet demand. Decisions related to place typically play an important role in determining the degree of vertical integration in a company, or how many activities in the distribution chain are owned and operated by the manufacturer. For example, some larger companies elect to own their trucks, the stores in which their goods are sold, and perhaps even the raw resources used to manufacture their goods.

Decisions about promotion, the third marketing mix decision area, relate to sales, advertising, public relations, and other activities that communicate information intended to influence consumer behavior. Often promotions are also necessary to influence the behavior of retailers and others who resell or distribute the product. Three major types of promotion typically integrated into a market strategy are personal selling, mass selling, and sales promotions. Personal selling, which refers to face-to-face or telephone sales, usually provides immediate feedback for the company about the product and instills greater confidence in customers. Mass selling encompasses advertising on mass media, such as television, radio, direct mail, and newspapers, and is beneficial because of its broad scope. A relatively new means of promotion involves the Internet, which combines features of mass media with a unique opportunity for interactive communication with customers. Publicity entails the use of free media, such as feature articles about a company or product in a magazine or related interviews on television talk shows, to spread the word to the target audience. Finally, sales promotion efforts include free samples, coupons, contests, rebates, and other miscellaneous marketing tactics.

Determination of price, the fourth major activity related to target marketing, entails the use of discounts and long-term pricing goals, as well as the consideration of demographic and geographic influences. The price of a product or service generally must at least meet some minimum level that will cover a company's cost of producing and delivering its offering. Also a firm would logically price a product at the level that would maximize profits. The price that a company selects for its products, however, will vary according to its long-term marketing strategy. For example, a company may underprice its product in the hopes of increasing market share and ensuring its competitive presence, or simply to generate a desired level of cash flow. Another producer may price a good extremely high in the hopes of eventually conveying to the consumer that it is a premium product. Another reason a firm might offer a product at a very high price is to discount the good slowly in an effort to maximize the dollars available from consumers willing to pay different prices for the good. In any case, price is used as a tool to achieve comprehensive marketing goals.

COMPETITIVE STRATEGIES

Often times, decisions about product, place, promotion, and price will be dictated by the competitive stance that a firm assumes in its target market. According to Michael Porter's classic book *Competitive Strategy*, the three most common competitive strategies are low-cost supplier, differentiation, and niche. Companies that adopt a low-cost supplier strategy are usually characterized by a vigorous pursuit of efficiency and cost controls. A company that manufactures a low-tech or commodity product, such as wood paneling, would likely adopt this approach. Such firms compete by offering a better value than their competitors, accumulating market share, and focusing on high-volume and fast inventory turnover.

Companies that adhere to a differentiation strategy achieve market success by offering a unique product or service. They often rely on brand loyalty, specialized distribution channels or service offerings, or patent protection to insulate them from competitors. Because of their uniqueness, they are able to achieve higher-than-average profit margins, making them less reliant on high sales volume and extreme efficiency. For example, a company that markets proprietary medical devices would likely assume a differentiation strategy.

Firms that pursue a niche market strategy succeed by focusing all of their efforts on a very narrow segment of an overall target market. They strive to prosper by dominating their selected niche. Such companies are able to overcome competition by aggressively protecting market share and by orienting every action and decision toward the service of its select group. An example of a company that might employ a niche strategy would be a firm that produced floor coverings only for extremely upscale commercial applications.

BUSINESS VERSUS CONSUMER MARKETS

An important micro-marketing delineation is that between industrial and consumer markets. Marketing strategies and activities related to transferring goods and services to industrial and business customers are generally very different from those used to lure other consumers. The industrial, or intermediate, market is made up of buyers who purchase for the purpose of creating other goods and services. Thus, their needs are different from general consumers. Buyers in this group include manufacturers and service firms, wholesalers and retailers, governments, and nonprofit organizations.

In many ways, it is often easier to market to a target group of intermediate customers. They typically have clearly defined needs and are buying the product for a very specific purpose. They are also usually less sensitive to price and are more willing to take the time to absorb information about goods that may help them do their job better. On the other hand, marketing to industrial customers can be complicated. For instance, members of an organization usually must purchase goods through a multi-step process involving several decision makers. Importantly, business buyers will often be extremely cautious about trying a new product or a new company because they do not want to be responsible for supporting what could be construed as a poor decision if the good or service does not live up to the organization's expectations.

A chief difference between marketing to intermediate and consumer markets is that members of the latter are typically considering purchasing goods and services that they might enjoy but are not absolutely necessary. As a result, they are more difficult to sell to than are business buyers. Consumers are generally less sophisticated than intermediate buyers, are less willing to spend time absorbing individual marketing messages of interest to them, and are more sensitive to the price of a good or service. Consumers typically make a buying decision on their own, however (or, for larger purchases, with the help of a friend or family member), and are much more likely to buy on impulse than are industrial customers.

Despite the differences, a dominant similarity between marketing to intermediate buyers and consumers is that both groups ultimately make purchases based on personal needs. Consumers typically act on their desires to belong, have security, feel high self-esteem, and enjoy freedom and status. Business and industrial consumers react more strongly to motivators such as fear of loss, fear of the unknown, the desire to avoid stress or hardship, and security in their organizational role.

INTERNET MARKETING

A discussion of marketing would not be complete without mentioning the emerging field of Internet marketing. Increasingly, small businesses have sought to take advantage of the global reach of the World Wide Web and the huge number of potential customers available online. Although it may seem like a completely new field, Internet marketing actually combines many of the basic elements of traditional marketing. ''Internet marketing employs the same methods and theory as traditional public relations and integrated marketing—the basic tools for any campaign,'' Maria Duggan and John Deveney wrote in *Communication World.*

In their article, Duggan and Deveney outline five steps for marketing managers to follow in putting together an Internet marketing campaign. Whether the campaign is intended to increase awareness of an existing brand, draw visitors to a Web site, or promote a new product offering, the first step involves identifying the target market. As is the case with any other type of marketing campaign, the small business must conduct market research in order to define the target audience for the campaign, and then use the information gathered to determine how best to reach them.

The next step is to develop a strategy for the campaign. This involves setting concrete and measurable goals and tying the campaign into the organization's traditional marketing efforts. The third step is to present the strategy to key decision makers in the small business. It is important at this stage to develop a timeline and budget, and also to be prepared to encounter resistance among colleagues not familiar with cyberspace. The fourth step is to implement the Internet marketing campaign. The final step, evaluation, should be conducted throughout the process. Online surveys of customers are one source of potential feedback.

MARKETING FOR SMALL BUSINESSES

In the early stages of forming a small business, a business plan is a vital tool to help an entrepreneur chart the future direction of the enterprise. A well-prepared business plan should include an extensive marketing component that explores the needs of the target market and lays out a marketing program to meet them. In fact, some experts claim that entrepreneurs should actually design their organizations in a way that gives the marketing function prominence. Once the needs of the target customers have been identified, these experts say, every aspect of the company's marketing program, as well as the basic image that the company develops, should be oriented toward satisfying these needs. For example, the company's selection of advertising, channels of distribution, packaging, price, and even vehicles and dress codes should all be coordinated to appeal to the target market.

As a small business grows, it may be helpful to create a separate marketing plan. While similar in format to the general business plan, a marketing plan focuses on expanding a certain product line or service rather than on the overall business. According to the *Entrepreneur Magazine Small Business Advisor,* creating a marketing plan helps a small business to define its markets, review its competitive position, develop goals and objectives, and determine the marketing tactics and financial resources needed to achieve its goals.

A number of resources are available to assist small businesses in marketing their products and services. It may be prudent to seek legal advice before implementing a marketing plan, for example. A firm with experience in consumer law could review the small business's product, packaging, labeling, advertising, sales agreements, and price policies to be sure that they meet all relevant regulations to prevent problems from arising later. In addition, many advertising agencies and market research firms offer a variety of means of testing the individual elements of marketing programs. Although such testing can be expensive, it can significantly increase the effectiveness of a company's marketing efforts.

FURTHER READING:

Duggan, Maria, and John Deveney. "How to Make Internet Marketing Simple." *Communication World.* April 2000.

The Entrepreneur Magazine Small Business Advisor. Wiley, 1995.

Homburg, Christian, John P. Workman, Jr., and Harley Krohmer. "Marketing's Influence within the Firm." *Journal of Marketing.* April 1999.

McCarthy, E. Jerome and William D. Perreault, Jr. *Basic Marketing.* Irwin, 1990.

Moorman, Christine, and Roland T. Rust. "The Role of Marketing." *Journal of Marketing.* December 1999.

Porter, Michael E. *Competitive Strategy.* Free Press, 1980.

Simkin, Lyndon. "Marketing Is Marketing—Maybe!" *Marketing Intelligence and Planning.* March 2000.

Stevens, Mark. *The Macmillan Small Business Handbook.* Macmillan, 1988.

Tracy, Joe. *Web Marketing Applied: Web Marketing Strategies for the New Millennium.* Advanstar Communications, 2000.

Zyman, Sergio. "Put the Petal to the Metal: Marketing and the Internet." *Brandweek.* October 2, 2000.

MARKUP

Markup is the amount that a seller of goods or services charges over and above the total cost of delivering its product or service in order to make a desired profit. For example, if the total cost of a manufacturer's product is $20, but its selling price is $29, then the extra $9 is understood to be the "markup." Markup is utilized by wholesalers, retailers, and manufacturers alike.

For entrepreneurs in the process of starting a business, establishing markup is one of the most important parts of pricing strategy. Markups must be sizable enough to cover all anticipated business expenses and reductions (markdowns, stock shortages, employee and customer discounts) and still provide the business with a good profit. The informed small business owner, then, is far more likely to arrive at a good markup price than the business owner who has a flawed understanding of the company's likely sales, its total operating expenses—including material, labor, and overhead costs—and its place in larger economic trends.

Entrepreneurs should also recognize that a flat markup percentage should not be blindly stamped on all of the company's products or services regardless of the frequency with which customers purchase those goods or services. As the Small Business Administration noted in its brochure *Pricing Your Products,* small business owners "should seriously consider different markup figures when some lines have very different characteristics. For instance, a clothing retailer might logically have different initial markup figures for suits, shirts, pants, and accessories. [The small business owner] may want those items with the highest turnover rates to carry the lowest initial markup."

Indeed, a small business may be able to realize a hefty profit even when it attaches a considerably smaller markup to one line of products, provided that the sales volume for that product line is high. For example, if company A and company B are selling the same $5 product, but company A insists on attaching a $4 markup on the product while company B limits itself to a $2 markup, the disparity in retail price may allow company B to register sales three or four times greater than the sales posted by company A. Company B thus realizes greater profits from the product than company A, even though the latter business had a higher markup.

MARKUPS IN SPECIFIC INDUSTRIES Markups vary enormously from industry to industry. In some industries, the markup is only a small percentage of the total cost of the product or service. Companies in other industries, however, are able to attach a far higher markup. Small appliance manufacturers can sometimes assign markups of 30 percent or more, while clothing is often marked up by as much as 100 percent. Even within industries, markups can vary widely. The automotive industry, for example, is usually limited to a 5-10 percent markup on new cars, but it realizes a far higher profit in the hugely popular sports utility vehicle market, where markups of 25 percent or more are not uncommon.

FURTHER READING:

Aguirregabiria, Victor. "The Dynamics of Markups and Inventories in Retailing Firms." *Review of Economic Studies*. April 1999.

Berry, Leonard L., and Manjit S. Yadav. "Capture and Communicate Value in the Pricing of Services." *Sloan Management Review*. Summer 1996.

Pricing Your Products. Small Business Administration, n.a.

Rugledge, John. "Pricing for Growth." *Forbes*. October 7, 1996.

Service Corps of Retired Executives (SCORE), Chapter 225. *Handbook for Small Business*. Small Business Administration, 1989.

Sinanoglu, Elif. "Want a Markdown? Learn the Markup." *Money*. February 1996.

SEE ALSO: Pricing

MATERIAL REQUIREMENTS PLANNING (MRP)

Material requirements planning (MRP) is a computer-based inventory management system designed to assist production managers in scheduling and placing orders for dependent demand items. Dependent demand items are components of finished goods—such as raw materials, component parts, and subassemblies—for which the amount of inventory needed depends on the level of production of the final product. For example, in a plant that manufactured bicycles, dependent demand inventory items might include aluminum, tires, seats, and derailleurs.

The first MRP systems of inventory management evolved in the 1940s and 1950s. They used mainframe computers to explode information from a bill of materials for a certain finished product into a production and purchasing plan for components. Before long, MRP was expanded to include information feedback loops so that production personnel could change and update the inputs into the system as needed. The next generation of MRP, known as manufacturing resources planning or MRP II, also incorporated marketing, finance, accounting, engineering, and human resources aspects into the planning process. A related concept that expands on MRP is enterprise resources planning (ERP), which uses computer technology to link the various functional areas across an entire business enterprise.

MRP works backward from a production plan for finished goods to develop requirements for components and raw materials. "MRP begins with a schedule for finished goods that is converted into a schedule of requirements for the subassemblies, component parts, and raw materials needed to produce the finished items in the specified time frame," William J.

Stevenson wrote in his book *Production/Operations Management*. "Thus, MRP is designed to answer three questions: *what* is needed? *how much* is needed? and *when* is it needed?"

MRP breaks down inventory requirements into planning periods so that production can be completed in a timely manner while inventory levels—and related carrying costs—are kept to a minimum. Implemented and used properly, it can help production managers plan for capacity needs and allocate production time. But MRP systems can be time consuming and costly to implement, which may put them out of range for some small businesses. In addition, the information that comes out of an MRP system is only as good as the information that goes into it. Companies must maintain current and accurate bills of materials, part numbers, and inventory records if they are to realize the potential benefits of MRP.

MRP INPUTS

According to Stevenson, the information input into MRP systems comes from three main sources: a bill of materials, a master schedule, and an inventory records file. The bill of materials is a listing of all the raw materials, component parts, subassemblies, and assemblies required to produce one unit of a specific finished product. Each different product made by a given manufacturer will have its own separate bill of materials. The bill of materials is arranged in a hierarchy, so that managers can see what materials are needed to complete each level of production. MRP uses the bill of materials to determine the quantity of each component that is needed to produce a certain number of finished products. From this quantity, the system subtracts the quantity of that item already in inventory to determine order requirements.

The master schedule outlines the anticipated production activities of the plant. Developed using both internal forecasts and external orders, it states the quantity of each product that will be manufactured and the time frame in which they will be needed. As Stevenson explained, the master schedule separates the planning horizon into time "buckets," which are usually calendar weeks. The schedule must cover a time frame long enough to produce the final product. This total production time is equal to the sum of the lead times of all the related fabrication and assembly operations. It is important to note that master schedules are often generated according to demand and without regard to capacity. An MRP system cannot tell in advance if a schedule is not feasible, so managers may have to run several possibilities through the system before they find one that works.

The inventory records file provides an accounting of how much inventory is already on hand or on order, and thus should be subtracted from the material requirements. "The inventory records file is used to store information on the status of each item by time period," Stevenson noted. "This includes gross requirements, scheduled receipts, and expected amount on hand. It also includes other details for each item, such as supplier, lead time, and lot size."

MRP PROCESSING

Using information culled from the bill of materials, master schedule, and inventory records file, an MRP system determines the net requirements for raw materials, component parts, and subassemblies for each period on the planning horizon. MRP processing first determines gross material requirements, then subtracts out the inventory on hand and adds back in the safety stock in order to compute the net requirements.

As Stevenson explained, the main outputs from MRP include three primary reports and three secondary reports. The primary reports consist of: planned order schedules, which outline the quantity and timing of future material orders; order releases, which authorize orders to be made; and changes to planned orders, which might include cancellations or revisions of the quantity or time frame. The secondary reports generated by MRP include: performance control reports, which are used to track problems like missed delivery dates and stock outs in order to evaluate system performance; planning reports, which can be used in forecasting future inventory requirements; and exception reports, which call managers' attention to major problems like late orders or excessive scrap rates.

Although working backward from the production plan for a finished product to determine the requirements for components may seem like a simple process, it can actually be extremely complicated, especially when some raw materials or parts are used in a number of different products. Frequent changes in product design, order quantities, or production schedule also complicate matters. "The importance of the computer becomes evident when you consider that a typical firm would have not one but many end items for which it needs to develop material requirements plans, each with its own set of components," Stevenson explained. "Differences in timing of demands and quantities needed, revisions caused by late deliveries, high scrap rates, and canceled orders all have an impact on processing."

BENEFITS AND DRAWBACKS OF MRP

MRP systems offer a number of potential benefits to manufacturing firms. Some of the main benefits include helping production managers to minimize inventory levels and the associated carrying costs, track material requirements, determine the most economi-

cal lot sizes for orders, compute quantities needed as safety stock, allocate production time among various products, and plan for future capacity needs. The information generated by MRP systems is useful in other areas as well. "A range of people in a typical manufacturing company are important users of the information provided by an MRP system," Stevenson wrote. "Production planners are obvious users of MRP. Production managers, who must balance work loads across departments and make decisions about scheduling work, and plant foremen, who are responsible for issuing work orders and maintaining production schedules, also rely heavily on MRP output. Other users include customer service representatives, who must be able to supply customers with projected delivery dates, purchasing managers, and inventory managers."

MRP systems also have several potential drawbacks, however. First, MRP relies upon accurate input information. If a small business has not maintained good inventory records or has not updated its bills of materials with all relevant changes, it may encounter serious problems with the outputs of its MRP system. The problems could range from missing parts and excessive order quantities to schedule delays and missed delivery dates. At a minimum, an MRP system must have an accurate master production schedule, good lead time estimates, and current inventory records in order to function effectively and produce useful information.

Another potential drawback associated with MRP is that the systems can be difficult, time consuming, and costly to implement. Many businesses encounter resistance from employees when they try to implement MRP. For example, employees who once got by with sloppy record keeping may resent the discipline MRP requires. Or departments that became accustomed to hoarding parts in case of inventory shortages might find it difficult to trust the system and let go of that habit.

The key to making MRP implementation work is to provide training and education for all affected employees. "It is vital to identify whose power base will be affected by a new system," William J. Sawaya wrote in *Industrial Management*. "These persons must be converted or the system will fail. Key personnel must be convinced that they personally will be better served by the new system than by any other alternative." One way to improve employee acceptance of MRP systems is to adjust reward systems to reflect production and inventory management goals. "People generally act in their own self-interest," Sawaya noted. "If the performance measures that are used in determining compensation and promotion do not adequately address materials management, then no system in the world can significantly improve the situation.''

MRP II

In the 1980s, MRP technology was expanded to create a new approach called manufacturing resources planning, or MRP II. ''The techniques developed in MRP to provide valid production schedules proved so successful that organizations became aware that with valid schedules other resources could be better planned and controlled,'' Gordon Minty noted in his book *Production Planning and Controlling*. ''The areas of marketing, finance, and personnel were affected by the improvement in customer delivery commitments, cash flow projections, and personnel management projections.''

Minty went on to explain that MRP II ''has not replaced MRP, nor is it an improved version of it. Rather, it represents an effort to expand the scope of production resource planning and to involve other functional areas of the firm in the planning process,'' such as marketing, finance, engineering, purchasing, and human resources. MRP II differs from MRP in that all of these functional areas have input into the master production schedule. From that point, MRP is used to generate material requirements and help production managers plan capacity. MRP II systems often include simulation capabilities so managers can evaluate various options.

FURTHER READING:

Goddard, Walter E. ''Focus on the Fundamentals of MRP II.'' *Modern Materials Handling*. December 1993.

Hasin, M. Ahsan A., and P.C. Pandey. ''MRP II: Should Its Simplicity Remain Unchanged?'' *Industrial Management*. May-June 1996.

''Manufacturing Execution Systems: Managing the Product through the Plant.'' *Industry Week*. September 18, 1995.

Minty, Gordon. *Production Planning and Controlling*. Goodheart-Willcox, 1998.

Orlicky, Joseph. *Material Requirements Planning*. McGraw-Hill, 1975.

Sawaya, William J., et al. ''Ten Guidelines for Implementing Manufacturing Systems.'' *Industrial Management*. January-February 1992.

Stevenson, William J. *Production/Operations Management*. 5th ed. McGraw-Hill, 1996.

SEE ALSO: Enterprise Resource Planning; Inventory Control Systems

MEDICARE AND MEDICAID

Medicare and Medicaid are health insurance programs sponsored by the federal government that cover medical expenses for elderly, disabled, and low-income Americans. Both programs took effect in 1965 and are administered by the Health Care Finance Administration (HCFA) of the Department of Health and Human Services. The U.S. government provides health care coverage to a variety of groups—including federal employees, military personnel, veterans, and Native Americans—but the Medicare and Medicaid programs account for the largest proportion of health care expenditures.

The cost of administering the programs has increased dramatically over the years with the rapid escalation in health care costs. In fact, the portion of overall government spending that went toward Medicare and Medicaid increased from 5 percent in 1970 to 12 percent in 1990 and was projected to reach 23 percent by 2000. As a result, many experts predict that Americans will not be able to depend upon the programs for their long-term health care needs in the future. For self-employed persons and small business owners, who are less likely to be covered by an employer's health insurance program, these statistics make obtaining private health insurance policies that much more important.

MEDICARE

Medicare is the nation's largest health insurance program, providing coverage for 39 million Americans who are age 65 or older or who have a disability. Medicare coverage consists of two parts. Part A, which is financed largely through Social Security taxes, provides hospitalization insurance. Intended to assist people who need long-term medical treatment, Medicare Part A covers inpatient hospital services, skilled nursing facilities, home health services, and hospice care. Part B, which is financed through premiums paid by those who choose to enroll in the program, provides supplemental insurance to help cover the cost of physician services, outpatient hospital services, and medical equipment and supplies.

Qualified people can enroll in the Medicare program by completing an application at their local Social Security Administration office. It is important to note that, once an employee becomes eligible for Medicare, a small business owner is no longer required to offer him or her health insurance continuation coverage under the provisions of the Consolidated Omnibus Budget Reconciliation Act (COBRA). Since Medicare does not cover all of an elderly or disabled person's health care costs, many insurance companies offer Medicare Supplemental Insurance (also known as Medigap coverage) to fill in the gaps. Medigap policies commonly take care of co-payments and over-limit expenses, for example, in exchange for a small premium. Due to past problems with disreputable Medigap providers, experts recommend that individuals shop carefully for this type of coverage.

MEDICAID

As the nation's second-largest health insurance program, Medicaid provides medical assistance to 36 million low-income Americans. It was established through Title XIX of the Social Security Act of 1965 to pay the health care costs for members of society who otherwise could not afford treatment. The program is jointly funded by the federal government and the state governments, but is administered separately by each state within broad federal guidelines. Medicaid recipients include adults, children, and families, as well as elderly, blind, and disabled persons, who have low or no income and receive other forms of public assistance. Medicaid also covers the "medically needy," or those whose income is significantly reduced by large medical expenses.

Medicaid covers the full cost of a wide range of medical services, including inpatient and outpatient hospital care, doctor visits, lab tests, X-rays, nursing home and home health care, family planning services, and preventative medicine. A large proportion of the Medicaid population is elderly or disabled, and thus also qualifies for Medicare. In these cases, Medicaid usually pays for Medicare premiums, deductibles, and co-payments, in addition to some non-covered services.

THE FUTURE

Although many Americans plan to rely on Medicare to meet their health insurance needs later in life, the program as it stood in the mid-1990s actually covered less than half of an average elderly person's medical costs, according to Lenore Janecek in her book *Health Insurance: A Guide for Artists, Consultants, Entrepreneurs, and Other Self-Employed.* It does not provide funds for dental, vision, or hearing care, for example, and 97 percent of the time it does not cover nursing home care. Most significantly for many seniors, Medicare does not cover outpatient prescription drugs. A 2000 article in *U.S. News and World Report* noted that health care costs account for 21 percent of senior citizens' income, with prescription drugs the second-largest expense after insurance premiums.

Even if the Medicare program remained basically the same beyond the year 2000, it would not provide adequate coverage for many Americans. But the program seemed likely to face significant changes to address the rising cost of health care and the increased need for coverage as the baby-boom generation neared retirement age. Both Medicare and Medicaid were featured prominently in discussions about the federal budget deficit, welfare reform, and health care reform. Various proposals to reduce the programs' budgets, introduce spending caps, and create new plans to cover children and prescription drugs may be adopted in the near future. As a result, Janecek noted, entrepreneurs may face even greater challenges in ensuring their financial and physical well-being upon retirement.

FURTHER READING:

Anastasio, Susan. *Small Business Insurance and Risk Management Guide.* U.S. Small Business Administration, n.d.

Cady, Donald F. "Medicare and Medicaid Defined." *National Underwriter Life and Health.* May 3, 1999.

Health Insurance. Council of Better Business Bureaus, 1995.

Janecek, Lenore. *Health Insurance: A Guide for Artists, Consultants, Entrepreneurs, and Other Self-Employed.* Allworth Press, 1993.

"Making Sense of Medicare." *Business Week.* November 1, 1999.

"Medicare Requires Serious Help." *Business Insurance.* September 11, 2000.

Retsinas, Joan. "Medicare, and the Statistical Good (and Maybe Not So Good) News." *Providence Business News.* December 6, 1999.

Shapiro, Joseph P. "Medicare's Drug Woes." *U.S. News and World Report.* February 21, 2000.

MEETINGS

Meetings, while disliked by many, are an essential part of myriad business operations. They are often the best venue for communications to take place, for issues to be discussed, for priorities to be set, and for decisions to be made in various realms of business management. Because it is more common for responsibility to be spread out across an organization these days, and because cross-functional efforts are common at almost every business, meetings are the best method for achieving organizational participation.

Holding successful meetings, then, is essential. Poorly run meetings waste time and fail to generate ideas, and unfortunately, far too high a percentage of business meetings are characterized by ineffective processes. Indeed, some analysts estimate that up to 50 percent of meeting time is wasted. Entrepreneurs and small business managers should thus take the appropriate steps to ensure that the meetings that they call and lead are productive.

PLANNING A SUCCESSFUL BUSINESS MEETING

The most important step in holding a successful meeting is planning. This includes determining who should attend, who will run the meeting, and what will be discussed. Before the meeting, finalize a list of attendees. This is especially important for meetings where a quorum is needed to conduct official business. Without a quorum, it is usually best to simply postpone the meeting until more group members can attend.

When determining who to include in a meeting, several criteria should be weighed. Charlie Hawkins pointed out in *Public Relations Quarterly* that the most important personnel to invite are those people who can best achieve the objective of the meeting. This can be people who are affected by a problem, those who will be most affected by the outcome of the meeting, experts on the subject at hand, or people who are known to be good problem-solvers or idea generators. Inviting people solely for political reasons should be avoided, although experts recognize that this may not always be possible. Avoid inviting disruptive people unless they absolutely have to be there. Finally, some meeting topics may benefit from the inclusion of an informed outsider who has no stake in the issue; sometimes a fresh, objective perspective can be most beneficial.

Once the meeting's moderator has determined who needs to be in attendance, he or she should develop an agenda and circulate it in advance of the meeting. There are two schools of thought on how to order the agenda. One school recommends starting the agenda with less-important items that can be handled quickly and easily. The theory is that this helps to build a positive atmosphere and makes it easier to move on to tougher issues later in the meeting. The other school of thought, however, feels that this is a waste of time and that the agenda should be prioritized, with the most important items coming first. This means jumping right into the most significant issue. Regularly scheduled meetings, such as staff meetings, lend themselves to the ''most important first'' style.

Many consultants, managers, and business owners contend that the traditional agenda model of ''old minutes, old business, new business, adjournment'' does not really work anymore. Agendas need to be more fluid and dynamic, yet still need to be structured and effective. Adhering to the following tips can help ensure that the meeting agenda can be addressed effectively:

- State the purpose of the meeting and write it clearly at the top of the agenda. If no clear goal or topic comes to mind, then perhaps the meeting is not even necessary. Consider using a memo, e-mail, conference call, or series of one-to-one meetings to canvas participants about meeting topics prior to creating the agenda.

- Set priorities. Reading the minutes from a past meeting is a colossal waste of time. It is ok to hand out the minutes from the previous meeting, but reading them is just not needed.

- Less is more. One of the fundamental meeting mistakes is tackling too many issues. Keep the agenda focused on a few key items.

If other group members are to play a role at the meeting, call or visit them once the agenda is established so that they clearly understand their role. Assign a time limit to each of the agenda items. Having time limits helps keep a meeting on track and prevents rambling discussions. Never include the agenda item ''Any Other Business.'' It encourages time-wasting at the end of the meeting and also serves as a method for a savvy (or sneaky) meeting participant to exploit the meeting by bringing up an item that is of importance to him or her alone.

Once an agenda has been established, many consultants recommend the appointment of a meeting facilitator in advance of the meeting itself. It is the facilitator's job to keep the meeting focused and on-schedule. He or she must remain ''issue neutral'' and encourage the free exchange of ideas without taking sides. The best facilitators are good listeners and communicators who successfully blend assertiveness with tact and discipline with humor, set a cooperative tone, and are achievement-oriented. The facilitator should remain focused and not allow side issues to distract from the agenda. Appointing a separate time-keeper who alerts the facilitator when agreed-upon time limits are approaching is recommended. Some professional meeting planners recommend using co-facilitators—this keeps one facilitator from falling in love with his or her own ideas. For small companies, this idea may not be feasible. However, if the company does hold a lot of meetings, perhaps several company members can be sent for formal training in meeting facilitation. This would make it easier to appoint co-facilitators.

For small companies, perhaps facilitators are not needed at every meeting. Indeed, small business owners often serve as facilitator, key information source, and chief strategist all in one. But some small businesses have successfully instituted systems in which meeting planning and leadership responsibilities are rotated among staff members.

CONDUCTING A SUCCESSFUL MEETING

Once the planning has been concluded, it is time to hold the meeting. Adhering to several simple rules can dramatically increase the likelihood that your meeting will be a productive one.

1) If you are facilitating the meeting, arrive early and be prepared. No exceptions to this rule are allowed. A late facilitator dampens the mood and gets the meeting off on the wrong foot because it makes it impossible for the meeting to start on time. Indeed, provided the facilitator is present, the meeting should begin at the time scheduled, even if other scheduled participants have not yet arrived. Waiting for latecomers rewards them for their behavior and implies that you value their time more than you value the time of those who showed up on time. If one of the latecomers is essential to the first agenda item, be flexible and move on to a later agenda item to keep things moving.

2) Facilitators interested in making certain that the meeting proceeds effectively should set the appropriate tone from the outset. Chit-chat should be kept to a minimum, especially at the start of the meeting. Do not be a dictator—social interaction is an important part of building a cohesive team—but do not let valuable meeting time be wasted either. ''Nothing saps the spirit like watching, powerless, as a meeting wanders into oblivion,'' observed Phaedra Hise in *Inc.*

3) Be sure to stick to the timed meeting agenda that was developed at the planning stage. This builds consensus for tabling discussions that are going nowhere. It also makes it easier to agree to send problems back to committees, and it keeps one long-winded group member from dominating the meeting. Using a phrase such as ''We would like to hear what you have to say, but in order for the group to be out on time we have to move on,'' is a very successful tactic.

4) If some members of the group are not participating, actively seek out their opinion. Groups tend to be dominated by the most outgoing or opinionated members, but the quiet members often have great ideas of their own. Do not let one person or group dominate the floor.

5) Stay focused on the purpose of the meeting. If the group that is meeting is a large board that is primarily responsible for delegating tasks to smaller committees, make sure the larger group does not make the mistake of doing the work for the smaller groups instead of passing it on.

6) Schedule meetings for times that are likely to encourage concentrate on agenda items. For example, facilitators may want to consider holding short meetings before lunch and quitting time, when staff are less likely to dawdle over non-work related subjects. Conversely, many analysts believe that meetings that are held immediately after lunch, when people are often at their least energetic, are apt to be less effective.

7) Stand-up meetings are often touted as a great way to ensure that meeting participants stay focused. Another way to stay focused is to use what Hawkins termed the ''parking lot'' strategy. During the course of one discussion, it is not unusual for important ideas or concerns to arise that are not related to the topic at hand. When that happens, the facilitator can call ''time out,'' identify the issue, and place it in a so-called ''parking lot'' so that it can be addressed at a later time. The group can then get back to the main focus of the meeting without losing topics or ideas that may be of importance to the firm.

8) Try to establish a consensus on business decisions that are arrived at in meetings. ''Building consensus does not mean caving in to conform with what the boss wants,'' said Hawkins. ''It does mean examining the plus and minus aspects of possible alternatives, and picking the one(s) that best meet the defined goals. The normal way of deciding—by voting—inevitably produces a win-lose situation. Those who are in the minority are liable to undermine the decision. Even if a voting process is used to pick the winners, a consensus process is recommended to isolate the concerns and address them. When this is done, the solution is refined to the point where everyone in the group can live with the recommendation and support it. A group that builds consensus in a constructive atmosphere is most likely a highly effective team.''

9) Ensure that decisions that are made in meetings are adequately disseminated, especially to staff members who are personally impacted by the decision. Make sure that company resources are appropriately redistributed to enable execution of decisions.

MEETING PITFALLS

Despite the best efforts and the strongest facilitator, meetings can quickly spin out of control. Following are some common pitfalls that beset meetings, launching them into downward spirals of inaction and/or flawed decision making:

- The facilitator puts aside the meeting agenda for his or her own personal agenda

- The facilitator allows interruptions such as telephone calls, etc.

- Loud group members are allowed to dominate the meeting

- Decisions are made based on generalizations, exaggeration, guesswork, and assumptions

- Discussions consistently wander off the topic

- Key members of the group are not present

- Overly ambitious agendas

- Meetings that exceed previously agreed-upon time limits

- Minutes that are inaccurate or biased

- Too many participants

- Waiting for latecomers to arrive

- An unclear, or inappropriate, decision-making process. For example, taking a vote when leadership and unilateral action by a company's CEO is clearly needed.

MEETINGS IN A FAMILY-OWNED BUSINESS

Many small businesses are family-owned. While it might seem that a family-operated business might not need to worry about holding successful meetings, that is not true. Family meetings can be an important means of keeping the business fresh, generating new ideas, and keeping grievances to a minimum.

Family meetings, when run properly, can help ensure business success and its continued survival into the next generation. The meetings do not need to be formal, but they should be structured and should be held on a regular basis. Because a family business affects all family members—not just those who are an active part of the business—some analysts contend that everyone in the family should be invited to the meetings. If everyone takes the meeting seriously and is willing to participate, the meeting can lead to greater cohesion, communication, and long-range planning.

Business experts say that the agenda for such a meeting can combine business and pleasure. Serious topics—creating a mission statement, strategy planning, setting a clear path of succession, professional growth and development, market analysis, and estate planning are some examples—typically need to be addressed during these meetings, but the agenda should also reflect a recognition of the family environment in which it is taking place. Meetings that include a meal (dinner, picnic, etc.) as a centerpiece are among the most popular options.

As with any other meeting, the family meeting should have a facilitator. An outside facilitator can be brought in if family members are concerned that objectivity might otherwise be hard to achieve, but be forewarned that hiring a facilitator can be expensive. It is possible to use a family member as a facilitator as long as that person is able to remain unbiased in the face of emotional discussions. Steering clear of long-time family conflicts is also a must if the facilitator is to succeed at his or her job, although admittedly this can sometimes be difficult. "Facilitating one's own family meeting can seem daunting because of the potential emotional intensity of family discussions," wrote John Ward and Sharon Krone in *Nation's Business*. "To be effective, a family member acting as a facilitator must overcome emotional barriers, dispel longtime family stereotypes, and curtail long-standing conflicts among family members. All are tough to do."

Ward and Krone provided several other tips for holding successful family meetings, including the following:

- Consider using co-facilitators as a safeguard to prevent one family member from wielding undue influence over the meeting's direction and tone.

- The facilitator must keep others involved. Assign jobs—keeping notes, creating charts or overheads, keying and distributing minutes, or chairing committees—and avoid the impression that one person is dominating the meeting.

- Provide formal training for the facilitator. While the person selected may have strong interpersonal and leadership skills, formal training in communications, conflict resolution, active listening, decision making, and group management can prove invaluable.

- Each person attending the meeting should reflect on his or her own strengths and weaknesses and personality style.

- Recognize when professional help *is* needed. Intense conflicts and domination by one person or a small group of people are examples of when it might be time to bring in a professional facilitator.

- Avoid surprises. Distribute agendas and notes in advance if possible.

- Set ground rules for the meeting.

- Have fun. Even if the business at hand is very serious, set aside some time for relaxation or fun.

- Use a well-lit meeting room with comfortable furniture. Make sure refreshments are provided and provide ample breaks.

- Do not rush things, and do not overload the agenda with too many heavy topics if at all possible.

FURTHER READING:

"Advanced Agenda Writing: Tactics to Use Before You Call the Meeting to Order." *Oregon Business.* December 1996.

Brokaw, Leslie. "The Model Meetings Agenda." *Inc.* July 1994.

Butler, Ava S. "Taking Meetings by Storm." *Management Review.* October 1996.

"Determine the Health of Your Company by the Meetings You Attend." *Sales and Marketing Management.* July 1999.

Gorup, Sharon R. "Conducting Productive Meetings: How to Stay on Track." *Association Management.* January 1997.

Hawkins, Charlie. "First Aid for Meetings." *Public Relations Quarterly.* Fall 1997.

Hise, Phaedra. "Keeping Meetings Brief." *Inc.* September 1994.

Jones, Becky, Midge Wilker, and Judy Stoner. "A Meeting Primer." *Management Review.* January 1995.

Krone, Sharon P., and John L. Ward. "Do-It-Yourself Family Meetings." *Nation's Business.* November 1997.

"Time's Up." *Industry Week.* June 9, 1997.

Williams, Kelly. "No More Boring Meetings." *Office Solutions.* February 2001.

Wyatt, Stuart. "How to Make Your Meetings More Effective." *Management Accounting.* April 1996.

MENTORING

Mentoring denotes a relationship between a more experienced person—the mentor—and a less experienced person—the protégé. The mentor's role is to guide, instruct, encourage, and correct the protégé. The protégé should be willing to listen to instruction and constructive criticism, and should also feel as though the mentor is concerned with his/her welfare. Mentor/protégé relationships are less structured and more personal than traditional teacher/student situations.

HOW MENTORING WORKS IN SMALL BUSINESSES

In many large corporations, formal systems of mentoring have been established in recent years. They are designed to quickly involve new employees in the work at hand, and to strengthen the work force in much the same way that other teambuilding strategies are designed to do. These systems pair experienced workers exhibiting (or needing to hone) strong leadership skills with new employees not yet acquainted with the nuances of the corporation, the work at hand, and/or their potential within the framework of the company.

But while mentoring is perhaps most closely associated with large corporate settings, the practice can be effectively utilized by small businesses as well. Small business owners themselves can become involved in mentoring relationships, on either the mentor or the protégé side. Entrepreneurs may seek out business owners or executives with more experience in certain areas, and approach them about beginning a mentoring relationship. Because this kind of approach acknowledges success, experience, and market savvy, a potential mentor will likely be flattered and appreciate the drive and initiative of the potential protégé. In other instances, more experienced small business owners may wish to initiate mentor/protégé relationships from the mentor angle, spurred by philanthropic instincts or a wish to strengthen the skills and knowledge of other people within his or her organization. These mentoring systems can be loosely or formally structured, either determined by the owner or simply encouraged by the owner and initiated by employees. In either case, attempts should be made to insure both diversity in the workplace, which can be strengthened by mentoring relationships, and a reasonable fit.

Protégés and mentors should feel relatively comfortable together, as the relationship ideally is one of trust and mutual growth. Mentors should not be expected to become drill sergeants or police; the mentor relationship is not intended to be one of management exerting its will over young or inexperienced employees. Rather, the relationship should reduce anxiety by clearly defining goals and boundaries, and should increase productivity as a result.

Small business owners seeking mentors have several structured alternatives to choose from. For example, the Small Business Administration can put potential protégés into contact with some groups. In addition, the Service Corps of Retired Executives (SCORE) includes mentoring among its various offerings.

BENEFITS OF MENTORING

Mentoring relationships can be beneficial to all parties. Any mentoring situation requires an investment of time, experience, and trust. But these investments will be rewarded in a strong tie between colleagues and the deepened experience of not just the protégé, but also the mentor.

BENEFITS FOR THE MENTOR

Mentors may receive great satisfaction from their experience with protégés. They feel respected and appreciated for their knowledge and skill. And mentors can become more invested in their work as a result: they have personal relationships to foster in the business setting, and they feel that the owner trusts and respects their judgment and talents. And as role models, mentors may even more closely evaluate their own performances and become more productive in their own business dealings and duties.

BENEFITS FOR THE PROTÉGÉ

The protégé, whether a new employee of a business or a new entrepreneur, will benefit from the transfer of knowledge and know-how that can be passed on by a mentor of greater experience. Perhaps the greatest benefit is being able to learn from other people's mistakes; a mentor can warn of pitfalls as yet unforeseen by the protégé, saving the time and the pain of having to make those mistakes in order to know they exist.

An employee who is a protégé also benefits by having a mentor trained in the management of a business, who can pass along the true meanings behind policy decisions, and the unwritten rules of the workplace. The mentoring relationship can make the transition into productive, comfortable employee a much smoother one; the protégés will quickly learn what is expected from them, their place within the framework of the business, and the responsibilities of other departments and personnel within the workplace. Career opportunities and areas of improvement can both be sensitively illustrated by a mentor, and transitions within the company and changes of business practice can be made less stressful with suitable guidance.

BENEFITS FOR THE BUSINESS OWNER

The business owner benefits from the mentor/ protégé relationship within their business in some very real ways. New employees can be thoroughly trained in technical aspects of the work by a mentor, resulting in employees who move quickly through the learning curve and into productive work. Business owners are able to practice more hands-off management of companies which have strong, capable mentors; and mentoring relationships have also been shown to promote employee satisfaction, leading to decreased turnover in the workforce and higher production rates.

FURTHER READING:

Benabou, Charles, and Raphael Banabou. "Establishing a Formal Mentoring Program for Organizational Success." *National Productivity Review.* Autumn 2000.

Boyett, Joseph H. and Henry P. Conn, *Workplace 2000*, Penguin, 1991.

Dortch, Thomas W., Jr. *The Miracles of Mentoring: The Joy of Investing in Our Future.* Cahners Publishing, 2000.

Eddy, Sandra E., "Computer Ease: Virtual Mentors," *Entrepreneur Online*, November 1997.

Graham, Anne. "A Mentoring Mindset." *Folio.* September 2000.

Kennedy, Danielle, "Guiding Light." *Entrepreneur*, July 1997.

Martin, Anya. "Mentoring Within." *Atlanta Business Chronicle.* August 4, 2000.

Roberts, Lee. "Mentoring May Develop Both Loyalty and Retention." *Minneapolis-St. Paul Business.* August 4, 2000.

MERCHANDISE DISPLAYS

Merchandise displays are special presentations of a store's products or services to the buying public. The nature of these displays may range somewhat from industry to industry, but all merchandise displays are predicated on basic principles designed to increase product purchases. Indeed, merchandise displays are an integral element of the overall merchandising concept, which seeks to promote product sales by coordinating marketing, advertising, and sales strategies.

Many business consultants believe that small business owners are among the leaders in innovative merchandise display strategies. W. Rae Cowan noted in *Chain Store Age Executive,* for example, that "in many instances, smaller specialty chains are leading the way in store ambience supporting their overall marketing strategy in a broad range of categories from fashion through hardware and housewares and building supplies areas. By their very nature, specialty stores depend on their fixturing to generate a differentiation or niche in the marketplace. And being physically smaller in some cases allows for faster response to market trends and conditions. . . . Successful retailers today are using their fixturing to productively dispense their merchandise and communicate an appropriate environment on the retail floor."

Merchandise displays generally take one of several basic forms:

- Storefront Window Displays—These typically open on to a street or shopping mall walk or courtyard and are intended to attract passerby that might not otherwise enter the store.

- Showcase Displays—These typically feature items that 1) are deemed to be too valuable for display in storefront set-ups, or 2) are niche items of high interest to the business's primary clientele. These display centers are usually located in high traffic areas and typically feature multiple tiers for product display and a sliding door on the clerk's side for access.

- "Found-Space" Displays—This term refers to product presentations that utilize small but nonetheless usable areas of the store, such as the tops of product carousels or available wall space.

Storefront window displays and "found space" displays are particularly popular tools for publicizing and selling sale items.

KEYS TO SUCCESSFUL MERCHANDISE DISPLAY

Trudy Ralston and Eric Foster, authors of *How to Display It: A Practical Guide to Professional Merchandise Display,* cited several key components of successful merchandise display that are particularly relevant for small business owners. First, displays should be economical, utilizing only space, materials, and products that are already available. Second, displays should be versatile, able to "fit almost anywhere, exhibit almost any merchandise, and convey almost any message. Finally, displays have to be effective. The ideal display, said Ralston and Foster, "is readily visible to any passer-by and [should be arranged so that] there is no time or space lag between when a potential buyer sees the design and when he or she can react to it. [The ideal display] also shows the customer what the product actually looks like, not some flat and intangible picture of it. Few other forms of promotion can give such a vivid presentation of both the merchandise and character of a store."

The effectiveness of these cornerstones of merchandising display strategy can be increased by remembering several other tips as well, including the following:

- Allocate merchandise display space and expenditures appropriately in recognition of customer demographics. If the bulk of your business's customers are males between the ages of 20 and 40, the bulk of your displays should probably be shaped to catch their interest.

- Be careful of pursuing merchandise display designs that sacrifice effectiveness for the sake of originality.

- Make certain that the cleanliness and neatness of the display is maintained.

- Do not overcrowd a display. Customers tend to pass over messy, busy-looking displays. Instead, Ralston and Foster affirm that "a display should feature a single item or point of interest. . . . Every primary article [in a display] must interact with every other so that they all come together as a group. If they don't it will look as if there is not one design, but several.

- Combine products that are used together in displays. For example, pairing ski goggles with other outdoor apparel is apt to be more effective than placing it alone or with some other product that is only tangentially related to skiing.

- Small items should be displayed so that would-be customers can get a good look at them without having to solicit the help of a member of the staff.

- Pay attention to details when constructing and arranging display backgrounds. For example, Foster and Ralston counsel business owners to "avoid dark backgrounds when customers will be looking through a window, since this makes the glass behave as a giant mirror."

- Merchandise displays can sometimes be utilized to educate customers. A well-conceived display could, for example, illustrate a product use that may not have occurred to most customers. "In addition to selling actual merchandise, display can be used to introduce a new product, a fashion trend, and a new 'look' or idea," explained Martin Pegler in *Visual Merchandising and Display.* "Display can be used to educate the consumer concerning what the new item is, how it can be worn or used, and how it can be accessorized. The display may also supply pertinent information, the price, and other special features."

All of these considerations need to be weighed when putting together a merchandise display. But ultimately, the final barometer of a display's worthiness is its ability to sell products. As Martin Pegler bluntly stated, "The test of a good display today is: *Does it sell?*"

FURTHER READING:

Areni, Charles S., et al. "Point-of-Purchase Displays, Product Organization, and Brand Purchase Likelihoods." *Journal of the Academy of Marketing Science.* Fall 1999.

Cowan, W. Rae. "Store Fixturing and Display—Retailer's Strategic Tool for Product Positioning and Productivity in the '90s." *Chain Store Age Executive.* December 1993.

Fox, Bruce. "Brand Erosion Potential." *Chain Store Age Executive.* February 1994.

Pegler, Martin M. *Visual Merchandising and Display.* Fairchild Publications, 1983.

Ralston, Trudy, and Eric Foster. *How to Display It: A Practical Guide to Professional Merchandise Display.* Art Direction Book Co., 1985.

Ray, Susan. "Merchandising Concepts are Solid as Rock." *Amusement Business.* September 27, 1993.

Reese, Shelly. "Congestion, Distractions Weaken Sales Value of Endcap Displays." *Stores.* February 1997.

MERGERS AND ACQUISITIONS

A merger occurs when one firm assumes all the assets and all the liabilities of another. The acquiring firm retains its identity, while the acquired firm ceases to exist. A majority vote of shareholders is generally required to approve a merger. A merger is just one type of acquisition. One company can acquire another in several other ways, including purchasing some or all of the company's assets or buying up its outstanding shares of stock.

In general, mergers and other types of acquisitions are performed in the hopes of realizing an economic gain. For such a transaction to be justified, the two firms involved must be worth more together than they were apart. Some of the potential advantages of mergers and acquisitions include achieving economies of scale, combining complementary resources, garnering tax advantages, and eliminating inefficiencies. Other reasons for considering growth through acquisitions include obtaining proprietary rights to products or services, increasing market power by purchasing competitors, shoring up weaknesses in key business areas, penetrating new geographic regions, or providing managers with new opportunities for career growth and advancement. Since mergers and acquisitions are so complex, however, it can be very difficult to evaluate the transaction, define the associated costs and benefits, and handle the resulting tax and legal issues.

"In today's global business environment, companies may have to grow to survive, and one of the best ways to grow is by merging with another company or acquiring other companies," consultant Jacalyn Sherriton told Robert McGarvey in an interview for *Entrepreneur.* "Massive, multibillion-dollar corporations are becoming the norm, leaving an entrepreneur to wonder whether a merger ought to be in his or her plans, too," McGarvey continued.

When a small business owner chooses to merge with or sell out to another company, it is sometimes called "harvesting" the small business. In this situation, the transaction is intended to release the value locked up in the small business for the benefit of its owners and investors. The impetus for a small business owner to pursue a sale or merger may involve estate planning, a need to diversify his or her investments, an inability to finance growth independently, or a simple need for change. In addition, some small businesses find that the best way to grow and compete against larger firms is to merge with or acquire other small businesses.

In principle, the decision to merge with or acquire another firm is a capital budgeting decision much like any other. But mergers differ from ordinary investment decisions in at least five ways. First, the value of a merger may depend on such things as strategic fits that are difficult to measure. Second, the accounting, tax, and legal aspects of a merger can be complex. Third, mergers often involve issues of corporate control and are a means of replacing existing management. Fourth, mergers obviously affect the value of the firm, but they also affect the relative value of the stocks and bonds. Finally, mergers are often "unfriendly."

TYPES OF ACQUISITIONS

In general, acquisitions can be horizontal, vertical, or conglomerate. A horizontal acquisition takes place between two firms in the same line of business. For example, one tool and die company might purchase another. In contrast, a vertical merger entails expanding forward or backward in the chain of distribution, toward the source of raw materials or toward the ultimate consumer. For example, an auto parts manufacturer might purchase a retail auto parts store. A conglomerate is formed through the combination of unrelated businesses.

Another type of combination of two companies is a consolidation. In a consolidation, an entirely new firm is created, and the two previous entities cease to exist. Consolidated financial statements are prepared under the assumption that two or more corporate entities are in actuality only one. The consolidated statements are prepared by combining the account balances of the individual firms after certain adjusting and eliminating entries are made.

Another way to acquire a firm is to buy the voting stock. This can be done by agreement of management or by tender offer. In a tender offer, the acquiring firm makes the offer to buy stock directly to the shareholders, thereby bypassing management. In contrast to a merger, a stock acquisition requires no stockholder voting. Shareholders wishing to keep their stock can simply do so. Also, a minority of share-holders may hold out in a tender offer.

A bidding firm can also buy another simply by purchasing all its assets. This involves a costly legal transfer of title and must be approved by the share-holders of the selling firm. A takeover is the transfer of control from one group to another. Normally, the acquiring firm (the bidder) makes an offer for the target firm. In a proxy contest, a group of dissident shareholders will seek to obtain enough votes to gain control of the board of directors.

TAXABLE VERSUS TAX-FREE TRANSACTIONS

Mergers and acquisitions can be either tax-free or taxable events. The tax status of a transaction may affect its value from both the buyer's and the seller's viewpoints. In a taxable acquisition, the assets of the selling firm are revalued or ''written up.'' Therefore, the depreciation deduction will rise (assets are not revalued in a tax-free acquisition). But the selling shareholders will have to pay capital gains taxes and thus will want more for their shares to compensate. This is known as the capital gains effect. The capital gains and write-up effects tend to cancel each other out.

Certain exchanges of stock are considered tax-free reorganizations, which permit the owners of one company to exchange their shares for the stock of the acquirer without paying taxes. There are three basic types of tax-free reorganizations. In order for a trans-action to qualify as a type A tax-free reorganization, it must be structured in certain ways. In contrast to a type B reorganization, the type A transaction allows the buyer to use either voting or nonvoting stock. It also permits the buyer to use more cash in the total consideration since the law does not stipulate a maxi-mum amount of cash that can be used. At least 50 percent of the consideration, however, must be stock in the acquiring corporation. In addition, in a type A reorganization, the acquiring corporation may choose not to purchase all the target's assets.

In instances where at least 50 percent of the bidder's stock is used as the consideration—but other considerations such as cash, debt, or nonequity securi-ties are also used—the transaction may be partially taxable. Capital gains taxes must be paid on those shares that were exchanged for nonequity consider-ation.

A type B reorganization requires that the acquir-ing corporation use mainly its own voting common stock as the consideration for purchase of the target corporation's common stock. Cash must comprise no more than 20 percent of the total consideration, and at least 80 percent of the target's stock must be paid for by voting stock by the bidder.

Target stockholders who receive the stock of the acquiring corporation in exchange for their common stock are not immediately taxed on the consideration they receive. Taxes will have to be paid only if the stock is eventually sold. If cash is included in the transaction, this cash may be taxed to the extent that it represents a gain on the sale of stock.

In a type C reorganization, the acquiring corpora-tion must purchase 80 percent of the fair market value of the target's assets. In this type of reorganization, a tax liability results when the acquiring corporation purchases the assets of the target using consideration other than stock in the acquiring corporation. The tax liability is measured by comparing the purchase price of the assets with the adjusted basis of these assets.

FINANCIAL ACCOUNTING FOR MERGERS AND ACQUISITIONS

The two principal accounting methods used in mergers and acquisitions are the pooling of interests method and the purchase method. The main difference between them is the value that the combined firm's balance sheet places on the assets of the acquired firm, as well as the depreciation allowances and charges against income following the merger.

The pooling of interests method assumes that the transaction is simply an exchange of equity securities. Therefore, the capital stock account of the target firm is eliminated, and the acquirer issues new stock to replace it. The two firms' assets and liabilities are combined at their historical book values as of the acquisition date. The end result of a pooling of inter-ests transaction is that the total assets of the combined firm are equal to the sum of the assets of the individual firms. No goodwill is generated, and there are no charges against earnings. A tax-free acquisition would normally be reported as a pooling of interests.

Under the purchase method, assets and liabilities are shown on the merged firm's books at their market (not book) values as of the acquisition date. This method is based on the idea that the resulting values should reflect the market values established during the bargaining process. The total liabilities of the com-bined firm equal the sum of the two firms' individual liabilities. The equity of the acquiring firm is in-creased by the amount of the purchase price.

Accounting for the excess of cost over the aggre-gate of the fair market values of the identifiable net assets acquired applies only in purchase accounting. The excess is called goodwill, an asset which is charged against income and amortized over a period that cannot exceed 40 years. Although the amortization "expense" is deducted from reported income, it cannot be deducted for tax purposes.

Purchase accounting usually results in increased depreciation charges because the book value of most assets is usually less than fair value because of inflation. For tax purposes, however, depreciation does not increase because the tax basis of the assets remains the same. Since depreciation under pooling accounting is based on the old book values of the assets, accounting income is usually higher under the pooling method. The accounting treatment has no cash flow consequences. Thus, value should be unaffected by accounting procedure. However, some firms may dislike the purchase method because of the goodwill created. The reason for this is that goodwill is amortized over a period of years.

HOW TO VALUE AN ACQUISITION CANDIDATE

Valuing an acquisition candidate is similar to valuing any investment. The analyst estimates the incremental cash flows, determines an appropriate risk-adjusted discount rate, and then computes the net present value (NPV). If firm A is acquiring firm B, for example, then the acquisition makes economic sense if the value of the combined firm is greater than the value of firm A plus the value of firm B. Synergy is said to exist when the cash flow of the combined firm is greater than the sum of the cash flows for the two firms as separate companies. The gain from the merger is the present value of this difference in cash flows.

SOURCES OF GAINS FROM ACQUISITIONS The gains from an acquisition may result from one or more of the following five categories: 1) revenue enhancement, 2) cost reductions, 3) lower taxes, 4) changing capital requirements, or 5) a lower cost of capital. Increased revenues may come from marketing gains, strategic benefits, and market power. Marketing gains arise from more effective advertising, economies of distribution, and a better mix of products. Strategic benefits represent opportunities to enter new lines of business. Finally, a merger may reduce competition, thereby increasing market power. Such mergers, of course, may run afoul of antitrust legislation.

A larger firm may be able to operate more efficiently than two smaller firms, thereby reducing costs. Horizontal mergers may generate economies of scale. This means that the average production cost will fall as production volume increases. A vertical merger may allow a firm to decrease costs by more closely coordinating production and distribution. Finally, economies may be achieved when firms have complementary resources—for example, when one firm has excess production capacity and another has insufficient capacity.

Tax gains in mergers may arise because of unused tax losses, unused debt capacity, surplus funds, and the write-up of depreciable assets. The tax losses of target corporations can be used to offset the acquiring corporation's future income. These tax losses can be used to offset income for a maximum of 15 years or until the tax loss is exhausted. Only tax losses for the previous three years can be used to offset future income.

Tax loss carry-forwards can motivate mergers and acquisitions. A company that has earned profits may find value in the tax losses of a target corporation that can be used to offset the income it plans to earn. A merger may not, however, be structured solely for tax purposes. In addition, the acquirer must continue to operate the pre-acquisition business of the company in a net loss position. The tax benefits may be less than their "face value," not only because of the time value of money, but also because the tax loss carry-forwards might expire without being fully utilized.

Tax advantages can also arise in an acquisition when a target firm carries assets on its books with basis, for tax purposes, below their market value. These assets could be more valuable, for tax purposes, if they were owned by another corporation that could increase their tax basis following the acquisition. The acquirer would then depreciate the assets based on the higher market values, in turn, gaining additional depreciation benefits.

Interest payments on debt are a tax-deductible expense, whereas dividend payments from equity ownership are not. The existence of a tax advantage for debt is an incentive to have greater use of debt, as opposed to equity, as the means of financing merger and acquisition transactions. Also, a firm that borrows much less than it could may be an acquisition target because of its unused debt capacity. While the use of financial leverage produces tax benefits, debt also increases the likelihood of financial distress in the event that the acquiring firm cannot meet its interest payments on the acquisition debt.

Finally, a firm with surplus funds may wish to acquire another firm. The reason is that distributing the money as a dividend or using it to repurchase shares will increase income taxes for shareholders. With an acquisition, no income taxes are paid by shareholders.

Acquiring firms may be able to more efficiently utilize working capital and fixed assets in the target firm, thereby reducing capital requirements and enhancing profitability. This is particularly true if the target firm has redundant assets that may be divested.

The cost of debt can often be reduced when two firms merge. The combined firm will generally have reduced variability in its cash flows. Therefore, there may be circumstances under which one or the other of the firms would have defaulted on its debt, but the combined firm will not. This makes the debt safer, and the cost of borrowing may decline as a result. This is termed the coinsurance effect.

Diversification is often cited as a benefit in mergers. Diversification by itself, however, does not create any value because stockholders can accomplish the same thing as the merger by buying stock in both firms.

VALUATION PROCEDURES The procedure for valuing an acquisition candidate depends on the source of the estimated gains. Different sources of synergy have different risks. Tax gains can be estimated fairly accurately and should be discounted at the cost of debt. Cost reductions through operating efficiencies can also be determined with some confidence. Such savings should be discounted at a normal weighted average cost of capital. Gains from strategic benefits are difficult to estimate and are often highly uncertain. A discount rate greater than the overall cost of capital would thus be appropriate.

The net present value (NPV) of the acquisition is equal to the gains less the cost of the acquisition. The cost depends on whether cash or stock is used as payment. The cost of an acquisition when cash is used is just the amount paid. The cost of the merger when common stock is used as the consideration (the payment) is equal to the percentage of the new firm that is owned by the previous shareholders in the acquired firm multiplied by the value of the new firm. In a cash merger the benefits go entirely to the acquiring firm, whereas in a stock-for-stock exchange the benefits are shared by the acquiring and acquired firms.

Whether to use cash or stock depends on three considerations. First, if the acquiring firm's management believes that its stock is overvalued, then a stock acquisition may be cheaper. Second, a cash acquisition is usually taxable, which may result in a higher price. Third, the use of stock means that the acquired firm will share in any gains from merger; if the merger has a negative NPV, however, then the acquired firm will share in the loss.

In valuing acquisitions, the following factors should be kept in mind. First, market values must not be ignored. Thus, there is no need to estimate the value of a publicly traded firm as a separate entity. Second, only those cash flows that are incremental are relevant to the analysis. Third, the discount rate used should reflect the risk associated with the incremental cash flows. Therefore, the acquiring firm should not use its own cost of capital to value the cash flows of

another firm. Finally, acquisition may involve significant investment banking fees and costs.

HOSTILE ACQUISITIONS

The replacement of poor management is a potential source of gain from acquisition. Changing technological and competitive factors may lead to a need for corporate restructuring. If incumbent management is unable to adapt, then a hostile acquisition is one method for accomplishing change.

Hostile acquisitions generally involve poorly performing firms in mature industries, and occur when the board of directors of the target is opposed to the sale of the company. In this case, the acquiring firm has two options to proceed with the acquisition—a tender offer or a proxy fight. A tender offer represents an offer to buy the stock of the target firm either directly from the firm's shareholders or through the secondary market. In a proxy fight, the acquirer solicits the shareholders of the target firm in an attempt to obtain the right to vote their shares. The acquiring firm hopes to secure enough proxies to gain control of the board of directors and, in turn, replace the incumbent management.

Management in target firms will typically resist takeover attempts either to get a higher price for the firm or to protect their own self-interests. This can be done a number of ways. Target companies can decrease the likelihood of a takeover though charter amendments. With the staggered board technique, the board of directors is classified into three groups, with only one group elected each year. Thus, the suitor cannot obtain control of the board immediately even though it may have acquired a majority ownership of the target via a tender offer. Under a supermajority amendment, a higher percentage than 50 percent—generally two-thirds or 80 percent—is required to approve a merger.

Other defensive tactics include poison pills and dual class recapitalizations. With poison pills, existing shareholders are issued rights which, if a bidder acquires a certain percentage of the outstanding shares, can be used to purchase additional shares at a bargain price, usually half the market price. Dual class recapitalizations distribute a new class of equity with superior voting rights. This enables the target firm's managers to obtain majority control even though they do not own a majority of the shares.

Other preventative measures occur after an unsolicited offer is made to the target firm. The target may file suit against the bidder alleging violations of antitrust or securities laws. Alternatively, the target may engage in asset and liability restructuring to make it an unattractive target. With asset restructuring, the target purchases assets that the bidder does not want or that will create antitrust problems, or sells off the assets that the suitor desires to obtain. Liability restructuring maneuvers include issuing shares to a friendly third party to dilute the bidder's ownership position or leveraging up the firm through a leveraged recapitalization making it difficult for the suitor to finance the transaction.

Other postoffer tactics involve targeted share repurchases (often termed "greenmail")—in which the target repurchases the shares of an unfriendly suitor at a premium over the current market price—and golden parachutes—which are lucrative supplemental compensation packages for the target firm's management. These packages are activated in the case of a takeover and the subsequent resignations of the senior executives. Finally, the target may employ an exclusionary self-tender. With this tactic, the target firm offers to buy back its own stock at a premium from everyone except the bidder.

A privately owned firm is not subject to unfriendly takeovers. A publicly traded firm "goes private" when a group, usually involving existing management, buys up all the publicly held stock. Such transactions are typically structured as leveraged buyouts (LBOs). LBOs are financed primarily with debt secured by the assets of the target firm.

DO ACQUISITIONS BENEFIT SHAREHOLDERS?

There is substantial empirical evidence that the shareholders in acquired firms benefit substantially. Gains for this group typically amount to 20 percent in mergers and 30 percent in tender offers above the market prices prevailing a month prior to the merger announcement.

The gains to acquiring firms are difficult to measure. The best evidence suggests that shareholders in bidding firms gain little. Losses in value subsequent to merger announcements are not unusual. This seems to suggest that overvaluation by bidding firms is common. Managers may also have incentives to increase firm size at the potential expense of shareholder wealth. If so, merger activity may happen for noneconomic reasons, to the detriment of shareholders.

FURTHER READING:

Auerbach, Alan J. *Corporate Takeovers: Causes and Consequences.* Chicago: University of Chicago Press, 1988.

"Business For Sale: No Sure Thing." *Inc.* July 1999.

Coffee, John C., Jr., Louis Lowenstein, and Susan Rose-Ackerman. *Knights, Raiders, and Targets: The Impact of the Hostile Takeover.* New York: Oxford University Press, 1988.

Gaughan, Patrick A. *Mergers and Acquisitions.* New York: HarperCollins, 1991.

Hoover, Kent. "Bill Would Aid Mergers of Small Businesses." *Sacramento Business Journal.* July 21, 2000.

Kilpatrick, Christine. "More Owners Put Small Businesses on the Sale Block." *San Francisco Business Times.* June 9, 2000.

McGarvey, Robert. "Merge Ahead: Before You Go Full-Speed into a Merger, Read This." *Entrepreneur.* October 1997.

Sherman, Andrew J. *Running and Growing Your Business.* New York: Random House, 1997.

SEE ALSO: Leveraged Buyout

METROPOLITAN STATISTICAL AREA (MSA)

A Metropolitan Statistical Area (MSA) is a designation the U.S. government uses to refer to a region that, broadly speaking, consists of a city and its suburbs, plus any surrounding communities that are closely linked to the city because of social and/or economical factors. MSAs were known as Standard Metropolitan Statistical Areas (SMSAs) from 1959 to 1983 and, before that, as Standard Metropolitan Areas (SMAs).

Familiarity with MSAs can be most useful to small business owners, for statistical data about the demographic character of these regions can be helpful in devising marketing strategies, delineating sales territories, and determining the appropriate locations of operating facilities. Such information can be invaluable not only for the entrepreneur seeking to launch a new business, but for the established small business owner seeking to expand operations or anticipate marketplace trends.

The government uses the designation MSA for the purpose of applying uniform and consistent standards to the wealth of data collected, analyzed, and published by its myriad departments and agencies. Official definitions for what constitutes an MSA are developed, issued, and periodically revised by the federal Office of Management and Budget (OMB), following public commentary and hearings. These revisions are made in conjunction with the Federal Executive Committee on Metropolitan Areas. In fact, since the MSA and similar designations figure prominently in the compilation of statistics for the national census, the U.S. Department of Commerce's Bureau of the Census also has a voice in determining MSA definitions.

Although the OMB's official standards for defining these regions are highly complex, detailed, and marked by qualifications, MSAs are commonly defined as regions composed of one or more counties containing either: 1) a city with a population of at least 50,000 people, or 2) a Census Bureau-defined "urbanized area" with a population that, when combined with that of its component county or counties, totals at least 100,000 people. An important exception to how

MSAs are defined exists in the New England states, however. In that region of the country, towns and cities rather than counties are used to designate regions as MSAs, and the total metropolitan population of the previously-mentioned "urbanized area" need only be 75,000 people. The Office of Management and Budget also notes that the MSA may include other "central" counties (any county with at least half of its population within the "urbanized" area) and "outlying" counties that satisfy specific criteria of metropolitan character and integration with the central counties, as indicated by population density, growth, urbanization, and levels of commuting.

A region that meets these requirements for recognition as an MSA and also has a population of one million inhabitants or more may be recognized as a Consolidated Metropolitan Statistical Area (CMSA) under the following conditions: 1) separate component areas can be identified within the entire area according to specific statistical criteria, and 2) local public opinion supports the idea of the component areas. If recognized, these component areas are designated as Primary Metropolitan Statistical Areas (PMSAs). As with the CMSAs, PMSAs are composed of one or more counties (except in New England). If no PMSAs are formally recognized, however, the entire area is designated as an MSA.

The largest city in each MSA or CMSA is formally designated a "central city." Additional cities qualify if specified requirements are met in areas such as population and commuting patterns. The title of each MSA consists of the names of up to three of its central cities and the name of each state into which the MSA extends. There is an exception to this, however. Unless local public opinion voices support for including the name in the MSA title, cities with fewer than 250,000 inhabitants and less than one-third of the population of the MSA's largest city will not be included in the title.

In 1999, there were 261 Metropolitan Statistical Areas in the United States and Puerto Rico. There were also 19 Consolidated Metropolitan Statistical Areas comprising 76 Primary Metropolitan Statistical Areas.

Information on the OMB's standards for defining MSAs and other such designations can be obtained from the Statistical Policy Office of the Office of Information and Regulatory Affairs, Office of Management and Budget in Washington, D.C. Information on the Census Bureau's application of these standards is available from the Secretary of the Federal Executive Committee on Metropolitan Areas, Population Division, U.S. Bureau of the Census, also in Washington, D.C.

FURTHER READING:

Cullen, Julie Berry, and Steven D. Levitt. "Crime, Urban Flight, and the Consequences for Cities." *Review of Economics and Statistics.* May 1999.

Purdum, Tracy, and Edward W. Hill. "Generating Wealth: 18 CMSAs Contribute a Huge Chunk of Manufacturing Value in the U.S." *Industry Week.* April 6, 1998.

MEZZANINE FINANCING

Mezzanine financing, also sometimes referred to as subordinated debt or financing, is a rarely used but viable financing option for small businesses in search of capital for rapid growth. Under this arrangement, an entrepreneur borrows some of the money that he or she requires to execute the next stage of company growth (whether through acquisition, expansion of existing operations, etc.), then raises additional funds by selling stock in the company to the same lenders. Mezzanine debt is usually unsecured or junior debt that is subordinate to traditional loans or senior debt. "Subordinated debt is an extremely flexible form of financing," wrote Lawrence M. Levine in *Business Credit.* "Because they are more concerned than senior lenders about their overall yield, mezzanine lenders are very liberal in tailoring their investment to meet the financial, operating, and long-term cash flow needs of the borrower. As long as the subordinated lender's anticipated yield is satisfied, they can be flexible as to the amortization of the loan and the interest rate." Major sources of mezzanine financing include private investors, insurance companies, mutual funds, pension funds, and banks.

Business experts point to mezzanine financing as a particularly provocative financing option for some companies that have moved beyond start-up status but do not yet have the wherewithal to finance big growth moves themselves or via traditional lending arrangements. Indeed, Juan Hovey observed in *Nation's Business* that mezzanine financing owes its very name to the fact that "it raises growth capital for firms that are well beyond the start-up stage but not yet far enough off the ground to go public." Entrepreneurs launching start-up businesses, though, should be aware that this method is not viable for them; lenders willing to make this kind of deal will require prospective borrowers to show a proven record of substantial cash flow before they will even entertain the idea.

But for growing companies with a strong cash flow, mezzanine financing may be the answer to securing business expansion funding. Certainly, the amounts that can be raised via mezzanine financing are substantial. According to *Private Placement Let-*

ter, mezzanine financing raised more than $820 million in 1996 for companies of all sizes, and other sources place the amount considerably higher. Larger companies account for some of this activity, but analysts indicate that even modest-sized companies ($10-12 million in revenues) can expect to raise as much as $15-$20 million through this route. As one investment executive told *Nation's Business,* "a company can leverage two to three times its cash flow in senior secured debt. It can raise total debt to four to five times cash flow with a mezzanine deal. So if the company is doing $2 million in cash flow, it can probably raise $4 million to $6 million in senior debt and $4 million to $5 million more in mezzanine financing, for a total debt of $10 million, or five times cash flow."

Most experts believe that the use of mezzanine financing will continue to grow among both small and large companies. "More and more U.S. companies are committed to financial restructuring in order to create the incentives to maximize business value," stated mezzanine investment executive Robert F. Perille in *Corporate Cashflow Magazine.* "In addition, as our economy has become increasingly service-oriented and entrepreneurial, thousands of excellent companies no longer meet the asset-based formulas of commercial banks. These companies need financing to grow or facilitate a change in ownership, but they do not want to issue relatively expensive equity. This growing demand, coupled with an increasing supply of mezzanine capital from a diverse base of institutional investors, will assure mezzanine financing a place in future capital structures."

HOW MEZZANINE FINANCING WORKS

In a mezzanine financing arrangement, the borrower negotiates an arrangement with a lender wherein the necessary capital is secured by combining a loan with a stock purchase to the lender.

"As a rule, you pay only interest on the money you borrow (at prime plus two to four points) for five years or so," explained Hovey. "At that point, you [the business owner] cash out your investors by going public or by recapitalizing your business in a new round of financing. Your investors, meanwhile, have earned interest on their loans, and if the value of your business has increased, they realize capital gains by selling their stock in your company."

Lenders that review mezzanine financing requests closely examine several facets of the prospective borrower's business when weighing the deal. The most important consideration examined by a mezzanine lender is the company's capacity to generate cash flow. As Levine stated, "because the primary concern of a subordinated lender is a company's abil-

ity to generate cash, if it is anticipated that the business' cash flow is sufficient to repay the loan, it is quite likely subordinated debt can be used." In addition to cash flow, lenders also examine ownership flexibility, company history, growth strategy, and acquisition targets (when applicable). Business owners in need of capital, meanwhile, should do some comparison shopping of their own. "In selecting a source for mezzanine financing, companies should pay attention to personnel turnover, commitment to the business, track record, and flexibility in structuring," indicated Perille. "Low turnover and commitment to the business are key because businesses rarely perform exactly according to plan. Therefore, you need an investor who understands the business and will respond consistently and appropriately."

ADVANTAGES AND DISADVANTAGES

As with most other types of financing, mezzanine financing includes both benefits and drawbacks for the small business owner.

ADVANTAGES

1) Even though the owner loses some independence, he or she rarely loses outright control of the company or its direction. Provided the company continues to grow and prosper, its owners are unlikely to encounter any interference from their lender.

2) The flexibility of the arrangement is often a big plus; "[mezzanine financing] offers considerably more flexibility to structure coupon, amortization and covenants to accommodate the specific cash flow requirements of the business," wrote Perille.

3) Lenders who are willing to enter into the world of mezzanine financing tend to be long-term investors rather than people looking to make a quick killing.

4) Mezzanine lenders can provide valuable strategic assistance. "Subordinated debt advisors often bring fresh insights to businesses because they are financially sophisticated and have a great deal of experience developing strategies to maximize long-term value," said Levine.

5) Mezzanine financing increases the value of stock held by existing shareholders, even though they will not have as great an ownership stake.

6) Most importantly, mezzanine financing provides business owners with the capital they need to acquire another business or expand into another production or market area.

DISADVANTAGES

1) Mezzanine financing does require the business owner to relinquish some measure of control over the firm. This can be difficult for entrepreneurs who have built a promising business in no small measure because of decision-making styles that run heavily toward independence and daring. Moreover, Perille pointed out that ''mezzanine investors with long-term incentives like co-investment plans or carried-interest plans, which provide their professionals with a meaningful stake in the business, are more likely to be there for the long term and take a partnership perspective.'' Finally, entrepreneurs should consider that lender of mezzanine funds will have a vote on the company's board of directors and significant abilities to take decisive action if the company does not meet its financial projections.

2) Subordinated debt agreements may include restrictive covenants. Writing in *Journal of Business Strategy,* Kent Gross and Amin Amiri pointed out that since mezzanine lenders usually do not have any direct security interest in the assets of the borrower, lenders typically incorporate restrictive covenants into the loans that the borrower has to abide by; these include agreements by the lender not to borrow more money, refinance senior debt from traditional loans, or create additional security interests in the assets, as well as the various financial ratios that the borrower must meet.

3) Similarly, business owners who agree to mezzanine financing may be forced to accept restrictions in how they spend their money in certain areas, such as compensation of important personnel (in such instances, a business owner may not be able to offer above-market packages to current or prospective employees). In some cases, business owners have even been asked to take pay cuts themselves and/or limit dividend payouts.

4) Mezzanine financing is more expensive than traditional or senior debt arrangements.

5) Arranging for mezzanine financing can be an arduous, lengthy process. Most mezzanine deals will take at least three months to arrange, and many will take twice that long to complete.

FURTHER READING:

Brooks, Rory, and Jim Read. ''Mezzanine Gains Ground.'' *Investors Chronicle.* October 21, 1994.

Campbell, Katharine. ''Development Capital is Industrial Strength.'' *Financial Times.* December 2, 1997.

Gross, Kent, and Amin Amiri. ''Flexible Financing with Mezzanine Debt.'' *Journal of Business Strategy.* March-April 1990.

Hoogesterger, John. ''Economic Trends Boost the Fortunes of Mezzanine Funds.'' *Minneapolis-St. Paul CityBusiness.* August 25, 2000.

Hovey, Juan. ''A Little-Known Pathway to Growth.'' *Nation's Business.* March 1998.

Levine, Lawrence M. ''The Role of Subordinated Debt in Financing.'' *Business Credit.* May 1995.

''Mezzanine: Refusing to be Overshadowed.'' *Acquisitions Monthly.* June 1998.

Perille, Robert F. ''Mezzanine: Efficient Financing for Recapitalization or Rapid Growth.'' *Corporate Cashflow Magazine.* May 1996.

MINIMUM WAGE

Minimum wage regulations, enacted by the federal government, set the lowest level at which workers may be compensated by their employers. For small business owners employing people other than themselves, compensation can be a complex issue. Creative compensation packages, such as performance-based compensation and others, are increasingly gaining acceptance and changing the way businesses pay their workers. But the minimum wage is still a ubiquitous form of compensation in many small businesses.

Changes in the minimum wage affect an estimated 11 million American workers. The overwhelming majority of minimum wage workers—90 percent—are employed in the private sector. Retail outlets, restaurants and hotels, and private households (which may employ housekeepers, gardeners, etc.) most often pay minimum wage. According to the Labor Department, of those likely to be affected by the increase in the minimum wage, about one-third are youths ages 16 to 19, and just over half are part-time workers.

THE WAGE BILL AND SMALL BUSINESS JOB PROTECTION ACTS

Two pieces of legislation enacted in the mid-1990s affected the way small business owners compensate their minimum wage workers. Passed concurrently and often jointly referred to as the Small Business Job Protection Act (SBJA) of 1996 (H.R. 3448), the acts misleadingly impact a much greater range of issues than simply wages. For instance, SBJA increases incrementally the amount a small business can deduct for equipment purchases from $17,500 to $25,000 in 2003. The bill also makes it easier for companies to avoid the problem of misclassifying an independent contractor as an employee, simplifies and liberalizes S corporation procedures, and makes it easier for small business owners to provide pension and retirement plans and spousal IRAs for their employees.

Most importantly however, it set the new minimum wage rate at $5.15 per hour, effective as of October 1996. This rate replaced the previous minimum of $4.75, which in turn had boosted the minimum wage from $4.25, where it had been for five years previously. Although the change meant an average increase in yearly earnings of nearly $2,000 for full time minimum wage workers, some estimates suggested that the minimum wage needed to be increased to $7.25 by the year 2002 to get families over the poverty line. Bills were being debated in Congress that would gradually increase the minimum wage to $7.25, but the prospects for their passage seemed uncertain at best. Instead, legislative efforts in 2000 appeared likely to increase the minimum wage by $1 in two incremental steps by 2002.

WEATHERING THE CHANGES

As a small business owner, it is important to build in budgetary adjustments in advance of wage changes, as one might for any planned raises. Keeping abreast of legislative trends may help keep accounting procedures flexible.

Of course, not all small business owners are impacted by changes in minimum wage to the same degree. Some businesses rely heavily on a minimum wage work force, while others utilize workers who make significantly more than that base wage. The industry in which a business operates is usually the most important factor in determining wages paid, but geographic location can also be a key component. As one McDonald's corporation franchisee in Vail, Colorado, noted in the *Wall Street Journal*, ''Supply and demand matter more than minimum wage.'' This Vail franchise operator paid his employees some seven dollars per hour, higher than the typical McDonald's wage, because area skiing venues, hotels, and retailers all compete for the same limited employment pool.

Some businesses are limited in their ability to make up for this reality in other parts of their operation, such as passing along higher workforce costs to the consumer in the form of higher prices. While this is an option for some companies, others operating in a competitive environment may simply have to accept diminished profit margin as a fact of life, at least for the near term, or cast about for savings elsewhere in the operation.

Still, some business analysts indicate that there are tangible advantages associated with paying employees above the minimum wage. In fact, according to a recent survey of small businesses conducted by National Small Business United and Arthur Andersen's Enterprise Group (in which 22 percent of respondents indicated that they paid at least a portion of their work force a minimum wage), higher-than-minimum wage structures have their advantages, including:

1) Fluctuations in the base wage, which is controlled by the federal government, will not impact a business that pays higher-than-minimum nearly as much as one that holds tightly to minimum wage to determine its payroll.

2) Employers that pay higher wages have better choices for new hires. Higher salaries mean better people because a larger group of candidates will be attracted to the open position(s).

3) Competitive salaries curb turnover. Workers are less tempted by other employers because they already make more than they would elsewhere. A stable workforce translates into fewer hours training and higher productivity.

OTHER STRATEGIES

Paying above the minimum wage is not the only way to cope, of course. The *Wall Street Journal* cites several other strategies that businesses use. They include:

1) Slash hours, but not jobs. This offsets the payroll impact, keeps workers' salaries stable, and perhaps most importantly prevents businesses from laying off workers they otherwise would not be able to afford.

2) Increase prices, but selectively. Businesses offering a variety of products or services can increase prices on a few, without giving customers the impression that they are getting hit at every turn.

3) Hire more carefully. Because wages comprise a very high proportion of a businesses budget, every dollar counts. For instance, the *Wall Street Journal* noted that one businessman, Edward R. Tinsey III, president of K-Bob's Steakhouses, prepared for the minimum wage increase by selectively raising menu prices and giving potential hires assessment profiles that are analyzed by a third party to make sure that his increased work force expenditures are well spent.

CONCLUSION

Increases in the minimum wage have a widely varying impact on businesses. This is due to the fact that the majority already pay more than minimum wage. In fact, an article in *Business Week* estimated that only 10 percent of the American work force earns within $1 of the minimum wage. For employers that pay more than the minimum, it is a subject of some debate whether increases in the minimum wage have a ripple effect that also boosts the salaries of those workers making higher wages. Employers who do pay minimum wage have to shift their resources creatively when the wage rate increases in order to offset short-falls.

In any case, small business consultants—and even many small business owners—have indicated that the minimum wage issue, while it does have an impact on some small business operations, is not the most important issue confronting the entrepreneur. A survey by the National Federation of Independent Businesses, for instance, indicated that although 82 percent of their members were against minimum wage hikes, they ranked a minimum wage increase as 62nd in importance on a list of 72 issues that concerned them.

FURTHER READING:

Carroll, Rick. "Minimum-Wage Hike: A Small Part of New Legislation." *Dallas Business Journal*. September 6, 1996.

"Debating the Minimum Wage." *Economist*. February 3, 2001.

Duff, Christina. "New Minimum Wage Makes Few Waves." *Wall Street Journal*. November 20, 1996.

"Federal Minimum Wage Increases to $5.15 an Hour." *Wall Street Journal*. September 2, 1997.

"Minimum Wage Debate May Escalate, with Bid to Boost Pay to $7.25 by 2002." *Wall Street Journal*. August 5, 1997.

"Minimum Wage: A Hike Won't Hurt." *Business Week*. October 9, 2000.

Mehta, Stephanie N., and Michael Selz. "New Proposals to Raise Minimum Wage Worry Some Small Employers." *Wall Street Journal*. Aug. 23, 1995.

Ramey, Joanna, and Dana Lenetz. "Democrats Promise Extensive Battle for Minimum Wage Hike." *Footwear News*. February 19, 2001.

MINORITY BUSINESS DEVELOPMENT AGENCY

Established in 1969 by executive order, the Minority Business Development Agency (MBDA) works to foster the creation, growth, and expansion of minority-owned businesses in the United States as a part of the Department of Commerce. The agency was originally called the Office of Minority Business Enterprise (OMBE), but its name was changed to its current incarnation in 1979.

The MBDA describes its mission as one of several facets, including 1) coordination of federal government plans, programs, and operations that affect minority business enterprises; 2) promotion and coordination of activities of government and private organizations that help minority businesses grow; 3) collection and dissemination of information that will help those interested in establishing or expanding a successful minority-owned firm; and 4) funding organizations to provide management and technical assistance to minority entrepreneurs. A wide range of individuals are eligible for MBDA assistance, including Hispanic Americans, Asian and Pacific Island Americans, Alaska Natives and Native Americans, African Americans, and Hasidic Jews.

The Minority Business Development Agency's primary headquarters are located in Washington, D.C., but it also maintains five regional offices (in Atlanta, Chicago, Dallas, New York, and San Francisco) and four district offices (in Miami, Boston, Philadelphia, and Los Angeles), as well as a group of local community-based outreach centers across the country. The centers are generally ensconced in regions that feature a large concentration of minority populations and large numbers of minority-owned businesses. These facilities include Minority Business Development Centers (MBDC), Native American Business Development Centers (NABDC), Business Resource Centers (BRC), and Minority Business Opportunity Committees (MBOC) that offer a variety of programs to assist minority entrepreneurs, including providing one-on-one assistance in writing business plans, marketing, management assistance, technical assistance, financial planning, and securing financing for business ventures. While these centers provide minority entrepreneurs with help in locating sources of financing and preparing loan proposals, they do not have any authority to make grants, loans, or loan guarantees to any qualified businessperson who wishes to purchase, start, or expand a small business. These centers are operated by private firms, government agencies (both state and local), educational institutions, and Native American tribes.

In recent years, the MBDA has also shown an increased emphasis on making certain that minority entrepreneurs are able to compete in the international marketplace. In 1992, for instance, it entered into an agreement with the International Trade Administration (ITA) to assist American minority entrepreneurs in their efforts to negotiate exporting hurdles and compete in foreign markets. Shortly after consummating this agreement, the MBDA launched its International Trade Initiative, which, according to *Business America*'s Linda L. Richardson, "closes the information gap for minority-owned firms having no direct knowledge or experience of exporting. The Agency's services initiatives provide basic data—export marketing plans, potential markets, trade leads, and technical assistance—to assist minority-owned firms in becoming 'export-ready' and to profit from the export assistance services provided by the U.S. Commercial Service.'' In addition, the MBDA has organized several ''Development Matchmakers'' delegations of minority business owners to foreign destinations. Minority-owned firms participating in the trade delegations have hailed from a wide range of industries, from medical supplies and waste management to retail, clothing manufacturing, engineering, and architecture sectors. ''In addition to practical information on how to do business overseas, the program puts Matchmaker participants in direct contact with prospective business partners, prescreened by the Commerce Department's overseas commercial staff,'' noted *Business America* contributor Judy Riendeau. ''Matchmakers are extremely cost competitive, and offer an excellent way to develop contacts with others in the minority business community. The synergies created by being part of a 30-member delegation make Matchmaker an ideal vehicle for companies to exchange information about business opportunities in the United States, as well as other overseas markets of interest.''

For more information on MBDA programs, minority entrepreneurs can contact the agency at its headquarters in Washington, DC or via the Internet (www.mbda.gov).

FURTHER READING:

''Frequently Asked Questions About the MBDA.'' Minority Business Development Agency, n.a.

Jones, Joyce. ''Second Time Around: The MBDA Gets Its Second New Director for the Year.'' *Black Enterprise*. September 1995.

Richardson, Linda L. ''Minority Business Development Agency Helps Minority-Owned Firms Overcome Export Hurdles and Compete in the International Marketplace.'' *Business America.* September 1995.

Riendeau, Judy. ''Matchmaker Events Planned for Minority Companies.'' *Business America.* June 1994.

MINORITY-OWNED BUSINESSES

Minority-owned businesses are among the most important elements in the unprecedented growth, in both number and stature, of small business enterprises in the United during the 1980s and 1990s. The African-American, Hispanic, Asian, and Native American communities all saw significant surges in small busi-

ness start-ups and growth during this period. This success has been attributed both to generally positive economic trends and to advances in the realms of education and access to capital.

Most observers agree, however, that minority entrepreneurs—like women entrepreneurs of all races—still face challenges that their white male counterparts are able to avoid. Racism remains a sad reality in some communities, industries, and corporate environments. In addition, many minority entrepreneurs believe that affirmative action programs and ''set-asides,'' which became a subject of considerable debate in the 1990s, remain an important factor in the success of many minority-owned businesses. They worry that if such programs are eliminated, countless minority-owned companies will be devastated.

Despite lingering racism and the uncertainty surrounding affirmative action, however, minority entrepreneurs have carved out significant business niches for themselves across the nation in both ethnic neighborhoods and majority-white communities. Indeed, members of Black, Hispanic, Asian, Native American, Arab, and other minority groups have pursued entrepreneurial dreams in record numbers, despite the challenges and pitfalls that lurk with any new small business venture. ''A number of challenges confront the courageous souls who aspire to be in business for themselves,'' wrote Suzanne Caplan, author of *A Piece of the Action.* ''The work is hard, the hours long, the pressures are great, and the rewards are sometimes elusive. When racism and sexism are added, an additional hurdle must be jumped. But even with these daunting obstacles, most [minority entrepreneurs] who have done it would do it again if they were asked. The desire to be creative and independent outweighs the prejudice and misconceptions.''

GROWTH OF MINORITY-OWNED ENTERPRISES

In the 1980s and 1990s, various surveys showed a pronounced increase in the number of minority business enterprises. This rapid growth, suggested *American Demographics,* ''is changing the profile of America's business owners.'' The magazine noted, for example, that the number of minority-owned businesses rose from less than 750,000 in 1982 to more than 1.2 million in 1987, nearly one-tenth of all of the nation's businesses. This marked an increase of 66 percent during a period when the total number of all American businesses grew by only 14 percent. ''The mid-1980s were good years for minority business owners,'' wrote *American Demographics* contributor William O'Hara. ''Every significant minority group experienced an increase in the number of businesses owned and in rates of business ownership. But some minority groups have much higher rates of business ownership than others, and the increases of the mid-1980s were not evenly shared.''

Indeed, studies indicated that Asians experienced the biggest increase in small business success. The number of companies owned by Asians (including people of Japanese, Korean, Vietnamese, and Chinese descent) grew by 89 percent from 1982 to 1987. ''The popular image of Asians as industrious immigrants is true,'' said O'Hara. ''Asians own 57 businesses for every 1,000 people, by far the highest business ownership rate of the four major [ethnic groups in America]. . . . The high rate of business ownership among Asians is due to several factors. First is their high level of educational attainment. In 1990, about 40 percent of adult Asian Americans had completed college, compared with only 23 percent of non-Hispanic whites. Asian Americans also have relatively high incomes, which provide them with more capital to launch small businesses.''

Finally, *American Demographics* pointed out that many recent immigrants from Asian countries come to the United States specifically to establish themselves in the business world, either as part of a larger company or as an entrepreneur. American government statistics indicated that whereas nearly 40 percent of immigrants from Asia and the Pacific Islands were engaged in professional or executive career areas, only 17 percent of immigrants from other parts of the world claimed such occupations. In addition, statistics have indicated that Asians—in large part because of their education and financial resources—tend to own larger companies with more employees than do other minorities. Finally, O'Hara noted that some Asian subgroups, such as Koreans—which have enjoyed perhaps the highest level of entrepreneurial success of any ethnic group—have shown a ''willingness to pool their resources to help other Koreans start or expand a business.''

Hispanic-owned businesses have also enjoyed significant increases in numbers and stature over the past several years. The number of Hispanic-owned firms grew by 81 percent from 1982 to 1987, due in large part to the tremendous success that entrepreneurs of Cuban descent have enjoyed. For that same period, business growth was comparatively weak among black-owned businesses (38 percent). And in the early 1990s statistics indicated that African Americans owned fewer than five percent of U.S. businesses even though they comprise about 12 percent of the nation's population. Nonetheless, business experts and economists have noted that black and Hispanic entrepreneurs were among the biggest beneficiaries of America's sustained economic growth in the 1990s. Indeed, *Hispanic Business* magazine estimated that the number of Hispanic-owned businesses in the United States increased from about 420,000 in 1987 to approximately 585,000 in the mid-1990s. *Black Enterprise* magazine, meanwhile, pointed out that when it published its first list of the top 100 black-owned industrial businesses in 1973, their combined annual sales totaled $473 million; conversely, the total from its 1995 listing of black-owned businesses was more than $6.7 billion.

The last major ethnic group in the United States are Native Americans. ''American Indians are the least likely of any major American racial and ethnic group to own their own businesses,'' stated O'Hara. He and other researchers note, however, that the relative scarcity of Native American small business owners can be traced in large part to the fact that many Indians live on remote, sparsely populated reservations in states that are themselves relatively lightly populated.

FACTORS IN MINORITY BUSINESS GROWTH

Analysts cite several reasons for the explosive growth in minority-owned businesses in the United States over the past two decades. Certainly, affirmative action programs and general economic trends have been significant influences. But observers also cite several other factors, including community support, increased networking, efforts to revitalize inner cities, increased levels of education and business experience, and improved access to capital.

- Community Support—Many entrepreneurial ethnic minorities benefit by instituting businesses within their communities that meet needs of that community. When these businesses succeed, the individual communities gain a greater measure of autonomy and financial health, thus laying the groundwork for additional businesses. Community banks have been among the most visible supporters of minority entrepreneurs seeking to revitalize moribund neighborhoods and business districts. Finally, many immigrant groups have done a laudable job of supporting entrepreneurs within their communities.

- Increased Networking—As the number of minority entrepreneurs has grown, so too has the number of organizations, associations, and other groups that have formed to provide assistance and information to minority-owned businesses. In addition, minority entrepreneurs have become adept at taking advantage of established business practices such as networking to assist them in opening their own firms. Networking—

interactions among business people for the purpose of discussing mutual problems, solutions, and opportunities—-is extremely important to minority business owners.

- Programs—In addition to federal set-aside programs, a variety of local, state, and federal agencies have extended help—whether in the form of legal expertise, grants, loans, or some other type of assistance—to encourage the establishment of minority-owned businesses.

- Corporate Acceptance—Observers point to increased corporate acceptance of minority-owned businesses as a key factor in the successes that minority-owned enterprises have registered over the past two decades. ''Well-established companies are buying from minority businesses as never before,'' wrote Sharon Nolton in *Nation's Business.* ''Corporations that are members of the National Minority Supplier Development Council now purchase more than $23 billion in goods and services annually from minority firms—compared with $86 million in 1972, when the council was chartered.''

- Urban Revitalization—Many minority entrepreneurs have established themselves as business owners in urban areas at a time when several large cities have experienced heartening signs of rebirth. Moreover, state and federal agencies have shown increased willingness to provide greater assistance to business owners and others who are intent on reversing declines in urban areas, which typically contain large minority populations. ''The breakthroughs being made in minority-business development could lead to solutions for breaking the cycles of poverty that so deeply affect minority communities,'' said Nolton.

- Higher Levels of Education and Business Experience—As one executive with the National Minority Supplier Development Council told *Nation's Business,* modern-day minority-owned businesses are significantly stronger than they used to be in several important respects: ''They're stronger, they're better financed, they're owners are better prepared, they're better business people in general than were their predecessors. They're better positioned to take advantage of any opportunities that are out there.'' Other analysts agree, noting that business schools and entrepreneurship programs have seen increases in minority enrollment.

- Access to Financing—Minority-owned businesses have benefited from several economic trends. Perhaps most importantly, black, Hispanic, Arab, Asian and other minority businesspeople have benefited from the financial community's belated recognition that small businesses are powering much of the nation's current economic growth, and that small companies will likely become an even more important component of the U.S. economy in the coming years. Moreover, the emergence of alternative financing sources friendly to minority entrepreneurs has made it easier for minority-owned businesses to secure funds for start-up costs or expansions. Finally, agencies such as the Small Business Administration (SBA) have increased the volume of loans to minorities (in fiscal year 1994, for example, the SBA increased the amount it loaned to minority business owners by nearly 60 percent over the previous year).

- Expansion Into Emerging Industries—Traditionally, minority business owners have been primarily involved in small-scale retailing and service industries such as restaurants, beauty parlors, dry cleaners, laundromats, grocery stores, etc. But increasing numbers of minority entrepreneurs have successfully ventured out into realms where minority owners had previously been less commonplace, such as manufacturing and high-technology industries. ''Minority entrepreneurs are also targeting larger markets, increasing their chances of success,'' wrote Nolton. ''Coupled with minority business owners' increased individual power is their greater sophistication in the use of group power and technology to accomplish economic goals.''

AFFIRMATIVE ACTION AND ''SET-ASIDE'' PROGRAMS

Affirmative Action and ''set-aside'' programs—which were first instituted more than 20 years ago to help minority-owned businesses survive in an economic world that was all too often colored by racial prejudice—have become subjects of fierce, sometimes impassioned debate across much of the United States over the past several years.

Set-asides were first created in 1953, when the U.S. government passed a law that set aside five percent of all procurement contracts for small businesses owned by socially and economically disadvantaged people. The SBA has defined and redefined the term ''socially and economically disadvantaged'' many times since then by adding different groups and deleting others. The core group under the original law included Black Americans, Hispanic Americans, Native Americans, Asian Pacific Americans, and other minorities.

By the early 1970s, the U.S. government passed a series of regulations and laws designed to ensure that private contractors with lucrative government contracts set aside a small percentage of their work for assignment to subcontractors owned by individuals from ''socially and economically disadvantaged'' backgrounds. ''The regulations in some government agencies were written specifically for minorities, and in some instances required a specific percentage of participation,'' wrote Caplan. ''The theory behind these laws was that when public (tax) money was being spent, all citizens should have an equal right to compete for contracts, and that minority- and women-owned companies needed special assistance to secure a fair share of the opportunities.'' In ensuing years, it became clear that such programs were a tremendous boon to many minority-owned businesses.

By the 1980s and 1990s, though, critics of affirmative action and set-aside policies argued that minority-owned businesses were coming of age and could compete in the mainstream economy. In fact, they said, ''set-asides'' impede minority-owned businesses' chances of success, because companies came to depend on them to the detriment of seeking contracts through competition. Finally, some critics contended that such policies discriminated against white business owners. ''Once seen as a redress for past discrimination, many now characterize affirmative action programs as reverse discrimination,'' summarized the *Pittsburgh Business Times*.

Many researchers and minority entrepreneurs reject these arguments, however. They point out that revenues of minority-owned businesses still fall short of those found in comparable white-owned firms. And as Rhonda Johnson noted, the combined revenues of *Black Enterprise*'s top 100 industrial and service companies still does not match the revenue of one Fortune 100 company. Finally, many supporters of affirmative action programs contend that ''public policy drives private behavior,'' and that any government decision to tear down programs designed to help minority-owned businesses would serve as a sort of tacit approval for companies to return to discriminatory behavior that they engaged in in the past.

SOURCES OF ASSISTANCE

Minority entrepreneurs have several sources of assistance that they can pursue in building and expanding their businesses. The Small Business Administration, for example, has provided billions of dollars in contracts, grants, and loans to minority businesses. In 1993 alone, the SBA guaranteed nearly 27,000 loans totaling more than $6.4 billion to small- and women-owned businesses. The number reached $7 billion in 1994 and $9 billion in 1995. In addition, the agency provides valuable information and assistance through programs like SCORE and its 8(a) contract program.

Several organizations have also been developed to help minorities in the world of business, including the National Black Chamber of Commerce, the U.S. Pan Asian American Chamber of Commerce, the U.S. Hispanic Chamber of Commerce, the National Indian Business Association, the National Association of Minority Contractors, the National Association of Black Women Entrepreneurs, and the National Minority Supplier Development Council.

FURTHER READING:

Caplan, Suzanne. *A Piece of the Action: How Women and Minorities Can Launch Their Own Successful Businesses.* AMACOM, 1994.

Fraser, George. *Success Runs in Our Race.* William Morrow & Co., 1995.

Green, Shelley, and Paul Pryde. *Black Entrepreneurship in America.* Transaction Publishers, 1990.

Griffin, Cynthia E. ''Where's the Dollar? Funding for Minority Owned Business Enterprises.'' *Entrepreneur.* February 1999.

Holdron, Don P. ''Perspectives on Minority Business.'' *Review of Black Political Economy.* Fall 1993.

Neese, Terry. ''Minority Owned Businesses Showing Explosive Growth.'' *LI Business News.* September 7, 1998.

Nolton, Sharon. ''Minority Business: The New Wave.'' *Nation's Business.* October 1995.

O'Hara, William. ''Reaching for the Dream.'' *American Demographics.* January 1992.

''Pushed to the Margins.'' *Pittsburgh Business Times.* April 15, 1996.

Whittemore, Mary. ''Expanding Opportunities for Minorities and Women.'' *Nation's Business.* December 1990.

MISSION STATEMENT

Mission statements are documents that are intended to serve as a summary of a business's goals and values. Their contents often reflect the fact that they are utilized both as an internal performance enhancer and as a public relations tool. Mission statements serve several purposes, but at their core, they are usually intended as a means by which a business's ownership or management attempt to attach meaning to an organization's operations beyond profit and loss statements.

The value of the mission statement is also sometimes thought to increase with the size of an organization. *Fortune* contributor Andrew Serwer, for instance, contended that entrepreneurial companies of relatively small size can sometimes thrive without a mission statement or explicit guiding principle, since the business owner/leader can communicate personally with each staff member. Expansion, however, can make it more difficult for entrepreneurs to communicate efficiently with individual staff members about their future plans, their vision of the company's goals, and the values that will guide the company's operation. "A mission statement not only provides that information, but it's also the foundation for any performance-enhancement initiative," wrote Karen Adler and Paul Swiercz in *Training & Development.*

When produced in a thoughtful and careful manner, mission statements can be superb vehicles for communicating the importance of an organization's activities and the overarching reasons why employees should value their work there. Unfortunately, *InfoWorld*'s Bob Lewis echoed a widespread sentiment with his contention that many of today's mission statements are produced in a formulaic, jargon-heavy manner that renders them bereft of vitality and meaning. Lewis and others argue that all too often, businesses of all shapes and sizes attach far greater weight to the mission statement's public relations function than to its value as a potential touchstone that can help the business maintain a steady course through the many obstacles and challenges of the modern business world.

CHARACTERISTICS OF EFFECTIVE MISSION STATEMENTS Small business owners, consultants, and researchers all agree that effective mission statements generally feature most of the following characteristics:

1) Simple, declarative statements—Mission statements that are cluttered with trendy buzz words and jargon rather than basic declarations of organizational goals and values tend to fall flat. Conversely, a mission that can be easily articulated is more likely to be remembered and to have resonance.

2) Honest and realistic—Observers agree that it is pointless—or worse, that it can actually turn into a negative—for a business enterprise to create and publicize a mission statement if it is at odds with its known operating philosophy. A company may espouse an abiding concern for the environment in its statement of mission, but if its everyday operations reflect a callous disregard for or outright hostility to established environmental protections, the statement may merely engender or deepen employee cynicism about management and generate negative public response. In short, hypocrisy often attracts greater attention than silence.

3) Communicates expectations and ethics—As Sharon Nelton noted in *Nation's Business,* a thoughtfully rendered mission statement can define not only what a company's business goals are, but also the methodologies it chooses to get there. A good mission statement often includes general principles to which a business's workers are expected to adhere, and in return, includes declarations of the business's obligations to its employees, its customers, and the community in which it operates.

4) Periodically updated—Just like other business documents, mission statements can lose their vitality and relevance over time if they are not reexamined on a regular basis. Mission statements should undergo continual review and refinement to ensure that they remain fresh and useful.

FURTHER READING:

Abrahams, Jeffrey. *The Mission Statement Book.* Ten Speed Press, 1999.

Adler, Karen, and Paul Swiercz. "Taming the Performance Bell Curve." *Training & Development.* October 1997.

Brown, Mark Graham. "Improving Your Organization's Vision." *Journal for Quality and Participation.* September-October 1998.

Drohan, William M. "Writing a Mission Statement." *Association Management.* January 1999.

Larson, Paul. "Strategic Planning and the Mission Statement." *Montana Business Quarterly.* Autumn 1998.

Lewis, Bob. "Mission Statements: Don't Write a Word Until Your Ideas are Clear to All." *InfoWorld.* January 29, 1996.

Nelton, Sharon. "Put Your Purpose in Writing." *Nation's Business.* February 1994.

O'Hallaron, Richard, and David O'Hallaron. *The Mission Primer: Four Steps to an Effective Mission Statement.* Mission Inc., 2000.

Serwer, Andrew. "Lessons from America's Fastest Growing Companies." *Fortune.* August 8, 1994.

Vander Weyer, Martin. "Mission Improvable." *Management Today.* September 1994.

MOBILE OFFICE

Advances in communication technology, entrepreneurial creativity, and the ever-more-hectic pace of modern life have all combined to encourage the development and refinement of mobile business offices. Indeed, entrepreneurs have been a driving force in the creation of computers, telephones, and other office equipment that are both effective and portable. "The goal of providing portability and adequate power to meet business people's needs also has led to a substantial degree of convergence among mobile computing, organizing, and communications technologies," wrote Tim McCollum and Albert Holzinger in *Nation's Business*. "This convergence now enables small-business people to compute and coordinate wherever they are, using one of a few coordinated devices and either traditional wired or new wireless telephone networks."

Mobile office technology allows entrepreneurs and other businesspeople to access data or information from their place of business in any location. This versatility can be vital in closing a deal, delivering a report, or saving a presentation. Of course, many businesspeople rely on portable office equipment primarily during transitional periods, such as at the airport or in a hotel room during a business trips. But observers have noted that mobile office technology has also become an essential performance tool for sales representatives, business planners, and busy entrepreneurs. Moreover, some enterprising small business owners have learned to synthesize communication technology with today's system of roadways to create truly mobile businesses that do not rely on a central office.

MOBILE BUSINESSES

In recent years, increasing numbers of small businesses—both start-ups and established ventures—have devised systems wherein they can successfully deliver their products or services through a mobile facility or office. "Many entrepreneurs find that packaging a business in a van, truck, bus, or car is a way to rejuvenate an existing firm or launch a new one," confirmed Carol Dilks in *Nation's Business*. Dilks noted that enterprises that are conducive to mobile office treatment are numerous, including optical services, maid services, lawn maintenance, veterinary services, and a host of others. Indeed, many observers suggest that any limitations in mobile businesses that currently exist are present only because the right entrepreneur has not yet come along to figure out how to deliver the product or service "on wheels" in a profitable way.

Entrepreneurs with mobile businesses also point to several major advantages associated with such arrangements. Mobile businesses do not have the expense of maintaining a store, which—with rent, furniture, utilities, and other costs—can be a very expensive part of operations. In addition, owners of mobile businesses report that they register savings because of reduced rates of theft and insurance. Finally, these business owners contend that by going to

the customer's home or business, they 1) immediately establish their interest in satisfying the client, and 2) create a dynamic wherein both the businessperson and the customer can concentrate on one another rather than peripheral distractions such as other customers. Business consultants warn, however, that mobile businesses need to adhere to a very high standard of professionalism to calm possible customer fears about legitimacy and quality. "People like to know there's an 'entity,'" one executive admitted to *BC Business*. "It makes them more comfortable and confident to know a business has a real office, not just a phone and a computer somewhere."

FURTHER READING:

Baker, Dean. "Desks on Wheels." *Oregon Business*. September 1997.

Bianchi, Alessandra. "Wheeling and Dealing." *Inc.* January 1995.

Dilks, Carol. "Business on the Move." *Nation's Business*. March 1984.

Findley, Nigel D. "The Great Communicators: Making the Most of the Mobile Office." *BC Business*. March 1993.

Kerven, Anne. "The Mobile Office." *Colorado Business Magazine*. December 1997.

McCollum, Tim, and Albert G. Holzinger. "Making a Move to Portability." *Nation's Business*. September 1997.

Nussbaum, Debra. "Taking the Office to the Highway." *New York Times*. September 14, 1997.

O'Brien, Kathleen. "Taking Advantage of the Mobile Office: Homeward Bound." *New York Times*. April 5, 2000.

Rabinovitch, Issie. "Mobile Office Still Not Reality for Most Users." *Computing Canada*. September 14, 1998.

MODEM

Modem, an acronym for modulator/demodulator, is a device that allows one computer to "talk" with another one over a standard telephone line. Modems act as a kind of interpreter between a computer and the telephone line. Computers transmit digital data, expressed as electrical impulses, whereas telephones transmit voice frequencies as analog signals. To transmit digital data, the sending modem must first *modulate,* or encode, a computer's digital signal into an analog signal that can travel over the phone line. The receiving modem must then *demodulate,* or decode, the analog signal back into a digital signal recognizable to a computer. A modem transmits data in bits per second (bps), with the fastest modems transmitting at 56K (kilobits per second). An *internal* modem is housed within the computer itself, while an *external* modem is a separate device that is connected to the computer via a cable.

A variety of different rules, called protocols, govern the conversion of data to and from digital and analog. These protocols also govern error correction and data compression. Error correction is necessary to detect and correct data that may have become lost or garbled as the result of a poor telephone connection. Data compression speeds the data transfer by eliminating any redundant data sent between two modems, which the receiving modem then restores to its original form. Individual modems vary in the types of protocols they support, depending on such factors as manufacturer and age.

Communications software enables a modem to perform the many tasks necessary to complete a session of sending and receiving data. To initiate a modem session, the user issues the command appropriate to the software being used, and then the software takes over and begins the complicated process of opening the session, transferring the data, and closing the session.

To open the session, the software dials the receiving modem and waits for an answering signal from it. Once the two modems have established a connection, they engage in a process called ''handshaking,'' wherein they exchange information about the types of protocols each uses, ultimately agreeing to use a set common to both. For example, if one modem supports a more recent set of protocols then does the other, the first modem will agree to use the earlier set so that each is sending data at the same rate, with error correction and data compression appropriate to those protocols. The handshaking process itself is governed by its own protocol.

In addition to transmitting and receiving data, the communications software may also automate other tasks for the user, such as dialing, answering, redialing, and logging onto an online service.

ALTERNATIVES TO THE TRADITIONAL MODEM

The functionality provided by a traditional dialup modem—the ability to send and receive information electronically—is also offered in other technologies that offer faster transmission speeds, although each is not without its disadvantages. Integrated Services Digital Network (ISDN), Asymmetric Digital Subscriber Lines (ADSL), and Digital Subscriber Lines (DSL) all use more capacity of the existing phone to provide services.

At 128K, ISDN is more than twice as fast as a dialup modem, but not nearly as fast as ADSL or DSL. ADSL can deliver data at 8mbps, but is available only in selected urban areas. DSL transmits at a high rate of speed, but to ensure reliable service, the user must be located near the phone company's central office. In addition, a DSL connection is always ''on,'' and so makes a computer more vulnerable to attacks from hackers. To secure a DSL connection, a user should install either a software package called a firewall or a piece of hardware called a router. With either of these in place, the DSL connection cannot be detected by outsiders.

Cable modems do not use phone lines. Instead, they utilize the same line that provides cable TV services to consumers. Offered by cable television companies, cable modems are about 50 times faster than a dialup modem, but transmission speed is dependent on the number of subscribers using the service at the same time. Because the service uses a shared connection, its speed decreases as the number of users increases. Satellite, or wireless, services are faster than a 56K modem, but slower than a DSL. In addition, the initial satellite installation is expensive. However, for users in rural areas who do not have access to other services, wireless service may be a viable option.

MODEMS AND THE WORKPLACE

As Bonnie Lund states in *Business Communication That Really Works!*, ''the speed with which we can exchange documents has revolutionized business communications,'' which in turn has enabled business to be done ''faster, cheaper, and more efficiently.'' Modems, along with the related technologies, facilitate this rapid transfer of information between colleagues or customers, regardless of their location. Communications that, in the past, may have taken several days or even weeks to complete, can now be accomplished in a fraction of the time. For example, during a typical work day, an employee could use a modem to facilitate sending an email message to a customer, transmitting a spreadsheet containing the annual budget to a manager for review, or downloading a file from the Internet.

Lund also notes that ''modems are changing the work style of corporate America'' by enabling workers to *telecommute* or *telework*. In many companies, employees are allowed to work from home one or more days per week, accomplishing their work by using modems or similar technology to access the company's computers. In survey results released in 2000, the International Telework Association and Council (ITAC), a nonprofit organization that promotes the benefits of telework, found that 9.3 million employees in the United States telecommute a least one full day each week. Of these, about half work for small- to medium-sized organizations, while the remainder work for organizations with a least 1,500 employees

FURTHER READING:

Freedman, Alan. *Computer Desktop Encyclopedia.* The Computer Language Company Inc., 1996.

Lund, Bonnie. *Business Communication That Really Works!* Affinity Publishing, Inc. 1995.

Rae-Dupree, Janet. ''Surfing the Web at Warp Speed with Minimal Expense.'' *U.S. News & World Report.* June 19, 2000.

Telework America 2000. International Telework Association & Council, 2000.

Terrell, Kenneth. ''Breaking the Speed Limit.'' *U.S. News & World Report.* August 10, 1998.

MONEY MARKET INSTRUMENTS

The money market is the arena in which financial institutions make available to a broad range of borrowers and investors the opportunity to buy and sell various forms of short-term securities. The money market is not a physical place, but an informal network of banks and traders linked by telephones, fax machines, and computers. Money markets exist both in the United States and abroad.

The short-term debts and securities sold on the money markets—which are known as money market instruments—have maturities ranging from one day to one year and are extremely liquid. Some examples of common money market instruments include treasury bills, federal agency notes, certificates of deposit (CDs), eurodollar deposits, commercial paper, bankers' acceptances, and repurchase agreements. The suppliers of funds for money market instruments are institutions and individuals with a preference for the highest liquidity and the lowest risk.

The money market is important for businesses because it allows companies with a temporary cash surplus to invest in short-term securities, and it also allows companies with a temporary cash shortfall to sell securities or borrow funds on a short-term basis. In essence, it acts as a repository for short-term funds. Large corporations generally handle their own short-term financial transactions, participating in the money market through dealers. Small businesses, on the other hand, often choose to invest in money-market funds, which are professionally managed mutual funds consisting only of short-term securities.

Although securities purchased on the money market carry less risk than long-term debt, they are still not entirely risk free. After all, banks do sometimes fail, and the fortunes of companies can change rather rapidly. But, as Richard A. Brealey and Stewart C. Myers explained in their book *Principles of Corporate Finance,* ''the range of possible outcomes is less for short-term investments. Even though the distant future may be clouded, you can usually be confident that a particular company will survive for at least the next month. Second, only well-established companies can borrow in the money market. If you are going to lend money for only one day, you can't afford to spend too much time in evaluating the loan. Thus you will consider only blue-chip borrowers.''

TYPES OF MONEY MARKET INSTRUMENTS

TREASURY BILLS Treasury bills (T-bills) are short-term notes issued by the U.S. government. They come in three different lengths to maturity: 90, 180, and 360 days. The two shorter types are auctioned on a weekly basis, while the annual types are auctioned monthly. T-bills can be purchased directly through the auctions or indirectly through the secondary market. Purchasers of T-bills at auction can enter a competitive bid (although this method entails a risk that the bills may not be made available at the bid price) or a noncompetitive bid. T-bills for noncompetitive bids are supplied at the average price of all successful competitive bids.

FEDERAL AGENCY NOTES Some agencies of the federal government issue both short-term and long-term obligations, including the loan agencies Fannie Mae and Sallie Mae. These obligations are not generally backed by the government, so they offer a slightly higher yield than T-bills, but the risk of default is still very small. Agency securities are actively traded, but are not quite as marketable as T-bills. Corporations are major purchasers of this type of money market instrument.

SHORT-TERM TAX EXEMPTS These instruments are short-term notes issued by state and municipal governments. Although they carry somewhat more risk than T-bills and tend to be less negotiable, they feature the added benefit that the interest is not subject to federal income tax. For this reason, corporations find that the lower yield is worthwhile on this type of short-term investment.

CERTIFICATES OF DEPOSIT Certificates of deposit (CDs) are certificates issued by a federally chartered bank against deposited funds that earn a specified return for a definite period of time. They are one of several types of interest-bearing ''time deposits'' offered by banks. An individual or company lends the bank a certain amount of money for a fixed period of time, and in exchange the bank agrees to repay the money with specified interest at the end of the time period. The certificate constitutes the bank's agreement to repay the loan. The maturity rates on CDs range from 30 days to six months or longer, and the amount of the face value can vary greatly as well. There is usually a penalty for early withdrawal of funds, but some types of CDs can be sold to another investor if the original purchaser needs access to the money before the maturity date.

Large denomination (jumbo) CDs of $100,000 or more are generally negotiable and pay higher interest than smaller denominations. However, such certificates are insured by the FDIC only up to $100,000. There are also eurodollar CDs, which are negotiable certificates issued against U.S. dollar obligations in a foreign branch of a domestic bank. Brokerage firms have a nationwide pool of bank CDs and receive a fee for selling them. Since brokers deal in large sums, brokered CDs generally pay higher interest rates and offer greater liquidity than CDs purchased directly from a bank.

COMMERCIAL PAPER Commercial paper refers to unsecured short-term promissory notes issued by financial and nonfinancial corporations. Commercial paper has maturities of up to 270 days (the maximum allowed without SEC registration requirement). Dollar volume for commercial paper exceeds the amount of any money market instrument other than T-bills. It is typically issued by large, credit-worthy corporations with unused lines of bank credit and therefore carries low default risk.

Standard and Poor's and Moody's provide ratings regarding the quality of commercial paper. The highest ratings are A1 and P1, respectively. A2 and P2 paper is considered high quality, but usually indicates that the issuing corporation is smaller or more debt burdened than A1 and P1 companies. Issuers earning the lowest ratings find few willing investors.

Unlike some other types of money-market instruments, in which banks act as intermediaries between buyers and sellers, commercial paper is issued directly by well-established companies, as well as by financial institutions. "By cutting out the intermediary, major companies are able to borrow at rates that may be 1 to 1 ½ percent below the prime rate charged by banks," according to Brealey and Myers. Banks may act as agents in the transaction, but they assume no principal position and are in no way obligated with respect to repayment of the commercial paper. Companies may also sell commercial paper through dealers who charge a fee and arrange for the transfer of the funds from the lender to the borrower.

BANKERS' ACCEPTANCES "A banker's acceptance begins life as a written demand for the bank to pay a given sum at a future date," Brealey and Myers noted. "The bank then agrees to this demand by writing 'accepted' on it. Once accepted, the draft becomes the bank's IOU and is a negotiable security. This security can then be bought or sold at a discount slightly greater than the discount on Treasury bills of the same maturity." Bankers' acceptances are generally used to finance foreign trade, although they also arise when companies purchase goods on credit or need to finance inventory. The maturity of acceptances ranges from one to six months.

REPURCHASE AGREEMENTS Repurchase agreements—also known as repos or buybacks—are Treasury securities that are purchased from a dealer with the agreement that they will be sold back at a future date for a higher price. These agreements are the most liquid of all money market investments, ranging from 24 hours to several months. In fact, they are very similar to bank deposit accounts, and many corporations arrange for their banks to transfer excess cash to such funds automatically.

FURTHER READING:

Black, Pam. "CDs That Try a Little Harder." *Business Week*, September 5, 1994.

Brealey, Richard A., and Stewart C. Myers. *Principles of Corporate Finance*. 4th ed. New York: McGraw-Hill, 1991.

Brostoff, Steven. "Stable Value Products Pushed for Pensions." *National Underwriter Property and Casualty*. September 1, 1997.

Dunnan, Nancy. *Dunn and Bradstreet Guide to Your Investments*. 1991.

Nayar, Nandkumar and Michael S. Rozeff. "Commercial Paper and the Cost of Capital, Rating, and Equity Returns." *Journal of Finance*. September 1994.

Retkwa, Rosalyn. "New CP-Funded Loans Broaden Market but Aren't Always Cheap." *Corporate Cashflow Magazine*. August 1993.

MULTICULTURAL WORK FORCE

A multicultural work force is one wherein a company's employees include members of a variety of ethnic, racial, religious, and gender backgrounds. Whereas past eras in American business saw few examples of multiculturalism, most of today's small business owners and corporate executives recognize that attention to the challenges and opportunities associated with the growing trend toward culturally diverse work forces can be a key factor in overall business success. "A combination of work force demographic trends and increasing globalization of business has placed the management of cultural differences on the agenda of most corporate leaders," wrote Taylor Cox Jr. "Organizations' work forces will be increasingly heterogeneous on dimensions such as gender, race, ethnicity, and nationality. Potential benefits of this diversity include better decision making, higher creativity and innovation, greater success in marketing to foreign and ethnic minority communities, and a better distribution of economic opportunity. Conversely, cultural differences can also increase costs through higher turnover rates, interpersonal conflict, and communication breakdowns.''

TRENDS IN CULTURAL DIVERSITY IN AMERICA

The United States has always been an immigrant culture. Aside from Native Americans, the entire population has immigrant origins. The traditional view toward immigrants was that they would wish to assimilate to the dominant Anglo-Saxon population of the nation's earliest colonial settlers. According to the traditional view, however, the assimilation process was never expected to be total. Each group would add a distinguishing contribution to the overall national culture so that in time the myriad immigrant groups would alter the cultural norms of the rest of the nation in subtle ways. This philosophy was summed up in the notion of the country as the ''American melting pot.'' But this conception of the nation was predicated on the willingness of the immigrant—and the demands of the dominant culture—to discard or at least sublimate unfamiliar cultural practices and attitudes, especially in work place settings. Additionally, during some periods, certain groups were deemed to be unable to assimilate no matter how much they were willing to bury their cultural differences with the dominant culture. A variety of peoples have been victimized by this attitude over the years, including African Americans, Asian Americans, and members of the Jewish religious faith.

The Civil Rights movement of the 1960s, however, had a direct effect on the assimilationist norm of the melting pot. It changed the view of the United States as a single culture welcoming those different from the dominant norm only if they would only drop their ethnic or cultural distinctiveness. The double standard as applied to certain groups of Americans came under scrutiny; the belief in integration into a dominant norm was questioned. Assuredly, such re-examination took place within the long-dominant native-born, white, non-Hispanic community. But perhaps the most significant impact of the Civil Rights movement was that immigrants and distinctive native-born minority groups began, as Stephen Steinberg argued in *The Ethnic Myth*, ''to affirm their right to a separate identity within the framework of a pluralist nation.''

The re-examination of the desirability of the domination of the work force by a culturally monolithic norm led to laws that required businesses to provide culturally diverse groups with greater opportunities to enter the work place. Title VII of the Civil Rights Act of 1964, for example, made it unlawful to discriminate on the basis of race, color, national origin, or religion. Equal opportunity for employment allowed for the entry into the American work force of increasing numbers of individuals from cultural groups that had historically been victims of discrimination. This, in turn, led groups that had attempted to assimilate to question their decision to subsume their own cultural values to the dominant norm. Thus, even within the historically favored white community, ethnic groups began to see benefits in returning to—or at least not hiding—their own cultural differences. Finally, as longstanding barriers to integrated work forces crumbled, increasing numbers of companies came to recognize both the business value of multicultural work forces and the negative repercussions associated with an inability or unwillingness to accommodate such demographic changes.

TODAY'S CHALLENGES Not all people in organizations value diversity. As a rule, people are most comfortable with those like themselves and emphasizing diversity may undermine that comfort level. Diversity tends to breed new approaches to old practices and long-standing problems. Individuals in organizations may find such change troubling. Moreover, individuals with strong prejudices against certain groups may find rapidly changing demographics in the work force threatening either because they find change itself disquieting or because they hold a position they feel they might not be able to maintain if groups historically excluded from their work place are allowed to compete in an unhindered way for their positions.

Given such realities, R. Roosevelt Thomas, Jr. indicated in *Beyond Race and Gender* that companies need to go beyond simple recognition of cultural diversity to active diversity management: ''Managing diversity is a comprehensive managerial process for developing an environment that works for all employees.'' Diversity management is an inclusive process since all employees belong to a culture, including those from the organization's traditionally dominant cultural group. Thomas indicated that diversity management must not be viewed as ''an us/them kind of problem to be solved but as a resource to be managed.'' Anthony Carnevale and Susan Carol Stone, authors of *The American Mosaic*, have emphasized that valuing diversity involves ''recognizing that other people's standards and values are as valid as one's own,'' and note that for most organizations, valuing and managing diversity requires nothing less than cultural transformation. This is a prodigious task, for it requires people—especially those of the dominant culture—to let go of their assumptions about the universal rightness of their own values and customary ways of doing things and to become receptive to other cultures.

In this regard, cultural diversity in the work place mirrors many of the same issues at play in the realm of international business. In international business interactions, people who have learned differing conceptions of normative behavior are forced to suspend judgment of one another. Cultural norms shift relative to language, technological expectations, social organization, face-saving, authority conception, nonverbal behavior and the perception of time.

ORGANIZATION TYPES

Taylor Cox Jr., an expert in the field of organization behavior, cited three primary organization types in the realm of cultural diversity development. Most U.S. businesses, he indicated, generally fall within one of the three models. The first of these types, called the monolithic organization, is characterized by a homogeneous work force composed primarily of while males with few women or minority men in management positions (although he contended that this type of organization can exist in any situation where one ''identity group''—blacks, Hispanics, etc.—is dominant). Moreover, many of these organizations feature high levels of occupational segregation, with women and minority men concentrated in lower-paying occupations. This environment, noted Cox, makes it a practical necessity for women, minority men, and foreign nationals who do enter the organization to accept the organizational norms already in place (which of course were put together by white males).

Cox pointed out that, ironically, ''one positive note [of the monolithic organization] is that intergroup conflict based on culture-group identity is minimized by the relative homogeneity of the work force.'' But he also noted that since this organization type generally places little importance on the integration of cultural minorities, discrimination and prejudice is likely to be prevalent: ''Aside from the rather obvious downside implications of the monolithic model in terms of under-utilization of human resources and social equality, the monolithic organization is not a realistic option for most large employers in the 1990s.'' But Barbara Jorgensen observed in *Electronic Business Buyer* that it can be difficult for owners and managers to turn such organizations around, especially if they are big and their work force is entrenched: ''Managing diversity is a lot like implementing quality: it's tough to define and it requires a massive culture change. You can't even apply statistical process control to it.''

The second organizational type is the plural organization. Cox contended that this model is an improvement over the monolithic organization in several important respects: ''It has a more heterogeneous membership than the monolithic organization and takes steps to be more inclusive of persons from cultural backgrounds that differ from the dominant group.'' Examples of such initiatives include hiring and promotion policies that may give preference to minorities, training on equal opportunity issues, and reviews of compensation systems to ensure fair treatment of all workers. These improvements also spur greater levels of social interaction between members of different backgrounds, and greater identification with the organization among minority members.

But many companies that have such precautions in place maintain management teams with little minority representation, an indication that principles of multicultural management have not infiltrated all levels of the company. And Cox suggested that this ''affirmative action approach to managing diversity'' has spurred charges from white males that such policies ''discriminate against white males and therefore perpetuate the practice of using racioethnicity, nationality, or gender as a basis for making personnel decisions. . . . This backlash effect, coupled with the increased number of minorities in the organization, often creates greater inter-group conflict in the plural organization than was present in the monolithic organization.''

The third organizational type described by Cox is the multicultural organization. Primary characteristics of this kind of organization include integration of minorities into all structural levels of the company, including management/executive positions; integration of informal/social networks of the business; absence of prejudice and discrimination; and a mindset that not only accommodates diversity (a hallmark of the plural organization) but also *values* that diversity.

KEYS TO EFFECTIVE CREATION AND MANAGEMENT OF A MULTICULTURAL WORK FORCE

Experts indicate that business owners and managers who hope to create and manage an effective, harmonious multicultural work force should remember the importance of the following:

- Setting a good example—This basic tool can be particularly valuable for small business owners who hope to establish a healthy environment for people of different cultural backgrounds, since they are generally able to wield significant control over the business's basic outlook and atmosphere.

- Communicate in writing—Company policies that explicitly forbid prejudice and discriminatory behavior should be included in employee manuals, mission statements, and other written communications. Jorgensen referred to this and other similar practices as ''internal broadcasting of the diversity message in order to create a common language for all members of the organization.''

- Training programs—Training programs designed to engender appreciation and knowledge of the characteristics and benefits of multicultural work forces have become ubiquitous in recent years. ''Two types of training are most popular: awareness and skill-building,'' wrote Cox. ''The former introduces the topic of managing diversity and generally includes information on work force demographics, the meaning of diversity, and exercises to get participants thinking about relevant issues and raising their own self-awareness. The skill-building training provides more specific information on cultural norms of different groups and how they may affect work behavior.'' New employee orientation programs are also ideal for introducing workers to the company's expectations regarding treatment of fellow workers, whatever their cultural or ethnic background.

- Recognize individual differences—Writing in *The Complete MBA Companion,* contributor Rob Goffee stated that ''there are various dimensions around which differences in human relationships may be understood. These include such factors as orientation towards authority; acceptance of power inequalities; desire for orderliness and structure; the need to belong to a wider social group and so on. Around these dimensions researchers have demonstrated systematic differences between national, ethnic, and religious groups.'' Yet Goffee also cautioned business owners, managers, and executives to recognize that differences between individuals can not always be traced back to easily understood differences in cultural background: ''Do not assume differences are always 'cultural.' There are several sources of difference. Some relate to factors such as personality, aptitude, or competence. It is a mistake to assume that all perceived differences are cultural in origin. Too many managers tend to fall back on the easy 'explanation' that individual behavior or performance can be attributed to the fact that someone is 'Italian' or 'a Catholic' or 'a woman.' Such conclusions are more likely to reflect intellectually lazy rather than culturally sensitive managers.''

- Actively seek input from minority groups— Soliciting the opinions and involvement of minority groups on important work committees, etc., is beneficial not only because of the contributions that they can make, but also because such overtures confirm that they are valued by the company. Serving on relevant committees and task forces can increase their feelings of belonging to the organization. Conversely, relegating minority members to superfluous committees or projects can trigger a downward spiral in relations between different cultural groups.

- Revamp reward systems—An organization's performance appraisal and reward systems should reinforce the importance of effective diversity management, according to Cox. This includes assuring that minorities are provided with adequate opportunities for career development.

- Make room for social events—Company-sponsored social events—picnics, softball games, volleyball leagues, bowling leagues, Christmas parties, etc.—can be tremendously useful in getting members of different ethnic and cultural backgrounds together and providing them with opportunities to learn about one another.

- Flexible work environment—Cox indicated that flexible work environments—which he characterized as a positive development for all workers—could have particularly ''beneficial to people from nontraditional cultural backgrounds because their approaches to problems are more likely to be different from past norms.''

- Don't assume similar values and opinions— Goffee noted that ''in the absence of reliable information there is a well-documented tendency for individuals to assume that others are 'like them.' In any setting this is likely to be an inappropriate assumption; for those who manage diverse work forces this tendency towards 'cultural assimilation' can prove particularly damaging.''

- Continuous monitoring—Experts recommend that business owners and managers establish and maintain systems that can continually monitor the organization's policies and practices to ensure that it continues to be a good environment for all employees. This, wrote Jorgensen, should include ''research into employees' needs through periodic attitude surveys.''

''Increased diversity presents challenges to business leaders who must maximize the opportunities that it presents while minimizing its costs,'' summarized Cox. ''The multicultural organization is characterized by pluralism, full integration of minority-culture members both formally and informally, an absence of prejudice and discrimination, and low levels of inter-group conflict. . . . The organization that achieves these conditions will create an environment in which all members can contribute to their maximum potential, and in which the 'value in diversity' can be fully realized.''

FURTHER READING:

Carnevale, Anthony Patrick, and Susan Carol Stone. *The American Mosaic.* McGraw-Hill, 1995.

Cox, Taylor, Jr. *Cultural Diversity in Organizations.* Berrett-Koehler Publishers, 1993.

Cox, Taylor, Jr. ''The Multicultural Organization.'' *Academy of Management Executive.* Vol. 5, no. 2, 1991.

Faird, Elashmawia, and Philip Harris. *Multicultural Management.* Gulf Publishing Company, 1993.

Fernandez, John P. *Managing a Diverse Work Force.* Lexington Books, 1991.

Fry, John M. ''A Firm Diversity Hiring Action Plan.'' *Public Relations Journal.* October 1993.

Goffee, Rob. ''Cultural Diversity.'' In *The Complete MBA Companion.* Pitman Publishing, 1997.

Jorgensen, Barbara. ''Diversity: Managing a Multicultural Work Force.'' *Electronic Business Buyer.* September 1993.

King, Albert S. ''Capacity for Empathy: Confronting Discrimination in Managing Multicultural Work Force Diversity.'' *Business Communication Quarterly.* December 1995.

Pollar, Odette, and Rafael Gonzalez. *Dynamic of Diversity: Strategic Programs for your Organization.* Crisp Publications, 1994.

Simons, George, Philip Harris, and Carmen Vasquez. *Transcultural Leadership: Empowering the Diverse Workforce.* Gulf Publishing Company, 1993.

Steinberg, Stephen. *The Ethnic Myth: Race, Ethnicity, and Class in America.* Atheneum, 1981.

Thomas, R. Roosevelt, Jr. *Beyond Race and Gender.* AMACOM, 1991.

MULTILEVEL MARKETING

Multilevel marketing (MLM) describes a type of business in which sales representatives not only sell products, but also attempt to recruit new sales representatives. Existing salespeople usually have a financial incentive to expand the sales force. ''In multilevel marketing, reps sell the company as well as the product, encouraging others to join the sales team,'' Ronaleen R. Roha noted in *Kiplinger's Personal Finance Magazine.* ''Then their recruits get others to come on board, and so on down the line. Their expanding army of salespeople—mostly women—is known as the 'downline.' The incentive to bring on potential competitors: The recruiter gets a cut, called an 'override,' of sales made by her recruits, and the sales of their recruits, too.''

Multilevel marketing—also known as network marketing, direct selling, and person-to-person marketing—is a rapidly growing industry. According to the Direct Selling Association, MLM businesses employed between 9 and 12 million people in 1999, up from 5 million in 1991. Some of the best-known companies that use MLM techniques include Amway, Mary Kay Cosmetics, Pampered Chef, and Longaberger Baskets.

MLM businesses appeal to people who want to work part-time and need a flexible schedule, like students and mothers of young children. They also attract people who are dissatisfied with their current job situation or who have come to believe that large corporations do not reward loyalty the way they did in the past. In an article for the *Business Journal,* Jeffrey Gitomer called MLM ''the least expensive, lowest risk, fastest path to achieving the American dream. It is at the core of the exploding 'home-based business' segment of the economy.''

CRITICISMS OF MLM

Despite its impressive growth, MLM suffers from a negative reputation in some quarters. In the past, many business ventures that used network marketing techniques were actually pyramid schemes. These illegal scams promised participants the chance to make huge amounts of money while doing very little work, provided they made a sizeable initial investment. The people who started the pyramid scheme were paid off by those who joined later, but most participants did not see any return on their investment. Roha noted that an MLM is more likely to be offering a legitimate business opportunity if it has low startup costs; charges a reasonable price for products; does not require sales representatives to purchase a lot of inventory; allows sales representatives to return unsold merchandise; and provides the majority of sales representatives' income from the sale of products.

Even legitimate MLM businesses have been criticized for employing hard-sell methods. ''To critics and turned-off erstwhile customers, MLM conjures up images of being hounded by door-to-door salesmen or pressured into hosting or attending 'parties' where pushy salespeople hawk products of dubious value amid peer pressure to buy something,'' Roha wrote. ''And, to top it off, you're subjected to an evangelical pitch to join the downline.'' Finally, some critics note that most people who become involved in network marketing businesses do not make much money. A 1991 study by the Direct Selling Association found that 90 percent of MLM sales representatives made less than $5,000 per year.

BENEFITS OF MLM

Despite these criticisms, MLM businesses have a great deal to offer their sales representatives. The primary reason people become involved in MLM is because they value flexibility. Sales representatives can usually work part-time from home and set their own hours. Direct Selling Association research shows that 90 percent of MLM sales representatives work less than 30 hours per week, and 50 percent work less than 10 hours per week. In addition, MLM businesses usually do not require a long-term commitment from their sales representatives.

Another reason for MLM's appeal is that it enables people to start their own businesses without making a large monetary investment. In fact, the average price of a startup kit for reputable MLM companies is about $100. Gitomer noted that many people value the opportunity to be their own boss and control their own destiny. ''The secret to successful network marketing is you—the messenger—and your willingness to dedicate and focus on preparation,'' he wrote. ''Your willingness to become a salesperson who believes in your own ability to succeed. Everyone wants success, but very few are willing to do what it takes to be successful.''

Of course, like any other entrepreneurial venture, becoming an MLM sales representative involves establishing goals and developing a plan to reach them. According to Kristine Ziwica, writing in *Success,* MLM sales representatives must master retailing techniques and understand the mechanics of compensation plans and distribution chains. Perhaps most importantly, they must also feel real enthusiasm about the product they are selling in order to be effective in creating downlines.

FURTHER READING:

Fuller, Karin. ''A New Vision for Network Marketing.'' *Success.* July 2000.

Gitomer, Jeffrey. ''Financial Freedom through Network Marketing.'' *Business Journal.* April 14, 2000.

Laymon, Rob. ''Multilevel Marketing Proves a Hit on Net.'' *Philadelphia Business Journal.* August 20, 1999.

Roha, Ronaleen R. ''Want to Buy a Potato Peeler? Want to Sell a Bunch of Them?'' *Kiplinger's Personal Finance Magazine.* March 1997.

Ziwica, Kristine. ''ABCD . . . MLM.'' *Success.* May 1999.

MULTIPLE EMPLOYER TRUST

A Multiple Employer Trust (MET) is a group of ten or more employers who form a trust in order to minimize the tax implications of providing certain types of benefits for their employees, particularly life insurance. The U.S. Congress authorized the formation of METs in 1984 under Section 419(A) of the Internal Revenue Code. The rules set forth for METs are stringent and require that no single employer contribute more than 10 percent of total funding for the benefit plan purchased by the MET. In addition, the MET must be an indivisible entity, with all participating employers sharing equally in the benefits forfeited by other members of the group. The employees of each participating employer are viewed as if they worked for a single company and are subject to the same requirements

A similar arrangement to a MET is a Multiple Employer Welfare Arrangement (MEWA). MEWAs include plans established by two or more employers to provide welfare benefits to their employees, including health care and pensions. The main difference between a MET and a MEWA is that a MEWA is generally subject to the requirements of the Employee Retirement Income Security Act of 1974 (ERISA), which regulates pension plans of businesses with more than 25 employees and imposes penalties on employers for breaches of fiduciary duty.

The main purpose of a MET is to give entrepreneurs and small business owners a tax-friendly way to provide life insurance benefits for themselves and their key employees. Under ordinary circumstances, life insurance is tax deductible for the employer in the current year, but any amounts that could be considered ''bonus'' life insurance must be reported as taxable income by the employee. Larger businesses are often able to get around this problem by funding life insurance benefits as part of a qualified retirement or profit-sharing plan. Although the benefits provided through such plans are usually tax free, there are a number of restrictions and complicated paperwork requirements associated with them that reduce the attractiveness of life insurance for smaller businesses. For example, the government requires companies that set up qualified plans to establish eligibility and vesting rules and then offer the benefits to all employees who meet them.

THE IMPORTANCE OF LIFE INSURANCE

It may seem odd for small businesses to go to the trouble of forming a MET just for the sake of providing life insurance for employees. But life insurance has a variety of uses that make it a very attractive benefit, particularly for key employees. A small business might need to provide life insurance to its workers in order to compete with larger companies in attracting and retaining qualified employees. For example, in addition to providing benefits upon the death or disability of the insured, some forms of life insurance can be used as a tax-deferred investment to provide funds during a person's lifetime for retirement or everyday living expenses. There are also a number of specialized life insurance plans that allow small business owners to reduce the impact of estate taxes on their heirs and protect their businesses against the loss of a key employee, partner, or stockholder.

Small businesses tend to depend on a few key people, some of whom are likely to be owners or partners, to keep operations running smoothly. Even though it is unpleasant to think about the possibility of a key employee becoming disabled or dying, it is important to prepare so that the business may survive and the tax implications may be minimized. In the case of a partnership, the business is formally dissolved when one partner dies. In the case of a corporation, the death of a major stockholder can throw the business into disarray. In the absence of a specific agreement, the person's estate or heirs may choose to vote the shares or sell them. This uncertainty could undermine the company's management, impair its credit, cause the flight of customers, and damage employee morale.

Life insurance can help small businesses protect themselves against the loss of a key person by providing a source of income to keep business running in his or her absence. Partnership insurance basically involves each partner acting as beneficiary of a life insurance policy taken on the other partner. In this way, the surviving partner is protected against a financial loss when the business ends. Similarly, corporate plans can ensure the continuity of the business under the same management, and possibly fund a repurchase of stock, if a major stockholder dies. Although life insurance is not tax deductible when the business is named as beneficiary, the business may deduct premium costs if a partner or owner is the beneficiary.

MET REQUIREMENTS

Participating in a MET enables a small business to provide life insurance to its key employees without subjecting them to negative tax implications. It does this by allowing tax-deductible contributions to a life insurance plan, made by the employer on behalf of employees, to be used for severance benefits. Basically, the cash value of the life insurance is available for severance benefits, while the mortality portion of the life insurance is payable to the beneficiary named by insured. A MET must be structured properly in order to comply with the tax laws, but the rules are significantly less extensive than with qualified pension and profit-sharing plans.

The rules that a MET must follow in order to gain tax benefits are laid out in IRS Notice 95-34. This notice states that severance benefits can only be paid when the termination of employment is beyond an employee's control. Otherwise, if the severance arrangements appear to be providing deferred compensation benefits to an employee, the employer's tax deduction will be denied. The notice also states that the deduction will not be allowed for "nondeductible prepaid expenses," which may include contributions to the plan that are made as lump sums or using accelerated funding techniques.

FURTHER READING:

Anastasio, Susan. *Small Business Insurance and Risk Management Guide.* U.S. Small Business Administration, n.d.

Budihas, John S. "Multiple Employer Trust Used for Fringe Benefits." *National Underwriter Life and Health.* September 4, 1995.

"Department of Labor Holds That a Health Care Program Is a MEWA." *Tax Management Compensation Planning Journal.* January 1, 1999.

White, Jane, and Bruce Pyenson. *Employee Benefits for Small Business.* Prentice-Hall, 1991.

MULTITASKING

Multitasking refers to the ability of an individual or machine to perform more than one task, or multiple tasks, at the same time. In the field of human resources, multitasking is a popular term that is often used to describe how busy managers or business practitioners are able to accomplish a growing amount of work in a limited time period. The term was popularized in the late 1990s with the increasing move to a 24-hours-per-day, seven-days-per-week work and service culture experienced in the U.S. The term has grown to define people in their roles as employees, parents, family members, and any number of other roles they perform simultaneously as they try to balance business and pleasure in a limited amount of time.

According to an article in *Manufacturing Engineering,* in the new world of project teams and multitasking, professionals often find relationships blurring as to the difference between activities inside and outside the organization. The multitasking abilities of both individuals and teams are important as companies stay connected with customers, suppliers, and partners, and as new products and services are continually developed. Multitasking is becoming the norm as the amount of information a manager or professional needs to process increases at a staggering rate.

Supporting this view is Arnold Brown in his article for *Across the Board.* He believes the phenomenon of multitasking that now pervades the workplace is also apparent in our personal lives. In the twenty-first century businesses are trying to turn employees into what he terms a hybrid of hedgehogs and foxes. Foxes do many things, while hedgehogs can do only one thing, but they do it very well. In organizations there is a drive for efficiency forced on businesses from outside competition. As companies are forced to downsize and reduce the number of layers of staff, the employees left behind are doing more work.

Technology is also creating the ability to leverage the efforts of employees more and more. As organizations use more team-building and decentralized decision-making, people are forced to become both specialists and generalists. Examples of multitasking include traditional grocery stores offering a variety of products and services outside food categories, including banking, catering, and wine; women juggling careers and family; and even people talking on cell phones while driving. The downside of multitasking is the level of stress and pressure on individuals.

Demanding more from machines is another part of the multitasking trend. For example, computers can now commonly perform or execute several programs at the same time, which is a form of multitasking or multiprocessing. In the computer arena, multiprocessing sometimes implies that more than one central processing unit (CPU) is involved. When only one CPU is involved, the computer may switch from one program to another quickly enough to give the appearance of simultaneous execution.

In another example of multitasking machines, people are demanding multitasking gasoline pumps. In addition to dispensing gasoline, new gas pumps are also giving travel directions, current weather reports, and stock quotes via an Internet link. Some pumps even let customers order food from neighborhood restaurants. Given the technologically complex and competitively intense environment in today's business world, the trend toward multitasking is expected to continue, for both individuals and machines.

FURTHER READING:

Brown, Arnold. ''The All Purpose Employee.'' *Across the Board*. May 2000.

Koucky, Sherri, and Stephan Mraz. ''Multitasking Gas Pump.'' *Machine Design*. August 3, 2000.

Molta, Dave. ''Balancing Act of Multitasking Managers.'' *Network Computing*. March 22,

1999.

''Surviving in the New World.'' *Manufacturing Engineering*. December 1999.

MYERS-BRIGGS TYPE INDICATOR (MBTI)

The Meyers-Briggs Type Indicator (MBTI) is an instrument designed to evaluate people and provide descriptive profiles of their personality types. Based on the theories of psychologist Carl Jung, it is widely used in the fields of business, education, and psychology.

MBTI was developed by Isabel Briggs Meyers and her mother, Katharine Cook Briggs, during World War II. The two women were acquainted with Jung's theories and sought to apply them to help civilians choose wartime jobs well-suited to their personality preferences. Meyers and Briggs felt that this would make people happier and more productive in their work. Consulting Psychologists, Inc. (www.cpp-db.com) bought the rights to MBTI in 1975. The company estimates that it administers MBTI testing to two million people per year worldwide.

The MBTI system begins with a test in which participants respond to questions that provide clues about their basic outlook or personal preferences. These responses are scored to see where participants' preferences lie within four sets of attributes: extroversion/introversion; sensing/intuiting; thinking/feeling; and judging/perceiving.

The attributes extroversion (E) and introversion (I) indicate whether a participant derives his or her mental energy primarily from other people or from within. Similarly, the attributes sensing (S) and intuiting (N) explain whether a participant absorbs information best through data and details or through general patterns. The attributes thinking (T) and feeling (F) show whether a participant tends to make decisions based on logic and objective criteria or based on emotional intelligence. Finally, the attributes judging (J) and perceiving (P) indicate whether a participant makes decisions quickly or prefers to take a more casual approach and leave his or her options open.

The MBTI system organizes the four sets of attributes into a matrix of sixteen different personality types. Each type is indicated by a four-letter code. For example, ESTJ would designate a person whose primary attributes were extroversion, sensing, thinking, and judging. For each personality type, the MBTI system includes a profile which describes the characteristics common to people who fit into that category.

For example, an article in the *Harvard Business Review* noted that people who fit into the category ISTP tend to be ''cool onlookers—quiet, reserved, and analytical; usually interested in impersonal principles, how and why mechanical things work; flashes of original humor,'' while people of type ENFJ are ''sociable, popular; sensitive to praise and criticism; responsive and responsible; generally feel real concern for what others think or want.''

MBTI is a popular evaluative tool. Many colleges and universities use it in career counseling to help guide students into appropriate fields for their personality types. In the business world, companies use it to make hiring decisions, identify leadership potential among employees, design training for specific employee needs, facilitate team building, and help resolve conflicts between employees. By giving people an increased understanding of their behavior and preferences, MBTI is said to help them increase their productivity, build relationships, and make life choices.

Proponents of MBTI see the testing system as a valuable aid to personal development and growth. But critics of MBTI argue that its personality profiles are so broad and ambiguous that they can be interpreted to fit almost anyone. Some also worry that, once a university career counselor or employer knows a person's ''type,'' that person might tend to be pigeonholed or pushed in a certain direction regardless of his or her desires. Finally, some psychologists have criticized the MBTI system on the grounds of ''confirmation bias,'' meaning that the results are self-fulfilling because people tend to behave in ways that are predicted for them. In other words, a person who learns that he or she is ''outgoing'' according to MBTI will be more likely to behave that way.

FURTHER READING:

Hirsh, Sandra Krebs, and Jean M. Kummerow. *Introduction to Type in Organizations.* Consulting Psychologists Press, 2000.

''Identifying How We Think: The Myers-Briggs Type Indicator and the Hermann Brain Dominance Instrument.'' *Harvard Business Review.* July-August 1997.

Leonard, Nancy H., Richard W. Scholl, and Kellyann Berube Kowalski. ''Information Processing Style and Decision Making.'' *Journal of Organizational Behavior.* May 1999.

Quenk, Naomi L. *Essentials of Myers-Briggs Type Indicator Assessment.* John Wiley, 1999.

''Type Talk.'' *Inc.* July 1998.

MYSTERY SHOPPING

Mystery shopping is a term that describes a field-based research technique of using independent auditors posing as customers to gather information about product quality and service delivery by a retail firm. The ''mystery shopper'' poses as a customer in order to objectively gather information on the business being studied. Getting a customer's view of one's business is a widely recognized tool in both the marketing and customer service arenas. When mystery shoppers are dispatched to visit a business, they use criteria developed by the client to evaluate the business and focus primarily on service delivery and the sales skills of employees. Their reports, usually written, are forwarded to the client and can be used in a number of ways. Mystery shoppers can also objectively evaluate competitors and their service delivery and product mix for comparisons and benchmarking.

Mystery shopping can allow a firm to create a competitive edge. It can also assist retailers in developing and evaluating strategies to retain current customers. The first step in mystery shopping is to identify your firm's important customer service characteristics and objectives—often flowing from your strategy and overall goals and objectives. Next a firm uses these variables to develop a mystery shopping questionnaire, either alone or with the help or a consultant or mystery shopping firm. The survey can include a mix of narrative and check-off questions. Typical areas of assessment are customer service, suggestive selling and up-selling techniques, teamwork, employee and management activities, headcount, store appearance and organization, merchandise displays and stock, cleanliness of the location, signage and advertising compliance, time in line and time elapsed for service, product quality, order accuracy, customer's preferences, cash handling, and return policies. After pre-testing the questionnaire, mystery shoppers are hired to do an assessment. Assessments can be on-site or via the telephone or even the Internet. A sample size as well as a period of time for the mystery shopping program is determined and results are used for feedback.

USE OF MYSTERY SHOPPING RESULTS

Managers can use the reports from mystery shoppers to evaluate their locations, and the results can be used to provide employee recognition and other positive reinforcements of loyalty and morale through incentive programs. Many restaurants, banks, supermarkets, and clothing retailers have used the techniques, along with hotels, furniture stores, grocery stores, gas stations, movie theaters, automotive repair shops, bars, athletic clubs, bowling alleys, and almost any business where customer service is important. As the service sector of the economy has increased, so has the demand for mystery shoppers.

Some retailers are large enough to have their own in-house program in place. Other smaller companies who do not have the resources to develop a quality mystery shopping program in-house use mystery shopping contractors. These contractors directly hire and train the mystery shoppers, who work as independent contractors.

The reports from mystery shoppers can measure training and levels of customer service pre- and post-training. Mystery shopping allows managers to determine if the services employees are providing are appropriate. Shopping reports can assess promotional campaigns and even verify employees' honesty in handling cash and charges.

Reports over time can yield a longitudinal database of averages. Some industries share findings so managers can know regional or national averages for an industry. At the Web site Managerspot.com, for example, restaurant owners can compare their numbers from mystery shopping reports with a pool of similar, but anonymous, restaurants.

The use of mystery shopping is just one part of a company-wide program to develop and augment employee performance. The idea is to learn from a consumer's point of view which areas of service and product quality are most important and what areas need improvement. Data from the shopping results can be used by the company to make necessary changes on a timely basis. The results should be used for developmental and reward purposes and not for punishment.

Mystery shopping is a valuable tool to businesses and is especially helpful for small, start-up businesses who need accurate and fast information to assess their employees and compare their products and services to the competition.

FURTHER READING:

Liddle, Alan J. ''Managerspot.com: It's Not Quite Like Any Other Potentially Useful Tool You Might Try This Year.'' *Nation's Restaurant News.* July 31, 2000.

Moore, Karen Gomes. ''Mystery Shopping.'' *Discount Merchandisers.* October 1999.

N

NATIONAL ASSOCIATION OF SMALL BUSINESS INVESTMENT COMPANIES (NASBIC)

The National Association of Small Business Investment Companies (NASBIC) is an organization of companies (SBICs) that have been specially licensed under the Small Business Investment Act of 1958, overseen by the Small Business Administration (SBA), to provide funding to start-up companies. NASBIC's primary concern, however, is with providing representation before government on behalf of the SBIC industry. The association is located in Washington, DC, and its Web site is at www.nasbic.org.

According to NASBIC, the several thousand SBICs operating in the United States and Puerto Rico are privately organized and managed financial institutions that invest capital in small independent businesses. They differ from venture capital firms in that they are licensed by the Small Business Administration. In exchange for investing only in small businesses, the SBA helps SBICs qualify for government-insured long-term loans. SBICs have complete control over their own lending policies and investment choices and are not bound by government regulation to make capital available to any particular type of business or business owner. The SBICs currently operating hold a combined $6 billion in assets under management. Among the companies that began with funding from an SBIC are Apple Computer, Federal Express, Outback Steakhouse, America Online, and Intel. According to the NASBIC, ''since 1958, the SBIC program has provided approximately $13 billion of long-term debt and equity capital to approxi-mately 80,000 small U.S. companies, with more than $1.6 billion invested in 1996.''

SSBICs, or Special Small Business Investment Companies, are identical to SBICs except in the respect that they tend to concentrate their lending in the area of socially and economically disadvantage entrepreneurs. However, all SBICs may consider applicants from all backgrounds.

FACTORS IN APPROACHING AN SBIC

NASBIC reports that small business owners contemplating a pitch to an SBIC should be mindful of the following considerations.

1) Amount of capital your business will need—SBIC policies differ and many have specific ranges they are willing to lend within.

2) Decide whether your business will be better served by a straight loan, an equity investment, or another kind of financing—SBICs offer different options, but these are not often found under the same roof.

3) Your business's industry—Some SBICs choose to lend only to businesses in a particular area, due to the expertise of the SBIC's officers or directors.

4) Geography—Although SBICs may operate regionally or even nationally, it is wise to look into the closest suitable SBIC, because they tend to lend to businesses in their general locale.

Seekers of financing should also note that SBICs may consider working in conjunction with one another to provide pooled capital if a special case merits a departure from standard policy, so no one company should be immediately ruled out.

REQUIREMENTS Your business qualifies as a ''small business'' according to NASBIC parameters if it has a net worth under 18 million dollars and average after-tax earnings of less than $6 million for the past two years. If your business fails these tests, it may qualify under employment or annual sales parameters.

When presenting your business to an SBIC for consideration, business owners must provide a business plan that includes information on every aspect of your operation, including detailed descriptions of the product or service and the facilities; an explanation of your customer base and distribution system; a description of your business's competition; an account of all key personnel and their qualifications; and financial statements, such as balance sheets and revenue projections. The ultimate acceptance or denial process will take a few weeks, although an indication will be made immediately of general interest or lack thereof.

When considering all sources of funding, a small business owner should weigh the appropriateness of each source with his or her needs. The wide variety of funding options provide many choices, with only a small number, perhaps, that will be suitable. Small Business Investment Companies provide a unique offering in that they have the security of the government behind them, but the flexibility of a private firm.

FURTHER READING:

Barlas, Stephen. ''Something Ventured.'' *Entrepreneur.* July 2000.

Beltz, Cynthia A. *Financing Entrepreneurs.* Aei Press, 1994.

Entrepreneur Magazine Guide to Raising Money. John Wiley & Sons, 1997.

Flanagan, Lawrence. *Raising Capital: How to Write a Financing Proposal.* Psi Research - Oasis Press, 1994.

Gillis, Tom S. *Guts & Borrowed Money: Straight Talk for Starting & Growing Your Small Business.* Bard Press, 1997.

Janecke, Ron. ''The National Association of Small Business Investment Companies.'' *St. Louis Business Journal.* November 1, 1999.

Ross, Duncan M., and Andrew Godley. *Banks, Networks, and Small Firm Finance.* Frank Cass & Co., 1996.

NATIONAL ASSOCIATION OF WOMEN BUSINESS OWNERS

As of 1996, there were nearly 8 million women-owned businesses in the United States. As the number of women-owned businesses grows, representation and support for this group becomes more and more critical. The National Association of Women Busi-

ness Owners (NAWBO), based in Washington D.C., provides women-owned businesses with a resource for such support and representation. Covering the many faceted interests of women entrepreneurs in all areas of business, the NAWBO has chapters all across the United States and maintains affiliate chapters around the world. Membership is available through annual dues paid to both the national organization and to a local chapter.

The NAWBO began as a small group of Washington, D.C., businesswomen who started meeting in 1974. They began as a networking group, meeting to discuss mutual experiences, exchange information, and help develop business skills for group members. They incorporated as the NAWBO on December 19, 1974. The first members in the newly formed organization were recruited in 1976, and in 1978, the first national chapters were formed. Today, its headquarters are in Washington, DC, and it maintains a Web site at www.nawbo.org.

The NAWBO's vision and mission statement states that the organization hopes to propel women entrepreneurs into ''economic, social and political spheres of power worldwide.'' Principle aims of the organization, as articulated in their mission statement, include:

1) Strengthen the wealth-creating capacity of members and promote economic development

2) Create innovative and effective changes in the business culture

3) Build strategic alliances, coalitions, and affiliations

4) Transform public policy and influence opinion makers

In addition, the NAWBO provides women entrepreneurs with assistance in gaining access to financial opportunities. For instance, the organization offers special loans, discount prices on certain equipment and services, and other opportunities which may translate into substantial savings on the start-up costs of business. The NAWBO also provides educational experiences and leadership training, and sponsors a wide range of special conferences, workshops, seminars, and counseling services. Finally, the organization's local, regional, national and international contacts provide networking opportunities that may be otherwise unavailable to small businesses.

In addition to its position as ''helping hand,'' the NAWBO has established a strong political presence, emerging as a strong voice of advocacy for small women-owned businesses. For example, the group was instrumental in supporting and helping to pass the 1988 Women's Business Ownership Act, which expanded women entrepreneurs' access to credit markets; instituted a three-year, $10 million training and technical support initiative for women business owners; and created a National Women's Business Council. A regular presence on Capitol Hill, members of the NAWBO work to make sure that the needs of women-owned businesses are represented.

AFFILIATIONS The NAWBO is the United States' representative in Les Femmes Chefs d'Entreprises Mondiales (FCEM, or The World Association of Women Entrepreneurs) with chapters in 33 countries, representing almost 30,000 businesses. This affiliation allows NAWBO members access to international business ideas and trends and provides networking opportunities throughout the world.

The National Foundation for Women Business Owners (NFWBO) is a nonprofit research and leadership development foundation established by NAWBO. This offshoot of the NAWBO gathers information about women-owned businesses and makes that information available to organizations around the globe.

NAWBO is also affiliated with the Small Business Technology Coalition (SBTC) and with the Women Business Owners Corporation (WBOC), which helps small women-owned businesses compete for government contracts. This organization helps women entrepreneurs and business owners to meet professional certification and training needs.

FURTHER READING:

Crowley, Lyle. "There's No Business Like Small Business." *Working Woman*. October 1996.

Gee, Sharon. "NAWBO Getting Serious About Women's Business." *Birmingham Business Journal*. August 11, 2000.

Henry, John. "Two Groups Give Women Career Support." *Arkansas Business*. August 18, 1997.

Reynolds, Rhonda. "On Our Own." *Black Enterprise*. July 1995.

Seglin, Jeffrey L. "The Best Little Advocacy Group in America." *Inc*. May 1994.

NATIONAL BUSINESS INCUBATION ASSOCIATION (NBIA)

The National Business Incubation Association (NBIA), founded in 1985, is a nonprofit organization comprising incubator developers and managers, corporate joint venture partners, venture capital investors, and economic development professionals. The association seeks to promote the growth of new business and educate the business and investor community about the benefits of incubators. NBIA offers information and training on how to form and manage incubators; conducts statistical research; provides a referral

service; and publishes a newsletter, membership directory, various reports and monographs, and a state of the industry analysis. The NBIA also hosts an annual convention where it bestows a number of industry awards.

Business incubators are facilities that provide shared resources for young businesses, such as office space, consultants, and personnel. They may also provide access to financing and technical support. These services provide the new businesses with a somewhat protected environment in which to grow before they becomes self-sustaining. The ultimate goal of any business incubator is to produce viable businesses, called "graduates" of the incubator. Today, there are an estimated 900 NBIA-affiliated business incubators in operation across the United States.

A business qualifying for incubator assistance must meet certain criteria, in much the same way it would for a venture capital firm. Some incubators have diversified interests, accepting different types of start-ups into the fold, whereas others concentrate in one particular area or industry. For instance, some special interest incubators exclusively support women and minority-owned businesses and others choose to focus on innovative software or medical applications.

A variety of sponsors support incubators. Some incubators are supported by government and nonprofit bodies. These incubators' main goals are job creation, tax base expansion, and economic diversification. Other incubators are affiliated with universities and provide faculty, alumni, and related groups with research and business opportunities. In addition, a number of incubators are hybrids combining resources from both government and the private sector. For-profit incubators, meanwhile, surged in popularity during the 1990s. This growth was fed in general by the decade's explosive economic expansion, and specifically by the advent of e-commerce. These incubators are operated by various types of investment groups and maintained to provide returns on funds invested by the group. Their main focus is usually on innovative applications for new technology and the development of commercial real estate. But many for-profit incubators can provide only limited leadership, guidance, and financing. Indeed, the NBIA estimates that the majority of for-profit incubators fail within two years of opening. For this reason, the NBIA encourages entrepreneurs to carefully research incubators before committing to membership. The remainder of incubators are sponsored by a variety of non-traditional organizations, such as Indian tribes, chambers of commerce, church groups, and others..

MEMBERSHIP Membership in the NBIA conveys a variety of benefits. They include a subscription to the *NBIA Review*, the association's newsletter; access to BatorLink, the NBIA's Internet discussion group; research, documentation, and dissemination services; support from NBIA staff for information and referrals; legislative and government program updates; and discounts on publications, educational materials, Microsoft products, insurance products from Biddle Insurance Services, and Paychex payroll services. Contact the organization by mail or phone for information on how to apply for membership. The National Business Incubator Association's headquarters are in Athens, Ohio. It also maintains a Web site at www.nbia.org.

FURTHER READING:

"Due Diligence Advised in Picking Business Incubator." *Business First-Columbus,* September 1, 2000.

Hayhow, Sally. *Business Incubation: Building Companies, Jobs and Wealth.* National Business Incubation Association, 1997.

Hayhow, Sally. *A Comprehensive Guide to Business Incubation.* National Business Incubation Association, 1996.

"Incubators Lay an Egg." *Business Week.* October 9, 2000.

Lichtenstein, Gregg A. and Thomas S. Lyons. *Incubating New Enterprises: A Guide to Successful Practice.* Aspen Institute, 1996.

Rice, Mark P., and Jana Matthews. *Growing New Ventures, Creating New Jobs: Principles and Practices of Successful Business Incubation.* Quorum Books, 1995.

NATIONAL LABOR RELATIONS BOARD (NLRB)

The National Labor Relations Board (NLRB) is a federal organization that oversees the establishment and conduct of union organizations as well as the conduct of businesses involved with unions. Its national headquarters are located in Washington, DC, and the organization maintains an informational Web site at www.nlrb.gov.

HISTORY AND PURPOSE OF THE NLRB The NLRB was created in 1935 by Congress to administer the National Labor Relations Act (NLRA). The NLRA is the law that governs relations between labor unions and employers whose operations involve interstate commerce. Though there are other federal and state laws which also protect the rights of employees, such as the Fair Labor Standards Act (FLSA), the NLRA is the Act specifically tied to the NLRB and to union organization.

The Act itself gives employees the right to organize and bargain collectively with their employers, as well as the right not to organize. In short, employees may join a union or not, as they so choose. Coverage of the law is relatively exclusive, covering only employees working for employers involved in interstate commerce with a few exceptions (airlines, railroads, agriculture and government). The act ensures that employees can choose their own representatives for the purpose of collective bargaining, establishes procedures for secret-ballot elections, and defines unfair labor practices, to which both employers and unions are subject.

The NLRB conducts elections and prevents and remedies unfair labor practices. It is made up of two different "arms." The Board is a group of five persons based in Washington, D.C., who act in a judicial capacity, though they are not judges. This group decides whether improper labor practices have actually occurred, either during an election campaign or during management-union bargaining sessions. The General Counsel is the prosecutorial side of the Board. It has offices throughout the country and is charged with the investigation and prosecution of those who engage in unfair labor practices. The NLRB is designed to be completely equitable, taking sides for neither management nor union, acting as a sort of "referee" in what is usually an emotionally charged action between employees and employers.

IMPACT ON BUSINESS The employees of any business may seek representation by filing a petition with the NLRB requesting an election. The NLRA requires that representation must be by a "labor organization," as defined by the NLRA. The definition of a labor organization is fairly liberal, and entrepreneurs should always be familiar with both large and smaller unions that might seek to organize a business' employees. The larger ones, such as the AFL-CIO or the United Auto Workers (UAW), are well known, but there are many smaller organizations as well.

Once an election has been held and employees have determined that they want representation by a union for the purposes of collective bargaining, the employer is required by law to bargain with no other organization for the workers in that business. All workers are covered by the decision, whether they become members of the union or not. Generally, such employment concerns such as wages, hours, and working conditions are included in the collective bargaining agreement, which is set up during meetings between the employer and the union representatives.

UNFAIR LABOR PRACTICES The judicial arm of the NLRB becomes involved when there is a dispute about the conduct of the employer or the union during a union election campaign or during bargaining. The General Counsel investigates the charge to determine if it is valid and should be pursued. The charge can become a local level complaint at this stage, or can be dismissed. The great majority of charges filed with the NLRB are settled or withdrawn at the stage when investigation has been completed, before a complaint has been issued.

If a complaint is filed, the case is heard before an Administrative Law Judge, part of the judicial arm of the NLRB. The Administrative Law Judge's decision on the case is adopted by the Board. If exceptions are made, the transcript, briefs, and other documentation of the case is sent to the Board in Washington for a decision. The NLRB rarely hears oral arguments; it usually making decisions based on the documentation from the Administrative Law Judge.

The NLRB decisions do not have the impact of law because the NLRB is an administrative agency. Their decisions are recommendations, but NLRB opinions carry a great deal of weight in courts of law. If either the union or employer is unwilling to follow the guidelines set down in the decision, the NLRB files a petition in the Court of Appeals—the level directly below the Supreme Court—for the district where the case arose. If this decision is contested, the Board will request that the United States Supreme Court hear the case.

FURTHER READING:

Gould, William B, IV. *Labored Relations: Law, Politics, and the NLRB.* MIT Press, 2000.

A Guide to Basic Law and Procedures Under the National Labor Relations Act. Revised ed. U.S. National Labor Relations Board, 1991.

''Managing American Labor.'' *Financial World.* June 25, 1991.

Miller, Edward B. *An Administrative Appraisal of the NLRB.* Labor Relations and Public Policy Series no. 16. University of Pennsylvania, 1977.

Weiler, Paul C. *Governing the Workplace: The Future of Labor and Employment Law.* Harvard University Press, 1990.

SEE ALSO: Labor Unions

NATIONAL VENTURE CAPITAL ASSOCIATION (NVCA)

The National Venture Capital Association (NVCA), founded in 1973, is an organization of venture capital firms, corporate backers, and individuals dedicated to professionally investing private capital in new companies. In their own words, they exist to ''define, serve, and represent the interests of the venture capital and private equity industries'' by, among other things, promoting the public policy interests of the venture capital and entrepreneurial communities. The group seeks to foster greater understanding of the necessity of investing in young companies and their role in the overall health of the United States economy. To that end, it works to stimulate the flow of risk equity capital to emerging and developing companies. It also aims to promote communication between venturing bodies throughout the United States and strives to improve the level of knowledge of the venturing process in government, universities, and the general business community. In support of these activities, the NVCA conducts research, hosts educational and networking programs, and serves as an information clearinghouse for its members. It makes available the results of its research in various publications, such as its *Annual Economic Impact of Venture Capital Study, Job Creation Survey, Expert Analysis of Legislative and Regulatory Issues,* and other scholarly works. Specific information available through the NVCA includes industry statistics, venture capital news, and listings of venture capital firms. NVCA headquarters are located in Arlington, VA. The association also maintains a Web site at www.nvca.org.

VENTURE CAPITAL

New business owners who lack the collateral and experience to garner traditional bank financing often must seek funds elsewhere. Many entrepreneurs seek ''venture capital'' informally, obtaining seed money from friends and family or wealthy individuals willing to risk an investment. Others, of course, seek funding by professional firms. In these cases, the firm assesses any number of business plans to determine which holds the greatest potential for success and then finances its construction. The venture capital firm will have an ongoing relationship with the start-up, providing coaching, training, management expertise, and other services, and often holding a seat on the young company's board of directors. Should your business be accepted for funding by a venture capital firm, expect the organization to take an active part in shaping your business.

According to the NVCA, funds used by venture capital firms come from a variety of sources, including institutional investors such as pension funds, foundations and endowments, insurance companies, wealthy individuals, professional money managers, foreign investors, and the venture capitalists themselves.

NVCA MEMBERSHIP

The NVCA actively advocates public policies that are beneficial to the entrepreneurial and venture communities. The association also provides educational programs accessible throughout the United States to its membership. Programs are conducted by industry scholars, practitioners, and analysts. In addition, the NVCA offers a director and officer insurance program intended for both members and their portfolio companies that provides risk management and loss control protection.

The Regional Member Committee program, a network of liaison groups that represents members from across the United States, works with the NVCA Board of Directors and staff to design and enhance the programs offered by the association. The committees, which are composed of members from each of the six regions, include Education, Public Relations, Research, Tax Policy and others. Finally, the NVCA's affiliate organization, the American Entrepreneurs for Economic Growth (AEEG), seeks to "serve as a united voice on public policy issues for entrepreneurs." It represents thousands of small business owners and executives across the country.

NVCA has several requirements of potential members. Those seeking membership (by invitation) must be capital organizations, investment advisors, corporate investors, or buyout funds. Members need not be full time venture capitalists, but they must have as their primary business the deployment of venture capital. They also must represent capital funds and utilize a professional approach before and after they make an investment, including the maintenance of a continuing interest in companies they sponsor. The managers of the business must be American citizens or resident aliens and operate from an office located in the United States. In addition, members must invest from a dedicated U.S.-based venture capital pool of funds of at least one million dollars. Finally, the members' business must be subject to U.S. taxation and laws. Dues are scalable and depend on the amount of capital under management.

FURTHER READING:

Flanagan, Lawrence. *Raising Capital: How to Write a Financing Proposal.* Psi Research - Oasis Press, 1994.

Gillis, Tom S. *Guts & Borrowed Money: Straight Talk for Starting & Growing Your Small Business.* Bard Press, 1997.

Lister, Kate, Tom Harnish, and Catherine E. Lister. *Directory of Venture Capital.* John Wiley & Sons, 1996.

Long, Mark H. *Financing the New Venture.* Adams Media, 2000.

Lundgren, Douglas A. *Venture Capital: An Authoritative Guide for Investors, Entrepreneurs, and Managers.* McGraw-Hill, 1998.

NEGOTIATION

Negotiation describes any communication process between individuals that is intended to reach a compromise or agreement to the satisfaction of both parties. Negotiation involves examining the facts of a situation, exposing the both the common and opposing interests of the parties involved, and bargaining to resolve as many issues as possible. Negotiation takes place every day in nearly every facet of life—from national governments negotiating border disputes, to companies negotiating work agreements with labor unions, to real estate agents negotiating the sale of property, to former spouses negotiating the terms of a divorce. Small business owners are likely to face negotiations on a daily basis when dealing with customers, suppliers, employees, investors, creditors, government agencies, and even family members. Many companies train members of their sales forces in negotiation techniques, and many others hire professional negotiators to represent them in business dealings. Good negotiation requires advance preparation, a knowledge of negotiating techniques, and practice.

Regardless of the type of negotiation, experts recommend entering into it with a cooperative rather than a competitive attitude. They stress that the point of negotiating is to reach agreement rather than to achieve victory. "Any method of negotiation may be fairly judged by three criteria," Roger Fisher and William Ury wrote in their book *Getting to Yes: Negotiating Agreement without Giving In.* "It should produce a wise agreement if agreement is possible. It should be efficient. And it should improve or at least not damage the relationship between the parties." When one of the parties uses "hard" negotiating techniques—or bullies and intimidates the other side in order to obtain a more favorable arrangement—it only creates resentment and poisons future negotiations. Instead, the idea should be to find a win/win solution that satisfies the needs and interests of both parties.

PREPARING FOR A NEGOTIATION

Good negotiation requires advance preparation, an understanding of the underlying assumptions and needs to be satisfied on both sides, a basic knowledge of human behavior, and mastery of a range of negotiating techniques, strategies, and tactics. In his book *Fundamentals of Negotiating,* Gerard I. Nierenberg outlined a number of steps toward adequately preparing for a negotiation. The first step is to "do your homework" about the other side. In nearly every negotiation, this will entail research to uncover their underlying motivations. In negotiating a business property lease, for example, it may be useful to find out the cost to the landlord of keeping the building vacant. The next step is to assess your own side's needs and establish objectives for the negotiation. It is important that the objectives remain relatively fluid, however, so as not to hinder the negotiation.

Another element of preparing for a negotiation involves deciding whether to use an individual or a team as your representative. This decision needs to be considered separately for every negotiation, and will always depend to some extent on what the other side is doing. A negotiating team offers a number of potential advantages. For example, it enables a small business to involve people with different areas of expertise in order to avoid misstatements of fact. Teams can also play into negotiating strategies and help gain concessions through consultation among team members. However, it is important to note that bringing extra people can be harmful to a negotiation when they do not have a distinct function. Using a single negotiator also offers some advantages. It prevents the weakening of positions that often occurs through differences of opinion within a team, and it also may help gain concessions through the negotiator's ability to make on-the-spot decisions.

The next step in preparing for a negotiation involves choosing a chief negotiator. Ideally, this person should have experience and training in negotiations, as well as a strong background in the area of the problem to be negotiated. Another important element of negotiation is selecting the meeting site. For a small business, holding the meeting on its own premises may provide a psychological advantage, plus will save on travel time and expense. It may also be helpful in enabling the negotiators to obtain approval from managers or use their own facilities to check facts and find additional information as needed. Holding a negotiation at the other side's offices, however, may help the negotiators to devote their full attention to the task at hand without distractions. It may also play into negotiating strategy by enabling the negotiators to temporarily withhold information by claiming a need to speak to higher level people or gather more information. A third alternative for a meeting site is a neutral location. Whatever site is chosen, it should be large enough to accommodate all parties and feature a telephone, comfortable chairs, visual aids, and available refreshments.

THE NEGOTIATION PROCESS

Fisher and Ury recommend conducting negotiations according to the process of ''principled negotiation.'' Their method has four main tenets:

1) Separate the people from the problem. The idea should be for both sides to work together to attack a problem, rather than attacking each other. To achieve this goal, it is necessary to overcome emotional responses and set aside egos.

2) Focus on interests rather than positions. The natural tendency in many negotiations—for example, dickering over the price to be paid for an antique—is for both sides to state a position and then move toward middle ground. Fisher and Ury warn against confusing people's stated positions with their underlying interests, and claim that positions often tend to obscure what people truly hope to gain through negotiation.

3) Generate a variety of options before deciding what to do. The pressure involved in any type of negotiation tends to narrow people's vision and inhibit their creativity, making it difficult to find optimal solutions to problems. Instead, Fisher and Ury suggest developing a wide range of possible solutions as part of the negotiating process. These possible solutions should attempt to advance shared interests and reconcile differences.

4) Base the result on objective criteria. No one will be happy with the result of a negotiation if they feel that they have been taken advantage of. The solution is to find and apply some fair standard to the problem in order to guarantee a mutually beneficial result.

Fisher and Ury's principles provide a good overall guide for the actual negotiation process. In his book, Nierenberg offered a number of other tips and strategies that may be effective in promoting successful negotiations. For example, it may be helpful to ask questions in order to form a better understanding of the needs and interests of the other side. The questions must be phrased diplomatically and timed correctly in order to avoid an antagonistic response. The idea is to gain information and uncover basic assumptions without immediately taking positions. Nierenberg stressed the importance of listening carefully to the other side's responses, as well as studying their facial expressions and body language, in order to gain quality information.

Nierenberg noted that good negotiators will employ a variety of means to accomplish their objectives. Small business owners should be aware of some of the more common strategies and techniques that they may see others apply or may wish to apply themselves. One common strategy is forbearance, or ''patience pays,'' which covers any sort of wait or delay in negotiations. If one side wishes to confer in private, or adjourn briefly, they are employing a strategy of forbearance. Another common strategy is to present a *fait accompli,* or come to a final offer and leave it up to the other side to decide whether to accept it. In a simple example, a small business owner may scratch out one provision in a contract that he or she finds unacceptable, then sign it and send it back. The other party to the contract then must decide whether to accept the revised agreement. Nierenberg warns that this strategy can be risky, and encourages those who employ it to carefully appraise the consequences first.

Another possible negotiating strategy is reversal, which involves taking a position that seems opposed to the original one. Similarly, feinting involves apparently moving in one direction in order to divert attention from the true goal. For example, a negotiator may give in on a point that is not very important in order to make the real objective more attainable. Another strategy involves setting limits on the negotiation, whether with regards to time, the people involved, or other factors. It is also possible to change the participation in the negotiation if it seems to be at an impasse. For example, a neutral third party may be enlisted to help, or one or two people from each side may be sent off to continue the negotiation separately. It may also be helpful to break down the problem into small pieces and tackle them one by one. Another strategy might be to trade sides for a short time and try to view the situation from each other's perspective. All of these techniques may be applied either to gain advantage or to push forward a negotiation that has apparently reached an impasse.

FURTHER READING:

Cohen, Herb. *You Can Negotiate Anything.* Bantam Books, 1980.

Fisher, Roger, and William Ury. *Getting to Yes: Negotiating Agreement without Giving In.* 2nd ed. Penguin, 2000.

Latz, Marty. "Are They Irrational or Are They Faking It? Negotiating a Business Deal with an Irrational Party." *Orlando Business Journal.* January 5, 2001.

Nierenberg, Gerard I. *Fundamentals of Negotiating.* New York: Hawthorn Books, 1977.

Whitaker, Leslie, and Elizabeth Austin. *The Good Girl's Guide to Negotiating: How to Get What You Want at the Bargaining Table.* Little, Brown, 2000.

NEPOTISM

In the business world, nepotism is the practice of showing favoritism toward one's family members or friends in economic or employment terms. For example, granting favors or jobs to friends and relatives, without regard to merit, might be considered nepotism. These practices can have damaging effects on businesses—such as eroding the support of non-favored employees or reducing the quality and creativity of management. In response, some larger companies have instituted "antinepotism" policies, which prevent relatives (by blood or marriage) from working in the same department or firm. But in many smaller, family-owned businesses, nepotism is viewed in more positive terms. Family members are trained in various aspects of management to ensure the continuity of the company when members of the earlier generation retire or die. In fact, in many small businesses nepotism is considered a synonym for "succession."

One of the most common arguments against nepotism is that the emotional ties between people who are related may negatively affect their decisionmaking abilities and professional growth. In the past, many businesses sought to avoid even the appearance of nepotism by forbidding relatives from working closely together. As women entered the work force in greater numbers and took on more significant jobs, however, rules regarding nepotism began to change. Both the man and the woman in a married couple were often too valuable for a company to lose. Instead of instituting strict antinepotism rules, many businesses decided that family members could be accommodated within a merit system, especially if there was no direct supervisory link between the positions of related employees.

NEPOTISM IN SMALL BUSINESSES

Nepotism has also traditionally had negative connotations in small business environments. "Business owners and their advisers have often feared that non-family employees would resent and possibly treat unkindly family members brought into the business or would see the family members as roadblocks to their own career success," noted Sharon Nelton in *Nation's Business.* "They also feared that some family members themselves might be incompetent or lazy yet have an attitude of entitlement."

But nepotism can be useful in smaller, family-owned businesses, when practiced in a reasonable way that rewards all employees for company successes. The emotional bonds between family members can actually have a positive effect on individual performance and company results. In addition, hiring family members can fill staffing requirements with dedicated employees. And it should not be forgotten that preparing a family member to carry on a business is a perfectly legitimate enterprise for the owner of a family business.

But in order to avoid potential pitfalls and ensure that relatives work together effectively, the company should establish formal guidelines regarding hiring, responsibilities, reporting structure, training, and succession. These guidelines will be different depending on the family's size, culture, history, and line of business, in addition to other factors. "How strict or liberal the rules . . . are is less important than clear communication of the rules before they are needed and fair application of the rules when timely," Craig E. Aronoff and John L. Ward wrote in *Nation's Business.* After all, most non-family employees recognize the legitimacy of preparing younger family members to assume the company's reins down the road. But experts agree that a widespread workforce perception that family members are not being held responsible for their performance can blossom into a major morale problem.

Regarding hiring, Aronoff and Ward recommend in *Family Business Succession* that family members meet three qualifications before they are allowed to join the family business on a permanent basis: an appropriate educational background; three to five years' outside work experience; and an open, existing position in the firm that matches their background. Of these qualifications, Aronoff and Ward stress that outside work experience is the most important for both the business and the individual. They claim that it gives future managers a wider experience base that makes them better equipped to deal with challenges, lets them learn and make mistakes before coming under the watchful eye of the family, makes them realize what other options exist and thus appreciate the family firm, and provides them with an idea of their market value.

Aronoff and Ward also suggest that family members begin their association with the business by working part-time during their school years or participating in internships. In addition, they stress that companies who hire family members should make it clear to the individuals that they will be fired for illegal or unethical behavior, regardless of their family ties. Finally, they recommend that family businesses encourage their employees to maintain outside associations in order to avoid problems associated with a lack of creativity or accountability in management. For example, future managers could participate in industry or civic groups, enroll in night school classes or attend seminars, take responsibility for a division or profit center, and have their job performance reviewed by outside consultants or directors. Such steps can improve the employee's self-confidence and preparation for an eventual leadership role in the business.

FURTHER READING:

Aronoff, Craig E., and John L. Ward. *Family Business Succession: The Final Test of Greatness.* Business Owner Resources, 1992.

Aronoff and Ward. ''Rules for Nepotism.'' *Nation's Business.* January 1993.

Lynn, Jacquelyn. ''Lawfully Wedded Employees.'' *Entrepreneur.* April 2000.

Milazzo, Don. ''All in the Family.'' *Birmingham Business Journal.* August 11, 2000.

Nelton, Sharon. ''The Bright Sight of Nepotism.'' *Nation's Business.* May 1998.

SEE ALSO: Family-Owned Business

NET INCOME

Net income is an accounting term that can be defined as the difference between a company's total revenues (money earned from sales or investments) and total expenses (money paid to produce goods or services, plus salaries, rent, depreciation, etc.) for a given period of time. Also known as net earnings, after-tax income, or profit, net income is the ''bottom line'' of the formal accounting report known as the income statement. If a company's total expenses exceed its total revenues for a certain period, it can be said to have experienced a net loss. If revenues and expenses should turn out to be equal, the company will have broken even.

Net income is one of the most important indicators of the financial health of a business. ''Some people view the income statement as the most important of the three required financial statements [the others are the balance sheet and the statement of changes in financial position] because it is designed to report the amount of net income and the details of how that amount was earned,'' according to Glenn A. Welsch, Robert N. Anthony, and Daniel G. Short in their book *Fundamentals of Financial Accounting.* ''The amount of net income for the period represents a net increase in resources (or a net decrease if a loss) that flowed into the business entity during that period as a result of operational activities.''

Most income statements will show three separate income figures. The first is pretax income, which is the amount the company earned before taking taxes into account. Reporting of this figure is optional. The second is income before extraordinary items, which is equal to ordinary revenues less ordinary expenses. Extraordinary items include any nonoperating gains or losses that are unusual in nature and infrequent in occurrence. They are separated from ordinary income in order to avoid confusing the readers of income statements. Reporting of this figure is mandatory whenever there are extraordinary items to be included.

The third and final income figure shown on an income statement is net income. It is the difference between total revenues and total expenses for the period, including taxes and extraordinary items. Net income always appears as the last figure in the body of the income statement, and its reporting is mandatory. Corporations (but not sole proprietorships or partnerships) are also required to divide the net income figure by the number of shares of stock outstanding in order to report the earnings per share (EPS) for the period.

In addition to providing information on its own, net income is also frequently compared to other figures in financial ratios in order to provide further information about a company's overall health. For example, financial analysts often divide net income by total sales in order to find a company's rate of return on sales. This figure provides a good indication of the amount of profit the company is able to earn for every dollar of sales. Another common ratio examined by financial analysts is return on stockholders' equity, which can be found by dividing net income by the average equity for the period. As Charles T. Horngren and Gary L. Sundem wrote in their book *Fundamentals of Financial Accounting,* ''This ratio is widely regarded as the ultimate measure of overall accomplishment.''

FURTHER READING:

Anthony, Robert N., and Leslie K. Pearlman. *Essentials of Accounting.* Prentice Hall, 1999.

Bragg, Steven M. *Accounting Best Practices.* Wiley, 1999.

Hilton, Ronald W. *Managerial Accounting.* McGraw-Hill, 1991.

Horngren, Charles T., and Gary L. Sundem. *Introduction to Financial Accounting.* 4th ed. Prentice Hall, 1990.

Welsch, Glenn A., Robert N. Anthony, and Daniel G. Short. *Fundamentals of Financial Accounting.* 4th ed. Irwin, 1984.

NET WORTH

Net worth is a basic measure of the value of a business. It can be defined as the difference between a company's assets and liabilities, as they are recorded on the balance sheet. Net worth is one of many terms used to describe the value of the equity held by owners of a business. The preferred term generally depends on the form of the business in question. Owner's equity is usually applied to the net worth of a sole proprietorship, partners' equity to that of a partnership, and shareholders' equity to that of a corporation. In contrast to these more specific terms, net worth can be used to describe the value of any business, as well as the financial position of an individual.

It is important to note that net worth measures only the book, or accounting, value of a business. This amount is not usually the same as the market value of a business, which is the amount an informed buyer would pay to acquire the business in an arm's-length transaction. Improving net worth is a matter of increasing assets or decreasing liabilities. If a business has liabilities in excess of its assets, it is said to have a negative net worth. This condition is considered detrimental for a business, and often prevents it from acquiring new funds through bank loans.

ELEMENTS OF THE BALANCE SHEET

Determination of a company's net worth comes from its balance sheet. The balance sheet outlines the financial and physical resources that a company has available for business activities at a particular point in time. It is important to note, however, that the balance sheet only lists these resources, and makes no judgment about how well they will be used by management. For this reason, the balance sheet is more useful in analyzing a company's current financial position than its expected performance.

The main elements of the balance sheet are assets, liabilities, and owners' equity. Assets generally include both current assets (cash or equivalents that will be converted to cash within one year, such as accounts receivable, inventory, and prepaid expenses) and noncurrent assets (assets that are held for more than one year and are used in running the business, including fixed assets like property, plant, and equipment; long-term investments; and intangible assets like patents, copyrights, and goodwill). The balance sheet also includes two categories of liabilities, current liabilities (debts that will come due within one year, such as accounts payable, short-term loans, and taxes) and long-term debts (debts that are due more than one year from the date of the statement).

The difference between assets and liabilities as reported on the balance sheet is recorded in owners' equity accounts. These accounts detail the permanent capital of the business, also known as its net worth. The total equity usually consists of two parts: 1) contributed capital, or the money that has been invested by shareholders; and 2) retained earnings, or the money that has been accumulated from profits and reinvested in the business. In general, the higher the net worth of a business, the better the ability of the business to borrow additional funds.

FURTHER READING:

Anthony, Robert N., and Leslie K. Pearlman. *Essentials of Accounting.* Prentice Hall, 1999.

Bangs, David H., Jr. *Managing by the Numbers: Financial Essentials for the Growing Business.* Upstart Publishing, 1992.

Bragg, Steven M. *Accounting Best Practices.* Wiley, 1999.

Welsch, Glenn A., Robert N. Anthony, and Daniel G. Short. *Fundamentals of Financial Accounting.* 4th ed. Irwin, 1984.

NETWORKING

Networking is the process of intentionally meeting people, making contacts, and forming relationships in hopes of gaining access to such business-related benefits as career advice, job leads, business referrals, useful information and ideas, and emotional support. For example, a small business owner's network might include clients, vendors, fellow members of trade or professional associations, bankers, accountants, professors at a local business school, friends who are employed in similar industries, and other small business owners. Each person that a small business owner adds to his or her network is at the center of their own network, so in actuality the network is expanded considerably with every new member. Ideally, networks serve both social and business functions and are mutually beneficial for their members. The relationships formed in networking help people create a larger world for themselves, with a variety of new relationships, opportunities, and resources.

BENEFITS OF NETWORKING

In an article for the *Training and Development Journal,* Frank K. Sonnenberg identified three main benefits that accrue to those who practice effective networking: referrals, relationships, and leads. Referrals, which are particularly important in growing a small business, take many forms. For example, a satisfied client might suggest others who may need the company's products or services. Similarly, a network member who is familiar with the company's offerings might provide an endorsement or allow the small business owner to mention his or her name in marketing efforts. It is good networking practice and a matter of professional courtesy to thank the person who provided the referral and to keep them informed of the results of the new contact. In addition, it is important never to use someone as a referral without first securing their permission. If a referral does result in a new client relationship, care should be taken to provide the new client with the same level of product or service quality that was enjoyed by the one that gave the referral. Otherwise, the small business risks ruining both client relationships.

Another benefit of networking is establishing relationships, which can have a number of positive outcomes for small businesses. Forming a close relationship with a client, for example, might provide invaluable insight into their needs. In addition to giving the small business a good opportunity to promote or develop products and services to meet those needs, this insight might also help the small business owner to fix small problems before they escalate into large ones. The insights gained from one client can often be applied to other clients in order to improve those relationships. Close client relationships can also provide information about competitors, their relative strengths and weaknesses, and what it takes to stay ahead of them.

Finally, networking can be an excellent source of leads, whether on new business opportunities, new career options, or further networking possibilities. For example, the head of a construction company that is erecting an office building might share a network with an interior designer. When the building is close to completion, the head of the construction company might provide the interior designer with leads on the occupants of the building and their furnishing needs. In turn, the interior designer might alert a network contact who sells office supplies when the new occupants are preparing to move into the building.

FINDING NETWORKING OPPORTUNITIES

Opportunities for networking abound. One well-known example of a possible contact is the person occupying the next seat on an airplane. But it is possible to take a more organized approach. In an article for *Entrepreneur,* Leann Anderson outlined several strategies for finding networking opportunities. First, she suggested making a list of specific groups of people that would be helpful to know for business purposes, from potential customers to other small businesses that offer complementary products or services. Then it is necessary to identify where best to find them. Perhaps they are likely to participate in certain activities, belong to certain organizations, or frequent certain places or events. The final step is to become involved in those organizations or activities.

A variety of organizations exist that are dedicated to providing business networking opportunities, like industry trade associations or chambers of commerce. In addition to these traditional groups, which cater mostly to larger businesses, there are hundreds of smaller and more intimate networking groups for small business owners. ''Networking groups, from nationwide organizations to single-chapter local outfits, bring together business owners on a regular, formal basis to promote one another's businesses,'' Kathleen Less wrote in the *Business Journal Serving Greater Sacramento.* ''The basic concept in all formal networking organizations is that members in a group of businesspeople, each in a different line of work, make referrals to each other from among their own friends, clients, and associates. They not only share customers, but develop a circle of businesses with which they do business and exchange expertise.''

Some networking organizations target specific geographic areas or particular demographic groups or industries. For example, there are groups catering to women and minority business owners, and groups consisting of entrepreneurs who run home-based businesses. These small business-oriented groups allow entrepreneurs to form stronger ties with one another than they might be able to do in larger groups with less stable membership. Small business owners can build relationships, provide and receive advice and moral support, and exchange sales leads with fellow members.

An article in *Business Week* recommended that small business owners begin the process of choosing a networking organization by deciding what their own goals are. They might locate potential groups by talking to other business owners or searching on the Internet. Once an entrepreneur has found several potential networking organizations, the next step is to talk to members and sit in on a meeting or two before deciding whether to join and paying any related fees. Finally, it may be possible to form a new group if an appropriate one cannot be found. Les emphasized that networking organizations have a great deal to offer entrepreneurs: "For small business owners who have little chance to get out of the store or office and interact, networking organizations can offer the regular discipline of meeting with other businesspeople to share free advice and offer support."

GUIDELINES FOR ESTABLISHING AND MAINTAINING A SUCCESSFUL NETWORK

Successful networking involves making it a personal practice to view every situation—both inside and outside of the business environment—as an opportunity to meet new people. In an article for *Manage,* Anna Boe suggested several key points in adding a new acquaintance to the network. First, when meeting people, it is important not to be afraid of rejection, and not to take it personally when it occurs. Second, it is helpful to exchange names, occupations, and other pertinent information shortly after meeting someone new. The best way to strike up a conversation is usually to ask questions to draw people out and get them talking about themselves.

But simply meeting and exchanging information with another person is not enough. Networking is a long-term strategy—not one that should be pursued only when contacts are urgently needed—and networks must be continually formed and improved upon over time. It is important to keep in touch with new acquaintances and nurture the relationships. It is also helpful to grant favors warmly when they are requested, and to be flexible when asking others for their time, information, advice, or a referral. In addition, merely attending conferences or meetings is not enough to establish and maintain a strong network. Instead, it requires one-on-one time with other people. Another factor in establishing networks is to become an active rather than passive participant in associations, clubs, or groups.

Networking has its own rules of etiquette that must be followed if it is to be practiced successfully. Most importantly, networking should consist of give-and-take relationships. People who only want to do one or the other quickly lose members from their networks. Boe noted that giving should be its own reward, and that people who grant favors should avoid the temptation to keep score or expect an immediate favor in return. On the other hand, it is important to allow others an occasional opportunity to reciprocate, or else they will become hesitant to ask for help.

The other common-sense rules of etiquette for successful networking include not smothering people or wasting their time, calling on contacts at convenient times, being reasonable and considerate with requests, spreading requests around among various contacts, not making promises that cannot be kept, and not revealing sensitive information that may be acquired through network contacts. Finally, networking should not be equated with sales. Instead, it should be considered an information-gathering exercise that can eventually lead to new business opportunities.

FURTHER READING:

Anderson, Leann. "Make the Connection: Networking Opportunities Are Everywhere. Don't Let Them Pass You By." *Entrepreneur.* July 1997.

Boe, Anna. "Making Networking Work for You." *Manage.* July 1993.

Les, Kathleen. "Networking: Pooled Efforts Help Owners Stalk the Mighty Sales Lead." *Business Journal Serving Greater Sacramento.* September 16, 1996.

"Schmooze Control." *Business Week.* March 1, 1999.

Shewmake, Brad. "Secrets of Successful Networking." *InfoWorld.* July 3, 2000.

Sonnenberg, Frank K. "The Professional (and Personal) Profits of Networking." *Training and Development Journal.* September 1990.

NEW ECONOMY

New economy is a term often used in the media to describe the changes that have taken place in the world of business since the widespread adoption of Internet technology. It has been applied to a wide range of situations and issues, most notably the rise and fall of high-tech and Internet startup companies. During the 1990s, as the United States experienced a long economic expansion and the stock market soared, many people started to think that basic economic principles no longer applied in the age of the Internet.

The basic idea behind the new economy was that computer and Internet technology had fundamentally changed the typical way of doing business. Analysts and investors alike focused on technology adoption and stock price valuation rather than revenues and long-term business plans when evaluating companies. As a result, high-tech startup firms staged public stock offerings before they had turned a profit and still attracted huge numbers of eager investors. Employees gave up the stability of traditional firms to work long hours at dot-coms in hopes of achieving a windfall in stock options. The workplace at high-flying tech companies evolved to include rooms full of toys and games to encourage employee creativity.

According to an article in *Business Week,* people made several assumptions about the new economy that ultimately proved to be false. First, they assumed that information technology was so important to business productivity that companies would always buy new systems and software, even in bad times. This belief caused big computer firms to give inflated earnings estimates which, when they were not met, contributed to the fall of the tech-heavy Nasdaq in 2000. Another popular assumption was that economic growth had become so stable that investors would no longer require a risk premium for stocks over bonds. Some analysts predicted that stock market averages would continue to increase indefinitely. In actuality, however, the high-tech driven expansion increased the risk and volatility of the stock market.

Another assumption concerning the new economy was that companies would no longer lay off workers during downtimes because high-tech labor is so scarce. As a result, many people were lulled into believing that they had greater job security than they actually did. Employees gave up the stability of employment at traditional companies for the big signing bonuses and stock options offered at dot-coms. "It used to be that when you went to a startup, you were an individual with a very high risk tolerance and probably had an ideal you were trying to achieve," technology company president Christine Heckart told Paul Prince in *Tele.com.* "But a lot of people with very low risk tolerance left very good, secure jobs at the height of the frenzy to get rich quick in the world of startupdom. And all of a sudden, before their dreams were achieved, the bubble burst."

When the Internet boom went bust and the U.S. economy slowed significantly in the early 2000s, many companies began laying off workers. As a result, employees began looking for jobs with more conservative companies once again. "Many [job seekers] are bent on finding a company with a future they can believe in, a dependable path to profitability, and a stable working environment where they won't be required to work around the clock for little more than stock options that may never pan out," Prince wrote. "Internet companies and technology startups in general must find a way to prove their stability and financial viability while giving employees some of what they gained in the new-economy environment. That includes room for creativity, as well as a sense of passion and ownership."

Some experts now claim that there is no such thing as a new economy. Others say that the new economy is actually the old economy, but with technological breakthroughs integrated into existing businesses. But some experts continue to insist that the Internet has fundamentally changed the rules of doing business, despite the stock market downturn. In an article for *Computerworld,* Don Tapscott argues that the Internet provides a new infrastructure that lowers transaction costs and encourages collaboration among firms. He says that it creates a new platform for strategic thinking that consists of suppliers, distributors, and customers, all using the Internet as their base of communications. "Some claim that there isn't a New Economy. E-business and the Internet are a bust, and it's time to go back to tried-and-true principles that have guided commerce and investing for decades, if not centuries," he wrote. "But heeding such advice would be a stunning mistake. There is a New Economy, with the Internet at its heart. Spurn this notion, and your company's failure is assured."

FURTHER READING:

Brock, Terry. "Old Principles, New Ideas Work in New Economy." *Atlanta Business Chronicle.* November 3, 2000.

"Educators Rethink Buzzwords Such as 'New Economy.'" *Knight-Ridder/Tribune Business News.* April 20, 2001.

"The New Economy's New Reality." *Business Week.* March 12, 2001.

Porter, Michael E. "Strategy and the Internet." *Harvard Business Review.* March 2001.

Prince, Paul. "Conventional Wisdom: Scarred by Dot-Bombs, Employees Are Fleeing New-Economy Flair for Traditional Nine-to-Fives." *Tele.com.* April 16, 2001.

Schwartz, Matthew. "Retire 'New Economy' Tag." *B to B.* March 19, 2001.

Suutari, Ray. "Organizing for the New Economy." *CMA Management.* April 2001.

Tapscott, Don. "Don't Doubt the Future of the New Economy." *Computerworld.* February 19, 2001.

SEE ALSO: Dot-Coms

NEWSGROUPS

Newsgroups are online discussion groups on a variety of topics. A common analogy used to describe newsgroups is "online bulletin boards." All newsgroups were originally part of a worldwide network of discussion groups known as Usenet. No one organization "owns" or manages Usenet—it is a self-regulating community of more than 13,000 newsgroups. Each newsgroup is comprised of a group of users who post public messages or articles to that group. These articles are then organized by subject category and tagged with a standard set of labels for the purpose of distribution from site to site. Each host site pays for its own transmission costs.

Newsgroups differ from discussion lists in that discussion lists are generated via e-mail while newsgroups require a special newsreader software in order to read and post messages. Like discussion lists, newsgroups can be active forums for the exchange of ideas and information, providing a small business with opportunities for networking, learning more about the industry and competition, and marketing and sales possibilities. Newsgroups also tend to be noncommercial (although commercial newsgroups do exist), so it is crucial that participants become aware of a group's purpose, makeup, and rules of etiquette.

Newsgroups are both moderated and unmoderated. A moderated newsgroup is monitored by an administrator who may screen posts to the group, on the basis of appropriateness of content. An unmoderated group is, obviously, not monitored. Articles posted by users appear ''as is.'' Prior to joining or posting to a newsgroup, review its file of frequently asked questions, also known as a FAQ. In addition, some newsgroups will have a charter, which establishes the newsgroup's purpose and general rules. Both the FAQ and the charter can be helpful in selecting a newsgroup to participate in.

Usenet does not allow commercial messages, and no advertising is allowed for most individual newsgroups. However, business newsgroups generally welcome and encourage commercial discussions, such as debate over products and services, and are useful for this purpose. Commercial information such as product announcements and price lists are commonplace here, providing a small business with the opportunity for free exposure without benefit of a website.

HOW TO USE NEWSGROUPS

Participation in a newsgroup requires a special type of software known as a newsreader. For most Internet users, this is a part of a web browser such as Netscape or Internet Explorer. If you do not have a web browser, you may need to acquire a newsreader. Check with your Internet service provider (ISP) for more details.

Other computer basics, which may be helpful in using newsgroups, are the concepts of a signature file (.sig) and a plan file (.plan). A signature file is a small file of text which automatically appends to the bottom of all outgoing e-mail messages. At the minimum, a signature file should include an individual's name, company name, and contact information, including e-mail address and URL. The signature file can also be used as a brief advertisement for a company. The key is to keep it short and to the point in order to prompt the reader each time he reads your messages. The signature file will then be appended to any message you post on a newsgroup.

A plan file (also called .plan or dot plan, plan.txt, or .profile) is a small information file which is automatically sent to other Internet users in response to a utility command called a ''finger.'' Usually, informa-tion sent in response to a finger is comprised of the account owner's name, login name, and some login details such as time of last login. You can provide a more detailed response to a finger by creating a plan file. Some ideas for inclusion in a plan file are the type of business, price and product information, and contact information. Contact your ISP or the maker of your web browser for more details.

Before using any newsgroups, begin by determining those newsgroups which may be helpful to your business and to which your company or product may be of interest. To ensure the newsgroup you wish to post to allows these types of posts, be sure to check the newsgroup's FAQ or file of frequently asked questions. Monitoring the newsgroup for a period of time prior to posting is also recommended, in order to ensure you are reaching the correct audience and not ruffling any feathers.

To identify appropriate newsgroups, use the domain or label found in the first part of the name. Business newsgroups are found under the *biz.* domain or label; for example, *biz.imports* might be a business newsgroup comprised of importers. Other newsgroups can serve as sources of information about computers and software (*comp.*), the Internet and networks (*news.*), and so on.

USING A NEWSGROUP FOR FUN AND PROFIT

Newsgroups can be an inexpensive method for a small business to learn more about its industry and competition, gain opportunities for networking, and generate marketing and sales possibilities.

Newsgroups can be a useful source of information about competitors. By reviewing postings and signatures and ''fingering'' plan files, a small business can determine who its competitors are and get a leg up on new product offerings. This information can also help a business to anticipate trends in the industry as well as to monitor related industries. According to Jill and Matthew Ellsworth, authors of *The New Internet Business Book*, newsgroups are ''popular for postings of business networking opportunities, including opportunities to form business partnerships.'' For a small business looking to expand, newsgroups offer the kind of information distribution that normally only big money can buy.

The Ellsworths suggest that prior to posting a message with commercial content, a small business user should begin by participating in a discussion with well reasoned and to the point comments. This can secure a business's standing in the newsgroup and generate interest within in further posts. The unobtrusive use of a signature or *.sig* with each message provides an opportunity for other individuals and business to make contact with the small business, without including commercial content in the message.

Commercial posts to a newsgroup should be short and to the point. Use the subject line to clarify the topic of the post. This will allow other users of the newsgroup to determine if the post is of use to them. Phaedra Hise, author of *Growing Your Business Online,* recommends keeping language simple and without ''sales'' emphasis, such as ''substantial business opportunity.'' As with most information online, recipients are not interested in wading through a lot of hyperbole to get to the facts. Hise also notes that it is important to be up front about being a company trying to sell a product, if that is your purpose, rather than posing as just another interested user. Her suggestion is to post a message asking if a specific commercial post would be acceptable to participants prior to posting the commercial article.

Using newsgroups can be a simple and rewarding method of finding out more about industry and competition. Used with sensitivity and purpose, they can also serve as an inexpensive path to marketing, sales, and business opportunities for a small business.

FURTHER READING:

Ellsworth, Jill H. and Matthew V. *The New Internet Business Book.* John Wiley & Sons, 1996.

Glossbrenner, Alfred, and John Rosenberg. *Online Resources for Business.* John Wiley & Sons, 1995.

Hise, Phaedra. *Growing Your Business Online.* Henry Holt and Co., 1996.

SEE ALSO: Electronic Bulletin Boards

NON-COMPETITION AGREEMENTS

Non-competition agreements are restrictive contracts between employers and employees that 1) prohibit workers from revealing proprietary information about the company to competitors or other outsiders, or 2) forbid workers from themselves competing with their ex-employer for a certain period of time after leaving the company. Non-competition agreements are important tools that small business owners may wield to ensure that key personnel do not walk off and establish a competing business on the strength of knowledge and contacts that they gained during their stint at the small business in question. These documents have significant deterrent value in many situations, and business owners are encouraged to secure such agreements with employees who have access to sensitive proprietary information company information (this may include any aspect of a business's operation, including production formulas, processes,

and methods; business and marketing plans; pricing strategies; salary structure; customer lists, contracts; intellectual property; and computer systems.).

These agreements, which are also sometimes called confidentiality or nondisclosure agreements, typically define confidential information, identify ownership rights, and detail employee obligations to ensure that confidentiality is maintained. But there are definite limits on the scope and duration of such covenants. ''Employers generally cannot use noncompete agreements to keep employees from practicing their trade or profession indefinitely,'' noted Susan Gaylord Willis in *HRMagazine.* ''Particularly if the former employees were experienced in the specified occupation before they were hired.'' But while employees generally have every right to make use of skills and experiences gained in one company when they set off on the next stage of their lives, it is illegal for them to make off with trade secrets of their former place of employment.

Nonetheless, business owners do not always win court cases against ex-employees who pilfer in this area. In some cases, they lose for the simple reason that the business owner ''never identified the company's confidential or trade secret information,'' noted the *Entrepreneur Magazine Small Business Advisor.* ''An ex-employee does not have the right to steal company confidential information or trade secrets that are identified as such; however, the ownership of information developed through company procedures must clearly differentiate what belongs to the employee and what to the company.''

More often, however, courts throw out non-competition agreements out of concerns that such clauses constitute restraints of trade or that they force prospective employees to choose between signing or continuing their job search elsewhere. ''In deciding whether to enforce a noncompete agreement,'' said Willis, ''courts generally focus on: Whether the covenant is ancillary to a valid employment contract [and] whether the agreement imposes reasonable restrictions in terms of time and geography.''

ENFORCING NON-COMPETITION AGREEMENTS
Non-competition covenants are usually enforced by the courts if they are reasonable with respect to time and place and do not unreasonably restrict the former employee's right to employment. Of course, different parties have different conceptions of what constitutes a ''reasonable'' restriction. Legal experts contend that the courts are far more likely to side with the business owner if he or she does not go overboard on imposing restrictions in the following areas:

- Nature of prohibition—Restrictive covenants often are shaped with an eye toward the type of position that was held by the employee. Companies are more likely to target high-level managers or executives for stringent noncompete measures than programmers, writers, architects or other staffers with specialized skills who have less overall knowledge of the company.

- Duration of agreement—Non-competition agreements are less likely to be enforced if they go beyond one year or so. In addition, Willis notes that businesses should consider imposing relatively short durations if the agreement stipulates a wide geographical scope "because the courts are unlikely to sustain a provision that leaves former employees with no way to earn a living in the field in which they are most experienced."

- Geographic area—While it is generally recognized that small business owners have a right to request competition protection from ex-employees in the immediate area in which they operate, stipulations that forbid ex-workers from setting up a similar business in some distant geographic area or region are likely to be overturned unless the company conducts business in a multi-state area or nationally.

- Restrictions on Solicitation—"Who is the employee prohibited from soliciting?" asked *Small Business Reports*. "Is it customers whom the employee personally acquired or any or your company's customers? The narrower your restriction, the more likely a court will enforce it."

- Restrictions on contacting other employees—The courts generally consider it unfair competition for one company to induce employees of another company who have acquired unique technical skills and secret knowledge during their employment to terminate their employment and use their skills and knowledge for the benefit of the competing firm. In such a case the plaintiff company could seek an injunction to prevent its former employees and the competing company from using the proprietary information.

Business owners should keep in mind, however, that attitudes toward noncompetition agreements vary considerably from jursidiction to jurisdiction. No federal statutes exist to regulate these types of agreements with former employees, unless the restrictions violate existing antidiscrimination laws. Instead, each state has its own unique state contract laws. Some courts adhere to a "blue pencil" rule, meaning that they have the authority to edit unduly restrictive agreements so that the scope and/or duration of the agreement is lessened without throwing out the entire contract. Jurisdictions without such options in place,

however, typically uphold the agreement in its entirety or strike it down entirely, leaving the employee free to pursue any course he/she wants. Given this reality, the smart business owner will make sure that he/she is cognizant of the legal philosophy that is prevalent in the state (or states) in which the company conducts its business.

One way in which the business owner can minimize the danger of having a noncompete agreement overturned in court is to create unique noncompetition agreements for each employee affected. "Rather than using a 'one-size-fits-all' covenant, analyze the danger that the restrictive covenant should be designed to protect against," advised Willis. "A company that performs services locally, such as a linen supply or janitorial company, may need protection against pirating of customers in its area of operation. In that case, the company would want a covenant that would be of long duration, perhaps two years, but limited geographically to the city, county, or metropolitan area. On the other hand, a company in a fast-moving field that sells nationally or internationally, such as a software publisher, might need a worldwide noncompete of only six months' duration. The reason is that by the end of six months, any proprietary information gleaned from the employer would be public knowledge and/or obsolete, and its disclosure would be harmless."

FURTHER READING:

Entrepreneur Magazine Small Business Advisor. John Wiley, 1995.

"How to Protect Yourself from Employees Who Become Competitors." *Profit-Building Strategies for Business Owners*. April 1993.

"Keeping Secrets Secret." *Small Business Reports*. February 1994.

Orr, Joel N. "The Employment Contract." *Computer-Aided Engineering*. May 2000.

Willis, Susan Gaylord. "Protect Your Firm Against Former Employees' Actions." *HRMagazine*. August 1997.

NONPROFIT ORGANIZATIONS

Nonprofit organizations are institutions that conduct their affairs for the purpose of assisting other individuals, groups, or causes rather than garnering profits for themselves. Nonprofit groups have no shareholders; do not distribute profits in a way that benefits members, directors, or other individuals in their private capacity; and (often) receive exemption from various taxes in recognition of their contributions to bettering the general social fabric of the community.

Nonprofit groups "are as diverse as the National Football League, Harvard University, and Fannie Mae. A third of these organizations are churches," Roz Ayres-Williams wrote in *Black Enterprise*. "Because nonprofits cover so many fields of interest—charity, religion, health, science, literature, wildlife protection, the arts, even sports—it's easy to find a niche, whatever your calling."

Nonprofit organizations are far more important to the overall U.S. economy than is generally recognized. Indeed, sources indicate that the sum total of nonprofit groups comprise a third sector of the American economy, along with the private (business) and public (government) sectors. According to *Black Enterprise*, there were 1.1 million nonprofit organizations in operation in the U.S. in 1998. These organizations were estimated to employ one out of every ten American workers on either a full-time or part-time basis.

TYPES OF NONPROFIT ORGANIZATIONS

A wide range of charitable and other institutions are classified as nonprofit organizations under the Internal Revenue Code. Many of these qualify under the definition provided in Section 501(c)(3) of the Code, which stipulates that all of the following qualify for tax-exempt status: "Corporations, and any community chest, fund or foundation, organized and operated exclusively for religious, charitable, scientific, testing for public safety, literary or educational purposes, to foster certain national or international amateur sports competition, or for the prevention of cruelty to children or animals," provided that the institutions adhere to basic standards of behavior and requirements of net earnings allocation.

CHARITABLE ORGANIZATIONS Charitable institutions comprise the bulk of America's nonprofit organizations. These include a wide variety of institutions involved in the realms of poverty assistance (soup kitchens, counseling centers, homeless shelters, etc.); religion (churches and their ancillary possessions, such as cemeteries, radio stations, etc.); science (independent research institutions, universities); health (hospitals, clinics, nursing homes, treatment centers); education (libraries, museums, schools, universities, and other institutions); promotion of social welfare; preservation of natural resources; and promotion of theatre, music, and other fine arts.

ADVOCACY ORGANIZATIONS "These groups attempt to influence the legislative process and/or the political process, or otherwise champion particular positions," explained Hopkins. "They may call themselves 'social welfare organizations' or perhaps 'political action committees.' Not all advocacy is lobbying and not all political activity is political campaign activity. Some of this type of program can be accomplished through a charitable organization, but that outcome is rare where advocacy is the organization's primary undertaking."

MEMBERSHIP GROUPS This kind of nonprofit organization includes business associations, veterans' groups, and fraternal organizations.

SOCIAL/RECREATIONAL ORGANIZATIONS Country clubs, hobby and garden clubs, college and university fraternity and sorority organizations, and sports tournament organizations all can qualify as nonprofit organizations, provided that they adhere to basic guidelines of net earnings distribution, etc. Unlike other tax-exempt organizations, however, their investment income is taxable.

"SATELLITE" ORGANIZATIONS Hopkins pointed out that "some nonprofit organizations are deliberately organized as auxiliaries or subsidiaries of other organizations." Such organizations include cooperatives, retirement and other employee benefit funds, and title-holding companies.

EMPLOYEE BENEFIT FUNDS Some profit-sharing and retirement programs can qualify for tax-exempt status.

ADVANTAGES AND DISADVANTAGES OF INCORPORATING

All nonprofit organizations are faced with the decision of whether or not to incorporate. As Ted Nicholas noted in *The Complete Guide to Nonprofit Corporations,* there are many benefits associated with incorporating: "Some are the same as those commonly enjoyed by *for-profit* business corporations. Others are unique to the nonprofit corporation. Perhaps the greatest advantages of all—granted exclusively to organizations with bona fide nonprofit status—is exemption from taxes at federal, state, and local levels." In addition to tax exemption, Nicholas cited the following as principle advantages of forming a nonprofit corporation:

- Permission to solicit funds—Many nonprofit organizations depend on their ability to solicit funds (in the form of gifts, donations, bequests, etc.) for their very existence. Nicholas noted that whereas some states bestow a fund-raising privilege on nonprofit corporations as soon as their articles of incorporation are filed, other states require groups to fulfill additional obligations before granting permission to solicit funds.

- Low postage rates—Many nonprofit corporations are able to use the U.S. mail system at considerably lower rates than private individuals or for-profit businesses. To secure these lower rates, nonprofits must apply to the Postal Service for a permit, but this is generally not a major hurdle, provided that the nonprofit group has its affairs in order. ''The importance of the mailing rate advantage is directly proportional to the volume of mail the nonprofit corporation generates in the course of its business,'' said Nicholas. ''Membership solicitations are usually mailed third class. Nonprofit corporations that rely on membership income can use the mail even more extensively to service their members. So potential savings from a special mailing permit are considerable.''

- Exemption from labor rules—Nonprofit organizations enjoy exemption from the various rules and guidelines of union collective bargaining, even if their work force is represented by a union.

- Immunity from tort liability—This advantage is not available in all states, but Nicholas observed that some states still provide nonprofit charitable organizations with immunity to tort liability. ''It is important to recognize, however, that where it exists, the immunity protects only the nonprofit corporation—not the agent or employee where negligence injures someone.''

In addition, nonprofit corporations enjoy certain advantages that are also bestowed on for-profit corporations. These include legal life (nonprofit corporations are guaranteed the same rights and powers of individuals), limited personal liability, continued existence beyond the involvement of original founders, increased public recognition, readily available information on operations, ability to establish employee benefits programs, and flexibility in financial recordkeeping.

But there are also certain disadvantages associated with incorporating. Nicholas cited the following as principle drawbacks:

- Costs associated with incorporation—Although these costs are usually not too excessive, especially for organizations of any size, incorporation does generally involve some extra costs.

- Additional bureaucracy—''An unincorporated nonprofit organization can be structured so informally that its operators could keep whatever records they chose on the backs of envelopes or as scribbled notes on paper napkins,'' said Nicholas. ''Not so in a nonprofit corporation. As a legal entity, the corporation is subject to some specific recordkeeping obligations set down by the state in which it is incorporated.'' In addition, there are certain activity guidelines to which incorporated organizations must adhere.

- Sacrifice of personal control—Depending on where incorporation takes place, the organization may have to appoint a board of directors to oversee operations (although founders of nonprofit groups can often exercise considerable control in influencing the composition of the board and the flavor of corporate bylaws and articles of incorporation). Founders and directors of unincorporated groups are under no such obligation.

''Generally, the advantages far outweigh the disadvantages,'' summarized Hopkins. ''The disadvantages stem from the fact that incorporation entails an affirmative act of the state government: It 'charters' the entity. In exchange for the grant of corporate status, the state usually expects certain forms of compliance by the organization, such as adherence to rules of operation, an initial filing fee, annual reports, and annual fees. However, these costs are frequently nominal and the reporting requirements are usually not extensive.''

ORGANIZING A NONPROFIT ORGANIZATION

''Being enthusiastic, imaginative, and creative about establishing a nonprofit organization is one thing,'' observed Hopkins. ''Actually forming the entity and making it operational is another. For better or worse, the exercise is much like establishing one's own business. It is a big and important undertaking, and it should be done carefully and properly. The label 'nonprofit' does not mean 'no planning.' Forming a nonprofit organization is as serious as starting up a new company.'' He recommended that individuals interested in forming a nonprofit organization begin by determining the organization's main purpose and functions. The next step involves choosing a category of tax-exempt status to match its functions. From there, would-be founders need to study a wide range of issues, many of which are also basic considerations for small business owners and other individuals involved in for-profit endeavors. Often, the counsel of a good attorney and/or accountant can be valuable at this stage. Primary issues include the following:

- Decide what legal form the organization will take (public charity or private foundation, incorporated or unincorporated, etc.)

- If incorporating, take necessary legal steps to make that decision a reality (devise bylaws, submit articles of incorporation, etc.)

- Investigate options and decide on principal organization programs and emphases

- Determine the leadership of the organization (directors, officers, primary staff positions)

- Define compensation for such positions

- Find a physical location for the organization (factors here can range from variations in state law to availability of reasonable office space)

- Put together a strategic plan for achieving organization goals at both community and larger levels

- Decide how to go about funding those goals (gifts, grants, unrelated income, etc.?)

- Determine which media avenues will be best for publicizing the organization's goals and securing volunteers

- Devise an ongoing business plan that 1) serves as a blueprint for institution goals and development, and 2) can be periodically reviewed and adjusted as appropriate.

FUNDRAISING

Nonprofit institutions can turn to several different methodologies to raise funds designed to support their mission. This is especially true for nonprofits that have tax-exempt status, because it permits donors to deduct their gifts from their own personal income tax liability. Major avenues of fundraising used by nonprofit organizations include the following: fundraising events (dinners, dances, charity auctions, etc.); direct mail solicitation; foundation grant solicitation; in-person solicitation (door-to-door canvassing, etc.); telemarketing; and planned giving (this includes bequests, which are given to the organization after the donor's death, and gifts made during the donor's lifetime through trusts or other agreements).

EFFECTIVE SOLICITATION AND REVENUE MANAGEMENT In order to prosper, nonprofit institutions not only need to know where the sources of funding are, they also need to know how to solicit those funds and how to effectively manage that revenue when it comes into their possession.

Certainly, solicitation of donors (whether they take the form of individuals, corporations, or foundations) is a vital component of many organization's operations. After all, most activities can only be executed with funding. But many nonprofit institutions are not accomplished in this area, either because they do not allocate adequate resources or because of problems with execution. Writing in *Fund Raising Management*, Robert Hartsook listed the following as common solicitation errors that nonprofit groups make:

- Not listening to donor expectations

- Unwarranted assumption of a donor's willingness to contribute

- Lack of follow-up after initial contact

- Inadequate research on potential donors and their ability to contribute

- Inability to close presentation with donor commitment

- Neglecting to establish rapport with potential donors prior to solicitation

- Framing solicitation as ''begging'' rather than as a reasonable request for help with a worthy cause

- Neglecting to tailor solicitation to individual donors

- Approaching potential donors without knowledge of how donations impact them in the realms of tax deductions, etc.

Of course, even the most effective solicitation campaigns will wither if the organization proves unable to allocate its financial and other resources wisely. ''Fundraising begins by determining exactly what financial and human resources are needed to accomplish the mission [of the organization],'' wrote Larry W. Kennedy in *Quality Management in the Nonprofit World*. ''In the short run, money can be raised on the organization's vision and the promises it makes to help its clients and, therefore, its community. It will not take long, though, for contributors to want to see results. . . . Performance is what counts.'' Indeed, an organization may be devoted to addressing a perfectly worthwhile cause, and its membership may be enthusiastic and dedicated, but most nonprofit organizations—and especially charitable ones—rely on funds from outside sources. And poorly run nonprofits will find that their revenue streams will dry up quickly if they do not leverage their funds wisely.

TRENDS IN THE NONPROFIT WORLD

Observers have pointed to several trends in the nonprofit community that are expected to continue or develop in the next few years. These range from changes in fundraising targets to expanded competition between nonprofit organizations to regulatory developments. The following is a listing of some issues that nonprofit organizations will be tracking in the coming years:

1) Increased emphasis on retaining donors—According to Robert F. Hartsook of *Fund Raising Management*, ''Non-profit organizations will focus on the renewal of donors rather than on the acquisition of new ones. As our country's population growth begins to plateau, it will be necessary for non-pro-

fits to more keenly target their marketing efforts.''

2) Corporate giving—Corporate giving to philanthropic causes has emerged as a major marketing tool for corporations in recent years, and this source of funds is expected to assume even greater importance as federal and state governments pare back their spending on various social programs.

3) Increased reliance on volunteerism—Reduced government expenditures on social programs is also expected to spur increased demand for volunteers who can meet the expected growth in organization activity. This need will be especially acute for nonprofit organizations primarily involved in charitable activities.

4) Competition with for-profit enterprises—Many analysts believe that this issue could have tremendous implications for nonprofit organizations in the future. Spurred by representatives of the for-profit small business community, regulatory agencies have undertaken more extensive reviews of ways in which some activities of tax-exempt groups allegedly damage the fortunes of for-profit businesses (who, of course, are subject to local, state, and federal taxes). Much of the controversy in this area centers around the definition and treatment of unrelated business income (income generated by tax-exempt organizations from ventures that are unrelated to their primary mission). ''There is a potential that all of this will lead to nothing,'' wrote Hopkins, ''or it could bring an in-depth inquiry into the federal and state law distinctions between for-profit and non-profit organizations, the rationale for the tax exemption of certain types of nonprofit organizations, and whether some existing tax exemptions are outmoded and some new forms of tax exemption are required.''

5) Continued emphasis on planned giving—''Nonprofit organizations will enjoy a significant increase in realized bequests,'' said Hartsook. ''This will happen as a result of planned giving programs put in place 10 to 15 years ago. With the evidence at hand of how successful planned giving can be, many institutions will increase their dependence on this methodology.''

6) Continued dominance of women in the non-profit community—According to *Fund Raising Management,* women occupied approximately two-thirds of all staff positions in nonprofit organizations in the mid-1990s,

a percentage that may increase in the coming years.

7) Increase in government regulation among nonprofits—Government oversight of fund-raising activities may continue to increase at both the state and federal levels, at least in part because of the solicitation practices of some ''fringe philanthropic groups,'' said Hartsook. ''Unfortunately, telemarketing for nonprofit organizations has received a bad name because of fringe philanthropic organizations that solicit and collect large sums of money—while dedicating most of those funds to the costs of fund raising and salaries.'' According to Hopkins, this increase in government regulation may be especially evident at the state level: ''States that have formerly foregone the desire for a fund-raising law have suddenly decided that their citizens now need one. States with fund-raising regulation laws are making them tougher. Those who administer these laws—the state regulators—are applying them with new vigor.''

8) Growth in self-regulation within the non-profit community—Self-regulation within various sectors of nonprofit operation underwent a noticeable increase in the late 1980s and early 1990s, and this trend is expected to continue with the introduction of new certification systems, codes of ethics, and watchdog groups.

9) Major donors will maximize benefits from contributions—According to Hartsook, major donors will increasingly incorporate aspects of planned giving into their philanthropic efforts in order to maximize their tax deductions. ''Significant gift giving will incorporate an aspect of planned gifts in order to afford the donor maximum tax deductions,'' he stated. ''As the level of tax recognition diminishes, major donors will turn to this methodology in order to maximize tax advantages.''

FURTHER READING:

Ayres-Williams, Roz. ''The Changing Face of Nonprofits.'' *Black Enterprise.* May 1998.

Drucker, Peter F. *Managing the Non-profit Organization: Principles and Practices.* Harper Business, 1990.

Hartsook, Robert F. ''Predictions for 1997.'' *Fund Raising Management.* January 1997.

Hartsook, Robert F. ''Top Ten Solicitation Mistakes.'' *Fund Raising Management.* March 1997.

Hopkins, Bruce R. *The Law of Tax-Exempt Organizations.* John Wiley & Sons.

Hopkins, Bruce R. *A Legal Guide to Starting and Managing a Nonprofit Organization.* 2d ed. John Wiley & Sons, 1993.

Kennedy, Larry W. *Quality Management in the Nonprofit World: Combining Compassion and Performance to Meet Client Needs and Improve Finances.* Jossey-Bass, 1991.

Krit, Robert L. *The Fund-Raising Handbook.* Scott Foresman, 1991.

Listro, John P. *Accounting & Reporting for Nonprofit Organizations.* Kendall/Hunt Publishing, 1992.

Nicholas, Ted. *The Complete Guide to Nonprofit Corporations.* Enterprise Dearborn, 1993.

Overton, G.W., ed. *Guidebook for Directors of Nonprofit Corporations.* American Bar Association, 1993.

Schoenhals, G. Roger. *On My Way in Planned Giving.* Planned Giving Today, 1995.

Warwick, Mal. "Outsider-In Marketing: A New Way to Look at Marketing for Nonprofits." *Nonprofit World.* September/October 1997.

NONPROFIT ORGANIZATIONS, AND HUMAN RESOURCES MANAGEMENT

Staffing decisions are among the most important decisions that nonprofit organizations make. Just as for-profit businesses of all different sizes and areas of operation rely on their personnel to execute their strategies and advance their goals, so too do nonprofit groups. It follows, then, that nonprofit organizations need to attend to the same tasks as profit-seeking companies do when they turn to the challenges of establishing and maintaining a solid work force. To accomplish this, nonprofit organizations have to address the following six personnel issues, as delineated in the Small Business Administration publication *Human Resources Management:*

- Assessing personnel needs
- Recruiting personnel
- Screening personnel
- Selecting and hiring personnel
- Orienting new employees to the organization
- Deciding compensation issues

"An effective non-profit manager *must* try to get more out of the people he or she has," wrote Peter F. Drucker in *Managing the Non-Profit Organization.* "The yield from the human resource really determines the organization's performance. And that's decided by the basic people decisions: whom we hire and whom we fire; where we place people, and whom we promote. The quality of these human decisions largely determines whether the organization is being run seriously, whether its mission, its values, and its objectives are real and meaningful to people rather than just public relations and rhetoric."

ASSESSING ORGANIZATION NEEDS

A key component of any endeavor to build a quality core of personnel is an honest assessment of current and future internal needs and external influences. Leaders and managers of nonprofit organizations should study workload history, trends in the larger philanthropic community, pertinent changes in the environment in which they operate (layoffs, plant closings, introduction of a new organization with a similar mission, legislative developments, etc.), personnel demands associated with current and planned initiatives, operating budget and costs, and the quality and quantity of the area worker pool, both for volunteer and staff positions. Moreover, all of these factors need to be studied within the framework of the organization's overarching mission statement. For as many nonprofit leaders have noted, adherence to other general business principles (sound fiscal management, retention of good employees through good compensation packages, etc.) is of little solace if the organization loses sight of its mission—its reason for being—in the process.

Writing in *Human Resources Management,* Gary Roberts, Carlotta Roberts, and Gary Seldon noted several fundamental business principles concerning assessment of personnel needs that apply to nonprofits as well. These principles include:

- Fill positions with people who are willing and able to take on the job.

- Providing accurate and realistic job and skill specifications for each position helps ensure that it is filled by someone capable of handling the responsibilities associated with that position.

- Written job descriptions are essential to communicating job expectations.

- Employees that are chosen because they are the best available candidate are far more likely to have a positive impact than those that are chosen on the basis of friendship or expediency.

- Performance appraisals, when coupled with specific job expectations, help boost performance.

"The process of selecting a competent person for each position is best accomplished through a systematic definition of the requirements for each job, including the skills, knowledge and other qualifications that employees must possess to perform each task," the authors concluded. "To guarantee that personnel needs are adequately specified, 1) conduct a job analysis, 2) develop a written job description, and 3) prepare a job specification."

RECRUITING, SCREENING, AND SELECTING ORGANIZATION WORK FORCE

RECRUITING For many nonprofit organizations, publicizing its very existence is the most important step that it can take in its efforts to recruit staff and volunteers alike. This is especially true of the latter element of the nonprofit organization work force. Volunteers are the life-blood of countless nonprofit organizations, for they attend to the basic tasks that need performing, from paperwork to transportation of goods and/or services to maintenance. Writing in *Quality Management in the Nonprofit World*, Larry W. Kennedy noted that "they supply valuable human resources which, when properly engaged, can be worth tens of thousands of dollars in conserved personnel costs to even the smallest organizations."

Nonprofit groups rely on two basic avenues to publicize their work and their staffing needs: local media (newspapers, newsletters, radio advertising, billboards, etc.) and other community organizations (municipal governments, churches, civic groups, other nonprofit organizations, etc.) Many nonprofit groups have found that contact with some community organizations, particularly churches and civic groups, can be particularly rewarding since these organizations already have members that may be predisposed toward lending a hand.

SCREENING AND SELECTION The interviewing process is another essential component of successful staffing for nonprofit groups. This holds true for volunteers as well as for officers, directors, and paid staff. Indeed, Larry W. Kennedy remarked in his book *Quality Management in the Nonprofit World* that "volunteers should be recruited and interviewed systematically the same way you would recruit paid staff. An orderly and professional approach to volunteer management will pay off handsomely for your organization. What you do in the recruitment phase of your work will set the standard for volunteer performance. If you are disciplined and well organized, you will often attract more qualified volunteers."

Managers of nonprofit organizations should make sure that they do the following when engaged in the process of staffing screening and selection:

- Recognize that *all* personnel, whether they are heading up your organization's annual fundraising drive or lending a hand for a few hours every other Saturday, have an impact on the group's performance. Certainly, some positions are more important than others, but countless nonprofit managers can attest that an underperforming, unethical, or unpleasant individual can have a disproportionate negative impact on organization morale and/or organization reputation in the community. This can be true of the occasional volunteer as well as the full-time staff member.

- Use an application form that covers all pertinent areas of the applicant's background.

- Ensure that your screening process provides information about an individual's skills, attitudes, and knowledge.

- Try to determine if the applicant or would-be volunteer is interested in the organization for legitimate reasons (professional development and/or advancement, genuine interest in your group's mission) or primarily for reasons that may not advance your organization's cause (loneliness, corporate burnout, etc.).

- Objectively evaluate prospective employees and volunteers based on criteria established in the organization's job specifications.

- Be realistic in putting together your volunteer work force. "Managers cause most of the problems with volunteers by making unreasonable assumptions about their intentions and capabilities," wrote Kennedy. An organization that sets the bar too high in its expectations of volunteers (in terms of services provided, hours volunteered, etc.) may find itself with a severe shortage of this potential valuable resource.

- Recognizing that would-be volunteers and employees bring both assets and negative attributes to your organization, nonprofit groups should be flexible in accommodating those strengths and weaknesses. "If you want people to perform in an organization, you have to use their strengths—not emphasize their weaknesses," said Drucker.

Organizations that pay attention to these guidelines will be far more likely to enjoy positive and lasting relationships with their volunteers and staff than those who fill their human resource needs in haphazard fashion. As Kennedy said, "the time to begin evaluating the probably reliability of human resources is prior to their insertion into your internal structure."

ORIENTING STAFF AND VOLUNTEERS TO THE ORGANIZATION

Training is a vital component of successful nonprofit organization management. But many nonprofit managers fail to recognize that training initiatives should be built for all members of the organization, not just those who are salaried employees. "Specialized training should be designed for every person in the organization, including board members and volunteers,'' contended Kennedy. ''The principles of quality management should be reinforced in each phase of training, with generous opportunities given to the trainees to talk about their questions and concerns. . . . If we select and train people with well-established and consistently implemented guidelines, we greatly increase the potential for team building. Beyond that, a common objective, a commitment to quality, a sincere concern for the team members, and a dedicated leader can cause wonderful things to happen. When those factors are not present, things can occur that are not so pleasant. . . . Volunteers who are shoddily intruded into an organization's processes or who are not well managed can create chaotic inconsistency in services. The additional, time, energy, and money needed to clean up well-intentioned but off-target volunteer efforts can quickly offset any gains provided by their services.''

POOR PERFORMERS Many nonprofit organizations find that at one point or another, they must address poor performance by a member of the organization. When that person is a paid member of the staff, dealing with the issue is in many respects no different than it would be in the for-profit world. Organizations of all types have a right to assume certain standards of performance from paid employees, and if that standard is not met, they should by all means take the steps necessary to ensure that they receive the necessary level of performance from that position, even if that means firing a poor worker.

The situation becomes more complex when the person is a volunteer, however. The volunteer worker is an essential element of many nonprofit organizations, and the primary characteristics of volunteerism—selfless service—make it difficult to remove poor performers. In addition, insensitive handling of one volunteer can have a negative impact on other volunteers upon which your organization relies. Nonetheless, Kennedy stated that ''volunteers should be held accountable just as though they were being paid top dollar to work. This does not mean that you can be careless about people's feelings. Even for-profit managers have learned that managing and supervising requires certain social graces and sensitivity to every individual. However, the reluctance of nonprofit managers to hold volunteers accountable to reasonable levels of performance or to terminate bad volunteer relationships can be their downfall.''

Drucker noted that most nonprofits will sooner or later have to deal with people ''who volunteer because they are profoundly lonely. When it works, these volunteers can do a great deal for the organization—and the organization, by giving them a community, gives even more back to them. But sometimes these people for psychological or emotional reasons simply

cannot work with other people; they are noisy, intrusive, abrasive, rude. Non-profit executives have to face up to that reality.'' If all else fails, such disruptive volunteers should be asked to leave. Otherwise, other members of the organization, including the executive, will find that their capacity to contribute is diminished.

Drucker agreed that dismissing an underperforming or otherwise undesirable volunteer can be a difficult task.''The non-profit executive is always inclined to be reluctant to let a non-producer go. You feel he or she is a comrade-in-arms and make all kinds of excuses,'' he granted. He contended that nonprofit managers should adhere to a basic guideline in such instances: ''If they try, they deserve another chance. If they don't try, make *sure* they leave. . . . An effective non-profit executive owes it to the organization to have a competent staff wherever performance is needed. To allow non-performers to stay on means letting down both the organization and the cause.''

COMPENSATING THE ORGANIZATION'S EMPLOYEES AND VOLUNTEERS

TANGIBLE BENEFITS As Ted Nicholas noted in *The Complete Guide to Nonprofit Corporations,* nonprofit corporations may establish fringe benefits programs for their employees. People that can be covered under these programs include not only staff personnel, but also directors and officers. ''The benefits,'' wrote Nicholas, ''can be as attractive as those provided by for-profit business corporations. In addition, the benefits can be far more economical for the corporation and beneficial to the employees than any program that could be offered by unincorporated organizations. The non profit corporation can establish an employee pension and retirement income plan. It can provide for sick pay and vacation pay. It may arrange for group life, accident and health insurance coverage for its officers and employees. It can elect to cover its employees' personal medical expenses that are not covered by the group insurance plans, provided that the corporation can pay all or part of the cost of the various employee benefits it sets up. It can require some contribution from the employees covered by the fringes.''

Bruce Hopkins observed in his *Legal Guide to Starting and Managing a Nonprofit Organization* that ''there is a tendency in our society to expect employees of nonprofit organizations to work for levels and types of compensation that are less than those paid to employees of for-profit organizations. Somehow, the nonprofit characteristics of the organization become transferred to the 'nonprofit' employee.'' Hopkins goes on to note that while this perception may indeed be a reality because of the budgetary constraints under which many nonprofit organizations operate, in other instances employees do not feel entitled to compensation levels that are offered to employees of for-profit businesses. In other cases, meanwhile, nonprofit groups feel no obligation to provide comparable levels of compensation in terms of salary, benefits, etc., relying instead on the altruistic leanings of some people. Organizations that operate under the assumption that their workers should accept compensation packages that are dramatically smaller than those offered by the corporate world simply because of the nature of their mission, however, run the risk of losing out on many talented people. Indeed, Hopkins pointed out that ''many nonprofit organizations, particularly the larger ones (universities, hospitals, major charities, and trade associations), require sophisticated and talented employees. Because these individuals are not likely to want to be 'nonprofit' employees, nonprofit and for-profit organizations compete for the same pool of talented persons. This competition extends not only to salaries but also to benefits and retirement programs.''

Experts indicate that although the compensation packages that are offered by nonprofit organizations are constrained by the so-called private inurement doctrine, which holds that the profits realized by a nonprofit organization can not be passed along to private individuals (as dividends are passed along to shareholders in a for-profit enterprise), they can still offer attractive compensation packages to employees provided that they are judged to be ''reasonable.'' When weighing whether it considers compensation to be reasonable, the Internal Revenue Service studies whether compensation arrangements exceed a certain percentage of the organization's gross revenues. Excessive compensation can be penalized by imposition of additional taxes and fines, but the most damage to organizations who do this can often be found in the realm of reputation; few allegations are more damaging to a nonprofit organization's community standing than the charge that it is bestowing excessive compensation (in the form of salary, country club memberships, etc.) to top executives or others.

INTANGIBLE BENEFITS Successful managers of nonprofit organizations recognize that the people who compose their organizations' work force— volunteers, employees, officers, and directors alike— are often participating in the group at least in part for altruistic reasons. Indeed, Drucker noted that ''although successful business executives have learned that workers are not entirely motivated by paychecks or promotions—they need more—the need is even greater in non-profit institutions. Even paid staff in these organizations need achievement, the satisfaction of service, or they become alienated and even hostile. After all, what's the point of working in a non-profit institution if one doesn't make a clear contribution?''

Leaders of nonprofit organizations, then, need to always be on the look out for ways in which they can show their paid staff, their volunteers, and their leadership how their involvement in the organization is making a difference, whether the group is involved with ministering to the economically disadvantaged or devoted to protecting a beloved natural resource. As Father Leo Bartel, Vicar for Social Ministry of the Catholic Diocese of Rockford, Illinois, told Drucker, ''We give [volunteers] opportunities to deepen in themselves and in each other the sense of how important the things are that they are doing.''

FURTHER READING:

Ayres-Williams, Roz. ''The Changing Face of Nonprofits.'' *Black Enterprise.* May 1998.

Drucker, Peter F. *Managing the Non-profit Organization: Principles and Practices.* HarperBusiness, 1990.

Hartsook, Robert F. ''Predictions for 1997.'' *Fund Raising Management.* January 1997.

Hopkins, Bruce R. *A Legal Guide to Starting and Managing a Nonprofit Organization.* 2d ed. John Wiley & Sons, 1993.

Kennedy, Larry W. *Quality Management in the Nonprofit World: Combining Compassion and Performance to Meet Client Needs and Improve Finances.* Jossey-Bass, 1991.

Nicholas, Ted. *The Complete Guide to Nonprofit Corporations.* Enterprise Dearborn, 1993.

Nichols, Judith E. ''Philanthropic Trends for the 1990s.'' *Fund Raising Management.* August 1990.

Roberts, Gary, Gary Seldon, and Carlotta Roberts. *Human Resources Management.* Small Business Administration, n.d.

NONPROFIT ORGANIZATIONS, AND TAXES

In recognition of the ''public good''-oriented goals and objectives of nonprofit organizations, U.S. law grants these groups a number of special privileges. Of these, perhaps none is more valuable than the bestowal of tax-exempt status. Such status basically means that the organization's income and assets are not subject to federal taxes, and federal exemptions often (though not always) pave the way for state and local tax exemptions as well. For-profit enterprises, on the other hand, are subject to local, state, and federal taxation.

Writing in his book *Quality Management in the Nonprofit World,* Larry W. Kennedy explained that ''the pursuit of profit for personal or individual gain is called private enterprise. Profits gained through private enterprise are taxable. Enterprise by tax-exempt organizations has as its goal for attaining profits the continued provision of services for the public good. Profits earned from public enterprise related to our tax-exempt mission are not taxable. Nonprofit organizations can engage in virtually any business enterprise in the fulfillment of their mission objectives and remain comfortably within the purposes of their tax-exempt status. Where the enterprise is *unrelated* to the stated mission, *only* that income that is generated by the unrelated enterprise is taxable. Gifts, contributions, and income generated by another enterprise related to the organization's mission statement would remain tax exempt." It should be noted, however, that complete exemption from federal taxation does not *automatically* mean that the organization avoids other kinds of taxation, such as state and/or local income taxes, sales taxes, and property taxes.

In addition, Bruce R. Hopkins noted in his *Legal Guide to Starting and Managing a Nonprofit Organization* that not all nonprofit organizations qualify as tax-exempt organizations: "Nearly every tax-exempt organization is a non-profit organization, but not all nonprofit organizations are eligible to be tax-exempt," he said. "The concept of a nonprofit organization is broader than that of a tax-exempt organization. Some types of non-profit organizations (such as mutual, self-help type entities) do not, as a matter of federal law, qualify for tax-exempt status." Ted Nicholas, author of *The Complete Guide to Nonprofit Corporations,* offered a similar assessment. He stated that "while the great bulk of nonprofit organizations are presumed to be tax-exempt in nature, there are exceptions to that premise." But he also went on to note that "the terms *nonprofit* and *charitable* are not interchangeable. A nonprofit organization is not necessarily charitably motivated, and, likewise, an organization that is truly charitable in nature may be a profit-making enterprise. And both kinds of organizations may be entitled to tax-exempt status from the IRS. For example, a religious and apostolic association or corporation, even if it is organized for profit, and a teacher's retirement fund association, which is operated to produce profits for its beneficiaries, are both eligible for tax exemptions."

DEVELOPMENT OF NONPROFIT TAX-EXEMPT STATUS

Until the end of the 19th century, all U.S. entities—whether they were private individuals or businesses—were exempt from taxation unless they were subject to a particular tax levy. The Tariff Act of 1894, however, changed that situation irrevocably. That legislation imposed a flat 2 percent tax rate on all U.S. corporations, but in recognition of the fundamentally different goals and objectives of for-profit businesses and charitable and educational groups, the bill exempted the latter organizations from the tax. "The important aspect of this legislation is that organizations involved in enterprise and whose profits would be used for altruistic purposes were specifically excluded from the requirement to share the profits of their work through taxation," wrote Kennedy. "The

initial emphasis of tax exemption was to protect the enterprises of nonprofit organizations from taxation, and it has remained as the central function of tax-exempt law to this day."

In recent years, the United States has seen a dramatic increase in the number of tax-exempt organizations operating around the country. Indeed, the rise in the number of churches, nursing homes, hospitals, chambers of commerce, charitable organizations, and social service agencies in many communities has led some observers to voice concern about the tax-base stability of some areas. "In some cities and towns, a substantial portion of the entire lot of privately held real estate is owned by tax-exempt organizations," wrote Nicholas. "This means there isn't any revenue flowing into local tax coffers from this sector." This state of affairs has led some corporate and individual taxpayers to register complaints about the "free ride" that some exempt organizations enjoy. "Even the tax-exempt status of churches, protected from the very beginning of the tax code, has been questioned in recent years, particularly in reference to church investments in secular properties," Nicholas said.

NONPROFITS AND PROFITABILITY

Many people operate under a fundamental misconception about nonprofit organizations and revenue. As Kennedy stated, "the word 'nonprofit' may carry with it an inference about profit that causes some people to think profitability by a nonprofit organization is illegal. To the contrary, we are free to do anything a for-profit company might do as we pursue our goals, *including making profits*. The law is designed to provide all the benefits of a free-market system plus the special favor of tax incentives for individuals and corporations who want to contribute financially to our efforts. Not only can we operate enterprises profitably as tax-exempt organizations but we can also prosper through the patronage of others."

But there are significant stipulations in place concerning the *distribution* of those profits that must be met for an organization to claim tax-exempt status. These are delineated in Section 501 of the Internal Revenue Code:

1) The organization must be organized and operated exclusively for one or more of the following purposes: for religious, educational, charitable, scientific, or literary purposes; to test for public safety; to encourage amateur sports competition (either national or international); to prevent cruelty to children or animals; to lessen the burdens of government (through creation and/or maintenance of public buildings, monuments, parks, natural attractions, etc.); and to maintain public confidence in the legal system.

Naturally, the organization may be involved in more than one of the above areas.

2) Net earnings garnered by the organization may not, under any circumstances, be distributed for the private benefit of individuals.

3) The organization may not participate in any way in any political campaigns, directly or indirectly (although it can use a political action committee or PAC to engage in political activities that are not political campaign activities).

4) The organization may not spend ''excessive'' time or energy on efforts to influence legislation. It is a common misconception that nonprofits may not engage in legislative activities, but as Hopkins stated, ''a charity is permitted to engage in far more lobbying efforts than most people realize. Indeed, under some circumstances, a charitable organization can spend more than one-fifth of its funds for legislative ends.''

FILING FOR TAX-EXEMPT STATUS

A wide variety of organizations are eligible for tax-exempt status because of their goals and activities. These include the following:

- Corporations organized under an Act of Congress (includes federal credit unions)
- Title-holding corporations for exempt organizations
- Religious organizations
- Educational organizations
- Charitable organizations
- Scientific organizations
- Literary organizations
- Public safety organizations
- Organizations devoted to national or international amateur sports competitions
- Organizations devoted to preventing cruelty to children
- Organizations devoted to preventing cruelty to animals
- Civic leagues
- Social welfare organizations
- Local associations
- Labor organizations
- Agricultural and horticultural organizations

- Business leagues, chambers of commerce, and real estate boards
- Social and recreational clubs
- Fraternal beneficiary societies and associations
- Voluntary employees' beneficiary associations
- Domestic fraternal societies and associations
- Teachers' retirement fund associations
- Benevolent life insurance associations
- Mutual irrigation or ditch companies
- Mutual or cooperative telephone companies
- Cemetery companies
- State-chartered credit unions and mutual reserve funds
- Mutual insurance companies or associations
- Cooperative agricultural organizations
- Supplemental unemployment benefit trusts
- Employee funded pension trusts (provided they were created prior to June 25, 1959)
- Organizations of past or present Armed Forces members
- Group legal services organizations
- Black lung benefit trusts
- Withdrawal liability payment funds
- Veteran's organizations (provided they were created prior to 1880)
- Religious and apostolic associations
- Cooperative hospital service organizations
- Cooperating service groups of operating educational organizations
- Farmer's cooperatives
- Political organizations (parties, committees, etc.)
- Homeowners' associations

Nicholas pointed out that ''some organizations such as churches, associations of churches, and auxiliary agencies of churches—mission societies and youth groups, for instance—are generally considered automatically tax-exempt. They are not required to request this status from the government taxing agencies. However, virtually all other kinds of organizations that fit legal definitions of eligibility for tax-exempt status due to their special benevolent purposes and goals cannot assume that status. They must ask the Internal Revenue Service to officially recognize their tax-exempt status.''

To do so, organizations have to file an application for tax exemption with the IRS (nonprofit organizations may also have to make separate applications to state and local tax agencies if they wish to secure exemptions from taxes imposed by those jurisdictions). In most instances, this filing step is a mere formality; approval of tax exemption is almost always based on the IRS's ruling on the organization's exemption application (the primary legal basis for all tax exemptions is Section 501 of the Internal Revenue Code of 1954). Organizations which have their exemption application approved, then, will often find that they are free from tax obligations at the local and state levels as well.

Experts note that while some nonprofit organizations are exempted from paying certain taxes, that does not mean that they have no filing obligations. "Despite the favoritisms the law frequently bestows on nonprofit organizations, the reporting requirements are not one of them, particularly when the organization is tax-exempt," said Hopkins. "The annual information return that most tax-exempt organizations have to file with the IRS is far more extensive than the tax returns most commercial businesses must file. Then, there may be several state annual reports (if the organization is doing business in more than one state) and the state annual charitable solicitation act reports (perhaps over 40 of them)." Given this reality, most nonprofit organizations choose to use the services of professional attorneys and accountants in compiling and delivering these reports.

UNRELATED BUSINESS INCOME

United States law has long differentiated between the activities of tax-exempt organizations that are related to the performance of tax-exempt functions and those that are not. Income garnered from these latter activities is subject to taxation. For incorporated organizations, net revenue from unrelated activities is subject to federal corporate income tax law, while for organizations that are not incorporated, this revenue—commonly referred to as "unrelated business income"—is subject to the canon of federal tax law on individuals. "The objective of the unrelated business income tax is to prevent unfair competition between tax-exempt organizations and for-profit, commercial enterprises," explained Hopkins. "The rules are intended to place the unrelated business activities of an exempt organization on the same tax basis as those of a nonexempt business with which it competes. . . . An organization's tax exemption will be denied or revoked if an inappropriate portion of its activities is not promoting one or more of its exempt purposes."

This area of tax law, noted Hopkins, has been one marked by upheaval and change in recent years. "As tax-exempt organizations struggle to generate additional income in these days of declining governmental support, proposed adverse tax reform, more sophisticated management, and greater pressure for more services, [tax-exempt organizations] are increasingly drawn to service-provider activities, some of which may be unrelated to their exempt purposes. The growth of service-provider activities, the increasing tendencies of the courts to find activities unrelated because they are 'commercial,' and the unrest over 'unfair competition' between tax-exempt organizations and for-profit entities—all of these are clear evidence that this aspect of the law of tax-exempt organizations is constantly evolving and will be reshaped." One emerging issue involves use of the Internet by nonprofit organizations. Some experts have expressed concern that linking to non-exempt sites, soliciting contributions online, or disseminating protected information could put an entity's exempt status at risk.

FURTHER READING:

Anderson, Alice M., and Robert A. Wexler. "Making Use of the Internet—Issues for Tax-Exempt Organizations." *Journal of Taxation.* May 2000.

Hopkins, Bruce R. *The Law of Tax-Exempt Organizations.* New York: John Wiley & Sons.

Hopkins, Bruce R. *A Legal Guide to Starting and Managing a Nonprofit Organization.* 2d ed. New York: John Wiley & Sons, 1993.

Jacobs, Jerald A., and Karen L. Cipriani. "Establishing an Affiliated Organization." *Association Management.* June 2000.

Kennedy, Larry W. *Quality Management in the Nonprofit World: Combining Compassion and Performance to Meet Client Needs and Improve Finances.* San Francisco: Jossey-Bass, 1991.

Moses, Nancy. "The Nonprofit Motive." *Wall Street Journal.* March 17, 1997.

Nicholas, Ted. *The Complete Guide to Nonprofit Corporations.* Enterprise Dearborn, 1993.

Schlesinger, Sanford J. "Unrelated Business Income and the Charitable Organization." *Estate Planning.* May 2000.

Wright, Carolyn D. "IRS Request for Comments on EO Web Activity: Good Start." *Tax Notes.* October 23, 2000.

NONQUALIFIED DEFERRED COMPENSATION PLANS

Nonqualified deferred compensation plans are used by businesses to supplement existing qualified plans. As Lawrence Bader and Yale Tauber noted in *Compensation & Benefits Management,* deferred compensation arrangements are proliferating in today's business and regulatory environment, and they are extending deeper into organizations. Small business owners, in particular, have made greater use of these deferred compensation plans in recent years, utilizing them to reward top executives and directors and woo top outside personnel. Another factor contributing to firms' efforts to defer compensation when possible, added Bader and Tauber, is the current limitations on deductible current compensation.

Companies have recognized other pluses associated with nonqualified deferred compensation plans as well. ''One big advantage to [nonqualified] deferred compensation plans is that they escape the non-discrimination rules imposed on qualified plans,'' explained John B. Connor Jr. in *Small Business Reports.* ''That means [small business owners] can offer the plan to a select group of employees, making it a more cost-effective benefit than a qualified plan. Administrative costs are lower as well because the plans are exempt from the U.S. Department of Labor's reporting requirements. All that's required is a one-time letter to the DOL stating that your plan is in place and has a given number of participants. In addition, small companies are discovering that deferred compensation plans can help them court executives from larger firms. In essence, your company can level the recruitment playing field by tailoring a benefits package comparable to that of big companies.''

There are two main types of nonqualified deferred compensation plans from which small business owners may choose: supplemental executive retirement plans (SERPs) and deferred savings plans. These two options share several common characteristics, but there are also important differences between the two. For example, eligibility for both plans may be based on the executive's salary, position, or both. But whereas deferred savings plans require employees to contribute their own earnings, executives that are placed in SERPs receive their compensation from their employers.

SUPPLEMENTAL EXECUTIVE RETIREMENT PLANS (SERPS)

''Executives consider SERPs to be an especially attractive plan because the company foots the bill for the benefits,'' wrote Connor. ''SERPs generally are structured to mirror defined-benefit pension plans that promise a stated benefit from the employer at retirement.'' SERP benefits, which can be allocated in conjunction with other benefit plans like qualified-plan savings and Social Security benefits, may be calculated in any number of ways. Employers may choose to pay their executives a flat dollar amount for an agreed-upon number of years; a percentage of their salary at retirement multiplied by their years with the company; or a fixed percentage of their salary at retirement for a given number of years. Companies also have the option of funding SERPs either through general assets (at the time of the employee's retire-

ment) or via sinking funds or corporate-owned life insurance (COLI).

SINKING FUNDS Businesses that utilize the sinking fund method allocate money on an annual basis to a fund that will cover benefit payments as they come due. This money can be invested by the company as it sees fit, but it is nonetheless earmarked for retirement payments.

CORPORATE-OWNED LIFE INSURANCE (COLI) Under the COLI funding method, businesses buy life insurance plans on those directors and executives that they wish to compensate. Each company pays the premiums on the purchased policies, and as each executive retires, the firm pays out his or her benefits from operating assets for a previously established period of time. The key benefit for the small business owner under the COLI arrangement is that his or her business would be ''designated the sole beneficiary of the insurance policy proceeds, which it would receive tax-free,'' explained Connor. ''At the executive's death, then, your company is reimbursed for some or all of the costs of the plan, including the actual benefits paid, the insurance premiums, and the loss of the use of your company's money for other purposes.'' Entrepreneurs should note, however, that their firm will not receive a tax deduction for its contributions to a SERP until the director or executive actually receives the benefit payments (businesses using qualified compensation plans, on the other hand, receive deductions in the current year).

DEFERRED SAVINGS PLANS

Deferred savings plans are similar to 401(k) plans in that affected employees are allowed to set aside a portion of their salary (usually up to 25 percent) and bonuses (as much as 100 percent) to put into the plan. This money is directly deducted from employee paychecks, and taxes are not levied on the money until the employee receives it. ''Over the years, the executive contributions accumulate earnings in one of two ways,'' stated Connor. ''Most commonly, the company simply guarantees a fixed rate of return on the deferrals, which would come from its general operating assets at the time of payout. A second option, which is becoming more popular, is to tie each executive's savings to the performance of a particular mutual fund; he or she would select the fund from among several offered by your plan.'' For those companies that set up a fixed rate of return on the deferrals, they may invest the monies in question however they wish, provided they ultimately meet their payout obligations. In addition, consultants note that some small businesses (and large ones as well) have established a policy wherein they will offer matching funds on employee deferrals or add profit-sharing or incentive-based contributions.

Experts point out that executives with deferred savings plans have a variety of payout options to choose from. They may choose to set up regular post-retirement payouts for five to ten years after retirement, but they also have the option of arranging for short-term deferrals to help them pay for a new house, college education for children, and other expenses. If an executive enrolled in this type of plan dies or is fired from the company prior to retirement, he or she (or their family) receives a lump-sum payout of their benefits. It should be noted, however, that nonqualified deferred compensation plans will not be protected from creditors if the company that created them files for bankruptcy.

PLANS FOR TAX-EXEMPT ORGANIZATIONS

Nonqualified deferred compensation plans may also be utilized by tax-exempt organizations, but managers of these entities should be aware that for tax-exempt organizations, such plans are subject to considerably more stringent Internal Revenue Service (IRS) regulations. Still, Janet Den Uyl stated in *Healthcare Financial Management* that "alternatives are available to tax-exempt organizations seeking to set up such plans. By subjecting employer-paid, tax-deferred compensation to risk of forfeiture or by paying the required taxes, tax-exempt organizations can develop workable alternatives for funding nonqualified deferred compensation plans."

FUNDING OPTIONS Tax-exempt organizations seeking to fund employer-paid deferred compensation plans can choose from a number of options:

1) Unfunded benefits that vest at retirement. Under this strategy, employers provide supplemental retirement benefit plans with assets that are not dedicated to funding the plan. If the employer runs into financial trouble before the employee or employees covered under the plan retire, it can use those assets to pay off its creditors.

2) Unfunded benefits that vest during employment. Den Uyl noted that with this plan, "Vesting occurs according to plan objectives as defined by the employer and, as vesting occurs, the employer provides a cash distribution to cover taxes. The ultimate benefit at retirement is reduced to reflect the annual distribution of a portion of the benefit to pay taxes."

3) Benefits funded with deferred annuities. Under this arrangement, the small business owner would acquire deferred annuities in the name of participating employees. Den Uyl pointed out that the employer that takes this tack usually provides cash distributions to cover the tax on both the contribution and the cash distribution, since contributions to the annuity are regarded by the IRS as taxable income.

Similarly, organizations looking to fund voluntary nonqualified deferred compensation plans may pursue the following funding alternatives:

1) Traditional deferred compensation plans with non-compete clauses. These do not pay out money until the end of a specified period of time. If an employee who is part of the plan leaves the company to join a competing business before that specified period of time elapses, then the employee forfeits the contributions. Analysts note, however, that this choice is often not a palatable one for employers, since employees will likely resent efforts to impose such restrictions.

2) Deferred annuities. Under this alternative, employees purchase deferred annuities with after-tax income, and they do not owe taxes on annuity earnings until payout.

3) Deferral using after-tax dollars. Under this plan, employees are immediately vested and taxed on the deferred compensation. After-tax compensation is subsequently placed in a mutual fund by the employer, but it is maintained for the benefit of the employee.

FURTHER READING:

Aisenbrey, Beverly W., and Michael A. Thompson. "Setting the Terms of the Deal: Restructuring Compensation Plans for Initial Public Offerings and Spinoffs." *Compensation and Benefits Review.* September-October 1996.

Bader, Lawrence, and Yale Tauber. "The High Cost (Sometimes) of Deferred Compensation." *Compensation & Benefits Management.* Summer 1997.

Brunetti, Frank L. "Small Business Tax Solutions." *Journal of Accountancy.* June 1995.

Connor, John B., Jr. "Pay Me Later." *Small Business Reports.* July 1994.

Den Uyl, Janet. "Options for Nonqualified Deferred Compensation Plans." *Healthcare Financial Management.* September 1996.

"The 401(k) Paper Chase." *Business Week.* March 27, 2000.

Galloway, Wesley. "Examining Reporting Standards Criteria: Many Deferred Compensation Plans Will Not Need to Be Reported." *American City & County.* February 1998.

Hall, Steven E., and Claude E. Johnston. "Designing State-of-the-Art Deferred Compensation Plans." *Compensation & Benefits Management.* Spring 1996.

"IRS Issues Long-Awaited Deferred Compensation Employment Tax Rules." *Tax Management Compensation Planning Journal.* March 1, 1996.

Jenks, James M., and Brian L.P. Zevnik. *Employee Benefits Plain and Simple.* Collier Books, 1993.

Madsen, Dawilla, and Domick Pizzano. ''The 401(k) Gamble.'' *Strategic Finance.* December 1999.

Morse, Charles T., William E. Hall Jr., and Brian J. Lake. ''More than Golden Handcuffs.'' *Journal of Accountancy.* November 1997.

Van Dyke, George. ''Examining Your 401 K.'' *Business Credit.* January 2000.

NONTRADITIONAL FINANCING SOURCES

Entrepreneurs can turn to a variety of sources to finance the establishment or expansion of their businesses. Common sources of business capital include personal savings, loans from friends and relatives, loans from financial institutions such as banks or credit unions, loans from commercial finance companies, assistance from venture capital firms or investment clubs, loans from the Small Business Administration and other government agencies, and personal or corporate credit cards. But for some businesspeople, these sources of financing are either unavailable, or available with restrictions or provisions that are either impossible for the company to meet or deemed excessive by the business owner. In such instances, the capital-hungry entrepreneur has the option of pursuing a number of nontraditional financing sources to secure the money that his or her company needs. Some of the more common nontraditional financing sources include selling assets, borrowing against the cash value of a life insurance policy, and taking out a second mortgage on a home or other property.

SELLING ASSETS Some entrepreneurs choose to sell some of their personal or business assets in order to finance the opening or continued existence of their enterprise. Generally, business owners who have already established the viability of their firm and are looking to expand their operations do not have to take this sometimes dramatic course of action, since their record will often allow them to secure capital from another source, either private or public. Whether selling personal or business assets, the small business owner should take a rational approach. Some entrepreneurs, desperate to secure money, end up selling business assets that are important to basic business operations. In such instances, the entrepreneur may end up accelerating rather than halting the demise of his or her business. Only nonessential equipment and inventory should be sold. Similarly, care should be taken in the selling of personal assets. Items like boats, antiques, etc. can fetch a decent price. But before embarking on this course of action, the entrepreneur should objectively study whether the resulting income will be sufficient, or whether the enterprise's financial straits are an indication of fundamental flaws.

BORROWING AGAINST THE CASH VALUE OF YOUR LIFE INSURANCE Entrepreneurs who have a whole life policy have the option of borrowing against the policy (this is not an option for holders of term insurance). This can be an effective means of securing capital provided that the owner has held the policy for several years, thus giving it some cash value. Insurers may let policyholders borrow as much as 90 percent of the value of the policy. As long as the policyholder continues to meet his or her premium payment obligations, the policy will remain intact. Interest rates on such loans are generally not outrageous, but if the policyholder dies during the period in which he or she has a loan on the policy, benefits are usually dramatically reduced.

SECOND MORTGAGE Some entrepreneurs secure financing by taking our a second mortgage on their home. This risky alternative does provide the homeowner with a couple of advantages: interest on the mortgage is tax deductible and is usually lower than what he or she would pay with a credit card or an unsecured loan. But if the business ultimately fails, this method of financing could result in the loss of your home. ''Second mortgages are best for people who want to borrow all the money they need at one time and secure fixed, equal payments,'' wrote Cynthia Griffin in *Entrepreneur.*

OTHER POSSIBLE SOURCES OF FINANCING Some entrepreneurs obtain financing for growth and expansion through franchising or licensing. Basically, they get money by selling the rights to a unique business or product to other companies. Other small business owners are able to form alliances or partnerships with other firms that have a vested interest in their success, such as customers, suppliers, or distributors. These business owners may obtain funds from their partners through cooperative work agreements, barter arrangements, or trade credit. The Internet provides another potential source of leads for loans from nontraditional sources. For example, America's Business Funding Directory, at http://www.businessfinance.com, includes a searchable database of nontraditional funding sources.

Experts recommend using nontraditional financing to start a business or provide funds during periods of rapid growth, but emphasize that small business owners should consider it a temporary arrangement. ''You should look at nontraditional financing,'' business loan broker Edward C. Hopson said in the *Knight-Ridder/Tribune Business News,* ''but look at it with an eye to when can I get out of this, not as permanent financing. . . . When you get strong, the banks will be calling you.''

FURTHER READING:

Andresky Fraser, Jill. "Show Me the Money: You Can Look for Money in All the Wrong Places." *Inc.* March 1997.

"Creative Financing." *Phoenix Business Journal.* September 29, 2000.

Entrepreneur Magazine Guide to Raising Money. John Wiley & Sons, 1998.

Financing for the Small Business. Small Business Administration, 1990.

Griffin, Cynthia. "Breaking the Bank." *Entrepreneur.* March 1998.

"Passing the Buck." *Entrepreneur.* May 1997.

Stolze, William J. *Start Up Financing: An Entrepreneur's Guide to Financing New or Growing Business.* Career Press, 1997.

Vanac, Mary. "Alternative *Financing Helps Small Businesses Bridge the Lending Gap.*" *Knight-Ridder/Tribune* Business News. August 15, 1999.

NONVERBAL COMMUNICATION

Nonverbal communication—such as facial expressions, gestures, posture, and tone of voice—is an important component of personal business interactions. Nonverbal communication can help a small business owner to get a message across, or to successfully interpret a message received from another person. On the other hand, nonverbal communication can also send signals that interfere with the effective presentation or reception of messages. "Sometimes nonverbal messages contradict the verbal; often they express true feelings more accurately than the spoken or written language," Herta A. Murphy and Herbert W. Hildebrandt noted in their book *Effective Business Communications.* In fact, studies have shown that between 60 and 90 percent of a message's effect may come from nonverbal clues. Therefore, it is important for small business owners and managers to be aware of the nonverbal messages they send and to develop the skill of reading the nonverbal messages contained in the behavior of others. There are three main elements of nonverbal communication: appearance, body language, and sounds.

APPEARANCE In oral forms of communication, the appearance of both the speaker and the surroundings are vital to the successful conveyance of a message. "Whether you are speaking to one person face to face or to a group in a meeting, personal appearance and the appearance of the surroundings convey nonverbal stimuli that affect attitudes—even emotions—toward the spoken words," according to Murphy and Hildebrandt. For example, a speaker's clothing, hairstyle, use of cosmetics, neatness, and stature may cause a listener to form impressions about her occupation, socioeconomic level, competence, etc. Similarly, such details of the surroundings as room size, furnishings, decorations, lighting, and windows can affect a listener's attitudes toward the speaker and the message being presented. The importance of nonverbal clues in surroundings can be seen in the desire of business managers to have a corner office with a view rather than a cubicle in a crowded work area.

BODY LANGUAGE Body language, and particularly facial expressions, can provide important information that may not be contained in the verbal portion of the communication. Facial expressions are especially helpful as they may show hidden emotions that contradict verbal statements. For example, an employee may deny having knowledge of a problem, but also have a fearful expression and glance around guiltily. Other forms of body language that may provide communication clues include posture and gestures. For example, a manager who puts his feet up on the desk may convey an impression of status and confidence, while an employee who leans forward to listen may convey interest. Gestures can add emphasis and improve understanding when used sparingly, but the continual use of gestures can distract listeners and convey nervousness.

SOUNDS Finally, the tone, rate, and volume of a speaker's voice can convey different meanings, as can sounds like laughing, throat clearing, or humming. It is also important to note that perfume or other odors contribute to a listener's impressions, as does physical contact between the speaker and the listener. Silence, or the lack of sound, is a form of nonverbal communication as well. Silence can communicate a lack of understanding or even hard feelings in a face-to-face discussion.

FURTHER READING:

Golen, Steven. *Effective Business Communication.* U.S. Small Business Administration, 1989.

Murphy, Herta A., and Herbert W. Hildebrandt. *Effective Business Communications.* 6th ed. McGraw-Hill, 1991.

"The Silent Factor." *Denver Business Journal.* August 18, 2000.

Strugatch, Warren. "More Than Words Can Say." *LI Business News.* May 26, 2000.

NORTH AMERICAN FREE TRADE AGREEMENT (NAFTA)

The North American Free Trade Agreement (NAFTA) is a treaty that was signed on August 12, 1991 by the United States, Canada, and Mexico; it went into effect on January 1, 1994. (Free trade had existed between the U.S. and Canada since 1989;

NAFTA broadened that arrangement.) On that day, the three countries became the largest free market in the world—the economies of the three nations at that time was more than $6 trillion and directly affected more than 365 million people. NAFTA was created to eliminate tariff barriers to agricultural, manufacturing, and services trade, remove investment restrictions, and protect intellectual property rights, all while addressing environmental and labor concerns (although many observers charge that the three governments have been lax in ensuring environmental and labor safeguards since the agreement went into effect). Small businesses were among those that were expected to benefit the most from the lowering of trade barriers since it would make doing business in Mexico and Canada less expensive and would reduce the red tape needed to import or export goods.

Highlights of NAFTA included:

- Tariff elimination for qualifying products. Before NAFTA, tariffs of 30 percent or higher on export goods to Mexico were common, as were long delays caused by paperwork. Additionally, Mexican tariffs on U.S.-made products were, on average, 250 percent higher than U.S. duties on Mexican products. NAFTA addressed this imbalance by phasing out tariffs over 15 years. Approximately 50 percent of the tariffs were abolished immediately when the agreement took affect, and the remaining tariffs were targeted for gradual elimination. Among the areas specifically covered by NAFTA are construction, engineering, accounting, advertising, consulting/management, architecture, health-care management, commercial education, and tourism.

- Elimination of nontariff barriers by 2008. This includes opening the border and interior of Mexico to U.S. truckers and streamlining border processing and licensing requirements. Nontariff barriers were the biggest obstacle to conducting business in Mexico that small exporters faced.

- Establishment of standards. The three NAFTA countries agreed to toughen health, safety, and industrial standards to the highest existing standards among the three countries (which were always U.S. or Canadian). Also, national standards could no longer be used as a barrier to free trade. The speed of export-product inspections and certifications was also improved.

- Supplemental agreements. To ease concerns that Mexico's low wage scale would cause U.S. companies to shift production to that country, and to ensure that Mexico's in-creasing industrialization would not lead to rampant pollution, special side agreements were included in NAFTA. Under those agreements, the three countries agreed to establish commissions to handle labor and environmental issues. The commissions have the power to impose steep fines against any of the three governments that failed to impose its laws consistently. Environmental and labor groups from both the United States and Canada, however, have repeatedly charged that the regulations and guidelines detailed in these supplemental agreements have not been enforced.

- Tariff reduction for motor vehicles and auto parts and automobile rules of origin.

- Expanded telecommunications trade.

- Reduced textile and apparel barriers.

- More free trade in agriculture. Mexican import licenses were immediately abolished, with most additional tariffs phased out over a 10-year period.

- Expanded trade in financial services.

- Opening of insurance markets.

- Increased investment opportunities.

- Liberalized regulation of land transportation.

- Increased protection of intellectual property rights. NAFTA stipulated that, for the first time, Mexico had to provide a very high level of protection for intellectual property rights. This is especially helpful in fields such as computer software and chemical production. Mexican firms will no longer be able to steal intellectual property from companies and create a ''Mexican'' version of a product.

- Expanded the rights of American firms to make bids on Mexican and Canadian government procurement contracts.

One of the key provisions of NAFTA provided ''national goods'' status to products imported from other NAFTA countries. No state, provincial, or local governments could impose taxes or tariffs on those goods. In addition, customs duties were either eliminated at the time of the agreement or scheduled to be phased out in five or 10 equal stages. The one exception to the phase out was specified sensitive items, for which the phase-out period would be 15 years.

Supporters championed NAFTA because it opened up Mexican markets to U.S. companies like never before. The Mexican market is growing rapidly, which promises more export opportunities, which in turn means more jobs. Supporters, though, had a difficult time convincing the American public that NAFTA would do more good than harm. Their main effort centered on convincing people that all consumers benefit from the widest possible choice of products at the lowest possible price—which means that consumers would be the biggest beneficiaries of lowered trade barriers. The U.S. Chamber of Commerce, which represents the interests of small businesses, was one of the most active supporters of NAFTA, organizing the owners and employees of small and mid-size businesses to support the agreement. This support was key in countering the efforts of organized labor to stop the agreement.

NAFTA AND SMALL BUSINESS

Analysts agree that NAFTA has opened up new opportunities for small and mid-size businesses. Mexican consumers spend more each year on U.S. products than their counterparts in Japan and Europe, so the stakes for business owners are high. (Most of the studies of NAFTA concentrate on the effects of U.S. business with Mexico. Trade with Canada has also been enhanced, but the passage of the trade agreement did not have as great an impact on the already liberal trade practices that America and its northern neighbor abided by.)

Some small businesses were affected directly by NAFTA. In the past, larger firms always had an advantage over small ones because the large companies could afford to build and maintain offices and/or manufacturing plants in Mexico, thereby avoiding many of the old trade restrictions on exports. In addition, pre-NAFTA laws stipulated that U.S. service providers that wanted to do business in Mexico had to establish a physical presence there, which was simply too expensive for small firms to do. Small firms were stuck—they could not afford to build, nor could they afford the export tariffs. NAFTA leveled the playing field by letting small firms export to Mexico at the same cost as the large firms and by eliminating the requirement that a business establish a physical presence in Mexico in order to do business there. The lifting of these restrictions meant that vast new markets were suddenly open to small businesses that had previously done business only in the United States. This was regarded as especially important for small businesses that produced goods or services that had matured in U.S. markets.

Still, small firms interested in conducting business in Mexico have to recognize that Mexican business regulations, hiring practices, employee benefit requirements, taxation schedules, and accounting principles all include features that are unique to that country. Small businesses, then, should familiarize themselves with Mexico's foundation of business rules and traditions—not to mention the demographics culture of the marketplace—before committing resources to this region.

OPPOSITION TO NAFTA

Much organized opposition to NAFTA centered on the fear that the abolishment of trade barriers would spur U.S. firms to pack up and move to Mexico to take advantage of cheap labor. This concern remains strong among labor unions and other worker organizations. Opposition to NAFTA was also strong among environmental groups, who contended that the treaty's anti-pollution elements were woefully inadequate. This criticism has not abated since NAFTA's implementation. Indeed, both Mexico and Canada have been repeatedly cited for environmental malfeasance.

Controversy over the treaty's environmental enforcement provisions remained strong in the late 1990s. In fact, North American business interests have sought to weaken a key NAFTA side accord on environmental protections and enforcement. This accord—one of the few provisions welcomed by environmental groups—allows groups and ordinary citizens to accuse member nations of failing to enforce their own environmental laws. A trinational Commission for Environmental Cooperation is charged with investigating these allegations and issuing public reports. "That process is slow, but the embarassment factor has proven surprisingly high," noted *Business Week*. As of mid-2000, the U.S. government has expressed opposition to revisions in the NAFTA agreement. But the Canadian government and many businesses in all three countries continue to work to change this accord.

THE EFFECTS OF NAFTA

Since NAFTA's passage, American business interests have expressed general satisfaction with the agreement. Employment, productivity, and trade have all surged in the 1990s, although analysts point out that these increases can be attributed to myriad factors, of which NAFTA is only one. Moreover, job losses in the U.S. that can be attributed to NAFTA have been minimal. As of 1997, only 117,000 Americans had signed up for the benefits offered to workers displaced by NAFTA.

Change has been most dramatic in Mexico. U.S. firms are setting up joint ventures in Mexico that, for the first time, use local firms for materials and parts. The quality of goods produced in Mexico has gone up, and the biggest beneficiaries are Mexican consumers. Wages and working conditions have also improved in many areas.

FURTHER READING:

Allen, Mike. "NAFTA Is a Good Treaty, But Could Be Better." *San Diego Business Journal.* July 21, 1997.

Edmond Jr., Alfred. "Making the Most of NAFTA: Here's What to Do when the Barriers to Mexico's Markets Come Down." *Black Enterprise.* February 1994.

"A Green Thumb in NAFTA's Eye?" *Business Week.* June 12, 2000.

Holzinger, Albert G. "Why Small Firms Back NAFTA." *Nation's Business.* November 1993.

Krueger, Anne O. "NAFTA's Effects: A Preliminary Assessment." *World Economy.* June 2000.

Ostroff, Jim. "Report: NAFTA Helped Both U.S. and Mexico." *WWD.* July 14, 1997.

"Taking the Green Out of NAFTA." *Business Week.* May 29, 2000.

"What NAFTA Means to Small Businesses: Mexico Is an Important Market for Small and Medium Sized U.S. Businesses." *Arkansas Business.* November 15, 1993.

"When Neighbours Embrace: the NAFTA Effect." *The Economist.* July 5, 1997.

NORTH AMERICAN INDUSTRY CLASSIFICATION SYSTEM (NAICS)

The North American Industry Classification System (NAICS) is a detailed industry coding system designed to facilitate the collection, analysis, and presentation of economic statistical data in the United States, Canada, and Mexico, which comprise the member nations of the North American Free Trade Agreement (NAFTA). First implemented in 1997, the NAICS is the successor to the Standard Industrial Classification (SIC) system, which had been used by U.S. agencies to compile and track national business data for more than six decades.

The U.S. Census Bureau touts the NAICS as "a unique, all-new system for classifying business establishments. It is the first economic classification system to be constructed based on a single economic concept. Economic units that use like processes to produce goods or services are grouped together. This 'production-oriented' system means that statistical agencies in the United States will produce data that can be used for measuring productivity, unit labor costs, and the capital intensity of production; constructing input-output relationships; and estimating employment-output relationships and other such statistics that require that inputs and outputs be used together. . . . NAICS is forward looking and flexible, anticipating increasing globalization and providing enhanced industry comparability among the NAFTA trading partners while recognizing important national industries and providing for periodic updates through three country review [the United States, Canada, and Mexico]. NAICS recognizes the structural and technological changes occurring in the economies of the three North American countries and provides the means to measure these changes well into the next millennium."

THE SIC SYSTEM

NAICS's predecessor—the Standard Industrial Classification system—was the first comprehensive classification system used by American government agencies to formulate economic statistics.

This information, available for study and use by both public and private entities, was arranged in a set of hierarchical numeric codes that sought to identify every single industry in the United States. The result was an establishment-based industry classification system that classified each establishment (defined as a single physical location at which economic activity occurs) according to its primary activity. For each of these recognized industries, the government kept detailed statistics in such areas as employment, payroll, receipts, profits, and capital investment.

After its unveiling in 1937, the SIC system's universe of economic data became a heavily utilized tool for conducting business research and tracking economic trends. Government agencies, nongovernmental organizations, and private businesses alike made extensive use of the data. But despite periodic updates and revisions to the SIC classification system, its inadequacies became more glaring with the passage of time.

The fundamental problem was that the SIC system was based on concepts developed in an era of American history—the 1930s and 1940s—when manufacturing was the dominant economic engine. Many service activities were not separately identified, and as service-oriented businesses became more important, SIC revisions did not keep pace. The economic statistics contained in the SIC system thus became progressively more obsolete and/or incomplete in some significant areas. This under representation of important economic sectors was further exacerbated by the SIC's framework, which lumped unrelated industries together into similar categories.

Despite its imperfections, however, the Standard Industrial Classification system continued to be widely used by business marketers through the 1980s. The SIC data did provide them with a method for classifying organizational customers and gauging industry trends (especially in manufacturing sectors), and it remained the only source of these important economic statistics. In addition, the 1987 revision added approximately 20 new service industries and tweaked several manufacturing industry classifications to reflect changing technological realities. Ultimately, however, the SIC system remained an outmoded one. For example, of the 1004 industries recognized in the 1987 Standard Industrial Classification program, nearly half (459) represented manufacturing, even though manufacturing's share of the U.S. Gross Domestic Product (GDP) has shrunk to less than 20 percent of the nation's total. "The SIC did a superb job of describing and detailing the structure of the footwear industry in the United States, but failed to recognize and account for the information age in which we live and work," summarized Carole Ambler in *Business America*. "The SIC scattered the production of high-tech products such as computers, semiconductors, and communications equipment in groupings of industrial machinery and electrical equipment, and included the reproduction of shrink-wrapped software in the same industry with software publishing."

The various inadequacies of the SIC system finally prompted America's public and private sectors to unite and call for a new industry classification system that would be based on the reality of today's service-based, Internet-driven, technology-powered global economy. The ultimate shape and character of this new system was dramatically influenced by the implementation of the North American Free Trade Agreement between the United States, Canada, and Mexico in 1994. This major trade treaty highlighted the need to develop a new industry classification system that would take into consideration the increased flow of goods, services, and capital between the three North American nations. Moreover, it emphasized the need for a system that could provide users with country-to-country comparability of statistical information.

CREATION OF THE NAICS

The North American Industrial Classification System was a cooperative effort that required the active involvement of U.S., Canadian, and Mexican government agencies. The primary U.S. body involved in NAICS creation and implementation was the Economic Classification Policy Committee (ECPC) of the Office of Management and Budget, but the Bureau of Economic Analysis, the Bureau of Labor Statistics, and the Census Bureau all contributed to the initiative. Statistics Canada and Mexico's Instituto Nacional de Estadistica, Geografia e Informatica (INEGI), meanwhile, worked with the ECPC to ensure that the new system would be able to provide comparable statistics for industries in place in all three countries, while simultaneously providing flexibility so that each country could accommodate industries unique to its own economy.

In 1997 the Office of Management and Budget (OMB) announced its decision to adopt the new NAICS as the industry classification system used by statistical agencies of the United States. During this same period, the nuts and bolts of the NAICS were unveiled to largely positive reviews. "NAICS recognizes new, emerging, and advanced technology industries; NAICS acknowledges the information age in which Americans live and work; NAICS considers over 150 new service industries; NAICS provides for comparability of data with other NAFTA trading partners; and NAICS is based on a production-oriented conceptual framework," observed *Energy Conservation News*. Marketing professionals were particularly pleased with the new proposed system. "NAICS is based on an entirely different concept than SIC," stated Suzanne Sabrosk in *Searcher*. "Its goals were not only to identify new industries but to acknowledge a more consistent economic principle—namely types of production activities performed, rather than the mix of production and market-based categories in the SIC. This process orientation, as opposed to an approach stressing supply and demand, accounts for the presentation of more detail in the service sector. NAICS classifies industries based on what the industries do, rather than whom the industries serve. For example, NAICS classifies bakeries that bake and sell on the premises under manufacturing, instead of as retailers, because of the way in which the bakeries produce their baked goods."

FRAMEWORK OF THE NAICS

The North American Industry Classification System defines a total of 1,170 industries in the United States. Nearly 360 of these industries are delineated for the first time (many in high-tech fields such as fiber optic cable manufacturing and satellite communications), while 565 are service-based. These industries are grouped in 20 industrial sectors that are progressively subdivided into three-digit subsectors, four-digit industry groups, and five-digit industries. The definition of most five-digit industries is the same in all three countries (the United States, Mexico, and Canada) so that they can produce comparable data, but some U.S. industries feature a sixth digit. The old SIC system was a four-digit one that did not have any linkages between the NAFTA-member economies. "NAICS allows each country to recognize activities that are important in the respective countries, but may not be large enough or important enough to recognize in all three countries. The sixth digit is reserved for this purpose," explained the Census Bureau.

The base two-digit NAICS Industry Sectors are as follows:

11 Agriculture, Forestry, Fishing and Hunting

21 Mining

22 Utilities

23 Construction

31-33 Manufacturing

42 Wholesale Trade

44-45 Retail Trade

48-49 Transportation and Warehousing

51 Information

52 Finance and Insurance

53 Real Estate and Rental and Leasing

54 Professional, Scientific, and Technical Services

55 Management of Companies and Enterprises

56 Administrative and Support and Waste Management and Remediation Services

61 Education Services

62 Health Care and Social Assistance

71 Arts, Entertainment, and Recreation

72 Accommodation and Food Services

81 Other Services (Except Publish Administration

92 Public Administration

Of these base sectors, five of them are primarily goods-producing (manufacturing) in nature, while the remaining 15 are services-oriented. This is a dramatic departure from the manufacturing-oriented perspective of the old Standard Industrial Classification system. Complete NAICS listings are available on the Census Bureau website at www.census.gov/naics.

Many of the NAICS sectors feature combinations of old SIC divisions, while others are long-neglected economic sectors. For instance, the NAICS has an information sector that includes all establishments that create, disseminate, or provide the means to distribute information. "So everything from data-processing services to motion pictures, broadcasting, and sound recording industries ended up here, as did newspaper, book, and periodical publishers, previously classified as manufacturing, and software publishers, previously included in SIC services," explained Sabrosk. "There are 34 industries in this sector, of which, 20 are new, such as paging, cellular, wireless, and satellite communications. In NAICS, publishing—including reporting, writing, and editing—appears as a major economic activity in its own right, whereas printing remains in NAICS manufacturing. Software publishing goes here because creating a copyrighted product and brining it to market equates to the creative process for other types of intellectual products." This sector's creation will enable the U.S. government and business (and other governments and business enterprises for that matter) to track the tremendous impact of information-based industries on the U.S., Canadian, and Mexican economies for the very first time.

Other important new or overhauled sectors in the North American Industry Classification System include:

Professional/scientific/technical services—This grouping consists of businesses whose major input is "human capital," such as physicians and attorneys.

Health care/social assistance—The number of industries classified in this sector nearly doubled from those listed under the old SIC system. Among the 27 new industries included in this sector, particularly notable ones include health maintenance organizations (HMOs), organ banks, and continuing care retirement facilities.

Computer and electronics manufacturing (including software reproduction, compact disc reproduction, and printed circuit assembly).

Arts, entertainment and recreation—This new sector includes a variety of ascendant industries that reflect our changing lifestyles, such as fitness and recreational sports centers, casinos, skiing facilities, and outfitting companies.

Insurance and real estate—the parameters of these important economic sectors have been expanded and extensively reshaped to reflect current realities.

Wholesale and retail trade—"The distinction between retail and wholesale trade is now based on how the establishment conducts its business rather than on the class of customer that it serves," wrote Ambler in *Business America*. "Those businesses that operate from a store-front, advertise to the general public, and provide retail-type services are considered retailers in NAICS regardless of whether they sell primarily to businesses or consumers. This new definition reflects the changing structure of retail trade."

DIFFERENCES BETWEEN NAICS AND SIC SYSTEMS

Analysts have pointed out a number of significant differences between the new NAICS system and the Standard Industrial Classification arrangement that it replaces. Key areas in which the two systems differ include:

Focus—The NAICS focused on services industries and new industries driven by advanced technology, whereas the SIC system was heavily weighted toward manufacturing. In addition, the NAICS benefits from a unified, production-oriented conceptual framework. "Businesses that use similar production processes to produce a good or service are grouped together," explained Ambler. "This single conceptual framework ensures that the classification system will produce data for improved analysis of input/output patterns, productivity, unit labor costs, and industrial performance. There was no consistent conceptual framework for the SIC.'' However, analysts note that the differing definitions that exist between the NAICS and the SIC will make historical trend analysis a difficult undertaking in many instances. ''Comparative statistics and bridge tables may help at the 2-digit SIC and 3-digit NAICS level of activity,'' noted Robert Haas and Thomas Wotruba in *Agency Sales Magazine*. ''[But] more detailed comparisons and links with past data may require what the Census Bureau calls 'synthetic estimates.' These involve applying proportions or trends from details making up one data set to the totals in a related data set or category.''

Nomenclature—Groupings within NAICS are known by different names than those in the SIC system. For example, the SIC called the highest level of aggregation in its system a ''division,'' whereas the NAICS calls it a ''sector.'' The SIC's next highest level of aggregation, meanwhile, was designated ''major group,'' but in the NAICS it is known as a ''subsector.''

Update-friendly—NAICS codes will be reviewed and updated on a regular five-year cycle by NAFTA member countries to make the system as useful and relevant as possible. The old SIC system, on the other hand, was only revised every 10 or 15 years.

Comparability—The Four-digit SIC system was not linked to the economic data tracking systems of Canada or Mexico in any way. The NAICS system, on the other hand, enables analysts to directly compare industrial production statistics collected and published by all three NAFTA members. In addition, NAICS provides for increased compatibility with the International Standard Industrial Classification System, developed and maintained by the United Nations and widely used in Europe.

The ECPC is currently working on revisions that are expected to be integrated into the 2002 version of the NAICS. New industries covered in this update will include data processing services and Internet service providers, and it is anticipated that the telecommunications industry will be further segmented into its service and manufacturing components. In addition, a North American Product Classification System (NAPCS) is also in development. This program will ultimately track economic activity by industry product.

In the meantime, the North American Industry Classification System continues to be regarded as a welcome development, despite the choppy conditions that may prevail during the transition away from the old SIC framework. ''The SIC system was dated and badly in need of revision,'' stated Haas and Watruba. ''The new system should provide much more detailed information on a wider spectrum of industries, which in the long run should prove more beneficial to all concerned. In addition, its application to Canadian and Mexican markets and its compatibility with the ISIC system should greatly facilitate more effective global marketing by U.S. marketers. Once NAICS has been adopted and implemented over an extended time period, the short-run problems may well be forgotten because of the long-run benefits of the new system.''

FURTHER READING:

Ambler, Carole A. ''NAICS: The 'S' Doesn't Stand for Services (But It Could).'' *Business America*. April 1998.

Blume, Eric R. ''A New Class of Classification.'' *Electric Perspectives*. September/October 1999.

''Good Bye to SIC, Hello to NAICS!'' *Energy Conservation News*. March 2000.

Haas, Robert W., and Thomas R. Wotruba. ''From SIC to NAICS—What Does It Mean for Business Marketers?'' *Agency Sales Magazine*. January 1998.

NAICS: New Data for a New Economy. U.S. Census Bureau, 2000.

Ott, Karalynn. ''New Industry Classification Gets a Code Shoulder.'' *Crain's Detroit Business*. March 23, 1998.

Sabrosk, Suzanne. ''NAICS Codes: A New Classification System for a New Economy.'' *Searcher*. November 2000.

Saunders, Norman C. ''The North American Industry Classification System: Change on the Horizon.'' *Occupational Outlook Quarterly*. Fall 1999.

''SIC Codes Get Revamped.'' *Quality*. December 1998.

O

OCCUPATIONAL SAFETY AND HEALTH ADMINISTRATION (OSHA)

The Occupational Safety and Health Administration (OSHA) was established by the Williams-Steiger Occupational Safety and Health Act (OSH Act) of 1970, which took effect in 1971. OSHA's mission is to ensure that every working man and woman in the nation is employed under safe and healthful working conditions. Nearly every employee in the United States comes under OSHA's jurisdiction. The only exceptions are people who are self-employed, workers in mining and transportation industries (which are covered by other agencies), and most public employees. Thus, nearly every private employer in the United States needs to be cognizant of OSHA rules and regulations. Because OSHA is an administrative agency within the United States Department of Labor, it is administered by an assistant secretary of labor.

OSHA OBJECTIVES AND STANDARDS

OSHA seeks to make workplaces safer and healthier by making and enforcing regulations, which the OSH Act calls ''standards.'' The OSH Act itself establishes only one workplace standard, which is called the ''general duty standard.'' The general duty standard states: ''Each employer shall furnish to each of his employees employment and a place of employment which are free from recognized hazards that are causing or are likely to cause death or serious physical harm to his [or her] employees.'' In the OSH Act, Congress delegated authority to OSHA to make rules further implementing the general duty standard.

Standards made by OSHA are published in the *Code of Federal Regulations (CFR)*. The three types of regulations are called interim, temporary emergency, and permanent. Interim standards were applicable for two years after OSH Act was passed. For this purpose, OSHA was authorized to use the standards of any nationally recognized ''standards setting'' organization such as those of professional engineering groups. Such privately developed standards are called ''national consensus standards.'' Temporary emergency standards last only six months and are designed to protect workers while OSHA goes through the processes required by law to develop a permanent standard. Permanent standards are made through the same processes as the regulations made by other federal administrative agencies.

As OSHA drafts a proposal for a permanent standard, it consults with representatives of industry and labor and collects whatever scientific, medical, and engineering data is necessary to ensure that the standard adequately reflects workplace realities. Proposed standards are published in the *Federal Register*. A comment period is then held, during which input is received from interested parties including, but not limited to, representatives of industry and labor. At the close of the comment period, the proposal may be withdrawn and set aside, withdrawn and re-proposed with modifications, or approved as a final standard that is legally enforceable. All standards that become legally binding are first published in the *Federal Register* and then compiled and published in the *Code of Federal Regulations*. It is important to note that many of OSHA's permanent standards originated as national consensus standards developed by private professional organizations such as the National Fire Protection Association and the American National

Standards Institute. Examples of permanent OSHA standards include limits for exposure of employees to hazardous substances such as asbestos, benzene, vinyl chloride, and cotton dust. See the OSHA Web site at www.osha.slc.gov for more information.

NATIONAL INSTITUTE OF OCCUPATIONAL SAFETY AND HEALTH The OSH Act of 1970 also established a research institute called the National Institute of Occupational Safety and Health (NIOSH). Since 1973, NIOSH has been a division of the U.S. government's Centers for Disease Control (CDC). The purpose of NIOSH is to gather data documenting incidences of occupational exposure, injury, illness and death in the United States. This information, which is highly valued by OSHA, is gathered from a wide variety of sources, ranging from industry groups to labor unions, as well as independent organizations.

OSHA RECORD-KEEPING REQUIREMENTS

OSHA requires all companies subject to its workplace standards to abide by a variety of occupational regulations. One of OSHA's major requirements is that companies keep records on facets of their operations relevant to employee safety and health. All employers covered by the OSH Act are required to keep four kinds of records:

- Records regarding enforcement of OSHA standards
- Research records
- Job-related injury, illness, and death records
- Job hazard records

OSHA ENFORCEMENT OF STANDARDS

OSHA inspectors conduct planned or surprise inspections of work sites covered by the OSH Act to verify compliance with the OSH Act and standards promulgated by OSHA. The OSH Act allows the employer *and* an employee representative to accompany OSHA's representative during the inspection. In 1978, in *Marshall v. Barlow*, the United States Supreme Court declared that in most industries, employers have a right to bar an OSHA inspector from his/her premises if the inspector has not first obtained a search warrant.

If violations are found during an inspection, an OSHA citation may be issued in which alleged violations are listed, notices of penalties for each violation are given, and an abatement period is established. The abatement period is the amount of time the employer has to correct any violation(s). Penalties for a violation can be civil or criminal and vary depending on the nature of the violation (minor or serious, willful or nonwillful, or repeated). Penalties are naturally more severe for serious, repeated, willful violations. Since

OSHA must refer cases to the United States Justice Department for criminal enforcement, it has not made extensive use of criminal prosecution as an enforcement mechanism. Instead, the agency has historically relied on civil penalties.

An employer has 15 days to contest an OSHA citation, and any challenge is heard by an Administrative Law Judge (ALJ) within OSHA. The ALJ receives oral and written evidence, decides issues of fact and law, and enters an order. If the employer is dissatisfied with that order, it can be appealed to the Occupational Safety and Health Review Commission, which will, in turn, enter an order. Finally, within 30 days of the issuance of that order, the employer or the Secretary of Labor can take the case to the United States federal court system by filing an appeal with a United States court of appeals.

OSHA AND ITS STATE COUNTERPARTS

Pursuant to the OSH Act, an individual state can pass its own worker health and safety laws and standards. Indeed, the 1970 legislation encouraged individual states to develop and operate their own job safety and health programs. If the state can show that its job safety and health standards are ''at least as effective as'' comparable federal standards, the state can be certified to assume OSH Act administration and enforcement in that state. OSHA approves and monitors state plans, and provides up to 50 percent of operating costs for approved plans.

To gain OSHA approval for a 'developmental plan,' the first step in the process of instituting a state plan for job safety and health, the applying state must first assure OSHA that it will, within three years, have in place all the structural elements necessary for an effective occupational safety and health program. These elements include: 1) appropriate legislation; 2) regulations and procedures for standards setting, enforcement, appeal of citations, and penalties; 3) adequate resources (both in number and qualifications of inspectors and other personnel) for enforcement of standards.

Once a state has completed and documented all its developmental requirements, it is eligible for certification. Certification is basically an acknowledgment that the state has put together a complete plan. Once the state has reached a point where it is deemed capable of independently enforcing job safety and health standards, OSHA may enter into an 'operational status' agreement with the state. Once this occurs, OSHA in effect steps aside and allows the state to enforce its laws.

The ultimate accreditation of a state plan is known as ''final approval.'' When OSHA grants final approval, it relinquishes its authority to cover occupational safety and health matters that are addressed by the state's rules and regulations. Final approval can not be given until at least one year after certification, and it is predicated on OSHA's judgment that worker protection is at least as effective under the state's standards as it is under the federal program. The state must meet all required staffing levels and agree to participate in OSHA's computerized inspection data system before being allowed to operate without OSHA supervision.

HISTORY OF THE RELATIONSHIP BETWEEN OSHA AND BUSINESS

OSHA has traditionally used ''command and control'' kinds of regulation to protect workers. ''Command and control'' regulations are those which set requirements for job safety (such as requirements for guard rails on stairs) or limits on exposure to a hazardous substance (such as a given number of fibers of asbestos per cubic milliliter of air breathed per hour). They are enforced through citations issued to violators.

In 1984 OSHA promulgated the Hazard Communication Standard (HCS), which was viewed as a new kind of regulation differing from ''command and control.'' The HCS gives workers access to information about long-term health risks resulting from workplace exposure to toxic or hazardous substances, and requires manufacturers, importers, and distributors to provide employers with evaluations of all toxic or hazardous materials sold or distributed to those employers. This information is compiled in a form known as a Material Safety Data Sheet (MSDS). The MSDS describes the chemical's physical hazards such as ignitability and reactivity, gives associated health hazards, and states the exposure limits established by OSHA. In turn, the employer must make these documents available to employees, and requires employers to establish hazard communication education programs. The employer must also label all containers with the identities of hazardous substances and appropriate warnings. Worker ''Right-to-Know,'' as implemented on the federal level through the HCS, is designed to give workers access to information so that they can make informed decisions about their exposure to toxic chemicals.

OSHA has been criticized by businesses and industry groups throughout its history. In the 1970s, it was criticized for making job-safety regulations that businesses considered to be vague or unnecessarily costly. For example, a 1977 OSHA regulation contained detailed specifications regarding irregularities in western hemlock trees used to construct ladders. In the Appropriations Act of 1977, Congress directed OSHA to get rid of certain standards that it described as ''trivial.'' As a result, in 1978 OSHA revoked 928

job-safety standards and increased its efforts to deal with health hazards.

On the other hand, OSHA has also been criticized by unions and other pro-worker groups throughout its history for doing too little to protect employees. Throughout its existence, OSHA has been criticized for issuing too few new standards, for failing to protect workers who report violations, for failing to adequately protect workers involved in the clean up of toxic-waste sites, and for failing to enforce existing standards. The latter charge has been a particularly frustrating one for OSHA. Funding for enforcement has dwindled in recent years, and over the last 20 years, both Congress and various presidential administrations have publicly supported efforts to keep OSHA and other agencies ''off the backs'' of business.

OSHA REFORMS

In recent years, critics of OSHA have become more vocal in their complaints. In fact, a 2000 survey of the National Association of Manufacturers cited OSHA as the nation's most intrusive federal agency (34 percent of responding manufacturers cited OSHA, while 18 percent pointed to the Environmental Protection Agency, the second-highest vote-getter; another 11 percent said no federal agency significantly impeded their efficiency). The most frequent complaint leveled against OSHA is that American workplace safety and health regulations are excessively burdensome on businesses of all shapes and sizes. Critics call for fundamental changes in OSHA's regulatory environment, insisting that changes should be made to encourage voluntary industry compliance on worker safety issues and reductions of penalties for nonserious violators of standards. OSHA itself has acknowledged that ''in the public's view, OSHA has been driven too often by numbers and rules, not by smart enforcement and results. Business complains about overzealous enforcement and burdensome rules. . . . And too often, a ''one-size-fits-all'' regulatory approach has treated conscientious employers no differently from those who put workers needlessly at risk.'' Worker advocates and others, however, point out that OSHA standards have been an important factor in the dramatic decline of injury and illness rates in many industries over the past few decades, and they express concern that reforms could put workers in a variety of businesses at greater risk.

OSHA's recent reform initiatives, then, have sought to address those issues raised by its critics while simultaneously ensuring that American workers receive adequate health and safety protection in the workplace. In 1995 OSHA announced a new emphasis on treating employers with aggressive health and safety programs differently from employers who lack such efforts. "At its core," said OSHA, "this new approach seeks to encourage the development of worksite health and safety programs. . . . OSHA will be looking for programs with these features: management commitment, meaningful participation of employees, a systematic effort to find safety and health hazards whether they are covered by existing standards or not, documentation that the identified hazards are fixed, training for employees and supervisors, and ultimately a reduction in injuries and illnesses." Those firms equipped with good safety programs will receive special recognition that will include: the lowest priority for enforcement inspections, the highest priority for assistance, appropriate regulatory relief, and major penalty reductions. Businesses that do not adequately provide for their workers' health and safety, however, will be subject to "strong and traditional OSHA enforcement procedures. . . . In short, for those who have a history of endangering their employees and are unwilling to change, OSHA will rigorously enforce the law without compromise to assure that there are serious consequences for serious violators."

OSHA announced its intention to pursue several initiatives to make the above changes possible. These include nationwide implementation of the "Maine 200" program, a highly successful initiative wherein 198 out of 200 Maine companies, when provided with a choice between stepped up enforcement or partnerships with government to realize workplace safety goals, chose partnerships. "The Maine program is extremely promising," said OSHA. "In two years, the employers self-identified more than fourteen times as many hazards as could have been cited by OSHA inspectors (in part, because OSHA's small staff could never have visited all 1,300 worksites involved). Nearly six out of ten employers in the program have already reduced their injury and illness rates, even as inspections and fines are significantly diminished. OSHA will expand the most successful features of this program nationwide."

OSHA also announced its plans to make more tightly focused inspections on companies that have effective safety and health programs. If a company with a strong record meets selected safety/health criteria, the OSHA inspector will conduct an abbreviated inspection. Conversely, in situations where a safety and health program is nonexistent or inadequate, a complete site inspection, including full citations, will be undertaken. OSHA also indicated that it planned to: target inspections at employers with poor worker safety and health records; conduct more inspections in industries with higher injury and illness rates; introduce additional incentives for employers with safety and health programs; promote greater worker participation in creating and maintaining workplace safety and health programs; streamline OSHA regulations;

increase use of technologies to streamline work; and adjust the criteria by which it evaluates inspectors ("inspectors have been told clearly that there are no numeric inspection goals and that their performance will not be judged by the number of citations and fines they issue but by their success in finding and reducing hazards associated with injuries and illnesses"). In addition, OSHA has expressed satisfaction with a pilot "quick-fix" program. "Using this model," noted OSHA, "compliance officers reduce penalties for violations that are abated—during the inspection. This policy encouraged employers to increase employee protection immediately, while freeing OSHA employees from monitoring abatement and follow-up paperwork." Finally, OSHA has proposed changes to federal regulations governing business record keeping on workplace injuries and illnesses, but the ultimate impact of some of these proposals is in dispute, and uncertainty exists as to when and how such changes might take place. In addition, OSHA and business interests clashed repeatedly during the late 1990s over proposed new regulations designed to identify and address workplace injuries and illnesses traced to the issue of ergonomics. "OSHA would require companies to implement permanent engineering controls and employ interim personal protective equipment," noted *Purchasing*. "Examples of engineering controls involve changing, modifying, or redesigning the following: workstations, tools, facilities, equipment, materials, and processes. . . . Many businesses have already adopted ergonomic design tools and workstations that reduce strain where repetitive motions, sitting for long periods, or reaching are required. It's not clear yet what companies will be required to do in the way of changes in processes and materials used."

OSHA AND SMALL BUSINESS

In recognition of the special challenges that often face small businesses—and the limited financial resources that they often have—the Occupational Safety and Health Administration administers a number of special programs specifically designed to help entrepreneurs and small business owners provide a productive yet safe environment for their employees. In addition, there are a number of situations in which OSHA has the discretion to reduce penalties for small businesses.

Among the special programs that OSHA has instituted for small businesses are the following:

- Penalty Reduction—OSHA may grant reductions of up to 60 percent for businesses that qualify as small firms.

- Penalty Reductions for Good Faith—OSHA has the option of granting a 25 percent penalty reduction if a small business has instituted an effective safety and health program for its employees.

- Flexible Requirements—OSHA gives smaller firms greater flexibility in certain safety areas in recognition of their limited resources (i.e., lead in construction, emergency evacuation plans, process safety management).

- Consultation Program—While not limited to small businesses, OSHA on-site consultation program has been particularly helpful to smaller companies (small firms accounted for about 40 percent of the program during the mid-1990s). This service, which is run by state agencies, provides businesses with the option of requesting a free on-site consultation with a state representative who helps them identify potential workplace hazards and improve or implement effective workplace safety and health programs.

- Training Grants—OSHA awards grant money to non-profit groups for the development of programs designed to help entrepreneurs and small business owners establish safety and health guidelines for their companies.

- Mentoring—OSHA and the Voluntary Protection Programs Participants Association (VPPA) operate a mentoring program to help small firms applying for entry into VPP refine their health and safety programs. The VPP is an OSHA program that is intended to recognize a firm's safety and health achievements. This mentoring program matches applicants with VPP members (often in the same or a related industry) who can help by sharing their experience with and knowledge about workplace safety and health programs.

In addition, many states with their own federally approved safety and health standards offer additional programs of assistance to small businesses.

THE VALUE OF CONSULTATION PROGRAMS OSHA and business consultants alike encourage small business owners to take advantage of available consultation programs. A comprehensive consultation can provide small business owners with a wide variety of information that can help ensure that they are in compliance with regulatory requirements.

Consultations will typically include appraisal of all mechanical and environmental hazards and physical work practices; appraisal of the firm's present job safety and health program; conference with management on findings; written report of recommendations and agreements; and training and assistance with implementing recommendations. "The consultant will then review detailed findings with you in a closing conference," noted OSHA. "You [the business owner] will learn not only what you need to improve, but also what you are doing right. At that time you can discuss problems, possible solutions and abatement periods to eliminate or control any serious hazards identified during the walk-through. . . . The consultant can help you establish or strengthen an employee safety and health program, making safety and health activities routine considerations rather than crisis-oriented responses."

FURTHER READING:

Bates, Steve. "OSHA Rethinks Implementation of Record-Keeping Proposal." *Nation's Business.* November 1997.

Boggs, Richard F. "OSHA Can't Do It All." *Safety & Health.* April 5, 1992.

"Ergonomics, S&H Rules on OSHA's Front Burner." *Purchasing.* April 22, 1999.

Kahn, James P., et al. *Fundamentals of Occupational Safety and Health.* Government Institutes, 1996.

Kerrigan, Karen. "OSHA Reforms Winding through Congress." *Washington Business Journal.* February 23, 1996.

"The New OSHA—Reinventing Worker Safety and Health." Occupational Safety and Health Administration, 1995.

"OSHA Most Intrusive Agency." *Products Finishing.* June 2000.

Yohay, Stephen C. "Recent Court Decisions on Important OSHA Enforcement Issues." *Employee Relations Law Journal.* Spring 1997.

OFFICE AUTOMATION

Office automation refers to the varied computer machinery and software used to digitally create, collect, store, manipulate, and relay office information needed for accomplishing basic tasks and goals. Raw data storage, electronic transfer, and the management of electronic business information comprise the basic activities of an office automation system.

The history of modern office automation began with the typewriter and the copy machine, which mechanized previously manual tasks. Today, however, office automation is increasingly understood as a term that refers not just to the mechanization of tasks but to the conversion of information to electronic form as well. The advent of the personal computer revolutionized office automation, and today, popular operating systems and user interfaces dominate office computer systems. This revolution has been so complete, and has infiltrated so many areas of business, that almost all businesses use at least one commercial computer business application in the course of daily activity. Even the smallest companies commonly utilize computer technology to maintain financial records, inventory information, payroll records, and other pertinent business information. ''Workplace technology that started as handy (but still optional) business tools in the 1980s evolved into a high-priority requirement in the 1990s,'' summarized Stanley Zarowin in *Journal of Accountancy.* ''As we enter the new millennium, it has taken another quantum leap, going from a priority to a prerequisite for doing business.''

THE BASICS OF OFFICE AUTOMATION

Generally, there are three basic activities of an office automation system: data storage of information, data exchange, and data management. Within each broad application area, hardware and software combine to fulfill basic functions.

Data storage usually includes office records and other primary office forms and documents. Data applications involve the capture and editing of files, images, or spreadsheets. Word processing and desktop presentation packages accommodate raw textual and graphical data, while spreadsheet applications provide users with the capacity to engage in the easy manipulation and output of numbers. Image applications allow the capture and editing of visual images.

Text handling software and systems cover the whole field of word processing and desktop publishing. Word processing, the most basic and common office automation activity, is the inputting (usually via keyboard) and manipulation of text on a computer. Today's commercial word processing applications provide users with a sophisticated set of commands to format, edit, and print text documents. One of the most popular features of word processing packages are their preformatted document templates. Templates automatically set up such things as font size, paragraph styles, headers and footers, and page numbers so that the user does not have to reset document characteristics every time they create a new record.

Desktop publishing adds another dimension to text manipulation. By combining the features of a word processor with advanced page design and layout features, desktop publishing packages have emerged as valuable tools in the creation of newsletters, brochures, and other documents that combine text and photographs, charts, drawings and other graphic images.

Image handling software and systems are another facet of office automation. Examples of visual information include pictures of documents, photographs, and graphics such as tables and charts. These images are converted into digital files, which cannot be edited the same way that text files can. In a word processor or desktop publishing application, each word or charac-

ter is treated individually. In an imaging system, the entire picture or document is treated as one whole object. One of the most popular uses of computerized images is in corporate presentations or speeches. Presentation software packages simplify the creation of multimedia presentations that use computer video, images, sound, and text in an integrated information package.

Spreadsheet programs allow the manipulation of numeric data. Early popular spreadsheet programs such as VisiCalc and Lotus 123 greatly simplified common business financial record keeping. Particularly useful among the many spreadsheet options is the ability to use variables in pro forma statements. The pro forma option allows the user to change a variable and have a complex formula automatically recalculated based on the new numbers. Many businesses use spreadsheets for financial management, financial projection, and accounting.

DATA EXCHANGE While data storage and manipulation is one component of an office automation system, the exchange of that information is another equally important component. Electronic transfer is a general application area that highlights the exchange of information between more than one user or participant. Electronic mail, voice mail, and facsimile are examples of electronic transfer applications. Systems that allow instantaneous or ''real time'' transfer of information (i.e. online conversations via computer or audio exchange with video capture) are considered electronic sharing systems. Electronic sharing software illustrates the collaborative nature of many office automation systems.

Office automation systems that include the ability to electronically share information between more than one user simultaneously are sometimes referred to as groupware systems. One type of groupware is an electronic meeting system. Electronic meeting systems allow geographically dispersed participants to exchange information in real time. Participants in such electronic meetings may be within the same office or building, or thousands of miles apart. Long-distance electronic sharing systems usually use a telephone line connection to transfer data, while sharing in the same often involves just a local area network of computers (no outside phone line is needed). The functional effectiveness of such electronic sharing systems has been one factor in the growth of telecommuting as an option for workers. Telecommuters work at home, maintaining their ties to the office via computer.

Electronic transfer software and systems allow for electronic, voice, and facsimile transmission of office information. Electronic mail uses computer-based storage and a common set of network communication standards to forward electronic messages from one user to another. Most of these systems allow users to relay electronic mail to more than one recipient. Additionally, many electronic mail systems provide security features, automatic messaging, and mail management systems like electronic folders or notebooks. Voice mail offers essentially the same applications, but for telephones, not computers. Facsimile transmissions are limited to image relay, and while usage of this communication option has declined somewhat with the emergence of electronic mail, fax machines remain standard in almost all business offices in America. In addition, new technologies continue to transform fax use, just as they have influenced other modes of corporate communication. For example, facsimile converters for the personal computer that allow remote printing of "faxed" information via the computer rather than through a dedicated facsimile machine are now available. Indeed, these facsimile circuit boards for the microcomputer are slowly replacing stand-alone fax machines. Simultaneously, other traditional office equipment continues to undergo changes that improve their data exchange capacities as well. Digital copiers, for example, are increasingly multifunctional (with copying, printing, faxing, and scanning capabilities) and connectable to computer networks.

DATA MANAGEMENT Office automation systems are also often used to track both short-term and long-term data in the realms of financial plans, workforce allocation plans, marketing expenditures, inventory purchases, and other aspects of business. Task management or scheduling systems monitor and control various projects and activities within the office. Electronic management systems monitor and control office activities and tasks through timelines, resource equations, and electronic scheduling. As in data exchange, groupware and network computer systems are gaining in popularity for data management. Under such arrangements, multiple members of the office environment are provided with access to a variety of information at a central electronic location.

OFFICE AUTOMATION CONSIDERATIONS: PEOPLE, TOOLS, AND THE WORKPLACE

Businesses engaged in launching or upgrading office automation systems must consider a wide variety of factors that can influence the effectiveness of those systems. These factors include budgetary and physical space considerations, changes in communication infrastructure, and other considerations. But two other factors that must be considered are employee training and proliferating office automation choices:

- Training—People involved with office automation basically include all users of the au-

tomation and all providers of the automation systems and tools. A wide range of people—including software and hardware engineers, management information scientists, executives, mid-level workers, and secretaries—are just a few of the people that use office automation on a daily basis. As a result, training of personnel on these office automation systems has become an essential part of many companies' planning. After all, the office automation system is only as good as the people who make it and use it, and smart business owners and managers recognize that workplace resistance to these systems can dramatically lessen their benefits. "It's true that as technology matures the need for special training will decline—because tomorrow's software and hardware will be much more intuitive and loaded with built-in teaching drills—that time is not here yet," wrote Zarowin. "Training is still essential."

- Choice—A dizzying array of office automation alternatives are available to businesses of all shapes, sizes, and subject areas. Such systems typically involve a sizable investment of funds, so it is wise for managers and business owners to undertake a careful course of study before making a purchase. Primary factors that should be considered include: cost of the system, length of time involved in introducing the system, physical condition of the facility into which the system will be introduced, level of technical support, compatibility with other systems, complexity of system (a key factor in determining allocations of time and money for training), and compatibility of the system with the business area in which the company is involved.

As the high-tech New Economy continues to evolve over the next several years, business experts warn small businesses not to fall too far behind. Some small businesses remain resistant to change and thus fall ever further behind in utilizing office automation technology, despite the plethora of evidence that it constitutes the wave of the future. The entrepreneurs and managers who lead these enterprises typically defend their inaction by noting that they remain able to accomplish their basic business requirements without such investments, or by claiming that new innovations in technology and automation are too expensive or challenging to master. But according to Zarowin, "those rationalizations don't acknowledge what many recent converts to technology are discovering: the longer one delays, the larger the gap and the harder it is to catch up. And though many businesses still can function adequately with paper and pencil, their customers—and their competition—are not sitting on their hands.''

FURTHER READING:

Bauroth, Nan. ''Selling Upper Management on New Equipment.'' *OfficeSolutions.* April 2000.

Dykeman, John. B. ''The State of Office Applications Software.'' *Managing Office Technology.* June 1993.

Laudon, Kenneth C., and Jane P. Laudon. *Management Information Systems: Organization and Technology.* Macmillan, 1994.

Lewers, Christine. ''A Keystroke Away.'' *Indiana Business Magazine.* September 1999.

Page, Heather. ''Branching Out: Network Computers Offer a Low-Cost Solution to Your Growing High-Tech Needs.'' *Entrepreneur.* September 1997.

Stevens, Tim. ''The Smart Office.'' *Industry Management.* January 17, 1994.

Zarowin, Stanley. ''Technology for the New Millennium.'' *Journal of Accountancy.* April 2000.

OFFICE ROMANCE

Office romances are situations in which two members of a business establishment—whether co-workers in an office or on a shop floor—become romantically linked with one another. For businesses of all sizes, such developments can complicate business operations. After all, office romances that go awry can not only result in emotional pain for one or both of the principals involved, but can also trigger losses of workplace productivity that directly impact on the business. Of course, office romances that go fabulously well can have the same bottom-line impact on a company if the couple spends an inordinate amount of work time courting one another. These concerns are often heightened in small business establishments, which feel such losses of personnel and productivity more acutely than do larger companies.

But most companies operating today recognize that attempts to neutralize or forbid office romances are probably doomed to failure. ''Concerns about invading individuals' privacy—as well as the recognition that, human nature being what it is, people are going to get involved with their co-workers no matter what their companies dictate—lead some employers to throw up their hands in despair,'' noted Judy Greenwald in *Business Insurance.* Moreover, some observers—consultants, small business owners, and CEOs alike—take a more benign view of the phenomenon, arguing that most office romances do not have an appreciable negative impact on business operations. In fact, defenders of office romance sometimes argue that the practice can actually improve workplace performance in such areas as morale, coop-

eration, and work force stability. They argue that the ultimate impact of an office romance on a business is often predicated on the fundamental nature of the relationship.

CONDITIONS THAT CONTRIBUTE TO OFFICE ROMANCE

The workplace's status as fertile territory for office romance is well-entrenched in American society, particularly in today's business and social climate. ''Work-related interaction gives people the rather unsuspecting opportunity to get acquainted with another's ideas, feelings, ambitions, interests, mannerisms, values, preferences, and personal habits—the very things we examine on a more conscious level when engaged in such mating rituals as dating,'' wrote Joseph D. Levesque in *The Human Resource Problem-Solver's Handbook.* ''When people's work bring them together in close association with each other, the stage can easily become set for unconscious development of attraction, whether it becomes the product of a lengthy and involved project, a singular business trip, or sporadic but intense contact with each other.'' Social scientist Marcy Crary, writing in *Organizational Dynamics,* concurred that the workplace is replete with conditions that foster intimacy: ''Most of us have been socialized into thinking of intimacy and work as two separate compartments in our lives; intimacy takes place at home and work takes place at our place of employment. But for many people the realities of day-to-day experiences belie these rational arrangements of our worlds. Working closely together can create a sense of intimacy between people, or the creation of intimate relationships may be essential to performing the task itself.''

Lisa A. Mainiero, author of *Office Romance: Love, Power, and Sex in the Workplace,* noted that larger societal factors also have come into play. One reason for the increase in workplace romance, she contended, ''concerns security, old-fashioned comfort, and safety. With the difficulties involved in meeting people of kindred spirit, and the rampant fear of sexually transmitted disease, we are more comfortable establishing relationships with those whom we already know well. We feel safer, more secure, and more knowledgeable about dating a coworker than, say, someone we meet at the local bar on a Saturday night. . . . Another reason is propinquity. The modern-day office has taken the place of church, neighborhood, and family networks in bringing people together. We choose employers today not only because we are challenged by a new and exciting job opportunity, but also because we genuinely will like the culture of the company and the people with whom we will work.'' Indeed, academic studies indicate that future spouses are more likely to meet at work than in school, neighborhood, or other social settings. Finally, feelings of attraction between coworkers are inevitable because of human nature. As one executive told Mainiero, "You don't turn off your feelings of sexual attraction just because you're walking through an office door. We are all human, and our hormones don't shut off between nine and five."

KINDS OF OFFICE ROMANCE

Each office romance is unique, but in general, business consultants and social scientists point to several basic types, each of which have are likely to have a different impact on business operations.

RELATIONSHIPS BETWEEN MENTORS/SUPERVISORS AND SUBORDINATES These kinds of office romances, which are often cited as among the most potentially damaging of workplace relationships, are also more likely to involve small business owners—who, after all, are usually the ultimate boss of a business enterprise. "Boss-subordinate relationships bring out the worst of the risks associated with office romance," observed Mainiero. "Hierarchical relationships—or any relationship where there is power inequity—can be exploited or manipulated. Sex can be traded for promotion. But it is only those with power who can recommend career assignments, promotions, raises, and favorable projects; peers cannot do so. It is for this reason that boss-subordinate or mentor relationships should be strictly avoided." She also pointed out that such relationships can cause morale problems among other employees in the small business, who may feel that the relationship is creating unequal treatment in terms of tasks, opportunities, etc. This perception of favoritism, *whether legitimate or not*, can have a devastating impact on a small firm's productivity and underlying health.

RELATIONSHIPS BETWEEN PEERS Office romances between peers in a business—whether they are partners in a business or entry-level employees—do not have the same perils as do boss/subordinate relationships, but they are obviously not without risk. Romances that end badly can result in strained office atmosphere, loss of productivity, and even, in some cases, the departure of valued employees.

FLINGS Flings are basically short-lived romantic entanglements. The repercussions of such behavior can vary tremendously within a business, depending on the emotions and goals of the principals involved, their "post-fling" attitudes, and the degree to which the fling becomes common knowledge, either within the office or in their personal lives (especially if a spouse is involved). Some flings may transpire with no ill effects, while others—especially if the small business owner is directly involved—can wreak heavy damage on a business.

LONG-TERM RELATIONSHIPS Most people—small business owners, managers, and employees alike—enter into office romances in the hopes of building a long-term relationship with the other individual, and in some instances this can actually take place. "This relationship," wrote Levesque, is "the one everyone admires and hopes . . . will flourish into a permanent, meaningful bond."

EXTRAMARITAL AFFAIRS The above-mentioned types of office romances can have a significant impact on the workplace, but the fallout from extramarital affairs is often most deeply felt in the homes of those involved (although they can often take a big toll in the office as well). Extramarital affairs, when discovered, often result in the dissolution of marriages, which in turn can cause significant havoc in a worker's (or a business owner's) relationship with children, living arrangements, state of mind, etc. Within the office, meanwhile, such affairs can cause considerable problems in terms of morale and productivity. Once again, the impact of this kind of office romance can vary considerably, depending on the identities, goals, and state of mind of those involved. The positions held by the principals involved is another vital factor. A business enterprise is far more likely to be damaged by an extramarital affair between the owner and a key employee than one in which the principals are two part-time employees.

DISPARATE VIEWS OF OFFICE ROMANCE

Assessments of the dangers of office romance vary dramatically. Some observers view it as a wholly undesirable condition that should be avoided by business owners and managers if at all possible, while others view it as a potential positive development, provided that the relationship lies within certain parameters. After all, a relationship that is marked by nepotism concerns or features a married person who is committing adultery is far more likely to raise eyebrows than one between two single people who have no reporting relationship with one another.

Some analysts, business owners, and managers view office romances in almost entirely negative terms. "While there may be a small percentage of workplace romance liaisons that have pleasant and fulfilling culminations (usually marriage), these situations are typically infrequent to those that become painful and end that way," claimed Levesque. "For the organization there is loss too. Inevitably there is a decline in performance, be it productivity, decisions, objectivity, or morale. There also evolves the disruption of working relationships, the emergence of rivalries, inappropriate disclosure of organizational information, damage to the company reputation, and all too frequently having to release an otherwise valued employee."

Other observers, however, are far less critical of the practice, and suggest that many such relationships can actually improve a company's performance. Management consultant Kaleel Jamison, for example, indicated in *Personnel Administrator* that "[sexual attraction] may be disruptive, but . . . if properly managed, it can be not disruptive but actually energizing and productive within the organization." Mainiero agreed, although she noted that "it is true, as popular opinion suggests, that there are a number of risks and disadvantages to a poorly conducted, unprofessional, [or exploitative] office romance. This cannot be denied. But it is equally true that some romances, under certain limited conditions, can be quite beneficial—in terms of corporate morale, employee motivation, and departmental productivity."

DEALING WITH OFFICE ROMANCES

Most experts believe that banning dating among employees is not a reasonable solution, although exceptions can certainly be made in instances where one of the principals involved has a supervisory role over the other. Restrictions against inter-office dating can be particularly hard to enforce in small business establishments, where the environment may be more relaxed and work-related interdependencies may be more pronounced, thus encouraging an atmosphere of social interaction.

But companies can still take steps to minimize the risk that an office romance will have a deleterious impact on workplace productivity or morale. Small business owners are encouraged to explore the following:

1) Recognize that employees follow your lead. If you are prone to becoming involved with employees or partners, you can hardly blame your employees if they interpret such behavior as a green light to engage in office romances of their own.

2) Use good judgement. Entrepreneurs who have established their own business may have more opportunities to enter into workplace romances, given their economic status and authority. Self-discipline may be necessary, especially if you are not looking for any long-term commitment (that may not be the case with the other person in the relationship)

3) Establish basic parameters of behavior through written policy guidelines. Policies that specifically outline the negative consequences of engaging in mentor/subordinate romantic relationships are a common example of this. Strongly worded anti-sexual-harassment policies are also encouraged.

4) Provide training for all supervisors/managers about sexual harassment in all its forms. Educate them on the various signs that an office romance is having a negative impact on the company's efficiency (these signs can range from increased workplace friction to unprofessional displays of affection, anger, or other emotions).

5) Do not overstep boundaries of employee privacy. Businesses that are overzealous in attempts to sever, repair, or otherwise react to office romances run the risk of attracting a lawsuit.

6) Do not flinch from intervening promptly in situations where a workplace relationship—either in full blossom or on the rocks—is having a detrimental effect on business productivity. Such intervention can range from informal discussions of performance problems to formal warnings and other disciplinary actions (including termination if serious violations of workplace professionalism have taken place). Consultants note that in many instances, prompt response to workplace issues that arise from an office romance gone sour can go far toward addressing the problem. Unfortunately, many managers and business owners wait until the situation has become messy before they intervene. This delay can result in the loss of valued employees, for some office romances turn so sour that the company faces the unpleasant prospect of removing one of the people from the work area. But whereas larger companies often have the option of transferring a person to another office location, smaller enterprises typically do not have this option; instead, they can only reassign one of the affected people to another project or area of the office, and adopt some sort of monitoring process to ensure that both people behave in a professional manner so as not to damage the business further. Basically, business owners need to make it abundantly clear that workplace performance is their primary concern.

DISTINGUISHING BETWEEN FLIRTING AND SEXUAL HARASSMENT

Given the increase in sexual harassment lawsuits that have been brought against companies in recent years, it is not surprising that small business owners have expressed concern about the sometimes blurry boundaries between office flirtations—which may lead to full-fledged office romances—and ugly instances of sexual harassment. While businesses can take certain steps to define inappropriate office conduct, many of them quite effective, stopping sexual harassment is often a more complicated issue if the two people involved were formerly romantically involved. Indeed, some people resort to harassment in the wake of a breakup, while others have been known to level false harassment charges after being jilted. If an office relationship degenerates to such a point, it is important for the business owner to maintain an impartial stance and make sure that decisions are made on the basis of the evidence at hand.

FURTHER READING:

Allen, Leilani. ''Work and Love can Become a Volatile Mixture.'' *Computerworld.* February 3, 1997.

Crary, Marcy. ''Managing Attraction and Intimacy at Work.'' *Organizational Dynamics.* Spring 1987.

''Cupid's Cubicles.'' *U.S. News and World Report.* December 14, 1998.

Greenwald, Judy. ''Office Romances May Court Trouble.'' *Business Insurance.* February 14, 2000.

Hymowitz, Carol. ''Drawing the Line on Budding Romances in Your Workplace.'' *Wall Street Journal.* November 18, 1997.

Jamison, K. ''Managing Sexual Attraction in the Workplace.'' *Personnel Administrator.* August 1983.

Levesque, Joseph D. *The Human Resource Problem-Solver's Handbook.* New York: McGraw-Hill, 1992.

Loftus, Mary. ''Frisky Business.'' *Psychology Today.* March/April 1995.

Mainiero, Lisa A. *Office Romance: Love, Power, and Sex in the Workplace.* New York: Rawson Associates, 1989.

Michaels, James W. ''Sex and Work.'' *Forbes.* May 6, 1996.

Powers, Dennis. *The Office Romance: Playing With Fire Without Getting Burned.* 1998.

OFFICE SECURITY

Office security can be broken down into two main areas: 1) protecting your office and employees from vandalism, theft, and personal attacks; and 2) protecting your office from corporate sabotage, both from inside the company and out. The first area deals more with the actual office itself—its layout, the use of security guards, alarm systems, and so on. The second area is primarily concerned with protecting a firm's intellectual property through the introduction and utilization of such measures as shredders, computer security, and employee surveillance.

PHYSICAL SECURITY: PROTECTING THE OFFICE AND EMPLOYEES

Office security is an issue for every business, no matter the size. ''There is not a business that's too small to consider the security issues that may effect them,'' contended one commercial security consultant in an interview with *Business First of Buffalo.* There are many steps that can be taken to improve security, many of which require relatively inexpensive outlays. To find out what is best for his or her company, a small business owner should hire a security consultant to visit the business premises and conduct a thorough security analysis. This review can identify weak spots and provide a clear plan for upgrading security.

The best place to start when examining office security is the physical layout of the office itself, or the layout of the larger building of which the office is a part. Office design should stress wide, open areas with clear sight lines. Hallways and offices should be open and have no nooks or crannies where an intruder could hide in the shadows. All areas should be well lit, especially after hours when employees might be working alone or in small groups. Mirrors in stairwells and inside and outside of elevators allow employees to see around corners or past obstructions.

Doors and windows are the most obvious access points to an office and should be secure. Avoid double doors because they are easily hinged open. Ideally, entranceway doors—particularly those used for deliveries, etc.—should be steel, or steel-sheathed. This helps with security and also aids in fire prevention. Door hinges should face inward whenever possible; use nonremovable pins and screws if it is not possible. Simply upgrading hinges and door locks is one of the cheapest and most effective security steps a business can take. Deadbolt locks are best, whether they are electronically controlled or manual in nature. Combination locks on washrooms and other common areas are also an excellent option. Employees don't have to carry keys and the combination can be changed frequently. All windows should use key locks, and windows near the ground level or fire escapes should have steel bars or lockable gates that meet local fire codes.

INCREASED USE OF ELECTRONICS

Improvements in electronics, computers, and other high-tech security features have given business owners new tools to fight crime in recent years. Perhaps the most common electronic tools are closed circuit surveillance systems and access control systems.

Closed circuit surveillance systems use television cameras to monitor specific areas of a company's work space. Signals from the cameras are fed back to a central monitoring post, where a security guard or company employee watches for signs of abnormal activity. These systems are effective both during business hours and after hours. But while video technologys can be an effective deterrent and investigative tool, a closed circuit system only works as well as the people monitoring it. The guard or employee must give the video monitors his or her complete attention.

Access control systems start with establishing "point of control" access over an office. That means that all tenants and guests are routed through a control area before admittance is authorized. The control point can be as low tech as a sign-in sheet or as high tech as an elaborate system to scan the fingerprints or retinas of visitors (most security experts understandably cite the former as an inadequate measure, in and of itself). Most common is the use of access cards, or "swipe" cards. These cards are electronic "keys"—the user passes a part of the card through an electronic reader stationed outside a door, and, if the person is authorized to enter, the door is unlocked. Newer versions of the swipe cards include video imaging. A central computer stores a photo of the employee and as much pertinent information as the company desires, including work hours, emergency contact numbers, license plate numbers and make of car, and other information. Electronic cards are preferable to metal keys because an electronic key can be deactivated at a moment's notice if an employee is fired or deemed a security risk. If metal keys are used, every lock in the building has to be replaced if a security breach is suspected.

Other electronic systems that are being used by security-conscious firms include tiny hidden cameras, panic buttons that summon security when pressed, and electronic door chimes that make it easy to tell when someone has entered a work space. The tiny cameras are perhaps the most popular innovation. They are small enough to be hidden in a clock face or a heating vent, yet provide a powerful tool for monitoring employees in areas where employee theft is suspected. Use of the cameras only works if their existence is kept a secret from the employees that are under suspicion.

Finally, identification tag systems are an increasingly popular tool in many businesses. Laminated photo identification cards are inexpensive to produce and update, and they can instantly identify employees and the department from which they hail. These photo ID cards can be particularly useful for larger, diversified enterprises in which employees may not know or interact with every other member of the workforce.

ALARM SYSTEMS

Alarm systems are another popular office security tool. There are two primary types of alarm systems: those that sound a loud siren or other noise when a break-in is detected, and those that send a silent alarm directly to a security company or to the police, who then respond to the alarm. The type of alarm chosen depends in large part where the business is located. Loud alarms work well in small towns or in low-crime areas, but businesses located in urban or high-crime areas have found that nearby residents have often become so used to alarms going off that they ignore them. In that case, a silent system linked directly to the police may be preferable.

Systems can range in complexity and price. However, any alarm system must cover all the doors and windows into a business to be effective. Most common are motion sensors that detect movement where it is not supposed to be occurring, or window glass bugs that are activated when glass is broken. Examples of advanced systems include combined audio and video alert systems that are triggered by noise. When the sounds of a break-in are detected, the security company is alerted and can listen in to what is occurring at the site. The security company can then activate video monitors to see what is happening at the site, or the cameras can be set up to begin recording automatically when the first sound is detected.

As with the closed circuit television systems, the key to a good alarm system is that it must be monitored at all times. If an alarm goes off and no one is there to notice, or if it is ignored, then office security has not been enhanced at all. In fact, the alarm may have provided a false sense of security that kept a company from pursuing other security measures.

SECURITY GUARDS

Using security guards is an increasingly popular form of office security. Guards can be used in two ways: to monitor the front desk of a company or building (the access control point); or, to patrol the grounds of a larger company or office complex.

The old image of the security guard—an elderly gentleman who slept as much as he monitored the grounds—is a thing of the past. Today's guards, especially those who monitor building access, should have good communication skills and be able to handle many roles. Guards often act as concierges and goodwill ambassadors, greeting the public as they come into a company and answering questions and providing directions. Ideally, they should present a positive public image for the company and/or building that employs them. With this in mind, traditional uniforms have given way to a casual but professional wardrobe of blazers and trousers at many security firms. Guards are almost never armed—the practice has come to be regarded as just too dangerous—and they are primarily expected to do four things at all times: deter, detect, observe, and report. Today's guards can also be expected to help out by arranging for building maintenance or even assisting in life-threatening situations.

The other type of security guard—the type that patrols the grounds of a larger company or an office park—receive conflicting marks from security experts. Some feel that simply driving or walking by each part of a office complex every hour or half-hour does little to prevent crime because such measures still leave large windows of time for criminal activity to occur. Others argue the very presence of the guards is enough to deter all but the most professional or determined criminals. The question of whether to use such guards is one that each company will have to answer for itself.

Small business owners should know that using security guards is not cheap. Round-the-clock coverage by a team of guards can cost upwards of $100,000 annually. Additionally, theft by the guards themselves has been a definite problem for some businesses. Many security firms pay minimum wage, so turnover is high, and background checks are not always thorough. To ensure that you are really hiring the best firm possible, screen prospective choices carefully. Look for firms that perform thorough background checks, pay better than minimum wage, and have low turnover. Fellow members of the local business community can be a valuable resource in this regard.

THE ROLE OF EMPLOYEES

It is common knowledge that a security system is only as secure as its weakest link. In many cases, that weak link is the company's employees. Untrained in security measures and prone to the attitude that "it can't happen to me," many employees are their own worst enemies when it comes to security. When a company installs a new security system, it should take the time to bring in a security consultant to speak to employees about what they can do to increase their own safety and improve the company's security. Among the measures the consultant will advise are:

- Do not leave valuables unattended.
- Lock doors after hours.
- Do not go into poorly lighted areas after dark.
- Bolt down or secure equipment if possible.
- Engrave identification numbers on office equipment and keep a list of serial numbers to give to the police and insurance companies in case of theft.
- Provide each employee with a drawer that locks.
- Verify identification and purpose of visit before letting non-employees into office space.
- Deposit checks and cash daily.
- Never leave visitors unsupervised.
- Try to leave with at least one other employee if working late.

- Do not advertise vacation plans.
- Keep emergency numbers posted at every phone.
- Make sure confidential files are secured when the office is closed.

CORPORATE SABOTAGE AND PROTECTING INTELLECTUAL PROPERTY

As computers have become an everyday part of almost every business, companies have found it harder and harder to protect their proprietary information and their money. The *Los Angeles Times* reported that the FBI estimates that commercial espionage, or the theft of information, costs U.S. companies and government agencies nearly $100 billion annually. Much of that theft is occurring electronically.

Unfortunately for most companies, the greatest risk of theft or sabotage (conventional or computer), often comes from the firm's employees themselves. In fact, many experts believe that a significant percentage of small business failures are directly related to internal theft of money, property, information, and time. "Few occurrences are as potentially destructive to a business as the theft, embezzlement, or misappropriation of company funds or other assets by its employees," said one Coopers and Lybrand executive in a *San Antonio Business Journal* article.

Business security experts warn that employee theft can take many forms. Examples include:

- Forgery of company checks for personal gain
- Using a "ghost payroll," which occurs when one or more employees create "phantom" employees, submit time cards for those employees, and then cash their paychecks themselves.
- Outright theft of cash from a register drawer
- "Sweethearting," at the cash register, which can mean granting a friend or other person a discount at the register when they pay, undercharging them, or ringing up fewer items than the person has actually bought.

Internal computer theft has become one of the most common forms of employee theft now that computers have become more common in nearly every industry sector. Indeed, employees often are more computer literate than their supervisors, which may strengthen the temptation to abscond with proprietary information or otherwise engage in illicit activities. Indeed, computer theft can take many forms, including false data entry, which is almost impossible to track; slicing off small amounts of data or money that add up over time; superzapping, which occurs when a computer network security bypass code falls into the wrong hands; and scanning, or using a high-speed computer to locate data that would be impossible to find by hand, then using that data for illegal purposes.

Sabotage, which can also cost millions, almost always involves disgruntled current or former employees and can take almost any form, from defacing company property to deleting or altering important company data. As mentioned above, using access control cards for employees that can be easily deactivated makes it easier to keep ex-employees out of the workplace and track the activities of current employees.

Because employee theft is so prevalent and so costly to businesses, a business owner needs to take every precaution and use every means possible to stop employee theft. Some of the steps that can be taken include:

- Making sure that security starts at the top. Executives must set a good and honest example. Establish a clear policy on theft and security and distribute it to all employees.

- Install a security program that meets your company's needs.

- Follow up on references provided by prospective new hires.

- Keep checkbooks locked up.

- Control cash flow and have good documentation on where money is spent.

- Do not leave bookkeeping to just one person without checks and balances.

- Audit internal financial documents frequently using independent auditors.

- Only allow a few people to have authority to sign checks.

- Check all invoices to make sure they match what was delivered.

FURTHER READING:

Bliss, Edwin C., with Isamu S. Aoki. *Are Your Employees Robbing You Blind?* Pfeiffer and Co. 1993.

Chanen, Jill Shachner. "Securing the Premises: Simple Changes in Office Policy, Setup Can Safeguard a Small Practice." *ABA Journal.* April 1997.

Jaffe, Susan Biddle. "Office Building Security Grows More Sophisticated." *Philadelphia Business Journal.* April 6, 1992.

Lombardi, John H. "Office and Office Building Security." *Security Management.* Nov. 1994.

Manis, Robert A. "Discouraging the Inside Job." *Inc.* April 1994.

Parent, Tawn. "Is Your Office Safe?" *Indianapolis Business Journal.* January 6, 1992.

Poling, Travis E. "A Thief Among Us: Employee Sabotage and Theft Leave Businesses Holding Hefty Tab." *San Antonio Business Journal.* January 2, 1993.

Rodriguez, Karen. "Virtual Office Raises Risks in Security." *Communications Week.* May 13, 1996.

Rosenthal, Tracy. "Keep Your Building and Your Employees Secure." *Business First of Buffalo.* July 25, 1994.

San Luis, Ed, et al. *Office and Office Building Security.* Butterworth-Heineman, 1994.

"Tighten Office Security for Yourself and Your Employees." *Profit-Building Strategies for Business Owners.* November 1992.

OFFICE SUPPLIES

Office supplies encompass a wide range of materials that are used on a regular, every-day basis by business owners and/or employees. Staple office supply items that are often utilized by even the smallest company or home office include pens, writing paper, notebooks, Post-It notes, scissors, erasers, computer diskettes, binders, slides, file folders, labels, basic reference materials (dictionaries, etc.), file cabinets, fax paper, envelopes, and a host of other items. In addition, equipment that is used in most office environments—printers, copy machines, fax machines, etc.—is often included under this umbrella term.

Despite the growth of technologies that supposedly herald the impending arrival of the "paperless office," offices in today's business environment would still be decidedly incomplete without paper, pens, file folders and other traditional office tools. Although their cost is small when purchased separately, in the aggregate they amount to a substantial portion of office expense. Small business owners should thus make sure that they pay attention to office supply costs and keep all receipts of such purchases, since office supplies are a legitiimate business deduction for tax purposes.

Entrepreneurs and business managers also need to take care to ensure that they get what they pay for. Most companies engaged in selling office supplies and equipment are scrupulous and reliable, but fraudulent suppliers do exist. For this reason, experts urge small businesses to proceed methodically, especially if dealing with a new supplier. "Prevent supplier swindles by adopting a written purchasing policy, which includes a list of your approved vendors," stated Scott Clark in *Pugent Sound Business Journal.* "A specific credit check procedure must be completed for a new vendor to be added to this list." Small business owners should also insist on written confirmation of all supplier claims and demand an opportunity to review sample goods before placing an order.

PROCUREMENT OPTIONS In recent years, office superstores and catalogue supply houses have emerged as the most efficient and inexpensive way to purchase various types of supplies. The average client of these superstores is the small- to medium-sized business, as well as the home office market. The convenience of being able to find virtually any office supply at one location is one of the primary reasons for the increased popularity of the superstores. In addition to convenience, these stores and catalogues offer merchandise that is very competitively priced since they are able to purchase their goods at bulk rates. Some of these savings are usually passed along to small business customers, especially if the stores are operating in a competitive environment.

The proliferation of Internet shopping has opened up a new avenue for office supply procurement as well. This option is expected to continue to grow in popularity, especially as technologies such as electronic fund transfer (EFT) evolve.

Finally, many small (and large) businesses are choosing suppliers who offer materials made from recycled materials This ''green'' trend in procurement can be seen in all types of paper products (computer paper, envelopes, tablets, file folders, etc.) as well as big-ticket items like office furniture. In the latter case, remanufactured, refurbished or reused furniture has emerged as a particularly attractive option for cash-strapped start-ups and growing businesses, who can register savings of 30-50 percent by pursuing this course of action. According to some experts, furniture recyclers now represent almost 10 percent of the $13.6 billion commercial furniture industry.

FURTHER READING:

Atkinson, William. ''Buyer Demand for Green Office Products Blossoms.'' *Purchasing.* July 13, 2000.

Belyea, Kathryn. ''Purchasing Exec Urges Peers to Embrace E-Buying.'' *Purchasing.* July 13, 2000.

Clark, Scott. ''Don't Let Fraudulent Suppliers Rip You Off.'' *Puget Sound Business Journal.* July 14, 2000.

Jeffress, Charles N. ''Ergonomics Standard Good for Business.'' *Business Insurance.* October 23, 2000.

Malik, Mary S. ''New Ways of Getting What You Need .'' *Managing Office Technology.* August 1994.

Reynolds, Rhonda. ''Setting Up at Home: To Get the Job Done, You Need the Right Space and Tools. *Black Enterprise,* July 1994.

ONLINE AUCTIONS

Online auctions are sales transactions involving competitive bidding that are conducted over the Internet. Whether the sales take place between individuals, between consumers and merchants, or between businesses, online auctions have enjoyed a rapid increase in popularity. The value of goods and services traded through consumer online auctions more than doubled from $3 billion in 1999 to $6.4 billion in 2000, according to a Jupiter Research study quoted by Joelle Tessler in the *Knight-Ridder/Tribune Business News.* In fact, some business analysts claim that online auctions—by giving both buyers and sellers access to a vast global marketplace—have created a whole new way of doing business. ''Online auctions are a method of commerce that did not really exist several years ago and couldn't exist offline on the scale it does online,'' Jeff Jordan of the leading Internet auction site eBay told Tessler.

As of 2000, the majority of traffic at online auctions consisted of transactions between individuals on hosted sites like eBay. The consumer online auction process has been described as being similar to a garage sale, with commonly offered items including collectibles, antiques, toys, clothing, and event tickets. Online auctions appeal to individuals who enjoy the competitive bidding process and like to feel as if they are getting a bargain. Most Web sites that host auctions allow buyers and sellers to negotiate payment methods and shipping details. Costs are usually limited to a small percentage of the final sales price.

Although individuals comprise the majority of current online auction participants, the future growth of the industry is expected to be driven by business-to-consumer and business-to-business auctions. Online auctions offer potential benefits to all types of businesses. ''Many companies wonder when and why they should use online auctions as part of their business trading strategy,'' Lori Mitchell wrote in *InfoWorld.* ''The short answer is, if you sell goods and services or if you purchase items to run your business, online auctions can work for you. . . . Companies of practically any size and within any industry can benefit from them.''

Internet analysts note that online retailers who incorporate auctions into their sales activities tend to see a higher level of repeat visits, more frequent purchases, and increased promotional opportunities compared to other online retailers. Auctions also offer advantages for those businesses interested in selling to or buying from other businesses. Some businesses choose to host closed or private auctions for their existing business contacts. But online auction companies may be able to assist companies in enlarging the audience for auctions by analyzing the bidding patterns of previous auctions to identify potential new customers.

BENEFITS OF ONLINE AUCTIONS

Online auctions offer small businesses a number of potential benefits with very few risks. After all, participating in online auctions does not prevent businesses from continuing to use traditional sales methods. In addition, companies can avoid financial losses on sale items by setting the minimum bid price high enough to cover costs. Among the few potential drawbacks are that buyers are not able to personally view and evaluate items before making a purchase, which raises the possibility of fraud. It can also be difficult to integrate online auction technology with the business's procurement systems. Finally, companies that decide to host auctions on their own Web sites may need to hire additional information technology staff.

Whether a small business participates in online auctions on a hosted site or sets up its own auction Web site, buying and selling items online offers a number of potential benefits. As Steffano Korper and Juanita Ellis noted in *The E-Commerce Book,* online auctions can help businesses reduce their distribution costs. Items to be sold online can be stored in one location until they are ready for shipping. This reduces the time and money spent packaging items for distribution to intermediaries, such as retail stores, and also helps eliminate the problems of damaged and missing goods.

Another major benefit of online auctions, according to Korper and Ellis, is that they enable small businesses to reduce their levels of surplus inventory, along with associated inventory carrying costs. Many businesses encounter problems disposing of seasonal, discontinued, or damaged goods. They either keep such items in inventory indefinitely, or end up marking down the prices until the items are sold at a loss. Online auctions provide a method for businesses to sell surplus inventory, often at a profit, and eliminate the expense of storing older merchandise.

Online auctions hold two other potential benefits for small businesses, as well. First, buying and selling over the Internet can help expand the global reach of a small business, opening international markets that would have been impossible to reach via normal marketing channels. Second, auctions can help new businesses—or those offering new products—to establish market prices based on supply and demand. Small businesses can use online auctions to gauge interest in their products and find out what customers are willing to pay. Furthermore, companies can collect such information quickly and informally, rather than investing in time-consuming and expensive market research.

HOSTED VERSUS IN-HOUSE AUCTION SITES

Small businesses interested in participating in online auctions have two basic choices about how to proceed. The first option is to join an existing online marketplace on a hosted auction site. A hosted site is usually a good choice for small to medium-sized companies that are interested in auctioning only occasionally. In contrast to creating a dedicated auction site, going through a host tends to give companies faster implementation and fewer start-up costs. In addition, this option requires little in the way of additional information technology staff to oversee the auctions. In general, buying and selling items through a hosted site is relatively simple. It only requires individuals and companies to have a Web browser and a digital image of any items they wish to sell. Fees are generally low, consisting of a small percentage of the sale price once a transaction is completed.

The second option for businesses looking to become involved in online auctions is to create a dedicated company auction site on the Internet. A dedicated site is the best approach for a larger company that plans to auction regularly and has adequate information technology staff to design and operate the site. Creating a site internally allows the company to exert greater control over the auctions and to integrate them into the overall marketing plan. The main drawback to this approach is that designing and maintaining an in-house site can be expensive. In fact, Mitchell reported that implementing an in-house auction site can cost upwards of $100,000.

A wide variety of software packages are available to help companies that wish to hold their own online auctions. Some of the leading auction software vendors include Microsoft, Netmerchants, OpenSite Technologies, and IBM. According to Korper and Ellis, Netmerchants' Auctioneer package is easy to install and administer. With options such as chat rooms, e-mail functions, and a built-in search engine, it is particularly appropriate for small businesses that plan to engage in consumer auctions. OpenSite Technologies offers three auction software packages for businesses seeking different levels of complexity. One is a complete package for entry-level auctioning, one is designed for merchants who wish to build auction capabilities into an existing Web site, and the third provides a completely integrated solution for businesses that plan to emphasize auctions. ''Auction software is starting to mature, making it far easier to manage the complicated transactional nature of these activities,'' Mitchell stated. ''Business-to-business auctions are no longer solely the domain of the Fortune 500. With planning, any company can use auctioning to add to the bottom line cost-effectively and without headaches.''

TYPES OF AUCTIONS

Whatever level of involvement a small business chooses, it is important to understand the various types of online auctions available. The most common type of auction is known as an open cry auction. In this type of auction, bidding typically begins low—either at zero or at a previously specified minimum bid—and proceeds upward quickly by increments. All potential buyers are usually made aware of the current bid and receive an equal chance to increase it. Open cry auctions tend to work best when buyers feel comfortable valuing the merchandise quickly.

Another type of auction is a sealed bid auction. In this case, the potential buyers receive no information about other bidders, including the amount bid. An example of a sealed bid auction is when a company takes bids from a number of vendors before awarding a contract. This type of auction is useful when potential buyers are unable to prepare bids quickly, or when the seller does not want bidders to have information about each other.

A Dutch auction basically works backward. Items are initially offered at a high price, and the price is gradually reduced until a bidder offers to buy at that price. The first person to bid is allowed to purchase the sale item. This type of auction is useful when a business is selling a few expensive items with high demand. In a second price auction, each potential buyer bids the most he or she is willing to pay for the item. Then the current bid amount is gradually adjusted downward until all the items have been sold. This type of auction generally works well when bidding is slow and the auction takes place over an extended time period.

In a forward auction, multiple buyers compete to buy things from an individual seller through a bidding process. In a reverse auction, however, one buyer requests a certain good or service from a number of sellers. The sellers then bid for the right to make the sale. Reverse auctions are expected to play a growing role in business-to-business transactions on the Internet, particularly for large, one-time purchases, such as a fleet of automobiles.

SETTING UP AN ONLINE AUCTION

Setting up an online auction requires a small business to make a number of choices in order to establish the rules and conditions under which the bidding will take place. Hosted auction sites usually offer sellers some options, while auction software packages vary greatly in the number of options they

provide. Either way, small businesses should have input into the basic parameters of the auction process. For example, a typical online auction requires the registration of both buyers and sellers and the collection of sale items, along with digital images and descriptions. The seller may be able to establish the start date and end date of the auction, as well as determine which auction method to use. It is also important to select preferred payment methods and establish a process for delivering items to customers.

A small business involved in an online auction may also have input into various settings that control the way the auction works. According to Korper and Ellis, auction settings are incorporated into most software packages and can be adjusted through most host sites. Sellers can thus specify the minimum bid, or the lowest acceptable starting price for a particular item; the bid increment, or the minimum amount by which a new bid must exceed the previous bid; the minimum current bid, or the lowest acceptable bid at any point in time, given the minimum bid and bid increment settings; the reserve price, or lowest price the seller will accept for the item; and the start and end date, which define the period when bids are accepted. It is also often possible to set the type of auction (open call or sealed bid, for example), and the process for resolving ties. The seller should always establish the settings prior to the beginning of the auction and never change them once the bidding process has begun.

FURTHER READING:

Baig, Edward C. ''Going Once. Going Twice. Cybersold!'' *Business Week.* August 11, 1997.

Hall, Diane Westbrook. ''Integrity of Online Auction Sites Questioned, Defended by Users.'' *Knight-Ridder/Tribune Business News.* July 21, 2000.

Korper, Steffano, and Juanita Ellis. *The E-Commerce Book: Building the E-Empire.* San Diego, CA: Academic Press, 2000.

Mitchell, Lori. ''Sold! On Online Auctions.'' *InfoWorld.* August 7, 2000.

Tessler, Joelle. ''Online Auction Sites Create Vast Global Marketplaces.'' *Knight-Ridder/Tribune Business News.* October 23, 2000.

SEE ALSO: Internet Payment Systems

OPERATIONS MANAGEMENT

Operations management is a multi-disciplinary field that focuses on managing all aspects of an organization's operations. ''The typical organization consists of the integration of many different functions,'' wrote Howard J. Weiss and Mark E. Gershon in *Production and Operations Management.* ''The two most obvious functions are to provide the product or service and to sell the product or service. Operations management focuses on the function of providing the product or service. It is concerned with the planning and controlling of all activities necessary for the provision of the firm's product or service.'' Aspects of operations management, then, include products or services to emphasize; facility size and location with respect to customers and suppliers; marketing strategies to attract clients/custmers; techniques and equipment to use to make the goods or to provide the services; work force management and training; and measurements of quality assurance. Operations managers apply ideas and technologies to increase productivity and reduce costs, improve flexibility to meet rapidly changing customer needs, enhance product quality, and improve customer service.

KEY ISSUES IN OPERATIONS

As an organization develops plans and strategies to deal with the opportunities and challenges that arise in its particular operating environment, it should design a system that is capable of producing quality services and goods in demanded quantities in acceptable time frames.

DESIGNING THE SYSTEM Designing the system begins with product development. Product development involves determining the characteristics and features of the good (or service if engaged in a service-oriented industry) to be sold. It should begin with an assessment of customer needs and eventually grow into a detailed product design. The facilities and equipment that will produce the product, as well as the information systems needed to monitor and control performance, are part of this system design process. In fact, manufacturing process decisions are integral to a system's ultimate success or failure. ''Of all the structural decisions that the operations manager faces, the one with the greatest impact on the manufacturing operation's success is the process/technology choice,'' said Thomas S. Bateman and Carl P. Zeithaml in *Management: Function and Strategy.* ''This decision addresses the question 'How will the product be made?' '' Product development should be a cross-functional decisionmaking process that relies on teamwork and communication to install the marketing, financial, and operating plans needed to successfully launch a product.

Product design is a critical task because it determines the characteristics and features of the product, as well as how the product functions. Product design determines a product's cost and quality, as well as its features and performance. These are important factors on which customers make purchasing decisions. In recent years, new design models such as Design for Manufacturing and Assembly (DFMA) have been implemented to improve product quality and lower costs.

DFMA focuses on operating issues during product design. This can be critical even though design costs are a small part of the total cost of a product, because, procedures that waste raw materials or duplicate effort can have a substantial negative impact on a business's operating profitability. Another innovation similar to DFMA in its emphasis on design is Quality Functional Deployment (QFD). QFD is a set of planning and communication routines that are used to improve product design by focusing design efforts on customer needs.

Process design describes how the product will be made. The process design decision has two major components: a technical (or engineering) component and a scale economy (or business) component. The technical component includes selecting equipment and selecting a sequence for various phases of operational production.

The scale economy or business component involves applying the proper amount of mechanization (tools and equipment) to make the organization's work force more productive. This includes determining: 1) If the demand for a product is large enough to justify mass production; 2) If there is sufficient variety in customer demand so that flexible production systems are required; and 3) If demand for a product is so small or seasonal that it cannot support a dedicated production facility.

Facility design involves determining the capacity, location, and layout for the production acility. Capacity is a measure of an organization's ability to provide the demanded services or goods in the quantity requested by the customer in a timely manner. Capacity planning involves estimating demand, determining the capacity of facilities, and deciding how to change the organization's capacity to respond to demand.

Facility location is the placement of a facility with respect to its customers and suppliers. Facility location is a strategic decision because it is a long-term commitment of resources that cannot easily or inexpensively be changed. When evaluating a location, management should consider customer convenience, initial investment necessary to secure land and facilities, government incentives, and operating transportation costs. In addition, qualitative factors such as quality of life for employees, transportation infrastructure, and labor environment should also be taken under consideration.

Facility layout is the arrangement of the work space within a facility. It considers which departments or work areas should be adjacent to one another so that the flow of product, information, and people can move quickly and efficiently through the production system.

PLANNING THE SYSTEM Planning the system describes how management expects to utilize the existing resource base created as a result of the production system design. One of the outcomes of this planning process may be to change the system design to cope with environmental changes. For example, management may decide to increase or decrease capacity to cope with changing demand, or rearrange layout to enhance efficiency.

Decisions made by production planners depend on the time horizon. Long-range decisions could include the number of facilities required to meet customer needs or studying how technological change might affect the methods used to produce services and goods. The time horizon for long-term planning varies with the industry and is dependent on both complexity and size of proposed changes. Typically, however, long-term planning may involve determining work force size, developing training programs, working with suppliers to improve product quality and improve delivery systems, and determining the amount of material to order on an aggregate basis. Short-term scheduling, on the other hand, is concerned with production planning for specific job orders (who will do the work, what equipment will be used, which materials will be consumed, when the work will begin and end, and what mode of transportation will be used to deliver the product when the order is completed).

MANAGING THE SYSTEM Managing the system involves working with people to encourage participation and improve organizational performance. Participative management and teamwork are an essential part of successful operations, as are leadership, training, and culture. In addition, material management and quality are two key areas of concern.

Material management includes decisions regarding the procurement, control, handling, storage, and distribution of materials. Material management is becoming more important because, in many organizations, the costs of purchased materials comprise more than 50 percent of the total production cost. Questions regarding quantities and timing of material orders need to be addressed here as well when companies weigh the qualities of various suppliers.

BUILDING SUCCESS WITH OPERATIONS

To understand operations and how they contribute to the success of an organization, it is important to understand the strategic nature of operations, the value-added nature of operations, the impact technology can have on performance, and the globally competitive marketplace.

Efficient organization operations are a vital tool in achieving competitive advantage in the daily contest for customers/clients. What factors influence buying decisions for these entities? For most services and goods, price, quality, product performance and features, product variety, and availability of the product are critical. All these factors are substantially influenced by actions taken in operations. For example, when productivity increases, product costs decline and product price can be reduced. Similarly, as better production methods are developed, quality and variety may increase.

By linking operations and operating strategies with the overall strategy of the organization (including engineering, financial, marketing, and information system strategy) synergy can result. Operations become a positive factor when facilities, equipment, and employee training are viewed as a means to achieve organizational objectives, rather than as narrowly focused departmental objectives. In recognition of this evolving viewpoint, the criteria for judging operations is changing from cost control (a narrowly defined operating objective) to global performance measurements in such areas as product performance and variety, product quality, delivery time, customer service, and operational flexibility.

In today's business environment, a key component of operational flexibility in many industries is technological knowledge. Advances in technology make it possible to build better products using fewer resources. As technology fundamentally changes a product, its performance and quality often increases dramatically, making it a more highly valued commodity in the marketplace. But the growth in high-tech business applications has created new competitiors as well, making it important for businesses to try to register advantages in any and all areas of operations management.

Over time, operations management has grown in scope and increased in importance. Today, it has elements that are strategic, it relies on behavioral and engineering concepts, and it utilizes management science/operations research tools and techniques for systematic decisionmaking and problem-solving. As operations management continues to develop, it will increasingly interact with other functional areas within the organization to develop integrated answers to complex interdisciplinary problems. Indeed, such interaction is widely regarded as essential to long-term business success for small business establishments and multinational corporations alike.

FURTHER READING:

Andrews, Katherine Zoe. ''Learning How to Learn.'' *Harvard Business Review.* March/April 1996.

Angell, Linda C., and Robert D. Klassen. ''Integrating Environmental Issues into the Mainstream: An Agenda for Research in Operations Management.'' *Journal of Operations Management.* August 1999.

Bateman, Thomas S., and Carl P. Zeithaml. *Management: Function and Strategy.* Richard D. Irwin, 1990.

Dyson, Robert G. "Strategy, Performance and Operational Research." *Journal of the Operational Research Society.* January 2000.

Krajewski, L.J., and L.P. Ritzman. *Operations Management: Strategy and Analysis.* Addison-Wesley Publishing, 1993.

Nie, Winter. "Waiting: Integrating Social and Psychological Perspectives in Operations Management." *Omega.* December 2000.

Ruffini, Frans A.J., Harry Boer, and Maarten J. Van Riemsdijk. "Organization Design in Operations Management." *International Journal of Operations and Production Management.* July 2000.

Weiss, Howard J., and Mark E. Gershon. *Production and Operations Management.* Allyn and Bacon, 1989.

OPPORTUNITY COST

Simply stated, an opportunity cost is the cost of a missed opportunity. Applied to a business decision, opportunity cost might refer to the profit a company could have earned from its capital, equipment, and real estate if these assets had been used in a different way. The concept of opportunity cost may be applied to many different situations. It should be considered whenever circumstances are such that scarcity necessitates the election of one option over another. Opportunity cost is usually defined in terms of money, but it may also be considered in terms of time, person-hours, mechanical output, or any other finite, limited resource.

Although opportunity costs are not generally considered by accountants—financial statements only include explicit costs, or actual outlays—they should be considered by managers. Small business owners should factor in opportunity costs when computing their operating expenses in order to provide a bid or estimate on the price of a job. Opportunity costs increase the cost of doing business, and thus should be recovered as a portion of the overhead expense charged to every job. Ignoring opportunity costs may lead small business owners to undercharge for their services and overestimate their profits.

EXAMPLES OF OPPORTUNITY COSTS

One way to demonstrate opportunity cost lies in the employment of investment capital. For example, a private investor purchases $10,000 in a certain security, such as shares in a corporation, and after one year the investment has appreciated in value to $10,500. The investor's return is 5 percent. The investor considers other ways the $10,000 could have been invested, and discovers a bank certificate with an an-

nual yield of 6 percent and a government bond that carries an annual yield of 7.5 percent. After a year, the bank certificate would have appreciated in value to $10,600, and the government bond would have appreciated to $10,750. The opportunity cost of purchasing shares is $100 relative to the bank certificate, and $250 relative to the government bond. The investor's decision to purchase shares with a 5 percent return comes at the cost of a lost opportunity to earn 6 or 7.5 percent.

Expressed in terms of time, consider a commuter who chooses to drive to work, rather than using public transportation. Because of heavy traffic and a lack of parking, it takes the commuter 90 minutes to get to work. If the same commute on public transportation would have taken only 40 minutes, the opportunity cost of driving would be 50 minutes. The commuter might naturally have chosen driving over public transportation because he could not have anticipated traffic delays in driving. Once the choice has been made to drive, it is not possible to change one's mind, thus the choice itself becomes irrelevant. Experience can create a basis for future decisions, however: the commuter may be less inclined to drive next time, knowing the consequences of traffic congestion.

In another example, a small business owns the building in which it operates, and thus pays no rent for office space. But this does not mean that the company's cost for office space is zero, even though an accountant might treat it that way. Instead, the small business owner must consider the opportunity cost associated with reserving the building for its current use. Perhaps the building could have been rented out to another company, with the business itself relocated to a location with a higher level of customer traffic. The foregone money from these alternative uses of the property is an opportunity cost of using the office space, and thus should be considered in calculations of the small business's expenses.

FURTHER READING:

Baumol, William J., and Alan S. Blinder. *Economics, Principles and Policy.* Harcourt Brace Jovanovich, 1982.

Miller, Bruce L., and A.G. Buckman. "Cost Allocation and Opportunity Costs." *Management Science.* May 1987.

Primeaux, Patrick, and John Stieber. "Managing Business Ethics and Opportunity Costs." *Journal of Business Ethics.* June 1997.

Sandoval-Chavez, Diego A., and Mario G. Beruvides. "Using Opportunity Costs to Determine the Cost of Quality: A Case Study in a Continuous-Process Industry." *Engineering Economist.* Winter 1998.

Vera-Munoz, Sandra C. "The Effects of Accounting Knowledge and Context on the Omission of Opportunity Costs in Resource Allocation Decisions." *Accounting Review.* January 1998.

OPTIMAL FIRM SIZE

Optimal firm size refers to the speed and extent of growth that is ideal for a specific small business. Optimal firm size is dependent on a variety of internal and external factors. For some home-based businesses, the optimal size may be the two founding partners—a husband and wife—if their primary operating goal is simply to bring in enough revenue for a comfortable standard of living, while leaving large blocks of time for family or travel. But most companies are intent on expanding their operations. "However wary a small business owner may be of the risks involved in expansion, growth of some kind—in revenues, profits, number of employees, or size of facilities—is essential for almost every business," stated Michael Barrier in *Nation's Business.* And for many companies competing in rapidly changing industries, expansion (of manufacturing capacity, geographic presence, market share, etc.) is usually imperative for survival. But smart growth strategies can be elusive, as many entrepreneurs have learned to their chagrin. As James A. Schriner explained in *Industry Week,* "Growing a company is like blowing up a balloon. Your first few breaths, though difficult, produce immediate results. Subsequent breaths expand the balloon proportionally until it nears capacity. Stop too soon and the balloon never reaches its potential. Stop too late and it bursts."

Successful entrepeneurs and business experts agree that the key to finding the optimal firm size is to grow in a controlled way. In some cases, restraining growth is simply a matter of saying "no," or turning down new business. This is particularly true for service businesses that depend on the personal attention of the founder. When turning down business becomes necessary, the entrepreneur may wish to provide referrals in order to maintain good relations with potential customers. Another strategy in restraining growth involves hiring employees who like working in a small company atmosphere. These people tend to enjoy the diversity of challenges they encounter in a small business, and they often have a strong interest in the product and can provide their expertise to customers. It is important to note, however, that restraining growth does not mean refusing to change. Small businesses are not likely to remain in business long if they cannot be creative and adapt to changes in customer tastes and competitors' tactics.

Schriner noted that one factor influencing the optimal size of a business is the availability of workers and other resources in the surrounding community. In fact, he suggested that it is possible for businesses to outgrow the communities in which they operate, particularly when they are located in a remote area. In this case, it may be difficult to attract talented workers from outside the immediate area, forcing the company to pay sharply higher wages to compete for labor. In addition, some communities cannot afford to provide services to growing companies (or provide top schools, parks, and other quality of life elements that attract high-quality employees necessary for successful business expansion). Finally, Schriner claimed that being too integral a part of a community can make it difficult for a growing company to adapt to a changing business environment. Some factors that may indicate a company has outgrown its community include: employing more than 10 percent of the local work force; growing at a faster rate than the community's labor force; providing more than one-third of the local government's funding through taxes; and being responsible for the death of the community if the company should shut down.

FURTHER READING:

Barrier, Michael. "Can You Stay Small Forever?" *Nation's Business.* October 1996.

Joaquin, Domingo Castelo, and Naveen Khanna. "Investment Timing Decisions Under Threat of Potential Competition: Why Firm Size Matters." *Quarterly Review of Economics and Finance.* Spring 2001.

Koretz, Gene. "Little Guys Are Making Plans: Small Businesses Are Set to Expand." *Business Week.* June 2, 1997.

Lawler, Edward E. III. "Rethinking Organization Size." *Organizational Dynamics.* Autumn 1997.

Orser, Barbara J., Sandy Hogarth-Scott, and Allan L. Riding. "Performance, Firm Size, and Management Problem Solving." *Journal of Small Business Management.* October 2000.

Schriner, James A. "How Big Is Too Big?" *Industry Week.* May 6, 1996.

ORAL COMMUNICATION

Oral communication describes any type of interaction that makes use of spoken words, and it is a vital, integral part of the modern business world. "The ability to communicate effectively through speaking as well as in writing is highly valued, and demanded, in business," Herta A. Murphy and Herbert W. Hildebrandt wrote in their book *Effective Business Communications.* "Knowing the content of the functional areas of business is important, but to give life to those ideas—in meetings or in solo presentations—demands an effective oral presentation." The types of oral communication commonly used within an organization include staff meetings, personal discussions, presentations, telephone discourse, and informal conversation. Oral communication with those outside of the organization might take the form of face-to-face meetings, telephone calls, speeches, teleconferences, or videoconferences.

Conversation management skills are essential for small business owners and managers, who often shoulder much of the burden in such areas as client/customer presentations, employee interviews, and conducting meetings. For oral communication to be effective, it should be clear, relevant, tactful in phrasology and tone, concise, and informative. Presentations or conversations that bear these hallmarks can be an invaluable tool in ensuring business health and growth. Unclear, inaccurate, or inconsiderate business communication, on the other hand, can waste valuable time, alienate employees or customers, and destroy goodwill toward management or the overall business.

ORAL PRESENTATIONS

The public presentation is generally recognized as the most important of the various genres of oral business communication. As is true of all kinds of communication, the first step in preparing a public speech or remarks is to determine the essential purpose/goal of the communication. As Hildebrandt and Murphy note, business presentations tend to have one of three general purposes: to persuade, to inform or instruct, or to entertain. Out of the purpose will come the main ideas to be included in the presentation. These ideas should be researched thoroughly and adapted to the needs of the audience.

The ideas should then be organized to include an introduction, a main body or text, and a summary or conclusion. Or, as the old adage about giving speeches goes, ''Tell them what you're going to tell them, tell them, and tell them what you told them.'' The introduction should grab the listener's interest and establish the theme of the remainder of the presentation. The main body should concentrate on points of emphasis. The conclusion should restate the key points and summarize the overarching message that is being conveyed.

Visual aids are an important component of many oral presentations. Whether they are displayed on chalkboards, dry-erase boards, flip charts, or presented using a slide projector, overhead projector, or computer program, visual aids should be meaningful, creative, and interesting in order to help the speaker get a message across. Visual aids should also be adapted to the size of the audience.

Once the presentation has been organized and the visual aids have been selected, the speaker should rehearse out loud and revise as needed to fit time constraints, cover points of emphasis, etc. It may help to practice in front of a mirror or in front of a friend in order to gain confidence. A good oral presentation will include transitional phrases to help listeners move through the material, and will not be overly long or technical. It is also important for the speaker to anticipate questions the audience might have and either include that information in the presentation or be prepared to answer afterward. Professional and gracious presentation is another key to effective communication, whether the setting is a conference, a banquet, a holiday luncheon, or a management retreat. ''Recognize that when you speak at a business event, you represent your company and your office in that company,'' stated Steve Kaye in *IIE Solutions*. ''Use the event as an opportunity to promote good will. Avoid complaints, criticism, or controversy. These will alienate the audience and destroy your credibility quickly. Instead, talk about what the audience wants to hear. Praise your host, honor the occasion, and compliment the attendees. Radiate success and optimism.''

Oral presentations can be delivered extemporaneously (from an outline or notes); by reading from a manuscript; or from memory. The extemporaneous approach is often touted as a method that allows the speaker to make eye contact and develop a rapport with the audience while simultaneously conveying pertinent information. Reading from a manuscript is more often utilized for longer and/or detailed communications that cover a lot of ground. Memorization, meanwhile, is usually only used for short and/or informal discussions.

The delivery of effective oral presentations requires a speaker to consider his or her vocal pitch, rate, and volume. It is important to incorporate changes in vocal pitch to add emphasis and avoid monotony. It is also helpful to vary the rate of speaking and incorporate pauses to allow the listener to reflect upon specific elements of the overall message. Finding the appropriate volume is crucial to the success of a presentation as well. Finally, speakers should be careful not to add extraneous words or sounds—such as ''um,'' ''you know,'' or ''okay''—between words or sentences in a presentation.

Nonverbal elements such as posture, gestures, and facial expression are also important factors in developing good oral communication skills. ''Your outward appearance mirrors your inner mood,'' Murphy and Hildebrandt confirmed. ''Thus good posture suggests poise and confidence; stand neither at rigid attention nor with sloppy casualness draped over the podium, but erect with your weight about equally distributed on each foot.'' Some movement may be helpful to hold listeners' attention or to increase emphasis, but constant shifting or pacing should be avoided. Likewise, hand and arm gestures can be used to point, describe, or emphasize, but they should be varied, carefully timed, and adapted to the audience. Finally, good speakers should make frequent eye contact with the audience, let their facial expression show their interest in the ideas they are presenting, and dress in a way that is appropriate for the occasion.

Small business owners reflect the general population in that their enthusiasm for public speaking varies considerably for individual to individual. Some entrepreneurs enjoy the limelight and thrive in settings that call for public presentations (formal or informal). Others are less adept at public speaking and avoid being placed in such situations. But business consultants urge entrepreneurs to treat public presentations and oral communication skills as a potentially invaluable tool in business growth. "You may consider hiring a presentation coach or attending a workshop on business presentations," counseled Kaye. "These services can show you how to maximize your impact while speaking. In fact, learning such skills serves as a long-term investment in your future as an effective leader."

FURTHER READING:

Hardingham, Alison. "Charged with Intent." *People Management.* March 30, 2000.

Holmes, Godfrey. "Tactical Blunder." *Accountancy.* June 2000.

Kaye, Steve. "Make an Impact with Style: Presentation Tips for Leaders." *IIE Solutions.* March 1999.

Murphy, Herta A., and Herbert W. Hildebrandt. *Effective Business Communications.* McGraw-Hill, 1991.

ORGANIZATION CHART

Organizational charts are detailed representations of organization structures and hierarchies. They are typically used to provide both employees and individuals outside the organization with a "snapshot" picture of it's reporting relationships, divisions of work, and levels of management. Obviously, smaller firms—whether they consist of a single owner of a home-based business, a modest shop of a few employees, or a family-owned business with a few dozen workers—are less likely to utilize organization charts, since the information that is gleaned from chart representations is typically pretty self-evident with such businesses. "Small organizations can get along very well without them as long as everyone understands what they are to do and who they are to do it with," stated James Gibson, John Ivancevich, and James Donnelly in *Organizations: Behavior, Structure, Processes.* But many consultants and small business owners contend that an organization chart can be a useful tool for growing firms.

Business owners endeavoring to allocate responsibilities, activities, and management authority to various employees also have to make certain that they coordinate the activities of those employees to avoid gaps and/or redundancies in operations and management. "It is helpful to think of organizational design elements as building blocks that can be used to create a structure to fulfill a particular purpose," stated Phyllis and Leonard Schlesinger in *The Portable MBA in Management.* "A structure is built by defining the requirements of each individual job and then grouping the individual jobs into units. These units are grouped into larger and larger units and coordinating (or integrating) mechanisms are established for these units. In this way, the structure has been built to support organizational goals and achieve the key factors for success." Ideally, a detailed organizational chart will provide the business owner or manager with an accurate overview of the relationships of these units/responsibilities to one another and a reliable indication as to whether the firm is positioned to meet the business's fundamental goals.

ADVANTAGES AND DISADVANTAGES ASSOCIATED WITH ORGANIZATION CHARTS

While organizational charts are commonly used by mid- and large-sized companies, as well as by significant numbers of smaller businesses with varied operations and a substantial workforce, their usefulness has been a subject of some debate.

ADVANTAGES Supporters of organization charts claim that they are tools that can effectively delineate work responsibilities and reporting relationships. "Managers of different organizational subunits," wrote Gibson, Ivancevich, and Donnelly, "do not understand how their work fits into the work of other subunits. In the absence of an organization chart to clarify relationships, illogical and confusing ones will develop. In fact, the very process of charting the organization is a good test of its soundness, because any relationship that cannot be charted is likely to be unsound and therefore confusing to those working in it."

Supporters also argue that org charts can be particularly useful as a navigational tool when small businesses expand their operations. "The argument that organization charts are necessary only when the organization becomes too big for any one individual to manage does not hold," claimed Gibson, Ivancevich, and Donnelly. "In many instances, small firms that do rather well in the early stages of their development begin to fail when the founders can no longer manage in their personal styles. The transition from successful small firm to successful large firm is impaired because the employees are doing jobs that fit their personality and unique skills rather than jobs necessary for organizational performance. Organization charts and supporting documents are necessary from the very beginning of a firm's existence, not just when it gets too big for one person to manage.''

DISADVANTAGES The above perspective is not universally accepted by business consultants, researchers, executives, and managers, however. Detractors point out that formal organization charts do not recognize informal lines of communication and influence that are quite vital in many business settings. Writing in *Perspectives on Behaviors in Organizations,* contributors David A. Nadler and Michael L. Tushman characterized organization charts as ''narrow and static in perspective. . . . It excludes such factors as leader behavior, the impact of the environment, informal relations, power distribution, etc. Such a model can only capture a small part of what goes on in an organization.''

Critics of organization charts also sometimes charge that the diagrams may paint a misleading picture of the importance and influence of various people within an organization. Charts are, out of necessity, somewhat streamlined representations that only provide so much detail to a user. In some instances, for example, an organization chart may depict two employees as being equal in power and influence, when in reality, one of the individuals is rapidly ascending through the ranks and has the ear of the firm's principal decisionmakers, while the other may be regarded as steady but unremarkable (or even worse, an individual whose position has deteriorated from a higher level over the previous years).

''Perhaps the most damaging criticism of organization charts is that they encourage individuals to take a very narrow view of their jobs,'' wrote Gibson, Ivancevich, and Donnelly. ''Job definitions imply what people will not do as well as clarifying what they will do. The result is an organization that is not responsive to change, that lacks flexibility. The organization chart and all the supporting documentation . . . become substitutes for action and creative responses. In fact, some managers adamantly oppose the creation of organization charts even when employees complain that they need some direction to understand what they should do. These managers respond by saying that it is better to go ahead and fail than to do nothing.''

USING ORGANIZATION CHARTS TO STUDY ORGANIZATION STRUCTURE

As alluded to earlier, the process of constructing an organization chart is sometimes cited as a valuable means by which a company can test its structural soundness. Proponents say that charts can be used to ensure that, as one executive told *Inc.*'s Teri Lammers, ''no one's productivity is constrained by the structure.''

Researchers, consultants, and executives note that this benefit can be even more pronounced in today's business world, which has seen dramatic changes in operating philosophies and management direction over the past few decades. Indeed, corporations are increasingly implementing innovative organizational redesigns in efforts to increase their productivity. The growth in cross-functional teams and reorganizations, for example, can easily blur reporting and operational relationships between various segments of a business. It is important, then, for businesses that do rely on organizational charts to continually examine and update those diagrams to ensure that they reflect current business realities. In fact, the changes in organizational structures have spurred innovative changes in the format of many organizational charts. Whereas traditional models have been formatted along general ''up-down'' lines, newer models sometimes utilize flattened or ''spoke'' frameworks.

FURTHER READING:

Austin, Nancy K. ''Reorganizing the Organizational Chart.'' *Working Woman.* September 1993.

Cherrington, David J. *Organizational Behavior: The Management of Individual and Organizational Performance.* Boston: Allyn and Bacon, 1994.

Doloff, Phyllis Gail. ''Beyond the Org Chart.'' *Across the Board.* February 1999.

Gibson, James L., John M. Ivancevich, and James H. Donnelly Jr. *Organizations: Behavior, Structure, Processes.* 8th ed. Boston: Irwin, 1994.

Lammers, Teri. ''The New, Improved Organizational Chart.'' *Inc.* October 1992.

LaZara, Vincent A. ''Put the Customer on Top: Updating Your Organizational Chart.'' *Manage.* October 1999.

Schlesinger, Phyllis F., and Leonard A. Schlesinger. ''Designing Effective Organizations.'' In *The Portable MBA in Management.* Allan R. Cohen, ed. John Wiley, 1993.

ORGANIZATION THEORY

An organization, by its most basic definition, is an assembly of people working together to achieve common objectives through a division of labor. An organization provides a means of using individual strengths within a group to achieve more than can be accomplished by the aggregate efforts of group members working individually. Business organizations are formed to deliver goods or services to consumers in such a manner that they can realize a profit at the conclusion of the transaction. Over the years, business analysts, economists, and academic researchers have pondered several theories that attempt to explain the dynamics of business organizations, including the ways in which they make decisions, distribute power and control, resolve conflict, and promote or resist organizational change. As Jeffrey Pfeffer summarized in *New Directions for Organization Theory,* organizational theory studies provide ''an interdisciplinary focus on a) the effect of social organizations on the behavior and attitudes of individuals within them, b) the effects of individual characteristics and action on organization, . . . c) the performance, success, and survival of organizations, d) the mutual effects of environments, including resource and task, political, and cultural environments on organizations and vice versa, and e) concerns with both the epistemology and methodology that undergird research on each of these topics.''

Of the various organizational theories that have been studied in this realm, the open-systems theory has emerged as perhaps the most widely known, but others have their proponents as well. Indeed, some researchers into organizational theory propound a blending of various theories, arguing that an enterprise will embrace different organizational strategies in reaction to changes in its competitive circumstances, structural design, and experiences.

BACKGROUND

Modern organization theory is rooted in concepts developed during the beginnings of the Industrial Revolution in the late 1800s and early 1900s. Of import during that period was the research of German sociologist Max Weber (1864-1920). Weber believed that bureaucracies, staffed by bureaucrats, represented the ideal organizational form. Weber based his model bureaucracy on legal and absolute authority, logic, and order. In Weber's idealized organizational structure, responsibilities for workers are clearly defined and behavior is tightly controlled by rules, policies, and procedures.

Weber's theories of organizations, like others of the period, reflected an impersonal attitude toward the people in the organization. Indeed, the work force, with its personal frailties and imperfections, was regarded as a potential detriment to the efficiency of any system. Although his theories are now considered mechanistic and outdated, Weber's views on bureaucracy provided important insight into the era's conceptions of process efficiency, division of labor, and authority.

Another important contributor to organization theory in the early 1900s was Henri Fayol. He is credited with identifying strategic planning, staff recruitment, employee motivation, and employee guidance (via policies and procedures) as important management functions in creating and nourishing a successful organization.

Weber's and Fayol's theories found broad application in the early and mid-1900s, in part because of the influence of Frederick W. Taylor (1856-1915). In a 1911 book entitled *Principles of Scientific Management,* Taylor outlined his theories and eventually implemented them on American factory floors. He is credited with helping to define the role of training, wage incentives, employee selection, and work standards in organizational performance.

Researchers began to adopt a less mechanical view of organizations and to pay more attention to human influences in the 1930s. This development was motivated by several studies that shed light on the function of human fulfillment in organizations. The best known of these was probably the so-called Hawthorn Studies. These studies, conducted primarily under the direction of Harvard University researcher Elton Mayo, were conducted in the mid-1920s and 1930s at a Western Electric Company plant known as the Hawthorn Works. The company wanted to determine the degree to which working conditions affected output.

Surprisingly, the studies failed to show any significant positive correlations between workplace conditions and productivity. In one study, for example, worker productivity escalated when lighting was increased, but it also increased when illumination was decreased. The results of the studies demonstrated that innate forces of human behavior may have a greater influence on organizations than do mechanistic incentive systems. The legacy of the Hawthorn studies and other organizational research efforts of that period was an emphasis on the importance of individual and group interaction, humanistic management skills, and social relationships in the workplace.

The focus on human influences in organizations was reflected most noticeably by the integration of Abraham Maslow's ''hierarchy of human needs'' into organization theory. Maslow's theories introduced two important implications into organization theory. The first was that people have different needs and therefore need to be motivated by different incentives to achieve organizational objectives. The second of Maslow's theories held that people's needs change over time, meaning that as the needs of people lower in the hierarchy are met, new needs arise. These assumptions led to the recognition, for example, that assembly-line workers could be more productive if more of their personal needs were met, whereas past theories suggested that monetary rewards were the sole, or primary, motivators.

Douglas McGregor contrasted the organization theory that emerged during the mid-1900s to previous views. In the 1950s, McGregor offered his renowned Theory X and Theory Y to explain the differences. Theory X encompassed the old view of workers, which held that employees preferred to be directed, wanted to avoid responsibility, and cherished financial security above all else.

McGregor believed that organizations that embraced Theory Y were generally more productive. This theory held that humans can learn to accept and seek responsibility; most people possess a high degree of imaginative and problem-solving ability; employees are capable of effective self-direction; and that self-actualization is among the most important rewards that organizations can provide its workers.

OPEN-SYSTEMS THEORY

Traditional theories regarded organizations as closed systems that were autonomous and isolated from the outside world. In the 1960s, however, more holistic and humanistic ideologies emerged. Recognizing that traditional theory had failed to take into account many environmental influences that impacted the efficiency of organizations, most theorists and researchers embraced an open-systems view of organizations.

The term ''open systems'' reflected the newfound belief that all organizations are unique—in part because of the unique environment in which they operate—and that they should be structured to accommodate unique problems and opportunities. For example, research during the 1960s indicated that traditional bureaucratic organizations generally failed to succeed in environments where technologies or markets were rapidly changing. They also failed to realize the importance of regional cultural influences in motivating workers.

Environmental influences that affect open systems can be described as either specific or general. The specific environment refers to the network of suppliers, distributors, government agencies, and competitors with which a business enterprise interacts. The general environment encompasses four influences that emanate from the geographic area in which the organization operates. These are:

- Cultural values, which shape views about ethics and determine the relative importance of various issues.

- Economic conditions, which include economic upswings, recessions, regional unemployment, and many other regional factors that affect a company's ability to grow and prosper. Economic influences may also partially dictate an organization's role in the economy.

- Legal/political environment, which effectively helps to allocate power within a society and to enforce laws. The legal and political systems in which an open system operates can play a key role in determining the long-term stability and security of the organization's future. These systems are responsible for creating a fertile environment for the business community, but they are also responsible for ensuring—via regulations pertaining to operation and taxation— that the needs of the larger community are addressed.

- Quality of education, which is an important factor in high technology and other industries that require an educated work force. Businesses will be better able to fill such positions if they operate in geographic regions that feature a strong education system.

The open-systems theory also assumes that all large organizations are comprised of multiple subsystems, each of which receives inputs from other subsystems and turns them into outputs for use by other subsystems. The subsystems are not necessarily represented by departments in an organization, but might instead resemble patterns of activity.

An important distinction between open-systems theory and more traditional organization theories is that the former assumes a subsystem hierarchy, meaning that not all of the subsystems are equally essential. Furthermore, a failure in one subsystem will not necessarily thwart the entire system. By contrast, traditional mechanistic theories implied that a malfunction in any part of a system would have an equally debilitating impact.

BASIC ORGANIZATIONAL CHARACTERISTICS

Organizations differ greatly in size, function, and makeup. Nevertheless, the operations of nearly all organizations—from the multinational corporation to a a newly opened delicatessen—are based on a division of labor, a decision-making structure; and rules and policies. The degree of formality with which these aspects of business are approached vary tremendously within the business world, but these characteristics are inherent in any business enterprise that utilizes the talents of more than one person.

Organizations practice division of labor both vertically and horizontally. Vertical division includes three basic levels—top, middle, and bottom. The chief function of top managers, or executives, typically is to plan long-term strategy and oversee middle managers. Middle managers generally guide the day-to-day activities of the organization and administer top-level strategy. Low-level managers and laborers put strategy into action and perform the specific tasks necessary to keep the organization operating.

Organizations also divide labor horizontally by defining task groups, or departments, and assigning workers with applicable skills to those groups. Line units perform the basic functions of the business, while staff units support line units with expertise and services. In general, line units focus on supply, production, and distribution, while staff units deal mostly with internal operations and controls or public relations efforts.

Decision-making structures, the second basic organizational characteristic, are used to organize authority. These structures vary from operation to operation in their degree of centralization and decentralization. Centralized decision structures are referred to as ''tall'' organizations because important decisions usually emanate from a high level and are passed down through several channels until they reach the lower end of the hierarchy. Conversely, flat organizations, which have decentralized decision-making structures, employ only a few hierarchical levels. Such organizations are typically guided by a management philosophy that is favorably disposed toward some form of employee empowerment and individual autonomy.

A formalized system of rules and policies is the third standard organizational characteristic. Rules, policies, and procedures serve as templates of managerial guidance in all sectors of organizational production and behavior. They may document the most efficient means of accomplishing a task or provide standards for rewarding workers. Formalized rules provide managers with more time to spend on other problems and opportunities and help ensure that an organization's various subsystems are working in concert. Ill-conceived or poorly implemented rules, of course, can actually have a negative impact on business efforts to produce goods or services in a profitable or satisfactory manner.

Thus, organizations can be categorized as informal or formal, depending on the degree of formalization of rules within their structures. In formal organizations, say researchers, management has determined that a comparatively impersonal relationship between individuals and the company for which they work is viewed as the best environment for achieving organizational goals. Subordinates have less influence over the process in which they participate, with their duties more clearly defined.

Informal organizations, on the other hand, are less likely to adopt or adhere to a significant code of written rules or policies. Instead, individuals are more likely to adopt patterns of behavior that are influenced by a number of social and personal factors. Changes in the organization are less often the result of authoritative dictate and more often an outcome of collective agreement by members. Informal organizations tend to be more flexible and more reactive to outside influences. But some critics contend that such arrangements may also diminish the ability of top managers to effect rapid change.

ORGANIZATIONAL THEORY IN THE 1980S AND 1990S

By the 1980s several new organizational system theories received significant attention. These included Theory Z, a blending of American and Japanese management practices. This theory was a highly visible one, in part because of Japan's well-documented productivity improvements—and the United States' manufacturing difficulties—during that decade. Other theories, or adaptations of existing theories, emerged as well, which most observers saw as indicative of the ever-changing environment within business and industry.

The study of organizations and their management and production structures and philosophies continued to thrive throughout the the 1990s. Indeed, an understanding of various organizational principles continues to be seen as vital to the success of all kinds of organizations—from government agencies to business—of all shapes and sizes, from conglomerates to small businesses. ''As we observe how different professionals working in different kinds of organizations and occupational communities make their case, we see we are still far from having a single 'theory' of organization development,'' wrote Jay R. Galbraith in *Competing with Flexible Lateral Organizations*. ''Yet, a set of common assumptions is surfacing. We are beginning to see patterns in what works and what does not work, and we are becoming more articulate about these patterns. We are also seeing the field increasingly connected to other organizational sciences and disciplines,'' such as information technology and coordination theory.

FURTHER READING:

Boje, D.M., R.P. Gephert Jr., and T.J. Thatchenkery, eds. *Postmodern Management and Organization Theory*. Sage, 1996.

Cherrington, David J. *Organizational Behavior: The Management of Individual and Organizational Performance*. Allyn and Bacon, 1994.

Galbraith, Jay R. *Competing with Flexible Lateral Organizations*. 2d ed. Addison-Wesley, 1994.

Gortner, Harold F., Julianne Mahler, and Jeanne Bell Nicholson. *Organization Theory: A Public Perspective*. 2d ed. Harcourt, 1997.

Hatch, Mary Jo. *Organization Theory: Modern, Symbolic, and Postmodern Perspectives*. OUP-USA, 1997.

Pfeffer, Jeffrey. *New Directions for Organization Theory: Problems and Prospects*. Oxford University Press, 1997.

ORGANIZATIONAL BEHAVIOR

Organizational behavior is an academic discipline concerned with describing, understanding, predicting, and controlling human behavior in an organizational environment. Organizational behavior has evolved from early classical management theories into a complex school of thought—and it continues to change in response to the dynamic environment and proliferating corporate cultures in which today's businesses operate. "The task of getting organizations to function effectively is a difficult one," wrote David A. Nadler and Michael L. Tushman in Hackman, Lawler, and Porter's *Perspectives on Behaviors in Organizations*. "Understanding one individual's behavior is a challenging problem in and of itself. A group, made up of different individuals and multiple relationships among those individuals, is even more complex. . . . In the fact of this overwhelming complexity, organizational behavior must be managed. Ultimately the work of organizations gets done through the behavior of people, individually or collectively, on their own or in collaboration with technology. Thus, central to the management task is the management of organizational behavior. To do this, there must be the capacity to *understand* the patterns of behavior at individual, group, and organization levels, to *predict* what behavior responses will be elicited by different managerial actions, and finally to use understanding and prediction to achieve *control*."

THE BEHAVIORAL SCIENCES

Organizational behavior scientists study four primary areas of behavioral science: individual behavior, group behavior, organizational structure, and organizational processes. They investigate many facets of these areas like personality and perception, attitudes and job satisfaction, group dynamics, politics and the role of leadership in the organization, job design, the impact of stress on work, decision-making processes, the communications chain, and company cultures and climates. They use a variety of techniques and approaches to evaluate each of these elements and its impact on individuals, groups, and organizational efficiency and effectiveness. "The behavior sciences," stated Gibson, Ivancevich, and Donnelly in *Organizations: Behavior, Structure, Processes,* "have provided the basic framework and principles for the field of organizational behavior. Each behavioral science discipline provides a slightly different focus, analytical framework, and theme for helping managers answer questions about themselves, nonmanagers, and environmental forces."

In regard to individuals and groups, researchers try to determine why people behave the way they do.

They have developed a variety of models designed to explain individuals' behavior. They investigate the factors that influence personality development, including genetic, situational, environmental, cultural, and social factors. Researchers also examine various personality types and their impact on business and other organizations. One of the primary tools utilized by organizational behavior researchers in these and other areas of study is the job satisfaction study. These tools are used not only to measure job satisfaction in such tangible areas as pay, benefits, promotional opportunities, and working conditions, but also to gauge how individual and group behavior patterns influence corporate culture, both positively and negatively.

ORGANIZATIONAL BEHAVIOR AND CORPORATE CULTURE

The terms "corporate culture" and "organizational behavior" are sometimes used interchangeably, but in reality, there are differences between the two. Corporate culture encompasses the shared values, attitudes, standards, and beliefs and other characteristics that define an organization's operating philosophy. Organizational behavior, meanwhile, can be understood in some ways as the academic *study* of corporate culture and its various elements, as well as other important components of behavior such as organization structure and organization processes. Organizational behavior, said Gibson, Ivancevich, and Donnelly, is "the field of study that draws on theory, methods, and principles from various disciplines to learn about *individual* perceptions, values, learning capacities, and actions while working in *groups* and within the total *organization;* analyzing the external environment's effect on the organization and its human resources, missions, objectives, and strategies. . . . Effective managers know what to look for in terms of structure, process, and culture and how to understand what they find. Therefore, managers must develop diagnostic skills; they must be trained to identify conditions symptomatic of a problem requiring further attention. Problem indicators include declining profits, declining quantity or quality of work, increases in absenteeism or tardiness, and negative employee attitudes. Each of these problems is an issue of organizational behavior."

FURTHER READING:

Connors, Roger, and Tom Smith. "Benchmarking Cultural Transition." *Journal of Business Strategy.* May 2000.

Egan, Gerard. "Cultivate Your Culture." *Management Today.* April 1994.

Gibson, James L., John M. Ivancevich, and James H. Donnelly Jr. *Organizations: Behavior, Structure, Processes.* 8th ed. Boston: Richard D. Irwin, 1994.

Gordon, George G. "Industry Determinants of Organizational Culture." *Academy of Management Review.* April 1991.

Hodgetts, Richard M. *Organizational Behavior: Theory and Practice.* New York: Macmillan Publishing Company, 1991.

Nijhof, Andre H.J., and Marius M. Rietdijk. "An ABC Analysis of Ethical Organizational Behavior." *Journal of Business Ethics.* May 15, 1999.

Phegan, Barry. *Developing Your Company Culture: The Joy of Leadership.* Context Press, 1996.

ORGANIZATIONAL DEVELOPMENT

Organizational development (OD) is an application of behavioral science to organizational change. It encompasses a wide array of theories, processes, and activities, all of which are oriented toward the goal of improving individual organizations. Generally speaking, however, OD differs from traditional organizational change techniques in that it typically embraces a more holistic approach that is aimed at transforming thought and behavior throughout an entity. Definitions of OD abound, but they are all predicated on the notion of improving organizational performance through proactive activities and techniques. It is also worth noting that organizational development, though concerned with improving workforce performance, should not be mistaken for human resource development. "Organization development is the planned process of developing an organization to be more effective in accomplishing its desired goals," wrote Rima Shaffer in *Principles of Organization Development.* "It is distinguished from human resource development in that HRD focuses on the personal growth of individuals within organizations, while OD focuses on developing the structures, systems, and processes within the organization to improve organizational effectiveness."

ORGANIZATIONAL DEVELOPMENT BASICS

Although the field of OD is broad, it can be differentiated from other systems of organizational change by its emphasis on process rather than problems. Indeed, traditional group change systems have focused on identifying problems in an organization and then trying to alter the behavior that creates the problem. But Margaret Neale and Gregory Northcraft observed in *Organizational Behavior: A Management Challenge* that OD initiatives focus on identifying the behavioral interactions and patterns that cause and sustain problems. Then, rather than simply changing isolated behaviors, OD efforts are aimed at creating a behaviorally healthy organization that will naturally anticipate and prevent (or quickly solve) problems.

OD programs usually share several basic characteristics. For instance, they are considered long-term efforts of at least one to three years in most cases. In addition, OD stresses collaborative management, whereby managers and employees at different levels of the hierarchy cooperate to solve problems. OD also recognizes that every organization is unique and that the same solutions cannot necessarily be applied at different companies—this assumption is reflected in an OD focus on research and feedback. Another common trait of OD programs is an emphasis on the value of teamwork and small groups. In fact, most OD systems use small teams—or even individuals—as a vehicle to implement broad organizational changes.

The catalyst—whether a group or individual—that facilitates the OD process is known as the "change agent." Change agents are often outside consultants with experience managing OD programs, although companies sometimes utilize inside managers. The advantage of bringing in outside OD consultants is that they often provide a different perspective and have a less biased view of the organization's problems and needs. The primary drawback associated with outside change agents is that they may lack an in-depth understanding of key issues particular to the company. In addition, outside change agents may have trouble securing the trust and cooperation of key players in the organization. For these reasons, some companies employ an external-internal team approach, which seeks to combine the advantages of internal and external change agents while minimizing the drawbacks associated with the two approaches. "Are change agents necessary for organizational development to take place?" queried Gibson, Ivancevich, and Donnelly, authors of *Organizations: Behavior, Structure, Processes.* "Once we recognize that organizational development involves substantial changes in how individuals think, believe, and act, we can appreciate the necessity of someone to play the role of change agent. But who should play the role? Existing managers? New managers? Or individuals hired specifically for that purpose? Depending upon the situation, any of these can be called upon to orchestrate the organizational development process. The point is that the role of the change agent is necessary for organizational development to occur."

MANAGING CHANGE THROUGH ORGANIZATIONAL DEVELOPMENT

Organization development initiatives do not automatically succeed. The benefits of effective OD programs are myriad, as many executives, managers, and business owners will attest. But OD interventions that are pursued in a sloppy, half-hearted, or otherwise faulty manner are far less likely to bring about meaningful change than those that have the full support of the people involved. Writing in the *Academy of Management OD Newsletter,* consultant William G. Dyer stipulated several conditions that had to be present if an OD intervention could have any meaningful chance of bringing about the desired change:

- Ownership and all involved personnel needed to be genuinely and visibly committed to the effort.

- People involved in OD have to be informed in advance of the nature of the intervention and the nature of their involvement in it.

- The OD effort has to be connected to other parts of the organization; this is especially true of such areas as the evaluation and reward systems.

- The effort has to be directed by appropriate managers and guided by change agents (which, if used, must be competent).

- The intervention should be based on accurate diagnosis of organizational conditions.

- Owners and managers should show their commitment to OD at all stages of the effort, including the diagnosis, implementation, and evaluation.

- Evaluation is key to success, and should consist of more than asking people how they felt about the effort.

- Owners and managers need to show employees how the OD effort relates to the organization's goals and overriding mission.

IMPLEMENTING OD PROGRAMS

OD efforts basically entail two groups of activities: ''action research'' and ''interventions.'' Action research is a process of systematically collecting data on a specific organization, feeding it back for action planning, and evaluating results by collecting and reflecting on more data. Data gathering techniques include everything from surveys and questionnaires to interviews, collages, drawings, and tests. The data is often evaluated and interpreted using advanced statistical analysis techniques.

Action research can be thought of as the diagnostic component of the OD process. But it also encompasses the intervention component, whereby the change agent uses action plans to intervene in the organization and make changes, as discussed below. In a continuous process, the results of actions are measured and evaluated and new action plans are devised to effect new changes. Thus, the intervention process can be considered a facet of action research.

OD interventions are plans or programs comprised of specific activities designed to effect change in some facet of an organization. Numerous interventions have been developed over the years to address different problems or create various results. However, they all are geared toward the goal of improving the entire organization through change. In general, organizations that wish to achieve a high degree of organizational change will employ a full range of interventions, including those designed to transform individual and group behavior and attitudes. Entities attempting smaller changes will stop short of those goals, applying interventions targeted primarily toward operating policies, management structures, worker skills, and personnel policies. Typically, organization development programs will simultaneously integrate more than one of these interventions. A few of the more popular interventions are briefly described below.

INTERPERSONAL INTERVENTIONS Interpersonal interventions in an OD program are designed to enhance individual skills, knowledge, and effectiveness. This type of program utilizes group dynamics by gathering individuals together in loosely structured meetings. Subject matter is determined by the group, within the context of basic goals stipulated by a facilitator. As group members try to exert structure on fellow members, group members gain a greater awareness of their own and other's feelings, motivations, and behaviors. Other types of interpersonal interventions include those designed to improve the performance review process, create better training programs, help workers identify their true wants and set complementary career goals, and resolve conflict.

GROUP INTERVENTIONS OD group interventions are designed to help teams and groups within organizations become more effective. Such interventions usually assume that the most effective groups communicate well, facilitate a healthy balance between both personal and group needs, and function by consensus as opposed to autocracy or majority rule.

Group diagnostic interventions are simply meetings wherein members of a team analyze their unit's performance, ask questions about what the team needs to do to improve, and discuss potential solutions to problems. The benefit of such interventions is that members often communicate problems of which their co-workers were unaware. Ideally, such communication will spur problem-solving and improved group dynamics.

Role analysis technique (RAT) is used to help employees get a better grasp on their role in an organization. In the first step of a RAT intervention, people define their perception of their role and contribution to the overall company effort in front of a group of coworkers. Group members then provide feedback to more clearly define the role. In the second phase, the individual and the group examine ways in which the employee relies on others in the company, and how they define his or her expectations. RAT interventions help people to reduce role confusion, which can result in either conflict or the perception that some people are not doing their job. A popular intervention similar to RAT is responsibility charting, which utilizes a matrix system to assign decision and task responsibilities.

INTERGROUP INTERVENTIONS Intergroup interventions are integrated into OD programs to facilitate cooperation and efficiency between different groups within an organization. For instance, departmental interaction often deteriorates in larger organizations as different units battle for limited resources or become detached from the needs of other units.

Conflict resolution meetings are one common intergroup intervention. First, different group leaders are brought together to secure their commitment to the intervention. Next, the teams meet separately to make a list of their feelings about the other group(s). Then the groups meet and share their lists. Finally, the teams meet to discuss the problems and to try to develop solutions that will help both parties. This type of intervention, say supporters, helps to gradually diffuse tension between groups that has arisen because of faulty communication.

Rotating membership interventions are used by OD change agents to minimize the negative effects of intergroup rivalry that arise from employee allegiances to groups or divisions. The intervention basically entails temporarily putting group members into their rival groups. As more people interact in the different groups, greater understanding results.

OD joint activity interventions serve the same basic function as the rotating membership approach, but these involve melding members of different groups to work together toward a common goal. Similarly, common enemy interventions achieve the same results by finding an adversary common to two or more groups and then getting members of the groups to work together to overcome the threat. Examples of common enemies targeted in such programs include competitors, government regulation, and economic conditions.

COMPREHENSIVE INTERVENTIONS OD comprehensive interventions are used to directly create change throughout an entire organization, rather than focusing on organizational change through subgroup interventions. One of the most popular comprehensive interventions is survey feedback. This technique basically entails surveying employee attitudes at all levels of the company and then disseminating a report that details those findings. The employees then use the data in feedback sessions to create solutions to perceived problems. A number of questionnaires developed specifically for such interventions have been developed.

Structural change interventions are used by OD change agents to implement organizational alterations related to departmentalization, management hierarchy, work policies, compensation and benefit incentives programs, and other cornerstones of the business. Often, the implemented changes emanate from feedback from other interventions. One benefit of change interventions is that companies can often realize an immediate and very significant impact in productivity and profitability (provided the changes are warranted and implemented appropriately).

Sociotechnical system design interventions are similar to structural change techniques, but they typically emphasize the reorganization of work teams. The basic goal is to create independent groups throughout the company that supervise themselves. This administration may include such aspects as monitoring quality or disciplining team members. The theoretic benefit of sociotechnical system design interventions is that worker and group productivity and quality is increased because workers have more control over (and subsequent satisfaction from) the process in which they participate.

A fourth OD intervention that became extremely popular during the 1980s and early 1990s is total quality management (TQM). TQM interventions utilize established quality techniques and programs that emphasize quality processes, rather than achieving quality by inspecting products and services after processes have been completed. The important concept of continuous improvement embodied by TQM has carried over into other OD interventions.

FURTHER READING:

Cherrington, David J. *Organizational Behavior: The Management of Individual and Organizational Performance*. Boston: Allyn and Bacon, 1994.

Dove, Rick. "The Principles of Change." *Automotive Manufacturing and Production*. March 1997.

Dyer, William G. "Team Building: A Microcosm of the Past, Present, and Future of O.D." *Academy of Management OD Newsletter*. Winter 1989.

Gibson, James L., John M. Ivancevich, and James H. Donnelly Jr. *Organizations: Behavior, Structure, Processes*. 8th ed. Boston: Richard D. Irwin, 1994.

Goodstein, Leonard D., and W. Warner Burke. "Creating Successful Organization Change." *Organizational Dynamics*. Spring 1991.

Ivancevich, John M., and Michael T. Matteson. *Organizational Behavior and Management*. Homewood, IL: Richard D. Irwin, Inc., 1990.

Lippitt, Gordon L., Peter Longseth, and Jack Mossop. *Implementing Organizational Change*. San Francisco: Jossey-Bass, 1985.

Northcraft, Gregory B., and Margaret A. Neale. *Organizational Behavior: A Management Challenge*. Chicago: The Dryden Press, 1990.

Recardo, Ronald J. "Best Practices in Organizations Experiencing Extensive and Rapid Change." *National Productivity Review.* Summer 2000.

Shaffer, Rima. *Principles of Organization Development.* American Society for Training and Development, 2000.

ORGANIZATIONAL GROWTH

Growth is something for which most companies, large or small, strive. Small firms want to get big, big firms want to get bigger. Indeed, companies have to grow, observed Philip B. Crosby, author of *The Eternally Successful Organization,* "if for no other reason than to accommodate the increased expenses that develop over the years. Inflation also raises the cost of everything, and retaliatory price increases are not always possible. Salaries rise as employees gain seniority. The costs of benefits rises because of their very structure, and it is difficult to take any back, particularly if the enterprise is profitable. Therefore cost eliminations and profit improvement must be conducted on a continuing basis, and the revenues of the organization must continue to increase in order to broaden the base."

Most firms, of course, desire growth in order to prosper, not just to survive. Organizational growth, however, means different things to different organizations. Indeed, there are many parameters a company can select to measure its growth. The most meaningful yardstick is one that shows progress with respect to an organization's stated goals. The ultimate goal of most companies is profit, so net profit, revenue, and other financial data are often utilized as "bottom-line" indications of growth. Other business owners, meanwhile, may use sales figures, number of employees, physical expansion, or other criteria to judge organizational growth.

WAYS IN WHICH ORGANIZATIONS ACHIEVE GROWTH

Many academic models have been created that depict possible growth stages/directions of a company, but management consultant Tom Peters suggested that there are several "real-world" ways in which both large and small companies may pursue a course of organizational growth.

- Joint Venture/Alliance—This strategy is particularly effective for smaller firms with limited resources. Such partnerships can help small business secure the resources they need to grapple with rapid changes in demand, supply, competition, and other factors. Forming joint ventures or alliances gives all companies involved the flexibility to move on to different projects upon completion of the first, or restructure agreements to continue working together. Subcontracting, which allows firms to concentrate on those aspects of their business that they do best, is sometimes defined as a type of alliance arrangement (albeit one in which the parties involved generally wield differing levels of power). Joint ventures and other business alliances can inject partners with new ideas, access to new technologies, new approaches, and new markets, all of which can help the involved businesses to grow. Indeed, establishing joint ventures with overseas firms has been hailed as one of the most potentially rewarding ways for companies to expand their operations. Finally, some firms realize growth by acquiring other companies.

- Licensing—"License your most advanced technology," advised Peters, who argued that truly proprietary technologies are quickly becoming extinct. Peters and other consultants contend that competitors will soon copy whatever a company develops in the realm of technology (and other areas), so it may make good sense for a company to turn to licensing. This creates cash flow for the company to fund future research and development.

- Sell Off Old Winners—Some organizations engaged in a concerted effort to grow divest themselves of mature "cash cow" operations to focus on new and innovative product or service lines. This option may sound contradictory, but analysts note that businesses can command top prices for such tried and true assets. An addendum to this line of thinking is the divestment of older technology or products. Emerging markets in Latin America and Eastern Europe, for instance, have been favorite places for companies to sell products or technology that no longer attract high levels of interest in the United States. These markets may not yet be able to afford large quantities of state-of-the-art goods, but they can still benefit from older models.

- New Markets—Some businesses are able to secure significant organizational growth by tapping into new markets. Creating additional demand for a firm's product or service, especially in a market where competition has yet to fully develop, can spur phenomenal growth for a small compan, although the competitive vacuum will generally close very quickly in these instances.

- New Product Development—Creation of new products or services is a primary method by which companies grow. Indeed, new product development is the linchpin of most organizations' growth strategies.

- Outside Financing—Many small companies turn to outside financing sources to fund their expansion. Smaller private firms search for capital from banks, private investors, government agencies, or venture capital firms.

PROBLEMS ENCOUNTERED WITH ORGANIZATIONAL GROWTH

Small business owners seeking to guide their organizations through periods of growth—whether that growth is dramatic or incremental—often encounter difficulties. After all, when a firm is small in size, the entrepreneur who founded it and usually serves as its primary strategic and operational leaders can often easily direct and monitor the various aspects of daily business. In such environments, added Theodore Caplow, author of *Managing an Organization,* the small business owner can also "understand a larger proportion of the relationships subordinates have with each other and with outsiders." Organizational growth, however, brings with it an inevitable dilution of that "hands-on" capability, while the complexity of various organizational tasks simultaneously increases. "As the organization grows," said Caplow, "control becomes more complex by the mere accretion of numbers. There are ways of reducing the complexity by delegating responsibility and installing better date systems but there is no way of avoiding it altogether."

According to Caplow, organizational growth also triggers an almost inevitable "diminution of consensus about organizational goals." He attributed this "in part to the inherent difficulty of getting a larger number of people who know each other less well to agree about anything, in part to the importation of new people and ideas, but mostly to the brute fact that as an organization grows, its relationships to its members and to the environment necessarily change." Oftentimes, organizational growth has a transformational effect on the business, especially if the growth has been realized via dramatic rather than incremental means (opening of a second store, a new promotional blitz for a popular product, major expansion of services, introduction of an online web site, etc.), and Caplow pointed out that such growth can be particularly disorienting for employee and owner alike: "often the people involved may not realize that anything significant has occurred until they discover by experience that their familiar procedures no longer work and that their familiar routines have been bizarrely transformed."

Small business owners, then, face a dizzying array of organizational elements that have to be revised in accordance with changing realities. Maintaining effective methods of communications with and between employees and departments, for example, become ever more important as the firm grows. Similarly, good human resource management practices—from hiring to training to empowerment—have to be implemented and maintained. Establishing and improving standard practices is often a key element of organizational growth as well. Indeed, a small business that undergoes a significant burst of growth will find its operations transformed in any number of ways. And often, it will be the owner's advance planning and management skills that will determine whether that growth is sustained, or whether internal constraints rein in that growth prematurely.

FURTHER READING:

Bildner, James L. "Hitting the Wall." *Inc.* July 1995.

Caplow, Theodore. *Managing an Organization.* New York: Holt, Rinehart and Winston, 1983.

Conner, Daryl R. "How to Create a Nimble Organization." *National Productivity Review.* Autumn 2000.

Crosby, Philip B. *The Eternally Successful Organization: The Art of Corporate Wellness.* New York: New American Library, 1990.

Dove, Rick. "The Principles of Change." *Automotive Manufacturing and Production.* March 1997.

Peters, Tom. "Get Innovative or Get Dead." *California Business Review.* Fall 1990.

Treen, Doug. "Vanishing Walls." *Ivey Business Journal.* September 2000.

ORGANIZATIONAL LIFE CYCLE

The organizational life cycle (OLC) is a model which proposes that over the course of time, business firms move through a fairly predictable sequence of developmental stages. This model, which has been a subject of considerable study over the years, is linked to the study of organizational growth and development. It is based on a biological metaphor—that business firms resemble living organisms because they demonstrate a regular pattern of developmental process. Organizations that are said to pass through a recognizable life cycle, wrote Gibson, Ivancevich, and Donnelly in *Organizations: Behavior, Structure, Processes,* are fundamentally impacted by external environmental circumstances as well as internal factors: "We're all aware of the rise and fall of organizations and entire industries. . . . Marketing experts acknowledge the existence of product-market life cycles. It seems reasonable to conclude that organizations also have life cycles.''

In a summary of OLC models, Quinn and Cameron wrote in *Management Science* that the models typically propose that ''changes that occur in organizations follow a predictable pattern that can be characterized by developmental stages. These stages are sequential in nature; occur as a hierarchical progression that is not easily reversed; and involve a broad range of organizational activities and structures.'' The number of life cycle stages proposed in various works studying the phenomenon have varied considerably over the years. Some analysts have delineated as many as ten different stages of an organizational life cycle, while others have flattened it down to as few as three stages. Most models, however, tout the organizational life cycle as a period comprised of four or five stages that can be encapsulated as start-up, growth, maturity, decline, and death (or revival).

TRENDS IN OLC STUDY

While a number of business and management theorists alluded to developmental stages in the early to mid-1900s, Mason Haire's 1959 work *Modern Organization Theory* is generally recognized as one of the first studies that used a biological model for organizational growth and argued that organizational growth and development followed a regular sequence. The study of organizational life cycles intensified, and by the 1970s and 1980s it was well-established as a key component of overall organizational growth.

Organizational life cycle is an important model because of its premise and its prescription. The model's premise is that requirements, opportunities, and threats both inside and outside the business firm will vary depending on the stage of development in which the firm finds itself. For example, threats in the start-up stage differ from those in the maturity stage. As the firm moves through the developmental stages, changes in the nature and number of requirements, opportunities, and threats exert pressure for change on the business firm. Baird and Meshoulam stated in the *Academy of Management Review* that organizations move from one stage to another because the fit between the organization and its environment is so inadequate that either the organization's efficiency and/or effectiveness is seriously impaired or the organization's survival is threatened. The OLC model's prescription is that the firm's managers must change the goals, strategies, and strategy implementation devices of the business to fit the new set of issues. Thus, different stages of the company's life cycle require alterations in the firm's objectives, strategies, managerial processes (planning, organizing, staffing, directing, controlling), technology, culture, and decision-making. For example, in a longitudinal study of 36 corporations published in *Management Science*, Miller and Friesen proposed five growth stages: birth, growth, maturity, decline, and revival. They traced changes in the organizational structure and managerial processes as the business firms proceeded through the stages. At birth, the firms exhibited a very simple organizational structure with authority centralized at the top of the hierarchy. As the firms grew, they adapted more sophisticated structures and decentralized authority to middle- and lower-level managers. At maturity, the firms demonstrated significantly more concern for internal efficiency and installed more control mechanisms and processes.

GROWTH PHASES Despite the increase in interest in OLC, though, most scholarly works focusing on organizational life cycles have been conceptual and hypothetical in content. Only a small minority have attempted to test empirically the organizational life cycle model. One widely-cited conceptual work, however, was published in the *Harvard Business Review* in 1972 by L. Greiner. He used five growth phases: growth through creativity; growth through direction; growth through delegation; growth through coordination; and growth through collaboration. Each growth stage encompassed an evolutionary phase (''prolonged periods of growth where no major upheaval occurs in organization practices''), and a revolutionary phase (''periods of substantial turmoil in organization life''). The evolutionary phases were hypothesized to be about four to eight years in length, while the revolutionary phases were characterized as the crisis phases. At the end of each one of the five growth stages listed above, Greiner hypothesized that an organizational crisis will occur, and that the business's ability to handle these crises will determine its future:

Phase 1—Growth through creativity eventually leads to a crisis of leadership. More sophisticated and more formalized management practices must be adopted. If the founders can't or won't take on this responsibility, they must hire someone who can, and give this person significant authority.

Phase 2—Growth through direction eventually leads to a crisis of autonomy. Lower level managers must be given more authority if the organization is to continue to grow. The crisis involves top-level managers' reluctance to delegate authority.

Phase 3—Growth through delegation eventually leads to a crisis of control. This occurs when autonomous employees who prefer to operate without interference from the rest of the organization clash with business owners and managers who perceive that they are losing control of a diversified company.

Phase 4—Growth through coordination eventually leads to a crisis of red tape. Coordination techniques like product groups, formal planning processes, and corporate staff become, over time, a bureaucratic system that causes delays in decision-making and a reduction in innovation.

Phase 5—Growth through collaboration, is characterized by the use of teams, a reduction in corporate staff, matrix-type structures, the simplification of formal systems, an increase in conferences and educational programs, and more sophisticated information systems. While Greiner did not formally delineate a crisis for this phase, he guessed that it might revolve around ''the psychological saturation of employees who grow emotionally and physically exhausted by the intensity of team work and the heavy pressure for innovative solutions.''

ORGANIZATION LIFE CYCLE AND THE SMALL BUSINESS OWNER

Entrepreneurs who are involved in the early stages of business creation are unlikely to become preoccupied with life cycle issues of decline and dissolution. Indeed, their concerns are apt to be in such areas as securing financing, establishing relationships with vendors and clients, preparing a physical location for business operations, and other aspects of business start-up that are integral to establishing and maintaining a viable firm. Basically, these firms are almost exclusively concerned with the very first stage of the organization life cycle. Small business enterprises that are well-established, on the other hand, may find OLC studies more relevant. Indeed, many recent examinations of organization life cycles have analyzed ways in which businesses can prolong desired stages (growth, maturity) and forestall negative stages (decline, death). Certainly, there exists no timeline that dictates that a company will begin to falter at a given point in time. ''Because every company develops at its own pace, characteristics, more than age, define the stages of the cycle,'' explained Karen Adler and Paul Swiercz in *Training & Development.*

Small business owners and other organization leaders may explore a variety of options designed to influence the enterprise's life cycle—from new products to new markets to new management philosophies. After all, once a business begins to enter a decline phase, it is not inevitable that the company will continue to plummet into ultimate failure; many companies are able to reverse such slides (a development that is sometimes referred to as turning the OLC bell curve into an ''S'' curve). But entrepreneurs and managers should recognize that their business is always somewhere along the life cycle continuum, and that business success is often predicated on recognizing where your business is situated along that measuring stick.

FURTHER READING:

Adler, Karen R., and Paul M. Swiercz. ''Taming the Performance Bell Curve.'' *Training & Development.* October 1997.

Churchill, N., and V. Lewis. ''The Five Stages of Small Business Growth.'' *Harvard Business Review.* May-June 1983.

Dodge, H. Robert, and John E. Robbins. ''An Empirical Investigation of the Organizational Life Cycle Model for Small Business Development and Survival,'' *Journal of Small Business Management.* January 1992.

Dodge, H. Robert, Sam Fullerton, and John E. Robbins. ''Stage of the Organizational Life cycle and Competition as Mediators of Problem Perception for Small Businesses.'' *Strategic Management Journal.* February 1994.

Fletcher, Douglas A., and Ian M. Taplin. ''Organizational Evolution: The American Life Cycle.'' *National Productivity Review.* Autumn 2000.

Gibson, James L, John M. Ivancevich, and James H. Donnelly, Jr. *Organizations: Behavior, Structure, Processes.* Irwin, 1994.

Greiner, L. ''Evolution and Revolution as Organizations Grow,'' *Harvard Business Review.* July-August 1972.

Hanks, S., C. Watson, E. Jansen, and G. Chandler, ''Tightening the Life-Cycle Construct: A Taxonomic Study of Growth Stage Configurations in High-Technology Organizations,'' *Entrepreneurship Theory and Practice.* Winter 1993.

Kazanjian, R. ''Relation of Dominant Problems to Stages of Growth in Technology-Based New Ventures.'' *Academy of Management Journal.* June 1988.

Miller, D., and P. Friesen, ''A Longitudinal Study of the Corporate Life Cycle,'' *Management Science.* October 1984.

Quinn, R., and K. Cameron, ''Organizational Life Cycles and Shifting Criteria of Effectiveness: Some Preliminary Evidence.'' *Management Science.* January 1983.

Smith, K., T. Mitchell, and C. Summer, ''Top Level Management Priorities in Different Stages of the Organizational Life Cycle,'' *Academy of Management Journal.* December 1985.

Tyebjee, T., A. Bruno, and S. McIntyre, ''Growing Ventures Can Anticipate Marketing Stages,'' *Harvard Business Review.* January-February 1983.

ORGANIZATIONAL STRUCTURE

An organizational structure is the pattern or arrangement of jobs and groups of jobs within an organization. This pattern pertains to both reporting and operational relationships, provided they have some degree of permanence. The individual elements of an organization structure typically include a variety of components that *Portable MBA in Management* contributors Phyllis and Leonard Schlesinger termed organizational ''building blocks'': 1) departments or divisions; 2) management hierarchy; 3) rules, procedures, and goals; and 4) temporary building blocks such as task forces or committees.

Ideally, organizational structures should be shaped and implemented for the primary purpose of facilitating the achievement of organizational goals in an efficient manner. Indeed, having a suitable organizational structure in place—one that recognizes and addresses the various human and business realities of the company in question—is a prerequisite for long-term success. But as Gibson, Ivancevich, and Donnelly noted in *Organizations: Behavior, Structure, Processes,* ''It is entirely reasonable to acknowledge that in many instances, organization structures do not contribute positively to organizational performance because managers are unable by training or intellect to design a structure that guides the behavior of individuals and groups to achieve high levels of production, efficiency, satisfaction, quality, flexibility, and development.'' Small business owners seeking to establish a beneficial organizational structure for their enterprise, then, need to recognize that the process is a complex one that requires considerable planning and research.

KEYS TO ERECTING AN EFFECTIVE ORGANIZATIONAL STRUCTURE

All sorts of different organizational structures have been proven effective in contributing to business success. Some firms choose highly centralized, rigidly maintained structures, while others—perhaps even in the same industry sector—develop decentralized, loose arrangements. Both of these organizational types can survive and even thrive. ''There is no one best way to design an organization,'' stated Phyllis and Leonard Schlesinger in *The Portable MBA in Management.* ''Organizational research has shown that the more we know about particular types of organizations, the less we can generalize about the optimal design for an effective organization. Generally, organizational theorists believe that no one structure, set of systems, or method of staffing is appropriate for every organization. Organizations operate in different environments with different products, strategies, constraints, and opportunities.''

But despite the wide variety of organizational structures that can be found in the business world, the successful ones tend to share certain characteristics. Indeed, business experts cite a number of characteristics that separate effective organizational structures from ineffective designs. Recognition of these factors is especially important for entrepreneurs and established small business owners, since these individuals play such a pivotal role in determining the final organizational structure of their enterprises.

As small business owners weigh their various options in this realm, they should make sure that the following factors are taken into consideration:

- Relative strengths and weaknesses of various organizational forms.

- Legal advantages and disadvantages of organizational structure options.

- Advantages and drawbacks of departmentalization options.

- Likely growth patterns of the company.

- Reporting relationships that are currently in place.

- Reporting and authority relationships that you hope will be implemented in the future.

- Optimum ratios of supervisors/managers to subordinates.

- Suitable level of autonomy/empowerment to be granted to employees at various levels of the organization (while still recognizing individual capacities for independent work).

- Structures that will produce greatest worker satisfaction.

- Structures that will produce optimum operational efficiency.

Once all these factors have been objectively examined and blended into an effective organizational structure, the small business owner will then be in a position to pursue his/her business goals with a far greater likelihood of success.

FURTHER READING:

Bateman, Thomas S., and Carl P. Zeithaml. *Management: Function and Strategy.* Boston: Richard D. Irwin, 1990.

Day, George. ''Aligning Organizational Structure to the Market.'' *Business Strategy Review.* Autumn 1999.

Gibson, James L., John M. Ivancevich, and James H. Donnelly Jr. *Organizations: Behavior, Structure, Processes.* 8th ed. Boston: Richard D. Irwin, 1994.

Schlesinger, Phyllis F., and Leonard A. Schlesinger. ''Designing Effective Organizations.'' *The Portable MBA in Management.* Allan R. Cohen, ed. New York: John Wiley & Sons, 1993.

ORIGINAL EQUIPMENT MANUFACTURER (OEM)

An original equipment manufacturer (OEM) is a company that produces products or major components of products that are sold to customers as new. Some companies and consumers, when choosing replacement parts for their products or equipment, prefer to purchase parts that were made by the same manufacturer that produced the original equipment. The view is that components and other processed items may work better or fit better if they come from the OEM and meet the original standards, tooling, and product specifications established for the product. OEM parts can be contrasted to other replacement parts that may be referred to as "functionally equivalent" or "of like kind and quality."

OEMS TODAY

Today, component parts and processed items are becoming branded, and as such their names are becoming well-known by consumers. In the past, these components were processed from raw materials and became part of a finished product without the consumer ever becoming aware of who made the component. In most cases, consumers did not care as long as the product worked as expected. But times have changed. Consumers upgrading their computers today, for example, may specify a new processor made by an OEM company that they respect, like Intel, and may request the processing power of the OEM's latest release, like the Pentium 4.

Component parts, like a computer's processor, include items that go into the assembly of the final product. Other examples include CD-ROM drives included in personal computers, air bags in cars, and motors for appliances. Consumers are also becoming interested in the component materials specifications and manufacturers of such items as wire, paper, textiles, or cement.

In another example, General Motors recommends that consumers request GoodWrench parts when replacements are needed for a GM vehicle. In fact, the GM Web site says, "GM parts are the highest-quality products for your GM vehicle and the only ones specifically designed, made, and tested to keep it running at peak performance and appearance. Heck, they're the same ones it was born with. So, whether you're restoring an old favorite or personalizing your newest baby, you can count on GM parts to provide genuine dependability." To stress the exact standards of OEM parts, they state, " It's reassuring to know you have a partner like GM Parts behind you. We offer a full line of products, all designed and manufactured to exacting standards specifically for your GM vehicle. So you know whenever you use GM parts, the feeling is genuine."

SETTING STANDARDS

Manufacturers must determine the quality and specify standards for components that go into their products. Some assembled products are not manufactured but put together from a variety of purchased component parts, like Dell computers. Some components may be custom made, requiring much teamwork between the engineering of both buyer and seller organizations as well as management involvement in negotiating prices and other terms.

Components are produced to accepted standards or specifications. Production personnel in the purchasing organization may specify quality. Because components become part of an organization's own product, quality is extremely important. The buyer's own name and entire marketing mix are at stake. Thus a buyer tries to buy from sources that help ensure a good product. In such a situation, a buyer may even find it attractive to develop a close partnership with a single supplier who is dedicated to the same objectives as the buyer and use this partner as a sole source supplier. As an example, Ford Motor Company forged a partnership with Firestone Tires. When the supplier's product was implicated in a series of accidents involving Ford sports utility vehicles, Ford took some responsibility for the problems and deaths that resulted.

If the co-branding and awareness of OEM manufacturers continues, more profitable replacement markets may develop for producers. Since component parts go into finished products, a replacement market often develops on its own. This after-market can be both large and very profitable. Car tires and batteries are two examples of components originally sold in the OEM market that become consumer products in the after-market. But because the target markets are different, different marketing and overall strategies may be necessary for selling OEM parts directly to final consumers.

FURTHER READING:

Convey, Mary Christine. "CAPA Refines Generic Auto Parts Definitions." *National Underwriter.* September 4, 2000.

Rayner, Bruce. "Some Industry Terms Need to Be Changed." *Electronic Buyers' News.* November 27, 2000.

OUTSOURCING

Outsourcing occurs when a company purchases products or services from an outside supplier, rather than performing the same work within its own facilities, in order to cut costs. The decision to outsource is a major strategic one for most companies, since it involves weighing the potential cost savings against the consequences of a loss in control over the product or service. Some common examples of outsourcing include manufacturing of components, computer programming services, tax compliance and other accounting functions, training administration, customer service, transportation of products, benefits and compensation planning, payroll, and other human resource functions. A relatively new trend in outsourcing is employee leasing, in which specialized vendors recruit, hire, train, and pay their clients' employees, as well as arrange health care coverage and other benefits.

The growth in outsourcing in recent years is partly the result of a general shift in business philosophy. Prior to the mid-1980s, many companies sought to acquire other companies and diversify their business interests in order to reduce risk. As more companies discovered that there were limited advantages to running a large group of unrelated businesses, however, many began to divest subsidiaries and refocus their efforts on one or a few closely related areas of business. Companies tried to identify or develop a "core competence," a unique combination of experience and expertise that would provide a source of competitive advantage in a given industry. All aspects of the company's operations were aligned around the core competence, and any activities or functions that were not considered necessary to preserve it were then outsourced. Today, outsourcing is embraced by companies of all sizes and industry orientations. As analysts Tom Osmond commented in *Employee Benefit News,* "many companies have decided that transactional and administrative functions are neither core competencies nor value-added activities. In fact, some companies are putting themselves at risk as a result of using outdated technology and not complying with government regulations. Vendors, by focusing on administration as part of their business model, provide better service enforced by contracts and service-level agreements."

Successful outsourcing requires a strong understanding of the organization's capabilities and future direction. As William R. King explained in *Information Systems Management,* "[d]ecisions regarding outsourcing significant functions are among the most strategic that can be made by an organization, because they address the basic organizational choice of the functions for which internal expertise is developed and nurtured and those for which such expertise is purchased. These are basic decisions regarding organizational design." Outsourcing based only upon a comparison of costs can lead companies to miss opportunities to gain knowledge that might lead to the development of new products or technologies.

Outsourcing can be undertaken to varying degrees, ranging from total outsourcing to selective outsourcing. Total outsourcing may involve dismantling entire departments or divisions and transferring the employees, facilities, equipment, and complete responsibility for a product or function to an outside vendor. In contrast, selective outsourcing may target a single, time-consuming task within a department, such as preparing the payroll or manufacturing a minor component, that can be handled more efficiently by an outside specialist.

Vendors providing outsourcing services are generally grouped into two models: Business Process Outsourcing (BPO) and Application Service Provider (ASP). In the BPO model, major resources and assets are transferred from the company to the vendor. Under the ASP model, on the other hand, vendors concentrate on providing selected services for multiple clients. But as Osmond told *Employee Benefit News,* many variations exist within these two models. "Each vendor has a particular focus and/or point of entry to the market, particularly in the ASP space," Osmond stated. "There is also a wide range of pricing models and option. The good news is that there is a seemingly endless combination of service, pricing, and delivery, providing a solution for most situations. The bad news is that it can be difficult to compare vendors on an apples-to-apples basis."

ADVANTAGES OF OUTSOURCING

Companies that decide to outsource do so for a number of reasons, all of which are based on realizing gains in business profitability and efficiency. Principal merits of outsourcing include the following:

Cost savings. Many businesses embrace outsourcing as a way to realize cost savings or better cost control over the outsourced function. Companies usually outsource to a vendor that specializes in a given function and performs that function more efficiently than the company could, simply by virtue of transaction volume.

Staffing levels. Another common reason for outsourcing is to achieve headcount reductions or minimize the fluctuations in staffing that may occur due to changes in demand for a product or service. Companies also outsource in order to reduce the workload on their employees (freeing them to take on additional moneymaking projects for the business), or to provide more development opportunities for their employees by freeing them from tedious tasks.

Focus. Some companies outsource in order to eliminate distractions and force themselves to concentrate on their core competencies. This can be a particularly attractive benefit for start-up firms. Outsourcing can free the entrepreneur from tedious and time-consuming tasks, such as payroll, so that he or she can concentrate on the marketing and sales activities that are most essential to the firm's long-term growth and prosperity. "What an outsourcing partner really sells is focus," wrote Adam Katz-Stone in *Baltimore Business Journal.* "In accounting for instance, that is something that typically is seen as necessary but not essential, not the core of the business. So you bring in an outsourcing partner and then you don't have to think about that any more. You can focus your energies on sales, marketing, all the other things that matter more."

Morale. This is an often-overlooked but still notable benefit that can sometimes be gained by initiating an outsourcing relationship. "Often a business's lack of internal expertise or dedication to non-core tasks results in poor attitudes and ultimately poor performance,'' wrote Kevin Grauman in *CPA Journal.* ''This can lead to overlap and duplication of internal efforts. An effectively designed and ongoing communication process emanating from one or more outsourcers can greatly reduce or eliminate these duplications.''

Flexibility. Still others outsource to achieve greater financial flexibility, since the sale of assets that formerly supported an outsourced function can improve a company's cash flow. A possible pitfall in this reasoning is that many vendors demand long-term contracts, which may reduce flexibility.

Knowledge. Some experts tout outsourcing of computer programming and other information technology functions as a way to gain access to new technology and outside expertise. This may be of particular benefit to small businesses, which may not be able to afford to hire computer experts or develop the in-house expertise to maintain high-level technology. When such tasks are outsourced, the small business gains access to new technology that can help it compete with larger companies.

Accountability. Outsourcing is predicated on the understanding—shared by business and vendor alike—that such arrangements require quality service in exchange for payment. ''Paying for a business service creates the expectation of performance,'' stated Grauman. ''Outsourcers are well aware that this accountability is both practical and legal, with fiscal implications. The same cannot be said for internally provided functions.''

DISADVANTAGES OF OUTSOURCING

Some of the major *potential* disadvantages to outsourcing include poor quality control, decreased company loyalty, a lengthy bid process, and a loss of strategic alignment. All of these concerns can be addressed and minimized, however, by companies who go about the outsourcing process in an informed and deliberate fashion. *InfoWorld*'s Maggie Biggs counsels businesses to define ''exactly what business processes and/or functions it makes sense to maintain via a service relationship. Unless you have a lot of resources to expend, it may make sense to prioritize outsourcing projects based on the number of benefits you expect to gain from the arrangement.'' There may also be inherent advantages of maintaining certain functions internally. For example, company employees may have a better understanding of the industry, and their vested interests may mean they are more likely to make decisions in accordance with the company's goals. Indeed, most analysts discourage companies from outsourcing core functions that directly affect the products or services that the business offers.

STEPS IN SUCCESSFUL OUTSOURCING

Once a company has made the decision to outsource, there are still a number of factors it must consider in making a successful transition and forming a partner relationship with the vendor. First, the company should determine what sort of outsourcing relationship will best meet its needs. ''Decide what's important,'' urged the *Journal of Accountancy.* ''If a function is not strategic to your business—for instance, payroll services or health insurance needs in a recruiting agency with only ten employees—consider outsourcing it to an expert provider.'' Some businesses share strategic decision-making with their vendors, while others only outsource on a limited, as-needed basis.

As Ethel Scully noted in *National Underwriter,* the company needs to obtain the support of key personnel during this time. Many companies encounter resistance from employees who feel that their jobs are threatened by outsourcing. Scully suggested forming a team consisting of an outsourcing expert, representatives from senior management and human resources, and the managers of all affected areas of the company to help address employee concerns about the decision.

Once your business has decided which functions to outsource, it should initiate a search process that utilizes referrals from other companies and service-provider directories. You can then begin contacting potential vendors and ask specific questions about the services they provide and their abilities to meet your company's unique and specific needs. Ideally, the vendor you select will have experience in handling similar business and will be able to give all of its clients' needs the priority they deserve. ''Consider the service company's knowledge of the entirety of your business, its willingness to customize service, and its compatibility with your firm's business culture, as well as the long-run cost of its services and its financial strength,'' said service provider Carl Schwenker in *Money.* During this period, you should also reexamine your own company culture and business needs to make sure that the outsourcing arrangement under consideration is a good fit. Many outsourcing experts counsel businesses to select vendors that can effectively integrate all their outsourced business functions so that they do not have to find individual vendors for each function.

Finally, you should select a vendor you trust in order to develop a mutually beneficial partner relationship. It is important to develop tangible measures of job performance before entering into an agreement, as well as financial incentives to encourage the vendor to meet deadlines and control costs. The contract should clearly define responsibilities and performance criteria, outline confidentiality rules and ownership rights to new ideas or technology. It should also include a means of severing the relationship if the service does not meet your expectations. Since the vendor is likely to have more experience in preparing outsourcing agreements than a small client company, it may also be helpful to consult with an attorney during contract negotiations.

FURTHER READING:

Biggs, Maggie. "Outsourcing Wisdom." *InfoWorld.* January 24, 2000.

Evans, David, Judy Feldman, and Anne Root. "Smart New Ways to Manage Subcontractors." *Money.* March 15, 1994.

"Examining the Ins and Outs of Outsourcing." *Employee Benefit News.* September 15, 2000.

Foxman, Noah. "Succeeding in Outsourcing." *Information Systems Management.* Winter 1994.

Grauman, Kevin. "The Benefits of Outsourcing." *CPA Journal.* July 2000.

Greaver, Maurice F. *Strategic Outsourcing: A Structured Approach to Outsourcing Decisions and Initiatives.* AMACOM, 1999.

Hammond, Keith H. "The New World of Work." *Business Week.* October 17, 1994.

Katz-Stone, Adam. "How to Use Outsourcing Firms." *Baltimore Business Journal.* April 28, 2000.

King, William R. "Strategic Outsourcing Decisions." *Information Systems Management.* Fall 1994.

Lacity, Mary, Rudy Hirschheim, and Leslie Willcocks. "Realizing Outsourcing Expectations: Incredible Expectations, Credible Outcomes." *Information Systems Management.* Fall 1994.

Meyer, N. Dean. "A Sensible Approach to Outsourcing: The Economic Fundamentals." *Information Systems Management.* Fall 1994.

Osmond, Thomas A., and Beth M. Schnaper. "Tips, Traps, and Travails: How to Hire the Right Outsourcing Vendor for Your Organization." *Benefits Quarterly.* Summer 2000.

"Outsourcing: Make It Work for Your Company." *Journal of Accountancy.* October 2000.

Scully, Ethel. "Many Factors to Weigh in Decision to Outsource." *National Underwriter.* January 16, 1995.

Springsteel, Ian. "Outsourcing Is Everywhere." *CFO: The Magazine for Senior Financial Executives.* December 1994.

OVERHEAD EXPENSE

Overhead expenses are those production and nonproduction costs not readily traceable to specific jobs or processes. Overhead expenses encompass three general areas: indirect materials, indirect labor, and all other miscellaneous production expenses, such as taxes, insurance, depreciation, supplies, utilities, and repairs. Therefore, overhead expense is part of the total costs of maintaining and staffing a business.

Production overhead includes such items as factory supplies and materials that are used in the production process, supervisors' salaries, maintenance and repairs of machinery, and utilities. Nonproduction overhead includes salaries of building maintenance, medical, and security personnel, rent or depreciation on plant and equipment, insurance on plant and equipment, the costs of meeting government regulations, and administrative salaries and expenses.

DETERMINING OVERHEAD RATES

The accurate accounting and allocation of overhead expenses are very important factors in calculating the true cost of goods and/or services soold and in setting a profitable selling price for those products and services. But since the exact amount of overhead expense that will need to be applied to products is not known at the time the products are manufactured or the service is provided, overhead expense must be estimated as part of the budget process. Accounting professionals (either in-house or outside) can, with the help of production supervisors and decision-point managers, develop projections of the volume of sales, the volume of production, and the cost of production for the coming year.

If the company produces only one product, the accountant merely divides the total estimated overhead by the expected volume of output to derive the standard overhead rate, burden rate, or indirect cost rate (an overhead rate per unit). During the fiscal year, the accountant keeps track of the number of finished goods going into inventory and allocates overhead for these units by multiplying by the standard overhead rate. The finished goods are then said to have absorbed a portion of the total overhead costs.

In a company that produces more than one product, however, the procedure is much more complex. The accountant's allocation of overhead is complicated by the variations in the production processes for different products. One item may require a labor-intensive finishing process, for example, while another relies more on machinery. As a result, the same standard overhead rate cannot be applied accurately to all products. Instead, the accountant must choose an activity base upon which to calculate the allocation of overhead to finished products. Commonly used activity bases include direct labor hours, direct labor costs, and machine hours. Other allocation formulas are based on sales dollars, gross-margin dollars, and employee count.

FURTHER READING:

Ansari, Shahid, et al. *Indirect Costs.* McGraw-Hill, 1996.

Hilton, Ronald W. *Managerial Accounting.* McGraw-Hill, 1991.

Leuth, M. Betsi. "Overhead Allocation." *Journal of Petroleum Marketing.* June 1999.

Meigs, Robert F., and Walter B. Meigs. *Accounting: The Basis for Business Decisions.* McGraw-Hill, 1990.

Rao, Srikumar S. "Overhead Can Kill You." Forbes. February 10, 1997.

SEE ALSO: Activity-Based Costing; Product Costing

OVERTIME

Overtime is work done by hourly employees beyond the regular work hours per week. Any work over forty hours per week for an hourly worker is considered overtime. Overtime and overtime compensation are provided under the federal Fair Labor Standards Act of 1938. It is required under the FLSA that employers pay employees working more that forty hours per week time-and-a-half, or 150 percent of the worker's salary for those hours exceeding the weekly average.

EXEMPT AND NON-EXEMPT EMPLOYEES

U.S. labor law distinguishes between "exempt" and "non-exempt" employees regarding overtime. Exempt employees do not have to be paid overtime if they work more than 40 hours a week. According to the FLSA, members of this class of employee include workers "employed in a bona fide executive, administrative, or professional capacity (including any employee employed in the capacity of academic administrative personnel or teacher in elementary or secondary schools) or in the capacity of outside [salesperson]." Any worker employed in the above caaegories who meets Department of Labor salary and duty tests is exempt from receiving overtime pay regardless of the number of hours they work.

In some businesses, employees attend to a wide variety of tasks that may include a blend of "exempt" and "non-exempt" duties. In these instances, their overtime status is dictated by their "primary duty" to their employer. Time spent on each task is an important but not decisive factor in determining exemption status. Instead, federal regulations dictate that the most relevant factor is "the relative importance of the [exempt] duties as compared with other types of duties . . . and the relationship between [the employee's] salary and the wages paid other employees for the kind of nonexempt work performed." For instance, the Code of Federal Regulations notes that "in some departments, or subdivisions of an establishment, an employee has broad responsibilities similar to those of the owner or manager of the establishment, but generally spends more than 50 percent of his time in production or sales work. While engaged in such work he supervises other employees, directs the work of warehouse and deliverymen, approves advertising, orders merchandise, handles customer complaints, authorizes payment of bills, or performs other management duties as the day-to-day operations require. He will be considered to have management as his primary duty." The Code of Federal Regulations also includes tests that can be used to determine the primary duties of other "white-collar" workers, including executives, professionals, computer programmers, and administrative personnel.

Employers should regularly review their staff classifications to make certain that all workers in their employ are properly classified. "As part of that process," wrote Jeffrey Pollack in *CPA Journal,* "employers should develop written job descriptions that delineate the duties of each position; the employee's actual duties—not the job description—will be the controlling factor."

DECIDING TO USE OVERTIME

Businesses with seasonal peaks, with quotas and deadlines, or with the possibility of rush orders, will at some point probably not be able to meet staffing needs with the regular hours worked by employees. It is at these crisis points that overtime becomes an invaluable tool for the employer.

Most business experts, however, counsel owners and managers to use overtime sparingly if possible. The ideal use of overtime is when employees are willing to work longer hours for increased pay, and the employer needs qualified, trained individuals who will not need excessive supervision while tackling an increased work load. An employer should not, however, rely on employees working many more hours per week to routinely make up for work not accomplished during the regular work week. If this is the case—if overtime becomes essential to the performance of a business, even during regular operating scenarios—there may be other factors, such as poor compensation, morale, or inadequate staffing levels, to be considered.

One serious consideration often cited in the routine use of overtime is the effect it can have on employees' regular production. Increased work hours during one period may lead to increased absenteeism during others, due to family commitments that were put off during "crunch" periods or to illness exacerbated by stress. Indeed, Cornell University's School of Industrial and Labor Relations conducted a late 1990s study that found that employees who work at least 11 and up to 20 hours over overtime weekly showed a much greater incidence of severe conflicts in the work-family realm. These conflicts manifested themselves in higher levels of stress, alcohol and drug use, and absenteeism. In addition, some analysts believe that employee productivity during regular business hours often undergoes a major downturn after periods of extensive overtime.

All overtime should be authorized by a manager or supervisor, preferably in writing. Consideration should be given to tracking the work accomplished during overtime hours; this ensures that employees are continuing to be productive at the increased pay rate, even with the stress of longer hours and increased sales or other pressures. Tracking what work is done on overtime will also aid the owner or manager of a business to better plan for staffing needs in the future.

ALTERNATIVES TO OVERTIME PAY

Because overtime can become very expensive, and can sometimes be draining for regular employees, some businesses have embraced alternate plans of human resource management.

Expanding workforce size. The first determination to be made is whether the amount of overtime used throughout the year is enough to justify the hiring of additional staff. This step should be very carefully considered, however, because while overtime is expensive, so are the costs (salary, payroll taxes, social security, benefits) associated with hiring additional employees.

Temps. Another alternative to overtime is to utilize temporary workers. This can be done independently by the owner or manager, or through a temporary employment agency. Depending on the task (and how much training and supervision is required), the temporary employee can save businesses significant overtime expenses. This alternative can be particularly attractive if increased staffing needs are seasonal and predictable, so that temporary employees can be hired in advance.

Stock options. Many employers have begun offering their workers stock options as compensation in lieu of actual overtime pay. In fact, studies show that as many as 10 million hourly workers in the United States had acquired stock options by the late 1990s. In 1999 employer rights to offer such stock options were codified into law with the passage and signing of the Worker Economic Opportunity Act. This act amends the Fair Labor Standards Act to exclude profits from stock options or purchase plans from the calculation of non-exempt employee's overtime if various requirements are met (such as full disclosure of terms and voluntary participation). Supporters of this new law contend that it will allow employers to offer stock options as incentives to hourly workers while safeguarding employees against businesses that might try to disseminate risky stock options in place of overtime pay.

EMPLOYEE REACTIONS TO OVERTIME

Many employees welcome the opportunity to augment their regular salaries with overtime pay. Some businesses can effectively use overtime as a kind of voluntary bonus: if the employees are willing to put in the added hours, they will be rewarded with increased pay. Because of the strong positive feelings many employees have about the opportunity to earn overtime pay, employers should carefully weigh the pros and cons of hiring temporary help; regular employees will recognize the loss of overtime, and morale may suffer, particularly if overtime has become an integral part of the business cycle.

But the prevailing feeling among many business owners and executives is that employees are placing ever greater value on leisure/family time, and that they are willing to make some sacrifices in the realm of compensation in order to enjoy personal interests. In addition, analysts point out that families that have both parents in the work force may not value overtime as much as employees of the past. Employers should remain sensitive to employees' needs and responsibilities outside of the workplace, and should recognize that employees may not always be willing to volunteer for overtime.

FURTHER READING:

Boyett, Joseph H., and Henry P. Conn. *Workplace 2000.* New York: Penguin, 1991.

Crawford, Dan. ''Option Law Frees Employers from Costly Overtime Issues.'' *Business First-Columbus.* July 7, 2000.

Employees: How to Find and Pay Them. U.S. Small Business Administration, n.a.

Pollack, Jeffrey D. ''Overtime and the White-Collar Exemptions.'' *CPA Journal.* October 2000.

Walsh, Mary Williams. ''As Overtime Rises, Fatigue Becomes Labor Issue.'' *New York Times.* September 17, 2000.

Weiss, Donald H. *Fair, Square, and Legal: Safe Hiring, Managing & Firing Practices to Keep You & Your Company Out of Court.* New York: AMACOM, 1991.

P

PACKAGING

Packaging refers to the container or wrapper that holds a product or group of products. Most commercial packaging serves two basic functions: protecting the product from damage during shipping, and promoting the product to the ultimate consumer. Some common types of packaging include shipping cartons, containers for industrial goods, and bags, boxes, cans, and other holders for consumer products. Packaging is of great importance to both sellers and buyers of products. It can prevent spoiling, breakage, tampering, or theft; enhance convenience in use or storage; and make products easier to identify. A significant improvement in packaging can even create a ''new'' product by expanding the ways in which it can be used, and thus its potential markets. For example, a soup that is packaged in a microwavable bowl might suddenly increase its sales to working people.

Prior to World War II, packaging was used primarily to surround and protect products during storage, transportation, and distribution. Some packages were designed with aesthetic appeal and even for ease-of-use by the end consumer, but package design was typically left to technicians. After World War II, however, companies became more interested in marketing and promotion as a means of enticing customers to purchase their products. As a result, more manufacturers began to view packaging as an integral element of overall business marketing strategies to lure buyers.

This increased attention to packaging coincided with socioeconomic changes taking place around the world. As consumers became better educated and more affluent, their expectations of products—and their reliance on them—increased as well. Consequently, consumers began to rely much more heavily on manufactured goods and processed food items. New technologies related to production, distribution, and preservatives led to a massive proliferation in the number and type of products and brands available in industrialized nations. Thus, packaging became a vital means of differentiating items and informing inundated consumers.

The importance of consumer packaging was elevated in the United States during the late 1970s and 1980s. Rapid post-war economic expansion and market growth waned during that period, forcing companies to focus increasingly on luring consumers to their product or brand at the expense of the competition. Package design became a marketing science. And, as a new corporate cost-consciousness developed in response to increased competition, companies began to alter packaging techniques as a way to cut production, storage, and distribution expenses. Furthermore, marketers began to view packaging as a tool to exploit existing product lines by adding new items and to pump new life into maturing products.

Today, good package design is regarded as an essential part of successful busines practice. Since many potential customers first notice a new product after it has arrived on the shelves of a store, it is vital that the packaging provide consumers with the information they need and motivate them to make a purchase. But packaging decisions involve a number of tradeoffs. While making a product visible and distinctive may be the top priority, for example, businesses must also comply with a variety of laws regarding product labeling and safety. Protecting products during transport is important, but businesses also need to keep their shipping costs as low as possible. The following provides an overview of some of the factors to consider in packaging products for consumer markets.

PACKAGE DESIGN

Consumer packaging serves to contain and communicate. A product's "packaging mix" is the result of several requirements that determine how a package accomplishes those two basic functions. Robert D. Hisrich identified eight major package requirements that dictate the mix. A package must: protect the product, be adaptable to production-line speeds, promote or sell the item, increase the product's density, help the consumer use the product, provide reusable value to the user, satisfy legal requirements, and keep packaging-related expenses low. Two classes of package design criteria are functional requirements and sales requirements.

FUNCTIONAL REQUIREMENTS Package design must meet five groups of functional criteria: in-home, in-store (or warehouse), production, distribution and safety, and legal. *In-home* requirements usually dictate that packaging be convenient to use and store, remind users when and what to repurchase, reinforce consumers' expectations of the product, and tell them how to safely and effectively use the product. In addition, increasing numbers of consumers expect packaging to be recyclable and environmentally sensitive.

In-store criteria require that packaging attract attention on the shelf, instill confidence in the buyer, identify the product or brand and differentiate it from the competition, communicate benefits and uses, and entice customers to actually purchase the item. The product must also be easy for retailers to store and stock on the shelves or the floor, and simple to process at a check-out counter or other final point of distribution. For instance, packaging that is oddly shaped and takes up a large amount of space may draw attention, but it may also be shunned by mail-order sellers concerned about shipping costs or by space-conscious store retailers.

Production demands, the third group of functional criteria influencing packaging, are primarily based on cost. A designer may create a fantastic package that would perform excellently in the marketplace, but if the company cannot find a way to produce the package cost-effectively, the design is useless. Among the most important considerations in this realm is production line speed. If a container is too long, wide, or short, it could significantly slow the speed of the production machines. Similarly, if the top or spout of a container is too small or is oddly shaped, the product may not flow easily into the package.

Packaging considerations related to *distribution and safety* are important and numerous. If an unacceptable portion of the goods are damaged during storage, transportation, or distribution, the package has failed. Likewise, if the package injures the user, future sales could be lost or the company could be liable for damages. As a result, packaging engineers face numerous technical considerations that have a residual impact on the final look and feel of the package. For instance, packages must be able to withstand the pressure of several other crates stored on top of them. They must also be able to resist moisture, adapt to temperature changes, and withstand rough handling. From a cost standpoint, packages must also be designed to suit standardized transportation requirements related to weight, size, and durability. Finally, they should be designed so that the bar code on the package is easily scanned.

Furthermore, packages should ideally be designed to handle normal use by consumers.Examples of packages that may result in harm to consumers include: those with sharp edges, such as some pull-top canisters; glass containers; and heavy item boxes which might break when the consumer is carrying them or cause strain or injury to the consumer when picked up or set down.

The fifth basic group of functional packaging requirements relate to *laws and legislation*. Various federal laws have been passed to protect consumers from misrepresentation and unsafe products. For instance, some laws require that potentially dangerous goods, such as gasoline or drugs, be stored in specially constructed containers. Other laws forbid producers from misrepresenting the quality or quantity of a product through misleading packaging. Perhaps the most influential class of laws that affect packaging, however, is that related to labeling.

PRODUCT LABELING The label is the text printed on a product package or, in the case of items like clothing, attached to the product itself. Legally, labels include all written, printed, or graphic material on the containers of products that are involved in interstate commerce or held for sale. The main body of legislation governing packaging and labeling is the Fair Packaging and Labeling Act of 1966. It mandates that every product package or label specify on its "principal display label" (the part of the label most likely to be seen by consumers) the following information: 1) the product type; 2) the producer or processor's name and location; 3) the quantity (if applicable); and 4) the number and size of servings (if applicable). Furthermore, several restrictions apply to the way that the label is displayed. For example, mandatory copy required by the act must be in boldface type. Also, if the company is not listed in the telephone book, the manufacturer's or importer's street address must be displayed.

Other information required by the act relates to specific foods, toys, drugs, cosmetics, furs, and textiles. For instance, under the act labels for edible products must provide sodium content if other nutritional information is shown. They must also show ingredients, in descending order from the one of highest quantity to the one of least quantity. Certain food items, such as beef, may also be required to display qualitative ''grade labels'' or inspection labels. Likewise, ''informative labeling'' may be required for products such as home appliances. Informative label requirements mandate information about use, care, performance capability, life expectancy, safety precautions, gas mileage, or other factors. Certain major home appliances, for example, must provide the estimated cost of running each make and model for one year at average utility rates.

Congress passed significant new labeling legislation, the Nutrition Labeling and Education Act of 1990, that became effective in the mid-1990s. This act is intended primarily to discourage misleading labeling related to health benefits of food items. Specifically, many package labels subjectively claimed that their contents were ''low-fat,'' ''high-fiber,'' or possessed some other health virtue when the facts indicated otherwise. Basically, the new laws require most food labels to specify values such as calorie and cholesterol content, fat and saturated fat percentages, and sodium levels.

SALES REQUIREMENTS In additional to functional requirements, product packaging must be designed in a way that will appeal to buyers. The four principal merchandising requirement areas are: apparent size, attention drawing power, impression of quality, and brand-name readability.

Apparent size entails designing packaging to look as large as possible without misrepresenting the actual contents. This objective can be achieved by ensuring that the panels or dimensions of the package most likely to be viewed by the consumer are the largest, and that the product or brand name is shown on the most visible areas in large letters. In addition, the package can be made to look larger by using solid colors and simple, bold designs free of borders, superfluous art work, and unnecessary print. The pretense of largeness is particularly important for packages containing commodity items, such as rice, driveway salt, and canned fruit or vegetables.

Attention drawing power refers to the aesthetics and obtrusiveness of the package design. Depending on the product and the goals of the marketers, the package may be made to appear attractive, exciting, pure, soft, sexy, scary, intriguing, or to evoke some other emotion. In most cases, though, the product is displayed on the front of the package in the form of a picture, art, or see-through window. In addition, bright colors, glossy stock, obtrusive carton displays, and other elements can garner positive attention if used prudently.

A *quality impression* is an important sales requirement for packaging because items that are perceived to be of low quality are usually assumed to be a poor value, regardless of price. Examples of packaging mistakes that convey low quality or poor value include: faded lettering or colors, tacky designs or strange typeface, outdated pictures and designs, and cheap construction.

Readability is the fourth basic sales requirement for successful package design. This element is of paramount importance for products like breakfast cereal that are shelved next to several competing brands and products. If the package attempts to convey too many messages, it will likely fail to connect with the consumer. Because of the mass of buying choices, buyers typically do not take time to absorb messages on packaging, with the possible exception of high-priced specialty items. Among other guidelines, letters or logos should be large and printed in the same type style as that used in complementary print and television advertising. The requirement of readability contributes to the difficulty in packaging completely new products.

PACKAGING STRATEGY

One of the most critical roles for packaging is promoting products. Indeed, just as ease-of-use and readability are elements of the strategic packaging mix, packaging is an important part of a company's strategic marketing mix. Most packages for consumer products are designed for one of three purposes: 1) to improve the packaging of an existing product; 2) to add a new product to an existing product line; or 3) to contain an entirely new product.

Redesign of packaging for existing products may be prompted by several factors. Many times, a company may simply want to breathe new life into a maturing product by updating its image or adding a new feature to the package, such as an easy-pour spout. Or, a company may redesign the package to respond to a competitive threat, such as a new product that is more visible on the shelf. Other strategic reasons for package redesign are: changes in the product; economics, which may require less or more expensive packaging; product line restructuring; alterations in market strategy, such as aiming the product at a different age group; trying to promote new uses for a product; or legal or environmental factors that lead to new materials or technology. Even small packaging changes for established brands and products typically require careful consideration, since a great deal of money is often at risk if a company alienates or confuses customers.

A second reason for package redesign is to extend a product or brand line. In these instances, the packaging strategy usually reflects an effort to closely mimic the established brand or product, but to integrate the benefits of the new feature into the existing package in such a way that customers will be able to easily differentiate it from other products in the line. The chief risks inherent in packaging for extensions are that the new package will confuse customers or frustrate retailers.

The third impetus for package design is the need to generate housing for an entirely new product. This is the most difficult type of packaging to create because it often requires the designer to instill consumer confidence in an unknown product or brand, and to inform the buyer about the product's uses and benefits. Packaging for products and brands that are entirely new to the marketplace are the most challenging to develop. In contrast, packaging for goods that are entering established product categories require less education, but they must overcome established competition. A common packaging strategy for such products entails mimicking the packaging of leading products, which helps to assure the buyer that the product is "normal."

FURTHER READING:

Boyd, Harper W., Jr., and Orville C. Walker, Jr. *Marketing Management: A Strategic Approach.* Irwin, 1990.

Clark, Ken. "Packaging for Profits." *HFN: The Weekly Newspaper for the Home Furnishing Network.* August 25, 1997.

Hisrich, Robert D. *Marketing.* Barron's Business Library, 1990.

McCarthy, E. Jerome, and William D. Perreault, Jr. *Basic Marketing.* Irwin, 1990.

McMath, Robert M. "Too Much of a Good Thing: A Perfectly Sound Product Idea can be Sidelined by Attractive but Impractical Packaging." *American Demographics.* December 1997.

"Packaging at the Turning Point." Consumer Network, 1999.

Quail, Jennifer. "Packaged for Profit." *Supermarket News.* October 18, 1999.

Schoell, William F., and Joseph P. Guiltinan. *Marketing: Contemporary Concepts and Practices.* Allyn and Bacon, 1992.

Sook Kim, Queena. "This Potion's Power is in Its Packaging." *Wall Street Journal.* December 21, 2000.

PARTNERSHIP

In the words of the Uniform Partnership Act, a partnership is "an association of two or more persons to carry on as Co-owners of a business for profit." The essential characteristics of this business form, then, are the collaboration of two or more owners, the conduct of business for profit (a nonprofit cannot be designated as a partnership), and the sharing of profits, losses, and assets by the joint owners. A partnership is not a corporate or separate entity; rather it is viewed as an extension of its owners for legal and tax purposes, although a partnership may own property as a legal entity. While a partnership may be founded on a simple agreement, even a handshake between owners, a well-crafted and carefully worded partnership agreement is the best way to begin the business. In the absence of such an agreement, the Uniform Partnership Act, a set of laws pertaining to partnerships that has been adopted by most states, govern the business.

There are two types of partnerships:

GENERAL PARTNERSHIPS In this standard form of partnership, all of the partners are equally responsible for the business's debts and liabilities. In addition, all partners are allowed to be involved in the management of the company. In fact, in the absence of a statement to the contrary in the partnership agreement, each partner has equal rights to control and manage the business. Therefore, unanimous consent of the partners is required for all major actions undertaken. Be advised, though, that any obligation made by one partner is legally binding on all partners, whether or not they have been informed.

LIMITED PARTNERSHIPS In a limited partnership, one or more partners are general partners, and one or more are limited partners. General partners are personally liable for the business's debts and judgments against the business; they can also be directly involved in the management. Limited partners are essentially investors (silent partners, so to speak) who do not participate in the company's management and who are also not liable beyond their investment in the business. State laws determine how involved limited partners can be in the day-to-day business of the firm without jeopardizing their limited liability. This business form is especially attractive to real estate investors, who benefit from the tax incentives available to limited partners, such as being able to write off depreciating values.

ADVANTAGES OF FORMING A PARTNERSHIP

Collaboration. As compared to a sole proprietorship, which is essentially the same business form but with only one owner, a partnership offers the advantage of allowing the owners to draw on the resources and expertise of the co-partners. Running a business on your own, while simpler, can also be a constant struggle. But with partners to share the responsibilities and lighten the workload, members of a partnership often find that they have more time for the other activities in their lives.

Tax advantages. The profits of a partnership pass through to its owners, who report their share on their individual tax returns. Therefore, the profits are only taxed once (at the personal level of its owners) rather than twice, as is the case with corporations, which are taxed at the corporate level and then again at the personal level when dividends are distributed to the shareholders. The benefits of single taxation can also be secured by forming an S corporation (although some ownership restrictions apply) or by forming a limited liability company (a new hybrid of corporations and partnerships that is still evolving).

Simple operating structure. A partnership, as opposed to a corporation, is fairly simple to establish and run. No forms need to be filed or formal agreements drafted (although it is advisable to write a partnership agreement in the event of future disagreements). The most that is ever required is perhaps filing a partnership certificate with a state office in order to register the business's name and securing a business license. As a result, the annual filing fees for corporations, which can sometimes be very expensive, are avoided when forming a partnership.

Flexibility. Because the owners of a partnership are usually its managers, especially in the case of a small business, the company is fairly easy to manage, and decisions can be made quickly without a lot of bureaucracy. This is not the case with corporations, which must have shareholders, directors, and officers, all of whom have some degree of responsibility for making major decisions.

Uniform laws. One of the drawbacks of owning a corporation or limited liability company is that the laws governing those business entities vary from state to state and are changing all the time. In contrast, the Uniform Partnership Act provides a consistent set of laws about forming and running partnerships that make it easy for small business owners to know the laws that affect them. And because these laws have been adopted in all states but Louisiana, interstate business is much easier for partnerships than it is for other forms of businesses.

Acquisition of capital. Partnerships generally have an easier time acquiring capital than corporations because partners, who apply for loans as individuals, can usually get loans on better terms. This is because partners guarantee loans with their personal assets as well as those of the business. As a result, loans for a partnership are subject to state usury laws, which govern loans for individuals. Banks also perceive partners to be less of a risk than corporations, which are only required to pledge the business's assets. In addition, by forming a limited partnership, the business can attract investors (who will not be actively involved in its management and who will enjoy limited liability) without having to form a corporation and sell stock.

DRAWBACKS OF FORMING A PARTNERSHIP

Conflict with partners. While collaborating with partners can be a great advantage to a small business owner, having to actually run a business from day to day with one or more partners can be a nightmare. First of all, you have to give up absolute control of the business and learn to compromise. And when big decisions have to be made, such as whether and how to expand the business, partners often disagree on the best course and are left with a potentially explosive situation. The best way to deal with such predicaments is to anticipate them by drawing up a partnership agreement that details how such disagreements will be dealt with.

Authority of partners. When one partner signs a contract, each of the other partners is legally bound to fulfill it. For example, if Anthony orders $10,000 of computer equipment, it is as if his partners, Susan and Jacob, had also placed the order. And if their business cannot afford to pay the bill, then the personal assets of Susan and Jacob are on the line as well as those of Anthony. And this is true whether the other partners are aware of the contract or not. Even if a clause in the partnership agreement dictates that each partner must inform the other partners before any such deals are made, all of the partners are still responsible if the other party in the contract (the computer company) was not aware of such a stipulation in the partnership agreement. The only recourse the other partners have is to sue.

The Uniform Partnership Act does specify some instances in which full consent of all partners is required:

- Selling the business's good will

- Decisions that would compromise the business's ability to function normally

- Assign partnership property in trust for a creditor or to someone in exchange for the payment of the partnership's debts

- Admission of liability in a lawsuit

- Submission of a partnership claim or liability to arbitration

Unlimited liability. As the previous example illustrated, the personal assets of the partnership's members are vulnerable because there is no separation between the owners and the business. The primary reason many businesses choose to incorporate or form limited liability companies is to protect the owners from the unlimited liability that is the main drawback of partnerships or sole proprietorships. If an employee or customer is injured and decides to sue, or if the business runs up excessive debts, then the partners are personally responsible and in danger of losing all that they own. Therefore, if considering a partnership, determine your assets that will be put at risk. If you possess substantial personal assets that you will not invest in the company and do not want to put in jeopardy, a corporation or limited liability company may be a better choice. But if you are investing most of what you own in the business, then you don't stand to lose any more than if you incorporated. Then if your business is successful, and you find at a later date that you now possess extensive personal assets that you would like to protect, you can consider changing the legal status of your business to secure limited liability.

Vulnerability to death or departure. Unlike corporations, which exist perpetually, regardless of ownership, general partnerships dissolve if one of the partners dies, retires, or withdraws. (In limited partnerships, the death or withdrawal of the limited partner does not affect the stability of the business.) Even though this is the law governing partnerships, the partnership agreement can contain provisions to continue the business. For example, a provision can be made allowing a buy out of a partner's share if he or she wants to withdraw or if the partner dies.

Limitations on transfer of ownership. Unlike corporations, which exist independently of their owners, the existence of partnerships is dependent upon the owners. Therefore, the Uniform Partnership Act stipulates that ownership may not be transferred without the consent of all the other partners. (Once again, a limited partner is an exception: his or her interest in the company may be sold at will.)

CHOOSING A PARTNER

Because of the need for compromise and the dynamics of shared authority that come along with sharing a business, partnerships can be very difficult to maintain and run efficiently. Therefore, the single most important decision a small business owner has to make when forming a partnership is the choice of a partner. In fact, warns Edward A. Haman, in *How to Write Your Own Partnership Agreement*, ''you should only take on a partner if you absolutely need that person's money or expertise.'' As an alternative, he advises, you could try to ''get the money as a loan, or hire the person as a consultant to get the expertise.'' But if you decide that forming a partnership is the best choice, consider the following when selecting a partner (anyone may become a partner, except minors and corporations):

ASSETS

- How much does your partner own in personal assets? If you own much more than your partner, then creditors will come after you in the event of extensive debts.

PERSONALITY

- Do you possess compatible personality types?
- How do you each deal with stress?
- How do you make decisions? Does your prospective partner tend to talk things through with others or make impulse decisions?

ROLES

- What role do each of you intend to take in the business? Are these roles compatible? Do you both hope to be in charge of the accounts or dealing with vendors, for example? Or can you split up the duties in a way that satisfies both of you?

SHARING RESPONSIBILITIES

- How much time will your partner contribute to the enterprise?
- Can you count on you partner to show up to work on time? Or you will be expected to cover for him?
- Is your prospective partner a hard worker, or will he or she routinely leave tasks for you to complete?

GOALS FOR THE BUSINESS

- How do each of you envision the future of the business? Do you hope to build up a solid business and then expand to other locations? Does your partner share that vision or does he or she hope only to be able to make a decent living out of one business with fewer responsibilities than would be required if running a chain of stores?

FORMING A PARTNERSHIP

RESERVING A NAME The first step in creating a partnership is reserving a name, which must be done with the secretary of state's office or its equivalent. Most states require that the words ''Company'' or ''Associates'' be included in the name to show that more than one partner is involved in the business. In all states, though, the name of the partnership must not resemble the name of any other corporation, limited liability company, partnership, or sole proprietorship that is registered with the state

THE PARTNERSHIP AGREEMENT A partnership can be formed in essentially two ways: by verbal or written agreement. A partnership that is formed at will, or verbally, can also be dissolved at will. In the absence of a formal agreement, state laws (the Uniform Partnership Act, except in Louisiana) will govern the business. These laws specify that without an agreement, all partners share equally in the profits and losses of the partnership and that partners are not entitled to compensation for services. If you would like to structure your partnership differently, you will need to write a partnership agreement.

It may be advisable to consult a lawyer before drafting the agreement, but you should at least research the issue on your own. A thorough partnership agreement should generally cover the following areas:

- Name and address

- Duration of partnership—You can specify a finite date on which all business will terminate or you can include a general clause that explains the partnership will exist until all partners agree to dissolve it or a partner dies.

- Purpose of business

- Partners' contributions—These may be in cash, property or services. Be sure to determine the value of all non-cash contributions.

- Partners' compensation—Determine how profits will be split up and how often. Also decide if any of the partners will receive a salary.

- Management Authority—Will partners be able to make some decisions on their own? Which decisions will require the unanimous consent of all partners?

- Work hours and vacation

- Kinds of outside business activities that will be allowed for partners

- Partner withdrawal—Decide how the death, retirement, withdrawal, disability, or death of a partner will be handled through a buy-sell agreement. Also determine whether or not a partner who has simply withdrawn will be allowed to operate a competing business.

- Disposition of the partnership's name if a partner leaves

- How to handle disputes—Decide whether or not mediation or arbitration will be provided for in the case of disputes that cannot be resolved amongst the partners. This is a way to avoid costly litigation.

RIGHTS AND RESPONSIBILITIES OF PARTNERS

The Uniform Partnership Act defines the basic rights and responsibilities of partners. Some of these can be changed by the partnership agreement, except, as a general rule, those laws that govern the partners' relationships with third parties. In the absence of a written agreement, then, the following rights and responsibilities apply:

RIGHTS

- All partners have an equal share in the profits of the partnership and are equally responsible for its losses.

- Any partner who makes a payment for the partnership beyond its capital, or makes a loan to the partnership, is entitled to receive interest on that money.

- All partners have equal property rights for property held in the partnership's name. This means that the use of the property is equally available to all partners for the purpose of the partnership's business.

- All partners have an equal interest in the partnership, or share of its profits and assets.

- All partners have an equal right in the management and conduct of the business.

- All partners have a right to access the books and records of the partnership's accounts and activities at all times. (This does not apply to limited partners.)

- No partner may be added without the consent of all other partners.

RESPONSIBILITIES

- Partners must report and turn over to the partnership any income they have derived from use of the partnership's property.

- Partners are not allowed to conduct business that competes with the partnership.

- Each partner is responsible for contributing his or her full time and energy to the success of the partnership.

- Any property that a partner acquires with the intention of it being the partnership's property must be turned over to the partnership.

- Any disputes shall be decided by a majority vote.

FURTHER READING:

Clifford, Denis. *The Partnership Book: How to Write a Partnership Agreement*. 5th ed. Nolo Press, 1997.

Edwards, Paul. *Teaming Up: The Small-Business Guide to Collaborating with Others to Boost Your Earnings and Expand Your Horizons*. G.P. Putnam's Sons, 1997.

Fay, Jack R. "What Form of Ownership is Best?" *CPA Journal*. August 1998.

Haman, Edward A. *How to Write Your Own Partnership Agreement*. Sphinx Publishing, 1993.

Handmaker, Stuart A. *Choosing a Legal Structure for Your Business*. Prentice Hall, 1997.

Selecting the Legal Structure for Your Business Small Business Administration. n.a.

Steingold, Fred S. *The Legal Guide for Starting and Running a Small Business.* Second Edition. Nolo Press, 1995.

PARTNERSHIP AGREEMENT

Partnership agreements are written documents that explicitly detail the relationship between the business partners, as well as their individual obligations and contributions to the partnership. Since partnership agreements should cover all possible business situations that could arise during the life of the partnership, the documents are often complex, and legal counsel in drafting and reviewing the finished contract is generally recommended. If a partnership does not have a partnership agreement in place when it dissolves, the guidelines of the Uniform Partnership Act and various state laws will determine how the assets and debts of the partnership are distributed.

RECOMMENDED ELEMENTS OF THE PARTNERSHIP AGREEMENT

1) Name and address of partnership

2) Duration of partnership—Partners can point to a specific termination date or include a general clause explaining that the partnership will exist until all partners agree to dissolve it or a partner dies.

3) Business purpose—Some consultants recommend that partners keep this section somewhat vague in case opportunities for expansion arise, while others, such as *Legal Handbook for Small Business* author Marc J. Lane, feel otherwise: "Avoid any conflict in entrepreneurial goals. Since a general partnership obligates you for the business acts and omissions of your copartners, it is wise to limit the scope of your business activities by contract."

4) Bank account information—This section should note which bank accounts are to be used for partnership purposes, and which partners have check-signing privileges.

5) Partners' contributions—Valuation of all contributions, whether in cash, property or services.

6) Partners' compensation—Determine in detail how and when profits (and salaries, if applicable) will be distributed.

7) Management authority—What are the operational responsibilities of each partner? Will partners be able to make some decisions on their own? Which decisions will require the unanimous consent of all partners? What are the voting rights of each partner? How will tie votes be resolved?

8) Circumstances under which new partners might be admitted into the partnership.

9) Work hours and vacation.

10) Kinds of outside business activities that will be allowed for partners.

11) Disposition of partnership's name if a partner leaves.

12) Dispute resolution—Stipulates what kinds mediation or arbitration will be utilized in the case of disputes that cannot be resolved amongst the partners. This is a way to avoid costly litigation.

13) Miscellaneous provisions—This portion of the agreement might delineate the circumstances under which the agreement could be amended, for example.

14) Buy-Sell Agreement.

THE BUY-SELL AGREEMENT The buy-sell agreement is one of the most important elements of any partnership agreement. It details what will happen to the partnership if one of its partners leave the business. In essence, it specifies the terms of a buyout in the event of death, divorce, disability, or retirement. "Having a buy/sell agreement in place makes a great deal of difference," commented Mary Rowland in *Nation's Business,* "to guarantee the smooth transition of a business and ensure that it need not be sold at an inopportune time." Indeed, the importance of this particular element of the partnership agreement is underlined by the fact that in recent years, loan institutions, companies that provide bonding for construction jobs, and other outside firms have begun to insist that small business clients have buy/sell agreements in place.

The two primary structures for buy/sell agreements are cross purchase agreements, in which the remaining partnership owners buy the departing partner's stock or partnership interest, and the stock redemption agreement, in which the company buys the stock of the departing owner. The advantage of the cross purchase agreement, wrote Rowland, is that "the purchasers get a tax saving 'step up' in basis to the market value of that portion of the business. . . . With a cross purchase agreement, the owners typically buy life insurance policies on one another to finance the agreement. If there are just two owners, it's pretty straightforward," but with multiple shareholders, this arrangement can get confusing and expensive.

With stock redemption agreements, on the other hand, "the company would own the life insurance policy and pay the premiums," said Rowland. "An advantage to this type of agreement is that if there are a number of owners, only one policy on each is necessary." Disadvantages of this type of buy/sell agreement include absence of 'step up' savings and the fact that in cases where the life insurance used to finance the redemption agreement is owned by a business structured as a C Corporation, the company might be liable for the alternative minimum tax (AMT) on any proceeds.

FURTHER READING:

Clifford, Denis, and Ralph E. Warner. *The Partnership Book.* Nolo, 1997.

Dunn, Ross. "Ye of Little Faith." *People Management.* April 27, 2000.

Jasper, Margaret C. *Law for the Small Business Owner.* Oceana Publications, 1994.

Lane, Marc J. *Legal Handbook for Small Business.* AMACOM, 1989.

Rowland, Mary. "The Importance of Buy/Sell Agreements." *Nation's Business.* March 1995.

Shapiro, Mort. "Get It in Writing." *CA Magazine.* August 1996.

Weisz, Richard L. "Breakup of Business Partnership isn't Easy Thing to Do." *Business First-Columbus.* December 1, 2000.

Williford, Jerry S., and Robin L. Imrie. "The Accountant's Role in Preparing and Amending Partnership or LLC Agreements." *Journal of Partnership Taxation.* Summer 1996.

PART-TIME BUSINESS

Thousands of American entrepreneurs supplement their income by starting and maintaining part-time small businesses. The circumstances and goals of these business owners run the gamut, but many are operated out of the home and are utilized to supplement income derived from other sources (a full-time job, retirement benefits, etc.). But not all people establish part-time enterprises out of economic necessity. Statistics also indicate that many individuals—and especially people which higher levels of education—launch part-time entrepreneurial ventures to make use of skills that may not be tapped in their full-time work. Finally, the ability and desire to launch a business on a part-time basis is often impacted by family considerations; in some instances, the cost of raising children may serve as an incentive to start a business on the side. In other cases, a parent may decide that the hours involved in looking after his or her children precludes the possibility of a part-time business. Many owners of part-time businesses, however, contend that if the desire is there, a part-time venture can be managed by most people.

Part-time businesses are also regarded by many entrepreneurs as a sensible option in situations where the ultimate success of the venture seems unclear. "Part-time entrepreneurs can . . . limit their risks compared with those taken by individuals who plunge in full-time," wrote David E. Gumpert in *Working Woman.* "For one thing, part-timers don't have the same pressure to produce cash flow, because they can hold down a job at the same time and operate out of their homes. For another, part-timers can go more slowly and learn the skills of running a business as they go along; they have the luxury of making errors and revising their business concept as they proceed."

KEYS TO ESTABLISHING A SUCCESSFUL PART-TIME BUSINESS

Experts point to several important factors in creating and maintaining a profitable and healthy part-time business venture:

Recognize importance of full-time job. It is vitally important for entrepreneurs who already have a full-time job to make sure that their part-time business does not interfere with their obligations to their employers. Moreover, it is important for part-time business owners to make sure that their employers do not begin to *perceive* that the side business is taking priority, for in the final analysis, your ability to meet the demands of both businesses is irrelevant if your employer begins to feel—fairly or not—that the arrangement is detracting from your job performance. For this reason, part-time business owners may want to weigh the likely reaction of their employer before even publicizing the existence of the part-time venture. Daugherty also noted that "your employer may well have rules on outside work. . . . If you don't know, ask. And if you value your job, do your best to comply with them."

Type of business. The nature of a part-time venture is often an important factor in its long-term viability. Certain businesses can be more easily maintained without unduly complicating regular job obligations. "Service businesses often allow for this kind of flexibility," explained Gumpert. "Men have for years carved out entrepreneurial opportunities as part-time plumbers, electricians, and carpenters. Women [are] discovering similar opportunities in such areas as consulting and teaching." Retail stores and manufacturing establishments, on the other hand, are far less conducive to part-time businesses.

Scheduling flexibility. The individual's full-time job is flexible enough to give him or her the time and resources to take care of the entrepreneurial business's needs during normal business hours or during particularly busy periods.

Realistic workloads. Entrepreneurs launching part-time business ventures should also be wary of overextending themselves. Many individuals tend to take on more part-time work than they can easily handle, especially during the first few months of operation, when they have less experience in estimating the time involved in executing various tasks. While finances are often a factor in establishing a part-time business, most part-time entrepreneurs do not begin a venture with the expressed intention of turning their life into a chaotic rush of impending deadlines. Complications associated with underestimating the amount of time a given project or assignment will take are also typically compounded if the entrepreneur in question has significant family obligations (child or elder care, for instance).

Scaling back existing businesses. Small business researchers also note that some of the most successful part-time businesses are those that were formerly full-time endeavors. Indeed, many full-time entrepreneurs choose to scale back their hours after a certain number of years. They may do this for any number of reasons; some simply reach retirement age and wish to relax a little more, others decide to start a family, and still others may decide that they wish to spend more of their time traveling or indulging other interests (including other promising entrepreneurial ventures). In many instances, switching a business from full-time status to part-time status can actually strengthen the enterprise's hourly productivity. For example, the entrepreneur who decides to turn his 50-hours-a-week venture into one that requires him to spend half that amount of time on the business each week will naturally do his best to maintain relations with his best clients, while letting less valuable or more problematic clients go. As many business owners will quickly attest, having greater freedom to pick and choose who you do business with can be a most valuable side benefit of going part-time.

Public perception of business. Some customers, especially if they are other businesses, may be wary of contracting with part-timers. The most effective way to counter the perception held in some quarters that part-time business owners are less reliable and responsive (because of obligations to their full-time employer) than full-time entrepreneurs is simply to not advertise your part-time status. Of course, you should also not lie about it if the issue comes up.

LEGAL AND TAX CONSIDERATIONS

Owners of part-time businesses should also consider the potential legal and tax ramifications of their activities. "Taxes may be one of the last things anyone thinks about when starting a part-time business, but they out to be high on the priority list for anyone who is serious about making money in a part-time venture,'' said *Los Angeles Business Journal* contributor Bob Howard. "Additional income from a part-time business means additional taxes, but those who wait until the end of the year may wind up paying penalties or not being able to take deductions they had counted on.'' Part-time business owners should thus consider doing one of the following: 1) have their regular employers take out more withholding taxes, or 2) file quarterly estimated tax payments. Either approach can go far toward helping the part-time entrepreneur avoid tax penalties or a big end-of-the-year tax blow.

In addition, owners of part-time enterprises should make sure that they take full advantage of available tax deductions. Gumpert noted that "part-timers get the same tax advantages [as full-time entrepreneurs], including deductions for travel, entertainment, home office, and related expenses, plus deductible retirement plans.'' Howard noted, though, that home-based business tax deductions can vary significantly, often depending on whether the business is a full- or part-time venture. "The IRS now requires that a home office be used 'exclusively and regularly as a place of business to meet or deal with patients, clients, or customers' in the normal course of the business. The world 'exclusively' is very important because it means any room or space designated as a home office must be used 100 percent for business in order to qualify for the deduction.''

MAKING THE LEAP TO FULL-TIME

Many part-time entrepreneurial ventures eventually expand into full-time businesses. Indeed, business owners who nurture their side-businesses into enterprises that are capable of covering their living and business expenses often waste little time in giving their employer two weeks notice and devoting their full attention to further expansion of their own business. But experts caution small business owners not to leave their long-time employer prematurely. For example, *Entrepreneur* pointed out that would-be full-time business owners can schedule health exams and other routine medical procedures while they are still covered by corporate insurance, and that they can sometimes convert existing health coverage to post-job use. In addition, entrepreneurs thinking about leaving their full-time job to devote their energies to their own business should first determine if they are enrolled in any benefit plans that will vest or increase in value in the near term.

Entrepreneurs are also urged to organize their credit situation to their greatest advantage before leaving the security of their job. "Pay off or pay down the balance on your credit cards while you're still generating a steady income,'' stated *Entrepreneur.* ''This helps your credit rating and enables you to finance various start-up costs.'' Finally, many entrepreneurs take out a home equity line of credit before leaving their full-time job. According to *Entrepreneur,* ''having a line of credit to draw upon is invaluable during the first two years you're in business, although you probably won't qualify for one once you leave your job until your business has been successful for more than two years.''

FURTHER READING:

Amirault, Thomas. ''Multiple Jobholders: What Else Do I Want to Do When I Grow Up?'' *Occupational Outlook Quarterly.* Winter 1996.

Anthony, Joseph A. *Kiplinger's Working for Yourself: Full Time, Part Time, Anytime.* Kiplinger Books, 1995.

Bowers, Brent. ''Finding the Best Part-Time Job for You.'' *New Choices for Retirement Living.* November 1994.

Daugherty, Greg. ''Part-Time Writing, Full-Time Success.'' *Writer's Digest.* July 1996.

Dunnan, Nancy. ''The Part-Time Solution.'' *Parents Magazine.* May 1996.

Edwards, Sarah, and Paul Edwards. ''On the Side.'' *Entrepreneur.* July 1999.

Gumpert, David E. ''Doing a Little Business on the Side: How Entrepreneurs Start Up a Business and Hold Down a Job.'' *Working Woman.* October 1986.

Howard, Bob. ''Part-Time Business Income Can Cause Tax Trouble for Wage Earners.'' *Los Angeles Business Journal.* December 23, 1996.

''Nurturing Part-Timers to be Entrepreneurs.'' *Nation's Business.* March 1996.

PART-TIME EMPLOYEES

Part-time employees are those who—whether by personal choice or due to employment conditions beyond their control—work fewer hours than the regular, full-time staff of a business over the course of a year. Many small business owners rely on a blend of full- and part-time employees to attend to basic operational needs, although some industries rely more heavily on one type or another. Retail sectors, for instance, utilize large percentages of part-time employees, while the work force of many manufacturers and service providers tends to be primarily composed of full-time employees.

Studies indicate, however, that there seems to be a general across-the-board trend toward part-time status in the American workplace. Small business establishments are an important component of this trend. As Elwood N. Chapman stated in *Human Relations in Small Business,* ''the majority of these part-timers will be recruited and managed by small business organizations.'' Business consultants indicate that each small business needs to determine for itself how to compose its work force in this areas, weighing the benefits and drawbacks associated with each type of employee.

TYPES OF PART-TIMERS

Federal law defines a part-time employee as one who works less than 1,000 hours a year for the same firm. This annual total averages out to about 17.5 hours per week. In reality, however, part-time employees may work more than 30 hours a week without gaining designation as full-time employees. Analysts admit, however, that the distinction between full- and part-time work grows quite hazy when an employee works more than 30 hours a week, and many consultants counsel small business owners who ask workers to put in weekly time above that threshold to consider making them full-time employees, especially if they are not providing any benefits to the employees when they work under ''part-time'' designations.

According to the U.S. Bureau of Labor Statistics, 18.3 percent of the work force in the United States in the mid-1990s consisted of part-time workers. Studies indicate that the overwhelming majority of these employees turned to part-time work not because of their inability to secure full-time employment, but because of the scheduling flexibility that part-time work offers. Some studies, for instance, state that more than three out of four part-time employees voluntarily work on that basis.

Analysts cite four primary demographic categories into which most part-time employees fall. These are: 1) Retirees, who may want to supplement a fixed income or ensure that they maintain a certain level of involvement in the world around them; 2) Parents, who choose to have one member of their partnership work on a part-time basis so that more time can be spent raising children; 3) Students, who embrace part-time employment as a way to make money without interrupting their education; and 4) Temporary agency workers, who sometimes become part-time employees of a particular establishment over time.

ADVANTAGES OF HIRING PART-TIMERS

Writing in *Human Relations in Small Business,* Chapman cited several advantages associated with utilizing part-time help:

- Costs are lower in terms of direct monetary compensation—''Some part-timers are paid less than half of what full-timers who do the same work are paid,'' he noted. ''Many small businesses would be forced to close without part-timers.'' And of course, many businesses save significant amounts of money in terms of benefits by hiring part-time workers.

- Energy and enthusiasm—Chapman contended that part-timers—especially college and high school students—can give businesses a needed injection of liveliness. Analysts state that this quality is particularly evident in retail clothing establishments and other businesses that survive on the expenditures of younger customers.

- In-house candidates for full-time job openings—Chapman said that ''when full-time positions open up, employers can make better choices from part-timers, whom they have had the opportunity to observe and test out.''

- Willingness to learn—Chapman and others indicate that young part-timers are often willing to learn new tasks and responsibilities.

- Availability during peak periods—Researchers note that many businesses that utilize part-time help have pronounced cycles of activity (for holidays, seasonal attractions, etc.). Students are particularly useful in meeting these periods of high demand because many of these periods coincide with times when they are not in school (Christmas vacation, summertime).

- Execution of mundane or unpleasant tasks—Analysts note that many part-time employees do not have the clout to refuse certain tasks, and they indicate that many young part-timers recognize that there is a ''paying your dues'' quality to worklife in many early employment experiences. This also frees up full-time employees to use their time to tackle more complicated, long-term challenges facing the business.

- Availability—Chapman indicated that ''some smaller and isolated communities offer a larger supply of responsible and hard-working part-timers, because fewer part-time jobs are available.''

DISADVANTAGES ASSOCIATED WITH PART-TIMERS

Chapman noted, however, that there are disadvantages associated with part-time employees as well. One of the major drawbacks, he wrote, is that ''part-timers are less committed to their jobs; they usually have a long-term goal that is more important. This causes them to be less stable and dependable.'' Indeed, it is a basic business reality that the turnover rate among part-time positions is significantly higher than the rate among full-timers.

Other disadvantages cited by Chapman included:

- Higher absenteeism rates.

- Inexperience, which can translate into higher training costs and/or unprofessional behavior.

- Mistakes in hiring decisions, since younger applicants for part-time positions have less of a track record.

- Excessive socializing (again, especially with younger employees).

- Increased risks in terms of workplace safety and security.

PART-TIME EMPLOYEES AND BENEFITS

Late 1990s studies of American businesses indicate that although part-time employees are more likely to receive benefits than they were even a few years before, many still are not compensated

with benefits packages. These reports also indicate that small business owners are less likely to offer additional benefits in such realms as paid vacation, health insurance, etc., than their larger counterparts, largely because of their more modest financial positions. Another key factor in determining the likelihood of a part-time worker receiving benefits was the number of hours worked, according to a survey of 505 employers by Hewitt Associates.

The Hewitt survey broke benefits down into several key areas: medical benefits, dental benefits, flexible benefits, life insurance, long-term disability, and paid sick leave.

- Medical Benefits—The Hewitt survey indicated that nearly 75 percent of respondent companies offered medical benefits to employees working 30 or more hours per week, but only one out of four offered medical coverage to part-timers who put in less than 20 hours per week.

- Dental Benefits—Although 69 percent of businesses surveyed offered dental insurance to part-timers working more than 30 hours a week, that percentage dropped significantly when the employees worked between 20 and 29 hours a week (56 percent) or less than 20 hours a week (23 percent).

- Flexible Benefits—Not all companies surveyed offered flexible work arrangements, but those that did overwhelmingly allowed their part-time employees to take part.

- Life Insurance—Life insurance was made available to fewer than one in four part-time workers who put in fewer than 20 hours a week, but for those employees who put in at least 30 hours a week, the percentage rose to nearly seven out of ten workers.

- Long-Term Disability—Employees working fewer than 20 hours a week rarely receive this benefit, but the Hewitt survey indicated that about half of employers were willing to provide this benefit to workers who put in more than 30 hours a week.

- Paid Sick Leave—Once again, the likelihood of receiving this benefit is directly dependent on number of hours worked; while 64 percent of respondent companies indicated that they provided paid sick leave to employees who worked 30 hours or more a week (and 57 percent of companies offered the benefit to employees working 20-29 hours a week), only 28 percent offered paid sick leave to workers who put in fewer than 20 hours a week.

Hewitt consultant Carol Sladek predicted that the trend toward increasing benefits for part-time workers would continue in the twenty-first century. "Employers have finally started to realize that the part-time work force is here to stay," she told Lee Fletcher in *Crain's Detroit Business.* "It's not something we're just doing to be nice, it's not something to help women come back from maternity leave, it's not just something that we do for shift workers to help with scheduling. There are a lot of good, talented people out there who are choosing to work fewer hours, for whatever reason."

In addition to offering benefits, *Entrepreneur* magazine provided several other tips for small businesses hoping to improve the morale and productivity of part-time employees. For example, experts suggest providing new part-time workers with an orientation to acquaint them with the company's operations and goals. It may also be helpful to give them a tour of the facility and introduce them to full-time staff members with whom they will be working. Experts also recommend that small businesses offer training to part-time workers in order to "enhance and expand their skills beyond basic job knowledge, and to groom part-timers for eventual full-time positions." Finally, small businesses may benefit from creating an inclusive environment that recognizes the value contributions of part-time workers. This may involve such simple tactics as celebrating part-time employees' birthdays or inviting them to participate in company social events or sports teams.

THE RETAIL INDUSTRY AND PART-TIME EMPLOYMENT

Many types of businesses rely on part-time employees to one degree or another, but historically, few industry sectors have counted on part-timers to the extent that the retail sector has. Indeed, the unique operational needs of retail establishments make the part-time employee an ideal one in many respects. "For retailers, seasonal buying patterns, year-round promotional activities, and ever-changing consumers demand a flexible work force," wrote Tracy Mullen in *Chain Store Age Executive with Shopping Center Age.* Retail stores also register major savings in benefits because of the composition of their work force.

But, as Mullen indicated, the retail industry would not be able to employ an estimated seven million part-time workers if those employees did not receive some rewards in return. "For most of these employees, the inherent value in part-time retail employment is [scheduling] flexibility," said Mullen. But she goes on to note that "another big draw for part-time retail employment is the discounts on merchandise. Part-time employees don't get a part-time discount on goods. While the average retail wage is far above the minimum wage at $8 per hour, who can say how much more that hourly wage is worth when you factor in the 20 percent to 40 percent discount part-timers enjoy?"

FURTHER READING:

Chapman, Elwood N. *Human Relations in Small Business.* Crisp Publications, 1994.

Clark, Scott. "Part-Time Employees Can Be a Smart Solution." *Birmingham Business Journal.* May 26, 2000.

Craver, Alan. "Welcome to the Full Time." *Baltimore Business Journal.* September 27, 1996.

Fletcher, Lee. "Part-Time Employees Find Better Benefits." *Crain's Detroit Business.* November 22, 1999.

Gruner, Stephanie. "The Benefits of Part-Time Work." *Inc.* December 1994.

Mullen, Tracy. "Part-Time Values Mean Full-Time Benefits." *Chain Store Age Executive with Shopping Center Age.* October 1997.

"Part-Time, Contingent Worker Benefits: Being Creative Doesn't Mean Being Expensive." *Employee Benefit Plan Review.* June 1997.

"Perks Work: Tips for Making Part-Time Employees Give Their Best." *Entrepreneur.* May 1999.

Sherer, Pamela D., and Lori A. Coakley. "Questioning and Developing Your Part-Time Employee Practices." *Workforce.* October 1999.

PATENT AND TRADEMARK OFFICE (PTO)

The Patent and Trademark Office (PTO) is responsible for administering all laws relating to trademarks and patents in the United States. It has thus been an important agency for several generations of entrepreneurs and small business owners, as well as for larger corporations and universities. The PTO describes itself thusly: ''Through the issuance of patents, we encourage technological advancement by providing incentives to invent, invest in, and disclose new technology worldwide. Through the registration of trademarks, we assist businesses in protecting their investments, promoting goods and services and safeguarding consumers against confusion and deception in the marketplace. By disseminating both patent and trademark information, we promote an understanding of intellectual property protection and facilitate the developments and sharing of new technologies world wide.''

In addition to handling the nation's patents and trademarks, the PTO also has a notable advisory function. It serves as both a developer of intellectual property policy and an advisor to the White House on patent/trademark/copyright policies. In addition, the PTO provides information and guidance on intellectual property issues to international commerce offices such as the International Trade Commission and the Office of the U.S. Trade Representative. In 1999 the PTO was established as an agency within the Department of Commerce.

By nearly all accounts, the PTO has historically done a laudable job of protecting the intellectual property rights of businesses and individuals while simultaneously encouraging the growth of business. ''Since its inception, the patent system has encouraged the genius of millions of inventors,'' wrote *Inventor's Desktop Companion* author Richard C. Levy. ''It has protected these creative individuals by allowing them an opportunity to profit from their labors, and has benefited society by systematically recording new inventions and releasing them to the public once the inventors' limited rights have expired. . . . Under the patent system, American industry has flourished. New products have been invented, new uses for old ones discovered, and employment given to millions.''

LEGAL UNDERPINNINGS OF THE PTO

The fundamental principles of the modern American patent system were first codified into law in 1790. Guided by Secretary of State Thomas Jefferson in its early years, the patent office grew quickly, and in 1849 the Department of the Interior was given responsibility for maintaining it. In 1870 the powers of the patent office were expanded dramatically; the commissioner of patents was given jurisdiction to register and regulate trademarks. The office thus came to be responsible for all American trademarks, even though the word ''trademark'' would not appear in its name for another 105 years (the Patent Office became the Patent and Trademark Office on January 2, 1975). In 1926 responsibility for the Patent Office was handed over to the Department of Commerce, where it remains today.

The PTO currently touts the following laws as the primary statutory authorities guiding its programs:

- 15 U.S.C. 1051-1127—Contains provisions of the Trademark Act of 1946, a law that governs the office's trademark administration

- 15 U.S.C. 1511—Establishes the PTO as a subordinate agency of the Department of Commerce

- 35 U.S.C.—Provides the PTO with its basic authority to administrate patent laws

- 44 U.S.C. 1337-1338—Gives the PTO authority to print trademarks, patents, and other material relevant to the business of the Office

In 1991 the PTO underwent a significant change in operation. The Omnibus Budget Reconciliation Act (OBRA) of 1990 included provisions to make the Office a self-supporting government agency that would not receive federal funding. In order to provide the PTO with needed operating funds, Congress raised the PTO's patent application fees to cover operating costs and maintain services for inventors. The PTO has been funded solely by fees since 1993. In 1999 it was formally established as an agency within the Department of Commerce.

As part of its efforts to process its patent applications in a timely manner, the Patent and Trademark Office established and opened an electronic patent application filing system open to all inventors in October 2000. The PTO's web site (www.uspto.gov) now allows inventors to assemble all components of a patent application online, including calculate fees, validate content, and encrypt and transmit the filing. At the same time, the PTO raised its patent fees to match current rates of inflation. This increase, the first since 1997, was needed to pay for the electronic system and other expenses associated with processing the huge volume of patent and trademark applications that pass through the PTO's doors every year (the Office experienced an annual 10 percent growth in patent applications during the 1990s, and in 1999 alone, the PTO issued more than 160,000 patents and registered more than 100,000 trademarks).

FURTHER READING:

Chun, Janean. ''Patent Leather.'' *Entrepreneur.* June 1997.

Hoover, Kent. ''Patent Office Opens Electronic Filing to All.'' *Sacramento Business Journal.* November 3, 2000.

Levy, Richard C. ''The Patent and Trademark Office.'' In *The Inventor's Desktop Companion.* Visible Ink, 1995.

SEE ALSO: Inventions and Patents

PAYROLL TAXES

Payroll taxes include a number of different taxes that must be withheld from wages by all businesses that have employees. Small businesses that employ persons other than the owner or partners are required to withhold payroll taxes from the wages paid to employees, remit these taxes to the Internal Revenue Service (IRS), and make regularly scheduled reports to the IRS about the amount of payroll taxes owed and paid. Businesses are not required to withhold payroll taxes on wages paid to independent contractors. It is important to be aware of the distinctions between independent contractors and employees, however, because the penalties for misclassification can be severe.

Many small businesses fall behind in paying these taxes or filing the associated reports at some time during their existence. This is a very bad practice, however, because significant interest and penalties apply for late payment or nonpayment of payroll taxes. In fact, the Trust Fund Recovery Penalty allows the IRS to hold a small business owner or accountant personally liable for 100 percent of the amount owed, even in cases where the business has gone bankrupt.

TYPES OF PAYROLL TAXES

Three main types of taxes fall under the category of payroll taxes:

1) The regular income tax that must be withheld from employees' paychecks. Employees can adjust their income tax withholding by filing Form W-4 with their employer and designating the number of withholding allowances they wish to claim. Ideally, the total income tax withheld should come close to equaling their overall tax liability at the end of the year. By adjusting their withholding allowances properly, employees can avoid owing large amounts in taxes or providing the government with an interest-free loan.

2) Federal Insurance Contribution Act (FICA) taxes, which include contributions to federal Social Security and Medicare programs. Employers are required to withhold 7.65 percent of the first $62,700 of an employee's income for FICA taxes. Employers are also required to match that amount for every employee, so that the total FICA contribution is 15.3 percent. Self-employed persons are required to pay both the employer and employee portions of the FICA tax.

3) Federal Unemployment Tax (FUTA), which is approximately 1 percent of the first $7,000 in wages paid to an employee. This tax is paid in full by the employer.

PAYROLL TAX REMITTANCE AND REPORTING

In addition to withholding payroll taxes for employees, employers must remit these taxes to the IRS in a timely manner. The regular income taxes and the portion of the FICA taxes that are withheld from employees' wages each pay period must be remitted to the IRS monthly, along with a Federal Tax Deposit Coupon (Form 8109-B). If the total withheld is less than $500, however, the business is allowed to make the payments quarterly. In 1996, the IRS began requiring businesses that owed more than $47 million in payroll taxes annually to make their monthly payments via telephone or computer through the Electronic Federal Tax Payment System. The threshold for electronic filing was scheduled to drop to $50,000 in annual payroll taxes by January 1, 1997, but the deadline was pushed back to June 30, 1998. In addition, two bills were introduced in Congress that would make electronic payments of payroll taxes voluntary for small businesses with few employees.

Employers must also file four different reports regarding payroll taxes. The first report, Form 941, is the Employer's Quarterly Federal Tax Return. This report details the number of employees the business had, the amount of wages they were paid, and the amount of taxes that were withheld for the quarter. The other three reports are filed annually. Form W-2—the Annual Statement of Taxes Withheld—must be sent to all employees before January 31 of the following year. It details how much each employee received in wages and how much was withheld for taxes over the course of the year. Copies of the W-2 forms for all employees also must be sent to the Social Security Administration. The third report, Form W-3, must be sent to the IRS by February 28 of the following year. It provides a formal reconciliation of the quarterly tax payments made on Form 941 and the annual totals reported on Form W-2 for all employees. The final report is the Federal Unemployment Tax Return, Form 940, which outlines the total FUTA taxes owed and paid for the year.

Most states—as well as some large cities—have their own income tax that businesses must withhold from employees' wages and report to the appropriate authorities. States may also have other payroll taxes that must be collected from employees, as well as unemployment taxes that must be paid by the company. The payment schedules and reporting procedures for state and local payroll taxes are usually consistent with those applied to federal payroll taxes.

EXCEPTIONS TO PAYROLL TAX RULES

There are certain situations in which small businesses can avoid owing payroll taxes. For example, special rules apply to sole proprietorships and husband-and-wife partnerships that pay their minor (under 18) children for work performed in the business. These small businesses receive an exemption from withholding FICA taxes from their children's paychecks, and are also not required to pay the employer portion of the FICA taxes. In this way, the parent and child each save 7.65 percent, for a total of 15.3 percent. In addition, the child's wages can still be deducted from the parents' income taxes as a business expense. Children employed in small family businesses also usually qualify for an exemption from the FUTA tax until they reach age 21.

There is no limit on how much children can earn and still receive the FICA tax exemption. However, it is important that the wages paid to the child are reasonable for the job performed, and that the hours worked by the child are carefully documented, so it will be clear to the IRS that the child has not been paid for nothing. In addition, parents should note that their child's financial aid for college may be reduced if they earn more than $1,750 per year.

Small businesses also are not required to withhold payroll taxes for persons who are employed as independent contractors. Using independent contractors rather than hiring employees can be a very attractive option for small businesses. By avoiding responsibility for payroll taxes and all the associated paperwork, as well as avoiding the need to pay benefits, businesses may find that using an independent contractors cost between 20 and 30 percent less than hiring an employee. But misclassifying an employee as an independent contractor can have dire consequences for a small business. The IRS examines such relationships very carefully, and in cases where an independent contractor must be reclassified as an employee, the business may be liable for back taxes plus a special penalty of 12 to 35 percent of the total tax bill.

The IRS uses a 20-step test to determine whether someone is an employee or an independent contractor. True independent contractors, according to the IRS definition, are in business for themselves with the intention of making a profit and are not under the direct control of the client company. To protect their companies from potential problems, small business owners should make sure that independent contractors are paid by the job rather than by the hour, set their own hours and rules, work on their own premises using their own equipment, sign a specific contract for each project, and make themselves available to multiple clients. Rather than withholding taxes, small businesses simply file an annual informational return—Form 1099, Statement of Miscellaneous Income—detailing the total amount paid to each contractor. No reporting is required for contractors that were paid less than $600 over the course of a year.

TRUST FUND RECOVERY PENALTY

"All too often in a small-business setting, the owner or executive finds himself/herself in a cash flow bind and must make a choice between paying essential suppliers and employees' salaries to stay in business or remitting employees' payroll taxes to the IRS on a timely basis," Ray A. Knight and Lee G. Knight explained in an article for *Management Accounting.* "A typical scenario is that, for short-term survival, the business owner or executive decides to meet current creditors' requirements and forces the IRS to become a creditor with the hope that in the long term the business can pay the IRS the delinquent taxes plus interest and penalties. Often, however, the business becomes insolvent and declares bankruptcy. To avoid a significant erosion of tax revenue and to address this problem, in 1954 Congress enacted a penalty—equal to the unpaid payroll taxes—against all responsible persons who willfully fail to collect and turn over the money."

This penalty for the failure to withhold or remit payroll taxes, known as the Trust Fund Recovery Penalty (TFRP), is included under Section 6672 of the Internal Revenue Code. It allows the IRS to hold individuals associated with a business personally liable for 100 percent of the unpaid amount when the business fails to meet its payroll tax obligations. The TFRP applies to employee funds that the employer holds in trust for the IRS—all of the regular income tax withheld and the employee half of the FICA tax—but not to the employer portions of payroll taxes. The penalty is particularly severe because the IRS considers an employer who fails to pay to be violating a trust. The TFRP can be applied in addition to civil and criminal penalties, including the seizure of business assets and forced closure of the business. And since it is a penalty rather than a tax, the TFRP is not erased by bankruptcy.

In order to apply the TFRP to an individual, the IRS must prove the person's responsibility (that he or she had the power to make the decision about whether or not to pay) and willfulness (that he or she knowingly failed to act rather than made an honest mistake) for the business's failure to remit payroll taxes. In making its determination about who to hold responsible, the IRS looks at who made the financial decisions in the business, who signed the checks, and who had the duty of tax reporting. Under these rules, a small business owner can be found personally liable even if a staff member or outside accountant was directly responsible for payroll tax compliance. In cases where both the business and the owner go bankrupt, the company's accountant may be tagged as the responsible party and held personally liable.

Because the law regarding payroll tax noncompliance is so sweeping, small business owners should pay particular attention to the trust fund taxes. It is vital to keep the taxes that are covered by the TFRP current, even when the business is experiencing cash flow problems. If it appears as if the small business is heading for bankruptcy, these taxes should be paid prior to filing, when management can still designate where the IRS should apply payments. After the company files for bankruptcy it loses this option, and the IRS will apply any payments elsewhere since they can collect the TFRP from individuals associated with the company. "Obviously, if a company is experiencing cash flow problems, accountants and other responsible persons are tempted to pay creditors who cry loudest and whose nonpayment will have an immediate negative impact, such as vendors who will stop shipping necessary supplies," Knight and Knight noted. "Not paying the IRS may solve short-term cash flow problems—but at the long-term personal expense of the responsible person who makes that decision."

FURTHER READING:

Barlas, Stephen. "Electronic Avenue: A New Deadline for Electronic Tax Filing Gives Small Businesses a Break—For Now." *Nation's Business.* October 1997.

Charles, Harry. "Avoiding the 100 Percent Penalty." *National Public Accountant.* June 1991.

Dailey, Frederick W. *Tax Savvy for Small Business.* 2nd ed. Berkeley, CA: Nolo Press, 1997.

DeJong, David S., and Ann Gray Jakabcin. *J.K. Lasser's Year-Round Tax Strategies.* New York: Macmillan, 1997.

Grassi, Carl. "Federal Withholding Rules Enforced with an Iron Fist." *Crain's Cleveland Business.* June 12, 2000.

Knight, Ray A., and Lee G. Knight. "Pay the IRS First, or Else!" *Management Accounting.* December 1993.

Marullo, Gloria Gibbs. "Hiring Your Child: Tax Breaks and Trade-Offs." *Nation's Business.* June 1997.

Raby, Burgess J.W., and William L. Raby. "Financial Hardship as Reasonable Cause." *Tax Notes.* December 6, 1999.

SEE ALSO: Tax Withholding

PENETRATION PRICING

Penetration pricing is a strategy employed by businesses introducing new goods or services into the marketplace. With this policy, the initial price of the good or service is set relatively low in hopes of "penetrating" into the marketplace quickly and securing significant market share. "This pricing approach," wrote Ronald W. Hilton in *Managerial Accounting,* "often is used for products that are of good quality, but do not stand out as vastly better than competing products."

Writing in *Basic Marketing,* E. Jerome McCarthy and William Perreault Jr. observed that "a penetration pricing policy tries to sell the whole market at one low price. Such an approach might be wise when the 'elite' market—those willing to pay a high price—is small. This is the case when the whole demand curve [for the product] is fairly elastic. A penetration policy is even more attractive if selling larger quantities results in lower costs because of economies of scale. Penetration pricing may be wise if the firm expects strong competition very soon after introduction. A low penetration price may be called a 'stay out' price. It discourages competitors from entering the market." Once the product has secured a desired market share, its producers can then review business conditions and decide whether to gradually increase the price.

Penetration pricing, however, is not the same as introductory price dealing, in which marketers attach temporary low prices to new products when they first hit the market. "These *temporary* price cuts should not be confused with low penetration prices," wrote McCarthy and Perreault Jr. "The plan [with introductory price dealing] is to raise prices as soon as the introductory offer is over."

SKIMMING VERSUS PENETRATION

Some manufacturers of new products, however, take a decidedly different tack when introducing their goods to the marketplace. Some choose to engage in skimming pricing, a strategy wherein the initial price for the product is set quite high for a relatively short time after introduction. Even though sales will likely be modest with skimming, the profit margin is great. This pricing approach is most often used for high-prestige or otherwise unique products with significant cache. Once the product's appeal broadens, the price is then reduced to appeal to a greater range of consumers. "The decision between skimming and penetration pricing," said Hilton, "depends on the type of product and involves trade-offs of price versus volume. Skimming pricing results in much slower acceptance of a new product, but higher unit profits. Penetration pricing results in greater initial sales volume, but lower unit profits."

FURTHER READING:

"Case Study: How to Price Your Products to Increase Profits." *Business Owner.* May-June 1995.

Clark, Scott. "Don't Miss the Boat with Strategic Pricing." *LI Business News.* June 4, 1999.

Cohen, William A. *The Entrepreneur and Small-Business Problem Solver.* Wiley, 1990.

Fishman, Arthur, and Rafael Bob. ''Experimentation and Competition.'' *Journal of Economic Theory*. February 1998.

Hilton, Ronald W. *Managerial Accounting*. McGraw-Hill, 1991.

McCarthy, E. Jerome, and William D. Perreault, Jr. *Basic Marketing: A Managerial Approach*. Irwin, 1990.

Winninger, Thomas J. *Price Wars: How to Win the Battle for Your Customer*. St. Thomas Press, 1994.

SEE ALSO: Pricing

PENSION PLANS

The term ''pension plan'' is now used to describe a variety of retirement programs that companies establish as a benefit for their employees—including 401(k) plans, profit-sharing plans, simplified employee pension (SEP) plans, and Keogh plans. In the past, however, pension plans were differentiated from other types of retirement plans in that employers were committed to providing a certain monetary level of benefits to employees upon retirement. These ''defined benefit'' plans, which were common among large employers with a unionized work force, have fallen into disfavor in recent years.

Some individuals also choose to establish personal pension plans to supplement their retirement savings. Making sound decisions about retirement is particularly important for self-employed persons and small business owners. Unlike employees of large companies, who can simply participate in the pension plans and investment programs offered by their employers, entrepreneurs must set up and administer their own plans for themselves and for their employees.

Though establishing and funding pension plans can be both time-consuming and costly for small businesses, such programs also offer a number of advantages. In most cases, for example, employer contributions to retirement plans are tax deductible expenses. In addition, offering employees a comprehensive retirement program can help small businesses attract and retain qualified people who might otherwise seek the security of working for a larger company.

The number of small firms establishing pension plans grew considerably during the 1990s, but small employers still lag far behind larger ones in providing this type of benefit for employees. According to a 1998 survey by the Employee Benefit Research Institute, 29 percent of small businesses (those with fewer than 100 employees) offered retirement plans, compared to 83 percent of businesses employing more than 100 workers. Small business owners reported uncertain company revenues, low worker demand, high administrative costs, and complex government regulations as some of the main reasons they did not sponsor retirement plans for their employees.

PENSION PLAN OPTIONS FOR SMALL BUSINESSES

Small business owners can set up a wide variety of pension plans by filling out the necessary forms at any financial institution (a bank, mutual fund, insurance company, brokerage firm, etc.). The fees vary depending on the plan's complexity and the number of participants. Some employer-sponsored plans are required to file Form 5500 annually to disclose plan activities to the IRS. The preparation and filing of this complicated document can increase the administrative costs associated with a plan, as the business owner may require help from a tax advisor or plan administration professional. In addition, all the information reported on Form 5500 is open to public inspection.

A number of different types of pension plans are available. The most popular plans for small businesses all fall under the category of defined contribution plans. Defined contribution plans use an allocation formula to specify a percentage of compensation to be contributed by each participant. For example, an individual can voluntarily deduct a certain portion of his or her salary, in many cases before taxes, and place the money into a qualified retirement plan, where it will grow tax-deferred. Likewise, an employer can contribute a percentage of each employee's salary to the plan on their behalf, or match the contributions employees make.

In contrast, defined benefit plans calculate a desired level of benefits to be paid upon retirement—using a fixed monthly payment or a percentage of compensation—and then the employer contributes to the plan annually according to a formula so that the benefits will be available when needed. The amount of annual contributions is determined by an actuary, based upon the age, salary levels, and years of service of employees, as well as prevailing interest and inflation rates. In defined benefit plans, the employer bears the risk of providing a specified level of benefits to employees when they retire. This is the traditional idea of a pension plan that has often been used by large employers with a unionized work force.

In nearly every type of qualified pension plan, withdrawals made before the age of 59 ½ are subject to an IRS penalty in addition to ordinary income tax. The plans differ in terms of administrative costs, eligibility requirements, employee participation, degree of discretion in making contributions, and amount of allowable contributions. Free information on qualified retirement plans is available through the

Department of Labor or on the Internet at www.dol.gov.

The most important thing to remember is that a small business owner who wants to establish a qualified plan for him or herself must also include all other company employees who meet minimum participation standards. As an employer, the small business owner can establish pension plans like any other business. As an employee, the small business owner can then make contributions to the plan he or she has established in order to set aside tax-deferred funds for retirement, like any other employee. The difference is that a small business owner must include all nonowner employees in any company-sponsored pension plans and make equivalent contributions to their accounts. Unfortunately, this requirement has the effect of reducing the allowable contributions that the owner of a proprietorship or partnership can make on his or her own behalf.

For self-employed individuals, contributions to a qualified pension plan are based upon the net earnings of their business. The net earnings consist of the company's gross income less deductions for business expenses, salaries paid to nonowner employees, the employer's 50 percent of the Social Security tax, and—significantly—the employer's contribution to retirement plans on behalf of employees. Therefore, rather than receiving pre-tax contributions to the retirement account as a percentage of gross salary, like nonowner employees, the small business owner receives contributions as a smaller percentage of net earnings. Employing other people thus detracts from the owner's ability to build up a sizeable before-tax retirement account of his or her own. For this reason, some experts recommend that the owners of proprietorships and partnerships who sponsor pension plans for their employees supplement their own retirement funds through a personal after-tax savings plan.

PERSONAL PENSION PLANS FOR INDIVIDUALS

For self-employed persons and small business owners, the tax laws that limit the amount of annual contributions individuals can make to qualified retirement plans, as well as the requirement that qualified plans established by an employer must cover all employees, may make these plans less desirable. ''If you're relying on a tax-qualified plan to fund your retirement, it's time to rethink that strategy,'' Arthur D. Kraus wrote in an article for *Small Business Reports.* ''You may want to use a non-qualified plan to supplement or even replace your qualified savings.'' Kraus recommended that small business owners consider setting up a personal pension plan to provide a source of income and security in their retirement. These plans have nearly unlimited annual contribu-

tions and do not have to be offered to employees. ''You can sock away as much money as you want each year and use the plan just to cover yourself—as most small business owners do—or offer it to a few top managers,'' Kraus stated. ''And that's not the best part. You can draw tax-free income in retirement from a personal pension plan.''

Establishing a personal pension plan involves purchasing a variable life insurance policy and paying premiums, which basically take the place of annual contributions to a retirement plan. The amount paid in is invested and allowed to grow tax-free. Both the premiums paid and the investment earnings can be accessed to provide the individual with an annual income upon retirement. The only catch is that, unlike qualified retirement plans, the annual payments made on a personal pension plan are not tax-deductible. However, Kraus claimed that the tax savings in retirement often offset the loss of the tax deduction during the working years.

Although other types of insurance policies—such as whole life or universal life—can also be used for retirement savings, they tend to be less flexible in terms of investment choices. In contrast, most variable life insurance providers allow individuals to select from a variety of investment options and transfer funds from one account to another without penalty. Many policies also allow individuals to vary the amount of their annual contribution or even skip making a contribution in years when cash is tight. Another worthwhile provision in some policies pays the premium if the individual should become disabled. In addition, most policies have more liberal early withdrawal and loan provisions than qualified retirement plans. The size of the annual contributions allowed depends upon the size of the insurance policy purchased. ''The bigger the policy, the higher the premiums—and thus, your plan contributions,'' according to Kraus. ''The IRS also sets a maximum annual contribution level for each size policy, based on your age, gender, and other factors.''

Upon reaching retirement age, an individual can begin to use the personal pension plan as a source of annual income. Withdrawals—which are not subject to income or Social Security taxes—first come from the premiums paid and earnings accumulated. After the total withdrawn equals the total contributed, however, the individual can continue to draw income in the form of a loan against the plan's cash value. This amount is repaid upon the individual's death out of the death benefit of the insurance. ''Is a personal pension plan right for you? That depends on whether other savings will meet your retirement needs,'' Kraus noted. ''But given the benefits of the plan—tax-free earnings, tax-free retirement income, protection for your heirs, and even disability benefits—it's clear that this savings strategy is well worth considering.''

FURTHER READING:

Battle, Carl W. *Senior Counsel: Legal and Financial Strategies for Age 50 and Beyond.* Alworth Press, 1993.

Blakely, Stephen. "Pension Power." *Nation's Business.* July 1997.

Blakely, Stephen. "Small Firm Gap Reflects Lack of Demand." *Nation's Business.* September 1998.

Connor, John B., Jr. "Pay Me Later." *Small Business Reports.* July 1994.

Corry, Carl. "Pension Tension Mounts." *LI Business News.* July 30, 1999.

Crouch, Holmes F. *Decisions When Retiring.* Allyear Tax Guides, 1995.

Gordon, Marcy. "Pensioners Go Underpaid." *Detroit Free Press.* June 17, 1997.

Kraus, Arthur D. "A Pension Plan of Your Own." *Small Business Reports.* March 1994.

Livingstone, Abby. "Ways to Expand Pension Savings." *Nation's Business.* October 1997.

Martin, Ray. *Your Financial Guide: Advice for Every Stage of Your Life.* Macmillan, 1996.

SEE ALSO: Employee Retirement Income Security Act; Retirement Planning

PER DIEM ALLOWANCES

The term "per diem" means "daily." In a business setting, the term has come to mean the daily rates employees use for expenses incurred while traveling on business-related activities. These rates are likely to differ based on whether the employee travels in their home area, away from home, or internationally. The per diem allowance is the amount given to a traveler to cover expenses such as lodging, meals, and entertainment in connection with the performance of service duties for a company.

Typically the human resources department of an organization will establish per diem rates for employee travel expense reimbursement as well as policies for submitting travel expense forms and for documenting all approved expenses. Per diem amounts are normally set in advance. Employees typically may either claim actual expenses incurred or use established per diem rates or combine these methods. For example, the employee may claim a per diem amount for meals and claim actual costs for lodging, as long as lodging expenses do not exceed the per diem allowance for lodging.

SETTING PER DIEM RATES

Per diem rates are established for a number of areas, including domestic air travel, international air travel, lodging, rental cars, vans, and trucks, other transportation, meals and entertainment, telephone us-age, miscellaneous reimbursable and non-reimbursable expenses, and travel insurance. Companies also may specify preferred travel agencies and programs and establish policies for payment of travel expenses and per diem rates.

Companies which do not set their own rates may use per diem amounts based on U.S. federal travel regulations. Per diem amounts vary by city. U.S. meal per diem rates are set every January. Foreign meal per diem rates are issued on a monthly basis. Organizations will normally pro-rate per diems for less than a full day's travel. IRS regulations and reporting requirements governing per diems vary. For employees, if the per diem requested exceeds the federal per diem rate for the given location and duration of the trip, the excess amount is considered reportable income and is added to the employee's W-2. For independent contractors, per diem payments made to such individuals are reportable income and will be reported on Form 1099M.

It is important for a company to establish clear per diem amounts and travel policies before employees are hired and begin to travel for the company. For example, a company must decide whether it will reimburse employees' personal phone calls while traveling, if it will reimburse employees for using airphones, etc. Other decisions include fees for currency conversion for international travel, ground transportation (taxi, bus, subway, etc.), hotel health club fees, laundry/dry cleaning/suit pressing, overnight delivery/postage, parking and tolls, tips, and visa/passport/consulate fees.

As a perk for employees, some firms consider paying for extra services to either reward, motivate, or retain employees in tight labor markets. Some per diem items to consider may include: airline club membership dues, annual fees for personal credit cards, hairdressers, clothing or toiletry items, country club dues, expenses related to vacation or personal days taken before, during, or after a business trip, golf fees, luggage and briefcases, magazines, books, newspapers, personal reading materials, mini-bar alcoholic refreshments, movies (including in-flight and hotel in-house movies), personal automobile routine maintenance/tune-ups, pet boarding, rental car upgrades, saunas, massages, shoe shines, or U.S. traveler's check fees.

PER DIEM EXAMPLES

The Per Diem, Travel and Transportation Allowance Committee exists to ensure that uniform travel and transportation regulations are issued for members of the seven branches of the U.S. military (Army, Navy, Air Force, Marine Corps, Coast Guard, National Oceanic and Atmospheric Administration, and Public Health Service). The objective of these regulations is fair and equitable reimbursement of uniformed members and civilian personnel.

The U.S. Government, through the U.S. Department of State, provides per diem allowance amounts for travel in foreign areas in lieu of reimbursement for actual subsistence expenses. The allowances are provided to employees and eligible dependents for daily expenses while on temporary travel status in the listed localities on official business away from an official post or assignment. The established rates are maximum amounts. Under travel regulations implemented by the General Services Administration and individual federal agencies, authorizing officials are required to reduce the maximum rates as needed to maintain a level of payment consistent with necessary travel expenses. Separate amounts are established for lodging and meals plus incidental travel expenses. The maximum lodging amount is intended to substantially cover the cost of lodging at adequate, suitable, and moderately priced facilities. The meals and incidental expenses portion is intended to substantially cover the cost of meals and incidental travel expenses such as laundry and dry cleaning.

FURTHER READING:

Luecke, Randall, et. al. ''Pros and Cons of Travel Per Diems.'' *Workforce.* March 1998.

Luecke, Randall, et. al. ''Should Your Company Use Travel Per Diems?'' *Journal of Compensation and Benefits.* March-April 1998.

Weaver, Peter. ''The IRS's Menu for Per Diem Dining Expenses.'' *Nation's Business.* May 1999.

SEE ALSO: Expense Accounts

PERSONAL SELLING

Personal selling is the process of communicating with a potential buyer (or buyers) face-to-face with the purpose of selling a product or service. The main thing that sets personal selling apart from other methods of selling is that the salesperson conducts business with the customer in person. Though personal selling is more likely to be effective with certain types of products or services, it has important applications for nearly all kinds of small businesses. In fact, most of history's successful entrepreneurs have been skilled salespeople, able to represent and promote their companies and products in the marketplace.

Personal selling is one part of a company's promotion mix, along with advertising, sales promotion, and public relations. Advertising is any form of paid sales presentation that is not done face-to-face. Television and radio commercials, newspaper and magazine advertisements, and direct mail inserts are well-known forms of advertising. Sales promotion is the use of incentives—such as coupons, discounts, rebates, contests, or special displays—to entice a customer to buy a product or service. Public relations is the act of building up a company's image in the eyes of the community in the hopes of translating the feelings of goodwill into sales. An example of public relations might include a company sponsoring a charity event.

Personal selling offers entrepreneurs both advantages and disadvantages in comparison with the other elements of the promotion mix. On the positive side, personal selling allows the salesperson to target the message specifically to the audience and receive immediate feedback. In this way, it is more precise than other forms of promotion and often has a greater persuasive impact. Conversely, personal selling cannot reach as many potential customers as advertising, plus the cost of each contact is much higher. Another advantage is that personal selling can be an important source of marketing information. Salespeople may learn about competitors' products, for example, or about emerging customer needs that may lead to the development of a new product. If the sales force is well trained—acting as problem solvers and advisors for customers rather than using hard-sell tactics—personal selling may help a small business build loyal, long-term relationships with customers.

A small business may choose to use any or all of the promotion mix elements in selling its products. Deciding how to allocate resources for each component involves a number of factors. Some of the things entrepreneurs should consider when deciding on the ideal promotion mix include the type of product or service, the value of the product or service, and the budget allotted for marketing.

WHEN TO USE PERSONAL SELLING

In general, if a product has a high unit value and requires a demonstration of its benefits, it is well suited for personal sales. For example, an encyclopedia is a high-priced item and most people do not feel they need one. After a demonstration, however, most people agree it would be a useful item to have. Therefore, encyclopedias are well suited to a promotion mix that emphasizes personal selling. Highly technical products, such as computers and copiers, are also primarily sold through personal sales methods. Products that involve a trade-in, like automobiles, are usually handled through personal selling to help facilitate the trade-in process. Finally, a company that cannot afford a mass-advertising campaign might consider personal selling as an alternative to advertising. Since sales force compensation is largely based on actual sales, personal selling may require less money up front than other parts of the promotion mix.

SELLERS' AGENTS

One method that many small manufacturers and wholesalers use to reduce the costs of personal selling—which can be the most critical aspect of the promotion mix for these types of businesses—is to hire an experienced selling agent. Selling agents are independent salespeople who work under contract with one or more companies and are usually paid a straight commission on sales. Hiring a selling agent allows a small business to save the time and money it would have to invest in recruiting and training an in-house sales force. In addition, an agent with experience in selling similar products may provide ready-made customers and quick entry into a sales territory. Selling agents are particularly helpful for businesses whose products experience seasonal or fluctuating sales, since they are only paid for the sales they make.

The main disadvantages of selling agents are that they usually work for several different firms, so they are unable to devote 100 percent of their attention to any one client, and that it may be difficult to retain the customers gained in this way once the relationship with the agent is severed. It is also difficult to control the selling methods used by agents, and they may not be able to provide the service that some customers require.

TYPES OF SALES POSITIONS

There are many different types of personal sales jobs. A driver-salesperson merely delivers the product and has few selling responsibilities. An inside order taker—such as a sales clerk in a retail store or a telephone representative with a catalog sales company—takes orders from within a selling environment and requires some selling skills. In contrast, an outside order taker goes to the customer's place of business to take orders. Some selling skills are required in this position, especially to establish new accounts. A missionary sales person, rather than selling an actual product or service, instead tries to make a customer feel good about the company and products he or she represents. The pharmaceutical and liquor industries frequently employ missionary salespeople.

A sales engineer might be found in technical industries such as computers and copiers. Sales engineers provide technical support, explain the product, and help adapt the product to the customer's needs. Finally, a creative salesperson may attempt to sell goods (such as vacuum cleaners or encyclopedias), but more often represents ideas, such as services (insurance) or causes (charities). These salespeople usually deal with customers who are unaware of their need for the service or product, so they must possess the most developed selling skills of all the types of salespeople.

STEPS IN COMPLETING A SALE

The many different types of salespeople all go through the same basic steps when making a sale: prospecting and qualifying, preapproach, approach, presentation and demonstration, handling objections, closing, and follow-up. Although training for personal sales forces may vary from one organization to another, the majority of the training will include some version of these steps.

Prospecting and qualifying involve locating potential customers and finding out if they are in a position to buy. Prospecting, or lead-generation, can be as simple as asking current customers for names of acquaintances who may also be interested, or as sophisticated as using a database or mailing list. Often the company provides leads, but a truly successful salesperson will also be able to generate his or her own leads. Prospecting usually involves an element of cold-calling—that is, calling an unknown potential customer and introducing oneself and the product. After possible customers have been located through prospecting, a salesperson must qualify them. This entails assessing their readiness and ability to buy. Personal selling almost always requires a salesperson to contact many prospects before completing a sale.

The preapproach step involves researching the prospective customer—often another company. The salesperson may read up on the company, talk to other vendors, or study the overall industry. At this stage, the salesperson will also try to determine the best time to make the sales call and establish sales call objectives. During the next step, the approach, it is crucial for a salesperson to make a positive first impression while introducing himself or herself, the company represented, and the product or service being offered. It is also important that the salesperson listen carefully to the prospect and respond appropriately.

Once the approach has been made, the salesperson should be ready to launch into the demonstration or presentation. Depending on the company and the product or service, there are generally three types of presentations. The prepared or ''canned'' approach involves a tightly scripted talk that is either memorized or read. The formula approach is less rigid. Depending on the buyer's response to some carefully asked questions, the seller will go to a formula presentation that he or she hopes will meet the customer's needs. The third presentation style is the need-satisfaction approach, in which the seller tries to uncover the customer's needs, mostly by listening. Presentations and demonstrations may involve any number of visual aids, such as flip-charts, or samples of the products themselves. One of the keys to a successful presentation is product knowledge. The more the salesperson knows about the product or service, the more relaxed he or she will be, and the more able to answer questions, shape his or her presentation to address customer concerns and desires, and handle objections.

Handling objections is the next phase of selling. Almost every customer will present objections to making a purchase. A good salesperson is not flustered by these objections and handles them in a positive, confident manner. One approach to handling objections, used frequently with canned presentations, is simply to acknowledge the objection then continue with the presentation.

The next step in the process of completing a sale—closing, or asking the buyer to make a purchase—is often identified by novice salespeople as the toughest step. In fact, some new salespeople are so reluctant to be perceived as aggressive that they never try to close the sale. Consequently, the customer may become annoyed and decide not to purchase just for that reason. Customers must be given the opportunity to purchase. Salespeople need to learn to look for signals that a closing is appropriate. Common signals that customers give include asking questions, making comments, leaning forward or nodding, or asking about price or terms.

The last step in completing a sale—following up—is often neglected, but is important for many reasons. The follow-up, which can be done in person or by telephone, gives the customer the chance to ask questions and reinforce his or her buying decision. The salesperson can review how to use the product, go over instructions and payment arrangements, and make sure the product has arrived in proper working order. This step ensures repeat business, is a good opportunity to obtain referrals, and increases the chances that subsequent payments will be made.

IMPROVING THE REPUTATION OF PERSONAL SELLING

Personal selling involves specific steps, requires training and experience, and employs some highly talented people. Unfortunately, personal selling is also commonly perceived as being a less than reputable field of work. Unethical salespeople, aggressive or hard sell tactics, and misleading sales pitches have made many buyers wary of personal sellers. Fortunately, much has been done to address this issue. Selling associations such as the Direct Selling Association have adopted codes of ethics that dictate standards of behavior that all members are to follow. Most organizations with personal sales forces also adopt their own codes of ethics that provide guidelines regarding the type of sales pitch that can be made, and

the hours during which a sales call may be made. Many companies also prohibit the use of misleading information or pressure tactics to make a sale.

FURTHER READING:

Bednarz, Shirley. ''The Selling Blues: Myths That Sabotage Positive Sales Outcomes.'' *American Salesman.* September 1998.

Cannon, Joseph P., and William D. Perreault, Jr. ''Buyer-Seller Relationships in Business Markets.'' *Journal of Marketing Research.* November 1999.

Comer, Lucette B., and Tanya Drollinger. ''Active Empathetic Listening and Selling Success.'' *Journal of Personal Selling and Sales Management.* Winter 1999.

Kimball, Bob. *AMA Handbook for Successful Selling.* NTC, 1994.

Kotler, Philip. *Marketing Management.* 8th ed. Prentice-Hall, 1994.

Stair, Lila B. *Careers in Marketing.* VGM Career Horizons, 1991.

Stanton, William J., Michael J. Etzel, and Bruce J. Walker. *Fundamentals in Marketing.* 10th ed. McGraw-Hill, 1994.

PHYSICAL DISTRIBUTION

Physical distribution is the set of activities concerned with efficient movement of finished goods from the end of the production operation to the consumer. Physical distribution takes place within numerous wholesaling and retailing distribution channels, and includes such important decision areas as customer service, inventory control, materials handling, protective packaging, order procession, transportation, warehouse site selection, and warehousing. Physical distribution is part of a larger process called ''distribution,'' which includes wholesale and retail marketing, as well the physical movement of products.

Physical distribution activities have recently received increasing attention from business managers, including small business owners. This is due in large part to the fact that these functions often represent almost half of the total marketing costs of a product. In fact, research studies indicate that physical distribution costs nationally amount to approximately 20 percent of the country's total gross national product (GNP). These findings have led many small businesses to expand their cost-cutting efforts beyond their historical focus on production to encompass physical distribution activities. The importance of physical distribution is also based on its relevance to customer satisfaction. By storing goods in convenient locations for shipment to wholesalers and retailers, and by creating fast, reliable means of moving the goods, small business owners can help assure continued success in a rapidly changing, competitive global market.

A SYSTEM APPROACH

Physical distribution can be viewed as a system of components linked together for the efficient movement of products. Small business owners can ask the following questions in addressing these components:

- Customer service—What level of customer service should be provided?

- Transportation—How will the products be shipped?

- Warehousing—Where will the goods be located? How many warehouses should be utilized?

- Order processing—How should the orders be handled?

- Inventory control—How much inventory should be maintained at each location?

- Protective packaging and materials handling—How can efficient methods be developed for handling goods in the factory, warehouse, and transport terminals?

These components are interrelated: decisions made in one area affect the relative efficiency of others. For example, a small business that provides customized personal computers may transport finished products by air rather than by truck, as faster delivery times may allow lower inventory costs, which would more than offset the higher cost of air transport. Viewing physical distribution from a systems perspective can be the key to providing a defined level of customer service at the lowest possible cost.

CUSTOMER SERVICE

Customer service is a precisely-defined standard of customer satisfaction which a small business owner intends to provide for its customers. For example, a customer service standard for the above-mentioned provider of customized computers might be that 60 percent of all PCS reach the customer within 48 hours of ordering. It might further set a standard of delivering 90 percent of all of its units within 72 hours, and all 100 percent of its units within 96 hours. A physical distribution system is then set up to reach this goal at the lowest possible cost. In today's fast-paced, technologically advanced business environment, such systems often involve the use of specialized software that allows the owner to track inventory while simultaneously analyzing all the routes and transportation modes available to determine the fastest, most cost-effective way to delivery goods on time.

TRANSPORTATION

The United States' transportation system has long been a government-regulated industry, much like its telephone and electrical utilities. But in 1977 the deregulation of transportation began with the removal of federal regulations for cargo air carriers not engaged in passenger transportation. The deregulation movement has since expanded in ways that have fundamentally altered the transportation landscape for small business owners, large conglomerates and, ultimately, the consumer.

Transportation costs are largely based on the rates charged by carriers. There are two basic types of transportation rates: class and commodity. The class rate, which is the higher of the two rates, is the standard rate for every commodity moving between any two destinations. The commodity rate is sometimes called a special rate, since it is given by carriers to shippers as a reward for either regular use or large-quantity shipments. Unfortunately, many small business owners do not have the volume of shipping needed to take advantage of commodity rates. However, small businesses are increasingly utilizing a third type of rate that has emerged in recent years. This rate is known as a negotiated or contract rate. Popularized in the 1980s following transportation deregulation, contract rates allow a shipper and carrier to negotiate a rate for a particular service, with the terms of the rate, service, and other variables finalized in a contract between the two parties. Transportation costs vary by mode of shipping, as discussed below.

TRUCKING—FLEXIBLE AND GROWING The shipping method most favored by small business (and many large enterprises as well) is trucking. Carrying primarily manufactured products (as opposed to bulk materials), trucks offer fast, frequent, and economic delivery to more destinations in the country than any other mode. Trucks are particularly useful for short-distance shipments, and they offer relatively fast, consistent service for both large and small shipments.

AIR FREIGHT—FAST BUT EXPENSIVE Because of the relatively high cost of air transport, small businesses typically use air only for the movement of valuable or highly-perishable products. However, goods that qualify for this treatment do represent a significant share of the small business market. Owners can sometimes offset the high cost of air transportation with reduced inventory-holding costs and the increased business that may accompany faster customer service.

WATER CARRIERS—SLOW BUT INEXPENSIVE There are two basic types of water carriers: inland or barge lines, and oceangoing deep-water ships. Barge lines are efficient transporters of bulky, low-unit-value commodities such as grain, gravel, lumber, sand, and steel. Barge lines typically do not serve small businesses. Oceangoing ships, on the other hand, operate in the Great Lakes, transporting goods among port cities, and in international commerce. Sea shipments are an important part of foreign trade, and thus are of vital importance to small businesses seeking an international market share.

RAILROADS—LONG DISTANCE SHIPPING Railroads continue to present an efficient mode for the movement of bulky commodities over long distances. These commodities include coal, chemicals, grain, non-metallic minerals, and lumber and wood products.

PIPELINES—SPECIALIZED TRANSPORTERS Pipelines are utilized to efficiently transport natural gas and oil products from mining sites to refineries and other destinations. In addition, so-called slurry pipelines transport products such as coal, which is ground to a powder, mixed with water, and moved as a suspension through the pipes.

INTERMODAL SERVICES Small business owners often take advantage of multi-mode deals offered by shipping companies. Under these arrangements, business owners can utilize a given transportation mode in the section of the trip in which it is most cost efficient, and use other modes for other segments of the transport. Overall costs are often significantly lower under this arrangement than with single-mode transport.

Of vital importance to small businesses are transporters specializing in small shipments. These include bus freight services, United Parcel Service, Federal Express, DHL International, the United States Postal Service, and others. Since small businesses can be virtually paralyzed by transportation strikes or other disruptions in small shipment service, many owners choose to diversify to include numerous shippers, thus maintaining an established relationship with an alternate shipper should disruptions occur. Additionally, small businesses often rely on freight forwarders who act as transportation intermediaries: these firms consolidate shipments from numerous customers to provide lower rates than are available without consolidation. Freight forwarding not only provides cost savings to small businesses, it provides entrepreneurial opportunities for start-up businesses as well.

WAREHOUSING

Small business owners who require warehousing facilities must decide whether to maintain their own strategically located depot(s), or resort to holding their goods in public warehouses. And those entrepreneurs who go with non-public warehousing must further decide between storage or distribution facilities. A storage warehouse holds products for moderate to long-term periods in an attempt to balance supply and demand for producers and purchasers. They are most often used by small businesses whose products' supply and demand are seasonal. On the other hand, a distribution warehouse assembles and redistributes products quickly, keeping them on the move as much as possible. Many distribution warehouses physically store goods for fewer than 24 hours before shipping them on to customers.

In contrast to the older, multi-story structures that dot cities around the country, modern warehouses are long, one-story buildings located in suburban and semi-rural settings where land costs are substantially less. These facilities are often located so that their users have easy access to major highways or other transportation options. Single-story construction eliminates the need for installing and maintaining freight elevators, and for accommodating floor load limits. Furthermore, the internal flow of stock runs a straight course rather than up and down multiple levels. The efficient movement of goods involves entry on one side of the building, central storage, and departure out the other end.

Computer technology for automating warehouses is dropping in price, and thus is increasingly available for small business applications. Sophisticated software translates orders into bar codes and determines the most efficient inventory picking sequence. Order information is keyboarded only once, while labels, bills, and shipping documents are generated automatically. Information reaches hand-held scanners, which warehouse staff members use to fill orders. The advantages of automation include low inventory error rates and high processing speeds.

INVENTORY CONTROL

Inventory control can be a major component of a small business physical distribution system. Costs include funds invested in inventory, depreciation, and possible obsolescence of the goods. Experts agree that small business inventory costs have dropped dramatically due to deregulation of the transportation industry.

Inventory control analysts have developed a number of techniques which can help small businesses control inventory effectively. The most basic is the Economic Order Quantity (EOQ) model. This involves a trade-off between the two fundamental components of an inventory control cost: inventory-carrying cost (which increases with the addition of more inventory), and order-processing cost (which decreases as the quantity ordered increases). These two cost items are traded off in determining the optimal warehouse inventory quantity to maintain for each product. The EOQ point is the one at which total cost is minimized. By maintaining product inventories as close to the EOQ point as possible, small business owners can minimize their inventory costs.

ORDER PROCESSING

The small business owner is concerned with order processing—another physical distribution function—because it directly affects the ability to meet the customer service standards defined by the owner. If the order processing system is efficient, the owner can avoid the costs of premium transportation or high inventory levels. Order processing varies by industry, but often consists of four major activities: a credit check; recording of the sale, such as crediting a sales representative's commission account; making the appropriate accounting entries; and locating the item, shipping, and adjusting inventory records.

Technological innovations, such as increased use of the Universal Product Code, are contributing to greater efficiency in order processing. Bar code systems give small businesses the ability to route customer orders efficiently and reduce the need for manual handling. The coded information includes all the data necessary to generate customer invoices, thus eliminating the need for repeated keypunching.

Another technological innovation affecting order processing is Electronic Data Interchange. EDI allows computers at two different locations to exchange business documents in machine-readable format, employing strictly-defined industry standards. Purchase orders, invoices, remittance slips, and the like are exchanged electronically, thereby eliminating duplication of data entry, dramatic reductions in data entry errors, and increased speed in procurement cycles.

PROTECTIVE PACKAGING AND MATERIALS HANDLING

Another important component of a small business physical distribution system is material handling. This comprises all of the activities associated with moving products within a production facility, warehouse, and transportation terminals. One important innovation is known as unitizing—combining as many packages as possible into one load, preferably on a pallet. Unitizing is accomplished with steel bands or shrink wrapping to hold the unit in place. Advantages of this material handling methodology include reduced labor, rapid movement, and minimized damage and pilferage.

A second innovation is containerization—the combining of several unitized loads into one box. Containers that are presented in this manner are often unloaded in fewer than 24 hours, whereas the task could otherwise take days or weeks. This speed allows small export businesses adequate delivery schedules in competitive international markets. In-transit damage is also reduced because individual packages are not handled en route to the purchaser.

FURTHER READING:

Artman Les. Clancy, David. "Distribution Follows Consumer Movement." *Transportation and Distribution*. June 1990.

Bowersox, Donald, et al. "How Supply Chain Competency Leads to Business Success." *Supply Chain Management*. September 2000.

Brenner, Gary, Joel Ewan, and Henry Custer. *The Complete Handbook for the Entrepreneur*. Englewood Cliffs, NJ: Prentice Hall, 1990.

Evans, James. *Production and Operations Management: Quality, Performance, and Value*. West Publishing Company, 1997.

Schmenner, Roger. *Production and Operations Management: From the Inside Out*. Macmillan, 1993.

"Supply Chain, Distribution, and Fulfillment." *International Journal of Retail and Distribution Management*. October 2000.

Wood, Donald, and James Johnson. *Contemporary Logistics*. Prentice Hall, 1996.

SEE ALSO: Distribution Channels; Transportation

POINT OF SALE SYSTEMS

Point of sale (POS) systems are electronic systems that provide businesses with the capability to retain and analyze a wide variety of inventory and transaction data on a continuous basis. POS systems have been touted as valuable tools for a wide variety of business purposes, including refining target marketing strategies; tracking supplier purchases; determining customer purchasing patterns; analyzing sales (on a daily, monthly, or annual basis) of each inventory item, department, or supplier; and creating reports for use in making purchases, reorders, etc. Basic point of sale systems currently in use include stand-alone electronic cash registers, also known as ECRs; ECR-based network systems; and controller-based systems. All function essentially as sales and cash management tools, but each has features that are unique.

Standalone ECRs. These electronic registers operate independently of one another, and are thus the most limited of the three POS system types. They cannot provide their owners with storewide reporting or file sharing; they can merely report the business activity at that particular register. Given its limitations, ECRs are usually used by small independent retailers that feature a limited number of register sites. Indeed, these systems are often well suited for small businesses because they are the least expensive of the POS system options, they nonetheless provide many helpful features, including automatic sales and tax calculation ability; calculation of change owed to the customer; sales report generation capability; capacity to sort food stamps and trading stamps (through programming of function keys); and scanning.

Network Systems. Network or ECR-based point-of-sale systems feature multiple terminals arranged into a primary/secondary configuration. One ECR in the store, equipped with extra memory capacity, serves as the primary terminal and receives data from the secondary terminals. These systems give businesses the added capacity to manage storewide data and transmit data to mainframe systems.

Controller-Based POS Systems. The top POS systems are controller-based systems in which each terminal is connected to a computer—the "controller" of the system—which receives and stores all sales, merchandise, and credit data. "The controller checks all data from the terminals for transmission errors and reformats the data for use by the headquarters computer," explained *Chain Store Age Executive.* "It may also perform sales analysis and price look-up. By having a dual-controller arrangement in which the computers back each other up, the chance for a total system failure can be reduced. Because of the importance of accurate data capture in sophisticated point-of-sale systems, retailers are increasingly turning to scanning as an alternative to error-prone keypunch entry." Indeed, scanning became a ubiquitous feature in many of the nation's most modestly-sized retail outlets during the 1990s.

Point of sale systems, like many other computer-based innovations, continue to change and develop at a rapid pace. In addition, the demand for POS systems has spawned many new manufacturers, each of which offer a dizzying array of standard and optional POS features to their customers. For example, some electronic POS systems now cover hand-held scanning devices, customer promotions, credit-card confirmations, counterfeit money checks, and staff scheduling. Given the expense involved and the proliferating number of POS software packages, small business owners should make sure that they adequately research both their current and future needs before making a purchase, so that they are able to acquire a customized POS system that best fills their current operating requirements and can accommodate future changes in the business. "Consider value—don't make your decision on price alone," counseled *National Petroleum News.* "Look for a high level of connectivity and compatibility with a multitude of peripherals. Demand customization capabilities. Don't accept a system that's almost what you want when today's technology makes it possible to customize one to exactly what you need."

FURTHER READING:

Blair, Adam. "POS Data to Power Efficient Distribution." *Supermarket News.* March 22, 1999.

Durocher, Joseph. "Point of Departure: Don't Think of Your POS System as Merely a Cashbox but Rather as a Management Tool." *Restaurant Business.* September 1, 1994.

Field, Christopher. "POS Man Always Rings Twice." *Computing.* October 22, 1998.

Murphy, Patricia A. "Cash Management Issues Foster Electronic Payments at Point of Sale." *Stores.* July 1999.

"Systems to Keep the Checkout Counter Humming." *Chain Store Age Executive.* October 1990.

PORTABILITY OF BENEFITS

The portability of benefits is a concept that is rapidly gathering support in the U.S. workforce. It refers to the idea that common job benefits—such as health insurance and pension plans—can be set up in such a way that they can travel with a worker as he or she moves from one job to the next. In many cases, these benefits would be paid for by the employee, which makes them attractive to employers. The portability factor would give the employee security that was never available in the past, which is attractive to the employee.

The current structure of employee benefits is not portable. In most employment sectors, each company offers a unique benefit plan that is established and administered by the company's human resources department. Most of the benefits are paid for by the company, and employees often have little, if any, choice about what benefits they receive and from whom they receive them. This is true mostly for pension and health plans, both of which are affected by numerous government regulations that make portability difficult. Even without the government interference, there are literally hundreds of pension and health plans for employers to choose from. Any given 100 employers in one geographic area may utilize 100 different plan providers, making portability practically impossible under such circumstances.

Portable benefits are gaining popularity in all segments of the business community, but two job sectors are leading the way—temporary work agencies and private, independent contractors. For temp agencies, portable benefits are an attractive new perk to lure in better workers in the current competitive employment environment. For temp workers, the thought of getting benefits that were previously unattainable is an extremely attractive proposition, even if they have to pay for part or all of the benefits. For independent contractors—specialized workers such as advertising designers or accountants who are hired to complete specific, time-bound, and/or goal-oriented projects—portable benefits would be a perfect tool to improve their financial security as they moved from one project to the next.

Several steps could be taken that would make portable benefits more likely. If numerous employers in the same geographic region banded together to offer the same benefits, it would make it easier for workers to change jobs and keep the level of seniority and money that they had accrued in their previous jobs. Also, if a government agency was established to oversee and encourage portable benefits, companies would have greater incentive to participate.

The most likely alternative, and one that is already happening at temp agencies and among independent contractors, is that employees would purchase their benefits themselves. They would pay for their own health insurance and make regular contributions to a pension plan that would travel with them from job to job. The government could offer tax credits that would provide workers with an incentive to participate in portable plans, which could help offset the cost. Tax savings would also help offset what workers might lose by participating in a portable plan instead of a more traditional plan, such as the higher rate of accrual and greater earnings that occur when large numbers of employees pool their resources together. The economies of scale of the large, traditional plans make them economically feasible for most employees to join. Without the reduced price gained by such economies, however, many employees could not afford to purchase benefits in the current work environment.

Even state governments are jumping on the portable benefits bandwagon. In the state of Michigan, for example, Governor John Engler spearheaded a move in 1997 to transition the state's pension plan for state workers from a traditional plan—which was organized, managed, and paid for by the state—to a portable plan that allowed workers to select from a number of private investment options and invest their own pension dollars. No matter what state job they took, the pension benefits traveled with the workers, gaining money at each stop along the way. "We have a defined contribution plan that empowers our employees to make critical investment decisions concerning their future," Engler told *Institutional Investor.* "They're also not tied to the state civil service, [as they were with] the old defined benefits, and that fits much more logically with the lifestyles we have today. This is a fully portable benefits plan that goes with them. And the rate of investment [return] over the long term is going to be far better for them than their state DB."

To many employment experts, the move to portable benefits is a positive one, and it is the wave of the future. As Frank Doyle, chairman of the Committee of Economic Development, said in *HR Magazine,* "Cor-

porate America found it couldn't deliver on those guarantees [of lifetime employment] in a highly competitive world economy. Companies that had job guarantees had to withdraw them. The substitute for this old form of job security—and frankly a much better alternative—is the security of having portable benefits and strong employability skills. If we can achieve those things, then we will have established the requisite security for maintaining a productive workforce into the next century."

FURTHER READING:

Bernhardt, Annette, and Thomas Bailey. "Improving Worker Welfare in the Age of Flexibility." *Challenge.* September-October 1998.

Benson, George P. "The Workplace Revolution." *Georgia Trend.* December 1999.

Cook, Christopher D. "Temps Demand a New Deal." *The Nation.* March 27, 2000.

"Cutting Edge Benefits for Growing Companies." *Inc.* February 1997.

Diaz, Scott. "Securing Prosperity—The American Labor Market: How It Has Changed and What to Do about It." *Government Finance Review.* June 2000.

Leonard, Bill. "The Economic State of the Union." *HR Magazine.* December 1996.

McNerney, Donald. "Life in the Jobless Economy." *HR Focus.* August 1996.

Rehfeld, Barry. "Michigan Redefines Public Pensions." *Institutional Investor.* October 1, 1998.

Rosen, Stephanie. "On Their Own: There's No Employer Match, But Self-Employed Individuals Do Have Access to a Host of Qualified Retirement Plans." *Bank Investment Marketing.* June 1, 1999.

Zabel, Gary. "A New Labor Movement in the Academy." *Dollars & Sense.* March 2000.

POSTAL COSTS

No business owner will escape postal costs entirely, no matter how small or technologically savvy his or her company is. From the occasional letter or invoice to large regular shipments, businesses continue to rely on some level of paper interaction to operate despite the ever-growing presence of e-mail and other high-tech modes of communication. The U.S. Postal Service remains the primary medium through which such paper communications go, and it provides a variety of services for businesses and individuals.

Express Mail Service. The Postal Service's most competitive alternative to other private delivery services, such as FedEx and UPS, is Express Mail. This service provides next day delivery by 12 p.m. to most destinations, even on weekends and holidays. Express

Mail costs several dollars less than the large private delivery services, making it the best option for frequent large shipments under 70 lbs., if cost is the only consideration. The cost for Express Mail is scaled up to 70 lbs., so business owners needing to send heavier packages for quick delivery should check with their local post office for details on larger shipments.

Priority Mail. Priority Mail is similar to Express Mail, provides two-day service to most domestic destinations. If an item can wait for two days to be delivered, this is the least expensive option. Again, this alternative is less expensive than those offered by privately owned delivery companies. Both Priority Mail and Express Mail rates end at 70 lbs, and packages must measure 108 inches or less in combined length and girth.

Standard Mail (A) and First-Class. Standard Mail (A) is the primary option used by retailers, catalogers, and other advertisers to promote products and services. Items must weigh less than 1 lb. to qualify under this designation. Although the charge per ounce on the single-piece rate is the same as First-Class mail, Standard Mail (A) bulk mailings (i.e. not single pieces) can, if pre-sorted by ZIP Code, save money. Pre-sorting saves the post office some processing time and the payoff for the mailer is a reduced·rate. However, if the bulk mailing contains errors, found by random sample checking by the postal staff, the charge increases. Then the mailer has the option of correcting the errors, or paying the additional fee. Standard Mail (B) is the same system, but it is applied to packages weighing more than 1 lb.

First-Class, on the other hand, allows the mailer the option of simply dropping mail into any mail drop box, provided it already has the correct amount of postage on each piece. Also, First-Class mail is the generally used option for post cards, regular mail such as bills or letters, and similar single items.

Postage Meters. Personal postal metering has long been an option for businesses that make heavy use of the mail system. It allows the user to pre-stamp their mailings according to precise weight, while still at their business location. The convenience of this item has made it a perennially popular one with many small business owners. According to many experts, however, electronic postal metering is the wave of the future. Electronic postal metering (sometimes referred to as E-postage) enables customers to download postage over the Internet.

SAVING ON POSTAL EXPENSES

Postal expenses can be a significant financial drain on business health and profitability, for small and large businesses alike. Direct marketers, periodical publishers, and other companies that make heavy use of the postal service for basic business operations can find themselves particularly vulnerable. But business owners and experts cite several steps that firms can investigate to reduce their expenses in this regard:

- Regularly update your customer mailing address data to eliminate outdated information and reduce unproductive mailings. ''List hygiene is critical to controlling postal costs,'' stated Kathy Reilly in *Folio.* ''Make sure your lists are clean, accurate and not redundant.''

- Take advantage of reduced rates for drop shipments. The U.S. Postal Service offers discounts for mail that is delivered to them further down its distribution pipeline. Destination discounts can be realized by dropping off mail at bulk mail centers (BMCs), sectional center facilities (SCFs), or destination delivery units (DDUs).

- Lighten weight of packages. All postage costs—for both domestic and international destinations—are based in part on weight. For bulk mailings, then, reductions in weight can produce big savings. Easy ways of doing so range from reducing the stock of letters and order forms that are being mailed to culling the number of pages in newsletters, correspondence, and other materials.

FURTHER READING:

''Applying Postage with a Keystroke.'' *Nation's Business.* December 1997.

D'Antonio, Mila, and Carol King. ''Minimizing International Postal Costs.'' *Circulation Management.* May 2000.

''Drop-Ship to Combat Costs of Postal Hike.'' *Folio: The Magazine for Magazine Management.* November 2000.

Fernandes, Lorna. ''E-Stamp may Lick Problem.'' *The Business Journal.* October 20, 1997.

McCarthy, Shawn P. ''Snail Mail via the Internet?'' *Logistics Management.* October 1997.

Mull, Angela. ''Required Postage Meter Change-Out Better Deal.'' *The Business Journal.* October 17, 1997.

Reilly, Kathy. ''Savvy Production Tips to Cut Postal Costs.'' *Folio: The Magazine for Magazine Management.* May 1, 1996.

PREGNANCY IN THE WORKPLACE

Most small business owners that maintain a paid staff will, at one time or another, have a pregnant employee in the workplace. In fact, Bureau of Labor Statistics figures indicate that fully 80 percent of all working women will become pregnant at some point in their working lives. Historically, this news has not always been welcomed by employers, and while research and highly publicized episodes indicated that mid-sized and large companies have been more likely to behave in a discriminatory fashion against pregnant employees than small businesses, which on the whole are more likely to cultivate a more relaxed, family-friendly atmosphere, the latter have also been known to look unkindly on news of an employee's pregnancy. Indeed, researchers have observed that attitudes toward pregnant employees have tended to be predicated more on company culture than on the size of the firm. For example, a small business headed by a driven entrepreneur who is determined to meet or exceed an ambitious agenda of growth may greet the news that his or her top salesperson is pregnant with far less equanimity than the leadership of a larger company that places greater weight on the long-term value of the salesperson.

For the most part, companies of all sizes have adopted more enlightened views of workplace pregnancy issues in recent years. This change can be traced in part to their need to comply with legal protections that have been established on behalf of pregnant workers, but it can also be attributed to increased recognition of the vital importance of women in the workplace and increased awareness of the negative impact that discriminatory practices can have on other women employees and on bottom-line performance. Nonetheless, unfair treatment of pregnant employees persists in some quarters. ''Despite the laws designed to protect workers who become pregnant, female employees increasingly believe they are unfairly denied promotions, proper medical leave, and even their jobs because they have become pregnant, or because they might become pregnant,'' wrote Amy Oakes Wren, Roland E. Caldwell, and Linda Ache Caldwell in *Business Horizons.* Wren, Caldwell, and Caldwell blame this festering problem in large measure on management inability to recognize the fundamental demographic changes taking place in the American workplace: ''The issue of pregnancy discrimination has become even more focused as women of childbearing age enter the work force at higher rates and corporate downsizing forces many managers to seek higher levels of productivity among remaining employees. Unfortunately, some managers have taken unlawful actions against pregnant workers because they perceive them as less productive, absent more often, or unable to perform their jobs.''

PREGNANCY DISCRIMINATION AND FEDERAL LAW

Over the past few decades, the United States has passed three major federal laws that provide legal protections to pregnant employees as well as employees who might become pregnant. These are Title VII of the 1964 Civil Rights Act, the Pregnancy Discrimination Act of 1978, and the Family and Medical Leave Act (FMLA) of 1993.

TITLE VII OF THE CIVIL RIGHTS ACT This legislation expressly forbids employers with 15 of more workers on their payroll from refusing to hire, discharge, or otherwise discriminate against any person in any way, shape, or form because of that person's gender. However, this law left a giant loophole for employers, because the Supreme Court ruled in a mid-1970s case that discrimination based on pregnancy was not the same as discrimination based on sex. In other words, a disability plan that provided benefits to both men and *non-pregnant* women was found to meet the criteria of Title VII. Such plans, said the Court, were simply insurance policies that covered some risks and not others. Pregnancy was ruled to be one of those risks that was not covered.

PREGNANCY DISCRIMINATION ACT OF 1978 This law was drawn up to close the above-mentioned loophole. This legislation stipulated that all employers treat pregnant and non-pregnant employees in the same way, both in terms of benefits received and all other respects.

FAMILY AND MEDICAL LEAVE ACT OF 1993 When it passed in 1993, the Family and Medical Leave Act (FMLA) was hailed as a ground breaking law that provided important federal protections for both men and women faced with issues related to pregnancy, childbirth, adoption, placement for foster care, and family sickness. It was bitterly opposed by some segments of the business community, but family advocates ultimately prevailed. The FMLA stipulates that men and women can take as many as 12 weeks of unpaid leave annually for the birth or adoption of a child, care of a sick child, placement for foster care, or because of morning sickness or other illness (the illness does not have to be pregnancy-related). Employers and employees alike should note, however, that the FMLA does not impact businesses with fewer than 50 employees.

AVOIDING DISCRIMINATORY BEHAVIOR

Wren, Caldwell, and Caldwell cited a number of ways in which employers—either intentionally or unintentionally—can run afoul of the various antidiscrimination rules that have been erected to protect women employees who are or may become pregnant. ''Examples range from intentionally eliminating pregnant applicants from the labor pool to unintentionally discriminating against a pregnant woman because of an apparently sex-neutral insurance policy,'' they wrote.

- Employers may not refuse to hire, refuse to promote, or fire a pregnant employee because of her pregnancy. Moreover, experts warn that the person's pregnancy can not be *any* factor in the action taken. If the pregnancy was a consideration in any way, shape, or form, then the employer is liable.

- Employers have to provide the same benefits to all employees, whether or not they are pregnant, although they do not have to provide additional benefits to pregnant workers.

- Employers may not refuse to adjust workloads for a pregnant employee if they do so for a worker who is not pregnant but claims some other disability or mitigating circumstance.

- Employers may not discriminate against staff members just because they might get pregnant.

- Employers may not discriminate against employees who 1) have had an abortion, or 2) are considering having an abortion.

- Employers may not forbid a pregnant employee from continuing to work if she wants to and is physically capable of doing all tasks associated with the work.

- Employers may not evaluate pregnant and non-pregnant employees differently. This is especially true, say Wren, Caldwell, and Caldwell, "when the employer has unilaterally lessened the employee's work load in response to the pregnancy."

- Employers have a responsibility to make sure that pregnant employees are not excluded from taking part in the normal office environment, since such exclusions can have a detrimental impact on the employee's cognizance of important work-related issues.

- Employers may not threaten to fire an employee because of her pregnancy or potential pregnancy.

- Employers are not allowed to reassign employees to lower-paying positions because of pregnancy. Similarly, employers may not change a worker's job description and then eliminate the new job via reorganization.

- Employers may not engage in discriminatory practices against men whose wives or partners become pregnant. It should be noted, however, that application of this law may vary from state to state, since states have different views of the rights of married and unmarried couples.

- Employers can not demand medical notes from a pregnant woman's doctor concerning her work status if they do not require similar documentation from doctors of other employees who have short-term disabilities.

The above guidelines add up to a very simple mandate for employers: Treat your pregnant employees no differently than you would any other employees.

MANAGING THE LOSS OF EMPLOYEES DURING PREGNANCY AND MATERNITY LEAVE

Obviously, pregnant employees should not have to endure discrimination from their employers. Indeed, many researchers, executives, and business owners contend that employers that are understanding and treat their pregnant employees fairly can often count on a heightened level of loyalty from that employee upon their return from maternity leave. But businesses also have to recognize that employee pregnancy means the loss—sometimes temporary, sometimes permanent—of workers, some of whom may be quite valuable to the firm's operation.

Businesses, then, have to figure out "how to balance the personal needs of a pregnant worker with the bottom-line imperatives of running a business," wrote Julia Lawlor in *Sales and Marketing Management.* She noted that effective management of this issue entails paying attention to the impact that pregnancy-related absences can have on important business areas, such as sales: "In a fiercely competitive marketplace, governed by even fiercer laws protecting women against discrimination at work, managers must be prepared to handle a host of difficulties surrounding pregnancies and maternity leave: How to accommodate a rep [sales representative] who's having a difficult pregnancy—severe morning sickness, backaches, complications that require bed rest—without seeming unfair to other reps; deciding who should cover a rep's territory while she's out, and how that person should be compensated; determining who will visit out-of-town customers when the salesperson is unable to travel; navigating antidiscrimination laws."

Not surprisingly, prior planning is often cited as an essential element of effectively managing the impact of pregnancies on business operations. Business owners and managers should study in advance how the pregnant person's responsibilities will be handled in her absence. Many experts encourage those owners and managers to talk openly with the pregnant employee about possible work dispersal options. The pregnant employee is often the person best equipped to make knowledgeable decisions about allocation of responsibilities. Moreover, opening and maintaining good communication with the pregnant employee can provide owners and managers with the information (anticipated length of maternity leave, restrictions on travel, etc.) they need to make informed decisions about business operations.

In addition, companies have to make sure that other employees that are impacted by a staffer's absence due to pregnancy are adequately compensated for the extra work that they take on. Employees that are asked to ''cover'' for a pregnant colleague for an extended period of time without receiving any parallel adjustment in compensation or recognition will quickly recognize that their employer is in essence trying to get something for nothing. Employers who do this may manage to keep all facets of the business running fairly smoothly, but it can also erode employee loyalty to the business and create needless friction between the pregnant employee and her co-workers.

FURTHER READING:

Compliance Guide to the Family and Medical Leave Act. U.S. Department of Labor, 1996.

Dessler, Gary. *Human Resource Management.* Prentice Hall, 2000.

Kenen, Regina H. *Reproductive Hazards in the Workplace: Mending Jobs, Managing Pregnancies.* Harrington Park Press, 1996.

Lawlor, Julia. ''Pregnant Pause.'' *Sales and Marketing Management.* February 1998.

''Managing a Salesperson's Pregnancy.'' *Sales and Marketing Management.* February 1998.

Oakes Wren, Amy, Roland E. Caldwell Jr., and Linda Ache Caldwell. ''Managing Pregnancy in the Workplace.'' *Business Horizons.* November-December 1996.

Shellenbarger, Sue. ''Pregnant Employees Worry About Effects of Workplace Stress.'' *Wall Street Journal.* July 26, 2000.

Wyld, David C. ''Morning Sickness: Testing the Proper Bounds of Employee Protection and Employer Prerogative Under the Pregnancy Discrimination Act.'' *Labor Law Journal.* February 1995.

SEE ALSO: Family and Medical Leave Act

PRESENT VALUE

Present value (PV) is an accounting term that measures how money money needs to be invested today in over to finance future business initiatives, projects, and obligations. In order to determine the present value of future costs, accountants use formulas based on the time value of money. These formulas features variables such as the length of time involved and the prevailing interest rate. In other words, the present value of an amount to be received in the future is the discounted face value considering the length of time the receipt is deferred and the required rate of return (or appropriate discount rate under the circumstances). Present value is the result of the time value of money concept, which recognizes that today's dollar is worth more than the same dollar received at a future point in time.

The standard formula for calculating the present value of a series of future receipts is:

$$PV = \text{cash flow } 1 / (1 + \text{interest rate})1 + \text{cash flow } 2 / (1 + \text{interest rate})2 + \ldots + \text{cash flow } n / (1 + \text{interest rate})n$$

Where cash flows 1 to n are the future receipts, the interest rate is the discount rate appropriate for the stated period, and n is the number of periods over which future receipts occur.

The interest, or discount, rate used in PV calculations is a key element in determining the PV. This importance is emphasized when the future amounts occur over an extended period of time, due to the power of compounding. For example, the final payment on a 30-year loan at 7 percent interest would be worth approximately 13.1 percent of its face amount on a present value basis at the date of loan origin $[1/(1 + .07)30]$. By contrast, the 30th payment on a loan with a 9 percent interest rate would be worth only 7.5 percent $[1/(1 + .09)30]$ of its face amount in present value terms at the origin. This example shows the power of compounding when time periods are long.

The discount rate used in a given circumstance must compensate the lender of funds for three elements of return:

Inflation. In order to remain even in terms of buying power, the return of money at a future date must be appended by the Consumer Price Index rate. In other words, if a person lends an amount of money adequate to buy a loaf of bread at $t = 0$, he will require repayment at $t = 1$ of the original amount plus the fraction of that amount representing the CPI increase over the period. That way he will be able to buy the same loaf of bread at $t = 1$.

Time value of money (TVM). In addition to keeping pace with inflation, the investor or lender has a natural inclination for consumption sooner rather than later. The cost of compensating for this aspect of human nature has been found to be about 1 to 2 percent per year.

Risk. In addition to postponing the preferred immediate consumption and having to reimburse for inflation's erosion of buying power, many types of investment involve a risk of default. Compensating for this element of required return can be the most expense of the elements under consideration.

FURTHER READING:

Baroum, Sami M., and James H. Patterson. ''The Development of Cash Flow Weight Procedures for Maximizing the Net Present Value of a Project.'' *Journal of Operations Management.* September 1996.

Brealey, Richard A., and Stewart C. Myers. *Principles of Corporate Finance.* McGraw Hill, 1991.

Finch, J. Howard, and John G. Fulmer. "Evaluating Ongoing Projects and Divisions." *Managerial Finance.* September 1997.

Pindyck, Robert S., and Daniel L. Rubinfeld. *Microeconomics.* Macmillan, 1992.

PRESS KITS

Press kits are packets of background information that are provided to members of the media at special events (conventions, press conferences, trade shows, etc.) or in conjunction with new product or service announcements. Businesses commonly utilize press kits as part of its overall public relations effort to disseminate new information about its products, services, operations, or other activities to the public. Typical elements of press kit packages include press/news releases, data sheets, glossy brochures, information on public relations contacts, general company information, and biographical information on relevant executives and/or employees. The appearance and content of all these materials should be designed and presented with an eye toward garnering positive press coverage for the business and its products and services.

Most press kits that are prepared in conjunction with new product releases continue to feature hardcopy data sheets and press releases. But the rise in Internet usage and other technological innovations has had an impact on press kit preparation. Some companies have utilized Internet sites to disseminate press kit contents, while others utilize an "electronic press kit," usually a video presentation that is a visual complement to written materials, suitable for television broadcast. *Los Angeles Business Journal* contributor Peter Berk noted that electronic press kits (EPKs) can be particularly effective if the product has a strong visual component: "Offering a ready-to-air [on television] EPK to those reporters attending your convention or trade show might soon yield exciting televised coverage that can directly help benefit your product and business both on the short and long-term levels."

Press kits are sometimes distributed in conjunction with press conferences that are called to bring attention to a new product or business initiative. However, business experts caution small business owners against arranging a press conference unless it concerns a major announcement, or the subject is so important that reporters will require the opportunity to ask questions, or a major dignitary or celebrity is involved. "Because what they are promoting is extremely important within the confines of their company, [businesses] get caught up in the excitement without realizing that outside of the company, the media and public may not share their enthusiasm," one analyst told *Los Angeles Business Journal.* "This often happens with the release of a new product, product line, or with a significant corporate announcement. Therefore, we ask our clients to 'externalize' the importance of their announcement, or step outside the company to see of, frankly, their announcement is truly newsworthy."

In most cases, a simple news release to industry media will be the preferred method of disseminating information to the public. If the news warrants a press conference, it should be timed to accommodate the release of the local papers (morning for an afternoon paper, afternoon for a morning paper) and held at a centrally located site with sufficient seating. When television coverage is expected, it is important to provide a visual element for the cameras. For example, a scale model of a new plant, a demonstration of a new process, or a sample of a new product might provide strong visual support at a press conference. The small business should also provide press kits to the members of the media in attendance at a press conference.

FURTHER READING:

Berk, Peter. "Electronic Press Kits: Getting Your Story Across to the Media." *Los Angeles Business Journal.*

Ryan, Michael. "Models Help Writers Produce Publishable Releases." *Public Relations Quarterly.* Summer 1995.

Soderberg, Norman R. *Public Relations for the Entrepreneur and the Growing Business.* Probus, 1986.

Zacek, Judith. "Using the Media: No News Isn't Good News." *Travel Weekly.* July 20, 1995.

SEE ALSO: Public Relations

PRESS RELEASES

Press releases—also known as news releases—are brief, printed statements that outline the major facts of a news story in journalistic style. As part of its overall public relations effort, a small business may need to prepare press releases in order to disseminate new information about its products, services, operations, or other activities. A steady flow of news helps to make a small business more visible to the public and creates favorable interest in its activities.

In his book *Public Relations for the Entrepreneur and the Growing Business,* Norman Soderberg lists several possible types of news stories that a small business could generate. For example, a small business might announce the promotion, transfer, retirement, or hiring of personnel, or the negotiation of a new labor contract. Building new facilities, planning a major expansion, installing new equipment, or offering a new product are other newsworthy events that might occur in a small business. In addition, human interest stories might arise from the unusual hobbies or avocations of employees, the success of company-sponsored sports teams or events, or the company's participation in charity or community activities. If a small business received an award or a visit from a celebrity, these events might provide impetus for a news story as well. In general, a newsworthy story should be timely, of general or human interest, and somewhat unusual.

PREPARING A NEWS RELEASE

In order to attract the attention of the media to anything but a vitally important story, a small business will probably have to prepare and send out a news release. Ideally, the news release will generate enough interest that the media will choose to cover the story themselves. A news release may also be useful as a handout to provide basic information to reporters who come to cover a story.

Soderberg explains that a well-written news release should include "five Ws and an H": who, what, when, where, why, and how. The lead, or first few lines of the news release, should address all of these questions, though not necessarily all in one sentence. The remainder of the news release should provide supporting information—such as facts and figures or quotes from people involved—in most-important to least-important order. Overall, a news release should be crisp and concise, never exceeding two pages in length, and similar to a newspaper article in content and style. It is important that a small business owner find someone to write the news release who has a good command of language, grammar, and punctuation.

News releases should be typed on company letterhead and include the name and address of the company, its trademark or logo, the name and telephone number of a contact person (usually the small business owner, even if the job of preparing the news release is delegated to another person), the date, and the words "News Release." The importance and scope of the story determines where it should be sent. In most cases, it would be appropriate to send it to the business editors of the local print media. Sometimes sending it to local radio and television contacts might be appropriate as well. A small business can create a mailing list of relevant addresses, which can be found in media and trade journals and some reference books, to simplify the process. Some publications have begun accepting press releases online. But small business owners should avoid the temptation to follow up a news release with a telephone call.

PRESS RELEASES IN THE AGE OF ELECTRONIC INFORMATION

The common press release has undergone several significant changes in recent years as the Internet has revolutionized the way news is delivered. The wide availability of online information allows average investors to receive business news at the same time as analysts and news services. While some investors have been able to use this instantaneous information to their advantage, it has also opened the door for some dubious practices. For example, many companies have been victimized by fake press releases issued by disgruntled former employees, unscrupulous investors, or competitors. Such "news" is usually intended to cause harm to the targeted company by convincing investors to sell its stock.

On the other hand, some companies have taken advantage of the technology to issue press releases of debatable merit, apparently with the intention of increasing their stock prices. "Once a relatively mundane communications device, a press release now has the might to dramatically drive the price of a stock," according to *Business Week*. "As a result, more companies are designing press releases with that goal in mind. But it's not just edgy or pushing-the-truth headlines from lesser-known companies that are designed to spike share prices. Stock analysts say established companies are also playing fast and loose with press-release language, especially those involving earnings reports. They may exclude entire unprofitable subsidiaries, or leave out key information—such as certain losses—in order to appear rosy to investors."

Some companies release information prematurely—for example, they might announce a planned merger or joint venture before the deal is completed—while others bombard the information highway with daily press releases in an attempt to keep their stocks in the minds of analysts and investors. "Apparently, some high-tech companies use press releases not only to inform the trade press but also to impress Wall Street analysts and business reporters and—through them—to impress investors who have no other way to get news because they don't read the trade press," Mark Ferelli noted in *Computer Technology Review*. In any case, the Securities and Exchange Commission (SEC) has begun taking notice of business news releases on the Internet. Experts recommend that investors look beyond companies' paid public relations efforts and review their filings with the SEC before making investment decisions.

FURTHER READING:

"Beware the Press Release." *Business Week*. April 24, 2000.

Dobkin, Jeffrey. "Getting Your Press Release into Print." *Direct Marketing*. August 1998.

Ferelli, Mark, and Hal Glatzer. "The Power of the Press Release: For Better or Worse . . . Much Worse." *Computer Technology Review.* September 2000.

Hall, Thomas C. "Press Release Snafu Puts Firms on Alert." *Business Journal.* September 1, 2000.

Pelham, Fran. "The Triple Crown of Public Relations: Pitch Letter, News Release, Feature Article." *Public Relations Quarterly.* Spring 2000.

Ryan, Michael. "Models Help Writers Produce Publishable Releases." *Public Relations Quarterly.* Summer 1995.

Saltz, Linda Citroen. "How to Get Your News Releases Published." *Journal of Accountancy.* November 1996.

Soderberg, Norman R. *Public Relations for the Entrepreneur and the Growing Business.* Probus, 1986.

Wilcox, Dennis L., and Lawrence W. Nolte. *Public Relations Writing and Media Techniques.* 3d ed. Addison Wesley, 1997.

SEE ALSO: Public Relations

PRICE/EARNINGS (P/E) RATIO

The price/earnings ratio (P/E ratio) provides a comparison of the current market price of a share of stock and that stock's earnings per share, or EPS (which is figured by dividing a company's net income by its number of shares of common stock outstanding). For example, if a company's stock sold for $30 per share and it posted earnings per share of $1.50, that company would have a P/E ratio of 15. A company's P/E ratio typically rises as a result of increases in its stock price, an indicator of the stock's popularity.

"The price-earnings ratio is part of the everyday vocabulary of investors in the stock market," noted Richard Brealey and Stewart Myers in *Principles of Corporate Finance*, because a company's P/E ratio is often viewed as an indicator of future stock performance. "The high P/E shows that investors think that the firm has good growth opportunities, that its earnings are relatively safe and deserve a low capitalization rate, or both." John B. Thomas observed in the *Indianapolis Business Journal*, however, that "while accepting that a high P/E ratio is usually a sign of high expectations, analysts and brokers nonetheless are quick to caution that the ratios are only part of the puzzle." A company may post an artificially high P/E ratio as a result of factors that can either boost stock prices or diminish earnings per share. Restructuring charges, merger and acquisition rumors (whether true or false), and high dividend yields all have the capacity to push a company's P/E ratio upward. In other instances, legitimately high P/E ratios can be adversely impacted down the road by such factors as market conditions, technology, and increased competition from new rivals (who may, in fact, be drawn to the industry by the company's previously posted P/E ratios).

Conversely, while a low P/E ratio is often a good indication that a company is struggling, appearances can again be deceiving. In addition, different industry sectors often have diverse P/E ratio averages. A company may have a fairly low P/E ratio when compared with all other corporations; when compared with the other companies within its industry, however, it may be a leader. Finally, a company that posts a loss has no earnings to compare with its stock price. As a result, no P/E ratio can be determined for the company. Still, these companies may remain viable choices for investment if an investor decides that the company under examination is headed toward future profitability. Since so many factors can influence a company's P/E ratio, industry analysts caution against relying on it too heavily in making investment decisions.

EARNINGS PER SHARE (EPS)

Earnings per share is one of the two factors that determine a company's P/E ratio; the other is the price of the company's stock. EPS is derived by dividing a corporation's net income by the number of shares of common stock that are outstanding. A company with 30,000 outstanding shares of common stock and a net income of $270,000 would thus have an earnings per share of $9.

An essential part of determining the P/E ratio, earnings per share has also come to be regarded as an important piece of information for the investment community in and of itself. "A primary concern of investors is how profitable a company is relative to their investment in the company," wrote Jay M. Smith, Jr., and K. Fred Skousen in *Intermediate Accounting*. "The investor is concerned with how net income relates to shares held and to the market price of the stock. . . . Only by converting the total amounts to per share data can a meaningful evaluation be made," because EPS figures can illustrate the degree to which a company's net income is keeping pace with its capital structure. In recognition of the importance of this information, corporations are required to report EPS amounts on their income statement (privately owned companies are under no such obligation).

FURTHER READING:

Brealey, Richard, and Stewart Myers. *Principles of Corporate Finance.* McGraw-Hill Book Company, 1984.

Smith, Jay M., Jr., and K. Fred Skousen. *Intermediate Accounting.* South-Western Publishing Co., 1987.

Smith, Richard L., and Janet Kiholm Smith. *Entrepreneurial Finance.* John Wiley, 2000.

Thomas, John B. "P/E Ratios Driven by Variety of Factors, Carry Variety of Meanings," *Indianapolis Business Journal.* May 23, 1994.

Intelligent pricing is one of the most important elements of any successful business venture. Yet many entrepreneurs fail to educate themselves adequately about various pricing components and strategies before launching a new business. Smart small business owners will weigh many marketplace factors before setting prices for their goods and services. As the Small Business Administration (SBA) indicated in *The Facts About Pricing Your Products and Services,* "you must understand your market, distribution costs, and competition. Remember, the marketplace responds rapidly to technological advances and international competition. You must keep abreast of the factors that affect pricing and be ready to adjust quickly."

COST FACTORS AND PRICING

There are three primary cost factors that need to be considered by small businesses when determining the prices that they charge for their goods or services. After all, price alone means little if it is not figured within the context of operating costs. A company may be able to command a hefty price for an item, only to find that the various costs of producing and delivering that item eliminate most or all of the profit that it realizes on the sale. It should also be noted that service businesses often find it more difficult to accurately gauge their costs, especially in the realm of employee hours. A freelance copyeditor may find that one 2,500-word article takes twice as long to complete as another article of the same size because of differences in quality that are often difficult to anticipate ahead of time.

LABOR COSTS Labor costs consist of the cost of the work that goes into the manufacturing of a product or the execution of a service. Direct labor costs can be figured by multiplying the cost of labor per hour by the number of employee-hours required to complete the job. Business owners, however, need to keep in mind that the "cost of labor per hour" includes not only hourly wage or salary of the relevant employees, but also the costs of the fringe benefits that those workers receive. These fringe benefits can include social security, retirement benefits, insurance, unemployment compensation, workers compensation, and other benefits.

MATERIAL COSTS Material costs are the costs of all materials that are part of the final product offered by the business. As with labor, this expense can apply to both goods and services. In the case of goods, material costs refer to the costs of the various components that make up a product, while material costs associated with services rendered typically include replacement parts, building parts, etc. A deck builder, for example, would include such items as lumber, nails, and sealer as material costs.

OVERHEAD COSTS Overhead costs are costs that cannot be directly attributed to one particular product or service. Some business consultants simply refer to overhead costs as those business expenses that do not qualify as labor costs or material costs. These costs include indirect expenses such as general supplies, heating and lighting expenditures, depreciation, taxes, advertising, rental or leasing costs, transportation, employee discounts, damaged merchandise, business memberships, and insurance. A certain percentage of employees usually fit in this category as well. While the wages and benefits received by an assembly line worker involved in the production of a specific product might well qualify as a labor cost, the wages and benefits accrued by general support personnel—janitors, attorneys, accountants, clerks, human resource personnel, receptionists—are included as overhead.

Overhead expenses are typically divided into two categories—fixed expenses and variable expenses. Fixed expenses are regular (usually monthly) expenses that will not change much, regardless of a company's business fortunes. Examples of fixed expenses include rent, utilities, insurance, membership dues, subscriptions, accounting costs, and depreciation on fixed assets. Variable expenses are those expenses that undergo greater fluctuation, depending on variables such as time of year (for seasonal businesses), competitor advertising, and sales. Expenses that are more heavily predicated on company revenues and business owner strategies include office supplies, mailing and advertising, communications (telephone and Fax bills), and employee bonuses.

COST OF GOODS SOLD One of the most important tools that accountants and entrepreneurs use to gauge the health of businesses is the "cost of goods sold." This figure is in essence the business's total cost of manufacturing the products it sells or—in the case of retail firms—its total expenditures to purchase products for resale. Delivery and freight charges are typically included within this equation. Cost of goods sold provides business owners with a rough measurement of their gross profit margin. The figure usually bears a close relationship to sales, but it may vary significantly if increases in the prices paid for merchandise cannot be offset by increases in sales prices, or if profit margins swell because of special purchase deals or sudden surges in product popularity.

PRICING STRATEGIES

Small businesses have many different pricing strategies from which they can choose, but they need to select carefully. An ill-considered decision can place a heavy burden on the business.

MANUFACTURER'S SUGGESTED RETAIL PRICE Many small businesses prefer to simply price their goods in accordance with the manufacturer's suggested retail price. They thus eliminate costs associated with making their own pricing decisions or pursuing more proactive pricing strategies. Critics note, however, that this strategy—such as it is—is utterly heedless of the competition, which may be able to offer a lower price for any number of reasons.

PRICE BUNDLING This is the practice of giving the customers the option of buying several items or services for one price. A furniture retailer, for example, might offer customers a sofa and love seat combination at a price that is somewhat lower than what the two goods would cost if bought separately. Similarly, a landscaper might lure customers by offering two free months of lawn maintenance with any major landscaping job. Leonard Berry and Manjit Yadav noted in *Sloan Management Review* that bundling has several advantages, especially for service-oriented businesses: "The cost structure of most service companies is such that providing an additional service costs less than providing the second service alone. . . . A second benefit of bundling that appeals to customers is purchasing related services from one service provider. They can save time and money by interacting with an paying one provider rather than multiple providers. Third, bundling effectively increases the number of connections a service company has with its customers."

MULTIPLE PRICING Similar to price bundling, multiple pricing is the practice of selling multiple units of an item for a single price. A grocery store that offers two boxes of macaroni and cheese at a single price, for instance, is engaged in multiple pricing. Whereas price bundling is more commonly employed for big-ticket items, multiple pricing is usually used to sell inexpensive consumable items such as razor blades, shampoo, household cleaning products, and food and beverages.

COST-PLUS PRICING This methodology, popular with manufacturers, involves adding together all labor, material, and overhead costs (the "cost") and then adding the desired profit (the "plus").

COMPETITIVE PRICING Some small business owners choose to base their own prices on the prices of their principal competitors. Business owners who choose to follow this course, however, should make sure that they look at competing businesses of similar size and strength. "It's very chancy to compete with a large store's prices," noted the SBA's *The Facts About Pricing Your Products and Services,* "because they can buy in larger volume and their cost per unit will be less. Instead, price products based on your local small-store analysis, then highlight other competitive factors, like personalized customer service and convenient location." Competitive pricing among service-oriented businesses, meanwhile, is a hazier proposition, since the nature and quality of services offered can vary so widely from business to business. Still, it is often employed, if only as a general pricing guideline.

PRICING ABOVE COMPETITION If a business is operating in a community in which low prices are most customers' primary concern, then this pricing strategy is obviously doomed to failure. In settings in which price is not the customer's most important consideration, however, some small businesses can do quite well employing this strategy. The key to making "pricing above competition" work, say experts, is to provide customers with added benefits that justify paying the higher price. These benefits can take the form of: 1) convenient or exclusive location; 2) social status; 3) exclusive merchandise; and 4) high level of service. The latter can take the form of home or office delivery of goods, service and/or product knowledge, speed of service, attractive return policies, and friendly atmosphere.

Some business owners also boost prices in markets that have few competitors, reasoning that the community has little choice but to buy from their businesses. Such prices rarely reach outrageous levels, but they can become sufficiently high that enterprising entrepreneurs will recognize an opportunity to undercut the business with more inexpensively priced goods or services.

PRICING BELOW COMPETITION Pricing below competition is the practice of setting one's prices below those of its competitors. Commonly employed by major discount chains such as Wal-Mart—which can do so because its purchasing power enables it to save on its costs per unit—this strategy can also be effectively used by smaller businesses in some instances (though not when competing directly with Wal-Mart and its ilk), provided they keep their operating costs down and do not spark a price war. Indeed, the smaller profit margins associated with this pricing strategy make it a practical necessity for participating companies to: exercise tight control over inventory; keep labor costs down; keep major operational expenses such as facility leases and equipment rental under control; obtain good prices from suppliers; and make effective use of its pricing strategy in all advertising.

PRICE LINING Companies that engage in this practice are basically hoping to attract a specific segment of the community by only carrying products within a specified price range. This strategy is often employed by businesses whose goods/services or location are likely to attract upscale buyers, though others use it as well. Advantages sometimes accrued through price lining practices include: reduced inventory and storage costs, ease of merchandise selection, and enhanced status. Analysts note, however, that this strategy frequently limits the company's freedom to react to competitors' pricing strategies, and that it can leave businesses particularly vulnerable to economic trends.

ODD PRICING Odd pricing is used in nearly all segments of the business world today. It is the practice of pricing goods and services at prices such as $9.95 (rather than $10) or $79.99 (rather than $80) because of the conviction that consumers will often round the price down rather than up when weighing whether to make a purchase. This little morsel of pricing psychology has become so universally employed that many observers question its value; still, the practice remains widespread across the United States (and elsewhere).

Other commonly used pricing policies include penetration pricing and skimming pricing (for manufacturers) and loss leader pricing (for retailers).

FACTORS IN ARRIVING AT A PRICING STRATEGY

Entrepreneurs encounter numerous considerations that should be weighed when assigning a price to their goods or services. These considerations range from the needs and desires of target consumers to general economic conditions. The SBA cited the following factors as among the most important to consider when arriving at a pricing strategy.

- Is the price of the good or service of significant importance to target consumers?

- How popular is the product or service being offered?

- What pricing and marketing strategies are compatible with the business's other characteristics (location, service reputation, promotions, etc.)

- Does the owner enjoy final pricing authority?

- Are there opportunities for special market promotions?

- What are competitors charging for similar goods or services?

- Should competitors' temporary price reductions be matched?

- What level of markup can be achieved for each product line or area of service?

- Will prices generate a satisfactory profit margin after calculating operating expenses and reductions?

- When reducing prices on goods or services, do you consider competitors' likely reactions?

- Are there legal factors to consider when establishing price?

- Should "odd pricing" or "multiple pricing" practices be introduced?

- Should marketing efforts highlight sales of selected high-profile products to attract customers?

- If coupons and other discount measures are offered, how will they impact on net profits?

- Will characteristics of the product sold (handling costs, installation requirements, alterations, etc.) meaningfully add to operating costs?

- Will product quantities be unduly reduced as a result of spoilage, breakage, employee theft, or shoplifting?

- Will services such as home/office delivery, gift wrapping, etc. be included in the purchase price?

- Are economic conditions in area of operation particularly good or bad?

- Will employees receive discounts on store items that they purchase?

- Will senior citizens or students receive discounts on goods or services?

- What markdown policies are in place?

REVISITING PRICING STRATEGIES

Since pricing is one of the single most important factors in determining whether a business will be successful, small business owners should continuously review their pricing policies to make certain that they remain in keeping with marketplace realities. Business environments can change quickly, and the successful entrepreneur will learn to change his or her pricing strategies accordingly. William Cohen, author of *The Entrepreneur and Small-Business Problem Solver,* described six different circumstances in which small business owners should review their pricing and make changes if necessary: 1) when introducing a new product or product line; 2) when testing for the best price; 3) when attempting to break into a new market; 4) when competitors change their prices; 5) when general economic conditions become inflationary or recessionary; 6) when weighing major changes in sales strategy. Indeed, any significant change in any aspect of a business's operations—from rising costs of raw materials to changing insurance premiums—should spark a review of company pricing strategies.

REAL PRICE AND NOMINAL PRICE

Economists, business owners, and other people engaged in the world of commerce have long recognized that historical events can help business owners evaluate current business plans and propose future strategies, including pricing strategies. Indeed, as Robert Pindyck and Daniel Rubinfeld observed in *Microeconomics,* ''we often want to compare the price of a good today with what it was in the past or is likely to be in the future.'' Such comparisons are meaningless, however, unless those prices are measured ''relative to the overall price level. In absolute terms, the price of a dozen eggs is many times higher today than it was 50 years ago, but relative to prices overall, it is actually lower. Therefore, we must be careful to correct for inflation when comparing prices across time. This means measuring prices in *real* rather than *nominal* terms.'' Pindyck and Rubinfeld go on to define the nominal price of a good (its ''current dollar'' price) as its absolute price, noting that the nominal price of a quart of milk was 40 cents in 1970 and about 80 cents in 1990. The real price, however, is defined as the price relative to an aggregate measure of prices (usually the Consumer Price Index-CPI). Percentage changes in the CPI measure the rate of inflation in the economy.

RAISING PRICES

Small business owners are often reluctant to raise prices once a good baseline price has been established. They worry that a price increase will alienate customers and drive them to the competition. ''Faced with such resistance, a lot of businesspeople are tempted to forgo price increases altogether, or at least put them off for as long as possible. If you do either one, however, you're making a big mistake,'' Norm Brodsky wrote in *Inc.* ''Your profit margins will be shrinking. . . . You're gradually undermining the perceived value of your services or products.'' Brodsky noted that many of a small business's costs—such as payroll, insurance, and utilities—tend to rise every year, slowly cutting into profit margins. In addition, customers tend to associate price with quality. A business that does not increase prices to keep up with the competition risks being regarded as the cheap alternative in the marketplace.

When price increases are implemented gradually and cautiously, small businesses may be able to keep their customers happy while also keeping their profit margins intact. After all, as Harry J. Plack wrote in the *Baltimore Business Journal,* customers typically base their purchase decisions on more than just price. Other factors influencing the decision process include quality, features, guarantees, and personal desires. In addition, people will always pay more for good, reliable customer service. In order to make an effective price increase, Howard Scott of *Nation's Business* recommended conveying the reasons for the increase to customers and giving them a perceived increase in value for their money. ''The message for companies is clear,'' Scott wrote. ''Those that differentiate their products from the competition's and are able to articulate that difference to customers are more likely to be able to raise prices—and keep them raised—above the competition's.''

SURVIVING COMPETITORS' DISCOUNT PRICING STRATEGIES

Major discount stores such as Wal-Mart, Sam's Club, Target, K-Mart, Office Depot, Staples, Best Buy, and Circuit City have gained control of large blocs of the American business world over the last several years on the strength of their one-stop shopping and discount prices, the latter a result of their ability to buy goods at bulk rates. Many small business owners have felt the impact of these stores—indeed, cautionary tales concerning the impact that such stores can have on formerly vibrant downtown shopping areas have proliferated in recent years.

Many observers believe, however, that some small business failures that occurred in the wake of these titans' arrivals could have been avoided if small business owners had adopted different strategies to deal with the new competitive environment in which they were operating. Indeed, economists and business analysts agree that most small businesses cannot compete with large chains in the area of price; the bulk-rate buying power advantage that the big stores enjoy is simply too great to overcome. But they contend that many small businesses can still co-exist with these titans if their owners outmaneuver the big stores in other areas. Effective strategies that can be used to help negate the discount pricing strategy employed at the big chains include:

- Emphasize value and personal service rather than price

- Offer attractive ancillary services (home and office delivery, generous return policies, etc.)

- Define your market segment or niche and devote energies accordingly

- Control inventory

- Streamline to eliminate less profitable areas of business

- Target advertising and promotions to reach the most likely customers

- Steer customers to the most profitable aspects of your business

- Establish your business's industry knowledge as an additional resource for customers

- Build strong relationships with vendors

- Meet or beat prices of big discounters on selected lead items or services

- Make intelligent use of price strategies such as price bundling.

Of course, pricing remains a very big component in determining a company's success or failure. "The key to success," concluded the SBA in its *Pricing Your Products* brochure, "is to have a well-planned strategy and established policies and to constantly monitor prices and operating costs to ensure a profit." Finally, the SBA cautioned entrepreneurs to "remember that the image of your business is crucial to obtaining and keeping the clientele and that your pricing structure and policies are a major component of your image."

FURTHER READING:

Brodsky, Norm. "Street Smarts: Raising Prices." *Inc.* May 2000.

"Case Study: How to Price Your Products to Increase Profits." *Business Owner.* May-June 1995.

Cohen, William A. *The Entrepreneur and Small-Business Problem Solver.* 2d ed. Wiley, 1990.

"The Delicate Art of Price Hikes." *Business Week.* November 6, 2000.

The Facts About Pricing Your Products and Services. Small Business Administration, 1996.

Marn, M.V., and R.L. Rosiello. "Managing Price, Gaining Profit." *Harvard Business Review.* September-October 1992.

Meyer, Peter. "Is the Price Right?" *Across the Board.* July 2000.

Pindyck, Robert S., and Daniel L. Rubinfeld. *Microeconomics.* 2d ed. Macmillan, 1992.

Plack, Harry J. "Price Hikes Not Always a Bad Thing." *Baltimore Business Journal.* July 14, 2000.

"The Power of Smart Pricing." *Business Week.* April 10, 2000.

Pricing Your Products. Small Business Administration, n.a.

Scott, Howard. "The Tricky Art of Raising Prices." *Nation's Business.* February 1999.

Walker, Bruce J. *A Pricing Checklist for Small Retailers.* Small Business Administration, n.a.

Winninger, Thomas J. *Price Wars: How to Win the Battle for Your Customer.* St. Thomas Press, 1994.

SEE ALSO: Loss Leader Pricing; Penetration Pricing

PRIVATE LABELING

Private labeling is when a retailer purchases products from various manufacturers and then markets those products under its own brand. Private label goods are often referred to as "store brands," as opposed to the "name brands" that are sold under the brand name of the manufacturer. For example, the consumer products giant Procter and Gamble manufactures peanut butter and sells it under the brand name Jif, while the supermarket chain Kroger purchases peanut butter from smaller manufacturers and sells it as Kroger brand peanut butter. Private label products tend to be less expensive than competing name brands, largely because of reduced advertising expenditures.

Private labeling gained prominence during the recession of the late 1980s, when many consumers chose to give up expensive name brand products in an effort to save money, and many retailers began to market store brands in an attempt to increase sales. But when consumer confidence in the economy rebounded in the 1990s, consumer loyalty to name brands did not. Today, private labeling is a widespread business practice among supermarkets, drugstore chains, and mass merchandisers. These retailers sell hundreds of different items under their own brand names, from basic household items and food to specialty items and even clothing. A survey by the Private Label Manufacturers Association indicated that sales of private label merchandise topped $43 billion in 1998. In addition, the market share held by private brands was expected to increase to 23 percent at large food retailers by 2004.

In the early days private label goods were essentially cheap imitations of the leading brands, even copying the colors and designs of the major competitors' packaging. Even though court rulings have supported right of private labelers to imitate the packaging of leading brands (unless there is documented confusion among consumers), private label retailers have now moved away from imitation and toward attractive packaging of their own design. Some retailers believe that they need eye-catching packaging because they do not do much advertising, and instead rely on consumers taking notice of their offerings as they walk through store aisles. Over time, many consumers began to consider store brands on the same level as national brands as far as quality, performance, and satisfaction.

Another emerging trend concerns the type of products that are sold as store brands. Whereas the majority of private label products used to be the most basic household goods, the areas of growth in recent years have been in premium and super-premium goods. "The growth in premium brands shows that while today's consumers are value-conscious, they're still picky about product quality," Jenny McCune wrote in an article for *Small Business Reports.* "Inferior goods aren't attracting consumers at any price, which is why sales of generic goods—the no-name, no-frills varieties—are actually down."

The continued growth of private labels has encouraged retailers to devote significantly more attention to developing store brands. "Eager to satisfy these value-conscious consumers and make higher margins to boot, many retailers are promoting their house brands as never before," McCune noted. "They've focused on improving the quality of store brands to better compete with name brands and other private-label lines. They're also lavishing the brands with marketing attention, rather than simply tossing the goods on the shelves and leaving them to fend for themselves."

McCune claimed that the recent growth of private labels has also provided new opportunities for small and medium-sized manufacturers in a whole spectrum of industries. Rather than competing directly with much larger companies and incurring the related advertising expenses, these small manufacturers can grow by marketing their products to retailers. "Despite the competition, the trends in private labeling present opportunities for small and midsize manufacturers that can meet the demands of this market," McCune stated. In essence, the small businesses who create private label goods serve as the manufacturing arm for their retail customers.

FACTORS IN SUCCESSFUL PRIVATE LABEL MANUFACTURING

In her article, McCune outlined three main factors that determine the potential for success of small businesses that wish to manufacture private label goods: the right product, a competitive price, and a strong marketing program. For products to be considered for private labels, they must have a large sales potential, because retailers are not usually interested in branding low-demand items. In addition, the manufacturer must be able to assure that the product quality is as good or better than the leading brands. As McCune explained, "A retailer puts its own name on the line when it private labels your product, and it won't want that name to be sullied by inferior or inconsistent quality." Small manufacturers may gain a marketing advantage if they are willing to assume responsibility for product quality, rather than leaving the retailer holding the bag. This might involve providing a toll-free number on product packaging for consumers to make complaints or suggestions, or giving the retailer a discount on future orders if the quality does not meet predetermined standards.

The type of manufacturing process involved is another important product-related aspect of private labeling. In general, private labels are most appropriate for products that can be manufactured on a tight schedule while maintaining high quality standards. Private label manufacturers must be able to assure their retail clients of reliable, on-time delivery. In addition, they must be flexible enough to ramp up production quickly to meet increases in demand or to change the product's formulation according to the retailer's wishes. "Given these demands, private labeling generally isn't for industry newcomers," McCune noted. "Retailers look for manufacturers, whether large or small, that are well-regarded in their fields. In a relatively young company, however, the owners' own reputation can compensate for the firm's short track record."

Price is another important component of successful private label manufacturing. The price must compare favorably to competing name brands while also enabling both the manufacturer and the retailer to make money. In general, private label sales provide high volume but tight margins, so price calculations are crucial. McCune claimed that private label goods are usually priced 20 percent or more below the market leader. In addition, the retailer generally expects to see a profit margin on private label goods that is 8 to 10 percent higher than it receives with name brands. When calculating the final sales price for private label items, manufacturers must be sure to consider any costs that are incurred especially for the private label line. These may include tailoring the product to meet retailer specifications, or designing special packaging for each retailer.

The third factor in successful private label manufacturing is a strong marketing program. The marketing program for private label goods consists of two parts: contracting with retailers to become their supplier for a certain product, and assisting the retailer in marketing that product to the final consumer. If a small business lacks expertise in dealing with retailers, it is possible to hire distributors or consultants who specialize in private-label selling. For small manufacturers who proceed on their own, however, McCune recommended getting all of the conditions of the contract in writing. It is particularly important to determine the amount of packaging that must be kept in stock, since extra packaging with a certain retailer's label becomes useless if the deal falls through. Manufacturers will want to keep the amount as low as possible and perhaps also include a clause that requires the retailer to reimburse them for unused packaging. It is also important that the contract specify realistic delivery dates, product design modifications, and the amount of notice required to terminate the contract. Finally, it may also be useful for private label manufacturers to contribute their product marketing expertise to their retail accounts. This may involve recommending specific promotions or even creating advertisements and writing ad copy.

Overall, McCune noted that private label manufacturing can present tremendous opportunities for small businesses, as well as significant challenges. For example, creating private label goods often requires developing a partnership with retail clients. "Private label veterans . . . warn newcomers to be prepared for some hand-holding, since the relationship between retailer and private-label supplier tends to be especially close," McCune wrote. Still, she recommended that small businesses who manufacture private label goods not allow any one retailer to account for more than 15 percent of their sales. After all, most contracts in this area are open-ended, which enables retailers to change suppliers at any time. Another potential challenge is that name-brand manufacturers are increasingly being attracted by the growth of private labeling. It has encouraged many to reduce prices, improve value, and in some cases even set up private-label divisions of their own to take advantage of their excess manufacturing capacity.

PRIVATE LABELS AND E-COMMERCE

An emerging trend in private labels is the rapid adoption of these brands by firms involved in Internet commerce. "While supermarkets and department stores in the brick-and-mortar world can take years before they venture into private label merchandise, e-tailers—in a development that echoes the rapid emergence of the medium itself—are developing private label programs as they approach the starting gate," Elaine Underwood wrote in *Brandweek*.

According to Underwood, some electronic retailers are attracted by the higher margins typically offered by private label merchandise. Others see it as a way to offer unique merchandise that helps differentiate them from competitors. For example, the online toy retailer eToys sold special cabinets and stands for customers to display their collections of toys under their own brand name. Some experts claim that offering private label merchandise gives substance to online brand names and reminds customers of e-commerce Web sites. Electronic retailers must be careful not to offend big name manufacturers by copying their products and packaging too closely, however, because they lack the leverage in the chain of distribution that is enjoyed by regular retail stores.

FURTHER READING:

Kaplan, Andrew. "A Name for Itself." *U.S. Distribution Journal.* March 15, 1995.

McAllister, Liane. "The Cachet of Private Labels." *Gifts and Decorative Accessories.* January 1997.

McCune, Jenny. "Catch a Growing Wave." *Small Business Reports.* June 1994.

Murray, Barbara. "Private Labels Pushed as Solutions." *Supermarket News.* February 14, 2000.

"The Store Brand Challenges Ahead." *Supermarket Business.* January 1998.

"Taking It Private." *Supermarket Business.* October 15, 1999.

Underwood, Elaine. "Store Brands, without the Store." *Brandweek.* June 19, 2000.

SEE ALSO: Brands and Brand Names

PRIVATE PLACEMENT OF SECURITIES

Private placement occurs when a company makes an offering of securities not to the public, but directly to an individual or a small group of investors. Such offerings do not need to be registered with the Securities and Exchange Commission (SEC) and are exempt from the usual reporting requirements. Private placements are generally considered a cost-effective way for small businesses to raise capital without "going public" through an initial public offering (IPO).

"Although most business owners dream of taking their company public someday, many have had to wait years for a traditional public offering," Gary D. Zeune and Timothy R. Baer explained in an article for *Corporate Cashflow Magazine.* "For them, a private placement of equity or debt has been a quicker, less expensive way to raise a limited amount of capital from a limited number of investors. A private placement has been appropriate when a company still lacks the financial strength or reputation to appeal to a broad base of investors and cannot afford the expense of a public offering."

ADVANTAGES AND DISADVANTAGES

Private placements offer small businesses a number of advantages over IPOs. Since private placements do not require the assistance of brokers or underwriters, they are considerably less expensive and time consuming. In addition, private placements may be the only source of capital available to risky ventures or start-up firms. "With loan criteria for commercial bankers and investment criteria for venture capitalists both tightening, the private placement offering remains one of the most viable alternatives for capital formation available to companies," Andrew J. Sherman wrote in his book *The Complete Guide to Running and Growing Your Business.*

A private placement may also enable a small business owner to hand-pick investors with compatible goals and interests. Since the investors are likely to be sophisticated business people, it may be possible for the company to structure more complex and confidential transactions. If the investors are themselves entrepreneurs, they may be able to offer valuable assistance to the company's management. Finally, unlike public stock offerings, private placements enable small businesses to maintain their private status.

Of course, there are also a few disadvantages associated with private placements of securities. Suitable investors may be difficult to locate, for example, and may have limited funds to invest. In addition, privately placed securities are often sold at a deep discount below their market value. Companies that undertake a private placement may also have to relinquish more equity, because investors want compensation for taking a greater risk and assuming an illiquid position. Finally, it can be difficult to arrange private placement offerings in multiple states.

RESTRICTIONS AFFECTING PRIVATE PLACEMENT

The SEC formerly placed many restrictions on private placement transactions. For example, such offerings could only be made to a limited number of investors, and the company was required to establish strict criteria for each investor to meet. Furthermore, the SEC required private placement of securities to be made only to ''sophisticated'' investors—those capable of evaluating the merits and understanding the risks associated with the investment. Finally, stock sold through private offerings could not be advertised to the public and could only be resold under certain circumstances.

In 1992, however, the SEC eliminated many of these restrictions in order to make it easier for small companies to raise capital through private placements of securities. The rules now allow companies to promote their private placement offerings more broadly and to sell the stock to a greater number of buyers. It is also easier for investors to resell such securities. Although the SEC restrictions on private placements were relaxed, it is nonetheless important for small business owners to understand the various federal and state laws affecting such transactions and to take the appropriate procedural steps. It may be helpful to assemble a team of qualified legal and accounting professionals before attempting to undertake a private placement.

Many of the rules affecting private placements are covered under Section 4(2) of the federal securities law. This section provides an exemption for companies wishing to sell up to $5 million in securities to a small number of accredited investors. Companies conducting an offering under Section 4(2) cannot solicit investors publicly, and the majority of investors are expected to be either insiders (company management) or sophisticated outsiders with a preexisting relationship with the company (professionals, suppliers, customers, etc.). At a minimum, the companies are expected to provide potential investors with recent financial statements, a list of risk factors associated with the investment, and an invitation to inspect their facilities. In most respects, the preparation and disclosure requirements for offerings under Section 4(2) are similar to Regulation D filings.

Regulation D—which was adopted in 1982 and has been revised several times since—consists of a set of rules numbered 501 through 508. Rules 504, 505, and 506 describe three different types of exempt offerings and set forth guidelines covering the amount of stock that can be sold and the number and type of investors that are allowed under each one. Rule 504 covers the Small Corporate Offering Registration, or SCOR. SCOR gives an exemption to private companies that raise no more than $1 million in any 12-month period through the sale of stock. There are no restrictions on the number or types of investors, and the stock may be freely traded. The SCOR process is easy enough for a small business owner to complete with the assistance of a knowledgeable accountant and attorney. It is available in all states except Delaware, Florida, Hawaii, and Nebraska.

Rule 505 enables a small business to sell up to $5 million in stock during a 12-month period to an unlimited number of investors, provided that no more than 35 of them are non-accredited. To be accredited, an investor must have sufficient assets or income to make such an investment. According to the SEC rules, individual investors must have either $1 million in assets (other than their home and car) or $200,000 in net annual personal income, while institutions must hold $5 million in assets. Finally, Rule 506 allows a company to sell unlimited securities to an unlimited number of investors, provided that no more than 35 of them are non-accredited. Under Rule 506, investors must be sophisticated. In both of these options, the securities cannot be freely traded.

DISCLOSURE

Although the 1992 SEC revisions eliminated the requirement for companies to prepare a Private Placement Memorandum for investors, experts suggest that it is still a good idea. The memorandum should describe the business, provide background information on management, discuss the terms of the offering (including the number of shares available, the price, and the intended use for the funds), outline the company's capital structure before and after the sale of securities, disclose the opportunities and risks involved in the investment, and provide copies of financial statements. Overall, the level of disclosure should be consistent with applicable state and federal securities laws, as well as with the sophistication of potential investors and the complexity of the terms of the offering.

A series of documents known as subscription materials should also be included with the information sent to potential investors in a private placement transaction. Subscription materials consist of two major documents that investors sign to indicate their desire to subscribe to purchase the securities offered. One of these documents is the offeree and purchaser questionnaire, which asks for background information about the investor to determine his or her level of sophistication. The second document is the subscription agreement, which is a contract showing that the investor has reviewed the offering information, is aware of the risks involved, and wants to invest.

FURTHER READING:

Lewis, Jakema. "2000: A See-Sawing Year for Private Deals." *Private Placement Letter.* January 29, 2001.

Sherman, Andrew J. *The Complete Guide to Running and Growing Your Business.* New York: Random House, 1997.

Steinberg, Carol. "The DPO Revolution: Direct Public Offerings Turn Customers into Investors." *Success.* March 1997.

Stolze, William J. *Start Up Financing: An Entrepreneur's Guide to Financing a New or Growing Business.* Franklin Lakes, NJ: Career Press, 1997.

Sweeney, Paul. "As Public Markets Fell, Equity Private Placements Filled the Gap." *Investment Dealers' Digest.* February 26, 2001.

Sweeney. "Staying Upbeat: Story Credits, Mezzanine Financing Boost Lackluster Private." *Investment Dealers' Digest.* August 21, 2000.

Taylor, Lon W. "Raising Capital through Private Placements." *Journal of Business Strategy.* July-August 1988.

Zeune, Gary D., and Timothy R. Baer. "Floating a Stock Offering: New Buoyancy from the SEC." *Corporate Cashflow Magazine.* August 1993.

SEE ALSO: Initial Public Offerings

PRIVATIZATION

Defined in the strictest of terms, privatization means the sale of public utilities to private concerns. But as *Public Works* magazine noted, "in the broader sense of the term . . . and the definition that applies to most contemporary discussions, privatization is the contract operation of a public utility or service by a private entity. It most often occurs in solid waste management, water/wastewater treatment, fleet maintenance, road/bridge building and maintenance, and municipal management." Small businesses that provide services in these and other areas (for-profit school academies, for instance) have been among the biggest winners in the growing national trend toward privatization. As *Public Works* commented, "opportunities abound for private concerns to offer to manage public services with a close eye on cost and efficiency."

Privatization efforts in America today are in large part a reaction to dissatisfaction with government performance and/or unhappiness with the level of taxation that is levied on individuals and businesses by municipal, state, and federal governments to pay for services. This trend has grassroots origins, with local governments in the forefront and state and federal levels of government trailing behind. The purpose of privatization is to take advantage of the perceived cost efficiencies of private firms. Indeed, proponents of the practice say that privatization results in better performance of needed services at lesser cost. "The government usually allows the firm to choose how it will satisfy the contract," wrote Simon Hakim and Edwin Blackstone in *American City and County.* "For example, a contract may specify trash removal services for the area residents a certain number of times per week. The firm is normally allowed to choose the methods it will use to perform the requirements of the contract, the trash trucks, used, and the number of workers on each trash truck. The profit motive will encourage the firm to produce the services efficiently at the least cost, a motive absent in government provision of services." Even after privatization, however, government monitoring is necessary in order to ensure that satisfactory services are provided to residents.

GROWTH OF PRIVATIZATION

"Privatization may be a popular buzzword today, but the concept has been around since the first municipality hired Joe and his wagon to pick up the trash instead of getting city employee Frank to do it," remarked *Public Works.* "The difference today is that privatization is encroaching into all areas of public administration. And governments are expecting public agencies to compete—dollar for dollar—with private operators or surrender management of services. For years, our country has supported the idea that a public workforce was the best provider of essential services. Public employees would reliably and efficiently protect the public safety and deliver water and power; maintain roads and bridges; collect refuse and treat sewage. . . . In return, public employees enjoyed a certain job stability and a wide range of desirable benefits." But proliferating responsibilities, fiscal belt-tightening, sometimes lackluster performance by workers, and—in the cases of larger cities, especially—festering problems with infrastructure led increasing numbers of city planners and public policy makers to look to privatization.

Today, several of the nation's largest cities, including New York, Indianapolis, Philadelphia, and Phoenix have contracted out a broad spectrum of services that were previously attended to exclusively by city employees. Indeed, New York City opened up bidding from private companies on 40 different municipal services in 1995 alone. Smaller cities and towns have instituted outsourcing philosophies as well, and many service businesses, both large and small, have garnered significant new contracts as a result. *American City and County* reported that various analyses indicate that this trend will likely continue. "Cost pressures, both internal and external, are rated as the most important reasons that officials decided to privatize a service," stated a report on privatization conducted by a coalition of Illinois academic, business, and municipal groups. "The main obstacle is the lack of information or evidence of the benefits of privatization. Many officials also report they would like more information on certain aspects of privatization. It can be deduced that providing additional information on privatization to city officials will lead to increased acceptance."

VARIATIONS IN PRIVATIZATION

The term privatization has been applied to three different methods of increasing the activity of the private sector in providing public services: 1) private-sector choice, financing, and production of a service; 2) public-sector choice and financing with private-sector production of the service selected; 3) and deregulation of private firms providing services. In the first case, the entire responsibility for a service is transferred from the public sector to the private sector, and individual consumers select and purchase the amount of services they desire from private providers. For example, solid-waste collection is provided by private firms in some communities. The third form of privatization means that government reduces or eliminates the regulatory restrictions imposed on private firms providing specific services.

The second version of privatization refers to joint activity of the public and private sectors in providing services. In this case, consumers select and pay for the quantity and type of service desired through government, which then contracts with private firms to produce the desired amount and category of service. Although the government provides for the service, a private firm carries out the actual execution of it. The government determines the service level and pays the amount specified in the contract, but leaves decisions about production decisions to the private firm.

ADVANTAGES AND DISADVANTAGES OF PRIVATIZATION

The merits and drawbacks of privatization have been subjects of considerable debate among businesspeople, city leaders, and public employees alike. Indeed, each element of privatization—from its apparent cost-saving properties to its possible negative impact on minority workers—provokes strong reaction. About the only thing that everyone can agree on is that the trend has been enormously beneficial to owners of small- and mid-sized businesses. Following are some privatization issues that communities, public providers, and private providers all need to consider:

COSTS AND PRODUCTIVITY

Proponents of privatization argue that whereas government producers have no incentive to hold down production costs, private producers who contract with the government to provide the service have more at stake, thus encouraging them to perform at a higher level for lower cost. The lower the cost incurred by the firm in satisfying the contract, the greater profit it makes. On the other hand, the absence of competition and profit incentives in the public sector is not likely to result in cost minimization. Of course, small- and mid-sized companies also need to make sure that they do not sacrifice an acceptable profit margin in their zeal to secure a contract.

Although private firms may pay lower wages and fringe benefits than local governments, the major cause of the cost differences between the private and governmental sectors is employee productivity. Lower labor costs may arise either from lower wages (which means that the government was paying wages higher than necessary for a given skill) or from less labor input (which means that the government retaining more employees than necessary to fulfill need). Private firms have more flexibility than governmental units to use part-timers to meet peak periods of activity, to fire unsatisfactory workers, and to allocate workers across a variety of tasks. Moreover, critics of municipal governments argue that they are less likely to reward individual initiatives or punish aberrant behavior when compared with their private sector counterparts.

Finally, supporters of privatization argue that the trend has spurred improvements in performance by public service providers. "Evidence shows that public agencies should be allowed to bid on contracts along with private operators," wrote Blackstone and Hakim, "since this exposure to competition has led many public agencies to improve their service delivery and significantly reduce costs."

Service. Expected quality of service varies from community to community, depending on a wide range of factors such as historical service levels, local taxation, and possible changes in service requirements. Moreover, *Public Works* observed that good service is sometimes defined differently by citizens, public service providers, and private service providers. "Response time and public confidence need to be taken into account when judging the pros and cons of private/public," stated *Public Works*. "Stability may be a concern in the eyes of the public; a government agency cannot walk away at the end of a contract period."

Operating Philosophies. Proponents of privatization state that private firms may be more likely to experiment with different and creative approaches to service provision, whereas government tends to stick with the current approach since changes often create political difficulties for elected officials. In addition, private firms may use retained earnings to finance research or to purchase new capital equipment that lowers unit production costs. On the other hand, government may not be able or willing to allocate tax revenues to these purposes as easily, given the many competing demands on the government's budget.

Regulatory Realities. In some cases, local, state, and federal regulations may determine whether a service can even be handed over to a private provider. Moreover, "the ultimate responsibility (in the eyes of the public, if not the courts) rests with the public agency that assigns operating rights to a private concern," stated *Public Works.* "The local government will still be held responsible for the cost and quality of the service under contract."

Competition. Supporters of privatization often cite the competitive environment that is nourished by the practice as a key to its success. Private owners have a strong incentive to operate efficiently, they argue, while this incentive is lacking under public ownership. If private firms spend more money and employ more people to do the same amount of work, competition will lead to lower margins, lost customers, and decreased profits. The disciplining effect of competition does not occur in the public sector. Still, even advocates of privatization agree that private ownership produces the public benefits of lower costs and high quality only in the presence of a competitive environment. Privatization cannot be expected to produce these same benefits if competition is absent. Given this reality, analysts strongly encourage municipal governments to make sure that the bidding process is an ethical one.

Monitoring and Enforcement. Critics of privatization of government services contend that problems sometimes arise in various aspects of the process, including the bidding process, the precise specification of the contract, and the monitoring and enforcement of the contract. For example, some observers have raised concerns that potential suppliers may initially offer a price to the government that is less than actual production costs to induce the government to transfer the service to the private sector or to win the contract. Subsequently, the contractor would then demand a higher price after the government has dismantled its own production system. Such "low-balling" in the bidding process may be reduced if the local government requires relatively long-term contracts, or constructs contracts that give them flexibility in hiring and firing outside firms.

Public Personnel Management magazine also noted that governments need to take several important precautions before handing out a contract in order to avoid litigation and legal liability. These precautions include detailed performance specifications for service providers, guidelines for the evaluation of competitive bids, and labor relations strategies. For their part, private bidders need to make certain that these precautions are reasonable ones that will not unduly impact their ability to perform both profitably and professionally.

Commonly utilized methods of contract monitoring, meanwhile, include performance appraisals, tracking complaints, citizen satisfaction surveys, reports from contractors, field observations, and ongoing cost comparisons.

Employment. Privatization is understandably viewed as an alarming trend by public employee groups. In some cases, privatization results in layoffs of public sector employees, although governments often reassign them to other government jobs, place them with private contractors, or offer them early retirement programs. These possibilities have been particularly upsetting to public employee unions, which have been at the forefront of efforts to block privatization. Indeed, one of the principal objections to privatization is that it replaces positions that featured compensation that could be used to support a family with private sector spots that offer modest compensation. Indeed, critics such as the *Journal of Commerce and Commercial*'s David Morris contend that private companies are only able to promise meaningful financial savings over public agencies because of the comparatively low salaries they pay their workers. Another charge leveled at privatization initiatives is that they too often have a disproportionate impact on minorities. "Governments often hire minorities in larger proportions than other workers," wrote Blackstone and Hakim. "Thus, if government size is reduced, relatively more minority workers are likely to lose their jobs." In recognition of these fears, some service contracts now require private contractors to hire affected public employees or give them hiring preference.

Demographic and Geographic Factors. Smaller municipalities may incur relatively high unit costs if they operate their own services as a result of not being able to achieve economies of scale. These localities may benefit from turning to a contractor that serves multiple communities. Privatization is also more acceptable in fast-growing communities. If services are being expanded to cover new residents, private contractors are less likely to displace existing public sector employees. Finally, contracting out varies with the number of services provided to residents. As the number of services increases, differences in the cost and effectiveness with which they are provided become more apparent. Therefore, municipalities providing diverse services may be more open to exploring private sector options than those localities where services are more limited.

FURTHER READING:

Blackstone, Edwin, and Simon Hakim. ''Private Ayes: A Tale of Four Cities.'' *American City and County.* February 1997.

Elam, L.B. ''Reinventing Government Privatization Style— Avoiding the Legal Pitfalls of Replacing Civil Servants with Contract Providers.'' *Public Personnel Management.* Spring 1997.

Kodrzycki, Yolanda. ''Privatization of Local Government Services: Lessons for New England.'' *New England Economic Review.* May/June, 1994.

Layne, Judy. ''An Overview of the Privatization Debate.'' *Optimum.* June 2000.

Lieberman, Ira W. ''Privatization: The Theme of the 1990s— An Overview.'' *Columbia Journal of World Business.* Spring 1993.

Morris, David. ''The Downside of Privatization.'' *Journal of Commerce and Commercial.* February 9, 1996.

''Private/Public Partnership: A Balancing Act.'' *Public Works.* September 1997.

Schine, Eric. ''America's New Watchword: If It Moves, Privatize It.'' *Business Week.* December 12, 1994.

Schriener, Judy, Stephen H. Daniels, and William J. Angelo. ''Gold in the Hills of Privatization.'' *ENR..* October 24, 1994.

Sturdivant, John N. ''Privatization: It Often Doesn't Work, Increases Costs and Lacks Accountability.'' *Site Selection.* April 1996.

PRO FORMA STATEMENTS

Pro forma, a Latin term meaning ''as a matter of form,'' is applied to the process of presenting financial projections for a specific time period in a standardized format. Businesses use pro forma statements for decision-making in planning and control, and for external reporting to owners, investors, and creditors. Pro forma statements can be used as the basis of comparison and analysis to provide management, investment analysts, and credit officers with a feel for the particular nature of a business's financial structure under various conditions. Both the American Institute of Certified Public Accountants (AICPA) and the Securities and Exchange Commission (SEC) require standard formats for businesses in constructing and presenting pro forma statements.

''Anyone thinking of going into business should prepare pro forma statements, both income and cash flow, before investing time, money, and energy,'' James O. Gill wrote in his book *Financial Basics of Small Business Success.* As a vital part of the planning process, pro forma statements can help minimize the risks associated with starting and running a new business. They can also help convince lenders and investors to provide financing for a start-up firm. But pro forma statements must be based upon objective and reliable information in order to create an accurate projection of a small business's profits and financial needs for its first year and beyond. After preparing initial pro forma statements and getting the business off the ground, the small business owner should update the projections monthly and annually.

USES OF PRO FORMA STATEMENTS

BUSINESS PLANNING A company uses pro forma statements in the process of business planning and control. Because pro forma statements are presented in a standardized, columnar format, management employs them to compare and contrast alternative business plans. By arranging the data for the operating and financial statements side-by-side, management analyzes the projected results of competing plans in order to decide which best serves the interests of the business.

In constructing pro forma statements, a company recognizes the uniqueness and distinct financial characteristics of each proposed plan or project. Pro forma statements allow management to:

- Identify the assumptions about the financial and operating characteristics that generate the scenarios.

- Develop the various sales and budget (revenue and expense) projections.

- Assemble the results in profit and loss projections.

- Translate this data into cash-flow projections.

- Compare the resulting balance sheets.

- Perform ratio analysis to compare projections against each other and against those of similar companies.

- Review proposed decisions in marketing, production, research and development, etc., and assess their impact on profitability and liquidity.

Simulating competing plans can be quite useful in evaluating the financial effects of the different alternatives under consideration. Based on different sets of assumptions, these plans propose various scenarios of sales, production costs, profitability, and viability. Pro forma statements for each plan provide important information about future expectations, including sales and earnings forecasts, cash flows, balance sheets, proposed capitalization, and income statements.

Management also uses this procedure in choosing among budget alternatives. Planners present sales revenues, production expenses, balance sheet and cash flow statements for competing plans with the underlying assumptions explained. Based on an analysis of these figures, management selects an annual budget. After choosing a course of action, it is common for management to examine variations within the plan.

If management considers a flexible budget most appropriate for its company, it would establish a range of possible outcomes generally categorized as *normal* (expected results), *above normal* (best case), and *below normal* (worst case). Management examines contingency plans for the possible outcomes at input/output levels specified within the operating range. Since these three budgets are projections appearing in a standardized, columnar format and for a specified time period, they are pro forma.

During the course of the fiscal period, management evaluates its performance by comparing actual results to the expectations of the accepted plan using a similar pro forma format. Management's appraisal tests and re-tests the assumptions upon which it based its plans. In this way pro forma statements are indispensable to the control process.

FINANCIAL MODELING Pro forma statements provide data for calculating financial ratios and for performing other mathematical calculations. Financial models built on pro form projections contribute to the achievement of corporate goals if they: 1) test the goals of the plans; 2) furnish findings that are readily understandable; and 3) provide time, quality, and cost advantages over other methods.

Financial modeling tests the assumptions and relationships of proposed plans by studying the impact of variables in the prices of labor, materials, and overhead; cost of goods sold; cost of borrowing money; sales volume; and inventory valuation on the company in question. Computer-assisted modeling has made assumption testing more efficient. The use of powerful processors permits online, real-time decision making through immediate calculations of alternative cash flow statements, balance sheets, and income statements.

ASSESSING THE IMPACT OF CHANGES A company prepares pro forma financial statements when it expects to experience or has just experienced significant financial changes. The pro forma financial statements present the impact of these changes on the company's financial position as depicted in the income statement, balance sheet, and the cash-flow statement. For example, management might prepare pro forma statements to gauge the effects of a potential merger or joint venture. It also might prepare pro forma statements to evaluate the consequences of refinancing debt through issuance of preferred stock, common stock, or other debt.

EXTERNAL REPORTING Businesses also use pro forma statements in external reports prepared for owners (stockholders), creditors, and potential investors. For companies listed on the stock exchanges, the SEC requires pro forma statements with any filing, registration statements, or proxy statements. The SEC and organizations governing accounting practices require companies to prepare pro forma statements when essential changes in the character of a business's financial statements have occurred or will occur. Financial statements may change because of:

- Changes in accounting principles due to adoption of a generally accepted accounting principle different from one used previously for financial accounting.

- A change in accounting estimates dealing with the estimated economic life and net residual value of assets.

- A change in the business entity resulting from the acquisition or disposition of an asset or investment, and/or the pooling of interests of two or more existing businesses.

- A correction of an error made in report or filing of a previous period.

Management's decision to change accounting principles may be based on the issuance of a new accounting principle by the Financial Accounting Standards Board (FASB); internal considerations taking advantage of revised valuations or tax codes; or the accounting needs of a new business combination. By changing its accounting practices, a business might significantly affect the presentation of its financial position and the results of its operations. The change also might distort the earnings trend reported in the income statements for earlier years. Some examples of changes in accounting principles might include valuation of inventory via a first-in, first-out (FIFO) method or a last-in, first-out method (LIFO), or recording of depreciation via a straight-line method or an accelerated method.

When a company changes an accounting method, it uses pro forma financial statements to report the cumulative effect of the change for the period during which the change occurred. To enable comparison of the pro forma financial statements with previous financial statements, the company would present the financial statements for prior periods as originally reported, show the cumulative effect of the change on net income and retained earnings, and show net income on a pro forma basis as if the newly adopted accounting principle had been used in prior periods.

A change in accounting estimate may be required as new events occur and as better information becomes available about the probable outcome of future events. For example, an increase in the percentage used to estimate doubtful accounts, a major write-down of inventories, a change in the economic lives of plant assets, and a revision in the estimated liability for outstanding product warranties would require pro forma statements.

THE SEC FORMAT

The SEC prescribes the form and content of pro forma statements for companies subject to its jurisdiction in circumstances such as the above. Some of the form and content requirements are:

1) An introductory paragraph describing the proposed transaction, the entities involved, the periods covered by the pro forma information, and what the pro forma information shows.

2) A pro forma condensed balance sheet and a pro forma condensed income statement, in columnar form, showing the condensed historical amounts, the pro forma adjustments, and the pro forma amounts. Footnotes provide justification for the pro forma adjustments and explain other details pertinent to the changes.

3) The pro forma adjustments, directly attributable to the proposed change or transaction, which are expected to have a continuing impact on the financial statements. Explanatory notes provide the factual basis for adjustments.

PRO FORMA STATEMENTS FOR CHANGES IN ENTITY AND FOR BUSINESS COMBINATIONS The FASB, the AICPA, and the SEC have provided significant directives to the form, content, and necessity of pro forma financial statements in situations where there has been a change in the form of a business entity. Such a change in form may occur due to changes in financial structure resulting from the disposition of a long-term liability or asset, or due to a combination of two or more businesses.

The purpose of pro forma financial statements is to facilitate comparisons of historic data and projections of future performance. In these circumstances users of financial statements need to evaluate a new or proposed business entity on a basis comparable to the predecessor business in order to understand the impact of the change on cash flow, income, and financial position. *Pro forma adjustments* to accounting principles and accounting estimates reformat the statements of the new entity and the acquired business to conform with those of the predecessor.

Occasionally, a partnership or sole proprietorship will sell all or part of the business interest. Sometimes it is necessary, especially if the business is ''going public,'' to reorganize into a corporation. The financial statements on a corporation with a very short history are not helpful in a thoughtful analysis of future potential. Similarly, because of the differences

in federal income tax liabilities, a restatement of the predecessor business in historical terms only confuses the picture. Since the financial statements of the predecessor business do not contain some of the expense items applicable to a corporation, the pro forma financial statements make adjustments to restate certain expenses on a corporate basis. In particular these would include:

- Stating the owners' salaries in terms of officers' salaries.

- Calculating the applicable federal taxes on the predecessor business as though it were a corporation.

- Including corporate state franchise taxes.

- For partnerships acquired through the pooling of interests, adding the balance of the partners' capital to contributed capital in the combined company rather than to retained earnings.

Subchapter S corporations exercise the tax-option of the shareholders to individually assume the tax liability rather than have it assumed by the corporation as a whole. If the shareholders choose to go public or change their qualifications, the corporation loses the tax-option. Therefore, in addition to the pro forma statement showing historical earnings, the new company will make pro forma provision for the taxes that it would have paid had it been a regular corporation in the past. When acquisition of a Subchapter S corporation is accomplished through the pooling of interests, the pro forma financial statement may not include any of the retained earnings of the Subchapter S corporation in the pooled retained earnings.

When presenting the historical operations of a business previously operated as a partnership, the financial information is adjusted to bring the statement in line with the acquiring corporation. Historical data listed in these instances includes net sales; cost of sales; gross profit on sales; selling, general, and administrative expenses; other income; other deductions; and income before taxes on income. Pro forma adjustments would restate partnership operations on a corporate basis, including estimated partnership salaries as officers and estimated federal and state taxes on income, as well as pro forma net income and pro forma net income per share. Accountants make similar adjustments to pro forma statements for businesses previously operated as sole proprietorships and Subchapter S corporations.

ACQUISITION OR DISPOSAL OF PART OF A BUSINESS For a company that decided to acquire part of a new business or dispose of part of its existing business, a meaningful pro forma statement should adjust the historical figures to demonstrate how the acquired part would have fared had it been a corporation. Pro forma statements should also set forth conventional financial statements of the acquiring company, and pro forma financial statements of the business to be acquired. Notes to the pro forma statements explain the adjustments reflected in the statements.

A pro forma income statement combines the historical income statement of the acquiring company and a pro forma income statement of the business to be acquired for the previous five years, if possible. Pro forma adjustments exclude overhead costs not applicable in the new business entity, such as division and head office expenses.

The purchase of a sole proprietorship, partnership, Sub-Chapter S corporation, or business segment requires pro forma statements for a series of years in order to reflect adjustments for such items as owners' or partners' salaries and income taxes. In this way, each year reflects the results of operations of a business organization comparable with that of the acquiring corporation. However, the pro forma statements giving effect to the business combination should be limited to the current and immediately preceding periods.

SUMMARY

Pro forma statements are an integral part of business planning and control. Managers use them in the decision-making process when constructing an annual budget, developing long-range plans, and choosing among capital expenditures. Pro forma statements are also valuable in external reporting. Public accounting firms find pro forma statements indispensable in assisting users of financial statements in understanding the impact on the financial structure of a business due to changes in the business entity, or in accounting principles or accounting estimates.

Although pro forma statements have a wide variety of applications for ongoing, mature businesses, they are also important for small businesses and start-up firms, which often lack the track record required for preparing conventional financial statements. As a planning tool, pro forma statements help small business owners minimize the risks associated with starting and running a new business. The data contained in pro forma statements can also help convince lenders and investors to provide financing for a start-up firm.

FURTHER READING:

Gill, James O. *Financial Basics of Small Business Success.* Menlo Park, CA: Crisp Publications, 1994.

Livingstone, John Leslie. *The Portable MBA in Finance and Accounting.* New York: Wiley, 1992.

Merrill, Ronald E., and Henry D. Sedgwick. *The New Venture Handbook: Everything You Need to Know to Start and Run Your Own Business.* AMACOM, 1987.

Mosich, A.N., and E. John. Larsen. *Intermediate Accounting.* McGraw-Hill Book Company, 1986.

Rappaport, Louis H. *SEC Accounting Practice and Procedure.* The Ronald Press Company, 1966.

Rutberg, Sidney. ''Pro Forma—The 'What If' Balance Sheet that Gives Companies a Second Chance.'' *WWD.* April 19, 1993.

Smith, Richard L., and Janet Kilholm Smith. *Entrepreneurial Finance.* John Wiley, 2000.

PROBATIONARY EMPLOYMENT PERIODS

When hiring new employees, many employers use probationary employment periods to ascertain whether the new workers will be able to handle the duties and challenges associated with their new job. ''The essential purpose of a probationary period,'' wrote William E. Lissy in *Supervision,* ''is to allow management to observe a new hire's performance before granting permanent status.''

Many consultants to small business owners believe that probationary employment periods—also sometimes known as trial periods—can be quite useful to both entrepreneurs hoping to get a start-up off the ground and established small business owners seeking to maintain or increase their current level of success. As countless small business owners and researchers will attest, the quality of a small company's work force can mean the difference between business success and failure. Indeed, personnel costs (wages, benefits, training, etc.) are among the most expensive elements of business operations; this cost becomes multiplied if your business is saddled with a poor worker. Probationary periods, which can range from two weeks to ninety days in length, are simply meant to give the small business owner the best possible chance of securing and retaining quality employees—and releasing substandard employees without legal penalty. ''[The probation period] gives both parties a chance to size up the situation,'' stated Elwood N. Chapman in *Human Relations in Small Business.* ''The employee can test the work environment, skills required, and future possibilities. The employer can test how the new person will product and fit into the team. Up to the day the trial period is over, either party can cancel the arrangement.''

Analysts do note, however, that companies that terminate probationary employees do not enjoy total protection from lawsuits. These terminated employees do have fewer legal rights than established workers, but they are not without recourse in certain situations. For example, the employement ''at-will'' doctrine that characterizes probationary periods is not a valid legal defense for employers it it can be proven that the work arrangement suggested that termination would only be made for cause. Business owners should consult with an attorney to minimize their exposure in this regard.

ELEMENTS OF AN EFFECTIVE PROBATIONARY PERIOD

Business experts state that small business owners should take the following steps when implementing a probationary period with a new hire:

- Make sure that the specifics of the probationary period (length of probation, for instance) are explicitly stated in company guidelines.

- Make certain that the new employee is aware that he or she will be ''on probation'' for the specified period.

- Monitor how well the new employee executes assigned tasks, using quantitative measurements whenever possible.

- Monitor the new employee's work habits; for example, a new worker who is consistently tardy in arriving at work or returning from lunch may well be a cause for concern.

- Monitor how well the new employee gets along with supervisors/managers.

- Monitor how well the new employee gets along with fellow staff.

- Determine whether the new hire is a ''self-starter,'' or one who needs continued guidance.

- Provide the new hire with feedback that will help him or her shape performance to business expectations; this will not only improve the likelihood of securing a good worker, but also provide the employer with possible legal protection in the event of an unfair dismissal legal action (documentation indicating a pattern of poor performance carries significant legal weight).

Of course, not every employee will be a superior one, and shortcomings in one (or even more) of the above areas does not necessarily mean that the employee should be let go. Factors such as availability of other workers, performance in critical areas, etc., usually have to be considered, and few companies are fortunate enough to be staffed entirely by workers of superior skills, excellent work habits, and healthy ambition.

But analysts indicate that new employees who perform poorly during probationary periods are rarely able to dramatically improve their performance after the trial period has ended. After all, if the worker did a bad job during a probationary period, when all parties were aware that performance would be monitored, why should the small business owner believe that the worker's performance would improve at the conclusion of that trial period, when pressure to ''be on one's best behavior'' would presumably be relieved somewhat. Ultimately, each business owner has to decide for him or herself whether the employee's performance during the trial period warrants continued employment.

FURTHER READING:

Aikin, Olga. ''The Trials of Working Life.'' *Personnel Management.* December 1991.

Chapman, Elwood N. *Human Relations in Small Business.* Crisp Publications, 1994.

Falcone, Paul. ''Using Employment at Will and Probationary Periods to Withstand Termination Challenges.'' *Employment Relations Today.* Summer 1998.

Lissy, William E. ''Probationary Employees.'' *Supervision.* April 1995.

Loh, Eng Seng. ''Employment Probation as a Sorting Mechanism.'' *Industrial and Labor Relations Review.* April 1994.

PRODUCT COSTING

Product costing is the process of tracking and studying all the various expenses that are accrued in the production and sale of a product, from raw materials purchases to expenses associated with transporting the final product to retail establishments. It is widely regarded as an extremely important component in evaluating and planning overall business strategies. As John A. Lessner indicated in the *Journal of Accountancy,* ''in today's hotly competitive business environment, accurate product costing has become critically important to a business's survival.''

Product costing has undergone a dramatic metamorphosis in America over the past 50 years, as *Textile World*'s Frank Wilson noted: ''In the 1940s, cost estimates normally included nothing more than total manufacturing costs. In the late '50s direct costing was implemented to separate variable [cost of materials, cost of transportation] and fixed [interest payments on equipment and facilities, rent, property taxes, executive salaries] costs.'' Indeed, Lessner remarked that ''fifty years ago, when manufacturing was far less automated than it is today, the costs of materials, labor and overhead were just about evenly divided. Now, production of a product's various components is often so synchronized on highly automated production lines that there is little or no need to maintain component inventories; thus, the old costing formulas, still used by many industries, are no longer applicable. . . . Further complicating the costing equation is the trend in manufacturing to focus more attention on quality, flexibility and responsiveness, to meet customer needs. This makes production-line cost analysis more difficult because each line requires small, but significant, changes in production techniques.'' As a result, today's managers and business owners have found that the limited information available through older job costing methods is inadequate for making informed decisions in the contemporary business environment.

With this in mind, companies have increasingly turned to detailed, long-range examinations that provide a more accurate representation of a product's true costs and benefits. ''Companies are discovering that their competitiveness is enhanced when purchasing, manufacturing, logistics, and product design groups begin using total life cycle costing,'' wrote Joseph Cavinato in *Chilton's Distribution*. ''Total life cycle cost recognizes that the purchase price of an item is only part of its total cost, just the beginning of a series of costs to be accumulated by the firm, its downstream customers, and users until the end of the product's life.'' This analysis is further enhanced when companies include suppliers/vendors in the process, because the costing process can help create a partnership relationship that enables both parties to move away from competitive stances on pricing, delivery dates, etc., toward cooperative initiatives that optimize the expense of creating and maintaining new products.

COSTS ASSOCIATED WITH MANUFACTURED PRODUCTS

As *Chilton's Distribution* observes, there are myriad potential costs associated with selling a product which may be directly or indirectly linked to the actual production process. Possible costs include:

- Developing and maintaining supplier relationships.

- Transportation costs, including carrier payment terms; special charges in the realms of packaging, handling, and loading and unloading; and loss and damage expenses.

- Sales and freight terms that define payment terms, sales, and title transfers.

- Payment terms—options here range from 15 days to as many as 90 days in some industries, and letter of credit terms provide additional options. These options, stated Cavinato, ''often are not considered by managers in purchasing, traffic, and sales. Instead, most firms mandate these terms and they become 'boiler plate' in purchase orders, carrier contracts, and invoices. It can

be mutually beneficial to negotiate these terms with suppliers and carriers.

- Costs to receive, process, or make ready, including unloading, counting, inspection, and inventory costs, as well as expenses associated with disposal of packaging and other product protection/transportation materials.

- Logistics expenses (warehousing, loading, unloading, handling, inventory control), which are typically lumped together under the catch-all title ''Overhead,'' despite the fact that costs for each of these can vary significantly depending on the arrangement.

- Production costs accrued in actual manufacture of goods.

- Warranty costs.

- Quality costs, including costs associated with defective products (what percentage and how far down the production line), inspections, product returns, chargebacks, cooperage, and storage.

- Lot size costs, including inventory and cash flow costs associated with lots of varying size.

- Supplier inventory.

- Overhead costs of supplier and customer transactions, including billing, collection, payment preparation, and receiving processes.

- Product improvement and modification, including costs of correcting defects and standardization of materials and packaging.

- Regulatory/environmental costs associated with meeting federal or state laws and community expectations on environmentally friendly production and packaging processes.

PRODUCT COSTING IN MULTI-PRODUCT ENVIRONMENTS

Some manufacturers distort true product costing results by evenly distributing costs for a certain aspect of production across all product lines, even though costs might vary with each specific product. In some instances, this practice might have little or no impact on a business's well being; a company that is enjoying record growth and profits on all three of its product lines, for instance, is unlikely to be seriously harmed by accounting practices that evenly divide transportation costs three ways, even though one of the product lines may account for, say, half of the firm's transportation expenses. Huge profits mask such inequities fairly well. But relatively few companies are in such a luxurious position. Most companies—and especially most small businesses, which typically have less margin for error than their larger cousins—need to work hard to arrive at true product costing figures. "As national and global competition increase," wrote Lessner, "even tiny costing disparities can have an overwhelming impact on whether a product—or an entire company, for that matter—survives. . . . Over the long term, product profitability analyses that use these distorted costs cause management to erroneously assume custom products generate better margins than they actually do," and top performing goods end up subsidizing other, less profitable, product lines.

PRODUCT COSTING IN NONMANUFACTURING FIRMS

Although product costing is primarily associated with manufacturing businesses, it also has applications in non-manufacturing industries. "Merchandising companies include the costs of buying and transporting merchandise in their product costs," observed Ronald W. Hilton in *Managerial Accounting*. "Producers of inventoriable goods, such as mining products, petroleum, and agricultural products, also record the costs of producing their goods. The role of product costs in these companies is identical to that in manufacturing firms." Business experts also note that while service-oriented companies (both service businesses and non-profit organizations) do not offer products that can be stored and sold in the manner of manufactured items, they nonetheless need to track the varied costs that they accrue in offering their services. After all, the services that they offer are in essence, their "product" line. "Banks, insurance companies, restaurants, airlines, law firms, hospitals, and city governments all record the costs of producing various services for the purposes of planning, cost control, and decision making," wrote Hilton.

FURTHER READING:

Cavinato, Joseph. "Product Costs From Cradle to Grave." *Chilton's Distribution*. January 1992.

Hilton, Ronald W. *Managerial Accounting*. New York: McGraw-Hill, 1991.

"The Ins and Outs of Target Costing." *Purchasing*. March 12, 1998.

Lessner, John A. "Traps to Avoid in Product Costing." *Journal of Accountancy*. July 1991.

Smith, Richard L., and Janet Kilholm Smith. *Entrepreneurial Finance*. John Wiley, 2000.

Wilson, Frank C. "How Modern is Your Company's Costing System?" *Textile World*. September 1991.

SEE ALSO: Activity-Based Costing; Overhead Costs

PRODUCT DEVELOPMENT

Product development is the process by which a company does one of two things: 1) creates an entirely new product that either adds to an existing product line or occupies an entirely new niche; 2) modifies or updates an existing product. Successful product development is essential for any business if it hopes to exist for any length of time.

IMPORTANCE OF NEW PRODUCT DEVELOPMENT

New products, whether they take the form of new applications, new innovations, or entirely new goods, are an essential component of business success. "Some entire industries are based on effectiveness in [new product development]," wrote George Gruenwald in *New Product Development: Responding to Market Demand*. "Everyone in industry knows that new products are essential for viability: If we do not continue to grow, we die. To grow, a company must continue to learn (research) and to make a difference in its industry (pioneer). . . . Business, whether it sells waste management or interstellar communications, janitorial services or gene-splicing, lives through new growth—not through clones of the past."

What this means is that new products are essential to survival. "Innovate or die" has become a rallying cry at small and large businesses as increasingly savvy consumers demand the newest and the best products. As one entrepreneur in the bicycle manufacturing industry told *Nation's Business*, "At trade shows, the first thing customers say is, 'What's new?' Every year you have to raise the ante. If you were not to do it, you'd be left in the dust." To prove his point, Sinyard admitted in the same article that he must revise the company's 37 products annually (from small changes to complete redesigns) and that fully 50 percent of a line of bike accessories the company also sells is totally replaced by new products each year.

NEW PRODUCT DEVELOPMENT FOR SMALL COMPANIES

As business experts, analysts, executives, and entrepreneurs all know, there is no one way to organize a company for effective new product development. As Gruenwald noted, the ultimate methodology that is chosen "depends on the nature of the corporation and its goals. It depends on the existing structural order of things. It depends on the corporation's management style. It depends on the caliber, motivations, and growth potential of the staff in place at the time of installing the new products organization. It depends on past performance by organizations charged with the responsibility. It depends on the orientation of the corporation, if this is not to change. (Are the present strengths or weaknesses centered in certain areas?).''

Nonetheless, analysts point to several factors that are fairly universal in determining whether a business will enjoy measurable success in new product development efforts. These include fundamentals like comprehensive market and cost analysis, support from top management, enthusiasm among workers, clear lines of authority, and past experience. Other qualities cited by marketing expert Kim Clark in *Industry Week* included focus, adequate resources, and leadership:

Focus. First, a small business needs to focus on its goals. Limited time and resources mean that hard decisions must be made and a strategic plan needs to be developed. Companies should ''do the right things right'' by using the best information available to choose the right technologies and decide on what new products to invest in. Small companies are often growing quickly and can pick and choose among many seemingly strong new product avenues, but the key is to decide what the company does very well and then concentrate on that area or areas.

Selecting the right focus can be a balancing act, however. A company needs to keep both short-term and long-term success in sight and needs to weigh rapid cash generation versus growth, business life cycles, and technology and market capabilities. All of these factors must come into play, and the risks associated with each must always be considered.

Clark notes that one way a company can stay focused is to develop a ''product-line architecture.'' Once a company creates its overall strategy and determines how it will reach its goal, it should map out exactly what product lines it will choose to achieve that goal. ''Product-line architecture tells you how your product line will look, what types of products you will have in what markets, how they will be positioned, and in what sequence they will be introduced.''

Defining a product-line architecture demands that correct decisions be made early in the product development process. Companies should be rigorous and quantitative when coming up with new product specifications or definitions. They should, as much as is possible, precisely define the product qualities and price points that a market will bear. Mistakes made early in the process will often not show up until it is far too late—either at the prototype or final product stage.

Customer feedback is essential at this stage and can eliminate mistakes in focus. As one executive told *Industry Week*, companies should ask themselves a series of questions when creating a new product-line vision: ''How would someone use this product? How would you articulate the benefit to the customer? Is this something a customer can really understand [as to] how it makes their life easier?''

Find the Resources. Another key to new product development for small businesses is to secure the resources and skills needed to create and market the new product. Small companies may lack the in-house resources needed to create a new product, making it seem out of reach, but analysts note that small business owners have other avenues that they can often pursue. If the product idea is good enough, the company may decide to look outside its own walls for partnership and outsourcing opportunities. ''When the need is not within the capability of your company,'' states Gruenwald, ''but beneficial arrangements can be made with other companies to joint-venture, contract-supply, license/acquire, or, in rare instances, to merge. . . . Pools of expertise can also be acquired by recruiting within the subject industry and by the use of technical and marketing consultants.''

One key to resource management is to not undertake too many projects at one time. Every company has a finite amount of resources to allocate to new product development, but small businesses often face especially tight budgets in this regard. And budget in this instance doesn't just mean money—it also means time. Too many projects means otherwise talented workers can't spend enough time on any one project, and as a result, all projects suffer and fall off schedule, leaving gaping openings for competitors or causing market windows to close.

Leadership. The third and final step a small company needs to follow is to find the leadership needed to bring a new product from the idea stage to completed product. This leader will often take the form of a ''product champion'' who can bring both expertise and enthusiasm to the project. (In small business environments, this product champion will often be the entrepreneur/owner himself.) A strong product champion will be able to balance all the issues associated with a product—economic factors, performance requirements, regulatory issues, management issues, and more—and create a winning new product.

The product champion has to guide the project through a predetermined series of viability tests—checkpoints in the development process at which a company evaluates a new product to determine if the product should proceed to the next development stage. If it is determined that the market has shifted, or technology has changed, or the project has become too expensive, then the product must be killed, no matter how much money has already been poured into it. This is where a strong product champion makes the difference—he or she has to have the honesty and authority to make the call to kill the product and convey the reasons for that decision to the product development team. If goals were clearly defined, resources properly allocated, and leadership was strong, then the decision to kill a project should not be a difficult one.

LAUNCHING A NEW PRODUCT

Once the product-line architecture has been established and a new product is being developed, it is time for a company to think about how to successfully launch the product in its target market. This is the stage where an advertising or public relations agency can come into play, especially for small businesses without the internal resources to handle such a job themselves. When using an outside agency to launch a product, a company should:

- Have a well-defined product concept (which is where product-line architecture comes into play).

- Provide the agency with background information on its products and goals.

- Conduct necessary patent research, applying for new patents as needed.

- Have the manufacturing process in place and ready to go, either internally or via outsourcing.

- Have a formal business plan in place that defines funding of the project.

- Determine who will approve the marketing or advertising plan that the agency creates (the fewer people communicating with the agency, the better).

- Determine the proper timing for the launch.

SPEED-TO-MARKET AND PRODUCT DEVELOPMENT

In today's technology-fueled business environment, the always-important speed to market factor has become perhaps the most critical factor in new product development. Today, however, speed to market is perhaps the most crucial part of product development. Improved communication (especially the Internet), increased globalization, and rapid changes in technology have put tremendous pressure on companies to get their product to market first. To improve speed to market, a company should first make sure that it is making the best possible use of available technology. If it is, then there are other steps that can be taken to speed product development through efficient, market-oriented product planning that takes the customer into account:

SERVICE COMPANIES AND NEW PRODUCTS

Service companies should take a disciplined, analytical approach to developing new services, relying on targeted customer input just as companies outside the service sector do. Companies in the service industry know that they are competing for customers based on perceived value as much as actual price. If a customer feels they are getting better treatment, or more service options, or more ''free'' services as part of their purchase, they are more likely to remain a client of that company. If, however, a company stops innovating and adding new services to its core business, then the service becomes a commodity and clients look at only one thing—price—when deciding on what company to choose.

Service companies should routinely ask themselves a series of questions:

- Could current services be presented in a different way?

- Could they be offered to new customer groups?

- Are their little things that can be tweaked to freshen or update a service?

- Could services be improved or changed?

Because by their very nature services are easy to copy (no materials or product knowledge is needed), service companies actually face more pressure to innovate and develop new products than manufacturers. By continually asking the above questions and by following the same models manufacturing companies follow when pursuing product development, service companies can stay ahead of their competitors and make their services clearly identifiable to consumers.

PITFALLS TO PRODUCT DEVELOPMENT

Finally, when embarking on the product development process, try to remember in advance what the obstacles to success are. These pitfalls are many and varied, and can include:

- Inadequate market analysis.

- Inadequate cost analysis.

- Strong competitor reaction.

- Undue infatuation with your company's own technology and expertise.

- Overreaching to make products beyond your company's financial and knowledge grasp.

- Technical staff too attached to a project and too proud to admit defeat, even when a project can not be justified according to preestablished criteria.

- Problems with patent, license, or copyright issues.

- No real criteria for deciding if a project is good or bad.

- Changes in strategy at the corporate level are not conveyed to the product development team.

- Low product awareness.

- Money and staff allocated to a project are hidden in the budget of another project.

- Company decision-makers blinded by the charisma or charm of the person presenting the new product idea.

- Project accepted on the basis of who gets it first.

FURTHER READING:

Berenson, Conrad, and Iris Mohr-Jackson. ''Product Rejuvenation: A Less Risky Alternative to Product Innovation.'' *Business Horizons.* November/December 1994.

De Young, Garrett. ''Listen, Then Design.'' *Industry Week.* Feb. 17, 1997.

Engineering Stages of New Product Development. National Society of Professional Engineers, 1990.

Gruenwald, George. *New Product Development: Responding to Market Demand.* NTC Publishing, 1995.

Henry, Walter, Michael Mesasco, and Hirokazu Takada. *New Product Development and Testing.* Lexington Books, 1989.

Kinni, Theodore B. ''Focus, Leverage, and Leadership.'' *Industry Week.* March 28, 1995.

Maynard, Roberta. ''Launching Your Product.'' *Nation's Business.* August 1995.

Stevens, Tim. ''Balancing Act: Product Development.'' *Industry Week.* March 17, 1997.

SEE ALSO: Prototypes

PRODUCT LIABILITY

Product liability comprises a number of laws and court rulings that apply to any business that makes or sells a product. Businesses that make or sell products are responsible for ensuring that those products are safe and do not pose a hazard to the public. Such businesses can be held liable for any damage or harm their products might cause.

According to Section 102(2) of the Uniform Product Liability Act, product liability includes ''all claims or action brought for personal injury, death, or property damage caused by the manufacture, design, formula, preparation, assembly, installation, testing, warnings, instructions, marketing, packaging, or labeling of any product.'' Product liability issues have become increasingly important to manufacturers and marketing managers, due to the spread of the doctrine of strict liability and the adoption of new theories that permit recovery in so-called ''delayed manifestation'' cases.

Because of their limited resources, small businesses must be particularly aware of their responsibilities under product liability laws. In addition to making safe products, this responsibility extends to prominently displaying warnings of any potential hazards on products and packaging. Experts recommend that small business owners consult with legal counsel experienced in the product liability field. An attorney can help the small business owner sift through the numerous federal and state laws that apply to different types of products. Small businesses are also encouraged to purchase product liability insurance. Unfortunately, the increasing number of lawsuits and large damage awards in this area have made such insurance very expensive and reduced the amount of coverage available. In fact, the expense of insuring against product liability has prevented small manufacturers from competing in certain product areas.

DEVELOPMENT OF PRODUCT LIABILITY LAWS

Product liability began to have meaning in the mid-1800s, when the American courts increasingly found that sellers of goods had a ''duty'' to use reasonable care in the production of those goods. Sellers were held liable to third parties for negligence in the manufacture or sale of goods ''inherently dangerous'' (the danger of injury arises from the product itself, rather than from a defect in the product) to human safety, ranging from food and beverages to drugs, firearms, and explosives. In the early 1960s, tort principles were first applied to product liability. During this time, the concept of ''inherently dangerous'' goods was still held to be significant, but there was a shift to negligence (tort) principles that held that producers of goods were required to apply ''due care'' in the marketing of goods to users.

Since that time, businesses have operated under an understanding that because they knowingly market products which affect the interests of consumers, they owe a legal duty of caution and prudence to consumers. Since manufacturers may foresee potentially harmful product effects, they are responsible for attempting to minimize harm. Establishing this legal duty between the manufacturer and the consumer made it possible for plaintiffs to argue the negligent breach of that duty. These principles are now accepted throughout the country and followed by all American courts. Eventually, the concept of ''inherently dangerous'' products fell into disuse and the concept of negligence was expanded beyond production to include labeling, installation, inspection, and design.

ELEMENTS OF PRODUCT LIABILITY

Four elements must be present for a product liability case to be considered under the negligent tort principles:

- The particular defendant owes a duty to the particular plaintiff to act as a reasonably prudent person under the same or similar circumstances.

- There is a breach of such a duty by the defendant—that is, a failure to act reasonably.

- There is an injury, including personal injury or property damage.

- There is a causal link between defendant's breach of duty and injuries sustained by the plaintiff.

The concept of negligence is applicable to every activity preceding a product's availability in the market. This encompasses everything from product design, the inspection and testing of materials, and the manufacture and assembly of the product to the packaging, the accompanying instructions and warnings, and the inspection and testing of the final product are all susceptible to negligence. Negligence can result from omission as well as commission—failure to discover a flaw is as negligent as creating one. Similarly, failing to provide adequate warnings about potential dangers in the use of a product is a violation of duty.

Still, it is often difficult to prove negligence in product liability cases. Defendants only must meet the general standards of reasonable behavior as judged against the behavior of a reasonably careful competitor who demonstrates the standard skills and expertise of the industry. In reality, a manufacturer must only show that ''ordinary care under the circumstances'' was applied to avoid liability for negligence. This is easy compared to the task of consumers showing evidence to the contrary.

Many products, even the most ordinary, pose some level of risk, and the law recognizes that it is often not possible to design a totally safe product. However, manufacturers are legally obligated to warn consumers about known dangers. Manufacturers may be found negligent if:

- They fail to warn users about recognized risk

- The warning is too vague to be adequate

- The warning is not brought to the user's attention

There is no duty to warn against misuse that is so rare or unusual that it cannot be foreseen. The obligation to warn consumers of potential dangers poses a unique difficulty for manufacturers who must not only provide warnings, but must communicate them such that a reasonable person will find and understand them. In some cases a warning buried in a product's instructions may be judged inadequate; in other situations, a warning sticker on the product itself may be considered sufficient.

STRICT PRODUCT LIABILITY

The most recent evolution in tort law, strict liability, has transformed the very nature of product liability because it eliminates the entire question of negligence. Strict liability only requires a plaintiff to demonstrate that a product caused an injury because it was defective; the reason for the defect is irrelevant. The product itself, not the defendant's use, is under investigation.

Under strict liability, the manufacturer is held liable for allowing a defective product to enter the marketplace. The issue is a matter of public policy, not the manufacturer's unreasonable or negligent conduct. The introduction of a defective product into the marketplace brings each member of the product's distribution channel into liability for negligence. The theory of strict liability holds that manufacturers: have the greatest control over the quality of their products; can distribute their costs by raising prices; and have special responsibilities in their role as sellers.

The tort of negligence at least provided the responsible person a standard by which to measure negligence, although it imposed the added burden of proving that the defendant was negligent. Although strict liability eases those burdens for the plaintiff and improves chances of recovery, it does not provide a universally accepted standard for measuring failure. Instead, it relies on what has become known as the ''consumer-expectation'' test: one who sells any product in a defective condition unreasonably dangerous to the user is subject to liability for physical harm caused to the user if: 1) the seller is engaged in the business of selling such a product, and 2) the product is expected to and does reach the user without substantial change in the condition in which it is used. ''Unreasonably dangerous'' is defined as dangerous beyond the expectations of the ordinary consumer who purchases it. Despite its great influence, this definition has not been universally accepted.

Tort law does recognize that some products beneficial to society cannot be made entirely safe. Prescription drugs and vaccines are notorious examples. Such products are not considered defective simply because of their inevitable hazards; something else must be wrong with them as well. Therefore, drug companies are not held strictly liable for a properly manufactured product accompanied by appropriate directions and warnings. In sum, design defects are not the same as manufacturing defects.

One defense manufacturers have employed with controversy is called "state of the art." This means that manufacturers should be held accountable only for information available to them at the time of manufacture. Flaws or defects which arose due to unavailable knowledge are not considered in questions of liability. The problem interpreting this defense concerns the variation of knowledge and its applications across the country.

FURTHER READING:

Gooden, Randall. "Reduce the Potential Impact of Product Liability on Your Organization." *Quality Progress.* January 1995.

Lane, Marc J. *Legal Handbook for Small Business.* AMACOM, 1989.

Siomkos, George, and Paul Shrivastava. "Responding to Product Liability Crises." *Long Range Planning.* October 1993.

Spiro, George W. *Legal Environment of Business.* Prentice Hall, 1993.

PRODUCT LIFE CYCLE

The theory of a product life cycle was first introduced in the 1950s to explain the expected life cycle of a typical product from design to obsolescence. Writing in *Marketing Tools,* Carole Hedden observed that the cycle is represented by a curve that can be divided into four distinct phases: introduction, growth, maturity, and decline. The goal is to maximize the product's value and profitability at each stage. It is primarily considered a marketing theory.

INTRODUCTION

This is the stage where a product is conceptualized and first brought to market. The goal of any new product introduction is to meet consumer's needs with a quality product at the lowest possible cost in order to return the highest level of profit. The introduction of a new product can be broken down into five distinct parts:

- Idea validation, which is when a company studies a market, looks for areas where needs are not being met by current products, and tries to think of new products that could meet that need. The company's marketing department is responsible for identifying market opportunities and defining who will buy the product, what the primary benefits of the product will be, and how the product will be used.

- Conceptual design occurs when an idea has been approved and begins to take shape. The company has studied available materials, technology, and manufacturing capability and determined that the new product can be created. Once that is done, more thorough specifications are developed, including price and style. Marketing is responsible for minimum and maximum sales estimates, competition review, and market share estimates.

- Specification and design is when the product is nearing release. Final design questions are answered and final product specs are determined so that a prototype can be created.

- Prototype and testing occurs when the first version of a product is created and tested by engineers and by customers. A pilot production run might be made to ensure that engineering decisions made earlier in the process were correct, and to establish quality control. The marketing department is extremely important at this point. It is responsible for developing packaging for the product, conducting the consumer tests through focus groups and other feedback methods, and tracking customer responses to the product.

- Manufacturing ramp-up is the final stage of new product introduction. This is also known as commercialization. This is when the product goes into full production for release to the market. Final checks are made on product reliability and variability.

In the introduction phase, sales may be slow as the company builds awareness of its product among potential customers. Advertising is crucial at this stage, so the marketing budget is often substantial. The type of advertising depends on the product. If the product is intended to reach a mass audience, than an advertising campaign built around one theme may be in order. If a product is specialized, or if a company's resources are limited, than smaller advertising campaigns can be used that target very specific audiences. As a product matures, the advertising budget associated with it will most likely shrink since audiences are already aware of the product.

Author Philip Kotler has found that marketing departments can choose from four strategies at the commercialization stage. The first is known as "rapid skimming." The rapid refers to the speed with which the company recovers its development costs on the product—the strategy calls for the new product to be launched at a high price and high promotion level. High prices mean high initial profits (provided the product is purchased at acceptable levels of course), and high promotion means high market recognition. This works best when the new product is unknown in the marketplace.

The opposite method, "slow skimming," entails releasing the product at high price but with low promotion level. Again, the high price is designed to recover costs quickly, while the low promotion level keeps new costs down. This works best in a market that is made up of few major players or products—the small market means everyone already knows about the product when it is released.

The other two strategies involve low prices. The first is known as rapid penetration and involves low price combined with high promotion. This works best in large markets where competition is strong and consumers are price-conscious. The second is called slow penetration, and involves low price and low promotion. This would work in markets where price was an issue but the market was well-defined.

Besides the above marketing techniques, sales promotion is another important consideration when the product is in the introductory phase. According to Kotler and Armstrong in *Principles of Marketing,* "Sales promotion consists of short-term incentives to encourage purchase or sales of a product or service. Whereas advertising offers reasons to buy a product or service, sales promotion offers reason to buy now." Promotions can include free samples, rebates, and coupons.

GROWTH

The growth phase occurs when a product has survived its introduction and is beginning to be noticed in the marketplace. At this stage, a company can decide if it wants to go for increased market share or increased profitability. This is the boom time for any product. Production increases, leading to lower unit costs. Sales momentum builds as advertising campaigns target mass media audiences instead of specialized markets (if the product merits this). Competition grows as awareness of the product builds. Minor changes are made as more feedback is gathered or as new markets are targeted. The goal for any company is to stay in this phase as long as possible.

It is possible that the product will not succeed at this stage and move immediately past decline and straight to cancellation. That is a call the marketing staff has to make. It needs to evaluate just what costs the company can bear and what the product's chances for survival are. Tough choices need to be made—sticking with a losing product can be disastrous.

If the product is doing well and killing it is out of the question, then the marketing department has other responsibilities. Instead of just building awareness of the product, the goal is to build brand loyalty by adding first-time buyers and retaining repeat buyers. Sales, discounts, and advertising all play an important role in that process. For products that are well-established and further along in the growth phase, marketing options include creating variations of the initial product that appeal to additional audiences.

MATURITY

At the maturity stage, sales growth has started to slow and is approaching the point where the inevitable decline will begin. Defending market share becomes the chief concern, as marketing staffs have to spend more and more on promotion to entice customers to buy the product. Additionally, more competitors have stepped forward to challenge the product at this stage, some of which may offer a higher quality version of the product at a lower price. This can touch off price wars, and lower prices mean lower profits, which will cause some companies to drop out of the market for that product altogether. The maturity stage is usually the longest of the four life cycle stages, and it is not uncommon for a product to be in the mature stage for several decades.

A savvy company will seek to lower unit costs as much as possible at the maturity stage so that profits can be maximized. The money earned from the mature products should then be used in research and development to come up with new product ideas to replace the maturing products. Operations should be streamlined, cost efficiencies sought, and hard decisions made.

From a marketing standpoint, experts argue that the right promotion can make more of an impact at this stage than at any other. One popular theory postulates that there are two primary marketing strategies to utilize at this stage—offensive and defensive. Defensive strategies consist of special sales, promotions, cosmetic product changes, and other means of shoring up market share. It can also mean quite literally defending the quality and integrity of your product versus your competition. Marketing offensively means looking beyond current markets and attempting to gain brand new buyers. Relaunching the product is one option. Other offensive tactics include changing the price of a product (either higher or lower) to appeal to an entirely new audience or finding new applications for a product.

DECLINE

This occurs when the product peaks in the maturity stage and then begins a downward slide in sales. Eventually, revenues will drop to the point where it is no longer economically feasible to continue making the product. Investment is minimized. The product can simply be discontinued, or it can be sold to another company. A third option that combines those elements is also sometimes seen as viable, but comes to fruition only rarely. Under this scenario, the product is discontinued and stock is allowed to dwindle to zero, but the company sells the rights to supporting the product to another company, which then becomes responsible for servicing and maintaining the product.

PROBLEMS WITH THE PRODUCT LIFE CYCLE THEORY

While the product life cycle theory is widely accepted, it does have critics who say that the theory has so many exceptions and so few rules that it is meaningless. Among the holes in the theory that these critics highlight:

- There is no set amount of time that a product must stay in any stage; each product is different and moves through the stages at different times. Also, the four stages are not the same time period in length, which is often overlooked.

- There is no real proof that all products must die. Some products have been seen to go from maturity back to a period of rapid growth thanks to some improvement or redesign. Some argue that by saying in advance that a product must reach the end of life stage, it becomes a self-fulfilling prophecy that companies subscribe to. Critics say that some businesses interpret the first downturn in sales to mean that a product has reached decline and should be killed, thus terminating some still-viable products prematurely.

- The theory can lead to an over-emphasis on new product releases at the expense of mature products, when in fact the greater profits could possibly be derived from the mature product if a little work was done on revamping the product.

- The theory emphasizes individual products instead of taking larger brands into account.

- The theory does not adequately account for product redesign and/or reinvention.

FURTHER READING:

Grantham, Lisa Michelle. "The Validity of the Product Life Cycle in the High-tech Industry." *Marketing Intelligence and Planning.* June 1997.

Gruenwald, George. *New Product Development: Responding to Market Demand.* NTC Business, 1995.

Hedden, Carole. "From Launch to Relaunch: The Secret to Product Longevity Lies in Using the Right Strategy for Each Stage of the Life Cycle." *Marketing Tools.* September 1997.

Rink, David R., Dianne M. Roden, and Harold W. Fox. "Financial Management and Planning with the Product Life Cycle Concept." *Business Horizons.* September 1999.

Ryan, Chuck, and Walter E. Riggs. "Redefining the Product Life Cycle: the Five-Element Product Wave." *Business Horizons.* September/October 1996.

PRODUCT POSITIONING

Product positioning involves tailoring an entire marketing program—including product attributes, image, and price, as well as packaging, distribution, and service—to best meet the needs of consumers within a particular market segment. In this way, product positioning is part of the overall process of market segmentation, but involves a narrowing of focus. "Segmentation analysis tells us how the market is defined and allows us to target one or more opportunities," Glen L. Urban and Steven H. Star wrote in their book *Advanced Marketing Strategy.* "Product positioning takes place within a target market segment and tells us how we can compete most effectively in that market segment."

The key to product positioning is understanding the dimensions consumers use to evaluate competing marketing programs and make purchase decisions. It may be helpful for small business managers to create a graph in order to map consumer perceptions along several different dimensions. Once consumer perceptions are understood, the next step is to select the best positioning for the product and take steps to align the marketing program behind this positioning choice. Some examples of possible positioning choices include quality, reliability, and unique features or benefits. Before delving into product positioning further, it may be helpful to understand the process and goals of market segmentation.

MARKET SEGMENTATION

Market segmentation is the science of dividing an overall market into key customer subsets, or segments, whose members share similar characteristics and needs. Because it involves significant market research, market segmentation can be costly. But it is particularly important for small businesses, which often lack the resources to target large aggregate markets or to maintain a wide range of differentiated products for varied markets. Market segmentation allows a small business to develop a product and a marketing mix that fit a relatively homogenous part of the total market. By focusing its resources on a specific customer base in this way, a small business may be able to carve out a market niche that it can serve better than its larger competitors.

In general, customers are willing to pay a premium for a product that meets their needs more specifically than does a competing product. Thus marketers who successfully segment the overall market and adapt their products to the needs of one or more smaller segments stand to gain in terms of increased profit margins and reduced competitive pressures. But the potential gains offered by market segmentation must be measured against the costs, which—in addition to the market research required to segment a market—may include increased production and marketing expenses.

In their book *The Portable MBA in Marketing,* Alexander Hiam and Charles D. Schewe identified six steps that companies should take in the market segmentation process. The first step is to determine the boundaries of the market. In completing this step, a marketer should use a formal business plan to develop a broad definition of their business, and then consider the offerings of both direct and indirect competitors to gain information about the basic needs of consumers in the market. The second step in the process is to decide which variables to use in segmenting the market. Many companies fall into the trap of collecting data on as many variables as possible and then attempting to sort through it later to draw meaningful conclusions. Instead, Hiam and Schewe recommend that marketers use their knowledge of the market to select a few relevant variables in advance. This approach is generally less expensive and will likely provide more useful results.

The third step in the market segmentation process is actually collecting and analyzing data, which involves applying market research tools. The goal in analyzing the data is to identify market segments that are internally homogeneous, yet are distinctly heterogeneous with respect to other segments. The fourth step is to develop a detailed profile of each market segment, which involves selecting those variables that are most closely related to consumers' actual buying behavior.

The fifth step in the market segmentation process is to decide which segment or segments to serve. In targeting a particular segment, a marketer should look for opportunities (i.e., customers with unsatisfied wants and needs) that provide a good match for the organization and its resources. It is important that the marketer consider not only the size and potential profitability of a market segment, but also whether the company's skills, technologies, and objectives would enable it to meet the needs of that segment better than its competitors.

UNDERSTANDING CONSUMER PERCEPTIONS

Product positioning—which is the sixth and final step in the market segmentation process—involves developing a product and marketing plan that will appeal to the selected market segment. In order to position a product effectively, a small business must identify the attributes that are most important to consumers in the segment, and then develop an overall marketing strategy that will attract consumers' attention. Positioning can be usefully applied during the earliest stages of product design, when a company first identifies who its target customer will be in terms of demographic, geographic, and behavioral characteristics.

A number of tools exist to help marketers understand the consumer perceptions that underlie purchase decisions. One such tool, a perceptual map, is a graph that can portray various product positioning options in a visual manner. Marketers can create perceptual maps from market research data in order to identify consumer needs that are not being fulfilled. For example, say that consumers were asked to rate home computers on the following attributes: 1) ease of use, 2) availability of service, 3) processing speed, and 4) data storage capacity. These four attributes could be combined into two perceptual dimensions: 1) utility (consisting of ease of use and availability of service), which would appeal to non-experts who needed a basic computer for business or personal use; and 2) technical (consisting of processing speed and storage capacity), which would appeal to experienced computer users who wanted the latest in technology. Then each brand of home computer could be represented on the graph according to consumers' perceptions of the product. If most computer manufacturers touted their products' technical attributes, there might be an opportunity for a new market entrant who emphasized ease of use and service.

However, it is also important to understand the relative importance that consumers place upon the different dimensions. In the home computer market, for example, consumers ultimately want both utility and technical characteristics, but vary in the importance they place upon each product dimension. "The implications of these importances for positioning are significant," according to Urban and Star. "It is necessary to understand preference differences within the targeted market segments because they are important in selecting a position for a brand and in determining the competitive structure within the segment. When preferences vary within a segment, positions and physical product features may vary considerably. If preferences are relatively homogeneous within a segment, the positions of competing brands will be relatively similar, and the quantity of advertising and promotion will be the critical competitive weapons."

It is also important to note that price is not represented in the home computer perceptual map, whereas price definitely has an effect on the final purchase decision made by consumers. Marketers can reflect the importance of price by adding a dimension to the perceptual map, so that it becomes a cube, or by dividing the dimensional coordinates of each brand by its average price. The resulting map would show "utility per dollar" and "technical attributes per dollar," or the tradeoffs consumers make between the original dimensions and price. Finally, small business owners need to consider the fact that perceptual maps show "overall dimensions of evaluation and not detailed features," as Urban and Star noted. "Feature selection is critical in positioning, however, because features are an important determinant of overall perception and choice." In fact, product features influence both consumer perceptions and product pricing.

POSITIONING OPTIONS

Once marketers have mapped consumer perceptions of competing brands and gained an understanding of the target segment, the next step is to select a position for their products. In positioning a product within a market segment, marketers should try to maximize the share of consumer choices attained by their product in order to achieve long-run profitability for the firm. Strategies that can help marketers to maximize share include adding features desired by consumers or advertising to improve consumer perceptions. Both of these strategies can be costly, however, so it is important for companies to balance the cost of making such expenditures with the payoff.

Marketers have several different positioning options available to them. One positioning option is quality emphasis, which includes not only defect-free production but also product design and customer service that meets or exceeds customer expectations. Another positioning option available to marketers involves offering unique features or benefits that consumers are unable to find in competing products, from environmentally-friendly production aspects to trendiness. Ideally, such features and benefits grow out of the company's unique sources of competitive advantage in the marketplace. This makes it difficult for competitors to match the features and benefits without incurring high costs. "If we develop a unique competitive advantage on a dimension of importance to a significant portion of the market, we can enjoy a substantial share and high margins," Urban and Star noted. Of course, continued market research and innovation are necessary to maintain such a competitive advantage.

In some cases, rather than selecting a product position within the accepted structure of a market segment, a company may instead try to create a new dimension of importance to consumers. But creating a new dimension is difficult and usually results from major product innovations. Another option available to marketers is to position products across different, yet overlapping, market segments. It is important to note, however, that since some consumers may belong to both segments, positioning claims for a product should never conflict. To avoid confusing consumers, it may be necessary to use a different brand name for the product in each segment, or to make a broad appeal to both segments and then change the positioning slightly within each segment.

FURTHER READING:

Gruenwald, George. *New Product Development: Responding to Market Demand.* NTC Publishing, 1995.

Hiam, Alexander, and Charles D. Schewe. *The Portable MBA in Marketing.* Wiley, 1992.

McCarthy, E. Jerome, and William D. Perreault, Jr. *Basic Marketing.* Irwin, 1990.

Urban, Glen L., and Steven H. Star. *Advanced Marketing Strategy.* Prentice Hall, 1991.

PRODUCTIVITY

In the simplest terms, productivity is the ratio between the quantity of goods and services produced and the quantity of resources used to produce them. Economists have come up with a number of intricate ways to measure productivity, but any business owner knows that if he or she is producing more of a product with the same number of resources, productivity has gone up. Of course, the opposite is true if fewer products are being produced.

Worker productivity is one of the key issues for any business, but for small businesses with limited resources, getting the most out of the least is an essential element in establishing and maintaining competitiveness. Small businesses need to have tools in place to measure productivity and must combine increased productivity with a commitment to quality and efficiency. Innovative goal setting, planning, and organizing are essential to improving productivity. Some of the major threats to productivity, as cited in *Industrial Management,* include an ineffective use of technology and lack of worker training and support, in addition to "an aging workforce, a declining labor supply, a lack of qualified workers, and rising wage and benefit costs."

STEPS IN MEASURING AND INCREASING PRODUCTIVITY

The first step in improving productivity is putting meaningful methodologies of measurement in place to evaluate and monitor the performance of a business operation. To be meaningful, productivity measurements must show a linkage with profitability; after all, it is the bottom line that is the ultimate barometer of a company's success. Measurements should clearly demonstrate how efficiently (or inefficiently) a company is using its resources to produce quality goods and services.

In the past, productivity was a stand-alone issue—a company could either improve it, or it could not. For most small businesses, increasing productivity has meant one thing—improving the output rate. When this is the only goal, improving quality is seen as a very expensive proposition that does nothing to boost output. In other words, improved quality and increased output are seen as mutually exclusive ideas. This way of thinking is a mistake. In fact, small business owners need to realize that just the opposite is true. An increase in quality most often results in lower costs as rework is eliminated and unnecessary inspections are eliminated. Improved quality should be seen as a strategic tool that can increase efficiency by improving resource utilization and increasing customer satisfaction while lowering costs.

Another tool to increase productivity is to improve communications between workers and management. This may be easier in a small firm than a large one since the total number of employees is lower. Managers must sell employees on their obligation to make things work better at the company, both in the work environment and the work product. By gathering input from more and more workers, that job can be made easier.

A business owner or CEO can begin gathering input from workers by starting at the top and letting the process filter down. Off-site retreats with top managers to discuss the company's values and goals are a good place to start. From there, those values and goals can be communicated to the whole work force at the same time it is conveyed to them that their input matters and that direct communication is valued throughout the organization. If something goes wrong, any employee should feel safe in stepping forward and identifying the problem without fear of reprisals. If one person has a conflict with another employee, they should be encouraged to go directly to that other person instead of ignoring the problem or complaining about it to people who cannot solve it. A high-level manager, or even the CEO or owner, can step in to solve disputes if there is still a conflict after communications have been initiated.

This improved and open communication eases tension in the workplace and fosters a cooperative, growth-oriented atmosphere. Employees feel that their problems will be listened to and that their suggestions will be taken seriously, which means they are more likely to work harder and to think creatively when initiating production improvements.

Improved communication can also lead to another step known to enhance productivity in small businesses—enabling the work force. Once communication channels are open, upper management may find that employees are as committed to improving the business as they are. They also realize that front-line employees are quite often the best source of ideas on how to improve productivity and the best source for implementing those ideas. In small businesses, employees are often forced to perform a greater variety of tasks than employees at large firms—it is up to small business owners to take advantage of that fact by empowering employees. As Jay Nathan observed in the *Review of Business,* ''empowerment in the small business environment enables employees and management to learn and implement new ways of working, thus improving business operations for increased profits and productivity.''

True empowerment also requires employers to provide their workers with the skills and knowledge to perform their jobs, as well as the unquestioned support of management. Upper management must provide ongoing training and skills development, while managers should act as coaches and leaders who make needed resources available. Finally, a mutual trust and caring must develop between associates and managers—such trust is essential if positive changes are to occur.

INCREASED PRODUCTIVITY THROUGH INCENTIVES

Another way to get employees to work harder and improve productivity is to let them share in any gains that result from the productivity improvements. Pay-for-performance bonus systems, or gain sharing, became a popular incentive in the 1990s with both large and small businesses. For example, one restaurant in Ohio offered to pay cash incentives to all employees if food costs dropped below 35 percent of total sales. The very first month, employees offered up several money-saving suggestions that resulted in a 1.7 percent drop in food costs and a $40 payout to everyone on staff. Payouts since then have gone as high as $95; in the two months where results did not meet the 35 percent goal, no payouts were made.

Gain sharing, and programs like it, have become successful because they increase employee awareness of the company's bottom line and their ability to have an impact on the firm's financial fortunes. From the employer's standpoint, gain sharing is a "win-win" proposition since employees work harder, feel more committed to the business, and profits (or some other measurable goal) improve.

How does a small business institute a gain-sharing program? First, keep things simple. Pick no more than five key business indicators that are important to the business's success. For example, a sales staff might focus on account growth, market penetration, and customer retention. Selecting more than five objectives complicates the issue and makes it harder for employees to understand. Likewise, it is important to select objectives that the employees have direct control over. Meeting goals that require actions outside their sphere of influence demoralizes employees and makes it far less likely that any improvements will be seen. The plan should be written in language that is easy to understand, with the bottom line goal clearly stated.

Once goals are determined, they have to be measured. Choose a realistic means of measuring progress, and, more importantly, choose realistic goals and performance targets that can be reached through productivity improvements. Employees have no problem spotting and ignoring unrealistic goals that they know they have no hopes of attaining. Goals should be both short-term (monthly) and long-range (annual). Also, it is important to note that goals will almost certainly change over time as employees become more efficient and meet the original goals.

Communication is an important part of the gain sharing process. Once management starts measuring productivity, it needs to share the data it gathers with employees so they can see the progress (or lack thereof) being made. This step—sharing financial or production data that was once considered confidential— might be new for many companies, but it must occur so that employees can make good decisions and sharpen their problem-solving skills. Communication should continue throughout the life of the program; business consultants counsel clients to use tools such as newsletters or memos to tell employees about success stories throughout the company. This lets employees know that their actions matter and provides other employees with examples of how to make improvements. Very visible means of communication such as large charts tracking progress against the goal are also very effective.

In addition to sharing information, management must enable employees to make decisions and act on them without too many layers of approval. Employees are the best source of ideas for improving productivity, and making them feel that they are in control of the program is a key part of making it work. Employees are sure to rebel against any program that they feel is being forced on them by upper management or by an outside consulting firm. One of the best ways to ensure employee buy-in is to form a cross-functional group made up of employees from throughout the company to help design and administer the plan.

Eventually, each department should come up with its own set of goals, but the initial plan must be a company-wide one with a big picture goal. Once that goal is stated, each department can look at its own operations and come up with a set of smaller goals that are all designed to help meet the larger goal. Departments should not set their smaller goals in a vacuum—quite often, the performance of one department is directly dependent on the performance of another department, so it is important that those two departments work together in establishing goals.

Once all the goals are set, the reward needs to be determined. The biggest caution that experts offer is to make sure the reward is worth the employee's efforts. If the incentive is too small, the plan might fail because employees simply do not care if they make the improvements needed to get what they view as inconsequential rewards. Experts recommend that employees be able to earn between four and eight percent of their annual salary as a reward for meeting gain sharing goals. Rewards can be paid as an increase in annual salary, or as a one-time bonus.

It should be noted that gain sharing can be an especially successful tool for a small business that is about to grow beyond the owner-several employee stage. When the company consists of the owner and just a few employees, the owner can control all operations and can rewards employees as he or she sees fit. As the company grows and is split into departments with managers who report to the owner, control is decentralized. The owner may step away from the day-to-day managerial responsibilities and therefore lose touch with the workflow. It is at that point that gain sharing can be an important tool to pull employees together and keep them working towards a common goal.

Finally, one note of caution about gain sharing or incentive based pay. Managers must make sure that employees do not become so focused on the targets needed to achieve gain sharing that they neglect other parts of their work or let quality slip. This is the most common criticism of gain sharing, and it is one of the most important reasons that short-term goals must be combined with long-range goals if the plan is to work. That way, workers will be able to see that if they commit too much effort to the short-term goal, the long-term goal may be lost.

USING TECHNOLOGY TO IMPROVE PRODUCTIVITY

From the time of the first factory, using machines to assist or even replace humans and improve productivity has been the norm. Using machines to create interchangeable parts, the creation of the assembly line, the use of robots to take over manual tasks—these are just a few of the dramatic improvements in productivity that came about as a result of technology. Today, that practice continues unabated. The giant leaps made in computer and robotic technology in the last decade have given business owners tremendous new options for improving productivity.

What is different about this wave of better productivity through technology is that it is directly impacting small businesses. In the past, leaps in technological know-how most often benefited large corporations that had the money to invest in expensive new systems. Today, when the most inexpensive laptop computer is more powerful than some of the behemoth mainframe computers that existed in the 1960s, even the smallest business can afford to take advantage of technology to make his or her business grow. Computers, voice mail, fax machines, e-mail—most people today would not dream of starting a business without these technological aids by their side.

Computers and other advances have simply let small businesses get more done in less time—the very essence of increased productivity. Examples of technological gains include database management software that make it easy to manage inventory, fax-back and e-mail services used by customer service departments to disseminate information that previously had to go through the mail, bar-coding technology that can be used to track customer purchases in a computer database that automatically sends a message to reorder a particular product when in-stock levels drop below a preset point, and "home pages" on the World Wide Web that allow small companies to go global for very little cost.

All of the above are examples of how technology was used to help a company grow; technology can also increase productivity and cut expenses by helping a company "stay small" in other areas. For example, instead of having to outsource bookkeeping operations or hire more customer support people, a small business can now look to computers (easy-to-use accounting software, for example) and communications technology to register significant savings in both time and money.

Communications tools, in fact, are the next wave of technology. Desktop videoconferencing, company intranets which can be linked to manufacturers and suppliers, paging and wireless communications—all are expected to explode in use in the coming years. At the center of this boom is the Internet. Even the smallest businesses are able to use the Internet to communicate with customers and suppliers, sell products, and advertise to both local and international audiences. Business-to-business communications have also increased as the Internet has expanded, making it easier for small firms to find partners to do business with.

While almost everyone concedes that small businesses must invest in technology to compete, there are still complaints about technology. The two most common are that it is still too expensive in many areas, and thus out of reach to many business owners. The second is that it is still too complicated and difficult to learn. The computer industry seems to be taking this complaint seriously and developing a new wave of "plug and play" products that are easy to install and easy to use. Computer networks designed just for small businesses are being marketed that have fewer bells and whistles, fewer set-up requirements, and more customized software.

FURTHER READING:

Aboganda, Wilfredo M. "Productivity Measurement Methodology." *Industrial Engineering.* November 1994.

Ibielski, Dieter. "So What About Small Business Productivity?" *National Productivity Review.* Winter 1997.

Livingston, Abby. "Gain-Sharing Encourages Productivity." *Nation's Business.* January 1998.

Longenecker, Clinton O., Deborah J. Dwyer, and Timothy C. Stansfield. "Barriers and Gateways to Workforce Productivity." *Industrial Management.* March-April 1998.

Maynard, Roberta. "Tapping Employee's Insights to Expand Productivity." *Nation's Business.* November 1996.

Nathan, Jay. "Empowerment As a Workplace Strategy in Small Business." *Review of Business.* Winter 1993.

Page, Heather. "Wired for Success: Entrepreneurs Reap the Rewards of the Technology Revolution." *Entrepreneur.* May 1997.

Parry, Thomas, and Phil Lacy. "Promoting Productivity and Workforce Effectiveness." *Financial Executive.* November 2000.

Wrennall, William. "Productivity: Reengineering for Competitiveness." *Industrial Engineering.* December 1994.

PROFESSIONAL CORPORATIONS

A professional corporation is a variation of the corporate form of business organization that is available to entrepreneurs who provide professional services—such as doctors, lawyers, accountants, consultants, and architects. "Professionals," Frederick W. Dailey explained in his book *Tax Savvy for Small Business,* "are treated as small businesses under the tax code. Most of them operate as sole proprietorships or partnerships, and are subject to the same tax rules as other similar businesses. However, certain professionals who offer services may form and operate a special type of entity, called a professional corporation.'' Some states require professionals to form this type of entity if they wish to incorporate. In a professional corporation, the owners perform services for the business as employees.

The first laws that permitted the formation of professional corporations were intended to give professionals some of the tax advantages enjoyed by corporations without also giving them the benefit of limited liability. If a regular corporation—which is a distinct entity under the law—becomes insolvent, its creditors can only claim business assets for the repayment of debts, not the personal assets of its owners. This is in contrast to regular proprietorships and partnerships, which are not legally distinct from their owners or partners. Since personal responsibility is a key factor in being a professional, the law could not allow professionals to escape liability for their own actions by incorporating. The lines between different forms of business organization have been blurred in recent years, however, as more tax advantages have become available to sole proprietorships and partnerships, and more limited liability has been granted to professional corporations.

PERSONAL SERVICE CORPORATIONS

Most professional corporations qualify as personal service corporations (PSC) for federal tax purposes, provided that they also qualify under state law. To qualify as a PSC under Internal Revenue Service (IRS) rules, a professional corporation must be organized under state law and then pass two federal tests: the function test and the ownership test. The function test requires that substantially all (95 percent) of the business activities of the professional corporation involve services within specific occupations in the fields of health, law, engineering, accounting, actuarial science, consulting, or performing arts. The ownership test requires that substantially all the professional corporation's outstanding stock be held directly or indirectly by qualified people, either: 1) employees who are currently performing professional services for the corporation; 2) retired employees who did so prior to their retirement; 3) or their heirs or estates. If a professional corporation organized under state law does not qualify as a PSC, then it is treated as a general partnership for federal tax purposes.

PSCs are taxed like regular C corporations, but with a flat corporate tax rate of 35 percent rather than a graduated rate depending on the level of income earned. The PSC files a corporate tax return and also issues Form K-1 to all shareholder/employees to show their individual shares of the corporation's profit or loss. Any income that is retained in the PSC is subject to the corporate tax rate, while any salaries paid to employees are considered tax-deductible business expenses. Like most small corporations, however, PSCs are likely to pay out all business income to shareholders in the form of salaries, bonuses, and fringe benefits, thus reducing corporate taxable income to zero. Of course, the shareholder/employees still must pay personal income taxes on the income they receive.

ADVANTAGES AND DISADVANTAGES

Organizing as a professional corporation offers many potential advantages to qualified small business owners. Some of the primary advantages involve tax breaks that are not available to unincorporated businesses. For example, professional corporations can create retirement plans and 401(k) plans for their employees that have higher contribution limits than plans available to individuals or unincorporated businesses. In addition, professional corporations can provide health and life insurance as a tax-free benefit to their employees by establishing a Voluntary Employees' Beneficiary Association (VEBA). They can also take tax deductions for disability insurance, dependent care, and other fringe benefits provided to employees. In most cases, such benefits are tax-deductible for the corporation, and also are not considered taxable income for the employees.

Another advantage available to professional corporations is perpetual existence. Unlike sole proprietorships and partnerships—which legally dissolve when an owner dies or leaves the company—professional corporations can continue operations without interruption if a shareholder/employee dies or withdraws. Another advantage is that professional corporations may enable shareholder/employees to avoid personal liability for another employee's negligence. In most cases, one owner is liable for another's actions only if he or she would have been liable as a shareholder of a regular corporation. In contrast, all members of a regular partnership are exposed to personal liability.

There are also a few potential disadvantages associated with the professional corporation form of organization. For example, passive loss limitations may apply that restrict the amount nonactive shareholders can deduct for tax purposes in the event of business losses. In the case of a partnership, all partners are able to deduct their share of business losses from their personal taxable income. Since most professional corporations have only active shareholders and do not experience losses, however, this tax liability is not usually an issue. The flat corporate tax rate that applies to professional corporations may be another source of disadvantage. Retaining earnings within the business will rarely make sense due to the higher tax bracket, and this may reduce the firm's flexibility in distributing income to shareholder/employees. In contrast, most regular corporations can "split income"—or adjust the amount paid out to shareholder/employees—so that both the company and the individual can gain the most favorable tax bracket possible.

CHOOSING AMONG THE ALTERNATIVES

Many states now provide professionals with several options about how to organize their businesses. The main alternatives to forming a professional corporation or personal service corporation include organizing as a limited liability company (LLC) or as a limited liability partnership (LLP). These options differ in the costs and tax benefits involved, as well as in the amount of liability protection afforded. For example, limited liability companies combine the liability protection afforded by professional corporations with the taxation flexibility provided by partnerships. LLCs are taxed similar to S corporations, so the income flows through to the shareholder/employees rather than accruing to the business and then being distributed to owners and employees. Limited liability partnerships are similar to regular partnerships except that they provide additional protection for partnership assets against malpractice suits. However, the partners in an LLP are required to carry hefty insurance or guarantee deposits in exchange for this protection.

The main advantages of organizing as a professional corporation, as outlined above, include tax benefits and transferability of ownership. However, the flat corporate tax rate prevents shareholder/employees from retaining earnings in the professional corporation, which may limit opportunities for expansion and growth. In addition, professional corporation owners may face the problem of double taxation upon liquidation of the business. Income from the sale of real estate or equipment might accrue to the business, for example, where it would be taxed at the corporate rate. If this income were then distributed to shareholders as dividends (since the company was no longer in business and thus could not pay it out as salaries and benefits to employees), then it would be subject to taxation again as personal income.

According to Roberta Schmalz in an article for *Outlook,* a professional or group of professionals should choose the type of business organization best for them by considering the following criteria:

- Which type of organization costs the least to form?

- Which type provides the best tax results?

- Which type offers the best liability protection?

- Which type is best suited for multi-state operations (if applicable)?

- And finally, which type is best for the professionals and their clients?

Of course, state laws differ regarding the types of business organizations that are available to professionals, so it is important to consult with an accountant familiar with the states in which the company will do business.

FURTHER READING:

Dailey, Frederick W. *Tax Savvy for Small Business: Year-Round Tax Advice for Small Businesses.* Nolo Press, 1997.

Malamud, Richard B. "In Search of a Definition of a Personal Service Corporation." *Tax Notes.* May 26, 1997.

Samelson, Donald P., Gary M. Cavett, and James W. Clifton. "Choosing the Form of Business for Professionals." *Taxation for Accountants.* January 1995.

Schmalz, Roberta. "PC, LLC, or LP? The Choice Is Yours." *Outlook.* Fall 1995.

Schutzer, A.I. "Blunders That Can Sink Your Professional Corporation." *Medical Economics.* April 10, 1995.

PROFIT CENTER

A profit center is a unit of a company that generates revenue in excess of its expenses. It is expected that, through the sale of goods or services, the unit will turn a profit. This is in contrast to a cost center, which is a unit inside a company that generates expenses with no responsibility for creating revenue. The only expectation a cost center has is to lower expenses whenever possible while staying with a specific budget that is determined at the corporate level.

Beyond that simple definition, the term "profit center" has also come to represent a form of management accounting that is organized around the profit center concept. Companies that have adopted the profit center system have organized all of their business units as either profit centers or cost centers, and all company financial results are reported in that manner. Adopting a profit center system often requires a radical shift in corporate philosophy and culture, but it can yield great returns in net before tax (NBT) profits. According to an article in *Business Solutions,* the data collection company Data Recognition, Inc. made the shift to a profit center-based system and was pleased with the results. "We saw the importance of evaluating, individually, areas of our business that are distinctly different," said Steve Terry, the company's vice president of systems. "The profit centers have allowed us to better identify specific gains and losses. And that's critically important for a growing business."

All companies, no matter what size, have both cost and profit centers (although, if it is a single-person company, that company would really have profit and cost activities, since all business "units" are the same person). For example, in most companies, units such as human resources and purchasing are strictly cost centers. The company has to spend money to operate those units, and neither has any means of producing a profit to offset those expenses. They exist solely to make it possible for other areas of the company to make money. However, without those two departments, the company could not survive. Examples of profit centers would be the manufacturing units that produce products for sale to consumers or other businesses. The sale of those products generates a profit that offsets the expense of creating the products.

All companies have profit centers and cost centers, but not all companies organize their accounting practices around the profit center concept. In fact, most companies do things the time-honored way, producing overall profit and loss statements for the company as a whole, without making each business unit accountable for generating a profit.

TURNING A COST CENTER INTO A PROFIT CENTER

A cost center may actually provide services that could generate a profit if they were offered on the open market. But in most corporate environments, cost centers are not expected to generate a profit and operation costs are treated as overhead. Departments that are typically cost centers include information technology, human resources, accounting, and others. However, the complacent acceptance that some departments will always be cost centers and can never generate a profit has changed at some companies. They recognize that cost centers can turn into profit centers by taking the services they used to automatically provide to the company's other business units and making those services available for a fee. The company's other business units are then required to pay for the services they used to get for free. But in return, they are allowed to go outside the company and contract with another firm to provide those services. Likewise, the former cost center may be allowed to sell its services to other companies. The expectation is that this free market system will improve performance through increased competition while increasing profits by turning former cost centers into profit centers.

"When a business firm becomes a corporate community of entrepreneurs who buy, sell, and launch new products and services internally as well as externally, it gains the same creative interplay that makes market economies so advantageous," said management professor William E. Halal when discussing making the move to profit center-based operations in *USA Today Magazine.*

As an example of how a cost center may be turned into a profit center, consider a company's information technology (IT) department. This department may provide such services as computer-aided design, network administration, or database development to other units of the company. These services have value, and they are important to the company's overall success, but they do not generate a profit. IT may charge the "cost" of its services back to the department that requested them, but it does not make a profit because it charges only for its actual costs incurred, without adding an extra margin for profit. The unit that requested the services absorbs the cost as part of its overhead; or, in some companies, the cost is not charged back and is simply part of the company's overall overhead.

There are two ways that the IT department could make the switch from cost center to profit center. First, instead of writing off its services to overhead or charging them at cost, the IT department could be allowed to bill other departments for its services at going market rates. The profit earned for the services would exceed the cost of providing the services. While all the money in this transaction would stay within the company, thus making it seem to be a meaningless way of creating a profit for the IT department, it is done for two reasons. One is to ensure that the IT department remains competitive with outside vendors providing the same services, and the other is to ensure that the company's other business units do not waste money on needless IT expenditures. Paying competitive market rates prevents the operating units from wasting money, thus making them more competitive.

If the IT department is turned into that type of profit center, it is considered to be a "zero profit center." In that situation, the department is expected to compete with outside vendors for the company's information technology budget. If a division of the company selects the IT department as its technology provider, it has done so because it feels it cannot purchase the same quality services for a lower price from an outside vendor. It will not actually "pay" the IT department for its services, but it will be charged by the IT department for services rendered, and those charges will be subtracted from the division's budget. Thus, the IT department does not really take in any revenue, but neither does it cost the company any money because the division that utilized its services would have had to spend money to hire an outside vendor. This, then, creates a zero profit center. Such a business model forces the IT department to be more competitive in its pricing and to provide high quality work if it hopes to survive as an operating unit.

The second way the IT department could become a profit center is if the company determined that the department was one of the best in the industry, better in fact than some companies that existed just to provide IT services. The company could then allow the department the freedom to sell its services to outside customers. Thus, the department would still operate as a cost center in its dealings with other units inside the company, but it would operate as a profit center when it provided services to outside companies. This method of operation has become far more common in the 1990s and beyond, as companies seek new revenue streams that have low start-up costs.

If the IT department exists only as a cost center, it faces enormous pressure to provide services at the lowest possible costs. Because it does not generate profits, it must constantly fight to remain in existence and must fight off attempts to slash its budget to free up cash for the company's profit centers. Just as the company's senior management could decide that the IT department was good enough to operate as a profit center by soliciting outside clients, so too could it decide that the department is behind the times and is not providing adequate services. This would result in management choosing to shut down the department and contract with an outside vendor for the company's IT needs.

PROFIT CENTERS AND THEIR CHANGING ROLE IN INDUSTRY

In large companies, especially manufacturing companies, it has become a fairly common occurrence to break the company into small pieces, with each piece operating as a profit center that has to compete for business. In this manner, a large business can suddenly find itself operating as a small business. For example, say the Acme Company produces a finished product that is composed of five smaller parts. Instead of operating as one large company that produces all five parts needed for the finished product, Acme has decided to split into six separate units—one that assembles and sells the finished product, and five smaller companies that each produce one of the parts needed for the finished product. Beyond Acme, there are other companies that produce those same five parts needed to produce the finished product.

Each of the five part manufacturers is now operating as a separate profit center, reporting to Acme's corporate office. Each has to determine its own methods of operation, and each has to determine how it is going to show a profit. There may be internal agreements in place that mandate that each of the five units will continue to work together to produce the finished product, or Acme may throw things wide open by stating that there is no corporate mandate forcing the five divisions to continue to work together.

If the latter model is chosen, the corporation may have decided that, while the company could continue making steady—but small—profits if it kept using the five units together as it had for decades, there was a chance that the company could make huge profits if it made each of the five units accountable for its own bottom line and opened up the manufacturing process to both internal and external competition. In such a radical environment, it was conceivable that one of the five units could go bankrupt and cost the company money, but senior management believed that the hugely increased profits in the other four units, and the resulting higher profit margin realized by the sale of the finished product, would more than offset the loss of one unit.

Thus, each of Acme's five units, formerly divisions within the larger company that were not accountable for directly generating profits, were now separate entities that had to show a profit to continue operating. Each of the units had gone from a cost center mentality—buying materials to produce part of a product that showed up on the company's overall bottom line—to a profit center mentality, responsible for showing a profit based solely on the production and sale of its one part. As part of the shift to becoming a profit center, each of the five units would also be free to sell its part on the open marketplace. Acme might make that freedom a restricted one that prevented sales to a direct competitor, or it might take the full plunge and make the unit a fully stand-alone company that was free to sell its part to any other company in the market, including direct competitors. That decision would dictate whether Acme's move was a small one, designed to encourage each of its five units to think creatively and work harder to perform at a high level, or a large one, designed to change the very core of the company's business in a bid for higher profits.

PROFIT CENTERS AND SMALL BUSINESSES

When operating a small business, it may not be practical to use the profit center concept initially because the business is so small. Fewer employees mean fewer business units, which means fewer opportunities to create profit centers. In addition, in a small business, the president or the chief financial officer is probably monitoring financial results very closely, which means that he or she knows exactly where profits and losses are occurring. However, as a small business begins to grow, establishing profit centers often makes sense. Data Recognition, Inc. found that switching to profit centers made sense as the company increased in size. "Establishing profit centers, and generating daily profit/loss statements, has allowed us to better identify, and correct, our weaknesses," said vice president Steve Terry.

Even without adopting the profit center accounting concept, the idea of profit centers has value for small businesses in that they should always be looking for new ways to generate revenue. When operating a small business, there are essentially two ways to create a new profit center. The first method is to create an extension of the original business—a new product related to existing products, or new services that build on services that are already offered. The second method is to create an entirely new business altogether that can operate using the first business's corporate infrastructure (at least initially) and that can be operated at the same time as the original business.

The rapid spread of the World Wide Web has created an unprecedented method for creating new profit centers. Almost every company today has a Web site to dispense public relations information and to make it easier for customers to contact the company, but more and more firms are recognizing that there is money to be made on the Web. Most corporate Web sites begin life as a cost center, since they are initially just used to disseminate information, but most can be transformed into a profit center.

When seeking new profit centers, small business entrepreneurs should avoid business models that have regularly failed on the Web. These include setting up an entertainment site that attempts to charge a fee for that entertainment; relying on advertising as a revenue stream, as banner advertisements are proving to be quite unsuccessful in bringing in new customers; charging subscription or other visitor fees; and biting off more than you can handle by attempting to establish business-to-business sales that may not be achievable.

FURTHER READING:

Auer, Joe. "IT as Profit Center? It Can Be Done." *Computerworld.* May 1, 2000.

Bickerstaffe, G. "The Perils of Being a Profit Centre." *International Management.* October 1982.

Coburn, Jeff, and Michael Preston. "Profit Center Management: The Wave of the Future?" *Legal Management.* July-August 1997.

Greco, Susan. "Are We Making Money Yet?" *Inc.* July 1996.

Feldman, Joan M. "Divide and Prosper." *Air Transport World.* May 1995.

Hoffman, Thomas. "Profit Centers vs. Cost Centers. *Computerworld.* August 2, 1999.

"Internal Competition Makes Firms Stronger." *USA Today Magazine.* December 1994.

O'Sullivan, Orla. "On-Line Markets Can Turn Web Site from Cost Center to Profit Center." *American Banker.* April 4, 2000.

Pronko, Nick. "Managing Your Business with Profit Centers." *Business Solutions.* January 1998.

Turner, Mary and Gavin Welbourn. "Turn a Cost Center into a Profit Center." *Communications News.* October 1, 1998.

Walker, Gordon and Laura Poppo. "Profit Centers, Single-Source Suppliers, and Transaction Costs." *Administrative Science Quarterly.* March 1991.

PROFIT IMPACT OF MARKET STRATEGIES (PIMS)

The Profit Impact of Market Strategies (PIMS) is a comprehensive, long-term study of the performance of strategic business units (SBUs) in thousands of companies in all major industries. The PIMS project began at General Electric in the mid-1960s. It was continued at Harvard University in the early 1970s, then was taken over by the Strategic Planning Institute (SPI) in 1975. Since then, SPI researchers and consultants have continued working on the development and application of PIMS data.

According to the SPI, the PIMS database is "a collection of statistically documented experiences drawn from thousands of businesses, designed to help understand what kinds of strategies (e.g. quality, pricing, vertical integration, innovation, advertising) work best in what kinds of business environments. The data constitute a key resource for such critical management tasks as evaluating business performance, analyzing new business opportunities, evaluating and reality testing new strategies, and screening business portfolios."

The main function of PIMS is to highlight the relationship between a business's key strategic decisions and its results. Analyzed correctly, the data can help managers gain a better understanding of their business environment, identify critical factors in improving the position of their company, and develop strategies that will enable them to create a sustainable advantage. PIMS principles are taught in business schools, and the data are widely used in academic research. As a result, PIMS has influenced business strategy in companies around the world.

THE PIMS DATABASE

The information comprising the PIMS database is drawn from member companies of SPI. These companies contribute profiles of their SBUs that include financial data as well as information on customers, markets, competitors, and operations. The SBUs in the database are separated into eight classifications: producers of consumer durables, consumer non-durables, capital goods, raw materials, components, or supplies; wholesale and retail distributors; and providers of services. Specific companies and industries are not identified. Each SBU profile includes financial data from the income statement and balance sheet, as well as information about quality, price, new products, market share, and competitive tactics. "It tracks the standard financial measures, plus many of the marketing and strategy variables thought to drive financial performance," Hiram and Schewe explained in *The Portable MBA in Marketing.*

From this database of SBU experiences and results, SPI researchers developed a set of strategic principles and a methodology for examining business problems and opportunities. Users of the data can look for statistical relationships and compare the experiences of similar businesses, but cannot access the individual SBU data files. For small business owners, PIMS provides an opportunity to obtain information about competitors, markets, market shares, prices, and financial performance. This information enables small business owners to see how their strategies might play out in the market by comparing the experiences of similar businesses profiled in the PIMS database.

For example, the owner of a business that is a high-quality producer in a declining market might analyze the PIMS data to find out how various strategic initiatives affected the performance of other high-quality producers in declining markets. However, the PIMS data cannot provide information about specific companies—such as levels of debt and equity—or about overall industries. ''The way to use PIMS effectively is not to simply run with the general findings,'' according to the SPI website. ''Rather, analyze the experience of comparables by 1) profiling the specific business situation and identifying the key issues, and then 2) accessing and analyzing the experience of a sample of PIMS businesses situationally comparable to this business.''

FURTHER READING:

Hagerty, Michael R., James M. Carman, and Gary J. Russell. ''Estimating Elasticities with PIMS Data.'' *Journal of Marketing Research*. February 1988.

Hiam, Alexander, and Charles D. Schewe. *The Portable MBA in Marketing*. John Wiley, 1992.

''The PIMS Database.'' Strategic Planning Institute. http://www.thespinet.org.

PROFIT MARGIN

The profit margin is an accounting measure designed to gauge the financial health of a business firm or industry. In general, it is defined as the ratio of profit earned to total sales receipts (or costs) over some defined period. The profit margin is a measure of the amount of profit accruing to a firm from the sale of a product or service. It also provides an indication of efficiency in that it captures the amount of surplus generated per unit of the product or service sold. In order to generate a sizeable profit margin, a company must operate efficiently enough to recover not only the costs of the product or service sold, operating expenses, and the costs of debt, but also to provide compensation for its owners in exchange for their acceptance of risk.

As an example of a profit margin calculation, suppose firm A made a profit of $10 on the sale of a $100 television set. Dividing the dollar amount of earnings by the product cost, that firm's profit margin would be .10 or 10 percent, meaning that each dollar of sales generated an average of ten cents of profit. Thus, the profit margin is very important as a measure of the competitive success of a business, because it captures the firm's unit costs.

A low-cost producer in an industry would generally have a higher profit margin. Since firms tend to sell the same product at roughly the same price (adjusted for quality differences), lower costs would be reflected in a higher profit margin. Lower cost firms also have a strategic advantage in a competitive price war, because they have the ability to undercut their competitors by cutting prices in order to gain market share and potentially drive higher cost firms out of business.

Firms clearly exist to expand their profits. But while increasing the absolute amount of dollar profit is desirable, it has minimal significance unless it is related to its source. This is why firms use measures such as profit margin and profit rate. Profit margin measures the flow of profits over some period compared with the costs, or sales, incurred over the same period. Thus, one could compute the profit margin on costs (profits divided by costs), or the profit margin on sales (profit margin divided by sales).

Other specific profit margin measures often calculated by businesses include: 1) gross profit margin—gross profit divided by net sales, where gross profit is the total money left over after sales and net sales is total revenues; and 2) net profit margin—net profit divided by net sales, where net profit (or net income) is profit after deducting costs such as advertising, marketing, interest payments, and rental payments.

RATE OF PROFIT

Profit margin is related to other measures such as the rate of profit (sometimes called the rate of return), which comprises various measures of the amount of profit earned relative to the total amount of capital invested (or the stock of capital) required to generate that profit. Thus, while the profit margin measures the amount of profit per unit of sales, the rate of profit on total assets indicates the efficiency of the total investment. Or, put another way, while the profit margin measures the amount of profit per unit of capital (labor, working capital, and depreciation of plant and equipment) consumed over a particular period, the profit rate measures the amount of profit per unit of capital advanced (the entire stock of capital required for the production of the good).

Using our previous example, if a $1,000 investment in plant and equipment were required to produce the $100 television set, then a profit margin of 10 percent would translate into a profit rate on total investment of only 1 percent. Thus, in this scenario, firm A's unit costs are low enough to generate a 10 percent profit margin on the capital consumed (assuming some market price) to produce the TV set; but in order to achieve that margin, a total capital expenditure of $1,000 must be made.

The difference between the profit margin measure and the profit rate concept then lies in the rate at which the capital stock depreciates, and the rate at which the production process repeats itself, or turnover time. In the first case, if the entire capital stock for a particular firm or industry is completely used up during one production cycle, then the profit margin would be exactly the same as the profit rate. In the case of turnover, if a firm succeeds in doubling the amount of times the production process repeats itself in the same period, then twice as much profit would be made on the same capital invested, even though the profit margin might not change. More formally, the rate of return = profit margin × sales / average assets, where average assets is the total capital stock divided by the number of times the production process turns over. Thus, the rate of return can be increased by increasing the profit margin or by shortening the production cycle. Of course, this will largely depend on the conditions of production in particular industries or firms.

If costs rise and prices do not rise to keep up, then the profit margin will fall. In times of business cycle upturns, prices tend to rise; in business cycle downturns, prices tend to fall. Of course, many factors, and not only costs, will affect the profit margin—namely, industry-specific factors that relate to investment requirements, pricing, type of market, and conditions of production (including production turnover time).

It is important for small business owners to remember that generating a profit margin does not guarantee that their business is healthy, or that they will have money in the bank. Rather, a small business must have a positive cash flow in order to pay its bills and compensate its employees. To use a profit margin figure to determine whether a start-up firm is doing well, an entrepreneur might compare it to the return that would be available from a bank or another low-risk investment opportunity.

FURTHER READING:

Anthony, Robert N., and Leslie K. Pearlman. *Essentials of Accounting*. Prentice Hall, 1999.

Bragg, Steven M. *Accounting Best Practices*. John Wiley, 1999.

Gill, James O. *Financial Basics of Small Business Success*. Menlo Park, CA: Crisp Publications, 1994.

Helfert, Erich A. *Techniques of Financial Analysis*. Homewood, IL: Irwin, 1987.

Raiborn, Cecily A., Jesse T. Barfield, and Michael R. Kinney. *Managerial Accounting*. West Publishing Company, 1993.

PROFIT SHARING

Profit sharing refers to the process whereby companies distribute a portion of their profits to their employees. Profit-sharing plans are well established in American business. The annual U.S. Chamber of Commerce Employee Benefits Survey indicates that somewhere between 19 and 23 percent of U.S. companies have offered some form of profit sharing since 1963. Other estimates place the number of companies offering profit-sharing plans in the 1990s somewhere between one-fourth and one-third of all U.S. firms. For small businesses, profit sharing provides an important means of increasing employee loyalty and tying employee compensation to company performance. Profit sharing is a particularly attractive option for newer small businesses with uncertain profit levels, as it allows business owners to share the wealth during good times without obligating them to do so during lean years.

The Employee Retirement Income Security Act of 1974 (ERISA) provided a boost in the use of profit-sharing plans. ERISA regulates and sets the standards for pension plans and other employee benefit plans. Many employers found that a simple profit-sharing plan avoided many of ERISA's rules and regulations that affected pension plans.

TYPES OF PROFIT-SHARING PLANS

Companies may use any number of different formulas to calculate the distribution of profits to their employees and establish a variety of rules and regulations regarding eligibility, but there are essentially two basic types of profit-sharing plans. One type is a cash or bonus plan, under which employees receive their profit-sharing distribution in cash at the end of the year. The main drawback to cash distribution plans is that employee profit-sharing bonuses are then taxed as ordinary income. Even if distributions are made in the form of company stock or some other type of current payment, they become taxable as soon as employees receive them.

To avoid immediate taxation, companies are allowed by the Internal Revenue Service (IRS) to set up qualified deferred profit-sharing plans. Under a deferred plan, profit-sharing distributions are held in individual accounts for each employee. Employees are not allowed to withdraw from their profit-sharing accounts except under certain, well-defined conditions. As long as employees do not have easy access to the funds, money in the accounts is not taxed and may earn tax-deferred interest.

Under qualified deferred profit-sharing plans, employees may be given a range of investment choices for their accounts, including stocks or mutual funds. Such choices are common when the accounts are managed by outside investment firms. It is becoming less common for companies to manage their own profit-sharing plans due to the fiduciary duties and liabilities associated with them. A 401(k) account is a common type of deferred profit-sharing plan, with several unique features. For example, employees are allowed to voluntarily contribute a portion of their salary, before taxes, to their 401(k) account. The company may decide to match a certain percentage of such contributions. In addition, many 401(k) accounts have provisions that enable employees to borrow money under certain conditions.

OTHER ISSUES CONCERNING PROFIT-SHARING PLANS

Deferred profit-sharing plans are a type of defined contribution plan. Such employee benefit plans provide an individual account for each employee. Individual accounts grow as contributions are made to them. Funds in the accounts are invested and may earn interest or show capital appreciation. Depending on each employee's investment choices, their account balances may be subject to increases or decreases reflecting the current value of their investments.

The amount of future benefits that employees will receive from their profit-sharing accounts depends entirely on their account balance. The amount of their account balance will include the employer's contributions from profits, any interest earned, any capital gains or losses, and possibly forfeitures from other plan participants. Forfeitures result when employees leave the company before they are vested, and the funds in their accounts are distributed to the remaining plan participants.

Employees are said to be vested when they become eligible to receive the funds in their accounts. Immediate vesting means that they have the right to funds in their account as soon as their employer makes a profit-sharing distribution. Companies may establish different time requirements before employees become fully vested. Under some deferred profit-sharing plans employees may start out partially vested, perhaps being entitled to only 25 percent of their account, then gradually become fully vested over a period of years. A company's vesting policy is written into the plan document and is designed to motivate employees and reduce employee turnover.

In order for a deferred profit-sharing plan to gain qualified status from the IRS, it is important that funds in employee accounts not be readily accessible to employees. Establishing a vesting period is one way to limit access; employees have rights to the funds in their accounts only when they become partially or fully vested. Another way to limit access is to establish strict rules for making payments from employees accounts, such as upon retirement, death, permanent disability, or termination of employment. Less strict rules may allow for withdrawals under certain conditions, such as financial hardship or medical emergencies. Nevertheless, whatever rules a company may adopt for its profit-sharing plan, such rules are subject to IRS approval and must meet IRS guidelines.

The IRS also limits the amount that employers may contribute to their profit-sharing plans. The precise amount is subject to change by the IRS, but 1996 tax rules allowed companies to contribute a maximum of 15 percent of an employee's salary to his or her profit-sharing account. If a company contributed less than 15 percent in one year, it may exceed 15 percent by the difference in a subsequent year to a maximum of 25 percent of an employee's salary.

Companies may determine the amount of their profit-sharing contributions in one of two ways. One is by a set formula that is written into the plan document. Such formulas are typically based on the company's pre-tax net profits, earnings growth, or some other measure of profitability. Companies then plug the appropriate numbers into the formula and arrive at the amount of their contribution to the profit-sharing pool. Rather than using a set formula, companies may decide to contribute a discretionary amount each year. That is, the company's owners or directors—at their discretion—decide what an appropriate amount would be.

Once the amount of the company's contribution has been determined, different plans provide for different ways of allocating the funds among the company's employees. The employer's contribution may be translated into a percentage of the company's total payroll, with each employee receiving the same percentage of his or her annual pay. Other companies may use a sliding scale based on length of service or other factors. Profit-sharing plans also spell out precisely which employees are eligible to receive profit-sharing distributions. Some plans may require employees to reach a certain age or length of employment, for example, or to work a certain minimum number of hours during the year.

Although profit sharing offers some attractive benefits to small business owners, it also includes some potential pitfalls. It is important for small business owners who wish to share their success with employees to set up a formal profit sharing plan with the assistance of an accountant or financial advisor. Otherwise, both the employer and the employees may not receive the tax benefits they desire from the plan. Also, small business owners should avoid making mentions of profit sharing or stock ownership to motivate employees during the heat of battle. Such mentions could be construed as promises and lead to lawsuits if the employees do not receive the benefits they feel they deserved.

FURTHER READING:

Blakely, Stephen. ''Pension Power.'' *Nation's Business.* July 1997.

Blencoe, Gregory J. ''Utilizing Profit Sharing to Motivate Employees: The Logic Behind Sharing a Piece of the Pie.'' *Business Credit.* September 2000.

Crouch, Holmes F. *Decisions When Retiring.* Allyear Tax Guides, 1995.

Hussain, Syed Asad. ''Impact of Profit Sharing on Productivity.'' *Economic Review.* April 2000.

PROGRAM EVALUATION AND REVIEW TECHNIQUE (PERT)

The Program Evaluation and Review Technique (PERT) is a widely used method for planning and coordinating large-scale projects. As William J. Stevenson explained in his book *Production/Operations Management,* PERT analysis provides managers with a graphical display of the various activities involved in a project, an estimate of how long each activity and the entire project will take to complete, an indication of which activities are most important to ensure a timely completion of the project, and an idea of how long certain activities can be delayed without necessitating an extension of the project deadline.

PERT was developed during the 1950s through the efforts of the U.S. Navy and some of its contractors working on the Polaris missile project. Concerned about the growing nuclear arsenal of the Soviet Union, the U.S. government wanted to complete the Polaris project as quickly as possible. The Navy used PERT to coordinate the efforts of some 3,000 contractors involved with the project. Experts credited PERT with shortening the project duration by two years. Since then, all government contractors have been required to use PERT or a similar project analysis technique for all major government contracts.

NETWORK DIAGRAMS

According to Stevenson, the main feature of PERT analysis is a network diagram that provides a visual depiction of the major project activities and the sequence in which they should be completed. Activities are defined as distinct steps toward completion of the project that consume either time or resources. The network diagram consists of arrows and nodes and can be organized using one of two different conventions. The arrows represent activities in the activity-on-arrow convention, while the nodes represent activities in the activity-on-node convention. For each activity, managers provide an estimate of the time required to complete it.

The sequence of activities leading from the starting point of the diagram to the finishing point of the diagram is called a path. The amount of time required to complete the work involved in any path can be figured by adding up the estimated times of all activities along that path. The path with the longest total time is known as the critical path. As Stevenson noted, the critical path is the most important part of the diagram for managers since it determines the completion date of the project. Delays in completing activities along the critical path will necessitate an extension of the final deadline for the project. If a manager hopes to shorten the time required to complete the project, he or she must focus on finding ways to reduce the time involved in activities along the critical path.

The time estimates managers provide for the various activities comprising a project involve different degrees of certainty. When time estimates can be made with a high degree of certainty, they are called deterministic estimates. When they are subject to variation, they are called probabilistic estimates. In using the probabilistic approach, managers provide three estimates for each activity: an optimistic or best case estimate; a pessimistic or worst case estimate; and the most likely estimate. A beta distribution can be used to describe the extent of variability in these estimates, and thus the degree of uncertainty in the time provided for each activity. Computing the standard deviation of each path provides a probabilistic estimate of the time required to complete the overall project.

PERT ANALYSIS

Managers can obtain a great deal of information by analyzing network diagrams of projects. For example, network diagrams show the sequence of activities involved in a project. From this sequence, managers can determine which activities must take place before others can begin, and which can occur independently of one another. Managers can also gain valuable insight by examining paths other than the critical path. Since these paths require less time to complete, they can often accommodate slippage without affecting the project completion time. The difference between the length of a given path and the length of the critical path is known as slack. Knowing where slack is located helps managers to allocate scarce resources and direct their efforts to control activities.

For complex problems involving hundreds of activities, computers are used to create and analyze the project networks. According to Stevenson, the project information input into the computer includes the earliest start time for each activity (ES), earliest finish time for each activity (EF), latest start time for each activity (LS), and latest finish time for each activity (LF) without delaying the project completion. From these values, a computer algorithm can determine the expected project duration and the activities located on the critical path. Managers can use this information to determine where project time can be shortened by injecting additional resources, like workers or equipment.

Stevenson remarked that PERT offers a number of advantages to managers. For example, it forces them to organize and quantify project information and provides them with a graphic display of the project. It also helps them to identify which activities are critical to the project completion time and should be watched closely, and which activities involve slack time and can be delayed without affecting the project completion time. Stevenson also mentioned a few limitations of PERT. For example, managers may omit activities when developing the network diagram, they may organize the activities in the wrong order, or they may include a fudge factor in their time estimates for certain activities.

FURTHER READING:

Minty, Gordon. *Production Planning and Controlling.* Goodheart-Willcox, 1998.

Stevenson, William J. *Production-Operations Management.* 5th ed. McGraw-Hill, 1996.

PROMISSORY NOTES

Quite simply, a promissory note is a promise to pay or an IOU. It is a formal commitment (also known as a loan agreement or contract) between two parties that is usually necessary when money is borrowed and lent between them. All business loans secured from a bank or other lending institution have some sort of promissory note, but they are also recommended for loans between two individuals (even if the loan is between family member or close friends) to avoid any misunderstandings or possible legal troubles.

A promissory note should have several essential elements, including the amount of the loan, the date by which it is to be paid back, the interest rate, and a record of any collateral that is being used to secure the loan. Other interest rate options, like discounting or compensating balance requirements, can also be included. When the promissory note is discounted, the interest is taken off the principal amount at the beginning of the loan. The borrower pays back the entire amount, even though he only received the principal minus the interest. This practice is not very common because it is a higher effective rate of interest than the stated rate for the borrower. A compensating balance is usually required for large loans or lines of credit. It requires that the borrower maintain an account with a specified minimum level account balance at the lending institution (usually a bank). This account balance earns little or no interest and also raises the effective interest rate of the loan. Default terms (what happens if a payment is missed or the loan is note paid off by its due date) should also be spelled out in the promissory note.

When signing a promissory note, both the lender and the person receiving the loan should be fully aware of the note's language. One obvious way to do this is to read the promissory note carefully and in its entirety before committing a signature to it. If there are any questions or confusion regarding the contents of the promissory note, a certified public accountant (CPA) or lawyer should be called on to make sure everything is understandable. When a casual promissory note is drawn up between two individuals, the IRS has a required interest rate. A CPA can help determine if the interest rate stated in the promissory note is too low and if it will result in penalties or automatically be raised. If the loan is interest free, the IRS may consider it a gift and require that a gift tax be paid on it.

Another point that businesses may want to consider when drafting a promissory note is what to do in case the business does not succeed. If the business is a corporation or limited liability company, it should be determined if the corporate shareholders or limited liability members will personally guarantee the loan. If this is not the case, they have no personal legal obligation to repay the loan in a worst case scenario.

FURTHER READING:

Contracts and Promissory Notes. LawPak, Inc. 1999.

McMillan, Dan. ''Notes Causing Headaches.'' *Business Journal-Portland.* July 28, 2000.

Nation III, George A. ''Promissory Notes in Commercial Lending: Selecting the Best Type of Note for Your Loan.'' *Commercial Lending Review.* Fall 1996.

PROPRIETARY INFORMATION

Proprietary information, also known as a trade secret, is information that a company wishes to keep confidential or protect from those outside the company. The Uniform Trade Secrets Act (UTSA) defines trade secrets as "information that derives independent economic value from not being generally known, and that is kept secret through reasonable actions." Proprietary information can include secret formulas, processes, and methods used in production. It can also include a company's business and marketing plans, salary structure, customer lists, contracts, and computer systems. In some cases, the special knowledge and skills that an employee has learned on the job are considered to be a company's proprietary information.

"Simply put, a trade secret is unpublished knowledge that, unlike a patent, can be kept forever if it is maintained as a secret," Keith Orum wrote in *Beverage World.* "One common characteristic of a trade secret is that it gives its owner an advantage over the competition in the marketplace. Other characteristics of a trade secret are that it can't be easily 'reverse-engineered,' and that its secrecy must be aggressively protected by its owners."

Although legal protections exist for inventions (patents), creative works (copyrights), and distinctive names and symbols (trademarks), no specific form of legal protection is available for trade secrets. In fact, there is no single standard by which to determine whether or not information is proprietary—some 39 U.S. states have different laws that define a trade secret and the conditions under which it is considered to have been stolen. But there is a significant body of case law covering proprietary information and trade secrets. This legal framework recognizes a company's right to have proprietary information and provides the company with remedies when its trade secrets have been misused or appropriated illegally.

In some ways, the lack of specific forms of protection makes it easier for small businesses to protect their proprietary information. No complicated forms or formal registration are required, for instance, and trade secret protection lasts indefinitely—or at least as long as the information remains secret. In other ways, however, the lack of specific forms of trade secret protection hurts small businesses. It does not prevent competitors from determining the trade secrets by examining products already on the market, for example, and it does not prevent others from using the proprietary information once it is uncovered. Compared to other legal forms of protection, it also makes it more difficult to prove a violation of rights.

PROTECTING TRADE SECRETS

In general, for information to be considered proprietary, companies must treat it as confidential. Thus, information that is readily available in public sources will not be treated by the courts as proprietary. In addition, proprietary information should give the firm some sort of competitive advantage and should not be generally known outside of the firm. A company must be able to demonstrate that it has taken every reasonable step possible to keep the information private if it hopes to obtain court assistance in protecting its rights. "Courts require that trade secret holders take 'reasonable' steps to maintain the secrecy of their trade secrets," Randy Kay wrote in the *San Diego Business Journal.* "Courts do not require that companies take all measures conceivable to maintain the secrecy, nor do courts require absolute secrecy. Rather, the confidentiality measures must be 'reasonable under the circumstances.'"

There are several steps a company can take to protect its proprietary information. Key employees with access to proprietary information may be required to sign restrictive covenants—also called confidentiality, nondisclosure, or noncompete agreements—that prohibit them from revealing that information to outsiders or using it to compete with their employer for a certain period of time after leaving the company. These restrictive covenants are usually enforced by the courts if they are reasonable with respect to time and place and do not unreasonably restrict the former employee's right to employment. In some cases the covenants are enforced only if the employee has gained proprietary information during the course of his or her employment.

In addition, the courts generally consider it unfair competition for one company to induce people who have acquired unique technical skills and secret knowledge during their employment at another company to terminate their employment and use their skills and knowledge for the benefit of the competing firm. In such a case the plaintiff company could seek an injunction to prevent its former employees and the competing company from using the proprietary information.

Companies may also develop security systems to protect their proprietary information from being stolen by foreign or domestic competitors. Business and industrial espionage is an ongoing activity that clandestinely seeks to obtain trade secrets by illegal methods. A corporate system for protecting proprietary information would include a comprehensive plan ranging from restricting employee access, to data protection, to securing phone lines and meeting rooms. In some cases a chief information officer (CIO) would be responsible for implementing such a plan.

As Kay noted, other means of demonstrating reasonable efforts at secrecy include marking documents as "confidential," prohibiting people from making photo copies of trade secret documents or removing them from company premises, limiting the access of employees to sensitive materials, creating a written trade secret protection plan, and bringing suit for the theft of trade secrets as required.

On the other hand, small businesses are unlikely to prevail in cases involving trade secret protection if they sell a product or publish technical literature that discloses the trade secret, expose the trade secret to employees or colleagues who have not signed confidentiality agreements, publish information about the secret in professional journals or on the Internet, or disclose the trade secret in public documents such as court records and government filings.

FURTHER READING:

"How to Protect Yourself from Employees Who Become Competitors." *Profit-Building Strategies for Business Owners.* April 1993.

Kay, Randy. "Guide to Trade Secret Protection—Maintaining Secrecy." *San Diego Business Journal.* June 5, 2000.

"Keeping Secrets Secret." *Small Business Reports.* February 1994.

Lickson, Charles P. *Legal Guide for Small Business.* Crisp Publications, 1994.

Lynn, Jacquelyn. "Shhh! Keep It Quiet: Revealing Trade Secrets Could Cost You Your Business." *Entrepreneur.* December 1995.

Orum, Keith. "Trade Secrets Made Simple." *Beverage World.* October 1995.

PROTOTYPE

Prototypes are working models of entrepreneurial ideas for new products. "A prototype is defined as an original model on which something is patterned," wrote Richard C. Levy in *The Inventor's Desktop Companion.* "If you do not have the time, money, skills, or commitment to build a prototype of your idea, the odds of your ever licensing it are reduced to practically zero." An entrepreneur armed with a good prototype, on the other hand, is able to show potential investors and licensees how the proposed product will work without having to rely exclusively on diagrams and his/her powers of description.

TYPES OF PROTOTYPES

There are three major types or stages of prototype creation, each of which can be used by the enterprising entrepreneur in securing financing and/or a licensee.

1) Breadboard—This is basically a working model of your idea, intended to serve the basic function of showing how the product will work, with less concern for aesthetics. "The breadboard doesn't have to look good or even work well," stated Jacquelyn Denalli in *Business Start-Ups.* "It simply proves your idea can be reduced to practice." Tomima Edmark, writing in *Entrepreneur,* added that a breadboard "is used in the early stages of product development to demonstrate functionality and communicate your idea to potential model makers or manufacturers so they can create a finished product for sale."

2) Presentation Prototype—-This type of prototype is a representation of the product as it will be manufactured. Often used for promotional purposes, it should be able to demonstrate what the product can do, but it is not necessarily an exact copy of the final product. "In building your model," said Denalli, "consider these issues: the item's sale price, materials, manufacturing costs, marketing details, safety factors, how it will be sold and distributed, and the profit margin. If you plan to license your invention to a manufacturer, you can often do so with a model."

3) Pre-Production Prototype—This type of prototype is for all practical purposes the final version of the product. It should be just like the finished product in every way, from how it is manufactured to its appearance, packaging, and instructions. This final-stage prototype is typically expensive to produce—and far more expensive to make than the actual unit cost once the product is in full production—but the added cost is often well worth it. It is most valuable because it enables inventors and producers to go over every aspect of the product in fine detail, which can head off potential trouble spots prior to product launch. In addition, Denalli pointed out that "you can make drawings or photographs of the sample to use in brochures, mailings, pamphlets, advertising, and so on. You can also use the prototype to show to potential buyers, whether manufacturers or buyers for department stores."

THINGS TO CONSIDER IN CREATING A PROTOTYPE

Prospective entrepreneurs with a new product idea should make sure that they consider the following when putting together a prototype:

- Adequately research the requirements of the product prototype. Edmark recommended that entrepreneurs follow these basic steps: 1) Write down all the materials, supplies, and tools that might be needed in creating the prototype; 2) Identify and order the various steps necessary to assemble the prototype; 3) Identify which parts can be easily purchased and/or found around the home, and which parts will need to be custom made.

- Make sure the prototype is well-constructed. ''Prototypes must be well made because often they take quite a beating at the hands of executives,'' warned Levy. ''Don't be surprised when prototypes come back broken because they were mishandled or poorly packed for shipment. It happens at the best of companies. It comes with the territory.''

- Do not shirk on presentation, even at the prototype stage. ''You must be as sophisticated and slick in your presentation to potential licensees as they will have to be in their pitch to the trade and/or the consumer,'' wrote Levy.

- Recognize that complex product ideas may require outside assistance from professional prototype makers. Universities, engineering schools, local inventor organizations, and invention marketing companies are all potential sources of information on finding a good person to help you make your prototype. But before hiring a prototype maker, entrepreneurs should make certain that they can meet your expectations. To help ensure that you are satisfied, conduct research on the maker's business reputation and make certain that you adequately communicate your concept.

- Consider making multiple submissions to potential licensees. Some inventors send prototypes to several manufacturers at the same time. Levy recommended, however, that ''if a company asks you to hold off further presentations until it has an opportunity to review the item at greater length, try to set guidelines. In all fairness, some products require a reasonable number of days to be properly considered. However, if you feel the company is asking for an unreasonable period of time, seek some earnest money to hold the product out of circulation.''

RAPID PROTOTYPING

A relatively recent development in the creation of prototypes is rapid prototyping (RP). Also known as desktop manufacturing, RP takes advantage of computer technology to turn designs into three-dimensional objects. Some older RP systems work by printing multiple layers of plastic ink to create a model of a computer-generated image. Some newer systems are able to freeze water into a three-dimensional ice sculpture model, while the most sophisticated systems can create metal molds. RP technology saves time in the product development process. It also improves product design by allowing various people to see a model and have input without creating a full-fledged prototype. It has been used by large companies like automakers and aircraft manufacturers for several years, and it is now becoming accessible to small businesses as well.

''Properly used, rapid prototyping can greatly accelerate product development and lead to high-quality, defect-free products. Fortunately, the new generation of rapid prototyping tools, variously known as conceptual modelers, desktop modelers, and 3D printers, are much faster than earlier versions. They lend themselves to use by engineers in office environments,'' G. Thomas Clay and Preston G. Smith wrote in *Machine Design*. ''Three-dimensional prototypes put engineers, managers, manufacturing staff, and marketers on equal footing in evaluating designs. All the interested parties can see, touch, and handle the design, just as the ultimate customers will.''

FURTHER READING:

Clay, G. Thomas, and Preston G. Smith. ''Rapid Prototyping Accelerates the Design Process.'' *Machine Design*. March 9, 2000.

Denalli, Jacquelyn. ''Inventor's Circle—Terms of Invention.'' *Business Start-Ups*. November 1993.

Edmark, Tomima. ''Model Approach: Creating a Prototype that will Wow Investors.'' *Entrepreneur*. October 1997.

''From Concept to Crystal Clear Prototype.'' *Business Week*. August 28, 2000.

Kochan, Detlef, Chee Kai Chua, and Du Zhaohui. ''Rapid Prototyping Issues in the 21st Century.'' *Computers in Industry*. June 1999.

Levy, Richard C. *The Inventor's Desktop Companion: The Guide to Successfully Marketing and Protecting Your Ideas.* Detroit: Visible Ink Press, 1995.

Schrage, Michael. ''How Prototypes Can Change Your Business.'' *Across the Board*. January 2000.

SEE ALSO: Product Development

PROXY STATEMENTS

A proxy statement is, according to the Securities and Exchange Commission (SEC), "a document which is intended to provide security holders with the information necessary to enable them to vote in an informed manner on matters intended to be acted upon at security holders' meetings." Publicly-traded companies are required to send proxy statements to all shareholders, each of whom has a vote in the operation of the business, in advance of annual and special meetings. It includes information pertaining to issues that require a shareholder vote as well as a ballot for voting. This ballot is used for the election of the Board of Directors for the next year and may be used for other issues requiring a vote as well.

Proxy statements also provide information on all other matters which will be discussed at the annual or special meeting, such as approval of company auditors, approval of employee bonus plans, approval of changes in the company's preferred stock, etc. In addition, proxy statements contain a wealth of financial information about a company's significant shareholders, composition of the board of directors (including background and investment holdings), and compensation (salary, bonuses, stock options) paid to its top executives.

Finally, proxy statements contain SEC-mandated performance graphs detailing the company's stock performance and shareholder return when stacked up against other industry indexes, such as a national market index (like the Standard & Poor's 500), and broad industry averages. This information, if studied with a discerning eye, can help stockholders discern the fortunes and priorities of a company's top management. It serves as a financial benchmark for comparing the relationship between executive compensation and company performance. For example, proxy statements are less likely to create controversy if the company is performing well and rewarding stockholders of publicly traded companies with profits, or if the company is struggling financially and the executives are limiting their compensation accordingly. However, if key executives are pulling in enormous compensation packages while the company founders, attentive shareholders will notice. "Examining compensation is especially important for young, fast-growing companies that have yet to begin generating profits," wrote Geoffrey Simon in *Business Journal of Tampa Bay.* This aspect of the proxy statement cannot be hidden from public view, so experts urge leaders of growing firms to exercise appropriate judgement when establishing executive compensation packages.

In the future, analysts believe that many proxy statements will be delivered to shareholders via the Internet. This methodology, while still uncommon in the late 1990s, is trending upward both for reasons of convenience and cost savings (in such realms as printing and postage expenses). Costs associated with converting to this delivery method can be significant for smaller companies, due to the expense of establishing/upgrading Internet sites and converting proxy documents to HTML format. But most observers agree that once an electronic delivery system has been put in place, the firm can register considerable annual savings.

FURTHER READING:

Q and A: Small Business and the SEC. Securities and Exchange Commission, 1997.

Roberts, Bill. "No Chads, No Rips, No Errors." *Electronic Business.* January 2001.

Simon, Geoffrey A. "Proxy Statements are Full of Highly Valuable Information." *Business Journal of Tampa Bay.*

Sosnoff, Martin. "Forget the Annuals, Read the Proxies." *Forbes.* May 4, 1998.

PUBLIC RELATIONS

Public relations describes the various methods a company uses to disseminate messages about its products, services, or overall image to its customers, employees, stockholders, suppliers, or other interested members of the community. The point of public relations is to make the public think favorably about the company and its offerings. Commonly used tools of public relations include news releases, press conferences, speaking engagements, and community service programs.

Although advertising is closely related to public relations—as it too is concerned with promoting and gaining public acceptance for the company's products—the goal of advertising is generating sales, while the goal of public relations is generating good will. The effect of good public relations is to lessen the gap between how an organization sees itself and how others outside the organization perceive it.

Public relations involves two-way communication between an organization and its public. It requires listening to the constituencies on which an organization depends as well as analyzing and understanding the attitudes and behaviors of those audiences. Only then can an organization undertake an effective public relations campaign.

Many small business owners elect to handle the public relations activities for their own companies, while others choose to hire a public relations special-ist. Managers of somewhat larger firms, on the other hand, frequently contract with external public rela-tions or advertising agencies to enhance their corpo-rate image. But whatever option is chosen, the head of a company is ultimately responsible for its public relations.

GOALS OF PUBLIC RELATIONS

Some of the main goals of public relations are to create, maintain, and protect the organization's repu-tation, enhance its prestige, and present a favorable image. Studies have shown that consumers often base their purchase decisions on a company's reputation, so public relations can have a definite impact on sales and revenue. Public relations can be an effective part of a company's overall marketing strategy. In the case of a for-profit company, public relations and market-ing should be coordinated to be sure they are working to achieve the same objectives.

Another major public relations goal is to create good will for the organization. This involves such functions as employee relations, stockholder and in-vestor relations, media relations, and community rela-tions. Public relations may function to educate certain audiences about many things relevant to the organiza-tion—including the business in general, new legisla-tion, and how to use a particular product—as well as to overcome misconceptions and prejudices. For ex-ample, a nonprofit organization may attempt to edu-cate the public regarding a certain point of view, while trade associations may undertake educational pro-grams regarding particular industries and their prod-ucts and practices.

STEPS IN A PUBLIC RELATIONS CAMPAIGN

Effective public relations requires a knowledge, based on analysis and understanding, of all the factors that influence public attitudes toward the organiza-tion. While a specific public relations project or cam-paign may be undertaken proactively or reactively (to manage some sort of image crisis), the first basic step in either case involves analysis and research to identify all the relevant factors of the situation. In this first step, the organization gains an understanding of its various constituencies and the key factors that are influencing their perceptions of the organization.

In the second step, the organization establishes an overall policy with respect to the campaign. This in-volves defining goals and desired outcomes, as well as the constraints under which the campaign will oper-ate. It is necessary to establish such policy guidelines in order to evaluate proposed strategies and tactics as well as the overall success of the campaign.

In step three, the organization outlines its strate-gies and tactics. Using its knowledge of the target audiences and its own established policies, the organi-zation develops specific programs to achieve the de-sired objectives. Finally, step four involves actual communication with the targeted public. The organi-zation then employs specific public relations tech-niques, such as press conferences or special events, to reach the intended audience.

In step five the organization receives feedback from its public. How have they reacted to the public relations campaign? Are there some unexpected de-velopments? In the final step, the organization as-sesses the program and makes any necessary adjust-ments.

AREAS OF PUBLIC RELATIONS

Public relations is a multifaceted activity involv-ing different audiences as well as different types of organizations, all with different goals and objectives. As a result, there are several specific areas of public relations.

PRODUCT PUBLIC RELATIONS Public relations and marketing work together closely when it comes to promoting a new or existing product or service. Public relations plays an important role in new product intro-ductions by creating awareness, differentiating the product from other similar products, and even chang-ing consumer behavior. Public relations can help in-troduce new products through staging a variety of special events and handling sensitive situations. For example, when the Prince Matchabelli division of Chesebrough-Pond's USA introduced a new men's cologne, there were twenty-one other men's fragran-ces being introduced that year. To differentiate its new offering, called Hero, Prince Matchabelli created a National Hero Awards Program honoring authentic male heroes and enlisted the participation of Big Brothers/Big Sisters of America to lend credibility to the program. Similarly, when Coleco introduced its Cabbage Patch Kids dolls, public relations helped in-crease awareness through licensed tie-in products, trade show exhibits, press parties, and even window displays in Cartier jewelry stores.

Public relations is often called on to give existing products and services a boost by creating or renewing visibility. For example, the California Raisins Advi-sory Board organized a national tour featuring live performances by the California Dancing Raisins to maintain interest in raisins during a summer-long advertising hiatus. The tour generated national and local publicity through media events, advance public-ity, trade promotions, and media interviews with per-former Ray Charles. Other public relations programs for existing products involve stimulating secondary demand—as when Campbell Soup Co. increased overall demand for soup by publishing a recipe booklet—or identifying new uses for the product. Public relations can interest the media in familiar products and services in a number of ways, including holding seminars for journalists, staging a special media day, and supplying the media with printed materials ranging from "backgrounders" (in-depth news releases) to booklets and brochures. Changes in existing products offer additional public relations opportunities to focus consumers' attention. An effective public relations campaign can help to properly position a product and overcome negative perceptions on the part of the general public.

EMPLOYEE RELATIONS Employees are one of the most important audiences a company has, and an ongoing public relations program is necessary to maintain employee good will as well as to uphold the company's image and reputation among its employees. The essence of a good employee relations program is keeping employees informed and providing them with channels of communication to upper levels of management. Bechtel Group, a privately held complex of operating companies, published an annual report for its employees to keep them informed about the company's operations. The company used surveys to determine what information employees considered useful. A range of other communication devices were used, including a monthly tabloid and magazine, a quarterly video magazine, local newsletters, bulletin boards, a call-in telephone service, and "brown bag" lunches where live presentations were made about the company. Suggestion systems are another effective way to improve employee-management communications.

Other public relations programs focusing on employees include training them as company public relations representatives; explaining benefits programs to them; offering them educational, volunteer, and citizenship opportunities; and staging special events such as picnics or open houses for them. Other programs can improve performance and increase employee pride and motivation. Public relations can also play a role in recruiting new employees; handling reorganizations, relocations, and mergers; and resolving labor disputes.

FINANCIAL RELATIONS Financial relations involves communicating not only with a company's stockholders, but also with the wider community of financial analysts and potential investors. An effective investor relations plan can increase the value of a company's stock and make it easier to raise additional capital. In some cases special meetings with financial analysts are necessary to overcome adverse publicity, negative perceptions about a company, or investor indifference. Such meetings may take the form of full-day briefings, formal presentations, or luncheon meetings. A tour of a company's facilities may help generate interest among the financial community. Mailings and ongoing communications can help a company achieve visibility among potential investors and financial analysts.

Annual reports and stockholder meetings are the two most important public relations tools for maintaining good investor relations. Some companies hold regional or quarterly meetings in addition to the usual annual meeting. Other companies reach more stockholders by moving the location of their annual meeting from city to city. Annual reports can be complemented by quarterly reports and dividend check inserts. Companies that wish to provide additional communications with stockholders may send them a newsletter or company magazine. Personal letters to new stockholders and a quick response to inquiries insure an additional measure of good will.

COMMUNITY RELATIONS A comprehensive, ongoing community relations program can help virtually any organization achieve visibility as a good community citizen and gain the good will of the community in which it operates. Banks, utilities, radio and television stations, and major retailers are some of the types of organizations most likely to have ongoing programs that might include supporting urban renewal, performing arts programs, social and educational programs, children's programs, community organizations, and construction projects. On a more limited scale, small businesses may achieve community visibility by sponsoring local sports teams or other events. Support may be financial or take the form of employee participation.

Organizations have the opportunity to improve good will and demonstrate a commitment to their communities when they open new offices, expand facilities, and open new factories. One company increased community awareness of its presence by converting a vacant building into a permanent meeting place. Another company built its new headquarters in an abandoned high school that it renovated. One of the more sensitive areas of community relations involves plant closings. A well-planned public relations campaign, combined with appropriate actions, can alleviate the tensions that such closings cause. Some elements of such a campaign might include offering special programs to laid-off workers, informing employees directly about proposed closings, and controlling rumors through candid and direct communications to the community and employees.

Organizations conduct a variety of special programs to improve community relations, including providing employee volunteers to work on community projects, sponsoring educational and literacy programs, staging open houses and conducting plant tours, celebrating anniversaries, and mounting special exhibits. Organizations are recognized as good community citizens when they support programs that improve the quality of life in their community, including crime prevention, employment, environmental programs, clean-up and beautification, recycling, and restoration.

CRISIS COMMUNICATIONS Public relations practitioners become heavily involved in crisis communications whenever there is a major accident or natural disaster affecting an organization and its community. Other types of crises involve bankruptcy, product failures, and management wrongdoing. In some cases, crises call for an organization to become involved in helping potential victims; in other cases, the crisis may require rebuilding an organization's image. In any case, experts recommend that business owners prepare a plan in advance to deal with potential crises in an honest and forthright manner. The main objective of such a plan is to provide accurate information quickly in order to reduce uncertainty. After the San Francisco earthquake of 1989, for example, the Bank of America utilized its public relations department to quickly establish communications with customers, the financial community, the media, and offices in 45 countries to assure them the bank was still operating.

GOVERNMENT AND POLITICAL RELATIONS Public relations in the political arena covers a wide range of activities, including staging debates, holding seminars for government leaders, influencing proposed legislation, and testifying before a congressional committee. Political candidates engage in public relations, as do government agencies at the federal, state, and local levels.

Trade associations and other types of organizations attempt to block unfavorable legislation and support favorable legislation in a number of ways. The liquor industry in California helped defeat a proposed tax increase by taking charge of the debate early, winning endorsements, recruiting spokespersons, and cultivating grassroots support. A speakers bureau trained some 240 industry volunteers, and key messages were communicated to the public through printed materials and radio and television commercials.

PUBLIC RELATIONS IN THE PUBLIC INTEREST Organizations attempt to generate good will and position themselves as responsible citizens through a variety of programs conducted in the public interest. Some examples are environmental programs (including water and energy conservation) and antipollution programs. Health and medical programs are sponsored by a wide range of nonprofit organizations, healthcare providers, and other businesses and industries. These range from encouraging other companies to develop AIDS-in-the-workplace policies to the American Cancer Society's Great American Smoke-

out. Other programs offer political education, leadership and self-improvement, recreational activities, contests, and safety instruction.

CONSUMER EDUCATION Organizations have undertaken a variety of programs to educate consumers, building good will and helping avoid misunderstandings in the process. Opportunities for educating consumers might include sponsoring television and radio programs, producing manuals and other printed materials, producing materials for classroom use, and releasing the results of surveys. In addition to focusing on specific issues or industries, educational programs may seek to inform consumers about economic matters and business in general.

OTHER PUBLIC RELATIONS PROGRAMS Other types of programs that fall under the umbrella of public relations include corporate identity programs, ranging from name changes and new trademarks to changing a company's overall image. Special events may be held to call attention to an organization and focus the public's good will. These include anniversary celebrations, events related to trade shows, special exhibits, or fairs and festivals. Speakers bureaus and celebrity spokespersons are effective public relations tools for communicating an organization's point of view. Speakers bureaus may be organized by a trade association or an individual company. The face-to-face communication that speakers can deliver is often more effective than messages carried by printed materials, especially when the target audience is small and clearly defined.

PUBLIC RELATIONS FOR SMALL BUSINESSES

Like other types of organizations, small businesses can benefit from public relations in terms of their relationships with customers, employees, investors, suppliers, or other interested members of the community. Since small business owners are the most visible representatives of their own companies, they frequently handle many of the public relations functions themselves. But experts caution small business owners against taking on this responsibility if they are unqualified, or if they are unable to give public relations the attention it deserves. In these cases, entrepreneurs may choose to hire a public relations specialist or contract with an outside agency.

In his book *Public Relations for the Entrepreneur and the Growing Business,* Norman R. Soderberg outlines the main qualifications for public relations professionals. An ideal candidate would be creative and enterprising, possess good communication skills and solid news judgment, have a thorough knowledge of the business, be sincere and considerate in dealing with people, and make a good impression as a representative for the company. Some of the skills required in public relations work include writing and editing, public speaking, graphic arts, public opinion polling, and advertising. The responsibilities of a public relations executive include interpreting public opinion, advising management, generating opportunities to increase public awareness and acceptance, disseminating good publicity, and evaluating the results of campaigns. In order to perform these duties effectively, the public relations professional must know what is going on in the business, which means that he or she requires access to management.

"Most companies need to seek outside help from a public relations agency at some point," Chad Kaydo wrote in *Sales and Marketing Management*. "Even if staff members handle most of your PR efforts, an independent firm can assist with a special project, or give occasional advice." There are a variety of reasons why a small business owner might decide to contract public relations work out to an external agency. For example, company personnel may be inexperienced in handling public relations; the company may be geographically distant from its main audiences; the company may not be able to afford to hire a full-time public relations executive with the needed skills; or the company may want the objective judgment of an outsider. A small business owner can locate reputable public relations firms through the Small Business Administration, the Public Relations Society of America, the trade press for their industry, or the recommendations of fellow business people or local news people. When choosing between several potential agencies, a small business owner should consider those that have experience in the industry, clients in similar industries, financial stability, and a compatible overall philosophy. Contracting with an outside firm can be costly—some charge their clients a monthly retainer, while others charge straight hourly rates for limited services.

While communication is the essence of public relations, an effective public relations campaign is based on action as well as words. Whether it is practiced formally or informally, public relations is an essential function for the survival of any organization. Small business owners cannot afford to neglect public relations. But lavish parties and gifts are not necessary—it is possible to vastly improve a small business's image within its community while also controlling public relations expenditures. Sponsoring a local softball team, speaking at a chamber of commerce meeting, and volunteering at a neighborhood clean-up are among the wide variety of public relations activities readily available to small businesses.

FURTHER READING:

Bianco, David, ed. *PR News Casebook: 1000 Public Relations Case Studies*. Gale Research, 1993.

Kaydo, Chad. "How to Hire a PR Firm." *Sales and Marketing Management*. April 2000.

Lesly, Philip, ed. *Lesly's Handbook of Public Relations and Communications*. AMACOM, 1991.

Nucifora, Alf. "Small Businesses Need Positive PR." *Dallas Business Journal*. May 19, 2000.

Soderberg, Norman R. *Public Relations for the Entrepreneur and the Growing Business*. Probus, 1986.

Young, Davis. *Building Your Company's Good Name*. AMACOM, 1996.

SEE ALSO: Community Relations; Press Kits; Press Releases

PURCHASING

Purchasing is the act of buying the goods and services that a company needs to operate and/or manufacture products. Given that the purchasing department of an average company spends an estimated 50 to 70 percent of every revenue dollar on items ranging from raw materials to services, there has been greater focus on purchasing in recent years as firms look at ways to lower their operating costs. Purchasing is now seen as more of a strategic function that can be used to control bottom-line costs. Companies are also seeking to improve purchasing processes as a means of improving customer satisfaction.

THE TRADITIONAL PURCHASING PROCESS

The traditional purchasing process involved several steps—requisition, soliciting bids, purchase order, shipping advice, invoice, and payment—that have come to be increasingly regarded as unacceptably slow, expensive, and labor intensive. Each transaction generated its own paper trail, and the same process had to be followed whether the item being purchased was a box of paper clips or a new bulldozer.

In this traditional model, purchasing was seen as essentially a clerical function. It was focused on getting the right quantity and quality of goods to the right place at the right time at a decent cost. The typical buyer was a shrewd negotiator whose primary responsibility was to obtain the best possible price from suppliers and ensure that minimum quality standards were met. Instead of using one supplier, the purchaser would usually take a divide-and-conquer approach to purchasing—buying small amounts from many suppliers and playing one against the other to gain price concessions. Purchasing simply was not considered to be a high-profile or career fast-track position—when surveys were taken of organizational stature, purchasing routinely rated in the lowest quartile.

That attitude has changed in recent years, in part because of highly publicized cases wherein companies have achieved stunning bottom-line gains through revamped purchasing processes. In addition, increased competition on both the domestic and global levels has led many companies to recognize that purchasing can actually have important strategic functions. As a result, new strategies are being used in purchasing departments at companies of all size.

Analysts observe that in this new purchasing environment, a guideline known as the total cost of ownership (TCO) has come to be a paramount concern in purchasing decisions. Instead of buying the good or service that has the lowest price, the buyer instead weighs a series of additional factors when determining what the true cost of the good or service is to his or her company. According to Anne Millen Porter in *Purchasing* magazine, these factors can include "price, freight, duty, tax, engineering costs, tooling costs, letter of credit costs, payment terms, inventory carrying costs, storage requirements, scrap rates, packaging, rebates or special incentive values, [and] warranty and disposal costs." To lower TCO, companies are taking a number of steps to improve purchasing.

STRATEGIC SOURCING

Strategic sourcing is one of the key methods that purchasing departments are using to lower costs and improve quality. Strategic sourcing involves analyzing what products the company buys in the highest volume, reviewing the marketplace for those products, understanding the economics and usage of the supplier of those products, developing a procurement strategy, and establishing working relationships with the suppliers that are much more integrated than such relationships were in the past. During this process, the team conducting the analysis should ask these questions:

- Why do we buy this product or service?
- What do we use it for?
- What market conditions do suppliers operate under?
- What profit margin do suppliers seek to obtain?
- What is the total price of purchasing from a particular vendor (in other words, the cost of the item plus the costs associated with quality problems)
- Where is the good or service produced?
- What does the production process look like?

The products that are purchased in the highest volume will be the best candidates for cost reductions. That is because once those products are identified, the company can then justify the time and expense needed to closely study the industry that supplies that product. It can look at the ways key suppliers operate, study their business practices to see where the most money is added to the final cost of the product, and then work with the supplier to redesign processes and lower production costs. This maximizes the contribution that suppliers make to the process.

By knowing the market and knowing how much it costs for a supplier to do business, the purchasing department can set "target prices" on goods. If the supplier protests that the price is far too low, the purchasing company can offer to visit the supplier's site and study the matter. As one purchasing executive explained in *Industry Week:* "We have 15 to 20 people who study the cost of everything we purchase. We know what it costs for a supplier to make a part, including all the overhead and the profit. So if a supplier comes in once we've given him a target price and says, 'You guys are crazy,' we send one of our engineers to visit the company. They look at the supplier's production process to see if they can spot a problem that's causing the supplier's prices to be higher. If necessary, our engineer helps the supplier rearrange the production line to make it more efficient." Proponents argue that these "supplier alliances" can result in improved buyer/seller communication, improved planning, reductions in leadtime, concurrent engineering, decreased paperwork, and better customer service.

The alliances also can sometimes register significant improvements in product quality. Buyers can build clearly-defined quality targets into their target prices. It will then work with the supplier to improve the manufacturing process until that quality target is met. Such a process can yield enormous benefits for buyers, including reduced inventory levels, faster time to market, significant cost savings, and reduced development costs.

Not all suppliers can meet the high standards demanded in this purchasing environment. Some studies indicate that companies that adapt strategic sourcing have lowered the number of suppliers they use by an average of nearly 40 percent. What characteristics makes a good supplier, then? If the supplier is willing to partner, then analysts have identified several traits that good suppliers share:

- Commitment to continuous improvement
- Cost-competitive
- Cost-conscious
- Customer-oriented
- Encourages employee involvement
- Flexible
- Financially stable

- Abe to provide technical assistance

Analysts indicate that suppliers receive some benefits in the emerging purchasing dynamic as well. Reduced paperwork, lower overhead, faster payment, long-term agreements that lead to more accurate business forecasts, access to new designs, and input into future materials and product needs have all been cited as gains. Other observers, meanwhile, point out that some buyer-supplier relationships have become so close that suppliers have opened offices on the site of the buyer, an arrangement that can conceivably result in even greater improvements in productivity and savings. Of course, companies are not going to form such ''partnerships''with all of their suppliers. Some form of the traditional purchasing process involving bidding and standard purchase orders and invoices will continue to exist at almost every company, and especially at smaller companies that do not have the financial weight to make large demands on their suppliers.

EMPOWERING TEAMS

In addition to strategic sourcing, there are other methods companies can use to improve purchasing. One is creating cross-functional teams that involve purchasing personnel in every stage of the product design process. In the past, purchasers were not involved at all in the design process. They were simply instructed to purchase the necessary materials once a new product had been created. Now, purchasers (and suppliers) are increasingly included from the start of the new product process to ensure that the products needed to create product are readily available and are not prone to quality problems. Suppliers tend to be experts in their field, so they bring a large knowledge base to the design process that would otherwise be missing. This can help prevent poor designs or manufacturing mistakes.

These teams have broken down barriers and helped abolish the old manufacturing method that was known as the ''over the wall'' method of productions—each business unit would work on a project until its portion of the job was completed. It would then ''throw the product over the wall'' to the next functional team that was waiting to perform its part of the manufacturing process. The new cross-functional teams often include personnel from purchasing, manufacturing, engineering, and sales and marketing.

Purchasing teaches other members of the team how to deal directly with suppliers, cutting the purchasing personnel out of the loop. This is important in that it eliminates much of the time-consuming work that buyers had to deal with (soliciting bids, creating purchase orders, etc.) and frees them to concentrate on the part of their job where their expertise most pays off: finding suppliers and negotiating prices and quality standards. ''Purchasing should be concerned with the strategic planning aspects of procurement process,'' purchasing director Ben Lapner told *Purchasing* magazine. ''Buying itself deals with the daily transactions and replenishment actions that should be performed as close to the company's end user as possible.''

JUST-IN-TIME PURCHASING

Just-in-time (JIT) manufacturing became one of the biggest trends in all facets of industry in the 1990s. JIT companies maintain only enough inventory to manufacture the products they need in the very near future. Parts are ordered on a near-continuous basis and often go directly from the loading dock to the assembly line. The benefits of this system include reduced inventory, improved quality, reduced leadtime, reduced scrap and rework, and reduced equipment downtime. However, when a company shifts to JIT manufacturing, it must also shift to JIT purchasing.

JIT purchasing requires a nearly 180-degree change in purchasing philosophy. Traditional purchasing meant building a supplier list over time by constantly adding new suppliers, spreading purchases around, and maintaining higher inventory levels in case demand for a product soared or quality from a supplier dipped suddenly. JIT purchasing demands that buyers narrow their supplier list to a chosen few who can deliver high-quality products on-demand and in a timely fashion.

Writing in *Industrial Management,* Bernhard Hadeler stated that JIT purchasers must look for a minimum of three things in suppliers: 1) demonstrated excellent quality; 2) ability to make frequent, on-time deliveries; and 3) ability to provide very large volume commitments or single sourcing arrangements. Quality may be the toughest of these standards for suppliers to meet; the JIT purchaser should deal only with companies that utilize statistical analysis to verify the quality of their output. Failure to do so should eliminate the supplier from even being asked to submit a bid.

For frequent, on-time deliveries, it often helps if the supplier is located in the same geographic region as the buyer. That way, it is easier for the supplier to react to a sudden, unexpected demand for its product, and it costs far less to make the frequent deliveries that are needed. Those lower costs can in part be passed on to the buyer.

In single sourcing arrangements, it is not uncommon for the buyer to exert some influence over the supplier's business processes. The buyer has made such a significant commitment to the supplier, and is such a large portion of the supplier's total business, that it has the right to expect some say in the supplier's business practices. For some suppliers, this is an uncomfortable arrangement.

PURCHASING CARDS

As transaction costs soar (some companies report spending as much as $300 per transaction in clerical and other costs), companies are looking to buy smarter and cut costs any way possible. One popular method is recent years is to supply certain employees with purchasing cards, or corporate procurement cards.

The cards are similar to credit cards; in fact the big three credit card companies—VISA, MasterCard, and American Express—are among the leaders in purchasing cards. In most cases, the cards are used to purchase small business items, and then a master bill is sent straight to the purchasing department. But Catherine Romano stated in *Management Review* that the cards do differ from true credit cards in key ways. In some cases, the cards work only between a buyer and suppliers identified in advance, eliminating the bank that is involved with credit cards. Additionally, the cards can be coded to include a variety of important transaction information that reduces the amount of paperwork needed to track the sale, including sales tax data, customer code (such as job number or cost center), taxpayer identification number, and more. This coding allows companies to receive valuable information about each transaction and greatly streamlines the purchasing process.

The cards are beneficial to suppliers as well. The most important advantage is that the vendor receives payment much more quickly than in the past—sometimes in as short a period as two or three days. Additionally, the supplier saves money by not having to issue and mail an invoice, and the supplier knows the credit worthiness of the customer before the transaction is even processed.

FURTHER READING:

Hadeler, Bernhard J. ''Supply Strategy: Capturing the Value.'' *Industrial Management.* July/August 1994.

Harrington, Lisa H. ''Buying Better: Strategic Sourcing Can Improve Suppliers' Productivity, Component and Product Quality—and Improve the Bottom Line.'' *Industry Week.* July 21, 1997.

Kulkarni, Shashank. ''A Supply-Side Strategy.'' *Journal of Business Strategy.* September/October 1997.

Meier, Ronald L., Michael A. Humphreys, and Michael R. Williams. ''The Role of Purchasing in the Agile Enterprise.'' *International Journal of Purchasing and Materials Management.* Fall 1998.

Minahan, Tim. ''Purchasing Rebuilds to Battle Poor Quality.'' *Purchasing.* January 16, 1997.

Porter, Anne Millen. ''Purchasing Pros Insist They Buy On Far More than Price.'' *Purchasing.* May 1, 1997.

''Purchasing Cards Change Corporate Buying Practices.'' *Corporate Cashflow Magazine.* November 1995.

Romano, Catherine. ''Purchasing Cards Save Money.'' *Management Review.* April 1994.

Stundza, Tom. ''Purchasing Evolves into Supply Management.'' *Purchasing.* July 17, 1997.

Wisner, Joel D., and Keah Choon Tan. ''Supply Chain Management and Its Impact on Purchasing.'' *Journal of Supply Chain Management.* Fall 2000.

Q

A quality circle is a participatory management technique that enlists the help of employees in solving problems related to their own jobs. In their volume *Japanese Quality Circles and Productivity,* Joel E. Ross and William C. Ross define a quality circle as "a small group of employees doing similar or related work who meet regularly to identify, analyze, and solve product-quality and production problems and to improve general operations. The circle is a relatively autonomous unit (ideally about ten workers), usually led by a supervisor or a senior worker and organized as a work unit." Employees who participate in quality circles usually receive training in formal problem-solving methods—such as brainstorming, pareto analysis, and cause-and-effect diagrams—and then are encouraged to apply these methods to either specific or general company problems. After completing an analysis, they often present their findings to management and then handle implementation of approved solutions.

Although most commonly found in manufacturing environments, quality circles are applicable to a wide variety of business situations and problems. They are based on two ideas: that employees can often make better suggestions for improving work processes than management; and that employees are motivated by their participation in making such improvements. Thus, implemented correctly, quality circles can help a small business reduce costs, increase productivity, and improve employee morale. Other potential benefits that may be realized by a small business include greater operational efficiency, reduced absenteeism, improved employee health and safety, and an overall better working climate. In their book *Production and Operations Management,* Howard J. Weiss and Mark E. Gershon called quality circles "the best means today for meeting the goal of designing quality into a product."

The interest of U.S. manufacturers in quality circles was sparked by dramatic improvements in the quality and economic competitiveness of Japanese goods in the post-World War II years. The emphasis of Japanese quality circles was on preventing defects from occurring rather than inspecting products for defects following a manufacturing process. Japanese quality circles also attempted to minimize the scrap and downtime that resulted from part and product defects. In the United States, the quality circle movement evolved to encompass the broader goals of cost reduction, productivity improvement, employee involvement, and problem-solving activities.

BACKGROUND

Quality circles were originally associated with Japanese management and manufacturing techniques. The introduction of quality circles in Japan in the postwar years was inspired by the lectures of W. Edwards Deming (1900-1993), a statistician for the U.S. government. Deming based his proposals on the experience of U.S. firms operating under wartime industrial standards. Noting that American management had typically given line managers and engineers about 85 percent of the responsibility for quality control and line workers only about 15 percent, Deming argued that these shares should be reversed. He suggested redesigning production processes to more fully account for quality control, and continuously educating all employees in a firm—from the top down—in quality control techniques and statistical control technologies. Quality circles were the means by which this continuous education was to take place for production workers.

Deming predicted that if Japanese firms adopted the system of quality controls he advocated, nations around the world would be imposing import quotas on Japanese products within five years. His prediction was vindicated. Deming's ideas became very influential in Japan, and he received several prestigious awards for his contributions to the Japanese economy.

The principles of Deming's quality circles simply moved quality control to an earlier position in the production process. Rather than relying upon post-production inspections to catch errors and defects, quality circles attempted to prevent defects from occurring in the first place. As an added bonus, machine downtime and scrap materials that formerly occurred due to product defects were minimized. Deming's idea that improving quality could increase productivity led to the development in Japan of the Total Quality Control (TQC) concept, in which quality and productivity are viewed as two sides of a coin. TQC also required that a manufacturer's suppliers make use of quality circles.

Quality circles in Japan were part of a system of relatively cooperative labor-management relations, involving company unions and lifetime employment guarantees for many full-time permanent employees. Consistent with this decentralized, enterprise-oriented system, quality circles provided a means by which production workers were encouraged to participate in company matters and by which management could benefit from production workers' intimate knowledge of the production process. In 1980 alone, changes resulting from employee suggestions resulted in savings of $10 billion for Japanese firms and bonuses of $4 billion for Japanese employees.

Active American interest in Japanese quality control began in the early 1970s, when the U.S. aerospace manufacturer Lockheed organized a tour of Japanese industrial plants. This trip marked a turning point in the previously established pattern, in which Japanese managers had made educational tours of industrial plants in the United States. Lockheed's visit resulted in the gradual establishment of quality circles in its factories beginning in 1974. Within two years, Lockheed estimated that its fifteen quality circles had saved nearly $3 million, with a ratio of savings to cost of six to one. As Lockheed's successes became known, other firms in the aerospace industry began adopting quality circles. Thereafter quality circles spread rapidly throughout the U.S. economy; by 1980, over one-half of firms in the Fortune 500 had implemented or were planning on implementing quality circles.

In the early 1990s, the U.S. National Labor Relations Board (NLRB) made several important rulings regarding the legality of certain forms of quality circles. These rulings were based on the 1935 Wagner Act, which prohibited company unions and management-dominated labor organizations. One NLRB ruling found quality programs unlawful that were established by the firm, that featured agendas dominated by the firm, and addressed the conditions of employment within the firm. Another ruling held that a company's labor-management committees were in effect labor organizations used to bypass negotiations with a labor union. As a result of these rulings, a number of employer representatives expressed their concern that quality circles, as well as other kinds of labor-management cooperation programs, would be hindered. However, the NLRB stated that these rulings were not general indictments against quality circles and labor-management cooperation programs, but were aimed specifically at the practices of the companies in question.

REQUIREMENTS FOR SUCCESSFUL QUALITY CIRCLES

In his book *Productivity Improvement: A Guide for Small Business,* Ira B. Gregerman outlined a number of requirements for a small business contemplating the use of quality circles. First, the small business owner should be comfortable with a participative management approach. It is also important that the small business have good, cooperative labor-management relations, as well as the support of middle managers for the quality circle program. The small business owner must be willing and able to commit the time and resources needed to train the employees who will participate in the program, particularly the quality circle leaders and facilitators. It may even be necessary to hire outside facilitators if the time and expertise does not exist in-house. Some small businesses may find it helpful to establish a steering committee to provide direction and guidance for quality circle activities. Even if all these requirements are met, the small business will only benefit from quality circles if employee participation is voluntary, and if employees are allowed some input into the selection of problems to be addressed. Finally, the small business owner must allow time for the quality circles to begin achieving desired results; in some cases, it can take more than a year for expectations to be met.

But successful quality circles offer a wide variety of benefits for small businesses. For example, they serve to increase management's awareness of employee ideas, as well as employee awareness of the need for innovation within the company. Quality circles also serve to facilitate communication and increase commitment among both labor and management. In enhancing employee satisfaction through participation in decision-making, such initiatives may also improve a small business's ability to recruit and retain qualified employees. In addition, many companies find that quality circles further teamwork and reduce employee resistance to change. Finally, quality circles can improve a small business's overall competitiveness by reducing costs, improving quality, and promoting innovation.

FURTHER READING:

Allender, Hans D. "Using Quality Circles to Develop an Action Plan Required for Leading Organizations." *Industrial Management.* September-October 1992.

Gregerman, Ira B. *Productivity Improvement: A Guide for Small Business.* New York: Van Nostrand Reinhold, 1984.

Gryna, Frank M., Jr. *Quality Circles: A Team Approach to Problem Solving.* AMACOM, 1981.

"New Rules on Employee Involvement." *Industry Week.* February 1, 1993.

Noble, Barbara Presley. "Worker-Participation Programs are Found Illegal." *New York Times.* June 8, 1993.

Ross, Joel E., and William C. Ross. *Japanese Quality Circles and Productivity.* Reston Publishing Company, 1982.

Uchitelle, Louis. "Workers Seek Executive Role, Study Says." *New York Times.* December 5, 1994.

Weiss, Howard J., and Mark E. Gershon. *Production and Operations Management.* Boston: Allyn and Bacon, 1989.

QUALITY CONTROL

Quality control refers to the process, most often implemented in manufacturing, of monitoring the quality of finished products through statistical measures and an overall corporate commitment to producing defect-free products. Quality control principles can also be utilized in service industries.

DEMING'S FOURTEEN POINTS

The term "quality control" came into common use in the 1950s thanks to W. Edward Deming, whose "Fourteen Points" have become the bible for quality control proponents. With the post-war world returning to normal manufacturing patterns, Deming preached that inspecting products for quality after they were manufactured was unacceptable. Instead, he proposed a process known as "statistical quality control" that would use closely monitored performance measures to gauge quality as a product was being manufactured. The goal of statistical quality control was to gather data that would allow for the constant improvement of manufacturing processes, which would in turn im-

prove quality control. Introducing such statistical controls could be expensive, but Deming argued that instituting quality measures ultimately saved companies money.

Another important tenet of Deming's beliefs was that upper management was largely to blame for quality failures. He firmly believed that, given the right tools and working environment, workers would strive to create the highest quality products possible. In Deming's own words, "the basic cause of sickness in American industry and resulting unemployment is failure of top management to manage." He believed that strong leadership led to an inspired work force that did not fear management and did not fear taking chances when seeking ways to improve quality.

If strong leadership is the buzzword for managers in a quality environment, then empowerment is the key concept for workers in Deming's system. Improved education and training are the key factors in reaching employees and making them believe that their increased participation in the work process is an essential part of improving quality. Involvement, participation, and teamwork are seen as absolute musts if a quality workplace is to be created.

The Japanese were the first to adopt Deming's Fourteen Points, and with great success. As an example, Deming learned of one Japanese factory that doubled production in just one year and was expecting to gain an additional 25 percent improvement the following year, with no increase in the amount of hours worked. All this occurred as a result of simply improving quality. What is most significant about this achievement is the year it happened—1951. Many American and European companies chose to ignore these dramatic results and nearly perished as a result. Critics contend that by the time American manufacturing plants realized that quality control was a significant issue, it was the late 1970s and Japanese firms such as Honda and Sony were taking over large portions of the American consumer market.

In the 1990s, most American firms have embraced quality control practices. Analysts indicate that when firms first began adopting these principles, many went too far, becoming bogged down in quality control charts and measurements of inconsequential operating factors. In too many cases, American industry went from ignoring statistical quality control to applying it to every single facet of a business, no matter how small. This overemphasis quickly disappeared, however, and has been replaced by a commitment to overall quality control that is unprecedented in the American workplace.

THE SCOPE OF JAPANESE INFLUENCE

Because they have been practicing quality management since the 1950s, the Japanese are still the leader in producing quality products in a number of industries and are still the role model for U.S. companies to emulate. For example, a study of the air conditioning industry in the early 1990s found that the worst Japanese air conditioning plant had an error rate that was less than one-half that of the *best* U.S. company.

This drastic difference is largely due to the Japanese adherence to one of Deming's most important ideas—that quality should be ''designed in'' to a product instead of ''inspected out.'' Japanese firms treat suppliers as equals, sharing information with them as if the supplier was an internal department of the company. This ensures that quality is already a part of the product before it is even manufactured.

Another common practice in Japan that has found its way to the United States are ''quality circles.'' Workers are brought together on a regular basis to brainstorm about quality and manufacturing processes, all with an eye towards improving quality. The circles are a success if management follows through on its end of the deal and incorporates the suggestions made in the quality circles into operations. When workers see their suggestions implemented, it increases their confidence in management and in the company as a whole, which in turn increases their commitment to the company and to producing high quality goods.

A highly trained work force is one of the keys to producing quality goods, and the training programs of many American companies reflect this recognition, for they are allocating more time and money to this area. Still, many U.S. companies lag behind in this respect. Researchers have stated that a higher commitment to training and lifelong learning are needed if the commitment to quality is to continue.

Today, the key components of quality control that were preached by Deming and practiced by the Japanese—including benchmarking, supplier partnering, and continuous improvement—have found their way into American industry. Each of these components demands a closer look.

BENCHMARKING

Benchmarking is a continuing process of measuring products, services, and practices against your strongest competitors. More simply stated, it means using the best companies as the yardstick against which your company measures itself. If your company comes up short, than improvements must be made to ensure that your products are just as high in quality as those of your competitor.

There are two types of benchmarking. The first, competitive benchmarking, entails benchmarking against direct competitors in the marketplace. This can include comparing specific numerical or statistical measurements—return on assets used, market share, etc. The more detailed information that can be obtained about a competitor, the better.

The second method, noncompetitive benchmarking, can take two forms. The first is measuring your company against the best companies in the world, regardless of industry. Companies such as 3M, Coca-Cola, and General Electric are considered to be trendsetters and leaders in quality, so companies from nearly every industry study them and copy their best practices. Business analysts note that noncompetitive benchmarking is a broader—and sometimes more useful—instrument of quality control. By only benchmarking against competitors, a company only ensures it will be as good as that competitor. By benchmarking against the best companies in the world, a company can aspire to be as good as those companies and can surpass the competition in its own industry. Additionally, companies may find it easier to gain access to information about companies they do not compete with because they are not seen as a threat to the well-being of the company.

The second type of noncompetitive benchmarking is internal benchmarking, which involves comparing functions or processes in different departments within the same organization. Internal benchmarking is often seen as a logical starting point for a business that is attempting to use benchmarking for the first time.

To successfully benchmark, a company must first look closely at its own practices and conduct a rigorous self-assessment. Once that self-assessment is completed, the company has a good idea of where it stands on each quality issue and can successfully compare itself to other companies. The self-assessment must be honest and thorough. It should identify weaknesses, but should also highlight strengths. Improving weaknesses that are identified should be tied to stated company strategic aims.

SUPPLIER PARTNERING

Supplier partnering is an increasingly common practice in the United States. Simply put, it means that manufacturers work directly with their parts and components suppliers to improve quality at the supplier's location. This can involve direct participation in the supplier's operations—that is, staff from the manufacturer might work on-site at the supplier's office or provide technical assistance and equipment—or simply a very close working relationship that more resembles a partnership rather than a simple business transaction between two unrelated companies.

One of the biggest methods of partnering with suppliers involves sharing the use of statistical controls. This is an underdeveloped area in the United States that should grow in the coming years. Most manufacturers have switched to outsourcing as a means of cutting the costs of production. This increased emphasis on outsourcing means that the companies that supply the parts or components must place just as much emphasis on quality as the manufacturer if the finished product is to be high quality.

Among the quality issues that still need to be addressed in the manufacturer-supplier relationship are:

- Inconsistent quality levels from suppliers, even from different plants of the same supplier.

- While most first-level, or Tier 1, suppliers have made a commitment to quality control, that commitment has yet to be made by Tier 2 suppliers (those companies that supply smaller parts or raw material to the Tier 1 supplier). The importance of quality must trickle all the way down the supply chain to be meaningful.

- In many industries, mergers are occurring at a record pace. Whenever a merger of two suppliers occurs, there is the chance that quality will suffer while the details of the merger are hammered out.

In many industries, especially the auto industry, manufacturers are overcoming these supplier problems by helping the suppliers meet quality standards.

The other facet of supplier partnering means that the manufacturer also actively seeks out feedback from the supplier on how the former's operations can be improved. Suppliers often have a unique perspective on the industry they work in and on the companies they supply and can provide valuable advice on how to make changes for the better. When this happens, it is important that the two companies have a framework in place to manage the partnering system. This can mean that the manufacturer's purchasing department would be deemed as the intermediary between the two companies, passing information from the supplier back to the appropriate internal customers.

CONTINUOUS IMPROVEMENT

Continuous improvement (CI) is a method for improving every facet of a company's operations and increasing competitiveness by developing a company's resources. The improvement can involve many goals—producing products with zero defects or achieving 100 percent customer satisfaction—but CI has the same basic principles no matter what the goal:

- Involve the entire company at all levels

- Find savings by improving existing processes, not by investing more money

- Gather data about company operations and quantify that data, which becomes the baseline against which improvements will be measured

- Do not forget that common sense is perhaps the most important component of CI

- Do not just give lip service to improvement—implement or practice ideas.

Continuous improvement most often involves creating a team that includes representatives from all areas of the company. The team first spends time learning—about the company they work for (looking at it in new ways) and about other companies (benchmarking is common during this phase). The necessary quantitative data is created. The team then proposes solutions to management and begins to implement those solutions. Once that is achieved, follow-up mechanisms must be put in place that seek additional improvements as time goes by. The team might change members with the passage of time, but hopefully it will become an established and accepted part of the company even as its roster changes. If the endeavor works as planned, the team will have improved quality to show as a result of its initial efforts. This can make even skeptical employees buy into the concept, which in turn leads to the continued search for even more improvements—hence the term continuous improvement. Follow-up mechanisms can include regular audits or regularly scheduled meetings to evaluate progress.

OTHER QUALITY BUZZWORDS

Quality control and literature about it have become a huge cottage industry in the business world. In addition to the terms outlined in this article, there are several other popular concepts and terms associated with quality control that are actually offshoots of the larger issue, or separate issues altogether. Among the most popular are:

- ISO 9000—This is a series of international standards that set out requirements and recommendations that specify how management operations are to be conducted at a company to ensure that quality is the end-result. ISO 9000 is part of the ''conformance to specifications'' school of quality control that believes that, by setting standards for companies to follow that the consumer is aware of, and ensuring that those standards are never deviated from, then quality is achieved. Essentially, its goal is to prevent nonconformity. Companies must undergo a comprehensive program to apply for ISO 9000 certification, reviewing and documenting management procedures, creating job descriptions from the ground up, preparing a quality manual, and submitting to periodic standards checks by an external body. The process is not cheap, but it does give a company that qualifies for the certification a badge to demonstrate its commitment to quality.

- Six Sigma—This defect-reduction program was pioneered by General Electric's Jack Welch. A sigma is a mark on a bell curve that measures standard deviation. In American industry today, most companies average between 35,000 and 50,000 defects per million operations; GE followed this trend by averaging 35,000, or 3.5 sigma. Welch determined that this was unacceptable—he wanted the error rate reduced to an almost nonexistent 3.4 errors per million operations, or "Six Sigma," a concept first introduced by Motorola in the early 1990s. Motorola was able to achieve six sigma quality, but it took eight years to go from three to six. Welch mandated that GE reach the mark in five years. More and more companies are expected to follow the lead of GE and Motorola, since both companies are considered world leaders.

- Quality awards—As quality control grows in popularity, companies strive to prove to customers that quality is their most important concern. One way they do this is to compete for the plethora of quality awards that are now available. The most famous of these is the Malcolm Baldridge National Quality Award, but others such as the European Quality Award and the Deming Award also exist. Additionally, there are hundreds of state, regional, and local quality awards. The awards, which are given to both large and small companies, carry a rigorous set of quality standards that a company must meet or exceed before it can even be considered for an award. Some companies coincide the launch of new quality control programs with announcements that they will be seeking one of the awards as a means of giving employees an incentive to improve quality and as a means of demonstrating to customers their commitment to quality.

- Mistake-proofing, or poka-yoke—"Poka-yoke" is a Japanese term that comes from two words that mean "avoid error." The concept was created by a Toyota engineer who felt that workers should always strive to avoid making any mistakes. The concept most often refers to "designing in" methods of avoiding mistakes—for example, putting guards on drill presses that prevent the machine from drilling a hole too deep and ruining a part. As a result, poka-yoke has come to have a second meaning. In addition to referring to the broad concept, it refers to any tool or process used to prevent a mistakes. Mistake-proofing is one of the easiest ways for small companies to reduce errors. It is easy and relatively inexpensive to perform an audit of existing poka-yokes and to draw up a flow chart of a production process to identify where other poka-yokes might be installed. Once the initial work is done, adding new poka-yokes can be an ongoing and continuous process. One warning to business owners—using the terms "mistake-proofing" or "fool-proofing" can anger workers, who may view the terms as being disparaging.

Finally, there is one term associated with the quality control movement that is too broad and too important to cover here. Total quality management, or TQM, has become an important quality movement in its own right and is fully explained in a separate entry in this book.

THE FUTURE OF QUALITY CONTROL

Despite the growing importance of quality control in the United States, there is still room for improvement in many areas. One of the most important is the attitude towards teams, especially cross-functional ones. Teams are recognized by quality experts as one of the best ways to increase speed to market and improve quality. Slowly, as American firms adopt other quality measures, they are also adopting the team philosophy. Still, improvements must be made. Too many firms still rely on the old styles of product development and production, handing off responsibility for a product from one department to the next with no interaction between the departments.

Another problem to be overcome in the future is downsizing. One of the key business principles of the 1990s, downsizing means improving technology and work processes so that the same amount of work can be done with fewer employees. While the move to downsize has improved the bottom line at many companies, it has also raised quality concerns. Some believe that there has been a marked reduction in the quality of some products because too many firms engaged in downsizing without making sure that their internal processes and infrastructure was adequately equipped to handle the loss of employees.

FURTHER READING:

Beard, Thomas L. "The Maturation of American Quality." *Modern Machine Shop.* April 1997.

Buttle, Francis. "ISO 9000: Marketing Motivations and Benefits." *International Journal of Quality & Reliability Management.* July 1997.

Calingo, Luis Maria R. "The Evolution of Strategic Quality Management." *International Journal of Quality & Reliability Management.* December 1996.

Conlin, Michelle. "Revealed at Last: The Secret of Jack Welch's Success." *Forbes.* January 26, 1998.

Davenport, Jerry Lee, Jr., and Thomas Li-Ping Tang. "Learning from Japanese Companies and Japanese Transplants in the United States." *Employment Relations Today.* Spring 1996.

Heller, Robert. "Fourteen Points that the West Ignore at Its Peril." *Management Today.* March 1994.

Henricks, Mark. "Make No Mistake." *Entrepreneur.* October 1996.

Hinckley, C. Martin. "The Quality Question." *Assembly.* November 1997.

Joiner, Brian L. "The Future of Quality in the United States." *National Underwriter Property & Casualty-Risk & Benefits Management.* December 16, 1997.

Kinni, Theodore B. "Lofty Goals: Superstructuring With Quality Standards and Awards." *Industry Week.* September 4, 1995.

McManus, Kevin. "Is Quality Dead?" *IIE Solutions.* July 1999.

Morgan, James. "The New Look of Quality." *Purchasing.* January 11, 1996.

Murphy, Elana Epatko. "Communicate Quality Standards on Every Level." *Purchasing.* January 11, 1996.

Murphy, Elana Epatko. "Look to Production for Tips on Boosting Quality." *Purchasing.* November 27, 1997.

Porter, Anne Millen. "In Some Companies Quality Culture Is Tangible." *Purchasing.* January 16, 1997.

Prado, J. Carlos. "Increasing Competitiveness with Continuous Improvement." *Industrial Management.* July-August 1997.

"Quality Revolution Not Over Yet." *Purchasing.* March 6, 1997.

Songini, Marc. L. "Setting Sights on Perfection." *Industrial Distribution.* August 1997.

Van de Vliet, Anita. "To Beat the Best." *Management Today.* January 1996.

"What Is Benchmarking?" *Food Manufacture.* May 1996.

Wilkinson, Adrian, and Hugh Willmott. "Quality Management, Problems and Pitfalls: A Critical Perspective." *International Journal of Quality & Reliability Management.* February 1996.

Wright, Richard B. "Why We Need ISO 9000." *Industrial Distribution.* January 1997.

SEE ALSO: ISO 9000; Total Quality Management

R

Racial discrimination is the practice of letting a person's race or skin color unfairly become a factor when deciding who receives a job, promotion, or other employment benefit. It most often affects minority individuals who feel they have been unfairly discriminated against in favor of a Caucasian (or white) individual, but there have been recent cases where whites have claimed that reverse discrimination has occurred—that is, the minority received unfairly favorable treatment at the expense of the white individual.

Court rulings handed down through the years have determined that a company's responsibility not to discriminate based on race begins even before an individual is hired. Companies can be held liable if pre-employment screening or testing is determined to be discriminatory, if applications ask unacceptable questions designed to screen for race, or if the overall selection process is deemed to be unfair. One of the main indicators that racial discrimination has occurred in the hiring process involves the qualifications of the job applicants. While a slight difference in qualifications between a minority and nonminority candidate do not automatically indicate racial bias (if the lesser qualified nonminority candidate is hired over the minority candidate), a drastic difference in qualifications has almost always been upheld by the courts as a sure sign of racial discrimination.

Racial discrimination is a high-profile issue in the business world and is a very real problem that still exists—and in some cases is getting worse. In a 1998 study by the nonprofit group Catalyst called "Women of Color in Corporate Management: A Statistical Picture," it was shown that minority women, while now accounting for almost a quarter of all women in the workplace, occupied only 15 percent of the management positions held by women. The study determined that a combination of racial discrimination and the glass ceiling (a term that describes the difficulty women in general have in reaching management positions) was responsible for the disparity in those numbers.

FEDERAL LAWS STRONGLY PROHIBIT RACIAL DISCRIMINATION

Since the social unrest of the 1960s, the federal government has been actively involved in preventing racial discrimination in the workplace. The most important law covering racial discrimination on the job is the Civil Rights Act of 1964—specifically, Title VII of that act, which strictly prohibits all forms of discrimination on the basis of race, color, religion, sex, or national origin in all aspects of employment. Written during a tumultuous period in American history when many people expected the federal government to right social wrongs, the law was a monumental piece of legislation that changed the American employment landscape.

The law stated that it was unlawful for an employer to "fail or refuse to hire or to discharge any individual, or otherwise discriminate against any individual with respect to his compensation, terms, conditions, or privileges of employment, because of such individual's race, color, religion, sex, or national origin." The law covers hiring, dismissals, compensation, and all other aspects of employment, while also covering actual employment opportunities that are available. Examples of racial discrimination that would fall under the scope of the act include:

I. An employee who alleges that his or her manager only promotes nonminority employees and keeps minorities in entry-level positions.

II. An employee who alleges that a manager or other person in power tells jokes or makes statements that are demeaning, insulting, or offensive to members of a minority group.

III. A manager who makes it clear that he or she believes in racial stereotypes by admitting that he or she refuses to promote a certain minority group because "all [members of that group] are lazy."

The law covers businesses with 15 or more employees and applies to all private, federal, state, and local employers. In many states, businesses with fewer than 15 employees face the same rules thanks to local or state statutes. In addition to the hiring provisions, the law dictates that employers cannot in any way limit or segregate employees based on race in any way that would adversely affect their chances at promotions. It does allow for two narrow exceptions to the law—businesses may use a "bona fide" seniority or merit system and measure performance and earnings based on a quantity or quality measuring system, and employers may use ability tests to determine the most qualified candidates for a job as long as the test does not discriminate racially in any way.

In 1991, the 1964 law was significantly amended for the first time by the passage of the Civil Rights Act of 1991. The law was passed to override several Supreme Court decisions that had made it much more difficult for employees to prove that racial discrimination had occurred. One of the many changes of the 1991 law is that it closed a loophole in the 1964 act that also involved a Civil War-era statute known as 42 U.S.C. Section 1981. The Supreme Court had held that Section 1981 applied to hiring and sometimes to promotions, but that it did not cover racial harassment that occurred in the workplace once a person was hired. The 1991 act said that all racial discrimination was covered by U.S. law, including post-hire harassment.

The other major enhancement under the 1991 act involved monetary damages. Before the law was passed, employees who sued an employer for discrimination and won could only recover lost wages or salary, lost benefits, attorney fees, other legal costs, and the costs associated with reinstatement. The 1991 law said that employees could also recover punitive monetary damages for pain and emotional suffering, mental anguish, future lost wages and benefits, and more. Those damages could only be collected if it was proven that the discrimination was intentional and there was clearly "malice" or "reckless indifference" exhibited, but this was a radical change from the previous legislation. To protect employers from overly large court settlements, the amount of punitive damages was capped at $300,000 for certain cases of discrimination, although no caps apply in cases of ethnic or racial discrimination.

Other changes in the 1991 law involve employment practices that have a "disparate impact" on racial groups (that is, affect them more than nonminority groups), make it easier for a plaintiff to receive damages in cases where a discriminatory practice *and* a nondiscriminatory practice both played a part in a hiring or promotion decision, and allow employees to challenge seniority systems that are put into place if the systems are later determined to be discriminatory (in the past, workers could only sue at the time the system was first put into place). Together, all of these changes made it easier for workers to prove discrimination claims, which has increased the number of lawsuits nationwide.

THE EQUAL EMPLOYMENT OPPORTUNITY COMMISSION

To oversee the federal civil rights legislation, a separate administrative body was created as part of the Civil Rights Act of 1964. The Equal Employment Opportunity Commission, or EEOC, was created to enforce laws that prevent discrimination based on race, sex, color, religion, national origin, disability, or age when hiring, firing, or promoting employees. Four groups—race, color, sex, and creed—were given "protected status" under the law, which was to be upheld by the EEOC. The commission is an independent regulatory body that has the power to launch investigations, file lawsuits, and create programs to eliminate discrimination.

The EEOC has been a controversial organization throughout its nearly 40-year history. Liberal politicians believe that the agency was long overdue and that it is absolutely imperative that the agency be proactive in identifying and fighting discrimination in the courts, while conservatives believe that the organization is a perfect example of "big government" that intrudes far too deeply into citizens' lives. The agency's strong enforcement of affirmative action policies (which actively seek to promote minorities over equally qualified nonminorities in order to address past discrimination) has been its most controversial action, as many Americans oppose affirmative action.

Even with political opposition, the EEOC continues to be effective in fighting racial discrimination. In 1997, for example, the agency collected $111 million in judgements for people who claimed to have been harmed by racial discrimination, including a $34 million settlement with Mitsubishi Motor Manufacturing. Each year, the EEOC handles nearly 50,000 claims.

STEPS TAKEN BY EMPLOYERS TO END DISCRIMINATION

Because racial discrimination can have disastrous results for a company—including lower morale, a divided workplace, expensive lawsuits, and public embarrassment—most companies are taking highly visible steps to curtail discrimination in the workplace. Steps taken include in-house workshops and training sessions on racial sensitivity and diversity in the workplace, training on employment laws, and adopting strict new rules against discrimination. *Training* magazine reported in 1998 that more than half of the approximately 137,000 companies in the United States with more than 100 employees had instituted some form of racial sensitivity training.

Unfortunately, many companies do not take action against racial discrimination until faced with an incident at their workplace or until they are named defendant in a large lawsuit. Instead of being proactive and instituting training programs before a problem arises, companies tend to be slow to act. In November of 2000, the Coca-Cola Company agreed to settle a racial discrimination suit by paying a penalty of $192.5 million. Sara Lee Corporation was forced to make a large cash settlement to a former employee who says that he was the butt of racist jokes, disparaging remarks, and was even forced to view a noose hanging in his workplace. In addition to the cash settlement, which was confidential, Sara Lee also agreed to establish training programs to raise awareness of the company's anti-discrimination policies.

To make sure that it is on the cutting edge of preventing racial discrimination, IBM has established individual employee task forces for almost every group that is employed by the huge company, including men, women, blacks, Hispanics, Asians, Native Americans, gays and lesbians, and disabled persons. The groups, which are established at many of the company's offices, meet regularly to discuss diversity and workplace concerns. This represents an extreme example of the steps companies are taking to prevent discrimination, but actions of this type are becoming more common.

Companies need to take steps to ensure that the training programs they adopt are appropriate and serve the purpose for which they are intended. For example, publishing giant R.R. Donnelly & Sons was sued in 1998 because elements of its training program were deemed discriminatory. Scenes from a training film that depicted the lynching of black slaves, as well as offensive questions from a questionnaire designed to make white workers confront racism, were challenged by a group of 3,500 black Donnelly employees that filed suit against the company. The training program had been instituted after the company was hit with a discrimination lawsuit in 1993. There are so many examples of diversity training gone bad that a new group of consultants has come into existence—their sole job is to visit companies to correct the damage caused by faulty diversity training programs.

AFFIRMATIVE ACTION

Affirmative action is a controversial policy that is intended to counteract racial discrimination. *West's Encyclopedia of American Law* defines affirmative action as referring "to both mandatory and voluntary programs intended to affirm the civil rights of designated classes of individuals by taking positive actions to protect them." In other words, affirmative action actively promotes the interest of minorities over nonminorities in order to correct past discrimination. For example, in a situation where a test is required before starting a particular job or to earn a promotion, minorities may be given preference over nonminorities for that job or promotion even though they score lower on the test than the nonminority worker. While this may seem wrong to some people, those who support affirmative action argue that past acts of discrimination have been so blatant that extraordinary steps are required to overcome those acts. At the start of the twenty-first century, however, affirmative action programs are under fire across the United States, with numerous court challenges occurring across the country.

One effect of affirmative action has been an increase in "reverse discrimination" lawsuits, in which nonminority workers allege that they have been discriminated against. In situations where companies have used affirmative action to help undo decades of blatant discrimination, white workers have become upset over being passed over for jobs and promotions. They claim that, if it is unfair to not hire a qualified worker just because he or she is a minority, then it should be equally unfair to not hire a qualified worker just because he or she is white. White employees have argued that, even though they have higher qualifications, experience, and skill, they are being passed over for jobs in favor of less-qualified candidates who are minorities.

In response to reverse discrimination lawsuits involving affirmative action programs, courts have recognized the need to overcome past racial bias, but have also sided with the nonminority workers in many cases. For example, in an attempt to redress past problems, a public university ruled that women and minorities would no longer have to take a test to qualify for a special employment program. As a result, for nine years, every job opening in the program went to a woman or a minority, even though white males represented half of the applicant pool. When the university's program was challenged in a lawsuit brought by white males, the courts ruled that the test exemption ensured that "the sole purpose of the affirmative action plan was to circumvent a lawful . . . preference program" and that the exemption violated Title VII because it caused white men to be excluded from the job in question. The school was forced to pay $113,000 to settle the case and correct the reverse discrimination.

Reverse discrimination does not always have to involve affirmative action, however. In 1999, five white instructors at traditionally black Livingstone College sued the college and charged it with racial discrimination. The five faculty members argued that documents proved that college administrators were attempting to fill all faculty positions with black teachers, going so far as to remove whites from department chairs and other positions. One of the plaintiffs in the case even filed a separate lawsuit, arguing that he had suffered "emotional pain and suffering" when he was passed over in favor of less-qualified black teachers.

RACIAL DISCRIMINATION STILL ON THE RISE

While great strides have been made to improve race relations in some areas, there is statistical evidence to show that racial discrimination in the workplace is still disturbingly commonplace. In 2000, the EEOC reported the results of a study of workplaces in North Carolina that showed that accusations of racial harassment on the job nearly quadrupled between 1996 and 2000, jumping from 16 reported incidents in 1996 to 62 in 2000 in just one region of the state. Mindy Weinstein, attorney at the EEOC office in Charlotte, North Carolina, was uncertain of what caused the increase, but she had some ideas. "There's a new generation of workers today who were not raised in the civil rights movement, who may not have been aware of the laws that came about because of that time," she said in the *Raleigh News & Observer*. "We think it's largely a reflection of what's going on in society as a whole."

Another potential cause of the increase is the fact that, thanks to earlier efforts to wipe out racial discrimination, there are more minorities than ever before in the workplace and also in high-level positions of power. Because minorities have been able to compete on a level playing field, they have been able to rise through the ranks more quickly, often taking jobs that were traditionally held by white workers. This can lead to resentment among the formerly dominant workers who are now lower on the employment ladder.

Another example of how racial discrimination is on the rise despite efforts to combat it involves wages. Traditionally, there has been a "wage gap" between minority and nonminority employees. That means

that, when a minority worker and a nonminority worker held the exact same job, the minority worker was paid less money for his or her efforts. From the 1940s to the 1970s, that gap between minority and nonminority workers actually narrowed as civil rights legislation was enacted and prevailing attitudes changed. However, in the 1980s and 1990s, the gap has actually reversed directions and begun to widen once again, according to *Nation's Cities Weekly*. The gap is increasing for both men and women and for all educational levels. In addition, the unemployment level for black workers has risen at the same time. A study by the Catalyst nonprofit group reported in *HR Focus* showed that men of color in management earned 75 cents for every dollar earned by white males in the same job in 1998, while women of color earned 57 cents.

FURTHER READING:

"Breaking the Color Barrier." *HR Focus*. July 1998.

"The Civil Rights Act of 1964 and the Equal Opportunity Employment Commission." National Archives and Records Administration website. http://www.nara.gov/education/cc/eeoc.html.

"Damned if You Do, Damned if You Don't." *Forbes*. December 15, 1998.

"Discrimination Laws Provide Protection to Job Applicants." *Supervision*. August 1999.

"Institutional Racism, Part II: Race, Skill, and Hiring in U.S. Cities." *Nation's Cities Weekly*. June 19, 2000.

Moss, Philip I., and Chris Tilly. *Stories Employers Tell: Race, Skill and Hiring in America (Multi-City Study of Inequality)*. Russell Sage Foundation, 2001.

"Reports of Racism at Work Increasing." *Raleigh News & Observer*. December 11, 2000.

SEE ALSO: Affirmative Action

REBATES

Rebates, widely known as refunds, are a popular tool used by businesses to promote their products and services. Rebates are distinct from coupons and other forms of discounting in that they reimburse a customer for part of the purchase price following, rather than at the time of, the sale. By offering consumers cash back on the purchase price, rebates provide an incentive to buy a particular product.

A relatively new method of promotion, rebating evolved from the marketing technique of offering coupons. They were initially offered by producers of grocery-store goods and subsequently by manufacturers of nonfood items. Currently, businesses making use of rebates are diverse and include the manufacturers of health and beauty aids, household supplies, and small and large appliances, as well as automakers, wine and liquor manufacturers, and segments of the computer industry.

The cash amounts these companies offer their customers is similarly wide-ranging; some rebates of less than a dollar are offered, while other rebates on ''big ticket'' items such as automobiles have reached several thousand dollars. The size of the rebate offered depends on the base retail price, the nature of the product being promoted, and the number of goods backed up in the production pipeline.

HOW REBATES WORK

The first step in rebating, as outlined by Susan J. Samtur in *Cashing in at the Checkout,* is for the manufacturer to issue an offer of a rebate to all who purchase its product; typically the offer carries an expiration date of six to eight months. The purchaser then completes a form provided by the manufacturer and mails it—along with any other items the manufacturer may require, such as a cash-register receipt or the Universal Product Code (UPC) snipped from the packaging—to the address specified on the form.

Most commonly, the purchaser sends the rebate form and related ''proof of purchase'' items not to the manufacturer but to one of several large clearinghouses hired by the manufacturer to handle these transactions—for instance, the Young America Corporation in Minnesota or the Nielson Clearing House in Texas. The clearinghouse then processes the form and sends the purchaser a check in the manufacturer's name, usually within four to eight weeks from the time the purchaser mails in the required information.

Companies use a number of means to get their rebate forms into the hands of customers. Many companies supply a pad of tear-off rebate forms to the stores selling their products; others print the form directly on the packaging or on a tag hanging from the merchandise. To announce the rebate offer and distribute the forms, companies may also place advertisements in newspapers and magazines, utilize home mailers, and/or place ads in the myriad refunders' newsletters developed by consumers to avail themselves of these offers. In addition, companies frequently use television and radio advertisements to publicize their rebate promotions. Finally, there are several Internet sites that direct consumers to rebate offers.

ADVANTAGES AND DISADVANTAGES OF REBATES

Rebates are highly attractive to most consumers, for they provide a partial cash reimbursement for their purchases that is tax-free (the Internal Revenue Service views rebates as a reduction in the price paid for a product, rather than as income). And for manufacturers, rebating provides numerous advantages: it induces prospective customers to try their products; it boosts company sales and visibility; it relieves problems of excess inventory; and it attracts interest from retailers, who often help promote the offer and expand the shelf space allotted to the manufacturer's goods accordingly. Rebate promotions can thus help a company increase its leverage with retailers and develop brand loyalty and repeat business among consumers over the long run. Indeed, a study conducted by United Marketing Services (UMS) found that rebates are an effective means of establishing product awareness with consumers. In addition, the information consumers provide on rebate forms can be used to target future promotions.

As rebates have increased in popularity, however, several common problems have emerged. For example, many companies have experienced problems honoring their rebate offers, largely due to an inability to keep up with demand. In fact, some companies offer rebates with the knowledge that only a small percentage of consumers bother to take advantage of them. ''Most . . . companies are hoping that although rebates will entice consumers to buy their products, most people will never actually get around to dealing with all the rigmarole required to redeem them,'' Roberta Furger wrote in *PC World.* These companies fail to anticipate the interest in a particular offer and thus plan their rebate processing poorly, resulting in long delays in sending checks to consumers.

Due to the frequent mix-ups and delays in processing rebate submissions, some consumers now tend to view rebate offers as a sleazy marketing tactic. This means that fewer consumers will base their purchase decisions on the availability of a rebate. Experts note that consumers can increase their chances of receiving rebates due by sending all the documentation requested in the rebate offer; keeping copies of all forms and receipts; checking on the status of overdue rebates with the company; and reporting any problems to the Federal Trade Commission, the Better Business Bureaus, or the state attorneys general. Finally, experts advise consumers to never buy anything just for the rebate.

FURTHER READING:

Furger, Roberta. ''The Trouble with Rebates.'' *PC World.* November 1997.

Kandra, Anne. ''Rebate, Rebate, Who's Got the Rebate?'' *PC World.* July 2000.

Royal, Leslie E. ''Reap the Rebates.'' *Black Enterprise.* July 2000.

Samtur, Susan J., with Tad Tuleja. *Cashing in at the Checkout.* Stonesong Press/Grosset & Dunlap.

SEE ALSO: Coupons; Discount Sales

RECIPROCAL MARKETING

Reciprocal marketing describes a situation in which two businesses promote each other in order to gain a mutual benefit. In the late 1990s and early 2000s, it has become a highly popular method of marketing for electronic retailers. In the online business world, reciprocal marketing is also known as reciprocal linking, because the most common application involves placing links on another company's Web site. A similar concept for Internet businesses is affiliate marketing, which occurs when one of the businesses involved in a reciprocal marketing arrangement pays the other for traffic or sales generated through a link. In the brick-and-mortar business world, reciprocal marketing is more commonly known as co-op marketing or cross-promotion.

Reciprocal marketing is equally popular among small, entrepreneurial Web sites and large, well-established ones. Writing in *Entrepreneur,* Melissa Campanelli called it "a reliable strategy employed by the most innovative dotcoms. . . . The tactic basically allows you to offer your paying customers discounts at your online partners' sites as well as provide discounts to your partners' customers on your site." As an example, a customer who spends $50 or more on your Web site might earn a coupon good for a discounted purchase on your partner's site. "These kinds of deals are the way the Internet will be working, going forward," Steven Bellach of the electronic florist site Proflowers told Campanelli. "The beauty of it is that no cash changes hands between merchants, and you get people when their wallets are still open."

Reciprocal marketing offers small business owners a number of potential benefits. For example, it helps reduce the cost of attracting new customers, adds value to customers' shopping experience, and is inexpensive to implement compared with many traditional marketing schemes. As Hollis Thomases explained in an article for the *Baltimore Business Journal,* the key to successful reciprocal marketing is to find the right partners. The most suitable companies will be complementary in terms of philosophy, product line, and brand image. It may also be helpful to target Web sites that see roughly the same number of visitors as your company's, since the arrangement should be mutually beneficial rather than self-serving. But small business owners should be careful not to clutter their Web sites with dozens of links offering discounts. In addition to confusing customers, including too many links might cause traffic to leave your site before making a purchase.

Small business owners can find potential partners for reciprocal marketing arrangements through traditional forms of networking, such as attending conferences. Thomases also recommended networking online. Some possible methods include contacting the Webmasters of sites you like, e-mailing the authors of message board postings that relate to your business, and subscribing to e-mail discussion groups on subjects that relate to your business. Before approaching potential partners, it may be helpful to define the value your site has to offer. Although experts state that Internet entrepreneurs should not depend on reciprocal marketing as their only form of promotion, they do admit it is a valuable way for e-businesses to grow. "At the core of a strategic online alliance is the desire to grow your e-business," Thomases wrote. "It will allow you to extend your reach and save on marketing costs."

FURTHER READING:

Campanelli, Melissa. "Give and Take: Why It Pays to Partner Up on Your Marketing Efforts." *Entrepreneur.* March 2001.

Nucifora, Alf. "Get Creative and Form That Marketing Partnership." *Orlando Business Journal.* January 26, 2001.

Thomases, Hollis. "Strategic Partnerships Drive Success on Internet." *Baltimore Business Journal.* March 24, 2000.

SEE ALSO: Banner Advertisements

RECORD RETENTION

Record retention refers to the practice of retaining copies of business or personal records over time. It is important for small business owners not only to keep good records, but also to know which ones to retain and for how long. Some aspects of record retention are determined by Internal Revenue Service (IRS) guidelines. Certain records that substantiate a small business's income, expenses, and withholding and payment of taxes must be retained for at least three years, or until the statute of limitations on an IRS audit expires. But good record retention is also in the best interest of companies. A poor system can not only prevent managers from retrieving the information they need to make sound business decisions, but can also pose a security risk.

The means chosen for record retention are also important for the simple reason that small businesses often suffer from a shortage of space. An article in *Purchasing* noted that paper records in an average business multiply at a rate of 7 percent per year, while electronic data stored on computer networks increases at a rate of 60 percent per year. Although some small businesses may find it adequate to keep their records in file folders, many find it helpful to use an electronic storage medium. The IRS issued new guidelines regarding electronic storage of business records in early 1997.

TYPES OF RECORDS

Businesses generate three main kinds of records: income, expenses, and capital expenditures. Income includes the revenue from sales of products or services, including both cash receipts and the collection of receivables. Expenses include cash disbursements and accounts payable that cover all operating expenses. These records should be maintained continuously. In the case of expenses, the records must not only prove that an expense was incurred, but also show how it was related to business. This is particularly important in the case of meals and entertainment expenses, for which the records must indicate the date, place, amount, and purpose of the expenses, as well as the type of business relationship with the person entertained.

It is also important for small business owners to keep records for major capital purchases to determine depreciation for tax purposes. These records must include the date and place of purchase, a complete description of the item, the amount paid, how it was purchased, and the date when it was put into service for the business. Keeping these basic business records enables business owners to track their progress, identify problems, and take advantage of all possible tax deductions.

Small businesses that employ people other than the owner or partners are required by the IRS to keep detailed payroll records. In fact, there are a total of 20 different types of records that must be kept for income tax withholding, FICA (Social Security) tax withholding, and FUTA (federal unemployment) taxes. These records—which include employees' names, addresses, and Social Security numbers, the amount and date of wages paid and withheld, and the amount of each type of tax paid, among other things—must be retained for at least four years from the time the relevant taxes were due or were paid, whichever was later. Experts also recommend that small businesses keep careful records regarding any automobile, life, fire, health, and other insurance coverage they hold. These records should list policy numbers and carriers, amounts of premiums and dates paid, and information on claims.

RECORD-RETENTION POLICIES

In addition to meeting legal and tax requirements, good record retention policies can help small businesses improve the efficiency and productivity of day-to-day operations and reduce their costs. "With a carefully considered, written record-retention policy in place," Kelly Hackett wrote in *Association Management,* a small business "accrues a number of business and legal benefits. Important records are on hand, while unimportant records are not allowed to consume precious storage space. Storage and maintenance

costs are reduced. With important files well-organized, staff easily find files. Moreover, a thorough record-retention policy helps ensure compliance with applicable regulations."

In developing a record-retention policy, Hackett recommends that small businesses begin by surveying their activities to see which records are most important to retain. The next step is to make sure that the policy meets all applicable legal and tax requirements. The record-retention policy should separate the business's records into categories, then specify the types of records retained for each category and the minimum retention periods. Finally, Hackett suggests that small businesses help employees understand the policy and know where to access records, and that management review the policy periodically to make sure it continues to meet business needs and legal requirements.

HOW LONG TO RETAIN VARIOUS TYPES OF RECORDS

There are a number of different types of records that small business owners should retain indefinitely—for the life of the business. These include copies of federal income tax returns, annual financial statements, general ledgers, fixed asset records, and corporate documents (charter, bylaws, stock records, patent and trademark applications, labor contracts, pension records, etc.). Regular business documents that support financial statements and tax payments—such as canceled checks, payroll checks, bank statements, invoices, purchase orders, and personnel records—should be retained for at least six years. These time periods allow for a margin of safety in meeting the IRS rules, which also address the means that may be used in retaining records.

Most of the IRS guidelines for record retention are included in Section 6001 of the Internal Revenue Code. "Virtually all taxpayers are required to keep records sufficient to establish the amount of gross income, deductions, credits, or any other relevant matters concerning their tax liability," Noelle Allen explained in an article for *The Tax Advisor.* These records can take the form of paper files or computerized data. Further IRS guidelines for record retention were issued in 1997 through Procedure 97-22, which allows taxpayers to transfer their paper files or computerized records to an adequate electronic storage media. "The general requirements are that an electronic storage system must ensure an accurate and complete transfer of the hard copy or computerized books and records to an electronic storage media, and the system must also index, store, preserve, retrieve, and reproduce the electronically stored books and records," Allen wrote. The procedure allows the IRS to test the storage system periodically without actually conducting an audit, and if it does not comply with the guidelines then the taxpayer may be subject to penalties.

More information about record retention is available in the IRS publications *Recordkeeping for Individuals* and *Guide to Record Retention Requirements*.

FURTHER READING:

Allen, Noelle. ''New Revenue Procedure Outlines Electronic Record Retention Rules and Allows for Destruction of Originals.'' *The Tax Advisor*. July 1997.

Dailey, Frederick W. *Tax Savvy for Small Business: Year-Round Tax Advice for Small Businesses*. Berkeley, CA: Nolo Press, 1997.

''Don't Underestimate the Need for Recordkeeping.'' *Purchasing*. November 9, 1995.

Jacobs, Jerald A., and Kelly P. Hackett. ''Record-Retention Policies.'' *Association Management*. September 1998.

Krumwiede, Tim, Raymond A. Zimmermann, and Patricia Eason. ''Record Retention Needed to Avoid Tax Redeterminations.'' *Taxation for Accountants*. December 1995.

Serchuk, David, and Jonathan Senft. ''Q & A: Record Retention.'' *Compliance Reporter*. December 18, 2000.

SEE ALSO: Internal Revenue Service Audits

RECRUITING

Recruiting describes the processes companies use to find qualified candidates to fill job openings. Some types of recruiting, such as college recruiting and networking, also serve to bolster the company's image among certain groups of potential employees. Effective recruiting is particularly important for small businesses, since finding and hiring talented employees is a key ingredient for growth. The Small Business Association publication *Human Resources Management* outlines three main steps in the recruiting process: assessing future personnel needs; developing a detailed description of the position to be filled and a corresponding profile of the person needed to fill it; and selecting the sources that will yield the best possible candidates. Throughout the recruiting process, small business owners must remain aware of the legal issues involved in hiring employees.

Assessing future personnel needs involves taking a close look at the company's expected workload, the capabilities of the current work force, the anticipated turnover, and the available labor supply. How the company stands in relation to these factors will help management to forecast future employment needs and develop a strategy to meet them. When a need has been identified, the next step is to perform a job analysis to collect information on all the tasks involved in the position and the types of skills, knowl-edge, and abilities required to do them. The job analysis leads directly to a job description, which defines all the duties and responsibilities of the position to be filled. Finally, the small business owner can use the job description to prepare a job specification—a written description of the person needed to fill the position. The job specification is the basis for recruiting, as it provides the standard against which applicants can be measured.

Next comes the actual search for candidates. In his book *Hiring Winners,* Richard J. Pinsker recommends that companies begin the search process as early as possible in order to generate a long list of candidates from which to choose. Even in the early stages of the hiring process, it is vital to consider the legal environment. The Civil Rights Act of 1964 and the Equal Employment Act of 1972 forbid discrimination based on race, color, national origin, sex, age, disability, veteran status, or religion. Therefore, it is illegal for recruiters to inquire about an applicant's age, marital status, children, nationality, or church, and employers must be careful to avoid any mention of such issues in employment ads. It is also illegal to require candidates to submit a picture along with their applications.

SOURCES OF QUALIFIED APPLICANTS

There are a wide variety of sources available for small business owners to use in finding qualified applicants to fill job openings. Some of the most common sources include:

- *Current employees.* Promoting someone from within the company helps keep employee morale high, but small business owners should take this approach only if the person meets the job specifications. In order to facilitate hiring from within, many companies maintain a skills bank on current employees, post notices about job openings and encourage employees to apply, and incorporate apprenticeship programs into employee training. Hiring from within may be difficult when there is a pressing need to fill a position and the required expertise does not exist in-house. Furthermore, Pinsker noted that it is a good idea for companies to fill at least 20 percent of job openings from outside, because outsiders tend to bring new ideas.

- *Employee referrals.* Many job openings in small businesses are best publicized by employees via word of mouth. Most employees will only recommend applicants with proven abilities. New hires can be an especially good source of referrals.

- *Networking.* Networking—developing a wide range of personal contacts within the industry and community—can provide a number of benefits to small business owners, including job candidates or referrals. Sources of networking connections include trade shows, associations, committee memberships, and charity functions. Pinsker suggests that business owners also encourage their employees to develop their own networks of contacts and to contribute names to the company list.

- *Unsolicited applications.* Most businesses receive unsolicited resumes and job applications when they are not hiring. All applicants should be treated courteously, but the materials submitted by qualified candidates should be kept on file for future reference.

- *Schools and colleges.* Depending on the type of position to be filled, high schools, trade and vocational schools, colleges, and universities can be good sources of candidates. Students are particularly good candidates for part-time positions or those in which prior experience is not needed. College recruiting is generally handled through a placement office. Companies usually send a representative to campus twice per year to meet with and interview students. Pinsker emphasizes that business owners should consider college recruiting as an opportunity to promote their company to both students and faculty.

- *Alumni placement offices.* Many colleges keep resumes on file for alumni who are seeking job or career changes. Alumni files can be a good source for companies seeking educated candidates with more work experience than recent graduates generally have.

- *Job fairs.* Job fairs can be useful for companies that need to hire several employees in a given specialty, such as engineering or computer programming. At a job fair, companies usually pay a booth fee and send representatives to collect resumes and pre-screen candidates. Like college recruiting, job fairs provide small businesses with an opportunity to promote themselves to potential hires.

- *Associations.* Most trade associations maintain a central clearinghouse of candidates who wish to change jobs. Trade shows, conventions, and seminars sponsored by associations can also provide valuable opportunities to meet potential employees.

- *Public employment offices.* The U.S. Department of Labor offers job placement services to some categories of workers free of charge. In many cases, public employment offices will provide small businesses with lists of pre-screened applicants for a certain opening.

- *Private employment agencies.* These organizations match job seekers with potential employers for a fee, usually paid by the employer once a candidate is hired.

- *Outplacement agencies.* Outplacement firms are similar to private employment agencies, but their fees are usually paid by former employers who have laid off or downsized workers. Small businesses with job openings can usually be placed on a mailing list free of charge to receive information on candidates who need a new job.

- *Temporary services.* These firms offer employees to fill a wide range of needs, from clerical to manufacturing to professional services. Hiring temporary employees can be a valuable method for companies to screen people before hiring them on a permanent basis.

- *Advertising.* Employment advertising includes everything from a ''help wanted'' sign in the window, to print ads in local newspapers or specialized publications like trade magazines, to classified ads on cable television or the Internet. For a small business, publicizing the fact that job openings exist is key to gaining access to a pool of applicants. Advertising can be expensive, however, so it is important to evaluate media carefully. It may be helpful to ask other business owners about their experiences advertising in various media. Small business owners must also be sure that their employment ads comply with equal opportunity employment laws and do not expose the company to charges of discriminatory hiring practices. Ads should concentrate on the skills and responsibilities of the position, rather than on the traits of applicants. In print ads, it is important to avoid nuances that suggest a certain gender or age of applicant is preferred. For example, the word ''salesman'' should be replaced with ''salesperson,'' ''waitress'' should be changed to ''wait staff,'' and ''young'' should be deleted in favor of ''energetic.'' In addition, the recruiter should make certain that all the qualifications listed are actually necessary for effective performance of the job.

- *Internet job banks.* There are a number of recruiting sites on the Internet that allow employers to screen candidates online. The Internet can be a valuable recruiting tool, particularly in terms of locating potential employees. Experts recommend that employers use several of the hundreds of available sites in order to find the ones that best meet their needs.

Other possible sources of recruiting leads include bankers, accountants, consultants, customers, competitors, and other professionals with whom the small business has regular contact. If the recruiting process is successful, the small business owner will have a substantial list of qualified candidates from which to select the one person who best matches the job specifications. The selection should be made through a formal screening process that may include an employment application, employment tests, and a personal interview. Each step in the process serves to narrow the field of candidates until a final selection can be made.

FURTHER READING:

Nicholas, Way. ''Talent War.'' *Business Review Weekly.* August 18, 2000.

Pinsker, Richard J. *Hiring Winners.* AMACOM, 1991.

Porter, Tom. ''Effective Techniques to Attract, Hire, and Retain 'Top Notch' Employees for Your Company.'' *San Diego Business Journal.* March 27, 2000.

Roberts, Gary, Gary Seldon, and Carlotta Roberts. *Human Resources Management.* Small Business Administration, n.d.

Shealy, Jane. ''Recruiting and Retaining Top Talent.'' *Success.* September 2000.

RECYCLING

Over the past few decades, recycling has become a central component of many business operations in the United States. Recycling is valued for the cost-savings associated with some programs as well as its general environment-friendly aspects. Recycling programs are comprised of three elements in a continuum represented by the well-known ''chasing arrows'' symbol that adorns recyclable products: 1) collection of recyclable materials from the waste stream; 2) processing of those materials into new products; and 3) purchasing of products containing recycled materials.

THE GROWTH OF RECYCLING IN THE BUSINESS WORLD

The importance of recycling programs in the business world to the environment can hardly be overstated. Businesses account for approximately one-third of the United States' total solid waste. As of 2000, for example, a study cited in the *Business Journal—Milwaukee* indicated that each office worker in America produced between 120 and 150 pounds of recyclable office paper per year, only 10 percent of which was typically recycled. Not surprisingly, paper accounts for a higher percentage (an estimated 40 percent) of the American waste stream than any other material. Many corporate recycling programs reflect this reality, and even businesses with exceedingly modest recycling programs sometimes take steps to collect wastepaper for recycling.

Recycling first emerged as an ongoing component of business operations in the late 1960s and early 1970s, as concerns about the pace at which the United States and other nations were consuming natural resources became widespread. (Previous recycling campaigns, such as the ones introduced in America during World War II, were relatively short-term efforts that were not predicated on environmental concerns.) The first national Earth Day celebration in 1970 heralded anti-litter campaigns, the creation of the federal Environmental Protection Agency (EPA), and the introduction of some of the first municipal and corporate recycling programs.

Legislation during that period provided an additional impetus for recycling programs, especially in the federal government. The Solid Waste Disposal Act had established resource recovery goals as a priority for U.S. environmental and energy conservation programs. The Resource Recovery Act of 1970 amended the previous legislation, mandating paper recycling and procurement of recycled products in federal agencies wherever economically feasible. The well-known Resource Conservation and Recovery Act of 1976 completely revised both acts, imposing requirements regarding hazardous waste disposal and mandating the recycling of non-hazardous waste in federal facilities. The legislation included the requirement that federal agencies ''purchase items that contain the highest percentage of recovered materials practicable given their availability, price and quality.'' Around the same time, deposit laws that encouraged recycling of glass beverage bottles were passed in several states around the country.

The Environmental Protection Agency and the General Services Administration (GSA), which were jointly charged with administration of the program, launched ''Use It Again, Sam,'' an earnest and widespread federal office paper recycling program, in 1976. Within two years, 90 federal agencies and their

115,000 employees were recycling, their efforts guided by a comprehensive, EPA-issued manual. The federal recycling program declined in the 1980s. Many state and local governments around the country stepped in to fill this void in the ensuing decade, but overall, low disposal costs relegated recycling to little more than an afterthought of solid waste management in the 1970s and early 1980s.

In the late 1980s, however, several factors converged to revive interest in recycling as an attractive alternative to traditional disposal. Growing concerns about both the proliferation and toxic characteristics of landfills around the country brought closures, increased regulation, higher costs, and public opposition to location and expansion of landfills. Other options, such as incinerators, were explored, but these proved controversial as well. Another important factor was a general increase in anxiety about the state of America's (and the world's) environment. Finally, growing numbers of companies came to see environmental friendliness as a viable means of attracting consumers.

By the late 1980s, a number of eastern states had adopted mandatory recycling legislation. This trend toward recycling legislation, combined with increasing consumer demand for environmental responsibility and corporate frustration with rising waste disposal expenses, prompted a modest revitalization of recycling programs in the 1990s.

DEFINING "RECYCLABLE" AND "RECYCLED CONTENT"

Given the popularity of recycled products and the various benefits that accrue from being known as a good corporate citizen, most businesses are eager to use terms like "recyclable" and "recycled content" on their packaging and in their advertising. But as J. Stephen Shi and Jane M. Kane pointed out in *Business Horizons,* the government has clearly defined those terms to prevent businesses from making misleading or fraudulent recycling claims. "For a product to be labeled recyclable," wrote Shi and Kane, "the product must be easily collected, separated, or otherwise recovered from what would generally be considered trash and then used for making a new package or product." They go on to note that companies also have a responsibility to qualify whether it is the product or the packaging (or both) that is recyclable, or to qualify claims of responsibility if the product is purchased in an area with limited recycling facilities.

"Recycled content," meanwhile, refers to goods made out of materials that would have otherwise been thrown out for good, relegated to a landfill or incinerator. "To qualify as having recycled content," wrote Shi and Kane, "the materials can come from waste produced in either the manufacturing process or post-consumer use [materials recycled by consumers]. . . . Again, manufacturers must be careful to indicate exactly what part—the product or the package—is made from recyclable material. If there is more than one component to the packaging, the manufacturer must indicate exactly which part of the packaging is made from recycled content. An example of this type of packaging is a paperboard box that is made of recycled materials covered by plastic shrink wrap that is not." Finally, they warn that manufacturers are guilty of misleading consumers if they claim that a product is composed of recycled content in instances where the company was merely following normal industry practice. "A manufacturer that routinely gathers spilled raw materials after trimming finished products and then adds the trimmings to virgin material for further production of the same product cannot claim that its product is made out of recycled content," they explained.

Business consultants, officials, and environmental groups all recognize that some of the regulations regarding permissible recycling/environmental claims are complex, but they urge business owners not to let this fact scare them off. Full descriptions of the rules governing recycling claims are available, and the potential benefits—both to the business and the environment—can often make the additional research an ultimately worthwhile endeavor.

INITIATING AND MAINTAINING EFFECTIVE RECYCLING PROGRAMS

The federal government's *Office Recycling Program Guide* notes five basic, interconnected components of a comprehensive recycling program: education, collection, marketing, procurement, and monitoring and evaluation.

EDUCATION Education encompasses training of both leaders and participants in recycling practices. Not surprisingly, the most successful recycling programs are ones that have the active involvement of business owners and managers and the full participation of employees. Observers of successful recycling initiatives note that this involvement is much more likely to occur if the company owners and work force are well-informed about the reasons for recycling and the ways in which recycling practices can be effectively instituted. There are a wide variety of resources available to businesses interested in organizing recycling programs. Regional Environmental Protection Agency (EPA) offices and state-affiliated natural resource departments throughout the country offer information packets and recycling kits.

After learning about recycling in general, business owners and managers should continue the education process by studying the operational factors that will be unique to their company's recycling efforts.

One of the most effective ways in which this can be accomplished is through the use of a "waste audit." A waste audit should note the sources, amounts, and types of trash generated; the current methods and cost of disposal; and the volume of potentially recyclable trash. Based on these findings, leaders of recycling programs can determine which materials to target. Some experts advise beginning recyclers to limit their programs to one type of waste, usually high-quality bond and computer paper. Once participants have grown accustomed to recycling, the program can be expanded to include aluminum, newspaper, plastics, glass, cardboard and other materials. The types and volumes of materials to be recycled will govern the methods of collection employed.

COLLECTION Collection comprises the nuts-and-bolts logistics of separating, gathering, and storing recyclables from trash at their source. The most common methods of collection employed in the workplace are the desktop container, a series of designated containers, or a central collection area, but some businesses employ vendor sorting, where mixed recyclables are stored together and sorted off-site by the waste hauler. These containers are usually brought by janitorial or mailroom staff to a storage area, where they are kept until they are picked up. Some companies dealing with sensitive, proprietary, or confidential information may also need to consider destruction (by shredding, for example) as part of this step.

Maintenance of quality standards is paramount to this facet of a successful recycling program. Similar materials, like white and colored paper, may have a market separately, but are nearly worthless when mixed. Processors of most types of paper discourage commingling of "stickies" (labels, stickers and tape), food, and other contaminants. Although source separation has proven to be the best collection method, new technological advances will almost certainly relieve some of this separation pressure in the future.

MARKETING Marketing recyclable materials to a processor involves research and contracting. Dealers in waste paper—the most commonly recycled material—can be found in local phone directories or through contact with the Paper Stock Institute of America. The *EI Environmental Services Directory*, "the nation's largest, most in-depth directory of environmental service providers," lists and describes over 2,000 vendors. There are many variables that entrepreneurs and small business owners should heed when seeking a buyer for their recyclable materials, however. Foremost among these is usually cost. "The quality of a particular collected material greatly affects the price that interested buyers are willing to pay," stated the *Encyclopedia of the Environment*. "Uncontaminated materials—for example, glass that is free of stones, ceramics, or other material—command prices substantially greater than contaminated materials. To help in evaluating the quality of a material, government and industry organizations have developed numerous quality standards. The actual price of a material depends on additional factors such as its relative abundance and the subsequent cost of transporting it to manufacturers."

PROCUREMENT Although it is sometimes overlooked, procurement is a vital component of recycling programs. Procurement helps "close the recycling loop," for it is the process whereby companies arrange to purchase and use supplies made from recycled materials. Most analysts of recycling programs contend that implementation of this stage of recycling often lags behind other stages. Recent studies indicate that while an overwhelming majority of businesses do have recycling collection systems of one kind or another in place, a far lower percentage of those businesses purchase recycled materials for use in their own operations.

This is due in part to the costs associated with developing additional capacity to use "secondary"—rather than virgin—materials. As the *Encyclopedia of the Environment* observed, "market conditions must be appropriate for companies to even consider new investments, credit must be available for financing projects, and sites have to be found and regulatory permits obtained."

MONITORING AND EVALUATION Each aspect of the recycling program should be monitored and evaluated for efficiency and progress. This is especially important for smaller companies, where flawed practices can have a more pronounced impact on fundamental business health. A cost-benefit analysis of the program can strengthen management support and encourage expansion to other areas of the company and/or other products in the waste stream.

FURTHER READING:

Cichonski, Thomas J., and Karen Hill. *Recycling Sourcebook.* Gale Research, Inc., 1993.

Curry, Gloria. "Increasingly Cost-Effective, Recycling Programs Continue to Grow." *Office.* August 1993.

Eblen, Ruth A., and William R. Eblen, eds. *The Encyclopedia of the Environment.* Houghton Mifflin, 1994.

Kimball, Debi. *Recycling in America: A Reference Handbook.* ABC-CLIO, 1992.

Office Recycling Program Guide. Office of Administrative and Management Services, 1993.

Ortbal, John. "How to Cultivate an Office Recycling Program." *Modern Office Technology.* April 1991.

"Set Up an Office Recycling System." *Business Journal—Milwaukee.* February 11, 2000.

Shi, J. Stephen, and Jane M. Kane. "Green Issues." *Business Horizons.* January-February 1996.

Steuteville, Robert. "Corporate Recycling Reaps Savings." *BioCycle.* August 1993.

Webb, Nan. "Recycling Tasks Are Part of the Job." *Purchasing World.* March 1991.

REENGINEERING

Reengineering is a management tool that became popular in the late 1980s and early 1990s. Like many such tools, it aims to cut costs while at the same time increasing productivity and providing higher levels of service. And while all this is true, reengineering still offers companies much more. The concept that is at the heart of all reengineering projects is the need to stay competitive in today's business world, and this broad concept involves costs, quality, productivity, and a host of other business elements. All of this is achieved by taking drastic steps to radically change an organization in areas like staffing, technology, and office culture.

When a business decides to reengineer, it often does so as a last resort because previous efforts to change have failed. The situation has become serious enough that drastic measures must be taken. When this decision is made, the company must first determine what the problems within the company are and what needs to be done about them. When this is determined, a basic reengineering model is developed. Next, the company's core processes are discussed and redesigned. The final stage is to adopt the new design.

While this seems like a simple plan, recent studies suggest that between 50 and 70 percent of reengineering projects ultimately fail within their first five years. This is usually the result of a faulty new design or the inability to implement one once it is created. Lack of support from management and employees also contribute to this surprisingly large rate of failure.

REENGINEERING TRAITS

One concept that is included in many reengineering models is downsizing or the reduction of staff. Getting rid of excess staff members is an obvious and many times painful way to cut costs. When this happens, the layoffs should be handled in such a fashion as to not strike fear into the main employee base, causing the company to lose its competitive edge while its most valuable assets (the employees) wonder what's going to happen next. If it is decided that the majority of the problems lie at the top of the company, then managers are often among the first to be let go. When this happens, the new business management team is expected to lead the company forward in their reengineering efforts. It is their job to get the rest of the company's employees on board with their new line of thinking. This participation involves trust, cooperation, and commitment from everyone involved.

In order to successfully achieve this goal, an internal reengineering team should be formed. The chances for success are greater if people with differing opinions are selected for the team. This can include people who are familiar with the inner workings of the company, those with little knowledge in this area, customers, and outside consultants. When choosing team members from within the company, it is best to consider people who have different areas of expertise in order to get more diverse and numerous ideas. Despite all these requirements, the team should not get too big, because it could become unmanageable. A team of no more than ten is suggested.

Because reengineering can be a drastic process, employees within the company can often experience a groundswell of emotions, including shock, fear, denial, anger, and anxiety. Most of these feelings can be attributed to the strong sense of change that is in the air. Management should be quick to notice these tendencies and work hard to calm any resentment that could be growing from within the company. They should also stress the excitement of the rebirth of the organization and try to muster enthusiasm from within. If they are successful, the fears of the employees could be replaced with anticipation as they help the company grow into a more competitive entity.

Many times reengineering involves reinventing the company from the ground up. While the concept of starting from scratch can be an exciting one, it can also be quite intimidating. Old habits should be abandoned and new ones adopted. This should be done in grand sweeping motions rather than small tiny steps, because the latter often offers the chance for the company to fall back into its old habits. This mind set can lead to things like liquidations, outsourcing of jobs, and mergers. Still, important things like customer relationships, company history, and the strengths of other past assets should not be forsaken during this period of starting over.

REENGINEERING ADVICE FROM THE OUTSIDE

Reengineering often tends to be a long, painful, and even confusing process. Many companies try to undertake reengineering internally, but with failed results. For these reasons, outside firms can be consulted to help develop the new business design. These firms offer their expertise on important matters that members of the internal management team need help on. The ideas that originate with outside reengineering consultants are often considered radical and fresh because they are not influenced by the history and current state of the company that is undergoing the reengineering effort.

For the most part, these outside consultants concentrate on the new business design and do not exhaust too much energy struggling to understand the current state of the company. Since one of the central reengineering ideas is to essentially start from scratch, this notion makes a lot of sense. These consultants are trained to take risks and create a sense of urgency in order to help make the sweeping changes necessary for reengineering success a reality. For this reason, most of the new business designs by outside firms happen rather quickly, while the overall implementation of the reengineering efforts can take a lot longer.

Reengineering can be a costly process. Outside consultants do not come cheaply and the implementation of a radically new business design can be expensive. Often a company under-budgets a reengineering effort and then is forced to go back and spend more than what was originally estimated.

WHY REENGINEERING OFTEN FAILS

As mentioned earlier, more than 50 percent of reengineering projects are unsuccessful within their first five years. With such a high rate of failure, it is curious why reengineering still exists as a management tool. Before totally condemning it, the main reasons for reengineering failures should be examined further.

Most reengineering projects fail because of a lack of support from upper management. While they are usually the ones who initiate the reengineering effort, they often fail to back it up because the changes are so great. Without proper management support, the necessary tools for a successful reengineering project (including money, leadership, and resources) may not be available.

Once the support from management becomes evident, the managers should keep the lines of communication open and honest so the necessary changes can successfully take effect. If everything is done amidst a cloud of secrecy, the chances for dissension and failure become greater.

A lack of strategy is another reason why reengineering fails. Before the project is undertaken, a lot of soul searching must be done within the organization. This most often requires that a simple, concise, business case study of the organization be written that identifies the problems, the goals of the reengineering effort, possible solutions, and how much time, money, resources, and people are needed for the project. The possible implications of standing pat and doing nothing should also be considered. This is a very important step in an reengineering project and if it is not done properly the results will almost certainly point to failure.

Of course, the possibility that those in charge are the main source of the company's problems is great. Many times management becomes too comfortable and out of touch with the ever-changing marketplace. They cannot see the problems with the company, because all too often they are responsible for them. This lack of objectivity and focus can sabotage even the most sincere reengineering efforts. Unfortunately, those that are not a part of upper management can do little to stop it.

When a company opts for changes that are just too radical, then the reengineering effort has a good chance of failure. All efforts should be in line with the company's previous goals and strategies, but different enough to make the necessary changes. While complex, reengineering should be simple enough that its goals are understandable by everyone involved.

REENGINEERING AND SMALL BUSINESSES

In the business world, large corporations often have large problems and seem to be the most likely candidates for a major overhaul through reengineering. That being said, reengineering can work for a small business too. With cost issues coming into play, an internal reengineering effort would seem like the logical choice for a small business. In order for this to be successful, a small business should scale their approach according to their size. They should become educated about reengineering and what it entails and study past cases to find an existing model or plan that could possibly work for them. If it is decided that outside help is needed, then the company should proceed carefully with a constant eye on their ultimate goal.

Since a smaller business would require a smaller reengineering plan, scrapping everything and starting from scratch may not necessarily be required. But as in larger businesses, reengineering requires careful planning, commitment, and an understanding of the company's goals. By reengineering its processes or functions, a small business has the chance to rebuild, grow, and remain competitive with their larger counterparts.

FURTHER READING:

Carr, David K., and Henry J. Johansson. *Best Practices in Reengineering.* McGraw-Hill, 1995.

Morris, Daniel C., and Joel S. Brandon. *Re-engineering Your Business.* McGraw-Hill, 1993.

REFINANCING

Refinancing is the refunding or restructuring of debt with new debt, equity, or a combination of both. The refinancing of debt is most often undertaken during a period of declining interest rates in order to lower the average cost of a firm's debt. Sometimes refinancing involves the issuance of equity in order to decrease the proportion of debt in the borrower's capital structure. As a result of refinancing, the maturity of the debt may be extended or reduced, or the new debt may carry a lower interest rate, or some combination of these options.

Refinancing may be done by any issuer of debt, such as corporations and governmental bodies, as well as holders of real estate, including home owners. When a borrower retires a debt issue, the payment is made in cash and no new security takes the place of the one being paid off. The term "refunding" is used when a borrower issues new debt to refinance an existing one.

CORPORATE OR GOVERNMENT DEBT REFINANCING

The most common incentive for corporations or governmental bodies to refinance their outstanding debt is to take advantage of a decline in interest rates from the time the original debt was issued. Another trigger for corporate debt refinancing is when the price of their common stock reaches a level which makes it attractive for a firm to replace its outstanding debt with equity. Aside from reducing interest costs, this latter move gives a firm additional flexibility for future financing; by retiring debt, the firm will have some unused debt capacity. Regardless of the reason for the refinancing, the issuer has to deal with two decisions: 1) Is the time right to refinance, and 2) What type of security should be issued to replace the one being refinanced?

If a corporation or governmental body wishes to refinance before the maturity date of the outstanding issue, they will need to exercise the call provision of the debt. The call provision gives the borrower the right to retire outstanding bonds at a stipulated price, usually at a premium over face amount, but never less than face value. The specific price which an issuer will need to pay for a call appears in the bond's indenture. The existence of a call premium is designed to compensate the bond holder for the firm's right to pay off the debt earlier than the holder expected. Many bond issues have a deferred call, which means the firm cannot call in the bond until the expiration of the deferment period, usually between five and ten years.

The cash outlay required by exercising the call provision includes payment to the holder of the bond for any interest which has accrued to the date of the call, and the call price, including premium (if any). In addition, the firm will need to pay a variety of administrative costs, including a fee to the bond's trustee. Of course, there will also be flotation costs for any new debt or equity that is issued as part of the refinancing.

Sometimes an issuer may be prohibited from calling in the bonds (e.g., during the deferred call period). In these instances, the issuer always has the opportunity to purchase its bonds on the open market. This strategy may also be advantageous if the outstanding bond is selling in the market at a price lower than the call price. Open market purchases involve few administrative costs. The corporation will recognize a gain on the repurchase if the market value is below the amount at which the corporation is carrying the bonds on its books (face value plus or minus unamortized premium or discount), or a loss on the repurchase if the market value is above the book value.

The major difficulty with open market purchases to effect a refinancing is that typically the market for bonds is "thin." This means that a relatively small percentage of an entire issue may be available on the market over any period of time. As a result, if a firm is intent on refinancing a bond issue, it almost always needs to resort to a call. This is why virtually every new bond that is issued contains a call provision. If an outstanding issue does not permit a call, another option available to the issuer is to seek tenders (offers to sell at a predetermined price) from current bond holders.

The new debt instrument issued in refinancing can be simple or complex. A corporation could replace an existing bond with traditional bonds, serial bonds (which have various maturity dates), zero-coupon bonds (which have no periodic interest payments), or corporate shares (which have no maturity date, but which may have associated dividend payments). One factor that a firm needs to consider is that the administrative and flotation costs of issuing either common or preferred shares are higher than for new debt. Furthermore, dividend payments, if any, are not tax deductible.

The decision to refinance is a very practical matter involving time and money. Over time the opportunity to refinance varies with changing interest rates and economic conditions. When a corporation anticipates an advantageous interest rate climate, it then analyzes the cash flows associated with the refinancing. Calculating the present value of all the cash outflows and the interest savings assists in comparing refinancing alternatives that have different maturity dates and capitalization schemes.

MORTGAGE REFINANCING

Owners of residential or commercial real estate use a similar method to analyze their refinancing decisions. In residential real estate the conventional wisdom applies the ''2-2-2 rule'': if interest rates have fallen two points below the existing mortgage, if the owner has already paid two years of the mortgage, and if the owner plans to live in the house another two years, then refinancing is feasible. However, this approach ignores the present value of the related cash flows and the effects of the tax deductibility of interest expense and any related points.

Therefore, a better analysis of a mortgage refinancing decision should be conducted as follows: 1) Calculate the present value of the after-tax cash flows of the existing mortgage; 2) Calculate the present value of the after-tax cash flows of the proposed mortgage; 3) Compare the outcomes and select the alternative with the lower present value. The interest rate to be used in steps one and two is the after-tax interest cost of the proposed mortgage.

FURTHER READING:

Arsan, Noyan, and Eugene Poindexter. ''Revisiting the Economics of Mortgage Refinance.'' *Journal of Retail Banking.* Winter 1993-1994.

Bierman, Harold, Jr., and Seymour Smidt. *Financial Management for Decision Making.* New York: Macmillan, 1986.

Freedman, Michael. ''The Right Way to Borrow.'' *Forbes.* December 11, 2000.

Hoeschen, Brad. ''Surge in New Home Mortgages Eases Loss of 'Refi' Business.'' *Business Journal—Milwaukee.* October 8, 1999.

Sharpe, William, F., and Gordon J. Alexander. *Investments.* 4th ed. New York: Prentice-Hall, 1990.

Tower, Jonathan. ''Rate Plunge Ignites a Boom in Refinancing Market.'' *American Banker.* August 8, 1997.

REGULATION D

Regulation D is a section of the U.S. federal securities law that provides the means for small businesses to sell stock through direct public offerings (DPOs). A DPO is a financial tool that enables a company to issue stock directly to investors—without using a broker or underwriter as an intermediary—and avoid many of the costs associated with ''going public'' through an initial public offering (IPO). Regulation D exempts companies choosing this form of offering from many of the registration and reporting requirements of the Securities and Exchange Commission (SEC).

DPOs, private placements of stock, and other exempt offerings provide small businesses with a quicker, less expensive way to raise capital than IPOs. The primary advantage of DPOs over IPOs is a dramatic reduction in cost. IPO underwriters typically charge a commission of 13 percent of the proceeds of the sale of securities, whereas the costs associated with a DPO are closer to 3 percent. DPOs also can be completed within a shorter time frame and without extensive disclosure of confidential information. Finally, since the stock sold through a DPO goes to a limited number of investors who tend to have a long-term orientation, there is often less pressure on the company's management to deliver short-term results.

DPOs and other exempt offerings also involve disadvantages, however. For example, the amount that a company can raise through a DPO within any 12-month period is limited. In addition, the stock is usually sold at a lower price than it might command through an IPO. Stock sold through exempt offerings is not usually freely traded, so no market price is established for the shares or for the overall company. This lack of a market price may make it difficult for the company to use equity as loan collateral. Finally, DPO investors are likely to demand a larger share of ownership in the company to offset the lack of liquidity in their position. Investors eventually may pressure the company to go public through an IPO so that they can realize their profits.

RULES 504, 505, AND 506

Regulation D—which was adopted in 1982 and has been revised several times since—consists of a set of rules numbered 501 through 508. Rules 504, 505, and 506 describe three different types of exempt offerings and set forth guidelines covering the amount of stock that can be sold and the number and type of investors that are allowed under each one. The most common type of DPO is the Small Corporate Offering Registration, or SCOR, which is included in Rule 504. SCOR gives an exemption to private companies that raise no more than $1 million in any 12-month period through the sale of stock. There are no restrictions on the number or types of investors, and the stock may be freely traded. The SCOR process is easy enough for a small business owner to complete with the assistance of a knowledgeable accountant and attorney. It is available in all states except Delaware, Florida, Hawaii, and Nebraska.

A related type of DPO is outlined in Rule 505. This option enables a small business to sell up to $5 million in stock during a 12-month period to an unlimited number of investors, provided that no more than 35 of them are non-accredited. To be accredited, an investor must have sufficient assets or income to make such an investment. According to the SEC rules, individual investors must have either $1 million in assets (other than their home and car) or $200,000 in net annual personal income, while institutions must hold $5 million in assets. Finally, a DPO conducted under Rule 506 allows a company to sell unlimited securities to an unlimited number of investors, provided that no more than 35 of them are non-accredited. Under Rule 506, investors must be sophisticated, or able to evaluate the merits and understand the risks of the transaction. In both of these options, the securities cannot be freely traded.

FURTHER READING:

Evanson, David R., and Art Beroff. "An Offer You Can't Refuse." *Entrepreneur.* April 1998.

Field, Drew. "Raising Equity through a Direct Public Offering." *Bankers Magazine.* March-April 1991.

Lowes, Robert L. "Try a Do-It-Yourself Public Offering." *Medical Economics.* April 14, 1997.

Sherman, Andrew J. *The Complete Guide to Running and Growing Your Business.* New York: Random House, 1997.

Steinberg, Carol. "The DPO Revolution: Direct Public Offerings Turn Customers into Investors." *Success.* March 1997.

Sutton, David P., and M. William Benedetto. *Initial Public Offerings: A Strategic Planner for Raising Equity Capital.* Chicago: Probus, 1988.

Taylor, Lon W. "Raising Capital through Private Placements." *Journal of Business Strategy.* July-August 1988.

Zeune, Gary D., and Timothy R. Baer. "Floating a Stock Offering: New Buoyancy from the SEC." *Corporate Cashflow Magazine.* August 1993.

REGULATORY FLEXIBILITY ACT

The Regulatory Flexibility Act (RFA) of 1980 is a law designed to make government agencies review all regulations that they impose to ensure that they do not place a disproportionate economic burden on small business owners and other small entities. The Regulatory Flexibility Act was intended to extend protection to three different types of small entities in the United States: small businesses (as defined by the Small Business Administration); small organizations (nonprofit establishments that are independently owned and operated and not dominant in their field); and small governmental jurisdictions (defined as governments of cities, counties, towns, townships, villages, school districts, and other districts with populations of less than 50,000).

In the years following the enactment of the RFA, however, many small business owners contended that agencies too often ignored the law. Periodic attempts to revise the RFA failed until March 1996, when the Small Business Regulatory Enforcement Fairness Act (SBREFA) became law. This new legislation cast the Regulatory Flexibility Act in an entirely new light, for it amended the 1980 law to allow for judicial review of government agencies' compliance with it.

Before the 1996 law was passed, small business owners had had no legal recourse when faced with regulations that they felt were unfair to smaller companies. "There was no statutory requirement that forces an agency to do an analysis," explained one spokesman for the Senate Committee on Small Business in *Nation's Restaurant News.* With the passage of the Small Business Regulatory Enforcement Fairness Act, however, "a small entity, including businesses—if an agency rule seems unfair—can challenge it in court. And if they prevail, they can modify it or strike it to reduce the impact on that entity."

LEGISLATIVE HISTORY OF THE RFA

Prior to 1980, American small businesses were forced to adhere to the same regulations as far larger companies, even though they did not have nearly the same resources to bring to bear. Entrepreneurs and directors of nonprofits repeatedly charged that when regulations put forth by the Environmental Protection Agency (EPA), the Occupational Safety and Health Administration (OSHA), and other agencies were applied evenly, without regard to the size of the enterprises affected, they sometimes did serious damage to smaller organizations. Such regulations had to do with taxes, workplace safety, and the environment, among other issues.

As the Small Business Administration noted in its *Guide to the Regulatory Flexibility Act,* "the costs of complying with a particular regulation . . . may be manageable for a business with 500 or more employees, or revenue in the millions of dollars. On the other hand, a smaller company may not have the ability to absorb the expenses as easily, to set competitive prices, to devise innovations or even to continue as a viable entity." The *Guide* added that as more businesspeople and politicians investigated the situation, "evidence indicated that uniform application of federal regulatory requirements imposed increases in the economies of scale and affected small entities' ability to compete effectively. Reports . . . cited these disproportionate economic burdens on small business as contributing to declines in productivity, competition, innovation, and the relative market shares of small business."

The passage of the RFA in 1980, then, was meant to blunt much of the burden that regulatory changes were laying on the shoulders of small businesses. According to the RFA, each agency was supposed to analyze how its regulations affected the ability of small businesses to compete. In addition, RFA directed agencies to balance the needs of small business with the benefits of the regulation being considered. The law called for agencies to propose regulatory alternatives for smaller companies that would be unduly hurt if forced to adhere to the original regulations. The Regulatory Flexibility Act still allowed agencies to put together needed regulatory measures in such realms as workplace safety and environmental protection, but it meant to give a greater voice to small businesses by encouraging agencies to listen to small business concerns and study ways in which regulations could be adjusted for them.

During the 1980s, however, many entrepreneurs and other members of the business community came to feel that the RFA was an unacceptably weak law. The law—which actually went into effect on January 1, 1981—included no legal penalties that could be imposed on agencies that did not follow the Act's guidelines, so some agencies paid little attention to the RFA. Observers felt that some agencies were simply recalcitrant, while others, burdened by inadequate budgets, did not have the resources to satisfactorily address the issues laid out in the RFA. Most observers granted that the Regulatory Flexibility Act was valuable in certain cases, but by the early 1990s there was a growing clamor in the small business community and Congress for an amended RFA.

In September 1993 President Clinton signed Executive Order 12866, which highlighted the responsibilities of government agencies to adhere to the principles of RFA. That same year, the Clinton administration's National Performance Review task force formally recommended that agency compliance with the RFA be subject to judicial review. Less than three years later, in March 1996, a number of major amendments to the RFA—including provisions adding judicial review—became law with the passage of the Small Business Regulatory Enforcement Fairness Act.

SMALL BUSINESS REGULATORY ENFORCEMENT FAIRNESS ACT

The 1996 act included several components that drew praise from small business owners. While the addition of judicial review of agency compliance with the RFA received the bulk of attention, the amendments also gave agencies additional responsibilities in the areas of policy review and outreach, and gave nonagency entities (small businesses, Congress) more influence in the regulatory process.

JUDICIAL REVIEW The Small Business Regulatory Enforcement Fairness Act amended the RFA so that small businesses finally had legal recourse when confronted with regulations that they felt did not adhere to the RFA. It created a complaint process whereby small businesses can seek review of the rule in court. Under the 1996 amendments, noted the SBA, "the court may review the final regulatory flexibility analysis, the agency's certification that the rule has no

impact on small entities, and the agency's compliance with periodic reviews of current rules. Under the amendment, judicial review also applies to interpretative rulemakings promulgated by the IRS [Internal Revenue Service]." (Prior to the 1996 legislation, interpretative rulemakings of the IRS had been exempt from the RFA because of provisions of the Administrative Procedure Act.) In addition, the RFA now includes a provision that reimburses small business operators for legal fees incurred if they successfully challenge a regulation as overly harsh.

PERIODIC REVIEWS SBREFA reinforced RFA review guidelines for government agencies. Under the amended RFA, agencies are required to review all existing regulations to see if they have a significant economic impact on meaningful numbers of small entities (businesses, nonprofits, small government bodies). In situations where a "significant" impact is found, the agency in question is directed to review the regulations and determine whether they should remain in place, be revised, or be rescinded. Factors to be evaluated include: continued need for the regulation; impact of industry and economic trends on the regulation; public comments on the regulation's strengths and weaknesses; complexity of the regulation; and extent to which the regulation overlaps, duplicates, or conflicts with already existing federal, state, or local laws.

OUTREACH RFA now requires both OSHA and EPA to put together small business advocacy review panels every time they propose a regulation that is likely to have a big economic impact on a large number of small businesses. This information-gathering step is designed to solicit small business input on both the likely compliance costs of the regulations and possible mutually acceptable regulatory alternatives. A report reflecting the results of the review panel meetings is then prepared.

In addition, federal agencies are directed under RFA to publish a listing of all proposed or final regulations expected to be implemented during the following year. This requirement, say proponents, provides small business owners with more time to study the regulations and their likely impact on their establishments. Finally, the RFA now requires agencies to prepare easily understandable guide books to help businesses comply with regulations.

EXPANDED AUTHORITY FOR CHIEF COUNSEL FOR ADVOCACY The 1996 amendments to the RFA expanded the authority of the SBA's chief counsel for advocacy. The RFA now allows the chief counsel—who has been formally designated to monitor agency compliance with the law—to file amicus briefs in situations where regulations are being reviewed in court.

LEGISLATIVE REVIEW A provision of the 1996 legislation established a 60-day review period during which Congress will be able to reject any new regulations that are held to be unnecessary.

Despite these changes, however, some critics contend that SBREFA has not lived up to expectations in its first two years of existence. ''The law was supposed to open up a new era of federal friendliness toward entrepreneurs,'' wrote Stephen Barlas in *Entrepreneur*. ''And while it's premature to call the law a bust, SBREFA's shortcomings are becoming readily apparent.'' Detractors argued that Congress showed little inclination to exercise its increased powers of legislative review, and they claimed that other review panels called for in SBREFA have been slow to take shape.

For further information on the Regulatory Enforcement Act, contact the Office of Advocacy of the Small Business Administration, Washington, DC.

FURTHER READING:

Allen, Robin Lee. ''Regulatory Bill Lets Small Operators Flex Muscles.'' *Nation's Restaurant News*. April 22, 1996.

Barlas, Stephen. ''In Limbo.'' *Entrepreneur*. December 1997.

Barlas, Stephen. ''Regulatory Relief: A New Bill to Ease Small-Business Burdens Just May Make It through Congress.'' *Entrepreneur*. April 1996.

Neese, Terry. ''Boosting Small Business Opportunities with RFA.'' *LI Business News*. June 11, 1999.

SBA Advocacy—Guide to the Regulatory Flexibility Act. Washington: U.S. Small Business Administration, 1997.

Warner, David. ''Putting the Brakes on Federal Rules.'' *Nation's Business*. March 1995.

RELOCATION

Relocation is the action of transferring a company's place of operation from one physical location to another. For small businesses, the act of relocating is often fraught with uncertainty, since the margin for error in companies with modest financial resources is so small. Indeed, the quality (or lack thereof) of a business relocation can be pivotal in determining the financial success or failure of all sorts of business ventures in a wide spectrum of industries, including retail, service, wholesale, and manufacturing efforts.

Small businesses look to relocate for many different reasons. Some business owners turn to relocation as a last resort, a final effort to reverse the fortunes of a floundering business. These efforts rarely succeed, though the reasons vary from business to business. In many cases, the source (or sources) of the business's financial difficulties lie in areas other than physical location. Inadequate capital, poor management, flawed marketing plans, wasteful production processes, lousy work habits, and a range of other maladies may be more directly responsible for a company's anemic performance than its physical location.

Of course, some small businesses struggle despite the presence of competent and hardworking management/ownership and sound business practices. In such cases, physical location might be a significant factor in the company's disappointing performance, and relocation could go far toward turning the business's financial fortunes around. But business experts note that relocation is generally an expensive process, and that small businesses that are struggling financially may find it difficult to stay afloat during this transition period.

After all, companies that decide to relocate must absorb several financial blows simultaneously: 1) They have to pay for the expense of moving their people, office furniture, and equipment into their new facilities; 2) They have to pay for necessary changes to the new facility (these changes can range from relatively minor rewiring to extensive reshaping of the facility's physical layout); 3) Before relocation, business owners and/or staff have to devote time to relocation research, negotiation, etc. that would otherwise be spent on attending to money-making tasks; and 4) During relocation, many businesses have to basically stop conducting their business until they are situated in their new place of business. This latter reality can cripple a fragile business, especially if the relocation process proves more problematic than anticipated (as it often is).

Of course, many successful businesses relocate as well, drawn by locales that feature high traffic, attractive physical attributes, proximity to needed transportation, advantageous financial terms, or, in some cases, a friendly community environment.

RELOCATION TRENDS

In recent years, business observers have pointed to a general trend in business relocations away from major metropolitan areas and toward small- and medium-sized communities. Certainly, some companies are limited in their relocation options by customer demographics and other factors, but many firms—especially those established by entrepreneurs—have forsaken large cities for smaller towns. Indeed, desires for quieter lifestyles away from pollution, crime, and other attributes often associated with large cities, coupled with the advances that have made telecommuting a reality, have led many entrepreneurs to relocate to more rural locations.

But although such settings have many positive aspects in terms of so-called ''quality of life'' considerations, entrepreneurs and other small business owners still need to weigh the potential drawbacks of making such a move on their livelihoods. As Brian Steinberg observed in *Entrepreneur,* "hurdles litter the track. [Entrepreneurs] must absorb the shock of adjusting to rural culture, navigate the difficulties of keeping family together, and discover new business practices necessitated by an out-of-the-way location."

Steinberg went on to describe several obstacles that small business owners may face when trying to make a successful relocation to a small-town setting. "The struggle to find employees constitutes one concern for rural entrepreneurs; getting along with the neighbors is yet another," he noted. "While the added tax dollars and employment opportunities a new company provides a small town are quite welcome, the success a firm might bring can also have some undesirable effects. A successful company may supersede existing firms in importance and influence, taking away employees and even driving up home prices. Towns sometimes offer economic incentives to lure new business owners—money local companies might view as ill-spent."

In addition, some entrepreneurs find that smaller communities do not provide the same level of services that can be found in larger cities. These inconveniences, noted Steinberg, can range from troublesome ones like unreliable electric service (perhaps necessitating the purchase of backup generators), lack of overnight delivery services (Federal Express, etc.), and an absence of local access numbers for Internet service (which can force businesses to pay exorbitant long-distance telephone costs to access the Internet), to downright crippling ones, like a dearth of qualified workers. "Preparation is the key to a successful move to the hinterlands," concluded Steinberg. "Location, available work force, proximity to transportation, local attitudes, and culture shock are all factors to consider."

LOCATION NEEDS OF VARIOUS BUSINESS TYPES

Small businesses will have different site needs that need to be considered when relocating, depending on their industry—retail, service, wholesale, or manufacturing—and their own financial and cultural factors. Whatever their area of business, however, small business owners need to make sure that they take the time to adequately examine all facets of a move. "A well organized site selection process should include research, planning, developing the transaction structure, analyzing the proposal, documenting the transaction, and negotiating for government incentives," wrote John R. Frazier in *Los Angeles Business Journal.*

When researching the merits and drawbacks of each potential relocation site, Frazier urged business owners to define each place by three primary measurements: specific location attributes, physical attributes, and occupancy cost parameters. "Specific location attributes might relate to transportation issues such as circulation patterns of surface streets and access to rail. Additional considerations would include corporate identity/image issues, attitudes regarding alternative government jurisdictions and any special utility needs for the proposed use," he wrote. "Physical attributes address structure and layout as they relate to form and function and include such on-site characteristics as topography, existing layout, ceiling heights and load bearing requirements. Goals with respect to occupancy costs will vary according to whether the firm plans to occupy on a fee ownership basis or as a tenant, but . . . could include special tenant improvement allowances, moving allowances, an option to purchase, a cash incentive, or even an ownership position as a tenant."

Business consultants and small business owners who have successfully undertaken relocation efforts urge managers and owners of small enterprises to examine a long list of specific concerns before making any relocation decisions. A relocation based on knowledge, after all, is far more likely to succeed than one that is predicated on assumptions and hopes. Following are some of the factors entrepreneurs should weigh in considering a relocation:

1) Determine if projected revenues will cover the cost of leasing or purchasing the site.

2) Research whether ancillary costs associated with the relocation can be absorbed by the company.

3) Honestly appraise the impact that relocation will have on the business's cash flow and productivity.

4) Determine whether it will be possible to secure lenders to help cover costs associated with moving into the new business site.

5) Investigate whether the targeted site is located in an area that has restrictive ordinances that will unduly interfere with your company's operations

6) Enlist the services of experts to determine if both the exterior and interior of the target building or facility are in good condition and adequately meet your business's layout and image requirements.

7) If refurbishment is necessary, find out how much it will cost and how long it will take.

8) Determine whether neighbor businesses complement your company, or whether they

might detract from your company's image or its ability to attract its primary demographic audience.

9) Gauge the attitudes of your workforce—and especially the feelings of key personnel—about relocation

10) If in an environment where you share maintenance, housekeeping, and other service costs with other companies, investigate whether the set-up is a good one for your company.

11) Check into the safety and security aspects of the facility.

12) Determine whether the site will be able to accommodate your company if it needs to expand.

13) Find out if competitors are located nearby. If so, try to determine how successful they are, and whether the region will be able to support your business and those of competitors.

14) Gauge whether the site is customer-friendly in terms of layout, parking, etc.

15) Is the area immediately surrounding the building in a state of flux? Development of vacant buildings or lots, construction sites, and other landmarks can dramatically change the complexion of an area.

16) Determine if leasehold improvements will need to be made.

17) Research whether existing or proposed government regulations might have an impact on the value of the facility.

18) Learn about the regulatory and tax climate of the area in which you are considering relocating.

19) Determine whether suppliers of raw materials and other goods and services necessary to your operation will be readily available.

Small business owners who take the time to inform themselves in these areas are far more likely to relocate successfully than those who do not attend to such issues.

FURTHER READING:

Ady, Robert M. ''Discussion: How to Select an Ideal Business Site.'' *New England Economic Review.* March-April 1997.

Bahls, Jane Easter. ''Love Thy Neighbor?'' *Entrepreneur.* July 1995.

Breuer, Nancy L. ''Company on Wheels.'' *Workforce.* December 2000.

Daly, Wadman. *Relocating Your Workplace: A User's Guide to Acquiring and Preparing Business Facilities.* Crisp Publications, n.d.

Frazier, John R. ''Keeping Goals in Site.'' *Los Angeles Business Journal.* May 25, 1992.

Karakaya, Fahri, and Cem Canel. ''Underlying Dimensions of Business Location Decisions.'' *Industrial Management and Data Systems.* July-August 1998.

Mihaly, Mary. ''Smart Moves.'' *Industry Week.* June 5, 1995.

Schriner, Jim. ''Picking Your Neighborhood.'' *Industry Week.* July 3, 1995.

Schriner, Jim. ''Where Will Employees Want to Live?'' *Industry Week.* March 3, 1997.

Steinberg, Brian. ''Green Acres: Why Some Entrepreneurs are Saying 'Goodbye, City Life.' '' *Entrepreneur.* October 1997.

Steingold, Fred S. *Legal Guide for Starting and Running a Small Business.* 3d ed. Nolo Press, 1997.

Venable, Tim. ''Getting Better Location Assistance: Here's How.'' *Site Selection.* April 1996.

Weber, Fred I., Jr. *Locating or Relocating Your Business.* Small Business Administration, n.d.

SEE ALSO: Site Selection

REMANUFACTURING

Remanufacturing is a process where a particular product is taken apart, cleaned, repaired, and then reassembled to be used again. Many different types of products can go through this process, including auto parts, tires, furniture, laser toner cartridges, computers, and electrical equipment. Essentially any product that can be manufactured can also be remanufactured. In order for a product to be considered remanufactured, most of its components should be used (although some of them can be new if the older parts are too defective to be salvaged).

As society continues to better understand the effects of pollution and the consequences that come with the depletion of our natural resources, different steps are being taken to ensure the health of the environment for future generations. This general awareness has led to many new developments to preserve our world. Remanufacturing is one such development. This process is responsible for large energy savings, extending the lives of landfills, and cutting down on the amount of air pollution that would normally occur when a product goes through a reprocessing procedure.

While the basic concept is quite simple, remanufacturing is actually an extensive process. It requires that a used product be completely disassembled in order to assess its actual condition. If it is determined that remanufacturing is worthwhile, various parts of the product are cleaned, restored, repaired, and replaced. Further refinements are then performed and the product is reassembled so that it once again operates in the manner for which it was intended. The product is then ready to be used again. Each step in this process is essential to the entire concept of remanufacturing and careful precautions must be taken to ensure that each step is carried out correctly.

MISCONCEPTIONS ABOUT REMANUFACTURING

Often, the process of remanufacturing gets confused with other similar activities. Rebuilt and recharged products are very close to remanufactured ones and the three terms can often be considered synonymous with each other. Rebuilt products usually refer to auto parts, while recharging is usually performed on imaging products like the aforementioned toner cartridges.

Other types of products are almost completely different from those that have been remanufactured. For example, a remanufactured product is not a recycled one. Recycling involves using a product or its parts as raw materials for a different product and is generally applied to consumable goods like newspapers, bottles, and cans. Very rarely are recycled products resold to be used as they were originally intended, and when they are, the quality is not as good as a remanufactured product.

In addition, a remanufactured product should not be confused with a repaired one. Usually when a product is repaired, the whole remanufacturing process is disregarded and only defective parts are investigated and replaced. Likewise, restored and reconditioned products are ones that are brought back to their original condition, but these changes are usually cosmetic and apply to things like antiques, rather than mass market consumer products. In addition, remanufactured products should not be classified as ''used.'' A used product is one that has not been repaired and therefore has no guarantees regarding its performance. Finally, demanufacturing and remanufacturing should not be confused with each other. Demanufacturing is simply the disassembly step that all products that are going to be remanufactured must go through.

REMANUFACTURING VS. RECYCLING

Although remanufacturing and recycling are two different things, many environmental groups are embracing the concept of remanufacturing over recycling because it cuts down on the use of energy and resources used for processing. While recycled goods are consumed, then returned to their original raw material form to be used again, remanufacturing ''recycles'' the value originally added to the raw material.

In the book *The American Edge: Leveraging Manufacturing's Hidden Assets*, Professor Robert T. Lund explained that ''Remanufacturing differs from recycling also, most importantly because it makes a much greater economic contribution per unit of product than does recycling. The essential difference arises in the recapture of value added. Value added is the cost of labor, energy, and manufacturing operations that are added to the basic cost of raw materials in the manufacture of a product. For all but the most simple durable goods, value added is by far the largest element of cost. Even in a product as simple as a beer bottle, the cost of the basic raw materials (sand, soda, and lime) is much less than 5 percent of the cost of a finished bottle. The rest is value added. For a product such as an automobile, the value of the raw materials that can be recovered by recycling is only in the order of 1.5 percent of the market value of the new car. Value added is embodied in the product. Recycling destroys that value added, reducing a product to its elemental value— its recoverable raw material constituents. Further, recycling requires added labor, energy, and processing capital to recover the raw materials. When all of the costs of segregation, collection, processing, and refining are taken into account, recycling has significant societal cost. Society undertakes recycling only because, for all nondurable and many durable products, the societal cost of any other disposal alternative is even greater.''

REMANUFACTURING AND SMALL BUSINESSES

Aside from environmental benefits, there are many other reasons why remanufactured goods exist. Like many good business decisions, remanufacturing simply saves money by prolonging the economic life of a product. A small business with a tight budget can save money by using remanufactured products because they often cost less (anywhere between 40 and 60 percent less) and come with warranties and extra services that guarantee their performance.

In recent years, remanufacturing has grown into a big business. Recent studies suggest that there are over 70,000 remanufacturing firms employing close to a half million people in the United States. Together, these firms make over $50 billion a year, proving that remanufacturing is a force to be reckoned with in today's economy. Because of this trend, it would seem that there are many opportunities for small businesses to get in on the action provided by the remanufacturing industry. For example, an auto repair business can easily branch out and start offering remanufactured goods as part of their services, or a small business that repairs office machines will gain the necessary knowledge to remanufacture related products at the same time as it conducts its normal business activities.

If a small business decides to get into the remanufacturing industry, it must first and foremost study and understand the market. Despite the recent success of remanufacturing, there is still a negative perception among consumers regarding products that contain used parts. Many consumers feel that a remanufactured product is not durable as a brand new one and may require additional maintenance in the future. This is a serious issue that must be addressed before a small business decides whether it is worth it to pursue remanufacturing as a vocation.

Like any business venture, remanufactured products must be properly marketed in order for the company producing them to ultimately succeed. Management must target consumers who will appreciate the fact that remanufactured goods are a great financial alternative to new ones, but educate them enough so that they understand they are not sacrificing quality for price. A sound warranty plan and follow-up calls that gauge the product's performance are also suggested. Like any product or service, a remanufactured product will benefit from positive word of mouth and grow into a solid business because of it.

Inexperienced remanufacturing firms must also be careful not to compete against themselves when marketing remanufactured and new goods at the same time. In addition, management must work with their own employees so that they understand the many benefits of the remanufacturing process. Many employees may be hesitant to offer remanufactured goods to their customers for fear of potential prejudices regarding the performance of the product.

Most importantly, a small business must have the means at its disposal to locate and recover the products and resources that will be used in the remanufacturing project and ultimately perform the task at hand. Once these products are found, they must be transported to the destination where disassembly will take place. After that, they will most likely be transported to another location that specializes in reassembly. Finally, any unusable parts and products must be collected and transported to recycling centers or other places that specialize in their disposal.

There are many legal and regulatory issues that affect the remanufacturing industry that businesses must be aware of. Intellectual property and anti-trust matters; federal, state and local recycling procedures; and government economic incentives are just a few of these issues. The Remanufacturing Institute is the watchdog organization for the entire industry and they are constantly monitoring these issues and representing the views of the businesses that are involved in remanufacturing. In addition, the federal government requires that all remanufactured goods must be labeled as such so that they cannot be passed off as new products.

FURTHER READING:

Ferrer, Geraldo, and D. Clay Whybark. "From Garbage to Goods: Successful Remanufacturing Systems and Skills." *Business Horizons.* November, 2000.

Lund, Robert T. *Remanufacturing: The Experience of the United States and Implications for Developing Countries.* World Bank, 1984.

RENOVATION

Renovation describes a series of planned changes and updates made to a facility where business is conducted. Office and building renovation is a common undertaking in today's competitive business environment, as businesses endeavor to keep up with infrastructure needs (especially those sparked by technology use) and provide aesthetically pleasing settings for customers.

Small business owners and consultants agree that a well-conceived and carefully planned renovation effort can revitalize a business and provide it with much-needed room to grow in the future. But they also note that renovation periods can have a negative impact on productivity and profitability. Often, the inconveniences associated with office and building renovation projects make it a practical impossibility for businesses to maintain the exact same level of operations that they met during non-renovation periods. But experts indicate that small business owners—whether they are building tenants or building owners—can take several steps to ensure that the negative aspects of renovation are minimized.

SMALL BUSINESS TENANTS AND RENOVATION

Many small business owners are co-tenants of a building with other businesses. These entrepreneurs may well find themselves faced with an impending renovation. This is especially true if they are operating their businesses in older buildings. Sometimes these renovations take place within the physical space of the business itself; on other occasions, the renovation may be limited to common areas—lobbies, outer building areas, stairways/elevator systems, etc.—that are shared by all the tenants. In either case, the impending arrival of a renovation crew should signal a period of preparation on the part of the small business owner.

"Tenants are usually very pleased with the modern conveniences and new environments that are created after a major office renovation project has been completed," wrote Lawrence Hearn in the *Journal of Property Management.* But during the period when the renovation is actually taking place, small business owners may find themselves feeling everything from anxiety to deep anger about the impact that it is (or seems to be) having on their company. The most effective way in which small business tenants can minimize these negative emotions is by establishing and maintaining good lines of communication with the building owner before and during the renovation process.

Hearn stated that good communication between building owners/managers and tenants is a priority whether the renovation is a minor capital improvement or a comprehensive rehabilitation project. "Almost any physical change in the work environment can be disruptive and potentially threatening to the tenant's business," he added. "It is management's, and ultimately ownership's, responsibility to make sure tenants are kept informed every step of the way during construction."

Hearn noted that smart building managers will take the initiative in talking with their business tenants so that they are more likely to "feel as if they are part of the renovation process, instead of becoming victims of the procedure. Retail tenants are particularly sensitive to signage and good access to their space." But if you are a small business owner and you feel that the facility's ownership is doing an inadequate job of informing you of renovation issues and schedules, it is entirely within your rights to demand more information and input. Business owners should make sure that they thoroughly review their leasing contract, soliciting legal assistance if necessary, to make sure that they are being treated fairly.

Some business owners inhabiting facilities that are undergoing renovation adopt a fatalistic sort of attitude toward the process, surrendering meekly to renovation strategies without offering any workable alternatives to plans that might unnecessarily hinder their operations. Other entrepreneurs, meanwhile, err on the other end of the spectrum by making unreasonable demands that may ultimately drag out the renovation process for several extra days or weeks. Small business experts counsel owners to instead adopt a middle ground. They have to recognize that renovation efforts almost inevitably bring about some measure of inconvenience for tenants and their customers, but that they ultimately increase the value of the location for business operation. On the other hand, if a business owner spots a problem during a review of upcoming or ongoing renovation plans, he or she should bring it to the attention of building management. A renovation strategy that would render a key loading dock unavailable during a big delivery period, for example, should immediately be brought to the attention of the landlord.

Small business owners should recognize that many facility managers want to help tenants out in whatever way they reasonably can. After all, they do not want to lose tenants and go to the trouble of finding new ones. As Hearn pointed out to facility owners, "although it may cost more, it is sometimes wiser to schedule work in high service areas at night or on the weekends. The same holds true for heavy pounding or other work that requires large equipment. You will certainly make up the cost difference if you keep your tenants happy and away from the construction headache as much as possible."

RENOVATING PROFESSIONAL OFFICES

Office and facility renovations may also be undertaken by small business enterprises that either own or are the sole tenants of the building in which they operate. Business owners that provide professional services are especially likely to renovate to meet changing internal demands, attract new clients, and keep existing ones. Indeed, doctors, dentists, attorneys, architects, engineers, and the like recognize that the appearance of their offices can be a significant component in their overall success. "With competition up and reimbursements down, a medical office that's shabby, impedes productivity, or can't accommodate expansion plans can be a big liability," cautioned Laura Clark in *Medical Economics*.

Analysts note that professional offices are more likely to renovate rather than relocate for two fundamental reasons: cost and client retention. Even a major renovation of an existing facility is likely to be considerably less expensive than the total costs associated with relocating to another facility. Perhaps even more importantly, existing patients and clients are accustomed to finding the office at a given location. "If you move, they may not follow you," warned one consultant in *Medical Economics*.

Renovation strategies can vary considerably, depending on the needs and concerns of the office in question. A medical practice or architectural firm may be amply equipped to integrate new technology with existing operations, only to recognize that its growth has been hampered because it is saddled with an unattractive waiting area. In this situation, the renovation may amount to little more than some new carpeting, wallpaper, and furniture. Other firms, however, may find that only a major rehabilitation effort will be sufficient to correct long-standing problems with infrastructure such as an ineffective floor plan, poor wiring to support information technology needs, or cramped office space.

Clark pointed to several other concerns that professional service firms (and many other businesses) have to consider when weighing renovation plans as well. For example, businesses have to be in compliance with the Americans with Disabilities Act of 1990. Much of the renovation work that took place in the early 1990s was undertaken specifically to address this law, which called on facilities to become fully accessible by widening hallways, installing ramps, and adapting drinking fountains and bathrooms for use by people in wheelchairs. Most buildings are now in compliance with the ADA, but building owners looking to renovate need to make sure that their new plans adhere to ADA parameters. In addition, professional service firms need to factor in their attractiveness to recent graduates when weighing their renovation strategies. ''Young men and women coming out of residencies are going to consider the attractiveness and efficiency of your office,'' one renovator told *Medical Economics.* ''They're simply not going to want to come to work in a dingy, 1940s-style medical building.''

Finally, before committing to a major renovation effort, professional service firms should discuss matters with appropriate experts, including architects, accountants, and lenders. Selecting a contractor should be done carefully as well; business owners are urged to check into the contractor's reputation for quality, timeliness, and financial soundness before making an agreement. Finally, firms should call in legal representation before signing a contract. As one renovation expert indicated in *Medical Economics,* ''[attorneys] should write all kinds of ceilings and floors into your contract so you don't get burned. Believe it or not, you can force your contractors to stay on schedule and within budget—or pay a penalty—but you've got to show them you're very serious about that right up front.''

FURTHER READING:

Clark, Laura. ''Revitalize Your Practice with an Office Renovation.'' *Medical Economics.* June 3, 1991.

Hearn, Lawrence. ''Retaining Tenants During Renovation.'' *Journal of Property Management.* July-August 1995.

Konz, Stephen. *Facility Design.* New York: John Wiley and Sons, 1985.

Kruk, Leonard B. ''Facilities Planning Supports Changing Office Technologies.'' *Managing Office Technology.* December 1996.

Pelland, Dave. ''Creating Buildings, Not Problems: Managing Construction Risk Effectively.'' *Risk Management.* November 1996.

''Re-Dressing Office Buildings for Success.'' *Building Design & Construction.* May 1993.

Sunoo, Brenda Paik. ''Redesign for a Better Work Environment.'' *Workforce.* February 2000.

''Too Much Togetherness: Is Your Office Design Hurting Productivity?'' *Managing Office Technology.* September 1998.

Vischer, Jacqueline C. ''Strategic Work-Space Planning.'' *Sloan Management Review.* Fall 1995.

REQUEST FOR PROPOSAL

Request for Proposal (RFP) is the process by which a corporate department or government agency prepares bid documents to acquire equipment or services. RFPs are frequently published in the legal documents section of pertinent newspapers or in trade journals covering the industry in which the department operates. The RFP can also be distributed to a list of qualified potential bidders that have already been contacted and prequalified as eligible by the agency or department. ''Qualified'' is a key word in answering or preparing any RFP. Qualification frequently depends on follow-up investigation on the part of the hopeful bidder, and careful wording of the original RFP.

RFPs are primarily associated with government agencies, since their responsibility to get equipment and consulting talent under the most beneficial circumstances possible is closely monitored by the press and tax watchdogs. Some private companies also employ RFPs, though, usually when purchasing commodities or services that do not bear directly on the company's own products or services.

ELEMENTS OF AN ATTRACTIVE RFP

Some RFP work requests are of a scale beyond the scope of small or mid-sized companies, but others provide such businesses with valuable opportunities to expand their client base and operations. Before bidding on an RFP, however, entrepreneurs and business owners should make sure they fully understand the nature of the work request.

For instance, some RFPs are decidedly more informative than others. When scanning an RFP, vendors should make certain that it specifically describes what needs to be delivered or executed to fulfill the needs of the company or agency that posted the notice. In order to do so, it is often necessary for potential vendors to educate themselves about the nature of the agency or corporation that has submitted the RFP. Vendors should also inquire whether the work request could translate into additional work on associated projects down the line. For instance, if the equipment will eventually be networked to a building that is not yet built, but is in the long range plans of the agency or company, a vendor may decide that a low price on the initial RFP is viable if it advances its prospects for a more long-term arrangement down the line.

Before making any bid, vendors should also check the RFP for other factors that might influence their response. Some possible questions follow:

- Will the asked-for equipment be subject to notable environmental conditions or regulations?

- If the equipment will be used in foreign countries, is the equipment compatible with the standards of those nations?

- Will ancillary costs associated with design, production, transportation, or some other aspect of delivery eat into the profit margin to an unacceptable extent?

- Are the RFP and the equipment or services it seeks legal under local, state, and federal laws?

- Is the RFP asking for both equipment and service? (Companies that sell equipment might not be able to adequately service it, yet that service performance may be written into the RFP in a separate section from the equipment specifications; responders must know they can fulfill the entire contract before answering it.)

- Are deadlines and performance clauses contained within the RFP reasonable?

- Will the RFP agency require the winning vendor to sign a performance bond that guarantees delivery of goods or services by a certain date?

Most companies and agencies that submit work requests provide prospective bidders with ample time to study the RFP before the deadline. Some companies give vendors as much as one month from the time the RFP is published before the bids are due. This allows bidders time to tinker with their bids, possibly allowing them to seek out new vendors of their own to help meet the needs of the RFP.

STAYING ON THE BID LIST

Companies wishing to bid on RFPs should monitor the legal notices in local newspapers and trade magazines, and contact the purchasing departments of corporations and government agencies likely to request services and equipment. They should investigate the requirements to be added to the ''bid list.'' Finally, once the company has fulfilled all obligations necessary to be added to the list, the company's leadership needs to make certain that it stays on that list.

Government agencies and corporate departments are sometimes reluctant to delete vendors from bid lists because of fears that such cuts will elicit favoritism charges. Nonetheless, establishments submitting RFPs do seek to keep bid lists to manageable size, since every bid requires scrutiny. One favored way to keep the bid list down is to require potential vendors to refile every few years. Another is to ask vendors to

provide certain information about their companies, such as past sales and experience or number of employees available to service the account. Such requirements cull the number of bidders down, eliminating companies that are too disorganized or feeble to keep up. Conversely, a small business that meets all such requirements in a timely fashion is essentially serving notice that it has its act together.

Companies seeking RFP business should also be cognizant of the fact that winning bids are not always exclusively a matter of providing the lowest cost or the highest level of customer service. Some corporations and government agencies give special consideration on their bid lists to minority- and women-owned companies.

FURTHER READING:

Harrington, Lisa H. ''The RFP Process: How to Hire a Third Party.'' *Transportation and Distribution*. September 1998.

''Preparing Your Request for Proposal.'' *Association Management*. July 2000.

Stein, Murry. ''Don't Bomb Out When Preparing RFPs.'' *Computerworld*. February 15, 1993.

SEE ALSO: Competitive Bids

RESEARCH AND DEVELOPMENT

Research and development (R & D) is a process intended to create new or improved technology that can provide a competitive advantage at the business, industry, or national level. While the rewards can be very high, the process of technological innovation (of which R & D is the first phase) is complex and risky. The majority of R & D projects fail to provide the expected financial results, and the successful projects (25 to 50 percent) must also pay for the projects that are unsuccessful or terminated early by management. In addition, the originator of R & D cannot appropriate all the benefits of its innovations and must share them with customers, the public, and even competitors. For these reasons, a company's R & D efforts must be carefully organized, controlled, evaluated, and managed.

OBJECTIVES AND TYPES OF R & D

The objective of academic and institutional R & D is to obtain new knowledge, which may or may not be applied to practical uses. In contrast, the objective of industrial R & D is to obtain new knowledge, applicable to the company's business needs, that eventually will result in new or improved products, processes, systems, or services that can increase the company's sales and profits.

The National Science Foundation (NSF) defines three types of R & D: basic research, applied research, and development. Basic research has as its objectives a fuller knowledge or understanding of the subject under study, rather than a practical application thereof. As applied to the industrial sector, basic research is defined as research that advances scientific knowledge but does not have specific commercial objectives, although such investigation may be in the fields of present or potential interest to the company.

Applied research is directed towards gaining knowledge or understanding necessary for determining the means by which a recognized and specific need may be met. In industry, applied research includes investigations directed to the discovery of new knowledge having specific commercial objectives with respect to products, processes, or services. Development is the systematic utilization of the knowledge or understanding gained from research toward the production of useful materials, devices, systems, or methods, including design and development of prototypes and processes.

At this point, it is important to differentiate development from engineering, which can be defined as utilization of state-of-the-art knowledge for the design and production of marketable goods and services. In other words, research creates knowledge and development designs, and builds prototypes and proves their feasibility. Engineering then converts these prototypes into products or services that can be offered to the marketplace or into processes that can be used to produce commercial products and services.

R & D AND TECHNOLOGY ACQUISITION

In many cases, technology required for industrial purposes is available in the marketplace, usually for a price. Before embarking on the lengthy and risky process of performing its own R & D, a company should perform a "make or buy" analysis and decide whether or not the new R & D project is strategically and economically justified. The following influencing factors should be considered: proprietariness, timing, risk, and cost.

PROPRIETARINESS If a technology can be safeguarded as proprietary—and protected by patents, trade secrets, nondisclosure agreements, etc.—the technology becomes exclusive property of the company and its value is much higher. In fact, a valid patent grants a company a temporary monopoly for 17 years to use the technology as it sees fit, usually to maximize sales and profits. In this case, a high-level of R & D effort is justified for a relatively long period (up to 10 years) with an acceptable risk of failure.

On the contrary, if the technology cannot be protected, as is the case with certain software programs, expensive in-house R & D is not justified since the software may be copied by a competitor or "stolen" by a disloyal employee. In this case, the secret of commercial success is staying ahead of competition by developing continuously improved software packages, supported by a strong marketing effort.

TIMING If the market growth rate is slow or moderate, in-house or contracted R & D may be the best means to obtain the technology. On the other hand, if the market is growing very fast and competitors are rushing in, the "window of opportunity" may close before the technology has been developed by the new entrant. In this case, it is better to acquire the technology and related know-how, in order to enter the market before it is too late.

RISK Inherently, technology development is always riskier than technology acquisition because the technical success of R & D cannot be guaranteed. There is always the risk that the planned performance specifications will not be met, that the time to project completion will be stretched out, and that the R & D and manufacturing costs will be higher than forecasted. On the other hand, acquiring technology entails a much lower risk, since the product, process, or service can be seen and tested before the contract is signed.

Regardless of whether the technology is acquired or developed, there is always the risk that it will soon become obsolete and be displaced by a superior technology. This risk cannot be entirely removed, but it can be considerably reduced by careful technology forecasting and planning. If market growth is slow, and no winner has emerged among the various competing technologies, it may be wiser to monitor these technologies through "technology gatekeepers" and be ready to jump in as the winner emerges.

COST For a successful product line with relatively long life, acquisition of technology is more costly, but less risky, than technology development. Normally, royalties are paid in the form of a relatively low initial payment as "earnest money," and as periodic payments tied to sales. These payments continue throughout the period of validity of the license agreement. Since these royalties may amount to 2 to 5 percent of sales, this creates an undue burden of continuing higher cost to the licensee, everything else being equal.

On the other hand, R & D requires a high front-end investment and therefore a longer period of negative cash flow. There are also intangible costs involved in acquiring technology—the license agreements may have restrictive geographic or application clauses, and other businesses may have access to the same technology and compete with lower prices or stronger marketing. Finally, the licensee is dependent upon the licensor for technological advances, or even for keeping up to date, and this may be dangerous.

MOVING AHEAD WITH R & D

Once the decision has been made to perform R & D, the company should decide where and how such R & D should be carried out. There are various possibilities: in-house R & D in the company laboratories, externally contracted R & D, and joint R & D. In-house R & D commands a strategic advantage, since the company is the sole owner of the technology and can protect it from unauthorized uses. In addition, since R & D is basically a learning process, the company can develop a group of experienced scientists and engineers that can be employed in developing more advanced products and processes and in transferring the results of their R & D to operations and to customers. However, since R & D personnel do not like to work alone and are stimulated by peers, the laboratory should have a critical mass in the core technologies and support services; this critical mass may exceed the company resources.

External R & D is usually contracted out to specialized nonprofit research institutions or to universities. The advantages are that these institutions may already have experienced personnel in the disciplines to be researched, as well as the necessary laboratory and test equipment. This will save money and especially time with respect to in-house R & D. The disadvantages are that the company will not benefit from the learning experience, and may become overly dependent on the contractor. Also, the technology transfer may be difficult, and there is always the possibility of leaks to competitors. In the case of universities, costs are usually lower, and there is the additional benefit of identifying graduate students who may be hired later and researchers who may be employed as consultants when needed.

Joint R & D became popular in the United States after antitrust laws were relaxed and tax incentives were offered to R & D consortia. In a consortium, several companies with congruent interests join together to perform R & D, either in a separate organization or in a university. The advantages are lower costs, since each company does not have to invest in similar equipment; a critical mass of researchers; and interchange of information among the sponsors. The disadvantages are that all the sponsors have access to the same R & D results. However, because of antitrust considerations, the R & D performed must be precompetitive, and each participant in the joint R & D must apply separately the information obtained to its products, processes, and services.

R & D PROJECT SELECTION, MANAGEMENT, AND TERMINATION

Industrial R & D is generally performed according to projects (i.e., separate work activities) with specific technical and business goals, assigned personnel, and time and money budgets. These projects can either originate ''top down'' (for instance, from a management decision to develop a new product) or ''bottom up'' (from an idea originated by an individual researcher). The size of a project may vary from a part-time effort of one researcher for a few months with a budget of thousands of dollars, to major five- or ten-year projects with large, multidisciplinary teams of researchers and budgets of millions of dollars. Therefore, project selection and evaluation is one of the more critical and difficult subjects of R & D management. Of equal importance, although less emphasized in practice, is the subject of project termination, particularly in the case of unsuccessful or marginal projects.

SELECTION OF R & D PROJECTS Normally, a company or a laboratory will have requests for a higher number of projects than can be effectively implemented. Therefore, R & D managers are faced with the problem of allocating scarce resources of personnel, equipment, laboratory space, and funds to a broad spectrum of competing projects. Since the decision to start on an R & D project is both a technical and a business decision, R & D managers should select projects on the basis of the following objectives, in order of importance:

1. Maximize the long-term return on investment;

2. Make optimum use of the available human and physical resources;

3. Maintain a balanced R & D portfolio and control risk;

4. Foster a favorable climate for creativity and innovation.

Project selection is usually done once a year, by listing all ongoing projects and the proposals for new projects, evaluating and comparing all these projects according to quantitative and qualitative criteria, and prioritizing the projects in ''totem pole'' order. The funds requested by all the projects are compared with the laboratory budget for the following year and the project list is cut off at the budgeted amount. Projects above the line are funded, those below the line delayed to the following year or tabled indefinitely. Some experienced R & D managers do not allocate all the budgeted funds, but keep a small percentage on reserve to take care of new projects that may be proposed during the year, after the laboratory official budget has been approved.

EVALUATION OF R & D PROJECTS Since R & D projects are subject to the risk of failure, the expected value of a project can be evaluated according to the following statistical formula:

$$EV = P \times pt \times pc \times pf$$

where P is the payoff if the project is successful; that is, the stream of net income accruing to the company over the life of the new product (or process, or service) resulting from the project. The payoff P is then multiplied by the probability of success, which is the product of three separate probabilities:

1. pt is the probability of technical success, i.e., that the new product or process will meet the technical and functional specifications

2. pc is the probability of commercial success, i.e., that the new product will be accepted by the marketplace and will achieve the forecasted market share

3. pf is the probability of financial success, i.e., that the new product will achieve the forecasted financial goals, in terms of profits, return on investment, and cash flow.

Consequently, project evaluation must be performed along two separate dimensions: technical evaluation, to establish the probability of technical success; and business evaluation, to establish the payoff and the probabilities of commercial and financial success. Once the expected value of a project has been determined, it should be divided by the forecasted cost C of the project, in order to obtain a benefit/cost ratio R of the form R = EV/C. Obviously the higher this ratio, the more desirable the project.

For more advanced and longer term projects, leading to major (rather than incremental) innovation, it may be difficult to establish reliable values of P, C, pt, pc, and pf. In this case, a relative comparison of projects is made based on their respective technical quality and potential business value. Technical quality is evaluated by analyzing and rating the clarity of the project goals; the extent of the technical, institutional, and market penetration obstacles that must be overcome; the adequacy of the skills and facilities available in the laboratory for carrying out the work; and how easily can the project results be transferred to an operation. Potential business value of a project is defined in terms of the market share of an existing market that can be captured by the new product; or by the size of a new market that can be developed by the new product; or by the value of new technology that can be sold by the company or transferred to its customers.

After the first tentative list of projects has been established in order of priority, it is "matched" with the existing laboratory human and physical resources to make sure that these resources are well utilized. In fact, creative human resources are the laboratory's most valuable asset, and these should not be wasted by asking researchers to do work outside their disciplines and interests. Also, it is difficult to change in a short time the "mix" of available disciplines and equipment, and to hire and fire researchers. Thus, a shift towards new disciplines should be done gradually, avoiding the underutilization or overloading of the existing resources.

Once the tentative list of prospects has been modified according to the above, the entire project portfolio of the R & D laboratory should be balanced, in order to control risk, according to three types of probabilities listed above. Technical risk is controlled in two ways: 1) by having a spectrum of projects ranging from low to medium-high technical risk; 2) by avoiding "bunching" too many projects in the same technology, particularly if the technology could be replaced by a superior technology during the expected lifetime of the new product.

Commercial risk can be controlled by not having "too many eggs in one basket," that is, by targeting different market segments (government, capital equipment, consumer, industrial, international, etc.) and attacking different competitors, since directly targeting a major competitor may trigger a dangerous counter offensive and a price war. Financial risk is controlled by having a majority of small- and medium-size projects (in terms of R & D expense), a few large projects, and no projects that, in case of failure, could bankrupt the company. Financial risk, in terms of cash flow, is also controlled by having a spectrum (in time-to-payoff) of more short- and medium-term projects than long-term projects. This type of spectrum is also psychologically important to maintain the credibility of the R & D laboratory in the face of upper-level executives who keep asking "What have you done for me lately?"

By definition, R & D is a risky activity, and there are no "zero risk" R & D projects, since these would then be engineering projects. While the majority of the projects in an R & D portfolio should be categorized as low-risk, some medium-risk projects are justified, and even a few high-risk projects, provided their expected value is high.

Finally, project evaluation and selection should be made objectively, in order to develop and maintain a favorable climate for creativity and innovation. Researchers will be naturally disappointed when their projects are not approved. Some may even suspect that other projects were preferred for subjective reasons, such as the "halo" effect (the past track record and prestige of other, more senior, researchers), the reluctance of management to terminate less deserving projects, and especially political influences to select "pet" projects of executives. If there is a feeling that project selection is not done objectively, many researchers, particularly the junior ones, will lose their enthusiasm and renounce proposing new projects of a high potential value for the company. Eventually, if this situation persists, the laboratory will lose its creativity and concentrate on routine low-risk (but also low-payoff) or "political" projects, and it will have difficulty in keeping and attracting the best researchers. Therefore, it is desirable that the project evaluation and selection criteria be properly explained and that all researchers be asked to participate in the evaluation process. Also, the finalized project portfolio should be presented to, and discussed with, all the researchers.

MANAGEMENT OF R & D PROJECTS The management of R & D projects follows basically the principles and methods of project management. There is, however, one significant caveat in relation to normal engineering projects: R & D projects are risky, and it is difficult to develop an accurate budget, in terms of technical milestones, costs, and time to completion of the various tasks. Therefore, R & D budgets should be considered initially as tentative, and should be gradually refined as more information becomes available as a result of preliminary work and the learning process. Historically, many R & D projects have exceeded, sometimes with disastrous consequences, the forecasted and budgeted times to completion and funds to be expended. In the case of R & D, measuring technical progress and completion of milestones is generally more important than measuring expenditures over time.

TERMINATION OF R & D PROJECTS Termination of projects is a difficult subject because of the political repercussions on the laboratory. Theoretically, a project should be discontinued for one of the following three reasons:

1. There is a change in the environment—for instance, new government regulations, new competitive offerings, or price declines—that make the new product less attractive to the company;

2. Unforseen technical obstacles are encountered and the laboratory does not have the resources to overcome them; or

3. The project falls hopelessly behind schedule and corrective actions are not forthcoming.

Due to organizational inertia, and the fear of antagonizing senior researchers or executives with pet projects, there is often the tendency to let a project continue, hoping for a miraculous breakthrough that seldom happens.

In theory, an optimal number of projects should be initiated and this number should be gradually reduced over time to make room for more deserving projects. Also, the monthly cost of a project is much lower in the early stages than in the later stages, when more personnel and equipment have been committed. Thus, from a financial risk management viewpoint, it is better to waste money on several promising young projects than on a few maturing "dogs" with low payoff and high expense. In practice, in many laboratories it is difficult to start a new project because all the resources have already been committed and just as difficult to terminate a project, for the reasons given above. Thus, an able and astute R&D manager should continuously evaluate his/her project portfolio in relation to changes in company strategy, should continuously and objectively monitor the progress of each R&D project, and should not hesitate to terminate projects that have lost their value to the company in terms of payoff and probability of success.

TAX ADVANTAGES FOR R & D

Since 1981, American companies engaging in R & D have been entitled to a federal tax credit equal to 20 percent of R & D expenditures over a base amount. The base amount is determined by the company's R & D spending patterns in prior years. This tax credit can be claimed every year, and there is no upper dollar limit. As Daniel Kadlec explained in *Fortune,* "The R & D tax credit is designed to spur innovation by reimbursing companies for some of the costs of engineering better mousetraps."

Some taxpayers resent subsidizing corporate R & D expenditures. After all, corporations that introduce successful new products based on R & D stand to reap huge financial rewards once their products reach the marketplace. Opponents of the tax credit argue that companies thus have ample incentives to fund their own R & D. "Yet there is a limit to how much money private industry is willing to gamble on products that may or may not pan out," Kadlec noted. "If a government kickback for research increases the amount of research being done, then it has value to the economy and society in ways that are hard to measure."

Supporters of the tax credit—which costs the federal government $2.2 billion per year—claim that it pays for itself by creating jobs and stimulating innovation and productivity. They also argue that it adds tangible net worth to small businesses engaged in developing new products and technologies, which makes them more attractive to investors and supports their growth. The R & D tax credit is scheduled to expire in 2004, but it seems likely to be made permanent by Congress before that time.

FURTHER READING:

Kadlec, Daniel. ''A Catalyst for Innovation—Both Presidential Candidates Agree: It's Time to Make the R & D Tax Credit Permanent.'' *Fortune.* September 18, 2000.

Martin, Michael J.C. *Managing Technological Innovation and Entrepreneurship.* Reston, 1984.

Roussel, Philip. A., Kamal N. Saad, and Tamara J. Erikson. *Third Generation R & D.* Harvard Business School Press, 1991.

Twiss, Brian. *Managing Technological Innovation.* 3rd ed. Pitman, 1985.

RÉSUMÉS

A résumé is a document presented by a job applicant to a prospective employer outlining and summarizing that person's qualifications for employment. A résumé generally includes data on education, previous work experience, and personal information, and well-crafted ones are composed in such a way as to maximize the applicant's attractiveness as a potential employee. A résumé is generally accompanied by a cover letter which introduces the applicant and the résumé to the employer. The purpose of a résumé is to obtain an interview, not to land a job. This is an important distinction. Whether or not a person is hired is largely determined by what transpires during the job interview, not by the résumé. A résumé is extremely important, however, because it provides the employer with a first impression of the job applicant. From this first impression a decision will be made as to whether or not an interview will be granted.

RÉSUMÉ APPEARANCE AND CONTENT

Résumés are read from two perspectives: the appearance of the physical document itself and the content of the résumé. Résumé appearance concerns the presence (or absence) of typographical errors, poor grammar usage, sloppy sentence structure, garish colors, unconventional typefaces, paper stains, etc.

The content of the résumé, as indicated earlier, is the actual information included in the document. The content of most résumés falls into four broad categories: education, previous work experience, personal data, and social data. The first two are self-explanatory. Personal data includes such things as address and telephone number. Social data includes military status, club memberships, references, etc.

Handbooks that provide detailed advice on compiling résumés are available in most bookstores and libraries. These guides generally agree on the types of information to include on a résumé but sometimes differ on the format and hierarchical arrangement of the résumé. Some authors feel that educational infor-

mation should be presented first while others feel previous work experience should be foremost. Other authors of such handbooks offer advice on tailoring a résumé to fit one's particular employment situation (looking for an entry-level position, re-entering the job market, or changing fields or vocations). Most of these handbooks, however, have one thing in common: they generally lack empirical data on what a prospective employer is looking for in a résumé. References in these handbooks to this aspect of the applicant, résumé, and employer scenario are often anecdotal.

EMPLOYERS AND RÉSUMÉS

When reading résumés, employers generally are looking for hard data and information. Functional résumés (résumés with no dates) are often viewed as indicators of excessive job movement or attempts to hide large gaps in one's career. Nebulous phraseology such as ''exposure to'' sometimes indicate a lack of depth of work experience, as does excess space devoted to education, personal, and social data. (Of course, recent college or high school graduates and other people relatively new to the work force often have little choice but to highlight such information, and the discerning employer will take this factor into account).

Many small business consultants urge their clients to study résumés closely, citing the unfortunate frequency with which some applicants include outright lies. A Massachusetts-based management consultant, for instance, told *Nation's Business* writer Peter Weaver that a résumé should only be used as a starting point for launching a thorough examination of an applicant's business, professional, and interpersonal skills. ''Hiring someone based on false claims in a résumé not only weakens a firm's work force but also can lead to costly legal action,'' said Weaver, who noted that many businesses are held legally responsible for the actions of all employees—even those who may have been placed in positions on the basis of fraudulent information.

Some employers have turned to automated résumé banks or reference checking firms to help them fill their workforce needs. Banks will, for a fee, mail out copies of résumés to prospective employers. Using technical terminology and job-related phrases a computer will match the résumés it stores in its data bank with job descriptions supplied by its clients. Résumé banks, however, are not professional recruiters; the latter are compensated for their services in terms of a percentage of a recruit's salary. Résumé banks charge a sliding fee for their services.

ELECTRONIC RÉSUMÉS

A 2000 survey reported in *Business Journal—Milwaukee* indicated that 48 percent of hiring executives preferred to receive résumés via e-mail. This result was a significant change from just two years earlier, when only 4 percent of executives preferred to receive résumés in electronic form. Some job applicants have found that the trend toward e-mailed résumés makes it more difficult for them to differentiate themselves in the eyes of prospective employers. As a result, many people have begun adding graphics and interactive elements to their electronic résumés. In fact, several Web sites exist to help users create résumés online. While including graphics and interactive elements can sometimes help applicants for some creative and technology-oriented positions, hiring executives emphasize that these features cannot make up for a lack of experience and achievements.

Job applicants who decide to create an electronic résumé and send it to potential employers via e-mail should keep a few factors in mind. First, it is generally considered bad form to use a current employer's e-mail system to send out résumés. Second, job applicants should make sure that their e-mail user name is professional and appropriate before sending out résumés. Third, applicants should consider using a standard ASCII format with a predictable layout and plain fonts, since fancy text may not be readable on some potential employers' computer systems. It may be helpful to send a test résumé to yourself and to several friends in order to check how the document appears on several systems. Fourth, experts recommend including a name, phone number, and e-mail address at the top of every page so the sender's identity will not get lost if the résumé is printed out or entered into a database. Finally, job applicants should be careful to include keywords referring to their job interests and experience in case hiring companies scan in résumés and search them to find candidates for later job openings.

FURTHER READING:

Asher, Donald. *The Overnight Résumé.* Ten Speed Press, 1999.

Meece, Mickey. "The E-Mail Résumé: Addressed for Success." *New York Times.* November 5, 2000.

Narain, R. Kamna. "Changing Face of Résumés." *Business Journal.* September 15, 2000.

Nemnich, Mary B., and Fred Edmund Jandt. *Cyberspace Résumé Kit: How to Make and Launch a Snazzy Online Résumé.* Jist Works, 1998.

"No Postage Necessary." *Business Journal—Milwaukee.* November 3, 2000.

Ream, Richard. "Rules for Electronic Résumés." *Information Today.* September 2000.

Roberts, Gary, Gary Seldon, and Carlotta Roberts. *Human Resources Management.* Small Business Administration, n.d.

Weaver, Peter. "Ignoring a Résumé Can Prove Costly." *Nation's Business.* September 1997.

SEE ALSO: Employee Hiring

RETAIL TRADE

Retailers are business firms engaged in offering goods and services directly to consumers. In most—but not all—cases, retail outlets are primarily concerned with selling merchandise. Typically, such businesses sell individual units or small groupings of products to large numbers of customers. A minority of retailers, however, also garner income through rentals rather than outright sales of goods (as in the case of enterprises that offer furniture or gardening tools for rent) or through a combination of products and services (as in the case of a clothing store that might offer free alterations with the purchase of a suit).

The retail industry is a massive part of the overall U.S. economy. In the mid-1990s, for example, retail establishments accounted for better than one out of five jobs in the country, and pulled in more than $2 trillion on an annual basis. Moreover, many retail niches are characterized by a healthy population of smaller enterprises; indeed, the vast majority of retail employees in the United States work at establishments with fewer than 20 employees.

Retail trade is widely known as a very competitive area of commercial endeavor, and observers note that many fledgling retail establishments do not survive for more than a few years. Indeed, competition for sales has become so great that consumers have seen a marked blurring of product lines among retailers. Increasingly, retailers have taken to stocking a much greater variety of goods than their basic industry classification would indicate (bookstores, for example, increasingly stock music products, while food, liquor, office supplies, automotive supplies, and other wares can all be found in contemporary drug stores). This development further complicates efforts to establish and maintain a healthy presence in the marketplace. But for the small business owner who launches a retail store on an adequate foundation of capital, business acumen, and attractive merchandise, involvement in the trade can be rewarding on both financial and personal fulfillment levels.

PRIMARY RETAIL TYPES

Retail enterprises can be either independently owned and operated or part of a "chain," a group of two or more stores whose activities are determined and coordinated by a single management group. Stores that are part of a chain may all be owned by a single company, but in other cases, the individual stores may be franchises that are independently owned by a small businessperson.

Many different types of retail establishments exist, and, as noted above, the overall industry has seen a significant blurring of the boundaries that had long separated the wide range of companies operating under the retail umbrella. Nonetheless, retailing establishments still generally fall into one of the following general categories:

- Specialty Stores—These establishments typically concentrate their efforts on selling a single type or very limited range of merchandise. Clothing stores, musical instrument stores, sewing shops, and party supply stores all fall within this category.

- Department Stores—These establishments are comprised of a series of departments, each of which specializes in selling a particular grouping of products. Under this compartmentalized arrangement, consumers go to one area of the store to purchase tableware and another area to acquire bedding, for example.

- Supermarkets—These retail establishments, which are primarily involved in providing food to consumers but have increasingly ventured into other product areas in recent years, account for the vast majority of total food-store sales in America.

- Discount Stores—These retail outlets offer consumers a trade-off: lower prices (typically on a broad range of products) in exchange for lower levels of service. Indeed, many discount stores operate under a basic ''self-service'' philosophy.

- Mail-Order Businesses and other Nonstore Retailing Establishments—Mail-order sales have become an increasingly ubiquitous part of the American retail landscape; indeed, some retail establishments subsist entirely on mail order, forsaking traditional stores entirely, while other companies maintain operations on both levels. In addition, this category includes sales made to end consumers through telemarketing, vending machines, the World Wide Web, and other nonstore avenues.

FURTHER READING:

Buss, Dale D. ''The Little Guys Strike Back.'' *Nation's Business.* July 1996.

Dolber, Roslyn. *Opportunities in Retailing Careers.* Lincolnwood, IL: VGM Career Horizons, 1989.

Du, Fanglan, and Ira Apfel. ''The Future of Retailing.'' *American Demographics.* September 1995.

Johnson, Walter E. ''Measuring Retail Performance: Category Sales and Productivity Benchmarks.'' *Do-It-Yourself Retailing.* April 1996.

Occupational Outlook: 1994-95. Scottsdale, AZ: Associated Book Publishers, Inc., 1994.

RETIREMENT PLANNING

Retirement planning describes the financial strategies individuals employ during their working years to ensure that they will be able to meet their goals for financial security upon retirement. Making sound decisions about retirement is particularly important for self-employed persons and small business owners. Unlike employees of large companies, who can simply participate in the pension plans and investment programs offered by their employers, entrepreneurs must set up and administer their own plans for themselves and for their employees.

Though establishing and funding retirement plans can be costly for small businesses, such programs also offer a number of advantages. In most cases, for example, employer contributions to retirement plans are tax deductible expenses. In addition, offering employees a comprehensive retirement plan can help small businesses attract and retain qualified people who might otherwise seek the security of working for a larger company. The number of small firms establishing retirement plans grew during the 1990s, but small employers still lag far behind larger ones in providing this type of benefit for employees. According to Connecticut-based consulting firm Access Research Inc., 24 percent of small businesses (those with fewer than 100 employees) offered retirement plans in 1996, compared to 51 percent of medium-sized businesses (between 100 and 1,000 employees) and 98 percent of large businesses (more than 1,000 employees).

Retirement planning is a topic of interest not only to older small business owners, but to young entrepreneurs as well. The debate over whether Social Security will be available for the younger members of the current work force adds legitimacy to the need for early retirement planning. Longer life expectancies mean that more money must be set aside for retirement, while the uncertainty of investment returns and inflation rates makes careful planning essential. In fact, some experts recommend that individuals invest a minimum of 10 percent of their gross income from the time they enter the work force to guarantee a comfortable retirement.

LAWS GOVERNING RETIREMENT PLANS

The Social Security Administration was created in the 1930s as part of President Franklin Roosevelt's New Deal. Private pension plans mushroomed shortly thereafter, offering coverage to millions of employees. In 1962 the Self-Employed Individuals Retirement Act established tax-deferred retirement plans with withdrawals starting between the ages of 59 ½ and 70 ½. These plans—also known as Keogh plans after their originator, New York Congressman Eugene J. Keogh—were intended for the self-employed and for those who have income from self-employment on the side. Embezzlement from pension plans by trustees led to the passage of the Employee Retirement Income Security Act of 1974 (ERISA). One of the main provisions of ERISA was to set forth vesting requirements—time periods over which employees gain full rights to the money invested by employers on their behalf. ERISA governs most large-employer-sponsored pension plans, but does not apply to those sponsored by businesses with less than 25 employees.

TYPES OF RETIREMENT PLANS

The two main categories of retirement plans are defined contribution and defined benefit. Defined contribution plans use an allocation formula to specify a percentage of compensation to be contributed by each participant. For example, an individual can voluntarily deduct a certain portion of his or her salary, in many cases before taxes, and place the money into a qualified retirement plan, where it will grow tax-deferred. Likewise, an employer can contribute a percentage of each employee's salary to the plan on their behalf, or match the contributions employees make.

In contrast, defined benefit plans calculate a desired level of benefits to be paid upon retirement—using a fixed monthly payment or a percentage of compensation—and then the employer contributes to the plan annually according to a formula so that the benefits will be available when needed. The amount of annual contributions is determined by an actuary, based upon the age, salary levels, and years of service of employees, as well as prevailing interest and inflation rates. In defined benefit plans, the employer bears the risk of providing a specified level of benefits to employees when they retire. This is the traditional idea of a ''pension plan'' that has often been used by large employers with a unionized work force. But defined benefit plans can also be useful for small business owners who are nearing retirement age and wish to put away as much money as possible.

Perhaps the most significant difference between defined benefit and defined contribution plans is the voluntary nature of defined contribution plans. Such plans are fully voluntary, so that hourly or salaried employees elect to have a certain percentage of money deducted—before taxes—from their paychecks. Conversely, defined benefit plans involve automatic contributions made by the employer, with no active participation on the part of the employee.

In the 1980s, defined benefit plans declined in popularity in favor of defined contribution plans. Part of this decline can be attributed to the fact that the work force became more mobile, and fewer people were willing to commit their entire working lives to a single employer in order to gain a pension. Employers, too, began moving away from defined benefit plans because of the financial pressure involved in funding them. Such pressure increased for some categories of employers in 1996, when nondiscrimination rules took effect. These rules state that public sponsors must offer the same benefits to all employees regardless of their compensation. Many state and local municipalities have moved to defined contribution plans to avoid this new mandate.

One significant advantage of defined contribution plans is that the amount invested by employees can be rolled over into another account with another employer. Rollover activity into similar tax-deferred plans has continued to increase as tax laws require a 20 percent withholding tax to be paid on the lump sum if it is not rolled over. Another reason for the growth of defined contribution plans was the emergence of 401(k) plans, in which employers can match contributions made by employees. But defined contribution plans continued to face scrutiny by many financial advisers for two reasons: 1) the investment decisions made by the company may be too restrictive for employees to meet individual goals; and 2) many times employees are not educated about the risk and returns associated with the investment vehicles available through the company plan. Similarly, the voluntary nature of defined contribution plans makes detractors wonder if ill-informed employees will have less money in their defined contribution accounts at retirement than they would have had under a defined benefit plan.

OPTIONS FOR SMALL BUSINESSES

Small business owners can set up a wide variety of retirement plans by filling out the necessary forms at any financial institution (a bank, mutual fund, insurance company, brokerage firm, etc.). The fees vary depending on the plan's complexity and the number of participants. Some employer-sponsored plans are required to file Form 5500 annually to disclose plan activities to the IRS. The preparation and filing of this complicated document can increase the administrative costs associated with a plan, as the business owner may require help from a tax advisor or plan administration professional. In addition, all the information reported on Form 5500 is open to public inspection.

The most important thing to remember is that a small business owner who wants to establish a qualified plan for him or herself must also include all other company employees who meet minimum participation standards. As an employer, the small business owner can establish retirement plans like any other business. As an employee, the small business owner can then make contributions to the plan he or she has established in order to set aside tax-deferred funds for retirement, like any other employee. The difference is that a small business owner must include all nonowner employees in any company-sponsored retirement plans and make equivalent contributions to their accounts. Unfortunately, this requirement has the effect of reducing the allowable contributions that the owner of a proprietorship or partnership can make on his or her own behalf.

For self-employed individuals, contributions to a retirement plan are based upon the net earnings of their business. The net earnings consist of the company's gross income less deductions for business expenses, salaries paid to nonowner employees, the employer's 50 percent of the Social Security tax, and—significantly—the employer's contribution to retirement plans on behalf of employees. Therefore, rather than receiving pre-tax contributions to the retirement account as a percentage of gross salary, like nonowner employees, the small business owner receives contributions as a smaller percentage of net earnings. Employing other people thus detracts from the owner's ability to build up a sizeable before-tax retirement account of his or her own. For this reason, some experts recommend that the owners of proprietorships and partnerships who sponsor plans for their employees supplement their own retirement funds through a personal after-tax savings plan.

Nevertheless, many small businesses sponsor retirement plans in order to gain tax advantages and increase the loyalty of employees. A number of different types of plans are available. The most popular plans for small businesses all fall under the category of defined contribution plans. In nearly every case, withdrawals made before the age of 59 ½ are subject to an IRS penalty in addition to ordinary income tax. The plans differ in terms of administrative costs, eligibility requirements, employee participation, degree of discretion in making contributions, and amount of allowable contributions. Brief descriptions of some of the most common types of plans follow:

SIMPLIFIED EMPLOYEE PENSION (SEP) PLANS SEP plans are employer-funded retirement accounts that allow small businesses to direct at least 3 percent and up to 15 percent of each employee's annual salary, to a maximum of $30,000, into tax-deferred individual retirement accounts (IRAs) on a discretionary basis. SEP plans are easy to set up and inexpensive to administer, as the employer simply makes contributions to IRAs that are established by employees. The employees then take responsibility for making investment decisions regarding their own IRAs. Employers thus avoid the risk and cost involved in accounting for employee retirement funds. In addition, employers have the flexibility to make large percentage contributions during good financial years, and to reduce contributions during hard times. SEP plans are available to all types of business entities, including proprietorships, partnerships, and corporations. In general, eligibility is limited to employees 21 or older with at least three years of service to the company and a minimum level of compensation. The maximum level of compensation for SEP eligibility is $170,000.

SAVINGS INCENTIVE MATCH PLAN FOR EMPLOYEES (SIMPLE) SIMPLE plans take two forms: a SIMPLE IRA and a SIMPLE 401(k). Both plans became available in January 1997 to businesses with less than 100 employees, replacing the discontinued Salary Reduction Simplified Employee Pension (SARSEP) plans. They were intended to provide an easy, low-cost way for small businesses and their employees to contribute jointly to tax-deferred retirement accounts. An IRA or 401(k) set up as a SIMPLE account requires the employer to match up to 3 percent of an employee's annual salary, up to $6,000 per year. Employees are also allowed to contribute up to $6,000 annually to their own accounts. Companies that establish SIMPLEs are not allowed to offer any other type of retirement plan. As of early 1997, most small businesses chose the SIMPLE IRA option, as the SIMPLE 401(k) proved more expensive than a regular 401(k) due to the company matching requirements. The main problem with the plans, according to Stephen Blakely in *Nation's Business,* was that ''Congress is already drafting legislation that would make SIMPLE less simple and more costly for the very businesses the plans were created to serve.''

PROFIT SHARING PLANS Profit sharing plans enable employers to make a discretionary, tax deductible contribution on behalf of employees each year, based on the level of profits achieved by the business. The total annual contribution is generally allocated among employees as a percentage of their compensation. Plan costs are tax deductible for the employer, and plan earnings are tax deferred for employees. Profit sharing plans are easy to implement, offer design flexibility, and provide a wide range of investment choices. Eligibility is typically limited to employees who are at least 21 years of age and who have at least one year of service. The employer's maximum deduction is 15 percent of the total annual salaries paid to nonowner employees (adjusted to 13.04 percent for the small business owner).

A common variation is the age-based profit sharing plan, in which contributions are based on an allocation formula that factors in the age or number of years to retirement of participants. Age-based profit sharing allows employers to reward valued older employees for their length of service. Another variation is the new comparability profit sharing plan, which allows employers to define classes of employees and set up the retirement plan so that certain classes benefit the most in terms of allocation. These types of profit sharing plans are similar to defined benefit plans, but the employer contributions are discretionary.

MONEY PURCHASE PENSION PLANS Money purchase pension plans are similar to regular profit sharing plans, but the employer contributions are mandatory rather than discretionary. The main advantage of money purchase plans is that they allow larger employer contributions than regular profit sharing plans. The employer determines a fixed percentage of profits that will be allocated to employee retirement accounts according to a formula. The maximum employer contribution jumps to 25 percent of payroll for nonowner employees (adjusted to 20 percent for the small business owner) or a total of $30,000 per employee. There are also combination money purchase-profit sharing plans that allow employers to select a fixed percentage for mandatory contribution and also retain the option of contributing additional funds on a discretionary basis when cash flow permits.

401(K) PROFIT SHARING PLANS The popular 401(k) plans are profit sharing plans that include a provision for employees to defer part of their salaries for retirement. The employer can make annual profit sharing contributions on behalf of employees, the employees can contribute up to $10,000 of pre-tax income themselves, and the employer can choose to match some portion of employee contributions. 401(k) plans offer a number of advantages. First, they allow both employer and employee to make contributions and gain tax advantages. Second, they can be set up in such a way that employees can borrow money from the plan. Third, 401(k) plans enable employees to become active participants in saving and investing for their retirement, which raises the level of perceived benefits provided by the employer. The main disadvantages are relatively high set up and administrative costs. Eligibility for 401(k) plans is typically limited to employees at least 21 years of age who have at least one year of service with the company.

Small businesses that establish 401(k)s must be careful to avoid liability for losses employees might suffer due to fluctuations in the value of plan investments. Under ERISA, plan sponsors can avoid liability by ensuring that their 401(k) meets three criteria: offering a broad range of investment options to employees; communicating sufficient financial information to employees; and allowing employees to exercise independent control over their accounts.

WHICH PLAN TO CHOOSE

Small business owners must carefully examine their priorities when selecting a retirement plan for themselves and their employees. If the main priority is to minimize administrative costs, a SEP plan may be the best choice. If it is important to have the flexibility of discretionary contributions, a profit sharing plan might be the answer. A money purchase plan would enable a small business owner to maximize contributions, but it would require an assurance of stable income, since contributions are mandatory. If the small business counts upon key older employees, an age-based profit sharing plan or a defined benefit plan would help reward and retain them. Conversely, an employer with a long time horizon until retirement would probably do best with a defined contribution plan. Finally, a small business owner who wants employees to be able to fund part of their own retirement should select a SIMPLE or a 401(k) plan. There are also many possibilities for combination plans that might provide a closer fit with a small business's goals. Free information on retirement plans is available through the Department of Labor or on the Internet at www.dol.gov.

FURTHER READING:

Blakely, Stephen. ''Pension Power.'' *Nation's Business.* July 1997.

Clifford, Lee. ''Getting Over the Hump before You're Over the Hill.'' *Fortune.* August 14, 2000.

Crouch, Holmes F. *Decisions When Retiring.* Allyear Tax Guides, 1995.

''Five Steps to a Great Retirement.'' *Money.* November 1, 1999.

Infante, Victor D. ''Retirement Plan Trends.'' *Workforce.* November 2000.

Korn, Donald Jay. ''Developing a Plan to Make Your Golden Years Brighter.'' *Black Enterprise.* October 2000.

Korn, Donald Jay. ''Tax-Deferred Vehicles That Will Last a Lifetime.'' *Black Enterprise.* October 2000.

Martin, Ray. *Your Financial Guide: Advice for Every Stage of Your Life.* Macmillan, 1996.

McHale, James. ''Will Retirement Planning Finally Be Cool?'' *LI Business News.* April 20, 1998.

Philip, Christine. ''Value of Defined Contribution Plans Debated.'' *Pensions and Investments.* February 20, 1995.

Szabo, Joan. ''Pension Tension.'' *Entrepreneur.* November 2000.

SEE ALSO: Estate Tax; 401(k) Plan; Individual Retirement Accounts; Keogh Plans; Pension Plans; Simplified Employee Pensions

RETURN ON ASSETS (ROA)

Return on assets (ROA) is a financial ratio that shows the percentage of profit that a company earns in relation to its overall resources. It is commonly defined as net income (or pretax profit) / total assets. ROA is known as a profitability or productivity ratio, because it provides information about management's performance in using the assets of the small business to generate income. ROA and other financial ratios can provide small business owners and managers with a valuable tool to measure their progress against predetermined internal goals, a certain competitor, or the overall industry. ROA is also used by bankers, investors, and business analysts to assess a company's use of resources and financial strength.

As James O. Gill noted in his book *Financial Basics of Small Business Success,* most entrepreneurs decide to start their own businesses in order to earn a better return on their money than would be available through a bank or other low-risk investments. If the ROA and other profitability ratios demonstrate that this is not occurring—particularly once a small business has moved beyond the start-up phase—then the entrepreneur should consider selling the business and reinvesting his or her money elsewhere.

It is important to note, however, that many factors can influence ROA, including a firm's degree of capitalization. ''ROA favors highly capitalized institutions,'' Steven Davidson noted in an article for *America's Community Banker.* ''Especially for such institutions, the ROA measure treats equity capital as 'free funds'—there is no 'cost' associated with them. Financial theory as well as common sense tells us that this is certainly not the case.'' As a result of this and other limitations, it is advisable to combine ROA with other measures of profitability and performance.

USES FOR ROA

Unlike other profitability ratios, such as return on equity (ROE), ROA measurements include all of a business's assets—including those which arise out of liabilities to creditors as well as those which arise out of contributions by investors. For this reason, ROA is usually of less interest to shareholders than some other financial ratios. However, the inclusion of liabilities makes ROA even more valuable as an internal measurement tool, particularly in evaluating the performance of different departments or divisions of companies.

''ROA is a good internal management ratio because it measures profit against all of the assets a division uses to make those earnings. Hence, it is a way to evaluate the division's profitability and effectiveness. It's also more appropriate here because division managers seldom get involved in raising money or in deciding the mix between debt and equity,'' James A. Kristy and Susan Z. Diamond wrote in their book *Finance without Fear.* ''One of the cardinal rules in managing business professionals is to hold them accountable for only those activities they control. ROA comes close to doing just that.''

Another common internal use for ROA involves evaluating the benefits of investing in a new system versus expanding a current system. The best choice will ideally increase productivity and income as well as reduce asset costs, resulting in an improved ROA ratio. For example, say that a small manufacturing company with a current sales volume of $50,000, average assets of $30,000, and a net profit of $6,000 (giving it an ROA of $6,000 / $30,000 or 20 percent) must decide whether to improve its current inventory management system or install a new one. Expanding the current system would allow an increase in sales volume to $65,000 and in net profit to $7,800, but would also increase average assets to $39,000. Even though sales would increase, the ROA of this option would be the same—20 percent. On the other hand, installing a new system would increase sales to $70,000 and net profit to $12,250. Because the new system would allow the company to manage its inventory more efficiently, the average assets would increase only to $35,000. As a result, the ROA for this option would increase to 35 percent, meaning that the company should choose to install the new system.

FURTHER READING:

Allred, James K. ''Looking at the Return on Assets.'' *Modern Materials Handling.* May 1997.

Bernstein, Leopold A., and John J. Wild. *Analysis of Financial Statements.* New York: McGraw-Hill, 2000.

Casteuble, Tracy. ''Using Financial Ratios to Assess Performance.'' *Association Management.* July 1997.

Davidson, Steven. ''Measuring Profitability.'' *America's Community Banker.* October 1997.

Gill, James O. *Financial Basics of Small Business Success.* Menlo Park, CA: Crisp Publications, 1994.

Kremer, Chuck, and Ronald J. Rizzuto. *The One-Page Financial Statement: How to Make Your Cash Flow, Profit, and Return on Assets Work Together.* International Thompson Publishing, 1999.

Kristy, James E., and Susan Z. Diamond. *Finance without Fear.* New York: American Management Association, 1984.

Larkin, Howard. ''How to Read a Financial Statement.'' *American Medical News.* March 11, 1996.

RETURN ON INVESTMENT (ROI)

Return on investment (ROI) is a financial ratio that compares the amount of income derived from an investment with the cost of the investment. ROI is known as a profitability ratio, because it provides information about management's performance in using the resources of the small business to generate income. ROI and other financial ratios can provide small business owners and managers with a valuable tool to measure their progress against predetermined internal goals, a certain competitor, or the overall industry. ROI is also used by bankers, investors, and business analysts to assess a company's use of resources and financial strength.

As James O. Gill noted in his book *Financial Basics of Small Business Success,* most entrepreneurs decide to start their own businesses in order to earn a better return on their money than would be available through a bank or other low-risk investments. If the ROI and other profitability ratios demonstrate that this is not occurring—particularly once a small business has moved beyond the start-up phase—then the entrepreneur should consider selling the business and reinvesting his or her money elsewhere. However, it is important to note that many factors can influence ROI, including changes in price, volume, or expenses, as well as the purchase of assets or the borrowing of money. In addition, ROI is limited by the fact that it focuses on one period of time and thus should be considered a short-term performance measure. Ignoring the long-term effects of investments can cause poor decision-making, so it is advisable to combine ROI with other measures of profitability and performance.

USES OF ROI

The general formula for computing ROI is income / invested capital. ROI can be computed on a company-wide basis by dividing net income by owners' equity. This measure indicates how well the overall company is utilizing its equity investment. Calculated in this way, ROI provides a good indicator of profitability that can be compared against competitors or an industry average. Experts suggest that companies usually need at least 10-14 percent ROI in order to fund future growth. If this ratio is too low, it can indicate poor management performance or a highly conservative business approach. On the other hand, a high ROI can either mean that management is doing a good job, or that the firm is undercapitalized.

ROI can also be computed for various divisions, product lines, or profit centers within a small business. In this way, it gives management a basis for comparing the performance of different areas. One large division may generate much higher profits than another, smaller division, for example, which might encourage management to consider investing further in that division. But an ROI analysis might reveal that a great deal more capital investment was required by the large division than by the smaller one. The smaller division may have generated a lower dollar amount of profit, but a greater percentage of profit on every dollar of investment. As Ronald W. Hilton wrote in his book *Managerial Accounting,* ''The important question is not how much profit each division earned, but rather how effectively each division used its invested capital to earn a profit.''

ROI can also be used to evaluate a proposed investment in new equipment by dividing the increase in profit attributable to the new equipment by the increase in invested capital needed to acquire it. For example, a small business may be able to save $5,000 in operating expenses (and thus raise profit by the same amount) by spending $25,000 on a piece of new equipment. This yields an ROI of $5,000 / $25,000 or 20 percent. If this figure is higher than the company's cost of capital (the interest paid on debt and the dividends paid to investors) prior to the investment, and no better investment opportunities exist for those funds, it may make sense to purchase the equipment.

In addition to the various uses ROI holds for a small business managers, it can also be a useful measure for investors. For example, a stockholder might calculate the return of investing in a company by the following formula: dividends + stock price change / stock price paid. This calculation of ROI measures the gain (or loss) achieved by placing an investment over a period of time.

FURTHER READING:

Bernstein, Leopold A., and John J. Wild. *Analysis of Financial Statements.* New York: McGraw-Hill, 2000.

Casteuble, Tracy. ''Using Financial Ratios to Assess Performance.'' *Association Management.* July 1997.

Friedlob, George T., and Franklin J. Plewa. *Understanding Return on Investment.* Chicago: Wiley, 1996.

Gill, James O. *Financial Basics of Small Business Success.* Menlo Park, CA: Crisp Publications, 1994.

Hilton, Ronald W. *Managerial Accounting.* New York: McGraw-Hill, 1991.

Larkin, Howard. ''How to Read a Financial Statement.'' *American Medical News.* March 11, 1996.

Murray, Barbara. ''Return on Investment.'' *Supermarket News.* October 2, 2000.

Spivey, John. ''Companies Searching for Ever-Elusive Internet ROI.'' *Mississippi Business Journal.* December 11, 2000.

RETURN POLICIES

Return policies are the rules retail merchants establish to manage the process by which customers return or exchange unwanted or defective merchandise that they have purchased previously. Return policies are an extension of the customer service retailers provide, and thus are often fairly liberal. "Retail stores in the U.S. tend to be generous in their return policies," Jodi Rodgers wrote in the *South Florida Business Journal*. "After all, if the customer is satisfied, the customer will come back." As a result of their experience with liberal return policies, many consumers hold the mistaken belief that they can always return merchandise for a full refund, regardless of the circumstances. But in reality, both regular and online merchants enjoy great leeway in establishing their own individual return policies. As returns have become more prevalent and more costly, some merchants have imposed tighter restrictions on merchandise returns.

The most generous return policies—which are usually found at large, upscale retailers—permit customers to return any merchandise at any time for a full refund, with or without a receipt. But most retailers place restrictions on one or more aspects of this process. For example, many merchants will not accept merchandise for return unless the customer can produce a dated receipt proving that he or she actually purchased the item at that store within a reasonable amount of time. Other merchants have slightly more liberal return policies and will accept items without a receipt as long as the sale tag is still attached. Still others will provide a store credit rather than a cash refund when no receipt is forthcoming. Some retailers have even tighter return policies and prohibit returns on sale merchandise or on certain types of items, like bathing suits, or impose a limited window of time when returns are accepted.

The goal for retailers is to balance the need to satisfy customers against the cost and hassle associated with merchandise returns. Setting too liberal policies may encourage customers to abuse the system. For example, a customer might purchase a dress for a formal occasion, wear it once, and then return it. Similarly, a consumer might purchase a top-of-the-line computer, use it for several months until an even faster model becomes available, and then return it. "So how do retailers strike the balance, protecting themselves from return abuses while at the same time maintaining customer satisfaction?" Rodgers asked. This can be a particularly important issue for small business owners, who depend on superior customer service to keep people coming back to their shops and Web sites. Larger merchants can generally afford to be more liberal in allowing returns, and smaller outfits may need to raise prices in order to compensate for the added expense. After all, returned items that cannot be resold must either be returned to the manufacturer or sold to a jobber, which costs the retailer extra in transaction and transportation fees.

There are several steps brick-and-mortar retailers can take to discourage abuse of their return policies. For example, they can attempt to reduce the volume of sales returns "by clearly posting return policies, spelling them out on tags, and training staff to explain them to each customer," according to Rodgers. In addition, a study reported in the *Journal of Economics and Business* found that it can be advantageous for retailers to vary their return policies from product to product. Policies can be more generous for items that hold their value for a long period of time or that can be resold at a high value. Conversely, policies can be tighter for items that lose their value quickly, like computers, or are difficult to resell or otherwise dispose of.

RETURNS IN E-COMMERCE

Establishing fair return policies while limiting the cost of returns is of particular importance to online retailers. After all, returns are a fact of life in electronic commerce. "How well you handle online returns will likely determine your future success—or failure—in the dotcom world," Melissa Campanelli wrote in *Entrepreneur*. "Unfortunately, returned merchandise is a major byproduct of increased Internet growth, especially as consumers become much more comfortable purchasing items over the Net." Some experts claim that the nature of electronic commerce invites large numbers of merchandise returns because consumers are not able to see and touch the items they purchase online. Recent technological developments promise to address this problem, however, and enhance the online shopping experience. "There's incredible technology at work in making touch, feel, color, look, size, and fit issues more user-friendly," Irwin Barkan of the data services organization e-BuyersGuide.com told Campanelli.

A 1999 survey by e-BuyersGuide.com found that 86 percent of online shoppers rated return policies of significant importance in choosing an online merchant. Consumers were especially concerned about whether the policies permitted them to receive a refund immediately after items were returned, return online purchases to a brick-and-mortar store, exchange items as needed, and have the convenience of postal pickup at their homes. But the number one priority of online shoppers was not having to pay return postage for items they ship back to e-tailers. In a survey of the top 50 online merchants, however, 85 percent said that they required customers to pay return postage. Requiring customers to pay for shipping tends to discourage frivolous returns, according to some online retailers.

According to the e-BuyersGuide.com survey reported in Entrepreneur, the main reasons online shoppers returned their purchases included: that the product was not what they expected (25 percent); that the product did not fit properly (17 percent); that the merchandise was damaged (17 percent); that the wrong items were delivered (16 percent); that the products were of poor quality (10 percent); and that they simply changed their minds and did not want the product (15 percent). Of the consumers who returned items purchased online, 78 percent said they were satisfied with the experience, while only 6 percent described it as unsatisfactory. Of those who had a bad experience returning merchandise, however, 62 percent said they would not return to the offending Web site afterward.

The most popular way to handle online returns is to provide postage-paid return labels. Both the U.S. Postal Service and United Parcel Service provide merchants with a service where customers can generate labels online and print them on their home computers. Retailers can open an account at a local post office to use the U.S. Postal Service's easy return system. There is a minimum charge of 30 cents per return for the merchant. The UPS system is similar but also separates merchandise that is returned because it is faulty or damaged from that returned because the customer changed their mind. Both systems allow retailers to track packages online.

Another option for electronic retailers is outsourcing returns to a return management solution (RMS) company. These firms handle all aspects of merchandise returns, from generating labels and return authorizations to the physical handling and processing of merchandise. Some RMS companies integrate their computer systems with retailers' in order to facilitate tracking and routing of packages. According to Campanelli, using an RMS firm generally involves an installation fee of around $10,000 plus a transaction fee for each package handled.

FURTHER READING:

Campanelli, Melissa. ''Many Happy Returns.'' *Entrepreneur.* January 2001.

Davis, Scott, Michael Hagerty, and Eitan Gerstner. ''Return Policies and the Optimal Level of 'Hassle.' '' *Journal of Economics and Business.* September-October 1998.

Kandra, Anne. ''Return to Sender—If You Can.'' *PC World.* February 2001.

Lin-Fisher, Betty. ''Online Return Policies Vary.'' *Knight-Ridder/Tribune Business News.* December 10, 2000.

Rodgers, Jodi. ''Being Slave to Fashion Isn't So Free.'' *South Florida Business Journal.* March 26, 1999.

REVENUE STREAMS

For organizations to make money and to survive in the long run, they must have constant sources or streams of revenue. Revenues come from sales, and the various categories of sales of a service or manufacturing firm are known as revenue streams. While measuring and reporting revenue is the domain of accounting and finance departments in organizations, determining new sources or streams of revenue is the responsibility of top management, strategic planners, and marketing forecasters.

INDUSTRY EXAMPLES OF REVENUE STREAMS

As one example, Internet Service Providers (ISPs) have earned sales revenue from providing fast Internet connections for individuals. An article entitled ''New Revenue Streams for Well-Targeted ISPs'' stresses that now ISPs should look for new revenue streams in three promising areas: the embryonic application service provider (ASP) market; the small- to-mid-sized business market; and the untapped international market. The article stresses that tapping these fields may be more difficult than providing connections to the Internet for individuals, but these are the only lucrative markets still open to new entrants. The market has moved along the industry and the product life cycle curves, and thus revenue streams are changing.

Many businesses today are looking at the World Wide Web as a potential new revenue stream. Dedicated e-businesses and traditional bricks-and-mortar businesses alike see the Internet as a way to grow a business and view having an Internet presence as a way to better serve customers or reach new customers. At the 2000 annual conference of the Vermont Captive Insurance Association in Burlington, Vermont, Fredrik Motzfeldt moderated a panel on the ''e-captive environment.'' He noted that some of the obvious e-business strategies for the captive insurance industry might include using the World Wide Web as an information facilitator and lead generator, or tapping into a Web-generated revenue stream with the Internet presence used as a way to promote business and generate quotes.

In another insurance example, banks are investigating a new and potentially large revenue stream that could come from selling insurance. To understand the importance of insurance to the current and future revenue stream of banks, the insurance division of Arthur Andersen surveyed 15 regional banks with assets ranging from $7 billion to $70 billion. As banks are faced with increased competition they must find more efficient ways to retain and grow their business. The key to their success is to find additional product lines that will allow a bank to use its existing structure and delivery channels. Many experts see insurance as a business that offers new and large revenue streams and ongoing potential for banks.

In a final example, restaurant managers and planners have discovered a new way to create additional revenue streams without a substantial capital investment. Instead of launching a second restaurant concept or adding new units to an existing portfolio of restaurants, these managers are turning to catering as a new tool to maximize existing assets as well as to increase public relations and awareness. Catering turns a restaurant's down time into preparation time for catering orders and allows a manger to use labor and facilities in a more efficient manner. Catering can include hosting events in on-site party rooms or in their own dining rooms when the restaurant would normally be closed.

Because product and service life cycles are shortening, businesses must be constantly planning strategy and determining where future revenue streams will come from to ensure their financial success and longevity.

FURTHER READING:

Heller, Al. ''The Pace Setters: New Products Infuse Vitality into the Marketplace and Create New Revenue Streams for Retailers.'' *Supermarket News.* June 7, 1999.

Heuton, Bruce. ''Banks Selling Insurance: Formulas for Success.'' *U.S. Banker.* October 2000.

LaVecchia, Gina. ''Profits on a Silver Platter.'' *Restaurant Hospitality.* October 2000.

Sanchez, Diane, et. al. *Selling Machine: How to Build Your Business to Maximum Revenue Growth.* Times Books, 1997.

Zolkos, Rodd. ''Web Holds Captive Uses.'' *Business Insurance.* August 28, 2000.

RIGHT-TO-KNOW (RTK) LAWS

Right-to-know laws are a group of rules and regulations at the state and national levels that mandate that employers share scientific information with workers and local communities about the toxicity and other characteristics of chemicals and materials used in business processes. This information encompasses all substances to which workers might be exposed in the workplace, including materials and chemicals utilized in producing goods or providing services, chemical releases into the environment, waste management, and long-term exposure to substances. Right to know laws place special emphasis on maintaining and disseminating information on the potential long-term

health effects (cancer, infertility, etc.) sometimes associated with longtime work exposure to high concentrations of industrial materials.

Experts in the fields of risk management and hazardous materials management generally separate employer obligations under ''right-to-know'' (RTK) into four broad categories: obligation to compile and retain relevant records; obligation to disclose any available information to workers, community members, or organizations on any potentially hazardous materials and processes used; obligation to provide adequate training to employees working with potentially dangerous materials; and obligation to disclose information on sudden health risks. This information, which must be presented even if it is not formally requested, should cover the potential risks of sudden and accidental chemical releases, explain the scope of the company's technological and human resources to effectively address such events; and identify other options that could also be considered.

THE MOVEMENT TOWARD RIGHT-TO-KNOW

The first U.S. efforts to inform workers and communities about hazardous substances used in the workplace were voluntary industry labeling practices. These labeling practices—now incorporated into the Federal Hazardous Substances Labeling Act—provided workers with basic information on hazardous materials, including descriptions of the nature of the hazard and instructions for safe handling (and medical treatment in case of exposure to the chemical in question). But as recognition increased of the potential long-term health effects of prolonged exposure to certain chemicals and materials, employee groups, companies, and government agencies all recognized that these safety measures needed to be bolstered.

In 1970 the federal Occupational Safety and Health Administration (OSHA) was formed to help assure that American workers enjoyed safe and healthy working environments. In subsequent years, the agency established a body of regulations designed to ensure that workers were adequately informed about workplace risks (both short- and long-term) through training programs, labeling, and material safety data sheets (MSDS), in which original manufacturers provide complete information on all hazardous substances shipped to customers (downstream users are also required to supply end-users with MSDSs. Contents of material safety data sheets must include the following for each chemical: identity, physical and chemical characteristics; primary routes of entry; health hazards; permissible exposure limits and control measures for reducing exposure; instructions for safe use, handling, and storage; emergency and first aid steps; name and address of manufacturer;

date of production; and date at which the information contained in the MSDS was last changed. This bounty of centralized information makes the MSDS a cornerstone of all right-to-know programs. Moreover, during the 1990s some states initiated efforts to make these information-crammed forms more concise and understandable to lay readers, making them even more valuable.

OSHA's mandate remains in place today. It requires employers to maintain safe workplaces and jobs for their workers and maintains exposure standards for a wide variety of substances that are used in all industry sectors. In addition, many states have also developed their own right-to-know programs. These programs, if certified by the OSHA, allow individual states to assume responsiblity for administration and enforcement. Observers agree that such programs are often difficult to implement, given the wide disparity of viewpoints typically exhibited by interested parties. ''Conflicts arise from the relative significance of 'subjective' versus 'objective' information and from the nature and degree of uncertainty, error, and/or risk that is tolerable,'' explained Nicholas Ashford in *UNESCO Courier.* ''Community residents, workers, and agency professionals may disagree about priorities: residents and workers worry about experts' ability to assess and control risk, while 'experts' fret about citizens' and workers' 'unreasonable demands' for certainty. All the members of a group will not necessarily share the same views on these matters. Conflicts occur between those trained and socialized in a technical field and those who identify more closely with humanistic traditions.'' But despite the challenges of accommodating these disparate concerns while simultaneously meeting the fundamental goal of ensuring workplace safety, many states that have established RTK programs have expressed satisfaction with the results.

COMPLIANCE WITH RTK PROGRAMS

Many employers erroneously believe that the nature of their business operation renders them immune to right-to-know regulations. Typical misconceptions include the belief that the workplace does not have any hazardous chemicals or that the quantities used in the workplace are so small that RTK rules do not appy. In reality, however, these regulations do not distinguish by quantity or size, and nearly every place of employment in the United States contains some substance that meets the definition of a hazardous chemical. For example, many paints, cleaning solutions, solvents, corrosives, compressed gases, glues, and other common substances fall under RTK regulations.

Business owners, though, can take a number of steps to ensure that they are in compliance with right-to-know rules and are promoting safety and healthy working conditions for all of their employees. Many of these steps can be undertaken quickly, and none require the knowledge or skills of a chemist or materials expert.

INVENTORY. Employers are encouraged to complete a comprehensive written inventory of all materials in the workplace that may be hazardous, irrespective of the quantity or size of the materials on hand. The written inventory should include chemicals used and/or stored in work areas outside the building proper. This inventory should also include by-products and intermediate products resulting from workplace processes. These materials inventories should include name of the product, contact information for the manufacturer and distributor, and general work area in which the material is used and/or stored (chemicals used throughout the facility can be so designated).

MATERIAL SAFETY DATA SHEETS Each substance noted as a result of the materials inventory should have a corresponding material safety data sheet, for manufacturers must provide MSDSs to each purchaser of a hazardous chemical when making the initial shipment (recipients of these information sheets, whether distributors or purchasers, must provide updated information with the first shipment after each update). If you do not have an MSDS for a chemical, immediately request a replacement data sheet from the manufacturer or distributor. Some businesses even stipulate delivery of an MSDS as a condition of purchase when ordering hazardous chemicals.

CHEMICAL INFORMATION LIST Once all material safety data sheets have been gathered, they should be reviewed to identify the substance and understand specific hazards associated with the material. The MSDS can also be used to prepare a chemical information list for the workplace. This list, required by law, must be 1) arranged in alphabetical order according to common name; 2) contain the chemical name; and 3) identify the area of the workplace in which it can be found. According to right-to-know regulations, employers must provide access to and copies of the chemical information list to employees and their representatives, OSHA inspectors, and other employers sharing the same workplace.

Not all chemicals used in the workplace are required on these information lists. For example, a chemical list in not required in situations where employees handle chemicals only in sealed, unopened containers under normal working conditions, such as in warehousing or retail sales.

CLEAR LABELING Businesses should make certain that all containers used to hold hazardous materials, whether on the factory floor or in the office, are labeled, tagged, or otherwise identified. This includes temporary portable containers if the container is going to be used by more than one person, utilized for an extended period of time (for example, more than one shift), or left unattended for any period of time. All hazardous substance container labels should clearly identify the material and detail potential hazards. Employers who receive unlabeled containers should either obtain an accurate label from the manufacturer or gather pertinent information from the manufacturer so that they can ready their own label.

Some businesses utilize commercially available labeling systems that use non-text methods to convey hazard warnings. These alternative systems may use icons, color coded numbers, or pictographs to describe levels of hazard and required personal protection equipment.

INSTITUTE UPDATING SYSTEM Employers should develop a system that allows them to efficiently update their chemical information list and MSDS holdings as each new substance arrives in their workplace. Updates should take place within 30 days of receiving the materials in question, as state and federal right-to-know programs require chemical lists to be updated regularly.

HAZARD ASSESSMENT Many employers use the hazard information contained in each MSDS to carefully review all processes in which the material is used. At this time, business owners can decide whether current workplace practices are adequate to ensure the safety and health of employees. Specific elements to review include level of engineering controls, adequacy of personal protective equipment, emergency procedures, and work practices.

HAZARD COMMUNICATION PROGRAM Employers should put together a written hazard communication program for their employees. This program should explain how the company is meeting state/federal right-to-know requirements. Effective hazard communication programs will also include detailed explanations of the company's system of identifying and labeling hazardous substances; information about the company's material safety data sheets and chemical information lists, including how they are maintained and how they can be accessed by workers; and detailed on policies and procedures that employees should follow when engaged in non-routine tasks that require usage of hazardous chemicals and other potentially dangerous materials.

TRAINING "If you approach the [hazard communication] training program as a means to enhance worker protection rather than as another burdensome requirement imposed by government, you may enjoy some positive results," noted the Maryland Department of the Environment, which enforces that state's right-to-

know laws. "Less absenteeism, a reduction of lost time accidents, a reduction of work related illnesses, a possible reduction in workers' compensation costs, and potentially, saved lives."

Effective training programs should be implemented in conjunction with RTK laws. Right-to-know training programs should provide guidance and information in several key areas, including the purpose and content of the law; the nature of the hazardous substances in the workplace; protection from hazards; location and usage of information on these workplace materials, including material safety data sheets, labels, and chemical information lists; and overall employee rights. In essence, all right-to-know training programs should be based on the knowledge that information that is not understood by workers will be of little utility to them in preventing or limiting their exposure to hazardous chemicals in the workplace.

Business experts and state and federal administrators cite several keys to shaping and implementing an effective training program for your workforce:

- Identify who needs training. Employers should utilize organizational charts and personnel records to identify the training needs of various staff. Assess each employee's actual and potential exposure to hazardous chemicals during normal working situations and in potential emergencies (for example, production and custodial workers are likely to have a higher level of training than salespeople and secretaries).

- Determine which chemicals your employees may be exposed to, either under normal working conditions or emergency situations.

- Ensure that employees are aware of the location of chemical information lists and material safety data sheets.

- Make sure that employees know how to use labels, MSDSs, and chemical information lists to obtain information on hazardous materials.

- Make sure that employees understand control programs and personal protective equipment.

- Institute measures to ensure that new and transferred workers receive training. Many businesses integrate Right-to-Know training into general orientation programs or existing departmental safety programs.

- Make contingency plans to provide additional training if new hazards are introduced into the workplace.

- Evaluate effectiveness of training programs after workers have completed them. This can be done through written tests, one-on-one meetings with employees who completed the program, or employee demonstrations of acquired skills and knowledge. Employee feedback on the training program should also be encouraged. Business owners and managers should ask workers which aspects of the program were most valuable and informative, and which aspects were least useful. In some cases, this feedback phase may reveal that the training program did not provide staff with the necessary level of knowledge to safely and effectively deal with hazardous materials they encounter in the workplace. In those cases, programs should be revised until they meet expectations.

Experts note that many facilities utilize literally thousands of chemicals in their operations. Training all employees about the characteristics of each one is an unrealistic burden for any employer. Over the years, OSHA policies have shown a general recognition of this reality. According to OSHA, ''information and training may be designed to cover categories of hazards (e.g., flammability, carcinogenicity) or specific chemicals. Chemical-specific information must always be available through labels and material safety data sheets. . . . If there are only a few chemicals in the workplace, then you may want to discuss each one individually. Where there are large numbers of chemicals, or the chemicals change frequently, you will probably want to train generally based on the hazard categories (e.g., flammable liquids, corrosive materials, carcinogens).'' In the late 1990s, however, employers increasingly charged that OSHA was inconsistent in defining the scope of this requirement and explaining its standards for chemical-specific training.

FURTHER READING:

Ashford, Nicholas A. ''The Right to Know.'' *UNESCO Courier.* May 1998.

Harris, Christopher. *Hazardous Chemicals and the Right to Know.* McGraw-Hill, 1994.

Hileman, Bette. ''Balancing the Right to Know with Security Issues.'' *Chemical and Engineering News.* March 16, 1998.

Lowry, George G, and Robert C. Lowry. *Lowry's Handbook of Right-to-Know and Emergency Planning: Handbook of Compliance for Worker and Community, OSHA, EPA, and the States.* Lewis, 1988.

Sapper, Arthur G. ''Chemical-Specific or Hazard-Category Training?'' *Occupational Hazards.* August 2000.

Stenzel, Paulette L. ''Right to Act: Advancing the Common Interests of Labor and Environmentalists.'' *Albany Law Review.* Vol. 57, no.1, 1993.

RISK MANAGEMENT

Risk management involves identifying, analyzing, and taking steps to reduce or eliminate the exposures to loss faced by an organization or individual. The practice of risk management utilizes many tools and techniques, including insurance, to manage a wide variety of risks. Every business encounters risks, some of which are predictable and under management's control, and others which are unpredictable and uncontrollable. Risk management is particularly vital for small businesses, since some common types of losses—such as theft, fire, flood, legal liability, injury, or disability—can destroy in a few minutes what may have taken an entrepreneur years to build. Such losses and liabilities can affect day-to-day operations, reduce profits, and cause financial hardship severe enough to cripple or bankrupt a small business. But while many large companies employ a full-time risk manager to identify risks and take the necessary steps to protect the firm against them, small companies rarely have that luxury. Instead, the responsibility for risk management is likely to fall on the small business owner.

The term risk management is a relatively recent (within the last 20 years) evolution of the term ''insurance management.'' The concept of risk management encompasses a much broader scope of activities and responsibilities than does insurance management. Risk management is now a widely accepted description of a discipline within most large organizations. Basic risks such as fire, windstorm, employee injuries, and automobile accidents, as well as more sophisticated exposures such as product liability, environmental impairment, and employment practices, are the province of the risk management department in a typical corporation. Although risk management has usually pertained to property and casualty exposures to loss, it has recently been expanded to include financial risk management—such as interest rates, foreign exchange rates, and derivatives—as well as the unique threats to businesses engaged in E-commerce. As the role of risk management has increased, some large companies have begun implementing large-scale, organization-wide programs known as enterprise risk management.

STEPS IN THE RISK MANAGEMENT PROCESS

According to C. Arthur Williams Jr. and Richard M. Heins in their book *Risk Management and Insurance,* the risk management process typically includes six steps. These steps are 1) determining the objectives of the organization, 2) identifying exposures to loss, 3) measuring those same exposures, 4) selecting alternatives, 5) implementing a solution, and 6) monitoring the results. The primary objective of an organization—growth, for example—will determine its strategy for managing various risks. Identification and measurement of risks are relatively straightforward concepts. Earthquake may be identified as a potential exposure to loss, for example, but if the exposed facility is in New York the probability of earthquake is slight and it will have a low priority as a risk to be managed.

Businesses have several alternatives for the management of risk, including avoiding, assuming, reducing, or transferring the risks. Avoiding risks, or loss prevention, involves taking steps to prevent a loss from occurring, via such methods as employee safety training. As another example, a pharmaceutical company may decide not to market a drug because of the potential liability. Assuming risks simply means accepting the possibility that a loss may occur and being prepared to pay the consequences. Reducing risks, or loss reduction, involves taking steps to reduce the probability or the severity of a loss, for example by installing fire sprinklers.

Transferring risk refers to the practice of placing responsibility for a loss on another party via a contract. The most common example of risk transference is insurance, which allows a company to pay a small monthly premium in exchange for protection against automobile accidents, theft or destruction of property, employee disability, or a variety of other risks. Because of its costs, the insurance option is usually chosen when the other options for managing risk do not provide sufficient protection. Awareness of, and familiarity with, various types of insurance policies is a necessary part of the risk management process. A final risk management tool is self-retention of risks— sometimes referred to as ''self-insurance.'' Companies that choose this option set up a special account or fund to be used in the event of a loss.

Any combination of these risk management tools may be applied in the fifth step of the process, implementation. The final step, monitoring, involves a regular review of the company's risk management tools to determine if they have obtained the desired result or if they require modification. *Nation's Business* outlined some easy risk management tools for small businesses: maintain a high quality of work; train employees well and maintain equipment properly; install strong locks, smoke detectors, and fire extinguishers; keep the office clean and free of hazards; back up computer data often; and store records securely off-site.

RISK MANAGEMENT IN THE INTERNET AGE

Small businesses encounter a number of risks when they use the Internet to establish and maintain relationships with their customers or suppliers. Increased reliance on the Internet demands that small business owners decide how much risk to accept and implement security systems to manage the risk associated with online business activities. ''The advent of the Internet has provided for a totally changed communications landscape. We communicate faster, more efficiently, and to a larger number of people,'' Gary Griffith wrote in the *Dallas Business Journal.* ''Shifting to Web sites and e-mail as forms of communication changes the scope, speed, and cost of advertising, customer/vendor communication, and employee-to-employee communication. Along with the advantages are liability issues which should not be ignored.''

Conducting business online exposes a company to a wide range of potential risks, including: liability due to infringement on copyrights, patents, or trademarks; charges of defamation due to statements made on a Web site or via e-mail; charges of invasion of privacy due to unauthorized use of personal information or excessive monitoring of employee communications; liability for harassment due to employee behavior online; and legal issues due to accidental noncompliance with foreign laws. In addition, businesses connected to the Internet also face a number of potential threats from computer hackers and viruses, including a loss of business and productivity due to computer system damage, and the theft of customer information or intellectual property.

As of the early 2000s, the insurance industry had not made policies widely available to protect businesses against the risks of E-commerce. As a result, business owners had to include Internet security among their risk analysis and management activities. As a minimum level of protection, experts recommend that companies conduct a legal review of their Web site content, establish clear policies on employees' Internet and e-mail usage, and install virus protection and security systems on all computers used to access the Internet.

ENTERPRISE RISK MANAGEMENT

In the 1990s, the field of risk management expanded to include managing financial risks as well as those associated with changing technology and Internet commerce. As of 2000, the role of risk management had begun to expand even further to protect entire companies during periods of change and growth. As businesses grow, they experience rapid changes in nearly every aspect of their operations, including production, marketing, distribution, and human resources. Such rapid change also exposes the business to increased risk. In response, risk management professionals created the concept of enterprise risk management, which was intended to implement risk awareness and prevention programs on a company-wide basis. "Enterprise risk management . . . seeks to identify, assess, and control—sometimes through insurance, more often through other means—all of the risks faced by the business enterprise, especially those created by growth," Griffith explained.

The main focus of enterprise risk management is to establish a culture of risk management throughout a company to handle the risks associated with growth and a rapidly changing business environment. Writing in *Best's Review,* Tim Tongson recommended that business owners take the following steps in implementing an enterprise-wide risk management program: 1) incorporate risk management into the core values of the company; *2)* support those values with actions; 3) conduct a risk analysis; 4) implement specific strategies to reduce risk; 5) develop monitoring systems to provide early warnings about potential risks; and 6) perform periodic reviews of the program.

Finally, it is important that the small business owner and top managers show their support for employee efforts at managing risk. "To bring together the various disciplines and implement integrated risk management, ensuring the buy-in of top-level executives is vital," Luis Ramiro Hernandez wrote in *Risk Management.* "These executives can institute the processes that enable people and resources across the company to participate in identifying and assessing risks, and tracking the actions taken to mitigate or eliminate those risks."

FURTHER READING:

Anastasio, Susan. *Small Business Insurance and Risk Management Guide.* U.S. Small Business Administration, n.d.

Blakely, Stephen. "Finding Coverage for Small Offices." *Nation's Business.* June 1997.

"The Changing Face of Risk Management." *Internal Auditor.* October 1998.

Conley, John. "Waves of the Future." *Risk Management.* July 1999.

Griffith, Gary. "Net Increases Need for Risk Management." *Dallas Business Journal.* September 22, 2000.

Head, George L., and Stephen Horn II. *Essentials of Risk Management.* Insurance Institute of America, 1991.

Hernandez, Luis Ramiro. "Integrated Risk Management in the Internet Age." *Risk Management.* June 2000.

Hovey, Juan. "Risky Business." *Industry Week.* May 15, 2000.

Tongson, Tim. "Turning Risk into Reward." *Best's Review.* December 2000.

Williams, C. Arthur, Jr., and Richard M. Heins. *Risk Management and Insurance.* McGraw-Hill, 1989.

SEE ALSO: Business Insurance

RISK AND RETURN

The term "risk and return" refers to the potential financial loss or gain experienced through investments in securities. An investor who has registered a profit is said to have seen a "return" on his or her investment. The "risk" of the investment, meanwhile, denotes the possibility or likelihood that the investor could lose money. If an investor decides to invest in a security that has a relatively low risk, the potential return on that investment is typically fairly small. Conversely, an investment in a security that has a high risk factor also has the potential to garner higher returns. Return on investment can be measured by nominal rate or real rate (money earned after the impact of inflation has been figured into the value of the investment).

Different securities—including common stocks, corporate bonds, government bonds, and Treasury bills—offer varying rates of risk and return. As Richard Brealey and Stewart Myers noted in their book *Principles of Corporate Finance,* "Treasury bills are about as safe an investment as you can get. There is no risk of default and their short maturity means that the prices of Treasury bills are relatively stable." Long-term government bonds, on the other hand, experience price fluctuations in accordance with changes in the nation's interest rates. Bond prices fall when interest rates rise, but they rise when interest rates drop. Government bonds typically offer a slightly higher rate of return than Treasury bills.

Another type of security is corporate bonds. Those who invest in corporate bonds have the potential to enjoy a higher return on their investment than those who stay with government bonds. The greater potential benefits, however, are available because the risk is greater. "Investors know that there is a risk of default when they buy a corporate bond," commented Brealey and Myers. Those corporations that have this default option, though, "sell at lower prices and therefore higher yields than government bonds." In the meantime, investors "still want to make sure that the company plays fair. They don't want it to gamble with their money or to take any other unreasonable risks. Therefore, the bond agreement includes a number of restrictive covenants to prevent the company from purposely increasing the value of its default option."

Investors can also put their money into common stock. Common stockholders are the owners of a corporation in a sense, for they have ultimate control of the company. Their votes—either in person or by proxy—on appointments to the corporation's board of directors and other business matters often determine the company's direction. Common stock carries greater risks than other types of securities, but can also prove extremely profitable. Earnings or loss of money from common stock is determined by the rise or fall in the stock price of the company.

There are other types of company stock offerings as well. Companies sometimes issue preferred stock to investors. While owners of preferred stock do not typically have full voting rights in the company, no dividends can be paid on the common stock until after the preferred dividends are paid.

RISK AND RISK AVERSION

Many types of risk loom for investors hoping to see a return on their money, noted Jae K. Shim and Joel G. Siegel in their *Handbook of Financial Analysis, Forecasting, & Modeling.* Business risk refers to the financial impact of basic operations of the company. Earnings variables in this area include product demand, selling price, and cost. Liquidity risk is the possibility that an asset may not be sold for its market value on short notice, while default risk is the risk that a borrower company will be unable to pay all obligations associated with a debt. Market risk alludes to the impact that market-wide trends can have on individual stock prices, while interest rate risk concerns the fluctuation in the value of the asset as a result of changes in interest rate, capital market, and money market conditions.

Individual risk aversion is thus a significant factor in the dynamics of risk and return. Cautious investors naturally turn to low-risk options such as Treasury bills or government bonds, while bolder investors often investigate securities that have the potential to generate significant returns on their investment. Certain types of common stock that fit this description include speculative stocks and penny stocks.

Many factors can determine the degree to which an investor is risk-averse. William Riley and K. Victor Chow contended in *Financial Analysts Journal* that "relative risk aversion decreases as one rises above the poverty level and decreases significantly for the very wealthy. It also decreases with age—but only up to a point. After age 65 (retirement), risk aversion increases with age." Riley and Chow note that decreases in risk aversion often parallel higher degrees of education as well, but speculate that "education, income and wealth are all highly correlated, so the relationship may be a function of wealth rather than education."

Economically disadvantaged families are, on the surface, often seen as risk-averse; in actuality, however, decisions by these households to avoid investment risk can be traced to a lack of discretionary income or wealth, rather than any true aversion. As Riley and Chow noted, "risk aversion can . . . be expected to decrease as an individual's wealth increases, independent of income. Someone whose stock of wealth is growing can be expected to become less risk-averse, as her tolerance of downside risk increases."

FURTHER READING:

Brealey, Richard, and Stewart Myers. *Principles of Corporate Finance.* 2d ed. New York: McGraw-Hill, 1984.

Brigham, Eugene F. *Financial Management: Theory and Practice.* Fort Worth: Dryden Press, 1991.

Dimson, Elroy, et. al. "Risk and Return in the 20th and 21st Centuries." *Business Strategy Review.* Summer 2000.

Riley, William B., Jr., and K. Victor Chow. "Asset Allocation and Individual Risk Aversion." *Financial Analysts Journal.* December, 1992.

Shim, Jae K., and Joel G. Siegel. *Handbook of Financial Analysis, Forecasting, & Modeling.* Englewood Cliffs, NJ: Prentice Hall, 1988.

Updegrave, Walter. "Why Diversification Pays: This Retro Concept Is Still the Best Way to Balance Risk and Return." *Money.* December 1, 1999.

ROBOTICS

The Robotic Industries Association defines *robot* as follows: "A robot is a reprogrammable, multifunctional manipulator designed to move material, parts, tools or specialized devices through variable programmed motions for the performance of a variety of tasks." Recently, however, the industry's current working definition of a robot has come to be understood as any piece of equipment that has three or more degrees of movement or freedom.

Robotics is an increasingly visible and important component of modern business, especially in certain industries. Robotics-oriented production processes are most obvious in factories and manufacturing facilities; in fact, approximately 90 percent of all robots in operation today can be found in such facilities. These robots, termed "industrial robots," were found almost exclusively in automobile manufacturing plants as little as 15 to 20 years ago. But industrial robots are now being used in laboratories, research and development facilities, warehouses, hospitals, energy-oriented industries (petroleum, nuclear power, etc.), and other areas.

The costs associated with establishing manufacturing processes that rely on industrial robots initially limited the number of companies that were able to fully employ robotics. Despite the cost, however, the *Handbook of Industrial Robotics* reported that the population of robots in North America nearly doubled between 1990 and 2000. In addition, the world robot population was expected to grow from 677,000 in 1996 to an estimated 950,000 in 2000. Many business experts expect that, as robotics technology develops and implementation costs drop, smaller companies will increasingly be able to make use of robotics in their production processes.

ROBOTICS TECHNOLOGY

Today's robotics systems operate by way of hydraulic, pneumatic, and electrical power. Electric motors have become progressively smaller, with high power-to-weight ratios, enabling them to become the dominant means by which robots are powered.

Robots are, of course, comprised of several different elements, depending on their purpose. The hand of a robot, for instance, is referred to in the industry as an "end effector." End effectors may be specialized tools, such as spot welders or spray guns, or more general-purpose grippers. Common grippers include fingered and vacuum types. Another central element of robotics control technology is the sensor. It is through sensors that a robotic system receives knowledge of its environment, to which subsequent actions of the robot can be adjusted. Sensors are used to enable a robot to adjust to variations in the position of objects to be picked up, to inspect objects, and to monitor proper operation (although some robots are able to adjust to variations in object placement without the use of sensors, provided they have sufficient end effector flexibility). Important sensor types include visual, force and torque, speed and acceleration, tactile, and distance sensors. The majority of industrial robots use simple binary sensing, analogous to an on/off switch. This does not permit sophisticated feedback to the robot as to how successfully an operation was performed. Lack of adequate feedback also often requires the use of guides and fixtures to constrain the motions of a robot through an operation, which implies substantial inflexibility in changing operations.

Robots are programmed either by guiding or by off-line programming. Most industrial robots are programmed by the former method. This involves manually guiding a robot from point to point through the phases of an operation, with each point stored in the robotic control system. With off-line programming, the points of an operation are defined through computer commands. This is referred to as manipulator level off-line programming. An important area of research is the development of off-line programming that makes use of higher-level languages, in which robotic actions are defined by tasks or objectives.

Robots may be programmed to move through a specified continuous path instead of from point to point. Continuous path control is necessary for operations such as spray painting or arc welding a curved joint. Programming also requires that a robot be synchronized with the automated machine tools or other robots with which it is working. Thus robot control

systems are generally interfaced with a more centralized control system.

COMMON USES OF ROBOTICS

Industrial robotics have emerged as a popular manufacturing methodology in several areas in recent years, including welding, materials transport, assembly, and spray finishing operations.

SPOT AND ELECTRIC ARC WELDING Welding guns are heavy and the speed of assembly lines requires precise movement, thus creating an ideal niche for robotics. Parts can be welded either through the movement of the robot or by keeping the robot relatively stationary and moving the part past the robot. The latter method has come into widespread use since it generally requires less expensive conveyor systems. The control system of the robot must synchronize the robot with the speed of the assembly line and with other robots working on the line. Control systems may also count the number of welds completed and derive productivity data.

PICK AND PLACE OPERATIONS Industrial robots also perform what are referred to as pick and place operations. Among the most common of these operations is loading and unloading pallets, used across a broad range of industries. This requires relatively complex programming, as the robot must sense how full a pallet is and adjust its placements or removals accordingly. Robots have been vital in pick and place operations in the casting of metals and plastics. In the die casting of metals, for instance, productivity using the same die-casting machinery has increased up to three times, the result of robots' greater speed, strength, and ability to withstand heat in parts removal operations.

ASSEMBLY Assembly is one of the most demanding operations for industrial robots. A number of conditions must be met for robotic assembly to be viable, among them that the overall production system be highly coordinated and that the product be designed with robotic assembly in mind. The sophistication of the control system required implies a large initial capital outlay, which generally requires production of 100,000 to one million units per year in order to be profitable. Robotic assembly has come to be used in the production of a wide range of goods, including circuit boards, electronic components and equipment, household appliances, and automotive subassemblies.

SPRAY FINISHING OPERATIONS Industrial robots are widely used in spray finishing operations, particularly in the automobile industry. One of the reasons these operations are cost-effective is that they minimize the need for environmental control to protect workers from fumes.

Robots are also used for quality control inspections, since they can be programmed to quantitatively measure various aspects of a product's creation. In addition, the use of robots in environmental applications, such as the cleaning of contaminated sites and the handling and analysis of hazardous materials, represents an important growth market for robotics producers. Non-industrial applications for robots in security, commercial cleaning, food service, and health care are also on the rise.

FUTURE OF ROBOTICS

Recent research and development has addressed a number of aspects of robotics. Robotic hands have been developed which offer greater dexterity and flexibility, and improvements have been made in visual sensors as well (earlier generations of visual sensors were designed for use with television and home video, and did not process information quickly for optimal performance in many robotics applications; as a consequence, solid-state vision sensors came into increased use, and developments were also made with fiber optics). The use of superconducting materials, meanwhile, offers the possibility of substantial improvements in the electric motors that drive robotic arms. Attempts have also been made to develop lighter robotic arms and increase their rigidity. Standardization of software and hardware to facilitate the centralization of control systems has also been an important area of development in recent years. Indeed, ''robots are simply more programmable and flexible than ever before,'' wrote *Tooling and Production* contributor Katina Z. Jones. ''Multiple cells can be more easily accommodated and cybernetic gadgetry such as virtual reality and computer simulation have added a new dimension to the sales and installation of robotics.'' Finally, the processing speed of robotic brains was expected to increase from 10 MIPS in 2000 to 1,000 MIPS by 2003.

FURTHER READING:

''Accuracy is Only Relative on Robotics, Automation.'' *Tooling & Production*. November 1996.

Alkhafaji, Abbas F. ''Strategic Applications of Robotics Technology.'' *Management Decision*. July 1991.

Anthes, Gary H. ''The Robots Are Coming!'' *Computerworld*. May 22, 2000.

Bergstrom, Robin P. ''Common Sense and Robot Use.'' *Production*. February 1993.

Donleavy, G.D. ''Evaluating the Potential of Office Robotics.'' *Long Range Planning*. April 1994.

''The Droid Void Is Ending.'' *Ward's Auto World*. January 1994.

Jones, Katina Z. ''Robots Serve Up New Directions.'' *Tooling & Production*. April 1995.

Nof, Shimon, ed. *Handbook of Industrial Robotics*. Chicago: Wiley, 1999.

''Robots on the Rise.'' *IIE Solutions*. March 2000.

Taylor, P.M. *Understanding Robotics*. CRC Press, 1990.

SEE ALSO: Automation

ROYALTIES

Royalties are payments made by one company (the licensee) to another company (the licensor) in exchange for the right to use intellectual property or physical assets owned by the licensor. For example, software giant Microsoft invented the Windows operating system for personal computers as a means of managing files and performing operations. Computer manufacturers such as IBM and Compaq pay a royalty to Microsoft in exchange for being allowed to use the Windows operating system in their computers. Other common situations in which royalties are paid include the following:

1. In the fashion industry, designers such as Ralph Lauren and Calvin Klein license the right to use their names on items of clothing in exchange for royalties. For example, they may sign a contract with a company that makes jeans that allows the company to place the designer's name on the jeans.

2. In book publishing, authors are commonly paid both a fee for their services and a royalty rate that entitles them to a percentage of their books' profits.

3. In the music industry, royalties are paid to music copyright holders and to songwriters by radio stations and anyone else who derives a commercial benefit from the copyrighted material.

4. In the television industry, popular satellite TV services such as Direct TV and cable television services pay network stations and superstations a royalty rate so that they can broadcast those channels over their systems.

5. In the oil and gas industry, companies pay landowners a royalty rate for the right to extract natural resources, such as petroleum and natural gas, from the landowner's property. Similar agreements exist in the mining industry for minerals such as copper and silver.

HOW RATES ARE ESTABLISHED

Royalty agreements are intended to benefit both the licensor (the person receiving the royalty) and the licensee (the person paying the royalty). For the licensor, signing a royalty agreement to allow another company to use its product or intellectual property can mean expanding into a new market, or increasing market share in an existing market. For the licensee, the agreement can mean gaining access to products that may have been too expensive or too difficult to produce on its own, or that were protected by patents it did not own. If done right, the royalty arrangement is a win-win situation.

Royalty agreements generally are one of two types. The fixed price per unit agreement pays the licensor a set price for every one of its products sold by the licensee. Often, this type of agreement is used when the licensor's product is one that will be a small part of a larger product produced by the licensee. An example of this might be a new type of windshield wiper motor developed by Company A. The motor drastically changes the way windshield wipers work and is granted a patent by the U.S. Patent Office. Company A approaches General Motors and offers to license the motor to the automaker so that it can be included in all GM cars and trucks. In return, GM agrees to pay Company A $10 per unit for every motor it purchases. This price would cover the materials and labor needed to produce the motor, as well as include an extra sum to cover Company's A investment in developing the motor. In fixed price arrangements, the amount per unit can be adjusted for inflation, or a minimum royalty amount can be specified.

The second type of agreement is a royalty that pays a percentage of revenues or operating profit that results from the sale of the licensed product. This is more likely to be used when the item covered by the royalty agreement stands alone or when the cost of using the item can be clearly itemized. Percentage agreements are generally more intricate than fixed price agreements because more terms must be defined—what rate will be paid for discounted items, what happens to items that are returned, whether sales commissions affect the percentage paid, whether updated versions of the item are covered by the agreement, and more. Agreements based on a percentage of the operating profit generally result in a more equitable settlement for both parties, but those agreements are also more complicated. As a result, it is more common for companies to agree on a percentage of revenues.

In percentage agreements, it is essential that the percentage chosen be fair to both sides. There are three areas to consider when determining a rate: 1) the specifications of the actual product or intellectual property being licensed; 2) the length and the geographic scope of the agreement; and 3) the capabilities of the licensor and licensee to live up to the agreement.

Factors related to the product that can affect the agreement include the uniqueness of the product, including any patents that may be included as well as any new versions of the product that may or may not be included in the agreement; the markets in which the product will be sold; and whether or not the product needs to be customized to meet the needs of the licensee. If customization is required, than the licensee should pay the licensor a higher percentage to cover additional manufacturing costs.

As for the agreement itself, it should clearly state the duration and should include the terms under which termination will occur. Whether or not the agreement can be renewed if certain goals are met should also be clearly spelled out. If a contract is too restrictive, the licensor may find at the end of the contract that it has limited itself in such a way that it can only renew the agreement with the current licensee, at less desirable financial terms. To try to find a new partner would be too cost intensive, so the licensor must renew with the original licensee. In addition to duration, the agreement should spell out the geographic rights granted to the licensee—does the agreement cover U.S. sales only, or are international rights included? Finally, the agreement should have a provision to handle ''third party assignment.'' That is, what happens if the licensee assigns the rights to the product to a third party, possibly as a means to lower production costs? In some cases, the contract is invalidated if a third party assignment occurs, so it is an important area to cover.

When approaching a licensor, a licensee should examine the company's business practices before signing an agreement. Things to watch for include the licensor's ability to keep up with technological advances and its financial stability. If the licensee feels there is a chance the licensor may not be able to keep up with industry shifts and may even go out of business during the life of the agreement, than the licensee should seek to negotiate more favorable royalty terms. The licensee should also expect the licensor to have a clear plan outlining research and development plans, goals for the product, and plans to develop new or related products that could possibly expand the agreement. Evidence of planning and clear goals for the future by the licensor should instill confidence in the licensee. Finally, does the licensor have the ability to provide the licensee (and consumers) with needed levels of customer service and support? This is especially important for high-tech products or for complex products. The better the support that is in place, the better the terms the licensor can expect to receive.

Conversely, the licensor should expect certain things from the licensee. Can the licensee live up to its promises as far as units sold and territory covered? Has the licensee sold products of this nature before, and does it have a strong history? Is the company financially viable, and does it show clear plans for future growth? Can the licensee offer something other than cash as part of the agreement—for example, does the licensee have the ability to enhance the original product with its own products, or does it offer the licensor a market credibility that was previously lacking? All of these situations can affect how much money the licensor expects in the royalty contract.

LICENSING INTELLECTUAL PROPERTY

Intellectual property that is owned by one company is considered to be an intangible asset of that company. An intangible asset is something abstract, such as a patent or copyright, as opposed to a tangible asset, such as a factory or manufacturing equipment, or even cash. As *Business Economics* reported, ''Intangible assets do not appear on the balance sheet. But they are quite real. Intangible assets contribute to revenue and growth. The stock market recognizes these assets and reflects their value in stock prices.''

Not all intangible assets are intellectual property, however. For example, a company's workforce has skills that make it an intangible asset, but it is not intellectual property. Intellectual property is protected by law and may be sold, licensed, or transferred. Patents are perhaps the most common form of intellectual property. A patent is essentially a license granted by the U.S. Patent Office that gives one company the exclusive right to make and sell a patented invention for a period of 17 years. Any other company that desires to use that invention must negotiate terms of use with the company that receives the patent. Most often, those terms of use will involve a royalty agreement.

The Internal Revenue Service of the United States has developed definitions of what qualifies as intellectual property and oversees the regulation of royalty payments involving intellectual property. Among the intangible assets that are considered to be intellectual property are:

1. Patents, inventions, formulas, processes, or designs;

2. Copyrights and artistic compositions, including books and music;

3. Trademarks, trade names, or brand names;

4. Franchises, licenses, or contracts;

5. Items specifically compiled or created by a company, such as methods, programs, systems, procedures, campaigns, surveys, studies, forecasts, estimates, customer lists, or technical data; and

6. Any other items that are not physical in nature, but rather intellectual.

Whenever any intangible assets that fit these criteria are sold or licensed from one company to another, a royalty must be paid. There are two types of transactions that may occur. The first involves the sale or license from one company to another, which is called a third-party transaction. In this type of transaction, Company A licenses the rights to its product or process to Company B, which pays a royalty rate for the right to use the product or process. This is the type of transaction that is most commonly thought of when royalties are considered. However, the second type of transaction, the intercompany transfer, is actually more common. The law in the U.S. makes it illegal for an American firm to transfer intellectual property rights to a foreign subsidiary unless royalties are paid. The IRS has very strict rules that it applies to all intercompany situations and has come up with a number of formulas that it uses to determine if a fair royalty rate is being paid.

The simplest formula used by the IRS is called the cost-based method. Using the cost-based method, a company can establish a royalty rate that recaptures the costs of developing the item that is being licensed while also providing a fair rate of return on the item. To use the cost-based method, a company must determine what it cost to develop the intellectual property, the life expectancy of the property, the total revenue generated by products that use the property, and a fair rate of return that will cover the risks the company took in developing the property.

The cost-based method is the most straightforward, but it has flaws that limit its effectiveness. In most cases, the costs of developing the intellectual property do not have a direct correlation to the actual value of the property, so the method will not produce accurate results. As a result, the most commonly used formula for determining a royalty rate is the ''comparable uncontrolled transaction (CUT)'' method. This method relies on historical data and the performance results for products or processes that are similar to the intellectual property that is being licensed. For example, a book publisher lining up an author to write a book may look at the rates that were paid to other authors to write similar books when they determine how much to pay an author for the new project. Similarly, a clothing designer may look at other licensing deals in the industry when it comes time to license his name for use on a line of handbags or accessories.

When applying the CUT method, the intellectual property in question can only be measured against other intellectual property that was used in similar products within the same basic industry or market, and that has similar profit potential. Additional factors, such as the length of the agreement, geographic restrictions, and the right to receive updates, also factor into determining if the CUT method can be utilized. The CUT method is preferred by the IRS and is used in most third-party licensing agreements.

Beyond the two most common methods of evaluating royalty rates, the IRS uses four other formulas that are less common. These include the comparable profits method (CPM), which compares the profits of companies that use the intellectual property in question to the profits of similar companies that do not use the intellectual property; the hybrid CPM, which uses a combination of the CUT method and the CPM method in order to take the profit-making potential of the intellectual property into account; the profit split method (PSM), which accounts for situations where the licensor takes the intellectual property and adds value to it through its own processes, thereby enhancing the profitability of the property at its own expense; and the residual market value (RSV) method, which recognizes that a company's financial performance can affect the value of intellectual property and thus uses stock market data to determine the estimated value of the intellectual property that is being licensed.

COPYRIGHTS, PATENTS, AND ROYALTIES

Perhaps the most common day-to-day application of royalties that most consumers can relate to involves those paid for the use of copyrighted material. Every time a song is played on the radio, a royalty fee is paid by the station for playing that song. Every time a cable television provider transmits the signal of a broadcast television channel, such as superstation WTBS out of Atlanta, it pays that station a royalty for the right to show it. Every book, magazine, and newspaper published in the United States is protected by a copyright, and royalties must be paid any time a portion of a print product is reproduced by anyone other than the publisher.

In the United States, several organizations are involved in the oversight and management of royalty agreements involving copyrighted material. These primarily consist of government agencies and non-profit associations that monitor intellectual property rights and, in some cases, actually collect royalties due to member companies.

The primary government agencies that are involved in royalty situations are the U.S. Copyright Office and the U.S. Patent Office. Neither agency is directly involved in royalty payments, but both play an important role in the process. The Copyright Office provides all original authored works (including literary, dramatic, music, and artistic works) with full protection under the law. When an author, artist, or publisher applies for a copyright, they receive the right to reproduce the work, to prepare derivative works based upon the work, to distribute copies of the work, to perform the work publicly, to display the work publicly, and, in the case of records, to perform the works by way of digital audio transmission. The length of time that a copyright lasts varies depending on the work and when it was published, but it is a minimum of several decades in every case. This means that only the person or company that holds the copyright for a work can license that work and receive royalties for it.

The Copyright Office determines when royalties are required, and its latest target is the Internet. Just as it requires cable and satellite television systems to pay licensing fees for content, the office is close to requiring Internet "webcasters" to pay royalties as well for broadcasting the copyrighted work of artists. Webcasters include online services that broadcast radio and television programming and movies over the World Wide Web.

Similarly, the Patent Office protects inventors and their inventions. Whenever a person or company invents a new product or process, they can apply for a patent to indicate that they did invent that product or process, which grants them full protection under the law. If the work they submit is found to already exist or to be too derivative of an existing patent, then the new patent is not granted. Like a copyright, a patent gives the holder of that patent the right to license the product or service under royalty agreements, in this case for 17 years.

In the private sector, one of the main royalty organizations is the American Society of Composers, Authors, and Publishers (ASCAP), an association that protects the rights of its members working in the music industry (primarily composers, songwriters, lyricists, and music publishers). ASCAP monitors all public venues where music is played and collects royalties for its members by negotiating licensing agreements and fees with those venues, mainly radio stations. In addition to radio, however, ASCAP also closely monitors network, local, and cable television; live concert venues; college radio stations; bars, clubs, and restaurants; and background music services such as MUZAK. Every single time a songwriter's song is played, ASCAP collects money for the songwriter. This greatly simplifies the process of collecting royalties for creative works, and other similar organizations exist for writers and other creative professionals.

Another example of an umbrella organization that gathers royalty payments for a large number of clients is the Copyright Clearance Center (CCC). Created by Congress in 1978, the CCC is a central body for licensing, recording, and paying royalty fees. Book and magazine publishers register their materials with the CCC (more than 9,600 publishers registering 1.75 million works by 1998 according to *Online* magazine), which then collects royalties whenever those materials are photocopied or used in print in some way. This service is not necessarily intended to capture royalties from the average person when they make a copy of an article at their local library; instead, the CCC is intended to ensure that large-scale copying is monitored so that publishers can be fairly compensated for their work.

More than 3,500 high-volume users are registered with the CCC as part of its Transactional Reporting Service so that their payments for copying materials can be easily processed (the alternative would be to contact each publisher individually and negotiate separate royalty agreements with each company). In 1997, according to *Online,* the CCC collected more than $50 million in payments from users and distributed more than $35 million in royalties to publishers. With the spread of the Internet and other digital sources, the CCC is working to expand its services beyond print documents.

FURTHER READING:

''The Copyright Clearance Center and Publishers.'' *Online.* March-April 1998.

''The E-Music Trap.'' *InfoWorld.* August 2000.

''Establishing Royalty Rates in Marketing Agreements.'' *CMA Management.* March 2001.

''Royalty Methods for Intellectual Property.'' *Business Economics.* April 1997.

''Royalty Payments Become Basis for Investment Securities.'' *San Antonio Business Journal.* March 10, 2000.

''Webcasters Face New Royalty Fee.'' *Billboard.* May 17, 1997.

SEE ALSO: Licensing

ROYALTY FINANCING

Royalty financing is a relatively new concept that offers an alternative to regular debt financing (loans and trade credit) and equity financing (venture capital and stock sales). In a royalty financing arrangement, a small business would receive a specific amount of funds from an investor or group of investors. This money might be put toward launching a new product or expanding the company's marketing efforts. In exchange, the investors would receive a percentage of the company's future revenues over a certain period of time, up to a specific amount. The investment can be considered an ''advance'' to the company, and the periodic percentage payments can be considered ''royalties'' to the investors.

Royalty financing arrangements offer a number of advantages to small businesses. Compared to equity financing, royalty financing enables entrepreneurs to obtain capital without giving up a significant ownership position in the company to outside investors. The founders of the company are thus able to preserve their equity position, which may help motivate them toward continued success. In addition, royalty financing arrangements—since they most resemble loans—are not subject to state and federal securities laws, as some equity financing deals are. Thus the company is able to save the time and money it might otherwise devote to complex filings and legal fees. Royalty financing also increases a company's ability to structure deals with individual investors, who might be attracted to the idea of receiving a monthly or quarterly yield over the life of their investment. In contrast, equity financing arrangements often show no yield until the stock is sold.

Compared to debt financing, royalty financing provides more convenient payback terms and less severe penalties for default. In addition, the infusion of cash may help the company increase sales, which may make it a better candidate to obtain more financing later. Finally, royalty financing enables a small business to keep its options open for later financing rounds. In contrast, a company that incurs significant debt or sells a great deal of equity in its early stages may find it difficult to attract investment later.

DETAILS OF ROYALTY FINANCING

As an example, suppose that a small business obtains an ''advance'' of $100,000 against future sales from individual investors or an economic development organization. In exchange, the investors would receive 3 percent of the company's total sales for a 10 year period, to a maximum of $300,000. If the company repaid the investment over 10 years, then the investors would earn a compound annual return of 11.6 percent. However, if the investors reached their maximum royalties of $300,000 in half that time, the initial investment would yield an annual return of 24.5 percent.

A small business interested in royalty financing may be able to negotiate a grace period, so that royalties will not begin to accrue for a quarter or more following the close of the deal. It may also be possible to establish a lag between the time revenues are realized by the company and the time royalties are paid to investors. This sort of arrangement can give the small business time to put the capital to work and increase sales before paying a percentage of sales as royalties. In most cases, these arrangements are acceptable to investors since they still offer a better deal than most equity financing arrangements, which only pay when the stock is sold.

In an article for *Entrepreneur,* David R. Evanson noted that royalty financing may tend to work best for small businesses that have some elasticity in pricing, so that they can raise prices to cover the percentage of royalties without losing customers. Royalty financing is also suitable for companies for which increased marketing efforts have an immediate impact on sales. However, royalty financing may not be a good option for companies with very tight profit margins. In summary, the capital gained through royalty financing can enable a fledgling business to launch a new product or expand its marketing efforts without having to give up too much equity in the early stages. In royalty financing, investors own a piece of the company's revenue stream rather than a piece of the company itself.

FURTHER READING:

Evanson, David R. "Cash Is King: Royalty Financing Keeps Investors Happy—and Keeps Your Company in Your Own Hands." *Entrepreneur.* December 1997.

Evanson, David R. "Lending Over Backwards: When the Bank Says Tough, the Tough Get Going—Five Alternative Ways to Raise Capital." *Success.* July 1998.

RURAL BUSINESSES

Rural businesses are those firms that are established and operate in rural settings, far from the metropolitan areas that have traditionally been the site of most non-agricultural business enterprises. Most businesses continue to conduct business in large cities or thriving suburbs, but analysts contend that technological advances, demographic changes, and increased attention to "quality of life" considerations have all combined to spur meaningful business growth in many rural areas as well. As of 1998, according to Terry Neese in *LI Business News,* about 20 percent of small businesses (defined as those having fewer than 500 employees) were located in rural areas.

Increased receptiveness to new businesses has also had an impact on the growth of commerce in some rural regions. As Brian Steinberg observed in *Entrepreneur,* "many small towns in states such as Iowa and Indiana are crying out for new businesses. Dependent for generations on sagging agricultural or manufacturing economies, these towns need entrepreneurs and the jobs they supply to stay economically viable."

CHARACTERISTICS OF RURAL BUSINESSES

In an article for the *OECD Observer,* Chantal Illouz-Winicki and Dennis Paillard discussed three special features of business creation in rural areas around the world that are not present in urban areas. For example, the majority of growth in rural econo-

mies comes from existing business enterprises rather than new ones, particularly in the industrial sector. This is by no means an indication that new businesses—industrial or otherwise—cannot survive in rural settings. It merely means that existing businesses are particularly well-equipped to continue once they have established themselves. Reasons for this include the higher percentage of family-owned businesses in smaller towns (which helps with issues of long-term continuity), less competition in local markets, and what Illouz-Winicki and Paillard described as "more determination when firms run into difficulties, through a genuine or perceived lack of alternatives."

Experts have also noted that businesses in rural areas tend to be characterized by their activities. Companies that specialize in providing personal services (propane delivery, rubbish removal, etc.) are commonplace, since there is a large and steady demand for these services, which in more metropolitan areas would be handled by companies armed with city contracts. Manufacturing establishments, on the other hand, are more scarce because of transportation and work force issues. "In isolated areas, business creation is usually aimed at local consumer markets (retailing, community services) or new market niches (products with a strong regional identity)," said Illouz-Winicki and Paillard. "In more accessible areas it is aimed more at services or intermediate goods (sub-contracting). It is notable that business services, from office maintenance to consulting, are still underrepresented in rural areas because local markets are so small."

FACTORS IN RURAL BUSINESS GROWTH

The growing appetite for a simpler, more relaxed way of life has long been touted as a primary reason for the increase in rural businesses in recent years. Certainly, this has been a factor, but several other considerations warrant mention as well, including general economic conditions, demographic changes, and new modes of communication such as the Internet. Of course, not all rural regions experience business growth at the same rate; indeed, some rural areas continue to flounder even as others blossom with new business opportunities. "It is not easy to explain why an area is dynamic, or backward," admitted Illouz-Winicki and Paillard. "Complex forces are at work: specific local factors, structures and aspects that are hard to assess precisely, such as cultural traditions, business networks, and an attractive natural setting."

DEMOGRAPHIC CHANGES Business experts believe that demographic changes will likely continue to encourage growth in rural businesses over the next few decades. As more and more "baby boomers" enter into retirement age with disposable income, analysts point to rural businesses as some of that trend's chief beneficiaries. Moreover, this trend transcends national boundaries, for it can be seen not only in the United States, but in Canada, Europe, and other regions of the world. "Catering for senior citizens is a potential source of activity whose scale has to be assessed without delay," said Illouz-Winicki and Paillard. "This social group, more mobile than earlier generations, often with more disposable income than the rest of the population, is of growing demographic and economic importance. Rural areas are already benefiting from this trend in tourism, in high season and at other periods; and senior citizens are also becoming new residents, either temporary or permanent."

TRAVEL AND TOURISM The tremendous growth in the travel industry has been a significant source of income for many small towns in rural settings. Indeed, economists cite the travel and tourism industry as an engine of terrific economic growth in many rural areas that are blessed with notable natural or cultural surroundings. Many small towns located near national parks, sites of historical interest, and scenic areas have seen a surge in businesses aimed at nabbing tourist dollars, and many rural regions have ridden the growth in travel and tourism to new levels of economic prosperity. Of course, this is not a meaningful factor for many rural areas that are not situated in the vicinity of a national park or other popular tourist destination. Still, many rural city planners have successfully spurred new levels of economic activity by marketing attractive elements of the region (lakes and rivers, festivals, historical sites, etc.) so as to draw tourists.

THE INTERNET AND OTHER TELECOMMUNICATIONS ADVANCES The amazing capacities of the Internet and other relatively new means of telecommunications have enabled business owners in even the most remote locations to dramatically expand their potential customer base. "Small remote communities are attempting to bridge their isolation by taking their businesses and even their local governments online," wrote David Goodman in *Inc.* " 'Community networking,' as the phenomenon is known, brings the Internet to people in far-flung outposts. Rural businesses have seized the opportunity to play in the big leagues, with entrepreneurs of every stripe now hawking their wares in cyberspace." Goodman cited the following as key steps for any rural business community hoping to establish an online presence:

1) Organize—This step could take the form of organizing Internet training for local business owners and managers.

2) Outreach—Talk to people and community organizations face-to-face to explain how the Internet can help their business.

3) Educate—According to Goodman, providing classes on Internet use to both em-

ployees and the larger community can help rural businesses "develop a critical mass of technoliterate citizens."

4) Target—Provide workshops and training seminars specifically tailored to individual business sectors so that their membership can see how an Internet presence can benefit them.

5) Provide Access—Small towns should follow the lead of their larger brethren, which often provide the public with free access to the Internet at local libraries or community centers.

Finally, the rise of telecommuting and other communication advances has made it increasingly possible for software developers, freelance writers, graphic artists, and others who maintain home-based businesses to establish themselves wherever they wish, provided they have reliable computer and/or postal resources at their disposal.

COMMON OBSTACLES TO BUSINESS GROWTH IN RURAL AREAS

A significant percentage of new businesses in rural areas are established businesses that relocate. Indeed, many entrepreneurs have established their business ventures in rural regions of the country in recent years. This trend has been especially evident among small business owners who have decided to relocate for "quality of life" reasons. These entrepreneurs are sometimes limited in their relocation options by customer demographics and other factors, but the desire for quieter, less hectic lifestyles has proven to be a potent one, as families search for homes that are not bedeviled by traffic, crime, and other attributes often associated with large cities.

Nonetheless, small business owners are urged to weigh the obstacles that often confront businesses that decide to relocate in rural locations. These hurdles range from different cultural standards and finding new friends to negotiating new ways of transporting goods or finding quality employees. In addition, services in rural areas often do not match those that can be routinely relied upon in more metropolitan areas. Unreliable electrical service, skimpy or nonexistent overnight delivery options, and increased telecommunications costs (for regular telephone service as well as Internet connections) can all complicate the efforts of businesses in rural locations. These difficulties can be particularly problematic for businesses that are involved in high-tech areas. "For technology-dependent businesses to thrive in remote areas, connecting a computer to the Internet is the easy part," wrote Goodman. "Finding employees who have the savvy to use the technology or . . . finding someone to fix your computer can be far more challenging.''

FURTHER READING:

Goodman, David. ''Small Town, Big Connections: Community Networking Gives Rural Business a Chance to Play in the Big Leagues.'' *Inc.* June 18, 1996.

Illouz-Winicki, Chantal, and Dennis Paillard. ''New Business in Rural Areas.'' *OECD Observer.* February-March 1998.

Neese, Terry. ''Rural Businesses Will Face Challenges in Global Market.'' *LI Business News.* December 25, 1998.

Steinberg, Brian. ''Green Acres: Why Some Entrepreneurs are Saying 'Goodbye, City Life.' '' *Entrepreneur.* October 1997.

Stickey, Marcia. ''Home-Grown Businesses Find Rural Niche: Rural States Need to Break Out of the Urban Economic Development Mold.'' *Successful Farming.* February 1995.

Venable, Tim. ''Getting Better Location Assistance: Here's How.'' *Site Selection.* April 1996.

Weber, Fred I., Jr. *Locating or Relocating Your Business.* Small Business Administration, n.d.

S

S CORPORATION

A small business has the option of incorporating at the beginning of its existence or after years of doing business. Once it incorporates, it has two choices: to be a regular C corporation by default or to elect S corporation status, a name derived from Subchapter S of the Internal Revenue Code. This status was derived in an effort to make incorporating more attractive to small businesses and allow them to enjoy some of the benefits of corporate status while avoiding some of the drawbacks. While most small businesses are eligible for S status, there are some requirements that must be met, such as limitations on the number and kind of stockholders the corporation may have.

In *Choosing a Legal Structure for Your Business*, Stuart Handmaker explains that ''Essentially, there isn't any difference between a C corporation and an S corporation. Each of them is a corporation, and each one has the same characteristics, shareholders, directors, officers, records, minute books, problems, and the like. The only real difference is that the S corporation has filed a special form with the Internal Revenue Service stating that it wants to be an S corporation.''

What makes the S corporation different from the C corporation, then, is that it has special status in the eyes of the IRS. In short, the S corporation is viewed as a partnership or sole proprietorship for taxation purposes. This means that the corporation itself is not taxed, as C corporations are; rather the S corporation's profits are passed on to its shareholders, who pay income tax on that money. In nearly all other respects, though, the S corporation is essentially the same as the C corporation. Most importantly, S corporations receive the benefit of limited liability that goes along with being a corporation. The combined benefits of limited liability (the lack of which is the main drawback of partnerships or sole proprietorships) and avoidance of double taxation (the main drawback of C corporations) makes the S corporation the most popular legal structure amongst small business owners.

BECOMING AN S CORPORATION

FILING WITH THE INTERNAL REVENUE SERVICE Once a business has gone through the procedure of becoming a corporation by filing the articles of incorporation, etc., it can elect S corporation status by filing form 2553 with the IRS. All of the corporation's shareholders must sign this form or file special shareholder consent forms. These rules apply to anyone who has held stock in the company during the current tax year. To be eligible for S corporation status for the current tax year, a corporation must file the form by the fifteenth day of the third month of the corporation's tax year. Once the form has been filed, it is not necessary to file every year.

ELIGIBILITY For a corporation to be eligible for S corporation status, the following conditions must be met and maintained:

- The business must have become a corporation prior to filing for S corporation status. See ''Incorporation'' for more information on this process.

- The business must also have no more than 75 stockholders. Until the Small Business Job Protection Act of 1996 was passed, corporations with more than 35 shareholders were disqualified, but now the limit is 75, allowing most small businesses to fall within the guidelines.

- All of the business's stock must be owned by individuals who reside in or are citizens of the United States. Estates or trusts may be allowed as stockholders, but corporate or foreign investors are not allowed. This includes other businesses that are not corporations, such as partnerships or sole proprietorships. This provision, therefore, excludes corporate subsidiaries from claiming S corporation status.

- The business must issue only one class of stock. This means that with the purchase of stock must come the same economic rights, such as receiving dividends or compensation in the event of liquidation at the same time and in the same amount per share as all other shareholders. Voting rights may differ amongst the shareholders without being considered a sign of the possession of different classes of stock.

INELIGIBLE BUSINESSES Those businesses that are ineligible for S corporation status include:

- All financial institutions, such as banks and savings and loans

- Insurance companies

- Businesses that receive 95 percent or more of their gross income from exports (also known as DISCs, Domestic International Sales Corporations)

- Corporations that use the possessions tax credit

- C Corporations that have been S corporations within the last five years

BENEFITS OF S CORPORATION STATUS

LIMITED LIABILITY Like C corporations, S corporations are considered to be separate entities apart from their owners for all purposes except taxation. This means that debts incurred by the corporation are the responsibility of the corporation, not its shareholders, who can only be held accountable up to the amount they invested in the corporation. If the corporation does not possess enough assets to pay its debts, the shareholders will not be required to make up the difference out of their own pockets. In addition, if the corporation is sued, liability rests on the shoulders of the corporation, not its shareholders.

AVOIDING DOUBLE TAXATION According to the Internal Revenue Service, an S corporation is not a separate taxable entity. Instead, the corporation's pro-

fits are considered to be the shareholders' income (whether the money is distributed or not). Therefore, the corporation's earnings turn up on the shareholders' personal federal tax returns, the amount of which must be proportional to their share of stock. This can be a beneficial arrangement for many small businesses, because the money is taxed only once on the federal level. (State and local taxes may still be levied against the corporation.)

C corporations, on the other hand, are required to pay a federal corporate tax on all profits, and then the shareholders must pay income taxes on their share of dividends that are distributed once the corporation tax has been deducted. In essence, then, that money has been taxed twice. In the case of businesses that intend to leave most of the profits in the corporation or reinvest significant portions of the profits back into the business, though, C corporation status may be preferential if the corporate tax bracket is lower that your personal tax rate. But for companies that plan to pay shareholders all or most of the profits, S corporation status helps them avoid double taxation.

Professional corporations may also desire to elect S corporation status as they are often taxed at a higher rate than a regular C corporation. In addition, corporations that plan to conduct business in more than one state will find it easier to register to do so as an S corporation than as a C corporation. In the case of asset liquidation, S corporation status can also be a benefit because the appreciated value is taxed only on the shareholders' personal income tax. In the case of C corporations, the sale of appreciated assets can result in double taxation because the profit is taxed to the corporation and then to the shareholders to whom it is distributed.

LOSSES AS PERSONAL DEDUCTIONS When an S corporation ends the year with a loss, that loss appears on the shareholders' personal income tax returns, just like profits do. This can mean substantial savings for shareholders, who will end up owing less (or even no) taxes after they deduct their share of the corporation's loss (proportional to their share of stock). In fact, many new small businesses that expect to start off with a loss elect S status so that they will receive this tax credit.

DRAWBACKS OF S CORPORATION STATUS

RECORDKEEPING AND ATTENTION TO DETAIL Because an S corporation is still a corporation, it requires owners to pay careful attention to the details of recordkeeping. In some cases, businesses that did file for S corporation status have not been viewed as such by the courts because they failed to act like corporations. In other words, some small businesses simply apply for the status in hopes of gaining limited liability protection, but they fail to keep separate personal and corporate accounts, for example, or to hold regular director's and shareholders' meetings and take minutes, all of which are requirements for corporations. They may also neglect to change their name to reflect their new corporate status in an effort to avoid the extra cost of ordering new stationary and business cards and changing their sign. As a result, the owners of such companies have been known to be found personally liable just as if their business was a sole proprietorship or partnership.

Simply filing the articles of incorporation does not guarantee limited liability. Moreover, an S corporation may be reverted to C corporation status if it fails to continually meet the eligibility requirements, another factor which requires attention to detail. The sale of stock to one foreign investor, for example, could mean the termination of S corporation status, and once a corporation reverts to C corporation status, it is not eligible to file for S status for another five years. This could be a costly error. Simply filing for S corporation status, therefore, does not guarantee protection from double taxation.

DOUBLE TAXATION FOR COMPANIES SWITCHING FROM C STATUS Businesses that start out as C corporations and change their status to that of S corporations may still be taxed as corporations if certain conditions exist. Corporations switching status from C to S and possessing capital gains, excessive passive investment gains, investment tax credits, or liquidations may be still be subject to double taxation.

FRINGE BENEFITS Unlike C corporations—but like partnerships—S corporations are not allowed to deduct fringe benefits given to shareholders who are employees as a business expense. As a result, shareholder-employees must pay taxes on those benefits. These rules apply to all shareholders who own more than two percent of the corporation's stock and are employees of the corporation. All non-shareholder employees, though, may receive benefits without paying taxes.

STOCK LIMITATIONS To remain eligible for S corporation status, a corporation is only allowed to issue one class of stock, which may be a deterrent to businesses that would like to issue preferred as well as common stock. In addition, a limit of 75 stockholders is placed on the S corporation, and all stockholders must be individuals who reside in or are citizens of the United States. The small business corporation, therefore, is denied the benefit of foreign investors in an increasingly global business world.

TERMINATING S CORPORATION STATUS

It is possible for an S corporation to voluntarily revoke its status if it finds that S status is no longer beneficial, or to lose the status involuntarily. In the first case, a majority of the stockholders is required to make the decision, and a simple notification to the IRS is all that is required. In the second case, any act which disqualifies the corporation's eligibility for S status will result in the termination of that status effective on the date that the infraction occurs. In either case, the corporation becomes a C corporation in the absence of S corporation status.

FURTHER READING:

Colville, John. ''Incorporation: Pros and Cons.'' *Accountancy*. July 2000.

Cooke, Robert A. *How to Start Your Own (Subchapter) S Corporation*. John Wiley & Sons, 1995.

Daughtrey, Zoel W., and Frank M. Messina. ''Entity Choice Comparisons.'' *CPA Journal*. November 2000.

Goldstein, Arnold S. *Starting Your Subchapter ''S'' Corporation*. John Wiley & Sons, 1988.

Handmaker, Stuart A. *Choosing a Legal Structure for Your Business*. Prentice Hall, 1997.

Lee, Mie-Yun. ''Incorporating Can Pave the Way to Profitability.'' *Washington Business Journal*. September 8, 2000.

Nichols, Ted. *How to Form Your Own ''S'' Corporation and Avoid Double Taxation*. Upstart Publishing, 1995.

Selecting the Legal Structure for Your Business Small Business Administration. n.d.

SEE ALSO: C Corporation; Incorporation; Professional Corporation

SALES COMMISSIONS

The sales commission is a method of compensating salespeople for the services they provide to their employer. Under so-called ''straight'' commission arrangements, the salesperson receives a previously agreed-upon percentage of the revenue brought in by a sale that he or she makes. Commission arrangements can be used for both service and product sectors. Some employers, however, choose to compensate their salespeople via straight salaries, thus compensating them in the same way as other employees, or via a combination of salary and commission.

The chief advantage associated with utilizing a straight commission arrangement is that it gives salespeople a major incentive to work hard on behalf of the company. But detractors contend that the compensation uncertainties associated with such plans sometimes make it difficult to secure good salespeople, and that their complete dependence on commissions may lead them into bad business habits. Even detractors, however, admit that commission set ups do provide salespeople with meaningful incentive to work hard. As a result, the majority of businesses that maintain a sales force use some combination of base salary and commission—also known as incentive pay—to compensate their salespeople.

"Because selling is so difficult, salespeople need to be trained, supported, and, above all, motivated," confirmed *The Portable MBA in Entrepreneurship.* "They need sales literature, administrative support to send out promotional material, and presentation graphics. They also need *incentives* that work—the right combination of commissions, prizes, stock, and whatever else you dream up. What are you doing in these areas and what do you plan for the future to upgrade your selling efforts?"

Some small- and mid-sized businesses have been known to balk at the size of the commissions that they pay to their top-level salespeople. Indeed, businesses that are engaged in industry sectors that are known for the sale and acquisition of so-called "big ticket" items, such as major equipment, or large-volume purchases may distribute commissions of several thousand dollars or more for a single sale. But most business consultants urge employers to remember that if they are doling out large commissions, that also means that those same salespeople are bringing in lots of business for the company. As the editors of *The Portable MBA in Entrepreneurship* indicated, "A good rule to follow is that when you find something that works, stay with it, even if it means paying what seems to be obscene amounts of cash. The best salespeople should earn top dollar."

BASIC COMPENSATION PLANS FOR SALESPEOPLE

Companies generally compensate their salespeople in one of three ways: straight commission, straight salary, or salary plus additional incentive (often commission).

STRAIGHT COMMISSION Under straight commission compensation arrangements, the salesperson receives a previously agreed-upon percentage of the selling price. The size of the percentage of the commission may vary from product to product. Business experts estimate that fewer than 15 percent of American firms pay their salespeople on a straight commission basis, although the majority of those companies that do choose this method of compensation indicate satisfaction with it. The primary benefit associated with this option, of course, is that it serves as a significant motivator to sales personnel. Moreover, companies that go this route are not forced to pay high salaries to salespeople during periods when sales are slow.

But Porter Henry and Joseph Callanan, authors of *Sales Management and Motivation,* indicated that there are potentially significant disadvantages associated with straight commission plans as well. In some cases, salespeople may concentrate on selling those products that are easiest to sell, paying comparatively little attention to high-profit specialty items or new products that are unfamiliar to prospective buyers. One solution to this problem is to pay higher commissions on those new or high-profit goods. Another problem associated with straight commissions is that salespeople may not put forth as much efforts after they reach a certain level of income. In such instances, Henry and Callanan recommend that businesses "adopt a sliding scale, with commissions increasing after a certain volume has been reached." Other potential disadvantages associated with straight commission compensation, say Henry and Callanan, include:

- Problems hiring new sales personnel— "Candidates for sales jobs are more security-conscious than they were in the past. Some quite desirable applicants may be unwilling or unable to face a few months of inadequate income before building up a satisfactory volume."

- High turnover—Another employee retention issue. Many good salespeople will choose to go to some other company that features a more secure employee compensation program, unless they are performing quite well under your arrangement. And even then, salespeople with families are may well decide that long-term security— embodied in a steady salary—is preferable to high levels of compensation that could dwindle away with the next industry downturn.

- Execution of nonselling tasks—Straight commission arrangements often encourage an environment wherein salespeople ignore non-sales related tasks that nonetheless need to be addressed. "You can't blame them," wrote Henry and Callanan. "Commission reps are in effect in business for themselves; they get paid for selling, and only for selling. Unless the nonselling jobs (such as taking inventory, setting up displays, collecting back debts) directly contribute to future sales, you're taking money right out of their pockets by asking reps to perform them. Some companies have found it advisable to pay salespeople a nominal fee for handling such duties."

STRAIGHT SALARY The most frequent criticism of compensation plans that pay sales representatives a straight salary is that they eliminate the employees' incentive to perform. As one sales executive told *Sales and Marketing Management,* companies that offer aggressive incentive structures create hunger among their salespeople, while those that offer comfortable base salaries foster an environment of complacency. Other analysts contend, however, that this admitted drawback can be neutralized to some degree by creating a company culture that rewards top-notch sales performances with prompt salary increases and/or promotions.

SALARY PLUS COMMISSION OR OTHER INCENTIVES
This arrangement is by far the most common one employed by organizations that use salespeople. Proponents tout several meaningful advantages associated with compensation plans that combine base salaries with commissions:

- Motivates sales force to expend greater effort.

- Provides company with a way to extend additional rewards to its best sales performers.

- Closely ties compensation to performance (though not to the same degree as straight commission arrangements).

- Generally easy to administer.

- Depending on the arrangement, the bestowal of increased security to employees may allow the company to take a greater percentage of sales profits.

Criticisms of compensation plans that combine salary with commissions or other incentives are usually framed not as rebukes of its philosophical underpinnings, but rather as laments concerning its execution. For example, some companies may offer only token commissions, which do little to foster aggressive salesmanship.

In addition to commissions, some companies choose to provide non-salary compensation to their sales force through expense accounts, automobile leasing, advances against future earnings (usually commission), or sales contests.

Expense accounts are common features in many industries. Indeed, salespeople in a wide range of industry sectors depend a great deal on business lunches, etc. to close deals. Moreover, salespeople often are responsible for large territories, which makes long hours of travel a fundamental element of their job description. Organizations that do not compensate such individuals with expense accounts—or free use of leased automobiles—are likely to have considerable difficulty finding and retaining gifted salespeople. Indeed, most prospective hires will view refusal to take care of expenses as a sure sign of company stinginess and an indication that the company's ownership may not be cognizant of basic business realities.

Sales contests are another popular tool used by business owners to encourage sales activities. Under these programs, sales personnel who meet certain sales goals are rewarded with cash bonuses, paid vacations, etc. But business experts contend that sales contests can have unintended consequences for organizations if they are poorly defined or structured so that only a small segment of the sales force is rewarded. Indeed, some organizations provide incentives only to a certain percentage of top-level performers. Such programs—whether commissions or sales contests—are usually implemented in hopes of creating a competitive environment, but all too often they have the opposite effect. ''Sure, your top salespeople are thrilled about the program—for them, it most likely means another trip to Hawaii or Europe,'' wrote Melanie Berger in *Sales and Marketing Management.* ''But for the vast majority of your sales force, the incentive is yet another opportunity to do one thing: lose. And nobody feels good about losing. All too often, executives planning incentive programs for their sales forces assume they need to motivate and reward their top performers—the ones who already generate the bulk of their business. Less successful—shall we say, average—players are ignored, left to remain, well, average.''

In order to counteract the negative characteristics associated with traditional sales contests, many business consultants recommend that businesses instead institute so-called ''open-ended'' incentive programs. These programs are designed so that participants compete against their own past performances rather than their fellow salespeople. As one sales manager told Berger, ''Very often with closed-ended programs [traditional programs in which salespeople compete against one another for a limited number of rewards], people use the excuse, 'Her territory is better than mine' or, 'They were lucky and closed a big sale; it was the right place at the right time.' The incentive programs that work the best are the ones that are considered fair. What's fair is to have people competing against themselves—that way you're being compared to what you've done in the past, not what the guy next to you is doing.'' In addition, Berger noted that open-ended programs can be shaped in two-tiered fashion so that a business's very best sales performers receive some extra recognition. For example, salespeople that increase their sales by 10 percent might receive a nice prize, while those that increase their sales by 20 percent would receive an even better one. Open programs, said Berger, can be used in place of closed programs so that ''rather than getting better results from just a small number of salespeople, companies can potentially inspire improved performance from all of them. And that translates into increased sales and a stronger bottom line.''

Berger did note, however, that there are two objections that are commonly raised to open-ended sales incentives. The first is that such initiatives cast greater uncertainty on sales budgeting efforts. After all, companies that offer an open program "don't know in advance how many winners they'll have or how many prizes they'll need to award." In addition, some observers contend that open programs actually can detract from the performance of a business's top salespeople. "If all reps have to do to win is increase sales by 15 percent, the top producers in an open-ended program could hit that mark well before the year is over, and coast the rest of the way," said Berger. But the impact of both of these negative attributes can be largely neutralized through careful planning (such as studying multi-tiered programs) and continuous monitoring.

FUTURE CHALLENGES

Business researchers believe that companies will have to continually adjust their sales commission/incentives packages in the coming years in order to remain competitive, since the overall business environment is changing with such rapidity. For example, salespeople are now seen as more likely to move not only from business to business but also from industry to industry. "Salespeople, despite their market specialization, have one thing in common: They want to make lots of money," observed Michele Marchetti in *Sales and Marketing Management.* "And these high-performing people will seek out companies with competitive pay plans—regardless of the industry."

In addition, increased emphasis on customer satisfaction and increasing market share with current customers is likely to broaden the responsibilities of salespeople, who will in turn expect to be compensated appropriately. "Today's selling environment is frustrating and fascinating," said Marchetti. "Technology is propelling us into a new way of thinking about business strategy and the way we define success. As always, though, salespeople will do what they're rewarded for doing. That's why compensation plans have to keep up with the changing selling methods. Sales managers must motivate their reps to build real relationships between customers and company, in order to increase the share of each customer's business and to increase the value of each customer to the company."

FURTHER READING:

Berger, Melanie. "When Their Ship Comes In: How to Create an Incentive Program that Motivates All of Your Salespeople—and Sends More Happy Winners on that Coveted Trip." *Sales and Marketing Management.* April 1997.

Bygrave, William D., ed. *The Portable MBA in Entrepreneurship.* 2d ed. New York: John Wiley & Sons, 1997.

Henry, Porter, and Joseph Callanan. *Sales Management and Motivation.* New York: Franklin Watts, 1987.

Keenan, Bill. "Moving Away from Commissions?" *Industry Week.* January 4, 1999.

Marchetti, Michele. "Developing a Competitive Pay Plan: the Key—Benchmarking Your Reps' Compensation Against Other Industries." *Sales and Marketing Management.* April 1997.

Marchetti, Michele. "Rewarding Team Players." *Sales and Marketing Management.* April 1996.

Meyer, Harvey R. "Linking Payday to Cash in Hand." *Nation's Business.* May 1996.

Peppers, Don, and Martha Rogers. "The Money Trap." *Sales and Marketing Management.* May 1997.

"Rethinking the Salesforce." *Management Today.* July 1995.

SALES CONTRACTS

A sales contract is an agreement between a buyer and seller covering the sale and delivery of goods, securities, and personal property other than goods or securities. In the United States, domestic sales contracts are governed by the Uniform Commercial Code. International sales contracts fall under the United Nations Convention on Contracts for the International Sale of Goods (CISG), also known as the Vienna Sale Convention.

Under Article 2 of the UCC, a contract for the sale of goods for more than $500 must be in writing in order to be enforceable (UCC 2-201). The sale of securities is a special case covered in Article 8 (UCC 8-319); to be enforceable a contract for the sale of securities must be in writing regardless of the amount involved. For the sale of other kinds of personal property, a minimum of $5,000 must be involved before an enforceable contract must be in writing. Otherwise, an oral agreement is enforceable as a binding contract.

Contracts that must be in writing to be enforceable are said to be within the Statute of Frauds. The Statute of Frauds dates back to 1677, when the English Parliament decreed that certain types of contracts must be in writing. The applicable parts of the UCC effectively define the types of sales contracts that must be in writing. In addition, every state has its own version of the Statute of Frauds.

Under the UCC a written sales contract should specify the parties involved, the subject matter to be sold, and any material or special terms or conditions. Some states also require that the consideration—the amount and type of payment—be specified. The UCC does not require a formal sales contract, though. In many cases a memorandum or collection of papers is sufficient compliance. The courts have held that a written check can be considered a written memorandum of a sales agreement. The UCC allows a written sales contract to be enforced even if it leaves out material terms and is not signed by both parties. However, one party may not create a sales contract on its own that is binding against another party, and an enforceable contract must be signed by the defendant or the one against whom the contract is sought to be enforced.

In many cases a purchase order, pro forma invoice, or order acknowledgment may serve in place of a formal sales contract. A purchase order is issued by the buyer and sent to the seller, stating the type and amount of goods to be purchased, the price, and any other material terms such as a time limit on filling the order. A pro forma invoice is issued by the seller and sent to the buyer, often in response to a purchase order or oral agreement. In international transactions, the pro forma invoice may enable the buyer to open a line of credit with which to pay for the goods ordered. The pro forma invoice typically includes relevant terms and conditions that apply to the sale.

A formal order acknowledgment is useful for establishing the seller's position in case a dispute should arise. The order acknowledgment is drawn up by the seller in response to a received purchase order. It does not necessarily repeat the details of the purchase order, but it may clarify details such as delivery schedules. When a formal order acknowledgment is countersigned by the buyer, it becomes a type of sales contract.

For international transactions, the Vienna Sale Convention is binding on signatory countries, of which the United States is one. Each of the nations that has signed the convention may state up to five reservations. For example, the United States has stipulated that it shall apply to U.S. companies only when the transaction involves another signatory country. Much of the convention parallels the UCC, with these notable exceptions:

- Acceptance of an offer that includes a request for additions or modifications constitutes a counteroffer.

- There is no provision requiring a contract be written in order to be enforceable.

- The period for discovering defective merchandise may be as long as two years.

Sales contracts are useful in providing for a common understanding between buyer and seller, thus minimizing disputes. When a dispute does occur, the sales contract can help provide for a fair settlement.

FURTHER READING:

Hough, Harry E. *Handbook for Buying and Purchasing Management*. Prentice Hall, 1992.

Lane, Marc J. *Legal Handbook for Small Business*. AMACOM, 1989.

Lickson, Charles P. *A Legal Guide for Small Business*. Crisp Publications, 1994.

Roberson, Cliff. *McGraw-Hill Complete Book of Purchasing Forms and Agreements*. McGraw-Hill, 1998.

World Class Selling: The Crossroads of Customer, Sales, Marketing, and Technology. Wiley, 1999.

SALES FORCE

A company's sales force consists of its staff of salespeople. The role of the sales force depends to a large extent on whether a company is selling directly to consumers or to other businesses. In consumer sales, the sales force is typically concerned simply with taking and closing orders. These salespeople are not responsible for creating demand for the product, since demand for the product has already been created by advertising and promotion. They may provide the consumer with some product information, but individuals involved in consumer sales are often not concerned with maintaining long-term customer relationships. Examples of consumer sales forces include automobile salespersons and the sales staffs found in a variety of retail stores.

The sales force takes on a completely different role in business-to-business sales. Industrial sales forces, for example, may be required to perform a variety of functions. These may include prospecting for new customers and qualifying leads, explaining who the company is and what its products can do, closing orders, negotiating prices, servicing accounts, gathering competitive and market information, and allocating products during times of shortages.

Within the business-to-business market, a distinction can be made between selling to retailers, industrial sales, and other types of business-to-business sales and marketing. The concerns and activities of the sales force tend to vary in each type of business market. What they have in common, however, is the desire of the sales force to establish a long-term relationship with each of its customers and to provide service in a variety of ways.

In selling to retailers, for example, the sales force is not concerned with creating demand. Since consumer demand is more a function of advertising and promotion, the sales force is more concerned with obtaining shelf space in the retailer's store. The sales force may also attempt to obtain more promotion support from the retailer. The sales force relies on sophisticated marketing data to make a convincing presentation to the retailer in order to achieve its sales and marketing objectives.

The largest sales forces are involved in industrial selling. An average industrial field sales force ranges in size from 20 to 60 people and is responsible for selling throughout the United States. The sales force may be organized around traditional geographic territories or around specific customers, markets, and products. An effective sales force consists of individuals who can relate well to decision makers and help them solve their problems. A sales manager or supervisor typically provides the sales force with guidance and discipline. Within the company the sales force may receive support in the form of specialized training, technical backup, inside sales staff, and product literature. Direct mail and other types of marketing efforts can be employed to provide the sales force with qualified leads.

In recent years, costs associated with making single business-to-business industrial sales calls have risen dramatically. As a consequence, many businesses have redoubled their efforts to make sure that they get the most possible efficiency out of their sales force (by expanding their territories, increasing their duties, etc.).

Sales managers and supervisors can measure the efficiency of their sales force using several criteria. These include the average number of sales calls per salesperson per day, the average sales-call time per contact, the average revenue and cost per sales call, the entertainment cost per sales call, and the percentage of orders per 100 sales calls. The sales force can also be evaluated in terms of how many new customers were acquired and how many customers were lost during a specific period. The expense of a sales-force can be measured by monitoring the sales-force-to-sales ratio, or sales force cost as a percentage of total sales.

Using such criteria to evaluate the effectiveness of the sales force allows companies to make adjustments to improve its efficiency. If the sales force is calling on customers too often, for example, it may be possible to reduce the size of the sales force. If the sales force is servicing customers as well as selling to them, it may be possible to shift the service function to lower-paid personnel.

In industrial and other business-to-business sales, the sales force represents a key link between the manufacturer and the buyer. The sales force is often involved in selling technical applications and must work with several different contacts within a customer's organization. Industrial salespeople tend, on average, to be better educated than their consumer counterparts, and to be better paid. However, their cost as a percentage of sales is lower than in consumer sales, because industrial and business-to-business sales generally involve higher-ticket items or a larger volume of goods and services.

The sales force may be compensated in one of three ways: straight salary, straight commission, or a combination of salary plus commission. The majority of today's businesses utilize a combination of salary plus commission to compensate their sales forces, and fewer companies based their sales force compensation on straight commission. It appears that, as a percentage of all sales forces, the use of straight salaries remains constant. Whatever type of compensation system is used for the sales force, the important consideration is that the compensation adequately motivates the sales force to perform its best.

FURTHER READING:

Churchill, Gilbert A., Jr., Neil M. Ford, and Orville C. Walker, Jr. *Sales Force Management: Planning, Implementation, and Control.* 3rd ed. Boston, MA: Irwin, 1990.

Newton, Derek A. *Sales Force Management: Text and Cases.* 2d ed. Boston, MA: Irwin, 1990.

Petrone, Joe. *Building the High Performance Sales Force.* Productivity Management Press, 1994.

Rackham, Neil. *Rethinking the Sales Force: Redefining Selling to Create and Capture Customer Value.* New York: McGraw-Hill, 1999.

Rich, Gregory. ''Fast Approximation Methods for Sales Force Deployment.'' *Journal of Personal Selling and Sales Management.* Summer 2000.

SALES FORECASTS

The sales forecast is a prediction of a business's unit and dollars sales for some future period of time, up to several years or more. These forecasts are generally based primarily on recent sales trends, competitive developments, and economic trends in the industry, region, and/or nation in which the organization conducts business. Sales forecasting is management's primary tool for predicting the volume of attainable sales. Therefore, the whole budget process hinges on an accurate, timely sales forecast.

These technical projections of likely customer demand for specific products, goods, or services for a specific company within a specific time horizon are made in conjunction with basic marketing principles. For example, sales forecasts are often viewed within the context of total market potential, which can be understood as a projection of total potential sales for all companies. Market potential relates to the total capacity of the market to absorb the entire output of a specific industry. On the other hand, sales potential is the ability of the market to absorb or purchase the output from a single firm.

Many agencies and organizations publish indexes of market potential. They base their findings on extensive research and analysis of certain relationships that exist among basic economic data—for example, the location of potential consumers by age, education, and income for products that demonstrate a high correlation between those variables and the purchase of specific products. This information allows analysts to calculate the market potential for consumer or industrial goods. *Sales and Marketing Magazine* publishes buying power indexes. Its commercial indexes combine estimates of population, income, and retail sales to derive composite indicators of consumer demand according to U.S. Census Bureau regions, by state, or by the bureau's organized system of metropolitan areas. The buying-power index (BPI) provides only a relative value which analysts adjust to determine the market potential for local areas.

Forecasting methods and levels of sophistication vary greatly. Each portends to assess future events or situations which will impact either positively or negatively on a business's efforts. Managers prepare forecasts to determine the type and level of demand for both current and potential new products. They consider a broad spectrum of data for indications of growing and profitable markets. Forecasting, however, involves not only the collection and analysis of hard data, but also the application of business judgment in their interpretation and application. For example, forecasting requires business owners and managers to not only estimate expected units sold, but also to determine what the business's production (materials, labor, equipment) costs will be to produce those items.

Computer-aided sales forecasting has revolutionized this process. Advances in computer technology, information highways, and statistical and mathematical models provide almost every business with the ability to execute complex data analyses, thus reducing the risks and pitfalls prevalent in the past. These advances have made the process and costs of forecasting practical and affordable for small- and mid-sized businesses.

FACTORS IN SALES FORECASTING

Sales forecasts are conditional in that a company prepares the forecast prior to developing strategic and tactical plans. The forecast of sales potential may cause management to adjust some of its assumptions about production and marketing if the forecast indicates that: 1) current production capacity is inadequate or excessive, and 2) sales and marketing efforts need revisions. Management, therefore, has the opportunity to examine a series of alternate plans that propose changes in resource commitments (such as plant capacity, promotional programs, and market activities), changes in prices and/or changes in production scheduling.

Through forecasting the company determines markets for products, plans corporate strategy, develops sales quotas, determines the number and allocation of salespeople, decides on distribution channels,

prices products or services, analyzes products and product potential in different markets, decides on product features, determines profit and sales potential for different products, constructs advertising budgets, determines the potential benefits of sales promotion programs, decides on the use of various elements of the marketing mix, sets production volume and standards, chooses suppliers, defines financing needs, and determines inventory standards. For the forecasting to be accurate, managers need to consider all of the following factors:

HISTORICAL PERSPECTIVE As a starting point, management analyzes previous sales experience by product lines, territories, classes of customers, and other relevant details. Management needs to consider a time line long enough to detect trends and patterns in the growth and the decline of dollar sales volume. This period is generally five to ten years. If the company's experience with a particular product class is shorter, management will include discernible experience of like companies.

The longer the view, the better management is able to detect patterns which follow cycles. Patterns which repeat themselves, no matter how erratically, are considered to be ''normal,'' while variations from these patterns are ''deviant.'' Some of these deviations may have resulted from significant societal developments that carried an impact that filtered all the way down to your business's sales performance. Management may compensate for these abnormalities by adjusting the figures to reflect normal trends under normal conditions.

BUSINESS COMPETENCE The ability of a company to respond to the results of a sales forecast depends on its production capacity, marketing methods, financing, and leadership, and its ability to change each of these to maximize its profit potential.

MARKET POSITION Forecasting also considers the competitive position of the company with respect to its market share; research and development; quality of service, pricing and financing policies; and public image. In addition, forecasters also evaluate the quality and quantity of the customer base to determine brand loyalty, response to promotional efforts, economic viability, and credit worthiness.

GENERAL ECONOMIC CONDITIONS Although consumer markets are often characterized as being increasingly susceptible to segmentation in recent years, the condition of the overall economy is still a primary determinant of general sales volume, even in many niche markets. Forecasters incorporate relevant data that correlate well or demonstrate a causal relationship with sales volume.

PRICE INDEX If the prices for products have changed over the years, changes in dollar volume of sales may not correlate well with volume of units. At one point in time when demand is strong, a company raises its prices. At another time, a company may engage in discounting to draw down inventories. Therefore, accountants devise a price index for each year which compensates for price increases. By dividing the dollar volume by the price indexes, a company can track its ''true'' volume growth. This process is similar to an inflation index, which provides prices in constant dollars. As a result, management is able to compare the price-adjusted dollar sales volumes.

SECULAR TRENDS The secular trend depicts: 1) general economic performance, or 2) the performance of the specific product for all companies. If a company's trend line rises more rapidly than the secular trend line, a company would be experiencing a more rapid growth in the rate of sales. Conversely, if a company's trend line is below the secular trend line, its performance is below the market's average. Management also uses this type of comparison to evaluate and control annual performance.

TREND VARIATIONS Although the secular trend represents the average for the industry, it may not be ''normal'' for a particular company. The comparison of company trends to secular trends may indicate that the company is serving a specialized market, or that the company is not faring well. Forecasters study the underlying assumptions of trend variations to understand the important relationships in determining the volume of sales. Although markets may be strong, the sales force might need to be adjusted.

"INTRA-COMPANY" TRENDS By analyzing month-to-month trends and seasonal variations over both the long and short terms, small business owners and managers can adjust the sales forecast to anticipate variations that historically repeat themselves during budget periods. Management may then construct a budget reflecting these variations, perhaps increasing volume discounts during traditionally slow periods, exploring new territories, or having sales representatives solicit product and service ideas from current customers.

PRODUCT TRENDS Forecasters also trend individual products, using indexes to adjust for seasonal fluctuations and price changes. Product trends are important for understanding the life cycle of a product.

SOURCES AND MAGNITUDE OF PRODUCT DEMAND In past eras, the introduction of new and improved products drove much of the demand. Currently, consumer attitudes and lifestyles anticipate product introductions and technological changes. Individual consumers are pushing technology to anticipate the needs of an increasingly segmented market. Demand based on anticipation is becoming the dominant feature of the technological age. The rapid pace of technological development and new product introduction have shortened product life-cycles. The combination of demographic considerations and technological change dominate consumer trends to a greater degree than in the past.

FORECASTING TECHNIQUES

There are a variety of forecasting techniques and methods from which the small business owner may choose. Not all of them are applicable in every situation. To allow for adequate forecasting, a business must choose those methods which best serve their purposes, utilize accurate and relevant data, and formulate honest assumptions appropriate to the market and product.

Sales forecasts may be general if they calculate aggregate sales attainable in an industry. Conversely, forecasts may be very specific, detailing data by individual products, sales territories, types of customers, and so forth. In recent decades market analysts have increased their use of focus groups, individual surveys, interviews, and sophisticated analytical techniques aimed at identifying specific markets.

APPROACHES TO FORECASTING In the causal approach forecasters identify the underlying variables that have a causal influence on future sales. The company has no influence over causal variables in the general society, such as population, gross national product, and general economic conditions. A company does, however, maintain control over its production lines, prices, advertising and marketing, and the size of its sales force. After studying the underlying causes and variables in depth, the analysts use a variety of mathematical techniques to project future trends. On the basis of these projections, management derives its sales forecast.

The non-causal approach involves an in-depth analysis of historical sales patterns. Analysts plot these patterns in graphs in order to project future sales. Because no attempt is made to identify and evaluate the underlying causal variables, the analysts assume that the underlying causes will continue to influence the future sales in the same manner as in the past. Although analysts may apply certain statistical techniques to extrapolate past sales into the future, this approach is sometimes criticized as simplistic or naive, especially since most business experts believe that rapid changes in technology are driving fundamental changes in many business operations.

Analysts employ the indirect method by first projecting industry sales. From this data they project the company's share of the industry total. The direct approach, however, skips the industry projection with a straightforward estimate of sales for the company. Either of these methods are applicable to the causal and non-causal approaches.

FORECASTING METHODOLOGIES

A variety of sales forecasting methodologies can be used by small and large businesses alike:

BOTTOM-UP FORECASTING Analysts using this methodology divide the market into segments, and then separately calculate the demand in each segment. Typically, analysts use sales force composites, industry surveys, and intention-to-buy surveys to collect data. They aggregate the segments to arrive at a total sales forecast. Bottom-up forecasting may not be simple because of complications with the accuracy of the data submitted. The usefulness of the data is contingent upon honest and complete answers from customers, and on the importance and priority given to a survey by the sales staff.

TOP-DOWN FORECASTING This is the method most widely used for industrial applications. Management first estimates the sales potential, then develops sales quotas, and finally constructs a sales forecast. Problems arise with this method, however, when the underlying assumptions of the past are no longer applicable. The correlation between economic variables and quantity demanded may change or weaken over time.

These two forecasting methods encompass a number of methodologies which can be divided into three general categories: qualitative, times-series analysis and regression, and causal.

QUALITATIVE METHODS Qualitative methods rely on non-statistical methods of deriving a sales forecast. A company solicits the opinion or judgment of sales executives, a panel of experts, the sales force, the sales division supervisors, and/or outside expert consultants. Qualitative methods are judgmental composites of expected sales. These methods are often preferred in the following instances: 1) when the variables which influence consumer buying habits have changed; 2) when current data is not available; 3) when none of the qualitative methods work well in a specific situation; 4) when the planning horizon is too far for the standard quantitative methods; and 5) when the data has not yet factored in technological breakthroughs taking place or forthcoming.

The Probability Assessment Method (PAM) forecasts sales volume by utilizing in-house expert opinion that provides probabilities between one and 99 percent, plus and minus, on certain target volumes. Analysts translate these estimates into a cumulative probability curve by plotting the volumes by the probability assigned to them. They use this curve to aid in forecasting.

The Program Evaluation and Review Technique (PERT) requires estimates of "optimistic," "pessimistic," and "most likely" future circumstances. Analysts weigh these three estimates to form an expected value from which they compute a standard deviation. In this way analysts convert the estimates of the small business owner and/or staff into measures of central tendency and dispersion. The standard deviation enables the forecaster to estimate a confidence interval around the expected value. While PERT is only an approximation, it is quick and easy to use. The forecaster can take into account the owner's opinion as a check on estimates produced by other methods.

The Delphi Technique relies on the assumption that several experts can arrive at a better forecast than one. Users of this method solicit a panel consensus and reprocess the results through the panel until a very narrow, firm median is agreed upon. By keeping the panel participants isolated, the Delphi excludes many aspects of group behavior, such as social pressure, argumentation, and domination by a few members, from causing undue influence. The expense associated with this method, however, precludes most small business enterprises from pursuing it.

A visionary forecast relies on the personal insights and judgment of a respected individual. Although often supplemented by data and facts about different scenarios of the future, the visionary forecast is characterized by subjective guesswork and imagination and is highly nonscientific. But while such forecasts are not based on reams of scientific information, many small business owners have achieved success by relying on such subjective data.

Historical analogy methodologies, meanwhile, attempt to determine future sales through an in-depth analysis of the introduction and sales growth of a similar product. Historical analogy seeks patterns applicable to the product considered for current introduction. This method requires several years' history for one or more products, and—when used—is generally applied to new product introductions.

The sales force composite gathers forecasts from each individual salesperson for a particular territory. The sales forecast is the aggregate of the individual forecasts. The usefulness of this method is dependent on the accuracy of the data submitted.

An intention-to-buy survey measures a target market's intention to buy within a specified future time period. Market analysts conduct such surveys prior to the introduction of a product or service. Analysts provide consumers with a description or explanation of the product or service with the hope that respondents will provide honest answers. If respondents tell analysts "what they want to hear," the survey will not be accurate. In addition, certain environmental factors, such as a competing technological breakthrough or a recession, may influence respondent buying habits between the time of the survey and the product introduction.

TIME-SERIES ANALYSIS AND PROJECTION Trend projection techniques may be most appropriate in situations where the forecaster is able to infer, from the past behavior of a variable, something about its future impact on sales. Forecasters look for trends that form identifiable patterns which recur with predictive frequency. Seasonal variations and cyclical patterns form more obvious trends, while random variables make projection more complex.

While time-series methods do not explicitly account for causal relationships between a variable and other factors, analysts find the emergent historical patterns useful in making forecasts. Analysts typically use time series for new product forecasts, particularly in the intermediate and long-term. The data required varies with each technique. A good rule of thumb is a minimum of five years' annual data. A complete history is very helpful.

Market research involves a systematic, formal, and conscious procedure for evoking and testing hypotheses about real markets. Analysts need at least two market research reports based on time series analyses of market variables, and a considerable collection of market data from questionnaires and surveys.

In its simplest form, trend projection analysis involves the examination of what has happened in the past. Analysts develop a specific linear percentage trend with the expectation that the trend will continue. The problem with the simple trend projection is the fact of randomness—that is, the random event or element that has a major impact on the forecast.

The moving average is a more sophisticated type of trend projection. It assumes the future will be an average of the past performance rather than following a specific linear percentage trend. The moving average minimizes the impact of randomness on individual forecasts since it is an average of several values rather than a simple linear projection. The moving average equation basically sums up the sales in a number of past periods and divides by the number of periods.

Industry surveys involve surveying the various companies that make up the industry for a particular item. They may include users or manufacturers. The industry survey method that uses a top-down approach of forecasting has some of the same advantages and disadvantages as the executive opinion and sales force composites.

A regression analysis may be linear or multiple. With linear regression, analysts develop a relationship between sales and a single independent variable and use this relationship to forecast sales. With multiple regression, analysts examine relationships between sales and a number of independent variables. Usually the latter is accomplished with the help of a computer that helps analysts to estimate the values of the independent variables and to incorporate them into a multi-regression equation. If analysts find a relationship among various independent variables, they can develop a multiple regression equation for predicting sales for the coming year.

Exponential smoothing is a time-series approach similar to the moving average. Instead of using a constant set of weights for the observation made, analysts employ an exponentially increasing set of weights so that more recent values receive more weight than do older values. More sophisticated models incorporate various adjustments for such factors as trends and seasonal patterns.

Analysts look at the leading indicators because the National Bureau of Economic Research has clearly demonstrated their value in forecasting. These indicators include prices of 500 common stocks, new orders for durable goods, an index of net business formation, corporate profits after taxes, industrial materials prices, and the change in consumer installment debt. Despite their widespread use, the leading indicators do not relate well with specific products. Nevertheless, when such relationships can be established, analysts construct multiple regression models with which to forecast sales.

CAUSAL METHODS When analysts find a cause-effect relationship between a variable and sales, a causal model may provide better forecasts than those generated by other techniques. Life-cycle analysis forecasts new product growth rates based on analysts' projections of the phases of product acceptance by various groups—innovators, early adapters, early majority, late majority, and laggards. Typically, this method is used to forecast new product sales. Analysts' minimum data requirements are the annual sales of the product being considered or of a similar product. It is often necessary to do market surveys to establish the cause-effect relationships.

THE SALES BUDGET

The sales forecast provides the framework for the detailed planning presented in the master budget. Based on planned strategies and its best business judgment, management converts a sales forecast into a sales plan through the commitment of resources and the establishment of control mechanisms. The sales budget provides an evaluative tool by presenting monthly indexes of volume of units and dollars as hard targets for the sales team. Deviations from these indexes indicate to small business owners and managers where they need to adjust their efforts to take advantage of hot products or to remedy difficult situations.

Management determines its sales policies and strategies within its ability to respond to customer needs, technological changes, and the financial pre-requisites of marketing. The sales budget projects that portion of potential sales the sales team believes it can achieve. The forecast, then, sets the parameters on the top side while the production capacity and sales acumen of the team sets the floor.

Although sales forecasts may accurately project significant changes in market conditions, a company needs to thoroughly examine its own resources to determine its ability to respond to these changes. A huge drop in demand may decrease the strain on the production process to where a company regains cost efficiencies, or a large increase in demand might be required by a company that needs cash for other projects. The sales budget, therefore, is predicated on a company's ability to meet expected demand at or near its maximum profit potential.

THE PRODUCTION BUDGET Both small and large businesses construct their production budgets within limitations of production, warehousing, delivery, and service capabilities. Subsequently, a company attempts to schedule production at maximum efficiency. By anticipating the variations in monthly sales, management can keep production at levels sufficient to provide adequate supply. Labor costs generally comprise the greatest single production cost. Therefore, management may adjust labor hours to production schedules.

Production levels remain rather constant if current inventory is sufficient to meet increases in sales. If management expects an increase, it may build inventories during the first quarter of the budget, and sell them down to planned levels during the remaining three quarters. From the production budget, a company estimates the mix of materials, labor, and production overhead needed to meet planned production levels.

DEVELOPING A SALES FORECAST

Forecasting sales is inherently more difficult than the construction of the subsequent sales budget. Although management exerts some degree of control over expenditures, it has little ability to direct the buying habits of individuals. The level of sales depends of the vagaries of the marketplace. Nonetheless, a sales forecast must attain a reasonable degree of reliability to be useful.

Fundamentally, sales forecasters follows steps similar to these in developing a forecast of sales potential:

- Determine the purposes for using the forecasts.
- Divide the company's products into homogeneous groups.

- Determine those factors affecting the sales of each product group and their relative importance.
- Choose a forecasting method or methods best suited for the job.
- Gather all necessary and available data.
- Analyze the data.
- Check and cross-check deductions resulting from the analyses.
- Make assumptions regarding effects of the various factors that cannot be measured or forecast.
- Convert deductions and assumptions into specific product and territorial forecasts and quotas.
- Apply forecasts to company operations.
- Periodically review performance and revise forecasts.

FURTHER READING:

Bolt, Gordon J. *Market and Sales Forecasting.* Franklin Watts, 1988.

Cohen, William A. *The Practice of Marketing Management.* Macmillan Publishing, 1988.

Crosby, John V. *Cycles, Trends, and Turning Points: Practical Marketing and Sales Forecasting Techniques.* NTC Publishing, 2000.

Henry, Porter, and Joseph A. Callanan. *Sales Management and Motivation.* Franklin Watts, 1987.

McCarthy, E. Jerome, and William D. Perreault, Jr. *Basic Marketing: A Managerial Approach.* Irwin, 1990.

Mentzer, John T., and Carol C. Bienstock. *Sales Forecasting Management: Understanding the Techniques, Systems, and Management of the Sales Forecasting Process.* Sage, 1998.

SALES MANAGEMENT

Sales management refers to the administration of the personal selling component of a company's marketing program. It includes the planning, implementation, and control of sales programs, as well as recruiting, training, motivating, and evaluating members of the sales force. In a small business, these various functions may be performed by the owner or by a specialist called a sales manager. The fundamental role of the sales manager is to develop and administer a selling program that effectively contributes to the organization's goals. The sales manager for a small business would likely decide how many salespeople to employ, how best to select and train them, what sort of compensation and incentives to use to motivate them, what type of presentation they should make, and how the sales function should be structured for maximum contact with customers.

Sales management is just one facet of a company's overall marketing mix, which encompasses strategies related to the "four Ps": products, pricing, promotion, and place (distribution). Objectives related to promotion are achieved through three supporting functions: 1) advertising, which includes direct mail, radio, television, and print advertisements, among other media; 2) sales promotion, which includes tools such as coupons, rebates, contests, and samples; and (3) personal selling, which is the domain of the sales manager.

Although the role of sales managers is multidisciplinary in scope, their primary responsibilities are: 1) setting goals for a sales force; 2) planning, budgeting, and organizing a program to achieve those goals; 3) implementing the program; and 4) controlling and evaluating the results. Even when a sales force is already in place, the sales manager will likely view these responsibilities as an ongoing process necessary to adapt to both internal and external changes.

GOAL SETTING

The overall goals of the sales force manager are essentially mandated by the marketing mix. The company coordinates objectives between the major components of the mix within the context of internal constraints, such as available capital and production capacity. The sales force manager, however, may play an important role in developing the overall marketing mix strategies. For example, the sales manager may be in the best position to determine the specific needs of customers and to discern the potential of new and existing markets.

One of the most critical duties of the sales manager is to estimate the market potential and sales potential of the company's offerings, and then to make realistic forecasts of sales. Market potential is the total expected sales of a given product or service for the entire industry in a specific market over a stated period of time. Sales potential refers to the share of a market potential that an individual company can reasonably expect to achieve. A sales forecast is an estimate of sales (in dollars or product units) that an individual firm expects to make during a specified time period, in a stated market, and under a proposed marketing plan.

Estimations of sales and market potential are often used to set major organizational objectives related to production, marketing, distribution, and other corporate functions, as well as to assist the sales manager in planning and implementing the overall sales strategy. Numerous sales forecasting tools and techniques, many of which are quite advanced, are available to help the sales manager determine potential and make forecasts. Major external factors influencing sales and market potential include: industry conditions, such as stage of maturity; market conditions and expectations; general business and economic conditions; and regulatory environment.

PLANNING, BUDGETING, AND ORGANIZING

After determining goals, the sales manager of a small business must develop a strategy to attain them. A very basic decision is whether to hire a sales force or contract with independent selling agents or manufacturers' representatives outside of the organization. The latter strategy eliminates costs associated with hiring, training, and supervising workers, and it takes advantage of sales channels that have already been established by the independent representatives. On the other hand, maintaining an internal sales force allows the manager to exert more control over the salespeople and to ensure that they are trained properly. Furthermore, establishing an internal sale force provides the opportunity to hire inexperienced representatives at a very low cost.

The type of sales force developed depends on the financial priorities and constraints of the organization. If a manager decides to hire salespeople, the next step is to determine the optimal size of the force. This determination typically entails a compromise between the number of people needed to adequately service all potential customers and the resources available to the company. One technique sometimes used to determine sales force size is the "work load" strategy, whereby the sum of existing and potential customers is multiplied by the ideal number of calls per customer. That sum is then multiplied by the preferred length of a sales call (in hours). Next, that figure is divided by the selling time available from one salesperson. The final sum is theoretically the ideal sales force size. A second technique is the "incremental" strategy, which recognizes that the incremental increase in sales that results from each additional hire continually decreases. In other words, salespeople are gradually added until the cost of a new hire exceeds the benefit.

A sales manager who is in the process of hiring an internal sales force also has to decide the degree of experience to seek and determine how to balance quality and quantity. Basically, the manager can either "make" or "buy" his force. "Green" hires, or those without previous experience whom the company must "make" into salespeople, cost less over the long term and do not bring any bad sales habits with them that were learned in other companies. On the other hand, the initial cost associated with experienced salespeople is usually lower, and experienced employees can start producing results much more quickly. But as Irving Burstiner noted in *The Small Business Handbook,* few star salespeople are ever unemployed, and a small business probably lacks the resources to find and hire those who are. Furthermore, if the manager elects to hire only the most qualified people, budgetary constraints may force him to leave some territories only partially covered, resulting in customer dissatisfaction and lost sales. Therefore, it usually makes more sense for small businesses to hire green troops and train them well.

After determining the composition of the sales force, the sales manager creates a budget, or a record of planned expenses that is (usually) prepared annually. The budget helps the manager decide how much money will be spent on personal selling and how that money will be allocated within the sales force. Major budgetary items include: sales force salaries, commissions, and bonuses; travel expenses; sales materials; training; clerical services; and office rent and utilities. Many budgets are prepared by simply reviewing the previous year's budget and then making adjustments. A more advanced technique, however, is the percentage of sales method, which allocates funds based on a percentage of expected revenues. Typical percentages range from about two percent for heavy industries to as much as eight percent or more for consumer goods and computers.

After a sales force strategy has been devised and a budget has been adopted, the sales manager should ideally have the opportunity to organize, or structure, the sales force. The structure of the sales force allows each salesperson to specialize in a certain sales task or type of customer or market, so that they will be more likely to establish productive, long-term relationships with their customers. Small businesses may choose to structure their sales forces by product line, customer type, geography, or a combination of these factors.

IMPLEMENTING

After setting goals and establishing a plan for sales activities, the next step for the sales manager is to implement the strategy. Implementation requires the sales manager to make decisions related to staffing, designing territories, and allocating sales efforts. Staffing—the most significant of these three responsibilities—encompasses recruiting, training, compensating, and motivating salespeople.

RECRUITING The first step in recruiting salespeople involves analyzing the positions to be filled. This is often accomplished by sending an observer into the field, who records the amount of time a salesperson must spend talking to customers, traveling, attending meetings, and doing paperwork. The observer then reports the findings to the sales manager, who uses the information to draft a detailed job description. The observer might also report on the characteristics and needs of the buyers, since it can be important for salespeople to share these characteristics.

The manager may seek candidates through advertising, college recruiting, company sources, and employment agencies. Candidates are typically evaluated through personality tests, interviews, written applications, and background checks. Research has shown that the two most important personality traits that salespeople can possess are empathy, which helps them relate to customers, and drive, which motivates them to satisfy personal needs for accomplishment. Other important traits include maturity, appearance, communication skills, and technical knowledge related to the product or industry. Negative traits include fear of rejection, distaste for travel, self-consciousness, and interest in artistic or creative originality.

TRAINING After recruiting a suitable sales force, the manager must determine how much and what type of training to provide. Most sales training emphasizes product, company, and industry knowledge. Only about 25 percent of the average company training program, in fact, addresses personal selling techniques. Because of the high cost, many small businesses try to limit the amount of training they provide. The average cost of training a person to sell industrial products, for example, commonly exceeds $30,000. Sales managers can achieve many benefits with competent training programs, however. For instance, research indicates that training reduces employee turnover, thereby lowering the effective cost of hiring new workers. Good training can also improve customer relations, increase employee morale, and boost sales. Common training methods include lectures, case studies, role playing, demonstrations, on-the-job training, and self-study courses. Ideally, training should be an ongoing process that continually reinforces the company's goals.

COMPENSATION After the sales force is in place, the manager must devise a means of compensating individuals. The ideal system of compensation reaches a balance between the needs of the person (income, recognition, prestige, etc.) and the goals of the company (controlling costs, boosting market share, increasing cash flow, etc.), so that a salesperson may achieve both through the same means. Most approaches to sales force compensation utilize a combination of salary and commission or salary and bonus. Salary gives a sales manager added control over the salesperson's activities, while commission provides the salesperson with greater motivation to sell.

Although financial rewards are the primary means of motivating workers, most sales organizations also employ other motivational techniques. Good sales managers recognize that salespeople have needs other than the basic ones satisfied by money. For example, they want to feel like they are part of a winning team, that their jobs are secure, and that their efforts and contributions to the organization are recognized. Methods of meeting those needs include contests, vacations, and other performance-based prizes, in addition to self-improvement benefits such as tuition for graduate school. Another tool managers commonly use to stimulate their salespeople is quotas. Quotas, which can be set for factors such as the number of calls made per day, expenses consumed per month, or the number of new customers added annually, give salespeople a standard against which they can measure success.

DESIGNING TERRITORIES AND ALLOCATING SALES EFFORTS In addition to recruiting, training, and motivating a sales force to achieve the company's goals, sales managers at most small businesses must decide how to designate sales territories and allocate the efforts of the sales team. Territories are geographic areas assigned to individual salespeople. The advantages of establishing territories are that they improve coverage of the market, reduce wasteful overlap of sales efforts, and allow each salesperson to define personal responsibility and judge individual success. However, many types of businesses, such as real estate and insurance companies, do not use territories.

Allocating people to different territories is an important sales management task. Typically, the top few territories produce a disproportionately high sales volume. This occurs because managers usually create smaller areas for trainees, medium-sized territories for more experienced team members, and larger areas for senior sellers. A drawback of that strategy, however, is that it becomes difficult to compare performance across territories. An alternate approach is to divide regions by existing and potential customer base. A number of computer programs exist to help sales managers effectively create territories according to their goals. Good scheduling and routing of sales calls can reduce waiting and travel time. Other common methods of reducing the costs associated with sales calls include contacting numerous customers at once during trade shows, and using telemarketing to qualify prospects before sending a salesperson to make a personal call.

CONTROLLING AND EVALUATING

After the sales plan has been implemented, the sales manager's responsibility becomes controlling and evaluating the program. During this stage, the sales manager compares the original goals and objectives with the actual accomplishments of the sales force. The performance of each individual is compared with goals or quotas, looking at elements such as expenses, sales volume, customer satisfaction, and cash flow. According to Burstiner, each salesperson should be evaluated using both subjective (i.e., product knowledge, familiarity with competition, work habits) and objective (i.e., number of orders compared to number of calls, number of new accounts landed) criteria.

An important consideration for the sales manager is profitability. Indeed, simple sales figures may not reflect an accurate image of the performance of the sales force. The manager must dig deeper by analyzing expenses, price-cutting initiatives, and long-term contracts with customers that will impact future income. An in-depth analysis of these and related influences will help the manager to determine true performance based on profits. For use in future goal-setting and planning efforts, the manager may also evaluate sales trends by different factors, such as product line, volume, territory, and market. After the manager analyzes and evaluates the achievements of the sales force, that information is used to make corrections to the current strategy and sales program. In other words, the sales manager returns to the initial goal-setting stage.

ENVIRONMENTS AND STRATEGIES

The goals and plans adopted by the sales manager will be greatly influenced by the company's industry orientation, competitive position, and market strategy. The basic industry orientations available to a firm include industrial goods, consumer durables, consumer nondurables, and services. Companies that manufacture industrial goods or sell highly technical services tend to be heavily dependent on personal selling as a marketing tool. Sales managers in those organizations characteristically focus on customer service and education, and employ and train a relatively high-level sales force. In contrast, sales managers that sell consumer durables will likely integrate the efforts of their sales force into related advertising and promotional initiatives. Sales management efforts related to consumer nondurables and consumer services will generally emphasize volume sales, a comparatively low-caliber sales force, and an emphasis on high-volume customers.

In his classic book *Competitive Strategy,* Michael Porter lists three common market strategies adopted by firms—low-cost supplier, differentiation, and niche. Companies that adopt a low-cost supplier strategy are usually characterized by a vigorous pursuit of efficiency and cost controls. Sales management efforts in this type of organization should generally stress minimizing expenses—by having salespeople stay at budget hotels, for example—and appealing to customers on the basis of price. Salespeople should be given an incentive to chase large, high-volume customers, and the sales force infrastructure should be designed to efficiently accommodate large order-taking activities.

Companies that adhere to a differentiation strategy achieve market success by offering a unique product or service. They often rely on brand loyalty or patent protection to insulate them from competitors, and thus are able to achieve higher-than-average profit margins. In this environment, selling techniques should stress benefits, rather than price. Firms that pursue a niche market strategy succeed by targeting a very narrow segment of a market and then dominating that segment. The company is able to overcome competitors by aggressively protecting its niche and orienting every action and decision toward the service of its select group. Sales managers in this type of organization would tend to emphasize employee training or to hire industry experts. The overall sales program would be centered around customer service and benefits other than price.

REGULATION

Besides markets and industries, another chief environmental influence on the sales management process is government regulation. Indeed, selling activities at companies are regulated by a multitude of state and federal laws designed to protect consumers, foster competitive markets, and discourage unfair business practices.

Chief among anti-trust provisions affecting sales managers is the Robinson-Patman Act, which prohibits companies from engaging in price or service discrimination. In other words, a firm cannot offer special incentives to large customers based solely on volume, because such practices tend to hurt smaller customers. Companies can give discounts to buyers, but only if those incentives are based on real savings gleaned from manufacturing and distribution processes.

Similarly, the Sherman Act makes it illegal for a seller to force a buyer to purchase one product (or service) in order to get the opportunity to purchase another product—a practice referred to as a "tying agreement." A long-distance telephone company, for instance, cannot require its customers to purchase its telephone equipment as a prerequisite to buying its long-distance service. The Sherman Act also regulates reciprocal dealing arrangements, whereby companies agree to buy products from each other. Reciprocal dealing is considered anticompetitive because large buyers and sellers tend to have an unfair advantage over their smaller competitors.

Several consumer protection regulations also impact sales managers. The Fair Packaging and Labeling Act of 1966, for example, restricts deceptive labeling, and the Truth in Lending Act requires sellers to fully disclose all finance charges incorporated into consumer credit agreements. Cooling-off laws, which commonly exist at the state level, allow buyers to cancel contracts made with door-to-door sellers within a certain time frame. Additionally, the Federal Trade Commission (FTC) requires door-to-door sellers who work for companies engaged in interstate trade to clearly announce their purpose when calling on prospects.

FURTHER READING:

Brown, Ronald. *From Selling to Managing: Guidelines for the First-Time Sales Manager.* AMACOM, 1990.

Burstiner, Irving. *The Small Business Handbook.* Prentice-Hall, 1989.

Churchill, Gilbert A., Jr., Neil M. Ford, and Orville C. Walker, Jr. *Sales Force Management: Planning, Implementation, and Control.* 3rd ed. Irwin, 1990.

Petrone, Joe. *Building the High Performance Sales Force.* Productivity Management Press, 1994.

Porter, Michael E. *Competitive Strategy.* Free Press, 1980.

Stafford, John, and Colin Grant. *Effective Sales Management.* Nichols, 1986.

Stanton, William J., and Richard H. Buskirk. *Management of the Sales Force.* 7th ed. Irwin, 1987.

Wilner, Jack D. *Seven Secrets to Successful Sales Management.* CRC Press, 1997.

SALES PROMOTION

Sales promotion is an important component of a small business's overall marketing strategy, along with advertising, public relations, and personal selling. The American Marketing Association (AMA) defines sales promotion as "media and nonmedia marketing pressure applied for a predetermined, limited period of time in order to stimulate trial, increase consumer demand, or improve product quality." But this definition does not capture all the elements of modern sales promotion. One should add that effective sales promotion increases the basic value of a product for a limited time and directly stimulates consumer purchasing, selling effectiveness, or the effort of the sales force. It can be used to inform, persuade, and remind target customers about the business and its marketing mix. Some common types of sales promotion include samples, coupons, sweepstakes, contests, in-store displays, trade shows, price-off deals, premiums, and rebates.

Businesses can target sales promotions at three different audiences: consumers, resellers, and the company's own sales force. Sales promotion acts as a competitive weapon by providing an extra incentive for the target audience to purchase or support one brand over another. It is particularly effective in spurring product trial and unplanned purchases. Most marketers believe that a given product or service has an established perceived price or value, and they use sales promotion to change this price-value relationship by increasing the value and/or lowering the price. Compared to the other components of the marketing mix (advertising, publicity, and personal selling), sales promotion usually operates on a shorter time line, uses a more rational appeal, returns a tangible or real value, fosters an immediate sale, and contributes highly to profitability.

In determining the relative importance to place on sales promotion in the overall marketing mix, a small business should consider its marketing budget, the stage of the product in its life cycle, the nature of competition in the market, the target of the promotion, and the nature of the product. For example, sales promotion and direct mail are particularly attractive alternatives when the marketing budget is limited, as it is for many small businesses. In addition, sales promotion can be an effective tool in a highly competitive market, when the objective is to convince retailers to carry a product or influence consumers to select it over those of competitors. Similarly, sales promotion is often used in the growth and maturity stages of the product life cycle to stimulate consumers and resellers to choose that product over the competition—rather than in the introduction stage, when mass advertising to build awareness might be more important. Finally, sales promotion tends to work best when it is applied to impulse items whose features can be judged at the point of purchase, rather than more complex, expensive items that might require hands-on demonstration.

GROWTH OF SALES PROMOTION

Sales promotion has grown substantially in recent years. There are several reasons for this dramatic growth in sales promotion. First, consumers have accepted sales promotion as part of their buying decision criteria. It provides reluctant decision makers with an incentive to make choices by increasing the value offered by a particular brand. Second, the increasing tendency of businesses to focus on short-term results has helped spur growth in sales promotion, which can provide an immediate boost in sales. Product managers also tend to view sales promotion as a way to differentiate their brand from that of competitors in the short term. Third, the emergence of computer technology has enabled manufacturers to get rapid feedback on the results of promotions. Redemption rates for coupons or figures on sales volume can be obtained within days. Finally, an increase in the size and power of retailers has also boosted the use of sales promotion. Historically, the manufacturer held the power in the channel of distribution. Mass marketers utilized national advertising to get directly to consumers, creating a demand for the heavily advertised brands that stores could not afford to ignore. With consolidation and the growth of major retail chains, however, retailers have gained the power to demand incentives from manufacturers to carry their products. Many sales promotions are designed to provide benefits to the retailers.

LIMITATIONS OF SALES PROMOTION

Although sales promotion is an important strategy for producing quick, short-term, positive results, it is not a cure for a bad product, poor advertising, or an inferior sales team. After a consumer uses a coupon for the initial purchase of a product, the product must then take over and convince them to become repeat buyers. In addition, sales promotion activities may bring several negative consequences, including ''clutter'' due to the number of competitive promotions. New approaches are promptly cloned by competitors, as each marketer tries to be more creative, more attention getting, or more effective in attracting the attention of consumers and the trade. Finally, consumers and resellers have learned how to milk the sales promotion game. Consumers may wait to buy certain items knowing that prices will eventually be reduced, for example, while resellers have become experts at negotiating deals and manipulating competitors against one another.

CONSUMER PROMOTIONS

Consumer sales promotions are steered toward the ultimate product users—typically individual shoppers in the local market—but the same techniques can be used to promote products sold by one business to another, such as computer systems, cleaning supplies, and machinery. In contrast, trade sales promotions target resellers—wholesalers and retailers—who carry the marketer's product. Following are some of the key techniques used in consumer-oriented sales promotions.

PRICE DEALS A consumer price deal saves the buyer money when a product is purchased. The main types of price deals include discounts, bonus pack deals, refunds or rebates, and coupons. Price deals are usually intended to encourage trial use of a new product or line extension, to recruit new buyers for a mature product, or to convince existing customers to increase their purchases, accelerate their use, or purchase multiple units. Price deals work most effectively when price is the consumer's foremost criterion or when brand loyalty is low.

Buyers may learn about price discounts either at the point of sale or through advertising. At the point of sale, price reductions may be posted on the package, on signs near the product, or in storefront windows. Many types of advertisements can be used to notify consumers of upcoming discounts, including fliers and newspaper and television ads. Price discounts are especially common in the food industry, where local supermarkets run weekly specials. Price discounts may be initiated by the manufacturer, the retailer, or the distributor. For instance, a manufacturer may "pre-price" a product and then convince the retailer to participate in this short-term discount through extra incentives. For price reduction strategies to be effective, they must have the support of all distributors in the channel. Existing customers perceive discounts as rewards and often respond by buying in larger quantities. Price discounts alone, however, usually do not induce first time buyers.

Another type of price deal is the bonus pack or banded pack. When a bonus pack is offered, an extra amount of the product is free when a standard size of the product is bought at the regular price. This technique is routinely used in the marketing of cleaning products, food, and health and beauty aids to introduce a new or larger size. A bonus pack rewards present users but may have little appeal to users of competitive brands. A banded pack offer is when two or more units of a product are sold at a reduction of the regular single-unit price. Sometimes the products are physically banded together, such as in toothbrush and toothpaste offers.

A refund or rebate promotion is an offer by a marketer to return a certain amount of money when the product is purchased alone or in combination with other products. Refunds aim to increase the quantity or frequency of purchase, to encourage customers to "load up" on the product. This strategy dampens competition by temporarily taking consumers out of the market, stimulates the purchase of postponable goods such as major appliances, and creates on-shelf excitement by encouraging special displays. Refunds and rebates are generally viewed as a reward for purchase, and they appear to build brand loyalty rather than diminish it.

Coupons are legal certificates offered by manufacturers and retailers. They grant specified savings on selected products when presented for redemption at the point of purchase. Manufacturers sustain the cost of advertising and distributing their coupons, redeeming their face values, and paying retailers a handling fee. Retailers who offer double or triple the amount of the coupon shoulder the extra cost. Retailers who offer their own coupons incur the total cost, including paying the face value. In this way, retail coupons are equivalent to a cents-off deal.

Manufacturers disseminate coupons in many ways. They may be delivered directly by mail, dropped door to door, or distributed through a central location such as a shopping mall. Coupons may also be distributed through the media—magazines, newspapers, Sunday supplements, or free-standing inserts (FSI) in newspapers. Coupons can be inserted into, attached to, or printed on a package, or they may be distributed by a retailer who uses them to generate store traffic or to tie in with a manufacturer's promotional tactic. Retailer-sponsored coupons are typically distributed through print advertising or at the point of sale. Sometimes, though, specialty retailers or newly opened retailers will distribute coupons door to door or through direct mail.

CONTESTS/SWEEPSTAKES The main difference between contests and sweepstakes is that contests require entrants to perform a task or demonstrate a skill that is judged in order to be deemed a winner, while sweepstakes involve a random drawing or chance contest that may or may not have an entry requirement. At one time, contests were more commonly used as sales promotions, mostly due to legal restrictions on gambling that many marketers feared might apply to sweepstakes. But the use of sweepstakes as a promotional tactic has grown dramatically in recent decades, partly because of legal changes and partly because of their lower cost. Administering a contest once cost about $350 per thousand entries, compared to just $2.75 to $3.75 per thousand entries in a sweepstake. Furthermore, participation in contests is very low compared to sweepstakes, since they require some sort of skill or ability.

SPECIAL EVENTS According to the consulting firm International Events Group (IEG), businesses spend over $2 billion annually to link their products with everything from jazz festivals to golf tournaments to stock car races. In fact, large companies like RJR Nabisco and Anheuser-Busch have special divisions that handle nothing but special events. Special events marketing offers a number of advantages. First, events tend to attract a homogeneous audience that is very appreciative of the sponsors. Therefore, if a product fits well with the event and its audience, the impact of the sales promotion will be high. Second, event sponsorship often builds support among employees—who may receive acknowledgment for their participation—and within the trade. Finally, compared to producing a series of ads, event management is relatively simple. Many elements of event sponsorship are prepackaged and reusable, such as booths, displays, and ads. Special events marketing is available to small businesses, as well, through sponsorship of events on the community level.

PREMIUMS A premium is tangible compensation that is given as incentive for performing a particular act—usually buying a product. The premium may be given for free, or may be offered to consumers for a significantly reduced price. Some examples of premiums include receiving a prize in a cereal box or a free garden tool for visiting the grand opening of a hardware store. Incentives that are given for free at the time of purchase are called direct premiums. These offers provide instant gratification, plus there is no confusion about returning coupons or box tops, or saving bar codes or proofs of purchase.

Other types of direct premiums include traffic builders, door openers, and referral premiums. The garden tool is an example of a traffic-builder premium—an incentive to lure a prospective buyer to a store. A door-opener premium is directed to customers at home or to business people in their offices. For example, a homeowner may receive a free clock radio for allowing an insurance agent to enter their home and listening to his sales pitch. Similarly, an electronics manufacturer might offer free software to an office manager who agrees to an on-site demonstration. The final category of direct premiums, referral premiums, reward the purchaser for referring the seller to other possible customers.

Mail premiums, unlike direct premiums, require the customer to perform some act in order to obtain a premium through return mail. An example might be a limited edition toy car offered by a marketer in exchange for one or more proofs-of-purchase and a payment covering the cost of the item plus handling. The premium is still valuable to the consumer because they cannot readily buy the item for the same amount.

CONTINUITY PROGRAMS Continuity programs retain brand users over a long time period by offering ongoing motivation or incentives. Continuity programs demand that consumers keep buying the product in order to get the premium in the future. Trading stamps, popularized in the 1950s and 1960s, are prime examples. Consumers usually received one stamp for every dime spent at a participating store. The stamp company provided redemption centers where the stamps were traded for merchandise. A catalog listing the quantity of stamps required for each item was available at the participating stores. Today, airlines' frequent-flyer clubs, hotels' frequent-traveler plans, retailers' frequent-shopper programs, and bonus-paying credit cards are common continuity programs. When competing brands have reached parity in terms of price and service, continuity programs sometimes prove a deciding factor among those competitors. By rewarding long-standing customers for their loyalty, continuity programs also reduce the threat of new competitors entering a market.

SAMPLING A sign of a successful marketer is getting the product into the hands of the consumer. Sometimes, particularly when a product is new or is not a market leader, an effective strategy is giving a sample product to the consumer, either free or for a small fee. But in order for sampling to change people's future purchase decisions, the product must have benefits or features that will be obvious during the trial.

There are several means of disseminating samples to consumers. The most popular has been through the mail, but increases in postage costs and packaging requirements have made this method less attractive. An alternative is door-to-door distribution, particularly when the items are bulky and when reputable distribution organizations exist. This method permits selective sampling of neighborhoods, dwellings, or even people. Another method is distributing samples in conjunction with advertising. An ad may include a coupon that the consumer can mail in for the product, or it may include an address or phone number for ordering. Direct sampling can be achieved through prime media using scratch-and-sniff cards and slim foil pouches, or through retailers using special displays or a person hired to hand out samples to passing customers. Though this last technique may build goodwill for the retailer, some retailers resent the inconvenience and require high payments for their cooperation.

A final form of sample distribution deals with specialty types of sampling. For instance, some companies specialize in packing samples together for delivery to homogeneous consumer groups, such as newlyweds, new parents, students, or tourists. Such packages may be delivered at hospitals, hotels, or dormitories and include a number of different types of products.

TRADE PROMOTIONS

A trade sales promotion is targeted at resellers—wholesalers and retailers—who distribute manufacturers' products to the ultimate consumers. The objectives of sales promotions aimed at the trade are different from those directed at consumers. In general, trade sales promotions hope to accomplish four goals: 1) Develop in-store merchandising support, as strong support at the retail store level is the key to closing the loop between the customer and the sale. 2) Control inventory by increasing or depleting inventory levels, thus helping to eliminate seasonal peaks and valleys. 3) Expand or improve distribution by opening up new sales areas (trade promotions are also sometimes used to distribute a new size of the product). 4) Generate excitement about the product among those responsible for selling it. Some of the most common forms of trade promotions—profiled below—include point-of-purchase displays, trade shows, sales meetings, sales contests, push money, deal loaders, and promotional allowances.

POINT-OF-PURCHASE (POP) DISPLAYS Manufacturers provide point-of-purchase (POP) display units free to retailers in order to promote a particular brand or group of products. The forms of POP displays include special racks, display cartons, banners, signs, price cards, and mechanical product dispensers. Probably the most effective way to ensure that a reseller will use a POP display is to design it so that it will generate sales for the retailer. High product visibility is the basic goal of POP displays. In industries such as the grocery field where a shopper spends about three-tenths of a second viewing a product, anything increasing product visibility is valuable. POP displays also provide or remind consumers about important decision information, such as the product's name, appearance, and sizes. The theme of the POP display should coordinate with the theme used in ads and by salespeople.

TRADE SHOWS Thousands of manufacturers display their wares and take orders at trade shows. In fact, companies spend over $9 billion yearly on these shows. Trade shows provide a major opportunity to write orders for products. They also provide a chance to demonstrate products, disseminate information, answer questions, and be compared directly to competitors. Related to trade shows, but on a smaller scale, are sales meetings sponsored by manufacturers or wholesalers. Whereas trade shows are open to all potential customers, sales meetings are targeted toward the company's sales force and/or independent sales agents. These meetings are usually conducted regionally and directed by sales managers. The meetings may be used to motivate sales agents, to explain the product or the promotional campaign, or simply to answer questions. For resellers and salespeople, sales contests can also be an effective motivation. Typically, a prize is awarded to the organization or person who exceeds a quota by the largest percentage.

PUSH MONEY Similarly, push money (PM)—also known as spiffs—is an extra payment given to salespeople for meeting a specified sales goal. For example, a manufacturer of refrigerators might pay a $30 bonus for each unit of model A, and a $20 bonus for each unit of model B, sold between March 1 and September 1. At the end of that period, the salesperson would send evidence of these sales to the manufacturer and receive a check in return. Although some people see push money as akin to bribery, many manufacturers offer it.

DEAL LOADERS A deal loader is a premium given by a manufacturer to a retailer for ordering a certain quantity of product. Two types of deal loaders are most typical. The first is a buying loader, which is a gift given for making a specified order size. The second is a display loader, which means the display is given to the retailer after the campaign. For instance, General Electric may have a display containing appliances as part of a special program. When the program is over, the retailer receives all the appliances on the display if a specified order size was achieved.

TRADE DEALS Trade deals are special price concessions superseding, for a limited time, the normal purchasing discounts given to the trade. Trade deals include a group of tactics having a common theme—to encourage sellers to specially promote a product. The marketer might receive special displays, larger-than-usual orders, superior in-store locations, or greater advertising effort. In exchange, the retailer might receive special allowances, discounts, goods, or money. In many industries, trade deals are the primary expectation for retail support, and the marketing funds spent in this area are considerable. There are two main types of trade deals: buying allowances and advertising/display allowances.

BUYING ALLOWANCES A buying allowance is a bonus paid by a manufacturer to a reseller when a certain amount of product is purchased during a specific time period. For example, a reseller who purchases at least 15 cases of product might receive a buying allowance of $6.00 off per case, while a purchase of at least 20 cases would result in $7.00 off per case, and so forth. The payment may take the form of a check or a reduction in the face value of an invoice. In order to take advantage of a buying allowance, some retailers engage in "forward buying." In essence, they order more merchandise than is needed during the deal period, then store the extra merchandise to sell later at regular prices. This assumes that the savings gained through the buying allowance is greater than the cost of warehousing and transporting the extra merchandise. Some marketers try to discourage forward buying, since it reduces profit margins and tends to create cyclical peaks and troughs in demand for the product.

The slotting allowance is a controversial form of buying allowance. Slotting allowances are fees retailers charge manufacturers for each space or slot on the shelf or in the warehouse that new products will occupy. The controversy stems from the fact that in many instances this allowance amounts to little more than paying a bribe to the retailer to convince them to carry your company's products. But many marketers are willing to pay extra to bring their products to the attention of consumers who are pressed for time in the store. Slotting allowances sometimes buy marketers prime spaces on retail shelves, at eye level or near the end of aisles.

The final type of buying allowance is a free goods allowance. In this case, the manufacturer offers a certain amount of product to wholesalers or retailers at no cost if they purchase a stated amount of the same or a different product. The allowance takes the form of free merchandise rather than money.

ADVERTISING ALLOWANCES An advertising allowance is a dividend paid by a marketer to a reseller for advertising their product. The money can only be used to purchase advertising—for example, to print flyers or run ads in a local newspaper. But some resellers take advantage of the system, so many manufacturers require verification. A display allowance is the final form of trade promotional allowance. Some manufacturers pay retailers extra to highlight their display from the many available every week. The payment can take the form of cash or goods. Retailers must furnish written certification of compliance with the terms of the contract before they are paid. Retailers are most likely to select displays that yield high volume and are easy to assemble.

FURTHER READING:

Blattberg, Robert C., and Scott A. Neslin. *Sales Promotion: Concepts, Methods, and Strategies.* Prentice Hall, 1990.

Lodish, Leonard M. *The Advertising and Promotion Challenge.* Oxford University Press, 1986.

Quelch, John A. *Sales Promotion Management.* Prentice Hall, 1989.

Schulz, Don, et. al. *Sales Promotion Essentials.* NTC Business Books, 1997.

Tellis, Gerald J. *Advertising and Sales Promotion Strategy.* Addison-Wesley, 1997.

SCALABILITY

In the dot-com industry, the ability for a Web site to grow at a rate comparable to that of the business itself is known as scalability. In order to stay competitive, a site must be able to add and drop merchandise and inventory from their online store in a relatively short period of time. The site must also be able to handle the increasing volume of online traffic that comes hand and hand with a successful Web business.

While specialized software exists for those who want to attempt scalability projects on their own, there are also many firms around that will help a business design their sites to become efficient models of scalability. These firms are experts in the latest technological innovations and specialize in tiered Internet architecture that allows the site to grow without having to rewrite mainframe systems, while at the same time making better use of existing servers. They also help larger sites set up subdirectories within the domain directory to help serve a large number of accounts simultaneously. By performing these functions, scalability experts can help prevent Web site crashes and save the company lost revenue and damaged reputations.

The inability for an e-commerce site to scale properly could cripple their business. As Nicholas G. Carr stated in an article that appeared in *The Standard:* ''On the Internet, if you can't scale—if you can't get really big really fast—you're nowhere. And

it's not enough for just your technology to be scalable. Your entire business model has to have scalability, as well; you need to be able to quickly extend your business into new markets, either horizontally or vertically. 'Will it scale?' is one of the first questions venture capitalists ask.''

While scalability is a critical issue for dot-coms, the actual advantage that comes with growing up to become a large Web site can still be debated. A larger site can appear to be more of a threat to a possible competitor that is thinking about entering the market, so much so that small sites are being bought up by larger sites in an effort cut down on the competition. This sort of consolidation can get pretty expensive, and presents a whole new set of scalability issues for the company that is doing the consolidating. Many dot-coms have learned the hard way about the problems that come with rapid and immense growth. A lot of the time, it is the consumer that gets hurt the most.

Carr sums it up by stating: ''While scalability will continue to be critical for e-businesses, I doubt scale itself will provide much of an advantage. Companies will need to be able to expand their businesses fast, but their bigness won't ensure lasting success. Rather, once they've scaled up in one market, they'll need to immediately look for new markets in which to replicate their growth. Defense was the name of the game in the old economy. In the new one, offense is everything.''

FURTHER READING:

Carr, Nicholas G. ''The Myth of Scalability.'' *The Standard.* January, 10, 2000.

Van Winkle, William. ''Setting Up Shop.'' *Home Office Computing.* October 2000.

West, Kelley. ''Managing Content on the Web.'' *Network Computing.* October 30, 2000.

SEE ALSO: Web Site Design

SEARCH ENGINES

Search engines are online services that allow users to scan the contents of the Internet to find Web sites or specific information of interest to them. A user inputs a search term, and the search engine attempts to match this term to categories or keywords in its catalog of World Wide Web sites. The search engine then generates a list of sites that match the search criteria, ranked in order of relevance. Search engines help organize the more than two billion pages of information on the World Wide Web and make them accessible to Internet users.

Search engines are the primary method Internet surfers use to locate information on the Web. In fact, Karl Greenberg noted in *Brandweek* that 85 percent of Internet surfers use search engines to locate information online. Search engines generate the largest percentage of new traffic to Web pages, followed by links from other sites, printed media, and word of mouth. For this reason, small businesses hoping to establish a presence on the Internet should make sure their Web sites are listed with a number of search engines.

Search engines ''catalog and list your Web site information so that when someone using the Internet searches for information pertaining to products or services that you sell, your potential customer locates your site,'' Steffano Korper and Juanita Ellis wrote in *The E-Commerce Book.* ''Search engines and directories function as listings of your site's theme and content, similar in function to a phone directory advertisement.''

HOW SEARCH ENGINES WORK

There are thousands of different search engines to help people navigate the Internet. These include major commercial search engines—like Yahoo!, Lycos, AltaVista, and Excite—as well as many smaller, industry-specific directories. There are even metasearchers, which work by querying a number of other search engines and processing the results. Many of the major search engines are created through an automated process in which a program called a spider ''crawls'' across the Web to gather information about existing sites. The spider captures this basic information and organizes its findings into categorizes, which are then used to generate search results for users. Small businesses hoping to list an existing Web site with a major search engine may find that the process has already been completed for them by an automated spider.

The largest and most popular search site, Yahoo!, is an exception to this rule. The Yahoo! listings are prepared by real people who actually look at each Web site, analyze its contents, and assign it to various classifications. Like most other commercial search engines, Yahoo! routinely seeks out new Web sites to include in its listings. However, small business owners may wish to change or add to the information that has been gathered about their sites. Many of the smaller directories are compiled using data submitted by individuals and businesses who want their site to be listed. Web page designers submit a form describing their sites, including keywords to describe the contents, in order to get a listing.

When a small business's potential customers use a search engine to scan the Internet for a particular type of information, they receive a list of matching Web sites ranked by relevance. The various search engines use different criteria to determine relevance. For example, Excite uses the number of links pointing to a particular site as a gauge of its popularity and ranks those sites higher. But regardless of the criteria used, the main idea of relevance rankings is to inform users how closely the contents of each site match their search criteria. As Vince Emery noted in *How to Grow Your Business on the Internet,* search engines generally rank Web sites higher if the keywords appear in the title of the page, as a headline in the body text, in the first 100 to 200 words of body text, or in the site's domain name. Another factor determining relevance rankings is the search term density, or how often the keywords appear in relation to other text on the Web site.

Since Web surfers generally have neither the time nor the inclination to examine hundreds of sites, small businesses need to achieve a high relevance ranking in order to attract visitors to their Web sites. ''Your goal with search engines is not just to have a listing in a database,'' Emery wrote. ''You need to rank in the first 50 listings returned, or even better, the first 25.''

''No company that wants to thrive on the Web can do so without a top ranking on the major search engines,'' Fredrick Marckini, founder of search engine positioning firm iProspect, told Greenberg. ''You can spend a million or two on a Web site, but if you don't do the things you need to do to make it found in the major search engines in the top 30 matches, your million-dollar Web site is a billboard in the woods.''

There are a few steps you can take while designing or registering your Web site to improve the odds of it appearing near the top of the list. Most important among these are making sure keywords appear early and often, and following the registration process for each search engine carefully. But experts caution against trying to trick the search engines into ranking your Web page highly. Known as ''search engine spamming,'' this practice is frowned upon and may cause your site to be rejected by some of the major search engines. The methods considered spamming include repeating a keyword multiple times on a Web page (for example, printing the word over and over in colored type that is invisible against the background of the page) and duplicating the same Web page with several different domain names in order to get multiple listings.

Korper and Ellis recommend that small business owners register their Web sites with a number of major search engines and directories. It may make sense to begin this process with the search engines that generate the most traffic, such as Yahoo!, Excite, and AltaVista, but it is also important to include smaller directories that may be popular within a specific industry. The registration process generally includes checking to see if your site is already listed, making any necessary changes to the automatically generated listing, finding out how the search engine organizes its listings, using this information to specify appropriate categories and keywords for your site, and then making sure that the keywords are placed in prominent positions on your site.

Several commercial services exist to help businesses register sites with search engines. Many of these services simplify the process by listing a Web site with a number of search engines at once. For example, Submit-It allows you to post the details of a Web site to 20 different directories from one central location. There are also search engine optimization firms whose purpose is to make Web pages more relevant in search engine results. For up-to-date information about search engines and directory listings—as well as tips on achieving high relevance rankings and links to online magazine articles—see www.searchenginewatch.com.

FURTHER READING:

Emery, Vince. *How to Grow Your Business on the Internet.* 3d Ed. Scottsdale, AZ: Coriolis Group, 1997.

Greenberg, Karl. "Search Patterns." *Brandweek.* September 11, 2000.

John, Lauren. "Wanted: As More of the IT Universe Moves to the Web, Search Engines Are Being Used to Take on Increasingly Complex Business Functions." *Computerworld.* July 3, 2000.

Korper, Steffano, and Juanita Ellis. *The E-Commerce Book: Building the E-Empire.* San Diego, CA: Academic Press, 2000.

Regan, Keith. "Does E-Commerce Need Search Engines?" *E-Commerce Times.* October 18, 2000.

Zetter, Kim, and Harry McCracken. "How to Stop Searching and Start Finding." *PC World.* September 2000.

SEE ALSO: Internet Domain Name; Web Site Design

SEASONAL BUSINESSES

Seasonal businesses are businesses that operate in one of two common business situations. The first situation is a business that is only open for operations during certain seasons of the year. Examples include vacation cottages, a lawn care service, or a snow removal service. These businesses either close down completely for part of the year or drastically scale back operations, managing only basic services such as accounts payable, during the off-season. The second situation is a business for which certain seasons of the year are far more profitable than others. In most cases, there are certain promotions or business techniques that can be used to increase profits during those seasons. A "season" in this sense can refer to the actual calendar season or to a specific business time period based on an event or holiday. The leading example of this type of seasonal business is a retail business that earns a large percentage of its annual profits during the Christmas "shopping season."

American Demographics magazine did a study of seasonal businesses and found that there are predictable events that can influence sales in every month of the year and that these events affect different industries. For example, the study showed that January is a good month for self-help books and programs. February is generally the slowest month of the year, but it does feature Valentine's Day, which triggers a great deal of seasonal business. In March, attendance at church and other religious activities jumps 60 percent. April is the month to market household cleaners and other spring cleaning products, while May features the cash cow that is Mother's Day. June features a lot of family activities, such as weddings, graduations, and vacations. July is the best month for all summer products. August is the busiest business and pleasure travel month of the year. September features back-to-school sales, while October is a marketing bonanza thanks to Halloween and the World Series. Finally, November and December are the biggest months of the year for almost every retailer thanks to the Thanksgiving and Christmas holidays.

BUSINESSES BASED ON THE ACTUAL SEASONS

Throughout the business world, there are numerous types of businesses that operate on a strictly seasonal basis, while many others stay open year-round but make a significant portion of their annual profits in one, or possibly two, seasons. Examples include vacation resorts, which in some regions of the United States are only open for part of the year (spring and summer in the northern U.S., fall and winter in the southern half of the country); cross-country and downhill skiing facilities; youth summer camps; lawn care and landscaping firms; golf courses; and sports leagues, from amateur all the way to the top professional leagues. Smaller-scale examples include snow removal services, pool cleaning services (in the northern U.S.), ice cream stands, golf driving ranges, and lifeguard positions, just to name a few.

If it is feasible, a business that relies heavily on one season at least tries to make some money during the remaining months of the year. If it absolutely cannot turn a profit, then the business often closes for the season to avoid paying employees and to reduce the cost of supplies and overhead. For example, in the northern United States, ice cream shops other than those located inside shopping malls simply close for the winter once the temperature dips down to the freezing level. On the other hand, some vacation resorts that might get 90 percent or more of their business in the summer months are trying to expand the length of their peak season and increasing their efforts to lure customers in the off-season.

Seasonal businesses can change drastically or even disappear as the demographics of a region or country change. An example of this phenomenon is the drive-in movie business, which in the 1950s and 1960s was thriving across the United States and Canada as a popular social event. By the 1990s, the advent of the VCR and the spread of plush, comfortable indoor ''movieplexes'' had all but vanquished the drive-ins. Adding to their demise was the fact that most people realized that, as urban growth occurred, the vast amount of land on which a drive-in was located was far more valuable for real estate development than it was for a seasonal business.

Above and beyond drive-ins, the movie industry remains one of the largest industries in the world that is driven by seasonal buying habits. The two biggest seasons of the year for the movie industry are summer and winter (mainly Christmas). Movie theaters do not shut down like other seasonal businesses, but they do hire extra employees for those two seasons and they do create budgets that reflect the dominance of those two seasons. Each year, the movie studios' most important releases are planned for those two times of year. High-budget, wide-appeal movies that have blockbuster potential are usually released in the summer, often at either the Memorial Day or Fourth of July holiday weekend. Around Christmas, the studios release serious pictures that are expected to gain Academy Award attention, together with big-budget films that are aimed at the entire family. A four-year study of monthly movie admissions revealed that, worldwide, December is the most popular movie-going month, with June finishing second in the United States.

According to the study, movies have become more like the leisure industry as a whole. ''Like all leisure industries, cinema is a highly seasonal business,'' said a summary of the study in *Screen Digest* magazine. ''The release strategies of the major studios are now very closely tied into the seasonal holidays and long weekends that divide and define the theatrical calendar. Pitching a film at the wrong month, week, or even day can mean the difference between success and failure.''

EVEN DURING BUSY SEASONS, THINGS CAN FLUCTUATE

For truly seasonal businesses, there are often situations beyond the business's control that cause sales to fluctuate wildly each year, with almost no way to predict what will happen in any given year. Perhaps the best example of this, in cold climates, is the amount of snow that falls each year. This can affect any number of businesses, from ski resorts to hardware stores that sell snowblowers, salt, and chemical de-icers. (The reverse of this situation for summer resorts is a summer that is colder and rainier than usual.) One winter can be extremely snowy, while the next can see almost no snowfall, with very little chance of consistently predicting which way a winter will turn out in advance.

Some businesses use this uncertainty to their advantage, offering unique sales pitches revolving around the snow, or lack of it. For example, it is not unusual for a creative hardware store to run a special on snowblowers late in the fall. As a gimmick to lure buyers, the store offers to refund the entire purchase price of a new snowblowers if a certain amount of snow does not fall that winter. If the snow does fall, then all sales are final, and the merchant was able to sell all his snowblowers at full price.

If the snow does not fall, then the merchant normally has taken out a special insurance policy that will cover most of his or her losses from the special sale, which has now turned out to be a worst-case scenario. Businesses that offer this kind of seasonal gimmick usually do their homework before they make what seems to be an outlandish offer. For example, the hardware store owner might know from studying statistical data that only twice in the last 100 years has the designated amount of snow not fallen, and therefore his odds of having to pay for the customers' snowblowers is extremely slim.

MAKE IT A YEAR-ROUND RESPONSIBILITY

For a businessperson who is used to working in traditional year-round occupations, the switch to a seasonal business might seem to require the use of different business practices. While there are a few things that will always be different, the changes can be minimized by treating the seasonal business as a year-round business. The business owner should take advantage of the downtime to make improvements to the business, attend industry seminars or conferences, recruit new employees, or other off-season activities.

In *Nation's Business* magazine, the experiences of an annual summer camp called Camp Echo Lake in upstate New York show how a seasonal business should be run year-round. At Echo Lake, the camp for 450 campers lasts only eight weeks during the summer. During that time, the camp employs 200 people. That leaves 44 weeks for owners Tony and George Stein to fill before the camp opens again. To make the most of their business, the brothers have devised a business plan that allows them to work on the camp all year. Following are some methods they recommend:

After the camp ends in August, the Steins prepare a newsletter for parents that is mailed in September; the letter provides a summary of the year's activities and highlights what campers can expect the following year.

During the winter months, the Steins study new literature on their industry, learning about new classes they can offer and new ways to market and promote the camp. Physical improvements to the camp are also made in the off-season.

They set up installment payment plans that allow parents to pay the camp tuition year-round. This makes it easier for parents to pay and ensures that the camp will have steady cash flow all year.

Additional cash is brought in by hosting off-season events, such as training camps for college athletic teams and wilderness getaways for adults and families.

The business owners also use the downtime to make sure that they hire the best possible staffers. Instead of filling staff positions in the few weeks leading up to the start of camp, the Steins hire a recruiter who begins interviewing candidates all the way back in May.

"Busy as it is, an advantage of the off-season is that it's a time when you have control over what you do," camp owner Tony Stein explained. "Once the new season begins, day-to-day operations occupy so much time that there is little left for any of the above activities."

SUCCEEDING AT A TRULY SEASONAL BUSINESSES

In a business that is truly driven by the seasons, there are steps that can be taken to ensure greater success. The two most important factors are managing cash flow and hiring the right employees. *Knight-Ridder/Tribune Business News* documented the case of Todd Binford, who owned a landscaping soil and stone company. Through the years Binford learned from his mistakes and determined how to manage money during his slow season. Tricks he used include not paying himself a salary during the winter months; paying employees well and letting them work 60 to 80 hours in the summer, then dismissing them each winter instead of paying them lower amounts to work 40 hours year-round; and rearranging bills so that most can be paid in the summer. "You just get used to trying to save money instead of spending every paycheck," said Binford.

Finding and keeping good employees is another key to succeeding in a seasonal business. Paying well and creating a positive work environment are obvious ways to gain good employees, but there are other tactics a small business owner can use. Keeping em-

ployees informed of how the seasonal shift affects the company is a good idea, as the employees feel as if they matter more and are an important part of the business. It also helps employees identify the best time to take a vacation. When hiring new employees, owners may neglect two sources of good seasonal employees—students and retirees. Students are perfect for summer jobs because their time off from school matches the business's busy season perfectly, and most students need to earn money in the summer to pay for school in the fall. Retirees tend to make good employees because they may have years of experience in their field, but they no longer desire to work full-time. Therefore, a job that lasts a few months each year is perfect.

One other tactic that seasonal business owners can use to succeed is to expand their business to include a new product line that is seasonal in the opposite way of their original line. For example, a lawn and garden company that sells lawn mowers and offers mowing and landscaping services can add snowblowers to their product mix and offer snow removal services to compliment their landscaping services. The new product should be similar to the existing product so that an owner does not have to learn a brand new business or invest a great deal of money.

EVENT- OR HOLIDAY-BASED SEASONAL BUSINESS

The second type of seasonal business is primarily set in the retail sector, although industry can also feel the seasonal boom as it strives to produce consumer goods for holiday-based retail sales. This type of seasonal business is driven by holidays or events that greatly influence consumer spending. Christmas is by far the largest holiday that creates seasonal shopping. In fact, Christmas has become so huge that a study of retail sales reported in the *Economist* showed that sales rise by 15 percent above normal months in December and drop 30 percent below normal in January each year. Other examples of event- or holiday-based seasonal periods include Halloween, Mother's Day, graduation, and back-to-school. These events are held at the same time each year, which makes it easy for a businessperson to establish an annual schedule.

One example that illustrates how event- or holiday-based seasonal business works is the candy industry. According to *Chain Drug Review*, "at mass retail stores . . . the bulk of sales [are] occurring around four holidays: Valentine's Day, Easter, Halloween, and Christmas." In the same article, the National Confectioners Association reports that it found that candy sales doubled during those four periods in 1997, illustrating how important those brief periods are to a candy manufacturer. Retail stores also take advantage of the seasonal increases in candy sales by targeting advertising toward holiday shoppers and presenting special displays of candy. Candy manufacturers have learned to take advantage of the holiday as much as retailers have. After offering nothing but the same colors of plain M&M candies for years, M&M/Mars Inc. now produces a number of holiday-themed candies, such as red and green for Christmas and pastel for Easter. Other candy manufacturers have followed suit and now offer candy with theme designs.

Outside the candy industry, those same four holidays are the biggest holidays or events in almost every other retail sector. Exceptions include the greeting card industry, which also sees huge sales on Mother's Day and Sweetest Day, and the office supply industry, which is responsible for meeting back-to-school needs.

Preparing for a seasonal event often begins months in advance of the event itself. For example, *Discount Store News* reports that ''superstores . . . in the past few years have steadily become more aggressive in their pursuit of the Back-to-School seasonal business. Almost as soon as school lets out for the summer, the superstores begin setting up merchandise displays in advance of television commercials touting superstores as destinations for Back-to-School shopping.'' Another example of this phenomenon is Christmas sales, which seem to start earlier and earlier with each passing year as stores try to expand the selling season and turn a greater profit. In the past, Christmas sales traditionally started on Thanksgiving weekend. Now, in most stores, the day the Halloween decorations come down, the Christmas decorations go up.

NON-ANNUAL EVENTS

The most extreme examples of holiday or event-based seasonal businesses are those involving a once-in-a-lifetime ''season,'' or one that is almost equally rare. An extreme example of this could be a type of solar eclipse that might be visible only from one-third of the Earth's surface and that will not occur again for 120 years. Tourism-related businesses in those regions where the eclipse was most visible could expect a large boost in bookings over a normal year, even if that boost might only last a single day (or several days at the most).

Just as sometimes happens in true seasonal businesses, events of this type can sometimes be ruined by actions that are out of the business owner's hands. Some insurance companies even offer a policy to businesses that protects them from unexpected losses if the unique event does not occur as planned. In the case of the eclipse, for example, if the day of the big event turns out to be overcast and rainy in the viewing area, then the expected increase in tourists that was hoped for on that day will never materialize. Money spent on advertising or increased inventory for that day could be recouped under the terms of the special insurance policy.

Perhaps the largest single ''unique event'' type of seasonal opportunity in history presented itself at the end of 1999, as businesses around the world prepared for the New Year's Eve that would signal the start of a new century (although the twenty-first century technically started on January 1, 2001, people generally celebrated the event as the calendar rolled to 2000). In addition to all of the worldwide panic over the Y2K computer bug, which created an almost ''seasonal'' event of staggering proportions for the computer industry, there was additional fallout from that one-time event in many business sectors. In the hospitality profession, for example, the initial reaction of hotels and restaurants was to charge exorbitant prices for special room and meal packages that evening. The thinking was that because the event was so unique, people would pay anything to experience it. In fact, just the opposite turned out to be true. Most people, worried about the computer problem and put off by the high prices, chose to stay home that night. Hotels, restaurants, and other businesses were left scrambling, desperate to drum up any amount of business at the last minute; many were forced to offer refunds to customers who purchased their packages early in the process.

FURTHER READING:

''Avoiding Seasonal Glitches.'' *Inc.* June 1996.

''Candy: Seasonal Tie-Ins Critical for Sales.'' *Chain Drug Review.* March 2, 1998.

Carlstrom, Charles T., and Timothy S. Fuerst. ''Interest Rates for Seasonal and Business Cycles.'' *Economic Commentary.* July 1996.

Carpenter, Robert E., and Daniel Levy. ''Seasonal Cycles, Business Cycles, and the Comovement of Inventory Investment and Output.'' *Journal of Money, Credit & Banking.* August 1998.

Gilbert, Sarah. ''Managers Learn to Weather Ups and Downs of Seasonal Business.'' *Knight-Ridder/Tribune Business News.* November 15, 1999.

Krummert, Bob. ''Peak Seasons Grow Longer at Resorts.'' *ID: The Voice of Food Service Distribution.* April 1998.

Maynard, Roberta. ''At Season's End, the Real Work Begins.'' *Nation's Business.* October 1995.

Sapers, Jonathan. ''In Season.'' *Entrepreneur.* September 1997.

''Stationery Offerings Find Little Room for Growth.'' *Discount Store News.* August 9, 1999.

''Summertime Arrives Early for U.S. Box Office.'' *Screen Digest.* August 1999.

''Tis the Season.'' *The Economist* (U.S.). December 14, 1996.

Waldrop, Judith. ''The Seasons of Business.'' *American Demographics.* May 1992.

Wilson, Richenda. ''Time Machines: The Conference and Exhibition Sector Is a Seasonal Business and as 2000 Nears, Many Event Organizers Are Feeling Anxious. Will the Turn of the Millennium Be a Help or a Hindrance?'' *Marketing Week.* December 2, 1999.

SEC DISCLOSURE LAWS AND REGULATIONS

Companies that are privately owned are not required by law to disclose detailed financial and operating information in most instances. They enjoy wide latitude in deciding what types of information to make available to the public. Small businesses and other enterprises that are privately owned may shield information from public knowledge and determine for themselves who needs to know specific types of information. Companies that are publicly owned, on the other hand, are subject to detailed disclosure laws about their financial condition, operating results, management compensation, and other areas of their business. While these disclosure obligations are primarily linked with large publicly traded companies, many smaller companies choose to raise capital by making shares in the company available to investors. In such instances, the small business is subject to many of the same disclosure laws that apply to large corporations. Disclosure laws and regulations are monitored and enforced by the U.S. Securities and Exchange Commission (SEC).

All of the SEC's disclosure requirements have statutory authority, and these rules and regulations are subject to changes and amendments over time. Some changes are made as the result of new accounting rules adopted by the principal rule-making bodies of the accounting profession. In other cases, changes in accounting rules follow changes in SEC guidelines. For example, in 2000 the SEC imposed new regulations to eliminate the practice of ''selective disclosure,'' in which business leaders provided earnings estimates and other vital information to analysts and large institutional shareholders before informing smaller investors and the rest of the general public. The regulation forces companies to make market-sensitive information available to all parties at the same time.

In any event, SEC regulations have a direct impact on what are known as generally accepted accounting principles (GAAP). The rule-making bodies of the accounting profession, most notably the Financial Accounting Standards Board (FASB) and the American Institute of Certified Public Accountants (AICPA), must rely on ''acceptance'' of their statements. While FASB and AICPA statements do not have the force of law, they are widely accepted in the accounting profession and in some cases influence subsequent SEC rules on disclosure.

SEC DISCLOSURE OBLIGATIONS

SEC regulations require publicly owned companies to disclose certain types of business and financial data on a regular basis to the SEC and to the company's stockholders. The SEC also requires disclosure of relevant business and financial information to potential investors when new securities, such as stocks and bonds, are issued to the public, although exceptions are made for small issues and private placements. The current system of mandatory corporate disclosure is known as the integrated disclosure system. By amending some of its regulations, the SEC has attempted to make this system less burdensome on corporations by standardizing various forms and eliminating some differences in reporting requirements to the SEC and to shareholders.

Publicly owned companies prepare two annual reports, one for the SEC and one for their shareholders. Form 10-K is the annual report made to the SEC, and its content and form are strictly governed by federal statutes. It contains detailed financial and operating information, as well as a management response to specific questions about the company's operations.

Historically, companies have had more leeway in what they include in their annual reports to stockholders. Over the years, however, the SEC has gained more influence over the content of such annual reports, primarily through amending its rules on proxy statements. Since most companies mail annual reports along with their proxy statements, they must make their annual stockholder reports comply with SEC requirements.

SEC regulations require that annual reports to stockholders contain certified financial statements and other specific items. The certified financial statement must include a two-year audited balance sheet and a three-year audited statement of income and cash flows. In addition, annual reports must contain five years of selected financial data, including net sales or operating revenues, income or loss from continuing operations, total assets, long-term obligations and redeemable preferred stock, and cash dividends declared per common share.

Annual reports to stockholders must also contain management's discussion and analysis of the firm's financial condition and results of operations. Information contained therein includes discussions of the firm's liquidity, capital resources, results of operations, any favorable or unfavorable trends in the industry, and any significant events or uncertainties. Other information to be included in annual reports to stockholders includes a brief description of the business covering such matters as main products and services, sources of materials, and status of new products. Directors and officers of the corporation must be identified. Specific market data on common stock must also be supplied.

REGISTRATION OF NEW SECURITIES Private companies that wish to become publicly owned must comply with the registration requirements of the SEC. In addition, companies floating new securities must follow similar disclosure requirements. The required disclosures are made in a two-part registration statement that consists of a prospectus as one part and a second section containing additional information. The prospectus contains all of the information that is to be presented to potential investors. It should be noted that SEC rules and regulations governing registration statements are subject to change.

In order to meet the disclosure requirements of new issue registration, companies prepare a basic information package similar to that used by publicly owned companies for their annual reporting. The prospectus, which contains all information to be presented to potential investors, must include such items as audited financial statements, a summary of selected financial data, and management's description of the company's business and financial condition. The statement should also include a summary of the company's material business contracts and list all forms of cash and noncash compensation given to the chief executive officer (CEO) and the top five officers. Compensation paid to all officers and directors as a group must also be disclosed. In essence, a company seeking to go public must disclose its entire business plan.

SECURITIES INDUSTRY REGULATIONS Additional disclosure laws apply to the securities industry and to the ownership of securities. Officers, directors, and principal stockholders (defined as holding 10 percent or more of the company's stock) of publicly owned companies must submit two reports to the SEC. These are Form 3 and Form 4. Form 3 is a personal statement of beneficial ownership of securities of their company. Form 4 records changes in such ownership. These reporting requirements also apply to the immediate families of the company's officers, directors, and principal stockholders. Individuals who acquire 5 percent or more of the voting stock of a SEC-registered company, meanwhile, must also submit notification of that fact to the SEC.

Securities broker-dealers must provide their customers with a confirmation form as soon as possible after the execution of an order. These forms provide customers with minimum basic information required for every trade. Broker-dealers are also responsible for presenting the prospectus to each customer for new securities issues. Finally, members of the securities industry are subject to reporting requirements of their own self-regulating organizations. These organizations include the New York Stock Exchange (for listed securities transactions) and the National Association of Securities Dealers (for over-the-counter traded securities).

DISCLOSURE RULES OF THE ACCOUNTING PROFESSION

Generally accepted accounting principles (GAAP) and specific rules of the accounting profession require that certain types of information be disclosed in a business's audited financial statements. As noted above, these rules and principles do not have the same force of law as SEC rules and regulations. Once adopted, however, they are widely accepted and followed by the accounting profession. Indeed, in some instances, disclosures required by the rules and regulations of the accounting profession may exceed those required by the SEC.

It is a GAAP that financial statements must disclose all significant information that would be of interest to a concerned investor, creditor, or buyer. Among the types of information that must be disclosed are financial records, accounting policies employed, litigation in progress, lease information, and details of pension plan funding. Generally, full disclosure is required when alternative accounting policies are available, as with inventory valuation, depreciation, and long-term contract accounting. In addition, accounting practices applicable to a particular industry and other unusual applications of accounting principles are usually disclosed.

Certified financial statements contain a statement of opinion from an auditor, in which the auditor states that it is his or her opinion that the financial statements were prepared in accordance with GAAP and that no material information was left undisclosed. If the auditor has any doubts, then a qualified or adverse opinion statement is written.

FURTHER READING:

Diamond, Michael R., and Julie L. Williams. *How to Incorporate: A Handbook for Entrepreneurs and Professionals.* John Wiley, 1996.

Fulkerson, Jennifer. "How Investors Use Annual Reports." *American Demographics.* May 1996.

Galinger, George W., and Jerry B. Poe. *Essentials of Finance.* Prentice Hall, 1995.

Nocera, Joseph. "No Whispering Allowed: Why the SEC's Crackdown on Selective Disclosure is Good News." *Money.* December 1, 2000.

Skousen, K. Fred. *An Introduction to the SEC.* SouthWestern Publishing, 1991.

SECURITIES AND EXCHANGE COMMISSION (SEC)

The U.S. Securities and Exchange Commission (SEC) is a federal agency responsible for administering federal securities laws that protect investors. The

SEC also ensures that securities markets are fair and honest and, if necessary, enforces securities laws through the appropriate sanctions. Basically, the SEC oversees the activities of all participants in the securities markets—including publicly held corporations, public utilities, investment companies and advisers, and securities brokers and dealers—to ensure that investors are adequately informed and their interests are protected. Small businesses are most likely to come into contact with the SEC when they decide to make a public offering of debt or securities. Any business wishing to issue stock must first file a registration statement with the SEC. Another role of the SEC is to serve as adviser to the federal courts in Chapter 11 cases (corporate reorganization proceedings under Chapter 11 of the Bankruptcy Reform Act of 1978).

ORGANIZATION AND RESPONSIBILITIES OF THE SEC

The SEC was created by Congress in 1934 under the Securities Exchange Act as an independent, nonpartisan, quasi-judicial regulatory agency. The commission is made up of five members: one chairman and four commissioners. Each member is appointed by the president to a five-year term, with the terms staggered. The commission's staff is made up of lawyers, accountants, financial analysts, engineers, investigators, economists, and other professionals. The SEC staff is divided into divisions and offices, which includes 12 regional and branch offices, each directed by officials appointed by the SEC chairman.

The chairman and commissioners of the SEC are responsible for ensuring that publicly held corporations, brokers or dealers in securities, investment companies and advisers, and other participants in the securities markets comply with federal securities law. These laws were designed to help public investors make informed investment analysis and decisions—principally by ensuring adequate disclosure of material information. The SEC does not, however, make any evaluations of the quality of the company making the IPO; it is concerned only with assuring that the registration statement and prospectus documents contain the information necessary for potential investors to make informed decisions. The SEC also has the authority to initiate legal penalties—both civil and criminal—against companies if the agency determines that the IPO materials contain serious omissions, misleading information, or outright falsehoods. "If the SEC finds mistakes during the registration process, it can delay your IPO," said Chuck Berg in *Cincinnati Business Courier*. "If it finds mistakes or omissions after your company goes public, your company may soon have a thorough—and unpleasant—understanding of legal liability."

There are six major laws that the SEC is responsible for administering:

- Securities Act of 1933
- Securities Exchange Act of 1934
- Public Utility Holding Company Act of 1935
- Trust Indenture Act of 1939
- Investment Company Act of 1940
- Investment Advisers Act of 1940

The Securities Act of 1933, also known as the "truth in securities" law, has two primary objectives: 1) to require that investors be provided with material information concerning securities offered for public sale; and 2) to prevent misrepresentation, deceit, and other fraud in the sale of securities. The SEC ensures that both of these objectives are met.

The Securities Exchange Act of 1934 extended the "disclosure" doctrine (from the Securities Act of 1933) to securities listed and registered for public trading on the U.S. securities exchanges. In 1964, the Securities Act Amendments extended disclosure and reporting provisions to equity securities in the over-the-counter market. The act seeks to ensure (through the SEC) fair and orderly securities markets by prohibiting certain types of activities and by setting forth rules regarding the operation of the markets and participants.

The SEC also administers the Public Utility Holding Company Act of 1935. Subject to regulation under this act are interstate holding companies engaged in the electric utility business or in the retail distribution of natural or manufactured gas. Reports to be filed with the SEC by these holding companies include detailed information concerning the organization, financial structure, and operations of the holding company and its subsidiaries. Holding companies are subject to SEC regulation in areas such as corporate structure, acquisitions, and issue and sales of securities.

The Trust Indenture Act of 1939 applies to bonds, debentures, notes, and similar debt securities offered for public sale and issued under trust indentures with more than $7.5 million of securities outstanding at any one time. Other provisions of the act prohibit the indenture trustee from having conflicts of interest; require the trustee to be a corporation with minimal combined capital and surplus; and impose high standards of conduct and responsibility on the trustee.

The SEC also ensures compliance with the Investment Company Act of 1940. This act seeks to regulate the activities of companies engaged primarily in investing, reinvesting, and trading in securities, and whose own securities are publicly offered. It is important for potential investors to understand that although the SEC serves as a regulatory agency in these cases, the SEC does not supervise a company's investment activities, and the mere presence of the SEC as a regulatory agency does not guarantee a safe investment.

The Investment Advisers Act of 1940—also overseen by the SEC—establishes a style, or a system, of regulating investment advisers. The main thrust of this act requires all persons, or firms, that are compensated for advising anyone about securities investment opportunities to be registered with the SEC and conform to the established standards of investor protection. The SEC has the power and ability to strip an investment adviser of his or her registration if a statutory violation has occurred.

Finally, the SEC is given some responsibility connected with corporate bankruptcy reorganizations, commonly referred to as Chapter 11 proceedings. Chapter 11 of the Bankruptcy Code grants the SEC permission to become involved in any proceedings, but the SEC is primarily concerned with proceedings directly involving significant public investor interest.

FURTHER READING:

Berg, Chuck. "To Avoid SEC's Wrath, Be Thorough, Accurate." *Cincinnati Business Courier*. April 17, 1995.

Skousen, K. Fred. *An Introduction to the SEC*. SouthWestern Publishing, 1991.

SEED MONEY

Seed money, or seed capital, is the financing an entrepreneur needs in the very early stages of launching a new business. It gets its name from the idea that early stage financing plants the seed that enables a small business to grow. Obtaining funding is one of the most critical aspects of starting a small business. In fact, many businesses fail or are prevented from even starting due to a lack of capital. Although obtaining financing can be difficult for any small business, it is particularly hard for new ventures; since they lack a track record, potential lenders and investors are often skeptical about their prospects for success. But the dedicated would-be entrepreneur, if armed with a sound business plan and the necessary skills, can usually obtain funding for his/her dream.

Many entrepreneurs approach their family, friends, and colleagues for seed money after exhausting their own finances. Since they know the entrepreneur, these investors are more likely to take a risk on funding a new venture than are traditional financing sources, such as banks or venture capital firms. "An entrepreneur needs vast quantities of commitment and enthusiasm in the seed-capital stage, since the venture has little else with which to entice investors," Reed Phillips III wrote in an article for *Folio*. "Because it is almost impossible to predict how successful the project might eventually become, the only outsiders likely to invest are those who respect the entrepreneur's judgment and abilities. And those are the people with whom the entrepreneur has had the longest relationships." By "getting in on the ground floor," the providers of seed money hope to participate in the entrepreneur's success and realize a healthy return as their investment appreciates over time. Still, Phillips noted, "Risking money in the early stages of a start-up is more like buying a lottery ticket than making an investment. Investors know the odds are against them and realize they may lose their entire investment."

In most cases, seed money takes the form of equity financing, so investors receive partial ownership of the fledgling company in exchange for their funds. As a result, it is important for the entrepreneur to take potential investors' personalities and business reputations into consideration when seeking seed money. Since these people will be part owners of the company—and may insist upon having some control over decision making—it is vital to ascertain whether their interests and personalities are compatible with those of the entrepreneur. Once suitable investors have been located, the entrepreneur must convince them that the new business venture has a good chance of success. The first step in this process is creating a formal, written business plan, including plausible projections of income and expenses.

The entrepreneur should also have a specific purpose in mind for the seed money. The purpose of seed capital usually involves moving the business out of the idea stage—by building a prototype product or conducting market research, for example—and gathering concrete evidence that it can succeed. In this way, seed money helps the entrepreneur to prove the merit of his or her idea in order to attract the interest of formal investment sources.

As far as the amount of seed money the entrepreneur should try to obtain, experts recommend targeting only what is needed to accomplish the business's initial objectives. Given its risk, seed capital is usually more expensive for the firm than later stage financing. Thus, raising a small amount at a time helps the entrepreneur to preserve equity for later financing rounds. Ideally, an arrangement can be made that links seed money to launch financing, so the entrepreneur can go back to the same investors for future funding needs. For example, the entrepreneur might set goals for a successful market test of a new product. If the goals are met, then the original investors agree to provide additional funds for a product launch. This approach protects the entrepreneur against the possibility of having a successful test and then running out of money before being able to launch the product. Even if the original investors cannot provide additional funds directly, their vested interest may encourage them to help the venture succeed in other ways.

There are other sources of seed money available to entrepreneurs besides friends and family members. For example, some venture capital firms reserve a limited amount of funds to finance new ventures or business ideas. Since start-ups involve greater risks than established businesses, however, the venture capital investors generally require a larger equity position in exchange. In his book *The Entrepreneur's Guide to Preparing a Winning Business Plan and Raising Venture Capital,* W. Keith Schilit estimated that venture capitalists providing seed money would expect a 50 to 100 percent higher return than in a standard venture capital arrangement. There are also nonprofit organizations dedicated to providing seed capital for new businesses. In many cases, these organizations will also assist the entrepreneur in creating a business plan or marketing materials, and establishing cash flow controls or other systems.

FURTHER READING:

Fraser, Jill Andresky. ''Seeking Seed Money.'' *Inc.* December 1995.

Phillips, Reed III. ''Raising Seed Money Is a Critical First Step.'' *Folio: The Magazine for Magazine Management.* February 15, 1995.

Schilit, W. Keith. *The Entrepreneur's Guide to Preparing a Winning Business Plan and Raising Venture Capital.* Prentice Hall, 1990.

Weinstein, Bob. ''On the Money: Figuring Out How Much Cash You Really Need to Start Your Business.'' *Entrepreneur.* September 1998.

''Where the Seed Money Is.'' *Industry Standard.* February 26, 2001.

SELF-ASSESSMENT

Self-assessment is a tool that involves performing a critical analysis of one's own goals, interests, skills, and experience. Among its many applications in the business world are employee development, team performance, and organizational change efforts. But self-assessment is perhaps most valuable for would-be entrepreneurs considering starting a new business. ''A business is merely an extension of the people managing it and mirrors their abilities,'' notes the *Entrepreneur Magazine Small Business Advisor.* ''As an entrepreneur, you have to know your strengths and weaknesses so you can compensate in some way for the areas where you will not be proficient. You can determine your strengths and weaknesses by evaluating the major accomplishments in your personal and professional life and the skills required to complete these tasks.'' In other words, entrepreneurs may be able to improve their chances of success in business by undertaking an honest and detailed self-assessment. By evaluating such personal traits as business skills, experience, and knowledge, financial goals, likes and dislikes, willingness to expend effort, and ability to meet challenges, entrepreneurs may be able to identify the business opportunities for which they are best suited. In some cases, self-assessment may even lead to innovative new business ideas. In addition, completing a self-assessment can help entrepreneurs recognize areas where they will need assistance or training. By increasing self-knowledge, it may also help entrepreneurs to attract investors and impress lenders.

A good place to start in performing a self-assessment is to prepare a detailed resume. This document should list the entrepreneur's educational background and professional experience—describing the requirements and responsibilities of each job in detail—along with hobbies and outside interests. Using the resume as a guide, it may then be helpful for the entrepreneur to separate his or her professional attributes by functional area—such as marketing, accounting, or human resource management—and assign a competency level to each one. Finally, the entrepreneur may wish to create a list of personal attributes—such as ability with numbers, common sense, communication skills, organization skills, people skills, etc.—that may be useful in starting and running a small business. The mere process of thinking about and categorizing one's skills and experience can be informative. Viewed objectively, these documents can assist the entrepreneur in myriad ways.

Not surprisingly, the tool of self-assessment can be applied to a wide variety of other business situations as well. For example, it can be used as an aid in employee development as part of a company's performance evaluation and training efforts. A common application is ''360-degree feedback'' systems—in addition to being evaluated by supervisors, peers, and subordinates, employees evaluate their own performance and participate in setting goals. Self-assessment can also be applied to teams of workers or even overall organizations to help identify strengths and weaknesses and improve performance. Teams might evaluate such elements of team performance as goal setting, communication, decision making, problem solving, and conflict management. At the organizational level, self-assessment performed with the participation of employees can help clarify a company's mission and goals, identify shortcomings, and generate ideas to increase competitiveness.

FURTHER READING:

Bygrave, William D., ed. *The Portable MBA in Entrepreneurship.* 2d ed. John Wiley, 1997.

Caffyn, Sarah. "Development of a Continuous Improvement Self-Assessment Tool." *International Journal of Operations and Production Management.* November 2000.

The Entrepreneur Magazine Small Business Advisor. New York: Wiley, 1991.

Halloran, James W. *The Right Fit: The Entrepreneur's Guide to Finding the Perfect Business.* Liberty House, 1989.

Maron, Rebecca M. "Self-Assessment: A Remedy for Dysfunctional Board Behaviors." *Association Management.* January 1997.

Meade, Jim. "Self-Assessment Tool Helps Target Training." *HR Magazine.* May 2000.

SELF-EMPLOYMENT

Self-employment refers to the status of an individual who—rather than accepting a position as an employee of another person or organization—chooses to go into business for him or herself. Self-employment offers individuals a number of advantages, from the freedom to work without supervision to the ability to deduct the costs of doing business for tax purposes. But it also has some potential drawbacks, including uncertain levels of income, long working hours, isolation, and the need to fund one's own health insurance and retirement plans. People choose self-employment for a wide variety of reasons. Some desire a change in lifestyle, some are unable to find other employment, some want to work at home in order to care for small children, and some are retirees seeking additional income. Regardless of the underlying motivation, however, there are ways for self-employed persons to overcome the potential drawbacks and increase their chances for success.

Individuals who choose self-employment must be aware of the rules governing the treatment of freelance employees (also known as independent contractors). Classification of someone as an employee or a self-employee is somewhat ambiguous and depends on several factors, including the degree of independence, the freedom to hire others to do the work taken on, the freedom to work for others, and the assumption of risks. Independent contractors typically accept no fringe benefits and pay Social Security, Medicare, and income tax installments directly. Employees have more statutory rights, benefits, and protections than subcontractors, who must generally provide these for themselves. But independent contractors have advantages in terms of freedom, flexibility, and tax deductions.

The IRS applies a 20-part test in order to determine whether a certain worker should be classified as an employee or an independent contractor. The main issue underpinning the test is who sets the work rules: employees must follow rules set by their bosses, while independent contractors set their own rules. For example, an individual who sets his own hours, receives payment by the job, and divides his time between work for several different employers would probably be classified as an independent contractor. Other criteria involve who provides the tools and materials needed to complete the work. For example, an individual who works at an employer's facility and uses the employer's equipment would be considered an employee, while one who works at a separate location and provides her own equipment would be classified as an independent contractor. Finally, an independent contractor usually pays his own expenses of doing business and takes the risk of not receiving payment when work is not completed in accordance with a contract, while an employee is usually reimbursed for business-related expenses by the employer and receives a paycheck whether his work is completed or not.

An individual's status as a self-employed, independent contractor can be reinforced by having multiple clients, being paid by the amount of work done rather than by the hour, or obtaining an employer identification number from the IRS. Working under a business name also helps reinforce this status. Printing invoices, business cards, and stationery can also help identify someone as a self-employed person. In general, the person must demonstrate that he or she is in business for the purpose of making a profit.

THE GROWTH OF SELF-EMPLOYMENT

The concept of self-employment received increased attention in the 1980s and early 1990s as many large firms responded to increased competition and a lingering recession by "downsizing," or reducing the size of their permanent staffs and hiring temporary employees and independent contractors to reduce overhead. The financial impact of workers' compensation, Social Security, and job protection laws also made employers more cautious about hiring full-time employees. While in the past a large company using free-lancers seemed to imply a crisis, it became a commonplace way to control costs and try out new talent in the 1990s. At the same time, many employees who were laid off chose to go into business for themselves rather than reenter an increasingly unstable work force. The growth of self-employed professionals, in turn, enabled smaller companies to enlist the services of people who have had experience at larger, more sophisticated companies, without the cost of hiring them full-time.

Another factor influencing the growth of self-employment was that personal computer and communications technology made working at home more feasible throughout the 1980s and 1990s. Mastering these technologies has become essential for those without staffs. Through cellular telephones and pagers, the self-employed professional can stay in touch with clients throughout the day. In addition, computer technology made instantaneous local, cross-country, and international networking and research feasible. The relatively low price of personal computers, peripherals, and communications equipment have enabled many more people to conduct business independently.

By 1993, one-fifth of all new jobs in the United States were created by self-employment, and self-employed persons accounted for 7.6 percent of the work force. In fact, job growth in this category increased almost twice as fast as overall job growth. The highest growth came in the finance, insurance, property, and business services industries—areas where professionals could expect to earn more by becoming independent. In the late 1990s, the number of self-employed Americans actually declined slightly as a percentage of the U.S. work force, and according to some studies, only 2 percent of people who go the entrepreneurial route stay self-employed 10 years later. But despite such sobering statistics, starting one's own business remains a dream that continues to be pursued by millions of individuals every year.

CONSIDERATIONS IN SELF-EMPLOYMENT

Self-employed individuals as a whole tend to work longer (an additional 17.5 hours per week, according to one study) and harder than their colleagues who are organizationally employed. Moreover, self-employed people often operate under uncertain payment schedules and must make outlays from personal earnings for insurance and retirement. In addition, their salaries and assets are dependent on their work contributions in a more intimate way than are those of their colleagues. The entrepreneurial role is also often more physically and psychologically stressful due to the investments in energy the jobs demand.

ISOLATION AND NETWORKING Isolation often proves to be an important source of psychological strain for self-employed individuals. The environment of the typical self-employed individual is quite different from the corporate environment where many professionals gain their experience. This is one reason contact with supportive colleagues becomes crucial. Mentors can provide advice regarding business aspects of a new business owner's operation. Trade and professional organizations can be an excellent way to establish contacts with peers. Tenacity in networking has been cited as a key to survival for business owners, some of whom maintain databases of thousands of contacts. These contacts are also vital in referring clients and providing market information. The role of the contact is made more important as the self-employed individual typically has no staff for marketing support.

It is difficult to exaggerate the importance of referrals to the typical independent professional. Since relationships are so vital, one must exercise the utmost delicacy in terminating employment with one's former employer or turning down a job. One's former employer can even become a good client, besides providing valuable referrals. When turning down clients, the self-employed person can protect those relationships by making referrals or even subcontracting to other colleagues in their network. Provided the work done is of quality, this can strengthen one's reputation as a purveyor of talent—whether one's own or an associate's. When the client calls back with a more appropriate assignment, the contractor has the choice of the business.

As they begin their enterprises, many self-employed individuals feel compelled to accept a variety of assignments due to sheer scarcity of work. However, specialization can help ensure their long-term survival. For one thing, corporate clients can often find a generalist's abilities in-house. Also, specialization may allow professionals to broaden their client base geographically, thus freeing their fortunes from fluctuations in the local economy. These factors can enable the specialist to earn higher fees and work more consistently. Paradoxically, one's work as a specialist can garner referrals outside one's specialty, so specialization might not be as limiting as a strict definition would imply. The self-employed should be cautioned against changing their specialties too often, as this can confuse clients and make their own operations inefficient.

TAX IMPLICATIONS Self-employment entails both tax advantages and disadvantages. In terms of advantages, individuals who are classified as independent contractors can deduct work-related expenses for tax purposes. In addition, independent contractors often qualify for tax deductions for using part of their home as an office and for salaries paid to other people, while employees usually do not. Independent contractors also can claim significant deductions for medical insurance, transportation, office supplies, and a host of other operating costs.

The main tax disadvantage for self-employed persons is that they must pay the full amount of Social Security and Medicare taxes themselves and make quarterly estimated tax payments to the federal government. For those who are organizationally employed, the employer withholds income taxes and pays half of their Social Security and Medicare taxes.

Although the payment of Social Security and Medicare increases the tax burden of self-employed individuals, these amounts are based on net, rather than gross, earnings. For this reason, it is essential for small business owners to keep an accurate record of expenses. Self-employed individuals also file quarterly taxes.

INCREASING THE CHANCE OF SUCCESS IN SELF-EMPLOYMENT

Self-employment, whether by choice or necessity, does not include any guarantee of success. In fact, nearly two out of every three new businesses fail within five years. But the chances of success can be greatly improved with careful planning, prior savings, and a sound marketing strategy. It may also be helpful to make the transition to full-time self-employment gradually. One option is to ''moonlight,'' or work part-time as a free-lancer while maintaining at least part-time employment on the side. Although some employers frown on this arrangement, it can provide an individual with time and money to develop a client base and a business plan. Those planning home-based businesses should also take time to prepare family members for the changes that will take place.

Some prospective new business owners also try to establish one stable client relationship that will provide steady income during the search for additional clients. A particularly attractive option may be an individual's former employer, which will already be familiar with the would-be entrepreneur's reputation and abilities. For this relationship to succeed, however, it is important that the individual use an honest and professional approach when severing ties with their employer. Of course, your employer may not react warmly to such an arrangement if your new business is a potential threat to its own financial fortunes.

Although one stable client relationship can help establish a new business, it is also important that the self-employed person develop a marketing strategy to find new clients and grow. Many new business owners become so busy serving their existing clients that they do not devote sufficient time to marketing. Sending out brochures, networking, and joining professional organizations are a few possible marketing strategies.

Finally, self-employed individuals should take an organized approach to all business activities in order to increase their chances of success. It may be helpful to draw up a business plan to follow when starting and growing a new business. This plan can help a self-employed person evaluate strategies, plan expenditures, and motivate him or herself. It is also important to keep careful records of income and expenses, set aside money for taxes, and insist upon contracts for all work performed.

FURTHER READING:

Bianchi, Alessandra. ''New Businesses.'' *Inc.* May 1993.

Edwards, Colin C. ''A Career in Contracting . . . Is It a Viable Alternative?'' *Management Services.* March 1992.

Eliason, Carol. *The Business Plan for Homebased Business.* U.S. Small Business Administration, 1991.

Ellis, Barbara. ''Tips for the Self-Employed Professional.'' *Accountancy.* January 1994.

Gutloff, Karen. ''Freelance!'' *Black Enterprise.* June 1997.

Hand, Larry E. *Freelancing Made Simple.* Doubleday, 1995.

McCarroll, Thomas. ''Starting Over.'' *Time.* January 6, 1992.

McGrath, Rita Gunther, and Ian MacMillan. *The Entrepreneurial Mindset.* Harvard Business School Press, 2000.

Murphy, Anne. ''Do-It-Yourself Job Creation.'' *Inc.* January 1994.

Nelton, Sharon. ''Putting Women into Business.'' *Nation's Business.* October 1992.

Oliver, Suzanne. ''Moonlighter's Delight.'' *Forbes.* June 21, 1993.

Robinson, Peter B., and Edwin A. Sexton. ''The Effect of Education and Experience on Self-Employment Success.'' *Journal of Business Venturing.* March 1994.

Steinhauer, Jennifer. ''Entrepreneurs' Golden Age Turns Out to be Mythology.'' *New York Times.* December 1, 2000.

SELF-EMPLOYMENT CONTRIBUTIONS ACT (SECA)

The Self-Employment Contributions Act (SECA) of 1954 is a tax law that requires the owners of small businesses—such as S corporations, partnerships, and sole proprietorships—to pay a tax of 15.3 percent of their net income from self-employment to cover their own Social Security, Medicare, and Old Age Survivors and Disability Insurance (OASDI) costs. Workers who are employed by a company or another person (rather than being self-employed) only have to pay half this amount, which is withheld from their paychecks. Their employer pays the other half. In effect, SECA requires self-employed persons to pay both the employer and employee portions of the Federal Insurance Contributions Act (FICA) tax (a combination of Social Security and Medicare). To make this situation more equitable, small business owners subject to SECA are allowed to deduct half of their SECA tax amount on their personal federal tax returns.

SECA taxes are computed on the basis of net earnings from self-employment. Net earnings are defined as the gross income derived from business activities, less the expenses incurred in the course of doing business. In this way, ordinary business expenses reduce the SECA tax paid by individuals. But some other expenses, such as the cost of contributions to Keogh or Simplified Employee Pension (SEP) retirement plans, are not deductible for the purposes of

SECA taxes. As a result, SECA makes it more expensive for the owner of a business to fund his or her own retirement plan than to fund the same plan for employees, because a larger percentage of employee contributions are tax deductible. After computing net earnings from self-employment, the business owner then applies a 15.3 percent rate (based on two separate rates for Social Security and Medicare) on income up to $60,600. A lower rate is applied to higher income amounts.

The application of SECA to various types of small business enterprises came under dispute in the late 1990s. ''Self-employment tax is just another area where the complexity of the tax law yields no easy solution,'' Jack Robinson noted in *Outlook*. One issue involved professional activities that were not classified as trades or businesses, and thus were not subject to self-employment tax. As Robinson explained, ''Carrying on a trade or business requires regularity of activities, frequency of transactions, and the production of income.'' Another issue involved people who were wrongly classified as independent contractors when the employer's level of control over their work actually made them employees. Finally, a number of questions existed regarding the application of self-employment taxes to members of limited liability corporations (LLCs). Members of non-professional service LLCs who are considered limited partners—meaning that they do not have personal liability for the company's debts, do not have the authority to enter contracts on behalf of the company, and do not participate in the company's trade for more than 500 hours during the tax year—are not subject to self-employment tax.

In general, SECA is believed to adversely affect the small business sector of the American economy. Many political leaders have indicated that they feel small businesses hold the key to employment and economic growth. But legislation increased the SECA rate significantly during the 1980s. Prior to 1984, the SECA rate was set at 50 percent of the regular FICA rate and 75 percent of the regular OASDI rate, giving self-employed individuals tax advantages similar to those enjoyed by individuals employed by others. But between 1984 and 1990, the SECA rate was increased to 100 percent of FICA. Since FICA rates were already increasing due to double-digit inflation at that time, SECA rates had to rise even more quickly to catch up. This increase reduced the after-tax earnings of small firms and thus the availability of capital for small business expansion. As John Brozovsky and A. J. Cataldo II wrote in *Management Accounting,* ''the small firm is taxed at higher rates on larger amounts, further hindering its efforts to expand facilities, increase employment, and provide economic stimulus.''

FURTHER READING:

Brozovsky, John, and A.J. Cataldo II. ''Inflation Indexing and Small Business.'' *Management Accounting.* November 1993.

Evanson, David R. ''Spare No Expense.'' *Entrepreneur.* August 1996.

Heatley, Warren. ''New Equipment Leasing LLCs May Avoid SE Tax.'' *Tax Adviser.* February 1999.

Nadel, Alan A. ''Self-Employment Tax Treatment of Keogh and SEP Contributions and Unreimbursed Business Expenses.'' *The Tax Adviser.* November 1995.

Phillips, Bernie. ''Self-Employment Tax Treatment of LLC Members.'' *National Public Accountant.* January-February 1999.

Raby, Burgess J.W., and William L. Raby. ''Partners, LLC Members and SE Tax.'' *Tax Notes.* May 1, 2000.

Robinson, Jack. ''Are You Filing Too Many Schedule Cs?'' *Outlook.* Winter 1999.

SELLING A BUSINESS

Many small business owners eventually decide to sell their companies, though the reasons for such divestments vary widely from individual to individual. Some owners may simply wish to retire, while others are impatient to investigate new challenges—whether in business or some other area—or tired of the frustrations of the business in which they find themselves. Others decide to sell for reasons more closely associated with the health of the business itself; disputes with partners, incapacitation or death of principals, or downturns in the company's financial performance can all spur business owners to ponder putting their business on the block. Whatever their ultimate reason for selling, though, business owners can get the most out of their company by carefully considering a number of factors.

TIMING THE SALE OF A BUSINESS

''External economic forces, together with internal financial performance, will dictate when you should put your company on the market so as to achieve the maximum results,'' wrote Lawrence W. Tuller in his book *Getting Out: A Step-by-Step Guide to Selling a Business or Professional Practice.* ''If the timing isn't right, it will take much longer to sell the business, and the price you negotiate will inevitably be less than you should get.''

The financial performance and history of the company in question is often the most important factor in determining price at the time of sale. A business owner who chooses to sell after posting several years of steady growth will naturally command a higher price than will the business owner who decides to sell only a year or two into that growth trend, even if the environment continues to appear friendly to the business for the foreseeable future.

The business environment in which the company operates is also an important factor in determining the asking price that the market will bear. If the company in question operates in an industry that is suffering through a downturn, the owner should delay selling the business if at all possible. Few companies are able to buck the tide when the industry in which they operate is stuck in a sluggish cycle, and even attractive businesses will not shine as brightly during such periods. For most business owners looking to sell their company, it is usually wise to ride out the trough and put the company up for sale after the industry enters a more robust cycle. Of course, some industries never post a recovery; business owners engaged in underperforming industries need to determine whether the downturns they experience are simply an inevitable part of the business cycle within a basically healthy industry, or whether changes in the marketplace are fundamentally altering the strength of the industry (establishments as varied as roller rinks and hat manufacturers have been relegated to the fringes of the American economy by the ever-changing tastes of U.S. consumers).

The stock market is a third factor that should be analyzed when pondering whether to put a company up for sale. "Stock market averages and trends reflect not only the current health of the national economy, but the projected conditions for the near future," pointed out Tuller. "Major corporate decisions for capital appropriations, expansion or contraction moves, and new product and service introductions are strongly influenced by the perceived well being of the economy. In turn, the magnitude of these corporate decisions affect investor confidence in the stock market. . . . The price an entrepreneur can get for his company will be heavily influenced by public investor attitudes."

STOCK SALES AND ASSET SALES

Another decision that some business owners need to make early in the selling process is whether to hand over the company through a stock sale or an asset sale. If a business has been incorporated, the owner has the option of making a stock sale or an asset sale. Under the terms of a stock sale, the seller receives an agreed-upon price for his or her shares in the company, and after ownership of those stocks has been transferred, the buyer steps in and operates the still-running business. Typically, such a purchase means that the buyer receives not only all company assets, but all company liabilities as well. This arrangement is often appealing to the seller because of its tax advantages. The sale of stock qualifies as a capital gain, and it enables the seller to avoid double taxation, since sale proceeds flow directly to the seller without passing through the corporation. In addition, a stock sale frees the seller from any future legal action that might be leveled against the company. Lawsuits and claims against the company become the sole responsibility of the new stock owner(s).

Partnerships and sole proprietorships, meanwhile, must change hands via asset sale arrangements, since stocks are not a part of the picture. Under asset sale agreements, the seller hands over business equipment, inventory, trademarks and patents, trade names, "goodwill," and other assets for an agreed-upon price. The seller then uses the money to pay off any debts; the remainder is his or her profit. Changes in ownership accomplished through asset transactions are generally favored by buyers for two reasons. First, the transaction sometimes allows the buyer to claim larger depreciation deductions on his or her taxes. Second, an asset sale provides the buyer with greater protection from unknown or undisclosed liabilities—such as lawsuits or problems with income taxes or payroll withholding taxes—incurred by the previous owner.

PREPARING TO SELL

When preparing to sell a business, owners need to gather a wide variety of information for potential buyers to review. Financial, legal, marketing, and operations information all need to be prepared for examination.

FINANCIAL INFORMATION Most privately held businesses are operated in ways that serve to minimize the seller's tax liability. As John A. Johansen observed in the SBA brochure *How to Buy or Sell a Business,* however, "the same operating techniques and accounting practices that minimize tax liability also minimize the value of a business. . . . It is possible to reconstruct financial statements to reflect the actual operating performance of the business, [but] this process may also put the owner in a position of having to pay back income taxes and penalties. Therefore, plans to sell a business should be made years in advance of the actual sale." Such a period of time allows the owner to make the accounting changes that will put his or her business in the best financial light. Certainly, a business venture that can point to several years of optimum fiscal success is apt to receive more inquiries than a business whose accounting practices—while quite sensible in terms of creating a favorable tax environment for the owner—blunt those bottom line financial numbers.

Would-be business sellers also need to prepare financial statements and other documents for potential buyers to review. These include a complete balance sheet (with detailed information on accounts receivable and payable, inventory, real estate, machinery and other equipment, liabilities, marketable securities, and schedules of notes payable and mortgages payable), an income statement, and a valuation report. The latter is an appraisal of the business's market value.

LEGAL INFORMATION The seller should also prepare the necessary information on legal issues pertaining to the company. These range from such basic operating documents as articles of incorporation, bylaws, partnership agreements, supplier agreements, and franchise agreements to data on regulatory requirements (and whether they are being adhered to), current or pending legal actions against the company, zoning requirements, lease terms, and stock status.

MARKETING INFORMATION Intelligent buyers will want detailed marketing information on the company as well, including data on the business's chief market area, its market share, and marketing expenditures (on advertising, consultants, etc.). In addition, product line information will also be expected. Buyers, for instance, will want to know whether any of the company's products are proprietary, or whether there are potentially valuable new goods in the production pipeline. Descriptions of pricing strategies, customer demographics, and competition should also be available for potential buyers to review.

OPERATIONS INFORMATION Finally, business owners looking to sell their company should be prepared to provide detailed information on various aspects of the business's day-to-day operations. The "operations" umbrella encompasses everything from company policies to historical hours of operation to personnel listings, including organizational charts (if applicable), job descriptions, rates of pay, and benefits. Other factors that can potentially impact one or more aspects of the company's operations, such as the presence or absence of an employee union, will also have to be detailed.

Once information on all facets of the business has been gathered, it should be organized into a comprehensive business presentation package. A complete business presentation package, remarked Johansen, should include the following:

- History of the business

- Description of business operations

- Description of physical facilities

- Discussion of suppliers (if any) and agreements with those suppliers

- Review of current and historical marketing practices

- Description of competition

- Coverage of personnel and employee issues

- Identification of owners

- Description of insurance coverage for business

- Discussion of pending legal issues or contingent liabilities

- Financial statements for the past three to five years

LOCATING PROSPECTIVE BUYERS

Most business owners sell their companies to external buyers—buyers who are not current partners or employees in the organization. There are three primary routes that sellers can take to notify these buyers of the availability of their companies: print advertising, industry sources, and intermediaries.

Many people hoping to sell their businesses make arrangements for advertisements in the Thursday edition of the *Wall Street Journal,* which produces several regional versions of its paper around the country. The *Journal* is a particularly popular option for owners of large, privately held businesses. Owners of smaller businesses, meanwhile, often turn to the classified sections of their own local newspapers to advertise the availability of their company for acquisition. When submitting a "business opportunity" advertisement for publication in the newspaper, however, sellers need to take a sensible approach. "There is a delicate balance to be struck in any kind of advertising between the need for confidentiality and giving enough information to attract potential buyers," wrote Michael K. Semanik and John H. Wade in *The Complete Guide to Selling a Business.* "When your ads describe too much, competitors and others can deduce who you are and find out information you don't want them to know. Give too little information and you won't attract any interest." Advertisements should provide a brief description of the type of business for sale, its primary assets (location, popularity, profitability, etc.), and a way for interested buyers to make contact. Sellers who wish to maintain some degree of anonymity while looking for a buyer may wish to arrange for a post office box rather than include their telephone number.

Industry sources also can be valuable when a business owner decides to sell his or her business. Suppliers, for instance, may know of potential buyers lurking elsewhere in the industry or community. In addition, trade associations and trade journals can be used to get the word out about a company's availability.

A third option that many sellers use is to secure the services of a business broker or merger and acquisition consultant to sell their business. Business brokers, who generally handle the sale of smaller companies (though this is by no means an absolute rule), typically charge the seller a fee of about 10% of the final purchase price. ''Business brokers are exactly what the name implies,'' wrote Tuller, ''firms that list businesses for sale, then advertise them for sale to the public. They are very similar to real estate brokers but not licensed. . . . A business broker will not usually investigate the businesses he lists but will rely entirely on data given to him by you, the Seller. Valuation of the business is usually left completely up to you, and although a reputable broker will make suggestions, he is generally either not qualified or not interested in spending much time analyzing the business to determine marketability.'' Merger and acquisition consultants, on the other hand, typically specialize in handling larger middle-market companies. ''Their coverage of the entrepreneurial market is usually very broad and they generally know, within specialized industries or regions, which larger companies are actively searching for additions to their product lines or industry groupings,'' said Tuller. Payments to ''M&A'' consultants are usually less than 10%, but this is in part because of the larger scale of the deals in which they are typically involved. In addition, many consultants ask for a monthly retainer fee. One of the benefits of securing the services of a merger and acquisition consultant is that he or she will typically provide help in preparing presentation packages, valuing businesses, and negotiating with prospective buyers.

A well chosen business broker or merger and acquisition consultant can save the seller of a business a considerable amount of time and effort. However, both groups include hucksters who prey on unwary business owners, so it is important for sellers to conduct the appropriate background research before soliciting services in these areas.

Another option sometimes available to business owners is to sell their company to ''internal'' buyers—employees, business partners, or family members. Selling to employees through employee stock ownership plans (ESOPs) or other arrangements are particularly attractive for business owners because they accrue significant tax advantages through such sales. Employees interested in assuming ownership of the company via a management buyout (MBO) could range from a single key employee, such as a general manager who already has a good grasp on many aspects of the enterprise, to a group of employees (or even all of the company's employees). ''This is fertile territory,'' claimed Tuller. ''Most employees yearn to have their own business. All employees are concerned about someone else buying the company and either being fired, or not being able to work for the new boss.'' Employee convictions that they could improve on the owner's performance often play a part as well. Finally, noted Tuller, ''when it comes time to finance the sale, bankers will bend over backwards to assist a [management buyout], although they might not be interested at all in an outside buyer.'' MBOs that rely on external financing, however, typically require that one or members of the purchasing group have management training in all aspects of the business; if such expertise is lacking, the seller will need to implement a training schedule for one or more employees to fulfill this requirement.

Business partners, meanwhile, are often ideal business buyers when an owner is ready to get out. Indeed, many business owners—especially in professional practices—bring in partners for this express purpose. The advantages of selling to a partner are numerous: the need to search for a buyer—or to use an intermediary—is obviated; terms of payment are often easier to arrange; and the business transition is eased because of the familiarity that already exists between the partner and the enterprise's suppliers, clients, and customers. Small business owners looking to hand over the reins of a company to a partner, however, need to adequately prepare for such a step. Locating a suitable partner, structuring a partnership buyout, and financing a partnership buyout are all important and complex issues that require care and attention.

Finally, business owners also groom people within their organization to take over the business upon their retirement (or death or disability). Family-owned businesses often hand over the reins from generation to generation in this fashion. In many cases this transfer of ownership is made as a gift or included as part of the owner's estate.

MAKING THE SALE

Once the seller has found a buyer for his or her company, the next step is to arrange the structure of the transaction. In addition to determining whether to make a stock or asset sale (in the case of corporations), the seller and the buyer need to reach agreement on other terms of the sale as well.

EARN-OUTS An earn out is an agreement wherein the seller takes a portion of the selling price each year for a fixed period of time out of the earnings of the company under its new ownership. These agreements are sometimes employed when a seller cannot get his or her full asking price because of buyer concerns about some aspect of the business. ''Most earn out plans are contingent on the level of profits a company earns,'' wrote Tuller. ''No profits, no payments.'' As a result, some sellers insist on minimum payment amounts. In addition, since the seller's total compensation under this arrangement depends on the company's performance during the specified earn-out period, sellers often require that they be involved in management decisions during this period. Earn-outs can be calculated as a percentage of gross profit, net profit, sales, or some other mutually agreed-upon figure. Sellers, however, need to make sure that the measurement used is fair and easily verifiable. As Semanik and Wade noted, ''profit is a very difficult word to define. A shrewd purchaser could allocate costs in such a way that profit expectations are repeatedly dashed.''

INSTALLMENT SALES Under this common arrangement, the seller of the business receives some cash, but the majority of the purchase price is received over a period of years. The down payment for small businesses may range from as little as 10 percent to as much as 40 percent or more, with the rest paid out— with interest—over a period of 3-15 years.

LEVERAGED BUYOUT A leveraged buyout or LBO is the purchase of a company through a loan secured by using the assets of the business as collateral. This option, however, places a greater debt burden on the company than do other types of financing.

STOCK EXCHANGES In instances where a large, publicly held company is the purchaser, business owners sometimes ask to be compensated with stock in the purchasing corporation. In such cases, the seller is usually required to hold on to the stock for a certain period of time—usually two years—before he or she has the option to resell it.

Buyers sometimes insist on a noncompetition clause as well. ''The noncompete agreement is a fair clause in any sales contract,'' wrote Semanik and Wade, ''because it prevents a seller from opening across the street (or town) and winning back the customers.'' This covenant not to compete with the buyer, which can be incorporated into the purchase and sale agreement or created as a separate document, usually stipulates a market area and/or a period of time (three to five years is common) in which the seller may not open a business that would compete with the enterprise that he or she previously sold.

CLOSING THE DEAL

Once a deal has been struck between the seller and the buyer of the business, various conditions of sale often have to be addressed before the deal is closed. These include verification of financial statements, transfer of licenses, obtaining financing, and other conditions. Most contracts call for these conditions of sale to be addressed by a specified date; if one or more of these conditions is not taken care of by that time, the agreement is no longer valid.

Provided that these conditions have been attended to, however, the parties can move on to the closing. Closings are generally done either via an escrow settlement or via an attorney performs settlement. In an escrow settlement, the money to be deposited, the bill of sale, and other relevant documents are placed with a neutral third party known as an escrow

agent until all conditions of sale have been met. The escrow agent then distributes the held documents and funds in accordance with the terms of the contract.

In an attorney performs settlement, meanwhile, an attorney—acting on behalf of both buyer or seller, or for the buyer—draws up a contract and acts as an escrow agent until all stipulated conditions of sale have been met. Whereas escrow settlements do not require the buyer and the seller to get together to sign the final documents, attorney-performed settlements do include this step.

Several documents are required to complete the transaction between business seller and business buyer. The purchase and sale agreement is the most important of these, but other documents often used in closings include the escrow agreement; bill of sale; promissory note; security agreement; settlement sheet; financing statement; and employment agreement.

FURTHER READING:

Currie, Phillip L. ''When Time is Right, Consider Selling the Business.'' *San Diego Business Journal.* October 2, 2000.

Johansen, John A. *How to Buy or Sell a Business.* Small Business Administration, n.a.

''Selling Your Business: How to Structure and Negotiate the Best Deal.'' *The Business Owner.* January-February 2001.

Semanik, Michael K., and John H. Wade. *The Complete Guide to Selling a Business.* AMACOM, 1994.

Tuller, Lawrence W. *Getting Out: A Step-by-Step Guide to Selling a Business or Professional Practice.* Liberty Hall Press, 1990.

Yegge, Wilbur M. *A Basic Guide to Buying and Selling a Company.* John Wiley & Sons, 1996.

SEE ALSO: Business Appraisers; Valuation

SENIORITY

Seniority is defined as the length of service by an employee in a continuing or temporary job or position. In some employment situations, time in supplemental positions may be added to an employee's seniority as well. Seniority is typically an issue for human resources managers and is important in managing resources, establishing compensation methods and policies, negotiating collective bargaining agreements with labor unions, and determining individual pay in some organizations.

Seniority may be used as a tie-breaker in overtime distribution, in hiring from a previous layoff list, or as a factor in consideration for vacant positions in a company. Seniority may be used to determine pay in organizations instead of or in addition to a merit-based pay system. If organizations do not pay employees on the basis of doing the same work and holding the same level or rank in the organization, they must determine a basis to make a pay distinction or differentiation. In a large organization, compensation specialists within the human resources area may make these determinations and may consider an employee's seniority in the pay decision.

SENIORITY TODAY

According to a recent article in *Fortune*, seniority no longer matters in most companies. In the past, when employees were fired, the younger or junior members were the first to be let go. Today this situation tends to be reversed, due to changes in the world and in the work place. Even with a good economy firms no longer respect the hierarchy and may eliminate jobs held by the most senior employees. The *Fortune* article suggests that companies have less tolerance for employees who are earning in excess of their output, and this is typically a characteristic of the most senior members of an organization. Today an older employee can be replaced by someone younger earning less than half as much salary.

While seniority was valued in the past, for many people today, the longer you have been with a company, the more your job may be in jeopardy. Technology is cited as the reason for the change. Younger workers are perceived as more creative and innovative and may have more relevant educational experiences and training. Just as the product life cycle has shortened, so too has the career cycle of employees. Today job change and diversity of experiences is valued more than seniority.

SENIORITY IN JAPAN

In the past, the seniority system in organizations was a measure of job security in the employment relationship. Even in Japan, where lifetime employment has long been the norm for large, traditional businesses, many companies are abandoning these plans and no longer offering lifetime employment.

Employment practices in Japan—which were once characterized by seniority, company unions, and lifetime employment—have been undergoing a structural transformation as the nation struggles to correct current economic issues. Since the collapse of the Japanese bubble economy early in the 1990s, Japanese companies, like their American counterparts, have been forced to restructure and have adopted a system of determining promotions and salaries not on seniority but on merit. This has dramatically changed their once-treasured code of seniority, according to *Focus Japan*.

In addition, the percentage of workers belonging to labor unions has steadily dropped, eroding the influence of the once-powerful Japanese company unions. Today's younger workers and new entrants to the job market are becoming less interested in the prospect of lifetime employment. As a result, many are considering entrepreneurship and self-employment as a more viable career choice.

FURTHER READING:

''The Growing Mobility of Labor.'' *Focus Japan* (Tokyo). October 2000.

Munk, Nina. ''Finished at Forty.'' *Fortune.* February 1, 1999.

Valletta, Robert G. ''Declining Job Security.'' *Journal of Labor Economics.* October 1999.

SERVICE BUSINESSES

Service businesses are enterprises that are established and maintained for the purpose of providing services (rather than or in addition to products) to private and/or commercial customers. The American Marketing Association defined services as ''activities, benefits, or satisfactions which are offered for sale or are provided in connection with the sale of goods.''

The overall service industry is regarded as an already robust one that should enjoy considerable healthy growth rates in the future as the United States and other nations continue to move from manufacturing-based economies to technologically advanced service economies. ''The service sector is a most attractive arena for the aspiring entrepreneur,'' confirmed Irving Burstiner in *Start & Run Your Own Profitable Service Business.* ''Many service enterprises can be launched with far less money than the amount of capital typically needed to open a manufacturing, wholesale, or retail business. Many new service operators are able to begin at home, thus avoiding the expense of renting, buying, or constructing business premises. Moreover, end-of-year earnings in the service sector compare favorably with the profit margins enjoyed by most other types of enterprise.'' In addition, service businesses enjoy several other advantages over their brethren in other business areas. For one thing, they tend to be local, and they often do not have to contend with the national or international corporate giants that roam across the manufacturing, retail, and wholesale industries. Moreover, they generally do not have to make the same levels of investment in inventory, raw materials, finished goods, operations, or production management as do firms engaged in manufacturing, wholesaling, or retailing.

Of course, initial investment requirements can vary significantly from sector to sector. While some service businesses, like bookkeeping, house painting, child care, lawn care, housekeeping, and tutoring, can all be launched with a modest investment by individuals with special skills or knowledge in those areas, other service businesses require a far greater investment of money. Attorneys, doctors, and other professionals who make their living by providing their services to clients make heavy up-front expenditures (tuition), while entrepreneurs interested in launching service businesses that require extensive investments in facilities and/or equipment (hotels, laundromats, car rental agencies, nursing care facilities, medical offices, etc.) have to make big up-front expenditures of their own, albeit in different form.

FACTORS IN SERVICE INDUSTRY GROWTH

Researchers point to a number of factors that have accounted for the surge in service business start-ups over the last few decades. Many of these factors reflect fundamental changes in societal structure and character. W. F. Schoell and J. T. Ivy, authors of *Marketing: Contemporary Concepts and Practices,* cited the following as major reasons for service industry expansion in North America:

1) Increased affluence—As consumers have raised their standard of living, they have increasingly chosen to purchase services such as lawn maintenance and carpet cleaning that they previously took care of themselves.

2) Increased leisure time—Some segments of the population have been able to garner larger chunks of free time; this trend, coupled with increased wealth, has spurred a higher demand for certain service businesses such as travel agencies and resorts, adult education courses, guide services, golf courses, health clubs, etc.

3) Changing work force demographics—Over the past few decades, increasing numbers of women have entered the work force. This has spurred greater demand for services in such realms as child care, housekeeping, drycleaning, etc.

4) Greater life expectancy—Another development that has had a particular impact on certain service sectors, particularly in the health care industries.

5) Increased complexity of products/technological advancement—High-tech products have created a corresponding increase in demand for specialists who can fix and maintain those products (computers, cars, electronic equipment, etc.).

6) Increased complexity of life—Many service sectors have enjoyed tremendous growth because of their orientation toward helping individuals and businesses stay on top of the many facets of today's fast-paced society. Tax preparers, psychiatrists and counselors, and legal advisors are good examples.

7) Increased environmental awareness—General trends toward increased ecological sensitivity and enlightened natural resource management practices have spurred growth in environmental service sectors (waste management, recycling, environmental advocacy).

8) Increased number of available products—Technological advances have spurred development of service industries in such areas as programming.

TYPES OF SERVICE INDUSTRIES

Following is a representative listing of service businesses in a range of commercial sectors that could conceivably be launched by an enterprising entrepreneur:

- Professional services (physicians, pharmacists, dentists, attorneys, architects, civil engineers)

- Business services (advertising, financial planning, mailing services, computer and data processing, consulting, training, recruiting)

- Counseling services (marriage, weight loss, career planning, pastoral, psychiatric)

- Transportation services (trucking, busing, taxicab service, limousine service, car rental)

- Personal services (pet grooming, health clubs, catering, beauticians, barbers, hairdressers, tailors and seamstresses, photography studios, realtors, funeral parlors, wedding planning)

- Restaurants and lodging (diners, family restaurants, taverns, hotels, cottages)

- Social services (individual and family services, child day care, residential care)

- Maintenance services (landscaping, plumbing and electrical, appliance, equipment, automobile, bicycle)

In addition, many service-oriented businesses are, by their very nature, slanted toward meeting the needs of one of two markets: individual consumers or other businesses/organizations. Of course, some service establishments, like carpet cleaning companies, can market their services to both client categories. But the majority of service businesses place their emphasis on meeting the needs of one market segment or the other. For example, a pet grooming establishment will not waste its advertising dollars trying to reach other businesses; its primary clients are going to be individual consumers simply because of the nature of the services they offer. Conversely, the primary target of a company that provides security personnel is going to be commercial establishments. Entrepreneurs that hope to market their services primarily to organizations rather than individuals should note that, on the whole, such businesses require greater capital investment at the outset.

KEYS TO SERVICE BUSINESS SUCCESS

"Service supplier skill should be distinguished on at least two levels," wrote Glenn Bassett, author of *Operations Management for Service Industries.* "The first is the technical product/service knowledge level. The service giver is expected to know the offering in depth and detail so that information about its utility and application can be provided on demand. He or she must also be technically competent to deliver the service expected, adapting as needed to varied or changing customer need. The second level of skill pertains to customer relationship. Here it is often as simple as whether the service-giver treats the customer as an object to be controlled and used, or as a unique, important individual to be served."

Entrepreneurs engaged in service businesses also need to recognize how service marketing differs from product marketing. "Service marketing," said Burstiner, "can be far more challenging than the marketing of products because of these three distinctive characteristics of service offerings: 1) Services are intangible; 2) Services are perishable; 3) Services cannot be separated from the service providers." Finally, service businesses need to consider the way in which they distribute their services. Most service businesses can be grouped according to the methodology with which they deliver their services. In other words, does the company bring its service to the customer, or does the customer go to the firm to receive the service? "In some cases," wrote Bateman and Zeithaml in *Management: Function and Strategy,* "there is no choice. The plumber or house painter has to go to the work. Conversely, the customer goes to the restaurant, and the patient has to go to the hospital for the operation. Some services have options. Either the TV repairperson can go to the customer or the customer delivers the TV to the back room (the repair shop). A service that has traditionally required the customer to come to its facility has a strategic advantage in changing that tradition." Indeed, owners of service businesses should examine this facet of their business closely to look for ways of realizing an advantage over competitors. In fact, customer convenience is—next to quality of service rendered—perhaps the single most important factor in securing and retaining new customers.

FURTHER READING:

Adams, Bob. *Adams Streetwise Small Business Start-Up: Your Comprehensive Guide to Starting and Managing a Business.* Adams Media, 1996.

Bateman, Thomas S., and Carl P. Zeithaml. *Management: Function and Strategy.* Richard D. Irwin, 1990.

Burstiner, Irving. *Start & Run Your Own Profitable Service Business.* Prentice Hall, 1993.

Crandall, Rick. *Marketing Your Services: For People Who Hate to Sell.* Contemporary Books, 1996.

Gronroos, Christian. *Service Management and Marketing: Managing the Moments of Truth in Service Competition.* D.C. Heath, 1990.

Lidsky, David. "Death of a Local Dream: Why the Web Has Failed Service Businesses." *FSB.* March 1, 2001.

SERVICE CORPS OF RETIRED EXECUTIVES (SCORE)

The Service Corps of Retired Executives (SCORE) is a national non-profit organization that counsels business owners and aspiring entrepreneurs. There are 389 SCORE chapters throughout the United States offering counseling services to small businesses in all areas at no charge to the client. There is no membership requirement to receive SCORE counseling—a phone call to make an appointment with a local SCORE chapter is sufficient to put the small business owner in touch with this valuable organization.

HISTORY SCORE was founded in 1964 specifically to provide business counseling to entrepreneurs. A national non-profit organization, SCORE is funded primarily by the U.S. Small Business Administration (founded in 1953). The group is made up of more than 13,000 active and retired business executives familiar with all areas of business management. This group donates their services, conducting one-to-one counseling, team counseling, and training sessions. It now provides assistance to an estimated 300,000 would-be entrepreneurs and business owners annually, and in 2000 it counseled 377,000 small businesses.

MISSION AND PROGRAMS According to SCORE, volunteers "serve as 'Counselors to America's Small Business.'" The volunteer members of the organization are "dedicated to entrepreneur education and the formation, growth and success of small business nationwide.''

SCORE counselors provide general business advice on all aspects of business formation and management. This service is provided free of charge and in confidential fashion. Counselors may assist in anything from investigating market potential for a product or service to providing guidance on cash flow management. They may provide insight into how to start or operate a business, how to buy a business or franchise, or how to sell a business. Volunteers also review business plans, often offering suggestions before the plans are submitted to a bank for financing consideration (in one survey of SCORE offices in 14 states, 27 percent of respondents indicated they delayed or canceled plans to start their own business after talking with a SCORE counselor, usually because the meetings illuminated shortcomings in training or strategy). Finally, individual SCORE offices offer free and confidential counseling and business advice via electronic mail on the Internet. According to the organization, these e-mail counseling sessions are its fastest growing service (SCORE offices conducted 75,000 such sessions in 2000).

SCORE also holds workshops throughout the country. Workshops and seminars on specialized areas of business training such as writing business plans, inventory control, advertising, financing and international trade are available at reduced cost (usually a nominal fee of $100 or so, to cover cost of facilities and materials). For more information on this and other SCORE services, the organization maintains a web site (www.score.org) detailing its offerings.

SCORE VOLUNTEERS SCORE volunteers (more than 13,000 in 2000) are usually between the ages of 60 and 70, but there is no age limit for a volunteer. Retired executives interested in joining SCORE fill out a formal application and usually supply a resume for consideration by their local chapter. There is a 90 day probation period during which performance is monitored. To insure quality, SCORE counselors are matched to cases according to the type of business or client seeking advice and the counselor's area of specialty. SCORE is not an employment service, however. Members may give advice, but may not accept positions with client companies, nor may they direct a business owner to individuals or firms which may provide employees. SCORE's main function is to provide free advice to small businesses.

FURTHER READING:

Aglar, Robert. ''SCORE: America's Small Business Counselors Score with Professional, Confidential, No-Cost Counseling.'' *Denver Business Journal.* May 26, 2000.

Broome, Jr., J. ''SCORE's Impact on Small Firms.'' *Nation's Business.* January 1999.

Campanelli, Melissa. ''Getting Good Advice.'' *Sales and Marketing Management.* March 1995.

Lindo, David K. ''Help Wanted: Part-time Manager.'' *Office Systems.* December 1994.

Watts, Christina F. ''SCORE Points to Success.'' *Black Enterprise.* January 1995.

SEXUAL HARASSMENT

Sexual harassment is a term used to describe a variety of illegal discriminatory actions—from unwelcome sexual advances to verbal conduct of a sexual nature—that create a hostile or abusive work environment. The Equal Employment Opportunity Commission (EEOC) defines sexual harassment as follows: ''Unwelcome sexual advances, requests for sexual favors, and other verbal or physical contact of a sexual nature constitute sexual harassment when: 1) Submission to such conduct is made either explicitly or implicitly a term or condition of an individual's employment. 2) Submission to or rejection of such conduct by an individual is used as the basis for employment decisions affecting such individuals. 3) Such conduct has the purpose or effect of unreasonably interfering with an individual's work performance or creating an intimidating, hostile, or offensive working environment.'' But legal experts warn managers and business owners that definitions of sexual harassment extend beyond the above borders. ''Most people think that sexual harassment necessarily involves conduct of a sexual nature,'' wrote Theresa Donahue Egler in *HRMagazine*. ''But sexual harassment includes conduct that is not overtly sexual but is directed at an individual based on his or her gender. Thus, conduct such as profanity and other rude behavior . . . may give rise to liability so long as it is based on gender.''

Some observers believe that small businesses are particularly susceptible to sexual harassment problems. ''Small businesses are especially vulnerable because the informal office atmosphere may seem to allow sexual banter and innuendos, and a small business is less likely to have an official sexual harassment policy and training program,'' wrote Steven C. Bahls and Jane Easter Bahls in *Entrepreneur*. Savvy small business owners, then, will adopt a proactive stance to make certain that his or her employees know that inappropriate behavior—whether it takes the form of displaying sexually explicit photographs, using offensive language, making suggestive or otherwise inappropriate comments, badgering an employee for dates or other interactions outside the workplace, or suggesting that one gender is inferior to another—will not be tolerated in their company. Indeed, firms that do not do so leave themselves open to financial loss via lawsuits as well as other problems (low morale, employee turnover, absenteeism, etc.) that can ultimately impact financial performance. As EEOC guidelines state, ''with respect to conduct between fellow employees, an employer is responsible for acts of sexual harassment in the workplace where the employer (or its agents or supervisory employees) knows or should have known of the conduct, unless it can show that it took immediate and appropriate corrective action.''

''The stakes are high and getting higher,'' concluded Ellen J. Wagner in *Sexual Harassment in the Workplace*. ''In an increasingly litigious society and in an era of ever-increasing employee rights and employer responsibilities, sexual harassment allegations are particularly hazardous.'' *Nation's Business* contributors Robert T. Gray and Donald H. Weiss agreed. ''All the signs point to sexual harassment becoming a more complex issue in the courts as well as in the workplace, and employers must be ready to respond accordingly,'' they wrote. ''While that response can be prolonged and even difficult, the experts say that the depth of a company's commitment to preventing such conduct can be determined by one step at the moment of the filing of a complaint. That step: Take it seriously.''

HARASSMENT AND EMPLOYEE RIGHTS

Over the past several years, sexual harassment has become a subject of considerable discussion. Previous generations of business owners and managers rarely had to address the issue. Business historians and social observers point to several possible factors for this. Some note that women used to comprise a much smaller component of the workforce, and that various societal pressures may have made them less likely to come forward with complaints. Others point out that many of the legal protections that are now in place against harassment have only developed over the last 30 years. Still other observers contend that the rise in sexual harassment claims simply reflects a general decline in civility in American society. Whatever the reasons, sexual harassment complaints have risen steadily in recent years. In fact, the EEOC reported that from 1990 to 1994, the number of sexual harassment cases that were filed in the United States more than doubled. ''Because an agency complaint is a prerequisite to suit under federal and many state laws, these numbers forecast a corresponding increase in sexual harassment lawsuits in the coming years,'' wrote Egler. ''When it is considered that many more potentially explosive situations are quietly resolved (some at substantial cost) before reaching the complaint stage, it is readily apparent that sexual harassment is a risk that requires proactive management.''

But small business owners and corporate executives alike need to make sure that in their zeal to protect the legitimate rights of employees not to be harassed in the workplace, they do not trample on the rights of those accused of misbehavior. ''While sexual harassment is clearly a pervasive reality, every case needs to be reviewed on its own merit,'' said Wagner. ''Just because harassment is a significant social and corporate problem does not mean it has in fact occurred in a particular instance.'' Indeed, an employee who is punished or dismissed on the basis of a frivolous sexual harassment claim has the same recourse to the law as the victim of sexual harassment who is left unprotected by indifferent managers/owners. Business owners and managers thus need to consider the rights of all parties involved when investigating sexual harassment complaints.

CHANGING DEMOGRAPHICS OF SEXUAL HARASSMENT VICTIMS

Over the past several years, human resource professionals and business consultants alike have pointed to some fundamental changes in sexual harassment demographics. The overwhelming number of employees who are victims of sexual harassment continue to be women, but increasing numbers of men have found themselves targeted as well. Same-sex harassment charges have been on the rise as well. Observers note that some companies have been slow to treat such complaints as seriously as the more prevalent woman-as-victim, man-as-harasser complaints, with sometimes disastrous financial consequences for the businesses.

Some analysts expect women-as-harasser complaints to continue to rise, as the number of women business owners and executives grows. ''Many would say that sexual harassment is nothing but an issue of power—that is, one person exercising power over another and using sex as the tool of power,'' attorney Gary Oberstein told *Industry Week*'s Michael Verespej. ''[Women are now] in a position to see this as a tool, just as men have seen it as a tool for years.'' Verespej points out, however, that the nature of sexual harassment does seem to vary with the gender of the harasser. ''When a male is the victim of harassment by a female, more than 50% of the cases allege a demand for sex—quid pro quo—in order to retain a job or receive a promotion,'' he reported. ''By contrast, less than 15% of the cases in which a female is the victim of harassment by a male is there a demand for sex; the majority allege a hostile work environment.''

DEVELOPING AND MAINTAINING SEXUAL HARASSMENT POLICIES

Ellen Wagner points out in *Sexual Harassment in the Workplace* that "a well-drafted, carefully thought-out policy statement on sexual harassment can be valuable to an organization in at least three major ways: 1) as an employee relations tool, 2) as basic education for both managers and employees on the subject of sexual harassment, and 3) as a way of minimizing legal liability to the organization in hostile-environment sexual harassment cases. . . . Not only is such a policy statement evidence of an organization's good-faith effort to provide a work environment free of harassment but, coupled with a proper investigation that successfully ends illegal or inappropriate conduct, it provides a major offensive weapon in employer efforts to demonstrate that all reasonable steps were taken and that they were effective."

Indeed, business consultants universally counsel both small businesses and multinational corporations to establish formal written policies that make it explicitly clear that no forms of sexual harassment will be tolerated. Some companies prefer to disseminate this information as part of their larger general policy statements because of their sensitivity to giving extra attention to a sometimes awkward subject. But others believe that doing so can have the effect of burying the company's sexual harassment policies under the weight of all its other statements. These observers claim that dissemination of a separate policy statement not only better informs employees of the policy itself, but also underlines the company's serious approach to the subject.

Whether a business chooses to distribute its policies on sexual harassment via general information sources (employee handbook) or separate statements, its policies should list all the various forms that sexual harassment can take (sexually loaded "compliments," sexual advances, denigration of a person's gender, etc.) and explain how the company proceeds when confronted with a sexual harassment complaint. The policy statement should also discuss possible disciplinary consequences for workers who are found guilty of engaging in harassment.

Other steps that businesses can take to establish an harassment-free workplace include: establishing internal procedures that address complaints promptly and thoroughly; establishing training programs that educate workers—and especially managers, supervisors, and other people wielding power—about components of sexual harassment and their responsibilities when exposed to such behavior; establishing alternative routes for workers to lodge complaints (in instances where his or her supervisor is the alleged harasser, for instance).

BUILDING A COMPREHENSIVE POLICY

Legal experts warn businesses that they need to make certain that their policies reflect a true understanding of the legal responsibilities of the employer, and a full recognition of the multitude of forms that sexual harassment can take. They point out that some companies have put together policies that, while sensible and effective in some or even most areas, are flawed in other areas, either because their policies did not adequately cover all the ways in which sexual harassment can occur, or because their understanding of sexual harassment was incomplete from the outset. For example, many people have long operated under the misconception that for sexual harassment to occur, the harasser must have a bad intent. The reality, however, is that "what may be viewed as perfectly harmless by most men, may be viewed as offensive by most women," wrote Egler. "In recognition of gender differences in perception, the courts have developed a new standard for analyzing claims of sexual harassment. In lieu of the traditional gender-neutral reasonable person standard, which is thought to be biased toward the male viewpoint, sexual harassment claims are analyzed in many jurisdictions from the perspective of a reasonable person of the same sex."

Another important factor that is not always sufficiently appreciated by employers is that they can be held liable for harassing conduct by a third party such as a customer or vendor. Egler explained that "even though these people are not employed by, and thus, not under the direction and control of the employer, the employer can be held responsible for harassment of its employees by such third parties." This mostly occurs in instances where the employer does not respond to such situations when they are brought to their attention. Finally, Egler pointed out that some companies have been slow to recognize that "what appears to be a consensual relationship by both parties may be regarded by the subordinate as an unwelcome obligation necessary for the protection of his or her job, whether or not this is actually the case."

INVESTIGATING SEXUAL HARASSMENT COMPLAINTS

Companies must investigate every sexual harassment complaint seriously and thoroughly, and take action accordingly. A key foundation of this process is to make certain that the person who will investigate the complaint has credibility with the workforce. Ideally, the individual will be knowledgeable about the legal dimensions of sexual harassments, experienced in handling employee issues, familiar with the organization's policies, and socially and organizationally distant from both the alleged victim and the alleged harasser (the investigator should not be friends with the alleged victim, nor directly report to the alleged harasser, or vice versa). With smaller companies, however, it can be more difficult to adhere to such guidelines. If a small business owner has only four employees, and two of them become embroiled in an harassment case, finding an investigator with the above qualities is next to impossible. The owner may be tempted to look into the complaint him or herself in such instances, but business advisors often counsel against this. Instead, they recommend that the owner turn to an outside counsel or external consultant to pursue the complaint.

Whether the person doing the investigating is a third party, an employee, or the owner of the business, he or she should have a focused, carefully thought out investigation plan designed to settle the issue in as timely a fashion as possible. This typically includes a review of relevant organizational records, including complainant's personnel file, alleged harasser's personnel file, performance reviews, and promotional and salary records. Such reviews can turn up everything from prior disciplinary warnings aimed at the accused to possibly relevant indications that the involved parties had previously competed against one another for promotions or other job opportunities. Such data may well be completely irrelevant to the legitimacy of the complaint, but it is the investigator's duty to check into all possible aspects of the complaint.

Every claim should be treated seriously, no matter how unusual or seemingly frivolous it might first appear, until an informed decision can be made. Conversely, an investigator should also suspend judgment on complaints that seem obviously legitimate until a thorough investigation has been completed. As Wagner remarked, "when sexual harassment is alleged, defamation is never very far away. . . . Since sexual harassment investigations almost always involve matters that might go to the heart of a person's reputation and good name, attention must be paid to minimizing the risks of defamation throughout the investigation and once it is concluded."

The first step in an investigation usually involves an in-depth interview of the complainant. Areas that should be pursued during this interview include the cultural background of the complainant (if dramatically different from that of the accused), a detailed reconstruction of the incident(s) that prompted the complaint, the context and circumstances in which it occurred, the involved parties' prior relationship (if any), the nature of the allegations against each individual in instances where incidents involved the participation of more than one person (common in hostile workplace complaints), and the complainant's expectations regarding how the alleged offender should be disciplined.

The investigation then turns to getting the accused's account of events. This step has different nuances, depending on whether the alleged harasser is a supervisor, a coworker, or a third party such as a customer, but basically this part of the investigation aims to secure the accused's perspective. In some instances, the accused may appear angry or shocked when confronted with a sexual harassment charge, so the investigator needs to allow time for the return of some measure of emotional equilibrium. When the initial reaction has subsided, wrote Wagner, the investigator should ask the worker to relate "what he believed happened during the incidents the complainant has cited. Allow him to relate his understanding of the situation through once, then return to it for specific, step-by-step review. As with the complainant, make sure the discussion is specific and detailed enough to provide the information you need to make an informed judgment later on. Note dates, times, places, circumstances, dress, words exchanged, as well as the specifics of the alleged acts." Again, issues such as prevailing work environment, prior relationships, etc. should be discussed.

Once the investigator has finished gathering information from the principal parties, he or she should then turn to possible witnesses. These could range from coworkers who were present when the alleged incident took place to those who have relevant information on either or both of the parties involved. The investigator should not be concerned with unsubstantiated rumors at this juncture; rather, he or she should concentrate on gathering factual data. This can be a very important part of the investigation, for accusations that turn into basic "he said, she said" disputes can be profoundly difficult for employers to resolve. "Immediate action may be difficult when an employer is faced with unsubstantiated accusation on one side and a categorical denial on the other," wrote Gray and Weiss. But experts point out that workplace behavior often can be corroborated by other staffers. Employers need to interview these witnesses carefully, however. "You must assess the credibility and believability of all persons corroborating some aspect of the complainant's or accused's contention," confirmed Wagner. "Consider the issue of witness motivation and the relationship between each witness and the individual whose word is being corroborated. Make sure you understand what each witness might stand to gain from the situation, as well as what genuine feelings are at work here." Witnesses also need to understand that the subject should not be discussed with coworkers or other individuals; sexual harassment charges are both serious and sensitive, and they should be regarded as such. Human resources experts also recommend that investigators not rely wholly on interviews. Ideally, the investigator should also secure written statements from all parties—

complainant, accused, and witnesses—as part of this information-gathering process.

Once the investigation into the sexual harassment complaint has been completed, corrective action (if any) needs to be implemented. When corrective action is warranted, it can range from counseling to transfer to dismissal. The key factors that usually determine the severity of the corrective action are: 1) the nature of the offense, 2) the desires of the complainant, and 3) the impact that the incident had on the workplace as a whole.

HARASSMENT OF THE SELF-EMPLOYED

Self-employed individuals who work as independent contractors enjoy fewer legal protections from sexual harassment at the hands of clients. Experts recommend that self-employed people confronted with such unpleasantness react strongly and decisively. They should make it immediately clear that the harassment (which in these situations typically takes the form of unwanted sexual advances) is unwelcome, and that they would prefer to keep their association with their client a professional one. If this line of defense does not work, the self-employed worker may wish to consult an attorney about their state's tort law, which regulates conduct between people and provides monetary damages. In addition, national women's organizations can often provide guidance and legal assistance in these matters.

FURTHER READING:

Bahls, Steven C., and Jane Easter Bahls. "Hands-Off Policy." *Entrepreneur.* July 1997.

Buhler, Patricia M. "The Manager's Role in Preventing Sexual Harassment." *Supervision.* April 1999.

Egler, Theresa Donahue. "Five Myths About Sexual Harassment." *HRMagazine.* January 1995.

"Facts About Sexual Harassment." Washington: U.S. Equal Employment Opportunity Commission, 1997.

Gray, Robert T., and Donald H. Weiss. "How to Deal with Sexual Harassment." *Nation's Business.* December 1991.

Lawlor, Julie. "Stepping Over the Line." *Sales and Marketing Management.* October 1995.

Petrocelli, William, and Barbara Kate Repa. *Sexual Harassment on the Job: What It Is and How to Stop It.* 4th ed. Nolo Press, 1998.

Risser, Rita. "Sexual Harassment Training: Truth and Consequences." *Training and Development.* August 1999.

Verespej, Michael J. "New Age Sexual Harassment: An Increasing Number of Victims are Men or Same-Gender Workers." *Industry Week.* May 15, 1995.

Wagner, Ellen J. *Sexual Harassment in the Workplace: How to Prevent, Investigate, and Resolve Problems in Your Organization.* AMACOM, 1992.

SEE ALSO: Gender Discrimination

SHARED SERVICES

Shared services is an operational philosophy that involves centralizing administrative functions that were once performed in separate divisions or locations. Services that can be shared among the various business units of a company include finance, purchasing, inventory, payroll, hiring, and information technology. For example, a central headquarters might control all the hiring for an entire chain of retail stores. The term "shared services" can also apply to partnerships formed between separate businesses. For example, the tenants of an office building might share telecommunications or maintenance service. Shared services are also available on the Internet. For example, Application Service Providers (ASPs) offer numerous business clients access to online applications so they can avoid purchasing special systems and software.

Ideally, companies that implement shared services enjoy significant cost savings by standardizing practices and procedures and by creating economies of scale. Proponents argue that performing a function in one location usually requires less investment in technology and office space, as well as up to 30 percent fewer employees, than performing the function in multiple locations. "Under shared services, a company centralizes back-office functions, such as accounting, warehousing, and even information technology, and treats them as internal vendors," Erik Sherman explained in *Computerworld.* "The rest of the company can use outside service providers instead, so competitive pressures promote responsive service, and reduced staffing saves money." In some cases, the centralized functions—or shared services organizations—charge the different divisions for the use of their services. Other shared services organizations even offer their services to outside firms on the open market.

Shared services is a popular business strategy. In fact, Elizabeth Ferrarini noted in *Computerworld* that it has been adopted by half of all Fortune 500 companies. "Centralizing company functions—in a manner now known as the 'shared services' model—is one of the hottest trends in business today," Mark Henricks wrote in *Entrepreneur.* "Those who practice it say they can cut costs while improving the quality of the services shared." The concept of shared services was introduced in the 1980s, when a number of large companies with multiple business units began looking for ways to reduce their administrative costs. Since then, Henricks noted, "Shared services has evolved into a more comprehensive and flexible tool for improving processes, enabling technology investment, generating profits, and reducing costs."

There are a number of potential drawbacks associated with shared services, however. For example, companies switching to a shared services model often incur the cost of hiring new people and installing new technology. In addition, implementing shared services takes time—often more than one year. Furthermore, as Henricks warned, centralization is not appropriate for every function. Companies should not centralize their core competencies or functions that involve direct customer contact, particularly if outside firms also use the shared services.

The implementation of shared services can also create problems within a company. For example, the employees who used to provide the services in various business units might be upset with the loss of control they experience under the new arrangement. In addition, the headquarters employees who provide shared services from a central location might be uncomfortable treating business units as customers. In fact, switching to a shared services environment requires employees to develop new skills, with an increased emphasis on flexibility and customer service. ''To be the preferred supplier—and even to have a secure corporate existence—the shared service has to cost-effectively deliver superior results,'' Sherman stated. As a result, shared services is not appropriate for every business. ''For many companies, shared services will remain an intriguing concept that just doesn't fit their needs,'' Henricks noted. ''For others, it will represent exactly the right model to take advantage of a promising opportunity to make the most of home-office skills that other divisions, locations, and even other companies can also use.''

FURTHER READING:

Ferrarini, Elizabeth. ''Shared Services.'' *Computerworld.* November 27, 2000.

Henricks, Mark. ''Learn to Share.'' *Entrepreneur.* March 2001.

Herman, Jim. ''Shared Business Services on the Net.'' *Business Communications Review.* June 2000.

Quinn, Barbara. *Shared Services: Mining for Corporate Gold.* Prentice-Hall, 2000.

Schulman, Donniel S., and Martin Hammer. *Shared Services: Adding Value to the Business Units.* John Wiley, 1999.

Sherman, Erik. ''The Shared Services Challenge: Retooling IT as an Internal Vendor to Deliver Better Service Works for Many, but It's Easy to Hit Snafus along the Way.'' *Computerworld.* August 2, 1999.

Whitehead, William T. ''Shared Services: A Business Strategy for Increasing Shareholder Value.'' *Site Selection.* July 2000.

SEE ALSO: Cost Sharing

SHOPLIFTING

Shoplifting is the practice of stealing merchandise from retail establishments. Unfortunately, shoplifting is a serious and persistent problem for most retailers. An annual National Retail Security Survey reported in *Providence Business News* found that shoplifting accounted for one-third of retail losses and cost a total of $8.5 billion in 1999. According to an article in *Pharmaceutical Technology,* 5 percent of retail customers have the potential to shoplift. Some of the most problematic are professional shoplifters, or boosters, who steal high-value items in order to resell them. Among the most commonly stolen items are tobacco products, athletic shoes, brand-name clothing, small appliances, jewelry, leather goods, and food items.

Shoplifting costs retailers a great deal of money in terms of lost inventory, increased security measures, and higher legal expenses. It also affects store location, causing stores in high-theft areas to relocate and contributing to the deterioration of urban centers. Finally, it costs consumers in terms of higher priced goods. ''The cost [of shoplifting] is very high,'' said business professor Ed Mazze in *Providence Business News.* ''It cuts into the profit margin of the retailer and is paid for by the consumer. It requires stores to invest in more complex security devices.''

PREVENTING THEFT

The first step for retailers hoping to reduce their losses to shoplifting is to create a strong antitheft policy and publicize it among customers and employees alike. In preparing a policy, it is important to note that deterring theft is usually less expensive than apprehending and prosecuting thieves. In addition, retailers must be familiar with the shoplifting laws in their states, particularly in light of recent incidents involving the assault of alleged shoplifters by store security guards. Some states require individuals to exit a store before they can be accused of shoplifting, for example. Experts suggest that small business owners consult with local police or their insurance company to obtain assistance in setting up an antitheft program.

In order to address the problem of employee theft, retailers can use integrity questionnaires and conduct reference checks when hiring new employees. In addition, software solutions exist to help retailers detect point-of-sale errors and fraud. Another way that small retailers can help prevent shoplifting is to buy merchandise from established sources. In many cases, professional shoplifters steal from major retail chains and then resell the merchandise to small, local stores. A good rule of thumb is that if you are able to buy merchandise less expensively than a big chain, then it is probably stolen merchandise.

SECURITY MEASURES

Retailers have a number of security measures available to them to help deter potential shoplifters. A good place to start is by training employees to recognize and report suspicious behavior. Visible security measures are another valuable way to deter shoplifters. Security gates in doorways, security cameras in obvious locations, and uniformed security guards patrolling the store are all strong deterrents. Many retailers choose to reduce the temptation to steal by putting items that have high theft rates behind counters or giving them electronic article surveillance (EAS) tags. These methods have drawbacks, however, because limiting customer access to items reduces sales, while applying antitheft tags to items is labor intensive.

A relatively new weapon in the fight against shoplifting is source tags. A source tag is a type of EAS tag that is applied by the manufacturer—usually inside the container or packaging—rather than by the retailer. The usage of source tags is growing, particularly in the areas of health and beauty aids and over-the-counter drugs. Some source tags can be used for both security and inventory control. In the future, the technology might even be used for tracing stolen merchandise that is resold to other stores. ''Source tagging helps us provide our valued customers with low-cost products and the perpetual inventory they are looking for,'' Tom Coughlin, CEO of Wal-Mart USA, told Hallie Forcinio in *Pharmaceutical Technology.* ''It allows us to enhance sales and focus our resources on how we can better serve our customers.''

FURTHER READING:

Forcinio, Hallie. ''Electronic Article Surveillance—Source Tag to Smart Tag.'' *Pharmaceutical Technology.* October 2000.

Guzzo, Maria. ''Security Measures.'' *Pittsburgh Business Times.* July 23, 1999.

Mavromatis, K. Alexa. '' 'Tis the Season—to Shoplift.'' *Providence Business News.* November 27, 2000.

''Protect High-Risk Items from Shoplifters.'' *Chain Store Age Executive with Shopping Center Age.* June 1998.

Weinstein, Steve. ''Loss Leaders.'' *Progressive Grocer.* September 1998.

Wilson, William. ''Being Prepared Is the Best Strategy against Shoplifters and Robbers.'' *Discount Store News.* April 3, 2000.

Sick leave and personal days are a form of time off afforded to employees who must miss work due to an illness or a personal situation. Since nearly all employees need such time off occasionally, all businesses should have a clear policy established regarding sick leave and personal days. A sick day is fairly self-explanatory and can be used for everything from a common cold to a more serious illness that could require hospitalization or even surgery. Personal days can cover things like the illness of a child, a death in the family, jury duty, military obligations, or religious holidays. Most companies also allow vacation time for employees in addition to their set amount of sick leave and personal days.

Most companies allocate only a certain number of days for sick leave and personal time. For example, in a calendar year an employee could have five sick days and three personal days. If the employee fails to use them in all in the given amount of time, the company must decide whether to allow employees to roll them over (that is, add or bank them to the number of sick days for the following year). The company could also reward the employee for not taking all available sick and personal days by offering cash bonuses, perks, or additional vacation days.

In an article for *Business First,* Dr. James D. Levy discussed employee attendance issues and described the three employee types that most businesses have to contend with. ''On average, a small portion of employees will rarely, if ever, be absent because of illness. They pride themselves on being the iron man or iron woman and prove that people can, and do fulfill their responsibilities even when they don't feel well,'' he explained. ''A second group, the great majority, will use a few sick days a year, well within most organizations' guidelines. The third group, usually only 5 percent or so, use their sick days plus most or all of their vacation time and additional lost time because of illness. It's this group that blurs the line between actual illness and the kind of 'not feeling well' that can be an excuse for poor performance or absences. Improvement in the attendance and performance of that small group would pay big dividends to organizations.''

PROBLEMS WITH SICK LEAVE AND PERSONAL DAYS

From a business standpoint, the main problem that companies face when an employee takes time off because of an illness or personal matter is the loss of production. This in turn leads to a loss of money (in most instances, an employee is paid when they take a sick or personal day). The loss of productivity occurs simply because the work that the employee was supposed to do that particular day has to be done by one or more other employees or by a temporary employee. There is also the chance that the work could not get done at all.

The existence of sick and personal days also leaves the door wide open for them to be abused by employees who are less than honest about their health or personal lives. Most everyone has played hooky by calling in sick to work at one time or another, but those who make a habit of it are costing their employers a lot of money over the long run. In addition, the other employees who have to cover for them while they are taking time off may start to build up resentment if this situation occurs over and over again with the same individuals. This dip in morale can also hurt the company over a long period of time.

WAYS TO COMBAT ABUSE OF SICK LEAVE AND PERSONAL DAYS

There are many ways employers can fight back and make sure that their employees are not abusing the sick and personal days that they have been allotted. The first step would be to examine the existing policy and determine if it encourages unscheduled absenteeism. Management and supervisors can also force themselves to become more aware of their employees' habits and be on the lookout for things like stress or specific types of lifestyles that may force an employee to take more time off. Single parents or recent divorcees would fall into this category.

In some instances, the company could consider providing counseling or other assistance to employees who suffer from problems that cause them to miss work (including alcoholism, drug abuse, and psychological problems). In addition, many employers can combat an attendance problem before it gets out of hand simply by confronting the employee and discussing the reasons why he or she has missed so much work. An official attendance record could be kept just in case the employee disputes the employer's claims. Policies requiring an employee to file a report stating why they missed work can also be helpful in these types of situations. Also, since many employees spend a lot of time in the workplace, an employer can also reduce the chances of them getting sick in the first place by promoting a clean, safe, and healthy office environment.

Another concept that many employers have found useful in cutting down on unscheduled absences is known either as a paid leave bank (PLB) or a paid time off program (PTO). This program requires employees to consider all of their vacation, sick, and personal days as one unit to be used either for PTO or serious catastrophic situations. This system forces an employee who is abusing their sick day privileges to subtract them from their vacation time or personal days if they continue to do so. Since the time that falls under the PTO plan is essentially the employee's time, they would be less likely to abuse it. This plan also helps to cut down on unscheduled absences that disrupt the workplace. On the positive side, a company is better able to control costs under this system while still allowing an employee to take additional time if something catastrophic happens to them. A reward system can also be built into this plan to encourage employees from taking unscheduled absences off.

If a company offers employment options like flextime or working at home, they also stand the chance of cutting back on unscheduled absences. With a flexible schedule, employees can rearrange their work times to attend to a personal situation like taking their child to the doctor in the morning. After their personal business is taken care of, they can still come in and put in a full day at the office and not have to use a personal day. The option to work at home can also cut down on an unscheduled absence if employees are too sick to report to work but healthy enough to perform their duties. Many such duties can be done at home with the help of a laptop or other device that is useful in telecommuting. Another benefit to this option is that other employees will stand less of a chance of coming down with an illness if the employee who is already sick just works from home.

If constant abuse of sick and personal days continue to be a problem between a company and a particular employee, more drastic measures can be taken. One tried and true method requires that the employer insist on a note from a doctor before allowing an employee who has been out for more than several days to return to work. Policies regarding raises or other rewards can also be tied directly to employees' attendance records, therefore encouraging them not to take an unscheduled absence.

In serious circumstances, an employee can be fired for taking too many days off. The employer should make sure that they have a legitimate case against the employee in this instance because many situations are covered by the Family and Medical Leave Act (FMLA) and other laws that protect employees. If an employer is found to have wrongfully terminated an employee under one of these laws, they could stand to lose a considerable amount of money in a settlement.

SICK LEAVE AND PERSONAL DAY POLICIES FOR SMALL BUSINESSES

Some small businesses do not have sick leave and personal day policies because many of their employees are paid by the hour rather than a set salary. In most cases, this discourages their employees from taking unnecessary time off, because if they do not show up for work, then they do not get paid. Time clocks or official attendance ledgers are also used to let employers know exactly how many hours a particular employee works per day so that they can be paid accordingly. Of course, things like extended illnesses, a death in the family, or religious holidays can always force an employee to miss work.

Small businesses should also be aware of possible legal entanglements that come with firing an employee who has taken more than their fair share of unscheduled absences. As Phillip M. Perry stated in *Industrial Distribution:* ''If your business is small enough that you operate as the sole supervisor, you are still open to legal problems if you don't have a written policy followed to the letter. Employees who are terminated for excessive absenteeism will sue, claiming discrimination over those employees— possibly the ones who are more vital to your business success—who are absent just as often.''

FURTHER READING:

Collis, Leighton. ''The Hidden Costs of Sniffles and Sneezes.'' *HR Magazine.* July 1997.

Kaiser, Carl P. ''What Do We Know About Employee Absence Behavior? An Interdisciplinary Interpretation.'' *The Journal of Socio-Economics.* January-February 1998.

Levy, Dr. James D. ''Employers Can Make Sick Leave Less Debilitating.'' *Business First-Columbus.* December 8, 2000.

Perry, Phillip M. ''Where's Jones? It's 9 A.M., Do You Know Where Your Employees Are?'' *Industrial Distribution.* June 1996.

SEE ALSO: Absenteeism; Employee Benefits

SIMPLIFIED EMPLOYEE PENSION (SEP) PLANS

Simplified employee pension (SEP) plans—also known as SEP/IRAs since they make use of individual retirement accounts—are pension plans intended specifically for self-employed persons and small businesses. Created by Congress and monitored by the Internal Revenue Service, SEPs are designed to give small business owners and employees the same ability to set aside money for retirement as traditional large corporate pension funds. SEP plans are available to all types of business entities, including proprietorships, partnerships, and corporations.

As employer-funded retirement plans, SEPs allow small businesses to direct at least 3 percent and up to 15 percent of each employee's annual salary into tax-deferred IRAs on a discretionary basis. SEP plans are easy to set up and inexpensive to administer, as the employer simply makes contributions to IRAs that are established by employees. The employees then take

responsibility for making investment decisions regarding their own IRAs. Employers thus avoid the risk and cost involved in accounting for employee retirement funds. In addition, employers have the flexibility to make large percentage contributions during good financial years, and to reduce contributions during hard times. Like other tax-deferred retirement plans, SEPs provide a tax break for employers and a valuable benefit for employees.

In many ways, SEPs can be more flexible and attractive than corporate pensions. They can even be used to supplement corporate pensions and 401(k) plans. Many people who are employed full-time use SEPs as a way to save and invest more money for retirement than they might normally be able to put away under IRS rules. In fact, an article in *Forbes* magazine called SEPs a ''moonlighter's delight,'' in that they enable full-time employees to contribute a portion of their self-employment income from consulting or free-lancing outside of their regular jobs.

RULES GOVERNING SEPS

The rules governing SEPs are fairly simple but are subject to frequent changes, so annual reviews of IRS publications 560 (retirement plans for the self-employed) and 590 (IRAs) are recommended. As of 2000, SEPs could be set up using a simple form (IRS Form 5305-SEP) and—unlike larger, more complicated pension plans—did not require a separate trustee. The maximum allowable tax-deductible SEP contribution per employee is 15 percent of net compensation or $30,000, whichever is lower. In general, eligibility is limited to employees 21 or older with at least three years of service to the company and a minimum level of compensation. The maximum level of compensation for SEP eligibility is $170,000.

A similar program is the Savings Incentive Match Plan for Employees (SIMPLE) IRA. SIMPLE plans became available in January 1997 to businesses with less than 100 employees, replacing the discontinued Salary Reduction Simplified Employee Pension (SARSEP) plans. They are intended to provide an easy, low-cost way for small businesses and their employees to contribute jointly to tax-deferred retirement accounts. An IRA set up as a SIMPLE account requires the employer to match up to 3 percent of an employee's annual salary, up to $6,000 per year. Employees are also allowed to contribute up to $6,000 annually to their own accounts. In this way, a SIMPLE IRA is similar to a 401(k), but it is generally less complex and has fewer administrative requirements.

Companies that establish SIMPLEs are not allowed to offer any other type of retirement plan. The main problem with the plans, according to Stephen Blakely in *Nation's Business,* was that ''Congress is already drafting legislation that would make SIMPLE less simple and more costly for the very businesses the plans were created to serve.''

OWNERS BENEFIT LESS THAN NONOWNER EMPLOYEES

A note of caution is in order. A small business owner who wants to establish a SEP—or any other qualified retirement plan—for him or herself must also include all other company employees who meet minimum participation standards. As an employer, the small business owner can establish retirement plans like any other business. As an employee, the small business owner can then make contributions to the plan he or she has established in order to set aside tax-deferred funds for retirement, like any other employee. The difference is that a small business owner must include all nonowner employees in any company-sponsored retirement plans and make equivalent contributions to their accounts. Unfortunately, this requirement has the effect of reducing the allowable contributions that the owner of a proprietorship or partnership can make on his or her own behalf.

For self-employed individuals, contributions to a retirement plan are based upon the net earnings of their business. The net earnings consist of the company's gross income less deductions for business expenses, salaries paid to nonowner employees, the employer's 50 percent of the Social Security tax, and—significantly—the employer's contribution to retirement plans on behalf of employees. Therefore, rather than receiving pre-tax contributions to the retirement account as a percentage of gross salary, like nonowner employees, the small business owner receives contributions as a smaller percentage of net earnings. Employing other people thus detracts from the owner's ability to build up a sizeable before-tax retirement account of his or her own. In the case of a SEP plan, the business owner's maximum annual contribution is reduced to 13.04 percent of income (compared to the 15 percent maximum that applies to nonowner employees), to a maximum of $25,500.

Still, a SEP plan offers significant advantages for self-employed persons and small business owners. It allows a much greater annual pre-tax contribution than a standard IRA (at $2,000 or less, depending on the individual's financial status and participation in other retirement plans). In addition, individuals can contribute to their existing IRAs and 401(k)s, and still participate in a SEP plan.

FURTHER READING:

Basi, Bart A. ''Look at SEP for Retirement Plan.'' *Supply House Times.* May 2000.

Blakely, Stephen. ''Pension Power.'' *Nation's Business.* July 1997.

Crouch, Holmes F. *Decisions When Retiring.* Allyear Tax Guides, 1995.

Lee, Mie-Yun. ''Retirement Plans Don't Have to Be Expensive.'' *Philadelphia Business Journal.* October 22, 1999.

Rowland, Mary. ''Pension Options for Small Firms.'' *Nation's Business.* March 1994.

SEE ALSO: Retirement Planning

SITE SELECTION

For many small businesses, business location is an essential component in its eventual success or failure. Site selection can be pivotal in all sorts of businesses, including retail, service, wholesale, and manufacturing efforts. In fact, studies conducted by the Small Business Administration (SBA) and other organizations indicate that poor location is one of the primary causes of business failure in America. Conversely, a good business location can be enormously beneficial to a small firm. As Fred I. Weber Jr. remarked in *Locating or Relocating Your Business,* ''sometimes a business that might otherwise be only marginal makes a good profit because of an excellent location. On the other hand, a poor location can often drag down a good business. It can affect sales adversely and help decrease the company's profit by adding to its cost.''

LOCATION NEEDS OF VARIOUS BUSINESS TYPES

Each of the above-mentioned business types—retail, service, wholesale, and manufacturing—have different site needs that need to be considered when settling upon a location for starting or relocating a business.

RETAIL BUSINESSES The success of retail establishments is often predicated to a large degree on their location. ''Real estate professionals are fond of saying that the three most important factors in choosing a business space are location, location, and location,'' wrote Fred S. Steingold in *Legal Guide for Starting and Running a Small Business.* ''For certain types of retail stores and restaurants, this may be true. For example, a sandwich shop requires a location with a high volume of foot traffic. Or maybe you'll benefit if you're near other businesses that are similar to yours; restaurants often like to locate in a restaurant district.''

Since location is so important to most retail operations, small business retailers often have to make significant expenditures to secure a good site on which to operate. Property owners that offer land or buildings or office space for lease or sale in already-thriving retail areas know that they can command a higher price because of the volume and quality of business that the location will bring to the company.

SERVICE BUSINESSES Many service-oriented businesses also need to operate in "high traffic" regions, but there are exceptions to this. Most home-based business owners, for example, package their talents in service-oriented businesses (software development, freelance writing, home improvement, etc.). Others, such as pest control services or landscaping services, secure the majority of their customers through the Yellow Pages, etc., and thus do not need to worry as much about their location (although location can become a problem because of other factors; for example, a service business that has to travel great distances to take care of the majority of its customers might consider relocating closer to its primary customer base). Still other service-oriented businesses, of course, rely to a great degree on their location. Dry cleaners, hair salons, and other businesses cannot afford to locate themselves on the outskirts of a business district. Many of their customers frequent their business precisely because of the convenience of their location; if that benefit dries up, so too do the customers.

WHOLESALE BUSINESSES Whereas the primary consideration for retailers and some service businesses is to locate themselves in high traffic areas—hence the ubiquity of such businesses in shopping centers and malls—the major location concern of wholesalers is to find a site that has good shipping and receiving facilities and close proximity to transportation routes. Zoning laws are also a consideration. Most communities maintain zoning laws that restrict where wholesalers can set up their businesses.

MANUFACTURING BUSINESSES As with wholesalers, businesses engaged in manufacturing usually have limited site location options because of local zoning laws. But manufacturers generally do not lack for options when the time comes to build or relocate a facility. Most communities have any number of sites to choose from. The key is to select the land or building that will be most beneficial to the company in the long run, taking into consideration the company's primary market, the available labor force, transportation factors, availability of raw materials, available buildings or building sites, community attitudes toward the industry, expense, and convenience of access for customers.

LOCATION OPTIONS

Small business have a number of different choices in the realm of site selection. The type of facility most often embraced by retail and many service establishments is the shopping center. The shopping center, which houses a variety of different stores (often including well-known chain stores), can take several different forms, but the best known of these is the mall. These establishments provide their tenants with large numbers of potential customers and professional marketing and maintenance services, but in return, tenants often pay high rent and additional fees (to cover maintenance costs, etc.) Many other small businesses, meanwhile, are located in smaller shopping centers that are sometimes known as strip malls or neighborhood shopping centers. These centers, which rely on a smaller customer base than their mega-mall cousins, are typically anchored by one or two large supermarkets or discount stores. The rest of the stores are usually small retail or service establishments of one type or another. The rent at strip malls is generally much less than it is at major malls, but of course, the level of traffic is generally not as high either. The small business owner who wishes to establish his or her store in a shopping center must carefully weigh the financial advantages and pitfalls of each of these options before moving forward. Other retailers or service businesses prefer to set up their businesses in freestanding locations. Restaurants, for instance, often choose to set up their business in a lone building, attracted by the lower fixed rent that often accompanies such arrangements.

Another facility option for the small business is the business park or office building. Indeed, many professionals (doctors, architects, attorneys) choose this option, attracted by the professional image that such trappings convey and the ability to share maintenance costs with other tenants. Some service businesses also operate from these facilities, especially if their primary clientele are other businesses.

OTHER FACTORS IN BUSINESS SITE SELECTION

There are myriad factors that need to be evaluated when deciding where to locate a business. Settling on a site that is both convenient and comfortable for the company's primary customers is, of course, vital, but that is only one piece of the site selection puzzle. These considerations include:

- Will projected revenues cover the total costs of leasing or purchasing the site?

- Will ancillary costs associated with business establishment or relocation (purchase and/or transportation of equipment, computer wiring requirements, etc.) be prohibitive?

- Will it be possible to secure lenders to help cover costs associated with moving into the new business site?

- Are there restrictive ordinances that will unduly interfere with business operations?

- Is the facility itself in good condition (including both exterior and interior), and does it meet layout requirements? If not, how expensive will refurbishment be?

- Are the grounds (landscaping, light fixtures, drainage, storage facilities) in good condition?

- If sharing costs of maintenance/housekeeping services, do other tenants view services favorably?

- How secure is the facility?

- Is the site large enough for your business?

- Can the site accommodate future growth?

- Are nearby business establishments successful, and are they likely to attract customers to your business?

- Are regional competitors successful?

- Does the site provide for adequate parking and access for customers?

- Might the area surrounding the facility (neighboring lots, parking facilities, buildings) undergo a dramatic change because of sale and/or construction?

- What sort of advertising expenditures (if any, in the case of malls, etc.) will be necessary?

- What sort of leasehold improvements (if any) will be necessary?

- Will customer service be interrupted by a relocation? If so, for how long?

- Will major system changes (addition or subtraction of equipment or processes) be necessary?

- What impact will the business site have on workforce needs?

- Should the choice of facility reflect changes in the industry or market in which you are operating?

- Are there any existing or proposed government regulations that could change the value of the facility?

- What is the climate as far as business taxation is concerned?

- Are important suppliers located nearby?

OWNERSHIP VS. LEASING

Whether starting up a new business or moving an already established one, small business owners are faced with the question of whether to lease or purchase the land and/or facility that they choose as the site for their company. Most small businesses operate under lease arrangements—indeed, many small business owners do not have the necessary capital to buy the facility where they will operate—but some do choose to go the purchase route, swayed by the following advantages:

- Increased sense of permanence and credibility in the marketplace

- Property taxes and interest payments are tax-deductible

- Facility improvements increase the value of the business's property rather than the landlord's property

- Increased net worth through appreciation of both the business and the facility (including land and buildings)

- No forfeiture of asset at the end of term

- Ability to liquidate (lessors often have far less freedom in this area)

Of course, there are also factors associated with ownership that either convince small business owners to stick with lease agreements or preclude ownership as a viable option.

- Risk that value of the land and/or facilities will actually go down over time because of business trends (a neighboring anchor store goes bankrupt) or regional events (a flood, massive layoffs)

- Financial risks associated with purchasing are greater, and put a greater financial drain on small establishments that often have other needs (purchasing typically requires greater initial capital investment and entails higher monthly costs)

- Property can be claimed by creditors as an asset if the business goes bankrupt

PLANNING FOR THE FUTURE

An important factor that small business owners need to consider when weighing various business location alternatives is the site's ability to address the company's future needs. ''You should keep in mind the danger of putting off relocating because you 'can't afford it now,' '' warned Weber. ''Some owner-managers find that, as time goes by and their competitive positions worsen, they can afford relocating even less. They learn the hard way that if a company stays too long in a location it can die in that location.'' Even a company that is performing satisfactorily can benefit from regular reviews of the pros and cons of its location. ''What about technological improvements?'' wrote Weber. ''Have you ever thought that, if you move, you could take advantage of the technological improvements that have come along in your industry since your present facility was built? If your facility has become a competitive liability because of such innovations, moving to another building may be the most economical way to become competitive again.''

Most business consultants counsel their clients to do two things to avoid getting stuck with an inadequate business facility and/or location: 1) plan for the future; and 2) pay attention to the tell-tale signs that are often buried in the business's balance sheet.''Facility costs are a normal everyday concern,'' wrote Wadman Daly in *Relocating Your Workplace,* ''but their relationship to other operating and overhead expenses can alter gradually in ways that, once perceived, suggest a facility change. Rent, operating expense, maintenance, taxes and insurance, etc., should be monitored as a percent of one or more preferred productivity measures to serve as a good indicator of the need for facility change.''

SOURCES TO CONSULT WHEN SELECTING A BUSINESS SITE

Local assistance in selecting a site for a new business can usually be found from a number of sources. These include local utilities, some of which have departments designed to provide help in this area; local Chambers of Commerce; banks and insurance agencies; real estate agents who specialize in commercial and industrial property; and state agencies. More informal networking with members of the local business community can also provide both leads and warnings about various regional properties.

FURTHER READING:

Ady, Robert M. ''Discussion: How to Select an Ideal Business Site.'' *New England Economic Review.* March-April 1997.

Daly, Wadman. *Relocating Your Workplace: A User's Guide to Acquiring and Preparing Business Facilities.* Crisp Publications, n.d.

Holmes, Thomas J. ''The Location of Industry: Do States' Policies Matter?'' *Regulation.* Winter 2000.

Porter, John. ''Nice Place You've Got There.'' *Grocer.* April 22, 2000.

Rappoport, James E., Robert F. Cushman, and Karen Daroff, eds. *Office Planning and Design Desk Reference.* Wiley, 1992.

Rice, Melinda. ''Picking the Spot: Firm's Location May Be Most Crucial Decision.'' *Baltimore Business Journal.* November 27, 1998.

Schriner, Jim. ''Picking Your Neighborhood.'' *Industry Week.* July 3, 1995.

Steinberg, Brian. ''Green Acres: Why Some Entrepreneurs are Saying 'Goodbye, City Life.' '' *Entrepreneur.* October 1997.

Steingold, Fred S. *Legal Guide for Starting and Running a Small Business.* 3d ed. Nolo Press, 1997.

Weber, Fred I., Jr. *Locating or Relocating Your Business.* Small Business Administration, n.d.

SEE ALSO: Relocation

SMALL BUSINESS ADMINISTRATION

The Small Business Administration (SBA), which was created in 1953, is an independent federal agency charged with aiding, counseling, and protecting the interests of American small businesses. The agency maintains a wide range of programs designed to address various aspects of this mandate. These programs, each of which seeks to assist small business owners in one or more areas of their enterprise, are maintained in the following areas: lending and investment; surety bonds; international expansion and development; disaster assistance; federal procurement contracts; minority small business assistance; veterans' assistance; research and development; business and training; and business information and counseling. The SBA also serves as an advocate for American small businesses in government.

STRUCTURE OF THE SBA

Most SBA programs and services are implemented through Small Business Administration district offices. District offices are maintained in all 50 states, as well as Washington, D.C., and Puerto Rico (some larger states, such as California, New York, and Texas, have as many as half a dozen offices). Personnel in these offices work directly with small business owners and various cooperating institutions to implement SBA programs.

These field offices report to regional offices of the SBA. In addition to their supervisory responsibilities, the regional headquarters are charged with educating small business owners, lending institutions, and others on issues that affect them; fostering regional economic development; and providing the Office of Field Operations (OFO) with information on SBA programs and small business developments at the district level. OFO is responsible for all aspects of the SBA's field operations, including communications, policy formation, and general performance. It reports directly to the SBA's chief administrator.

Collateral offices maintained by the Small Business Administration include administration; comptroller; personnel; external affairs; marketing and customer service; public communications, congressional and legislative affairs; Hearings and Appeals; Inspector General; Office of Information Resources Management (OIRM); Equal Employment Opportunity and Civil Rights Compliance; and Office of General Counsel.

Finally, the SBA maintains several departments devoted to providing advocacy services on behalf of American small business owners. The Office of Interagency Affairs oversees enforcement of the Regulatory Flexibility Act, analyzes small business issues, develops governmental policy options, and prepares testimony for use before various legislative and regulatory bodies. The Office of Economic Research oversees the SBA's research contracting program, and compiles and interprets various economic data on small businesses. The Office of Information publishes books and economic reports on small business issues, and serves as a distributor of advocacy publications and other materials. Finally, the Office of Advocacy attempts to evaluate the effect of proposed legislation and other policy issues on small businesses. The chief counsel for advocacy acts as the primary spokesperson for America's small business community and represents its views before Congress, local governments, and other agencies. The Office of Advocacy also utilizes regional advocates who work directly with local communities and small businesses, gathering information on policies and regulations that are helping and hurting small businesses and the communities in which they operate.

SMALL BUSINESS ADMINISTRATION PROGRAMS

LENDING PROGRAMS The SBA provides a number of lending options to small business owners. The best known of these is the 7(a) Loan Guaranty, but there are many others that are widely used as well. In all of these cases, the loan is actually delivered through commercial lending institutions and other intermediaries. The SBA helps secure the loans, though, by consenting to cover the cost of the loan should the borrower be unable to pay. Lending institutions value this added protection very highly.

The 7(a) Loan Guaranty Program, which was authorized by the passage of the Small Business Act, is primarily designed to address the long-term funding needs of small businesses by guaranteeing loans to qualified enterprises. These loans can be used for all sorts of purposes, including inventory, working capital, equipment, and real estate. Maturities are up to 10 years for working capital and up to 25 years for fixed assets. The SBA can guarantee 80 percent of loans of $100,000 or less, and 75 percent of loans between $100,000 and $750,000. There are several other loan programs available through the 7(a) Loan Guaranty plan as well.

The Low Documentation Loan (LowDoc) program is a streamlined version of the 7(a) loan for businesses seeking less than $150,000. Limited to applicants with a strong credit history, LowDoc loans can be secured with a one-page application (in cases where the loan request is for $50,000 or less). The SBA has made a strong effort to improve response time under this plan, in large measure because it had

long been criticized for the bureaucratic red tape associated with even the smallest of its loan programs.

The CAPLines program is an option designed to meet the short-term and cyclical working capital needs of small businesses. There are several different loan options available under this program, which replaced the SBA's earlier GreenLine program. Loans under CAPLines are generally limited to $750,000.

The SBAExpress program is shaped to increase the capital available to small businesses seeking loans up to $150,000; it is currently offered as a pilot program, with a limited number of participating lenders.

SBA MicroLoans, meanwhile, are short-term loans of up to $25,000. Disseminated through non-profit groups, MicroLoans are intended for the purchase of machinery and other equipment, office furniture, inventory, supplies, and working capital.

The SBA also offers several targeted lending programs for small businesses. These include the Defense Loan and Technical Assistance (DELTA) program, which provides financial assistance to defense-dependent small businesses impacted by defense cuts (maximum loan amount under the DELTA plan through the 7(a) Program is $1.25 million, usable for working capital, acquisition of assets, raw materials or inventory, capital improvements, or refinancing of current debt); prequalification pilot loan programs for women and minorities; the Export Working Capital Program (EWCP), which guarantees loans for qualified small businesses engaged in export transactions; the International Trade Loan (ITL), which provides long-term financing assistance to small businesses engaged in international trade and/or hurt by imports; and the Pollution Control Program, which gives loan guarantees to eligible small businesses proposing to design and install pollution control facilities.

The SBA also maintains a loan program known as the 504 CDC (Certified Development Companies), which makes available up to $1 million to qualified applicants. Under this system, long-term, fixed-rate financing is made available to small businesses interested in expanding or modernizing their operations through the purchase of new machinery, equipment, and/or real estate. DELTA loans are available through this program as well.

Another SBA loan program is the U.S. Community Adjustment and Investment Program (CAIP), created to help communities that suffered economic and workforce losses due to changing trade patterns following implementation of the North American Free Trade Agreement (NAFTA). According to the SBA, this program utilizes both the SBA 7(a) Program and the SBA 504 Program to ''promote economic implementation of the adjustment [to NAFTA] by increasing the availability and flow of credit and [encourage] business development and expansion in impacted areas. Through the CAIP, credit is available to businesses in eligible communities to create new, sustainable jobs or to preserve existing jobs.'' Small companies interested in pursuing CAIP assistance should contact their local CDC for more information.

The Small Business Administration relies on lending institutions and other intermediaries (such as non-profit organizations, in the case of MicroLoans). But the SBA is careful about the banks and savings and loans companies with which it does business. The most reliable of these lending institutions are eventually designated as ''preferred lenders.'' This status gives them increased powers of loan approval and processing (although the SBA still conducts a final review of loan applications). To become a preferred lender, an institution needs to have established a reputation for solid community lending (to small businesses and minority- and women-owned firms) and a strong history of being repaid by loan applicants.

INVESTMENT The SBA also maintains investment programs for small businesses. The Main Street Investment Program, for example, is described by the SBA as ''a public/private partnership between the SBA and state governments to make capital more available to lenders who, in turn, make loans to small businesses. Participating states invest tax revenues in community banks that agree to make LowDoc loans.'' Small Business Investment Companies (SBICs), meanwhile, are SBA-licensed investment firms who—armed with U.S. government-guaranteed debentures or participating securities—make investments and loans to small businesses. Indeed, SBICs exist for the express purpose of funding start-up companies. They operate under extremely stringent guidelines, however, and turn down many applicants. Similar to SBICs are Minority Enterprise Small Business Investment Companies (MESBICs), which provide funding to businesses owned or operated by minorities.

SURETY BONDS In recognition of the fact that contractors to construction projects must post surety bonds on federal construction projects valued at $25,000 or more, the SBA established a program wherein they guarantee bid, performance, and payment bonds for contracts up to $1.25 million for eligible small firms unable to secure surety bonds through commercial lenders. Under this program, bonds may be obtained either via prior approval, in which contractors apply through a surety bonding agent; or preferred sureties, authorized by the SBA to issue, monitor, and service bonds without prior SBA approval.

INTERNATIONAL TRADE The SBA's International Trade Loan Program is designed for small companies engaged or preparing to engage in international commerce. Under this program, the SBA guarantees up to $1.25 million for a combination of fixed asset financing and Export Working Capital Program (EWCP) assistance. The fixed-asset portion of the loan may not exceed $1 million, while the EWCP segment may not exceed $750,000. In order to qualify, the small business applicant must, according to the SBA, ''establish that the loan will significantly expand or develop an export market, is currently adversely affected by import competition, will upgrade equipment or facilities to improve competitive position, or must be able to provide a business plan that reasonably projects export sales sufficient to cover the loan.''

In addition to maintaining loan programs for small businesses engaged in international commerce, the Small Business Administration provides a number of other services to these enterprises. The Export Legal Assistance Network (ELAN), for instance, is the product of an agreement between the SBA, the Federal Bar Association, and the U.S. Department of Commerce. Under this program, trade attorneys provide free legal consultations to small business exporters.

The SBA also operates information centers called U.S. Export Assistance Centers (USEACs). As with ELAN, the USEACs are the product of an alliance between the SBA and other organizations (in USEACs' case, the Department of Commerce and the Export-Import Bank). These centers are designed to disseminate trade promotion and export financing information to small businesses engaged in international trade. In addition, the SBA maintains a computer database known as the Small Business Automated Trade Locator Assistance System (SBAtlas), which includes market data of interest to exporters.

ASSISTANCE PROGRAMS The SBA makes available Physical Disaster Business Loans to businesses of any size that need to repair or replace business property to ''pre-disaster'' conditions. These loans, which can be used for equipment, fixtures, and inventory, are limited to $1.5 million and are not available to businesses who were insured for their losses. Economic Injury Disaster Loans (EIDLs), meanwhile, are targeted at businesses that have ''sustained economic injury as a direct result of a disaster,'' said the SBA. ''These working capital loans are made to help businesses pay ordinary and necessary operating expenses which would have been payable barring disaster.'' The maximum amount of an EIDL loan is $1.5 million, but small business experts note that businesses can receive no more than $1.5 million in combined EIDL and physical disaster business loans. An exception to this stipulation is made, however, for those places of business that qualify as major sources of employment. Under the SBA's Major Source of Employment (MSE) program, the $1.5 million loan limit is waived for those businesses that employ 250 or more people in an affected area.

FEDERAL PROCUREMENT The Small Business Administration maintains several programs designed to help small businesses secure government contracts. These include:

- Breakout Procurement Program—promotes the breakout of historically sole-source contracts for open competition with the aim of aiding small businesses and effecting government savings.

- Prime Contracting Program—designed to help small businesses interested in securing federal contracts; services include support for small business set-asides, counseling, identification of new small business sources, and "assessment of compliance with the Small Business Act through surveillance reviews."

- Subcontracting Program—designed to aid small businesses in their efforts to secure federal contracts as suppliers and subcontractors.

- Certificates of Competency—appeal process that can be used by small businesses that have been denied government contracts because of alleged lack of ability to fulfill job requirements.

The most recent program in this area introduced by the SBA is the HUBzone Empowerment Contracting Program. This initiative, unveiled in 1997, provides federal contracting opportunities for qualified small businesses located in economically distressed areas.

MINORITY ASSISTANCE The SBA has several programs intended to provide support to small businesses owned and operated by minorities. Programs maintained by the SBA's Minority Enterprise Development office include 8(a) Small Disadvantaged Business Development, which arranges federal procurement opportunities for minority- and disadvantaged-owned firms, and initiatives which provide management and technical assistance to those firms. The SBA also operates an Office of Native American Affairs (ONAA), which works to provide Native American communities with business development and job creation opportunities.

BUSINESS TRAINING AND COUNSELING SBA-sponsored training and counseling services are available through the following programs:

- Small Business Development Centers—provides management and technical assistance to both current and prospective small business owners through an alliance of educators, the private sector, and federal, state, and local governments. All areas of business are covered, from market research and accounting systems to inventory control and cost-benefit analysis.

- Business Information Centers (BICs)—specializes in providing technology information to small businesses. Subjects covered include advances in telecommunications, software, and computers.

- Service Corps of Retired Executives (SCORE)—matches retired business executives with small businesses seeking advice on business issues. SCORE includes more than 12,300 members in hundreds of chapters around the country.

WOMEN'S BUSINESS OWNERSHIP SBA programs specifically directed at women small business owners include the Women's Demonstration Program, which provides women with training and advice on all aspects of business ownership and management, and the Women's Network for Entrepreneurial Training (WNET), wherein established women business owners serve as mentors to other women entrepreneurs.

VETERANS' AFFAIRS The SBA maintains several programs intended to provide information and training to veterans. These include the VET (Veterans' Entrepreneurial Training) Program, the Transition Assistance Program (TAP), and "business opportunity conferences," which helps veteran-owned companies previously reliant on the defense industry to secure other clients.

RESEARCH AND DEVELOPMENT The two principal programs administered by the SBA in this area are the Small Business Innovation Research (SBIR) Program and the Small Business Technology Transfer (STTR) Program. STTR is a program that seeks to form research and development partnerships between small firms and nonprofit research institutions. It provides up to $100,000 to companies for the first phase of research, though there are stipulations attached to that figure. SBIR, meanwhile, provides financial rewards to small businesses who propose innovative ideas to problems faced by participating federal agencies. Initially established in the early 1980s, as a result of the 1982 Small Business Innovation Development Act, SBIR has been warmly received by many small companies with expertise in science and high-technology areas.

ONE-STOP CAPITAL SHOP (OSCS) The SBA expects to contribute to the Empowerment Zone/Enterprise Communities Program initiative headed by the Department of Housing and Urban Development and the Department of Agriculture through its "One-Stop Capital Shops." These centers, located in federally designated empowerment zones and enterprise communities, are expected to be headed up by local nonprofit organizations, but they are intended to include access to complete information on various SBA programs and offerings. ''A One Stop Capital Shop is a partnership between SBA and a local community designed to offer small business assistance from an easy to access, retail location, all under one roof,'' explained the SBA. ''Small business clients require a wide range of assistance, from the simple: accessing the Internet or gathering basic information on writing a business plan, to the complex: learning how to compete for a federal contract or applying for a city permit. Whether a small business needs information or has to complete a transaction, requires training or counseling, is applying for a loan or seeking a government contract, a One Stop Capital Shop is designed to make all those services available in one location. . . . No other SBA program or federal agency plays a more prominent role in generating economic revitalization in distressed communities than the One Stop Capital Shop Initiative.''

BUSINESS INFORMATION SERVICES A comprehensive range of business development booklets is published by and made available from the SBA. A diverse range of topics are covered in these brochures; sample titles include *Strategic Planning for Growing Businesses, Budgeting in a Small Service Firm, Inventory Management,* and *Evaluating Franchise Opportunities.* SBA also maintains SBA Online, a computer-based electronic bulletin board of small business information, and a toll-free answer desk for small business owners with questions about aspects of their operation. The Small Business Administration maintains a page on the World Wide Web at http://www.sba.gov.

FURTHER READING:

Barlas, Stephen. ''Looking Ahead: Three SBA Programs Face Closer Scrutiny.'' *Entrepreneur.* January 1997.

Emerich, Amy, ed. *Small Business Sourcebook.* Gale, 1996.

SBA Profile: Who We Are and What We Do. Small Business Administration, 2000.

SMALL BUSINESS CONSORTIA

Business consortia are alliances of individual business enterprises. These firms are often in the same broad field or industry, though they are rarely in direct competition with one another. Instead, members usually offer products or services that are complementary to those available through other consortium members. Unlike associations and other similar organizations, which engage in efforts to shape legislation and present a unified industry front, business consortia ally themselves for basic business functions, such as marketing. These alliances are not commonplace, but some analysts indicate that in the future, increasing numbers of small business owners may investigate consortiums as a way of sharing common costs, increasing purchasing power, and competing with larger companies.

Business consortia that do form usually come into being for specific reasons, such as competitive threats from a common enemy (whether another business or an unwelcome economic trend), changes in competitive structures, or deregulation. Writing in *Acquisitions Monthly,* John Eric Bigbie observed that by forming a consortium, the companies that are involved are usually admitting that—for the time being, at least—competitive pressures are so great that the business's ability to survive as a completely independent entity is in question.

Participants in business consortia admit that striking such alliances can sometimes curb a firm's ability to act independently, since it's words and actions will reflect on other consortia members. This can be difficult for some entrepreneurs to handle. Moreover, consortia can become crippled if their membership grows too large and unwieldy to make quick decisions, or if individual members fall victim to squabbling or worse as a result of personality conflicts, similar customer bases, or other business disputes. But proponents point out that a business consortium can provide several meaningful advantages to members as well. These include:

Increased clout. Whereas individual small businesses sometimes do not enjoy the same name recognition or respect as do larger companies, the collective bargaining and purchasing power of a consortium as well as the individual marketing efforts of members can provide individual businesses with increased recognition and stature in the community.

Savings of time and money. Joint marketing and advertising efforts save members money because they can pool their resources for better rates; they also save member businesses time because they do not have to undertake as much work themselves.

Expanded customer base. Membership in business consortia can provide participating businesses with increased exposure to new revenue streams.

FURTHER READING:

Bigbie, John Eric. ''Consortia Back in Business.'' *Acquisitions Monthly.* April 1994.

Doz, Yves L., and Gary Hamel. *Alliance Advantage: The Art of Creating Value Through Partnerships.* Harvard Business School Press, 1998.

Smith, Jerd. ''Strength in Their Number.'' *Denver Business Journal.* March 3, 1995.

Vaanderdorpe, Laura. ''Capitalizing on Consortia: Cooperation Bolsters Research.'' *R & D.* October 1997.

SMALL BUSINESS DEVELOPMENT CENTERS (SBDC)

One of many programs administered by the Small Business Administration (SBA), the Small Business Development Center (SBDC) program is intended to provide management assistance to both established and prospective small business owners. The SBA characterizes the program, which was established in 1976, as a "cooperative effort of the private sector, the educational community, and federal, state, and local governments. It enhances economic development by providing small businesses with management and technical assistance."

The SBA maintains small business development centers in all 50 states, as well as Puerto Rico, Guam, the U.S. Virgin Islands, and the District of Columbia. Many of these centers have satellite service locations to aid small businesses as well. These satellite locations are housed primarily at colleges, universities, and community colleges, but they are also maintained at vocational schools, chambers of commerce, and economic development corporations.

SBDCs are typically headed up by a director and include paid staff members, but the services of volunteers—qualified individuals from professional and trade associations, members of the legal, banking, and academic community, chambers of commerce representatives, and members of the Service Corps of Retired Executives—are integral to most SBDCs. In addition, SBDCs commonly compensate consultants, consulting engineers, and testing laboratories for services rendered on behalf of SBDC clients.

While SBDCs are administered by the SBA, that organization is prevented by law from providing more than 50 percent of the operating funds for each state SBDC. The centers turn to state legislatures, private sector foundations and grants, state and local chambers of commerce, economic development corporations, public and private universities, vocational and technical schools, and community colleges for the remainder of their operating funds. In recent years, non-SBA sponsors have accounted for more than 50 percent of their required matching share at a number of centers.

THE SBDC PROGRAM

According to the SBA, Small Business Development Centers are designed to deliver timely and accurate counseling, training, and technical assistance in all aspects of small business management, including financial management, marketing, production and operations, organization, engineering and technical issues, personnel management, and feasibility studies. Some centers also offer assistance in such areas as venture capital formation, rural development, exporting and importing, and procurement of funding (including Small Business Innovation and Research grants), depending on the needs of their business clients and the communities in which the centers operate.

SBDC assistance to small business owners takes many forms, from counseling on legal issues to seminars on business finance to aid in putting together a business plan. Many centers also maintain extensive business libraries that contain a great deal of information of value to entrepreneurs and small business owners.

Anyone interested in starting a small business or making improvements to an existing small business is free to make use of the SBDC program, provided that they do not have the financial resources to secure the services of a private consultant. Indeed, the SBDC centers regard their primary clientele to be businesspeople from disadvantaged socioeconomic backgrounds. The SBDC program also makes special efforts to provide assistance to women, the disabled, and military veterans. To locate the SBDC nearest you, see the Small Business Administration website at www.sba.gov/sbdc.

FURTHER READING:

SBA Profile: Who We Are and What We Do. Small Business Administration, 1996.

Tiffany, Laura. "Show Me the Way: SBDCs Put You on the Road to Success." *Entrepreneur.* July 1998.

SMALL BUSINESS INNOVATION RESEARCH (SBIR) PROGRAM

The Small Business Innovation Research Program (SBIR) is the federal government's most important research and development funding program for small businesses. It was established by the passage of the Small Business Innovation Development Act of 1982. SBIR, at the time of its passage, required by law that any federal government agency with an extramural research and development budget of more than $100 million set aside 1.25 percent of those funds for the development of high tech small businesses. When the original law expired after ten years, Congress reauthorized SBIR and increased the agencies' contributions to 2.5 percent in 1992. By the latter part of the 1990s, total SBIR funding had reached some $1.2 billion. In December 2000 the program was reauthorized—with $1.5 billion in annual funding—for another seven years.

The Small Business Administration (SBA) serves as the coordinating agency for the SBIR program. It directs implementation of the program among participating agencies, reviews their progress, and reports annually to Congress on the status of the program. The SBA is also the information link to the program, collecting solicitation information from participating agencies and publishing it in quarterly Pre-Solicitation Announcements (PSA). These announcements are the single source for the topics and anticipated release and closing dates for each federal agency's solicitations.

By 2000, ten federal agencies were participating in SBIR, bestowing research and development funds to small businesses in an array of industries. Participating agencies include the Departments of Agriculture, Commerce, Defense, Education, Energy, Health and Human Services, and Transportation, as well as the Environmental Protection Agency, the National Aeronautics and Space Administration, and the National Science Foundation. According to *Science* magazine, 96 percent of the total SBIR budget from all agencies comes from the Departments of Defense and Energy, the National Institutes of Health, National Aeronautics and Space Administration, and the National Science Foundation.

These agencies set aside seed funds to help small businesses develop innovative high-tech ideas whose commercial appeal may by some time in coming. Each year the agencies release for consideration more than 3,000 technology topics under which businesses may apply. The topics speak to specific program problems or needs and may be found in the quarterly *Pre-Solicitation Announcement (PSA)*, which is only provided online.

SBIR ELIGIBILITY AND FRAMEWORK

To be eligible for SBIR funding, a small business concern must be American-owned, independently operated, for-profit, and employ fewer than 500 people. Nonprofit organizations are not eligible for SBIR awards.

The SBIR program comprises three phases. This approach allows the government agency to invest a small amount in the beginning and then increase their financial support later should the idea show promise. Once the project nears completion, funding drops off and the business must solicit capital from other sources.

Phase One - The Concept Stage. In this stage, individual awards of up to $100,000 are distributed to enable businesses to conduct approximately six months of preliminary investigations into the feasibility of their proposed project. At this point, business owners must have a well-formed idea for an innovative product and a specific plan for how to transform it into a commercially viable form.

Phase Two - The Prototype Development Phase. This phase, for which only Phase One entrepreneurs are eligible, provides additional monies (up to $750,000 over 24 months) to be used toward developing a prototype. From here, determinations are made about whether the product is a success or a failure and whether or not it is commercially viable. About 40 percent of Phase One ideas reach this second stage.

Phase Three - The Commercialization Stage. In this stage, states the SBA, "Phase Two innovation moves from the laboratory into the marketplace." No SBIR funds are used in this stage. Instead, funding must be secured from the private sector or other non-SBIR federal agency funding.

For more information on the SBIR program, contact the Small Business Administration's Office of Technology in Washington, DC. The SBA's web site is www.sba.gov.

FURTHER READING:

Barlas, Stephen. "Teaming Up: Universities and Businesses Come Together in a Pilot Program to Fund Innovation." *Entrepreneur*, August 1996.

Giannone, Michael A. "A Wealth of New Ideas." *Environmental Technology.* November-December 1999.

Gillis, Tom S. *Guts & Borrowed Money: Straight Talk for Starting & Growing Your Small Business.* Bard Press, 1997.

Rushmeyer, Sheila. "SBIR Grants Technical Projects." *Corporate Report-Minnesota*, March 1995.

Wallsten, Scott J. "The Effects of Government-Industry R&D Programs on Private R&D: The Case of the Small Business Innovation Research Program." *RAND Journal of Economics.* Spring 2000.

"What Do You Call a Federal Program that Requires No Additional Federal Spending, Costs Virtually Nothing to Administer, and Yields Venture Capital-Like Returns?" *Inc.*, January 1993.

SMALL BUSINESS INVESTMENT COMPANIES (SBIC)

The Small Business Investment Company (SBIC) program was created in 1958 with the passage of the Small Business Investment Act of 1958. Licensed by the Small Business Administration (SBA), SBICs are privately organized and privately managed investment firms that provide venture capital to small independent businesses. These loans, which are available both to new and established business establishments, consist of funds borrowed (at favorable rates) from the U.S. government or their own capital.

Two different kinds of SBICs operate in the United States. In addition to regular SBICs, investment firms known as Specialized Small Business Investment Companies (SSBICs) also exist; this latter type of firm emphasizes service to entrepreneurs who ''have been denied the opportunity to own and operate a business because of social or economic disadvantage,'' according to the SBA. Formerly known as Minority Enterprise Small Business Investment Companies (MESBICs), SSBICs are now officially called Section 301(d) SBICs. Since the differences between SSBICs and regular SBICs are minor, though, they are generally lumped together under the SBIC heading.

THE SBIC ORGANIZATION

Ownership of SBICs generally takes two different forms. The majority of SBICs are relatively small, privately owned and operated firms, but many others are firms owned by commercial banks or insurance companies. For banks, establishment of an SBIC subsidiary is often an attractive proposition, because it enables them to make small business investments that would otherwise be closed to them because of U.S. banking laws and requirements. United States law places few restrictions on SBIC ownership. As the SBA itself said, ''almost any person or organization with a minimum initial private capitalization of $5 million and an SBA-approved full time manager who will be in charge of the licensee's operations and who is able to serve the licensee's small business concerns, may be approved for ownership.'' Indeed, the SBA's interest in encouraging SBICs is evident in the relatively hands-off regulatory environment that they have established for such enterprises. Those regulations that the SBA does enforce are concerned with ensuring the continued financial and ethical health of the SBIC program.

SBICs, then, range from limited partnerships to subsidiaries of multinational corporations. Whatever their ownership situation, however, their ultimate goal is to realize a profit from their various business transactions. Some SBICs make most of their revenue from straight debt financing, with their profit coming from the differential between its borrowing costs from the Small Business Administration and the interest rate they charge its small business clients. Other SBICs take a more aggressive tack in seeking profits by making equity-participation loans.

According to the SBA, prospective SBICs (and SSBICs) must have a minimum private capital investment of $5 million to form (the minimum requirement for those firms wishing to utilize participating securities is $10 million). The amount of private capital that an SBIC has at its disposal is important, for the SBA limits its loan guarantees to SBICs to 300 percent of its private capital. The SBA notes, however, that an SBIC ''with at least 50 percent of its 'total funds available for investment' invested or committed in 'venture capital' may receive an additional tier of leverage per dollar of private capital for total leverage

of 400 percent of private capital. However, in no event may any SBIC or SSBIC draw down leverage in excess of $90 million.'' An SBIC that engages in leveraging is in essence borrowing additional investment funds from the U.S. Treasury. Only those SBICs that have invested the bulk of its initial private capital and are in full compliance with state and federal regulations are eligible to do this.

Small Business Investment Companies have several different options to choose from in providing financing to small businesses. Most provide long-term loans to qualified small businesses that need funding for needs that range from expansion of existing facilities to modernization of operation. Sometimes this loan will take the form of equity or debt securities.

OPERATING RESTRICTIONS FOR SBICS

While the SBA provides SBICs with considerable freedom to operate, they do require that these organizations adhere to certain rules. For example, SBICs are not permitted to invest in the following entities: companies with less than one-half of their assets and operations in America; unimproved real estate; finance and investment companies; or companies seeking to purchase or improve farmland, cemeteries, or certain other stipulated types of real estate (exceptions are made for subdividers and developers, title abstract companies, and real estate agents and brokers. Small Business Investment Companies also are forbidden from investing in other SBICs, or in business enterprises that do not fit federal definitions of a ''small business.''

The SBA also has established regulations in the following areas:

- Conflict of Interest—SBICs are not allowed to make business transactions with any of its associates, which are defined as officers, directors, employees, key ''control persons,'' and certain shareholders.

- Control—the SBA has stipulated that no SBIC may exercise either direct or indirect control over the operations of any small business on a permanent basis. The SBA has, under some circumstances, permitted SBICs to assume temporary control of a business enterprise in order to protect its investment. Before doing so, however, the SBIC and the small business must submit a plan of divestiture for SBA approval.

- Overline Limitations—The SBA has established investment ceilings for both SBICs and SSBICs in their dealings with individual small businesses. SBICs are not allowed to invest more than 20 percent of its private capital with any one small business, while the limit for SSBICs is 30 percent. The SBA does, however, occasionally grant waivers to this rule.

- Cost of Money—The SBA regulates the cost of money on SBIC loans and debt securities issued by SBIC clients.

- Financing Proceeds—The SBA has established regulations designed to ensure that investment funds that are used to purchase securities go directly to the small business that has offered those securities.

- Length of Financing Agreements—SBA rules stipulate (in most cases) that SBIC loan agreements with small business enterprises be made for at least five years, and that the small business taking the loan be given adequate opportunity to fulfill its obligations ahead of schedule if it is able to do so. According to the SBA, loan and debt securities of less than five years' duration are permissible only on those occasions when they are necessary to protect existing financing agreements, are made in contemplation of long-term financing, or are made to finance a change in ownership.

BORROWING FROM AN SBIC

''As is true with venture capitalists in general, SBICs have divergent philosophies and operating policies,'' wrote Art DeThomas in *Financing Your Small Business.* ''Some specialize in equity financing while other provide debt financing in several different forms. This latter group of SBICs is the richest source of debt financing for small businesses outside commercial banks.'' Small business owners, however, need to weigh several factors before making a loan arrangement with an SBIC.

Entrepreneurs and small business owners seeking financing from SBICs first need to determine how many options they have. Regional SBA offices maintain information on SBICs that operate in their areas, and while they do not provide guidance in directing businesses to particular SBICs, they can give information on the industries and types of investments in which area SBICs have historically shown interest. In addition, a free directory of SBICs is available through the National Association of SBICs.

As many experts note, small businesses should narrow their search for a suitable SBIC by eliminating those that do not provide the business's desired financing route or display adequate management experience in the industry in which the business is involved. Analysts also caution small business owners not to rush through the decision making process. Given the latitude that SBICs have in shaping their loan policies, individual SBICs often maintain dramatically varied lending policies. Entrepreneurs and small business owners should thus take the time to find the program that best meets their needs.

Business consultants also encourage prospective borrowers to negotiate the best possible loan agreement for themselves when talking with SBICs. ''Aside from the specifics of SBIC lending that are mandated by existing law or regulation,'' noted DeThomas, ''particulars such as interest rate, maturity, equity participation, and collateral requirements can be negotiated. In general, the more attractive your firm as a financing opportunity—that is, the stronger the business plan—the more negotiating leverage you possess.''

FURTHER READING:

DeThomas, Art. *Financing Your Small Business: Techniques for Planning, Acquiring & Managing Debt.* Oasis Press, 1992.

SBA Overview of SBIC Program. Small Business Administration, n.a.

SBA Profile: Who We Are and What We Do. Small Business Administration, 1996.

Timmons, Jeffrey A. *Planning and Financing the New Venture.* Brick House, 1990.

SMALL BUSINESS JOB PROTECTION ACT

The Small Business Job Protection Act (SBJPA), signed into law in 1996, contains a number of provisions impacting various aspects of small business operations, from retirement plans to changes in S Corporation structures. The small business community greeted many of the changes contained in SBJPA with considerable enthusiasm, since it was widely interpreted as an act that eliminated a number of unnecessarily burdensome provisions. The act touched on a wide variety of areas relevant to small businesses, especially in the area of pensions. Changes made by the law can be found in such areas as the definition of highly compensated employees, deferred compensation arrangements, family aggregation rules, minimum pension participation rules, ''safe harbor'' rules for qualified cash or deferred arrangements (CODAs), notice requirements, limits on matching contributions, distributions of excess contributions, elective deferrals includible as compensation, early participation nondiscrimination rules, plan distributions and QJSA waivers, employee leasing provisions, and modification of GATT interest and mortality rate rules. Small business consultants strongly advise business owners who wish to take full advantage of the myriad changes included within SBJPA to consult with a tax advisor or other accounting professional.

IMPACT ON SUBCHAPTER S CORPORATIONS

Some observers estimate that the Small Business Job Protection Act has directly impacted as many as two million small businesses currently structured as Subchapter S corporations. For instance, the law allows S corporations to increase its shareholders from 35 to 75, giving businesses heightened capacity to attract additional investors and capital. Another change that benefited small business owners concerned an expansion in the kinds of organizations that can be shareholders. Under the SBJPA, qualified pension plans became eligible to be shareholders in S corporations after January 1998. Since many pension plans are willing to invest in promising young businesses, S corporation owners have been able to turn to these entities as a source of significant capital.

The SBJPA also provided S corporation owners with greater flexibility in structuring their businesses. Prior to the passage of the SBJPA, S corporations could not own more than 79 percent of another company, but with the new law, they may now own 100 percent of affiliated companies. Finally, business experts note that the SBJPA expands the number of allowable beneficiaries when an S corporation puts together a small business trust.

CHANGES TO RETIREMENT PLANS

The SBJPA established a simplified retirement plan for small businesses that is known as the SIMPLE retirement plan. Under these plans, which are designed for employers with 100 or fewer employees who do not maintain another employer-sponsored plan, employers and employees work together to help ensure that workers have adequate financial security when they reach retirement age. Under the law, employees may make elective contributions of up to $6,000 annually. The employer is required to make matching contributions and do so every year. The SBJPA also requires that businesses contribute at least 1 percent of all employee's compensation or be subject to significant penalties.

The law also impacts other elements of pension plans. For example, for the years 1997, 1998, and 1999, the 15 percent excise tax on excess distributions from pension plans was suspended. Moreover, the act introduced safe-harbor formulas for 401(k) salary deferral and matching contributions that eliminated requirements that employers conduct annual nondiscrimination testing. "Under the 1996 act, small employers can adopt matching 401(k) plans without concern about whether non-HCEs [highly compensated employees] elect to participate," wrote Michael Collins and Charles Sherman Jr. in *Journal of Accountancy*. "Depending on how attractive non-HCEs find the safe-harbor matching formula, the use of the safe harbors may reduce substantially the employer contributions businesses must make on behalf of these employees. . . . The safe-harbor formulas provide a way for employers to avoid nondiscrimination testing by adopting a plan with a relatively generous employer match—one that includes a contribution of at least 4 percent of pay on behalf of all eligible employees (depending on employee contributions). Safe-harbor matching contributions must be 100 percent vested at all times. Such contributions generally may not be distributed to employees until the earlier of when they terminate employment or reach age $59\frac{1}{2}$." In addition, under the SBJPA, distributions from a qualified plan must begin by April of the calendar year following the later of: 1) the calendar year in which the employee reaches $70\frac{1}{2}$ years of age, or 2) the calendar year in which the worker retires.

FURTHER READING:

Mulleneaux, Natasha M. "Retirement Plan Reform: The Aftermath of the Small Business Job Protection Act of 1996." *Taxes: The Tax Magazine.* August 1997.

Schneider, Mark N., and Marilyn C. Doolittle. "Small Business Job Protection Act Adds Simplicity (and Complexity)." *The Tax Advisor.* June 1997.

Sharp, Jr., Joel, and Hewitt D. Shaw Jr. "Subchapter S Reform: The Small Business Job Protection Act of 1996." *Journal of Corporate Taxation.* Spring 1997.

Sherman, Jr., Charles W., and Michael J. Collins. "The Safe-Harbor Solution." *Journal of Accountancy.* July 1999.

West, Diane. "401(K)s Catch on at Small Companies." *National Underwriter Life & Health.* June 9, 1997.

SMALL BUSINESS/LARGE BUSINESS RELATIONSHIPS

Many small business owners see large businesses exclusively in competitive terms. And for some small enterprises, that characterization is an accurate one. An independent record store owner, for example, will undoubtedly—and legitimately—regard the arrival of a new record store operating under the banner of a national chain as a threat. Similarly, a small plastics manufacturer will view larger firms engaged in the same industry sector as competition. But small businesses should recognize that large regional, national, or even international companies can take on other, decidedly more attractive, identities as well. Larger companies also may assume roles as business partners, product distributors, or customers. Indeed, large enterprises wear different hats to different observers. One small business's aggressive competitor may be another small firm's business ally, distributor, or client.

LARGE BUSINESSES AS PARTNERS

The 1990s has seen a general increase in business partnerships between small and large companies. Alliances between large companies are still more prevalent, and many large firms continue to prefer to simply swallow up smaller enterprises via acquisition, but analysts and consultants alike contend that growing numbers of large companies are recognizing the benefits that can accrue from establishing partnerships with nimble, entrepreneurial firms. Small but growing companies can offer mature partners access to new customers, innovative products and management practices, and opportunities to bask in the glow of the small business's innovative, contemporary image. This is especially true in biotechnology sectors and other industries characterized by rapid change and innovation. But as Myron Gould noted in *Direct Marketing,* "Partnerships can be formed in the profit and nonprofit sectors, in the same or different industries, within different divisions of the same company, and in similar market segments/demographics in non-competitive industries."

Indeed, many observers believe that in recent years, festering suspicions and stereotypes in both the large- and small-business camps about the motivations and abilities of the other have begun to give way to an increasing recognition of the positives that they can bring to the table. James W. Botkin and Jana B. Matthews, authors of *Winning Combinations: The Coming Wave of Entrepreneurial Partnerships Between Large and Small Companies,* stated that "entrepreneurs and corporate executives now need each other more than ever. Their needs and their strengths are often opposite and complementary. Both large corporations and small companies can brighten their global prospects by forming collaborative partnerships that capitalize on their complementary strengths while respecting the independence of each party."

Over the past number of years, well-managed smaller companies have proven themselves to be very adept at anticipating market trends, capitalizing on new technologies, and using their lean structures to outpace larger companies. But while their small size enables them to evade the lumbering bureaucracies that hamper the actions of all but the most progressive larger companies, small companies are also limited by certain realities that can be easily addressed by big firms, and these impediments are often emphasized if the small firm hopes to establish a presence beyond its domestic borders. "Increasing globalization . . . makes it difficult for small entrepreneurial companies to act alone effectively," wrote Botkin and Matthews. "Their marketing and distribution channels are frequently inadequate for getting their innovative products and services to an international marketplace. The continual need of small companies for capital also

limits their maneuverability. The time and attention of their entrepreneurial management is often diverted to finding and negotiating financing instead of developing markets and distribution systems. . . . Though their innovations may be exactly what the marketplace needs and wants, they are likely to be handicapped in reaching it."

Large firms are an obvious source of assistance in many of the above areas—distribution, financing, marketing, etc.—but small businesspeople have a tendency to regard large corporations with suspicion. After all, many entrepreneurs come from corporate environments that were not necessarily characterized by adherence to any code of business ethics, and American corporations have not always shown respect for small business autonomy. "Given the 'big fish eats little fish' history of large-to-small encounters, founders of small companies may understandably be leery of forming partnerships that they fear will destroy their company's autonomy and identity," admitted Botkin and Matthews. "But this need not be the case. We suggest that any partnership offer be examined critically and carefully. Entrepreneurs must learn to discriminate between corporate sharks with a bite and swallow mentality and those suitors who have a mutually beneficial arrangement in mind. It's natural to be suspicious. However, many founders of small businesses write off strategic alliances altogether, closing off what might be an increasingly important avenue of rapid growth."

KEYS TO SUCCESSFUL PARTNERSHIPS WITH LARGER COMPANIES Following are several tips that entrepreneurs should consider when negotiating and maintaining a partnership with a larger company:

Research. Some partnership offers sound great on the surface, but are fraught with unpleasantness under the surface. Entrepreneurs should make sure that they undertake diligent research so that they can best assure themselves of finding the right partner, for as Botkin and Matthews admitted, "not every partnership yields happy results; ill-conceived partnerships can leave your company in worse shape than before. Bad partnerships, like bad marriages, can drain resources, end up in costly litigation, and sour both partners on future relationships." Typically, however, warning signs will be there for the small business owner who takes the time to look.

Fundamentally sound business practices. Entrepreneurs hoping to secure a partner to bankroll their R&D efforts or market their products are wasting their time if they do not have a viable business already in place. If the small company's business practices are shoddy, disorganized, or incomplete, large companies will be sure to notice.

Recognition of own responsibilities. Entrepreneurial companies can reap many benefits from partnering with large firms, but they need to recognize that those big companies are for-profit enterprises; they expect something in return for their financial, marketing, and/or management help.

Monitor requirements of successful partnership. Many partnerships with larger companies require entrepreneurs to make a greater commitment to their business in order to meet the obligations and conditions explicated in the partnership agreement. If the entrepreneur in question launched his or her business for the express purpose of realizing greater personal wealth or establishing a significant presence in a given industry, finding the desire to meet those partnership obligations should not be a problem. If, however, the entrepreneur launched his or her venture in order to stake out a lifestyle of independence and travel, that person may want to weigh the sort of impact that the partnership could have on those aspects of his or her life.

Do not be intimidated. The trappings of the corporate world (high-rise buildings, cavernous conference rooms, legions of blue suits, etc.) can be intimidating, but small business owners have to remember that they run viable businesses of value themselves, and they should negotiate accordingly.

Maintain independence. Autonomy is assured if you maintain ownership, so be leery of turning over too much equity in the business in exchange for financial help.

Establish clear and open lines of communication. Good communication practices are essential to all business relationships, both internal and external, and alliances with large companies are no exception.

LARGE BUSINESSES AS PRODUCT DISTRIBUTORS

Myriad small manufacturers rely on major mass merchandisers (regional, national, or international) to sell their goods. Indeed, these distributors can dramatically heighten a small business's fortunes in a matter of weeks or months. But entrepreneurs seeking to establish such relationships will find that 1) competition to secure a place on the shelves of major retail outlets is fierce, and 2) some mass merchandisers will be better suited for the small business's product than others.

COMPETITION The single most important factor in securing a distribution agreement with a major retailer is, of course, having a quality product that will sell. But small business owners seeking to establish themselves with a major mass merchandiser also need to make sure that they attend to myriad other business matters every step of the way. After all, the mass merchandiser in question has plenty of product options from which to choose; if your company stumbles at any point, there are plenty of other competitors waiting to take your place on the merchandiser's shelf. Given that reality, entrepreneurs have to make sure that they have a dependable production/delivery operation in place. In addition, small business owners should be prepared to provide prospective distributors with information on the firm's management and financial situation.

COMPATIBILITY Moreover, entrepreneurs need to make sure that they concentrate their efforts on finding mass merchandisers that already sell products to the new product's probable demographic audience. For example, an expensive, "high-end" home furnishing product is more likely to be compatible with the existing product lines of an upscale retailer than one of the major discount retailers (K-Mart, Wal-Mart, etc.). Conversely, an inexpensive but functional item that would be commonly used might be better suited to discount outlets rather than Nordstrom's or some other high-end retailer.

LARGE BUSINESSES AS CUSTOMERS

Many small businesses, whether involved in retail, wholesale, manufacturing, or service sectors, count fellow businesses as significant or primary customers. Pleasing corporate clients is in many fundamental respects no different than pleasing individual customers. As Richard Gerson observed in *Great Customer Service for Your Small Business,* "much of customer service comes down to plain old common sense. Simply put, customer service involves everything you and your employees do to satisfy customers. That means you give them what they want and make sure they are happy when they leave. If you just manage complaints, offer refunds or exchanges on returns, and smile at customers, you only provide a small part of excellent customer service. Customer service also means going out of your way for the customer, doing everything possible to satisfy the customer, and making decisions that benefit the customer—sometimes even at the expense of the business [depending on the customer's future potential]."

However, corporate customers sometimes have different needs and priorities than do private individuals, and small businesses that do not recognize these differences are unlikely to provide service that will be acceptable in the long term. For example, delivery deadlines are often far more important for businesses than they are for regular customers. Late delivery of a service or product may constitute no more than a minor convenience to a private-sector customer, but it might mean significant monetary loss for a corporate customer that was depending on that delivery to meet deadlines imposed by its own customers.

Small business owners servicing fellow businesses also need to recognize that the loss of a single corporate customer often constitutes a much more severe blow to a business's health than does the loss of a single retail consumer. Whereas businesses that provide goods or services to the general public will have many customers, establishments that provide their goods or services to corporate clients will in all likelihood have far fewer customers. The loss of even one such client, then, can have a significant impact because of the percentage of total business that the customer represents. Finally, businesses that rely on corporate clients are more likely to encounter higher levels of paperwork and bureaucracy to satisfy the recordkeeping apparatus of their clients.

FURTHER READING:

Botkin, James W., and Jana B. Matthews. *Winning Combinations: The Coming Wave of Entrepreneurial Partnerships Between Large and Small Companies.* John Wiley & Sons, 1992.

Buvik, Arnt, and Kjell Gronhaug. ''Inter-firm Dependence, Environmental Uncertainty, and Vertical Coordination in Industrial Buyer-Seller Relationships. *Omega.* August 2000.

Doz, Yvez L., and Gary Hamel. *Alliance Advantage: The Art of Creating Value through Partnerships.* Harvard Business School Press, 1998.

Gerson, Richard F. *Great Customer Service for Your Small Business.* Crisp Publications, 1996.

Gould, Myron. ''Partnering for Profit—How to Achieve Impressive Cost-Benefit Results.'' *Direct Marketing.* February 1997.

Lancaster, Hal, and Marj Charlier. ''Bigger Partners Can Cause Problems for Small Firms.'' *Wall Street Journal,* March 4, 1991.

Paajanen, George. ''Customer Service: Training, Sound Practices, and the Right Employee.'' *Discount Store News.* September 15, 1997.

Weinstein, Steve. ''Rethinking Customer Service.'' *Progressive Grocer.* May 1995.

Wilhelm, Wayne, and Bill Rossello. ''The Care and Feeding of Customers.'' *Management Review.* March 1997.

SMALL BUSINESS TECHNOLOGY TRANSFER (STTR) PROGRAM

The Small Business Technology Transfer (STTR) Program is an initiative, coordinated by the Small Business Administration (SBA), to provide small businesses with greater access to funding in the federal innovation research and development arena. ''Central to the program,'' notes the SBA, ''is expansion of the public-private sector partnership to include the joint venture opportunities for small business and the nation's premier nonprofit research institutions. STTR's most important role is to foster the innovation necessary to meet the nation's scientific and technological challenges in the 21st century.''

STTR is a parallel program to the Small Business Innovation Research (SBIR) Program, and was created by Congress when it reauthorized SBIR in 1992. The STTR program is a cooperative research partnership between small business concerns and research institutions. It differs from SBIR in two ways. First, it places a greater emphasis on the potential for commercial success. This has spurred participating agencies to be more stringent in their evaluations of applicants. Secondly, it requires that universities, federal laboratories, or nonprofit research centers team with businesses to get products into the marketplace. These research partnerships between small businesses and nonprofit institutions enable participants to combine entrepreneurial initiative and creativity with the expertise, equipment, and other assets of nonprofit research laboratories.

STTR QUALIFICATIONS

In order to be considered for the STTR program, interested small businesses must meet several criteria. For instance, they must be American-owned and independently operated for-profit enterprises. In addition, the size of the company may not exceed 500 employees. There is no workforce size limit for participating nonprofit research institutions, but they must also meet certain parameters of the program. They must be principally located in the United States, and they must meet one of the following three definitions: nonprofit college or university, domestic nonprofit research organization, or federally funded research and development center.

Five federal departments and agencies—the departments of Defense, Energy, and Health and Human Services, along with the National Science Foundation and the National Aeronautics and Space Administration—are required by STTR rules to reserve a portion of their research and development funds for the program. As the distributors of STTR funding, they also designate those subjects suitable for additional R&D and determine whether to accept or reject STTR proposals.

These agencies make STTR awards based on the following factors: qualifications of the nonprofit research institution and its small business partner; degree of innovation; and future market potential. Small businesses that secure STTR funding are then routed through a three-phase program.

Phase One: Startup. In this initial stage, awards of up to $100,000 are given to pay for approximately one year's worth of study and research into the scientific, technical, and commercial feasibility of an idea or technology.

Phase Two: Development. These awards, available to Phase One participants, reach up to $500,000 for two years. During this period, business/research partnerships engage in research and development work with an eye toward commercial potential.

Phase Three: Introduction to Market. During this phase, the completed project is introduced into the commercial marketplace to succeed or fail. No STTR funds support this phase. Instead, participants must secure funding from private parties or other federal agencies that do not allocate STTR monies.

For more information on the STTR program, contact the Small Business Administration's Office of Technology in Washington, DC, or visit the SBA's Web site at www.sba.gov.

SMALL BUSINESS-DOMINATED INDUSTRIES

The United States supports many industries that are dominated by or heavily populated with small firms. The majority of these are in service industries, a fact that reflects the growing dominance of the service sector in the overall American economy. According to the U.S. Small Business Administration, the fastest-growing small business-oriented industries in the country in the mid-1990s were as follows:

1) Employment Agencies

2) Real Estate

3) Automotive Dealers and Service Stations

4) Building Materials and Garden Supplies

5) Automotive Services, Except Repair

6) Millwork, Veneer, and Plywood Manufacturing

7) Paint, Paper Hanging, and Decorating

8) Meat Markets and Freezer Provisioners

9) Retail Stores

10) Agricultural Services

These industries are expected to see continued growth over the coming years, as increasing numbers of small businesses enter the marketplace. But many analysts, citing studies conducted by the SBA's Small Business Advocate office, believe that some other industries friendly to small business are poised for even greater growth. Indeed, statistics compiled by the SBA, the Department of Labor, the Bureau of Labor Statistics, and *Monthly Labor Review* indicated that high rates of growth can also be expected in such business areas as residential care, collection agencies, child day care services, travel arrangement services, equipment rental companies, accounting and book-keeping services, public relations, and family services.

SELECTED HIGH-GROWTH INDUSTRIES FOR SMALL BUSINESS

RESIDENTIAL CARE Residential care encompasses a variety of facilities, including those devoted to caring for emotionally disturbed adolescents and mentally retarded individuals, but government data indicates that the area in which residential care will see its greatest growth is in the realm of elder care. Analysts expect growth in assisted-living facilities—which range from domiciliary care homes and personal care homes to adult congregate living facilities—to serve as the engine that drives this industry forward over the next number of years, as the American population ages and workers explore various elder care options. "These facilities," wrote Jenny McCune in *Journal of Business Strategy,* "are a bridge between traditional nursing homes, which offer round-the-clock, skilled medical care in an institutional setting, and independent retirement housing, in which residents receive no outside help. In assisted living, the elderly live as independently as possible—usually in suites or cottages—but also have access to meal and laundry facilities and get assistance with daily chores such as bathing and dressing." Business consultants and current participants in the industry warn, however, that while demand for these services will continue to grow in the coming years, entrance into this business area is costly.

CHILD CARE The child care services industry has enjoyed steady growth for a number of years, due to population increases and the growing presence of women in the business world. And as McCune noted, the popularity of child care facilities in recent years has also been driven by the increased professionalism of the industry, as evidenced by the development of accreditation standards. The sheer demand for child care services is expected to insure the continued health of many businesses engaged in this area for years to come, but entrepreneurs should be aware of the hazards that lurk here as well. Business experts note that concerns about child welfare have sparked increased calls for regulation of the industry by OSHA and other government agencies, and that participants face a host of competitors. "A for-profit center may be competing with non-profit centers sponsored by religious organizations, the local Head Start program, family members who baby-sit for little or no cost, caregivers who work in the home, and even after-hours programs run by local elementary schools." Finally, professional day care centers have to grapple with liability issues, encroaching involvement of larger firms, and historically high levels of turnover both among clients and employees.

COLLECTION AGENCIES The surge in credit availability in American households has sparked a corresponding increase in demand for businesses willing to pursue collections for clients. As one industry participant told *Journal of Business Strategy,* establishing a business in this area is attractive to some entrepreneurs "because the cost of entry is low—someone can start out with a phone and a personal computer in a spare bedroom—and clients generally accept smaller vendors." Another business owner in the industry observed that effective collection agencies will particularly benefit from increasing demands from clients such as credit card companies; doctors, lawyers, and other professionals; and health care firms. Moreover, many observers believe that privatization initiatives by local, state, and federal government agencies will provide collection agencies with additional business.

TRAVEL AGENCIES Travel and tourism is a huge business area both in the United States and around the world, and independent travel agencies have benefited accordingly. Both business and recreational travel continue to rise in all geographic regions of America, but the hectic pace of modern life has made many of these travelers look to agencies to take care of the specifics of their journeys, from itinerary planning to plane reservations. McCune noted that travel agents do face some challenges today, including slimmer profit margins (because of competitive fares, etc.) and what amounts to a mandate to provide top-level service (since travelers can either go to competitors or make travel arrangements themselves). But she added that travel agencies that are able to improve productivity through available technology can dramatically increase their prospects for success, and noted that "becoming a specialist in a particular type of travel also gives agencies an edge. [In the mid-1990s], cruises, adventure travel, and eco-tours are what's hot. In addition to being in demand by consumers, such packaged tours also offer better margins. Of course, the key to succeeding in the long run is an ability to uncover the next trendy market in travel. That requires a study of demographics—like the aging of the population and the rise of dual-income families—to identify up-and-coming niches."

FURTHER READING:

Bregger, John. "Measuring Self-Employment in the United States." *Monthly Labor Review.* January-February 1996.

Goff, Lisa. "They're In the Money." *Crain's New York Business.* September 23, 1996.

McCune, Jenny. "The Face of Tomorrow." *Journal of Business Strategy.* May-June 1995.

Porter, Michael E. *Competitive Strategy: Techniques for Analyzing Industries and Competitors.* Free Press, 1998.

"Top 10 Small-Business-Dominated Industries." *Journal of Accountancy.* January 1995.

SMALL CLAIMS COURT

Small claims court is a legal court of law designed to resolve disputes involving small amounts of money in an expeditious manner. Unlike other legal courts, small claims court does not operate by formal rules of evidence, and attorneys are (generally) not utilized. Instead, plaintiffs and defendants simply go before the court and present their respective perspectives on the dispute, and the court makes a judgement based on the evidence presented. Claims made in small claims court, noted writer Sandra R. Bell, typically "involve purchases made by consumers, disputes over shared property, failure to honor contracts or invoices involving small business, investments that have gone under, and expenses that employees accrued from employers." Given the parameters of small claims court, then, it is little wonder that many small business owners sooner or later find themselves involved in a proceeding there, either as a defendant or plaintiff.

APPEARING AS A PLAINTIFF Most small business owners that appear in small claims court as plaintiffs do so because they are having difficulty securing payment for some product or service that they have provided to the defendant. To file a small claims action, the owner needs to first find out if he or she has a case that can even be heard in the court. State limits vary considerably in this regard; some place a ceiling of several hundred dollars, while others will hear claims for as much as $5,000.

If the plaintiff has a complaint that can be legitimately heard in small claims court, he or she should then check with the local county clerk's office for information on procedures for bringing suit. Again, guidelines vary from state to state, although the basic set-up is consistent. The plaintiff also needs to file the claim in the jurisdiction where the defendant resides.

Once the business owner has familiarized him or herself with the basic procedures, he/she should proceed with the filing. This is a fairly basic document, usually only one page in length, that briefly delineates the main reasons for the suit. The document, known as a summons or complaint, should describe the dispute; the time, date, and location that it took place; names of witnesses (if any); and desired compensation. The plaintiff should also try to name the defendant as accurately as possible when filing. "It's very important to have the exact legal listing for a business (named as a defendant)," said one county clerk in an interview with *Business First of Buffalo* contributor Jane Schmitt. "If it's a DBA (doing business as), you want to list them as a DBA if its is responsible for the loss you have incurred. If it's a corporation, make sure you have the exact corporate name. Because while it is not going to make a difference to us, it is going to make a difference to the claimant. . . . If they are successful and want to collect their money, they could hit a snag if they have sued them under an improper legal listing.'' When the complaint has been filed, the court clerk will inform the plaintiff when the case will be tried. The cost of filing a complaint ranges from about $5 to $25.

In the weeks leading up to the court date, the plaintiff should gather whatever evidence is available to bolster his or her claims, including photographs, written agreements, itemized bills and invoices, written cost estimates for service or repairs, receipts, canceled checks, and other correspondence.

APPEARING AS A DEFENDANT When a small business owner receives notice of claim (this is usually sent via both certified mail and first-class mail), he or she should study the summary of the plaintiff's claims, the amount that is being sought, and begin preparing for the trial date (which is also included in the notification). If the copy of the claim that is sent via regular mail is not returned to the court as undeliverable within 21 days, then it is assumed that the defendant has received notice of the claim.

Once the defendant receives notice of the claim, he or she can either try to reach a mutually satisfactory agreement with the plaintiff prior to the trial date or begin preparing for the case by gathering all favorable evidence available (itemized bills or invoices, written agreements, etc.). ''If the claim is not true, you must deny it in no uncertain terms,'' wrote Bell. ''If the basic facts are true, explain why you haven't made restitution. If you are counter-claiming for damages, this must generally be done when you answer the suit. Do not ignore a complaint, and be sure to file your response or counterclaim within the allowable time frame.'' This time frame, it should be noted, varies from state to state.

RESOLVING SMALL CLAIMS COURT CASES

Small claims court cases are resolved in one of four ways: trial, arbitration, settlement, or default judgement.

Trial. This is the method that is most familiar to most Americans. Under this arrangement, the plaintiff makes his case, the defendant offers a rebuttal, and the presiding judge makes a judgement based on the evidence presented by both sides. If either the plaintiff or the defendant is unhappy with the judge's verdict, he or she can file an appeal. This step is rarely taken, however, because of the added expense involved (filing an appeal is more expensive than filing an initial claim, and it sometimes requires soliciting the services of an attorney).

Arbitration. If both sides agree, the dispute can be resolved via arbitration rather than by going to trial. ''The advantage of arbitration is that it occurs the same night and is less formal than a trial,'' said Carol J. Steinberg in *Back Stage.* ''The disadvantage is that you cannot appeal the arbitrator's decision so that if you are unhappy with the result, you have no recourse.''

Settlement. Plaintiffs and defendants also have the option of settling the case out of court prior to the trial. But as Steinberg indicated, small business owners who consent to a settlement need to be very careful about the various provisions of the agreement, especially if you are owed money: ''Your opponent may agree to pay you $150 a month for a year, but if the payments are not made, you have no recourse. If you want to settle the case, make sure that the settlement amount is paid in one lump sum on a certain date. Ask the court to adjourn your case for some time after that. If at that point you have not been paid, you will go forward either with a trial or with arbitration. Be sure that your settlement agreement is in writing and is signed off by a judge.''

Default Judgement. A default judgement—also sometimes referred to as a liquidated complaint—can be handed down in the event that one of the sides involved in the dispute does not appear at the scheduled trial time. In such instances, the judge is presented with the evidence provided by whichever side is present. If the person adequately proves his or her case, a default judgement for the amount claimed is entered, or (in instances wherein the plaintiff does not show up) the case may be dismissed.

COLLECTING MONEY THAT IS OWED

Consultants to small business enterprises warn that winning a small claims case does not necessarily mean that the dispute has been wholly settled. Certainly, if the small business owner mounts a successful defense of a claim, then he or she can return to his business secure in the knowledge that the affair is over. But if the small business owner was a successful plaintiff, he or she still needs to make sure that the amount owed is turned over.

There are a variety of enforcement techniques available to successful plaintiffs, but most people owed money can follow basic steps that are generally effective. ''The first thing that you do after you win is send a demand letter to your opponent, advising that you will begin judgment enforcement techniques immediately if the full amount of the judgment is not sent to you within 20 days of the date of the letter,'' wrote Steinberg. ''You will have an easier time collecting if while you were in court you asked the judge to order the defendant to disclose the assets that would cover the judgment and not to dispose of them until the judgment is paid. The most effective enforcement technique, guaranteed to get the defendant's attention, is to restrain his or her bank account.'' Plaintiffs can do this, stated Steinberg, by locating the defendant's bank and account number on a canceled check (if available). The court then can then impose a restraining order upon the bank, which serves to freeze the account in the amount of the judgement. ''If you do not know where the assets are,'' added Steinberg, ''the court can help you serve information subpoenas upon banks and any institutions or persons who may have knowledge of your opponent's assets.''

FURTHER READING:

Bell, Sandra R. ''Represent Yourself: Here's How You Can Stay One Step Ahead in Small Claims Court.'' *Black Enterprise.* October 1997.

Schmitt, Jane. ''Small Claims Need Not be Big Headache.'' *Business First of Buffalo.* January 17, 1994.

Steinberg, Carol J. ''The Performing Artist's Guide to Small Claims Court.'' April 28, 1995.

Zervos, Michelle. ''Collecting Your Small Claims Court Judgement.'' *Business Credit.* September 1997.

SMOKE FREE ENVIRONMENT

The term smoke free environment is sometimes used indiscriminately to discuss both 100 percent smoke free areas as well as ventilated ones. A truly smoke free environment in a business is one in which no smoking is allowed within any company building or vehicle. Depending on the company, smoking may be permitted in certain outdoor areas designated for that purpose. In other companies, the smoke free policy prohibits *any* smoking on company property. Employees who smoke either have to leave company grounds to do so, or must abstain from smoking while at work. Other companies allow smoking in special rooms or areas dedicated to that purpose. For smoking areas within the building, a special and separate ventilation system must be installed in order to prevent smoke from leaking into other areas of the company.

The concept of creating a smoke free workplace has gained many supporters over the last decade. According to the U.S. Department of Health and Human Services, 79 percent of workplaces with 50 or more employees had formal policies restricting or prohibiting smoking as of 2000. In a Centers for Disease Control (CDC) study published in *JAMA,* the number of respondents reporting that smoking was not allowed in public or work areas at their companies

increased from 46.5 percent in 1992-93 to 63.7 percent in 1995-96. The CDC also noted that in 1999, 43 states and the District of Columbia had laws restricting smoking in governmental work areas. Eleven of these states completely prohibited smoking in these areas. Yet the CDC also noted that only one state (Utah) had achieved a CDC national health objective (under the Healthy People 2000 program) of reducing the prevalence of adult cigarette smoking to 15 percent or less.

HEALTH RISKS OF SMOKING

The 1990 publication of *Risk Assessment on Environmental Tobacco Smoke* by the Environmental Protection Agency ushered in the beginnings of restrictions on smoking in public areas. The EPA report classified environmental tobacco smoke (ETS) as a Group A carcinogen. This designation means that a substance has been determined to present the greatest possible cancer risk for humans. Another Group A carcinogen is asbestos.

According to a 1999 study by the CDC published in *JAMA,* the use of tobacco in the U.S. causes roughly 430,000 deaths each year, including an estimated 3000 deaths from lung cancer among nonsmokers exposed to ETS. The CDC also estimates that 62,000 coronary heart disease deaths annually among nonsmokers are due to their exposure to ETS. ETS can also contribute to allergies, asthma, and other pulmonary disorders, as well as physical discomfort such as eye, nose, throat, and stomach irritation. Despite these findings, the CDC also noted that the percentage of adult smokers in the U.S. ranges from 13.1 percent to 31.5 percent between state lines.

The CDC's national public health goals for 2010 focus more extensively on reducing the number of nonsmokers exposed to environmental smoke. There are specific objectives to increase the number of work sites that have smoking restrictions, and to address ETS in more restrictive clean indoor air laws. According to the CDC, the existence of smoke free work environments will increase the likelihood that affected employees will either reduce or eliminate cigarette use.

DEVELOPING AND IMPLEMENTING A SMOKE FREE WORK ENVIRONMENT

In addition to its impact on employee health and welfare, there are a number of costs associated with smoking. According to Lin Grensing-Pophal in *HR Magazine,* expenditures in the United States related to smoking equal roughly $72 billion every year. These include property loss from fires started by smoking products (over $500 million), work productivity loss

($40 billion), and the costs of additional tobacco-related cleaning and maintenance ($4 billion).

Despite the many reasons to help reduce the incidence of employee smoking, the implementation of a smoke free workplace policy needs to be considered carefully. Between the 1960s and the 1990s, the number of smokers in the U.S. dropped steadily. However, the number leveled off during the 1990s, despite increased numbers of smoke free work sites. Smokers have rights too, as has been proven by litigation attempts. Human resources director Arthur Friedson, quoted in *HR Magazine,* stated that developing a smoke free policy rooted in ''the basic respect of one co-worker to another'' can be most successful, from both an ethical and a legal standpoint.

Prior to establishing a smoke free policy, a company should investigate any existing local and state laws on smoking. Despite highly publicized trials and settlements between the federal government and tobacco companies, there is no federal oversight with respect to the institution of a smoke free environment. *HR Magazine* quotes a figure of over 560 local governments which have enacted ordinances dealing with the rights of nonsmokers. These tend to be stricter than state laws and generally address smoking in public areas such as restaurants, grocery stores, and malls.

On the other side, a careful review of Occupational Safety and Health Administration (OSHA) regulations, protections under the Americans with Disabilities Act (ADA), and state and local law with regards to the rights of smokers and nonsmokers is also warranted. Litigation in which a smoker claims that his or her addiction to tobacco is a disability covered by state and federal laws has occurred with more frequency, although not usually successfully. However, given that any litigation, successful or not, is an enormous burden both financially and emotionally for a small business, it is important to proceed carefully. Work closely with your lawyer to determine applicable laws and regulations.

It may also be helpful to determine how many other businesses in your area are addressing the issue of smoking in the workplace. This can serve as support for your own policies in the case of litigation. You can also get a good idea of what has been successful in other organizations in order to establish a smoke free environment of your own. Other sources for ideas on how to develop or update a nonsmoking policy include a report published by the CDC, *Best Practices for Comprehensive Tobacco Control Programs,* as well as organizations such as the American Cancer Society.

The most important factor in creating a smoke free business environment is having a solid understanding of the workforce. By factoring in the needs of each employee segment, smokers and nonsmokers, and achieving some ''buy-in,'' a small business can reduce or avoid problems down the road. From the very beginning, the involvement of individual employees (again, smokers and nonsmokers alike) in the development of a nonsmoking policy is crucial. Be supportive of employee efforts to stop smoking as well. Many businesses have found the investment in or reimbursement for smoking cessation programs and tools to be money well spent. Some companies even provide a monetary award to successful quitters.

Depending on the elements of your policy, you may need to establish a designated area for smoking. Placing the area outdoors eliminates the expense of a separate ventilation system but may have undesired consequences such as longer break times, and possibly the additional expense of building a shelter, if this is needed.

Be sure to focus efforts on how employee habits, such as frequent breaks, impact an employee's job. In other words, keep policy and discussions steered toward job performance, rather than the issue of smoking. It is important to establish guidelines that impact all employees, such as those regarding breaks, and then enforce them on a consistent basis for the entire staff. Any discussions of violations to these guidelines should address the impact of employee actions on performance. Leave smoking out of the discussion entirely.

Once a small business has developed its nonsmoking policy, it should provide early notice of the policy, prior to implementation. This allows employees to consider the consequences of behavior and, if need be, to make efforts to quit smoking. At this time, the company should also publicize any assistance in quitting smoking, such as a cessation program or monetary rewards. It may be more successful to implement a smoke free policy in stages. For example, smoking might first be restricted to a designated area, then eliminated from company property entirely. However, the success of gradual implementation can vary from workplace to workplace.

Once established, a small business's smoke free environment should also take into account new employees. While there are no laws prohibiting discrimination against smokers, questioning prospective staff as to their smoking habits is ill advised. Not hiring smokers may be defensible for an organization such as the American Cancer Society, but not for most small employers. A more acceptable position is to alert candidates at the time of the interview to the small business's nonsmoking policy and its associated standards of acceptable behavior.

Finally, it is especially important for a small business to regularly revisit its smoking policy, along with other human resources policies. Local, state, and federal laws and regulations are in a constant state of flux over this issue. It pays to review these laws regularly and in conjunction with a legal advisor. The burden of litigation over such issues is a heavy one for a small business to bear. In addition, a shifting employee population may make some changes necessary. Seeking input from employees helps to both promote and refine the policy.

EFFECTS OF A SMOKE FREE ENVIRONMENT ON CUSTOMERS

The implications of a smoke free environment in small businesses such as restaurants, bars, and shops also extend to customers. For these types of businesses, local and state laws and regulations may also be more straightforward. Many states and municipalities already limit or eliminate smoking in the public areas of these businesses. In the state of California, for example, no smoking is permitted in any public establishment. California lawmakers alerted the public of the change six months prior to implementing this legislation to allow businesses time to address the issue in their workplace policies and to provide consumers with time to get used to the idea. There also may be legal issues to consider. According to an article in *Business-First Columbus,* the National Restaurant Association states that employers can be held liable if staff members become ill from second-hand smoke.

Other states require a public establishment to have both smoking and nonsmoking areas within a restaurant, with space and sometimes ventilation requirements for each. As noted with work environments, a separate ventilation system may be used to divert smoky air. Working with local authorities as well as reviewing policies from similar businesses in the area can help a small business to determine its needs.

If the institution of a smoke free environment at a small business is not tied to any governmental regulations or requirements that are already known by the general public, a small business should consider giving advance notice of the new policy to their customers. A simple posting at the door as well as personal verbal or written notice to regular clients can go a long way to ensure customers' responsiveness and compliance. Finally, in cases where customers ignore the policy, it is important to courteously but consistently administrate it, even at the risk of losing those customers.

The implementation of a smoke free environment is a complex process for any small business. By using legal counsel to wade through the maze of pertinent laws and regulations, working with employees to develop a policy, and communicating the policy regularly to both employees and customers, a small business can ensure its efforts are successful.

FURTHER READING:

Bellotti, Mary. ''Who's Taking the Hit?'' *Business Journal-Portland.* September 22, 2000.

Cronan, Carl. ''Cancer Society Offers 'How-To' Help On Smoking Policies.'' *Tampa Bay Business Journal.* January 26, 2001.

''DOD to Phase Out Smoking at Recreation Facilities.'' *All Hands.* August 2000.

Downey Grimsley, Kirstin. ''Dumped, Stiffed and Delinquent.'' *Washington Post.* May 31, 2000.

Grensing-Pophal, Lin. ''Smokin' in the Workplace.'' *HR Magazine.* May 1999.

Linn, Diane. ''Ordinance 937: A Business-Friendly Smoking Ban.'' *Business Journal-Portland.* September 22, 2000.

Pavilkey, Susan. ''Clearing the Air.'' *Business First-Columbus.* February 2, 2001.

''State-Specific Prevalence of Current Cigarette Smoking Among Adults and the Proportion of Adults Who Work in a Smoke Free Environment—United States, 1999.'' *JAMA, The Journal of the American Medical Association.* December 13, 2000.

Sullum, Jacob. *For Your Own Good.* The Free Press, 1998.

Weis, William L. and Bruce W. Miller. *The Smoke Free Workplace.* Prometheus Books, 1985.

SOLE PROPRIETORSHIP

The sole proprietorship is both the simplest and most common type of business operating in the United States today. Most businesses that are owned and operated by one person take this form; in fact, small business owners who have sole ownership of their enterprises are automatically categorized under this business type if they do not take steps to legally establish themselves as another type of business.

ADVANTAGES OF SOLE PROPRIETORSHIP

Many aspects of sole proprietorship are attractive to entrepreneurs. Primary reasons why small business owners choose to operate in this fashion include:

- Sole proprietors enjoy a great deal of independence and autonomy. As Janet Attard remarked in *The Home Office and Small Business Answer Book,* the sole proprietor makes all the decisions: ''You alone can decide what to sell and how to sell it, when to expand the business and when to pull back, when to look for financing, when to buy new equipment, when and how long to work, and when to take the day off—without having to justify your decision to anyone.'' In some instances, sole proprietorships can benefit enormously as a result of this streamlined management structure. An entrepreneur who keeps abreast of business trends, community events, and other factors that can impact on a company's fortunes may, in some cases, be able to adjust to changing business realities far more quickly than a partnership or corporation, where multiple owners and/or managers need to reach agreement on appropriate responses to changes in their business environment.

- Figuring taxes is fairly straightforward. Unlike other business types, sole proprietorships do not have to file separate income tax returns. In addition, FICA (Federal Insurance Contributions Act) taxes for such businesses are less than they are for partnerships or other legal operating forms.

- Accounting is a relatively simple affair, although small business experts encourage the owners of even the most modest business ventures to establish separate bank accounts and record keeping practices for their enterprise.

- Business operations, too, are generally simpler in a sole proprietorship. Other forms of business often have to contend with more cumbersome or time-consuming regulatory requirements in conducting or reporting on their operations.

- Start-up costs are often modest. This is due in part to the fact that entrepreneurs who intend to establish sole proprietorships do not need to secure the services of an attorney to prepare documents required by state or federal agencies, since none are needed.

- Business losses can be used to offset other income on personal tax returns. Conversely, business profits do not have to be shared with any other owners.

- Sole proprietors are not forbidden from securing and building a work force. Indeed, many businesses that qualify as sole proprietorships (delicatessens, landscaping firms, canoe liveries, flower shops, etc.) have employees.

DISADVANTAGES OF SOLE PROPRIETORSHIP

But while business owners who choose sole proprietorship understandably enjoy their autonomy and their freedom from the paperwork that can be considerable in other, more complicated, business types, they still need to consider the following drawbacks in the areas of liability and business financing.

''In a sole proprietorship,'' warned Jocelyn West Brittin in *Selecting the Legal Structure for Your Business,* ''the business and the owner are one and the same. There is no separate legal entity and thus no separate legal 'person.' This means that as a sole proprietor you will have unlimited personal responsibility for your business's liabilities. For example, if your business cannot pay for its supplies, the suppliers can sue you individually. The business creditors can go against both the business's assets, including your bank account, car or house. . . . The reverse is also true; i.e., your personal creditors can make claims against your business's assets.'' She does note that some states offer sole proprietors protection of their personal assets from business risks through legal designations that involve the owner's spouse and/or children, but such arrangements are complex and should not be entered into without first consulting with an attorney. Business owners can also elect to purchase liability insurance for protection from lawsuits and other threats. In addition to general liability insurance, producers or sellers of goods may also want to consider securing product liability insurance. The cost of such insurance varies considerably depending on the type of business under consideration.

Raising capital for a sole proprietorship can be quite difficult as well (though many businesses that operate as sole proprietorships are of modest size and thus are not impacted by this reality). Many lenders are reluctant to provide financing to owners of sole proprietorships—in large part because of fears about their ability to recover the funds should the owner die or become disabled—and even those who make such loans require borrowers to provide personal guaranties on the loan. Sole proprietors who consent to such arrangements are in effect pledging their personal assets as collateral on the loan. Small business advisors counsel clients who are considering these stipulations to proceed cautiously. If a potential lender is taking extra measures to protect itself from default, it may be an indication that the prospective borrower's business plan is viewed—legitimately, perhaps—as flawed or risky. In addition, even well-conceived businesses sometimes fail as a result of circumstances beyond the owner's control. An entrepreneur might, for example, establish a store that is enormously successful for its first few years of operation, only to see it suffer a dramatic downturn in performance with the arrival in town of a much larger competitor that provides its customers with a wider variety of services and goods. Banks and other lending institutions are aware that such scenarios occur, and they plan accordingly.

CONTINUITY AND TRANSFERABILITY Unlike other businesses that can be passed down from generation to generation or continue to exist long after the passage of its original board of directors, sole proprietorships have a limited life. As Brittin wrote, ''a sole proprietorship can exist as long as its owner is alive and desires to continue the business. When the owner dies, the sole proprietorship no longer exists. The assets and liabilities of the business become part of the owner's estate.''

A sole proprietor is free to sell all or a portion of his or her business to a buyer, but any transaction that transfers ownership or turns the business into one with two or more owners puts an end to the sole proprietorship that had been in existence.

STARTING A SOLE PROPRIETORSHIP

Sole proprietorships often operate under the name of the owner of the business, but this is not a requirement. If the owner decides to select a fictitious name, however, he or she may be required to file a certificate explaining the arrangement in the region in which he or she is operating the business in question (this requirement also gives the sole proprietor legal protection, for it serves to protect them from other persons who might otherwise use the name for their own business enterprises). In addition, many states forbid business establishments from using words like ''incorporated,'' ''Co.,'' or ''Inc.'' unless they actually qualify as corporations. Some cities and counties also require sole proprietorships to secure a business license before launching their business. Owners who subsequently change their business location or add new locations to their operation are often required to obtain new business licenses for those sites as well.

Many sole proprietorships also will need to obtain federal and state payroll ID numbers. These numbers are required for any businesses that will have employees or will do business with establishments that have employees. Finally, owners of sole proprietorships will, like all other business owners, have to obtain the appropriate operating licenses and certificates, if any, for the area in which they will be conducting business. Business licenses and zoning permits are among the types of licenses that are sometimes required. Once these few minor licensing issues have been addressed, the sole proprietor is free to conduct business.

Once a sole proprietorship has been established and proven viable, many business owners eventually choose to incorporate. Incorporation is both more expensive and more time-consuming than sole proprietorship, but it also affords the business owner considerably more legal protection from lawsuits and other liabilities than does sole proprietorship, and it also makes it easier to secure financing for business expansion.

FURTHER READING:

Attard, Janet. *The Home Office and Small Business Answer Book.* Holt, 1993.

Brittin, Jocelyn West. *Selecting the Legal Structure for Your Business.* Small Business Administration, n.a.

The Entrepreneur Magazine Small Business Advisor. Wiley, 1995.

Fraser, Jill Andresky. ''Perfect Form.'' *Inc.* December 1997.

Hawkins, Carole. ''Beyond the Sole Proprietorship.'' *Home Office Computing.* March 2001.

How to Set Up Your Own Small Business. American Institute of Small Business, 1990.

Schneeman, Angela. *The Law of Corporations, Partnerships, and Sole Proprietorships.* West Legal Studies, 1996.

Sitarz, Daniel. *Sole Proprietorship: Small Business Start-Up Kit.* Nova, 2000.

SEE ALSO: Incorporation; Partnership

SPAM

Spam is a slang term that describes unsolicited commercial advertisements sent by e-mail over the Internet. Spam, which can be used as a noun or as a verb, is also known as junk e-mail or unsolicited bulk e-mail. According to Heather Newman in the *Detroit Free Press,* the term comes from a skit by the Monty Python comedy troupe, in which a group of Vikings chants ''spam, spam, spam'' to drown out all other conversation. It was adopted by early Internet users to describe annoying, unsolicited e-mail advertisements that crowd out legitimate communication. ''Spam is an overwhelming fact of life for nearly every e-mail user,'' Newman wrote. ''Some Internet postmasters say that more than half the traffic their computers handle is spam.''

THE COSTS OF SPAM

''The financial and psychological costs of spam are eroding the Internet's goodwill,'' Karen Rodriguez wrote in the *Phoenix Business Journal.* Spam causes problems for both e-mail users and the Internet Service Providers (ISPs) that offer access to the Internet to customers for a fee. Most e-mail users resent receiving spam messages because they fill up electronic mailboxes and are time-consuming to sort through. In addition, a large proportion of spam messages contain material that could be considered offensive or fraudulent. A survey of spam content conducted on behalf of Representative Gary Miller of California, co-sponsor of proposed legislation to ban spam, found that 30 percent consisted of pornographic materials, another 30 percent consisted of get-rich-quick schemes, and the remainder included a variety of questionable business proposals and gambling opportunities.

Companies that send out bulk e-mail defend the practice on several grounds. For example, they say that some small businesses cannot afford other forms of marketing. Sending bulk e-mail helps these businesses reach potential customers and compete with larger firms. Proponents of e-mail marketing also claim that their advertisements are a constitutionally protected form of free speech. "Spammers try to justify their actions by claiming that companies have the right to take advantage of the online market and that people have no right to filter their mail," Maria O'Daniel wrote in *Computimes*.

But opponents of spam argue that Internet users end up paying to receive unwanted advertisements. By sending bulk e-mail to thousands of recipients, spammers create an increase in the load placed on ISP mail servers. O'Daniel explained that ISPs must purchase bandwidth in order to connect their servers to the Internet. They buy bandwidth based on expected usage by their paying customers, and the cost accounts for a large percentage of their operating budgets. Spam ties up bandwidth and reduces processing speed, which causes an increase in costs for ISPs and a decrease in performance for their customers. So while it may cost a spammer only a few dollars to create and send an advertisement via e-mail, it may cost an ISP thousands of dollars to accommodate the spam. These costs are usually passed on to the ISP's customers, most of whom did not want to receive the spam in the first place.

Complaints from ISPs and Internet users have prompted several states to pass laws regulating spam. But many people claim that, due to the interstate reach of the Internet, federal action is also required. The U.S. government has considered various proposals to reduce spam. One such proposal would allow ISPs to sue in civil court and claim damages as high as $50 per message or $25,000 per day against companies that send unsolicited commercial e-mail over their servers. Other bills would require spammers to include a "reply to sender" option to allow recipients to opt out of receiving future e-mails, or would prohibit spammers from sending e-mail to people who register their addresses on a "global opt out" list compiled by the Federal Communications Commission.

Some experts claim that such laws might facilitate claims by large Internet companies like America Online, which can afford to take legal action against spammers, but would do little to help smaller, local ISPs. "Although state anti-spam legislation is designed to encourage ISPs to sue every time spammers clog e-mail servers and harass ISP customers, the providers have filed few if any lawsuits because the cost of litigation is too high and such cases are hard to prosecute," Rodriguez noted. "Spam is easy to create, and its purveyors are hard to find."

WAYS TO REDUCE SPAM

Most reputable ISPs have "acceptable use" policies that prohibit users from sending bulk commercial e-mail over their systems. Since spam is against the rules, some people think that spammers operate by breaking into an ISP's mail system and sending e-mail to everyone on the system. In reality, spammers obtain e-mail addresses from a wide range of legal sources, including business cards, newspaper articles, Web pages, member lists, customer lists, and message postings. They even collect jokes, chain letters, and other frequently forwarded e-mail messages that have hundreds of addresses on the top.

The first rule of reducing spam, according to Newman, is to limit the ways in which your e-mail address is exposed to the public. One possible method is to create a free e-mail account to use in situations where you must make your address public, such as posting messages to newsgroups. It is also a good policy to hide the addresses of recipients if you forward e-mail messages to large groups of people. Newman emphasized that you should never respond to spam or select an option that allows you to opt out of receiving future messages, because this proves that your e-mail is a working address and makes it more valuable to spammers.

Since sending spam is against the rules of most ISPs, it may be helpful to notify the originating ISP that someone is using their service to send spam. The best way to do this involves sending a copy of the offending message to the ISP's system administrator. "The administrators are the ones who are best able to deal with it," O'Daniel noted. "They will be grateful to hear from you—no one wants to be associated with spammers." Most ISPs will respond by terminating the spammer's account. This strategy is not always effective, however, because spammers are often difficult to locate. The worst offenders will "spoof" or create a false address for their messages, change identity frequently, and send spam from a number of different addresses.

It may also be helpful to inform your own ISP when you receive spam, so that the system administrator can filter out future messages from that address. Many e-mail programs also feature filtering capabilities. Finally, if you are bombarded with e-mail from a company with which you have done business, or you find out that such a company has sold your e-mail address to a spammer, you can boycott the company's products or send an e-mail of protest to the company president.

FURTHER READING:

Hinde, Stephen. ''Smurfing, Swamping, Spamming, Spoofing, Squatting, Slandering, Surfing, Scamming, and Other Mischiefs of the World Wide Web.'' *Computers and Security.* May 2000.

Hoover, Kent. ''Spamming: Marketing Opportunity for Small Business or Costly Annoyance?'' *Pittsburgh Business Times.* November 12, 1999.

Newman, Heather. ''Do a Little Work to Give Spammer Unhappy Returns.'' *Detroit Free Press.* February 28, 2001.

Newman, Heather. ''How to Can Net Spam—The Real Junk Mail.'' *Detroit Free Press.* February 21, 2001.

O'Daniel, Maria. ''How to Handle E-Mail Spamming.'' *Computimes.* April 3, 2000.

Rodriguez, Karen. ''Federal Lawmakers Propose Bill to End Spamming.'' *Phoenix Business Journal.* May 12, 2000.

SEE ALSO: Electronic Mail

SPAN OF CONTROL

Span of control, also known as span of management, is a human resources management term that refers to the number of subordinates a supervisor can effectively manage. It is a particularly important concept for small business owners to understand. ''Span of control is widely taught in management schools and widely employed in large organizations like the military, government agencies, and educational institutions,'' Mark Hendricks wrote in an article for *Entrepreneur.* ''Yet few entrepreneurs know the term or are willing to admit any limit to the number of people they directly oversee.'' When a small business owner's span of control becomes too large, it can limit the growth of his or her company. Even the best managers tend to lose their effectiveness when they spend all their time managing people and their issues and are unable to focus on long-term plans and competitive positioning for the business as a whole.

The concept of span of control was developed in the United Kingdom in 1922 by Sir Ian Hamilton. It arose from the assumption that managers have finite amounts of time, energy, and attention to devote to their jobs. In studies of British military leaders, Hamilton found that they could not effectively control more than three to six people directly. These figures have been generally accepted as the ''rule of thumb'' for span of control ever since. More than a decade later, A.V. Graicumas illustrated the concept of span of control mathematically. His research showed that the number of interactions between managers and their subordinates—and thus the amount of time managers spent on supervision—increased geometrically as the managers' span of control became larger. For example, as George P. Hattrup and Brian H. Kleiner noted in *Industrial Management,* the addition of a fifth subordinate under one manager raises the manager's potential interactions from 44 to 100, while the addition of an eighth subordinate increases the potential interactions from 490 to 1,080. At some point, the demands of these interactions with subordinates creates serious problems for the manager.

It is important to note that all managers experience a decrease in effectiveness as their span of control exceeds the optimal level. In other words, the limitations implied by span of control are not shortcomings of certain individual managers but rather of managers in general. In addition, it is important to understand that span of control refers only to direct reports, rather than to an entire corporate hierarchy. Even though a CEO may technically control hundreds of employees, his or her span of control would only include the department heads or functional managers who reported to the CEO directly. ''When given enough levels of hierarchy, any manager can control any number of people—albeit indirectly,'' Hendricks noted. ''But when it comes to direct reports, the theory [of span of control] suggests entrepreneurs must respect managers' inborn limits.''

Entrepreneurs and small business owners are particularly susceptible to overextending their span of control. After all, many of these people have started a business from the ground up and are wary of losing control over its operations. They thus choose to manage lots of people directly, rather than delegating tasks to middle managers, in an effort to continue being involved in key decisions as the business grows. But this strategy can backfire, as Hendricks explained: ''Extending span of control beyond the recommended limits engenders poor morale, hinders effective decision making, and may cause loss of the agility and flexibility that give many entrepreneurial firms their edge.''

ORGANIZING TO OPTIMIZE MANAGERS' SPAN OF CONTROL

In their article, Hattrup and Kleiner noted that establishing the optimal span of control for managers is one of the most important tasks in structuring organizations. Finding the optimal span involves balancing the relative advantages and disadvantages of retaining responsibility for decisions and delegating those decisions. In general, studies have shown that the larger the organization, the fewer people should report to the top person. Managers should also have fewer direct reports if those subordinates interact with each other frequently. In this situation, the supervisor ends up managing both his or her relationship with the subordinates and the subordinates' relationships with one another.

Some other factors affecting the optimal span of control include whether workers perform tasks of a routine nature (which might permit a broader span of control) or of great variety and complexity (which might require a narrower span of control), and whether the overall business situation is stable (which would indicate a broader span) or dynamic (which would require a narrower span). Other situations in which a broader span of control might be possible include when the manager delegates effectively; when there are staff assistants to screen interactions between the manager and subordinates; when subordinates are competent, well-trained, and able to work independently; and when subordinates' goals are well-aligned with those of other workers and the organization.

Hattrup and Kleiner also outlined a number of advantages and disadvantages to different spans of control. A narrow span of control tends to give managers close control over operations and to facilitate fast communication between managers and employees. On the other hand, a narrow span of control can also create a situation where managers are too involved in their subordinates' work, which can reduce innovation and morale among employees. A wide span of control forces managers to develop clear goals and policies, delegate tasks effectively, and select and train employees carefully. Since employees get less supervision, they tend to take on more responsibility and have higher morale with a wide span of control. On the other hand, managers with a wide span of control might become overloaded with work, have trouble making decisions, and lose control over their subordinates.

With all of these factors to consider, small business owners might become overwhelmed with the task of finding the optimal span of control. But Hendricks claimed that evaluating the situation and making a decision should not be too difficult. ''The rule of thumb that an executive should supervise three to six people directly held up fairly well against challenges from efficiency experts, team-building zealots, technology buffs, empowerment boosters, megalomaniacs, and others determined to increase the accepted span of control,'' Hendricks wrote. ''If the calculations are too much for you, just take a look at the amount of hours you're working. When workdays for the people at the top are twice what they are for others, span of control is out of whack.''

For small business owners who feel that they have too many direct reports and need to reduce their span of control, the solution may involve either hiring middle managers to take on a portion of the owner's responsibilities, or reorganizing the reporting structure of the company. In either case, small business owners must balance their own capabilities and workload against the need to control costs. After all, reducing the entrepreneur's span of control may involve the costs of paying additional salaries for new hires or training existing employees to take on supervisory responsibilities. Despite the potential costs involved, Hendricks argued that adjusting span of control toward the optimal level can can lead to vast improvements for small businesses. ''There's the real possibility that paying attention to span of control could usher your business into a new era of rapid, sustained, profitable growth,'' he told entrepreneurs. ''You could even find running your business easier and more fun.''

FURTHER READING:

Hattrup, George P., and Brian H. Kleiner. ''How to Establish the Proper Span of Control for Managers.'' *Industrial Management.* November-December 1993.

Hendricks, Mark. ''Span Control.'' *Entrepreneur.* January 2001.

Visser, Bauke. ''Organizational Communication Structure and Performance.'' *Journal of Economic Behavior and Organization.* June 2000.

SEE ALSO: Delegation; Manager Recruitment

STANDARD MILEAGE RATE

The standard mileage rate (SMR), also known as mileage per diem, is the amount per mile that the Internal Revenue Service (IRS) allows small businesses and self-employed persons to use to calculate their vehicle expenses for tax deduction purposes. Businesses that choose to use the standard mileage rate do so because it is easier to use than the actual costs method, which requires keeping complete records of expenses like gasoline, maintenance, tires, insurance, and license and registration fees. The standard mileage rate can be used for all mileage accumulated for work-related trips, but commuting between home and work does not qualify for this type of deduction.

The standard mileage rate is determined by the IRS and is routinely adjusted, but not more often than once a year. Most recently, the IRS raised the standard mileage rate to 34.5 cents per mile (up from 32.5 cents the previous year) for small business owners. This adjustment took effect on January 1, 2001. The federal government cited fluctuating gas prices and a desire to provide relief for businesses as the main reasons for adjusting the rate. Other current standard mileage rates include 14 cents per mile for the use of a car that provides services to a charity, 12 cents per mile for cars used for medical reasons, and 12 cents per mile for deductible moving expenses.

The standard mileage rate can be used for vehicles that a business owns. In addition, the IRS decided in 1998 that the SMR can also be used for leased vehicles, provided that one uses the standard mileage rate for the duration of the lease (or the balance of the lease if it began before 1998).

RESTRICTIONS ASSOCIATED WITH THE STANDARD MILEAGE RATE

While the standard mileage rate is quite practical, it may not be used in several situations. One instance would include taxis and other vehicles for hire that charge for mileage in the first place. Also, if a fleet-type business is using more than one vehicle at the same time, they cannot use the standard mileage rate, although they can use it if they own two or more vehicles that aren't being used concurrently. Rural mail carriers that already receive a qualified reimbursement are also not eligible for the standard mileage rate.

In addition, small businesses that decide to use the standard mileage rate for a vehicle must do so in the first year that the vehicle is placed into service. In later years, a business can switch to the actual cost method if they so desire. However, a straight line method of depreciation, which yields a smaller deduction, must be used in all subsequent years for vehicles that initially used the standard mileage rate.

The standard mileage rate already has vehicle depreciation built into it, meaning that one cannot claim additional depreciation when using this form of deduction. Also, businesses that sell a car that has used the standard mileage rate will have to figure out whether any taxable gains were made on the sale and adjust the tax basis of the vehicle for each year the SMR was applied. Finally, the standard mileage rate and the actual costs method cannot be used at the same time.

FURTHER READING:

Tax Guide for Small Business. Internal Revenue Service, n.d.

SEE ALSO: Business Travel

STOCKS

Securities issued by a corporation are classified as debt, equity, or some hybrid of these two forms. Debt usually takes the form of a loan and must be repaid, while equity usually takes the form of an ownership claim upon the corporation. The two main types of equity claims are common stock and preferred stock, although there are also related claims, such as rights, warrants, and convertible securities. Growing companies, which tend to lack the assets

necessary to secure debt, often decide to issue equity securities. Although issuing common stock can be traumatic for a small business—because it can be costly, and because it causes a dramatic redistribution of ownership and control—it can also provide a solid foundation upon which to build a company. Preferred stock offers holders priority in receiving dividends and in claiming assets in the event of business liquidation, but it also lacks the voting rights afforded to common stockholders. Many venture capitalists require convertible preferred stock—which can be converted to common stock at some time in the future at a favorable price—as incentive to invest in start-up ventures.

COMMON STOCK

A share of common stock is quite literally a share in the business, a partial claim to ownership of the firm. Owning a share of common stock provides a number of rights and privileges. These include sharing in the income of the firm, exercising a voice in the management of the firm, and holding a claim on the assets of the firm.

DIVIDENDS Sharing in the income of the firm is generally in the form of a cash dividend. The firm is not obligated to pay dividends, which must be declared by the board of directors. The size and timing of the dividends is uncertain. In a strictly rational economic environment, dividends would be considered as a ''residual.'' In this view, the firm would weigh payment of dividends against other uses for the funds. Dividends would be paid only if the firm had no better use for the funds. In this case, declaring or increasing dividends would be a negative signal, since the firm would be admitting that it lacked possibilities for growth.

For widely held, publicly traded firms there are a number of indications that this is not the case, and that shareholders and investors like dividends and dividend increases. In these contexts, dividends are taken as a signal that the firm is financially healthy. A decrease in dividends would indicate inability to maintain the level of dividends, signaling a decline in prospects. An increase would signal an improvement in prospects. The signal from a dividend decrease is strong because management will wish to give only positive signals by at least maintaining the dividend, making cuts only when absolutely necessary. The signal from a dividend increase is also strong because management would be hesitant to increase dividends unless they could be maintained. The signaling nature of dividends is supported by cases in which the dividend is maintained in the face of declining earnings, sometimes even using borrowed funds. It is also supported by the occurrence of ''extraordinary'' or one-time-only dividends, a label by which management attempts to avoid increasing expectations.

This signaling approach is not applicable to closely held firms. In this situation, communication between management and shareholders is more direct and signals are not required. When owners are also the managers, sharing in earnings may take the indirect form of salaries and fringe benefits. In fact, shareholders in closely held firms may prefer that dividends be reinvested, even in relatively low return projects, as a form of tax protection. The investment is on a pretax (before personal tax) basis for the investor, avoiding immediate double taxation and converting the income to capital gains that will be paid at a later date.

Dividends are declared for stockholders at a particular date, called the date of record. Since stock transactions ordinarily take five business days for completion, the stock goes ''ex-dividend'' four days before the date of record, unless special arrangement is made for immediate delivery. Since the dividend removes funds from the firm, it can be expected that the per share price will decrease by the amount of the dividend on the ex-dividend date.

Stock dividends are quite different in form and nature from cash dividends. In a stock dividend, the investor is given more shares in proportion to the number already held. A stock split is similar, with a difference in accounting treatment and a greater increase in the number of shares. The use of the word ''dividends'' in stock dividends is actually a misuse of the word, since there is no flow of cash, and the proportional and absolute ownership of the investor is unchanged. The stockholder receives nothing more than a repackaging of ownership: the number of shares increases, but the price per share will drop. There are, however, some arguments in favor of stock dividends. One of these is the argument that investors will avoid stocks of unusually high price, possibly due to required size of investment and round lot (100 share) trading. On the other hand, stocks with unusually low price are also avoided, perhaps perceived as ''cheap.'' The price drop accompanying stock dividends can be used to adjust price. Stock dividends have also been suggested as a way to make cash dividends elective while also providing tax-advantaged reinvestment.

With a cash dividend, an investor who wishes to reinvest must pay taxes and then reinvest the reduced amount. With a stock dividend, the entire amount is reinvested. Although taxes will ultimately be paid, in the interim a return is earned on the entire pretax amount. This is the same argument as that for low dividends in a closely held firm. Investors who want cash dividends can simply sell the stock. Using stock dividends in this way faces restrictions from the Internal Revenue Service.

CONTROL The corporate form allows the separation of management and ownership, with the manager serving as the agent of the owner. Separation raises the problem of control, or what is termed the agency problem. Stockholders have only indirect control by voting for the directors. The directors in turn choose management and are responsible for monitoring and controlling management's conduct. In fact, the stockholders' ability to influence the conduct of the firm may be quite small, and management may have virtually total control within very broad limits.

Voting for the directors takes either of two forms. The first form is majority voting. In this form, each stockholder receives votes for each open position according to the number of shares held, and may cast those votes only for candidates for that position. The winning candidate is the candidate winning a majority of the votes cast. The second form is called cumulative voting. In this form, stockholders again receive votes for each open position according to the number of shares held, but may apportion the votes among the positions and candidates as desired. The candidates receiving the most votes are elected.

Excluding minority stockholders from representation on the board is more difficult under cumulative voting. For example, if there are four directors to be elected and one million shares eligible to vote at one vote per share, a stockholder with 500,001 shares would control the election. Under majority voting a dissident stockholder with 200,001 shares could cast only 200,001 votes apiece for candidates for each of the four positions, which would not be sufficient to ensure representation on the board. Under cumulative voting, a dissident stockholder with a minimum of 200,001 shares could be sure of representation by electing one candidate of choice, casting a cumulative 800,004 votes for that candidate. The remaining 799,999 shares could be sure of electing three chosen candidates, but could not command sufficient votes to exceed the cumulative dissident vote four times.

Although the board of directors is supposedly independent of management, the degree of independence is sometimes small. Typically, some members of the board are ''insiders'' drawn from management, while others are ''outside'' directors. Even the outside directors may not be completely independent of management for several reasons. One reason is that few shareholders can afford the time and expense to attend the annual meetings, so that voting is done through the mail. This usually takes the form of a ''proxy'' giving management the power to vote for the shareholder, as instructed. While the shareholder may instruct management on how to vote, the choices may be few and are controlled by management. Management will tend to nominate safe candidates for directorship, who will not be likely to challenge the status quo. As a result, directorship is at times an honor or sinecure, treated as having few real obligations.

Dissidents may mount opposition and seek the proxy votes, but such opposition is liable to face legal challenges and must overcome both psychological barriers and shareholder apathy. Many shareholders either do not vote or routinely vote for existing management. Further, dissidents must spend their own money, while management has the resources of the firm at its disposal.

In addition to controlling the proxy system, managements have instituted a number of other defensive mechanisms in the face of takeover threats. It is not unusual to find several ''classes'' of stock with different voting power, with some classes having no voting power at all. A number of firms have changed from cumulative to majority voting. Staggered boards, in which only a portion of the board terms expire in a given year, and supermajority voting policies have also been used. Takeover defenses include the golden parachute, or extremely generous severance compensation in the face of a takeover, and the poison pill, an action that is triggered by a takeover and has the effect of reducing the value of the firm. All of these measures act to make stockholder power appear more tenuous.

There has been some recent movement towards greater stockholder power. One factor in this movement is the increasing size of institutional investors such as pensions and mutual funds. This has led to a more activist stance, and a willingness to use the power of large stock positions to influence management. Another factor is a renewed emphasis on the duties of the directors, who may be personally liable for management's misconduct.

RESIDUAL OWNERSHIP The common stockholder has a claim on the assets of the firm. This is an undifferentiated or general claim which does not apply to any specific asset. The claim cannot be exercised except at the breakup of the firm. The firm may be dissolved by a vote of the stockholders, or by bankruptcy. In either case, there is a well-defined priority in which the liabilities of the firm will be met. The common stockholders have the lowest priority, and receive a distribution only if prior claims are paid in full. For this reason the common stockholder is referred to as the residual owner of the firm.

PREEMPTIVE RIGHT The corporate charter will often provide common stockholders with the right to maintain their proportional ownership in the firm, called the preemptive right. For example, if a stockholder owns 10 percent of the stock outstanding and 100,000 new shares are to be issued, the stockholder has the right to purchase 10,000 shares (10 percent) of the new issue. This preemptive right can be honored in a rights offering. In a rights offering, each stockholder receives one right for each share held. Buying shares or subscribing to the issue then requires the surrender of a set number of rights, as well as payment of the offering price. The offering is often underpriced in order to assure its success. The rights are then valuable because possession of the rights allows subscription to the underpriced issue. The rights can be transferred and are often traded.

A rights offering may be attractive to management because the stockholders, who thought enough of the firm to buy its stock, are a pre-sold group. The value of the preemptive right to the common stockholders, however, is questionable. The preemptive right of proportional ownership is important only if proportional control is important to the stockholder. The stockholder may be quite willing to waive the preemptive right. If the funds are used properly, the price of the stock will increase, and all stockholders will benefit. Without buying part of the new issue, the stockholder may have a smaller proportional share, but the share will be worth more. While rights are usually valuable, this value arises from underpricing of the issue rather than from an inherent value of rights. The value of the rights ultimately depends on the use of the funds and whether or not the market views that use as valuable.

VALUATION In investment practice, decisions are more often expressed and made in terms of the comparative expected rates of return, rather than on price. A number of models and techniques are used for valuation. A common approach to valuation of common stock is present value. This approach is based on an estimate of the future cash dividends. The present value is then the amount which, if invested at the required rate of return on the stock, could exactly recreate the estimated dividends. This required rate of return can be estimated from models such as the capital asset pricing model (CAPM), using the systematic risk of the stock, or from the estimated rate of return on stocks of similar risk. Another common approach is based on the price-earnings ratios, or P/E. In this approach, the estimated earnings of the firm are multiplied by the appropriate P/E to obtain the estimated price. This approach can be shown to be a special case of present value analysis, with restrictive assumptions. Since various models and minor differences in assumptions can produce widely different results, valuation is best applied as a comparative analysis.

In some cases, such as estate valuation, the dollar value of the stock must be estimated for legal purposes. For assets that are widely publicly traded, the market price is generally taken as an objective estimate of asset value for legal purposes, since this is sale value of the stock. For stock that is not widely traded, valuation is based on models such as present value, combined with a comparison with similar publicly traded stock. Often, however, a number of discounts are applied for various reasons. It is widely accepted that, compared to publicly traded stock, stock that is not publicly traded should be valued at a discount because of a lack of liquidity. This discount may be 60 percent or more. Another discount is applied for a minority position in a closely held stock or a family firm, since the minority position would have no control. This discount does not apply if the value is estimated from the value of publicly traded stock, because the market price of a stock is traded already at the price of a minority position. There is an inverse effect for publicly traded stock in the form of a control premium. A large block of stock which would give control of the firm might be priced above market.

Finally, it should be noted that the accounting book value is only rarely more than tangentially relevant to market value. This is due to the use of accounting assumptions such as historic cost. While accounting information may be useful in a careful valuation study, accounting definitions of value differ sharply from economic value.

PREFERRED STOCK

Preferred stock is sometimes called a hybrid, since it has some of the properties of equity and some of the properties of debt. Like debt, the cash flows to be received are specified in advance. Unlike debt, these specified flows are in the form of promises rather than of legal obligations. It is not unusual for firms to have several issues of preferred stock outstanding, with differing characteristics. Other differences arise in the areas of control and claims on assets.

DIVIDENDS Because the specified payments on preferred stock are not obligations, they are referred to as dividends. Preferred dividends are not tax-deductible expenses for the firm, and consequently the cost to the firm of raising capital from this source is higher than for debt. The firm is unlikely to skip or fail to declare the dividend, however, for several reasons. One of the reasons is that the dividends are typically (but not always) cumulative. Any skipped dividend remains due and payable by the firm, although no interest is due. One source of the preferred designation is that all preferred dividends in arrears must be paid before any dividend can be paid to common stockholders (although bond payments have priority over all dividends). Failure to declare preferred dividends may also trigger restrictive conditions of the issue. A very important consideration is that, just as for common dividends, preferred dividends are a signal to stockholders, both actual and potential. A skipped preferred dividend would indicate that common dividends will also be skipped, and would be a very negative signal that the firm was encountering problems. This would also close off access to most lenders.

There is also a form of preferred stock, called participating preferred stock, in which there may be a share in earnings above the specified dividends. Such participation would typically only occur if earnings or common dividends rose over some threshold, and might be limited in other ways. A more recent innovation is adjustable-rate preferred stock, with a variable dividend based on prevailing interest rates.

CONTROL Under normal circumstances, preferred stockholders do not have any voting power. As a result, they have little control over or direct influence on the conduct of the firm. Some minimal control would be provided by the indenture under which the stock was issued, and would be exercised passively— i.e., the trustees for the issue would be responsible for assuring that all conditions were observed. In some circumstances, the conditions of the issue could result in increased control on the part of the preferred stockholders. For instance, it is not unusual for the preferred stockholders to be given voting rights if more than a specified number of preferred dividends are skipped. Other provisions may restrict the payment of common dividends if certain conditions are not met. Preferred stockholders also may have a preemptive right.

CLAIM ON ASSETS AND OTHER FEATURES Another source of the preferred designation is that preferred stock has a prior claim on assets over that of common stock. The claim of bondholders is prior to that of the preferred stockholders. Although preferred stock typically has no maturity date, there is often some provision for retirement. One such provision is the call provision, under which the firm may buy back or recall the stock at a stated price. This price may vary over time, normally dropping as time passes. Another provision is the sinking fund, under which the firm will recall and retire a set number of shares each year. Alternately, the firm may repurchase the shares for retirement on the open market, and would prefer to do so if the market price of the preferred is below the call price. Preferred stock is sometimes convertible, i.e., it can be exchanged for common stock at the discretion of the holder. The conversion takes place at a set rate, but this rate may vary over time.

VALUATION The par value of a preferred stock is not related to market value, except that it is often used to define the dividend. Since the cash flow of dividends to preferred stockholders is specified, valuation of preferred stock is much simpler than for common stock. The valuation techniques are actually similar to those used for bonds, drawing heavily on the present value concept. The required rate of return on preferred stock is closely correlated with interest rates, but is above that of bonds because the bond payments are contractual obligations. As a result, preferred stock prices fluctuate with interest rates. The introduction of adjustable-rate preferred stock is an attempt to reduce this price sensitivity to interest rates.

FOREIGN STOCK

Purchases of foreign stock have greatly increased in recent years. One motivation behind this increase is that national economies are not perfectly correlated, so that greater diversification is possible than with a purely domestic portfolio. Another reason is that a number of foreign economies are growing, or are expected to grow, rapidly. Additionally, a number of developing countries have consciously promoted the development of secondary markets as an aid to economic development. Finally, developments in communications and an increasing familiarity with international affairs and opportunities has reduced the hesitance of investors to venture into what once was unfamiliar territory.

Foreign investment is not without problems. International communication is still more expensive and sometimes slower than domestic communication. Social and business customs often vary greatly between countries. Trading practices on some foreign exchanges are different than in the United States. Accounting differs not only in procedures, but often in degree of information disclosed. Although double taxation is generally avoided by international treaties, procedures are cumbersome. Political instability can be a consideration, particularly in developing countries. Finally, the investor faces exchange rate risk. A handsome gain in a foreign currency can be diminished, or even turned into a loss, by shifting exchange rates. These difficulties are felt less by professional managers of large institutions, and much of the foreign investment is through this channel.

An alternative vehicle for foreign investing is the American Depositary Receipt (ADR). This is simply a certificate of ownership of foreign stock that is deposited with a U.S. trustee. The depository institution also exchanges and distributes any dividends, and provides other administrative chores. ADRs are appealing to individual investors. It has also been suggested that the benefits of international investing can be obtained by investing in international firms.

INVESTMENT CHARACTERISTICS

Stocks are diverse in nature and can be classified many ways for investment purposes. For example, stocks can be classified according to the level of risk. Risky stocks are sometimes referred to as aggressive or speculative. They may also be growth stocks, which are expected to experience high rates of growth in size and earnings. If risk is measured by the beta (systematic or nondiversifiable risk), then the term applies to a stock with a beta greater than one. These stocks are quite sensitive to economic cycles, and are also called cyclical. Contrasted are the blue-chip stocks—high-quality stocks of major firms that have long and stable records of earnings and dividends. Stocks with low risk, or a beta of less than one, are referred to as defensive. One form of investment strategy, called timing, is to switch among cyclical and defensive stocks according to expected evolution of the economic cycle. This strategy is sometimes refined to movement among various types of stock or sectors of the economy. Another stock category is income stocks—stocks that have a long and stable record of comparatively high dividends.

Common stock has been suggested as a hedge against inflation. This suggestion arises from two lines of thought. The first is that stocks ultimately are claims to real assets and productivity, and the prices of such claims should rise with inflation. The second line of thought is that the total returns to common stock are high enough to overcome inflation. While this is apparently true over longer periods, it has not held true over shorter periods.

Preferred stock is generally not considered a desirable investment for individuals. While the junior position of preferred stockholders as compared to bondholders indicates that the required rate of return on preferred will be above that of bonds, observation indicates that the yield on bonds has generally been above that of preferred stock of similar quality. The reason for this is a provision of the tax codes that 70 percent of the preferred dividends received by a corporation are tax exempt. This provision is intended to avoid double taxation. Because of the tax exemption, the effective after-tax yield on preferred stock is higher for corporations, and buying of preferred stock by corporations drives the yields down. The resulting realized return for individuals, who cannot take advantage of this tax treatment, would generally be below acceptable levels.

FURTHER READING:

Arkebauer, James B. *Going Public: Everything You Need to Know to Take Your Company Public.* Dearborn, 1998.

Bodie, Zvi, Alex Kane, and Alan J. Marcus. *Investments.* 2nd ed. Irwin, 1993.

Cottle, Sidney, Roger F. Murray, and Frank E. Block. *Graham and Dodd's Security Analysis.* McGraw-Hill, 1988.

Gitman, Lawrence J., and Michael D. Joehnk. *Fundamentals of Investing.* 5th ed. HarperCollins, 1993.

Petty, J. William, Arthur J. Keown, David F Scott, Jr., and John D. Martin. *Basic Financial Management.* Prentice Hall, 1993.

Pinches, George E. *Essentials of Financial Management.* HarperCollins, 1992.

STRATEGY

As James Brian Quinn indicated in *The Strategy Process: Concepts and Contexts,* "a strategy is the pattern or plan that integrates an organization's major goals, policies, and action sequences into a cohesive whole. A well-formulated strategy helps to marshal and allocate an organization's resources into a unique and viable posture based on its relative internal competencies and shortcomings, anticipated changes in the environment, and contingent moves by intelligent opponents." All types of businesses require some sort of strategy in order to be successful; otherwise their efforts and resources will be spent haphazardly and likely wasted. Although strategy formulation tends to be handled more formally in large organizations, small businesses too need to develop strategies in order to use their limited resources to compete effectively against larger firms.

Formulation of an effective business strategy requires managers to consider three main players—the company, its customers, and the competition—according to Kenichi Ohmae in his book *The Mind of the Strategist.* These three players are collectively referred to as the strategic triangle. "In terms of these three key players, strategy is defined as the way in which a corporation endeavors to differentiate itself positively from its competitors, using its relative corporate strengths and weaknesses to better satisfy customer needs," Ohmae explained.

Quinn noted that an effective business strategy should include three elements: 1) a clear and decisive statement of the primary goals or objectives to be achieved; 2) an analysis of the main policies guiding or limiting the company's actions; and 3) a description of the major programs that will be used to accomplish the goals within the limits. In addition, it is important that strategies include only a few main concepts or thrusts in order to maintain their focus. They should also be related to other strategies in a hierarchical fashion, with each level supporting those above and below. Finally, strategies should attempt to build a strong yet flexible position for the company so that it may achieve its goals whatever the reaction of external forces. "Strategic decisions are those that determine the overall direction of an enterprise and its ultimate viability in light of the predictable, the unpredictable, and the unknowable changes that may occur in its most important surrounding environments," Quinn stated.

LIMITS ON STRATEGIC CHOICES

The strategic choices available to a company are not unlimited; rather, they depend upon the com-

pany's capabilities and its position in the marketplace. "At the broadest level formulating competitive strategy involves the consideration of four key factors that determine the limits of what a company can successfully accomplish," Michael E. Porter wrote in his classic book *Competitive Strategy.* Two of these limiting factors are internal, and the other two are external. The internal limits are the company's overall strengths and weaknesses and the personal values of its leaders. "The company's strengths and weaknesses are its profile of assets and skills relative to competitors, including financial resources, technological posture, brand identification, and so on," Porter stated. "The personal values of an organization are the motivations and needs of the key executives and other personnel who must implement the chosen strategy."

The external factors limiting the range of a company's strategic decisions are the competitive environment and societal expectations under which it operates. "Industry opportunities and threats define the competitive environment, with its attendant risks and potential rewards," Porter noted. "Societal expectations reflect the impact on the company of such things as government policy, social concerns, evolving mores, and many others. These four factors must be considered before a business can develop a realistic and implementable set of goals and policies."

Once a company has analyzed the four factors, it may then begin developing a strategy to compete under or attempt to change the situation it faces. The approach to strategy development recommended by Porter involves identifying the company's current strategy; revealing underlying assumptions about the company's position, its competitors, or industry trends affecting it; analyzing the threats and opportunities present in the external environment; determining the company's own strengths and weaknesses given the realities of its environment; proposing feasible alternatives; and choosing the one that best relates the company's situation to its environment.

GENERIC STRATEGIES

The number of potential business strategies are probably as great as the number of different businesses. Each distinct organization must develop a strategy that best matches its internal capabilities and its situation with regard to the external environment. Still, many of the numerous strategies pursued by businesses can be loosely grouped under three main categories—cost leadership, differentiation, and focus. Porter termed these categories "generic strategies," and claimed that most companies use variations of them, either singly or in combination, to create a defensible position in their industry. On the other hand, companies that fail to target their efforts toward any of the generic strategies risk becoming "stuck in the middle," which leads to low profitability and a lack of competitiveness.

COST LEADERSHIP The first generic strategy, overall cost leadership, can enable a company to earn above average profits despite the presence of strong competitive pressures. But it can also be difficult to implement. In a company pursuing a low-cost strategy, every activity of the organization must be examined with respect to cost. For example, favorable access to raw materials must be arranged, products must be designed for ease of manufacturing, manufacturing facilities and equipment must continually be upgraded, and production must take advantage of economies of scale. In addition, a low-cost strategy requires a company to implement tight controls across its operations, avoid marginal customer accounts, and minimize spending on advertising and customer service. Implemented successfully in a price-sensitive market, however, a low-cost strategy can lead to strong market share and profit margins.

Of course, a low-cost strategy—like any other strategy—also involves risks. For example, technological changes may make the company's investments in facilities and equipment obsolete. There is also the possibility that other competitors will learn to match the cost advantages offered by the company, particularly if inflation helps narrow the gap. Finally, low-cost producers risk focusing on cost to such an extent that they are unable to anticipate necessary product or marketing changes.

DIFFERENTIATION Companies that pursue a strategy of differentiation try to create a product or service that is considered unique within their industry. They may attempt to differentiate themselves on the basis of product design or features, brand image, technology, customer service, distribution, or several of these elements. The idea behind a differentiation strategy is to attract customers with a unique offering that meets their needs better than the competition, and for which they will be willing to pay a premium price. This strategy is intended to create brand loyalty among customers and thus provide solid profit margins for the company. Although the company may not be able to achieve a high market share using a differentiation strategy—because successful differentiation requires a perception of exclusivity, and because not all customers will be willing or able to pay the higher prices—the increased profit margins should compensate. Naturally, there are risks associated with committing to a differentiation strategy. For example, competitors may be able to imitate the unique features, customers may lose interest in the unique features, or low-cost competitors may be able to undercut prices in a way that erodes brand loyalty.

FOCUS Companies undertaking a focus strategy direct their full attention toward serving a particular market, whether it is a specific customer group, product segment, or geographic region. The idea behind the focus strategy is to serve that particular market more effectively than competitors on the basis of product differentiation, low cost, or both. Since focusing on a small segment of the overall market limits the market share a company can command, it must be able to make up for the lost sales volume with increased profitability. The focus strategy, too, entails risks. For example, there is always a possibility that competitors will be able to exploit submarkets within the strategic target market, that the differences between the target market and the overall market will narrow, or that the high costs associated with serving the target market will eliminate any advantage gained through differentiation.

Each of the three generic strategies identified by Porter requires a company to accumulate a different set of skills and resources. For example, a company pursuing a low-cost strategy would likely have a much different organizational structure, incentive system, and corporate culture than one pursuing a differentiation strategy. The key to successful implementation of one of the three generic strategies is to commit to it fully, rather than take half-measures that do not distinguish the company in any way.

NEW APPROACHES TO STRATEGY DEVELOPMENT

In the past, the formulation of strategy—at least in large corporations—was the domain of upper-level management. The traditional approach involved top managers coming up with a strategic direction for the company, setting it forth in an annual written strategic plan, and then disseminating the plan to various departments and employees, who were expected to contribute only within their own spheres of influence. This approach seemed to work fairly well for slow-moving companies in a stable external environment. In recent years, however, the process of developing strategy has changed dramatically in response to changes in the overall business world. "There is little question that the traditional approach to strategic planning, formulated in a different era, is often inadequate to deal with the rapid and continuous changes taking place in today's marketplace; it also fails to take into account the increased demand for autonomy in today's work force," Stephen J. Wall and Shannon Rye Wall wrote in *Organizational Dynamics*.

Traditional approaches to strategy development have been criticized for being too rigid, inflexible, and authoritative. Experts claim that these approaches were too concerned with analysis and quantification to be able to predict and adapt quickly to market changes. As a result, new approaches have emerged that no longer relegate strategy to top management; instead, the strategy formulation process involves all individuals in an organization, particularly those who are in direct contact with customers. ''A new approach to the strategic planning process, one that involves managers at all levels, can result in a dynamic process that increases competitive advantage,'' Wall and Wall wrote. ''Strategic planning is evolving due to the increasingly urgent need for responsiveness to market changes.''

In large measure, the changes that have taken place in business strategy have come as a result of changes in the environment. As the global marketplace has become increasingly volatile and competitive, companies have had to adjust by reducing their time frames for responding to changing customer needs. In addition, the changes in business strategy have come in part because today's workers tend to want and even demand more control over their work lives. The combination of these two factors has resulted in a new value being placed on employee participation in the strategy process. ''In an environment in which change is the norm, the insights of those on the front lines take on a new importance, since those close to the action—salespeople and others who deal directly with outside clients—are first to get wind of changes in customer needs,'' according to Wall and Wall. With this in mind, many companies are now choosing to develop strategy through the creation of multifunctional teams. Combining employees from various functional areas in this way tends to promote strategic thinking, because the groups are able to focus on broad company goals rather than on more limited functional, department, or individual goals. In addition to establishing cross-functional teams within the organization, some companies are beginning to solicit strategic input from their external customers and suppliers as well.

BENEFITS FROM THE NEW APPROACHES

Employee participation in the strategy process not only helps the company to develop a more responsive strategy, but also improves employee morale and commitment to the organization. Companies that encourage such participation are creating a more knowledgeable workforce, which is particularly important for small businesses since intellectual capital is often one of their most valuable assets.

The new, participative approaches to strategy formulation can also enable companies to improve their focus on customer needs by increasing the access of line employees to top management. In fact, hierarchies are designed to filter the information that goes to upper-level managers. But this lack of information can lead to overconfidence and myopic decision mak-

ing. Similarly, the new approaches can also help companies to remain flexible and responsive to market changes. The greater amount of information that managers receive about the market enables them to adapt the company's strategic direction to take advantage of new circumstances.

Participative strategic development also may help companies to retain key employees, because employees gain satisfaction by being able to direct and see the results of their efforts. ''Retaining these highly skilled and trained professionals will become increasingly important as knowledge has more and more to do with the company's ability to build and maintain a competitive advantage,'' Wall and Wall noted. Finally, participating in strategy formulation may enable managers to make better use of their time. This benefit is particularly helpful because time is always limited as companies try to do more with less people.

FURTHER READING:

Eccles, Robert, and Nitin Nohria. *Beyond the Hype: Rediscovering the Essence of Management.* Harvard Business School Press, 1992.

Eisenhardt, Kathleen M. ''Strategic Decisions and All That Jazz.'' *Business Strategy Review.* Autumn 1997.

Hamel, Gary, and C.K. Prahalad. *Competing for the Future.* Harvard Business School Press, 1994.

Markides, Constantinos C. *All the Right Moves: A Guide to Crafting Breakthrough Strategy.* Harvard Business School Press, 1999.

McGrath, Rita Gunther, and Ian MacMillan. *The Entrepreneurial Mindset.* Harvard Business School Press, 2000.

Mintzberg, Henry, and James Brian Quinn. *The Strategy Process: Concepts and Contexts.* Prentice-Hall, 1992.

Ohmae, Kenichi. *The Mind of the Strategist: Business Planning for Competitive Advantage.* Penguin, 1982.

Porter, Michael E. *Competitive Strategy: Techniques for Analyzing Industries and Competitors.* Free Press, 1980.

Wall, Stephen J., and Shannon Rye Wall. ''The Evolution (Not the Death) of Strategy.'' *Organizational Dynamics.* Autumn 1995.

SEE ALSO: Business Planning

SUBCONTRACTING

Subcontracting refers to the process of entering a contractual agreement with an outside person or company to perform a certain amount of work. The outside person or company in this arrangement is known as a subcontractor, but may also be called a free-lance employee, independent contractor, or vendor. Many small businesses hire subcontractors to assist with a wide variety of functions. For example, a small business might use an outside firm to prepare its payroll, an accountant to help with its record keeping and tax compliance, or a free-lance worker to handle a special project. Subcontracting is probably most prevalent in the construction industry, where builders often subcontract plumbing, electrical work, drywall, painting, and other tasks.

Hiring subcontractors offers a number of advantages for small businesses. For example, subcontracting mundane but necessary tasks can free up time and resources to enable the small business owner to concentrate on making money and growing the business. In addition, hiring a subcontractor is usually less expensive than hiring a full-time employee, because the small business is not required to pay Social Security taxes, workers' compensation benefits, or health insurance for independent contractors. Subcontracting does pose some potential pitfalls, however, such as a loss of control over the quality and timeliness of work. But small business owners can take several steps to help ensure that their relationships with subcontractors are productive and beneficial for all concerned.

SUBCONTRACTORS VS. EMPLOYEES

Although hiring an independent contractor to handle a special project or help out during a busy season may be cheaper than hiring a full-time employee, a small business cannot simply call someone an independent contractor in order to avoid paying Social Security taxes and benefits. The U.S. Internal Revenue Service (IRS) scrutinizes employer-subcontractor relationships carefully, and any misrepresentation may be subject to severe financial penalties. To avoid confusion, small business owners should be aware of the distinctions between independent contractors and employees and consult IRS guidelines when making subcontracting decisions. Most importantly, all subcontractors hired by a small business should present themselves as being in business for the purpose of making a profit. In addition, all work and pay arrangements should be spelled out in a contract that specifically mentions that the work is being performed by an independent contractor.

The IRS applies a 20-part test in order to determine whether a certain worker should be classified as an employee or an independent contractor. The main issue underpinning the test is who sets the work rules: employees must follow rules set by their bosses, while independent contractors set their own rules. For example, an individual who sets his own hours, receives payment by the job, and divides his time between work for several different employers would probably be classified as an independent contractor. Other criteria involve who provides the tools and materials needed to complete the work. For example, an individual who works at an employer's facility and uses the employer's equipment would be considered an employee, while one who works at a separate location

and provides her own equipment would be classified as an independent contractor. Finally, an independent contractor usually pays his own business expenses and takes the risk of not receiving payment when work is not completed in accordance with a contract, while an employee is usually reimbursed for business-related expenses by the employer and receives a paycheck whether his work is completed or not.

To be safe, a small business may wish to include some of these factors in the contract provided to subcontractors. For example, the contract should specify a certain amount of work to be performed by a given deadline, but should not specify how that work should be performed in terms of working hours or tools and materials used. In addition, payment should be made by the job rather than by the hour, and the subcontractor should not be prohibited from working simultaneously with other clients.

WORKING WITH SUBCONTRACTORS

Small business owners can take a series of steps to help ensure that the subcontracting process provides the desired benefits. First, it is important to assess the needs of the small business to make sure that outside help is needed, decide which specific tasks or projects to subcontract, and determine what sort of subcontractor could best perform the work. The small business owner should also give some thought to the type of relationship he or she wants to have with the subcontractor. Some businesses choose to share control of the project or process with a trusted subcontractor, even including the vendor in strategic decision-making. Indeed, subcontractors in many industries are often sources of valuable information and insight on ways in which small business owners can save time and money or improve quality. Other companies choose to maintain a high degree of control internally and subcontract only minor projects on a limited, as-needed basis.

The next step in the subcontracting process involves preparing in-house staff and obtaining the support of key personnel for the decision. Many companies encounter resistance from employees who feel that their jobs are threatened by subcontracting. Other companies may even find that turnover increases when the most interesting or fulfilling jobs are outsourced, leaving employees to perform less attractive tasks. To avoid these problems, in-house employees should be informed of the plans to subcontract work and told the rationale behind the decision. The small business owner may also wish to get employee input about what work is appropriate for subcontracting, and take steps to make sure that employees continue to receive rewarding, interesting, career-building responsibilities.

The next step is to begin contacting potential subcontractors, either formally or informally, and asking specific questions about the services provided and the terms of the contract. The questions should also seek to assess the subcontractor's intentions, or what they hope to gain from the relationship. Some subcontractors may be seeking a long-term business relationship, while others may simply wish to gather information in order to complete their work in a timely, professional fashion. Overall, the questions should establish whether the subcontractor will provide a good fit with the small business client. Ideally, the subcontractor will have experience in handling similar business and will be able to give the small business's needs the priority they deserve. ''Consider the service company's knowledge of the entirety of your business, its willingness to customize service, and its compatibility with your firm's business culture, as well as the long-run cost of its services and its financial strength,'' recommended service provider Carl Schwenker in *Money*.

Once a subcontractor has been selected, the small business owner should then negotiate a contract in order to help ensure a mutually beneficial relationship. This document should include tangible measures of job performance, as well as financial incentives to encourage the subcontractor to meet deadlines and control costs. The contract should also clearly define responsibilities and performance criteria, so that no questions arise later about whether the subcontractor or the client was supposed to handle a certain task or pay any extra charges incurred. The contract should also outline the procedures for changing the subcontractor relationship, including the means for renewal, cancellation, or termination. Finally, the contract should set strict confidentiality rules if needed and specify who owns the rights to any new ideas, inventions, or materials that are created from the business arrangement.

The next step is to prepare the subcontractor to interact efficiently with the client company during performance of the contract. The small business owner may wish to introduce the subcontractor to key employees, for example, and establish reporting relationships. It is also important to arrange to receive periodic progress reports from the subcontractor, as well as feedback about both the project at hand and the overall relationship. At the conclusion of the project, the small business owner should conduct a post-mortem and provide the subcontractor with an evaluation of their work.

When it is all said and done, the use of subcontractors can be a tremendous boon or a terrible bane to a small company. Skilled, professional subcontractors with a strong work ethic can help boost your company's financial success and burnish its reputation with clients and community alike. Conversely, sub- contractors who turn in sloppy or tardy work or behave in an unprofessional manner can quickly stain your company's name, and leave business owners (and any staff) with a heavier, messier workload. Given these factors, the wise business owner will choose her subcontractors judiciously and take special steps if necessary (such as sweetened financial compensation) to hold on to those with proven records of reliability and performance.

FURTHER READING:

Evans, David, Judy Feldman, and Anne Root. ''Smart New Ways to Manage Subcontractors.'' *Money*. March 15, 1994.

Foxman, Noah. ''Succeeding in Outsourcing.'' *Information Systems Management*. Winter 1994.

Hammond, Keith H. ''The New World of Work.'' *Business Week*. October 17, 1994.

Kelly, Joseph M. ''A Bad Sub Can Harm a Good Reputation.'' *Home Improvement Market*. February 1997.

King, William R. ''Strategic Outsourcing Decisions.'' *Information Systems Management*. Fall 1994.

Lacity, Mary, Rudy Hirschheim, and Leslie Willcocks. ''Realizing Outsourcing Expectations: Incredible Expectations, Credible Outcomes.'' *Information Systems Management*. Fall 1994.

Schwolsky, Rick. ''20 Ways to Keep Your Subs.'' *Builder*. January 1996.

Springsteel, Ian. ''Outsourcing Is Everywhere.'' *CFO: The Magazine for Senior Financial Executives*. December 1994.

SUBSTANCE ABUSE

Substance abuse in the workplace is a subject of concern to many small business owners, to one degree or another. Oftentimes the issue is a sensitive one to confront, but business owners and researchers alike agree that if left unchecked, substance abuse has the capacity to cripple or destroy a company.

IMPACT IN THE WORKPLACE

Substance abuse is a hard problem to eradicate in any business setting, but it can be particularly difficult to address in small business settings. After all, many small business owners develop close—or at least friendly—relationships with their employees because they often work together on projects and share smaller work areas. ''Because many small business owners have one-on-one relationships with each employee, dealing with an employee who is addicted to alcohol or drugs is a personal as well as a personnel problem,'' wrote Barbara Mooney in *Crain's Cleveland Business*.

But substance abuse experts and business researchers alike warn that substance abuse problems are not the sort of problems that tend to go away by themselves. Rather, they often continue to grow and fester, further strangulating the business's productivity and profitability. Indeed, substance abuse often ends up being a tremendous drain on a company's fiscal well-being. This drain takes many forms, including decreased productivity, increased absences, rising numbers of accidents, use of sick leave, and jumps in workers' compensation claims. Indeed, *HR Focus* reported in 1997 that "alcohol and drug abusers are absent from work two-and-a-half times more frequently than nonusers; they use three times the amount of sick leave as nonusers; their worker's compensation claims are five times higher; and they are generally less productive." This latter factor—what *HR Focus* termed "the less dramatic, day-to-day financial losses that accrue in a company when its workers are impaired and performing below potential"—can be particularly deadly to a business precisely because its impact is so hard to detect and quantify. Finally, substance abusers often compromise the efficiency of other workers within the business. Co-workers are often hampered by the substandard work of the abuser, and in many cases their effectiveness may be further curtailed by a sense of obligation to cover for their co-workers—who, after all, are often their friends as well.

Substance abuse problems also open companies up to greater legal liability. According to *Occupational Medicine,* studies indicate that 1) alcohol and drug abusers are two to four times as likely to have an accident as people who do not use drugs and alcohol, and 2) substance abusers can be linked to approximately 40 percent of American industrial fatalities. Moreover, business consultant Tim Plant indicated to *HR Focus* that drug- or alcohol-addled employees can also wreak harm on people and places outside the company: "When drivers come to work under the influence of drugs or alcohol," he said, "accidents could happen, causing the disruption of deliveries or other activities. Vehicles could be damaged; people could be hurt or killed. These have an immediate impact on the bottom line for a small- or medium-sized company."

Finally, in situations where a partner or owner of the business is the one with the substance abuse problem, the very life of the company is often jeopardized. Such people obviously wield a tremendous amount of influence over a company, and if their ability to make reasonable, intelligent decisions in a timely manner is compromised, the financial health of the company will likely deteriorate as well.

CHARACTERISTICS OF SUBSTANCE ABUSERS

Substance abuse experts and business owners who have been forced to deal with drug and/or alcohol abusers in their workplace cited a variety of warning signs that owners and managers should look for if they suspect a problem:

- Increased absenteeism and tardiness, especially immediately before and after weekends and holidays
- Deteriorating work performance, as manifested in big changes in work quality and/or productivity
- Frequent colds, flus, headaches, and other ailments
- High rates of mishaps, both on and off the job
- Unusually high medical claims
- Excessive mood swings, which may manifest themselves in immoderate levels of talking, anxiety, or moodiness
- Overreactions to criticism, both real or imagined
- Avoidance of supervisors
- Deterioration in physical appearance or grooming
- Financial problems

Researchers also note that certain industries and business dynamics seem especially prone to substance abuse problems. One substance abuse counselor flatly told Barbara Mooney of *Crain's Cleveland Business* that the extent of substance abuse problems in small businesses often depends on the makeup of its work force: "It's a problem prevalent among employers who hire a lot of entry-level people in industries with high turnover rates and high stress levels." Such conditions can be found in some retail establishments and especially in the restaurant industry, where late working hours, proximity to liquor, and demographic characteristics (prevalently young and single) provide a fertile atmosphere for substance abuse. Family-owned businesses are also cited as being particularly vulnerable to substance abuse problems, in part because family members may have a more difficult time being objective about a relative's work performance.

POLICIES AND STRATEGIES TO CURB SUBSTANCE ABUSE

Although tackling the problem of substance abuse can be a daunting one for small business enterprises, substance abuse experts and business researchers note that affected businesses can utilize a variety of steps that have a track record of effectiveness in curbing workplace drug and alcohol abuse.

One of the most commonly practiced policies employed by businesses of all sizes is random drug testing, wherein employees (and prospective employees) are required to submit to scientific tests to determine whether they have been using illegal drugs. Many experts cite the growing popularity of such policies for the apparent downturn in workplace substance abuse incidents in recent years. Drug testing remains controversial, however, as opponents argue that it violates individual privacy rights and sometimes hurts employee morale.

Another option for small business owners is to actively utilize the hiring/interviewing process to screen for substance abusers. ''You get what you ask for,'' contended Gregory Lousig-Nont and Paul Leckinger in *Security Management.* ''If you want people who are free from substance abuse problems—just ask for them in your ad.'' They point out that studies and anecdotal evidence suggests that want ads that include phrases like ''Applicant must have a clean drug history'' effectively dissuade many applicants with substance abuse problems from submitting an application. ''Another commonsense approach to screening applicants,'' say Lousig-Nont and Leckinger, ''is to broach the subject on the application form'' by bluntly inquiring whether the applicant has used illicit drugs in the past. ''Surprisingly, many people will actually list the drugs they have used. People who use drugs but do not want to tell you about it will leave the answer blank or put a dash on the answer line. People who have not used drugs will usually write a bold 'NONE' in the space provided.'' They note, however, that even though federal laws do not restrict asking questions about drug abuse, companies should check with their state employment commission to see if any state laws might apply in this area.

With current employees, business owners are encouraged to establish clear, written guidelines that explicitly detail the company's stance on substance abuse. ''The policy should take a clear stand against the use, possession, sale or distribution (particularly on company time) of any mood altering substances,'' stated *HR Focus.* ''It should also outline a very clear sequence of events that will ensue if the rules are broken.'' Small business owners need to make sure that their substance abuse policies abide by various state and federal laws.

Small business owners should also make an effort to enlist the support of employees in establishing a drug-free workplace. ''Everyone . . . has an interest in securing a safe workplace and making sure that colleagues pull their loads,'' commented *HR Focus.* ''One of the most effective ways to fight substance abuse is for employees to unite against it,'' concurred W.H. Weiss in *Supervisor's Standard Reference Handbook.* ''Supervisors can spur such a move by making it clear to their people that alcohol or drug use on the job is absolutely unacceptable.''

Business owners should also consider providing an employee assistance program (EAP) for its workers. ''Adopting an employee assistance program is viewed favorably by both management and employees,'' wrote Lousig-Nont and Leckinger. ''Under such a policy, the company agrees to assist employees who have a substance abuse problem. Assistance generally comes in the form of granting the employee sick leave and paying for a rehabilitation program, and a promise by the company that there will be no retribution against the employee.'' The responsibility for initiating enrollment in such programs, however, rests with the employee. If management discovers that a worker who has not pursued help through an EAP has a substance abuse problem, he or she may face termination. Employee assistance programs have been hailed by substance abuse experts and businesspeople alike as an effective tool in curbing workplace drug and alcohol abuse, and proponents point out that the cost of such programs is usually far less than the costs that often accrue when a substance-abusing employee is not dealt with.

Finally, when confronted with evidence of workplace substance abuse, managers and owners of small companies are urged to intervene immediately and determine whether a problem exists. If a problem is found, then the business needs to document the performance of the employee. This will offer the company a greater measure of legal protection in case they need to fire the employee or the employee's performance spurs legal claims from outside parties.

FURTHER READING:

''Drug Trends: A Shot in the Arm?'' *Security Management.* August 1996.

Gray, George R., and Darrel R. Brown. ''Issues in Drug Testing for the Private Sector.'' *HR Focus.* November 1992.

Humphreys, Richard M. ''Substance Abuse: The Employer's Perspective.'' *Employment Relations Today.* Spring 1990.

Lousig-Nont, Gregory M., and Paul M. Leckinger. ''Alternatives to Drug Testing.'' *Security Management.* May 1990.

Martin, Lynn. ''Drug Free Policy: Key to Success for Small Businesses.'' *HR Focus.* September 1992.

Mooney, Barbara. ''Addiction: A Downer for All; Substance Abuse can be an Owner's Toughest Problem.'' *Crain's Cleveland Business.* August 8, 1994.

''Substance Abuse in the Workplace.'' *HR Focus.* February 1997.

SUCCESSION PLANS

A succession plan is a written document that provides for the continued operation of a business in the event that the owner—or a key member of the management team—leaves the company, is terminated, retires, or dies. It details the changes that will take place as leadership is transferred from one generation to the next. In the case of small businesses, succession plans are often known as continuity plans, since without them the businesses may cease to exist. Succession plans can provide a number of important benefits for companies that develop them. For example, a succession plan may help a business retain key employees, reduce its tax burden, and maintain the value of its stock and assets during a management or ownership transition. Succession plans may also prove valuable in allowing a business owner to retire in comfort and continue to provide for family members who may be involved with the company.

Despite the many benefits of having a succession plan in place, many companies neglect to develop one. This oversight may occur because the business owner does not want to confront his or her own mortality, is reluctant to choose a successor, or does not have many interests beyond the business. Although less than one-third of family businesses survive the transition from the first generation to the second—and only 13 percent remain in the family for more than 60 years—just 45 to 50 percent of business owners establish a formal succession plan. "Succession and the planning it entails is equivalent to planning one's own wake and funeral," observed one family business consultant in *Industrial Distribution*. "But the fact is that the transfer of power from the first to the second generation seldom happens while the founder is alive and on the scene." Yet it is one that must be prepared for, if the business owner hopes to avoid having hard-earned assets go to unwanted individuals and institutions. "The economic costs are significant," agreed James Bieneman in *Business First-Columbus*. "[But] the human costs are even greater in terms of spoiled family relationships, missed career opportunities, and the discomfort of living in a state of misalignment."

PREPARING FOR SUCCESSION

Experts claim that the succession planning process should ideally begin when the business owner is between the ages of 45 and 50 if he or she plans to retire at 65. Since succession can be an emotionally charged issue, sometimes the assistance of outsider advisors and mediators is required. Developing a succession plan can take more than two years, and implementing it can take up to ten years. The plan must be carefully structured to fit the company's specific situation and goals. When completed, the plan should be reviewed by the company's lawyer, accountant, and bank.

"One of the main reasons business owners should take the time to create a successful continuity plan is that they should want to get out of the business alive, with as much money as possible," Joanna R. Turpin noted in *Air Conditioning, Heating, and Refrigeration News*. To do this, the business owner has a few basic options: sell the company to employees, family members, or an outsider; retain ownership of the company but hire new management; or liquidate the business. An Employee Stock Ownership Plan, or ESOP, can be a useful tool for the owner of a corporation who is nearing retirement age. The owner can sell his or her stake in the company to the ESOP in order to gain tax advantages and provide for the continuation of the business. If, after the stock purchase, the ESOP holds over 30 percent of the company's shares, then the owner can defer capital-gains taxes by investing the proceeds in a Qualified Replacement Property (QRP). QRPs can include stocks, bonds, and certain retirement accounts. The income stream generated by the QRP can help provide the business owner with income during retirement.

In *Family Business Succession: The Final Test of Greatness*, Craig E. Aronoff and John L. Ward outline a number of steps companies should follow in preparing for succession. These steps include: 1) Establishing a formal policy regarding family participation in the business; 2) Providing solid work experience for all employees, to ensure that succession is based on performance rather than heredity; 3) Creating a family mission statement based on the members' beliefs and goals for the business; 4) Designing a leadership development plan with specific job requirements for the successor; 5) Developing a strategic plan for the business; 6) Making plans for the preceding generation's financial security; 7) Identifying a successor or determining the selection process; 8) Setting up a succession transition team to keep decision-makers informed about their role in the changes; and 9) Completing the transfer of ownership and control.

In the Small Business Administration publication *Transferring Management in the Family-Owned Business*, Nancy Bowman-Upton also emphasizes that succession should be viewed as a process rather than as an event. She describes four main stages in the succession process: initiation, selection, education, and transition. In the initiation phase, possible successors learn about the family business. It is important for the business owners to speak openly about the business, in a positive but realistic manner, in order to transmit information about the company's values, culture, and future direction to the next generation.

The selection phase involves actually designating a successor among the candidates for the job. Because rivalry often develops between possible successors—who, in the case of a family business, are likely to be siblings—this can be the most difficult stage of the process. For this reason, many business owners either avoid the issue or make the selection on the basis of age, gender, or other factors besides merit. Instead, Bowman-Upton recommends that the business owners develop specific objectives and goals for the next generation of management, including a detailed job description for the successor. Then a candidate can be chosen who best meets the qualifications. This strategy helps remove the emotional aspect from the selection process and also may help the business owners feel more comfortable with their selection. The decision about when to announce the successor and the schedule for succession depends upon the business, but an early announcement can help reassure employees and customers and enable other key employees to make alternative career plans as needed.

Once a potential successor has been selected, the company then enters the training phase. Ideally, a program is developed through which the successor can meet goals and gradually increase his or her level of responsibility. The owner may want to take a number of planned absences so that the successor has a chance to actually run the business for limited periods of time. The training phase also provides the business owner with an opportunity to evaluate the successor's decision-making processes, leadership abilities, interpersonal skills, and performance under pressure. It is also important for the successor to be introduced to the business owner's outside network during this time, including customers, bankers, and business associates.

The final stage in the process occurs when the business owner retires and the successor formally makes the transition to his or her new leadership role. Bowman-Upton stresses that the business owner can make the transition smoother for the company by publicly committing to the succession plan, leaving in a timely manner, and eliminating his or her involvement in the company's daily activities completely. In order to make the transition as painless as possible for himself or herself, the business owner should also be sure to have a sound financial plan for retirement and to engage in relationships and activities outside of the business.

Business owners that fail to adhere to the above steps may end up cobbling together succession plans that do not reflect the best interests of the company or of its stakeholders (valued staffers, family members, partners, etc.). "Why and how often do succession plans fail?" wrote Bieneman. "Succession plans fail when serious conflict (some call it dysfunctional behavior) cannot be overcome, when family members have and cannot abandon unrealistic expectations, or when the family business has run its course and should be sold but isn't. Succession plans are an exercise in compromise, tough love, forthrightness, and making difficult but necessary decisions."

FURTHER READING:

Aronoff, Craig E., and John L. Ward. *Family Business Succession: The Final Test of Greatness.* Business Owner Resources, 1992.

Bieneman, James N. "Succession Plans Provide Blueprint for Peace of Mind." *Business First-Columbus.* October 6, 2000.

Bowman-Upton, Nancy. *Transferring Management in the Family-Owned Business.* U.S. Small Business Administration, 1991.

Frieswick, Kris. "Successful Succession." *Industrial Distribution.* April 1996.

Shanney-Saborsky, Regina. "Why It Pays to Use an ESOP in a Business Succession Plan." *The Practical Accountant.* September 1996.

Turpin, Joanna R. "Succession Planning Requires Long-Term Strategy, Implementation." *Air Conditioning, Heating, and Refrigeration News.* April 28, 1997.

SEE ALSO: Estate Tax; Family-Owned Business

SUPPLIER RELATIONS

Good purchasing practices are integral to small business success, and few factors are as vital in ensuring sound purchasing methodologies as the selection of quality suppliers. Indeed, finding good suppliers and maintaining solid relations with them can be an invaluable tool in the quest for business success and expansion. As James Morgan observed in *Purchasing,* "for a surprisingly large number of procurement organizations, suppliers have become an important factor in their planning. In fact, for many procurement organizations, suppliers have become their secret competitive weapon, their hidden resource, their competitive edge." These competitive gains can manifest themselves in a wide range of areas, from better prices and delivery times to increased opportunities to consider and implement innovative practices. But management consultant Paul Inglis noted in *Purchasing* that such improvements will not be realized without meaningful leadership from business owners and executives. "Leading companies develop tailored supply strategies that are directly linked to their corporate strategies," he said. These leaders emphasize shareholder-value creation, revenue growth, and cost competitiveness, and establish specific programs with their key suppliers in order to ensure that these priorities are addressed. Smart business leaders, he added, "use suppliers to maximize their own product competitiveness, going beyond the narrow focus of cost reduction. Leaders exceed traditional sourcing practices, adopt new models to fully leverage supplier capabilities, and further their own position in the marketplace.''

SUPPLY CHAINS AND PARTNERSHIPS

In recent years, countless management experts and analysts have touted the benefits that businesses of all sizes can realize by establishing ''partnerships'' with their suppliers. Under such a plan, which is also sometimes referred to as ''supply chain management,'' distribution channels are set up across organizations so that all the members of the channel, from suppliers to end users, coordinate their business activities and processes to minimize their total costs and maximize their effectiveness in the marketplace. But while this trend has become more prevalent in today's business environment, it is still practiced in only spotty fashion in many industries. According to a 1997 A.T. Kearney survey of business executives, common impediments to establishing true business partnerships with suppliers include: attachment of greater importance to other initiatives; comfortable relationships with existing suppliers; dearth of cross-business unit cooperation; doubts about the benefits of instituting such practices; lack of cross-functional cooperation; poor monitoring and control systems; inexperience at managing improvement programs; and distrust of suppliers. Companies that feature many of these characteristics typically cling to old competitive bidding practices that center on perfectly legitimate concerns about price, but at the exclusion of all else.

As a result, these businesses miss out on the many benefits that can accrue when effective partnering initiatives are established with suppliers. As Morgan indicated, suppliers can be an important source of information on ways in which both small and large businesses can improve performance and productivity. After studying a major mid-1990s buyer survey, he cited five general categories in which supplier involvement can help buyers compete in the marketplace:

1) Improvement of products through contributions to product design, technology, or ideas for producing new products. In most such instances, suppliers help buyers by pointing out ways in which designs can be improved or more desirable materials can be used.

2) Improvements in product quality. In addition to providing design recommendations that result in improved products, suppliers are often sources of suggestions that allow buyers to hold consistent tolerances in production.

3) Improvements in ''speed to market.'' ''Some of the most significant contributions

in this area came from suppliers to OEM [original equipment manufacturer] manufacturers,'' said Morgan. ''Typical is the instance of an equipment maker whose supplier helped cut 30 months from the design to market schedule.''

4) Reductions in total product cost, either through streamlining of work processes (inventory management, new product design, scheduling, etc.) or replacement of costly components with less expensive—but still effective—ones.

5) Improvements in customer satisfaction.

Analysts indicate that suppliers receive some benefits in the emerging purchasing dynamic as well. Reduced paperwork, lower overhead, faster payment, long-term agreements that lead to more accurate business forecasts, access to new designs, and input into future materials and product needs have all been cited as gains. Other observers, meanwhile, point out that some buyer-supplier relationships have become so close that suppliers have opened offices on the site of the buyer, an arrangement that can conceivably result in even greater improvements in productivity and savings. Of course, companies are not going to form such ''partnerships'' with all of their suppliers. Some form of the traditional purchasing process involving bidding and standard purchase orders and invoices will continue to exist at almost every company, and especially at smaller companies that do not have the financial clout to pressure suppliers for price or delivery concessions.

But many management consultants and business experts contend that even those businesses that are not ideally positioned to create partnerships with suppliers can benefit from the establishment of effective supply chain management practices. Management theorist Jordan Lewis, for example, told *The Economist* that buyer-seller alliances unleash a capacity for innovation that far outweighs the short-term cost savings offered by arm's-length competitive bidding. He added that businesses should explain their overarching needs to several dedicated suppliers and open lines of communication with them rather than simply defining their requirements and waiting for a flurry of bids that are primarily—or exclusively—concerned with submitting the lowest bid.

POTENTIAL DRAWBACKS OF SUPPLIER PARTNERSHIPS Establishing close relationships with suppliers, though, means that buyers have to conduct the necessary research to make sure that they select the right companies. ''Purchasing needs to know a great deal more about supplier capabilities than it did when everything depended on a bid/buy relationship,'' confirmed *Purchasing's* Ernest L. Anderson. ''Today's emphasis on partnership requires suppliers who can become part of a whole supply system. In fact, major suppliers need to be critically screened and evaluated before they are brought into any new system.'' Thriving small- and mid-sized businesses that are already well-established will be better able to take on such tasks than will fledgling businesses, but even start ups should take the time to learn more about their suppliers than their prices.

Of course, desired supplier traits vary somewhat depending on who is being surveyed. For example, design engineers tend to place the most weight on product quality when analyzing suppliers, while purchasing professionals place greater importance on cost considerations in conjunction with product quality. Anderson noted that criteria to be evaluated will also vary depending on product category. ''There's a difference, for instance, between how you evaluate suppliers for MRO and how you evaluate raw materials suppliers,'' he said. ''Whether an item is proprietary or generic will make a difference in what gets stressed in selection of significant suppliers. Still, the objective of all evaluations is the same: To compare all potential suppliers in a market segment to determine the one best qualified to be your partner. It's important to evaluate strengths and weaknesses of potential suppliers in terms of which one can best help purchasing meet prime objectives. Typical objectives include inventory reduction, quality improvement, elimination of paperwork, and improved handling of incoming goods.''

Companies that do not do the necessary legwork, on the other hand, may find themselves linked to a poor or untrustworthy supplier that can erode a business's financial fortunes and industry/community reputation in a remarkably short span of time. ''Poor supplier performance is not the only risk a purchaser faces'' in situations where it has linked with a bad supplier, noted *The Economist*. ''It must also worry about the possibility of a supplier passing trade secrets to competitors, or, with its newfound abilities, venturing out on its own. A company that abdicates too many things [to suppliers] may 'hollow' itself out. All of these risks are especially great in fast-moving, knowledge-intensive industries, which are precisely those for which integrated supply chains otherwise make the most sense.'' Given these potential pitfalls, businesses seeking to establish partnerships with suppliers are urged to proceed with caution.

EVALUATING SUPPLIERS

Whether searching out new suppliers or benchmarking the performance of current suppliers, businesses are urged to consider the following when evaluating their options:

- Commitment to quality—Not surprisingly, product quality is regarded as an essential factor in selecting a supplier. Specifics in this realm include the suppliers' statistical process control methods, its QS-9000 registration, its approaches to problem solving and preventive maintenance, and its methods of equipment calibration. ''What gets looked at varies by whether the supplier is a distributor or manufacturer,'' pointed out Anderson. ''With a distributor, the team wants to determine whether it carries mainly Grade A lines or B lines in a particular group. With a manufacturer it's important to have QC people on the team to realistically appraise the supplier's control standards and methods of measuring quality.''

- Cost-competitive—Competitive pricing is another huge factor, especially for businesses that are smaller or experiencing financial difficulties.

- Communication—Suppliers that do not maintain a policy of open communication—or even worse, actively practice deception—should be avoided at all costs. The frustrations of dealing with such companies can sometimes assume debilitating dimensions. Moreover, constant exposure to such tactics can have a corrosive effect on internal staff.

- Timely service—Businesses strategies are predicated on schedules, which in turn are based on receiving shipments at agreed-upon times. When those shipments slip, business strategies suffer. The blow can be particularly severe if the supplier is negligent or late in reporting the problem. ''Reliable delivery is first among the basics of what we expect [from suppliers],'' one executive told *Industrial Distribution*. ''It doesn't have to be instantaneous—it just needs to get there when they promised it would.''

- Flexibility and special services—Many purchasers express appreciation for suppliers that take extra measures to satisfy their customers. These ''perks'' can range from after-hours accessability to training or inventory support.

- Market knowledge—Suppliers with extensive knowledge of market conditions and mastery of contemporary issues impacting your business can be immensely valuable in helping small companies chart a course to sustained financial success.

- Production capabilities—the supplier's capacity for program management and production should be considered, including its ability to integrate design and manufacturing functions, its approach to design changes, and its program measurement features.

- Financial stability—Businesses that allocate large sums for purchasing materials often prefer to make long-term deals with suppliers that are financially stable. Such arrangements not only convey security, but they allow companies to learn about one another and gain a fuller understanding of each business's needs, desires, operating practices, and future objectives. Moreover, *The Economist* noted that "being in a meaningful relationship instead of a one-part stand encourages suppliers to make investments that are tailored to the purchasing firm's needs— and to be more thrifty. . . . A trusted supplier is more likely to think about the purchasing firm's own customers."

- Logistics/Location—Supplier capabilities in this area include transportation capacity, sourcing capabilities, and 'just-in-time' performance.

- Inventory—According to *Purchasing,* evaluation of this consideration is dependent somewhat on the supplier's business. "If the supplier is a distributor, the emphasis will be on how well his inventory is set up to avoid stockouts. With a manufacturer, emphasis has to be on inventory accessability. If the supplier has a [just in time] program with 24-hour assured delivery, it's in better condition than the manufacturer with a lot of raw material inventory and an eight-week leadtime for raw material."

- Ability to provide technical assistance— Suppliers with top research and development capacities can be quite valuable to buyers, providing them with significant savings in both price and quality.

OTHER KEYS TO SUCCESSFUL SUPPLIER RELATIONSHIPS

A common lament of suppliers is that buyer organizations all too often have unrealistic expectations about the supplier's ability to anticipate buyer needs. As one purchasing executive admitted to *Purchasing,* "In new technology areas we have great difficulty getting the users in our own company to define what they want. Most have an attitude of 'I'll know it when I see it.' And many of these users keep changing their minds."

Honesty on both sides is another important quality in effective buyer-supplier relations. Small business owners hate being misled by their suppliers, yet they are often less than above-board in their own communications with suppliers. This is most common when the business is grappling with past-due payments, but entrepreneurs should avoid subterfuge and be upfront with suppliers about their situations. "Instead of lying and saying the check's in the mail, tell suppliers what's happening and what you propose to do about it," one small business owner told *Nation's Business.* "If you have a note that's due, you call them, instead of waiting for them to call you. They appreciate that. Business people are afraid to make that phone call; they want to make it all sound rosy. But . . . if you owe them, suppliers are eager to find a way to work with you."

FURTHER READING:

Anderson, Ernest L. "Evaluate Critical Suppliers." *Purchasing.* July 14, 1994.

Fitzgerald, Kevin R. "What OEM Engineers Want from Suppliers." *Purchasing.* August 14, 1997.

Forbes, Christine. "Creating the Super Supplier." *Industrial Distribution.* September 1993.

Harrington, Lisa H. "Buying Better: Strategic Sourcing Can Improve Suppliers' Productivity, Component and Product Quality—and Improve the Bottom Line." *Industry Week.* July 21, 1997.

"Holding the Hand that Feeds." *The Economist.* September 9, 1995.

McIvor, Ronan, Paul Humphreys, and Eddie McAleer. "Implications of Partnership Sourcing on Buyer-Supplier Relations." *Journal of General Management.* Autumn 1997.

Morgan, James. "Five Areas Where Suppliers Can Be Your Competitive Edge." *Purchasing.* November 25, 1993.

Munson, Charles L., Meir J. Rosenblatt, and Zehava Rosenblatt. "The Use and Abuse of Power in Supply Chains." *Business Horizons.* January-February 1999.

"The Nuts and Bolts of Supplier Relations." *Nation's Business.* August 1997.

Porter, Anne Millen. "Purchasing Pros Insist They Buy On Far More than Price." *Purchasing.* May 1, 1997.

"Strong Supply Relationships Reduce Cost, Spark Innovation." *Purchasing.* January 15, 1998.

SUPPLY AND DEMAND

Supply and demand is a fundamental factor in shaping the character of the marketplace, for it is understood as the principal determinant in establishing the cost of goods and services. The availability, or "supply," of goods or services is a key consideration in determining the price at which those goods or services can be obtained. For example, a landscaping company with little competition that operates in an area of high demand for such services will in all likelihood be able to command a higher price than will a business operating in a highly competitive environment. But availability is only one-half of the equation that determines pricing structures in the marketplace. The other half is "demand." A company may be able to produce huge quantities of a product at low cost, but if there is little or no demand for that product in the marketplace, the company will be forced to sell units at a very low price. Conversely, if the marketplace proves receptive to the product that is being sold, the company can establish a higher unit price. "Supply" and "demand," then, are closely intertwined economic concepts; indeed, the law of supply and demand is often cited as among the most fundamental in all of economics.

FACTORS IMPACTING SUPPLY AND DEMAND

"When we speak about demand," wrote Robert Heilbroner and Lester Thurow in *Economics Explained*, "most people think the word just means a certain volume of spending, as when we say that the demand for automobiles has fallen off or the demand for gold is high. But that is not what the economist has in mind when he defines demand as part of his explanation of markets. Demand means not just how much we are spending for a given item, but how much we are spending for that item *at its price,* and how much we would spend *if its price changed.*"

The demand for products and services is predicated on a number of factors. The most important of these are the tastes, customs, and preferences of the target market, the consumer's income level, the quality of the goods or services being offered, and the availability of competitors' goods or services. All of the above elements are vital in determining the price that a business can command for its products or services, whether the business in question is a hair salon, a graphic arts firm, or a cabinet manufacturer.

The supply of goods and services in the marketplace is predicated on several factors as well, including production capacity, production costs (including wages, interest charges, and raw materials costs), and the number of other businesses engaged in providing the goods or services in question. Of course, some factors that are integral in determining supply in one area may be inconsequential in another. Weather, for example, is an important factor in determining the supplies of wheat, oranges, cherries, and myriad other agricultural products. But weather rarely impacts the operations of businesses such as bookstores or auto supply stores except under the most exceptional of circumstances.

"When we are willing and able to buy more, we say that demand rises, and everyone knows that the effect of rising demand is to lift prices," summarized Heilbroner and Thurow. "Of course the mechanism works in reverse. If incomes fall, so does demand, and so does price." They point out that supply can also dwindle as a result of other business conditions, such as a rise in production costs for the producer or changes in regulatory or tax policies. "And of course both supply and demand can change at the same time, and often do," added Heilbroner and Thurow. "The outcome can be higher or lower prices, or even unchanged prices, depending on how the new balance of market forces works out."

SUPPLY AND DEMAND ELASTICITY

Robert Pindyck and Daniel Rubinfeld observed in their book *Microeconomics* that "the demand for a good depends on its price, as well as on consumer income and on the prices of other goods. Similarly, supply depends on price, as well as on variables that affect production cost. . . . Often, however, we want to know *how much* supply or demand will rise or fall." This measurement of a product or service's responsiveness to market changes is known as elasticity. Todd G. Buchholz, writing in his book *From Here to Economy: A Shortcut to Economic Literacy,* used an example from the world of sports business to provide an example of economic elasticity: "Will football fans buy the same number of tickets if the team jacks up the prices? If they do, then demand is *inelastic.* If higher prices lead the fans to cut back their attendance, then demand is *elastic,* or sensitive to change."

The quality and degree of marketplace reaction to price changes depends on several factors. These include: 1) the presence or absence of alternative sources for the product or service in question; 2) the time available to customers to investigate alternatives; 3) the size of the investment made by the purchaser. Elasticity, then, is an important factor for small business owners to consider when entertaining thoughts about changing the prices of the goods or services that they offer.

FURTHER READING:

Buchholz, Todd G. *From Here to Economy: A Shortcut to Economic Literacy.* Dutton, 1995.

Heilbroner, Robert, and Lester Thurow. *Economics Explained: Everything You Need to Know About How the Economy Works and Where It's Going.* Revised ed. Touchstone, 1994.

Langabeer II, Jim R. "Aligning Demand Management with Business Strategy." *Supply Chain Management Review.* May 2000.

Pindyck, Robert S., and Daniel L. Rubinfeld. *Microeconomics.* 2d ed. Macmillan, 1992.

SUSTAINABLE GROWTH

The sustainable growth rate (SGR) of a firm is the maximum rate of growth in sales that can be achieved, given the firm's profitability, asset utilization, and desired dividend payout and debt (financial leverage) ratios. Variables typically include the net profit margin on new and existing revenues; the asset turnover ratio, which is the ratio of sales revenues to total assets; the assets to beginning of period equity ratio; and the retention rate, which is defined as the fraction of earnings retained in the business.

Sustainable growth models assume that the business wants to: 1) maintain a target capital structure without issuing new equity; 2) maintain a target dividend payment ratio; and 3) increase sales as rapidly as market conditions allow. Since the asset to beginning of period equity ratio is constant and the firm's only source of new equity is retained earnings, sales and assets cannot grow any faster than the retained earnings plus the additional debt that the retained earnings can support. The sustainable growth rate is consistent with the observed evidence that most corporations are reluctant to issue new equity. If, however, the firm is willing to issue additional equity, there is in principle no financial constraint on its growth rate. Indeed, the sustainable growth rate formula is directly predicated on return on equity. "Assuming asset growth broadly parallels sales growth, the SGR is calculated as the retained [return on equity], i.e. your company's [return on equity] minus the dividend payout percentage," wrote John Costa in *Outlook*. "Just as the break-even point is the 'floor' for minimum sales required to cover operating expenses, so the SGR is an estimate of the 'ceiling' for maximum sales growth that can be achieved without exhausting operating cash flows. Think of it as a growth break-even point."

THE CHALLENGE OF ATTAINING SUSTAINABLE GROWTH

Creation of sustainable growth is a prime concern of small business owners and big corporate executives alike. Obviously, however, achieving this goal is no easy task, given rapidly changing political, economic, competitive, and consumer trends. Jayne Buxton and Mike Davidson pointed out in *Strategy and Leadership* that each of these trends present unique challenges to business leaders searching for the elusive grail of sustainable growth. Customer expectations, for example, have changed considerably over the last few generations. Modern consumers have less disposable wealth than their parents, which makes them more discriminating buyers. "This fact, coupled with the legacy of a decade of quality and cost reduction programs, means that companies will have to attract customers by redefining value based on unique customer insights and keep customers by beating their competitors in enhancing value," said Buxton and Davidson. Similarly, competition is keen in nearly all industries, which have seen unprecedented breakdowns in the barriers that formerly separated them.

"Companies now must look widely afield to identify their competitors and their available option in the search for creating sustainable competitive advantage," they said.

In addition, Buxton and Davidson noted that "the growth challenge is articulated differently by different leaders. For some, developing and launching new products and services to meet the evolving needs of their customers is the issue; for others, capitalizing on global opportunities is key; for still others, the challenge is identifying the one new business that will represent the next major thrust for the company. And for a few, all of these strategic challenges are simultaneously top-of-mind, along with the enormous task of rebuilding organizational capabilities."

Economists and business researchers contend that achieving sustainable growth is not possible without paying heed to twin cornerstones: growth strategy and growth capability. Companies that pay inadequate attention to one aspect or the other are doomed to failure in their efforts to establish practices of *sustainable* growth (though short-term gains may be realized). After all, if a company has an excellent growth strategy in place, but has not put the necessary infrastructure in place to execute that strategy, long-term growth is impossible. The reverse is true as well.

USING THE SUSTAINABLE GROWTH RATE

The concept of sustainable growth can be helpful for planning healthy corporate growth. This concept forces managers to consider the financial consequences of sales increases and to set sales growth goals that are consistent with the operating and financial policies of the firm. Often, a conflict can arise if growth objectives are not consistent with the value of the organization's sustainable growth.

According to economists, if a company's sales expand at any rate other than the sustainable rate, one or more of the above-mentioned ratios must change. If a company's actual growth rate temporarily exceeds its sustainable rate, the required cash can likely be borrowed. When actual growth exceeds sustainable growth for longer periods, management must formulate a financial strategy from among the following options: 1) sell new equity; 2) permanently increase financial leverage (i.e, the use of debt); 3) reduce dividends; 4) increase the profit margin; or 5) decrease the percentage of total assets to sales.

In practice, companies are often reluctant to undertake these measures. Firms dislike issuing equity because of high issue costs, possible dilution of earnings per share, and the unreliable nature of equity funding on terms favorable to the issuer. A firm can only increase financial leverage if there are assets that can be pledged and if its debt/equity ratio is reasonable in relation to its industry. The reduction of dividends typically has a negative impact on the company's stock price. Companies can attempt to liquidate marginal operations, increase prices, or enhance manufacturing and distribution efficiencies to improve the profit margin. In addition, firms can source more activities from outside vendors or rent production facilities and equipment, which has the effect of improving the asset turnover ratio. Increasing the profit margin is difficult, however, and large sustainable increases may not be possible. Therefore, it is possible for a firm to grow too rapidly, which in turn can result in reduced liquidity and the unwanted depletion of financial resources.

The sustainable growth model is particularly helpful in situations in which a borrower requests additional financing. The need for additional loans creates a potentially risky situation of too much debt and too little equity. Either additional equity must be raised or the borrower will have to reduce the rate of expansion to a level that can be sustained without an increase in financial leverage.

Mature firms often have actual growth rates that are less than the sustainable growth rate. In these cases, management's principal objective is finding productive uses for the cash flows that exist in excess of their needs. Options available to business owners and executives in such cases including returning the money to shareholders through increased dividends or common stock repurchases, reducing the firm's debtload, or increasing possession of lower earning liquid assets. Note that these actions serve to decrease the sustainable growth rate. Alternatively, these firms can attempt to enhance their actual growth rates through the acquisition of rapidly growing companies.

Growth can come from two sources: increased volume and inflation. The inflationary increase in assets must be financed as though it were real growth. Inflation increases the amount of external financing required and increases the debt-to-equity ratio when this ratio is measured on a historical cost basis. Thus, if creditors require that a firm's historical cost debt-to-equity ratio stay constant, inflation lowers the firm's sustainable growth rate.

FURTHER READING:

Buxton, Jayne, and Mike Davidson. "Building a Sustainable Growth Capability." *Strategy and Leadership*. November-December 1996.

Costa, John. "Challenging Growth: How to Keep Your Company's Rapid Expansion on Track." *Outlook*. Summer 1997.

Daly, Herman E. *Beyond Growth: The Economics of Sustainable Development*. Beacon Press, 1997.

Gallinger, George W. "Tax Effects on Profitability and Sustainable Growth." *Business Credit*. April 2000.

Moore, Darrell M. "Growing Broke: Sustainable Growth as a Factor in Financial Analysis." *Business Credit*. September 1988.

SYNDICATED LOANS

Syndicated loans are loans made by two or more lenders and administered by a common agent using similar terms and conditions and common documentation. According to *Business Credit,* most loan syndications take the form of a direct-lender relationship, in which the lead lender is the agent for the other lenders in the origination and administration of the loan, and the other lending banks are signatories to the loan agreement. In the last several years the popularity of this type of loan has exploded. By 2000, the total annual volume of syndicated loan issuance had risen to $1.2 trillion, a $100 billion increase over the year before. The businesses that are choosing this option to finance their growth have expanded beyond the Fortune 500 companies that were its first users. Initially developed to address the needs of huge, acquisition-hungry companies, they have now become a flexible funding source for both mid-sized companies and smaller companies that are on the cusp of moving into mid-sized status. In fact, syndicated loans for as little as $10 million have become commonplace.

Most successful small companies that have evolved to the point where they are straining at the boundaries of that "small" designation have always dealt with one or a few individual banks, negotiating individual loans and lines of credit separately with each institution. The next financing step, however, may be to consolidate banking activity through one syndicated facility. *Corporate Cashflow Magazine*'s Thomas Bunn noted that while business owners and executives are sometimes loathe to run the risk of alienating banks with which they have long done business, the simple reality is that "companies can outgrow their traditional banks and need new capabilities or an expanded bank group to fund their continued growth."

Of course, businesses can always choose to simply increase their stable of lending institutions, but this has several drawbacks. "Managing multiple bank relationships is no small feat," said Michael Fidler and Patricia Neumeyer in *Business Credit*. "Each bank needs to come to an understanding of your business and how its financial activities are conducted. A comfort level must be established on both sides of the transaction, which requires time and effort. . . . Negotiating a document with one bank can take days. To negotiate documents with four to five banks separately is a time-consuming, inefficient task.

Staggered maturities must be monitored and orchestrated. Moreover, multiple lines require an inter-creditor agreement among the banks, which takes additional time to negotiate.''

Given these obstacles, business owners and executives often express interest in syndicated loans, which offer consolidation of effort and the possibility of making new banking contacts. Lenders support their use as well. ''Lenders like syndications because they permit them to make more loans, while limiting individual exposures and spreading their risk within portfolios more widely,'' explained Fidler and Neymeyer. ''Moreover, administration of the loan is extremely efficient, with the agent managing much of the process on behalf of the participants.''

Syndicated loans hinge on the creation of an alliance of smaller banking institutions who, by joining forces, are able to meet the credit needs of the borrower. This creation is spurred by selection of an agent who manages the account. ''In consultation with the borrower, the arranger will assemble a group of banks to form a syndicate, with each bank lending portions of the required amount,'' explained John Tsui in *Lodging Hospitality.* ''The loan normally is signed six to eight weeks after the mandate has been awarded, and after signing, the borrower can draw down funds.''

Borrowers taking out syndicated loans pay up-front fees and annual charges to the participating banks, with interest accruing (on a quarterly, monthly, or semiannual basis) from the initial draw-down date. ''One advantage of syndication loans is that this market allows the borrower to access from a diverse group of financial institutions,'' said Tsui. ''In general, borrowers can raise funds more cheaply in the syndicated loan market than they can borrowing the same amount of money through a series of bilateral loans. This cost saving increases as the amount required rises.''

OTHER ADVANTAGES OF SYNDICATED LOANS

In addition, economists and syndicate executives contend that there are other, less obvious advantages to going with a syndicated loan. These benefits include:

- Syndicated loan facilities can increase competition for your business, prompting other banks to increase their efforts to put market information in front of you in hopes of being recognized.

- Flexibility in structure and pricing. Borrowers have a variety of options in shaping their syndicated loan, including multicurrency options, risk management

techniques, and prepayment rights without penalty.

- Syndicated facilities bring businesses the best prices in aggregate and spare companies the time and effort of negotiating individually with each bank.

- Loan terms can be abbreviated.

- Increased feedback. Syndicate banks sometimes are willing to share perspectives on business issues with the agent that they would be reluctant to share with the borrowing business.

- Syndicated loans bring the borrower greater visibility in the open market. Bunn noted that ''For commercial paper issuers, rating agencies view a multi-year syndicated facility as stronger support than several bilateral one-year lines of credit.''

SYNDICATE FORMATION

A borrower's ability to secure a syndicated loan, though, is predicated on its ability to spur the creation of a syndicate in the first place. ''No two syndications are identical,'' wrote Bunn. ''The market changes every day. Many intangibles influence the structure and pricing of a credit, including the experience and depth of a company's management team; trends in the industry and market; and financial trends within a company.''

The first thing the company has to do is select an agent to facilitate communications and transactions between the borrower and the banking institutions that will form the syndicate. ''The first place to look for an agent is among your existing relationships,'' said Fidler and Neumeyer. ''Certainly you will want a bank that has the necessary syndication capability and experience to obtain market credibility. Although the agent need not always be the largest participant in the syndication, the agent should have sufficient capital strength to be the anchor for the credit. Most important, however, is that you are comfortable with the bank. Because the agent is acting on your behalf, they must fully understand your business and share your attitudes and priorities.''

Once an agent has been selected, the process of finding willing banks is undertaken. This phase of the process can vary considerably in terms of complexity. Some agents gauge the interest level of other lenders by simply sending them necessary financial information on the borrower and the intended shape and size of the syndicate group, as well as data on borrower operations, background, management, and marketing. Bunn noted that in other cases, however, this process can be more complex, involving extensive due diligence, the preparation of a complete syndication offering memorandum (including financial projections), and a formal bank presentation.

By and large, the length of time necessary to form a bank group is roughly equivalent to the complexity of the proposed deal. Creation of a syndicate can take place over the course of a few weeks or a few months. Analysts note, however, that the length of time necessary to conclude the deal is usually less if the banks are already familiar with the borrower's operations. Once the membership of the group has been determined, the relationship quickly assumes the character that the borrowing business would expect when dealing with a single lending institution. ''This is not to say that the borrower relinquishes control over the process and the participants will still actively call on the borrower,'' noted Fidler and Neumeyer. ''It is merely the interaction between the participating banks that should diminish—to your benefit. The agent should educate you about the market and help you navigate the specifics of pricing and structuring the transaction.''

Indeed, the agent's responsibilities are many and varied. The agent is charged with administering the syndicated facility itself, as well as all borrowings, repayments, interest settlements, and fee payments. A chief component of the administration function is to make sure that communications between the lending institutions and the borrower remain open so that both sides remain informed about changing business and market realities. In return for providing these services, the agent is compensated with an annual fee.

FURTHER READING:

Bunn, Thomas. ''What Borrowers Need to Know About Loan Syndication.'' *Corporate Cashflow Magazine.* October 1995.

Fidler, Michael, and Patricia Neumeyer. ''Vindication of Syndication—Why Borrowers Should Consider Agented Transactions.'' *Business Credit.* May 1996.

''Syndicated Loans.'' *Wall Street Journal.* November 22, 2000.

Tsui, John F. ''The Appeal of Syndicated Loans.'' *Lodging Hospitality.* February 1992.

Wienke, Robert O. ''Loan Syndications and Participations: Trends and Tactics.'' *Commercial Lending Review.* Spring 1994.

T

TARGET MARKETS

A target market is a group of customers with similar needs that forms the focus of a company's marketing efforts. Similarly, target marketing involves tailoring the company's marketing efforts to appeal to a specific group of customers. Selecting target markets is part of the process of market segmentation—dividing an overall market into key customer subsets, or segments, whose members share similar demographic characteristics and needs. Demographic characteristics that are analyzed for target marketing purposes include age, income, geographic origins and current location, ethnicity, marital status, education, interests, level of discretionary income, net worth, home ownership, and a host of other factors. The company then selects from among these segments the particular markets it wishes to target. "Small businesses that identify the needs of specific target markets—existing and potential customers who are the focus of marketing efforts—and work to satisfy those needs, are more effective marketers," according to Gloria Green and Jeffrey Williams in *Marketing: Mastering Your Small Business.*

Target marketing can be a particularly valuable tool for small businesses, which often lack the resources to appeal to large aggregate markets or to maintain a wide range of differentiated products for varied markets. Target marketing allows a small business to develop a product and a marketing mix that fit a relatively homogenous part of the total market. By focusing its resources on a specific customer base in this way, a small business may be able to carve out a market niche that it can serve better than its larger competitors.

Identifying specific target markets—and then delivering products and promotions that ultimately maximize the profit potential of those targeted markets—is the primary function of marketing management for many smaller companies. For instance, a manufacturer of fishing equipment would not randomly market its product to the entire U.S. population. Instead, it would conduct market research, using such tools as demographic reports, market surveys, and trade shows, to determine which customers would be most likely to purchase its offerings. It could then more efficiently spend its limited resources in an effort to persuade members of its target group(s) to buy. Advertisements and promotions could then be tailored for each segment of the target market.

There are infinite ways to address the wants and needs of a target market. For example, product packaging can be designed in different sizes and colors, or the product itself can be altered to appeal to different personality types or age groups. Producers can also change the warranty or durability of the good or provide different levels of follow-up service. Other influences, such as distribution and sales methods, licensing strategies, and advertising media, also play an important role. It is the responsibility of the marketing manager to take all of these factors into account and to devise a cohesive marketing program that will appeal to the target customer.

Small business enterprises are also encouraged to continually examine their marketing efforts to make sure that they keep pace with changing business realities. For example, business start-ups typically accept any kind of legitimate business in order to pay the bills and establish themselves as a viable entity. But long after the start-up has blossomed into a solid member of the local business community, it may continue to rely on these early accounts rather than casting its net for more promising clients. ''Are you happy with the makeup of your customer base and the nature of the work you do now?,'' asked Kim Gordon in *Entrepreneur.* ''Altering the types of accounts you serve, their size, location or other criteria can have a big impact on your bottom line. . . . Instead of letting your current customer base define you, use target marketing to determine who your next customers or clients should be.'' The process of redefining ideal clients and customers can be painstaking and time-consuming, for creating profiles of your new target audience necessitates extensive research into ideal prospects and the marketing measures that will be most effective in reaching them, as well as your own desires for your company's future direction. But for many small business owners, the effort is worthwhile. ''By targeting your ideal prospects, you'll avoid detours and grow your business in all the right directions,'' wrote Gordon. ''Soon you'll have the kind of company that matches your vision and grows increasingly profitable over time.''

FURTHER READING:

Cohen, Eric. ''How to Target Smarter.'' *Target Marketing.* May 1998.

Durden, Jonathan. ''Questioning the Term 'Targeting' is Fundamental.'' *Marketing.* November 3, 1994.

Field, Anne. ''Precision Marketing.'' *Inc.* June 18, 1996.

Gordon, Kim T. ''Cream of the Crop.'' *Entrepreneur.* January 2001.

Green, Gloria, and Jeffrey Williams. *Marketing: Mastering Your Small Business.* Upstart Publishing, 1996.

Weinstein, Art. *Market Segmentation: Using Niche Marketing to Exploit New Markets.* Probus, 1989.

SEE ALSO: Market Segmentation

TARIFFS

A tariff is a tax or duty imposed by one nation on the imported goods or services of another nation. Tariffs have been used throughout history to control the amount of imports that flow into a country and to determine which nations will be granted the most favorable trading conditions. High tariffs create protectionism, shielding a domestic industry's products against foreign competition. High tariffs usually ensure that a given product will not be imported into a country because the high tariff would lead to a high price for the customers of that product, be they other businesses or consumers.

Throughout the 1990s, the trend has been decreased tariffs on a global scale, as evidenced by the passage of well-known treaties such as the General Agreement on Tariffs and Trade (GATT) and the North American Free Trade Agreement (NAFTA), as well as the lowering of trade barriers in the European Economic Community, reducing or even abolishing tariffs. These changes reflect the conviction among some politicians and economists that lower tariffs spur growth and reduce prices.

For the most part, the issue of tariffs is of greater concern to businesses in the United States than those outside it. That is because the U.S. generally has lower tariffs for goods coming into this country than other countries do for U.S. goods being imported there. Prior to the passage of NAFTA, for example, Mexican tariffs on U.S. goods entering that country were, on average, 250 percent higher than U.S. duties on Mexican goods.

Lower tariffs especially benefit small businesses because they level the playing field and make it easier for them to compete with larger companies. The majority of small business owners, then, tend to lobby hard for them. As one small manufacturer told *Nation's Business:* ''Anytime you make a movement toward more free trade, I know we're going to benefit from it.'' Conversely, large corporations are in the best position to absorb higher tariffs for the sake of gaining market share—they have the cash to spend up front, even if it means initially taking a loss. Small companies cannot afford making such large initial investment in the hopes that their product will eventually prove successful.

GATT is especially beneficial to the small businessman. This treaty has spurred significant drops in tariff rates in many areas of the globe. This trend makes it easier for U.S. companies to sell their products abroad, and gives them more options when purchasing products or materials here in the United States. Even small businesses that do not engage in exporting themselves can benefit from this environment, for they can register increased sales to companies engaged in higher volumes of itnernational trade. It is important to note that the current move towards lower tariffs is a gradual one, however. While NAFTA and GATT did eliminate some tariffs immediately, most are designed to be phased out over a period of years, even decades. Every small businessperson should study the provisions of major trade agreements that pertain specifically to their industry before moving ahead with plans to increase exports.

One key area to keep an eye on in the coming year is the idea of Internet tariffs. The United States is pushing hard for international agreements that will ensure that there are no tariffs on equipment used to build the Internet nor on products or services sold over it. This would make the Internet a duty-free zone, which has huge implications for small businesses engaged in business activities on the Net.

FURTHER READING:

DeMott, John S. "What GATT Means to Small Business." *Nation's Business.* March 1995.

Holzinger, Albert G. "Why Small Firms Back NAFTA." *Nation's Business.* November 1993.

Jacobson, Ken. "U.S. Pushing for Accord Heading Off Internet Tariffs." *New Technology Week.* August 4, 1997.

Santinelli, Angelo. "Achieving Cost Savings Through Tariff Management." *Telecommunications.* December 1997.

Wilhelm, Steve. "Banning Tariffs Sector-by-Sector." *Puget Sound Business Journal.* November 7, 1997.

SEE ALSO: Exporting

TAX DEDUCTIBLE BUSINESS EXPENSES

Tax deductible business expenses include a variety of costs that can be subtracted from a company's income before it is subject to taxation. By reducing taxable income, these deductions reduce a company's tax liability and thus improve its bottom line. The standard business deductions—which include general and administrative expenses, business-related travel and entertainment, automobile expenses, and employee benefits—are outlined in Section 162 of the Internal Revenue Code. Although the tax law is complex, virtually any expense that is considered ordinary, reasonable, and necessary to the business can be tax deductible. Some expenses are considered "current" and are deducted in the year that they are paid, while others are considered "capitalized" and must be spread out or depreciated over time.

The significant tax deductions available to self-employed persons and small business owners often provide one of the main sources of motivation for going into business. However, it is important for small business owners to maintain a personal awareness of tax-related issues in order to save money. Even if they employ a professional bookkeeper or accountant, small business owners should keep careful tabs on their own tax preparation in order to take advantage of all possible opportunities for deductions and tax savings. "Whether or not you enlist the aid of an outsider, you should understand the basic provisions of the tax code," Albert B. Ellentuck wrote in the *Laventhol and Horwath Small Business Tax Planning Guide.* "Just as you would not turn over the management of your money to another person, you should not blindly allow someone else to take complete charge of your taxpaying responsibilities." In addition, as Frederick W. Dailey wrote in his book *Tax Savvy for Small Business,* "Tax knowledge has powerful profit potential. Knowing what the tax law has to offer can give you a far better bottom line than your competitors who don't bother to learn."

Taking advantage of allowable tax deductions can also offer other benefits to small business owners. "Knowing how to maximize your deductible business expenses lowers your taxable profit," Dailey noted. "To boot, you may enjoy a personal benefit from a business expenditure—a nice car to drive, a combination business trip/vacation and a retirement savings plan—if you follow the myriad of tax rules." Solid record-keeping is vital for small businesses that hope to claim their allowable tax credits and deductions. After all, deductions can be disallowed for even legitimate business expenditures if those expenditures are not adequately supported by business records. Some of the major categories of tax deductible business expenses are described below.

GENERAL AND ADMINISTRATIVE EXPENSES

All of the basic expenses necessary to run a business are generally tax-deductible, including office rent, salaries, equipment and supplies, telephone and utility costs, legal and accounting services, professional dues, and subscriptions to business publications. Education expenses are deductible if they are necessary to improve or maintain the skills involved in one's present employment or are required by an employer. However, education costs cannot be deducted when they are incurred in order to qualify for a different job. Some other miscellaneous expenses that may be deductible in this category include computer software, charitable contributions, repairs and improvements to business property, bank service charges, consultant fees, postage, and online services.

In most cases, general and administrative business expenses are deductible in the year in which they were incurred. An exception applies to the costs of starting a business that are incurred prior to beginning operations. These expenses must be capitalized over five years, which may seem strange since they are deductible immediately once the business is open. Depreciating the costs of starting a business might be preferable if the business is expected to show a loss for the first year or two. Otherwise, it may be possible to avoid the need to capitalize these expenses by delaying payment on invoices until the business opens or by doing a trivial amount of business during the startup period.

HOME OFFICE DEDUCTION The use of part of a home as a business office may enable an individual to qualify for significant tax deductions. The "home office deduction" allows individuals who meet certain criteria to deduct a portion of mortgage interest or rent, depreciation of the space used as an office, utility bills, home insurance costs, and cleaning, repairs, and security costs from their federal income taxes. Although the Internal Revenue Service (IRS) has set strict regulations about who qualifies for the deduction, about 1.6 million people claim the deduction each year. According to Gloria Gibbs Marullo in an article for *Nation's Business,* the savings can be considerable: a sole proprietor living in a $150,000 home stands to save about $2,500 in actual taxes annually.

Home office operators may claim a deduction for those offices on IRS Form 8829 (Expenses for Business Use of Your Home), which is filed along with Schedule C (Profit or Loss From Your Business). There are restrictions, however, which are covered in IRS Publication 587 (*Business Use of Your Home*). The restrictions were eased somewhat with the passage of the Taxpayer Relief Act of 1997, which will take effect beginning with returns filed in 2000.

In general, a home office deduction is allowed if the home office meets at least one of three criteria: 1) the home office is the principal place of business; 2) the home office is the place where the business owner meets with clients and customers as part of the normal business day; or 3) the place of business is a separate structure on the property, but is not attached to the house or residence. The 1997 changes expanded the definition of "principal place of business" to include a place that is used by the taxpayer for administrative or management activities of the business, provided there is no other fixed location where these activities take place.

The deduction is figured on the size of the home office as a percentage of the total house or residence. For example, if the total house size is 2,400 square feet and the home office is 240 square feet, 10 percent of the total house is considered used for business. That would allow the business owner to deduct 10 percent of the household's costs for electricity, real estate taxes, mortgage interest, insurance, repairs, etc. as business expenses. The total amount of the deduction is limited to the gross income derived from the business activity, less other business expenses. In other words, the home office deduction cannot be used to make an otherwise profitable business show a loss.

AUTOMOBILE EXPENSES

Most people have occasion to drive a car while conducting business. Business-related automobile mileage is tax deductible, with the exception of commuting to and from work. Any other mileage from the place of business to another location can be considered a business expense as long as the travel was made for business purposes. The IRS allows the mileage deduction to be calculated using two different approaches. The straight-mileage approach multiplies the cents-per-mile allowed by the IRS (31.5 cents in 1997) by the number of miles attributable to business use of the automobile. For example, a small business owner who drove 1,000 miles at .315 per mile would gain a deduction of $315.

In contrast, the actual-expense approach adds up all the costs of operating the car for a year—such as gasoline, insurance, maintenance, and depreciation—and multiplies that total by the percentage of the annual mileage that was attributable to business purposes. For example, a small business owner who paid a total of $3,000 in operating costs and drove a total of 15,000 miles, only 1,500 of which were business-related, would gain a deduction of $3,000 x .10 or $300. Businesses are required to use the actual-expense approach under certain circumstances—if the vehicle is leased, if more than one vehicle is used for the business, or if the approach was used for that vehicle during its first year of service—but otherwise can choose the approach that yields the larger deduction. In either case, it is necessary to maintain an accurate log of business mileage and associated automobile expenses.

ENTERTAINMENT AND TRAVEL

Reasonable travel and entertainment costs are tax deductible if they are: 1) directly related to business, meaning that business took place or was discussed during the entertainment; or 2) associated with business, meaning that business took place or was discussed immediately before or after the entertainment (i.e., a small business owner took a client out to dinner or to a sporting event following a meeting). Because they include a personal element, only 50 percent of meals and entertainment expenses are deductible as business expenses. Business-related travel, however, is fully deductible.

Careful records are necessary to substantiate the deductions. For business-related meals and entertainment, these records should include the amount, place, date, reason for entertainment, nature of business discussion, and name and occupation of the person being entertained. It is not necessary to retain receipts for expenditures less than $75. Entertainment that is done within the home is also deductible in some cases. Company parties that involve all employees are 100 percent deductible, although they must be infrequent and not overly extravagant. In addition, gifts to clients and customers are deductible to maximum of $25 per year, or $400 if the business name is imprinted on them.

The costs of reasonable and necessary business travel—including meetings with clients and suppliers as well as conferences and seminars intended to expand a business person's expertise—are fully deductible as business expenses. The costs that can be deducted include airfare, bus or train fare, car rental, and taxi fare, hotels and meals, and incidentals such as tips and dry cleaning expenses. Restrictions apply to travel in foreign countries or on cruise ships. In addition, travel to investment-related seminars are not deductible, though the cost of the seminars may be. A variety of rules apply to deducting business travel expenses, so it is necessary to review them in detail or enlist the help of a tax professional.

DEPRECIATION

According to Section 179 of the Internal Revenue Code, small business owners can write off the first $18,000 of equipment purchased for business use each year during the year in which it was purchased. In many cases, it makes sense to take advantage of this tax break immediately, particularly if purchases will be fairly regular from year to year. If the item is a one-time purchase or if the total amount spent is greater than the limit, however, the business owner may wish to depreciate the cost over future time periods. Depreciation is a tax-deductible business expense.

Depreciation for tax purposes is determined by an IRS formula and has nothing to do with the actual value of equipment at year end. Instead, the amount claimed as depreciation is designed to spread the cost of the equipment over time and maximize the annual tax deductions associated with it. Most companies use a straight-line depreciation method for their financial statements, because the even amounts approximate the rate at which the equipment is used up and will need to be replaced. However, they tend to use accelerated depreciation methods for tax purposes in order to deduct a larger portion of the equipment's cost sooner. The IRS applies different ''life spans'' to different types of equipment for the purposes of depreciation. For example, it applies a five-year life to telecommunications equipment and automobiles, and a seven-year life to computers and office equipment like desks, chairs, and fixtures.

EMPLOYEE BENEFITS

The cost of providing employees with a wide variety of fringe benefits is considered a tax deductible business expense for employers. Most of these benefits are not considered income for employees, so they receive a tax break as well. Certain types of benefits—particularly retirement and pension plans—are also deductible for self-employed persons and small business owners. However, it is important to keep up with the rapidly changing tax laws regarding these matters. Some of the types of employee benefits that may be considered tax deductible business expenses include: retirement plans, health insurance, disability and life insurance, company cars, membership in clubs and athletic facilities, dependent care

assistance, education assistance, employee discounts, and business meals, travel, and lodging.

RETIREMENT AND PENSION PLANS Small business owners can set up a wide variety of retirement plans in order to gain tax advantages. In most cases, employer contributions are tax-deductible business expenses, and the money is allowed to grow tax-deferred until employees reach retirement age, at which point they will likely be in a lower tax bracket than during their working years. The most important thing to remember is that a small business owner who wants to establish a qualified plan for him or herself must also include all other company employees who meet minimum participation standards. As an employer, the small business owner can establish retirement plans like any other business. As an employee, the small business owner can then make contributions to the plan he or she has established in order to set aside tax-deferred funds for retirement, like any other employee. The difference is that a small business owner must include all nonowner employees in any company-sponsored retirement plans and make equivalent contributions to their accounts. Unfortunately, this requirement has the effect of reducing the allowable contributions that the owner of a proprietorship or partnership can make on his or her own behalf.

For self-employed individuals, contributions to a retirement plan are based upon the net earnings of their business. The net earnings consist of the company's gross income less deductions for business expenses, salaries paid to nonowner employees, the employer's 50 percent of the Social Security tax, and—significantly—the employer's contribution to retirement plans on behalf of employees. Therefore, rather than receiving pre-tax contributions to the retirement account as a percentage of gross salary, like nonowner employees, the small business owner receives contributions as a smaller percentage of net earnings. Employing other people thus detracts from the owner's ability to build up a sizeable before-tax retirement account of his or her own. For this reason, some experts recommend that the owners of proprietorships and partnerships who sponsor plans for their employees supplement their own retirement funds through a personal after-tax savings plan.

Nevertheless, many small businesses sponsor retirement plans in order to gain tax advantages and increase the loyalty of employees. A number of different types of plans are available. In nearly every case, withdrawals made before the age of 59 ½ are subject to an IRS penalty in addition to ordinary income tax. The plans differ in terms of administrative costs, eligibility requirements, employee participation, degree of discretion in making contributions, and amount of allowable contributions.

HEALTH INSURANCE Health insurance benefits provided to employees are also tax deductible. However, self-employed persons are only able to deduct a portion of their own payments for health insurance (40 percent in 1997, gradually increasing to 80 percent in 2006). An exception to this rule is included under Section 105 of the Internal Revenue Code. This loophole allows a small business owner whose spouse works in the business to fully deduct his or her health insurance and unreimbursed medical expenses by creating a medical reimbursement plan for employees. The spouse is then covered under the plan, the small business owner is covered under his or her spouse's insurance, and the entire bill is a tax-deductible business expense. Many tax professionals and insurance providers offer this sort of plan to their clients. It is important to note, however, that the same plan must be available to all of the business's employees.

FURTHER READING:

Cash, L. Stephen, and Thomas L. Dickens. ''New Home Office Rule Applies for 2000 Filing Season.'' *Strategic Finance.* February 2000.

Dailey, Frederick W. *Tax Savvy for Small Business.* 2nd ed. Berkeley, CA: Nolo Press, 1997.

DeJong, David S., and Ann Gray Jakabcin. *J.K. Lasser's Year-Round Tax Strategies.* New York: Macmillan, 1997.

Ellentuck, Albert B. *Laventhol and Horwath Small Business Tax Planning Guide.* New York: Avon Books, 1988.

The Entrepreneur Magazine Small Business Advisor. New York: Wiley, 1995.

Harrington, Phillip. ''Small Firms Get Help from Section 105.'' *National Underwriter and Health.* July 7, 1997.

Keating, Peter. ''Can I Deduct That?'' *Money.* March 1997.

Korn, Donald J. ''Deducting Home Office Expenses.'' *Black Enterprise.* September 1996.

Marullo, Gloria Gibbs. ''Redefining the Home-Office Deduction.'' *Nation's Business.* September 1997.

Szabo, Joan. ''Found Money: Capture Increased Tax Savings with These Ten Business Deductions.'' *Entrepreneur.* June 1997.

Wiener, Leonard. ''How to Keep One Step Ahead: Hot Tips for Turning an Annual Chore into Many Happy Returns.'' *U.S. News and World Report.* March 9, 1998.

TAX PLANNING

Tax planning involves conceiving of and implementing various strategies in order to minimize the amount of taxes paid for a given period. For a small business, minimizing the tax liability can provide more money for expenses, investment, or growth. In this way, tax planning can be a source of working capital. According to *The Entrepreneur Magazine Small Business Advisor,* two basic rules apply to tax planning. First, a small business should never incur additional expenses only to gain a tax deduction. While purchasing necessary equipment prior to the end of the tax year can be a valuable tax planning strategy, making unnecessary purchases is not recommended. Second, a small business should always attempt to defer taxes when possible. Deferring taxes enables the business to use that money interest-free, and sometimes even earn interest on it, until the next time taxes are due.

Experts recommend that entrepreneurs and small business owners conduct formal tax planning sessions in the middle of each tax year. This approach will give them time to apply their strategies to the current year as well as allow them to get a jump on the following year. It is important for small business owners to maintain a personal awareness of tax planning issues in order to save money. Even if they employ a professional bookkeeper or accountant, small business owners should keep careful tabs on their own tax preparation in order to take advantage of all possible opportunities for deductions and tax savings. ''Whether or not you enlist the aid of an outsider, you should understand the basic provisions of the tax code,'' Albert B. Ellentuck wrote in the *Laventhol and Horwath Small Business Tax Planning Guide.* ''Just as you would not turn over the management of your money to another person, you should not blindly allow someone else to take complete charge of your taxpaying responsibilities.'' In addition, as Frederick W. Dailey wrote in his book *Tax Savvy for Small Business,* ''Tax knowledge has powerful profit potential. Knowing what the tax law has to offer can give you a far better bottom line than your competitors who don't bother to learn.''

GENERAL AREAS OF TAX PLANNING

There are several general areas of tax planning that apply to all sorts of small businesses. These areas include the choice of accounting and inventory-valuation methods, the timing of equipment purchases, the spreading of business income among family members, and the selection of tax-favored benefit plans and investments. There are also some areas of tax planning that are specific to certain business forms—i.e., sole proprietorships, partnerships, C corporations, and S corporations. Some of the general tax planning strategies are described below:

ACCOUNTING METHODS Accounting methods refer to the basic rules and guidelines under which businesses keep their financial records and prepare their financial reports. There are two main accounting methods used for record-keeping: the cash basis and the accrual basis. Small business owners must decide which method to use depending on the legal form of the business, its sales volume, whether it extends credit to customers, and the tax requirements set forth by the Internal Revenue Service (IRS). The choice of accounting method is an issue in tax planning, as it can affect the amount of taxes owed by a small business in a given year.

Accounting records prepared using the cash basis recognize income and expenses according to real-time cash flow. Income is recorded upon receipt of funds, rather than based upon when it is actually earned, and expenses are recorded as they are paid, rather than as they are actually incurred. Under this accounting method, therefore, it is possible to defer taxable income by delaying billing so that payment is not received in the current year. Likewise, it is possible to accelerate expenses by paying them as soon as the bills are received, in advance of the due date. The cash method is simpler than the accrual method, it provides a more accurate picture of cash flow, and income is not subject to taxation until the money is actually received.

In contrast, the accrual basis makes a greater effort to recognize income and expenses in the period to which they apply, regardless of whether or not money has changed hands. Under this system, revenue is recorded when it is earned, rather than when payment is received, and expenses recorded when they are incurred, rather than when payment is made. The main advantage of the accrual method is that it provides a more accurate picture of how a business is performing over the long-term than the cash method. The main disadvantages are that it is more complex than the cash basis, and that income taxes may be owed on revenue before payment is actually received. However, the accrual basis may yield favorable tax results for companies that have few receivables and large current liabilities.

Under generally accepted accounting principles (GAAP), the accrual basis of accounting is required for all businesses that handle inventory, from small retailers to large manufacturers. It is also required for corporations and partnerships that have gross sales over $5 million per year, though there are exceptions for farming businesses and qualified personal service corporations—such as doctors, lawyers, accountants, and consultants. Other businesses generally can decide which accounting method to use based on the relative tax savings it provides.

INVENTORY VALUATION METHODS The method a small business chooses for inventory valuation can also lead to substantial tax savings. Inventory valuation is important because businesses are required to reduce the amount they deduct for inventory purchases over the course of a year by the amount remaining in inventory at the end of the year. For example, a business that purchased $10,000 in inventory during the year but had $6,000 remaining in inventory at the end of the year could only count $4,000 as an expense for inventory purchases, even though the actual cash outlay was much larger. Valuing the remaining inventory differently could increase the amount deducted from income and thus reduce the amount of tax owed by the business.

The tax law provides two possible methods for inventory valuation: the first-in, first-out method (FIFO); and the last-in, first-out method (LIFO). As the names suggest, these inventory methods differ in the assumption they make about the way items are sold from inventory. FIFO assumes that the items purchased the earliest are the first to be removed from inventory, while LIFO assumes that the items purchased most recently are the first to be removed from inventory. In this way, FIFO values the remaining inventory at the most current cost, while LIFO values the remaining inventory at the earliest cost paid that year.

LIFO is generally the preferred inventory valuation method during times of rising costs. It places a lower value on the remaining inventory and a higher value on the cost of goods sold, thus reducing income and taxes. On the other hand, FIFO is generally preferred during periods of deflation or in industries where inventory can tend to lose its value rapidly, such as high technology. Companies are allowed to file Form 970 and switch from FIFO to LIFO at any time to take advantage of tax savings. However, they must then either wait ten years or get permission from the IRS to switch back to FIFO.

EQUIPMENT PURCHASES Under Section 179 of the Internal Revenue Code, businesses are allowed to deduct a total of $18,000 in equipment purchases during the year in which the purchases are made. Any purchases above this amount must be depreciated over several future tax periods. It is often advantageous for small businesses to use this tax incentive to increase their deductions for business expenses, thus reducing their taxable income and their tax liability. Necessary equipment purchases up to the limit can be timed at year end and still be fully deductible for the year. This tax incentive also applies to personal property put into service for business use, with the exception of automobiles and real estate.

WAGES PAID TO FAMILY MEMBERS Self-employed persons can also reduce their tax burden by paying wages to a spouse or to dependent children. Wages paid to children under the age of 18 are not subject to FICA (Social Security and Medicare) taxes. Under normal circumstances, employers are required to withhold 7.65 percent of the first $62,700 of an employee's income for FICA taxes. Employers are also required to match the 7.65 percent contributed by every employee, so that the total FICA contribution is 15.3 percent. Self-employed persons are required to pay both the employer and employee portions of the FICA tax.

But the FICA taxes are waived when the employee is a dependent child of the small business owner, saving the child and the parent 7.65 percent each. In addition, the child's wages are still considered a tax deductible business expense for the parent—thus reducing the parent's taxable income. Although the child must pay normal income taxes on the wages he or she receives, it is likely to be at a lower tax rate than the parent pays. Some business owners are able to further reduce their tax burden by paying wages to their spouse. If these wages bring the business owner's net income below $62,700—the threshold for FICA taxes—then they may reduce the self-employment tax owed by business owner. It is important to note, however, that the child or spouse must actually work for the business and that the wages must be reasonable for the work performed.

BENEFITS PLANS AND INVESTMENTS Tax planning also applies to various types of employee benefits that can provide a business with tax deductions, such as contributions to life insurance, health insurance, or retirement plans. As an added bonus, many such benefit programs are not considered taxable income for employees. Finally, tax planning applies to various types of investments that can shift tax liability to future periods, such as treasury bills, bank certificates, savings bonds, and deferred annuities. Companies can avoid paying taxes during the current period for income that is reinvested in such tax-deferred instruments.

TAX PLANNING FOR DIFFERENT BUSINESS FORMS

"The first step in tax planning—for small business owners and professionals, at least—is to select the right form of organization for your enterprise," according to Albert B. Ellentuck in the *Laventhol and Horwath Small Business Tax Planning Guide.* "You'll end up paying radically different amounts of income tax depending on the form you select. And your odds of being audited by the IRS will change, too." Many aspects of tax planning are specific to certain business forms; some of these are discussed below:

SOLE PROPRIETORSHIPS AND PARTNERSHIPS Tax planning for sole proprietorships and partnerships is in many ways similar to tax planning for individuals. This is because the owners of businesses organized as sole proprietors and partnerships pay personal income tax rather than business income tax. These small business owners file an informational return for their business with the IRS, and then report any income taken from the business for personal use on their own personal tax return. No special taxes are imposed except for the self-employment tax (SECA), which requires all self-employed persons to pay both the employer and employee portions of the FICA tax, for a total of 15.3 percent.

Since they do not receive an ordinary salary, the owners of sole proprietorships and partnerships are not required to withhold income taxes for themselves. Instead, they are required to estimate their total tax liability and remit it to the IRS in quarterly installments, using Form 1040 ES. It is important that the amount of tax paid in quarterly installments equal either the total amount owed during the previous year or 90 percent of their total current tax liability. Otherwise, the IRS may charge interest and impose a stiff penalty for underpayment of estimated taxes.

Since the IRS calculates the amount owed quarterly, a large lump-sum payment in the fourth quarter will not enable a taxpayer to escape penalties. On the other hand, a significant increase in withholding in the fourth quarter may help, because tax that is withheld by an employer is considered to be paid evenly throughout the year no matter when it was withheld. This leads to a possible tax planning strategy for a self-employed person who falls behind in his or her estimated tax payments. By having an employed spouse increase his or her withholding, the self-employed person can make up for the deficiency and avoid a penalty. The IRS has also been known to waive underpayment penalties for people in special circumstances. For example, they might waive the penalty for newly self-employed taxpayers who underpay their income taxes because they are making estimated tax payments for the first time.

Another possible tax planning strategy applies to partnerships that anticipate a loss. At the end of each tax year, partnerships file the informational Form 1065 (Partnership Statement of Income) with the IRS, and then report the amount of income that accrued to each partner on Schedule K1. This income can be divided in any number of ways, depending on the nature of the partnership agreement. In this way, it is possible to pass all of a partnership's early losses to one partner in order to maximize his or her tax advantages.

C CORPORATIONS Tax planning for C corporations is very different than that for sole proprietorships and partnerships. This is because profits earned by C corporations accrue to the corporation rather than to the individual owners, or shareholders. A corporation is a separate, taxable entity under the law, and different corporate tax rates apply based on the amount of net income received. As of 1997, the corporate tax rates were 15 percent on income up to $50,000, 25 percent on income between $50,000 and $75,000, 34 percent on income between $75,000 and $100,000, 39 percent on income between $100,000 and $335,000, and 34 percent on income between $335,000 and $10 million. Personal service corporations, like medical and law practices, pay a flat rate of 35 percent. In addition to the basic corporate tax, corporations may be subject to several special taxes.

Corporations must prepare an annual corporate tax return on either a calendar-year basis (the tax year ends December 31, and taxes must be filed by March 15) or a fiscal-year basis (the tax year ends whenever the officers determine). Most Subchapter S corporations, as well as C corporations that derive most of their income from the personal services of shareholders, are required to use the calendar-year basis for tax purposes. Most other corporations can choose whichever basis provides them with the most tax benefits. Using a fiscal-year basis to stagger the corporate tax year and the personal one can provide several advantages. For example, many corporations choose to end their fiscal year on January 31 and give their shareholder/employees bonuses at that time. The bonuses are still tax deductible for the corporation, while the individual shareholders enjoy use of that money without owing taxes on it until April 15 of the following year.

Both the owners and employees of C corporations receive salaries for their work, and the corporation must withhold taxes on the wages paid. All such salaries are tax deductible for the corporations, as are fringe benefits supplied to employees. Many smaller corporations can arrange to pay out all corporate income in salaries and benefits, leaving no income subject to the corporate income tax. Of course, the individual shareholder/employees are required to pay personal income taxes. Still, corporations can use tax planning strategies to defer or accrue income between the corporation and individuals in order to pay taxes in the lowest possible tax bracket. The one major disadvantage to corporate taxation is that corporate income is subject to corporate taxes, and then income distributions to shareholders in the form of dividends are also taxable for the shareholders. This situation is known as ''double taxation.''

S CORPORATIONS Subchapter S corporations avoid the problem of double taxation by passing their earnings (or losses) through directly to shareholders, without having to pay dividends. Experts note that it is often preferable for tax planning purposes to begin a new business as an S corporation rather than a C corporation. Many businesses show a loss for a year or more when they first begin operations. At the same time, individual owners often cash out investments and sell assets in order to accumulate the funds needed to start the business. The owners would have to pay tax on this income unless the corporate losses were passed through to offset it.

Another tax planning strategy available to shareholder/employees of S corporations involves keeping FICA taxes low by setting modest salaries for themselves, below the Social Security base. S corporation shareholder/employees are only required to pay FICA taxes on the income that they receive as salaries, not on income that they receive as dividends or on earnings that are retained in the corporation. It is important to note, however, that unreasonably low salaries may be challenged by the IRS.

FURTHER READING:

Dailey, Frederick W. *Tax Savvy for Small Business.* 2nd ed. Berkeley, CA: Nolo Press, 1997.

DeJong, David S., and Ann Gray Jakabcin. *J.K. Lasser's Year-Round Tax Strategies.* New York: Macmillan, 1997.

Ellentuck, Albert B. *Laventhol and Horwath Small Business Tax Planning Guide.* New York: Avon Books, 1988.

The Entrepreneur Magazine Small Business Advisor. New York: Wiley, 1995.

Hoover, Kent. ''Critics Blast IRS Rule Change.'' *Triangle Business Journal.* April 21, 2000.

Marullo, Gloria Gibbs. ''Hiring Your Child: Tax Breaks and Trade-Offs.'' *Nation's Business.* June 1997.

Wiener, Leonard. ''How to Keep One Step Ahead: Hot Tips for Turning an Annual Chore into Many Happy Returns.'' *U.S. News and World Report.* March 9, 1998.

Wiener, Leonard. ''Tricks to Trim Taxes.'' *U.S. News and World Report.* December 7, 1998.

TAX PREPARATION SOFTWARE

Faced with a tax code which inevitably changes from year to year, many small business owners choose to use one of the many tax preparation software packages which are now widely available. These packages are available for both PCS and Apple computers, and most use a spreadsheet format.

Using tax preparation software will almost certainly result in a more complete and more correct tax return. As Keith Higginbotham reported in the *Knight-Ridder/Tribune News Service,* typical paper tax returns have an error rate of 20 percent. Thanks to built-in math calculators and other automatic checks, electronic tax preparation and filing reduces this error rate to less than 1 percent. Tax preparation software packages may also steer the taxpayer toward greater savings or little-known deductions, paying for themselves with the returns they yield. Even if no direct tax savings are realized through the use of the software, many analysts believe that business owners can save themselves a considerable amount of time by using the packages, thus freeing them to use their talents in other business areas.

Purchasing the software to prepare tax returns, no matter which package is purchased, will undoubtedly be less expensive than hiring an accountant. Of course, a CPA can be creative and intuitive about individual circumstances in a way that a computer program can never be. But unless the finances for the year are extremely complicated, the best of these software programs should be sufficient to meet the requirements of most small enterprises. "For people who have done their returns and feel comfortable doing them, software can be an excellent tool, as opposed to doing them by hand," CPA Bruce Bernard said in the *Business Courier-Cincinnati/Northern Kentucky*. "But you have a garbage-in, garbage-out problem. If you put bad information in, you're going to get a bad return." A major drawback associated with using one of the available packages, however, is that in the event of an audit, the small business owner will have to face the IRS without the expert knowledge of the CPA that originally prepared the tax return.

COMPONENTS OF THE PACKAGES

DATA ENTRY All of the software packages have more than one option for entering data into the IRS-accepted forms. The user can always opt for the simple method of entering figures into the forms without assistance from the program, using the software mainly to double-check figures and calculate final amounts. All of the software packages also have an interview function, which asks easily understandable questions to which the user responds by clicking yes or no boxes. This function specifies which schedules are required by the IRS, and which sections of the basic 1040 and schedules can be bypassed. Depending on the program, there may be a third route—a "fast track" interview, through which the user can select specific parts of the interview to fill out, speeding up the process and avoiding the sections which are not pertinent to the case at hand.

Many of the programs also have importing features, which allow the user to pull data from other programs directly into the tax preparation. Generally, these work primarily with Quicken and QuickBooks. If the small business owner already uses one of these applications to calculate tax-related expenses, it is relatively quick and easy to transfer information, cutting down on duplicated work. Almost all of the packages also allow the user to import last year's tax information, provided it was prepared with the same package.

FILING When it comes to methods of filing, most of the packages provide several options for the user to choose between. The forms can be filled out electronically and then printed and mailed to the IRS to be processed in a paper version. Some of the packages offer the abbreviated Form 1040PC, which is also submitted as a hard copy. And some of the packages allow the user to file electronically, although some charge an additional fee for this option (around $10).

FEATURES AND HELP All of the software packages automatically check for mathematical mistakes and warn of possible errors when questionable data is entered into a field. Most of the programs can offer advice—some from specific tax experts—about how to maximize the return and minimize taxes paid. Some of the programs offer complete IRS tax guides which can be directly accessed, and some offer only abbreviated versions of this information. Some of the programs even alert the user to potential audit flags resulting from data entered. Several packages offer a review option after the forms are completed; this option can provide advice on what to do differently to pay less taxes the next time around.

Most of the packages offer state tax preparation in addition to the federal forms. Some offer only a few states, while others offer all the states which provide electronic forms. These supplements may be included in the price, or may be priced separately. Prices for the packages range from around $20 to more than $50, plus state supplements and filing fees.

DECIDING WHICH PACKAGE TO USE

Choosing a package will depend on how involved the tax return is. A few of the products can manage even very complicated scenarios, while the few at the bottom of the price range tend to be better for simple personal tax returns. For the small business owner, who may be dealing with self-employment taxes, home-work environments, and partnerships, it is probably worthwhile to purchase one of the more detailed programs. As of 2000, the two most popular tax software packages were Kiplinger Tax Cut by H&R Block, and Turbo Tax by Intuit.

With the advent of high-speed Internet connections and improved Internet security, more and more tax preparation is taking place online. Growing numbers of small businesses are contracting with application service providers (ASPs) that specialize in tax preparation. ASPs provide tax preparation applications on their Web sites and also maintain huge databases to store clients' data. Users connect to the ASP's remote computer over the Internet, access their files with a password, and use the software provided to prepare their taxes online.

FURTHER READING:

Dailey, Frederick W. *Tax Savvy for Small Business.* 2nd ed. Berkeley, CA: Nolo Press, 1997.

DeJong, David S., and Ann Gray Jakabcin. *J.K. Lasser's Year-Round Tax Strategies.* New York: Macmillan, 1997.

Frees, John. "Tax Software Can Be a Help, But Isn't a Cure-All Solution. *Business Courier-Cincinnati/Northern Kentucky.* February 25, 2000.

Higginbotham, Keith. "IRS Expands Electronic Tax Filing." *Knight-Ridder/Tribune Business News.* January 5, 2001.

Needleman, Ted. "Business Tax Prep Preview." *Practical Accountant.* October 2000.

Zarowin, Stanley. "Expanding into Cyberspace." *Journal of Accountancy.* September 2000.

SEE ALSO: Electronic Tax Filing

Tax returns include all the required paperwork that accompanies the remittance of taxes to the appropriate government agency, usually the Internal Revenue Service (IRS). The IRS issues more than 650 different forms for taxpayers to use in calculating and paying their taxes (the complete list is available through IRS publication 676, *Catalog of Federal Tax Forms*). Each form applies to a different situation or purpose. For example, Form 1065 details the income received by a business operating as a partnership, and Form 8826 relates to expenses claimed for business use of a home. Perhaps the most familiar type of tax form is the annual personal tax return, Form 1040, that must be completed by millions of taxpayers each year.

Considering that the laws have undergone no fewer than seven major revisions in the past two decades, as well as numerous minor changes, it can be exceedingly difficult for small business owners to prepare their own tax returns. But, as Frederick W. Dailey noted in his book *Tax Savvy for Small Business,* "The average small business person can't afford to call a tax pro with every question." Fortunately, a great deal of information is available through other sources, such as IRS publications and help lines, self-help tax preparation guides and software, trade associations, periodicals, and online services.

It is important for small business owners to maintain a personal awareness of tax-related issues in order to save money. Even if they employ a professional bookkeeper or accountant, small business owners should keep careful tabs on their own tax preparation in order to take advantage of all possible opportunities for deductions and tax savings. "Whether or not you enlist the aid of an outsider, you should understand the basic provisions of the tax code," Albert B. Ellentuck wrote in the *Laventhol and Horwath Small Business Tax Planning Guide.* "Just as you would not turn over the management of your money to another person, you should not blindly allow someone else to take complete charge of your taxpaying responsibilities." In addition, as Dailey noted, "Tax knowledge has

powerful profit potential. Knowing what the tax law has to offer can give you a far better bottom line than your competitors who don't bother to learn."

COMMON BUSINESS TAX FORMS AND FILING DEADLINES

Small businesses that employ persons other than the owner or partners are required to withhold payroll taxes from the wages paid to employees, remit these taxes to the Internal Revenue Service (IRS), and make regularly scheduled reports to the IRS about the amount of payroll taxes owed and paid. Payroll taxes include regular income taxes, FICA (Social Security and Medicare) taxes, and FUTA (federal unemployment) taxes. In addition to withholding payroll taxes for employees, employers must remit these taxes to the IRS in a timely manner. The regular income taxes and the portion of the FICA taxes that are withheld from employees' wages each pay period must be remitted to the IRS monthly, along with a Federal Tax Deposit Coupon (Form 8109-B). If the total withheld is less than $500, however, the business is allowed to make the payments quarterly.

Employers must also file four different reports regarding payroll taxes. The first report, Form 941, is the Employer's Quarterly Federal Tax Return. This report details the number of employees the business had, the amount of wages they were paid, and the amount of taxes that were withheld for the quarter. The other three reports are filed annually. Form W-2—the Annual Statement of Taxes Withheld—must be sent to all employees before January 31 of the following year. It details how much each employee received in wages and how much was withheld for taxes over the course of the year. Copies of the W-2 forms for all employees also must be sent to the Social Security Administration. The third report, Form W-3, must be sent to the IRS by February 28 of the following year. It provides a formal reconciliation of the quarterly tax payments made on Form 941 and the annual totals reported on Form W-2 for all employees. The final report is the Federal Unemployment Tax Return, Form 940, which outlines the total FUTA taxes owed and paid for the year.

Since they do not receive an ordinary salary, the owners of sole proprietorships and partnerships are not required to withhold income taxes for themselves. Instead, they are required to estimate their total tax liability and remit it to the IRS in quarterly installments, using Form 1040 ES. It is important that the amount of tax paid in quarterly installments equal either the total amount owed during the previous year or 90 percent of their total current tax liability. Otherwise, the IRS may charge interest and impose a stiff penalty for underpayment of estimated taxes. At the end of the tax year, the income for sole proprietorships is simply reported on the personal tax return of the business owner. Partnerships must file the informational Form 1065 (Partnership Statement of Income) with the IRS, and then report the amount of income that accrued to each partner on Schedule K1.

Corporations must prepare an annual corporate tax return on either a calendar-year basis (the tax year ends December 31, and taxes must be filed by March 15) or a fiscal-year basis (the tax year ends whenever the officers determine). Most Subchapter S corporations, as well as C corporations that derive most of their income from the personal services of shareholders, are required to use the calendar-year basis for tax purposes. Most other corporations can choose whichever basis provides them with the most tax benefits. At the end of their tax year, corporations file either Form 1120, the U.S. Corporate Income Tax Return, or the shorter Form 1120A. If they expect to owe taxes, corporations are required to make quarterly estimated payments, like other businesses.

FURTHER READING:

Dailey, Frederick W. *Tax Savvy for Small Business.* 2nd ed. Berkeley, CA: Nolo Press, 1997.

DeJong, David S., and Ann Gray Jakabcin. *J.K. Lasser's Year-Round Tax Strategies.* New York: Macmillan, 1997.

Ellentuck, Albert B. *Laventhol and Horwath Small Business Tax Planning Guide.* New York: Avon Books, 1988.

The Entrepreneur Magazine Small Business Advisor. New York: Wiley, 1995.

Guttman, George. ''How Simple Can a Simple Form Be?'' *Tax Notes.* November 6, 1995.

McTague, Jim. ''Tax Man or Father Time: The New Forms Are Supposed to Be Friendlier, and You Get to Stay with Them Longer.'' *Barron's.* January 2, 1995.

Rieschick, Jacqueline. ''Taxpayers Will Spend Less Time on 1997 Form 1040, IRS Predicts.'' *Tax Notes.* September 22, 1997.

''Top Errors Preparers Make.'' *Journal of Accountancy.* June 2000.

Wiener, Leonard. ''How to Keep One Step Ahead: Hot Tips for Turning an Annual Chore into Many Happy Returns.'' *U.S. News and World Report.* March 9, 1998.

TAX WITHHOLDING

Tax withholding refers to the portion of an employee's wages that are retained by an employer for remittance to the Internal Revenue Service (IRS). Two main types of taxes are typically withheld—regular income taxes and Federal Insurance Contribution Act (FICA) taxes, which include contributions to federal Social Security and Medicare programs—although most states and some cities apply their own taxes as well.

Employers are required to withhold 7.65 percent of the first $62,700 of an employee's income for FICA taxes. Employers are also required to match that amount for every employee, so that the total FICA contribution is 15.3 percent. Self-employed persons are required to pay both the employer and employee portions of the FICA tax. The amount of regular income tax that must be withheld from an employee's paycheck depends on the individual's tax status. Ideally, the total income tax withheld should come close to equaling the employee's overall tax liability at the end of the year. Employees can adjust their income tax withholding by filing Form W-4 with their employer and designating the number of withholding allowances they wish to claim.

Tax withholding can affect entrepreneurs and small business owners in two ways. First, small business owners who have employees other than themselves and their partners must withhold payroll taxes for those employees. Second, entrepreneurs who are employees of a company and also have income from self-employment must designate the amount of wages that are withheld from their paychecks.

Withholding is usually done in standard amounts based on formulas provided by the IRS. Employees designate the number of withholding allowances they wish to claim based on their expected tax liability, which depends on their filing status, family circumstances, other sources of income, and available deductions or tax credits. It is not advisable to overpay taxes—even though the extra amount is eventually refunded to the taxpayer—because it is like giving the government an interest-free loan. At the same time, it is not advisable to underpay taxes because it may be difficult to come up with a lump-sum payment when it is due on April 15. In addition, a taxpayer who underpays his or her income taxes by more than 10 percent may face a penalty and have to pay the government interest on the funds owed.

Unfortunately, the IRS guidelines for withholding can cause problems with overpayment or underpayment of taxes even in simple cases, as Michael M. Watts and James E. Gauntt explained in an article for *National Public Accountant.* For example, a single taxpayer with no dependents and only one source of income would be instructed to claim two withholding allowances to best approximate the total tax owed. But Watts and Gauntt found that this strategy would cause the taxpayer in question to owe between $180 and $190 on April 15. Similarly, a married couple with one income would be instructed to claim three withholding allowances, but this would cause a balance due for the year of $370. The situation was even worse for married couples who both work outside the home.

In addition, many people supplement their regular employment income with interest, dividends, capital gains, rental property, or self-employment income. In many cases, this means that regular withholding from employment income—based on the IRS formulas—is not enough to cover the taxes owed. Instead, these taxpayers should try to estimate their total tax liability and adjust their withholding accordingly. "Wage earners should monitor their expected tax liability versus withholding throughout the year and make adjustments as needed," David S. DeJong and Ann Gray Jakabcin wrote in *J.K. Lasser's Year Round Tax Strategies.*

Taxpayers are required to pay at least 90 percent of their total tax liability in installments prior to April 15, or they may be subject to a penalty. However, the penalty is waived for taxpayers who pay at least as much in total taxes as they had owed the previous year, or for whom the amount underpaid is less than $500. Since the IRS calculates the amount owed quarterly, a large lump-sum payment in the fourth quarter will not enable a taxpayer to escape penalties. On the other hand, a significant increase in withholding in the fourth quarter may help, because tax that is withheld by an employer is considered to be paid evenly throughout the year no matter when it was withheld. For this reason, taxpayers who see a significant underpayment problem looming should have additional taxes withheld by their employers. "Many people don't realize that they may have as much withheld from their pay as they want, up to the full amount of their salary," according to DeJong and Jakabcin. To avoid a penalty, the total tax withheld must reach 90 percent of what will be owed in the current year or 100 percent of what was owed in the previous year.

This strategy can also work for a self-employed person who falls behind in his or her estimated tax payments. By having an employed spouse increase his or her withholding, the self-employed person can make up for the deficiency and avoid a penalty. The IRS has also been known to waive underpayment penalties for people in special circumstances. For example, they might waive the penalty for newly self-employed taxpayers who underpay their income taxes because they are making estimated tax payments for the first time.

FURTHER READING:

Dailey, Frederick W. *Tax Savvy for Small Business.* 2nd ed. Berkeley, CA: Nolo Press, 1997.

DeJong, David S., and Ann Gray Jakabcin. *J.K. Lasser's Year-Round Tax Strategies.* New York: Macmillan, 1997.

The Entrepreneur Magazine Small Business Advisor. New York: Wiley, 1995.

Grassi, Carl. "Federal Withholding Rules Enforced with an Iron Fist." *Crain's Cleveland Business.* June 12, 2000.

Halphen, Christine. "Revised Withholding Regulations—A Race to the Finish?" *Tax Notes.* July 10, 2000.

Watts, Michael M., and James E. Gauntt. "Beware the Withholding Tax Trap." *National Public Accountant.* September 1994.

"When and How to Change Withholding on Wages." *Taxes: The Tax Magazine.* May 1996.

Wiener, Leonard. "Squaring Your Account with the IRS." *U.S. News and World Report.* August 29, 1988.

SEE ALSO: Payroll Taxes

TELECOMMUTING

Telecommuting is a practice in which an employee works at a location—usually, but not always, one's home—that is remote from the actual business facility at which he/she is employed. Under this arrangement, the employee maintains close contact with coworkers and supervisors via various forms of computer, Internet, and communication technology (i.e, electronic mail, telephone, computer disks, etc.)

Telecommuting is an increasingly popular work option in many businesses and industries, and its usage is expected to increase in the future, boosted by new innovations in computer and communication technology. This trend is driven by several factors. Linda Shaw, author of *Telecommute! Go to Work without Leaving Home,* wrote that "the labor pool of employees with specific talents will shrink, making employers more willing to make concessions to keep valued employees happy. A smaller labor pool combined with an increasing demand for highly skilled laborers has fueled employee-driven change in working environments. Scarce, highly skilled workers have begun to demand more flexible work arrangements, especially as they choose to live farther and farther from their employers." Shaw and other observers also note demographic changes within the American work force as a factor in the growth of telecommuting. These analysts contend that new generations of workers are less willing to sacrifice time with family than their counterparts of previous eras. This desire to spend more time at home and avoid long commutes is touted as a key factor in making telecommuting an attractive benefit. Finally, new technologies have made working from home a viable alternative. With the advent of high speed modems, fax machines, voice mail, powerful personal computers, electronic mail and the like, workers can now perform their jobs without losing touch with employers and customers.

ADVANTAGES OF TELECOMMUTING

Both employers and employees have found telecommuting to be a mutually beneficial arrangement in many instances. Proponents cite several positive factors in particular:

Happier employees. Telecommuting arrangements can help workers realize a general improvement in their personal "quality of life." They avoid long, stressful commutes, thus gaining more time for pleasurable activities and more flexibility for changeable tasks like child and elder care.

Increased retention of valued employees. Many businesses lose workers when those employees undergo significant life changes, such as starting a family or relocating to another region or state because of a spouse's career. Telecommuting is one way in which a business may be able to continue to utilize the services of an otherwise unavailable worker. It is also touted as a tool that permits workers to minimize use of "personal days" in instances where they have to stay home and care for a sick child, etc.

Increased employee productivity. Business studies and anecdotal evidence both suggest that employees are often much more productive at home, where "drop-in" interruptions and meetings are not distractions. Instead, the teleworker can focus on the job at hand. Of course, productivity at home is directly related to the employee's level of self-discipline and abilities.

Cost savings. Businesses can often gain significant savings in facilities costs like office space and parking space requirements when staff members telecommute.

DISADVANTAGES OF TELECOMMUTING

But while telecommuting programs have been highly successful for many businesses of all shapes, sizes, and industry orientations, there are potential pitfalls associated with them. Commonly cited drawbacks include the following:

Lack of oversight. Direct supervision of teleworkers is not possible.

Diminished productivity. Some people are unable to be productive in at-home work settings, either because of family distractions or their own limited capacity to focus on tasks when more pleasurable activities (bicycling, gardening, watching television, etc.) beckon.

Security problems. "The remote access needs of telecommuters and other mobile staff . . . create a hole in security walls with every connection," cautioned Kevin McNeely in *Providence Business News.* "Procedures should be implemented to allow employee access while keeping out unwanted intruders. This includes periodically updated password protection and informing employees concerning the need for remote access security."

Isolation. "The freedom of working alone comes with a price—the burden of solitude," commented one executive in *Association Management.* "We all have wished for days where people would just leave us alone, and with telework, we get our wish—in spades." Partial teleworking arrangements, in which the employee spends a portion of each week (1-3 days) in the office and the remainder working from home, can sometimes be an effective means of addressing this problem.

Erosion of company culture and/or departmental morale. Many businesses include certain employees who have a major positive impact on the prevailing office environment. When these employees enter into telecommuting programs, their absence is often deeply felt by the staff members left behind. In some cases, this departure from the company's everyday operations can even have a deleterious effect on the operation's overall culture.

Loss of "brainstorming" ability. "Given that much of the value added to the production process in Western economies is at the 'knowledge' end of the spectrum, the dispersal of brains could be a problem," wrote Richard Thomas in *Management Today.* "The informal bouncing around of ideas is difficult, or even impossible, without the face-to-face contact of a shared workplace."

Perceived damage to career. A common perception among employees of businesses that embrace teleworking options is that telecommuters are placed at a disadvantage in terms of career advancement and opportunity. Certainly, some professional avenues—such as supervisor positions—may be shut off to workers who want to continue telecommuting, but employers should make every effort to avoid an "out of sight, out of mind" perspective from taking shape.

Legal vulnerability. Some analysts have expressed concern that some employer liability issues regarding telecommuting practices have yet to be completely settled. They cite issues such as employer liability for home-office accidents under common law; applicability of the employer's insurance coverage when they work at home; and responsibility for equipment located in the home as particular concerns.

INSTITUTING A TELECOMMUTING PROGRAM

Experts cite several key elements in creating and maintaining a successful telecommuting policy in your business. First, business owners and/or managers should make sure that such a program will actually benefit their company's ability to efficiently address its various operational needs. For example, some positions require an extensive on-site presence. These range from management positions to those in which face-to-face communication with clients or other members of the workforce is imperative. Consultants urge employers to consider telecommuting proposals on a position-by-position basis, rather than adopting "one size fits all" parameters.

Companies should also conduct extensive research before buying and implementing new technologies necessary to institute a telecommuting program. Information technology (IT) personnel can be particularly useful in shaping program policies and anticipating remote workplace needs of teleworkers. In addition, you should consider the impact of telecommuting on other departments, both in terms of operational efficiency and morale.

Business owners should draft specific guidelines and policies for any telecommuting program. These policies may delineate reporting guidelines, delivery schedules for completing and submitting work, selected hours during which employee guarantees availability, employee performance evaluation criteria, and telecommuting work option evaluation criteria. Once such a program has been put in place, it is essential that it be actively monitored. Analysts urge business owners and managers to maintain open lines of communication with teleworkers, so that problems can be addressed in a timely manner.

Finally, business owners and managers need to recognize that some employees are better suited than others to thrive in a telecommuting program. Prospective workers should be self-motivated; self-disciplined; and possessed of good problem-solving skills and communication skills (both written and verbal). They should also have a home environment which will enable them to maintain or exceed the levels of productivity they attain in an office setting.

FURTHER READING:

Bray, Laura. "Consider the Alternatives." *Association Management.* November 1999.

Ditlea, Steve. "Home is Where the Office Is." *Nation's Business,* November 1995.

Dunham, Kemba J. "Telecommuters' Lament: Once Touted as the Future, Work-at-Home Situations Lose Favor with Employers." *Wall Street Journal.* October 31, 2000.

"Flexible Working Practices Boost Business Success." *Leadership and Organization Development Journal.* February-March 1997.

Kugelmass, John. *Telecommuting: A Manager's Guide to Flexible Work Arrangements.* Lexington Books. 1995.

Leveen-Sher, Margery. "Flexibility is the Key to Small Business Benefits." *Washington Business Journal.* February 16, 1996.

McNeely, Kevin. "Pitfalls of an Electronic Workplace." *Providence Business Journal.* March 27, 2000.

Schepp, Brad. *The Telecommuter's Handbook: How to Work for a Salary Without Ever Leaving the House.* Pharos Books, 1990.

"Seize the Future; Making Top Trends Pay Off Now." *Success.* March 1990.

Shaw, Linda. *Telecommute! Go to Work Without Leaving Home!.* John Wiley & Sons, 1996.

Thomas, Richard. "The World is Your Office." *Management Today.* July 1999.

SEE ALSO: Flexible Work Arrangements

TELEMARKETING

Telemarketing is the process of using the telephone to generate leads, make sales, or gather marketing information. Telemarketing can be a particularly valuable tool for small businesses, in that it saves time and money as compared to personal selling, but offers many of the same benefits in terms of direct contact with customers. In fact, experts have estimated that closing a sale through telemarketing usually costs less than one-fifth of what it would cost to send a salesperson to make a sale in person. Though telemarketing is more expensive than direct mail, it tends to be more efficient in closing sales and thus provides a greater yield on the marketing dollar.

Telemarketing is especially useful when the customers for a small business's products or services are located in hard-to-reach places, or when many prospects must be contacted in order to find one interested in making a purchase. Although some small businesses operate exclusively by telephone, telemarketing is most often used as part of an overall marketing program to tie together advertising and personal selling efforts. For example, a company might send introductory information through the mail, then follow-up with a telemarketing call to assess the prospect's interest, and finally send a salesperson to visit.

Telemarketing can be either inbound or outbound in scope. Inbound telemarketing consists of handling incoming telephone calls—often generated by broadcast advertising, direct mail, or catalogs—and taking orders for a wide range of products. Representatives working in this type of telemarketing program normally do not need as much training as outbound reps because the customer already has shown an interest by calling in.

Outbound telemarketing can be aimed directly at the end consumer—for example, a home repair business may call people in its community to search for prospects—or can be part of a business-to-business marketing program. Representatives working on this side of the industry generally require more training and product knowledge, as more actual selling is involved than with inbound operations.

Major applications of business-to-business telemarketing include selling to existing accounts, outbound new account development, inbound order processing and inquiry handling, customer service, and supporting the existing field sales force. As the costs of field sales continue to escalate, businesses are using telemarketing as a way to reduce the cost of selling and give more attention to marginal accounts. Telemarketing programs can be either handled in-house by a company or farmed out to service bureaus. Operations range in size from a one-person in-house staff member at a small business to a major corporation or service center that may have as many as 1,000 telephone stations.

One of the advantages telemarketing has over other direct marketing methods is that it involves human interaction. According to Robert J. McHatton in *Total Telemarketing,* ''used correctly and by professionals, the telephone is the most cost-efficient, flexible and statistically accountable medium available. At the same time, the telephone is still very intimate and personal. It is individual to individual.''

Although telemarketing has been the center of some controversies—ranging from scams run over the phone to a number of legal issues that have been the center of debate at both the state and national levels—the industry continues to grow. In fact, the American Telemarketing Association found that spending on telemarketing activities increased from $1 billion to $60 billion between 1981 and 1991. By the mid-1990s, telemarketing accounted for more than $450 billion in annual sales, a figure that is expected to continue to rise through the foreseeable future.

TYPICAL TELEMARKETING USES

Although telemarketing can be used as a stand-alone operation, it often works best as part of an overall marketing effort. Companies considering the use of telemarketing have to look at such factors as: which products and services are candidates to be sold by phone; whether telemarketing can be used to increase volume through upgrading the sale; how the process can help qualify prospects, define the market, and service existing accounts; and whether telemarketing can help generate new business. Some of the roles telemarketing can be used to fulfill include: selling, generating leads, gathering information, and improving customer service.

SELLING Telemarketing can either supplement or replace face-to-face selling to existing accounts. It can complement the field sales effort by reaching new customer bases or geographic markets at relatively low cost. It can also be used to sell goods and services independently, with no field sales force in place. This method often is used for repetitive supply purchases or readily identifiable products, though it can be effectively applied to other products as well.

The inside sales force can be used to replace direct contact for marginally profitable customers. A general rule of thumb in business says that 20 percent of customers account for 80 percent of sales, so conversely the remaining 80 percent of customers generate just 20 percent of sales. But businesses must keep in mind that marginal does not necessarily mean unprofitable. And the existing customer base is perhaps the most important asset in any business; sales increases most often come from current accounts, and it generally is less costly to maintain current customers than to search out new business. Telemarketers can give these reliable customers the attention they deserve. The reps can phone as often as needed, determine the customers' purchasing cycles, and contact them at appropriate reorder times.

In making such a consolidation between a direct and inside sales force, the company must be careful in determining which accounts should stay with field sales and which should be handled by telemarketing. Some businesses start their telemarketing operations with just small or inactive accounts, gradually increasing the size of accounts handled.

LEAD GENERATION Through telemarketing, a company can compile and update lists of customer prospect leads and then go through these lists searching for sales leads. Telemarketing can screen the leads and qualify them according to priority, passing the best leads to the field sales force for immediate action. The inside sales force also can identify the decision maker with the buying power and set up appointments for the outside sales force.

GATHERING INFORMATION Telemarketing can provide accurate information on advertising effectiveness, what customers are buying, from whom they're buying, and when they will buy again. It is also commonly used in conducting surveys.

IMPROVING CUSTOMER SERVICE Studies show it costs five times more to win over a new customer than to keep an existing one. By using telemarketing as a main facet of customer service, companies can go a long way toward keeping customers happy.

In addition, when used in conjunction with current computer technology, a telemarketing program can be analyzed in terms of costs and benefits, using quantitative data on the number of contacts, number of presentations, total sales, cost per sale, and income per sale.

ESTABLISHING A SUCCESSFUL PROGRAM

Not all telemarketing programs are successful. Improper execution, unrealistic goals over a short time period, oversimplification, and lack of top management support have caused the ultimate failure of more telephone sales programs than can be imagined. Like any marketing strategy, telemarketing takes time to plan and develop. It takes time to gain confidence in the message, to identify weak areas, and to predict bottom-line results. Some of the most common telemarketing mistakes include: not considering telemarketing as an option; not giving it a total commitment; not utilizing the proper expertise; failing to develop a proper database; improper human resource planning; lack of proper scripts and call guides; lack of quality control; and failing to understand the synergy with other direct marketing disciplines. As Richard L. Bencin wrote in *Strategic Telemarketing,* ''management must understand and agree to the necessary personnel and financial resources, as well as the time required for program development and testing. Telemarketing and related direct marketing techniques can work astoundingly well. But they need a real chance to demonstrate that success. It doesn't happen over a couple of weekends.''

Experts agree that companies must be careful in forming telemarketing goals and objectives. Some of the most important factors for success include: developing a complete marketing plan with built-in criteria for accounting and analysis; writing scripts, sales outlines, and presentations to be performed; establishing training and hiring procedures for both supervisors and sales personnel; analyzing and evaluating campaigns, personnel, and cost effectiveness; having support and commitment from management for the telemarketing's role in the overall marketing effort; establishing reachable goals; and placing a continuous emphasis on follow-up.

IN-HOUSE VS. OUTSIDE SERVICE BUREAU

When establishing a telemarketing program, a company has the option of setting up the operation in-house, or subcontracting it to an outside service bureau. Both have advantages and disadvantages. In-house programs usually are better if products and/or services require extensive technical expertise to explain. They also can be better for firms making a long-term commitment to telemarketing. Service bureaus, on the other hand, can help firms that need around-the-clock coverage for inbound programs, are supporting television ad campaigns, or are running a seasonal marketing program.

SERVICE BUREAUS One of the main advantages of service bureaus is that they can likely offer lower costs. By grouping programs from several different companies, service bureaus can generate sufficient volume to reduce labor and telephone costs, which make up a majority of total costs. They can also get a program started more quickly because they have experienced telephone reps on staff, along with necessary equipment.

When 24-hour coverage is needed on an inbound telemarketing program, it probably is more cost effective to go with a bureau. When setting up an outbound program, the experienced managers at a bureau can help a company avoid making mistakes and often can accurately project call volumes and sales per hour. Service bureaus also can help with testing new programs and have a greater ability to handle demand peaks.

On the downside, several client companies often must compete for a service bureau's attention, and for firms that share service with a broadcast advertiser whose response rates are underestimated, that can be a decided drawback. Stability of service bureaus has also been a problem at times.

IN-HOUSE OPERATIONS The main reason companies decide to run their own telemarketing campaign is that they can maintain total control over all facets, including hiring and firing, scripts and presentations, budgets, advertising, and compensation and incentive policies. When telemarketing programs are kept in-house, phone reps have ready access to company information, so they can confirm delivery, authorize credit, and suggest alternatives to out-of-stock items.

Since in-house reps are trained on individual product lines, they can handle highly technical calls no service bureau likely would attempt. Such technical expertise also helps companies maintain effective customer service programs through observation (such as via call monitoring). In addition, it is easier to gain company loyalty from actual employees than from people employed by an outside bureau. The biggest drawback to taking a program in-house is the large capital investment needed to get a telemarketing program started. It involves hiring and training new personnel, purchasing new communications equipment, and dealing with a process that is unfamiliar to many in business.

TECHNOLOGICAL AND HUMAN ELEMENTS

Computers have played an important role in the growth of telemarketing. Access to databases provides phone reps with account histories, stock status, order-taking formats, and other vital information. Besides analyzing data, computers are used for scheduling, scripting, and follow-ups. Computers also can be programmed to automatically dial phone numbers and connect the calls to telemarketers only if they are answered, screen out answering machines, and guide the phone rep through the telemarketing presentation.

While technology plays a vital role in keeping telemarketing cost-effective, the human element is critical in making the effort successful. Unfortunately, many firms still view telemarketing positions as clerical-level jobs staffed by people with few skills, no training, and little understanding of the product or service being sold. Often, the manager of a telemarketing operation is the only person in an organization familiar with the discipline. Some firms, though, have come to realize the importance of the telemarketers, as the firm's image is on the line with every call. They realize the position needs skilled, trained professionals who must be adequately compensated.

For compensation, most companies use a combination of salary, commission, and/or bonuses. Studies indicate that incentives generally aid in sales success, but it is important to link the inducements to the performance desired, be it total sales, calls completed, or presentations given. Some form of quotas also are common so sales reps know what is expected of them. Firms should be reasonable in setting quotas. If the goals are too high, the reps will become frustrated, leading to morale and worker retention problems. Conversely, low quotas can create an environment in which effort is lacking, especially if the compensation package in place is heavily weighted toward base salary.

Telemarketing positions typically show high levels of turnover, in large measure because the majority of interactions with potential customers end in rejection. Working shorter shifts or using computers to prescreen customers can help reduce the amount of rejection telemarketers experience. Training is another important factor. If the individuals that comprise your telemarketing staff are trained to be specific, control the time and pace of conversation, ask questions and listen without interrupting or rushing the customer's response, and respond to objections or concerns in a positive manner, they will experience greater levels of success—and hence, a more positive outlook on their duties.

CONTROVERSIES AND FUTURE OUTLOOK

Unfortunately, telemarketing has been the basis for numerous scams over the years. Federal authorities estimate that con artists using the phone bilk people out of least $1 billion annually. Some analysts contend that the figure may even be closer to $10 billion, as many embarrassed victims shy away from filing complaints. These frauds have given the telemarketing industry much bad press.

Legislators, on both the state and federal levels, have debated a number of proposed laws that could affect telemarketing in the future. For example, some proposed laws would require registration of telephone solicitors in a state. Registration often includes bonding requirements, submission of scripts and/or names of employees, and other administrative devices designed to create a paper trail to track fraudulent marketers. Another type of proposed legislation, known as ''asterisk bills,'' would require the telephone company or state government to keep a list of people who object to receiving unsolicited phone sales calls. Marketers would be required to obtain the list and not call these people. A similar law passed in 1996 mandated that marketers remove from their calling lists the name of anyone who requests that the marketer not contact him or her again.

A number of other proposed bills seek to restrict the hours available to telemarketers, generally limiting calls to no later than nine o'clock in the evening, local time. Still other laws under discussion would prohibit the completion of some types of phone sales unless a written contract is signed and returned by the consumer. Telemarketers generally favor an alternative allowing firms that offer consumers a right of examination and promise a refund to be exempt from such legislation. Finally, many states have considered enacting legislation that would prohibit or restrict the practice of monitoring customer service employees who work over the phone. The telemarketing industry considers monitoring vital to maintaining quality control and protecting consumers, so many firms ask employees to sign a release allowing such monitoring.

FURTHER READING:

Eisenhart, Tom. ''Telemarketing Takes Quantum Leap.'' *Business Marketing*. September 1993.

Everett, Martin. ''It's Jerry Hale on the Line.'' *Sales & Marketing Management*. December 1993.

Gottlieb, Mag. ''Telemarketing and The Law.'' *Direct Marketing*. February 1994.

McHatton, Robert J. *Total Telemarketing*. Wiley, 1988.

McLuhan, Robert. ''Warm Calling Builds Results.'' *Marketing*. August 5, 1999.

Moretti, Peggy. ''Telemarketers Serve Clients.'' *Business Marketing*. April 1994.

Rosen, Judith. ''Telemarketing: Pros and Cons.'' *Publishers Weekly*. January 11, 1999.

Stern, Aimee L. ''Telemarketing Polished Its Image.'' *Sales & Marketing Management*. June 1991.

TEMPORARY EMPLOYMENT SERVICES

Temporary employment services (often referred to as temporary employment agencies or firms) provide employees who possess specific skills to client companies for brief and often fixed periods of time. This arrangement can provide a client company with needed help during peak demand periods, staffing shortages, or vacations of regular employees, without requiring the time, expense, and long-term commitment of hiring a new employee. Temporary employment firms typically undertake hiring and firing decisions, issue paychecks, withhold payroll taxes, and make contributions for unemployment insurance, workers' compensation, and Social Security for their own employees. Client companies simply describe their staffing needs and time frame, then pay a set hourly rate to the temporary employment agency for the services of a "temp." The business scenarios in which temporary staff can be useful are virtually endless, noted *Arkansas Business*. "A large staffing service can bring in any number of temporaries to work days, nights, weekends, or holidays—and not just to perform low-skill tasks. Specialized temporary services can routinely handle specific, time-sensitive and highly skilled projects. In fact, very often temporary workers are so qualified, employers end up adding them to the full-time staff, saving the high cost of hiring and training. Additionally, a temporary employee allows you to judge whether you need a full-time person for a particular job or if ongoing temporaries can complete the tasks."

The use of temporary employment grew rapidly in the 1980s and early 1990s during the trend toward business downsizing and restructuring, in which many companies reduced the size of their core work forces. Companies began to substitute temporary for permanent employees for cost savings in payroll administration and fringe benefits, and to gain greater flexibility in the face of changing business conditions. Today, most temporary employment services continue to specialize in providing general secretarial and clerical help to client companies. In fact, office, clerical, and industrial temps comprise an estimated 70 percent of total industry placements. But use of temporary workers has also expanded in the manufacturing sector—coinciding with the advent of "just-in-time" production systems—and in professional occupations, such as executives, lawyers, and engineers. Growth in these areas enabled the temporary staffing industry to register annual double-digit gains in revenue throughout the 1990s.

Some changes in the nature of the work force—such as an increase in the number of working mothers—have contributed to the popularity of temporary employment arrangements. Part-time workers who are employed as "temps" enjoy a great deal of flexibility in setting schedules and choosing assignments. For example, a mother with young children in school might opt to work fairly consistently during the school year, but not at all during the summer months. Some professional workers use temporary assignments as a way to add variety to their jobs, while recent college graduates might view temp work as a stepping stone to permanent employment. But even though temporary employment offers advantages for some workers, many others—who have been laid off or are unable to find permanent positions—work as temps out of necessity rather than preference.

In his book *Alternative Staffing Strategies,* David Nye argued that the expanded use of temporary employment was likely to persist. He wrote: "The forces that gave rise to increased use of temporary workers as an alternative to permanent employment are generally expected to stay with us, if not accelerate. These forces include the shift from production of goods to processing of information and other service industries; employer reluctance to add permanent staff in the face of possible business downturns; increased technology that both requires special expertise and facilitates its deployment; and the availability of capable individuals who either must, or prefer to, enter the temporary labor market."

Nonetheless, there are potential drawbacks associated with going the "temp service" route that must be weighed. One factor commonly cited is the greater allocation of time and resources to training that may be necessary if a company receives several different temp workers in succession for one job. Another criticism that is sometimes raised in conjunction with reliance on temp services is that some temporary staffers do not feel a connection to the company for which they are working, which can have a deleterious impact on effort and effectiveness. Companies can do much to address these potential problem areas, however, by establishing and maintaining a program that continually monitors and reviews the contributions of temp workers.

CHOOSING A TEMPORARY SERVICE

Temporary employment services are a particularly attractive option for small businesses, which often need help on a limited basis but lack the resources to recruit, screen, and pay new, full-time employees. A small business considering the services of a temporary employment agency should first consider several factors:

Gauge need. Business owners should examine production schedules, composition of employee benefits (number of sick days and vacation days, etc.), and seasonal workloads when weighing whether to pursue temporary staff. Shortcomings in specific areas of business knowledge should be factored in as well. Another key factor that should be weighed is less quantifiable but even more important: quality of customer service. "Check the quality of the work not just during the times when employees are covering for another worker, but on a regular basis," said Don Owens in *Sacramento Business Journal*. "Judge the way employees react when asked to do more from each other and from managers. Most importantly, look at how employees treat people outside the company—from the vendors and suppliers to the customers themselves. Are they harried, short and tense?" If so, temporary additions to the workforce may be in order.

Put an effective screening process in place. It is important to understand the temporary services firm's screening process for temporary employees. Though minimal screening is acceptable for low-level jobs, the process should include more sophisticated screening methods—such as personal interviews, computer testing, or psychological evaluations—for positions requiring specialized skills. Existing employee job descriptions can be used to determine temp staffers' suitability for jobs and to measure their performance once they have begun work.

Evaluate potential temporary staffing services. Experts urge business owners to seek out recommendations for temp services from other members of the business community. Once you have targeted specific services for consideration, conduct extensive interviews with management to explain your company's needs and determine their ability to meet those needs. "The natural inclination is to look for the lowest rate," observed *Arkansas Business*. "Yet quality of service is just as important. . . . A firm that carefully screens and evaluates the skills of all its temporaries will provide you with workers who do the job right the first time."

Establish partnership with the temp service. The temporary services firm your company selects should be able to evaluate the client company's project requirements, time frame, budget, and working environment, and provide temporary employee who have the appropriate skills, availability, and personality to meet its client's needs. Ideally, the temp services firm should be flexible in accepting last-minute requests for temps or in changing temps in the middle of a project if the first one does not work out. Payment rates should be negotiable, based on the skill level required and the quantity of work.

Make your workplace one in which temporary workers can succeed. Companies should make sure that temporary workers are made to feel welcome upon arrival, and that they receive solid training. Do not abandon temporary workers to "sink or swim" on their own.

Monitor temporary staffing initiatives. Put programs in place to monitor and review temp staff performance and determine the impact of the temp service on bottom-line financial performance and customer service.

FURTHER READING:

"Business Gives in to Temptation." *U.S. News and World Report*. July 4, 1994.

"Business and the Temp Temptation: A Permanent Situation." *Washington Post*. October 20, 1993.

Lee, Mie-Yun. "Temp Choices Put Longtime Mark on Firms." *Crain's Cleveland Business*. September 9, 1996.

Owens, Don L. "Employees Know if You Need Temporary Staffing." *Sacramento Business Journal*. February 11, 2000.

Rowland, Mary. "Your Own Account; Temporary Work: The New Career." *New York Times*. September 12, 1993.

"Temporary Employees Take Up Slack, Save the Day With a Variety of Skills." *Arkansas Business*. December 27, 1999.

TESTING LABORATORIES

Testing laboratories are utilized by all manner of businesses to provide objective analytical data on the quality of a product or process. Some companies look to testing labs for product certification, which can be a significant marketing tool, while others use testing labs to analyze the results of employee drug tests. Still others secure the services of environmental testing laboratories to check on water and soil quality before making a major land and/or facility purchase. Whatever the reason, the services offered by testing laboratories are often of great usefulness to businesses in a wide range of industry sectors.

The number and size of testing laboratories operating in the United States and many other industrialized nations has increased significantly over the last number of years. There are myriad reasons for this growth, but observers generally point to the rise in product testing for the bulk of the increase. "It's the significant diversity in products, growth in consumer demand, and the globalization of sourcing that are providing the major thrust behind testing and certification," claimed a testing industry executive in *Appliance Manufacturer*. Experts agree that these product analysis factors have had a significant impact, but several other trends have also been cited as key to the increased reliance on external testing labs. The rising expense of product liability insurance, for instance, has led many companies to utilize testing labs to check out new or "improved" products prior to general release. "Small to mid-sized companies," wrote

Food Processing contributor Robert Morgan, ''often are looking for a lab to serve as what amounts to their quality control department.'' Testing laboratories have assumed this role with smaller companies in large measure because of the expense of maintaining comparable facilities in-house. Still, many big firms use them as well in order to secure independent results in areas of quality control and failure analysis.

It should be noted, however, that testing laboratories generally limit themselves to one specific testing area. For example, a company that conducts analysis of employee drug tests will rarely offer services in the realm of environmental analysis; similarly, a company that conducts tests on soil or water will not be of use to a small business owner who is seeking product quality testing services.

ADVANTAGES OF USING A TESTING LABORATORY

Business analysts, laboratory managers, and business owners—both large and small—agree that there are several significant advantages associated with utilizing the services of an independent testing lab. Morgan cited three primary reasons why businesses choose off-site independent labs: objectivity, economic considerations, and safety.

OBJECTIVITY ''The independent off-site testing laboratory focuses on its testing procedures to ensure accurate results,'' stated Morgan. '' 'Third-party testing' or 'tested by an independent laboratory' is a common advertising claim that guarantees the test results are objective and free from the influence, guidance or control of interested parties. The independent laboratory exists for only one purpose: to provide objective analytical data on the quality of a product or process. The laboratory management invests considerable time, money and effort to ensure this objectivity.'' In keeping with this agenda, testing labs usually keep copious documentation on the internal processes that they follow to ensure objectivity and accuracy. Such information, said Morgan, usually includes requirements for: training of personnel, especially analysts; maintenance and calibration of equipment; standardization and adoption of analytical methods; verification of results; sample recovery and handling procedures; quality control measurement procedures; internal and external proficiency programs and certifications; and accreditations.

ECONOMIC CONSIDERATIONS Economics play a central role in the decision of many firms—and especially smaller businesses—to utilize an outside lab to conduct quality and safety tests. Indeed, small business owners engaged in establishing or fortifying their enterprises will likely have a host of things on which they will want to spend their money, from new equipment to new advertising campaigns to work force or facility expansion. These businesses may well be better off financially by securing the services of an outside entity, despite the expense involved there, rather than setting up internal testing facilities. Moreover, many businesses that decide to establish internal testing facilities do so without fully factoring in the ancillary costs associated with such activity. Morgan noted that laboratory activities are rife with such ''hidden costs,'' including corporate or upper management salaries and benefits; liability insurance; additional professional services (legal or accounting); office supplies, accounts payable salaries, depreciation and interest expense; and ''last but not least, lost opportunity for profits had the money been invested in profit-making activities.''

SAFETY Many companies engaged in producing potentially hazardous materials prefer to utilize an outside testing firm to minimize the danger of in-house exposure to hazardous agents.

CHOOSING A TESTING LABORATORY

There are many criteria to consider when selecting a testing laboratory. These criteria will be shaped to some degree by the situation of the company making the selection; for example, a smaller company that needs only limited testing done may well make its selection exclusively on the basis of price and quality. But for many companies of varying sizes, several other factors are usually considered as well. As Raymond Luce wrote in *Business First of Buffalo,* ''it's important to take as much care in selecting a lab as you would a financial advisor—the accuracy of the results may affect decisions worth thousands or even millions of dollars.''

According to Luce, there are several basic criteria upon which testing laboratories should be selected:

- Quality and accuracy of testing
- Turnaround time
- Nature of analysis services provided
- Additional services
- Cost
- Certification/accreditation

QUALITY This is the most vital consideration in judging any testing lab. Small business owners should look for labs that maintain and adhere to documented quality control programs. ''A good laboratory should be eager to discuss its quality control program and have a quality assurance manager whose sole responsibility is to implement and monitor proper use of the program,'' said Luce, who added that quality control programs should also: perform multi-point calibrations; analyze control standards; use analytical methods in testing; test for inadvertent skewing of results; and test for reproducible results.

TURNAROUND The amount of time necessary to get results on tests from independent labs depends to a large extent on the area in which the labs are involved. Product testing labs, for example, typically take months to complete their tests, and environmental analyses take longer than do medical or clinical tests. Still, most environmental tests can be completed in one or two weeks, and some environmental, clinical, or medical labs are able to speed up analyses in exchange for additional compensation.

NATURE OF SERVICES Businesses requiring environmental, clinical, or medical tests should find out about the following before committing to a testing laboratory:

- Can the laboratory supply the necessary sample collection equipment and/or guidance?

- Can the laboratory take the sample itself?

- Do the samples have to be delivered or will the lab pick them up?

- Are you given the opportunity to communicate with personnel directly involved in the testing process?

- If the laboratory can not offer a certain kind of test, will it provide good referrals to other facilities that can do so?

EXPENSE Cost is always a concern, especially for smaller businesses with more modest financial resources. But small business owners should make sure that they fully understand the extent of the testing and other services that they are receiving before signing an agreement.

CERTIFICATION ''You should ask what certifications or accreditations a laboratory has,'' said Luce. ''Certification differs from state to state. The consequences of a poor choice range from worthless data to the potential staggering costs associated with correction actions based on incorrect data.''

Companies preparing a product for testing and certification should make arrangements with a reliable testing laboratory early in the process, so that all procedural issues can be addressed in advance and so both sides are on the same page regarding such issues as timeline and necessary information exchange. ''Communication is probably the most important aspect of dealing with an outside certification agency,'' stated one executive in *Appliance Manufacturer*.

FUTURE CHALLENGES

Several challenges loom for both the testing industry and those companies that utilize its services in the next few years. For example, the rapid expansion of the global marketplace has brought with it a corresponding expansion in the testing and certification offerings of laboratories. Most observers believe that American firms' ability to make inroads into international markets will partially depend on the pace at which the international business community is able to settle on common testing and certification standards. Observers point to the European Community's CE Mark as a key component of any harmonization. ''[Harmonization is] becoming a major thrust mainly because testing and certification are built into the CE-Marking approach created by the Europeans,'' one American executive told *Appliance Manufacturer*. ''The CE Mark is the EU-required safety mark that must be affixed in order for products to travel freely throughout the EU.'' Most experts agree that the development of one globally accepted mark of certification lies some time off because of the lack of a single international legal system that can ensure compliance.

Another factor that is expected to have a significant impact on independent laboratory practices is the Internet. ''The laboratory-services industry is eyeing the Internet as a potential tool for expansion,'' said Sue Robinson in *Seafood Business*. She noted that many analysts believe that testing companies will become even more vital as products are sold online because such sight-unseen transactions will place an even greater premium on third-party assurances of quality.

FURTHER READING:

''Circling the Globe.'' *Appliance Manufacturer*. August 1997.

Cook, Robert C. ''A Tale of UL Testing.'' *Security Management*. July 1995.

Crowe, Michelle. ''Testing Lab Provides Other Firms With a Competitive Edge.'' *The Business Journal*. February 9, 1998.

Litsikas, Mary. ''Put Products Through Their Environmental Paces.'' *Quality*. February 1997.

Luce, Raymond. ''Selecting a Testing Lab: Questions You Should Ask.'' *Business First of Buffalo*. April 1, 1991.

Morgan, Robert. ''Off-Site Labs Right on Target: An Independent Lab May Be Better than Doing Your Own Testing.'' *Food Processing*. August 1995.

Munzer, Michael. ''Research: Outsourcing of R&D, Testing Seen Increasing in Popularity.'' *American Metal Market*. May 14, 1996.

Robinson, Sue. ''Lab Services.'' *Seafood Business*. December 2000.

Wingo, Walter S. ''A Boom Time for Product Testing.'' *Design News*. March 9, 1992.

Winter, Drew. ''Tough Quality Demands Spur Testing Business.'' *Ward's Auto World*. April 1992.

Zuckerman, Amy. ''Sorting Out the Seals of Approval.'' *New York Times*. July 16, 2000.

TOLL-FREE TELEPHONE NUMBERS

Toll-free telephone numbers are a staple of business efforts to garner new customers and retain existing ones. By utilizing toll-free phone numbers, businesses provide clients and others with a means of communicating with them at no charge; instead, the business that maintains the toll-free line pays all costs associated with the line.

At one time, toll-free telephone numbers were a novelty. Since their inception in 1967, however, the U.S. economy has become increasingly service-based and competitive, creating an environment in which toll-free numbers have come to be expected by customers seeking to make purchases of all kinds of goods and services. But the popularity of toll-free numbers has created a growing shortage of the numbers in recent years. Indeed, reports indicate that the mid-1990s saw the same number of new toll-free numbers introduced as were assigned during the first two and a half decades of toll-free usage. This increase can be attributed both to improved technologies, which gave rise to pager, modem, and cellular phone usage (many of which have 800 numbers); the ease in obtaining toll-free telephone numbers through promotional packages; 800 number portability from carrier to carrier; and the growth in use of ''vanity'' numbers (i.e., 800-FLOWERS, 800-HOLIDAY). Another key factor in the explosion of toll-free numbers was an FCC ruling that took effect in 1993, granting companies ownership of their toll-free numbers. ''Before that time, a company with an 800 number that wanted to change from AT&T to Spring for long-distance had to have its number deleted from the AT&T database, then see if Sprint had the same toll-free number available, which was unlikely,'' wrote *Telephony*'s Phil Britt. ''So rather than change toll-free numbers, the company would stay with its original long-distance carrier. After the ruling took effect, the toll-free numbers were maintained . . . on a centralized database rather than on separate databases by each of the long-distance companies. . . . That meant lower cost and keener competition.''

Toll-free telephone numbers became so popular that the Federal Communications Commission (FCC) was forced to issue a new prefix (888) in anticipation of the exhaustion of all possible 800 numbers. The 800 prefix ran out in 1996, but the new 888 prefix lasted only two years beyond that before becoming nearly depleted itself. As a result, the FCC imposed a new plan capping the number of toll-free numbers that carriers could allocate on a weekly basis. These measures slowed the distribution of the numbers, but analysts expect that the FCC will introduce a string of new toll-free prefixes (877, 866, etc.) over the coming years to accommodate demand.

ADVANTAGES OF TOLL-FREE NUMBERS

Toll-free service offers several advantages to small business owners that traditional toll phone service cannot provide. First and foremost, a toll-free telephone number makes your company more accessible to clients, customers, employees, and business associates. It enhances a business's image as a successful, professional company, and many experts contend that it shows clients that customer service is an important component of the business's operating philosophy. Additionally, toll-free service can help lower business costs if you are currently accepting collect calls or are finding it expensive to keep in touch with the home office while on the road. Lastly, toll-free service usually details incoming calls on your statement, with names and numbers allowing easier customer tracking.

Obtaining a toll-free number is a relatively simple process. Consumers can simply request one from their local or long-distance phone company. The cost of securing and maintaining a toll-free line will vary depending on geographic region and the amount of calls that are transmitted through the line. Some small business owners who request vanity toll-free numbers have reported tremendous success with them, but other experts counsel small business owners to avoid vanity numbers altogether, saying that customers may become frustrated by being forced to hunt and peck their way through an alphabetic toll-free number. Firms that do choose to secure a vanity number can eliminate much of this frustration by advertising both the spelled-out and numeric versions of the number.

FURTHER READING:

Britt, Phil. ''Toll-Free Help Is On the Way: But 888 Numbers Must Last a Little Longer.'' *Telephony*. November 17, 1997.

De Marco, Donna. ''Residences Can Now Get Toll-Free 1-800 Numbers.'' *Knight-Ridder/Tribune Business News*. April 21, 1999.

Gable, Robert A. ''Establishing a Corporate Toll-Free Strategy.'' *Telecommunications*. October 1996.

Harder, Jerry. ''The Brave New World of Toll-Free Service.'' *Business Communications Review*. February 1996.

Kirvan, Paul. ''800 vs. 888: Next Generation Toll-Free Service.'' *Communications News*. November 1995.

Toth, Victor J. ''Preparing for a New Universe of Toll-Free Numbers.'' *Business Communications Review*. November 1995.

Turner, Dan. ''Telemarketers Contend with New Number Woes.'' *Los Angeles Business Journal*. April 15, 1996.

Whitefield, Mimi. ''New Toll-Free Prefixes.'' *Knight-Ridder/Tribune Business News*, March 1, 1996.

TOTAL PREVENTIVE MAINTENANCE

Total Preventive Maintenance (TPM) is a production management approach that places the responsibility for routine maintenance on the workers who operate the machinery, rather then employing separate maintenance personnel for that function. Used in many Japanese companies, TPM gives employees "a sense of responsibility and awareness of the equipment they use and [cuts] down on abuse and misuse of the equipment," William J. Stevenson wrote in his book *Production/Operations Management*. TPM is increasingly being used in manufacturing environments in the United States. It holds particular appeal for small manufacturers.

The term *maintenance* is used to describe the various efforts businesses make toward keeping their facilities and equipment in good working order. It encompasses both breakdown maintenance—a policy that involves dealing with problems as they occur and attempting to reduce their impact on operations—and preventive maintenance—a policy that involves using such measures as inspecting, cleaning, adjusting, and replacing worn parts to prevent breakdowns from occurring in the first place.

Preventive maintenance is performed periodically in order to reduce the incidence of equipment failure and the costs associated with it. These costs include disrupted production schedules, idled workers, loss of output, and damage to products or other equipment. Preventive maintenance can be scheduled to avoid interfering with production. Common methods of planning preventive maintenance are based on the passage of time, on the amount of usage the equipment receives, and on an as-needed basis when problems are uncovered through inspections. Ideally, preventive maintenance will take place just before failure occurs in order to maximize the time that equipment is in use between scheduled maintenance activities.

As Stevenson explained, the goal for production managers is to find a balance between preventive maintenance and breakdown maintenance that will minimize the company's overall maintenance costs. "Decision makers try to make a trade-off between these two basic options that will minimize their combined cost," he noted. "With no preventive maintenance, breakdown and repair costs would be tremendous. Furthermore, hidden costs, such as lost production and the cost of wages while equipment is not in service, must be factored in. So must the cost of injuries or damage to other equipment and facilities or to other units in production. However, beyond a certain point, the cost of preventive maintenance exceeds the benefit."

The decision of how much maintenance to perform involves the age and condition of the equipment, the complexity of technology used, the type of production process, and other factors. For example, managers would tend to perform more preventive maintenance on older machines because new ones have only a slight risk of breakdown and need less work to stay in good condition. It is also important to perform routine maintenance prior to beginning a particularly large or important production run.

In TPM, production employees are trained in both operating procedures and routine maintenance of equipment. They perform regular inspections of the machinery they operate and replace parts that have become worn through use before they fail. Since the production employees spend so much time working with the equipment, they are likely to pick up small signals that a machine is in need of maintenance. Among the main benefits of TPM is that employees gain a more complete understanding of the functioning of the system. TPM also gives them increased input into their own productivity and the quality of their work.

FURTHER READING:

Hall, Robert W. "Total Productive Maintenance—Essential to Maintain Progress." *Target.* Fall 1987.

Minty, Gordon. *Production Planning and Controlling.* Goodheart-Willcox, 1998.

Stevenson, William J. *Production/Operations Management.* 5th ed. McGraw-Hill, 1996.

Wireman, Terry. *Preventive Maintenance.* Reston Publishing, 1984.

TOTAL QUALITY MANAGEMENT (TQM)

Total Quality Management (TQM) refers to management methods used to enhance quality and productivity in organizations, particularly businesses. TQM is a comprehensive system approach that works horizontally across an organization, involving all departments and employees and extending backward and forward to include both suppliers and clients/customers.

TQM is only one of many acronyms used to label management systems that focus on quality. Other acronyms that have been used to describe similar quality management philosophies and programs include CQI (continuous quality improvement), SQC (statistical quality control), QFD (quality function deployment), QIDW (quality in daily work), TQC (total quality control), etc. Like many of these other systems, TQM provides a framework for implementing effective quality and productivity initiatives that can increase the profitability and competitiveness of organizations.

ORIGINS OF TQM

Although TQM techniques were adopted prior to World War II by a number of organizations, the creation of the Total Quality Management philosophy is generally attributed to Dr. W. Edwards Deming. In the late 1920s, while working as a summer employee at Western Electric Company in Chicago, he found worker motivation systems to be degrading and economically unproductive; incentives were tied directly to quantity of output, and inefficient post-production inspection systems were used to find flawed goods.

Deming teamed up in the 1930s with Walter A. Shewhart, a Bell Telephone Company statistician whose work convinced Deming that statistical control techniques could be used to supplant traditional management methods. Using Shewhart's theories, Deming devised a statistically controlled management process that provided managers with a means of determining when to intervene in an industrial process and when to leave it alone. Deming got a chance to put Shewhart's statistical-quality-control techniques, as well as his own management philosophies, to the test during World War II. Government managers found that his techniques could be easily taught to engineers and workers, and then quickly implemented in overburdened war production plants.

One of Deming's clients, the U.S. State Department, sent him to Japan in 1947 as part of a national effort to revitalize the war-devastated Japanese economy. It was in Japan that Deming found an enthusiastic reception for his management ideas. Deming introduced his statistical process control, or statistical quality control, programs into Japan's ailing manufacturing sector. Those techniques are credited with instilling a dedication to quality and productivity in the Japanese industrial and service sectors that allowed the country to become a dominant force in the global economy by the 1980s.

While Japan's industrial sector embarked on a quality initiative during the middle 1900s, most American companies continued to produce mass quantities of goods using traditional management techniques. America prospered as war-ravaged European countries looked to the United States for manufactured goods. In addition, a domestic population boom resulted in surging U.S. markets. But by the 1970s some American industries had come to be regarded as inferior to their Asian and European competitors. As a result of increasing economic globalization during the 1980s, made possible in part by advanced information technologies, the U.S. manufacturing sector fell prey to more competitive producers, particularly in Japan.

In response to massive market share gains achieved by Japanese companies during the late 1970s and 1980s, U.S. producers scrambled to adopt quality and productivity techniques that might restore their competitiveness. Indeed, Deming's philosophies and systems were finally recognized in the United States, and Deming himself became a highly-sought-after lecturer and author. The ''Deming Management Method'' became the model for many American corporations eager to improve. And Total Quality Management, the phrase applied to quality initiatives proffered by Deming and other management gurus, became a staple of American enterprise by the late 1980s. By the early 1990s, the U.S. manufacturing sector had achieved marked gains in quality and productivity.

TQM PRINCIPLES

Specifics related to the framework and implementation of TQM vary between different management professionals and TQM program facilitators, and the passage of time has inevitably brought changes in TQM emphases and language. But all TQM philosophies share common threads that emphasize quality, teamwork, and proactive philosophies of management and process improvement. As Howard Weiss and Mark Gershon observed in *Production and Operations Management,* ''the terms quality management, quality control, and quality assurance often are used interchangeably. Regardless of the term used within any business, this function is directly responsible for the continual evaluation of the effectiveness of the total quality system.'' They go on to delineate the basic elements of total quality management as expounded by the American Society for Quality Control: 1) policy, planning, and administration; 2) product design and design change control; 3) control of purchased material; 4) production quality control; 5) user contact and field performance; 6) corrective action; and 7) employee selection, training, and motivation.

For his part, Deming pointed to all of these factors as cornerstones of his total quality philosophies. In his book *Out of the Crisis,* he contended that companies needed to create an overarching business environment that emphasized improvement of products and services over short-term financial goals. He argued that if such a philosophy was adhered to, various aspects of business—ranging from training to system improvement to manager-worker relationships—would become far more healthy and, ultimately, profitable. But while Deming was contemptuous of companies that based their business decisions on statistics that emphasized quantity over quality, he firmly believed that a well-conceived system of statistical process control could be an invaluable TQM tool. Only through the use of statistics, Deming argued, can managers know exactly what their problems are, learn how to fix them, and gauge the company's progress in achieving quality and organizational objectives.

MAKING TQM WORK

Joseph Jablonski, author of *Implementing TQM,* identified three characteristics necessary for TQM to succeed within an organization: participative management; continuous process improvement; and the utilization of teams. Participative management refers to the intimate involvement of all members of a company in the management process, thus de-emphasizing traditional top-down management methods. In other words, managers set policies and make key decisions only with the input and guidance of the subordinates that will have to implement and adhere to the directives. This technique improves upper management's grasp of operations and, more importantly, is an important motivator for workers who begin to feel like they have control and ownership of the process in which they participate.

Continuous process improvement, the second characteristic, entails the recognition of small, incremental gains toward the goal of total quality. Large gains are accomplished by small, sustainable improvements over a long term. This concept necessitates a long-term approach by managers and the willingness to invest in the present for benefits that manifest themselves in the future. A corollary of continuous improvement is that workers and management develop an appreciation for, and confidence in, TQM over a period of time.

Teamwork, the third necessary ingredient for the success of TQM, involves the organization of cross-functional teams within the company. This multidisciplinary team approach helps workers to share knowledge, identify problems and opportunities, derive a comprehensive understanding of their role in the overall process, and align their work goals with those of the organization.

Jablonski also identified six attributes of successful TQM programs:

- Customer focus (includes internal customers such as other departments and coworkers as well as external customers)

- Process focus

- Prevention versus inspection (development of a process that incorporates quality during production, rather than a process that attempts to achieve quality through inspection after resources have already been consumed to produce the good or service)

- Employee empowerment and compensation

- Fact-based decision making

- Receptiveness to feedback.

IMPLEMENTING TQM

Jablonski offers a five-phase guideline for implementing total quality management: preparation, planning, assessment, implementation, and diversification. Each phase is designed to be executed as part of a long-term goal of continually increasing quality and productivity. Jablonski's approach is one of many that has been applied to achieve TQM, but contains the key elements commonly associated with other popular total quality systems.

- Preparation—During preparation, management decides whether or not to pursue a TQM program. They undergo initial training, identify needs for outside consultants, develop a specific vision and goals, draft a corporate policy, commit the necessary resources, and communicate the goals throughout the organization.

- Planning—In the planning stage, a detailed plan of implementation is drafted (including budget and schedule), the infrastructure that will support the program is established, and the resources necessary to begin the plan are earmarked and secured.

- Assessment—This stage emphasizes a thorough self-assessment—with input from customers/clients—of the qualities and characteristics of individuals in the company, as well as the company as a whole.

- Implementation—At this point, the organization can already begin to determine its return on its investment in TQM. It is during this phase that support personnel are chosen and trained, and managers and the work force are trained. Training entails raising workers' awareness of exactly what TQM involves and how it can help them and the company. It also explains each worker's role in the program and explains what is expected of all the workers.

- Diversification—In this stage, managers utilize their TQM experiences and successes to bring groups outside the organization (suppliers, distributors, and other companies have impact the business's overall health) into the quality process. Diversification activities include training, rewarding, supporting, and partnering with groups that are embraced by the organization's TQM initiatives.

FURTHER READING:

Deming, W. Edwards. *Out of the Crisis.* MIT Center for Advanced Engineering Study, 1982.

Hiam, Alexander. *Closing the Quality Gap: Lessons from America's Leading Companies.* Prentice Hall, Inc., 1992.

Hunt, V. Daniel. *Quality in America: How to Implement a Competitive Quality Program.* Business One Irwin, 1992.

Jablonski, Joseph R. *Implementing TQM.* 2nd ed. Technical Management Consortium, Inc., 1992.

McManus, Kevin. "Is Quality Dead?" *IIE Solutions.* July 1999.

Roberts, Harry V., and Bernard F. Sergesketter. *Quality Is Personal: A Foundation for Total Quality Management.* The Free Press, 1993.

Weiss, Howard J., and Mark E. Gershon. *Production and Operations Management.* Allyn and Bacon, 1989.

Youngless, Jay. "Total Quality Misconception." *Quality in Manufacturing.* January 2000.

SEE ALSO: ISO 9000; Quality Control

TRADE SHOWS

A trade show is an event where companies that are involved in a certain industry gather to exhibit their products, learn about current trends in their industry, and gain knowledge about their competitors. Trade shows provide opportunities for selling, reinforcing existing business relationships, and launching new products. These events can range in size from a small regional show featuring fewer than two dozen participants to massive national shows, which may draw hundreds of exhibitors and tens of thousands of visitors over a period of several days to a week.

During the early and mid-1990s, business analysts, consultants, and participants alike debated whether the surge in electronic commerce and Internet purchasing options might soon render the trade show an irrelevant relic of a bygone business era. But by the beginning of the 21st century, the continued importance of trade shows had been reinforced. In fact, *Tradeshow Week* reported that the number of commercial exhibitions in the United States grew at an annual rate of more than 4 percent during the 1990s, with more than 4,500 exhibitions in 1998 alone. These trade shows accounted for more than $100 billion in annual direct spending and attracted nearly 125 million individuals. "In many industries, the trade show has become a must-seize marketing opportunity," stated *Business Week.* "It's a time to meet prospective customers, get valuable feedback on your product or service, and close sales."

The continued vitality of trade show exhibitions provide small businesses with excellent opportunities to stand on equal footing with far larger competitors. For small companies with limited marketing budgets, trade shows can serve as an economical and effective pathway to new clients and increased industry visibility. Moreover, trade shows provide entrepreneurs and their small business managers with priceless opportunities to gather information about new industry innovations and competitor products and/or services.

SELECTING THE APPROPRIATE TRADE SHOW

The first step in establishing a presence at a trade show is choosing the right show. Finding the show that best meets your company's needs is crucial, since exhibiting is a costly proposition. Attending the wrong show is a frustrating waste of time and money. In order to avoid committing to a trade show that provides little in the way of new business or contacts, companies can take several precautions:

Crunch the Numbers. Businesses should request detailed statistical and other information on past trade shows from the organizers.

- What was last year's attendance? Was the show visited most by serious buyers or by browsers? Savvy small business owners are aware that some trade shows pad their attendance numbers by counting every person who walks through the doors, including exhibitors and repeat visitors.

- Is there demographic data available on attendees? For example, how old is the average attendee? Male or female? What is his or her income?

- Who else will be exhibiting? Will your competitors be there?

- How stable and successful is the show promoter? Are they experienced in managing a show and delivering an audience, or is this a new, untested exhibition?

- What will the cost be? Expenses include booth space (typically about 25 percent of your expenses); furnishings, equipment, and other exhibit expenses (30 percent); utilities (20 percent); transportation of staff and materials to and from the trade show (15 percent); and pre-show promotions (10 percent). Booths that incorporate new electronic technologies (Webcasts, videoconferencing, etc.) will add to the expense as well. Some companies that exhibit infrequently rent displays—typically portable booths that come in easy-to-assemble kits—rather than invest in booths.

Identify target audience. If you are a small vendor with a new and exciting product seeking national distributors, then the goal would be to attend a national show with high visibility and attendance by all key players. If, on the other hand, you have an existing product that you want to expose to new markets, you would target potential buyers. For example, if a company decides that one of its software packages—originally designed for and used by the publishing industry—also would be useful to teachers and educators, the sensible strategy would be to attend trade shows aimed at teachers instead of computer software industry shows.

Scout potential shows. Experts counsel entrepreneurs to scout potential trade shows before committing resources to a booth. Business owners can often get an accurate sense of a trade show's value simply by visiting a show, sponsoring a show-related event, or participating in a show-related seminar or conference. All of these avenues can be excellent ways of gauging the quality of the attendees.

Weigh value of exhibiting. Business owners are also urged to consider whether or not he/she should even be exhibiting at trade shows. A very small business with limited funds and a clear business model might decide that the best route to go is direct mail and promotions to a well-defined target audience. On the other hand, a business that is attempting to publicize an established product with low profit margins might well decide that attendance at large national and regional shows with heavy traffic is a good strategic move. And some industry sectors—such as high tech, transportation, communications, and manufacturing—place a heavy emphasis on trade shows.

PREPARING FOR A SUCCESSFUL TRADE SHOW EXHIBIT

Once a small business owner has decided to attend a specific trade show, there are steps that he or she can take to ensure that it is a successful and profitable endeavor. Of course, shows will vary in content, character, and tone from industry to industry, but for the most part, these guidelines can be followed no matter what field your small business is in.

Set specific and measurable goals. Perhaps the most important first step to take is to approach the show with enthusiasm and treat it as a sales opportunity and not a money drain. To take advantage of the opportunity, set specific goals. If the purpose of the show is to gather leads, then set a number in advance that would make the show, in your mind, a success. Compare actual leads gathered to that target number to gauge whether or not the show was worthwhile.

Publicize your involvement. According to the Trade Show Bureau, 45 percent of trade show attendees are drawn to a company's exhibit as the direct result of a personal invitation (via direct mail, e-mail, or telephone), trade journal publicity, or pre-show

advertising. A trade show is worthless unless prospective customers visit the booth, and the best way to ensure that those visits occur is to make them aware of your location on the floor. Indeed, industry surveys indicate that about 75 percent of all trade show attendees make out their schedules in advance of arrival. This is an important step, then, so companies should make sure that they allocate sufficient funds for marketing needs.

Prepare personnel. Staffers manning trade show booths should be personable, well-informed, and well-trained to demonstrate and sell your product and/or service. Conduct a preshow meeting with all key personnel who will be a part of the show, from employees who will spend their time at the booth to the shipper who will send your products to the show and be responsible for set-up. Let each person know what is expected of them at the show, and make sure that they know about all pertinent facets of the effort, from the location of promotional brochures to products that should be highlighted. Other assignments, like observation of competitor's booths and materials or breaking down the booth at the end of the show, may be assigned to specific people.

SUCCESSFUL EXHIBITING

"Getting attention on a crowded show floor isn't easy for a newcomer," admitted *Business Week*. "However, you can create a respectable-looking booth inexpensively without being tacky: Buy good quality, three-sided skirts for your tables and portable banner stands for signage, and make flyers on your computer to set on plastic literature racks. Don't clutter the space with lots of giveaways, but do hand out your business card and a small gift with your logo and phone number on it to qualified leads."

There are two types of booths you can set up at a show, with different sales techniques needed for each. One is designed to make sales at the show, so salespeople should be trained in "one interview selling"—quickly identifying a customer's needs and selling him or her your product to meet that need. At such a booth, it is common to have smaller and less expensive items on display and for sale at the show. Larger and more expensive items can be sold at the show and delivered later. All sales at the show should be at a discount over the regular list price, at least 20 percent. If sales are your goal, be prepared to deal with cash, credit cards, and checks.

The other kind of booth is more informational and less sales-oriented. It is primarily designed to meet people, to demonstrate a presence in the industry, to promote customer relations, or to generate new business leads. It can also serve as an excellent meeting point for people you are hoping will invest in your company or join you in a partnership. Since the focus of this type of booth is not sales, the booth personnel should approach their role differently than that of a pure salesperson. Interaction produces valuable feedback. ''Unlike the social vacuum of the Web, you can see immediately what customers think of your product,'' observed *Business Week.*

In the booth itself, try to have at least two people on duty at all times so that visitors receive a healthy measure of personal attention. Arrange the booth to maximize flow of traffic, for overcrowded booths will lead many potential visitors to pass on by. Booth staff should not hover over visitors. Instead, they should encourage browsing and be attentive to signals of interest in products/services from visitors. Make sure everyone who will be manning the booth understands the rules of etiquette at trade shows. There should be no eating or drinking in the booth, and no smoking. Do not spend time talking to the other salespeople in the booth. Assume friendly body posture and look receptive to questions. Perhaps most importantly, do not be in a hurry to get out of the show, since many people wait until the end of the show to make their purchases.

POST-EXHIBITION FOLLOW UP

Small businesses that maintain a quality presence at a trade show are likely to obtain a number of business leads during the show's duration. Yet many companies never follow up on these leads. According to the Trade Show Bureau, as many as 83 percent of exhibitors do not engage in any sort of organized post-exhibition marketing to trade show visitors. This is a terrible oversight that blunts much of the business potential of trade shows. With this in mind, trade show experts offer a variety of tips to make sure that small business owners make the most of their trade show experiences:

- Allocate money wisely. Many analysts believe that businesses should devote at least one third of their total trade show budgets to post-exhibition follow-up.

- Separate hot leads from those that seemed lukewarm or ambivalent and concentrate on those.

- Use a lead sheet to collect information on prospective customers who visit the booth.

- If applicable, send new leads back to the home office every night.

- Make sure that salespeople follow up on a lead within one or two weeks after the show; time is often of the essence in these cases.

- Do not gather more leads than you can follow up on. Analysts contend that many businesses owners or representatives that gather a surplus of leads at trade shows are likely to break promises made (sending literature, following up with an answer to a question, etc.) at the show, which will reflect badly on the company.

- Do not let new leads keep you from servicing existing customers. If you cannot handle new leads without neglecting the existing customer base, then maybe you should not be at the trade show.

ATTENDING A SHOW

Even if a small business owner considers trade shows to be an important part of his or her marketing strategy, there will be some trade shows that are not worth exhibiting at but that would still be useful to attend. For those shows, there are tips to follow to make the most out of the show.

The most important step is to find a good show that is worth the time and trouble it takes to attend. Watch the local papers or industry journals for leads. The biggest shows are typically held in major metropolitan areas, so concentrate on the largest cities in your region. Once you have identified a list of potential shows, contact each and ask for information.

Once you have identified a show to attend, good planning is the key to a successful trip. Make your travel arrangements and submit the show registration far in advance. Allow at least 90 days to avoid snags and delays. Decide in advance what you are hoping to get out of the show—if it is a buying trip, know in advance what you hope to purchase.

Once you arrive at the show, review the list of exhibitors to see which companies interest you the most. Highlight those companies and check them off as you visit each one. Some people like to make one general trip around the entire exhibit floor, highlighting interesting exhibits as they go and making a second, more serious trip to those booths. Be warned that this approach may not be practical for the largest national trade shows, which are often spread over several floors of a huge convention center. Also, do not ignore the seminars that are offered as part of most trade shows. These may be just as useful as the booths in the exhibit hall. The seminars are educational and are also a great way to meet people.

Prepare to spend the entire day at the show. It is often helpful to take a tote bag along with supplies you might need—a notepad and pens, a personal tape recorder to record notes along the way, traveler's checks and credit cards, business credentials (a list of creditors, for example, if this is a buying trip), business cards, and personal identification. The tote bag will also hold all the product literature you gather at the show. Finally, trade show visitors should make certain that they pack comfortable walking shoes. This sounds like a minor issue, but after eight hours on your feet walking the floor, it will seem like a very important item to remember.

FURTHER READING:

Blackwood, Francy. ''Show and Sell.'' *Working Woman.* May 1998.

Boone, Mary E. ''Beefing Up Booth Traffic.'' *Sales and Marketing Management.* May 1999.

Caffey, Andrew A. ''It's Showtime.'' *Entrepreneur.* February 1996.

Demetros, Valeria A., ed. *More Secrets of Successful Exhibiting.* Aviva, 1998.

''For Small Firms, a Really Big Show.'' *Nation's Business.* November 1996.

''How to Plan a Trade Show Booth.'' *South Florida Business Journal.* June 27, 1997.

Lipman, Jim. ''So Many Conferences, So Little Time.'' *EDN.* January 1, 1998.

Miller, Steve. *How to Get the Most Out of Trade Shows.* NTC Publishing, 2000.

Test, Alan. ''Trade Show Success.'' *American Salesman.* September 1995.

''Trade Secrets.'' *Business Week.* August 16, 1999.

Tradeshow Week's 1999 Data Book, 1999.

TRADEMARKS

A trademark is a word, phrase, symbol or design—or a combination of words, phrases, symbols, or designs—adopted and used by a manufacturer or merchant to identify its goods and distinguish them from those manufactured or sold by its competitors. In recent years, colors (such as John Deere green), sounds (such as the National Broadcasting Company's use of distinctive chimes), and scents have also been registered as trademarks. Service marks, meanwhile, are identical to trademarks except that they identify and distinguish the source of a *service* rather than a product. The term ''trademark,'' however, is commonly utilized to refer to both trademarks and service marks.

Whereas exclusive rights to other items of intellectual property such as copyrights and patents eventually expire, trademark rights can last indefinitely, provided the owner of the mark continues to use it to identify its goods or services. The initial term for a federal trademark registration is ten years, but the owner has the option to renew for additional ten-year terms. The Patent and Trademark Office (PTO), however, has stipulated that between the fifth and sixth years of the initial registration term, the registrant must file an affidavit confirming the need to keep the registration alive. If no affidavit is filed, the registration is canceled, and other companies can pursue the mark for their own use if they so desire.

OTHER TYPES OF TRADEMARKS

In addition to trademarks and service marks, there are two other kinds of marks that generally fit under the generic ''trademark'' umbrella: certification marks and collective marks.

CERTIFICATION MARK A certification mark, explained Richard Levy in his *Inventor's Desktop Companion,* ''is a mark used upon or in connection with the products or services of one or more persons other than the owner of the mark to certify regional or other origin, material, mode of manufacture, quality, accuracy, or other characteristics of such goods or services, or that the work or labor on the goods or services was performed by members of a union or other organization.'' Examples of certification marks include the UL symbol of Underwriters Laboratories (for quality), ''Made in the U.S.A.'' designations (for place of origin), and the Motion Picture Association of America's movie ratings (for service).

COLLECTIVE MARK Collective marks are trademarks or service marks used by members of an association, cooperative, or other group. Organizations as diverse as the National Rifle Association, the Big Ten Athletic Conference, and the Sierra Club all utilize collective marks.

TRADEMARK RIGHTS

Trademark rights to an identifying word, phrase, symbol, design, sound, or color can be secured either by actually using the mark in commerce or by registering the mark with the Trademark Office, a division of the Patent and Trademark Office (PTO). ''Federal registration [with the PTO] is not required to establish rights in a mark, nor is it required to begin use of a mark,'' noted the PTO in its booklet, *Basic Facts About Registering a Trademark.* ''However, federal registration can secure benefits beyond the rights acquired by merely using a mark. For example, the owner of a federal registration is presumed to be the owner of the mark for the goods and services specified in the registration, and to be entitled to use the mark nationwide.'' In addition, owners of federal registration for a trademark often enjoy an advantage if legal disputes over use of a trademark arise.

THE ''RIGHT TO REGISTER'' According to the Patent and Trademark Office, the ultimate right to register a trademark generally belongs to the first party—whether it is a small business or a large corporation—to use a trademark ''in commerce'' or file a trademark application with the PTO. (''Commerce'' in this situation means commerce regulated by the U.S. Congress, i.e., interstate commerce or commerce between America and another nation; use of a trademark in purely local commerce within a state does not qualify as ''use in commerce.'')

THE "RIGHT TO USE" As the PTO itself admitted in its *Basic Facts About Registering a Trademark,* ''the right to use a mark can be more complicated to determine. This is particularly true when two parties have begun use of the same or similar marks without knowledge of one another and neither has a federal registration. Only a court can render a decision about the right to use, such as issuing an injunction or awarding damages for infringement.'' As indicated above, possession of federal registration can be a valuable weapon if a court fight erupts over use of a disputed trademark.

TRADEMARK SEARCHES

A small business owner who has come up with a trademark that he or she wishes to use may want to conduct a trademark search before going to the trouble and expense of sending an application to the PTO. As Thomas Field remarked in *Avoiding Patent, Trademark and Copyright Problems,* ''one can infringe on another's marks without copying them or even being in direct competition with their owner. All that is necessary is to use the same or a similar mark under circumstances in which consumers may be confused as to the source or sponsorship of the goods or services.'' A trademark search can uncover whether the mark (or a similar one) has already been registered with the PTO. But even if a search turns up nothing, that does not necessarily mean that the business owner is guaranteed untroubled use of the mark. ''In the United States, it is unnecessary for a firm to do more than use a good mark to have trademark rights in its market area,'' explained Field. ''Consequently, a search may not locate all such prior users. Second, people may be able to prevent the use of a potential mark without having used it as a mark themselves; for example, when a trademark can be associated with others in such a way that consumers might presume that some kind of relationship might exist.''

APPLICATIONS FOR FEDERAL REGISTRATION

There are two primary ways in which a U.S. applicant can apply to register his or her trademark with the PTO, depending on whether or not the mark has already been used in commerce. An applicant who has already begun using the trademark in commerce may file with the PTO based on that use. This is commonly known as a ''Use'' application. If an applicant has not yet used the trademark in question in commerce, but has an honest intention to do so, he or she may file an ''Intent-to-Use'' application with the

PTO. A third option, which can only be used by applicants from outside the United States, allows the applicant to file in the United States based on an application or registration made in another country.

Applications for federal registration should include the following:

- PTO Form 1478—this application, also known as ''Trademark/Service Mark Application, Principal Register, with Declaration,'' should be carefully completed and fully signed.

- Drawing of the mark—this drawing must be included on a separate piece of paper; the specifications for the drawing—and the paper itself—are quite extensive, so make sure that the drawing adheres to all guidelines. If a separate drawing page is not included, then the application will be returned to the applicant without a filing date.

- Filing fee—For current information on the application filing fee for trademarks, call the Patent and Trademark Office or consult its Web site (''Intent-to-Use'' applications are more expensive). If the full amount of the fee is not included in the application, then the application will not be considered. Fees are not refundable, even in instances where trademark ownership applications are turned down.

- Specimens—These are actual samples of how the mark is actually used—or will be used—in commerce. ''If the mark is used on goods,'' wrote Levy, ''examples of acceptable specimens are tags or labels which are attached to the goods, containers for the goods, displays associated with the goods, or photographs of the goods showing use of the mark on the goods themselves. . . . If the mark is used for services, examples of acceptable specimens are signs, brochures about the services, advertisements for the services, business cards or stationery showing the mark in connection with the services, or photographs which show the mark as it is used either in the rendering or advertising of the services.'' Each application must include three specimens, but they do not necessarily have to be of three different uses.

PTO ACCEPTANCE AND REJECTION The federal registration of trademarks is governed by the Trademark Act of 1946 (and amendments thereof), the Trademark Rules, 37 C.F.R. Part 2, and the Trademark Manual of Examining Procedure. When the PTO receives an application for trademark registration, it checks the application in accordance with the above-mentioned guidelines. First, the Office reviews it to see if it meets the minimum requirements for receiving a filing date. If it meets those requirements, the PTO assigns it a serial number and sends the applicant a notification of receipt. If the minimum requirements are not met, the entire thing (including the filing fee) is returned to the applicant.

Applications that pass this first stage are then reviewed by an examining attorney at the PTO, who determines if there are any reasons why the mark cannot be registered. Levy noted that a mark may be turned down for any of the following reasons:

- The mark too closely resembles a mark already registered in the PTO

- The mark's capacity for causing confusion among relevant consumers with goods or services associated with other parties

- The mark includes a name, portrait, or signature identifying a particular living individual except by his written consent, or the name, signature, or portrait of a deceased president of the United States during the life of his wife, except in instances where the widow has given her written consent to such use

- The mark includes the flag or coat of arms or other insignia of the United States or any of its states or municipalities, or of any foreign nation, or any simulation thereof

- The mark has immoral, deceptive, or scandalous connotations

- The mark disparages or falsely suggests a connection with persons (living or dead), institutions, beliefs, or national symbols

- The mark brings such persons, institutions, beliefs, or national symbols into contempt or disrepute

Objections raised during this stage of the review are sent along to the applicant. Remedies that might make the mark acceptable are sometimes suggested in these letters as well. The application will be deemed abandoned if the applicant does not respond within six months of the mailing date of that letter. In cases in which the applicant's response does not sway the PTO examiner to give approval for the mark, the applicant can turn to the PTO's Trademark Trial and Appeal Board.

"If there are no objections, or if you [the applicant] overcome all objections, the examining attorney will approve the mark for publication in the *Official Gazette,* a weekly publication of the PTO," wrote Levy. "Any party who believes it may be damaged by the registration of the mark has 30 days from the date of publication to file an opposition to registration. An opposition is similar to a formal proceeding in the federal courts, but is held before the Trademark Trial and Appeal Board. If no opposition is filed, the application enters the next stage of the registration process.''

If the application is approved and no opposition is filed, applicants may have a little or a lot to do, depending on their situation. For applicants who filed "Use" applications, most of the work is over. The PTO will register the trademark and issue a registration certificate a few months after the date the mark was published in the *Gazette.* Applicants who filed based on their intent to use the trademark down the line, though, need to attend to several matters to make sure that their rights do not slip away. In situations where it has approved an "Intent-to-Use" application, the PTO issues a Notice of Allowance approximately 12 weeks after the mark was published. After receiving the Notice, the applicant has six months to either use the trademark in commerce and submit documentation of that use or request a six-month extension. If the documentation of use—called the Statement of Use—is filed and approved, then the PTO will issue the registration certificate for the trademark.

Even if the PTO grants an applicant a trademark registration, however, business experts warn that such registration only provides protection to the owner in the United States and its territories. "If the owner of a mark wishes to protect a mark in other countries, the owner must seek protection in each country separately under the relevant laws," warned the PTO in its *Basic Facts About Registering a Trademark.* "The PTO cannot provide information or advice concerning protection in other countries.''

FURTHER READING:

Basic Facts About Registering a Trademark. U.S. Patent and Trademark Office, 1995.

Field, Thomas. *Avoiding Patent, Trademark and Copyright Problems.* Small Business Administration, 1992.

Levy, Richard C. *The Inventor's Desktop Companion.* Visible Ink, 1995.

Miller, Arthur R., and Michael H. Davis. *Intellectual Property: Patents, Trademarks and Copyright.* West/Wadsworth, 2000.

Schoell, William F., and Joseph P. Guiltinan. *Marketing: Contemporary Concepts and Practices.* Allyn and Bacon, 1992.

SEE ALSO: Brands and Brand Names; Copyrights; Corporate Logos

TRAINING AND DEVELOPMENT

Training and development describes the formal, ongoing efforts of organizations to improve the performance and self-fulfillment of their employees through a variety of methods and programs. In the modern workplace, these efforts have taken on a broad range of applications—from instruction in highly specific job skills to long-term professional development. In recent years, training and development has emerged as a formal business function, an integral element of strategy, and a recognized profession with distinct theories and methodologies. More and more companies of all sizes have embraced "continual learning" and other aspects of training and development as a means of promoting employee growth and acquiring a highly skilled work force. In fact, the quality of employees, and the continual improvement of their skills and productivity through training, are now widely recognized as vital factors in ensuring the long-term success and profitability of small businesses. "Create a corporate culture that supports continual learning," counseled Charlene Marmer Solomon in *Workforce*. "Employees today must have access to continual training of all types just to keep up. . . . If you don't actively stride against the momentum of skills deficiency, you lose ground. If your workers stand still, your firm will lose the competency race."

For the most part, the terms "training" and "development" are used together to describe the overall improvement and education of an organization's employees. However, while closely related, there are important differences between the terms that center around the scope of the application. In general, training programs have very specific and quantifiable goals, like operating a particular piece of machinery, understanding a specific process, or performing certain procedures with great precision. On the other hand, developmental programs concentrate on broader skills that are applicable to a wider variety of situations, such as decision making, leadership skills, and goal setting.

TRAINING IN SMALL BUSINESSES

Implementation of formal training and development programs offers several potential advantages to small businesses. For example, training helps companies to create pools of qualified replacements for employees who may leave or be promoted to positions of greater responsibility. It also helps ensure that companies will have the human resources needed to support business growth and expansion. Furthermore, training can enable a small business to make use of advanced technology and to adapt to a rapidly changing competitive environment. Finally, training can improve employees' efficiency and motivation, leading to gains in both productivity and job satisfaction. According to the U.S. Small Business Administration (SBA), small businesses stand to receive a variety of benefits from effective training and development of employees, including reduced turnover, a decreased need for super-

vision, increased efficiency, and improved employee morale. All of these benefits are likely to contribute directly to a small business's fundamental financial health and vitality

Effective training and development begins with the overall strategy and objectives of the small business. The entire training process should be planned in advance with specific company goals in mind. In developing a training strategy, it may be helpful to assess the company's customers and competitors, strengths and weaknesses, and any relevant industry or societal trends. The next step is to use this information to identify where training is needed by the organization as a whole or by individual employees. It may also be helpful to conduct an internal audit to find general areas that might benefit from training, or to complete a skills inventory to determine the types of skills employees possess and the types they may need in the future. Each different job within the company should be broken down on a task-by-task basis in order to help determine the content of the training program.

The training program should relate not only to the specific needs identified through the company and individual assessments, but also to the overall goals of the company. The objectives of the training should be clearly outlined, specifying what behaviors or skills will be affected and how they relate to the strategic mission of the company. In addition, the objectives should include several intermediate steps or milestones in order to motivate the trainees and allow the company to evaluate their progress. Since training employees is expensive, a small business needs to give careful consideration to the question of which employees to train. This decision should be based on the ability of the employee to learn the material and the likelihood that they will be motivated by the training experience. If the chosen employees fail to benefit from the training program or leave the company soon after receiving training, the small business has wasted its limited training funds.

The design of training programs is the core activity of the training and development function. In recent years, the development of training programs has evolved into a profession which utilizes systematic models, methods, and processes of instructional systems design (ISD). ISD describes the systematic design and development of instructional methods and materials to facilitate the process of training and development and ensure that training programs are necessary, valid, and effective. The instructional design process includes the collection of data on the tasks or skills to be learned or improved, the analysis of these skills and tasks, the development of methods and materials, delivery of the program, and finally the evaluation of the training's effectiveness.

Small businesses tend to use two general types of training methods, on-the-job techniques and off-the-job techniques. On-the-job training describes a variety of methods that are applied while employees are actually performing their jobs. These methods might include orientations, coaching, apprenticeships, internships, job instruction training, and job rotation. The main advantages of on-the-job techniques is that they are highly practical, and employees do not lose working time while they are learning. Off-the-job training, on the other hand, describes a number of training methods that are delivered to employees outside of the regular work environment, though often during working hours. These techniques might include lectures, conferences, case studies, role playing, simulations, film or television presentations, programmed instruction, or special study.

On-the-job training tends to be the responsibility of supervisors, human resources professionals, or more experienced co-workers. Consequently, it is important for small businesses to educate their seasoned employees in training techniques. In contrast, off-the-job tends to be handled by outside instructors or sources, such as consultants, chambers of commerce, technical and vocational schools, or continuing education programs. Although outside sources are usually better informed as to effective training techniques than company supervisors, they may have a limited knowledge of the company's products and competitive situation. In addition, the cost of some off-the-job training methods may be too high for many small businesses to afford.

Actual administration of the training program involves choosing an appropriate location, providing necessary equipment, and arranging a convenient time. Such operational details, while seemingly minor components of an overall training effort, can have a significant effect on the success of a program. In addition, the training program should be evaluated at regular intervals while it is going on. Employees' skills should be compared to the predetermined goals or milestones of the training program, and any necessary adjustments should be made immediately. This ongoing evaluation process will help ensure that the training program successfully meets its expectations.

COMMON TRAINING METHODS

While new techniques are under continuous development, several common training methods have proven highly effective. Good continuous learning and development initiatives often feature a combination of several different methods that, blended together, produce one effective training program.

ORIENTATIONS Orientation training is vital in ensuring the success of new employees. Whether the training is conducted through an employee handbook, a lecture, or a one-on-one meeting with a supervisor, newcomers should receive information on the company's history and strategic position, the key people in authority at the company, the structure of their department and how it contributes to the mission of the company, and the company's employment policies, rules, and regulations.

LECTURES A verbal method of presenting information, lectures are particularly useful in situations when the goal is to impart the same information to a large number of people at one time. Since they eliminate the need for individual training, lectures are among the most cost-effective training methods. But the lecture method does have some drawbacks. Since lectures primarily involve one-way communication, they may not provide the most interesting or effective training. In addition, it may be difficult for the trainer to gauge the level of understanding of the material within a large group.

CASE STUDY The case method is a non-directed method of study whereby students are provided with practical case reports to analyze. The case report includes a thorough description of a simulated or real-life situation. By analyzing the problems presented in the case report and developing possible solutions, students can be encouraged to think independently as opposed to relying upon the direction of an instructor. Independent case analysis can be supplemented with open discussion with a group. The main benefit of the case method is its use of real-life situations. The multiplicity of problems and possible solutions provide the student with a practical learning experience rather than a collection of abstract knowledge and theories that may be difficult to apply to practical situations.

ROLE PLAYING In role playing, students assume a role outside of themselves and play out that role within a group. A facilitator creates a scenario that is to be acted out by the participants under the guidance of the facilitator. While the situation might be contrived, the interpersonal relations are genuine. Furthermore, participants receive immediate feedback from the facilitator and the scenario itself, allowing better understanding of their own behavior. This training method is cost effective and is often applied to marketing and management training.

SIMULATIONS Games and simulations are structured competitions and operational models that emulate real-life scenarios. The benefits of games and simulations include the improvement of problem-solving and decision-making skills, a greater understanding of the organizational whole, the ability to study actual problems, and the power to capture the student's interest.

COMPUTER-BASED TRAINING Computer-based training (CBT) involves the use of computers and computer-based instructional materials as the primary medium of instruction. Computer-based training programs are designed to structure and present instructional materials and to facilitate the learning process for the student. A main benefit of CBT is that it allows employees to learn at their own pace, during convenient times. Primary uses of CBT include instruction in computer hardware, software, and operational equipment. The last is of particular importance because CBT can provide the student with a simulated experience of operating a particular piece of equipment or machinery while eliminating the risk of damage to costly equipment by a trainee or even a novice user. At the same time, the actual equipment's operational use is maximized because it need not be utilized as a training tool. The use of computer-based training enables a small business to reduce training costs while improving the effectiveness of the training. Costs are reduced through a reduction in travel, training time, amount of operational hardware, equipment damage, and instructors. Effectiveness is improved through standardization and individualization. In recent years, videodisc and CD-ROM have been successfully integrated into PC-platforms, increasing the flexibility and possibilities of CBT.

SELF-INSTRUCTION Self-instruction describes a training method in which the students assume primary responsibility for their own learning. Unlike instructor- or facilitator-led instruction, students retain a greater degree of control regarding topics, the sequence of learning, and the pace of learning. Depending on the structure of the instructional materials, students can achieve a higher degree of customized learning. Forms of self-instruction include programmed learning, individualized instruction, personalized systems of instruction, learner-controlled instruction, and correspondence study. Benefits include a strong support system, immediate feedback, and systematization.

AUDIOVISUAL TRAINING Audiovisual training methods include television, films, and videotapes. Like case studies, role playing, and simulations, they can be used to expose employees to ''real world'' situations in a time- and cost-effective manner. The main drawback of audiovisual training methods is that they cannot be customized for a particular audience, and they do not allow participants to ask questions or interact during the presentation of material.

TEAM-BUILDING EXERCISES Team building is the active creation and maintenance of effective work groups with similar goals and objectives. Not to be confused with the informal, ad-hoc formation and use of teams in the workplace, team building is a formal process of building work teams and formulating their objectives and goals, usually facilitated by a third-party consultant. Team building is commonly initiated to combat poor group dynamics, labor-management relations, quality, or productivity. By recognizing the problems and difficulties associated with the creation and development of work teams, team building provides a structured, guided process whose benefits include a greater ability to manage complex projects and processes, flexibility to respond to changing situations, and greater motivation among team members. Team building may include a broad range of different training methods, from outdoor immersion exercises to brainstorming sessions. The main drawback to formal team building is the cost of using outside experts and taking a group of people away from their work during the training program.

APPRENTICESHIPS AND INTERNSHIPS Apprenticeships are a form of on-the-job training in which the trainee works with a more experienced employee for a period of time, learning a group of related skills that will eventually qualify the trainee to perform a new job or function. Apprenticeships are often used in production-oriented positions. Internships are a form of apprenticeship which combine on-the-job training under a more experienced employee with classroom learning.

JOB ROTATION Another type of experience-based training is job rotation, in which employees move through a series of jobs in order to gain a broad understanding of the requirements of each. Job rotation may be particularly useful in small businesses, which may feature less role specialization than is typically seen in larger organizations.

APPLICATIONS OF TRAINING PROGRAMS

While the applications of training and development are as various as the functions and skills required by an organization, several common training applications can be distinguished, including technical training, sales training, clerical training, computer training, communications training, organizational development, career development, supervisory development, and management development.

Technical training describes a broad range of training programs varying greatly in application and difficulty. Technical training utilizes common training methods for instruction of technical concepts, factual information, and procedures, as well as technical processes and principles.

Sales training concentrates on the education and training of individuals to communicate with customers in a persuasive manner. Sales training can enhance the employee's knowledge of the organization's products, improve his or her selling skills, instill positive attitudes, and increase the employee's self-confidence. Employees are taught to distinguish the needs and wants of the customer, and to persuasively communicate the message that the company's products or services can effectively satisfy them.

Clerical training concentrates on the training of clerical and administrative support staffs, which have taken on an expanded role in recent years. With the increasing reliance on computers and computer applications, clerical training must be careful to distinguish basic skills from the ever-changing computer applications used to support these skills. Clerical training increasingly must instill improved decision-making skills in these employees as they take on expanded roles and responsibilities.

Computer training teaches the effective use of the computer and its software applications, and often must address the basic fear of technology that most employees face and identify and minimize any resistance to change that might emerge. Furthermore, computer training must anticipate and overcome the long and steep learning curves that many employees will experience. To do so, such training is usually offered in longer, uninterrupted modules to allow for greater concentration, and structured training is supplemented by hands-on practice. This area of training is commonly cited as vital to the fortunes of most companies, large and small, operating in today's technologically advanced economy.

Communications training concentrates on the improvement of interpersonal communication skills, including writing, oral presentation, listening, and reading. In order to be successful, any form of communications training should be focused on the basic improvement of skills and not just on stylistic considerations. Furthermore, the training should serve to build on present skills rather than rebuilding from the ground up. Communications training can be taught separately or can be effectively integrated into other types of training, since it is fundamentally related to other disciplines.

Organizational development (OD) refers to the use of knowledge and techniques from the behavioral sciences to analyze an existing organizational structure and implement changes in order to improve organizational effectiveness. OD is useful in such varied areas as the alignment of employee goals with those of the organization, communications, team functioning, and decision making. In short, it is a development process with an organizational focus to achieve the same goals as other training and development activities aimed at individuals. OD practitioners commonly practice what has been termed "action research" to effect an orderly change which has been carefully planned to minimize the occurrence of unpredicted or unforeseen events. Action research refers to a systematic analysis of an organization to acquire a better understanding of the nature of problems and forces within it.

Career development refers to the formal progression of an employee's position within an organization by providing a long-term development strategy and designing training programs to achieve this strategy as well as individual goals. Career development represents a growing concern for employee welfare and their long-term needs. For the individual, it involves the description of career goals, the assessment of necessary action, and the choice and implementation of necessary steps. For the organization, career development represents the systematic development and improvement of employees. To remain effective, career development programs must allow individuals to articulate their desires. At the same time, the organization strives to meet those stated needs as much as possible by consistently following through on commitments and meeting the employee expectations raised by the program.

Management and supervisory development involves the training of managers and supervisors in basic leadership skills, enabling them to effectively function in their positions. For managers, training initiatives are focused on providing them with the tools to balance the effective management of their employee resources with the strategies and goals of the organization. Managers learn to develop their employees effectively by helping employees learn and change, as well as by identifying and preparing them for future responsibilities. Management development may also include programs for developing decision-making skills, creating and managing successful work teams, allocating resources effectively, budgeting, business planning, and goal setting.

FURTHER READING:

Goldstein, Irwin L., ed. *Training and Development in Organizations.* Jossey-Bass, 1989.

Kim, Nancy J. "Continuing Education is No Longer an Option." *Puget Sound Business Journal.* August 15, 1997.

Roberts, Gary, Gary Seldon, and Carlotta Roberts. *Human Resources Management.* Washington, D.C.: U.S. Small Business Administration, n.a.

Scarpello, V.G., James Ledvinka, and Thomas J. Bergmann. *Human Resource Management: Environments and Functions.* Southwestern, 1995.

Solomon, Charlene Marmer. "Continual Learning: Racing Just to Keep Up." *Workforce.* April 1999.

TRANSACTION PROCESSING

Transaction processing is a type of computer processing that takes place in the presence of a computer user. It allows for an immediate response to a user request (or transaction). When a large number of transactions are taken and then stored to be dealt with at a later time (without the presence of a user), the process is known as batch processing. Different examples of transaction processing include automated teller machines, credit card authorizations, online bill payments, self-checkout stations at grocery stores, the trading of stocks over the Internet, and various other forms of electronic commerce.

Every business has to deal with some form of transactions. How a company decides to manage these transactions can be an important factor in its success. As a business grows, its number of transactions usually grows as well. Careful planning must be done in order to ensure that transaction management does not become too complex. Transaction processing is a tool that can help growing businesses deal with their increasing number of transactions.

TRANSACTION PROCESSING AND THE INTERNET

One place where transaction processing has made a big splash is on the Internet. The advent of online technology has made the international distribution of goods and information a quick and often simple process. Customers have grown accustomed to placing orders online. The emergence of features like secure servers, one-click shopping, and tracking of packages over the Internet have helped make them feel more at ease with the process.

Transaction processing on the Internet includes several options for those who want to use a credit card or a checking account to pay for goods that do not originate from a typical e-business site, almost as if it is digital cash. One example of this type of service is PayPal, which touts itself as the world's first instant and secure online payment service. With PayPal, anyone can register to send and receive payments through the Internet. This service has gained most of its popularity on auction sites like eBay, but can also be used for simple transactions between any two people in the world that have email accounts. Users have found this to be a safe, fast, easy, convenient, and inexpensive way to distribute money in the digital world. PayPal's service is free to most consumers, although there can be small service fees to businesses that decide to use it for a large number of transactions. PayPal only requires that users have either a valid credit card or active checking account.

Retailers have also enjoyed the benefits of jumping on the Internet bandwagon to help with the processing of their transactions. A company can set up a web site for their customers to purchase merchandise and the order can taken, fulfilled, and processed by someone else (for example, Yahoo handles the distribution of products for many online companies). If a business decides to go this route, they may want to make themselves totally aware of the shipping charges that a particular firm will charge to send their goods. Many times, the shipping charges for products purchased over the Internet have a tendency to become inflated, causing consumers to become annoyed and even angry because they feel like they are being taken advantage of. A smart business would do anything in their power to keep this from happening and possibly alienating their loyal customer base. Other possible problems that often plague online world—such as computer system outages, slow servers, and security issues—should also be considered.

THE TRANSACTION PROCESSING PERFORMANCE COUNCIL

The Transaction Processing Performance Council (TPC) is a non-profit corporation that defines transaction processing and provides database benchmarks that distribute information to the industry. The TPC emerged in the early 1980s just as ATMs, gasoline pumps that accepted credit cards, and other electronic payment devices began to gain popularity. Today they are as busy as ever as the online transaction processing industry registers billions of dollars in yearly sales. The TPC also monitors and measures transaction processing and database performance in terms of how many transactions a system can perform in a given amount of time of time. Many businesses can benefit from the work of the TPC, including retail stores, online businesses, electronic stock brokers, and travel agencies. Their dedication will only ensure that the quality of conducting transactions remains at the highest possible level. For more information on what they do, visit www.tpc.org.

SMALL BUSINESSES AND TRANSACTION PROCESSING

The growth in the transaction processing industry can only mean good things for small businesses. For example, a company that distributes and manages coin operated video games and vending machines can expand its business by teaming up with a transaction processing firm that will help allow the machines to accept credit cards. A small antique store can increase business by marketing its goods over the Internet and then accepting payments through PayPal or another similar service. As is the case with most sound business decisions, managers should acquire proper education and knowledge about transaction processing before committing to it.

FURTHER READING:

Guerrisi, Joseph. ''Making Money Move Faster.'' *Supply Chain Management Review.* January 2001.

Hapgood, Fred. ''Online Transaction Processing Takes a Bow.'' *CIO.* February 15, 2001.

Hunt, Clair. ''In the Blink of an Eye.'' *Computer Weekly.* March 31, 1994.

Overton, Rick. ''Signed, Sealed, Delivered . . . Online.'' *PC World.* November 1999.

TRANSPORTATION

Transportation concerns the movement of products from a source—such as a plant, factory, or workshop—to a destination—such as a warehouse, customer, or retail store. Transportation may take place via air, water, rail, road, pipeline, or cable routes, using planes, boats, trains, trucks, and telecommunications equipment as the means of transportation. The goal for any business owner is to minimize transportation costs while also meeting demand for products. Transportation costs generally depend upon the distance between the source and the destination, the means of transportation chosen, and the size and quantity of the product to be shipped. In many cases, there are several sources and many destinations for the same product, which adds a significant level of complexity to the problem of minimizing transportation costs. Indeed, the United States boasts the world's largest and most complex transportation system, with four million miles worth of roads, a railroad network that could circle the earth almost seven times if laid out in a straight line, and enough oil and gas lines to circle the globe 56 times.

The decisions a business owner must make regarding transportation of products are closely related to a number of other distribution issues. For example, the accessibility of suitable means of transportation factors into decisions regarding where best to locate a business or facility. The means of transportation chosen will also affect decisions regarding the form of packing used for products and the size or frequency of shipments made. Although transportation costs may be reduced by sending larger shipments less frequently, it is also necessary to consider the costs of holding extra inventory. The interrelationship of these decisions means that successful planning and scheduling can help business owners to save on transportation costs.

BASIC MEANS OF TRANSPORTATION

There are five basic means of transporting products utilized by manufacturers and distributors: air, motor carrier, train, marine, or pipeline. Many distribution networks consist of a combination of these means of transportation. For example, oil may be pumped through a pipeline to a waiting ship for transport to a refinery, and from there transferred to trucks that transport gasoline to retailers or heating oil to consumers. All of these transportation choices contain advantages and drawbacks.

Air transport. Air transportation offers the advantage of speed and can be used for long-distance transport. However, air is also the most expensive means of transportation, so it is generally used only for smaller items of relatively high value—such as electronic equipment—and items for which the speed of arrival is important—such as perishable goods. Another disadvantage associated with air transportation is its lack of accessibility; since a plane cannot ordinarily be pulled up to a loading dock, it is necessary to bring products to and from the airport by truck.

According to *Transportation and Distribution,* air cargo remains a comparatively small segment of total freight transportation volume when measured by tonnage (12.5 billion domestic ton-miles of freight annually). But L. Clinton Hoch noted in the magazine that ''access to air transportation is expected to become increasingly important since a growing number of customers (such as hospitals and electronic manufacturers) depend upon 'just in time' delivery systems as well as the increasing number of high-tech industries (such as computer manufacturers) adopting the 'build-to-order' strategy.'' These trends, coupled with increased pressure on consumer goods manufacturers to deliver products quickly to 1) meet customer expectations and 2) reduce inventory and other supply chain costs, are expected to ''fuel the demand for expedited services,'' wrote Hoch. ''Accordingly, competition is heating up among the major air cargo and express carriers who are building specialized hubs to handle larger aircraft and major sorting facilities.''

Railways. The rail transportation network in the United States included about 120,000 miles of major rail lines in the late 1990s, on which carriers transported an estimated 1.3 million tons of freight annually. Trains are ideally suited for shipping bulk products, and can be adapted to meet specific product needs through the use of specialized cars—i.e., tankers for liquids, refrigerated cars for perishables, and cars fitted with ramps for automobiles.

Rail transportation is typically used for long-distance shipping. Less expensive than air transportation, it offers about the same delivery speed as trucks over long distances and exceeds transport speeds via marine waterways. In fact, deregulation and the introduction of freight cars with larger carrying capacities has enabled rail carriers to make inroads in several areas previously dominated by motor carriers. But access to the network remains a problem for many businesses.

Motor carriers. Accessible and ideally suited for transporting goods over short distances, trucks are the dominant means of shipping in the United States. In fact, motor carriers account for approximately $120 billion in annual revenue, much of it due to local shipments (shipments to and from business enterprises in the same community or local region). This industry sector underwent tremendous change in the 1990s with the introduction of deregulation measures that removed most state and federal regulations in the areas of pricing and operating authority. ''With few exceptions, motor carriers are now free to operate wherever they wish and to charge any rates that are agreeable to the shipper and the carrier,'' wrote Hoch, although he noted that trucks are still subject to federal laws on vehicle specifications and the parameters of the sanctioned truck routes of the Surface Transportation Assistance Act of 1982.

Water transport. Water transportation is the least expensive and slowest mode of freight transport. It is generally used to transport heavy products over long distances when speed is not an issue. Although accessibility is a problem with ships—because they are necessarily limited to coastal area or major inland waterways—piggybacking is possible using either trucks or rail cars. However, industry observers note that port terminal accessibility to land-based modes of transportations is lacking in many regions. The main advantage of water transportation is that it can move products all over the world.

Pipeline facilities. Most pipeline transportation systems are privately owned. Generally used for transport of petroleum products, they can also be used to deliver certain products (chemicals, slurry coal, etc.) of other companies. According to *Transportation and Distribution,* the nation's natural gas line networks include 276,000 miles of transmission pipe and more than 919,000 miles of distribution lines, which combine to deliver nearly 20 trillion cubit feet of gas on an annual basis.

FURTHER READING:

Ewing, Reid. ''Measuring Transportation Performance.'' *Transportation Quarterly.* Winter 1995.

Gordon, Cameron. ''Putting Transportation Investments in Context.'' *Transportation Quarterly.* Summer 1997.

Hoch, L. Clinton. ''Find the Best Ways to Your Markets.'' *Transportation and Distribution.* March 1998.

Weiss, Howard J., and Mark E. Gershon. *Production and Operations Management.* Allyn and Bacon, 1989.

TRANSPORTATION OF EXPORTS

An important part of the international trade process for exporters of any size is ensuring that the goods that are shipped reach their destination intact and in timely fashion. Appropriate packaging and proper documentation are essential in meeting these goals.

INTERNATIONAL FREIGHT TRANSPORTATION OPTIONS

The exporter's options for transporting goods are dictated in large measure by their final destination. American exporters preparing goods for shipment to Mexico or Canada, for instance, will often make arrangements to transport their merchandise over land routes via trucks, while exports that are headed for destinations unreachable via land routes have to be transported by air or water.

Exporters who are faced with the choice of air or water modes of transport need to be cognizant of the advantages and disadvantages of those two options. While shipping by water is generally less expensive than transporting by air, the difference in cost is narrowed somewhat by ancillary costs associated with sea transport, such as the cost of transporting goods to the dock. Merchandise shipped over water also takes longer to reach its ultimate destination, and since some export transactions do not require the importer to pay until they are in possession of the goods, exporters in immediate need of cash infusions will need to weigh this factor carefully. Of course, the sheer size and tonnage of some export shipments render air transportation impractical.

EXPORT PACKAGING

Consultants to companies who engage in exporting note that the merchandise they ship will generally be subject to more handling and potentially damaging forces during transport than will goods headed for domestic destinations. Intelligent packaging, then, is a key component of the exporting process. Ideally, exporters should use a packaging approach that minimizes the cost of transportation while simultaneously ensuring that the goods reach their destination intact. Many small exporting companies that do not have the financial or operating resources to take care of packaging themselves utilize firms that specialize in providing such services.

Exporting firms need to keep abreast of labeling and marking requirements on goods intended for international destinations as well. Pharmaceutical products, for instance, require special labeling that varies from country to country. In addition, many countries enforce regulations requiring that imported goods bear the name of the country of origin on the outside of their packaging. Packaging containing merchandise intended for foreign ports also typically includes markings indicating the height and weight of the packages, as well as any additional handling instructions.

NECESSARY EXPORT DOCUMENTS

The documentation required for international trade is quite extensive (and potentially confusing), but exporters need to make certain that they have their papers in proper order if they wish to avoid potentially damaging delays in shipment. Documents required for the export of goods include the following:

Export License. While most merchandise can be shipped to overseas customers without benefit of an actual license, some goods are subject to additional regulations and require an Individually Validated Export License (IVL). "Should your particular export be subject to export controls," explained the Small Business Administration, "then a 'validated' license must be obtained. In general, your export would require a 'validated' license if export of the goods would: threaten United States national security; affect certain foreign policies of the United States; or create short supply in domestic markets."

Shipper's Export Declaration (SED). This important document is required for mail shipments of $500 or more, all shipments of more than $2500 value, and any shipment that is covered by an IVL. SEDs are utilized by the U.S. Bureau of the Census to track export trends in the United States.

Commercial Invoice. The commercial invoice is used by both exporters and importers. Exporters use the document as proof of ownership and an aid in securing payment for goods delivered, while importers use it to confirm that the merchandise they have received matches what they ordered. Commercial invoices are also used by Customs officers to figure the correct duty on the goods being imported, so U.S. exporters generally provide translated copies of the invoice when shipping goods to destinations for which English is not the primary language spoken.

Consular Invoice. This kind of invoice serves the same general purpose as the commercial invoice, but it must be worded in the language of the nation for which the goods are intended. Consular invoices are so named because they can be obtained from the destination country's consulate.

Bill of Lading. This document serves as evidence of ownership of the goods being exported, and also specifies the responsibilities of the transporting company. Two types of ocean bills of lading can be used.

The first, known as the straight bill of lading, provides for delivery of merchandise *only* to the person named in the bill of lading. Under the second bill of lading option, called the shipper's order, goods can be delivered not only to the person named in the bill but also to other designated people. Under the latter option, financing institutions are empowered to take possession of the goods being exported if the buyer defaults; they retain title on the merchandise until all payments and conditions of sale have been fulfilled. For exports that are transported by air, documents known as air waybills serve the same general purpose.

Certificate of Origin. Some countries require shipments of goods from foreign ports to include certificates that indicate where the merchandise originated. In instances wherein the importing country has trade agreements in place with the country that is doing the exporting, lower tariffs on those goods can sometimes be imposed.

Export Packing List. This highly involved document provides a detailed description of the contents being shipped. It covers the material in each individual package, providing information such as individual net, legal, tare and gross weights and measurements for each package. This data is typically measured by both metric and U.S. systems of measurement. Export packing lists are used by the shipper (or the freight forwarder) to confirm the shipment's contents and figure the total weight and volume of the shipment.

Inspection Certificate. This documentation is bestowed by independent inspection firms, whose services are required when foreign purchasers ask for independent corroboration that the goods meet agreed-upon specifications.

Insurance Certificate. Some international transactions require the exporting firm to provide insurance on the shipment. The insurance certificate describes the type and amount of merchandise contained in the shipment, and confirms that the shipment has been insured.

Inland Bill of Lading. These documents—known as "waybills on rail" in the railroad industry and "pro-forma" bills within the trucking industry—provide information on the inland transportation of goods and the port that will eventually send the exporter's goods on their way.

Dock Receipt. This paper is the international carrier's acknowledgment that goods have been received. It serves to transfer responsibility for those goods from the domestic to the international carrier.

Shipper's Instructions. This document serves to provide transporters of exports with any other information necessary to ensure the effective movement of goods to their final destination.

THE FREIGHT FORWARDER

International freight forwarders are important figures in the exporting process for American firms. Knowledgeable about all aspects of international trade—including international and U.S. regulations, import and export rules, and shipping options—freight forwarders serve as agents for exporting businesses, overseeing the transportation of their cargo to overseas destinations.

As the Small Business Administration noted in its *Breaking into the Trade Game,* many freight forwarders provide services at the very beginning of the exporting process by advising exporting firms about freight costs, port charges, insurance costs, consular fees, handling fees, and other expenses. They can also advise small exporters about packaging options, and in some cases can make arrangements to have goods containerized or packed at the port. Freight forwarders also have the power to reserve space on freighters and other ocean vessels in accordance with client specifications.

In order to represent their exporter clients as effectively as possible, freight forwarders may review the wide array of documentation necessary for international business transactions, including letters of credit, commercial invoices, and packing lists. Exporters can also ask freight forwarders to prepare necessary documentation for the exporting process, including bills of lading. Once this documentation has been taken care of, they can be forwarded as needed. Finally, the exporter can also ask the freight forwarder to make arrangements with the customs broker to ensure that their merchandise is in compliance with customs export documentation regulations. Given the wide array of services that they provide, and the importance of those services to the exporting process, trade experts view freight forwarders as an extremely valuable resource for small exporting firms. ''The cost for their services,'' contended the Small Business Administration (SBA), ''is a legitimate export cost that should be figured into the price charged to the customer.''

FURTHER READING:

Branch, Alan E. *Elements of Export Marketing and Management.* Chapman and Hall, 1990.

Breaking into the Trade Game: A Small Business Guide. Small Business Administration, n.a.

Ewing, Reid. ''Measuring Transportation Performance.'' *Transportation Quarterly.* Winter 1995.

Gordon, Cameron. ''Putting Transportation Investments in Context.'' *Transportation Quarterly.* Summer 1997.

Hoch, L. Clinton. ''Find the Best Ways to Your Markets.'' *Transportation and Distribution.* March 1998.

Sandhusen, Richard L. *Global Marketing.* Barron's Educational Series, 1994.

Sletten, Eric. *How to Succeed in Exporting and Doing Business Internationally.* Wiley, 1994.

TUITION ASSISTANCE PROGRAMS

Tuition assistance programs are a type of employee benefit in which an employer reimburses employees for the costs associated with continuing education, such as tuition, fees, and books. Many progressive companies pay for an unlimited number of courses that may or may not be directly related to an employee's current job. In fact, a 1999 survey conducted by the Society for Human Resource Management indicated that approximately 90 percent of employers offer financial assistance to their workforce in the form of tuition assistance or related practices such as on-site training and admission into professional seminars and/or conferences. These companies reason that today's rapidly changing work environment requires employees to possess a wide variety of skills, and that education provides a way for them to improve their skills and adapt to the new realities of the business world. Other companies adopt tuition assistance programs on a smaller scale, providing partial reimbursement of certain costs associated with job-related courses.

Although tuition assistance programs can be costly for businesses, there are a number of proven strategies that can be applied to help keep costs down. In addition, tuition assistance programs offer companies a number of important benefits. For example, companies that provide their employees with tuition assistance are building a more educated work force by encouraging workers to pursue higher education. Tuition assistance programs can also provide companies with an effective recruiting tool, enabling them to attract highly motivated people. Finally, tuition assistance can lead to reduced employee turnover and increased loyalty to the company.

COMMON CONCERNS ABOUT TUITION ASSISTANCE

HIGH COSTS Many companies resist instituting tuition assistance programs because of the cost involved. In fact, poorly planned tuition assistance programs do waste money. But as Heather Kirkwood observed in *Kansas City Business Journal,* ''experts say a well-designed tuition reimbursement program can turn what seems like a cash-sucking recruiting tool into a revenue-increasing program that creates loyal employees.''

Writing in *HR Magazine,* Kathryn Tyler noted a number of different strategies that businesses can take to limit the expense of tuition assistance programs. The first step is to determine the specific educational goals of employees in order to better focus their course selections. Outside educational advisory services can help employees understand their goals and thus decrease the chance that they will begin one course of study only to quit and start another. Similarly, specialists within the company can be made available to advise employees about their educational options, rather than simply explaining the features of the tuition assistance program to them. These individuals can help guide employees in educational directions that will benefit both themselves and the company for which they work.

Experts also recommend that employers reimburse fees as well as tuition in order to reduce costs. State-supported universities tend to charge lower tuition rates but higher additional fees than private colleges, which might cause some employees to choose to attend the more expensive private colleges in order to save on out-of-pocket expenses. Another way companies can save money in their tuition assistance programs is to investigate negotiating discounts with the schools. Larger companies or even smaller ones with specific educational needs may be able to save money by providing a certain number of students for a course. If, for example, a dozen employees from one company need to take a basic class, that company may be able to arrange a reduced rate or even a special class just for employees. Employers may also find it beneficial to arrange to pay certain local colleges and universities directly in order to reduce paperwork and other hassles for their employees.

Another way for companies to save money, as well as make the idea of continuing education more attractive to employees, is to provide nontraditional education options, such as correspondence, television, videotape, or Internet classes. Thousands of accredited courses are available through these alternative means, which allow busy employees with family responsibilities to fulfill course requirements on their own time without having to sit in a formal classroom. Collectively known as "distance learning," these options offer employees a great deal of flexibility. However, it is important to make sure that such programs are regionally accredited so any credits earned will transfer to traditional schools if necessary.

Employers can also save money on tuition assistance programs by helping employees receive college credit for skills and knowledge they may already possess. For example, about 600 colleges offer students the opportunity to demonstrate their knowledge of various subjects through a life-experience portfolio. When employees have mastered the content of a course through work experience, they may be able to obtain college credit without actually having to spend time or money on a class. This option might enable a person employed as a bookkeeper to pass out of an intermediate accounting course, for instance.

Assessment tests, offered by college testing services, provide a similar, relatively inexpensive, option. Such testing enables some employees to reduce the amount of formal education they need to obtain a degree, which also reduces the time and cost involved in their education. In addition, gaining credit for skills and knowledge can enhance employees' self-esteem and bring them recognition for their skills at work.

EMPLOYEES WILL NOT APPLY THEMSELVES AS STUDENTS "One of the most common fears related to offering a liberal tuition reimbursement policy is that an employee will enroll in a course, the company will pay for it, and the person won't invest the effort required to earn a passing grade," according to Tyler. "Clear reimbursement guidelines can reduce the likelihood of that happening. For instance, companies can tie reimbursement to grades—a certain percentage for an A, a B, and so on, or 100 percent reimbursement for a passing grade." Employers can also avoid this potential problem by requiring students who fail a course to either repeat it or pay back the company for related tuition and fees.

EMPLOYEES MAY TAKE THE EDUCATION AND THEN LEAVE THE COMPANY Many businesses providing tuition assistance to employees fear that the worker will depart for greener pastures after taking advantage of the program. In order to reduce the likelihood of losing newly educated employees, some companies require participants in their tuition assistance programs to remain at the company for a certain length of time or else reimburse the company for part of the tuition paid on their behalf. Many businesses also limit enrollment in such programs to individuals who have already been with the company for a certain amount of time (typically six months to one year). Other companies take the more positive step of rewarding employees who earn their degrees with a gift of company stock. The stock can be set up to mature over a few years, thus giving the employee added incentive to remain at the company.

COMPLEX TAX IMPLICATIONS Finally, some companies are reluctant to establish tuition assistance programs for their employees because of the paperwork related to tax compliance. Some forms of tuition assistance to workers are tax-deductible, though, especially if the coursework is necessary to maintain professional licenses or otherwise ensure that the employee in question can adequately fulfill his/her workplace obligations and responsibilities. Businesses interested in establishing tuition assistance programs for their employees should first consult with an accounting/tax professional to discuss these and other potential factors.

FURTHER READING:

Burzawa, Sue. ''Employers Can Use State Programs to Help Employees Save for College Education.'' *Employee Benefit Plan Review*. December 2000.

Jenks, James M., and Brian L.P. Zevnik. *Employee Benefits Plain and Simple*. Collier Books, 1993.

Kirkwood, Heather. ''Education Perks Benefit Employers, Too.'' *Kansas City Business Journal*. January 14, 2000.

Roberts, Gary, Gary Seldon, and Carlotta Roberts. *Human Resources Management*. Washington, D.C.: U.S. Small Business Administration, n.d.

Rubis, Leon. ''Legislation Echoes in the Workplace.'' *HR Magazine*. October 1996.

Tyler, Kathryn. ''Expanded Tuition Policies Save in the Long Run.'' *HR Magazine*. September 1997.

U

UNDERCAPITALIZATION

Undercapitalization is a situation in which a business has insufficient funds, or capital, to support its operations. Although undercapitalization can affect any business, it is particularly common and problematic for small businesses. In fact, undercapitalization is one of the warning signs of major financial trouble for small businesses, as well as a significant cause of small business failures. Undercapitalization also acts to limit the growth of many small businesses, because without sufficient capital they cannot afford to make the investments necessary for expansion. In this way, undercapitalization can pose a problem even for profitable small businesses. "What separates the successful entrepreneur from the unsuccessful? In many cases, it seems to be whether the prospective business owner has access to sufficient funds," Brian Hamilton wrote in the Small Business Administration publication *Financing for the Small Business*. "Without sufficient capitalization, companies do not have the staying power to withstand intense competition or downturns in the business cycle," Richard Hamilton added in an article for *Manitoba Business*.

The amount of capitalization needed by a small business depends upon a number of factors. Businesses that offer a service usually require less funds than those that manufacture a product. Similarly, businesses in which the owners perform most of the work tend to need less up-front capital than those that must hire employees. A company's initial capitalization also depends on the entrepreneur's ability to invest personal funds and institute a sound business plan.

In order to avoid future problems with undercapitalization, entrepreneurs need to perform a realistic assessment of their expenses and financial needs. Some of the major expenses facing a new business include facility rental, equipment, supplies, utilities, insurance, advertising, business licenses, and salaries. Based upon this information, the entrepreneur should prepare a cash flow projection on a monthly basis for the first year. The difference between the funds the entrepreneur is able to contribute, the amount of income the business is expected to generate, and the amount of expenses the business is projected to incur provides a rough estimate of the business's financial needs. The entrepreneur must approach various sources for debt or equity financing to make up the difference and provide the business with sufficient capitalization.

Although more than 50 percent of small business failures can be attributed to undercapitalization, it is important for entrepreneurs not only to raise enough money but also to use that money wisely. In an article for *Inc.,* Norm Brodsky noted that many entrepreneurs fall into an "image trap," trying to present an image of success with fancy offices, expensive but unnecessary equipment, and personal perquisites. Spending valuable funds on such luxury items is a sure invitation to business failure. Instead, Brodsky recommends that entrepreneurs put off such expenditures until the business is successful, and instead concentrate on making good decisions to build the business while making their capital last.

UNDERCAPITALIZATION AND CORPORATE LIABILITY

A little-known problem associated with undercapitalization is that it can increase the likelihood of the owners of a corporation being held personally liable for business-related matters. One of the main reasons that entrepreneurs choose the corporate form of business organization is to protect themselves against personal liability for business debts and court judgments. Incorporation does not afford automatic protection, however. Corporate owners can be held personally liable in a number of situations, including cases where personal and corporate assets are commingled, the corporation does not keep adequate records, or corporate owners intentionally defraud their creditors.

But perhaps the most critical factor in determining whether there should be personal liability for corporate debts is whether the owners provided sufficient capitalization for the business. ''This issue is so important that owners risk personal liability even if it is the only factor a court finds,'' according to *Nation's Business* contributor Anthony J. Mohr. ''The ultimate test is whether there are enough corporate assets to satisfy corporate obligations.'' For example, an entrepreneur could not contribute only $500 to start a new business, knowing that it actually required an initial capital outlay of $10,000, and expect his or her personal assets to be protected in case the business became insolvent. In this instance, a court would be likely to rule that the extreme undercapitalization of the corporation made the owner personally liable for its debts.

FURTHER READING:

Brodsky, Norm. ''Why Start-Ups Fail.'' *Inc.* December 1995.

Ellison, Mitch, and Neil E. Seitz. *Capital Budgeting and Long-Term Financing Decisions.* HBJ, 1999.

Hamilton, Brian. *Financing for the Small Business.* Washington, DC: Small Business Administration, 1990.

Hamilton, Richard. ''Will Your Company Survive?'' *Manitoba Business.* May 1996.

Mohr, Anthony J. ''Take Care to Avoid Liability Traps.'' *Nation's Business.* November 1997.

UNDERWRITERS LABORATORIES (UL)

Underwriters Laboratories (UL) is the largest and best known independent, not-for-profit testing laboratory in the world. Based in Northwood, Illinois, UL conducts safety and quality tests on a broad range of products, from fire doors to CCTV cameras. The laboratory provides a full spectrum of conformity and quality assessment services to manufacturers and other organizations. It also assists jurisdictional and provincial authorities, offers educational materials to consumers, and works to strengthen safety systems around the world.

UL provides comprehensive diagnostic testing services in the following areas: fire testing; medical device testing; EPH services (food service equipment, drinking water certification, plumbing equipment); audio/video; home electronics; Source Verification and Inspection Services (SVIS); electric vehicle components and systems; EMC testing and certification; information technology equipment (ITE) industry services; and telecom industry services. It conducts tests on products in these areas to see whether they meet standards set by UL engineers in conjunction with input from manufacturers and product users, but it will also test products to see whether they meet standards set by outside entities, such as a city (in the case of building codes, for instance). In 1999, 16.1 billion products and components received passing grades from the laboratory's 35 facilities, which are located around the world.

In addition to its work in the U.S. market, Underwriters Laboratories maintains services for companies looking to test products for international markets. This division of UL studies international product certification standards, assists clients with the application process, helps with correspondence and translation, and can coordinate the exchange and review of test data. In order to increase its efficiency in these international realms, Underwriters Laboratories has also launched a sustained effort to establish common standards for safety requirements, testing protocols, and certifications around the world. The impetus for this effort, according to UL, is a recognition that companies seeking to establish a presence in multiple overseas markets sometimes need as many as 20 separate safety certifications for a single product, a requirement that ''can cost as much as $8,000 per safety mark per product. Many companies have annual certification budgets of $5 million or more.'' UL hopes to first establish common standards between the United States and Canada, then turn its attention to other markets.

UL DESIGNATIONS ''Underwriters Laboratories, which has been in existence for more than 100 years, is very sensitive to the prevalent but mistaken belief that it approves products,'' wrote Robert C. Cook in *Security Management.* ''The only entity that can actually approve or reject a product is a federal, state, or local government agency—known generally as the 'Authority Having Jurisdiction' or AHJ.'' However, an AHJ—whether it is a local health code inspection department or the federal Occupational Safety and Health Administration—often requires products to be tested by Underwriters Laboratories or another lab before the agency will approve its use.

UL hands out one of three different designations to products that pass its tests: UL listed, UL recognized, or UL certified. Businesses should note that there is no such designation as ''UL approved''; companies that mistakenly tout their products with such a designation will arouse the ire of Underwriters Laboratories, which will insist that the company clarify the matter immediately.

UL Listed. This designation means that the tested product meets the laboratory's standards and can be used by itself.

UL Recognized. This designation is granted to equipment components that are used in combination with other pieces of equipment to create a finished product.

UL Certified. This designation is used by UL when it has been successfully tested to the standards of an outside authority, such as a city's building code requirements.

In 2000 UL announced its intention to transition to usage of Standard Technical Panels (STPs) in its development of diagnostic processes. The STPs will include representatives from consumer protection organizations (such as the National Consumer League), manufacturers, industry trade associations (like the Association of Home Appliance Manufacturers), and regulatory authorities (including government agencies like the Consumer Product Safety Commission). According to UL, these forums will work together to establish consensus opinions on diagnostic standards and will vote on proposed standards before they are adopted.

Businesses considering enlisting the services of Underwriters Laboratories (or similar labs) should be aware that testing can be both expensive and time-consuming. Bills of several thousand dollars per product tested are not unusual in many industry sectors, and the testing procedures usually take about six months to complete, with some tests extending well beyond that time frame. But the importance of UL acknowledgment is very significant to marketplace image in many industries.

FURTHER READING:

Cook, Robert C. ''A Tale of UL Testing.'' *Security Management.* July 1995.

Jancsurak, Joe. ''New Standards for Standards.'' *Appliance Manufacturer.* August 2000.

Strom, Shelly. ''Underwriters Laboratories Gives Seal of Approval.'' *Business Journal-Portland.* August 4, 2000.

''The Underwriters Labs' Faster Seal of Approval.'' *Business Week.* December 20, 1993.

''Underwriters Labs Pursues Single Worldwide Standard.'' *Manufacturing News.* August 25, 2000.

Wingo, Walter S. ''A Boom Time for Product Testing.'' *Design News.* March 9, 1992.

UNIFORM COMMERCIAL CODE (UCC)

The Uniform Commercial Code (UCC) is a collection of modernized, codified, and standardized laws that apply to all commercial transactions with the exception of real property. Developed under the direction of the National Conference of Commissioners on Uniform State Laws, the American Law Institute, and the American Bar Association (ABA), it first became U.S. law in 1972. Since that time, it has undergone a process of constant revision.

The Uniform Commercial Code arose out of the need to address two growing problems in American business: 1) the increasingly cumbersome legal and contractual requirements of doing business, and 2) differences in state laws that made it difficult for businesses from different states to do business with one another. Businesspeople and legislators recognized that some measures needed to be taken to ease interstate business transactions and curb the trend toward exhaustively detailed contracts. They subsequently voiced support for the implementation of a set of standardized laws that would serve as the legal cornerstone for all exchanges of goods and services. These laws—the Uniform Commercial Code—could then be referred to when discrepancies in state laws arose, and freed companies from painstakingly including every conceivable business detail in all of their contractual agreements.

DEVELOPMENT OF THE UNIFORM COMMERCIAL CODE

Work on the UCC began in earnest in 1945. Seven years later, a draft of the code was approved by the National Conference of Commissioners on Uniform State Laws, the American Law Institute, and the American Bar Association. Pennsylvania became the first state to enact the UCC, and it became law there on July 1, 1954. The UCC editorial board issued a new code in 1957 in response to comments from various states and a special report by the Law Revision Commission of New York State. By 1966 48 states had enacted the code. Currently, all 50 states, the District of Columbia, and the U.S. Virgin Islands have adopted the UCC as state law, although some have not adopted every single provision contained within the code.

BUSINESS ISSUES ADDRESSED IN THE UCC

Many important aspects of business are covered within the UCC, and several of them are of particular import to entrepreneurs and small business owners. The Code provides detailed information on such diverse business aspects as: breach of contract (and the options of both buyers and sellers when confronted with breach); circumstances under which buyers can reject goods; risk allocation during transportation of goods; letters of credit and their importance; legal methods of payment for goods and services; and myriad other subjects.

ARTICLES The UCC consists of ten articles. Article 1, titled General Provisions, details principles of interpretation and general definitions that apply throughout the UCC. Article 2 covers such areas as sales contracts, performance, creditors, good faith purchasers, and legal remedies for breach of contract; given its concern with the always important issue of contracts, small business owners should be thoroughly acquainted with this section. Article 3, which replaced the Uniform Negotiable Instruments Law, covers transfer and negotiation, rights of a holder, and liability of parties, among other areas. Article 4 covers such areas as collections, deposits, and customer relations; it incorporated much of the Bank Collection Code developed by the American Bankers Association.

Article 5 of the Uniform Collection Code is devoted to letters of credit, while Article 6 covers bulk transfers. Article 7 covers warehouse receipts, bills of lading, and other documents of title. Article 8, meanwhile, is concerned with the issuance, purchase, and registration of investment securities; it replaced the Uniform Stock Transfer Act. Article 9 is another provision that is particularly important to small business owners. Devoted to secured transactions, sales of accounts, and chattel paper, it supplanted a number of earlier laws, including the Uniform Trust Receipts Act, the Uniform Conditional Sales Act, and the Uniform Chattel Mortgage Act.

Finally, Article 10 provides for states to set the effective date of enactment of the code and lists specific state laws should be repealed once the UCC has been enacted (Uniform Negotiable Instruments Act, Uniform Warehouse Receipts Act, Uniform Sales Act, Uniform Bills of Lading Act, Uniform Stock Transfer Act, Uniform Conditional Sales Act, and Uniform Trust Receipts Act). In addition, Article 10 recommends that states repeal any acts regulating bank collections, bulk sales, chattel mortgages, conditional sales, factor's lien acts, farm storage of grain and similar acts, and assignment of accounts receivable, for all of these areas are covered in the UCC. Individual states may also add to the list of repealed acts at their own discretion.

The UCC has a permanent editorial board, and amendments to the UCC are added to cover new developments in commerce, such as electronic funds transfers and the leasing of personal property. Individual states then have the option of adopting the amendments and revisions to the UCC as state law. For current information on changes within and interpretations of the Uniform Commercial Code, consult the *Business Lawyer's* "Uniform Commercial Code Annual Survey."

FURTHER READING:

Stone, Bradford. *The Uniform Commercial Code in a Nutshell.* West, 1995.

White, James J., and Robert Summers. *Uniform Commercial Code.* West/Wadsworth, 1999.

U.S. CHAMBER OF COMMERCE

The U.S. Chamber of Commerce is a national not-for-profit business federation devoted to promoting business interests in the United States and around the globe. Founded as a national federation in 1912 and headquartered in Washington, D.C., the U.S. Chamber of Commerce has long championed the cause of large and small businesses alike. Primary areas of activity by the Chamber include efforts to: ease perceived overregulation of business activities; cut taxes on businesses; strengthen trade relations with other nations; improve labor relations; increase productivity and innovation in all industry areas; develop new markets; study major business policy issues; improve socioeconomic conditions in communities; and reduce business-related litigation.

In 2000 the membership of the U.S. Chamber of Commerce included 830 business associations, approximately 3,000 local and state chambers of commerce; 87 American Chambers of Commerce based in foreign markets; and 3 million individual business enterprises. Of the latter members, the Chamber counts most of the United States' largest corporations. But according to Chamber of Commerce data, more than 96 percent of the federation's members are small businesses with 100 or fewer employees.

In addition to its intensive lobbying activities on behalf of its membership, the U.S. Chamber of Commerce boasts several affiliated organizations engaged in policy areas of interest to small and large businesses alike. The National Chamber Foundation (NCF), for instance, is a public and business policy research institution dedicated to exploring issues and solving problems found in the modern business world. The Chamber also supports two organizations devoted to legal issues. Its National Chamber Litigation center

(NCLC) represents businesses in legal proceedings, while the Institute for Legal Reform (ILR) is dedicated to tort reform and other pro-business changes to the U.S. legal system. Other foundations associated with and supported by the Chamber include the Center for International Private Enterprise (CIPE), which promotes business development in Third World countries, and the Center for Workforce Preparation (CWP), which endeavors to boost workforce education and training initiatives in all industries. In 2000 the Chamber also announced its intention to establish a humanitarian aid foundation called the Center for Corporate Citizenship Foundation. This organization's mandate will be to channel corporate donations to victims of natural disasters and other groups and individuals in need.

The national offices of the U.S. Chamber of Commerce are located in Washington, DC. The Chamber also maintains an Internet presence at www.uschamber.org.

FURTHER READING:

Mack, Charles S. *Business, Politics, and the Practice of Government Relations.* Quorum, 1997.

SEE ALSO: Chambers of Commerce

U.S. DEPARTMENT OF COMMERCE

The Department of Commerce, which was established in 1903, is one of the main government agencies intended to assist businesses—large and small—and represent their interests domestically and abroad. The agency states that its broad range of responsibilities include expanding U.S. exports, developing and promoting innovative technologies, gathering and disseminating statistical data and other important economic information, measuring economic growth, granting patents, promoting minority entrepreneurship, and providing stewardship. The department promotes these goals by encouraging job creation and economic growth through exports, free and fair trade, technology and innovation, entrepreneurship, deregulation, and sustainable development.

One of the key offices within the Department of Commerce is the Office of Business Liaison. That office serves as the intermediary between the business community and the agency. Its objectives include:

- To be pro-active in its dealings with the business community and to be responsive and effective in its outreach efforts.

- To keep the current administration aware of problems and issues facing the business community.

- To keep the business community abreast of key administration decisions and policies.

- To regularly meet with members of the business community.

- To help businesses navigate their way through all the federal agencies and regulations through its Business Assistance Program. In addition to producing a wide variety of published materials, the Assistance Program also provides specialists who are available to answer specific questions on government policies, programs, and services.

Another office that is of interest to small business owners is the Office of Small and Disadvantaged Utilization. This office is responsible for ensuring that the department purchases goods and services from small businesses. It helps small businesses identify which bureaus small businesses should pursue as potential buyers, clarifies who the key individuals at that bureau are, and provides small businesses with basic information on the procurement process and helps them develop marketing strategies.

Following is a list of other key offices, departments, and programs at the Department of Commerce that are also of interest to small business owners:

- Bureau of the Census—every 10 years, collects a wide variety of information on all people living in the United States. It makes this information publicly available, and business owners often use the information for demographic or marketing purposes.

- Economic Development Administration—responsible for creating new jobs, retaining existing jobs, and stimulating industrial and commercial growth in economically challenged areas of the United States.

- International Trade Administration—helps U.S. businesses compete in the global market by assisting exporters, helping businesses gain equal access to foreign markets, and making it easier to compete against unfairly traded imports. Includes separate units for trade development and import administration.

- Minority Business Development Agency—Devoted to fostering the creation, growth, and expansion of minority businesses in the United States.

- Office of Consumer Affairs—exists to bridge the gap between businesses and consumers, to help businesses improve the quality of the services they offer consumers, to educate consumers, and to speak for the consumer in regards to each administration's economic policy development. The Office also works with American businesses to help them become more competitive in the global marketplace.

- Patent and Trademark Office—protects innovation in the marketplace by providing inventors and authors with exclusive rights to their creations.

- National Institute of Standards and Technology—promotes economic growth by working with businesses to develop and apply technology, measurements, and standards. Of growing interest to U.S. businesses because of the growing influence of the International Standards Organization (ISO) and international emphasis on quality standards.

- National Trade Data Bank—provides the public with access, including electronic access, to export and international economic information.

- Trade Compliance Center—monitors foreign compliance with trade agreements and provides businesses with information about their rights and obligations under existing trade agreements with other nations.

Extensive information on the Department and its various bureaus and programs is available on the World Wide Web at www.doc.gov.

FURTHER READING:

U.S. Department of Commerce Handbook. USA International Business Publications, n.a.

U.S. SMALL BUSINESS ADMINISTRATION GUARANTEED LOANS

The U.S. Small Business Administration (SBA) is a major source of financing for small businesses in the United States. The SBA's various loan programs have provided needed funding for thousands of small enterprises who were unable to secure loans from lending institutions on their own; indeed, businesses cannot solicit loans from the SBA unless they are unable to get funding independently.

Some of today's most successful businesses, including Intel, Apple, and Federal Express, were given much needed boosts in their early days by SBA loans. This record of success, coupled with the trend toward small-business start-ups and entrepreneurship in

America, has encouraged both the SBA and its lending partners to continue to expand its loan programs. The SBA has subsequently set new records in various loan guarantee categories since the mid-1990s. In fiscal year (FY) 1996, it made $10.2 billion in loan guarantees through its primary commercial lending programs, and a year later it made a record $10.9 billion in loan guarantees. By fiscal year 2000, the total amount of approved SBA loans reached $12.34 billion. The main component of the SBA loan system—its 7(a) programs—annually accounts for the vast majority of the loan guarantees distributed to small businesses. Loan guarantees made through the 7(a) programs totaled $10.5 billion in FY 2000, accounting for approximately 91 percent of the total of all SBA loans made during that time.

TYPES OF SBA GUARANTEED LOANS

The SBA's 7(a) Loan Program is the most popular of the agency's programs (more than 43,000 of these loans were bestowed upon small businesses in FY 2000). Under this program, the SBA does not actually make direct loans to small businesses. Instead, it assures the institution that is making the business loan—usually a bank—that it will make payment on the loan if the business defaults on it. Since the SBA is taking responsibility for the loan, it is usually the final arbiter of whether a loan application will be approved or not.

The 7(a) Loan Program was formed to meet the long-term financing needs of small businesses. The primary advantage of 7(a) loans is that business enterprises are able to repay the loan over a very long period of time. Ten-year maturities are available for loans for equipment and working capital (though seven-year terms are more commonplace), and loans for real estate and major equipment purchases can be paid back over as long as 25 years. The SBA can guarantee 75 percent of loans up to $750,000, and 80 percent of loans of less than $100,000. The interest rate of 7(a) loans does not exceed 2.75 over the prime lending rate.

The SBA maintains several individual loan programs under the 7(a) umbrella. These include CAPLines, LowDoc, SBAExpress, EWCP, DELTA, and an assortment of other lending initiatives targeted at specific sectors of the small business world.

CAPLINES Limited to $750,000, CAPLines loans are given to small businesses with short-term working capital needs. "Under CAPLines," notes the SBA, "there are five distinct short-term working capital loans: the Seasonal, Contract, Builder's, Standard Asset-Based, and Small Asset-Based lines. For the most part, the SBA regulations governing the 7(a) Program also govern this program."

LOWDOC The Low Documentation Loan (LowDoc) Program is a simplified version of the 7(a) loan for businesses with strong credit histories seeking less than $150,000. It combines a streamlined application process (for many loan requests, the application is only one page long) with the elimination of several bureaucratic steps to improve response time to requests. Any small business that posted average annual sales over the previous three years of $5 million or less and employs 100 or few individuals (including all owners, partners, and principals) is eligible to apply for a Low Documentation Loan. Since its inception, the LowDoc Program has proven enormously popular with small business owners and entrepreneurs.

SBAEXPRESS This relatively new pilot program is only available through selected lending institutions. It makes loans of up to $150,000 to qualified businesses.

EWCP The Export Working Capital Program (EWCP) guarantees loans for qualified small businesses engaged in export transactions. It replaced another SBA program known as the Export Revolving Line of Credit Program. Most of the SBA regulations governing the 7(a) Program also govern this program. Loan maturities, however, may be for up to three years, with an option for annual renewals. EWCP loans can be extended for either single or multiple export sales.

DELTA The Defense Loan and Technical Assistance (DELTA) Program was implemented to help ease the impact of national defense cuts on defense-dependent small businesses. According to the SBA, DELTA loans of up to $1.25 million must be used to retain jobs of defense workers, create new jobs in impacted communities, or to make operating changes with the aim of remaining in the "national technical and industrial base." While listed under the 7(a) umbrella of loan programs, DELTA actually uses the 504 CDC program as well.

MICROLOANS SBA MicroLoans are short-term loans of up to $25,000. Disseminated through non-profit groups, MicroLoans are intended for the purchase of machinery and other equipment, office furniture, inventory, supplies, and working capital.

INTERNATIONAL TRADE LOAN (ITL) The ITL provides long-term financing assistance to small businesses who are involved in international trade or who have been hurt by imports. Under this program, the SBA guarantees loans for up to $1.25 million for a combination of fixed-asset financing and working capital needs (though the working capital portion of the guarantee is limited to $750,000).

POLLUTION CONTROL PROGRAM This program extends loans to small businesses engaged in the planning, design, or installation of pollution control facilities.

The Small Business Administration's other major loan program is the 504 CDC (Certified Development Companies) Program. CDCs are nonprofit corporations established to aid communities in their economic development efforts. The 504 CDC Program is designed to provide growing businesses with long-range, fixed-rate financing (up to $1 million for qualified applicants) for major expansion expenditures in the realm of fixed-asset projects. These include: real estate purchases and improvements, including existing buildings, grading, street improvements, parking lots and landscaping, and utilities; long-term machinery and equipment; renovation of existing facilities; and building construction. Monies from the 504 CDC Program cannot be used for refinancing, working capital or inventory, or consolidating or repaying debt.

The SBA describes the program thusly: "Typically, a 504 project includes a loan secured with a senior lien from a private-sector lender covering up to 50 percent of the project cost, a loan secured with a junior lien from the CDC (a 100 percent SBA-guaranteed debenture) covering up to 40 percent of the cost, and a contribution of at least 10 percent equity from the small business being helped. The maximum SBA debenture generally is $750,000 (up to $1 million in some cases). . . . The CDC's portfolio must create or retain one job from every $35,000 provided by the SBA."

Finally, the SBA offers Physical Disaster Business Loans to businesses that have been victimized by various natural disasters (fires, floods, hurricanes, earthquakes, etc.). These loans, limited to $1.5 million and not available to firms that were insured for their losses, are available to businesses of any size that need to repair or replace facilities to "pre-disaster" condition. Economic Injury Disaster Loans are also made available to companies that suffered severe economic damage as a result of a given disaster. These loans, which are capped at $1.5 million, are meant to help businesses cover ordinary operating expenses "which would have been payable barring disaster," according to the SBA. It is worth noting that businesses can apply for either type of disaster loan assistance, but they can be awarded no more than a total of $1.5 million from the two programs unless they qualify as a major source of employment for the region in which they operate.

INTEREST RATES ON SBA LOANS

The interest rates on SBA-guaranteed loans are negotiated between the borrowing business and the lending institution, but they are subject to SBA-imposed rate ceilings, which are linked to the prime rate.

Interest rates on SBA loans can be either fixed or variable.

According to the SBA, fixed rate loans are not allowed to exceed the prime rate plus 2.25 percent if the loan matures in less than seven years. If the maturity of the loan is seven years or more, however, the rate can be boosted to the prime rate plus 2.75 percent. For SBA loans totaling less than $25,000, the maximum interest rate cannot exceed the prime rate plus 4.25 percent for loans with a maturity of less than seven years (for loans that mature after seven years, the interest rate can be as much as the prime rate plus 4.75 percent). For SBA loans between $25,000 and $50,000, maximum rates are not permitted to exceed 3.25 percent (for loans that mature in less than seven years) and 3.75 percent (for loans with longer terms of maturity).

Variable rate loans, notes the SBA, may be pegged to either the SBA optional peg rate or the lowest prime rate (the optional peg rate is a weighed average of rates that the federal government pays for loans with maturities similar to the average SBA loan). Under variable rate loan plans, the lender and borrower negotiate the amount of the spread to be added to the base interest rate. Such agreements also provide for regular adjustment periods wherein the note rate can be changed as needed. Some agreements call for monthly adjustment periods, while others provide for quarterly, semiannual, or annual adjustments.

ELIGIBILITY ISSUES

The Small Business Administration defines businesses eligible for SBA loans as those that: operate for profit; are engaged in, or propose to do business in, the United States or its possessions; have reasonable owner equity to invest; and use alternative financial resources (such as personal assets) first. In addition, to secure SBA assistance, a company must qualify as a ''small business'' under the terms of the Small Business Act. That legislation defined an eligible small business as one that is independently owned and operated and not dominant in its industry.

Since the passage of the Small Business Act, the SBA has developed size standards for every industry to gauge whether a company qualifies as a ''small business'' or not. Size standards are arranged by Standard Industrial Classification (SIC) code, but in general, the following guidelines apply for major industry groups:

- Manufacturing—A key criteria for manufacturing establishments is the size of their work force. Generally, 1,500 employees is the cut-off point for SBA consideration, but even establishments that have between 500 and 1,500 employees may not qualify as small businesses; in such instances the SBA bases its determination on a size standard for the specific industry in which the business under consideration operates.

- Wholesaling—Generally, wholesale establishments seeking SBA financial assistance should not have more than 100 employees.

- Retail and Service—Financial information is the key consideration here; ideally, retail and service industry businesses seeking SBA assistance should not have more than $3.5 million in annual receipts, although the requests of larger establishments are considered (depending on the industry). Establishments engaged in construction or agriculture industries are also evaluated on the basis of their financial reports.

The Small Business Administration also considers other factors in determining whether an establishment qualifies as a small business. For example, if a business is affiliated with another company, the owners must determine the primary business activity of both the affiliated group and the applicant business before submitting a request for SBA assistance. If the applicant business and the affiliated group do not both meet the SBA's size standards for their primary business activities, then the loan request will not be considered.

The SBA also has a number of eligibility rules that apply to specific kinds of businesses. Franchisees, for example, are often favored by the SBA because their businesses enjoy a higher success rate than do other businesses. Nonetheless, SBA officials will examine a franchisee's franchise agreement closely before extending any loan guarantees to him or her. If the officials decide that the franchisor wields so much control over the franchise's operations that the franchisee is basically an employee, then the SBA will turn down the request. Other types of businesses, such as those in agriculture or the fishing industry, are free to apply for SBA assistance, but they are directed to first look to government agencies that deal directly with their industries. Farmers, for example, are supposed to first explore loan programs available through the Farmers Home Administration (FHA), while some members of the fishing industry—depending on the nature of their need—should first consult with the National Marine Fisheries Service (NMFS). The SBA also notes that some businesses are disqualified from consideration from the outset by the industry in which they operate. Businesses that operate in gambling, investment, or media-related fields, for example, are all ineligible for SBA loans.

Finally, the SBA notes that loans that they guarantee are only to be used for specific business purposes, including ''the purchase of real estate to house the business operations; construction, renovation, or leasehold improvements; acquisition of furniture, fixtures, machinery, and equipment; purchase of inventory; and working capital.'' Using the money for other purposes—payment of delinquent withholding taxes, acquisition of another business, refinancing of debt, and a whole host of other actions—is not allowed.

APPLYING FOR AN SBA LOAN

The chief challenge of any business seeking to secure a loan from the Small Business Administration is to convince the SBA that it has the ability to be successful in its chosen field. To do so, the small business owner should be equipped with a complete understanding of his or her operation (whether existing or proposed) and the benefits that a loan, if granted, will bring to the business. Of course, it is also necessary to effectively articulate this information to the SBA. Business owners disseminate this data through a variety of documents.

Principal documents that should be submitted by the entrepreneur who hopes to start a new business include: resume (and resumes of any other key people involved in the proposed enterprise); current financial statement of all personal assets and liabilities; summary of collateral; proposed operating plan; and statement detailing revenue projections. Perhaps the most important document, however, is the loan request statement itself, for it is this document that should detail all aspects of the proposed business. For established business owners seeking an SBA loan, the most important documents—besides the loan application—are the company balance sheet, personal financial statements, and business income statements. Consultants urge small business owners to be both careful and realistic in preparing these records. They also caution entrepreneurs and small business owners not to distort figures or facts in their presentation. The SBA does not look kindly on misrepresentations in financial statements or any other part of the loan application.

THE LOAN APPLICATION The SBA loan application form serves to summarize much of the information detailed elsewhere in the total application package. Applicants are directed to furnish basic information about themselves and their businesses, including personal information (full legal name, street address); basic business information (employer ID number, type of business, number of employees, banking institution used); names and addresses of management personnel; estimated business expenditures and costs (including details on the SBA loan request); summary of collateral; summary of previous government financing; and listing of debts.

The SBA loan application form also provides a complete listing of the various other items of information that must be provided for a business's application to be considered. These include a personal history statement; personal and business financial statements; business description; listing of management personnel; equipment list; cosigners; summary of bankruptcies, insolvencies, and lawsuits (if any); listing of any familial relationships with SBA employees; subsidiaries, either proposed or in existence; franchise agreements; and statements of financial interest in any establishments with which applicant business does business, if applicable.

FURTHER READING:

Cohen, William. *The Entrepreneur and Small Business Problem Solver.* Wiley, 1990.

Emerich, Amy, ed. *Small Business Sourcebook.* Gale, 1996.

SBA Profile: Who We Are and What We Do. Small Business Administration, 2000.

SEE ALSO: 8(A) Loan Program

V

VALUATION

Valuation is the process of putting a price on a piece of property. The value of businesses, personal property, intellectual property (such as patents, trademarks, and copyrights), and real estate are all commonly determined through the practice of valuation. In the context of a business valuation, the appraiser considers many factors, including the following:

- Financial attributes (sales and profitability trends, noncash expenses, capital expenditures, tangible and intangible assets and liabilities, contracts, contingent liabilities, and others)

- Marketing attributes (location, competition, barriers to entry, distributor and supplier relationships, current demand for products or services offered, likely future profit potential for the business)

- General condition of the business and its assets (including state of bookkeeping, equipment, facilities, work environment, etc.)

- General economic factors in industry which the business operates (regulatory environment, labor relations, interest rates, consumer confidence, the stock market, etc.).

APPROACHES TO VALUATION

Several different valuation approaches can be used to determine the value of a business. Some are better suited to certain business types than others, and as Lawrence Tuller noted in *Getting Out: A Step-by-Step Guide to Selling a Business or Professional Practice,* "everyone has his own theory about the most equitable and accurate method [of valuation]." Tuller noted that each business interest naturally tends to favor the valuation method that best suits his own self-interests: "Finance companies value a business at what the assets will bring at liquidation auction. Investment bankers and venture capitalists, interested in rapid appreciation and high returns on their investment, value a business at discounted future cash flow. Statisticians have devised complex deviation curves based on historical performance to project future earnings. Corporate America looks to the prevailing P/E ratios, unless the market is depressed, in which case they use book value."

BALANCE SHEET METHODS OF VALUATION These methods of valuation are most often employed when the business under examination generates most of its earnings from its assets (rather than the contributions of its employees). It is also used, wrote John A. Johansen in *How to Buy or Sell a Business*, "when the cost of starting a business and getting revenues past the break-even point doesn't greatly exceed the value of the business's assets."

- Liquidation Approach—This method assesses the value of a business by gauging its value if were to cease operations and sell its individual assets. Under this approach, the business owner would receive no compensation for business "goodwill"—nontangible assets such as the company's name, location, customer base, or accumulated experience. This method is further divided into forced liquidations (as in bankruptcies) and orderly liquidations. Values are typically figured higher in the latter instances. Asset-based lenders and banks tend to favor this method, because they view the liquidation value of a company's tangible assets to be the only valuable collateral to the loan. But it is unpopular with most business owners because of the lack of consideration given to goodwill and other intangible assets.

- Asset Value Approach—This approach begins by examining the company's book value. Under this method, items listed on a business's balance sheet (at historical cost levels) are adjusted to bring them in line with current market values. In essence, this method calls for the adjustment of an asset's book value to equal the cost of replacing that asset in its current condition. This method is most often used to determine the value of companies which feature a large percentage of commodity-type assets. The net asset value method, also referred to as net worth or owner's equity, is one of the most commonly employed of all valuation approaches. While flawed in some respects, the net asset value method is popular because this approach can be easily figured from existing financial records.

INCOME STATEMENT METHODS OF VALUATION
These valuation methods are perhaps the most frequently used of the myriad valuation approaches that exist.

- Historical Cash Flow Approach—This is the most commonly used of all valuation methods. Many buyers view this method as the most relevant of all valuation approaches for it tells them what the business has historically provided to its owners in terms of cash. As Tuller observed, "the value of assets might be interesting to know, but hardly anyone buys a business only for its balance sheet assets. The whole purpose is to make money, and most buyers feel that they should be able to generate at least as much cash in the future as the business yielded in the past." This method typically takes financial data from the company's previous three years in drawing its conclusions.

- Discounted Future Cash Flow (DCF) Approach—This method uses projections of future cash flows from operating the business to determine company value. The DCF approach requires detailed assumptions about future operations, including volumes, pricing, costs, and other factors. DCF usually starts with forecast income, adding back

non-cash expenses, deducting capital expenditures, and adjusting for working capital changes to arrive at expected cash flows. The future cash flow method also is notable for its recognition of industry reputation, popularity with customers, and other "goodwill" factors in its assessment of company value. Once the value of the business's assets has been settled upon, the appropriate discount rate must be determined and used to bring the future cash flows back to their present value at the as-of date of the valuation. DCF in its single period form is known as capitalization of earnings, which usually involves "normalizing" a recent measure of income or cash flow to reflect a steady-state or going forward amount that can be capitalized at the appropriate multiple.

MARKET COMPARABLE APPROACH This approach looks to comparable companies—in terms of industry, size, growth rates, capitalization, and other factors—for which a market value is known or observable (e.g., publicly traded companies) to establish a value for the company under examination. This approach, contended Johansen, is inherently flawed since "rarely if ever are two businesses truly comparable. However, businesses in the same industry do have some characteristics in common, and a careful contrasting may allow a conclusion to be drawn about a range of value."

VALUING PERSONAL SERVICE BUSINESSES

Different valuation methods and emphases are required when assessing the value of a personal service business such as a medical practice. While equipment, supplies, real estate and other assets that are typically included in assessing the value of companies are also included in assessing personal service business values, they are often of little consequence to potential buyers of the business in question. After all, a buyer may have an entirely new location in mind for the business, and costs associated with leases, utilities, and taxes often change dramatically with relocation. Instead, wrote Tuller, the most important consideration in valuing any personal service business "is how much gross billings can be generated from the customer/client base, not what profits have been recorded or how much cash [the owner has] taken out. . . . A key consideration to keep in mind if you are selling a professional practice is that the goodwill you have built up over the years is really what you are selling. Sometimes, it is called customer or client lists, or client files, but it is really just goodwill."

VALUATION ISSUES AND STANDARDS

It is important to recognize and deal properly with certain subtleties and standards in the field of valuation. Issues and standards to keep in mind include:

TREATMENT OF DEBT If the method used to determine company value uses a pre-debt-service income measure, then debt must usually be subtracted from the resulting figure.

CONTROL PREMIUMS If the valuation methodology used is based on price-earnings ratios of comparable public companies and the interest being valued is the entirety of a company, a control premium may be imposed.

DISCOUNT FOR LACK OF MARKETABILITY This discount, also known as the liquidity discount, comes into play in situations where the business owner's ability to readily sell his or her business is questionable. For example, publicly traded companies are highly marketable, and their shares can be quickly turned into cash. Closely held companies, however, are sometimes far more difficult to sell. Depending on the valuation, it may be necessary to subtract a discount for lack of marketability, or add a premium for the presence of marketability.

STANDARD OF VALUE When determining valuation of a company, the standard of value must be clearly defined. That is, it must be clear whether the valuation is based on book value, fair market value, liquidating versus going concern value, investment value, or some other definition of value. Defining the standard of value is important because of adjustments that are necessary under some, but not all, of these standards.

"AS-OF" DATES Valuation methods determine the value of a company at a given point in time. Thus, businesses that undergo a valuation process are said to be worth X dollars ''as of'' a certain date. Values of businesses inevitably change over time, so it is critical to state the date for any valuation. In addition, the information used by the appraiser should be limited to that which would have been available at the as-of date.

FORM OF ORGANIZATION The legal definition of the organization under examination is an important factor in any valuation. Different legal forms of entity—corporations, S corporations, partnerships, and sole proprietorships—are all subject to different tax rules which impact the value of the enterprise being appraised.

FOCUS OF VALUATION The focus of the valuation must be clearly identified. The portion of the business enterprise being acquired, the type(s) of securities involved, the nature of the purchase (asset purchase or stock purchase), and the possible impact of the transaction on existing relationships (such as related party transfers) can all affect the value of the entity under examination.

FURTHER READING:

Buchanan, Doug. ''Business Valuators Must 'Dig Behind the Hype.' '' *Washington Business Journal.* September 15, 2000.

Johansen, John A. *How to Buy or Sell a Business.* Small Business Administration, n.a.

Medaglia, Arthur. ''Corporate Valuation: Is There Room for Improvement?'' *Fordham Business Review.* January 1999.

Semanik, Michael K., and John H. Wade. *The Complete Guide to Selling a Business.* AMACOM, 1994.

Slee, Robert. ''How Much is Your Small Business Worth to a Roll-Up?'' *Triangle Business Journal.* August 20, 1999.

Tuller, Lawrence W. *Getting Out: A Step-by-Step Guide to Selling a Business or Professional Practice.* Liberty Hall, 1990.

''Twelve Ways to Multiply the Value of Your Business.'' *The Business Owner.* May-June 1994.

Yegge, Wilbur M. *A Basic Guide to Buying and Selling a Company.* Wiley, 1996.

SEE ALSO: Selling a Business

VALUE-ADDED TAX

A value-added tax (VAT) is a fee that is assessed against businesses by a government at various points in the production of goods or services—usually any time a product is resold or value is added to it. For tax purposes, value is added whenever the value of a product increases as a result of the application of a company's factors of production, such as labor and equipment. VAT must be paid by every company that handles a product during its transition from raw materials to finished goods. For example, tax is charged when a manufacturer sells to a wholesaler and again when a wholesaler sells to a retailer.

With VAT, the taxable amount is based on the value added at each stage of the process of producing goods and bringing them to market. As an example, say that a company that makes socks buys cotton yarn for $1,000; adds $500 to its value in terms of labor, depreciation of knitting machines, and profits; then sells the completed socks for $1,500. VAT would be calculated as a percentage of the $500 value added by turning cotton yarn into socks. Of course, the sock company would also get credit for the amount of VAT it paid on the purchase of inputs, like cotton yarn.

In general, the total VAT accrued during the production of goods is reflected in the price of items sold to final consumers, because each reseller along the way usually passes along its VAT costs. In this way, VAT is somewhat similar to a national sales tax, and the two forms of taxation are often compared by governments. Experts claim that VAT entails higher administrative costs but is easier to enforce than a national sales tax.

The concept of VAT was first adopted by France in 1954. By 2000, it was used by Canada and 40 other industrialized countries. In most cases, the percentage of tax charged varies based on the necessity of the particular product, so the tax on food would generally be less than the tax on luxury items like boats. In recent years, VAT has been proposed for use in the United States as a way to simplify business and personal income tax laws. Proponents claim that VAT would replace other forms of taxation and reduce the costs of tax compliance. In fact, some people say that adopting VAT would eliminate tax returns for individuals and make the Internal Revenue Service obsolete. On the other hand, opponents argue that VAT would be more complicated to implement than other tax-reform options, such as a national sales tax. They also worry that it would increase the cost of food, medicine, and other necessities, which would hurt the poor.

VAT AND E-COMMERCE

VAT is a common form of taxation in the European Union (EU). In fact, VAT rates are as high as 25 percent in some EU countries. In 2000, a group of these countries proposed implementing a VAT for online businesses. The proposed tax would cover all digital products downloaded over the Internet in member countries, including software, videos, and music. Since the products of electronic retailers were not previously subject to VAT, EU leaders felt that these businesses gained an unfair advantage over domestic, brick-and-mortar retailers. In addition, they argued that the EU nations were being deprived of tax income on goods sold in their countries by what were essentially foreign corporations.

As E-commerce expands in popularity, it may create hardships for some traditional retailers. As these brick-and-mortar businesses earn lower profits and hire fewer employees, they are likely to generate less tax revenue for their governments. If the new Internet competitors were based in the same country, then the tax situation would likely balance out. But the nature of online businesses often means that they can locate anywhere with sufficient technology and telecommunications capacity. Experts predict that increasing numbers of Internet businesses will base their operations in countries where taxes are low. Some low-tax jurisdictions, like Bermuda, have begun to enact favorable laws to attract such businesses. "Thus governments have to face the prospect of permanent flows of taxable profits out of their jurisdictions," Christine Sanderson wrote in *International Tax Review*. "Taking a European view, there is

clearly a potential issue for tax authorities, since E-commerce and Internet development is likely to mean a flow of tax profits away from Europe."

The basic problem facing EU leaders is to determine how to apply VAT laws—which were developed with physical products and traditional retail markets in mind—to new types of goods and services delivered over the Internet. In 2000, representatives of 29 countries got together to develop the Ottawa Framework for dealing with these issues. Although the guidelines have not been finalized, they are expected to bring a higher level of certainty and consistency to the tax situation for E-commerce.

FURTHER READING:

"EU to Consider Internet Tax." *eWeek.* October 23, 2000.

Sanderson, Christine. "EU Forges Ahead on E-Commerce." *International Tax Review.* September 2000.

Tagliabue, John. "From Europe, Creative Taxation." *New York Times.* September 28, 2000.

VARIABLE PAY

Variable pay programs are an increasingly popular mode of compensation in today's business world. These programs, which are also sometimes referred to as "pay-for-performance" or "at-risk" pay plans, provide some or all of a work force's compensation based on employee performance or on the performance of a team. Variable pay proponents contend that providing tangible rewards for superior performance—a true merit system—encourages hard work and efficiency and serves as an effective deterrent to mediocre or otherwise uninspired work performance.

Variable pay programs can take a range of forms, including annual incentives or bonus payments; individual incentive plans; lump-sum payments; technical achievement awards; cash profit-sharing plans; small group incentives; gainsharing; and payments for skill and knowledge. Some analysts disagree about whether some of the above offerings are true variable pay programs, but most agree that all of the above share a common emphasis on recognizing achievement, which is the ultimate goal of variable pay plans. (All agree that standardized merit programs, in which individual performance is a negligible factor in determining compensation changes, do not qualify.) Business experts say that small business owners seeking to increase productivity should consider variable pay as an option, but they are also discouraged from implementing a plan without first engaging in an appropriate examination of current company issues and future company goals. "In establishing merit increase programs or any other cash bonus incentives, companies should keep in mind the type of work force they have, what the competition in their industry is doing, what the company philosophy is—and have a strong plan in place to set company goals and ensure all business units or departments of the organization are clear about the goals,'' wrote Brenda Paik Sunoo in *Personnel Journal.*

Indeed, businesses that adopt variable pay have to recognize the importance of tailoring the program to account for different circumstances. Factors that have to be considered, said Sunoo, include:

- Achievement of business and personal growth goals

- Compensation packages that are available to employees if they decided to look elsewhere for work

- Current level of pay based on salary range relative to skills and experience

- Eligibility of variable pay as an ingredient in total cash compensation

''In a pay-for-performance environment, we expect true differentiation based on these types of factors,'' wrote Sunoo. ''Managing a performance-based salary program requires a strong commitment to goal setting and measurement.''

VARIABLE PAY AND THE MODERN BUSINESS ENVIRONMENT

The growing prevalence of variable pay alternatives in business compensation strategies has been attributed in part to a couple of other business trends. ''Employers are facing up to a new reality about the way jobs should be valued and compensated in an age of rapid technological change,'' wrote Paul J. Williamson in *Small Business Reports.* ''Gone are the days when employees' skills lasted a lifetime and companies could predict the future value of jobs— and thus a fixed pay increase—based on past performance. Today, as customer needs shift rapidly due to advances in technology, the skills you need to make a profit may change almost before the ink is dry on your job descriptions.'' At the same time, business observers point out that increased emphasis on quick reactions to changing competitive conditions have triggered a growth in movement toward employee empowerment. And as employees become more empowered, employers have had to find new ways to compensate them for their contributions to the overall enterprise.

Other analysts of variable pay frame the issue in terms of return on investment (ROI). ''To minimize today's heightened business risk, you must reduce your investment in fixed costs and maximize the use of variable costs, which the company incurs only if it achieves certain results,'' stated Williamson. ''Nowhere is this mandate more essential than in the balance between fixed and variable pay, since compensation often is a company's single largest expense.''

ADVANTAGES AND DRAWBACKS OF VARIABLE PAY

Most criticisms of variable pay can be traced to concerns about the nature, implementation, and execution of such programs rather than the theories upon which they are based. *Inc.*'s Jack Stack, for instance, argued that many companies fail to make variable pay programs meaningful to individual employees, which in turn robs the program of much of its power to facilitate increased productivity. ''Most [variable pay] programs provide no incentive to anyone and never deliver the promised results,'' he charged. ''Why not? Because in 9 cases out of 10, they are not true bonus programs at all. They are simply profit-sharing programs, and there is a world of difference between the two.'' By profit-sharing, I mean the practice of taking a percentage of a company's profits, putting it into a pool, and disbursing it to the company's employees, usually sometime after the close of the year.'' Stack and other analysts contend that such distribution plans are unlikely to encourage employees toward greater productivity because they do not get an adequate sense of how their personal contributions helped generate the business's profits. ''Many of the failures to date [in variable pay plans] have occurred because companies simply reshuffled the same amount of compensation in a new plan, offering some through fixed pay and some through incentives,'' commented Williamson. ''But they didn't use the plan to create reach change in the way they organize and value work.''

But business consultants agree that variable pay programs that truly reward individual performance can be helpful. The purpose of a good bonus program, Stack said, should be ''to make the company stronger, more competitive, able to survive and prosper in the months and years ahead. . . . A good bonus program draws people into that process. It drives the value of the company by educating people, not with formal training programs but through the work they do every day on the job. It gives them the tools they need to make and understand decisions. It provides them with business knowledge they can use to enhance their own standard of living and job security as they're making a measurable difference to the company as a whole.''

ESTABLISHING A VARIABLE PAY SYSTEM

Proponents of variable pay programs contend that implementation of such a system is far more likely to be successful if the following conditions are met:

- Employees must have control over their performance. If employees are overly dependent on the actions and output of other employees or processes, they may have little control over their own performance. Variable pay programs that are not based on principles of employee empowerment are almost certainly doomed to fail.

- Differences in performance must mean something to the business. Employees must see that mediocre and high performances are not rewarded equally, and that results count.

- Business goals must be clearly defined and adequately disseminated to employees, and they should be arrived at with their assistance.

- Performance must be measured regularly and reliably. A clear system of performance appraisal and feedback must be put in place, with regularly scheduled meetings as one component.

- Employers should use variable pay as a tool in reaching ambitious business goals. ''You need targets that require some effort,'' argued Stack. ''I'm not talking about having stretch goals, which are almost always demotivators, but neither should the targets be so easy that people can take them for granted.''

- Businesses should make sure that their variable pay plans reward employees for actions or skills that actually further the aims of the company.

FURTHER READING:

Abosch, Kenan S. ''Variable Pay: Do We Have the Basics in Place?'' *Compensation and Benefits Review.* July/August 1998.

Beatty, L. Kate. ''Pay and Benefits Break Away from Tradition.'' *HRMagazine.* November 1994.

Clark, Amy W. ''Aligning Compensation with Business Strategy.'' *Employment Relations Today.* Winter 1995.

Ganzel, Rebecca. ''What's Wrong with Pay for Performance?'' *Training.* December 1998.

Hay Group. *People, Performance, & Pay: Dynamic Compensation for Changing Organizations.* The Free Press, 1996.

Milkovich, George T., and Alexandra K. Wigdor. *Pay for Performance: Evaluating Performance Appraisal and Merit Pay.* National Academy Press, 1991.

Stack, Jack. ''The Problem with Profit Sharing.'' *Inc.* November 1996.

Sunoo, Brenda Paik. ''Tie Merit Increases to Goal-Setting and Employer Objectives.'' *Personnel Journal.* November 1996.

''Variable Pay Growth in US.'' *Financial Times.* September 22, 1999.

Williams, Valerie L., and Stephen E. Grimaldi. ''A Quick Breakdown of Strategic Pay.'' *Workforce.* December 1999.

Williamson, Paul J. ''How to Shake Up Your Pay.'' *Small Business Reports.* August 1994.

VARIANCE

A variance has several meanings in business. In an accounting sense, a variance is the difference between an actual amount and a pre-determined standard amount. In a statistical sense, a variance is a measure of the amount of spread in a distribution. It is computed as the average squared deviation of each number from its mean.

ACCOUNTING VARIANCES

In accounting, a variance could be a cost variance, where actual costs may be different from the estimated standards for costs. Variances can be favorable or unfavorable. A variance from standard cost is considered favorable if the actual cost is less than the standard cost, and it is considered unfavorable if the actual cost is more than the standard cost. It is also possible to break down the cost variance into the factors that may have caused it to occur—such as a quantity variance, or the difference between the actual quantity and the standard quantity; and a price variance, or the difference between the actual price and the standard price.

When a variance occurs, like the cost variance in this example, top management should examine the circumstances to determine the factors that created it. By doing so, management should be able to identify who or what was responsible for the variance and take steps to correct the problem. For example, assume that the standard material cost for producing 1,000 units of a product is $8,000, but that materials costing $10,000 were actually used. The $2,000 unfavorable variance may have resulted from paying a price for the material that was higher than the standard price. Alternatively, the process may have used a greater quantity of material than standard. Or, there may have been some combination of these factors.

The purchasing department is usually responsible for the price paid for materials. Therefore, if the variance was caused by a price higher than standard, responsibility for explaining the problem rests with the purchasing manager. On the other hand, the production department is usually responsible for the amount of material used. Thus, the production department manager is responsible for explaining the problem if the process used more than the standard amount of materials. However, the production department may have used more than the standard amount of material because its quality did not meet specifications, with the result that more waste was created. Then the purchasing manager is responsible for explaining why the inferior materials were acquired. On the other hand, the production manager is responsible for explaining what happened if the analysis shows that the waste was caused by inefficiencies.

Thus variances—like the cost variance in the example above—trigger questions to be answered within the organization. These questions call for answers that, in turn, should lead to changes designed to correct the problem and minimize or eliminate the variances for the next reporting period. A performance report may identify the existence of the problem, but it can do no more than point the direction for further investigation of what can be done to improve future results. Other common variances in accounting include overhead rate and usage variances.

STATISTICAL VARIANCES

In statistics, a variance is also called the mean squared error. The variance is one of several measures that statisticians use to characterize the dispersion among the measures in a given population. To calculate the variance, it is necessary to first calculate the mean or average of the scores. The next step is to measure the amount that each individual score deviates or is different from the mean. Finally, you square that deviation by multiplying the number by itself. Numerically the variance equals the average of the squared deviations from the mean.

FURTHER READING:

Hunter, Katharine. "Variances: The Three-Step Method." *Accountancy*. January 1995.

Larson, K.D. *Fundamental Accounting Principles*. 14th ed. McGraw-Hill, 1997.

Yeldon, Elizabeth. "Variances—Words and Numbers." *Accountancy*. April 1999.

VENTURE CAPITAL

Venture capital refers to funds that are invested in an unproven business venture. Venture capital may be provided by wealthy individual investors, professionally managed investment funds, government-backed Small Business Investment Corporations (SBICs), or subsidiaries of investment banking firms, insurance companies, or corporations. Such venture capital organizations generally invest in private startup companies with a high profit potential. In exchange for their funds, venture capital organizations usually require a percentage of equity ownership of the company, some measure of control over its strategic planning, and payment of assorted fees. Due to the highly speculative nature of their investments, venture capital organizations expect a high rate of return. In addition, they often wish to obtain this return over a relatively short period of time, usually within three to seven years. After this time, the equity is either sold back to the client company or offered on a public stock exchange.

Venture capital is somewhat more difficult for a small business to obtain than other sources of financing, such as bank loans and supplier credit. Before providing venture capital to a new or growing business, venture capital organizations require a formal proposal and conduct a thorough evaluation. Even then, they tend to approve only a small percentage of the proposals they receive. Perhaps the most important thing an entrepreneur can do to increase his or her chances of obtaining venture capital is to plan ahead.

Venture capital offers several advantages to small businesses, including management assistance and lower costs over the short term. In addition, venture capital is more likely to be available to startup or concept businesses than other forms of financing. The disadvantages associated with venture capital include the possible loss of effective control over the business and relatively high costs over the long term. Overall, experts suggest that entrepreneurs should consider venture capital to be one financing strategy among many, and should seek to combine it with debt financing if possible.

THE EVALUATION PROCESS

Since it is often difficult to evaluate the earnings potential of new business ideas or very young companies, and investments in such companies are unprotected against business failures, venture capital is a highly risky industry. As a result, venture capital firms set rigorous policies and requirements for the types of proposals they will even consider. Some venture capitalists specialize in certain technologies, industries, or geographic areas, for example, while others require a certain size of investment. The maturity of the company may also be a factor. While most venture capital firms require their client companies to have some operating history, a small number handle startup financing for businesses that have a well-considered plan and an experienced management group.

In general, venture capitalists are most interested in supporting companies with low current valuations, but with good opportunities to achieve future profits in the range of 30 percent annually. Most attractive are innovative companies in rapidly accelerating industries with few competitors. Ideally, the company and its product or service will have some unique, marketable feature to distinguish it from imitators. Most venture capital firms look for investment opportunities in the $250,000 to $2 million range, although some are willing to consider smaller or larger projects. Since venture capitalists become part owners of the companies in which they invest, they tend to look for businesses that can increase sales and generate strong profits with the help of a capital infusion. Because of the risk involved, they hope to obtain a return of three to five times their initial investment within five years.

Venture capital organizations typically reject the vast majority—90 percent or more—of proposals quickly because they are deemed a poor fit with the firm's priorities and policies. They then investigate the remaining 10 percent of the proposals very carefully and at considerable expense. Whereas banks tend to focus on companies' past performance when evaluating them for loans, venture capital firms tend to focus instead on their future potential. As a result, venture capital organizations will examine the features of a small business's product, the size of its markets, and its projected earnings.

As part of the detailed investigation, a venture capital organization may hire consultants to evaluate highly technical products. They also may contact a company's customers and suppliers in order to obtain information about the market size and the company's competitive position. Many venture capitalists will also hire an auditor to confirm the financial position of the company, and an attorney to check the legal form and registration of the business. Perhaps the most important factor in a venture capital organization's evaluation of a small business as a potential investment is the background and competence of the small business's management. Hosmer noted that ''many venture capital firms really invest in management capability'' rather than a small business's product or market potential. Since the abilities of management are often difficult to assess, it is likely that a representative of the venture capital organization would spend a week or two at the company. Ideally, venture capitalists like to see a committed management team with experience in the industry. Another plus is a complete management group with clearly defined responsibilities in specific functional areas, such as product design, marketing, and finance.

VENTURE CAPITAL PROPOSALS

In order to best ensure that a proposal will be seriously considered by venture capital organizations, an entrepreneur should furnish several basic elements. After beginning with a statement of purpose and objectives, the proposal should outline the financing arrangements requested, i.e., how much money the small business needs, how the money will be used, and how the financing will be structured. The next section should feature the small business's marketing plans, from the characteristics of the market and the competition to specific plans for getting and keeping market share.

A good venture capital proposal will also include a history of the company, its major products and services, its banking relationships and financial milestones, and its hiring practices and employee relations. In addition, the proposal should include complete financial statements for the previous few years, as well as pro forma projections for the next three to five years. The financial information should detail the small business's capitalization—i.e., provide a list of shareholders and bank loans—and show the effect of the proposed project on its capital structure. The proposal should also include biographies of the key players involved with the small business, as well as contact information for its principal suppliers and customers. Finally, the entrepreneur should outline the advantages of the proposal—including any special and unique features it may offer—as well as any problems that are anticipated.

If, after careful investigation and analysis, a venture capital organization should decide to invest in a small business, it then prepares its own proposal. The venture capital firm's proposal would detail how much money it would provide, the amount of stock it would expect the small business to surrender in exchange, and the protective covenants it would require as part of the agreement. The venture capital organization's proposal is presented to the management of the small business, and then a final agreement is negotiated between the two parties. Principal areas of negotiation include valuation, ownership, control, annual charges, and final objectives.

The valuation of the small business and the entrepreneur's stake in it is very important, as it determines the amount of equity that is required in exchange for the venture capital. When the present financial value of the entrepreneur's contribution is relatively low compared to that made by the venture capitalists—for example, when it consists only of an idea for a new product—then a large percentage of equity is generally required. On the other hand, when the valuation of a small business is relatively high—for example, when it is already a successful company—then a small percentage of equity is generally required. Hosmer warns that entrepreneurs are likely to find that the valuation of their businesses provided by a venture capital organization will not be as high as they would like.

The percentage of equity ownership required by a venture capital firm can range from 10 percent to 80 percent, depending on the amount of capital provided and the anticipated return. But most venture capital organizations want to secure equity in the 30-40 percent range so that the small business owners still have an incentive to grow the business. Since venture capital is in effect an investment in a small business's management team, the venture capitalists usually want to leave management with some control. In general, venture capital organizations have little or no interest in assuming day-to-day operational control of the small businesses in which they invest. They have neither the technical expertise or managerial personnel to do so. But venture capitalists usually do want to place a representative on each small business's board of directors in order to participate in strategic decision-making.

Many venture capital agreements include an annual charge, typically 2-3 percent of the amount of capital provided, although some firms instead opt to take a cut of profits above a certain level. Venture capital organizations also frequently include protective covenants in their agreements. These covenants usually give the venture capitalists the ability to appoint new officers and assume control of the small business in case of severe financial, operating, or marketing problems. Such control is intended to enable the venture capital organization to recover some of its investment if the small business should fail.

The final objectives of a venture capital agreement relate to the means and time frame in which the venture capitalists will earn a return on their investment. In most cases, the return takes the form of capital gains earned when the venture capital organization sells its equity holdings back to the small business or on a public stock exchange. Another option is for the venture capital firm to arrange for the small business to merge with a larger company. The majority of venture capital arrangements include an equity position, along with a final objective that involves the venture capitalist selling that position. For this reason, entrepreneurs considering using venture capital as a source of financing need to consider the impact a future stock sale will have on their own holdings and their personal ambition to run the company. Ideally, the entrepreneur and the venture capital organization can reach an agreement that will help the small business grow enough to provide the venture capitalists with a good return on their investment as well as to overcome the owner's loss of equity.

THE IMPORTANCE OF PLANNING

Although there is no way for a small business to guarantee that it will be able to obtain venture capital, sound planning can at least improve the chances that its proposal will receive due consideration from a venture capital organization. Such planning should begin at least a year before the entrepreneur first seeks financing. At this point, it is important to do market research to determine the need for a new business concept or product idea and establish patent or trade secret protection, if possible. In addition, the entrepreneur should take steps to form a business around the product or concept, enlisting the assistance of third-party professionals like attorneys, accountants, and financial advisors as needed.

Six months prior to seeking venture capital, the entrepreneur should prepare a detailed business plan, complete with financial projections, and begin working on a formal request for funds. Three months in advance, the entrepreneur should investigate venture capital organizations to identify those that are most likely to be interested in the proposal and to provide a suitable venture capital agreement. The best investor candidates will closely match the company's development stage, size, industry, and financing needs. It is also important to gather information about a venture capitalist's reputation, track record in the industry, and liquidity to ensure a productive working relationship.

One of the most important steps in the planning process is preparing detailed financial plans. Hosmer claimed that strong financial planning demonstrates managerial competence and suggests an advantage to potential investors. A financial plan should include cash budgets—prepared monthly and projected for a year ahead—that enable the company to anticipate fluctuations in short-term cash levels and the need for short-term borrowing. A financial plan should also include pro forma income statements and balance sheets projected for up to three years ahead. By showing expected sales revenues and expenses, assets and liabilities, these statements help the company to anticipate financial results and plan for intermediate-term financing needs. Finally, the financial plan should include an analysis of capital investments made by the company in products, processes, or markets, along with a study of the company's sources of capital. These plans, prepared for five years ahead, assist the company in anticipating the financial consequences of strategic shifts and in planning for long-term financing needs.

Overall, experts warn that it takes time and persistence for entrepreneurs to obtain venture capital. But venture capital is becoming more widely available than ever before because of the strong American economy, rising trends of private investment, and the rapid emergence of new technology in areas such as the Internet, telecommunications, and health care. Finally, another trend in the industry involves foreign venture capital. Under this arrangement, overseas companies provide financing to small U.S. firms in exchange for royalties, a percentage of profits, a license for technology, or overseas sales agreements. Basically, these foreign companies try to form strategic partnerships with young American companies that are producing things needed in overseas markets.

FURTHER READING:

Bartlett, Joseph W. *Fundamentals of Venture Capital.* Madison, 1999.

Clark, Scott. "Business Plan Basics: Who Most New Ventures Fail to Raise Capital." *Houston Business Journal.* March 17, 2000.

Evanson, David R. "Venture Capital, Networks Proliferate." *Nation's Business.* September 1996.

Geer, John F., Jr. "The Venture Capital Boom: It's Gold Medal Time for the Venture Capitalists." *Financial World.* November 18, 1996.

Hamilton, Brian. *Financing for the Small Business.* Washington, D.C.: U.S. Small Business Administration, 1990.

Hosmer, LaRue T. *A Venture Capital Primer for Small Business.* Washington, D.C.: U.S. Small Business Administration, 1990.

Parmar, Simon, J. Kevin Bright, and E.F. Peter Newson. "Building a Winning E-Business." *Ivey Business Journal.* November 2000.

Schilit, W. Keith. *The Entrepreneur's Guide to Preparing a Winning Business Plan and Raising Venture Capital.* Prentice Hall, 1990.

Taylor, Charlotte. "Cash from Investors." *Executive Female.* July-August 1997.

SEE ALSO: Angel Investors

VENTURE CAPITAL NETWORKS

Venture capital networks, or clubs, are groups of individual and institutional investors that provide financing to risky, unproven business ventures. Like other providers of venture capital—which may include professionally managed investment funds, government-backed Small Business Investment Corporations (SBICs), or subsidiaries of investment banking firms, insurance companies, and corporations—members of these networks generally invest in private startup companies with a high profit potential. In exchange for their funds, the venture capitalists usually require a percentage of equity ownership of the company, some measure of control over its strategic planning, and payment of assorted fees. Due to the highly speculative nature of their investments, venture capitalists hope to achieve a high rate of return over a relatively short period of time.

The main difference between venture capital networks and other venture capital providers is their degree of formality. Venture capital networks are informal organizations that exist to help entrepreneurs and small businesses connect with potential investors. Before the advent of networks, it was extremely difficult for entrepreneurs to gain access to wealthy private investors, also known as "angels" or "adventure capitalists." The networks—which may take the form of computer databases or document clearinghouses—basically provide "matchmaking" services between people with good business ideas and people with money to invest. In contrast, formal venture capital firms are professionally managed organizations that exist to earn a high return on funds by investing in new and growing companies. These firms are typically highly selective about the companies in which they invest, meaning that venture capital from these sources is not available to the vast majority of startup businesses.

According to *Nation's Business,* wealthy private investors provided American small businesses with $10 to $20 billion annually during the mid-1990s, an amount that easily outdistanced the investments of traditional venture capital partnerships. The membership of venture capital networks consists primarily of wealthy entrepreneurs who recognize both the financial potential of new businesses and the importance of capital in the early stages of a business's life. In many cases, these investors wind up sitting on the boards of the companies they fund, where they can provide valuable, firsthand management advice based on their own experiences.

HOW NETWORKS WORK

In the past, it was extremely difficult for entrepreneurs to find and make contact with private investors. In response to this problem, many business groups and universities created networks to help entrepreneurs gain access to interested investors. One of the earliest such efforts was the Venture Capital Network, a computer database that was established by a professor at the University of New Hampshire. This and other computerized networks are similar to computer matchmaking services. Each entrepreneur posts a business plan and a set of financial projections on the network, while each investor submits information describing his or her interests and investment criteria. Due to their previous business experience, different investors may be most interested in investing in companies of a certain size, in a certain industry, or with certain capital requirements. The computer then provides participants with a list of possible matches. Interested parties are left to make contact with one another and try to reach an agreement.

Non-computerized venture capital networks operate in basically the same way. A central clearinghouse solicits business plans from companies seeking capital, then distributes profiles of the companies to private investors who belong to the network. If a certain investor wants to know more about a particular company, he or she might arrange for a formal presentation. In many cases, both business and investor profiles are distributed anonymously—without names attached—until both parties express an interest in proceeding further. Another similar type of arrangement can be found in a private investment club. These are community-based organizations in which several individuals pool their resources to invest in new and existing businesses on a local level. Such clubs generally solicit business plans and then distribute them to members, but then invest as a group.

The financing provided through venture capital networks can range dramatically in size from investments of $25,000 to more than $1 million (the majority of financing deals are under $100,000). Entrepreneurs searching for venture capital assistance usually pay a small fee to participate in a network—typically less than $500 annually—and institutional investors may pay a somewhat higher fee. Although venture capital networks are usually better sources of funding for startup companies than formal venture capital firms, merely joining a network does not guarantee that a small business will obtain financing. There are usually at least two companies for every one investor listed in databases. In addition, even if a match is made, the entrepreneur still must sell the investor on the proposal and negotiate a mutually beneficial agreement.

FURTHER READING:

Bartlett, Joseph W. *Fundamentals of Venture Capital.* Madison, 1999.

Brown, Carolyn R. ''Matchmaking for Venture Capital: Database Networks Can Help Your Business Connect with Willing Investors.'' *Black Enterprise.* June 1994.

Evanson, David R. ''Venture Capital, Networks Proliferate.'' *Nation's Business.* September 1996.

Geer, John F., Jr. ''The Venture Capital Boom: It's Gold Medal Time for the Venture Capitalists.'' *Financial World.* November 18, 1996.

Schilit, W. Keith. *The Entrepreneur's Guide to Preparing a Winning Business Plan and Raising Venture Capital.* Englewood Cliffs, NJ: Prentice Hall, 1990.

VERTICAL MARKETING SYSTEM

A vertical marketing system (VMS) is one in which the main members of a distribution channel—producer, wholesaler, and retailer—work together as a unified group in order to meet consumer needs. In conventional marketing systems, producers, wholesalers, and retailers are separate businesses that are all trying to maximize their profits. When the effort of one channel member to maximize profits comes at the expense of other members, conflicts can arise that reduce profits for the entire channel. To address this problem, more and more companies are forming vertical marketing systems.

Vertical marketing systems can take several forms. In a corporate VMS, one member of the distribution channel owns the other members. Although they are owned jointly, each company in the chain continues to perform a separate task. In an administered VMS, one member of the channel is large and powerful enough to coordinate the activities of the other members without an ownership stake. Finally, a contractual VMS consists of independent firms joined together by contract for their mutual benefit. One type of contractual VMS is a retailer cooperative, in which a group of retailers buy from a jointly owned wholesaler. Another type of contractual VMS is a franchise organization, in which a producer licenses a wholesaler to distribute its products.

The concept behind vertical marketing systems is similar to vertical integration. In vertical integration, a company expands its operations by assuming the activities of the next link in the chain of distribution. For example, an auto parts supplier might practice forward integration by purchasing a retail outlet to sell its products. Similarly, the auto parts supplier might practice backward integration by purchasing a steel plant to obtain the raw materials needed to manufacture its products. Vertical marketing should not be confused with horizontal marketing, in which members at the same level in a channel of distribution band together in strategic alliances or joint ventures to exploit a new marketing opportunity.

As Tom Egelhoff wrote in an online article entitled ''How to Use Vertical Marketing Systems,'' VMS holds both advantages and disadvantages for small businesses. The main advantage of VMS is that your company can control all of the elements of producing and selling a product. In this way, you are able to see the whole picture, anticipate problems, make changes as they become necessary, and thus increase your efficiency. However, being involved in all stages of distribution can make it difficult for a small business owner to keep track of what is happening. In addition, the arrangement can fail if the personalities of the different areas do not fit together well.

For small business owners interested in forming a VMS, Egelhoff recommended starting out by developing close relationships with suppliers and distributors. ''What suppliers or distributors would you buy if you had the money? These are the ones to work with and form a strong relationship,'' he stated. ''Vertical marketing can give many companies a major advantage over their competitors.''

FURTHER READING:

Baker, Sunny, and Kim Baker. ''Going Up! Vertical Marketing on the Web.'' *Journal of Business Strategy.* May 2000.

Egelhoff, Tom. ''How to Use Vertical Marketing Systems.'' http://www.smalltownmarketing.com.

Mullich, Joe. "Vertical Segmentation Gets More Emphasis." *Advertising Age.* June 10, 1996.

VIRTUAL PRIVATE NETWORKS

Virtual private networks (VPNs) are systems that use public networks to carry private information. Some of the earliest examples of virtual private networks were developed in the 1980s by phone companies and included business voice services. The voice VPNs provided a multitude of features, such as teleconferencing, toll-free numbers, private numbering plans, and call management. With the growth of the Internet, the definition of virtual private networks has started to expand. The emergence of information sharing technologies like local area networks (LANs) has allowed Internet service providers (ISPs) and information technology (IT) managers to get in on the action. Equipment and software manufacturers also have a hand in reshaping the future of virtual private networks.

Now, many companies are using the Internet and turning to virtual private networks to cut down on costs and increase performance and security. VPNs can connect remote users and other off-site users (such as vendors or customers) to a larger centralized network. In previous years, this was an expensive venture that required large equipment and maintenance costs for the extra servers and private lines that virtual private networks required. Mounting phone charges were also a financial concern. This is no longer an issue because ISPs are a lot more affordable (usually a flat monthly fee) than long-distance and toll-free services. This fact, along with the universal appeal of the Internet, has revolutionized thinking and made VPN technology more accessible and financially viable for large corporations and small businesses alike. The result is remote access that is quicker, more secure, and wider in scope.

THE COST OF VIRTUAL PRIVATE NETWORKS

When a company decides to transfer from a remote access server to a virtual private network, it should first and foremost consider the financial impact of the decision. If there is an opportunity to save money, then VPNs should definitely be considered an option.

One of the main cost concerns hinges on whether the virtual private network will be housed on site or outsourced to an independent service provider. When a business decides to use an outside provider, it is immediately eliminating any costs for purchasing and maintaining the necessary equipment. The most the business will have to do is maintain security measures (usually a firewall) as well as provide the servers that will help authenticate users. Of course, this too can be done by an outside provider for an additional price. Outsourcing also cuts down on the number of employees that would be required to manage and maintain the virtual private network.

Today, there are a greater number of providers who help companies service their virtual private networks than ever before. This has forced many of the providers to be more competitive and therefore develop the communication and management skills necessary to keep their customers happy. This in turn has led to better all around service for the companies who decide to outsource their VPNs.

There are several disadvantages to outsourcing virtual private networks. There is an obvious loss of control when an outside provider is running things. Remote users that are in different cities, states, or even countries may also experience difficulty dialing in to the VPN. Several roaming services are available to help eliminate this problem, but they can often be costly solutions.

If a business decides to run a virtual private network in house, it is looking at larger startup costs upfront because the proper equipment must be purchased and a trained staff must be hired to maintain it. The advantage is that once this is done, the company has more control over features like authentication and access. A large corporation may find this more beneficial than a small business because it may already have the staff in place to take on such a project. Still, the potential for retraining the staff to properly operate the VPN exists, and this is another cost that should be considered.

VIRTUAL PRIVATE NETWORKS AND SECURITY

Virtual private network systems are constantly evolving and becoming more secure through four main features: tunneling, authentication, encryption, and access control. These features work separately, but combine to deliver a higher level of security while at the same time allowing all users (including those from remote locations) to access the VPN more easily.

Tunneling is what creates the connection between a user (either from a remote location or separate office) to the main LAN. This connection is called a tunnel and is essentially the circuit-like path that transfers private information through the Internet (which is a public forum). This requires a corporate address to be programmed into the dial-up network to ensure privacy.

To avoid crowded connections, a tunneling feature called "switching" was developed. This feature helps differentiate between direct and remote users to determine which connections should receive the highest priority. The switching can either be programmed directly into the virtual private network or upgraded so that the hardware recognizes each connection on an individual basis.

Incoming callers to the virtual private network are identified and approved for access through features called authentication and access control. These features are usually set up by the IT manager who enters a user's individual identification code or password into the main server, which cuts down on the chances that the network can manipulated from outside the company. Authentication also offers the chance to regulate access to the material on the LAN so that select users can only view certain information.

Encryption is the security measure that allows information on a virtual private network to be scrambled so that it becomes meaningless to unauthorized users. Encrypted data is eventually unscrambled at the end of the tunnel by a user with the proper authorization. This process is usually done via a private IP address that encrypts the information before it leaves the LAN or a remote location.

Despite these precautions, some companies are still hesitant to transfer highly sensitive and private information over the Internet via a virtual private network and still resort to tried and true methods of communication for such data.

THE PERFORMANCE OF VIRTUAL PRIVATE NETWORKS

The latest wave of virtual private networks feature self-contained hardware solutions (whereas previously they were little more than software solutions and upgrades to existing LAN equipment). Since they are now self-contained, this VPN hardware does not require an additional connection to a network and therefore cuts down on the use of a file server and LAN, which makes everything run a bit more smoothly. These new VPNs are small and easy to set up and use, but still contain all of the necessary security and performance features.

In order for a virtual private network to perform properly, the server must have enough bandwidth to accommodate the number of users (which usually grows over time). The number of remote users can also affect a VPN's performance. In addition, new technology that requires more bandwidth is bound to come out from time to time, and this should be planned for in advance to avoid a potential disruption in performance. Many virtual private network service providers are able to relegate more bandwidth as it is needed to keep up with their customers' needs.

High volumes of traffic are also known to adversely affect the performance of a virtual private network, as is encrypted data. Since encryption technology is often added on via software, this often causes the network to slow down, therefore hindering performance. A more desirable solution is to incorporate encryption technology that uses hardware solutions to keep the network running at the proper speed. New technologies are also constantly emerging that help to decide just how sensitive certain material is (and therefore how intensive the encryption needs to be).

THE FUTURE OF VIRTUAL PRIVATE NETWORKS

As virtual private networks continue to evolve, so do the number of outlets that can host them. Several providers have experimented with running VPNs over cable television networks. This solution offers high bandwidth and low costs, but less security. Other experts see wireless technology as the future of virtual private networks. While bandwidth is the critical issue here, the evolution of the mobile work force could create significant changes in the VPN market. Users who wish to take advantage of the added convenience that would likely be provided by wireless VPNs could increase the demand in this area. Still, wireless virtual private networks will probably not take off until technology is developed that is both convenient and reliable.

VIRTUAL PRIVATE NETWORKS AND SMALL BUSINESSES

The growing number of options as well as solutions that are more affordable make virtual private network technology that much more attractive to small business owners. Some VPN software is even available on a trial basis so that businesses can find the solution that works best for them. Another option would be ISPs and NSPs (network service providers), which are also starting to provide more VPN services at better rates.

Still, virtual private networks do not always eliminate the need to maintain a company's remote access system. Toll-free-number services should be kept as backups to an ISP in case it is determined that they a better fit either financially or performance-wise for the company and its users.

FURTHER READING:

Binsacca, Rich. "Virtual Private Networks." *Builder*. June 2000.

Hayes, Jim. "Managed Data Services." *Communicate.* July 2000.

Kosiur, Dave. "VPN Buyers Need to Make the Right Call." *PC Week.* December 14, 1998.

VIRUS

A virus is a program designed to infect and potentially damage files on a computer that receives it. The code for a virus is hidden within an existing program—such as a word processing or spreadsheet program—and when that program is launched, the virus inserts copies of itself into other programs on the system to infect them as well. Because of this ability to reproduce itself, a virus can quickly spread to other programs, including the computer's operating system. A virus may be resident on a system for a period of time before taking any action detectable to the user. The impact of other viruses may be felt immediately. Some viruses causes little or no damage. For example, a virus may manifest itself as nothing more than a message that appears on the screen at certain intervals. Other viruses are much more destructive and can result in lost or corrupted files and data. At their worst, viruses may render a computer unusable, necessitating the reinstallation of the operating system and applications.

Viruses are written to target program files and macros, or a computer's boot sector, which is the portion of the hard drive that executes the steps necessary to start the hardware and software. Program viruses attach themselves to the executable files associated with software programs, and can then attack any file that is used to launch an application, usually files ending with the "exe" or "com" extensions. Macro viruses infect program templates that are used to create documents or spreadsheets. Once infected, every document or spreadsheet opened with the infected program becomes corrupted. Boot sector viruses attack the computer's hard drive and launch themselves each time the user boots, or starts, the computer. Viruses are often classified as Trojan Horses or Worms. A Trojan Horse virus is one that appears harmless on the surface but, in reality, destroys files or programs. A Worm attacks the computer's operating system and replicates itself again and again, until the system eventually crashes.

VIRUSES AND THE INTERNET

The Internet, with its global reach and rapid delivery times, provides the ideal breeding ground for viruses. Typically, someone who wants to spread a virus does so by sending out an email message containing an infected attachment. The subject line on such a message sounds innocuous, so unsuspecting recipients open the message, unwittingly infecting their computers.

An email message was used to spread the so-called Love Bug virus in 2000. The most destructive virus to date, it targeted users of Microsoft's Outlook email program. Originating in the Philippines, the Love Bug message's subject line was the inviting "ILOVEYOU." If a user opened the message's attachment, the virus quickly began to destroy files, targeting digital pictures and music files. The Love Bug virus also perpetuated itself by forwarding the original message to all email addresses listed in the current recipient's Outlook address book. In this way, the virus was able to circle the globe in just two hours. The virus brought businesses to a standstill as companies, large and small, were forced to shut off incoming Internet email messages and repair infected systems. In all, the Love Bug virus is estimated to have cost up to $10 billion in lost work hours.

VIRUS PROTECTION

With an estimated 40,000 viruses already identified and some 300 new viruses created each month, keeping a computer free of viruses is a daunting but not impossible task. The following are steps every computer user should follow to protect his or her computer from viruses.

1) Install an anti-virus software program to identify and remove viruses before they can cause any damage. These programs scan, or review, files that may come from floppy diskettes, the Internet, email attachments, or networks, looking for patterns of code that match patterns in the anti-virus software vendor's database of known viruses. Once detected, the software isolates and removes the virus before it can be activated.

2) Because the number of viruses is increasing all the time, it is important to keep anti-virus software up to date with information on newly identified viruses. Anti-virus software vendors are constantly updating their databases of information on viruses and making this information available to their customers via their web sites or email.

3) Do not open email from unknown recipients or messages that contain unexpected attachments. A user should delete these types of messages. As a general rule, a user should scan every email attachment for viruses before opening it—even an expected attachment—as the sender may have unknowingly sent an infected file.

FURTHER READING:

''Attack of the Love Bug.'' *Time*. Mary 15, 2000.

Cavanah, Cassandra. ''Bug Off! Protect Against Invaders with Antivirus Software.'' *Entrepreneur*. November 1998.

Freedman, Alan. *Computer Desktop Encyclopedia*. The Computer Language Company Inc., 1996.

Goldberg, Cheryl J. ''Safety Net: Does Using the Internet Put Your Business at Risk?'' *Entrepreneur*. September 1996.

SEE ALSO: Internet Security

W

WARRANTIES

A product or service warranty (also known as a guarantee) is an assurance of performance and reliability given to the purchaser of a product or service by the company that provides that product or service. Such warranties have become standard practice in most U.S. industries, although opinions vary somewhat regarding their impact on sales. But misleading language in these guarantees has the capacity to spark significant legal troubles for small businesses that run afoul, however inadvertently, of legal guidelines. As the magazine *Profit-Building Strategies for Business Owners* noted, ''consumers and business buyers alike can ask the courts to enforce warranties, whether they're express, implied, written, verbal, or given any other way. So be careful not to overstate your case. In addition to a printed warranty, watch your ads and brochures and keep tabs on your salespeople.'' Most warranties are covered by local, state and federal laws. The Federal Trade Commission (FTC) is the ultimate arbiter of warranty law in the United States. The FTC's primary tool in monitoring product and service guarantees is the Magnuson-Moss Consumer Warranty Act.

ELEMENTS OF A WARRANTY

The Federal Trade Commission requires that written warranties bestowed in connection with the sale of a product or service explicitly detail the following information:

- Who is covered by the warranty
- Length of warranty
- Description of the products, parts, properties, or characteristics covered by or excluded from the warranty
- Steps for customer in the event that warranty coverage comes into play
- Warrantor's response when confronted with product/service malfunctions, defects, or failures
- Any exclusions of or limitations on relief such as incidental or consequential damages
- Statement that indicates that some states do not allow such exclusions or limitations
- Statement of consumer legal rights
- Any limitations on the length of implied warranties, if possible

FULL AND LIMITED WARRANTIES

The Magnuson-Moss Act does not require businesses to provide warranties to customers. Indeed, some business owners decide that written warranties are not even necessary to enjoy success in their chosen field of endeavor. But other manufacturers and retailers are convinced that warranties help sell their products, pointing to the popularity of service contracts and the like.

Businesses that choose to provide written warranties may choose from two types: full and limited. FTC regulations concerning full warranties are considerably more stringent than those that apply to limited warranties. According to the Magnuson-Moss Act, ''fully guaranteed'' products or services must meet the following five criteria:

- Customer receives full money back or replacement or repair of any defective part of product in the event of a complaint

- Prompt and free repairs

- If repairs are not fully satisfactory to the buyer, a prompt refund is available

- Customer has no responsibility beyond reporting the defect to the company

- Acknowledgment of all implied warranties

"If you're reading to stand by those assurances," said *Profit-Building Strategies for Business Owners,* " 'fully guaranteed' accurately describes your conditions of sale. But if your policy falls short in any way, you can be penalized for making that claim when you're really making a 'limited warranty.' " Limited warranties, which must be prominently labeled as such, limit the liability of the manufacturer or service provider. A limited warranty may offer to replace defective parts for free, but only for a limited length of time, or require that the consumer ship the product to a manufacturer-approved service center. The distinctions between full and limited warranties and the obligations of manufacturers to honor them vary from state to state, so it is up to the consumer to carefully read the literature and understand what is covered before the purchase.

EXPRESS AND IMPLIED WARRANTIES

"Express warranties arise from statements you make about a product or service, from a picture, sample, or brochure, while implied warranties arise by automatic operation of law," wrote Marc J. Lane in the *Legal Handbook for Small Business.* "Although the Magnuson-Moss Consumer Warranty Act supersedes state laws regarding express warranties in the sale of products, it does not supersede the Uniform Commercial Code (UCC) provisions on implied warranties or state laws applicable to express warranties in the sale of services." The provisions of the UCC, which cover all products, basically stipulate that products should look like they do in advertisements, and perform as they do in demonstrations, so express warranties vary in accordance with the nature of the advertising campaign launched on behalf of that product or service

In addition, states require that the manufacturer or seller of a product offer an implied warranty— some sort of guarantee that the product will work as advertised once it is out of the box and that it will work under ordinary circumstances in the manner that its manufacturer says it will. This implied warranty is known as the "implied warranty of merchantability." A second implied warranty—known as the "warranty of fitness for a particular purpose"—is described by *Profit-Building Strategies for Business Owners* as a warranty that "provides assurance that your product will do the job buyers have in mind, assuming they've explained their purposes to you. . . . Your degree of vulnerability to legal claims depends in part on how clearly buyers explain what they want and in part on who they are. If you're a supplier of institutional dinnerware, your customers are expected to have enough knowledge and sophistication to judge fitness of purpose for themselves. They'd need a strong case to prove you sold them the wrong dishes for their needs. But regular customers can't be expected to know much about various kinds of dinnerware, or even the right questions to ask. So with them you're more accountable." The length of time that these implied warranties are in effect varies from state to state.

DISCLAIMERS Vulnerability to express and/or implied warranties can be lessened somewhat through the use of disclaimers. "A disclaimer may wholly deny that you are making one or more express or implied warranties, or it may limit warranty coverages," wrote Lane. "In the absence of a disclaimer, a breach of warranty will usually give a purchaser of the item the right to recover the cost of the item together with any additional damages caused by that breach."

Small business consultants note that warranties—both express and implied—can be negotiated with buyers, but they urge business owners to use specific language when adding such disclaimers to a sales contract. The term "exclusive remedy," for instance, can give a seller of products or services significant legal protection when it is used to explicitly limit a buyer's legal options in the event of complaints about product defects or workmanship. "But take care also to see that the buyer receives genuine protection," noted *Profit-Building Strategies for Business Owners.* "If your customer is left in the end without a working product, you can be sued no matter what agreement you signed, on the grounds that it's a remedy that 'fails of its essential purpose.' " Obviously, the obligations imposed by law in the areas of warranty are extensive, so small business owners should make sure that they consult a legal expert so that they can develop the most effective disclaimer possible.

EXTENDED WARRANTIES

Extended warranties are somewhat controversial, but often profitable, warranty packages offered by manufacturers and service providers. Manufacturers sell these warranties, which are basically extensions of basic warranty packages, in hopes that the extended warranty will not be needed or used, thereby resulting in profits. Consumers buy them for peace of mind, reasoning that they are protecting their initial outlay of money. The controversy revolves around what the warranties cover. Some extended warranties are actually service agreements, resulting in higher charges than might be expected under a warranty. In other cases the fine print in the warranties exclude the very things that the consumer assumes would be covered.

FURTHER READING:

Hollis, Aidan. ''Extended Warranties, Adverse Selection, and Aftermarkets.'' *Journal of Risk and Insurance.* September 1999.

Lane, Marc J. *Legal Handbook for Small Business.* AMACOM, 1989.

Lewis, Jeff. ''Extended Warranties Help Pay the Bill.'' *HFN: The Weekly Newspaper for the Home Furnishing Network.* April 27, 1998.

Pratt, Eddy. ''Will the Digital Surge Bring Happier Times for Extended Warranties?'' *ERMagazine.* August 2000.

''What You Promise the Buyer When You Warranty Your Product.'' *Profit-Building Strategies for Business Owners.* January 1992.

WEB SITE DESIGN

Web site design is the process of creating a site, or homepage, on the World Wide Web, which is one part of the international series of computer networks collectively known as the Internet. Computer users use a software program known as a web browser to visit those homepages, each of which has a distinct address and can consist of text, graphics, audio, video, and animation. For businesses, these Web sites are virtual ''storefronts'' that enable companies to sell products and services to customers and clients around the world at a relatively small price.

The most common way that small companies establish a presence on the Web is by setting up a simple homepage that provides potential customers with information on the company and its products. The essentially limitless storage space of the computer network means that businesses are free to post as much information as they wish about themselves—computerized versions of brochures and press releases; product catalogs, complete with photos; a company overview; news and notes related to the industry the company serves; and contact and technical support information. This makes it easy for consumers to locate information about the company 24 hours a day.

Business Web sites also provide visitors with the means to order goods and services electronically. With direct online purchasing, customers identify an item they wish to purchase from the company, fill out an order form and provide their credit card number, and then transmit that information electronically to the company. The product is then shipped directly to the customer. The advantages to this method of selling are obvious. Instead of being restricted to a local market, even the smallest company can now reach users around the world. Customers can locate information about the company or order a product 24 hours a day. Customers with questions can now find very specific information about a company's products or services.

HOW TO DESIGN A WEB PAGE

When designing a Web page, certain information should always be included:

- Basic Company Information—This can include vision or mission statements, a history of the business, a summary of business philosophy, etc. The key is to sell the customer on the company.

- Product Line Information—Commercial Web pages should include photos and text descriptions outlining the benefits of the products. Features, applications, and examples can also be highlighted. Consultants often recommend that businesses establish separate pages or sections for each major product line—connected, of course, to the main company Web site.

- Technical support—Frequently asked questions, parts information, product diagrams, and technical specifications are just some of the ways a company can provide support from its Web site.

- Ordering information—Companies should include an electronic mail or hardcopy form with instructions on how to order a product.

- Service section—Free information that is of interest to potential customers, designed to keep them coming back to the site. Industry news and trends are good examples of this kind of information, which is a feature of increasing numbers of business-oriented sites.

- ''What's New''—This section is essentially intended to inform visitors of new initiatives, products, etc., that are covered on the Web site.

Once you decide what to put on your homepage, it is time to actually create the site. Web pages are written using a language called the Hypertext Markup Language. HTML, as it is more commonly known, is a series of tags and codes that instruct a Web browser on how the text on that page should be displayed. Once a page has been written using HTML, the page must be placed on the host computer, or server, of an Internet provider. HTML can be created using any common word processing package or via any one of the proliferating HTML editor software packages available in the marketplace.

One of the most important features of HTML is the "hypertext" feature. This means that text can be highlighted on a Web page so that when a customer clicks on a word or an image, a link to a new page on that site (or even another site altogether) is called up on the computer screen. This allows customers to move freely on a site and allows for design creativity and flexibility.

Learning the basics of HTML coding is not difficult, and an ambitious business owner who has the time and the initiative may create his or her own homepage from scratch. However, as the Web has continued to grow, pages have become far more sophisticated in appearance, convincing some businesses to outsource the design and creation of the site to firms that specialize in providing such services.

Small business owners should also recognize that the development of a Web site does not constitute an ironclad guarantee of e-commerce success. "It takes a lot of market support [to maintain a site]," said Dawn Dayton of the Michigan Small Business Development Center in *Entrepreneur* magazine. "If you put up a site and nobody knows [about it], it's not going to do you any good." Web design firms will make sure people know about your site by advertising it in other Internet locations and by registering the site with the dozens of Internet directory services that exist.

Another trap that snares some small businesses is the flawed Web site. Company e-sites with errors in content, structure, or navigation have the capacity to plunge businesses far behind their competitors and obliterate painstaking calculations of return on investment. "Making changes to a Web site once it's finished can be a costly and painful experience," warned Lisa Schmeiser in *Macworld*. "But you can avoid this scenario by first creating and testing a prototype of your site—a scaled-down working model of the finished product. A prototype lets you get a first look at what users will see as they click through your site, and it can expose unforeseen flaws in your structure and navigation. This gives you a chance to fix glitches before they send your site—and your reputation—up in flames."

Whether you choose to create your company's Web site yourself or outsource it, the expense of creating a basic informational site is relatively modest. Small business owners should also keep several other cost factors in mind when weighing an entrance onto the Web, however. For instance, businesses who do not serve as their own Web server are required to pay a monthly charge to a professional Internet hosting firm. Some companies choose to serve as their own host for control and security reasons, but others prefer to enlist a professional hosting firm, which can provide technical support and e-commerce experience at a relatively modest price (hosting fees vary from $10 to $100 a month).

Once the site is on a host computer, users from around the world can then access the homepage, which is given an address that is unique to the entire Web. That address is one part of naming your site. The chosen name can be secured through a domain provider, if the company chooses to go the in-house route. Otherwise, the contracted outside server will purchase the domain name.

POSITIONING AND MAINTAINING A BUSINESS HOMEPAGE

Sites can be freestanding, or they can be a part of a larger online "mall." Hundreds of retail malls have opened on the Web, some more successful than others. Before choosing an Internet provider to store your homepage, do some research on popular online malls and see where your company might best fit in. Visit the sites yourself, and see what you like and do not like. This research step can be an essential component of Internet success for companies, because location can be just as important on the Web as it is in real life.

Even after your Web site has been successfully launched and is up and running, the work does not end. The site needs to be updated on a regular basis to ensure continued content integrity. Areas to monitor include:

- Price changes
- Product changes
- Adding pages to describe other parts of your business
- Adding new links and eliminating obsolete links
- Updating images
- Overhauling the entire site when it becomes tired looking

Once again, you will have to decide if you want to undertake the updating yourself or if you want to hire a firm to handle the work for you.

FURTHER READING:

Dickman, Steven. "Catching Customers on the Web ." *Inc.* Summer 1995.

"How to Build Your Firm's Web Site." *Baltimore Business Journal.* March 23, 2001.

McCarthy, Paul. "Small Firms Can Succeed in the E-Business Game." *Computer Weekly.* November 30, 2000.

Neelakatan, Shailaja. "We Do Web Work." *Forbes.* Jan. 27, 1997.

Niederst, Jennifer. *Web Site Design in a Nutshell: A Desktop Quick Reference.* O'Reilly, 1998.

Page, Heather. ''Tech Smarts.'' *Entrepreneur.* June 1997.

Reynolds, Janice, and Roya Mofazali. *The Complete E-Commerce Book: Design, Build and Maintain a Successful Web-Based Business.* CMP Books, 2000.

Schmeiser, Lisa. ''Test Drive Your Web Site.'' *Macworld.* May 2001.

SEE ALSO: HTML; Internet Domain Name; Search Engine

WHOLESALING

Wholesaling is the selling of merchandise to anyone—either a person or an organization—other than the end consumer of that merchandise. Wholesalers, who are sometimes referred to as middle agents, represent one of the links in the chain along which most goods pass on their way to the marketplace. As intermediaries between producers and consumers of goods, wholesalers facilitate the transport, preparation of quantity, storage, and sale of articles ultimately destined for customers. Wholesalers are extremely important in a variety of industries, including such diverse product areas as automobiles, grocery products, plumbing supplies, electrical supplies, and raw farm produce. They are particularly vital to the operations of small retailers. Whereas large retail companies buy directly from the manufacturer and often have their own intermediate warehousing operations, the limited resources of independent retail outlets makes alliances with wholesalers a practical necessity.

Strictly speaking, although a wholesaler may own or control retail operations, wholesalers do not sell to end-customers. Indeed, many wholesale operations are themselves owned by retailers or manufacturers. Even in these instances, however, the enterprise's wholesaling branch exists to facilitate the movement of goods from one area to a market demand in another area. Wholesaling provides manufacturers with an expanded consumer market potential in terms of geographical locations and consumer purchasing power while at the same time providing a cash flow for the manufacturer.

Wholesalers are successful only if they are able to serve the needs of their customers, who may be retailers or other wholesalers. Some of the marketing functions provided by wholesalers to their buyers include:

- Provide producer's goods in an appropriate quantity for resale by buyers.

- Provide wider geographical access and diversity in obtaining goods.

- Ensure and maintain a quality dimension with the goods that are being obtained and resold.

- Provide cost-effectiveness by reducing the number of producer contacts needed.

- Provide ready access to a supply of goods.

- Assemble and arrange goods of a compatible nature from a number of producers for resale.

- Minimize buyer transportation costs by buying goods in larger quantities and distributing them in smaller amounts for resale.

- Work with producers to understand and appreciate consumerism in their production process.

TYPES OF WHOLESALERS

Although there are a number of ways to classify wholesalers, the categories used by the Census of Wholesale Trade are employed most often. The three types of wholesalers are 1) merchant wholesalers; 2) agents, brokers, and commission merchants; and 3) manufacturers' sales branches and offices.

MERCHANT WHOLESALERS Merchant wholesalers are firms engaged primarily in buying, taking title to, storing, and physically handling products in relatively large quantities and reselling the products in smaller quantities to retailers; industrial, commercial, or institutional concerns; and other wholesalers. These types of wholesaling agents are known by several different names, including wholesaler, jobber, distributor, industrial distributor, supply house, assembler, importer, and exporter, depending on their services.

According to E. Jerome McCarthy and William D. Perreault Jr., authors of *Basic Marketing,* merchant wholesalers account for the large majority of wholesaling establishments and wholesale sales. ''As you might guess based on the large number of merchant wholesalers, they often specialize by certain types of products or customers,'' added McCarthy and Perreault. ''They also tend to service relatively small geographic areas.... Merchant wholesalers also differ in how many of the wholesaling functions they provide. There are two basic kinds of merchant wholesalers: 1) service (sometimes called full-service wholesalers) and 2) limited-function or limited-service wholesalers.'' The latter category of wholesalers, which itself is divided up into little niches, offer varying levels of service in such areas as product delivery, credit bestowal, inventory storage, provision of market or advisory information, and sales.

AGENTS, BROKERS, AND COMMISSION MERCHANTS Agents, brokers, and commission merchants are also independent middlemen who do not (for the most part) take title to the goods in which they deal, but instead are actively involved in negotiating and other functions of buying and selling while acting on behalf of their clients (commission merchants typically are limited to agricultural goods). They are usually compensated in the form of commissions on sales or purchases. Agents, brokers, and commission merchants usually represent the non-competing products of a number of manufacturers to several retailers. This category of wholesaler is particularly popular with producers with limited capital who can not afford to maintain their own sales forces.

MANUFACTURERS' SALES BRANCHES AND OFFICES Manufacturers' sales branches and offices are owned and operated by manufacturers but are physically separated from manufacturing plants. They are used primarily for the purpose of distributing the manufacturers' own products at the wholesale level. Some have warehousing facilities where inventories are maintained, while others are merely sales offices. Some of them also wholesale allied and supplementary products purchased from other manufacturers.

THE CHANGING LANDSCAPE OF WHOLESALING

The future of wholesaling appears somewhat ambiguous. One major force affecting wholesaler activity is growth in the power of retail chain stores. The continued mergers and acquisitions taking place between similar regional chains since 1970 means that independent retailers will have a lesser need for wholesalers. The emergence of the Internet as a sales tool has also impacted wholesalers, many of whom are struggling to adopt profitable methodologies that make use of this new medium. Another negative factor has been an increased emphasis, on the part of both manufacturers and end users, on cutting distribution costs. However, there is a countervailing force at work in that retailing is becoming increasingly fragmented as more and more specialized retailers cater to specialized market niches. As this specialization continues, using wholesalers becomes the most cost-efficient way for manufacturers to cover fragmented retailer market segments. The wholesaler is able to bundle several manufacturers' items into combinations that can all be sold through the specialist outlet. In most cases, wholesalers will capitalize on market opportunities among specialized, independent retailers while they lose ground to chains buying directly from manufacturers. Many wholesalers have adapted nicely by becoming efficient importers, upgrading their operations with computers, improving inventory handling, and automating their warehouses.

KEYS TO SUCCESSFUL WHOLESALING

Industry observers contend that for many wholesalers, the ultimate key to success will be an ability to establish closer alliances with retail specialists that offer solid, long-term growth prospects or concentrate on merchandise categories where chains still must use wholesalers because of needed buying efficiencies. ''Most wholesalers are busy changing quickly to offer much more to their retailers than the assembly and conveyance of products,'' wrote David Merrefield in *Supermarket News.* ''Most are mobilizing groups of independent retailers into virtual chains of stores that use a common banner and hew to uniform standards. . . . Wholesalers must actively collect sales data from affiliated retailers to aggregate and make it known to manufacturers. Wholesalers must also make known to their retailer affiliates that the retailers are partners with their wholesaler, their vendors, and even their fellow retailers, all of whom must join the quest for overall low-cost operation.''

In addition to establishing good working relationships with independent retailers, wholesalers can also take several other steps to give them the best chance of surviving—and even thriving—in today's competitive marketplace. These include smart, customer-oriented marketing programs, superior customer service, efficient operations management processes, and innovative business strategies for expanding into new product lines, industries, or geographic territories. ''Error-free management of a wholesale operation is impossible,'' admitted the editors of *How to Run a Small Business,* ''due to the wide variety of items that most wholesalers handle, and the many imponderables (such as delays in shipments from vendors, unforeseeable spurts in consumer demands, and even the vagaries of weather) that wholesalers are subject to. But all wholesalers have the same problems. What distinguishes successful wholesalers is how well they manage the variables under their control.''

FURTHER READING:

J.K. Lasser Institute. *How To Run a Small Business.* McGraw-Hill, 1994.

Matthews, Ryan. ''Zen and the Art of Wholesaling.'' *Progressive Grocer.* January 1996.

McCarthy, E. Jerome, and William D. Perreault, Jr. *Basic Marketing: A Managerial Approach.* Irwin, 1990.

Merrefield, David. ''Wholesaling's Future: Product or Support?'' *Supermarket News.* March 10, 1997.

''Wholesaling.'' *Do-It-Yourself Retailing.* November 2000.

WIDE AREA NETWORKS (WANS)

A wide area network (WAN) is a telecommunications network, usually used for connecting computers, that spans a wide geographical area. WANs can by used to connect cities, states, or even countries. WANs are often used by larger corporations or organizations to facilitate the exchange of data, and in a wide variety of industries, corporations with facilities at multiple locations have embraced WANs. Increasingly, however, even small businesses are utilizing WANs as a way of increasing their communications capabilities.

Although WANs serve a purpose similar to that of local area networks (LANs), WANs are structured and operated quite differently. The user of a WAN usually does not own the communications lines that connect the remote computer systems; instead, the user subscribes to a service through a telecommunications provider. Unlike LANs, WANs typically do not link individual computers, but rather are used to link LANs. WANs also transmit data at slower speeds than LANs. WANs are also structurally similar to metropolitan area networks (MANs), but provide communications links for distances greater than 50 kilometers.

WANs have existed for decades, but new technologies, services, and applications have developed over the years to dramatically increase their efficacy for business. WANs were originally developed for digital leased-line services carrying only voice, rather than data. As such, they connected the private branch exchanges (PBXs) of remote offices of the same company. WANs are still used for voice services, but today they are used more frequently for data and image transmission (such as video conferencing). These added applications have spurred significant growth in WAN usage, primarily because of the surge in LAN connections to the wider networks.

HOW WANS WORK

WANs are either point-to-point, involving a direct connection between two sites, or operate across packet-switched networks, in which data is transmitted in packets over shared circuits. Point-to-point WAN service may involve either analog dial-up lines, in which a modem is used to connect the computer to the telephone line, or dedicated leased digital telephone lines, also known as ''private lines.'' Analog lines, which may be either part of a public-switched telephone network or leased lines, are suitable for batch data transmissions, such as nonurgent order entry and point-of-sale transactions. Dedicated digital phone lines permit uninterrupted, secure data transmission at fixed costs.

Point-to-point WAN service providers include both local telephone companies and long distance carriers. Packet-switched network services are typically chosen by organizations which have low volumes of data or numerous sites, for which multiple dedicated lines would be too expensive.

Depending on the service, WANs can be used for almost any data sharing purpose for which LANs can be used. Slower transmission speeds, however, may make some applications less practical for WANs. The most basic uses of WANs are for electronic mail and file transfer, but WANs can also permit users at remote sites to access and enter data on a central site's database, such as instantaneously updating accounting records. New types of network-based software that facilitate productivity and production tracking, such as groupware and work-flow automation software, can also be used over WANs. Using groupware, workers at dispersed locations can more easily collaborate on projects. WANs also give remote offices access to a central office's other data communications services, including the Internet.

FURTHER READING:

Chappell, Laura A., and Roger L. Spicer. *Novell's Guide to Multiprotocol Internetworking.* Novell Press, 1994.

Pecar, Joseph A., Roger J. O'Connor, and David A. Garbin. *The McGraw-Hill Telecommunications Factbook.* McGraw-Hill, 1993.

Sharp, Duane E. ''Wide Area Networks: The Key to Enterprise Productivity.'' *Canadian Manager.* Summer 1996.

SEE ALSO: Local Area Networks

WOMEN ENTREPRENEURS

According to the National Association of Women Business Owners, there were 6.5 million women entrepreneurs in the United States in the late 1990s. In addition, many analysts predict that more than 50 percent of all self-employed people in the United States will be women in the first years of the twenty-first century. These statistics reflect a sea change in American conceptions of gender roles and abilities over the past half-century.

Women have owned and operated businesses for decades, but they were rarely recognized or given credit for their efforts. Often women entrepreneurs were ''invisible'' as they worked side by side with their husbands, and many only stepped into leadership positions when their husbands died. But a variety of factors have combined in recent years to contribute to the visibility and numbers of women who start their own businesses. As more women joined the work force, for example, they gained the professional and managerial skills and experience they would need as entrepreneurs. In addition, many women felt as if they were discriminated against in large companies, which provided them with an incentive to be their own bosses. Some women also have found entrepreneurship to be an ideal way to juggle the competing demands of career and family, while some single mothers have started businesses as a way out of poverty.

Although the small businesses owned by women have traditionally focused on fashion, food, and other service sectors, in recent years women entrepreneurs have been moving rapidly into manufacturing, construction, and other industrial fields. Women business owners still face greater difficulties in gaining access to commercial credit and bidding on government contracts than do their male colleagues, and pockets of resistance to women entrepreneurs remain strong in some industries and geographic regions. But millions of successful businesses launched and managed by women now dot America's business landscape, each a testament to the legitimacy of the aspirations and talents of the woman entrepreneur.

REASONS WOMEN BECOME ENTREPRENEURS

Many studies indicate that women start businesses for fundamentally different reasons than their male counterparts. While men start businesses primarily for growth opportunities and profit potential, women most often found businesses in order to meet personal goals, such as gaining feelings of achievement and accomplishment. In many instances, women consider financial success as an external confirmation of their ability rather than as a primary goal or motivation to start a business, although millions of women entrepreneurs will grant that financial profitability is important in its own right.

Women also tend to start businesses about ten years later then men, on average. Motherhood, lack of management experience, and traditional socialization have all been cited as reasons for delayed entry into entreprneurial careers. In fact, over 30 percent of women entrepreneurs reported that they started a business due to some traumatic event, such as divorce, discrimination due to pregnancy or the corporate glass ceiling, the health of a family member, or economic reasons such as a layoff. But a new talent pool of women entrepreneurs is forming today, as more women opt to leave corporate America to chart their own destinies. Many of these women have developed financial expertise and bring experience in manufacturing or nontraditional fields. As a result, the concentration of women business owners in the retail and service sectors—and in traditional industries such as cosmetics, food, fashion, and personal care—is slowly changing.

PROBLEMS FACED BY WOMEN ENTREPRENEURS

One of the main problems facing women entrepreneurs is obtaining financing. In the early 1990s, study after study confirmed that women business owners did not receive equal treatment at financial institutions. Over one half of women business owners believed that they faced gender discrimination when dealing with a loan officer. And 67 percent of women business owners reported difficulty in working with financial institutions. But this figure had declined by 15 percent by 1997, according to a study conducted by the National Association of Women Business Owners (NAWBO). "There's been improvement on both sides," said Julie Weeks, research director for NAWBO. "Not only have women business owners become more savvy about these matters and boast businesses that are more stable and mature, but the banking community has experienced an awakening. They've made tremendous efforts to reach out to women business owners and have taken a proactive role in making the relationship better."

Part of the improvement can be attributed to the success of the Small Business Administration's Women's Prequalification Pilot Loan Program. Introduced in 1994 and expanded nationwide in 1997, the program helps women seeking loans of under $250,000 to complete their loan applications, and also provides an SBA guarantee for repayment of their loans. Women are prequalified based on their character, credit rating, and ability to repay the loan from future business earnings, rather than on collateral. The prequalification statement from the SBA enables the women to obtain funding much more readily.

Another area in which women business owners have been historically shortchanged is procurement, or the selling of their goods and services to city, state, and federal governments. In the past, fewer than 5 percent of the women-owned firms in the United States were certified to do business with their state government and only 1.5 percent of the billions of dollars in federal contracts went to women-owned firms. Some efforts have been undertaken to rectify this situation. If a company is 51 percent owned and controlled by a woman, it can obtain certification and bid on government contracts. In addition, many government agencies at the state and federal levels have created set-aside programs which specifically help women-owned businesses in the bidding process. Nonetheless, the percentage of government contracts going to women-owned firms remained a meager 2.5 percent as recently as 2000.

RESOURCES

A number of resources now exist to support women entrepreneurs. In 1988, Congress authorized the Small Business Administration Office of Women's Business Ownership, which created a "Low-Doc" loan program which makes it easier for women entrepreneurs to obtain SBA financing. The SBA also has established a Women's Network for Entrepreneurial Training (WNET) which links women mentors with protegees. Small Business Development Centers (SBDC) are also co-sponsored by the SBA and operate in every state. They offer free and confidential counseling to anyone interested in starting a small business. In addition, many states now have a Women's Business Advocate to promote women entrepreneurs within the state. These advocates are represented by an organization, the National Association of Women Business Advocates.

A number of trade associations also represent women entrepreneurs. The National Association of Women Business Owners is the largest group throughout the country. There are also some smaller regional groups, which can be located through the Yellow Pages or local chambers of commerce. The American Business Women's Association provides leadership, networking, and educational support. The National Association of Female Executives makes women aware of the need to plan for career and financial success. As women-owned businesses continue to create jobs and become an increasingly important factor in the American economy, the resources to support them will continue to grow as well.

FURTHER READING:

Duff, Carolyn. *When Women Work Together.* Conari Press, 1993.

Eckert, Toby. "Female-Owned Firms Growing at Fast Clip." *Indianapolis Business Journal.* September 16, 1996.

Godfrey, Joline. *Our Wildest Dreams.* Harper Business, 1992.

Maitland, Alison. "From Female Upstarts to Start-Ups: Women Entrepreneurs." *Financial Times.* October 19, 2000.

Pinson, Linda, and Jerry Jinnett. *Women Entrepreneurs, 33 Personal Stories of Success.* Upstart Publishing, 1992.

Silver, A. David. *Enterprising Women.* Amacom, 1994.

Zuckerman, Laurie. *On Your Own: A Women's Guide to Building a Business.* Upstart Publishing, 1990.

WORK FOR HIRE

Work for hire is a concept of intellectual property protection outlined in Section 101 of the 1976 Copyright Act. In most cases, the person who creates a copyrightable work—such as a story, poem, song, sculpture, graphic design, or computer program—holds the copyright for that work. A copyright is a form of legal protection which gives the holder sole rights to exploit the work for financial gain for a certain period of time, usually 35 years. In contrast, the copyright for a work for hire is owned by the company that hires the person to create the work or pays for the development of the work. The creator holds no rights to a work for hire under the law. Instead, the employer is solely entitled to exploit the work and profit from it. The concept of work for hire is different from the creator transferring ownership of a copyrightable work, because the latter arrangement allows the creator to reacquire rights to the work after the copyright period expires.

There are two main categories of copyrightable materials that can be considered works for hire. One category encompasses works that are prepared by employees within the scope of their employment. For example, if a software engineer employed by Microsoft writes a computer program, it is considered a work for hire and the company owns the program. The second category includes works created by independent contractors that are specially commissioned by a company. In order to be considered works for hire, such works must fall into a category specifically covered by the law, and the two parties must expressly agree in a contract that it is a work made for hire.

"If you show up to a job where somebody tells you what to do and when to do it, and for that you're rewarded with a paycheck, then your work product is classified as a work for hire and you don't own the copyright on it. Instead, it automatically becomes copyrighted in the name of the company," Michael Bertin explained in the *Austin Chronicle*. In the situation of independent contractors, he added, "There are two criteria for works for hire. It has to fit into one of nine specific categories, and there has to be a contract stipulating that it's a 'work for hire.' If one of those two elements is missing, then the work in question is not, repeat not, a work for hire."

The nine categories of materials eligible to be considered works for hire, as outlined in the Copyright Act, include works commissioned for use as: a contribution to a collective work; a part of a motion picture or other audiovisual work or sound recording; a translation; a supplementary work; a compilation; an instructional text; a test; answer material for a test; or an atlas.

Work for hire arrangements affect small businesses in a variety of ways. For example, a small business that hires a Web page design firm to create a company site must make certain that the contract stipulates that the design is a work made for hire. Otherwise, the company may find that it does not hold copyright to various elements of its own Web page, and the design firm may decide to use those elements in pages created for other clients. On the other hand, entrepreneurs who do occasional work for large companies as independent contractors will want to be careful signing work for hire contracts. A consultant who develops a framework for problem solving under contract with one client may be unable to use that framework with any other clients if it was developed under a work for hire arrangement.

FURTHER READING:

Bertin, Michael. ''Mastering Intellectual Property Rights: Work for Hire.'' *Austin Chronicle.* August 25, 2000.

Fishman, Stephen. *The Copyright Handbook: How to Protect and Use Written Works.* Nolo Press, 2000.

Halpern, Sheldon W., Craig Allen Nard, and Kenneth L. Port. *Fundamentals of United States Intellectual Property Law: Copyright, Patent, and Trademark.* Kluwer, 1999.

SEE ALSO: Copyrights; Intellectual Property

WORKERS' COMPENSATION

Workers' compensation is a mandatory type of business insurance that provides employees who become injured or ill while on the job with medical coverage and income replacement. It also protects companies from being sued by employees for the workplace conditions that caused such an injury or illness.

Businesses are required by law in all fifty states to pay for the medical treatment and lost wages of employees who suffer job-related injuries or illnesses. In order to avoid crippling expenses in this regard, companies purchase workers' compensation insurance policies of one kind or another. Most states give businesses the choice of buying workers compensation policies either directly from the state or from a private insurer. Each state determines its own system's payment schedules, employee eligibility requirements, and rehabilitation procedures. Although provisions of each state's laws differ greatly, the underlying principle is the same—that employers should assume the costs of injuries, illnesses, and deaths that occur on the job, without regard to fault, and partially replace wage income lost. While income replacement under workers' compensation is usually a percentage of the actual wage, it is counted as a transfer payment and thus is not subject to federal income tax. Some state laws exempt certain categories of employees from coverage. Those most likely to be excluded are domestics, agricultural workers, and manual laborers.

Given the mandatory nature of workers' compensation coverage and the potential expense involved, the cost of workers' compensation insurance policies is a huge concern for small business owners. In fact, workers' compensation premiums stand as most companies' second largest operating expense, after payroll. These rates are based on the employer's total payroll, the classification of the employees (the relative riskiness of their work activities), and the employer's accident record.

Small business owners have less control over the cost of workers' compensation coverage than they do over health insurance costs. State legislatures set the level of benefits and employers pay the full cost, so medical cost-containment strategies like co-payments do not apply. Some insurers avoid handling workers' compensation policies for small businesses because they feel that smaller companies lack the funds to provide a safe working environment. In general, the rates depend upon the type of business, number of employees, and company safety record.

Penalties for failing to carry workers comp insurance policies can be severe. In general, business owners who are neglectful in this manner can be held liable for the medical expenses incurred by the worker in their employ. Nonetheless, many businesses engage in what is known as ''premium fraud,'' in which they either do not carry policies or lower the costs of their policy premiums through fraudulent recordkeeping (underreporting their employee count or the wages they pay them, paying workers under the table in order to falsify the number of employees they have, misclassifying the kind of work engaged in by employees in order to reduce premiums, etc.). However, momentum is building to beef up penalties for these kinds of fraudulent actions, which injure insurers and honest employers alike. ''Honest employers pick up . . . additional costs [of fraud committed by other companies] in the form of higher premiums,'' noted Rebekah Young in *Washington Monthly.* ''But even if honest employers are able to pass along the costs of their higher premiums, that doesn't mean they aren't adversely affected by premium fraud. For example, honest construction companies lose out on projects to premium fraud-committing companies because they are underbid by these crooked companies, which have lower overhead costs thanks to their lower premium costs.''

TYPES OF COVERAGE AVAILABLE

There are three basic methods available for employers to obtain the required workers' compensation protection: state insurance funds, private insurance, and self-insurance through insurance pools. The latter option—which involves setting aside funds in anticipation of workers' compensation claims, rather than purchasing insurance—is seen as a cost-saving method for safety-oriented firms. In the states that permit it, many large employers now self-insure, and many small businesses form groups to insure themselves and decrease the risks.

In *Employee Benefits for Small Business,* Jane White and Bruce Pyenson tout group self-insurance plans as a good option for small businesses with better-than-average workplace safety records. Such plans work best when the companies involved are in the same or similar industries, so that their level of risk is roughly equivalent. The companies can then join together to purchase stop-loss coverage to protect themselves against claims over a certain amount. Though self-insurance can be less expensive than private workers' compensation policies, small businesses should make sure that they have the financial resources to withstand potential losses.

Small businesses can explore a variety of other measures to reduce their workers' compensation premiums as well. These include:

Select the right insurer. Business owners seeking workers' comp insurance policies should seek out insurers with proactive claims adjusting policies. In addition, *Occupational Hazards* contributor Shawn Adams counsels companies to give preference to insurers who assign specific adjusters for accounts. "[When] claims are . . . handled on a file basis . . . your account is handled by whatever adjuster happens to be assigned the file for your claim. An assigned adjuster is one who can take responsibility for your account, as opposed to having different adjusters handle different claims against your policy but not coordinating the claims in a comprehensive manner."

Pay attention to your own claims trends. Businesses should take steps to monitor all aspects of their work safety record and insurance coverage, and ensure that all subcontractors carry workers' comp coverage.

Adopt policies and programs to reduce exposure to workers' comp claims. Companies can reduce premiums by minimizing the number of claims made by their workforce. This requires the implementation of safety programs in such areas as materials handling and ergonomics. "Few companies know how to prevent workers' compensation claims, or how affordable and effective ergonomic training can be in preventing such claims," wrote Mary Murray in *Occupational Hazards.* "Businesses don't know that ergonomic training and redesign can almost entirely be paid for with 'found' dollars that otherwise would be wasted in overfeeding their workers' compensation policy."

FURTHER READING:

Adams, Shawn. "Risk Management Methods to Reduce Your Workers' Compensation Rates." *Occupational Hazards.* March 2001.

Blakely, Stephen. "Costly Numbers in Workers' Comp." *Nation's Business.* September 1997.

Blakely, Stephen. "Finding Coverage for Small Offices." *Nation's Business.* June 1997.

Lynn, Jacquelyn. "A Quick Guide to Insurance." *Entrepreneur.* June 1997.

Murray, Mary. "Dispelling the Myths of Workers' Compensation." *Occupational Hazards.* August 1998.

White, Jane, and Bruce Pyenson. *Employee Benefits for Small Business.* Prentice-Hall, 1991.

Young, Rebekah. "Cheap Tricks." *Washington Monthly.* September 1998.

WORKPLACE ANGER

Workplace anger and hostility often manifests itself in ways that have received a great deal of attention from business owners, researchers, legislators, and members of the business press in recent years. Workplace violence and sexual harassment are probably the two best known examples of workplace anger and hostility. But anger and hostility can manifest themselves in other less dramatic ways that can nonetheless have a tremendously negative impact on a business by producing an environment marked by poor or nonexistent communication, lousy morale, excessive employee absenteeism or turnover, and a host of other undesired conditions. Business owners, managers, and employees who are unable to control their own anger or effectively respond to the angry outbursts of others will likely find that their business and/or career suffers as a result. "Organizations which fail to recognize and deal effectively with this problem will suffer as a result," wrote Andrea Adams in *Personnel Management.* "They may be in breach of their legal duty to ensure their employees' health, safety and welfare, or guilty of unlawful discrimination, or open to a claim of constructive dismissal. Their costs will rise because of poor morale and productivity, higher absenteeism and staff turnover. They will find it difficult to attract new staff, and in extreme cases the damage to their image or reputation will mean loss of business."

Of course, not all small businesses that utilize employees are confronted with the challenge of addressing and correcting problem workers who behave in an angry or hostile manner toward coworkers or customers. Many enterprises feature a positive work environment and employ staff that enjoy their jobs and relate to one another in a professional manner. But most small business owners that have a payroll will eventually encounter someone who exhibits angry or hostile behavior and looms as a potential threat to the financial and/or spiritual health of the organization. ''One of the more obvious conditions in the workplace is that people, in their roles as employees, are distinguished by their vast differences,'' wrote Joseph D. Levesque, author of *The Human Resource Problem-Solver's Handbook.* ''They come to us in all forms, divergent experiences and backgrounds, and in remarkably unique psychological makeup. Some are quite stable in their values, lifestyles, reasoning, actions, and direction. Others may be self-serving, deceptive, rebellious, or in many other ways problematic.''

Entrepreneurs, then, need to prepare themselves for the day when an employee's actions or words seem to be based on feelings of anger or hostility. Some small business owners underestimate the impact that workplace anger and hostility can have on their business and on their staff, and they do so at their peril. ''One nasty crack that receives minimal attention from management can get half your work force stewing, not only creating low morale and an unpleasant work environment, but also severely cutting productivity,'' wrote Robert McGarvey in *Entrepreneur.*

Small business owners should be aware that failure to address workplace hostilities can also open them up to legal liability. Moreover, the person who engages in hostile workplace behavior does not have to be an owner or supervisor for the business owner to be vulnerable to charges concerning that person's behavior, because in the eyes of the law, business owners have the power and obligation to control their employees.

CAUSES OF WORKPLACE ANGER AND HOSTILITY

Workplace hostility can often be traced to attitudes that have little to do with the current employment situation in which workers find themselves. Deep-seated feelings of hostility toward other people because of their gender, skin color, sexual orientation, political beliefs, or other factors are often firmly in place long before the person begins working at your company. Often, the small business owner faced with such an employee will have limited options available to deal with such problems; instead, he or she will concentrate efforts on making sure that those undesired attitudes do not disrupt the workplace.

Factors that cause workplace anger, on the other hand, can sometimes be addressed directly. While workplace anger sometimes can be traced back to prejudices that are at the root of deep-seated hostility, on many other occasions, work-oriented factors serve as the primary catalysts. Common causes of workplace anger include:

- General harassment, whether sexual or some other form.
- Favoritism of one employee over another.
- Rejection (whether arbitrary or for good reason) of a proposal or project in which employee has big emotional investment.
- Insensitivity by owners or managers.
- Criticisms of employees in front of staff or clients.
- Depersonalized workplace environment.
- Unfair (or tardy) performance appraisals or criticism.
- Lack of resources for the employee to meet his/her objectives.
- Inadequate training.
- Lack of teamwork.
- Withdrawal of earned benefits.
- Betrayal of trust extended to manager or owner.
- Unreasonable demands on employees.
- Does not keep promises.
- Lack of flexibility on part of owner or manager.
- Poor communication.
- Feedback is wholly or primarily negative in tone.
- Absentee leadership (such as instances wherein needed disciplinary action is absent).
- Micromanagerial environment in which staff decisionmaking opportunities are limited.

Of course, sometimes a distinction must be made between legitimate and illegitimate catalysts of workplace anger. For example, an employee may express great anger over a negative performance review even though the appraisal was conducted fairly and honestly. Small business owners and managers cannot jettison basic principles of management simply to avoid making one of their employees angry.

WARNING SIGNS Workplace anger is often sublimated by employees until they reach a point where they suddenly burst. This ''bursting'' point may manifest itself in a variety of ways. One employee may just yell at his manager, while another may impetuously decide to quit. Still others may resort to workplace violence or vandalism. Small business owners and managers should acquaint themselves with the warning signs of hidden anger so that they can address the causes for that anger and hopefully head off an incident before it occurs. Other employees, meanwhile, may exhibit behavior that is more obviously troubling. Following are a range of behaviors that may signal a need for intervention:

- Sarcastic, irritable, or moody behavior
- Apathetic and/or inconsistent work performance
- Prone to making direct or veiled threats
- Aggressive and antisocial behavior
- Overreaction to company policies or performance appraisals
- Touchy relationships with other workers
- Obsessive involvement and/or emotional attachment to job

"BULLYING" Explicit workplace violence, sexual harassment, and episodes of discrimination garner the most headlines and receive the bulk of attention from consultants because of their potential legal impact on business enterprises. But researchers contend that simple bullying behavior may be a greater threat to business health and productivity than any of the above-mentioned problems. Sometimes bullying takes place between employees, but it often is most evident in supervisor-worker relationships, in which one person is perceived to wield greater power. "Bullying is not just the problem of an individual, however, but, where it exists, of the organization and its culture as a whole," stated Andrea Adams in *Personnel Management*. "Whether it is a bully's persistent intimidation or their devious efforts to make a colleague appear professionally incompetent, these menacing tactics can be difficult to identify." She also notes that organization bullying is often disguised by euphemisms that avoid calling the behavior what it really is. "In America employee abuse, as it is called, is also referred to as 'workplace trauma,' " wrote Adams. "It has been identified in research carried out by one psychologist in the USA as a more crippling and devastating problem for both staff and employers than all the other work-related stresses put together. There are always those who will put forward the argument that the making of snide remarks or jokes at other people's expense is 'a part of human nature,' but office banter which is not really designed to offend is undoubtedly different to the persistent downgrading of people by any individual in a position of power."

Adams noted that confronting bullies about their behavior is often difficult: "Where bullying exists and someone is willing to tackle it, the bully will have to be addressed in some way and prevailed on to change. The way in which they see themselves will rarely tally with the view of those who are placed under attack." Small business owners and managers, however,

should stand fast. Bullying behavior generally does not take place in a vacuum; other employees are usually aware of the situation, and they should be consulted. Finally, owners seeking to eliminate bullying behavior need to make it clear that anyone who is the victim of bullying tactics will receive their full support.

PEER CONFLICT Another common cause of workplace anger and hostility is peer conflict. Unlike instances of bullying, wherein one employee makes a conscious decision to engage in behavior that is hurtful or uncomfortable for another employee, peer conflict is characterized by mutual feelings of animosity toward the other individual. "Peer conflicts are typically caused by personality or perception differences, moodiness, impatience, or sensitive emotional states such as jealousy, annoyance, and embarrassment," wrote Levesque. "When these rivalries evolve into skirmishes or outbursts, the conflict erupts and people are damaged. Since work relies heavily on the ability of people to interact in a cooperative and harmonious fashion, conflict between employees represents a serious breakdown of those two vital ingredients to effective work relationships."

According to management theorist Peter Drucker, managers can pursue one of the following routes when attempting to resolve peer conflicts:

1) Convince both workers to accept a mutually agreeable view or agreement about the issue that was the cause of the conflict.

2) Support the position of one employee and reject the position of the other.

3) Make your own decision about the issue and force both people to comply with your perception.

"What is important for the manager to keep in perspective," wrote Levesque, "is that the problem belongs to those in conflict and only they can resolve it, but they will need someone to help—you."

Small business owners who find themselves mediating a peer conflict should avoid taking sides (especially if both workers' views have merit), provide an objective viewpoint, keep the discussion from bogging down in tangents or name-calling, and help each worker to understand the perspective of the other. Finally, the small business owner's overriding concern should be to explicitly restate his or her expectations of staff performance, including the ways in which staff members should behave toward one another.

KEYS TO STOPPING OR PREVENTING EXPRESSIONS OF WORKPLACE HOSTILITY AND ANGER

Attempts to address inappropriate workplace behavior through negotiation and mediation are not always effective. In some instances, an employee's conduct and/or performance will leave the small business owner with no alternative but to resort to disciplinary action. This discipline can take a variety of forms, from suspension to negative comments in the employee's personnel file to yanking the worker off a plum project. Reports on the effectiveness of such steps vary considerably. Some firms contend that such measures inform the employee that his or her problematic behavior will not be tolerated and can be an effective tool in triggering behavioral reforms, especially if the punishment has a financial dimension. But others insist that such measures—especially if used without first pursuing other options—may only deepen feelings of animosity and hostility.

No two small business enterprises or employees are alike. Researchers agree, however, that there a number of steps that employers can take to address the issues of workplace anger and hostility before they erupt into full-blown crises.

1) Explicitly state your absolute opposition to inappropriate behavior in writing. This can often be included as part of a new hire's employee guidelines package, but small business owners should also consider displaying such ''zero tolerance'' statements in public areas. Such statements should also clearly delineate which types of comments and actions are regarded as offensive.

2) Encourage an environment that values diversity. ''There must be vision and commitment to the ideal of valuing diversity demonstrated by an underlying respect toward everyone in the organization,'' wrote Charlene Marmer Solomon in *Personnel Journal*.

3) Recognize that incidents of workplace hostility tend to get worse over time if they are not addressed. For example, remarks that might at first seem to be merely in mildly bad taste can eventually escalate into full-fledged racist, sexist, or otherwise mean-spirited harassment. ''Learning to deal with [workplace anger] issues is critical to creating a workplace that is comfortable—and therefore productive—for employees,'' wrote McGarvey. ''An all-too-common reaction, and one that often creates bigger problems down the road, is shrugging off such incidents.'' Instead, business owners should respond to incidents of workplace anger or hostility promptly and decisively.

The whole workforce will likely be watching, looking for some signal about whether management takes such transgressions seriously, or whether it implicitly gives the green light to further incidents.

4) Learn to recognize the symptoms of workplace anger, and try to provide employees with constructive avenues to express frustrations and/or concerns.

5) Monitor workplace culture to ensure that it does not provide fertile ground for unwanted behavior.

6) Make sure you have all the facts before confronting an employee with a charge of workplace discrimination or otherwise unprofessional behavior. This is especially true if the identity of the transgressor is in any doubt.

7) Make sure that your own actions and deeds are a good model for your employees.

8) Recognize that your primary imperative is not to change an employee's mindset about minorities, women, or other co-workers, but rather to ensure that the employee does not engage in offensive behavior in his or her interactions with co-workers or customers. ''We won't change what a person says at a bar, after work, but we can impact how he carries out his job in the workplace,'' one consultant told *Entrepreneur*. ''We won't change attitudes, but we can manage behaviors—and that's your responsibility as an employer.''

WHEN THE SMALL BUSINESS OWNER IS ANGRY

Small business owners should also be aware of the challenges of managing their own anger in the workplace. Entrepreneurship brings with it a host of responsibilities and pressures that can make it difficult for them to manage strong emotions such as anger. But it is important for small business owners to handle their anger in an effective manner. ''Expressing anger can be constructive when your true intent is to maintain, reestablish, or restore a positive relationship with the person who has offended you,'' wrote Eugene Raudsepp in *Machine Design*. ''When done properly, constructive confrontations assure future harmony, better performance, and improved productivity. . . . When confronting the person who sparked your anger, don't underestimate the value of courtesy. Express your feelings in a reasonable, calm and controlled way. Back your statements with specifics. State the problem as you see it and then give the other party a chance to express his or her side. Listen, empathize, and try to understand what caused the conflict. Make it clear it's the behavior, not the person, that caused the problem.''

FURTHER READING:

Braverman, Mark. *Preventing Workplace Violence: A Guide for Employers and Practitioners.* Sage, 1999.

Levesque, Joseph D. *The Human Resource Problem-Solver's Handbook.* McGraw-Hill, 1992.

McGarvey, Robert. ''Foul Play: Battling Hostilities in the Workplace.'' *Entrepreneur.* October 1997.

McShulskis, Elaine. ''Workplace Anger: A Growing Problem.'' *HRMagazine.* December 1996.

Meyer, Pat. ''Preventing Workplace Violence Starts with Recognizing Warning Signs and Taking Action.'' *Nation's Restaurant News.* February 28, 2000.

Neville, Haig. ''Workplace Violence Prevention Strategies.'' *Memphis Business Journal.* September 8, 2000.

Solomon, Charlene Marmer. ''Keeping Hate Out of the Workplace.'' *Personnel Journal.* July 1992.

SEE ALSO: Workplace Violence

WORKPLACE SAFETY

Workplace safety refers to the working environment at a company and encompasses all factors that impact the safety and health of employees. This can include environmental hazards, unsafe working conditions or processes, drug and alcohol abuse, and workplace violence. Workplace safety is monitored at the national level by the Occupational Safety and Health Administration (OSHA). OSHA has three stated goals that serve as the cornerstones of its policies and regulations: 1) Improve the safety and health for all workers, as evidenced by fewer hazards, reduced exposures, and fewer injuries, illnesses, and fatalities; 2) Change workplace culture to increase employer and worker awareness of, commitment to, and involvement in safety and health; 3) Secure public confidence through excellence in the development and delivery of OSHA's programs and services. The federal guidelines imposed by this agency are complemented by state regulations that are often tougher than those proposed by OSHA.

IMPROVING WORKPLACE SAFETY AT A SMALL BUSINESS

Some small business owners erroneously believe that the modest size of their enterprise makes them immune from following OSHA regulations. In reality, even though there may be different standards for some regulations, small businesses do have to pay attention to safety. Indeed, workplace safety is an important consideration on a number of levels. Attention to

safety issues can not only help businesses avoid legal penalties, but also improve employee morale, productivity, and retention. Moreover, effective workplace safety programs often have a tremendous impact on a company's bottom-line financial performance. In addition to the hidden benefits in retention and productivity that go hand-in-hand with such programs, businesses armed with solid workplace safety policies and records realize enormous benefits in the realm of insurance. ''An employer's workers' compensation premium is based on several factors,'' noted *Arkansas Business.* ''Among them are classification code, payroll, and accident history. No factor has more control over insurance premium or is less understood by policy holders than the experience modification or 'mod.' The mod is an indicator of how an individual operation's accident rate compares to other businesses within its industry. Three consecutive years of actual workers' compensation claims provide the statistical basis for an employer's mod.'' Under this system, companies that are determined to have a higher accident rate (as determined by workers' compensation claims over a three-year period) than the industry average pay higher premiums. Conversely, companies that boast a claim rate lower than the industry average will benefit by paying less expensive premiums.

Workplace safety programs can take many forms and cover many potential areas of concern. Such disparate measures as provision of personal safety equipment, installation of equipment controls, creation and dissemination of operational manuals, policies of hazardous materials handling, adoption of drug and alcohol testing policies, introduction of employee counseling services, and implementation of safety training programs are all utilized by companies to minimize their workforce's exposure to workplace injuries.

Following are several avenues that small firms can pursue when implementing or updating a workplace safety program.

SAFETY MANAGERS AND COMMITTEES One method that many firms have had success with is to appoint one person in the organization as the safety coordinator. The ideal candidate has a background in safety, but if no one fits that profile, then choose the candidate who best relates to workers and management, has strong communication skills, and has an interest in and commitment to safety. A common title for this person is ''safety manager.''

For the safety manager to do his or her job, he or she must have direct access to the top manager in the company. Without management buy-in, safety initiatives will not last long. The manager must also have access to every department and work area, and must be able to question people freely for the purpose of gathering information. Regular status reports should be prepared that update management on current safety initiaves and identify areas that still need improvement. Ideally, the safety manager's role will remain an advisory one: responsibility for implementing the manager's suggestions should fall to upper management and the individuals or teams that are singled out by the safety manager. The safety's manager's mandate is to facilitate change, not implement it.

Many analysts believe that businesses should make certain that safety managers are adequately educated on workplace safety issues as well. Business owners are thus often encouraged to send managers to training and education seminars or classes as part of an overall policy of ongoing education. Additionally, management should encourage the manager to seek out safety professionals at other companies to help him or her build a network of contacts and information. Upper management is also responsible for ensuring that safety performance is made a part of every employee's job responsibility and performance reviews. Only when every employee is held accountable for safety will it become a part of a company's culture.

The best starting point for a new safety manager is often to review company records of past safety problems. By drawing up a list of areas that are known problems, the manager can identify the best place to begin implementation of new safety measures. Of course, it is also important that the manager immediately follow up on any disquieting patterns or dangerous situations that are discovered and implement action steps to correct the problems. Unfortunately, in some instances safety managers will find that workplace safety reports are scant or nonexistent. In such instances, the manager should start from ground zero and establish a formal accident/safety reporting system to gather data.

Documentation and record keeping serves two additional purposes—it provides written evidence that the new safety program is providing positive results and it can be used to protect the firm in the event that a lawsuit is filed or safety inquiry launched. Documentation of employee training sessions is especially important, including the topics covered, the date and time at which the sessions were held, and any test scores earned by employees at the sessions. Consultants cite testing as a potentially valuable way of determining employee retention of safety information.

The safety manager should seek to involve all employees and managers in safety initiatives. Inspections should be conducted by the personnel of each department, not the safety manager. In fact, the manager should let each department handle most of its own safety problems—if proper training has been given to all employees, the safety manager should only have to address serious problems that require his or her knowledge and authority.

Studies have shown that safety committees can be valuable tools in implementing and maintaining safety programs as well. Safety committees, which typically feature representation from all operational areas, have been shown to reduce the injury rate at companies, which in turn can boost morale and efficiency. Companies that use committees have also reported some unexpected benefits, including an increased sense of teamwork, better sharing of information, and a drop in absenteeism, discrimination claims, grievances, and sick days. Not all small business enterprises reach a size that warrant creation of such committees. But for growing businesses with a significant payroll, safety and health committees can provide important benefits. The committees, which ideally will include a cross-section of employees, should serve as a central gathering and dissemination point for all information related to safety.

OUTSIDE SAFETY ANALYSIS Another potentially useful option for entrepreneurs interested in determining workplace safety is to have an outside firm conduct a safety analysis. These firms specialize in safety and hazardous materials and can offer many suggestions on how to improve safety. Analysts note that reports submitted by these organizations often range from warnings of regulatory breaches to suggestions on alternative production methods, etc. Not all safety improvement suggestions are implemented, of course. Some courses of action may be deemed excessively expensive, while others are dismissed because of employee resistance or skepticism about their ultimate impact on workplace safety.

SAFETY INCENTIVES Business owners and consultants alike agree that safety managers and consultants will likely not have a meaningful impact on a company's safety records if the employees are not willing to do their part to help make things better. One of the best ways to ensure employee cooperation is to offer incentives tied to improvements in safety, although observers are quick to add that safety incentives are not an adequate substitute for a strong safety program. In fact, only companies that have a strong program already in place should even think of using incentives. Cash and non-cash awards should only be used to motivate employees to practice what the already-in-place program preaches, which reinforces behavior and encourages participation.

Incentives should reward behaviors that prevent injury by eliminating unsafe work practices. Reward employees who achieve ''zero accidents,'' but be sure to use a broad definition of accident (such as one that would cause an employee to miss time on the job) so that employees do not try to cover up minor injuries in order to keep their zero accident rating. Once the behaviors to be rewarded are identified, then determine allocation of awards (individual, department, or companywide).

To make an incentive program really work, several things must be done. First, the incentives must be an ongoing element of the workplace. One-time incentive programs tend to get employees interested for a short time, then cause them to lose interest and fall back into bad habits once the period has passed. Second, meaningful incentives should be chosen. Many experts believe that non-cash incentives can be most effective, warning that under cash-based reward systems, employees too often pocket the cash and forget about the ongoing message. Some companies do believe that cash works best, while others feel using cash sends people the wrong message by paying them extra for practices that they should already be doing. Good examples of non-cash incentives include recognition awards, token gifts that build morale, customized items (clothing, for example), and, most effective of all, professional advancement. Finally, goals and results must be clearly communicated to employees at every step of the process.

Small business owners should not be scared of the costs associated with running an incentive program. Even if the program costs several thousand dollars annually, many economists and business experts contend that the expense is insignificant compared to the productivity lost as a result of poor safety practices.

WORKPLACE VIOLENCE AS A SAFETY ISSUE

Every act of workplace violence leaves scars on every person in the organization. One act of violence can change an entire company permanently. The working environment can become so toxic that no work gets done—all employees can think about is what happened. From the company perspective, violence also leaves the company exposed to lawsuits and liability that can cost millions of dollars.

There are steps that can be taken to prevent or at least minimize the chances of workplace violence. The most important step is for the company's leadership to communicate a zero-tolerance policy for workplace violence and behaviors (bullying, harassment, defiance of management, etc.) that can lead to such events. At the same time, businesses should display a corresponding determination to create and maintain a safe workplace for employees by examining their existing security, hiring, and performance appraisal policies.

FURTHER READING:

Arkin, Alan. "Safer Workplaces Are No Accident." *People Management.* July 25, 1996.

"Creating Safe Workplace, Educating Employees Saves Time and Money." *Arkansas Business.* December 27, 1999.

Friend, Mark A. "Safety in the Small Business: Getting Started." *Occupational Hazards.* July 1994.

Goldberg, Carol. "Workplace Safety Is a Wise Investment." *LI Business News.* August 19, 1996.

Pasher, Victoria S. "Small Businesses Split Over Safety." *National Underwriter Property & Casualty-Risk & Benefits Management.* July 17, 1995.

Quilty, Michelle. "Safety Takes the Prize." *Small Business Reports.* March 1994.

Ronca, Theodore J. "Be On the Safe Side." *Small Business Reports.* September 1994.

Synett, Robert J. "Achieving Safety Excellence: 6 Keys to Success." *Risk Management.* October 1996.

"What Causes Accidents?" *Monthly Labor Review.* December 1996.

SEE ALSO: Ergonomics; Industrial Safety

WORKPLACE VIOLENCE

Workplace violence is an act of aggression, physical assault, or threatening behavior that occurs in a work setting and causes physical or emotional harm to customers, coworkers, or managers. Broad definitions of workplace violence also often include acts of sabotage on work-site property.

Workplace violence has emerged as a subject of considerable interest to both small and large businesses in recent years. Some small business owners deny that this grim issue is a concern for them, but in reality, workplace violence can strike even tiny start-up firms. And as many analysts and business owners have charged, even the threat of violence can have a dreadful impact on the culture and productivity of a small business. Whereas employees of larger firms generally have more avoidance options to choose from when forced to share workspace with a volatile employee, the more modest facilities and resources of smaller businesses do not provide the same level of protection.

Certainly, recent statistics indicate that workplace violence is an issue that all businesses need to address. A U.S. Department of Justice survey indicated that 709 workplace homicides took place across America in 1998 alone, and that nearly two million violent incidents occurred in U.S. businesses from 1993 to 1998, including one million simple assaults and 400,000 aggravated assaults. A 2000 study conducted by Northwestern National Life Insurance, meanwhile, stated that 2,500 of every 100,000 American workers have been attacked on the job, with a full 30 percent of those assaults made by coworkers, supervisors, or ex-employees. In addition, most experts agree that these statistics do not adequately convey the scale of the problem, for most incidents of workplace violence and aggression are never reported. As Donald W. Myers' observed in *Business Horizons,* murders and suicides are the only categories of workplace violence that have been documented in any meaningful way: "Similar categories of data on other types of violent acts committed against employees, such as aggravated assaults, simple assaults, and rape, are not available. In addition, data on these acts are not recorded on a consistent basis, so yearly trends cannot be determined. Furthermore, information is not maintained on workplace violence involving property, such as arson or sabotage. In sum, with the exception of workplace fatalities, no one really knows the magnitude of workplace violence."

According to the Workplace Violence Research Institute, workplace aggression also takes a heavy financial toll on businesses. An Institute study estimated the aggregate cost of workplace violence to U.S. employers to be more than $36 billion as a result of expenses associated with lost business and productivity, litigation, medical care, psychiatric care, higher insurance rates, increased security measures, negative publicity, and loss of employees. Problems in any of these areas can create a difficult financial environment for companies, especially those that are in the small or mid-sized range, but prohibitive legal expenses and penalties have become a source of particular concern in recent years. "Workplace violence has become a breeding ground for litigation wherein victims seek compensation for their injuries," explained Kari Johnson in *Business North Carolina.* "Gone are the days when businesses were able to have such claims dismissed as a matter of course based upon the unforeseeable criminal acts of third parties. Today, victims of workplace violence are recovering substantial jury verdicts and hefty settlements."

ADDRESSING WORKPLACE VIOLENCE BEFORE IT ERUPTS

Small business owners can take several steps to address the spectre of workplace violence. Hiring and interviewing practices should reflect the company's desire to establish and maintain a good workforce, and the owner should do his or her best to establish a company culture that does not tolerate non-violent forms of intimidation. After all, insulting and intimidating behavior—which may lead to physically violent behavior if left unchecked—can wreak significant mental harm on its victims, and may even provoke a violent response by victims who feel that they have no other recourse. Indeed, some studies have indicated that victims of harassment actually become less productive than employees who suffer from physical assaults.

"The best solution to avoiding workplace violence is to discuss it with your employees and have a plan to deal with it—before you need it," stated business writer Jane Applegate. "Business owners should have a written workplace violence-prevention plan to show they are dealing with the problem." Other options, albeit unpleasant to contemplate, include boosting security precautions by adding security personnel or installing metal detectors. Some security consultants urge their clients to make it clear that employee desks and lockers are company property that can be looked through at any time, and they should be encouraged to report all violent acts to legal authorities. Finally, business consultants and security experts counsel small business owners to recognize that workplace violence does not always stem from internal sources. Indeed, the majority of homicides that take place in workplace settings are actually perpetuated by non-employees (angry customers, robbers, irate spouses, or romantic partners).

STOPPING WORKPLACE VIOLENCE

Experts believe that businesses can take a number of steps to dramatically reduce their likelihood of an employee carrying out an act of workplace violence. Many of these are proactive in nature, designed to minimize the business's exposure to violent acts by employees:

Maintain and disseminate detailed policies on workplace behavior. "Adopt a zero-tolerance policy that addresses signs of potential violence," counseled *Security Management*'s Michael Gips. "Such a policy should clearly state that threats, intimidation, destruction of company property, and violence in any form will not be tolerated and provide for progressive disciplinary action for such conduct." These guidelines should also clearly delineate violations that may result in discharge or other disciplinary action so that workers are cognizant of behavioral boundaries. In addition, these policies should explicitly state the company's determination to protect victims and/or informants of violent acts against any form of retaliation.

Maintain and disseminate workplace violence prevention programs. This plan should cover everything from investigatory steps to take when an employee exhibits questionable behavior to the manner in which problem employees are dismissed. "These training programs should focus on teaching employees how to recognize and report suspicious activity and should provide written information on whom to contact in an emergency," wrote Gillian Flynn in *Workforce.* This aspect of the program needs to be addressed with particular care, for staff participation will only occur if they can express concerns about coworkers in a safe and confidential way. Other elements of these programs typically include disciplinary training for managers, security plans, pre-employment screening, and media relations of an incident of workplace violence does take place.

Screen applicants. Every company's workplace violence prevention program should include a thorough investigation of applicants' background (including employment history and possible criminal record) and qualifications for the job opening. Many experts believe that incidents of workplace violence are more likely to occcur when an employee is struggling with his/her responsibilities, so ability to fulfill the responsibilities of the position in question is a particularly relevant consideration. In addition, interviews should include questions that can help identify potential risky hires. According to Gips, such questions include: ''What would you do if a fellow employee called you a bad name? Embarrassed you in front of others? What did your previous boss do that made you mad? Tell me about a past supervisor you admired. It is a clear warning sign that a person has problems getting along with others if he can not identify a single past supervisor he liked.'' In addition to the above background and interviewing techniques, many companies have also adopted drug and alcohol testing, aptitude testing, and honesty testing as part of their overall interviewing process.

Recognize warning signs. Law enforcement and security experts agree that employees who engage in violent acts often—though not always—exhibit behaviors that serve as ''red flags'' indicating potential problems. These include: engaging in direct or veiled threats against coworkers, paranoid behavior, unreciprocated romantic interest in a coworker, obsession with weapons, pronounced mood swings, excessive anger over company policies or decisions, decreased productivity, and deteriorating relations with fellow staff, customers, or vendors.

Be cognizant of potential trigger events. Business owners should remember that workplace violence does not erupt for no reason, and that if it takes place within the walls of the company, the chances are pretty good that it was triggered by a workplace issue or event. Demotions, critical performance appraisals, layoffs, disciplinary actions, and other professional disappointments can all trigger violent behavior.

Counseling. Employee assistance programs can be very valuable to workers who are struggling with stress at home and/or in the office. Applegate noted that ''when confronted with a volatile employee, the nature tendency is to fire the troublemaker, which often exacerbates the situation and can provoke a violent episode. The better approach is to suggest the troubled employee get professional counseling. Paying for it out of your own pocket, if necessary, is worth it, if it will avert a disaster.'' In addition, some

employers have instituted policies designed to give employees an outlet for them to relay their grievances and concerns. These avenues range from regular meetings with managers to comment boxes or surveys.

Terminate with dignity. Employers can reduce their exposure to workplace violence by instituting and carrying out policies that treat terminated employees with respect. In addition, some consultants encourage companies to offer outplacement counseling for ex-employees as part of their severance packages. Before doing so, however, business owners and managers should discuss possible legal ramifications with a qualified attorney.

Address ex-employees who pose a potential threat. Many businesses erroneously believe that once an employee has been discharged and is no longer in the workplace, the worker no longer poses a threat. But this is not necessarily the case. A study by Northwestern National Life Insurance, for example, stated that 3 percent of the total number of reported incidents of workplace violence were perpetrated by ex-employees. Restraining orders, password changes, and other special security measures may be necessary in some situations.

PROVIDING REFERENCES FOR EX-EMPLOYEES

''The mere act of helping a violent or potentially violent ex-employee gain new employment raises problems, according to legal experts,'' wrote Gips. He noted that according to legal consultants, ''there is no legal duty to warn a prospective employer of another company's experiences with an employee. But if the company purports to say something positive about the employee without revealing negative information, [it] might be interpreted as an endorsement of that employee, which could trigger the duty to tell the whole truth—including the violence or threatened violence.'' Other potential legal pitfalls await business owners who are asked to comment on ex-employees who engaged in questionable behavior that nonetheless never became violent in nature. Business owners and managers can not simply speculate that an ex-employee *might* be a violence risk, if there is no confirmed behavior upon which to base that opinion. Statutes governing defamation liability in this area vary considerably from state to state, so business owners who are asked about ex-employees who are seen as security risks should seek legal advice before responding.

FURTHER READING:

Applegate, Jane. ''Workplace Violence Threatens Every Firm: Even Small Companies Need a Plan.'' *Detroit Free Press.* August 25, 1997.

Bensimon, Helen Frank. "Violence in the Workplace." *Training and Development.* January 1994.

Braverman, Mark. *Preventing Workplace Violence: A Guide for Employers and Practitioners.* Sage, 1999.

Flynn, Gillian. "Employers Can't Look Away from Workplace Violence." *Workforce.* July 2000.

Fogleman, Dannie B. "Minimizing the Risk of Violence in the Workplace." *Employment Relations Today.* Spring 2000.

Gips, Michael A. "Transitioning Problem Employees." *Security Management.* November 2000.

Johnson, Kari R. "Workplace Violence: Is Your Business at Risk?" *Business North Carolina.* September 2000.

Labig, Charles. *Preventing Violence in the Workplace.* AMACOM.

Lipman, Ira A. "Violence at Work." *Business Perspectives.* Summer 1994.

Meyer, Pat. "Preventing Workplace Violence Starts with Recognizing Warning Signs and Taking Action." *Nation's Restaurant News.* February 28, 2000.

Myers, Donald W. "The Mythical Work of Workplace Violence—Or is it?" *Business Horizons.* July-August 1996.

Neville, Haig. "Workplace Violence Prevention Strategies." *Memphis Business Journal.* September 8, 2000.

Taylor, Robert. "Firm Response to Violence at Work." *Financial Times.* August 28, 1996.

Thornburg, Linda. "When Violence Hits Business." *HR Magazine.* July 1993.

SEE ALSO: Workplace Anger

WORKSTATION

Workstation is a general term used to describe two different types of computer systems. At its most sophisticated, a workstation is a high-end, typically expensive, computer used for computer-aided design (CAD), computer-aid engineering (CAE), graphics, simulation, and other applications requiring significant computing resources. At its most basic, a workstation is any personal computer used for business, professional, home, or recreational purposes. A workstation typically includes a combination of a mouse, keyboard, monitor, and central processing unit. It may also include peripheral devices such as a modem, scanner, or printer. In a business setting, a workstation PC is often linked with other computers to a local area network (LAN), which enables it to use the resources of other larger computers in the LAN. A PC, if it has its own hard drive for storage and its own applications installed on it, can be used independently even if it is part of a network.

WORKPLACE WORKSTATIONS: POTENTIAL FOR INJURY

PCs are a fixture in any business, large or small, and are used for word processing, data entry, and other functions. PCs bring with them the expected potential for improved productivity and efficiency. But what some business owners may not realize is that extensive use of PCs by their employees may also result in the employees developing ailments that, in turn, have the potential to lower a business's productivity and increase its healthcare and workers' compensation costs.

The most commonly reported problem associated with computer use is eyestrain. James Sheedy of the University of California—Berkeley estimates that ten million cases of eyestrain are reported each year. As Don Sellers noted in *Zap!: How Your Computer Can Hurt You and What You Can Do About It,* "The computer is a much more visually demanding environment than people think." To reduce employee eyestrain, employers should adjust lighting to reduce glare on computer screens and encourage workers to take regular breaks to look away from the screen and refocus on a distant object. Employees, particularly those who already wear bifocals, may also want to invest in eyeglasses designed specifically to be worn while working with a computer.

Computer users also face the risk of developing more serious repetitive stress injuries, or cumulative trauma disorders (CTDs). These injuries are disorders of the musculo-nervous system that involve nerve compression and wear and tear on muscles and tendons. The U.S. Department of Labor reports that all CTDs—not just those related to computer use—account for 61 percent of occupational illness cases. The direct cost of a CTD is placed at about $27,500 by the National Council on Compensation Insurance, while the indirect costs may include wages for temporary help, overtime pay, and retraining.

According to Sellers, repetitive stress injuries "could possibly be the most serious effect of using a desktop computer and can be very debilitating." Perhaps the best-known type of repetitive-stress injury is carpal-tunnel syndrome, which is usually related to keyboard use. The syndrome is the result of putting pressure on the nerves that run from the hand to the arm and is characterized by pain and weakness in the hand, arm, and even the shoulder.

AN EMPLOYEE-FRIENDLY WORKSTATION AND ENVIRONMENT

Dr. Bruce Bernard of the U.S. National Institute of Occupational Safety and Health encourages employers to evaluate the nature and extent of keyboard use. "Generally," he says, "carpal tunnel syndrome is not found in the workplace unless tendonitis appears there first. You don't want to wait until tendonitis presents itself. You really need to take seriously employee complaints of discomfort." Sellers echoes this approach, urging employers "to examine the workstation environment. Just simply look at how a person is using a workstation: Is he or she comfortable?''

To ensure a comfortable workstation, employers need to be aware of workplace ergonomics, which is the effective and safe interaction between people and things. When reviewing the current work environment, employers should look to see if employees have already made their own adjustments to improve comfort. For example, has an employee placed his monitor on a stack of books, added a cushion to his chair, or placed the legs of his desk on blocks? If so, then clearly the original workstation configuration is not effective. Employers may then consider investing in ergonomically designed furniture and computer accessories that can be adjusted to meet the needs of an individual employee.

Employers should also encourage employees who work extensively with computers to take regular breaks. Marvin Dainoff, director of the Center for Ergonomics Research at Miami University of Ohio, urges employers to ''remember that people are not machines.'' Dainoff also recommends stretching as a means of eliminating musculoskeletal problems. Finally, Bernard and other experts urge employers to create an environment where employees feel they can speak up when they are experiencing any pain or discomfort. The sooner a problem is identified, the greater the employer's chance of controlling related costs.

FURTHER READING:

Cady, Eric. ''Is Your Workplace a Trauma Center?'' *Small Business Reports.* October 1994.

Freedman, Alan. *Computer Desktop Encyclopedia.* The Computer Language Company Inc., 1996.

Lewin, David L. ''Preventive Medicine at Work.'' *Nation's Business.* March 1995.

SEE ALSO: Ergonomics; Hoteling

WRITTEN COMMUNICATION

Written communication involves any type of interaction that makes use of the written word. It is one of the two main types of communication, along with oral/spoken communication. Written communication is very common in business situations, so it is important for small business owners and managers to develop effective written communication skills. Some of the various forms of written communication that are used internally for business operations include memos, reports, bulletins, job descriptions, employee manuals, and electronic mail. Examples of written communication avenues typically pursued with clients, vendors, and other members of the business community, meanwhile, include electronic mail, Internet Web sites, letters, proposals, telegrams, faxes, postcards, contracts, advertisements, brochures, and news releases.

Ironically, the importance of good writing skills in the business world has become more evident even as companies rely increasingly on computers and other new technologies to meet their obligations. Indeed, business experts warn that any business's positive qualities—from dedication to customer service to high-tech expertise—will be blunted to some degree if they are unable to transfer that dedication and knowledge to the printed page. ''Whether you are pitching a business case or justifying a budget, the quality of your writing can determine success or failure,'' wrote Paula Jacobs in *InfoWorld.* ''Writing ability is especially important in customer communication. Business proposals, status reports, customer documentation, technical support, or even e-mail replies all depend on clear written communication.''

THE COMMUNICATION PROCESS

The basic process of communication begins when a fact or idea is observed by one person. That person (the sender) may decide to translate the observation into a message, and then transmit the message through some communication medium to another person (the receiver). The receiver then must interpret the message and provide feedback to the sender indicating that the message has been understood and appropriate action taken.

As Herta A. Murphy and Herbert W. Hildebrandt observed in *Effective Business Communications,* good communication should be complete, concise, clear, concrete, correct, considerate, and courteous. More specifically, this means that communication should: answer basic questions like who, what, when, where; be relevant and not overly wordy; focus on the receiver and his or her interests; use specific facts and figures and active verbs; use a conversational tone for readability; include examples and visual aids when needed; be tactful and good natured; and be accurate and nondiscriminatory. Unclear, inaccurate, or inconsiderate business communication can waste valuable time, alienate employees or customers, and destroy goodwill toward management or the overall business.

ADVANTAGES AND DISADVANTAGES OF WRITTEN COMMUNICATION

In their book *Management: Function and Strategy,* Thomas S. Bateman and Carl P. Zeithaml described several advantages and disadvantages of using written forms of communication. One advantage is that written messages do not have to be delivered on the spur of the moment; instead, they can be edited and revised several times before they are sent so that the content can be shaped to maximum effect. Another advantage is that written communication provides a permanent record of the messages that have been sent and can be saved for later study. Since they are permanent, written forms of communication also enable recipients to take more time in reviewing the message and providing appropriate feedback. For these reasons, written forms of communication are often considered more appropriate for complex business messages that include important facts and figures. Other benefits commonly associated with good writing skills include increased customer/client satisfaction; improved interorganizational efficiency; and enhanced image in the community and industry.

There are also several potential pitfalls associated with written communication, however. For instance, unlike oral communication, wherein impressions and reactions are exchanged instantaneously, the sender of written communication does not generally receive immediate feedback to his or her message. This can be a source of frustration and uncertainty in business situations in which a swift response is desired. In addition, written messages often take more time to compose, both because of their information-packed nature and the difficulty that many individuals have in composing such correspondence. Many companies, however, have taken a proactive stance in addressing the latter issue. Mindful of the large number of workers who struggle with their writing abilities, some firms have begun to offer on-site writing courses or enrolled employees in business writing workshops offered by professional training organizations, colleges, and community education programs.

E-MAIL COMMUNICATIONS

Electronic mail has emerged as a highly popular business communication tool in recent years. Indeed, its capacity to convey important corporate communications swiftly and easily has transformed it into a communications workhorse for business enterprises of all sizes and orientations. But many users of e-mail technology pay little attention to basic rules of grammar and format when composing their letters, even when they are penning business correspondence addressed to clients, customers, vendors, business partners, or internal colleagues. This sloppy correspondence reflects an ''astonishing'' lack of professionalism, wrote Sana Reynolds in *Communication World:* ''We seem to have been seduced by the ease and informality of the medium to produce messages that ignore the rules and conventions usually in place when producing hard copy. We send out messages with grammar, usage or spelling errors. . . . In the name of speed, we throw caution to the winds and forget sentence patterning, paragraphing, and other conventions that make messages intelligible, creating unattractive and impenetrable data dumps.''

Given this unfortunate trend, many business experts counsel companies to install firm guidelines on tone, content, and shape of e-mail correspondence. These guidelines should make it clear that all employees are expected to adhere to the same standards of professionalism that (presumably) remain in place for traditional postal correspondence. Proper spelling and grammar and the ability to frame correspondence in suitably diplomatic language should be hallmarks of electronic mail as well as regular mail, especially if the communication is directed at a person or persons outside the company.

FURTHER READING:

Bateman, Thomas S., and Carl P. Zeithaml. *Management: Function and Strategy.* Irwin, 1990.

Golen, Steven. *Effective Business Communication.* Washington, DC: U.S. Small Business Administration, 1989.

Jacobs, Paula. ''Strong Writing Skills Essential for Success, Even in IT.'' *InfoWorld.* July 6, 1998.

Murphy, Herta A., and Herbert W. Hildebrandt. *Effective Business Communications.* McGraw-Hill, 1991.

Reynolds, Sana. ''Composing Effective E-Mail Messages.'' *Communication World.* July 15, 1997.

Schafer, Sarah. ''Office E-Mail: It's Fast, Easy and All Too Often Misunderstood.'' *International Herald Tribune.* November 1, 2000.

Y

YOUNG ENTREPRENEURS' ORGANIZATION (YEO)

The Young Entrepreneurs' Organization (YEO) is perhaps the best known of several groups that emerged during the 1990s to offer educational opportunities and other kinds of support to young business owners. Membership in such groups has increased dramatically in recent years, as more and more young people have abandoned traditional corporate career paths in favor of the increased autonomy and financial rewards that are possible through entrepreneurship. "Times have changed, and today entrepreneurship has become a key career choice for young Americans," wrote Tariq K. Muhammad in *Black Enterprise*. "Highly publicized corporate downsizings have cast a pall over the traditional path to success, and fueled a general perception that well-paying jobs with room for advancement are scarce. The days when professionals could expect to stay with the same company for a lifetime are long gone. Human resources professionals estimate that today's worker will have an average of five to ten career changes in their lifetime. As a result, interest in entrepreneurship has grown."

YEO was founded in 1987 by a group of five successful young entrepreneurs, including the founders of I Can't Believe It's Not Yogurt, the California Closet Company, and Redgate Communications Corporation. By the late 1990s, the group included 2,500 business founders based in 30 countries around the world. YEO member companies represented more than $130 billion in revenues and employed an estimated 1.3 million people in the late 1990s. The YEO is managed by an international board of directors that oversees local community chapters.

The mission of YEO is to provide its members with mentoring, peer networking, and educational opportunities. Membership is open to individuals who are under the age of 40 and are the founders, cofounders, or majority shareholders of companies grossing over $1 million annually (special exceptions also exist for venture-backed firms). Annual membership fees are $1,300. Local chapters hold monthly meetings and sponsor regular educational events or presentations. In addition, the national organization regularly sponsors tours of other countries to study new business strategies, methods, and innovations. Many chapters also feature "self-help" forums where groups of 10 to 12 entrepreneurs from noncompeting industries get together to work on common problems faced by small business owners, such as hiring good employees or international expansion. Personal issues are also sometimes explored in these private, confidential settings, which are facilitated by trained moderators.

Another popular YEO program is its so-called Inventory of Skills (IOS), in which members can turn to fellow members to solve business problems or garner information on business issues they are facing. "YEO lets me benefit from the experience of my peers, who are also entrepreneurs and have already gone through situations I may be going through," one entrepreneur told *Black Enterprise*. "When I'm looking to enter new markets, I already have a contact in any part of the world because of my affiliation with YEO." The YEO can be contacted via its web site at www.yeo.org.

FURTHER READING:

Applegate, Jane. ''Entrepreneurs Have Support of Peer Groups.'' Triangle Business Journal. April 30, 1999.

Henderson, Barry. ''Join the Club.'' Kansas City Business Journal. May 26, 1995.

Mitseas, Catherine. ''Organization Focuses on Young Leaders.'' January 21, 2000.

Muhammad, Tariq K. ''From Buppie to Biz-Wiz: Forget Corporate America—Generation X Is Choosing the Entrepreneurial Path to Success.'' Black Enterprise. January 1997.

Z

ZONING ORDINANCES

Zoning ordinances are laws that govern activities in townships and other municipalities. Most cities and towns are composed of regions that are zoned for residential, commercial, or industrial development, and often these zones are subdivided by additional use restrictions (type of business permitted, etc.). Zoning laws and ordinances may affect such varied issues as parking for customers, setbacks, access for deliveries, the number and types of employees permitted, and the use of signs or other forms of advertising. These ordinances have to be considered by entrepreneurs/business owners wishing to set up, expand, or relocate business establishments. They should check with their city's zoning office and licensing board for restrictions that may apply to the city, or even to their particular neighborhood, prior to finalizing any business plan.

ZONING AND COMMERCIAL BUSINESSES Review of zoning ordinances for areas designated for commercial and/or industrial use is a standard procedure for entrepreneurs seeking to establish a business in such places. In most cases, establishing a business in a building that was previously used for commercial purposes will not run afoul of zoning ordinances for the area. Experts warn, however, that businesses seeking to construct a new facility, acquire an existing building for a new use, or launch extensive remodeling efforts should closely examine local zoning and building codes. In instances where local zoning laws present a problem, the business owner has the option of filing for a zone variance, a conditional-use

permit, or a zone change. All three of these options have their drawbacks.

A zone change amounts to a permanent change in the zoning classification of the property. This is obviously desirable, but the procedure to successfully trigger such a change is generally a cumbersome one that goes through City Hall. After all, bids for reclassification are based on claims that current zoning is in error or no longer reflects the character of the neighborhood. Many municipalities are reluctant to accept such arguments. Variances and conditional-use permits, meanwhile, are in essence requests for special permission to use the property for a purpose other than for which it was zoned. Such permits are often expensive to obtain and can take two to four months to go through if they are even approved. But they are usually easier to obtain that outright zoning changes.

ZONING AND HOME BUSINESSES Checking into local zoning ordinances is a step often overlooked by owners of home-based businesses as well. Such neglect can prove troublesome down the line, for as Janet Attard noted in *The Home Office and Small Business Answer Book,* ''zoning laws are established locally, often at the township, city, or village level. Furthermore, each town or village decides for itself what types of home businesses it will allow. Thus in one community you might be able to run a home business that has up to two employees while in another community the same business might be restricted from having any employees. In still another community you might be able to have a homebased business if you are a fisherman or carpenter but not if you are a real estate agent or insurance broker.''

Most zoning ordinances restricting home offices in residential neighborhoods were originally designed to protect residential neighborhoods from becoming cluttered with commercial activity and thus maintain the family-friendly flavor and atmosphere of the area. In the past, these laws often were strictly interpreted to keep residents from conducting any sort of business from their home, even if it did not have a visible impact on the rest of the neighborhood. Today, the explosion in home-based business start-ups has sparked a reevaluation of zoning laws in residential areas, but many of the old zoning laws remain on the books.

It is widely recognized that millions of home-based businesses operate for years in violation of zoning laws, and that many of those businesses prosper without ever running into problems. Indeed, many communities simply ignore violations unless a neighborhood resident or someone else complains. These complaints may be triggered by utterly trivial factors—unhappiness with the frequency with which you mow your lawn, for instance, or anger about some real or imagined social slight—but in the eyes of the law, the motivations behind the complaint will generally be of little consequence. ''You cannot assume . . . that it is OK for you to disregard local law because *some* town boards don't enforce regulations and *some* people get away with operating on the sly,'' said Attard. ''If there are laws prohibiting your type of home business, it will only take one complaint to plunge you into a pot of legal hot water.''

FURTHER READING:

Attard, Janet. *The Home Office and Small Business Answer Book*. Henry Holt, 1993.

Barhight, G. Scott, Jennifer R. Busse, and David K. Gildea. ''Get the Lay of the Land Before Buying Property.'' *Baltimore Business Journal.* December 8, 2000.

Barlas, Stephen. ''Zone Defense.'' *Entrepreneur.* February 1998.

Hardin, Pamala M. ''Keep Your Firm from Zoning Out: Running Your Business from Your Basement May Get You Zapped with Hefty Fines.'' *Black Enterprise.* March 1996.

A

Deferred annuities, I:51–52

Deferred savings plans, II:794–795

Defined benefit plans, II:974

Defined contribution plans, II:864, II:974

Delaware, incorporation law, I:589

Delegation, **I:312–314**

Delivery services, **I:315–316**

Delphi technique, I:524, II:1007

DELTA (Defense Loan and Technical Assistance) Program, II:1149

Deming, W. Edwards, II:933–934, II:935, II:1123

Demographics, **I:316–318**

See also Metropolitan Statistical Areas (MSAs)

Department stores, II:973

Depreciation, I:58, **I:318–319**, II:740, II:1103

See also Accelerated Cost Recovery System

Descriptive bases, II:721

Design patents, I:632

Desktop publishing, **I:319–320**, II:810

Developing countries and globalization, I:541

Development, organizational, **II:833–836**

"Development Matchmakers," II:748

Development stage companies, **I:508**

Differentiation market strategy, II:1013

Difficult customers, **I:320–322**

Difficult employees, **I:322–324**

Digital cash, I:616

Digital Millennium Copyright Act (1998), I:250

Direct costs, I:266

Direct exporting, **I:471–472**

Direct-labor budgets, I:111

Direct mail, I:24, **I:324–327**, I:329

See also Direct marketing; Mail-order businesses; Mailing lists

Direct marketing, I:324, **I:327–331**

See also Mail-order businesses

Direct-materials budgets, I:110–111

Direct premiums. *See* Premiums

Direct public offerings, **I:331–334**

See also Regulation D

Direct selling. *See* Multilevel marketing

Disability insurance, **I:334–336**, I:383

Disability insurance pools, I:603–604

Disabled customers, **I:336–337**

Disaster assistance loans, **I:337–338**

Disaster planning, **I:338–341**

Disclaimers, II:1170

Discontinued operations, I:584

Discount for lack of marketability, II:1155

Discount rate, I:607

Discount sales, **I:341–344**, II:1014–1015

Discount stores, II:973

Discounted cash flow, **I:344–345**

Discounted future cash flow approach valuation, II:1154

Discounts, advertising, I:18

Discretionary income, **I:345–346**

Discrimination

affirmative action, **I:29–32**, II:943–944

age, **I:32–34**

AIDS, I:36

gender, **I:537–540**, II:1176

Pregnancy Discrimination Act (1978), II:876

racial, **II:941–944**

See also specific legislation and court cases

Display loaders. *See* Deal loaders

Display merchandise, as collateral, I:203

Disposable income, I:345

Dissolution. *See* Business failure and dissolution

Distress liquidation value, II:690

Distribution channels, **I:346–349**, I:353

Distribution of annuities, I:53

Distributions to owners, I:5

Distributorships and dealerships, **I:349–352**

Diversification, **I:352–353**

Diversity and cross-cultural communication, I:606

See also Multicultural work force

Dividends, **I:353–354**, II:1076–1077, II:1079

Division of labor, II:830–831

Dock receipts, II:1138

"Dog companies," II:722

"Doing business as" forms, I:141–142

Domain names, **I:614–615**

Dot-coms, **I:354–356**, I:601, II:690

Double- and triple-net leases, II:671

Double taxation, I:164, **I:356–357**, I:587, II:687, II:998

See also C corporations

Downloading issues, **I:357–359**

Downsizing. *See* Layoffs and downsizing

Downturn. *See* Economic decline

Dress codes. *See* Casual business attire

Drug abuse. *See* Substance abuse

Drug testing, **I:359–361**, I:401, I:415

DSL (Digital Subscriber Lines) connections, II:754

Due diligence, **I:361–362**

Duke Power Co., Griggs v. (1971), I:31

Dutch auctions, II:821

Dynamic budgets, I:109

Dynamic HTML, I:573

E

E-commerce insurance, I:138

E-mail, I:218, **I:374–376**, I:555, I:619, II:811, II:1190

See also Viruses

E-mail advertising, I:23

Early-payment discounts, I:343–344

Earn-outs, II:1035–1036

"Earned" discounts, I:343

Earnings per share, I:503, II:881

Earnings ranking (Fortune 500), I:525

Ease of entry (into industry), I:594

Eco-labeling, I:549

Eco-sponsoring, I:549

Economic decline, I:117

Economic Development Administration, II:1147

Economic injury disaster loans, I:338

Economic Order Quantity model, II:871–872

Economic Recovery Tax Act (1981), I:526–527

Economies of scale, I:85, **I:364–365**

Economies of scope, **I:365–366**

Economy Order Quantity, **I:363–364**

Education

AIDS awareness, I:37

apprenticeship programs, **I:54–55**, II:663, II:1133

automation, I:71

business education, **I:120–121**

cross-training, **I:289–291**

customer service, I:292

employee motivation, I:397

flexible work programs, I:518–519

hazardous materials, II:983–984

human resources' role, I:577

internships, I:120, **I:624–626**, II:1133

multicultural work force, II:759

orientation programs, I:391, II:1132

recycling, II:951–952

sales force, II:1011

training and development, **II:1130–1134**

EEOC. *See* Equal Employment Opportunity Commission (EEOC)

Effective rate of interest, I:47

Efficiency curves. *See* Learning curves

Efficiency ratios, I:505

8(A) Program, **I:366–368**

Elasticity, **I:369**, II:1093

Eldercare, **I:369–371**

Electronic article surveillance tags, II:1046

Electronic banking, I:81

Electronic bill presentment and payment, I:304

Electronic bulletin boards, **I:371–372**, I:628

Electronic checks, **I:616–617**

Electronic data interchange, **I:372–374**, II:872

Electronic mail. *See* E-mail

Electronic résumés, II:972

Electronic scanners, I:84

Electronic tax filing, **I:376–377**

Eligibility rules for SBA loans, II:1150–1151

Ellerth, Burlington Industries, Inc. v. (1998), I:539

Emergency preparedness. *See* Disaster planning

Emerging markets, **I:377–378**

Employee abuse. *See* Bullying

Employee assistance programs, **I:378–382**, II:1087

Employee benefits, **I:382–385,** I:387, I:397, II:1103–1104
  childcare, I:191–192
  comp time, **I:210–211**
  cross-functional teams, I:288
  disability insurance, **I:334–336,** I:383
  eldercare, I:370–371
  employee assistance programs, **I:378–382**
  employee reward and recognition systems, **I:409–412,** I:420
  employee stock ownership plans, **I:415–417**
  fiduciary duty, I:496–497
  flexible benefit plans, **I:513–514**
  flexible spending accounts, I:193, I:513–514, **I:514–516**
  401(K) plans, **I:526–529**
  health promotion programs, **I:562–563**
  job sharing, II:653
  nonqualified deferred compensation plans, **II:793–796**
  part-time employees, II:858–859
  pension plans, **II:864–866,** II:975, II:1061
  portability of benefits, **II:873–874**
  sales commissions, **II:999–1002**
  sick leave and personal days, **II:1046–1048**
  tuition assistance programs, **II:1139–1141**
  See also Health insurance
Employee compensation, I:39, **I:386–388,** II:1011–1012
  See also Variable pay
Employee hiring, **I:388–391**
  See also Probationary employment periods; Résumés
Employee-initiated reviews, I:400
Employee leasing programs, **I:391–394**
Employee manuals, **I:394–395,** I:628
Employee motivation, **I:395–398**
Employee performance appraisals, **I:398–400,** I:576, II:650
Employee privacy, **I:401–403**
Employee references, **I:403–405,** I:414
Employee registration procedures, **I:405–406**
Employee reinstatement, **I:406**
Employee relations, II:927
Employee retention, **I:406–408**
Employee Retirement Income Security Act (1974), **I:408–409,** I:496–497, II:918
Employee reward and recognition systems, **I:409–412,** I:420, I:577, II:759
Employee rights, **I:412–413**
  See also Employee privacy
Employee screening programs, **I:413–415**
Employee stock ownership plans, **I:415–417**
Employee strikes, **I:417–419**

Employee suggestion systems, **I:419–421**
Employee termination, I:324, **I:421–424,** II:651
Employee theft, **I:424–426**
Employees
  alien, **I:38–40**
  difficulty with, **I:322–324**
  drug testing, **I:359–361**
  hiring, **I:388–391**
  mentally disabled, I:44
  part-time, **II:857–859**
  seasonal, II:1022
Employer identification number, **I:426–427**
Employer's Quarterly Federal Tax Return, II:861
Employment advertising, II:949
Employment applications, **I:427–428**
Employment-at-will, I:421
Employment contracts, **I:428–430**
Employment interviews, **I:430–432,** II:1087
Employment of minors, **I:432–435**
Employment practices liability insurance, **I:435–436**
Empowerment, employee, I:397
Empowerment zones, **I:436–438,** II:1055–1056
Encryption, I:617
Ending inventory budgets, I:110
Endorsements and testimonials, **I:438–440**
Endorsers, I:203
Enterprise resource planning, **I:440–443**
Enterprise risk management, II:985–986
Enterprise zones. *See* Empowerment zones
Entrepreneurial couples, **I:443–445**
Entrepreneurship, **I:445–449**
  See also "Angel" investors; Intrapreneurship; Women entrepreneurs
Environment and cross-cultural communication, I:283
Environmental agencies, I:453
Environmental audits, **I:449–452**
Environmental law and business, **I:452–454**
  See also Environmental Protection Agency (EPA); *specific laws*
Environmental Protection Agency (EPA), I:452–453, **I:455–456**
Environmental site assessments, I:217
Environmentally-responsible products. *See* Green products
Equal Employment Opportunity Act (1972), I:31
Equal Employment Opportunity Commission (EEOC), I:30, **I:456–457,** I:539, II:942–943, II:1040
Equal Pay Act (1963), I:386, I:538, I:539
Equifax, I:274
Equipment leasing, **I:457–459**

Equity, I:5, I:164
Equity capital, I:168
Equity financing, **I:459–462**
Ergonomics, **I:462–463,** II:1188
Erie County Retirees Association v. County of Erie, I:33
Escrow, I:160
"Estate freeze," I:490
Estate planning and family-owned businesses, I:484, I:485, I:490
Estate tax, **I:463–464**
Ethical practices audits, I:67
Ethics, **I:121–123**
Ethnocentrism, I:282
Euro (currency), I:466
European Commission, I:465
European Community. *See* European Union
European Union, **I:464–466**
Evaluation, research and development projects, II:969–970
Event marketing. *See* Corporate sponsorship
Excess inventory, donation of, I:638
Exclusivity clauses (leases), II:672
Executive Order 10925 (1961), I:30
Exempt and nonexempt employees, II:845
Exhibits. *See* Trade shows
Expanded leave, I:516–517
Expansion, business, **I:123–127**
Expansion capital, I:124–125
Expedited arbitration, I:41
Expense accounts, **I:467–468,** II:1001
Expenses, I:5, I:583–584, I:585
  See also Tax deductible business expenses
Experian, I:274
Experience curves. *See* Learning curves
Expert endorsements, I:439
Exponential smoothing, II:1008
Export Credit Insurance Program, I:468–469
Export-Import Bank, **I:468–469**
Export licenses, II:1138
Export packing lists, II:1138
Exporting, I:119, **I:469–473, II:1137–1139**
  See also International marketing
Exporting, indirect, **I:472–473**
Exporting financing and pricing, **I:473–476**
Express and implied warranties, II:1170
Express contracts, I:245
Express Mail Service, II:874–875
Extended warranties, II:1170–1171
eXtensible Markup Language. *See* XML
External audits, **I:60–63,** I:66
External reporting and *pro forma* statements, II:894
Extramarital affairs, II:813
Extraordinary gains and losses, I:584
Eyestrain, II:1188

Grievance mediation, I:42
Grievance procedures, **I:551–553,**
II:662–663
Griggs v. Duke Power Co. (1971), I:31
Gross leases, II:670
Gross profitability, I:503
Group-based reward systems, I:411
Group interventions, II:834
Groupthink, I:309, **I:553–554**
Groupware, **I:554–556**
Growth, economic, I:117
Growth, of businesses. *See* Business
expansion
Growth, organizational, **II:836–837,**
II:838–839
Growth, sustainable, **II:1093–1095**
Growth stage, I:596, II:905
Growth strategies, I:149
Guarantees. *See* Warranties
GUI (Graphical user interface), **I:546–547**

H

Hacking, I:221, I:222, I:618–619
Harassment. *See* Sexual harassment;
Workplace anger and hostility;
Workplace violence
Hard assets. *See* Fixed assets
Hawthorn Studies, II:829
Hazardous substance cleanup. *See*
Comprehensive Environmental
Response Cleanup and Liability
Act (CERCLA) (1980)
Hazards, industrial, I:592–593, II:807
Hazen Paper Co. v. Biggins (1993),
I:33
Health care reform, I:562
Health insurance, I:137, I:383–384,
I:557–560, II:1104
COBRA, **I:229–232,** I:515
insurance pools, I:603
Medicare and Medicaid, **II:730–731**
See also HMOs and PPOs
Health Maintenance Organizations
(HMOs). *See* HMOs and PPOs
Health promotion programs, **I:562–563**
''Hierarchy of human needs,'' II:829
High-tech businesses, **I:563–565**
Hispanic-American business owners,
II:749
Historical analogy methodologies,
II:1007
Historical cash flow approach valuation,
II:1154
HIV and pre-employment screening,
I:37
HMOs and PPOs, I:137, I:384, I:559–
560, **I:560–562**
Holding companies, I:80–81
Holiday-based seasonal businesses,
II:1022–1023
Home-based businesses, I:172–173,
I:568–571, II:1193–1194
Home offices, **I:565–568**
Homepages. *See* Web site design
Homes, sale of, I:169

Horizontal acquisitions, II:738
Horizontal and vertical division of
labor, II:830–831
Hostile acquisitions, II:741–742
Hoteling, **I:571–572**
Hotels and business travel, I:152
Hours of operation. *See* Business hours
Housebrokers, I:598
HTML, **I:572–574,** II:1171–1172
HUBZone Empowerment Contracting
Program, **I:574–575**
Human resource policies, **I:580–581**
Human resources management, **I:575–
579, II:787–790**
Human resources management and the
law, **I:579–580**
Hypertext Markup Language. *See*
HTML

I

ICANN (Internet Corporation for
Assigned Names and Numbers),
I:615
Idea validation, II:904
Illegal Immigration Reform and
Immigrant Responsibility Act
(1996), I:39
Imaging software, II:810
Immediate annuities, I:51
Immigrant visas, I:38
Immigration laws, I:38
Impairment of capital rule, I:353
Implied contracts, I:245
Importing and business cycles, I:119
Imputed costs, I:267
Income, I:585
Income protection benefits, I:383
Income statements, I:5, I:499, **I:583–
585**
Income tax. *See* Audits, Internal
Revenue Service; Internal
Revenue Service (IRS); Tax
fraud; Tax preparation software;
Tax returns
Incorporation, **I:585–589**
Incorporation, articles of, **I:55–56**
Incorporation of nonprofit
organizations, II:783–784
Incremental costs, I:267
Independent contractors. *See* Freelance
employment; Subcontracting
Independent laboratories, II:1119
See also Underwriters Laboratories
(UL)
Indirect costs, I:266
Indirect exporting, **I:472–473**
Individual branding, I:103
Individual retirement accounts (IRAs),
I:526, **I:589–591,** II:975
Industrial analysis, **I:593–595**
Industrial safety, **I:591–593**
Industrial unions, II:660–661, II:662
Industrial *versus* consumer markets,
II:725–726
Industry life cycle, **I:595–597**
Industry survey method, II:1008

Infomercials, **I:21–22**
Informal communications, I:207
Information brokers, **I:597–598**
Information systems audits, I:67
Initial public offerings, **I:598–602**
Innovation, **I:602–603**
Inspection certificates, II:1138
Installment plans, I:278
Installment sales, II:1036
Insurance
business insurance, **I:135–138**
business interruption insurance,
I:137–138, **I:139–140**
corporate-owned life insurance,
II:794
disability insurance, **I:334–336,**
I:383
employment practices liability
insurance, **I:435–436**
insurance pooling, **I:603–604**
life insurance, I:137, **II:685–687,**
II:761–762
property leasing, II:672
See also Health insurance
Insurance certificates, II:1138
Insurance pooling, **I:603–604**
Intangible assets. *See* Goodwill
Intellectual property, **I:604–605,**
II:991–992
See also Copyright; Inventions and
patents; Work for hire
Intention-to-buy surveys, II:1007
Interactive television advertising, I:25
Intercompany transfers, II:991
Intercultural communication. *See* Cross-
cultural communication
Interest arbitration, I:41
Interest coverage ratio, I:504
Interest rates, I:270, **I:607–609,**
II:1149–1150
Intergenerational care facilities, I:371
Intergroup interventions, II:835
Intermediaries, distribution, I:347
Intermediate-term loans, II:693
Internal audits, **I:64–68**
Internal benchmarking, II:936
''Internal'' buyers (of businesses),
II:1035
Internal Revenue Code. *See* Internal
Revenue Service (IRS)
Internal Revenue Service (IRS), **I:609–
610**
approval of accounting methods, I:8
audits, **I:644–645**
barter income, I:86
cost-sharing arrangements, I:264
depreciation, II:1103
electronic tax filing, **I:376–377**
equipment purchases, II:1105
FICA taxes, **I:495,** II:861, II:862
flexible benefit plans, I:513
flexible spending accounts, I:514
freelance worker status, I:533–534
home office deductions, I:565–566
intangible assets and intellectual
property, II:991
payroll taxes, **II:861–863**

National Association of Small Business Investment Companies (NASBIC), **II:767–768**

National Association of Women Business Owners (NAWBO), **II:768–769**

National Business Incubation Association (NBIA), **II:769–770**

National Environmental Policy Act (1970), I:453

National Exchange of Industrial Resources (NAEIR), I:638

National Foundation for Women Business Owners (NFWBO), II:769

National Institute of Occupational Safety and Health (NIOSH), II:806

National Institute of Standards and Technology, II:1148

National Labor Relations Act (1935), I:579, II:661, II:662, II:665, II:770

National Labor Relations Board (NLRB), **II:770–771**
See also Labor unions

National Labor Relations Board supervised elections, II:666–667

National Pollutant Discharge Elimination System, I:199

National Trade Data Bank, II:1148

National unions, II:663–664

National Venture Capital Association (NVCA), **II:771–772**

Native American business owners, II:749

NAWBO (National Association of Women Business Owners), **II:768–769**

NBIA (National Business Incubation Association), **II:769–770**

Negligence, II:903

Negotiation, **II:772–774**

Nepotism, **II:774–775**

Net gain and loss, I:170, I:584

Net income, I:584, **II:775–776**

Net leases, II:670–671

Net profitability, I:503

Net worth, **II:776**

Network marketing. *See* Multilevel marketing

Network Solutions, Inc., I:615

Networking, **II:776–778**
bartering, I:87
"boundaryless" organizations, I:97
business appraisers, I:113
business incubators, I:131
business information sources, I:135
minority-owned businesses, II:749–750
reciprocal marketing, II:946
self-employment, II:1030

Networks, computer. *See* Local area networks (LANs); Wide area networks (WANs)

Neutral evaluations, I:42

New Coke market research, II:717

New economy, **II:778–779**

News releases. *See* Press releases

Newsgroups, **II:779–781**

Newspaper advertising, I:24

Newspaper direct marketing, I:330

NFWBO (National Foundation for Women Business Owners), II:769

Niche market strategy, II:1013

NIOSH (National Institute of Occupational Safety and Health), II:806

NLRB (National Labor Relations Board), **II:770–771**

"No-fault" absenteeism policies, I:2

No-layoff policies, II:669

Nominal price and real price, II:885

Non-annual events, II:1023

Noncash transactions, I:180

Noncausal approach (sales forecasts), II:1006

Noncompetition agreements, **II:781–782**, II:1036

Noncompetitive benchmarking, II:936

Nonimmigrant visas, I:38

Nonmanufacturing firms and product costing, II:899

Nonprofit corporations and taxes, **II:790–793**

Nonprofit organizations, **II:782–787**, II:795

Nonprofit organizations and human resources management, **II:787–790**

Nonqualified deferred compensation plans, **II:793–796**

Nontraditional financing sources, **II:796–797**

Nonverbal communication, I:206–207, I:284, **II:797**, II:826–827
See also Written communication

Norris-Laguardia Act (1932), I:579

North American Free Trade Agreement (NAFTA), **II:797–800**, II:1100

North American Industry Classification System (NAICS), **II:800–803**

Notebook and laptop computers, I:227

Numerically controlled machines, I:71

Nutrition Labeling and Education Act (1990), II:849

NVCA (National Venture Capital Association), **II:771–772**

O

Object-related database management systems, I:297

Objective and task method budgeting, I:17

Occupational Safety and Health Act (1970), I:579, I:591–592, II:665

Occupational Safety and Health Administration (OSHA), **II:805–809**

Odd pricing, II:884

Off-the-job training, II:1132

Office automation, **II:809–812**

Office of Consumer Affairs, II:1147–1148

Office romance, **II:812–815**

Office security, **II:815–818**

Office supplies, **II:818–819**

Older Workers Benefit Protection Act (1990), I:33

Ombuds, I:42

On-site childcare facilities, I:192

On-the-job training, II:1132

Oncale v. Sundower Offshore Services (1998), I:540

One-Stop Capital Shop (OSCS), II:1055–1056

Online auctions, **II:819–821**

Online direct public offerings, I:333

Online focus groups, I:522

Open accounts (exporting), I:476

Open and closed shops, II:661

Open computer systems, I:227

Open cry auctions, II:821

Open-end leases, I:73

Open-end questionnaires, II:719

"Open-ended" incentive programs, II:1001–1002

Open-systems theory, II:830

Operating activities, I:178–179

Operating and long-term leases, I:458

Operating budgets, I:109–110

Operational audits, I:67

Operations information, I:1034

Operations management, **II:821–824**

Opportunity costs, I:267, **II:824**

Optimal firm size, **II:825**

Optional benefits, I:382–383

Oral communication, I:206, **II:825–827**

Order acknowledgments, II:1003

Order processing, II:872

Orderly liquidation value, II:689–690

Organization endorsements, I:439

Organization theory, **II:828–831**

Organizational behavior, **II:832–833**

Organizational charts, I:628, **II:827–828**

Organizational development, **II:833–836**, II:1134

Organizational growth, **II:836–837**

Organizational life cycle, **II:837–839**

Organizational structure, **II:839–840**

Orientation programs, I:391, II:1132

Original equipment manufacturers, **II:840–841**

OSCA (One-Stop Capital Shop), II:1055–1056

OSHA (Occupational Safety and Health Administration), **II:805–809**, II:1183

Out-of-pocket costs, I:266

Outdoor advertising, I:24–25

Outplacement agencies, II:949

Outsourcing, **II:841–844**

Overhead expenses, **II:844–845**, II:882

Overpayments, I:10

Overtime, II:650–651, **II:845–846**

Owner's equity, I:77

Ownership, change in roles, I:126

Ownership, disagreements among, I:125

P

Packaging, I:326, **II:847–850,** II:1137–1138

Part-time businesses, **II:855–857**

Part-time employees, **II:857–859**

Partial retirement, I:517

Participative audits, I:67

Partnership agreements, II:852–853, **II:854–855**

Partnerships, **II:850–854,** II:1106

Passwords, I:92–93, I:619

Patent attorneys, I:634

Patent drawings, I:634

Patent searches, I:633

Patents. *See* Inventions and patents

Pay for applied services, I:288

Pay for performance, I:387, I:410, II:909–910

Payment systems, Internet, **I:615–618**

PayPal, II:1135

Payroll taxes, **II:861–863**

Peer conflict, II:1181

Penetration pricing, **II:863–864**

Pension plans, **II:864–866,** II:975, II:1061

Per diem allowances, **II:866–867**

Percentage agreements, II:990

Percentage leases, II:671

Percentage of sales method budgeting, I:17

Performance reviews. *See* Employee performance appraisals

Period and product costs, I:266

Person-to-person marketing. *See* Multilevel marketing

Personal computers. *See* Microcomputers

Personal financial statements, I:508

Personal property disaster loans, I:338

Personal selling, **II:867–869**

Personal service business valuation, II:1154

Personnel. *See* Employees

PERT (Program Evaluation and Review Technique), **II:920–921,** II:1007

Phased retirement, I:517

Physical disaster business loans, I:337–338, II:1149

Physical distribution, **II:869–872**

Pick and place operations and robotics, II:988

''Piggyback'' exporting, I:472

PIMS (Profit Impact of Market Strategies), **II:916–927**

Pipeline shipping, II:871, II:1137

Place (''Four Ps''), II:725

Plaintiffs, small claims court, II:1066–1067

Plant patents, I:632

Plural organizations, II:758

Point-of-purchase (POP) displays, II:1016–1017

Point of sale (POS) systems, **II:872–873**

Poka-yoke. See Mistake-proofing

Politics and business cycles, I:118–119

Polls, online, I:628

Pollution. *See* Clean Air Act (1970); Clean Water Act (1972); Environmental law and business

Pollution Control Program, II:1149

Pooling of interests method of accounting, II:739

POP (Point-of-purchase) displays, II:1016–1017

Portability of benefits, **II:873–874**

Post-sales/customer satisfaction research, II:718

Postage meters, II:875

Postal costs, **II:874–875**

Potential foreign markets, marketing factors, I:612–613

Potentially responsible parties, hazard cleanup, I:216

PPOs. *See* HMOs and PPOs

Pre-employment screening and HIV, I:37

Pre-production prototypes, II:923

Preemptive right, II:1078

Preferred Provider Organizations (PPOs). *See* HMOs and PPOs

Preferred stock, II:1079–1080

Pregnancy Discrimination Act (1978), II:876

Pregnancy in the workplace, **II:875–878**

Premiums, II:1015–1016

Prepaid insurance plans. *See* HMOs and PPOs

Prepaid legal services, II:674–675

Present value, **II:878–879**

Presentation prototypes, II:923

Presentations, II:826–827

Press kits, **II:879**

Press releases, **II:879–881**

Preventive mediation, I:42

Price bundling, II:883

Price deals. *See* Discount sales

Price/earnings ratio, **II:881**

Price (''Four Ps''), II:725

Price index and sales forecasts, II:1005–1006

Price lining, II:883–884

Pricing, **II:882–886,** II:887

Pricing above/below competition, II:883

Primary and secondary market information, II:716–717

Prime Contracting Program, II:1055

Prime rate, I:47, I:607

Print advertising, **I:23–25**

Print information sources, I:133–134

Priority Mail, II:875

Privacy, employee, **I:401–403**

Privacy and drug testing, I:360

Private accountants. *See* Accountants

Private labeling, **II:886–888**

Private placement of securities, **II:888–890**

Privatization, **II:890–893**

Pro forma invoices, II:1003

Pro forma statements, **II:893–896**

Probability Assessment Method, II:1007

Probationary employment periods, **II:896–897**

Problem identification, I:307–308

Problem solving, I:308–309

Process costing, I:267

Process design, II:822

Producers' cooperatives, I:248–249

Product, II:724–725

   concept, I:27

   demonstration, I:641

   design, I:219, I:336, II:822

   development, **II:899–902**

   differentiation, I:85

   labeling, II:848–849

   launching, II:901

   life cycle, **II:904–906**

   positioning, **II:906–908**

   public relations, II:926–927

   research, II:717

   samples, II:1016

   substitution, I:594

Product and period costs, I:266

Product costing, **II:897–899**

Product demand and sales forecasts, II:1006

Product liability, I:136, I:243, **II:902–904**

Product safety laws. *See* Product liability

Production budgets, I:110, II:1009

Production costs. *See* Production overhead budgets

Production overhead budgets, I:111

Productivity, **II:908–911**

Productivity curves. *See* Learning curves

Productivity loss and desktop publishing, I:319–320

Productivity ratio. *See* Return on assets

Professional corporations, **II:911–913**

Professional unions, II:660

Profit. *See* Net income

Profit centers, **II:913–916**

Profit Impact of Market Strategies (PIMS), **II:916–927**

Profit margins, **II:917–918**

Profit sharing, I:410–411, **II:918–920,** II:975–976

Profitability, I:500, I:503–504

Program audits, I:67

Program Evaluation and Review Technique (PERT), **II:920–921,** II:1007

Promissory estoppel, I:245

Promissory notes, **II:921**

Promotion (''Four Ps''), II:725

Promotion from within, II:709, II:948

Promotional tools mix, I:19

Property depreciation, I:3

Property leasing, **II:670–673**

Property losses, I:136

Proposals. *See* Business proposals

Proprietary information, **II:922–923,** II:967

Prospective buyers (of businesses), II:1034–1035

Prototypes, **II:923–925**

Proxy servers, I:510
Proxy statements, **II:925**
Psychological research, II:717–718
Public domain, I:250
Public interest relations, II:928
Public relations, **II:925–929**
Public sector employees and
  privatization, II:892
Public Utility Holding Company Act
  (1935), II:1026
Pull method of advertising, I:28
Purchase method of accounting, II:739–
  740
Purchase money security interest, I:203
Purchase orders, II:1003
Purchasing, **II:929–932**
Purchasing cards, II:932
Push method of advertising, I:28
Push money, II:1017
Pyramid schemes, II:760

Q

Qualitative forecasting methods, I:523–
  524, II:1007
Quality
  awards, II:938
  control, **II:935–939**
  desktop publishing, I:320
  ISO 9000, **I:645–648**
  licensing, II:683
  quality circles, **II:933–935**
  testing laboratories, II:1119–1120
  Total Quality Management, II:835,
    II:1122–1125
Quantitative forecasting methods, I:524
Quasi-contracts, I:245
"Question marks," II:723
Quick ratio, I:500, I:504

R

R. R. Donnelly & Sons, II:943
R & D (Research and development),
  II:966–971
Racial discrimination, **II:941–944**
  See also Workplace anger and
    hostility
Radio advertising, **I:20–21**
Railroad shipping, II:871, II:1136–1137
Raising prices, II:885
Random drug testing, II:1087
Rapid and slow penetration, II:905
Rapid and slow skimming, II:904–905
Rapid prototyping, II:924
Rate of profit, II:917–918
Rate of return. *See* Rate of profit
Reach, I:14
"Readily achievable" modifications,
  I:43
Reagan Administration and affirmative
  action, I:31
Real estate, as collateral, I:203
Real estate transactions and
  environmental audits, I:450
Real price and nominal price, II:885
"Reasonable accommodations," I:43

Rebates, **II:944–945,** II:1015
Receipts. *See* Cash inflows
Recession, I:117
Reciprocal dealing. *See* Sherman Act
Reciprocal linking and affiliate
  marketing, II:946
Reciprocal marketing, **II:946**
Recognition programs, I:411–412
Record retention, **II:946–948**
Recordkeeping, I:124, II:998–999
Recovery, economic, I:117
Recovery, from business failure, I:129
Recovery, from disasters. *See* Disaster
  planning
Recruiting, I:388–389, **II:709–710,**
  II:788, **II:948–950,** II:1011
"Recyclable" and "recycled content,"
  II:951
Recycling, **II:950–953,** II:962
Redemption agreements. *See* Buy-sell
  agreements
Reengineering, **II:953–954**
*Reeves v. Sanderson Plumbing
  Products, Inc.* (2000), I:34
Referrals and networking, II:777,
  II:948–949
Refinancing, **II:955–956**
Refunds. *See* Rebates
*Regents of the University of California
  v. Bakke* (1978), I:31
Registration, copyright, I:252
Regression analysis, II:1008
Regulation A, I:333
Regulation D, I:332–333, II:889,
  II:956–957
Regulatory Flexibility Act (1980),
  II:957–959
Related diversification, I:365
Relational database management
  systems, I:296–297
Relinquishing style communication,
  I:627
Relocation, **II:959–961,** II:995
Remanufacturing, **II:961–963**
Removal action (hazard cleanup),
  I:217–218
Renovation, **II:963–965**
Repayment schedules, I:270
Repetitive strain injuries. *See*
  Ergonomics
Representations and warranties liability
  insurance, I:362
Repurchase agreements, II:756
Reputation. *See* Corporate image
Request for Proposal (RFP), **II:965–
  966**
Research and development programs
  (SBA), II:1055
Research and development (R & D),
  II:966–971
Research departments, advertising
  agencies, I:13
Residential care industry, II:1065
Residual ownership, II:1078
Resistance to change, II:711
Response and complied lists, I:330
Response mailing lists, II:699

Responsibility centers, I:261
Restrictions on minor employees,
  I:433–434
Résumés, **II:971–972**
Retail industry and part-time
  employment, II:859
Retail trade, **II:972–973**
Retirement
  benefits and assumptions, I:59–60,
    I:384
  Employee Retirement Income
    Security Act (1974), **I:408–409,**
    I:496–497, II:918
  employee stock ownership plans,
    I:415–417
  pension plans, **II:864–866,** II:975,
    II:1061, II:1103
  phased and partial retirement, I:517
  planning, **II:973–976**
  protection from age discrimination,
    I:33, I:35
  supplemental executive retirement
    plans, II:794
Retrenchment. *See* Defensive strategies
Return on assets, I:503, **II:977**
Return on equity ratio, I:500–501
Return on investment, I:503, **II:978**
Return policies, **II:979–980**
Revenue streams, **II:980–981**
Revenues, I:5, I:583, I:584–585
Reverse auctions, II:821
Reverse discrimination, II:943–944
Revolving credit, I:270
RFP (Request for Proposal), **II:965–
  966**
Riders and options, life insurance,
  II:686
"Right to Know" laws, I:453–454,
  II:981–984
"Right to register" (trademarks),
  II:1128–1129
"Right to use" (trademarks), II:1129
Risk, credit, I:272
Risk, research and development
  projects, II:969
Risk and return, **II:986–987**
Risk assessment, I:196–197
Risk management, **II:984–986**
  See also Business insurance
Risk-purchasing groups. *See* Disability
  insurance pools
Risk Retention Act (1986), I:604
Risky and riskless assets, I:58–59
Robinson-Patman Act, II:1013
Robinson v. Shell Oil Co., I:33
Robotics, I:71, **II:987–989**
Rochdale Principles, I:247
Role analysis technique, II:834–835
Role playing training method, II:1132
Routers, I:510
Royalties, **II:989–993**
Royalty financing, **II:993–994**
RSA encryption program, I:296
Rule 404(c), I:528
Rules 504, 505, and 506. *See*
  Regulation D
Rural businesses, **II:994–996**

Web site scalability, **II:1018**
Weber, Max, II:829
Welch, Jack, II:938
Welding and robotics, II:988
Wellness programs. *See* Health
    promotion programs
Wheaton Glass Co., Schultz v. (1970),
    I:538
Whole life insurance, II:686
Wholesale businesses and site selection,
    II:1050
Wholesalers and wholesaling, I:350,
    II:1173–1174
Wide area networks (WANs), I:228,
    II:697, **II:1175**
Women entrepreneurs, **II:1175–1177**
Women's organizations
    National Association of Women
        Business Owners (NAWBO),
        II:768–769
    National Foundation for Women
        Business Owners (NFWBO),
        II:769
    SBA programs, II:1055
    World Association of Women
        Entrepreneurs (Les Femmes Chefs
        d'Entreprises Mondiales), II:769

Word processing packages, II:810
Work and family programs, I:517
Work for hire, I:251, **II:1177–1178**
Work force, maintenance of, I:576
Work sharing, I:516
Worker Adjustment and Retraining
    Notification Act (1988), I:423
Workers' compensation, I:136, I:591,
    II:1178–1179
Workers' cooperatives, I:249
Working capital financing, I:473
Working Capital Guarantee Program,
    I:468
Workplace anger and hostility,
    II:1179–1183
    See also Workplace violence
Workplace safety, **II:1183–1185**
Workplace violence, **II:1185–1188**
Workstations, **II:1188–1189**
World Association of Women
    Entrepreneurs (Les Femmes Chefs
    d'Entreprises Mondiales), II:769
World Trade Organization (WTO),
    I:541–542
World Wide Web. *See* Internet

Written communication, I:206, I:207,
    II:1189–1190
    See also E-mail; Nonverbal
    communication
WTO (World Trade Organization),
    I:541–542

X

XML, I:573–574

Y

Yahoo!, I:94, II:1019
Year 2000 (Y2K), II:1023
Yellow Pages, I:24
Young Entrepreneurs' Organization,
    II:1191–1192

Z

Zero tolerance policies and
    discrimination, I:539
Zoning ordinances, **II:1193–1194**